THE OFFICIAL®
PRICE GUIDE TO

Movie/TV Soundtracks
and
Original Cast Albums

THE OFFICIAL®
PRICE GUIDE TO

Movie/TV
Soundtracks
and
Original Cast Albums

FIRST EDITION

JERRY OSBORNE

Editor: Ruth Maupin

HOUSE OF COLLECTIBLES • NEW YORK

© 1991 by Jerry Osborne

This is a registered trademark of Random House, Inc.

Published by: House of Collectibles
                 201 East 50th Street
                 New York, New York 10022

Distributed by Ballantine Books, a division of Random House, Inc., New York, and simultaneously in Canada by Random House of Canada Limited, Toronto.

Manufactured in the United States of America

ISBN: 0-876-37846-7

First Edition: May 1991

10 9 8 7 6 5 4 3 2

CONTENTS

ACKNOWLEDGMENTS

The single most important element in the updating and revision of a price and reference guide is reader input.

From dealers and collectors, based in every state and in nearly every country around the globe, we receive suggestions, additions, and corrections. Every single piece of data we acquire from readers is carefully reviewed, with all appropriate and usable information utilized in the next edition of this guide.

As enthusiastically as we encourage your contribution, let us equally encourage that when you write, you'll either type or print your name clearly. It's as frustrating for us to receive a mailing of useful information, and not be able to credit the sender, as it probably is for the sender to not see his or her name in the Acknowledgments section.

In compiling this edition, information supplied by the people whose names appear below was of great importance. To these good folks, listed alphabetically, our deepest gratitude is extended. The amount of data and investment of time, of course, varied, but without each and every one of them this book would have been something less than it is.

Special gratitude is extended to Ruth Maupin, editor and data coordinator, Denise Brown, editorial assistant, and George Maupin, whose computer programs were invaluable.

Here then, alphabetically listed, is the board of advisors and contributors to this edition:

Jerry P. Abbott
Dan Alvino
Christina Babonni
Cecelia Bayes
Douglas E. Beebe
Robert Bennett
Mary Estelle Benton
Mel Berlin
Ronald L. Bohn
Richard Bozeman Jr.
Denise Brown
Pat Brown
Ralph Bukofzer
Kenneth Burden
Tom Carroll
Bruce Chilstrom
Alan K. Collins
Scott Copenhaver
Perry Cox
G.B. Cyrus
T. Darcy
Vernon A. Davis
James Daye
Rene de la Salle
Cindy Dodd
Cliff Dodd
Jim Doherty
Roger Dorfman
William Drell
Tony Duncan
Judith Ebner
Rick Edgcomb
John Ellis
Trevie Emery

Frank Falsken
John Patrick Feeney
Conrad P. Felber
Stan Feldman
Bob Furmanek
Bruce Garthe
Lina Gaynor
Charles T. Gray
Jan Grefstad
Butch Guest
Philip Haldeman
William Hansen
Dennis Hartman
Ross Hartsough
Tom Hendrick
David Hummel
Susan Jacob
George Jenkins
Bill Johnson
Jeff Jones
Jeff Joseph
Jack Kabin
George Kappral
Alan Kemp
Dave Kressley
Ronald Krieger
Walt Kubis
Mark Langley
Howard Levine
Ron Lewko
Joe Lindsay
Dennis Locantore
A.J. Lutsky
Al Madden

Carol Marston
George Maupin
Frank J. Mente
Kevin Moltner
Anne Morrison
Tim Murphy
Mike Murray
Steve Naperstick
Charlie Neu
Todd R. Norris
Tony Palumbo
Dennis J. Pauly
Gareth Pawlowski
S.N. Perry
Patrick Phillips
Ronald Piell
Michael R. Pitts
Joan M. Polizotto
Chester Prudhomme
Gary W. Radovich
Bill Raoul
Mike Reams
Bob Richards
Freddie Richards
David Robertson
Tim Robinson
April Rogers
Eileen Rogers
Tim Rogers
R.K. Rose
Ann Ruby
Walter Ryland
Alfred Sandberg Jr.
Louis S. Sarog

Mel Schelich
Laura Serra
Gerald Skagfjord
Louie E. Sloan
Curtis Smith
Frank Smith
Mark Smith
Dr. Robert L. Smith
Wayne Stanley
Janis Stearns
Tom Stein
Gerald Stone
Ann Tamboline
A.A. Temperley
J.K. Temperley
Robert Temple
Jeff Thompson
Frank Tinari
Gilbert R. Turcotte
Katherine M. Turney
Dan and Diana Valois
Steve Vanghel
Johnny Ward
Jack Waxman
Jim Weaver
Eric Welch
Bruce Wemett
Joel Whitburn
Brian D. Wilder
Barbara Williams
John Winfrey
Terry Wycuff
Bruce Yeko
Stan Zadroga

Movie/TV Soundtracks
and
Original Cast Albums

INTRODUCTION

Collecting original cast and soundtrack recordings is an area quite unlike any other in music collecting — truly a world of its own.

Most of us who are cast and soundtrack collectors developed our interest in the hobby as members of the audience. From box seats at the lavish Broadway show palaces to the rickety ones at the nearly extinct downtown local theatres, we came into the fold. While watching the show or film, we heard this magical music that added immeasurably to the overall enjoyment of the spectacle. Our subsequent purchase of the cast or soundtrack album allowed us to relive those cherished moments of escapism over and over on our turntables, to our heart's delight.

If the music of a certain show is truly overwhelming, one might be inclined to seek out other recordings by that same composer, conductor, or performer. When that happens it is safe to say you've become a collector!

Sometimes the scenario is reversed. We hear a piece of music that steals our hearts, then can't wait to see the show from which this wonderful music came. Then, after seeing the show, we go home and play the album again.

Like a train on a circular track, it doesn't matter where you climb on board, sooner or later you're going to come full circle — and in the process you will multiply your appreciation of this fascinating genre.

Unlike the bottomless pit that most areas of record collecting can turn out to be — no one is likely to ever have a truly *complete* collection of Elvis Presley or Beatles recordings — collectors of soundtracks can, in many cases, amass a complete collection. Likewise, this is one book in our series of record guides that we feel can eventually be complete. There are only so many records of show tunes, and our goal is to list every one released in the United States on LP or EP.

By sticking to records issued in the United States, or widely distributed here, we feel we can lay the best foundation. This is not to say we will not include foreign listings in a future edition, rather that our first priority is to offer a genuinely comprehensive guide to domestic releases.

With approximately 8,000 separate cast and soundtrack entries in this first edition, we have already documented nearly every significant recording within our established boundaries. It's an excellent foundation upon which we can build.

COMING TO TERMS

Many releases are original soundtracks or original cast recordings, and many others contain music actually recorded in a studio and merchandised in such a way as to appear to be *original* recordings. Such recordings, often as collectible as the original recording of the show, are designated as "Studio Casts" or "Studiotracks" in this guide. Although there is really not much difference in the two terms, the preferred format of listing casts before soundtracks (if any), created the need for having two terms meaning the same thing. Either way, these recordings were done at a studio recording session and are from neither the film score nor from a live stage show in front of an audience.

With the more popular shows, many studio session albums were made — far more than were issued with the music of the original cast. A highly successful show with great music has always been a bandwagon on which many others couldn't wait to jump upon. We have included as many of these studio cast releases as possible, realizing that a fan of a particular show may want to own or at least know about other renditions of that show.

included as many of these studio cast releases as possible, realizing that a fan of a particular show may want to own or at least know about other renditions of that show.

There are only two types of soundtracks in this guide: movie soundtracks and television soundtracks. TV soundtracks are identified as such, which is to say that any soundtrack not shown as a TV soundtrack is from a motion picture release.

Not to be confused with studiotrack releases is the type of LP where an artist performs an assortment of tunes, one of which is a popular show tune. We have made no attempt to be comprehensive in this area since there are probably a million albums of this type, though a few are sprinkled throughout the guide for one reason or another. An exception might be records where the title is the same as that of a show. Such albums are listed in the guide more for identification purposes than actual content, as well as to inform collectors that a particular LP is not exactly what its title might indicate.

Another borderline type of cast album is one made during a live performance. If the concert was broadcast via radio, television, or film, then it clearly belongs in this guide. The gray area involves significant concerts issued only on records, such as a Madison Square Garden or Hollywood Bowl performance. Feeling such recordings are usually outside the boundaries of this book, few live appearance albums are included. Those we have listed appear not because they contain a live show, but based on other factors — such as a Broadway theatre performance or to complete the section of a certain artist.

WHAT ABOUT REISSUES?

One area of endless complexities is the matter of original pressings vs. reissues. Many of the successful show albums have never gone out of print, which may result in a considerably lower value for the original issues than other releases of the same vintage. For some of these, it may be the death of vinyl recordings in favor of compact discs and cassettes, more than just because they are old, which will ultimately increase their value .

Prices in the guide are for the first pressing, even if means the first pressing of a reissue. As often as possible, we will provide the information necessary to identify each pressing. If a reissue uses the exact same prefix, catalog number, and packaging, it may create a situation where collectors are not overly concerned about having the first pressing. After all, reissues do contain the exact same music. Sometimes only by having an original and reissue in hand can one discover some little detail that can be documented as the key to identifying which is which. In this area, the slight premium placed on these first pressings is more token than authentic.

An $8 or $10 reissue that is easily available will likely have a noticeably different label design than its original pressing. We may then show the original pressing at $10 to $12, knowing that any collector who was particularly seeking a first pressing would gladly pay the token premium.

Looking at any of the Elvis Presley soundtracks, for example, will reveal how prices can vary from original to reissue, to later reissue. While these are accurate prices among Presley collectors, who in many cases do not collect soundtracks per se, they may not be representative of prices paid by collectors of soundtracks for the sake of film music. Still, if offered to the proper market, these prices can be obtained. Many similar examples exist with other albums by artists, such as the Beatles, that have their own following outside the realm of soundtrack collecting. None of the prices in this guide were determined by what people who *do not* want the records would be willing to pay.

THIS GUIDE IS JUST THAT: A GUIDE

It is important to remember that this book is merely a *guide,* not a gospel of absolutes and undeniable, unflexible, truths. Used properly, it can be of immense help to the record collector. Our position is to reflect existing trends and values, not to establish them. Use it with an element of flexibility.

IT SAYS "STEREO," BUT IS IT?

Opinions certainly do vary with regard to rechanneled stereo. Some feel that a rechanneled (electronically simulated) stereo album is absolutely worthless — tantamount to the commission of an audio felony on the part of the record company. Their position is that the pure, original monaural sound is ruined by the fake stereo process, which, depending on the skill of the engineers, often makes the artists sound as though they were performing at the bottom of a well.

Then there are those who actually prefer rechanneled stereo to monaural. They admit that while nearly everyone prefers *true* stereo, the rechanneled stereo tracks have an enhanced sound. They also point out that, because they didn't sell well, many of the rechanneled issues from the late '50s and early '60s are quite a bit rarer than their mono counterparts. This we know is true.

When the dust settles, we will likely find most rechanneled stereo releases priced about the same, if they were released simultaneously. Individual tastes can and ultimately will dictate any variances.

An exception would be a rechanneled stereo release that appeared several years after the original monaural issue, in which case the mono LP would usually have the higher value.

When an album is known to be in rechanneled stereo, the designation "SE" (Stereo is Electronic) is used in parenthesis ahead of the catalog number.

"M" indicates a monaural release and "S" means either true stereo, or that we believe the LP to be true stereo. Having not auditioned each and every one of the 8,000+ records in this guide, we know there are likely to be some that we show as "S" (stereo), that actually make use of some form of electronic stereo. It is also possible we may show an LP as "SE," when it does, in fact, contain true stereo. If you discover such a flaw, please bring it to our attention.

RECORD COLLECTING GUIDELINES: HOW PRICES ARE DETERMINED

Record values shown in this new *Official® Price Guide to Movie/TV Soundtracks and Original Cast Albums* were averaged using information derived from a number of reliable sources, one of the most influential being our long-established price review board, with dozens of the country's top dealers and collectors pricing each listing within their area of interest. Then, assisted by some sophisticated computer software, we averaged all of the input to arrive at the most accurate price range possible.

Besides the review board, we receive an abundance of mail throughout the year from folks like yourself, suggesting corrections and changes for the next edition of the guide.

Another extremely important source of pricing information is *DISCoveries* magazine, the monthly publication where hobbyists buy, sell, and trade assorted music collectibles. We painstakingly review each issue, carefully comparing prices being asked to those shown in our data base. If trading in *DISCoveries* indicates guide prices need to be increased or decreased, such changes are made.

What makes this step in the pricing process so vital is that nothing more verifiably illustrates the out-of-print record marketplace than the everyday sales lists placed in *DISCoveries* by dealers from both around the country and around the globe.

Record prices, as with most collectibles, can vary drastically from one area of the country to another. Having reviewers and annotators in every state, as well as in Europe, Asia, and beyond, enables us to present a realistic average of the highest and lowest current asking prices for an identically graded copy of each record.

Other sources of consequential information include set sales and auction lists in other magazines, as well as private sales list mailings, record convention trading, personal visits with collectors and to retail locations around the country, and hundreds of hours on the telephone with key advisors.

Although the record marketplace information in this edition was believed accurate at press time, it is ever subject to market changes. At any time, major bulk discoveries, quantity dumps, sudden price increases wrought by a singer or composer's death, overnight stardom that creates a greater demand for earlier material, and other such events and trends can easily affect scarcity and demand. Through diurnal research, keeping track of the day-to-day changes and discoveries taking place in the fascinating world of record collecting is a relatively simple and ongoing procedure.

To ensure the greatest possible accuracy, the prices in this guide are averaged from data culled from all of the aforementioned sources.

HOW YOU CAN HELP

Obviously, we can never get too much input or too many reviewers. We wholeheartedly encourage you to submit whatever information you feel would be useful in building a better record guide. The quantity of data is not a factor. No amount is too little or too much.

When preparing additions for the next edition, please try to list records in generally the same format as is used in the guide: show or film title, type (soundtrack, original cast, etc.), year of actual performance, label name, mono or stereo designation, catalog number, year of release of record (if known), and an estimated price range.

WAX FAX

One frequently used method of forwarding data to us is by FAX. For your convenience, we now have a full-time, dedicated FAX line: (206) 385-6572. Use this service to quickly and easily transmit additions, corrections, price updates, and suggestions. Be sure to include your name, address, and phone number so we can acknowledge your contribution and, if necessary, contact you.

Whether mailing or faxing, please print or type your name so we may accurately credit you in the next edition. Submit all written additions, corrections, and suggestions to:

Jerry Osborne
P.O. Box 255
Port Townsend, WA 98368

RECORD GRADING AND
THE PRICE RANGE

The pricing shown in this edition represents the PRICE RANGE for NEAR-MINT condition copies. The value range allows for the countless variables that affect record pricing. Often, the range will widen as the dollar amount increases, making a $200-$300 range as logical as an $8-$10 range.

The standardized system of record grading, used and endorsed by Osborne Enterprises, the House of Collectibles, *DISCoveries* magazine, and buyers and sellers worldwide, is as follows:

MINT: A *mint* item must be absolutely perfect. Nothing less can be honestly described as mint. Even brand-new purchases can easily be flawed in some manner and not qualify as mint. To allow for tiny blemishes, the highest grade used in our record guide series is *near-mint*. An absolutely pristine, or still sealed, item may carry a slight premium above the near-mint range shown in this guide.

VERY GOOD: Records in *very good* condition should have a minimum of visual or audible imperfections, which should not detract much from your enjoyment of owning them. This grade is halfway between good and near-mint.

GOOD: Practically speaking, the grade of *good* means that the item is good enough to fill a gap in your collection until a better copy becomes available. Good condition merchandise will show definite signs of wear and tear, probably evidencing that no protective care was given the item. Even so, records in good condition should play all the way through without skipping.

Most older records are going to be in something less than near-mint condition. It is very important to use the near-mint price range in this guide only as a starting point in record appraising. Be honest about actual condition. Apply the same standards to the records you trade or sell as you would want one from whom you were buying to observe. Visual grading may be unreliable. Accurate grading may require playing the record (play-grading).

Use the following formula to determine values on lesser condition copies:

For VERY GOOD condition, figure about 60% to 80% of the near-mint price range given in this guide.

Some dealers now report that a VG+ record priced at $8 (or 80% of near-mint) will sell ahead of another copy of that same item in near-mint condition priced at $10. Also, with many of the older pieces that cannot be found in near-mint, VG or VG+ may be the highest grade available. This significantly narrows the gap between VG and the near-mint range.

For GOOD condition, figure about 20% to 40% of the near-mint price range given in this guide.

A plus or minus sign following the grade (G+, VG+, etc.) indicates an appreciation or depreciation of that grade, equivalent to about half the distance between grades. In other words, there's very little difference between G+ (good plus) and VG- (very good minus).

THE BOTTOM LINE

All the price guides and reporting of previous sales in the world won't change the rudimentary fact that true value is nothing more than what one person is willing to accept and what another is prepared to pay. Actual value is based on scarcity and demand. It's always been that way and always will.

A recording — or anything for that matter — can be 50 or 100 years old, but if no one wants it, the actual value will certainly be minimal. Just because something is old does not necessarily make it valuable. Someone has to want it!

On the other hand, a very recent release can have exceptionally high value if it has already become scarce and is by an artist whose following has created a demand. A record does not have to be old to be valuable.

BOOTLEGS AND COUNTERFEITS

Bootleg and counterfeit records are not listed in this guide. Fortunately, counterfeiting is less a problem in the field of soundtracks and original cast albums than with rock and roll and rhythm and blues singles.

For the record, a bootleg recording is one illegally manufactured, usually containing material not previously available in a legitimate form. Often, with the serious collector in mind, a boot will package previously issued tracks that have achieved some degree of value or scarcity. If the material is easily available, legally, then there would be no gain for the bootlegger.

The counterfeit record is one manufactured as close as possible in sound and appearance to the source disc from which it was inspired. Not all counterfeits were created to fool an un-suspecting buyer into thinking he or she was buying an authentic issue, but some were. Many were designated in some way, such as with a special marking or design variance, so as not to allow them to be confused with originals. Such a fake record primarily exists to fill a gap in the collection until the real thing comes along.

With bootleg and counterfeit records, the appropriate and deserving recipients of royalties are, of course, denied remuneration for their works.

Since many of the most valuable records have been counterfeited, it is always a good idea to consult with an expert when there is any doubt. The trained eye can usually spot a fake.

Not listing boots and counterfeits does not mean *unauthorized* releases are excluded from the book. There are many legitimate, private label releases that are unauthorized by one en-tity or another; records that are neither bootleg, or counterfeit. Unauthorized does not neces-sarily mean illegal.

USING THIS GUIDE: ADDITIONAL POINTS

- Names are listed in the alphabetical order of the first word. This means you'll find **Red Tent** before **Redhead.**

- The articles "A" and "The" have been dropped from the beginning of show titles in this guide even though they may appear on the records as part of the name. Because it makes for so many awkward titles to delete the article "An," we have chosen to leave those shows as is. This means you will find *An American in Paris* listed exactly that way, but *A Hard Day's Night* will be under "H."

- Equally as important as the composers and conductors in determining the collectibility of a record is the cast — the performers actually heard on the disc. For this reason, we list as many of the performers as known for each separate record, with special notations of interesting information occasionally included. The major source of confusion in this area is based on the way music is marketed by the record companies. Usually, and in large lettering, the stars of the *show* or *film* are billboarded on the front cover of the jacket. Often, however, the stars of the show are not the same cast that is heard on the record. It is only the performers who appear *on the record* that we want listed in the cast section. When a film star is not a singer, but must appear to be singing in the film, a qualified singer will go into a studio and record the songs. The film star will then simply lip sync the lyrics. When this is done, it is the actual vocalist whose name we want to list. For this reason, many a well-known star is not listed in our cast, even though commonly associated with the show.

- For the sake of consistency, we have narrowed the many different descriptive job titles down to two: composer and conductor. Both in the listings and in the composer/conductor index, you will find those names who may actually be shown on the album cover as "lyricist," "musical director," "musical arranger," etc.

- The index has the names of all individuals known to have contributed to the records listed in this guide only. It is not intended to provide a complete filmography of its personnel.

- With few exceptions, all titles listed are those of the record release and not necessarily the exact title of the show (though in most cases they are identical). When a likelihood exists that you might first look elsewhere for a show, a cross-reference should be there to point you in the right direction.

- If a show was recorded from both stage and screen performances, the stage (Original Cast, Original Revival Cast, etc.) listings are first. Following those are Movie and TV Soundtracks, and then Studiotracks.

- We believe the year of release given in the guide to be accurate — for both year of performance and year of actual record release. If we don't know the correct year, the column is left blank. Any assistance to help fill in the blanks would be appreciated.

- When the release date of a *reissue* is not known, the designation "Re" will appear in the year of release column, thus identifying the album as a reissue.

- Comments and information notes placed on the line directly below the record listing generally apply only to the release above the note. When the note describes more than just that one record above, appropriate wording, such as "The above two albums have a gatefold cover," is used.

- Unusual though it may seem, some show albums have been issued on discs without a label name; some without a catalog number; and, in some cases, they have neither. When a label name is either not shown or is just not known to us, the standard wording is "No Label Shown," even though there may be a label shown. If the catalog number is either missing or is not known to us, we'll just say "No Number Used." Again, if a label name or catalog number was in fact used on any of these, please contact us with the appropriate data and we will make the change.

- There are hundreds of multi-disc albums and extended plays documented in the guide, and most are identified as such. If there are ones we've missed, please let us know. The same goes for any other noteworthy details, such as boxed sets, inserts, bonus booklets, and posters.

WHAT TO EXPECT WHEN SELLING YOUR RECORDS TO A DEALER

As nearly everyone in the hobby knows, there is a significant difference between the prices reported in this guide and the prices that one can expect a dealer to pay when buying records for resale. Unless a dealer is buying for a personal collection and without thoughts of resale, he or she is simply not in a position to pay full price. Dealers work on a percentage basis, largely determined by the total dollar investment, quality, and quantity of material offered as well as the general financial condition and inventory of the dealer at the time.

Another very important consideration is the length of time it will take the dealer to recover at least the amount of the original investment. The greater the demand for the stock and the better the condition, the quicker the return and therefore the greater the percentage that can be paid. Our experience has shown that, day-in and day-out, most dealers will pay from 25% to 50% of *guide* prices. And that's assuming they are planning to resell at guide prices. If they traditionally sell below guide, that will be reflected in what they can pay for stock.

If you have records to sell, it would be wise to check with several shops. In doing so you'll begin to get a good idea of the value of your collection to a dealer.

Also, consult the Directory of Buyers and Sellers in this guide for the names of many dealers who not only might be interested in buying, but from whom many collectible records are available for purchase.

Whether you wish to sell the records you have or add out-of-print discs to your collection, you'll want *DISCoveries* magazine. Each issue is jam-packed with ads, features, discographies, collecting tips, and more. *DISCoveries* is prepared by collectors . . . for collectors. If getting into the record marketplace is important to you, *DISCoveries* is essential (*DISCoveries*, P.O. Box 255, Port Townsend, WA 98368. Phone: 1-800-666-DISC, a toll-free call. Sample issue available upon request).

CONCLUDING THOUGHTS

The purpose of this guide is to report as accurately as possible the most recent prices asked and paid for records within the area of its coverage. There are two key words here that deserve emphasis: **Guide** and **Report**.

We cannot stress enough that this book is only a guide. There always have and always will be instances of records selling well above and below the prices shown within these pages. These extremes are recognized in the final averaging process; but it's still important to understand that just because we've reported a 30-year-old record as having a $50-$75 near-mint value doesn't mean that a collector of that material should be hesitant to pay $100 for it. How badly he or she wants it and how often it's possible to purchase it *at any price* should be the prime factors considered, not the fact that we last reported it at a lower price. Of course, we'd like to know about sales of this sort so that the next edition can reflect the new pricing information.

Our objective is to report and reflect record marketplace activity; not to *establish* prices. For that reason, and if given the choice, we'd prefer to be a bit behind the times rather than ahead. With this guide being regularly revised, it will never be long before the necessary changes are reported within these pages.

We encourage record companies, artist management organizations, talent agencies, publicists, and performers to make certain that we are on the active mailing list for new release information, press releases, bios, publicity photos, and anything pertaining to recordings.

There is an avalanche of helpful information in this guide to aid the collector in determining what is valuable and what may not be worth fooling with, but the wise fan will also keep abreast of current trends and news through the pages of the fanzines and publications devoted to his/her favorite forms of music.☐

A

ACTION JACKSON
Soundtrack (1988) ....*Lorimar (S) 90886-1*   88   **$8-10**
Cast: Various artists.

ADDAMS FAMILY
TV Soundtrack (1964) .... *RCA Victor (M) LPM-3421*   64   **30-50**
TV Soundtrack (1964) ....*RCA Victor (S) LSP-3421*   64   **40-60**
Composer: Vic Mizzy.

ADIOS AMIGO
Soundtrack (1976) .... *London (S) PS-666*   76   **10-12**
Composer: Luchi DeJesus. Cast: Infernal Blue Machine.

ADRIFT
Soundtrack (1964) ....*MPO (S) 1001*   71   **50-75**
Composer: Zdenek Liska. Conductor: Frantisek Belfin. Cast: Prague Symphony Orchestra.

ADVANCE TO THE REAR
Soundtrack (1964) .... *Columbia (M) CL-2159*   64   **20-25**
Soundtrack (1964) .... *Columbia (S) CS-8959*   64   **25-30**
Composer: Randy Sparks. Cast: New Christy Minstrels.

ADVENTURERS
Soundtrack (1970) .... *Paramount (S) 6001*   70   **20-25**
Composer: Antonio Carlos Jobim.
Soundtrack (1970) .... *Symbolic (S) SYS-9000*   70   **10-12**
Actual title: *Harold Robbins Presents Music from the Adventurers.*
Composer: Antonio Carlos Jobim. Conductor: Ray Brown. Cast: Sally Kellerman; Morgan
Ames; Peter Christlieb.

ADVENTURES OF A YOUNG MAN:
see HEMINGWAY'S ADVENTURES OF A YOUNG MAN

ADVENTURES OF BARON MUNCHAUSEN
Soundtrack (1988) .... *Warner Bros. (S) 1-25826*   88   **8-10**
Composer: Michael Kamen. Conductor: Michael Kamen.

ADVENTURES OF BULLWHIP GRIFFIN
Soundtrack (1967) ....*Disneyland (M) DQ-1291*   67   **10-15**
Composer: Richard M. Sherman; Robert B. Sherman.

ADVENTURES OF DON JUAN
Soundtrack (1948) ....*TT (Tony Thomas) (SE) MS-11*   **40-50**
Composer: Max Steiner. Conductor: Max Steiner.

ADVENTURES OF HUCKLEBERRY FINN:
see BIG RIVER

ADVENTURES OF MARCO POLO
TV Soundtrack (1956) .... *Columbia (M) ML-5111*   56   **20-30**
Composer: Clay Warnick; Mel Pahl. Conductor: Charles Sanford. Cast: Alfred Drake;
Doretta Morrow.

ADVENTURES OF RIN TIN TIN
TV Soundtrack (1959) ....*Harmony (M) HL-9502*   59   **35-45**
Composer: Ray Carter. Cast: Original TV cast. (With dialogue.)

ADVENTURES OF ROBIN HOOD
Studiotrack (1938) .... *Delos (M) DEL/F2540*   75   **10-12**
Also contains *Requiem for a Cavalier* (biography of Errol Flynn in sound, with interview by Tony
Thomas). Composer: Erich Wolfgang Korngold. Conductor: Erich Wolfgang Korngold.
Cast: Basil Rathbone (narrator).

Studiotrack (1938) .... *Varese Sarabande (SE) 704-180*   83   **$8-10**
  Composer: Erich Wolfgang Korngold. **Conductor:** Varujan Kojian. **Cast:** Utah Symphony
  Orchestra.

ADVENTURES OF SHERLOCK HOLMES
Original Radio Cast .... *Golden Age (M) 5030*   78   **8-10**

ADVENTURES OF THE LONE RANGER:
see LONE RANGER

ADVENTURES OF ZORRO
TV Soundtrack (1956) .... *Disneyland (EP) DEP-3601*   56   **15-25**
  Composer: William Lava; George Bruns and Norman Foster (theme). **Conductor:** William
  Lava. **Cast:** Guy Williams; Henry Calvin.

ADVISE AND CONSENT
Soundtrack (1962) .... *RCA Victor (M) LOC-1068*   62   **35-45**
Soundtrack (1962) .... *RCA Victor (S) LSO-1068*   62   **45-60**
  Composer: Jerry Fielding. **Conductor:** Jerry Fielding.

AFFAIR TO REMEMBER:
see AN AFFAIR TO REMEMBER

AFRICA
TV Soundtrack (1967) .... *MGM (M) E-4462*   67   **35-40**
TV Soundtrack (1967) .... *MGM (S) SE-4462*   67   **40-45**
  Composer: Alex North.

AFRICA ADDIO
Soundtrack (1966) .... *United Artists (M) UAL-4141*   66   **25-30**
Soundtrack (1966) .... *United Artists (S) UAS-6141*   66   **30-35**
  Composer: Riz Ortolani. **Conductor:** Riz Ortolani.

AFTER THE BALL
Original London Cast (1954) .... *AMR (M) 301*   **50-60**
  Composer: Noel Coward. **Conductor:** Philip Martell.

AFTER THE FALL
Original Cast (1962) .... *Mercury (S) OCS-4-620*   65   **40-60**
  Four LP set. A dramatic play by Arthur Miller with the Lincoln Center Repertory Theatre Production Cast.
  Composer: David Amram. **Cast:** Jason Robards Jr.; Barbara Loden; Faye Dunaway; Michael
  Strong; Ralph Meeker.

AFTER THE FOX
Soundtrack (1966) .... *United Artists (M) UAL-4148*   66   **15-20**
Soundtrack (1966) .... *United Artists (S) UAS-5148*   66   **20-30**
Soundtrack (1966) .... *United Artists (S) UA-LA286-G*   74   **8-10**
  Composer: Burt Bacharach. **Conductor:** Burt Bacharach. **Cast:** Peter Sellers; Hollies.

AGAINST A CROOKED SKY
Soundtrack (1975) .... *Embryo (Q) EM-1005-S*   75   **15-20**
  Composer: Lex de Azevedo. **Conductor:** Lex de Azevedo.

AGAINST ALL ODDS
Soundtrack (1984) .... *Atlantic (S) 80152-1*   84   **8-10**
  Composer: Michel Colombier; Larry Carlton. **Cast:** Phil Collins; Stevie Nicks; Peter Gabriel;
  Big Country; Mike Rutherford; Kid Creole and the Coconuts; Larry Carlton; Michel Colombier.

AGATHA
Soundtrack (1975) .... *Casablanca (S) NBLP-7142*   75   **15-25**
  Composer: Johnny Mandell; Paul Williams (lyrics). **Cast:** Pattie Brooks.

AGE OF TELEVISION
Studio Cast (1972) .... *RCA Victor (S) LL-8*   72 $10-20
Full title: *The Age of Television–A Chronicle of the First 25 Years.* From NBC. Includes 32-page booklet.
Cast: Narrated by Milton Berle, Hugh Downs, and Arlene Francis.

AGES OF MAN
Studio Cast (1959) .... *Columbia (M) OL-5390*   59   **15-20**
John Gielgood recites Shakespeare.
Cast: John Gielgood.

AGNES OF GOD
Soundtrack (1985) .... *Varese Sarabande (S) STV-81257*   85   **8-10**
Composer: Georges Delerue. **Conductor:** Georges Delarue.

AGONY AND THE ECSTASY
Soundtrack (1965) ....: *Capitol (M) MAS-2427*   65   **60-70**
Soundtrack (1965) .... *Capitol (S) SMAS-2427*   65   **80-90**
Composer: Alex North. **Conductor:** Alex North.

AIN'T MISBEHAVIN'
Original Cast (1978) .... *RCA Victor (S) DBL2-2965*   78   **10-15**
Double LP set.
Composer: Fats Waller; others. **Conductor:** Luther Henderson. **Cast:** Nell Carter; Andre
DeShields; Armelia McQueen; Ken Page; Charlaine Woodard.

AIN'T SUPPOSED TO DIE A NATURAL DEATH
Original Cast (1972) .... *A&M (S) SP-3510*   72   **25-30**
Double LP set.
Composer: Melvin Van Peebles. **Conductor:** Harold Wheeler. **Cast:** Arthur French; Gloria
Edwards; Ralph Wilcox; Marilyn Coleman; Joe Fields; Carl Gordon; Madge Wells; Barbara
Alston; Toney Brealond; Bill Duke; Clebert Ford; Minnie Gentry; Albert Hall; Jimmy Hayeson;
Sati Jamal; Lauren Jones; Garrett Morris; Dick Williams; Beatrice Winde.

AIR POWER
TV Soundtrack (1957) .... *Columbia (M) ML-5214*   57   **45-55**
TV Soundtrack (1957) .... *Columbia (SE) MS-6029*   58   **70-80**
Composer: Norman Dello Joio. **Conductor:** Eugene Ormandy. **Cast:** Eugene Ormandy and
the Philadelphia Symphony Orchestra.

AIRBORNE SYMPHONY
Original Cast (1946) .... *Columbia (SE) M-34136*   76   **15-20**
Composer: Marc Blitzstein. **Conductor:** Leonard Bernstein. **Cast:** Orson Welles; New York
Philharmonic.

AIRPLANE!
Soundtrack (1980) .... *Regency (S) RY-9601*   80   **8-10**
Also includes themes from: *Jaws, Stayin' Alive, Everything's Coming Up Roses, River of Jordan,
Notre Dame Victory March* and the *Love Theme from Airplane.*
Composer: Elmer Bernstein. **Conductor:** Elmer Bernstein. **Cast:** Shadoe Stevens (narrator);
Robert Hays; Julie Hagerty; Peter Graves; Lloyd Bridges; Lorna Patterson. (With dialogue.)

AIRPORT
Soundtrack (1970) .... *Decca (S) DL-79173*   70   **25-30**
Composer: Alfred Newman. **Conductor:** Alfred Newman. **Cast:** Dean Martin; Burt Lancaster;
Van Heflin; George Kennedy; Jean Seberg; Maureen Stapleton; Jacqueline Bisset.

AIRPORT 1975
Soundtrack (1975) .... *MCA (S) 2082*   75   **10-12**
Composer: John Cacavas. **Conductor:** John Cacavas.

ALADD
TV Soundtrack (1976) .... *Bag-A-Tale (S) BAT-1000* 76 **$15-20**
Composer: Jo Adler; Hannah Price. **Conductor:** Jo Adler. **Cast:** Original Stage Cast - Beverly Cohen; Debra DeLuca; Kathy DeSalvo; Michelle Kahan; Erwin Kaufman; Trish Kondra; Justin Paul; Joyce Schulman.

ALADDIN
TV Soundtrack (1958) .... *Columbia (M) CL-1117* 58 **40-50**
Composer: Cole Porter. **Conductor:** Robert Emmett Dolan. **Cast:** Sal Mineo; Cyril Ritchard; Dennis King; Basil Rathbone; Anna Maria Alberghetti.

ALAKAZAM THE GREAT
Soundtrack (1961) .... *Vee Jay (M) LP-6000* 61 **50-60**
Composer: Les Baxter. **Conductor:** Ian Freebairn-Smith; Albert Harris. **Cast:** Bobby Adano.

ALAMO
Soundtrack (1960) .... *Columbia (M) CL-1558* 60 **10-20**
Soundtrack (1960) .... *Columbia (S) CS-8358* 60 **15-25**
Composer: Dimitri Tiomkin. **Conductor:** Dimitri Tiomkin. **Cast:** Marty Robbins; Brothers Four; John Wayne (with dialogue).
Studiotrack (1960) .... *RCA Victor/Camden (M) CAL-655* 60 **10-15**
Studiotrack (1960) .... *RCA Victor/Camden (S) CAS-655* 60 **10-20**
Cast: Tex Beneke and His Orchestra.

ALAMO BAY
Soundtrack (1985) .... *Slash (S) 1-25311* 85 **8-10**
Composer: Ry Cooder. **Cast:** Ed Harris; Amy Madigan.

ALBERT PECKINGPAW'S REVENGE
Soundtrack (1967) .... *Sidewalk (M) T-5907* 67 **15-20**
Soundtrack (1967) .... *Sidewalk (S) ST-5907* 67 **20-25**
Composer: Harley Hatcher. **Conductor:** Harley Hatcher. **Cast:** Don Epperson; Jimmy August; Lydia Marcelle; Davie Allan and the Arrows; Jan Sweet.

ALBUM OF THE SOUNDTRACK OF THE TRAILER OF THE FILM OF MONTY PYTHON AND THE HOLY GRAIL:
see MONTY PYTHON

ALEXANDER THE GREAT
Soundtrack (1956) .... *Mercury (M) MG-20148* 56 **250-275**
Composer: Mario Nascimbene. **Cast:** Dennis Lotis. (With dialogue.)

ALFIE
Soundtrack (1966) .... *Impulse (M) 9111* 66 **25-30**
Soundtrack (1966) .... *Impulse (S) 9111* 66 **30-35**
Composer: Sonny Rollins. **Conductor:** Oliver Nelson.

ALFRED NEWMAN CONDUCTS HIS GREAT FILM MUSIC
Soundtrack . . . .*Angel (S) S-36066*   73   **$15-20**
Composer: Alfred Newman. Conductor: Alfred Newman. Cast: Hollywood Bowl Symphony
Orchestra.

ALI BABA AND THE 40 THIEVES
Studio Cast (1952) . . . .*MGM (M) E-110*   52   **20-35**
Cast: Lionel Barrymore.

ALICE IN WONDERLAND
Soundtrack (1952) . . . .*Disneyland (M) DQ-1208*   59   **10-12**
Studio Cast (1949) . . . . *Columbia (M) ML-4148*   49   **50-75**
10-inch LP.
Studio Cast (1949) . . . . *Columbia (M) CL-986*   57   **20-30**
Composer: Carmen Dragon. Conductor: Carmen Dragon. Cast: Jane Powell.
Studio Cast (1949) . . . . *Decca (M) DL-5040*   49   **50-75**
Cast: Ginger Rogers.
Studio Cast (1952) . . . .*Mercury (M) MG-25096*   52   **25-50**
Studio Cast . . . .*Disneyland (M) ST-3909*   **15-20**
Includes story booklet.
Also see PETER PAN; TREASURE ISLAND

ALICE THROUGH THE LOOKING GLASS
TV Soundtrack (1966) . . . . *RCA Victor (M) LOC-1130*   66   **25-35**
TV Soundtrack (1966) . . . . *RCA Victor (S) LSO-1130*   66   **30-40**
Composer: Moose Charlap. Conductor: Harper MacKay. Cast: Roy Castle; Robert Coote;
Jimmy Durante; Nanette Fabray; Judi Rolin; Jack Palance; Agnes Moorehead; Ricardo
Montalban.

ALICE'S ADVENTURES IN WONDERLAND
Soundtrack (1972) . . . . *Warner Bros. (S) BS-2671*   72   **15-25**
Composer: John Barry. Conductor: John Barry. Cast: Peter Sellers; Dudley Moore; Fiona
Fullerton; Davy Kaye; Michael Crawford.
Studio Cast (1957) . . . . *Riverside (M) SDP-22*   58   **45-65**
Four LP boxed set, with hardbound book.
Composer: Alec Wilder. Conductor: Barrett Clark. Cast: Cyril Ritchard (vocals and narration).

ALICE'S RESTAURANT
Soundtrack (1969) . . . .*United Artists (S) UAS-5195*   69   **8-12**
Composer: Arlo Guthrie; Garry Sherman. Conductor: Garry Sherman. Cast: Arlo Guthrie;
Tigger Outlaw; Al Schookman.

ALIEN
Soundtrack (1969) . . . .*20th Century-Fox (S) T-593*   79   **8-10**
Composer: Jerry Goldsmith. Conductor: Lionel Newman. Cast: National Philharmonic
Orchestra.
Also see FREUD

ALIENS
Soundtrack (1986) . . . . *Varese Sarabande (S) STV 81283*   86   **10-15**
Composer: Jack Horner. Conductor: Jack Horner. Cast: London Symphony Orchestra.

ALIKI MY LOVE
Soundtrack (1963) . . . .*Fontana (M) MGS-27523*   63   **15-20**
Soundtrack (1963) . . . .*Fontana (S) SRF-67523*   63   **20-25**
Composer: Manos Hadjidakis. Conductor: Manos Hadjidakis.

ALL ABOUT LIFE
Original Cast . . . . *Industrial OC Life XTV 89424/5*   **40-50**
Composer: Jerry Powell. Conductor: Rod Warren. Cast: Michaeil Allinson; Gloria Bleezarde;
Bill Linton; Eliza Ross; Jay Stuart; Ronny Whyte.

ALL AMERICAN
Original Cast (1962) ....*Columbia (M) KOL-5760*   62 $20-25
Original Cast (1962) .... *Columbia (S) KOS-2160*   62   30-35
Original Cast (1962) .... *Columbia (S) AKOS-5760*   8-10
  Conductor: John Morris. **Cast:** Ray Bolger; Eileen Herlie; Ron Husmann; Anita Gillette; Fritz
  Weaver.
Soundtrack (1962) .... *Challenge (M) CHL-614*   62   15-20
Soundtrack (1962) .... *Challenge (S) CHS-2514*   62   20-25
  Cast: Champs; Lionel Hampton; Les Elgart.
Studiotrack (1962) .... *MGM (M) E-4034*   62   10-12
Studiotrack (1962) .... *MGM (S) SE-4034*   62   12-18
  Composer: Charles Strouse; Lee Adams. **Conductor:** LeRoy Holmes. **Cast:** LeRoy Holmes
  and His Orchestra.
Studiotrack (1962) .... *Mercury (M) MG-20707*   62   10-15
Studiotrack (1962) .... *Mercury (S) SR-20707*   62   10-15

ALL AMERICAN BOY
Original Radio Cast .... *Golden Age (M) 5033*   78   5-10

ALL BY MYSELF:
  see ANNA RUSSELL'S LITTLE SHOW

ALL DOGS GO TO HEAVEN
Soundtrack .... *Curb (S) CRB-10403*   8-10
  Cast: Irene Cara; Freddie Jackson.

ALL HANDS ON DECK
Soundtrack (1961) .... *Dot (EP) DEP-1098*   61   10-15
  Composer: Jay Livingston; Ray Evans. **Cast:** Pat Boone; Buddy Hackett.

ALL IN LOVE
Original Cast (1961) .... *Mercury (M) OCM-2204*   61   25-35
Original Cast (1961) .... *Mercury (S) OCS-6204*   61   35-45
  Composer: Jacques Urbont; Bruce Geller. **Conductor:** Jacques Urbont. **Cast:** David Atkinson;
  Lee Cass; Gaylea Byrne; Dom DeLouise; Christina Gillespie; Mimi Randolph; Michael Davis.

ALL IN ONE:
  see TROUBLE IN TAHITI

ALL IN THE FAMILY
TV Soundtrack (1971) .... *Atlantic (S) SD-7210*   71   10-12
  Includes four-page booklet.
  Cast: Carroll O'Connor; Jean Stapleton.

ALL IN THE FAMILY - 2ND ALBUM
TV Soundtrack (1971) .... *Atlantic (S) 7232*   72   10-12
  Cast: Carroll O'Connor; Jean Stapleton.

ALL NIGHT LONG
Soundtrack (1962) .... *Epic (M) LA-16032*   62   25-30
Soundtrack (1962) .... *Epic (S) BA-17032*   62   30-35
  Cast: Philip Green; Johnny Scott; Dave Brubeck; Johnny Dankworth.

ALL NIGHT STRUT
Original Cast (1976) .... *Playhouse Square (S) PHS-CLE 1S-1001*   76   40-60
  Composer: Various. **Conductor:** Tom Fitt. **Cast:** Robert Chidsey; Dean Hill; Elaine Psihountas;
  Laura Robinson.

ALL THAT JAZZ
Soundtrack (1979) .... *Casablanca (S) NBLP-7198*   79   10-12
Soundtrack (1979) .... *Casablanca (S) 822869-1*   Re   8-10
  Composer: Various. **Conductor:** Ralph Burns. **Cast:** George Benson; Peter Allen; Ben Vereen.

ALL THAT MONEY CAN BUY:
see GREAT FILM CLASSICS

ALL THE LOVING COUPLES
Soundtrack (1969) .... *GNP/Crescendo (S) 2051*   69   **$25-30**
  Composer: Casanova (Les Baxter).

ALL THE RIGHT MOVES
Soundtrack (1983) .... *Casablanca (S) 422-81444*   83   **8-10**
  Cast: Jennifer Warnes; Frankie Miller; Junior; others.

ALL THE RIGHT NOISES
Soundtrack (1971) .... *Buddah (S) BDS-5132*   71   **20-25**
  Composer: Melanie Safka.

ALL THIS AND WORLD WAR II
Soundtrack (1977) .... *20th Century-Fox (S) T2-540*   77   **20-25**
  Double LP boxed set. Includes 36-page booklet and T-shirt ad flyer.
  Cast: Ambrosia; Elton John; Bee Gees; David Essex; Paul McCartney and Wings; Frankie Laine;
  4 Seasons; Henry Gross; Tina Turner; Leo Sayer; Rod Stewart; Keith Moon; Helen Reddy; Status
  Quo; Frankie Valli; Bryan Ferry; Jeff Lynne; Roy Wood; Brothers Johns Johnson; Richard
  Cocciante; London Symphony Orchestra.

ALLEGRO
Original Cast (1947) .... *RCA Victor (M) LOC-1099*   65   **40-50**
  LP release of material originally issued on 78 rpm singles.
Original Cast (1947) .... *RCA Victor (SE) LSO-1099*   65   **50-60**
Original Cast (1947) .... *RCA Victor (SE) CBM1-2758*   78   **8-10**
  Composer: Richard Rodgers; Oscar Hammerstein. Conductor: Salvatore Dell'Isola.
  Cast: John Battles; Annamary Dickey; John Conti; Lisa Kirk; Patricia Bybell; William Ching;
  Julia Humphries; Roberta Jonay; Sylvia Karlton; Kathryn Lee; Muriel O'Malley; Robert Reeves;
  Gloria Wills.

ALLEN, STEVE:
see STEVE ALLEN

ALLNIGHTER
Soundtrack (1987) .... *Chameleon (S) CHST-9601*   87   **8-12**
Soundtrack (1979) .... *Chameleon (S) D1-74792*   Re   **8-10**

ALMOST PERFECT AFFAIR
Soundtrack (1979) .... *Varese Sarabande (S) STV-81132*   79   **8-12**
  Composer: Georges Delerue. Conductor: Georges Delerue.

ALMOST SUMMER
Soundtrack (1978) .... *MCA (S) 3037*   78   **8-12**
  Composer: Ron Altbach; Charles Lloyd; Brian Wilson; Mike Love; Al Jardine. Cast: Mike
  Love and Celebration; Fresh; High Inergy.

ALOHA FROM HAWAII VIA SATELLITE:
see ELVIS - ALOHA FROM HAWAII VIA SATELLITE

ALTERED STATES
Soundtrack (1980) .... *RCA Victor (S) ABL1-3983*   80   **8-10**
  Composer: John Corigliano. Conductor: Christopher Keene. Cast: Various artists.

ALVIN SHOW
TV Soundtrack (1961) .... *Liberty (M) LRP-3209*   61   **10-15**
TV Soundtrack (1961) .... *Liberty (S) LST-7209*   61   **15-20**
  Composer: Ross Bagdasarian (David Seville). Cast: David Seville and the Chipmunks (Alvin,
  Theodore, and Simon).

ALWAYS
   Soundtrack (1990) ....*MCA (S) 8036* 90   **$8-10**
     Composer: John Williams (original music); others. **Conductor:** John Williams; others.
     Cast: J.D. Souther; Jimmy Buffett; Lyle Lovett; Denette Hoover; Michael Smotherman;
     Platters; John Williams and His Orchestra.

AMADEUS
   Soundtrack (1984) ....*A&M (S) SP-91001* 84   **10-12**
     Double LP set.
     Composer: Wolfgang Amadeus Mozart. **Conductor:** Neville Marriner.

AMAHL AND THE NIGHT VISITORS
   TV Soundtrack (1951) ....*RCA Victor (EP) ERA-1701* 52   **10-20**
   TV Soundtrack (1951) ....*RCA Victor (M) LPM-1701* 52   **20-40**
     10-inch LP.
   TV Soundtrack (1951) ....*RCA Victor (M) VIC-1512* 57   **15-25**
     Conductor: Thomas Schippers. **Cast:** Chet Allen; Rosemary Kuhlmann (NBC-TV cast).
   TV Soundtrack (1963) ....*RCA Victor (M) LPM-2762* 63   **10-15**
   TV Soundtrack (1963) ....*RCA Victor (S) LSC-2762* 63   **15-20**
     Composer: Gian-Carlo Menotti. **Conductor:** Herbert Grossman. **Cast:** Kurt Yaghijian;
     Martha King; NBC Opera Co.

AMARCORD
   Soundtrack (1975) .... *RCA Victor (S) ARL1-0907* 75   **15-20**
     Composer: Nino Rota. **Conductor:** Carlo Savina.

AMAZING GRACE AND CHUCK
   Soundtrack (1987) ....*Varese Sarabande (S) STV-81312* 87   **10-12**
     Composer: Elmer Bernstein. **Conductor:** Elmer Bernstein.

AMBASSADOR
   Original London Cast (1972) .... *RCA Victor (S) SER-5618* 72   **40-50**
     Composer: Don Gohman; Hal Hackady. **Conductor:** Gareth Davies. **Cast:** Howard Keel;
     Danielle Darrieux; Margaret Courtenay; Toni-Sue Burley; Blain Fairman; Neville Jason; Judith
     Paris; Isobel Stuart; Nevil Whiting.

AMERICA, AMERICA
   Soundtrack (1963) ....*Warner Bros. (M) W-1527* 63   **20-25**
   Soundtrack (1963) ....*Warner Bros. (S) WS-1527* 63   **25-30**
     Composer: Manos Hadjidakis. **Conductor:** Manos Hadjidakis.

AMERICA THE BEAUTIFUL
   Studio Cast (1962) ....*Columbia (M) ML-5668* 61   **10-20**
     Cast: Vincent Price.

AMERICAN ANTHEM
   Soundtrack (1986) ....*Atlantic (S) 81661-1* 86   **8-10**
     Cast: John Parr; Stevie Nicks; Graham Nash; Andy Taylor; Chris Thompson; Alan Silvestri;Inxs.

AMERICAN DREAMER
   Soundtrack (1971) ....*Mediarts (S) 41-12* 71   **10-15**
     Cast: Gene Clark; Hello People; John Manning; John Buck Wilkin; Abbey Road Singers.

AMERICAN FLYERS
   Soundtrack (1985) ....*GRP (S) AP-2001* 85   **8-10**
     Composer: Lee Ritenour; Greg Mathieson; others. **Cast:** Creedence Clearwater Revival; Glenn
     Shorrock; Danny Hutton; Chris Isaak.

AMERICAN GAME
   Soundtrack (1980) ....*Buddah (S) BDS-5724* 80   **10-12**
     Composer: Jeffrey Kaufman. **Conductor:** Jeffrey Kaufman. **Cast:** Richie Havens; Gail Wynters.

AMERICAN GIGOLO
Soundtrack (1980) . . . .*Polydor (S) PD-1-6259*   80   **$8-10**
  Composer: Giorgio Moroder. **Conductor:** Giorgio Moroder. **Cast:** Blondie; Cheryl Barnes;
  Giorgia Moroder; Harold Faltermeyer (keyboards).

AMERICAN GRAFFITI
Soundtrack (1973) . . . . *MCA (S) 2-8001*   73   **10-12**
  Double LP set.
  Composer: Various. **Cast:** Buddy Holly; Crests; Beach Boys; Fats Domino; Buster Brown;
  Chuck Berry; Platters; Flamingos; Silhouettes; Five Satins; Bobby Freeman; Buddy Knox;
  Del-Vikings; Johnny Burnette; Lee Dorsey; Mark Dinning; Continental Kids; Monotones; Big
  Bopper; Sonny Til and the Orioles; Spaniels; Booker T. and the MGs; Fleetwoods; Diamonds;
  Clovers; Joey Dee and the Starliters; Tempos; Heartbeats; Frankie Lymon and the Teenagers;
  Regents; Skyliners; Del Shannon; Wolfman Jack (dialogue).

AMERICAN HOT WAX
Soundtrack (1978) . . . .*A&M (S) SP-6500*   78   **15-20**
  Double LP set.
  Composer: Various. **Cast:** Chuck Berry; Buddy Holly; Jerry Lee Lewis; Bobby Darin; Little
  Richard; Jackie Wilson; Delights; Chesterfields; Planatones; Clark Otis; Tammy and the Tulips.

AMERICAN IN PARIS:
see AN AMERICAN IN PARIS

AMERICAN POP
Soundtrack (1981) . . . .*MCA (S) 5201*   81   **8-10**
  Cast: Pat Benatar; Big Brother and the Holding Company; Mamas and the Papas; Peter, Paul, and
  Mary; Marcy Levy; Jimi Hendrix Experience; Dave Brubeck Quartet; Sam Cooke; Fabian; Doors.

AMERICAN RABBIT
Soundtrack . . . .*Rhino (S) RNEP-70614*   **8-10**
  Cast: Flo and Eddie.

AMERICAN TAIL
Soundtrack (1986) . . . .*MCA (S) 39096*   86   **8-10**
  Composer: James Horner. **Conductor:** James Horner. **Cast:** Linda Ronstadt; James Ingram;
  Dom Deluise; Philip Glasser; Nehemiah Persoff; John Guarnieri; Warren Hays; Christopher
  Plummer; Betsy Cathcart.

AMERICAN WEREWOLF IN LONDON
Soundtrack (1981) . . . .*Casablanca (S) NBLP-7260*   81   **8-10**
  Composer: Elmer Bernstein; others. **Cast:** Meco.

AMERICANIZATION OF EMILY
Soundtrack (1964) . . . . *Reprise (M) R-6151*   64   **20-30**
Soundtrack (1964) . . . . *Reprise (S) RS-6151*   64   **25-35**
  Composer: Johnny Mandel.

AMERICATHON
Soundtrack (1979) . . . .*Lorimar (S) JS-36174*   79   **10-12**
  Cast: Beach Boys (with their otherwise unavailable *It's a Beautiful Day*); Elvis Costello; Nick
  Lowe; Eddie Money; Tom Scott; Harvey Korman; Zane Buzby.

AMITYVILLE HORROR
Soundtrack (1979) . . . . *American Int'l (S) AILP-3003*   79   **8-10**
  Composer: Lalo Schifrin. **Conductor:** Lalo Schifrin.

AMO NON AMO:
see I LOVE YOU, I LOVE YOU, I LOVE YOU NOT

AMONG FRIENDS - WAA-MU SHOW OF 1960

Original Cast (1960) . . . . *RCA Victor Custom (M) L70P-5670*   60   **$100-150**
  By the cast of Northwestern University. One of the dancers in the cast was Ann-Margret Olson, better
  known as Ann-Margret.
  Composer: Lawrence Grossman. **Conductor:** John Paynter. **Cast:** Hal Warren; Show Girls;
  Choral Girls; Martha Stickney; Suzanne Lehman; James Rusk; Scott Smith; Gary Crabb; David
  Soltzer; Thomas Phillips; Robin Deck; Ann Fraser; Mimi Romann; Jill Milliken; Lawrence
  Gossman (orchestra); Ann-Margret (dancer).
  Also see BE MY GUEST

AMORE IN 4 DIMENSIONI:
see LOVE IN 4 DIMENSIONS

AMOROUS ADVENTURES OF MOLL FLANDERS

Soundtrack (1965) . . . . *RCA Victor (M) LOC-1113*   65   **35-50**
Soundtrack (1965) . . . . *RCA Victor (S) LSO-1113*   65   **65-80**
  Composer: John Addison. **Conductor:** John Addison.

AN ACTION HISTORY

Studio Cast (1957) . . . . *Columbia (M) KL-5270*   57   **20-30**
  Cast: Buddy Blattner (narrator).

AN AFFAIR TO REMEMBER

Soundtrack (1957) . . . . *Columbia (M) CL-1031*   57   **50-75**
  Composer: Hugo Friedhofer; Harry Warren. **Conductor:** Lionel Newman.

AN AMERICAN IN PARIS

Soundtrack (1951) . . . . *MGM (EP) X-93*   51   **10-20**
Soundtrack (1951) . . . . *MGM (M) E-93*   51   **45-55**
  10-inch LP.
Soundtrack (1951) . . . . *MGM (M) E-3232*   55   **25-35**
Soundtrack (1951) . . . . *MGM (M) E-3767*   59   **20-25**
  One side has music from *Show Boat*.
Soundtrack (1951) . . . . *Metro (M) M-552*   66   **12-18**
Soundtrack (1951) . . . . *Metro (SE) SM-552*   66   **15-20**
Soundtrack (1951) . . . . *MCA (SE) 1427*   **8-10**
  Composer: George Gershwin (music); Ira Gershwin (lyrics). **Conductor:** Johnny Green; Saul
  Chaplin. **Cast:** Gene Kelly; Leslie Caron; Oscar Levant; MGM Studio Orchestra.

AN ELEPHANT CALLED SLOWLY

Soundtrack (1970) . . . . *Bell (S) B-1202*   70   **15-20**
  Composer: Howard Blake. **Conductor:** Howard Blake.

AN EVENING WITH ALAN JAY LERNER

Original Cast (1971) . . . . *Laureate Records (S) LL-602*   77   **10-12**
  Issued as part of the "Lyrics and Lyricists Series."
  Cast: Alan Jay Lerner; Bobbi Baird; J.T. Cromwell; Barbara Williams.

AN EVENING WITH BEATRICE LILLY
Original Cast (1952) . . . . *London (M) 1373*   56   **$40-50**
Original Cast (1952) . . . . *London (M) 5212*   Re   **15-20**
Cast: Beatrice Lilly; Eadie and Rack (pianos).

AN EVENING WITH BORIS KARLOFF AND HIS FRIENDS
Soundtrack (1967) . . . . *Decca (M) DL-4833*   67   **15-20**
Music from: *Dracula* (1931), *Frankenstein* (1932), *Bride of Frankenstein* (1935), *Son of Frankenstein* (1939), *The Wolfman* (1941), and *House of Frankenstein* (1944).
Composer: William Loose; Frank Skinner; Hans J. Salter; Charles Previn; Franz Waxman.
Cast: Boris Karloff (narrator).

AN EVENING WITH DIANA ROSS
Original Cast (1976) . . . . *Motown (S) M7-877R2*   76   **10-12**
Double LP set.
Conductor: Gil Askey. Cast: Diana Ross; Brenda Jones; Shirley Jones; Valorie Jones.

AN EVENING WITH FRED EBB AND JOHN KANDER
Original Cast (1973) . . . . *Laureate Records (S) LL-605*   78   **10-12**
Issued as part of the "Lyrics and Lyricists Series."
Cast: Fred Ebb; John Kander.

AN EVENING WITH JEROME KERN
Original Cast (1959) . . . . *United Artists (M) UAL 3039*   59   **20-25**
Composer: Jerome Kern; Oscar Hammerstein II; Otto Harbach; E.Y. Harburg; Ira Gershwin; others. Conductor: Joseph Ricardel. Cast: Wilbur Evans; Dolores Perry; Bill Tabbert.

AN EVENING WITH JERRY HERMAN
Original Cast (1974) . . . . *Laureate Records (S) LL-606*   78   **10-12**
Issued as part of the "Lyrics and Lyricists Series."
Cast: Jerry Herman; Lisa Kirk: Joe Masiell; Carol Dorian.

AN EVENING WITH JOHNNY MERCER
Original Cast Live (1971) . . . . *Laureate Records (S) LL-601*   77   **10-12**
Issued as part of the "Lyrics and Lyricists Series."
Cast: Johnny Mercer; Margaret Whiting; Robert Sands.

AN EVENING WITH LERNER AND LOEWE
Studio Cast (1959) . . . . *RCA Victor (S) LSP-6005*   59   **15-25**
Double LP set. Has selections from *My Fair Lady* and *Paint Your Wagon*.
Composer: Alan J. Lerner; Frederick Loewe. Cast: Jane Powell; Phil Harris; Jan Peerce; Robert Merrill.

AN EVENING WITH MIKE NICHOLS AND ELAINE MAY
Original Cast (1960) . . . . *Mercury (M) OCM-2200*   60   **30-35**
Original Cast (1960) . . . .*Mercury (S) OCS-6200*   60   **45-50**
Above two LPs have a gatefold cover.
Original Cast (1960) . . . .*Mercury (M) MG-20865*   64   **15-20**
Original Cast (1960) . . . . *Mercury (S) SR-60865*   64   **25-30**
Original Cast (1960) . . . .*Mercury (S) 2-628*   Re   **10-15**
Has Nichols and May material previously unissued on LP.
Cast: Mike Nichols; Elaine May.

AN EVENING WITH QUENTIN CRISP
Original Cast (1978) . . . . *DRG (S) S26-5188*   78   **20-30**
Double LP set.
Cast: Quentin Crisp (dialogue).

AN EVENING WITH RICHARD NIXON
Original Cast (1972) . . . . *Ode (S) SP-77015*   72   **20-30**
An original play by Gore Vidal.
Cast: Saliva Sisters; Gene Rupert; Humbert Allen Astredo; Phillip Sterling; George S. Irving; Robert King.

AN EVENING WITH SAMMY CAHN
Original Cast (1972) .... *Laureate Records (S) LL-604*   78   **$10-12**
  Issued as part of the "Lyrics and Lyricists Series."
  Composer: Sammy Cahn. **Cast:** Sammy Cahn; Bobbi Baird; Shirley Lemmon; Jon Peck.

AN EVENING WITH SHELDON HARNICK
Original Cast (1971) .... *Laureate Records (S) LL-603*   77   **10-12**
  Issued as part of the "Lyrics and Lyricists Series."
  Cast: Sheldon Harnick; Margery Gray; Mary Louise.

AN EVENING WITH W.S. GILBERT
Original Cast .... *Original Cast (S) OC-8026*   **8-12**
  Composer: Arthur Sullivan; Osmond Carr; Edward German; W.S. Gilbert. **Cast:** Lloyd
  Harris; Alfred Heller (piano).

ANASTASIA
Soundtrack (1956) .... *Decca (M) DL-8460*   56   **40-50**
Soundtrack (1956) .... *MCA (S) 7137*   73   **8-12**
Soundtrack (1956) .... *Varese Sarabande (SE) STV 81125*   82   **8-10**
  Composer: Alfred Newman. **Conductor:** Alfred Newman. **Cast:** Ingrid Bergman.

ANASTASIA - THE MYSTERY OF ANNA
Soundtrack .... *Southern Cross (S) SCRS-1015*   **8-10**
  Conductor: Rosenthal. **Cast:** Munich Philharmonic Orchestra.

ANATOMY OF A MURDER
Soundtrack (1959) .... *Columbia (EP) B-13601*   59   **10-20**
Soundtrack (1959) .... *Columbia (M) CL-1360*   59   **35-45**
Soundtrack (1959) .... *Columbia (S) CS-8166*   59   **45-60**
Soundtrack (1959) .... *Columbia Special Products (S) JCS-8166*   82   **8-10**
  Composer: Duke Ellington. **Conductor:** Duke Ellington. **Cast:** Ben Gazzara; Lee Remick;
  James Stewart.
Soundtrack (1959) .... *Coronet (M) CX-99*   **10-15**
  Composer: Duke Ellington. **Conductor:** Bob Friedman. **Cast:** Bob Friedman Orchestra.

ANCHORS AWEIGH
Soundtrack (1979) .... *Sandy Hook (S) SH-2024*   79   **8-10**
  Composer: Jule Styne. **Cast:** Frank Sinatra; Gene Kelley; Kathryn Grayson.

AND AWA-A-Y WE GO
TV Cast (1954) .... *Capitol (M) EBF-511*   54   **40-60**
  Double EP, boxed set.
TV Cast (1954) .... *Capitol (M) H-511*   54   **50-75**
  10-inch LP. Jackie Gleason performs as the following characters, popularized on his television show:
  Ralph Kramden; Joe the Bartender; Reggie Van Gleason III; The Poor Soul; The Loud Mouth; and
  Fenwick Babbit.
  Cast: Jackie Gleason.

AND GOD CREATED WOMAN
Soundtrack (1957) .... *Decca (M) DL-8685*   57   **$60-75**
    Composer: Paul Misraki. Cast: Bridget Bardot (French dialogue).

AND GOD SAID
Studio Cast (1959) .... *Epic (M) 5LN-3534*   59   **10-15**
Studio Cast (1959) .... *Epic (S) 6BN-511*   59   **10-15**
    Biblical stories.
    Composer: God. Cast: Dana Andrews (narrator).

ANDERSONVILLE TRIAL
Original Cast (1960) .... *20th Century-Fox (M) FDX-4000*   60   **40-50**
Original Cast (1960) .... *20th Century-Fox (S) SFX-4000*   60   **50-60**
    A dramatic play by Saul Levitt, produced by Jose Ferrer.
    Composer: Henry Nemo. Conductor: Hugo Montenegro. Cast: George C. Scott; Albert Dekker;
    Herbert Berghot; Russell Hardie; Robert Carroll; Robert Gerringer; James Greene.

ANDRE PREVIN - COMPOSER, CONDUCTOR, ARRANGER:
see INVITATION TO THE DANCE

ANDROCLES AND THE LION
TV Soundtrack (1967) .... *RCA Victor (M) LOC-1141*   67   **30-35**
TV Soundtrack (1967) .... *RCA Victor (S) LSO-1141*   67   **40-45**
    Composer: Richard Rodgers. Conductor: Jay Blackton. Cast: Noel Coward; Ed Ames; Inga
    Swenson; John Cullum; Kurt Kasznar; Norman Wisdom.

ANDROMEDA STRAIN
Soundtrack (1971) .... *Kapp (S) KRS-5513*   71   **35-50**
    Standard, square cover.
Soundtrack (1971) .... *Kapp (S) KRS-5513*   71 · **75-100**
    Hexagon cover.
    Composer: Gill Melle.

ANDY GRIFFITH SHOW
TV Soundtrack (1961) .... *Capitol (M) T-1611*   61   **15-20**
TV Soundtrack (1961) .... *Capitol (S) ST-1611*   61   **20-25**
    Composer: Earle Hagen. Conductor: Earle Hagen. Cast: Andy Griffith.

ANDY WARHOL'S FRANKENSTEIN
Soundtrack (1974) .... *Varese Sarabande (S) STV 81157*   82   **8-12**
    Composer: Claudio Gizzi.

ANDY WILLIAMS SHOW
TV Soundtrack (1971) .... *Columbia (S) KC-30105*   71   **8-12**
    Includes illustrated booklet.
    Cast: Andy Williams.

ANGEL
Original Cast (1978) .... *Angel (S) GUA-001*   78   **10-20**
    Broadway show, recorded privately by producers.
    Composer: Gary Geld; Peter Udell. Conductor: William Cox. Cast: Don Scardino; Joel
    Higgens; Frances Sternhagen; Fred Gwynne.

ANGEL, ANGEL, DOWN WE GO
Soundtrack (1970) .... *Tower (S) ST-5161*   70   **15-25**
    This film is also known as *Cult of the Damned.*
    Composer: Barry Mann; Cynthia Weil; Fred Karger.

ANGEL HEART
Soundtrack (1987) .... *Antilles New Directions (S) 91035*   87   **8-10**
    Composer: Trevor Jones. Conductor: Trevor Jones. Cast: Bessie Smith; Brownie McGhee;
    Courtney Pine; LaVern Baker; Lilian Boutte; Glen Gray and the Casa Loma Orchestra.

ANGEL UNCHAINED
Soundtrack (1970) .... *American Int'l (S) A-1037* 70   **$10-15**
    Composer: Randy Sparks. **Conductor:** Randy Sparks. **Cast:** Randy Sparks; Don Stroud; Luke
    Askew; Larry Bishop; Tyne Daly.

ANGELS DIE HARD
Soundtrack (1970) .... *UNI (S) 73091* 70   **20-25**
    Composer: Various. **Conductor:** Richard Hieronymous. **Cast:** Fever Tree; Sylvanus; Dewey
    Martin and Medicine Ball; East-West Pipline; Mark Eric; Rabbit MacKay.

ANGELS FROM HELL
Soundtrack (1968) .... *Tower (S) ST-5128* 68   **20-25**
    Composer: Stu Phillips. **Conductor:** Stu Phillips. **Cast:** Peanut Butter Conspiracy; Lollipop
    Shoppe; Ted Marckland.

ANIMAL HOUSE
Soundtrack (1978) .... *MCA (S) 3046* 78   **8-10**
    Composer: Elmer Bernstein; others. **Conductor:** Elmer Bernstein. **Cast:** John Belushi; Sam
    Cooke; Bobby Lewis; Lloyd Williams; Paul and Paula; Stephen Bishop; Chris Montez; Elmer
    Bernstein; National Lampoon. (With dialogue.)

ANIMALYMPICS
Soundtrack (1980) .... *A&M (S) SP-4810* 80   **8-10**
    Composer: Graham Gouldman.

ANKLES AWEIGH
Original Cast (1955) .... *Decca (M) DL-9025* 55   **75-85**
Original Cast (1955) .... *AEI (M) 1104* 76   **8-10**
    Composer: Sammy Fain; Dan Shapiro. **Cast:** Betty Kean; Jane Kean; Lew Parker; Mark Dawson;
    Gabriel Dell; Betty George; Ray Mason.

ANNA / HELL RAIDERS OF THE DEEP
Soundtrack (1951) .... *MGM (EP) X-1108* 54   **10-20**
    Cast: Silvana Mangano.

ANNA RUSSELL'S LITTLE SHOW (ALL BY MYSELF)
Original Cast (1953) .... *Columbia (M) ML-4594* 53   **25-30**
Original Cast (1953) .... *Columbia (M) ML-4733* 53   **25-30**
Original Cast (1953) .... *Columbia (M) ML-4928* 54   **25-30**
Original Cast (1956) .... *Columbia (M) ML-5036* 56   **20-25**
Original Cast (1957) .... *Columbia (M) ML-5195* 57   **20-25**
Original Cast (1958) .... *Columbia (M) ML-5295* 58   **20-25**
Original Cast (1953-1958) .... *Columbia (M) MG-31199* 72   **10-12**
    Double LP set, with excerpts. A 1964 revival was titled *All By Myself* (though there is no LP with this title).
    Each of the original six LPs is different, as the show was regularly changed. For example, each show has a
    different pianist.
    Composer: Anna Russell; others. **Cast:** Anna Russell.

ANNE OF GREEN GABLES
Canadian Studio Cast (1971) .... *Dominion (S) LP-1368* 71   **20-30**
    Side two has one song from each of the following Canadian musicals: *The Navy Show, Mr. Scrooge,*
    Turvey, The Pied Piper, Willie the Squouse and *Wild Rose.*
    Composer: Norman Campbell; Donald Harron. **Conductor:** John Fenwick; Al Baculis.

ANNE OF THE THOUSAND DAYS
Soundtrack (1970) .... *Decca (S) DL-79174* 70   **30-35**
    One side has samples of Tudor Court music, by the New York Pro Musica, arranged by John Reeves
    White and Noah Greenberg.
    Composer: Georges Delerue; John Hale. **Cast:** Gary Bond.

ANNETTE (AND OTHER WALT DISNEY SERIALS)
TV Soundtrack (1958) .... *Mickey Mouse (M) MM-24* 58   **40-50**
    Cast: Annette Funicello; others.

ANNIE

Original Cast (1977) .... *Columbia (S) PS-34712*	77	**$8-10**
Original Cast (1977) .... *Columbia (S) HS-44712*	79	**10-15**

Half-speed mastered.

Composer: Charles Strouse; Martin Charnin. **Conductor:** Peter Howard. **Cast:** Andrea McArdle; Dorothy Loudon; Reid Shelton; Laurie Beechman; Edie Cowan; Donald Craig; Barbara Erwin; Sandy Faison; Robert Fitch; Raymond Thorne; Penny Worth.

Original Cast (1977) .... *Columbia (S) JS-34712*	Re	**8-10**
Soundtrack (1982) .... *Columbia (S) JS-38000*	82	**8-10**

Composer: Charles Strouse; Martin Charnin. **Conductor:** Ralph Burns. **Cast:** Aileen Quinn; Carol Burnett; Albert Finney; Ann Reinking; Tim Curry; Bernadette Peters.

ANNIE GET YOUR GUN

Original Cast (1946) .... *Decca (EP) ED-805*	49	**15-20**
Original Cast (1946) .... *Decca (M) DL-8001*	49	**30-40**
Original Cast (1946) .... *Decca (M) DL-9018*	55	**15-20**
Original Cast (1946) .... *Decca (SE) DL7-9018*	59	**15-20**
Original Cast (1946) .... *MCA (SE) 2031e*	73	**10-12**
Original Cast (1946) .... *MCA (SE) 37092*	81	**5-8**

Composer: Irving Berlin. **Conductor:** Jay Blackton. **Cast:** Ethel Merman; Ray Middleton; Robert Lenn; Garth, Turner and Bibb; Kathleen Carnes.

Original Revival Cast (1966) .... *RCA Victor (M) LOC-1124*	66	**10-15**
Original Revival Cast (1966) .... *RCA Victor (S) LSO-1124*	66	**8-15**

Conductor: Franz Allers. **Cast:** Ethel Merman; Bruce Yarnell; Benay Venuta; Jerry Orbach; Ronn Carrol; Rufus Smith.

Studio Cast (1963) .... *Columbia (M) OL-5960*	63	**10-15**
Studio Cast (1963) .... *Columbia (S) OS-2360*	63	**15-20**
Studio Cast (1963) .... *Columbia (S) PC-2360*	Re	**8-10**
Studio Cast (1963) .... *Harmony (S) KH-30396*	71	**10-12**
Studio Cast (1963) .... *Columbia Special Products (S) CS-2360*	76	**8-10**

Conductor: Franz Allers. **Cast:** Doris Day; Robert Goulet; Kelly Brown; Renee Winters; Leonard Stokes; Jack and Jill Little People; Malcolm Dodds Quartet.

Studio Cast (1973) .... *London (S) XPS-905*	73	**15-20**

Conductor: Stanley Black. **Cast:** Ethel Merman; Neilson Taylor; Neil Howlett; London Festival Orchestra and Chorus; Leslie Fyson; Benay Venuta.

Soundtrack (1950) .... *MGM (M) E-3227*	55	**25-30**

One side has music from *Easter Parade*.

Soundtrack (1950) .... *MGM (M) E-509*	50	**40-50**

10-inch LP.

Soundtrack (1950) .... *MGM (M) E-3768*	60	**20-25**

One side has music from *Three Little Words*.

Soundtrack (1950) .... *MGM (EP) X-50*	50	**15-20**
Soundtrack (1950) .... *Metro (M) M-548*	65	**15-20**
Soundtrack (1950) .... *Metro (SE) MS-548*	65	**15-20**

Soundtrack (1950) .... *MCA (SE) 1626*   Re   **$8-10**
   Conductor: Adolph Deutsch. **Cast:** Betty Hutton; Howard Keel; Louis Calhern; Keenan Wynn.
Studiotrack (1953) .... *RCA Victor (M) LM-1798*   53   **20-30**
Studiotrack (1961) .... *Columbia (M) CL-1623*   61   **15-20**
   Actual title: *(Hit Songs from) Annie Get Your Gun.* One side has music from *Do Re Mi.*
   Conductor: Luther Henderson. **Cast:** Polly Bergen.
TV Soundtrack (1957) .... *Capitol (EP) EDM-913*   57   **10-20**
   Composer: Irving Berlin.
TV Soundtrack (1957) .... *Capitol (M) W-913*   57   **25-30**
   Conductor: Louis Adrian. **Cast:** Mary Martin; John Raitt.
Soundtrack (1949) .... *Sandy Hook (M) SH-2053*   81   **8-10**
   Previously unreleased soundtrack music.
   Composer: Irving Berlin. **Cast:** Judy Garland; Howard Keel; Louis Calhern; Keenan Wynn;
   Benay Venuta; Frank Morgan.
Studiotrack (1954) .... *RCA Victor (EP) ERA-1798*   54   **10-15**
Studiotrack (1954) .... *RCA Victor (M) LM-1798*   54   **15-25**
   Conductor: Arthur Fiedler. **Cast:** Boston Pops Orchestra.
Studiotrack (1955) .... *RCA Victor/Camden (M) CL-154*   55   **15-25**
   Actual title: *Annie Get Your Gun Gems (and Others).*
   Conductor: Harold Coates (Al Goodman). **Cast:** Harold Coates and His Orchestra.
   Also see DO RE MI; OKLAHOMA

ANNIE'S CHRISTMAS
Studio Cast (1982) .... *Columbia (S) CC-38361*   82   **8-10**

ANONYMOUS VENETIAN
Soundtrack (1971) .... *United Artists (S) UAS-5218*   71   **20-25**
   Composer: Stelvio Cipriani. **Conductor:** Stelvio Cipriani.

ANOTHER TIME, ANOTHER PLACE
Soundtrack (1958) .... *Columbia (M) CL-1180*   58   **75-85**
   Composer: Douglas Gamley. **Conductor:** Muir Mathieson.

ANTHONY ADVERSE
Soundtrack (1936) .... *Warner Bros. (M) W-1438*   62   **40-50**
Soundtrack (1936) .... *Warner Bros. (SE) WS-1438*   62   **50-60**
   Composer: Erich Wolfgang Korngold. **Conductor:** Lionel Newman.

ANY WEDNESDAY
Soundtrack (1966) .... *Warner Bros. (M) W-1669*   66   **20-25**
Soundtrack (1966) .... *Warner Bros. (S) WS-1669*   66   **25-35**
   Composer: George Duning. **Conductor:** George Duning.

ANY WHICH WAY YOU CAN
Soundtrack (1980) .... *Warner Bros. (S) HS-3499*   80   **8-10**
   Conductor: Steve Dorff. **Cast:** Ray Charles; Clint Eastwood; Glen Campbell; David Frizell;
   Shelly West; Fats Domino; Sondra Locke; Jim Stafford; Johnny Duncan; Gene Watson; Cliff
   Crofford; John Durrill; Texas Opera Company.

ANYA
Original Cast (1965) .... *United Artists (M) UAL-4133*   65   **20-25**
Original Cast (1965) .... *United Artists (S) UAS-5133*   65   **25-30**
   Composer: Robert Wright; George Forrest. **Conductor:** Harold Hastings. **Cast:** Constance
   Towers; Michael Karmoyan; Lillian Gish; Barbara Alexander; Boris Aplon; George S. Irving;
   John Michael King; Irra Petina; Michael Quinn; Karen Shepard; Ed Steffe.

ANYONE CAN WHISTLE
Original Cast (1964) .... *Columbia (M) KOL-6080*   64   **35-40**
Original Cast (1964) .... *Columbia (S) KOS-2480*   64   **40-45**
Original Cast (1964) .... *Columbia (S) S-32608*   73   **12-18**

ANYONE CAN WHISTLE (continued)
Original Cast (1964) .... *Columbia Special Products (S) AS-32608* $8-10
  Composer: Stephen Sondheim. Conductor: Herbert Greene. Cast: Lee Remick; Angela
  Lansbury; Harry Guardino; Sterling Clark; Gabriel Dell; Harvey Evans; James Frawley; Larry
  Roquemore; Arnold Soboloff; Tucker Smith.

ANYTHING GOES
Original Cast (1934) .... *Smithsonian (M) R-007*   77   8-10
  With members of the original London cast.
  Cast: Ethel Merman; Jack Whiting; Jeanne Aubert; Cole Porter.
Original Revival Cast (1962) .... *Epic (S) FLS-15100*   62   10-15
Original Revival Cast (1962) .... *Epic (S) JS-15100*   Re   8-10
  Composer: Cole Porter. Conductor: Julian Stein. Cast: Eileen Rodgers; Hal Linden; Mickey
  Deems; Margery Gray; Kay Norman; Barbara Lang; Kenneth Mars.
Studio Cast (1950) .... *Columbia (M) ML-2159*   51   40-50
Studio Cast (1950) .... *Columbia (M) ML-4751*   53   20-25
  One side has music from *Bandwagon*.
Studio Cast (1950) .... *Columbia (M) DL-193*   56   15-20
Studio Cast (1950) .... *Columbia Special Products (M) AML-4751*   8-10
  Conductor: Lehman Engel. Cast: Mary Martin.
Studio Cast (1953) .... *RCA Victor (EP) EPA-489*   53   10-20
Studio Cast (1953) .... *RCA Victor (M) LPM-3157*   53   35-45
  10-inch LP. One side has music from *Kiss Me Kate*.
  Cast: Helena Bliss; George Britton; Lisa Kirk.
Soundtrack (1936) .... *Decca (M) DL-6009*   50   45-55
  One side has music from *Two for Tonight*.
  Composer: Cole Porter; Robin Whiting. Conductor: George Stoll. Cast: Bing Crosby; Ethel
  Merman.
Soundtrack (1956) .... *Decca (EP) ED-845*   56   10-20
Soundtrack (1956) .... *Decca (M) DL-8318*   56   30-35
Soundtrack (1956) .... *Decca (M) DL-4264*   56   20-25
  Also has music from *Little Boy Lost* and *The Country Girl*. Issued as part of *Bing's Hollywood Series*.
  Composer: Cole Porter; Jimmy Van Heusen; Sammy Cahn (Van Heusen and Cahn provided
  additional songs specifically for this remake of the film). Conductor: Joseph J. Lilley.
  Cast: Bing Crosby; Donald O'Connor; Jeanmarie; Mitzi Gaynor.
Revival Cast .... *RCA Victor (S) 7769-1*   88   8-10
  Composer: Cole Porter. Cast: Patti LuPone; Howard McGillin; Bill McCutcheon.
TV Soundtrack (1954) .... *Sandy Hook (M) SH-2043*   81   10-12
TV Soundtrack (1954) .... *Larynx Disc (M) 567*   8-10
  On above two LPs, one side has music from *Panama Hattie*.
  Composer: Cole Porter. Cast: Ethel Merman; Art Carney; Jack Leonard.
  Also see PENNIES FROM HEAVEN

APARTMENT
Soundtrack (1960) .... *United Artists (M) UAL-3105*   60   35-40
Soundtrack (1960) .... *United Artists (S) UAS-6105*   60   45-50
Soundtrack (1960) .... *Ascot (M) UM-13500*   64   15-20
Soundtrack (1960) .... *Ascot (S) US-16500*   64   20-35
  Also has selections from *Some Like It Hot, Exodus* and *Odds Against Tomorrow*.
  Composer: Adolph Deutsch; Charles Williams. Theme by Ferrante and Teicher.
  Conductor: Mitchell Powell. Cast: Shirley MacLaine; Fred MacMurray; Hollywood
  Symphony Orchestra.

APOCALYPSE NOW
Soundtrack (1979) .... *Elektra (S) DP-90001*   79   **$8-12**
  Composer: Carmine Coppola; Francis Coppola; others. **Cast:** Marlon Brando; Robert Duvall;
  Martin Sheen; Doors; Frederic Forrest; Albert Hall; Sam Bottoms; Dennis Hopper; Vienna
  Philharmonic Orchestra; Flash Cadillac; Harrison Ford. (With dialogue.)

APPEARING NIGHTLY
Original Cast (1977) .... *Arista (S) AB-4142*   77   **8-10**
  Cast: Lily Tomlin.

APPLAUSE
Original Cast (1970) .... *ABC (S) OCA-11*   70   **15-20**
Original Cast (1970) .... *MCA (S) OC-11*   **8-10**
  Composer: Charles Strouse; Lee Adams. **Conductor:** Donald Pippin. **Cast:** Lauren Bacall; Len
  Cariou; Robert Mandan; Bonnie Franklin; Penny Fuller; Brandon Maggart; Lee Roy Reams;
  Ann Williams.

APPLE
Soundtrack (1980) .... *Cannon (S) 1001*   80   **8-10**
  Composer: Coby Recht; others. **Cast:** Grace Kennedy; Allan Love; Mary Hylan; George
  Gilmour; Joss Ackland; Vladek Sheybal; Ray Shell.

APPLE TREE
Original Cast (1966) .... *Columbia (M) KOL-6620*   66   **15-20**
Original Cast (1966) .... *Columbia (S) KOS-3020*   66   **20-25**
  Conductor: Elliot Lawrence. **Cast:** Barbara Harris; Larry Blyden; Alan Alda; Marc Jordan.
Original Canadian Cast (1966) .... *Trillium (S) TR-2000*   66   **30-35**
  Act I only.
  Composer: Jerry Bock; Sheldon Harnick. **Conductor:** Hank Monis. **Cast:** Tom Kneebone;
  Dinah Christie.

APRIL FOOLS
Soundtrack (1969) .... *Columbia (S) OS-3340*   69   **20-25**
  Composer: Marvin Hamlisch; Burt Bacharach. **Cast:** Chambers Brothers; Mongo Santamaria;
  Taj Mahal; Robert John; Percy Faith; Jack Lemmon; Catherine Deneuve; Sally Kellerman;
  Peter Lawford. (With dialogue.)

APRIL LOVE
Soundtrack (1957) .... *Dot (M) DLP-9000*   57   **$35-40**
Composer: Sammy Fain; Paul Francis Webster (musical adaptation by Alfred Newman and Cyril J. Mockridge). **Conductor:** Lionel Newman. **Cast:** Pat Boone; Shirley Jones.

ARABESQUE
Soundtrack (1966) .... *RCA Victor (M) LPM-3623*   66   **20-30**
Soundtrack (1966) .... *RCA Victor (S) LSP-3623*   66   **25-35**
Composer: Henry Mancini. **Conductor:** Henry Mancini.

ARABIAN NIGHTS
Original Cast (1954) .... *Decca (EP) ED-816*   54   **15-20**
Original Cast (1954) ......,................... *Decca (M) DL-9013*   54   **60-70**
Conductor: Pembroke Davenport. **Cast:** Lauritz Melchior; Helena Scott; Ralph Herbert; William Chapman; James McCracken; Hope Holiday; Gloria Van Dorp.
Studio Cast (1954) .... *Decca (EP) ED-687*   54   **15-20**
Studio Cast (1954) .... *Decca (M) DL-5542*   54   **40-50**
10-inch LP.
Composer: Carmen Lombardo; John Jacob Loeb. **Conductor:** Guy Lombardo. **Cast:** Guy Lombardo and the Royal Canadians; Bill Flanagan; Kenny Gardner.

ARCHIES
TV Soundtrack (1968) .... *Calendar (S) KES-101*   68   **15-25**
Composer: Jeff Barry. **Conductor:** Don Kirshner.

ARCHY AND MEHITABEL:
see SHINBONE ALLEY

ARIA
Soundtrack (1988) .... *RCA Victor (S) 6587-1*   88   **8-10**
Cast: Various artists.

ARISTOCATS
Soundtrack (1971) .... *Disneyland (S) DQ-1333*   71   **8-10**
Composer: Various. **Cast:** Mike Sammes Singers; Robbie Lester; Susan Novack; Victor Sweier; Phil Harris; Wellingtons; Louis Prima.
Studiotrack (1971) .... *Disneyland (S) STER-3995*   71   **8-10**
Composer: Richard M. Sherman; Robert B. Sherman; Terry Gilkyson; Floyd Huddleston; Al Rinker. **Cast:** Sterling Holloway (narration); Phil Harris; Robbie Lester; Susan Novack; Gregory Novack; Victor Sweier and the Mike Sammes Singers.

ARMED AND DANGEROUS
Soundtrack (1986) .... *Manhattan (S) SJ-53041*   86   **8-10**
Composer: Various. **Cast:** Atlantic Starr; Escapades; Maurice White; Cheryl Lynn; Tito Puente and His Latin Ensemble; Glenn Burtrick; Eve; Sigue Sigue Sputnik; Michael Henderson; Bill Meyers.

ARMS AND THE GIRL
Original Cast (1950) ....*Decca (M) DL-5200*   50   **$125-150**
10-inch LP.
Composer: Morton Gould; Dorothy Fields. **Conductor:** Frederick Dvonch. **Cast:** Nanette
Fabray; George Gustaray; Pearl Bailey; Florenz Ames.

AROUND THE WORLD IN 80 DAYS
Soundtrack (1957) ....*Decca (EP) ED-836*   57   **15-20**
Soundtrack (1957) ....*Decca (M) DL-9046*   57   **30-35**
Soundtrack (1957) .... *MCA (SE) 2062*   74   **8-10**
Composer: Victor Young. **Conductor:** Victor Young.
Studiotrack (1956) ....*Tops (M) L-1591*   57   **10-20**
Conductor: Lew Raymond.
Studiotrack .... *Valiant (M) V-4926*   **8-12**
Cast: Hollywood Orchestra.
Studiotrack .... *Mayfair (S) 9591*   **15-25**
Yellow vinyl.
Conductor: Lew Raymond.
Studiotrack (1957) .... *Masterseal (M) No Number Used*   **10-15**
Conductor: Jack Hansen. **Cast:** Hollywood Transcription Orchestra.
Studiotrack (1958) ....*Specialty (M) SP-2101*   58   **20-35**
Studiotrack (1958) ....*Specialty (M) SP-2101*   87   **8-10**
Has a 1987 copyright date on back cover.
Composer: Victor Young. **Cast:** Gerald Wiggins Trio: Gerald Wiggins (piano); Eugene Wright
(bass); Bill Douglass (drums).
Studiotrack ....*Everest (M) LPBR-4001*   **10-15**
Studiotrack .... *Everest (S) SDBR-4001*   **10-15**
Conductor: Jack Saunders. **Cast:** Jack Saunders Orchestra.
Studiotrack ....*Grand Award (S) 214-SD*   **10-15**
Composer: Victor Young. **Conductor:** Enoch Light. **Cast:** Enoch Light Orchestra.

AROUND THE WORLD, UNDER THE SEA
Soundtrack (1966) ....*Monument (M) 8050*   66   **25-40**
Soundtrack (1966) .... *Monument (S) 18050*   66   **35-50**
Composer: Harry Sukman. **Conductor:** Harry Sukman.

ARRANGEMENT
Soundtrack (1968) ....*Warner Bros. (S) WS-1824*   68   **25-30**
Composer: David Amram. **Conductor:** David Amram.

ARRIVEDERCI, BABY!
Soundtrack (1966) .... *RCA Victor (M) LOC-1132*   66   **20-25**
Soundtrack (1966) .... *RCA Victor (S) LSO-1132*   66   **25-35**
Composer: Dennis Farnon. **Conductor:** Dennis Farnon. **Cast:** Vic Damone.

ART OF LOVE
Soundtrack (1965) .... *Capitol (M) T-2355*   65   **25-30**
Soundtrack (1965) .... *Capitol (S) ST-2355*   65   **30-35**
Composer: Cy Coleman. **Conductor:** Cy Coleman.

ARTHUR (OR THE DECLINE AND FALL OF THE BRITISH EMPIRE)
TV Soundtrack (1970) ....*Reprise (S) RS-6366*   70   **10-15**

ARTHUR (THE ALBUM)
Soundtrack (1981) ....*Warner Bros. (S) BSK-3582*   81   **8-10**
Composer: Christopher Cross; Nicolette Larson; others. **Cast:** Liza Minnelli.

ARTHUR 2: ON THE ROCKS
Soundtrack (1988) ....*A&M (S) SP-3916*   88   **8-10**

ARTHUR GODFREY
TV Soundtrack (1954) .... *Columbia (M) CL-540*   54   **$25-35**
   Full title: *Christmas With Arthur Godfrey.*
   Composer: Various. **Conductor:** Archie Bleyer. **Cast:** Arthur Godfrey; Jeanette Davis; Mariners;
   Julius LaRosa; McGuire Sisters; Frank Parker; Marion Marlowe; Haleloke Kahauolopua;
   Lu Ann Simms.
Studio Cast (1953) .... *Columbia (M) CL-521*   53   **25-35**
   Full title: *Arthur Godfrey's TV Calendar Show.*
   Composer: Joan Edwards; Lyn Duddy. **Conductor:** Archie Bleyer. **Cast:** Arthur Godfrey; Julius
   LaRosa; Lu Ann Simms; Marion Marlowe; Frank Parker; Jeanette Davis; Mariners; Haleloke
   Kahauolopua; Chordettes.

ARTISTS AND MODELS
Studiotrack (1955) .... *Capitol (EP) EAP 1-702*   55   **25-50**
   Composer: Jack Brooks; Harry Warren. **Conductor:** Dick Stabile. **Cast:** Dean Martin.

AS YOU LIKE IT:
see ROSENCRANTZ AND GUILDENSTERN ARE DEAD

ASPECTS OF LOVE
Original London Cast (1989) .... *Polydor (S) 422-841-126-1*   89   **10-20**
   Double LP. Gatefold cover. Custom inner sleeves. Includes 24-page lyrics booklet.
   Composer: Andrew Lloyd Webber (music); Don Black and Charles Hart (lyrics).
   Conductor: Michael Reed. **Cast:** Ann Crumb; Michael Ball; Kevin Colson; Kathleen Rowe
   McAllen; Paul Bentley; Diana Morrison; Sally Smith.

ASSAULT OF THE KILLER BIMBOS
Soundtrack (1988) .... *Rhino (S) R1-70311*   88   **8-10**
   Composer: Various. **Cast:** Knight and Day; Fierce; Linda Strick; Attila the Hun; Billion Dollar
   Babies; Lois Blaisch; Andy Landis and Rockslide; Third Language; Mavis Vegas Davis; Idolls.

AT HOME AT THE PALACE
Original Cast (1967) .... *ABC (S) ABCS-620*   67   **15-20**
   Conductor: Bobby Cole. **Cast:** Judy Garland; Joe Luft; Lorna Luft.

AT HOME WITH ETHEL WATERS
Original Cast (1951) .... *Monmouth Evergreen (SE) MES-6812*   **15-20**
   Cast: Ethel Waters; Reginald Bean (piano).

AT HOME WITH THE MUNSTERS
Studiotrack (1964) .... *Golden Records (M) LP-139*   64   **10-15**
   Composer: Jack Marshall; Bob Mosher. **Cast:** Fred Gwynne; Yvonne De Carlo; Al Lewis;
   Pat Priest; Butch Patrick.
   Also see MUNSTERS

AT LONG LAST LOVE
Soundtrack (1975) .... *RCA Victor (S) ABL2-0967*   75   **15-20**
   Double LP set.
   Composer: Cole Porter. **Conductor:** Artie Butler. **Cast:** Burt Reynolds; Cybill Shepherd;
   Madeline Kahn; Duilio Del Prete; Eileen Brennan; John Hillerman; Mildred Natwick.

AT THE DROP OF A HAT
Original London Cast (1959) .... *Angel (M) 65042*   59   **20-25**
Original London Cast (1959) .... *Angel (M) 35797*   59   **15-20**
Original London Cast (1959) .... *Angel (S) S-35797*   59   **20-25**
   Composer: Michael Flanders; Donald Swann. **Cast:** Michael Flanders; Donald Swann (piano).

AT THE DROP OF ANOTHER HAT
Original Cast (1966) .... *Angel (M) 36388*   66   **15-20**
Original Cast (1966) .... *Angel (S) S-36388*   66   **20-25**
   Composer: Michael Flanders; Donald Swann. **Cast:** Michael Flanders; Donald Swann (piano).

ATHENA
Soundtrack (1954) ....*Mercury (EP) EP-2-3284*   54   **$25-50**
Double EP set.
Soundtrack (1954) .... *Mercury (M) MG-25202*   54   **100-125**
Composer: Ralph Blane; Hugh Martin. **Conductor:** George Stoll. **Cast:** Jane Powell; Debbie
Reynolds; Vic Damone.

ATHENIAN TOUCH
Original Cast (1964) .... *Broad Way East (M) OC-101*   64   **130-140**
Original Cast (1964) .... *Broad Way East (S) OCS-101*   64   **150-160**
Composer: Willard Straight; David Eddy. **Conductor:** Glen Clugston. **Cast:** Marion Marlowe;
Butterfly McQueen; Robert Cosden; Alice Cannon; Ken Cantril; Ron Hansen; James Harder;
Mark Holliday; Richard Ianni; Janet McCall; Peter Sands.

ATHENS, GA. - INSIDE/OUT
Soundtrack ......................................*I.R.S. (S) RS-6185*   **8-10**
Composer: Various. **Cast:** Squalls; Flat Duo Jets; R.E.M.; Love Tractor; Kilkenny Cats; Time
Toy; Pylon; Bar-B-Q Killers; Dreams So Real.

ATLANTIC CITY
Soundtrack (1982) ....*DRG (S) DRG-6104*   81   **8-10**
Composer: Michel Legrand. **Conductor:** Michel Legrand.

ATLANTIS IN HI-FI (FORBIDDEN ISLAND)
Soundtrack (1959) .... *Carlton (M) 106*   59   **60-70**
Composer: Alexander Laszlo.

AUNTIE MAME
Soundtrack (1958) ....*Warner Bros. (M) W-1242*   58   **55-60**
Soundtrack (1958) ....*Warner Bros. (S) WS-1242*   58   **70-75**
Also contains music from other Kaper films: *Green Dolphin Street, Invitation* and *The Glass Slipper.*
Composer: Bronislau Kaper. **Conductor:** Ray Heindorf. **Cast:** Rosalind Russell; Forrest Tucker.
Soundtrack (1974) ....*Warner Bros. (S) WS-2773*   74   **10-12**
Composer: Jerry Herman. **Conductor:** Fred Werner. **Cast:** Lucille Ball; Beatrice Arthur; Robert
Preston; Jane Connell; Bruce Davidson; Kirby Furlong.

AVALANCHE
Soundtrack (1978) ....*Delos (S) DLS-25452*   78   **8-10**
Composer: William Kraft. **Conductor:** William Kraft. **Cast:** National Philharmonic Orchestra.

AVENGERS
TV Soundtrack (1966) .... *HBR (M) 8506*   66   **35-45**
TV Soundtrack (1966) .... *HBR (S) 9506*   66   **50-60**
Conductor: Laurie Johnson. **Cast:** Laurie Johnson Orchestra.
Studiotrack (1982) ....*Starlog/Varese Sarabande (S) SV-95003*   82   **8-10**
Also has music from *The New Avengers* and *The Professionals.*
Composer: Laurie Johnson. **Conductor:** Laurie Johnson. **Cast:** Laurie Johnson Orchestra.

AVIATOR
Soundtrack (1985) .... *Varese Sarabande (S) STV 81240*   85   **12-15**
Composer: Dominic Frontiere. **Conductor:** Dominic Frontiere.

AWAKENING
Soundtrack (1980) .... *Entr' acte (S) ERS-6520-ST*   80   **8-10**
Composer: Claude Bolling. **Conductor:** Claude Bolling.

B

B.S. I LOVE YOU
Soundtrack (1971) .... *Mercury (S) SRM1-610*   71   **$15-20**
Composer: Mark Shekter; Jim Dale. **Conductor:** Jim Dale. **Cast:** Stouffville Grit.

BABES IN ARMS
Studio Cast (1951) .... *Columbia (EP) A-1024*   52   **15-20**
Studio Cast (1951) .... *Columbia (M) ML-4488*   52   **25-35**
Studio Cast (1951) .... *Columbia (M) CL-823*   56   **20-25**
Studio Cast (1951) .... *Columbia (M) OL-7070*   65   **30-40**
Studio Cast (1951) .... *Columbia (SE) OS-2570*   65   **50-60**
Studio Cast (1951) .... *Columbia Special Products (SE) AOS-2570*   Re   **8-10**
Composer: Richard Rodgers; Lorenz Hart. **Conductor:** Lehman Engel. **Cast:** Mary Martin;
Mardi Bayne; Jack Cassidy.
Studio Cast (1953) .... *RCA Victor (EP) EPA-478*   53   **15-20**
Studio Cast (1953) ..../.. *RCA Victor (M) LPM-3152*   53   **30-40**
10-inch LP. One side has music from *Jumbo*.
Composer: Richard Rodgers; Lorenz Hart (both). **Conductor:** Jay Blackton. JUMBO: Lehman
Engel. **Cast:** Lisa Kirk (both); William Tabbert; Sheila Bond. JUMBO: Jack Cassidy; Jordon
Bentley.
Also see PANAMA HATTIE

BABES IN TOYLAND
Original Cast (1979) .... *Bit (S) 91550*   79   **12-18**
Composer: Victor Herbert; Glen MacDonough. **Conductor:** Bob Christiansen.
Studio Cast (1950) .... *Decca (EP) 9-165*   50   **20-30**
Triple EP, boxed set.
Studio Cast (1950) .... *Decca (M) DLP-7004*   50   **40-50**
10-inch LP.
Studio Cast (1950) .... *Decca (M) DL-8458*   57   **25-35**
One side of this LP contains music from *The Red Mill*.
Conductor: Alexander Smallens. **Cast:** Kenny Baker; Karen Kemple.
Soundtrack (1961) .... *Buena Vista (M) BV-4022*   61   **15-20**
Soundtrack (1961) .... *Buena Vista (S) BVS-4022*   61   **25-30**
Composer: Victor Herbert; George Bruns. **Conductor:** Tutti Camarata. **Cast:** Ray Bolger;
Henry Calvin; Tommy Sands; Annette; Ed Wynn; Mary McCarty; Kevin Corcorah; Ann Jillian.
Studiotrack (1961) .... *Disneyland (M) 1219*   62   **8-12**
Studiotrack (1961) .... *Disneyland (M) ST-3913*   62   **10-15**
With music tracks and chorus numbers identical to the Buena Vista issues, but with unidentified vocalists
and the stars' voices added.
Composer: Victor Herbert; George Bruns.

BABY
Original Broadway Cast .... *Polydor (S) 422-821593-1*   84   **8-10**
Composer: David Shire; Richard Maltby. **Conductor:** B. Howard. **Cast:** Liz Callaway; James
Longdon; Catherine Cox; Beth Fowler; Todd Graff; Martin Vidnovic; Kim Criswell; Philip
Hoffman; Dennis Warning.

BABY DOLL
Soundtrack (1956) .... *Columbia (M) CL-958*   57   **50-60**
Composer: Kenyon Hopkins. **Conductor:** Ray Heindorf. **Cast:** Carroll Baker; Karl Malden;
Smiley Lewis.
Studiotrack .... *Columbia (EP) B-2114*   **10-15**
Composer: Kenyon Hopkins. **Conductor:** Percy Faith. **Cast:** Percy Faith and His Orchestra.

BABY FACE NELSON
Soundtrack (1957) .... *Jubilee (M) 2021*   57 $75-90
  Composer: Van Alexander. Conductor: Van Alexander.

BABY MAKER
Soundtrack (1972) .... *Ode '70 (S) 77002*   72   20-25
  Composer: Fred Karlin. Cast: Ole Blue.

BABY, THE RAIN MUST FALL
Soundtrack (1965) .... *Ava (M) A-53*   65   30-40
Soundtrack (1965) ....*Ava (S) AS-53*   65   40-50
  Conductor: Elmer Bernstein.
Soundtrack (1965) ....*Mainstream (S) S-6056*   Re   35-40
  Composer: Elmer Bernstein. Conductor: Elmer Bernstein.
Soundtrack (1965) ....*Mainstream (M) 56056*   Re   30-35

BACHELOR PARTY
Soundtrack (1984) ................................*I.R.S. (S) 70047*   84   8-10
  Composer: Various. Cast: Fleshtones; Oingo Boingo; R.E.M.; Jools Holland; Alarm.

BACK STREET
Soundtrack (1961) ....*Decca (M) DL-9097*   61   40-60
Soundtrack (1961) ....*Decca (S) DL7-9097*   61   60-80
  Composer: Frank Skinner. Conductor: Joseph Gershenson. Cast: Universal-International
  Orchestra.

BACK TO SCHOOL
Soundtrack (1986) ....*MCA (S) 6175*   86   8-10
  Composer: Various. Cast: Jude Cole; Bobby Caldwell; Tyson and Schwartz; Michael Bolton;
  Philip Ingram; Rodney Dangerfield; Aretha Franklin.

BACK TO THE BEACH
Soundtrack (1987) .... *Columbia (S) JS-40892*   87   10-12
  Composer: Various. Cast: Annette Funicello; Frankie Avalon; Eddie Money; Stevie Ray
  Vaughan; Dick Dale; Aimee Mann; Private Domain; Pee-Wee Herman; Marti Jones; Fishbone;
  Herbie Hancock; Dweezil Zappa; Terry Bozzio; Dave Edmunds.

BACK TO THE FUTURE
Soundtrack (1985) ....*MCA (S) 6144*   85   8-10
  Composer: Alan Silvestri; others. Cast: Huey Lewis and the News; Outatime Orchestra; Eric
  Clapton; Lindsay Buckingham; Etta James; Marvin Berry and the Starlighters.

BACK TO THE FUTURE, PART 2
Soundtrack (1979) ....*Chameleon (S) D1-74792*   Re   8-10

BACKGROUND TO VIOLENCE:
see LUST FOR LIFE

BACKSTAGE AT "TWO BY TWO":
see TWO BY TWO

BAD AND THE BEAUTIFUL:
see LAURA

BAD BOYS
Soundtrack (1983) ....*Capitol (S) ST-12272*   83   8-10
  Cast: Ebonee Webb; Melba Moore; T-Connection; others.

BAD COMPANY
Soundtrack (1972) .... *Private Label (S) STK-1069*   76   **$50-60**
One side has music from *A Texas Romance, 1909*.
Composer: Harvey Schmidt. **Cast:** Harvey Schmidt (piano).

BAD DREAMS
Soundtrack (1988) .... *Varese Sarabande (S) 704-560*   88   **10-15**
Composer: Jay Ferguson.

BAD GUYS
Soundtrack (1986) .... *Casablanca (S) 826610-1*   86   **8-10**
Composer: William Goldstein; others. **Cast:** Spyder Turner; Precious Metal; Kane Gang; Paul Chiten; Redskins; Hand Tools; William Goldstein; Robert John; Stars on 45; Jeff Tyzik.

BAD INFLUENCE
Soundtrack (1990) .... *Mango (S) MLPS-9860*   90   **5-10**
Composer: Trevor Jones (original music); others. **Conductor:** Trevor Jones; others. **Cast:** Toots; Nana Vasconcelos and the Bushdancers; Lloyd Cole; Etta James; Chaba Fadela; Thomas Mapfump; Skinny Puppy; Les Negresses Vertes; Gavin Friday and the Man; Trevor Jones.

BAD SEED
Soundtrack (1956) .... *RCA Victor (EP) EPA-4010*   56   **40-50**
Soundtrack (1956) .... *RCA Victor (M) LPM-1395*   56   **250-300**
Composer: Alex North. **Conductor:** Ray Heindorf.

BAJOUR
Original Cast (1964) .... *Columbia (M) KOL-6300*   64   **20-25**
Original Cast (1964) .... *Columbia (S) KOS-2700*   64   **30-35**
Composer: Walter Marks. **Conductor:** Lehman Engel. **Cast:** Chita Rivera; Nancy Dussault; Hershel Bernardi; Robert Burr; Herbert Edelman; Mae Questel; Gus Trikonis.

BAKER STREET
Original Cast (1965) .... *MGM (M) E-7000*   65   **15-20**
Original Cast (1965) .... *MGM (S) SE-7000*   65   **25-30**
Composer: Marian Grudeff; Raymond Jessel. **Conductor:** Harold Hastings. **Cast:** Fritz Weaver; Inga Swenson; Martin Gabel; Teddy Green; Patrick Horgen; Daniel Keyes; Peter Sallis; Virginia Vestoff; Martin Wolfson.

BAKER'S WIFE
Original Cast (1976) .... *Take Home Tunes (S) THT-772*   76   **8-10**
Original Cast (1976) .... *Take Home Tunes (S) THT-773*   76   **15-20**
7-inch LP. Stephen Schwartz is heard on piano on the 7-inch disc only. This LP also has five tracks not heard on THT-772.
Composer: Stephen Schwartz; Carol Schwartz. **Cast:** Paul Sorvino; Portia Nelson; Darlene Conley; Carol Schwartz; Stephen Schwartz (piano).

BAL, LE:
see LE BAL

BALLAD FOR BIMSHIRE
Original Cast (1963) .... *London (M) AM-48002*   63   **40-50**
Original Cast (1963) .... *London (S) AMS-78002*   63   **60-75**
Composer: Irving Burgie. **Conductor:** Sammy Benskin. **Cast:** Frederick O'Neal; Christine Spencer; Jimmy Randolph; Ossie Davis; Robert Dolphin; Eugene Edwards; Clebert Ford; Alyce Webb.

BALLAD OF BABY DOE
Original Cast (1958) .... *MGM (S) 3GC-1*   58   **100-125**
Triple LP set.
Original Cast (1958) .... *Heliodor (S) 250-35-3*   Re   **25-35**
Original Cast (1958) .... *Deutsche Grammophon (S) 3-DG-2709*   Re   **10-20**
Composer: Douglas Moore; John Latouche. **Conductor:** Emerson Buckley. **Cast:** New York City Opera Company; Beverly Sills; Walter Cassell; Frances Bible.

BALLET MUSIC FROM WEST SIDE STORY:
see WEST SIDE STORY

BALLET ON BROADWAY
Studiotrack .... *Painted Smiles (S) PS-1364*   **$8-12**

BALLROOM
Original Cast (1978) .... *Columbia (S) JS-35762*   78   **15-20**
   Composer: Billy Goldenberg; Marilyn and Alan Bergman. **Conductor:** Dan Jennings.
   Cast: Dorothy Loudon; Vincent Gardenia; Bernie Knee; Lynn Roberts.

BAMBI
Soundtrack (1942) .... *Disneyland (EP) DEP-4010*   57   **10-15**
Soundtrack (1957) .... *Disneyland (M) WDL-4009*   57   **10-20**
   One side has music from *Cinderella*.
   Conductor: Tutti Camarata. **Cast:** Camarata and His Orchestra.
Studio Cast (1954) .... *RCA Victor (M) LBY-1012*   54   **15-25**
Studio Cast (1954) .... *RCA Victor/Camden (M) CAL-1012*   62   **10-15**
   Composer: Frank Churchill; Ed Plumb; Larry Morey. **Cast:** Shirley Temple.

BANANA SPLITS
TV Soundtrack (1969) .... *HBR (EP) 34578*   69   **8-12**
   Special products issue for Kellogg's, sponsor of the NBC-TV series.
TV Soundtrack (1969) .... *Decca (S) DL-75075*   69   **25-30**
   Full title: *(We're the) Banana Splits*.
   Composer: Various. **Conductor:** Jack Eskew. **Cast:** Banana Splits.

BAND OF ANGELS
Soundtrack (1957) .... *RCA Victor (M) LPM-1557*   57   **100-125**
Soundtrack (1957) .... *Entr' acte (M) ERM-6003*   Re   **8-10**
   Composer: Max Steiner. **Conductor:** Max Steiner. **Cast:** Warner Bros. Orchestra.

BAND OF THE HAND
Soundtrack (1986) .... *MCA (S) 6165*   86   **8-10**
   Composer: Various. **Cast:** Bob Dylan with the Heartbreakers; Shriekback; Reds; Andy
   Summers; Tiger Tiger; Michael Rubini.

BAND WAGON
Original Cast (1931) .... X (M) LVA-1001	55	**$50-60**
Original Cast (1931) .... RCA Victor (M) LSA-3082	Re	**20-25**
Original Cast (1931) .... Smithsonian (M) R-021	Re	**8-10**

Composer: Arthur Schwartz; Howard Dietz. Conductor: Leo Reisman. Cast: Fred Astaire; Adele Astaire; Arthur Schwartz.

Studio Cast (1953) .... RCA Victor (EP) EPA-484	53	**15-20**
Studio Cast (1953) .... RCA Victor (M) LPM-3155	53	**30-40**

One side has music from *The Little Shows*.

Composer: Arthur Schwartz. Conductor: Jay Blacton. Cast: Harold Lang; George Britton; Edith Adams.

Soundtrack (1953) .... MGM (EP) X-1013	53	**15-20**

Actual title: *The Girl Hunt Ballet*.

Cast: Fred Astaire.

Soundtrack (1953) .... MGM (EP) X-207	53	**10-15**
Soundtrack (1953) .... MGM (M) E-3051	53	**35-45**
Soundtrack .... MCA (S) 25015		**8-10**

Composer: Arthur Schwartz; Howard Deitz. Conductor: Adolph Deutsch. Cast: Fred Astaire; Nanette Fabray; Jack Buchanan; India Adams. (With dialogue.)

Studio Cast (1953) .... Clef (EP) CL-183	53	**10-15**

Cast: Fred Astaire.

Studiotrack (1951) .... Decca (EP) ED-2094	54	**8-15**

Conductor: Tommy Dorsey. Cast: Tommy Dorsey Orchestra.

Studiotrack (1951) .... Decca (M) DL-5317	51	**15-25**

10-inch LP.

Conductor: Tommy Dorsey. Cast: Tommy Dorsey Orchestra.

Studio Cast .... Monmouth Evergreen (SE) MRS-6605		**15-20**

Composer: Arthur Schwartz. Conductor: Paul Trueblood. Cast: Nancy Dussault; Clifford David; Karen Morrow.

Studio Cast (1951) .... Columbia (M) ML-2160	51	**20-35**

10-inch LP.

Composer: Adolph Schwartz. Conductor: Lehman Engle. Cast: Mary Martin.
Also see ANYTHING GOES

BANDOLERO!
Soundtrack (1968) .... Project 3 (S) 5026-SD	68	**30-40**

Composer: Jerry Goldsmith. Conductor: Lionel Newman.

BANG THE DRUM SLOWLY
Soundtrack (1973) .... Paramount (S) PAS-1014	73	**15-20**

Composer: Stephen Lawrence. Conductor: Stephen Lawrence.

BANJOMAN
Soundtrack (1977) .... Sire (S) SA-7527	77	**12-18**

Composer: Bob Dylan; Earl Scruggs; Jimmy Driftwood; others. Cast: Byrds; Joan Baez; Nitty Gritty Dirt Band; Earl Scruggs Revue; Doc and Merle Watson; Jack Elliot.

BARABBAS
Soundtrack (1962) .... Colpix (M) CP-510	62	**50-60**
Soundtrack (1962) .... Colpix (S) SCP-510	62	**75-90**

Composer: Mario Nascimbene.

Soundtrack (1962) .... Citadel (S) CT 7034	81	**8-10**

Composer: Mario Nascimbene; Ennio Morricone. Conductor: Mario Nascimbene. Cast: Chuck Bruce (narration).

BARBARA COOK AT CARNEGIE HALL
Original Cast (1975) .... Columbia (S) M-33438	75	**8-10**

Conductor: Wally Harper. Cast: Barbara Cook.

BARBARELLA
Soundtrack (1968) .... *Dyno Voice (M) DV-1908*   68 $25-30
Soundtrack (1968) .... *Dyno Voice (S) DV-31908*   68   30-35
    Composer: Charles Fox; Bob Crewe. **Conductor:** Bob Crewe. **Cast:** Glitter House; Bob Crewe.

BARBARIAN AND THE GEISHA
Soundtrack (1958) .... *20th Century-Fox (M) 3004*   58   150-175
    Composer: Hugo Friedhofer. **Conductor:** Kurt Graunke.

BAREFOOT ADVENTURE
Soundtrack (1961) .... *Pacific Jazz (M) PJ-35*   61   20-30
Soundtrack (1961) .... *Pacific Jazz (S) PJS-35*   61   30-40
    Composer: Bud Shank. **Conductor:** Bud Shank. **Cast:** Bob Cooper; Shelly Manne; Carmell Jones.

BAREFOOT IN THE PARK
Soundtrack (1967) .... *Dot (M) DLP-3803*   67   20-25
Soundtrack (1967) .... *Dot (S) DLP-25803*   67   25-30
    Composer: Neal Hefti.

BARNUM
Original Cast (1980) .... *Columbia (S) JS-36576*   80   8-10
    Composer: Cy Cloeman; Michael Stewart. **Conductor:** Peter Howard. **Cast:** Jim Dale; Glenn Close; Leonard John Crofoot; Terri White; Marianne Tatum; William C. Witter.

BARRY LYNDON
Soundtrack (1975) .... *Warner Bros. (S) BS-2903*   75   8-10
    Conductor: Leonard Rosenman.

BATMAN
TV Soundtrack (1966) .... *20th Century-Fox (M) 3180*   66   20-25
TV Soundtrack (1966) .... *20th Century-Fox (S) TFS-4180*   66   25-30
    Composer: Nelson Riddle. **Conductor:** Nelson Riddle. **Cast:** Adam West; Burt Ward; Frank Gorshin; Burgess Meredith; George Sanders; Anne Baxter; Jack Kruschen.
TV Soundtrack (1966) .... *RCA Victor (M) LPM-3573*   66   15-20
TV Soundtrack (1966) .... *RCA Victor (S) LSP-3573*   66   20-25
    Composer: Neal Hefti. **Conductor:** Neal Hefti. **Cast:** Neal Hefti and His Orchestra.
Studiotrack (1966) .... *Design (S) SDLP-249*   66   8-12
    Cast: Bat Boys.
Studio Cast (1966) .... *MGM/Leo (M) CH-1027*   66   10-15
    Actual title: *More Official Adventures of Batman.*
Soundtrack (1989) .... *Warner Bros. (S) 1-25977*   89   8-10
    Composer: Danny Elfman. **Conductor:** Shirley Walker. **Cast:** Sinfonia of London Orchestra.

BATTERIES NOT INCLUDED
Soundtrack (1987) .... *MCA (S) 6225*   87   8-12
    Composer: James Horner. **Conductor:** James Horner. **Cast:** James Horner.

BATTLE BEYOND THE STARS
Soundtrack (1980) .... *Rhino (S) RNSP-300*   80   8-10
    Composer: Jack Horner.

BATTLE OF ALGIERS
Soundtrack (1967) .... *United Artists (M) UAL-4171*   67   20-30
Soundtrack (1967) .... *United Artists (S) UAS-5171*   67   30-40
Soundtrack (1967) .... *United Artists (S) UA-LA293-G*   74   8-10
    Composer: Ennio Morricone; Gillo Pontecorvo. **Conductor:** Bruno Nicolai.

BATTLE OF BRITAIN
Soundtrack (1969) ....*United Artists (S) UAS-5201*   69   **$25-30**
Soundtrack (1969) ....*MCA (S) 25008*   Re   **8-10**
  Composer: Ron Goodwin; Sir William Walton. Conductor: Ron Goodwin.

BATTLE OF NERETVA
Soundtrack (1971) ....*Entr' acte (Q) ERQ-7001-ST*   75   **10-12**
Soundtrack ....*Southern Cross (S) SCAR-5005*   **8-10**
  Composer: Bernard Herrmann. Conductor: Bernard Herrmann. Cast: London Philharmonic
  Orchestra.

BATTLE OF THE BULGE
Soundtrack (1965) ....*Warner Bros. (M) W-1617*   65   **45-50**
Soundtrack (1965) ....*Warner Bros. (S) WS-1617*   65   **55-65**
  Composer: Benjamin Frankel. Conductor: Benjamin Frankel. Cast: New Philaharmonia
  Orchestra of London.

BATTLEFIELD EARTH
Soundtrack (1984) ....*BPI (S) BPILS-01*   84   **8-10**

BATTLESTAR GALACTICA
Soundtrack (1978) ....*MCA (S) 3051*   78   **8-10**
  Composer: Stu Phillips. Conductor: Stu Phillips.
Soundtrack (1978) ....*Casablanca (S) NBLP 7126*   78   **8-10**
  Disco version.
  Composer: Stu Phillips. Conductor: Giorgio Moroder.

BATTLESTAR GALACTICA (THE SAGA OF BATTLESTAR GALACTICA)
Soundtrack (1978) ....*MCA (S) 3078*   78   **10-15**
  Story with dialogue.
  Composer: Stu Phillips. Conductor: Stu Phillips. Cast: Lorne Greene; Richard Hatch; Dirk
  Benedict; Ray Milland; Lew Ayres; Jane Seymour; Laurette Spang; Terry Carter.

BE MY GUEST
Original Cast (1959) ....*XCTV (M) 10303*   59   **150-200**
  Full title: *Lagniappe '59 Presents Be My Guest.* From the cast of New Trier High School in Chicago,
  which includes Ann-Margret, then known as Ann-Margret Olson, singing *Tropical Heat Wave.*
  Cast: Ann-Margret (Olson); others.
  Also see AMONG FRIENDS - WAA-MU SHOW OF 1960

BEACH BLANKET BINGO
Soundtrack (1965) ....*Capitol (M) T-2323*   65   **20-25**
Soundtrack (1965) ....*Capitol (S) ST-2323*   65   **25-30**
  Composer: Jerry Styner; others. Conductor: H.B. Barnum. Cast: Donna Loren.

BEACH PARTY
Soundtrack (1963) .... *Buena Vista (M) BV-3316* 63 $20-30
Soundtrack (1963) .... *Buena Vista (S) ST-3316* 63 35-50
Cast: Annette Funicello.

BEACHES
Soundtrack (1988) .... *Atlantic (S) 81933-1* 8-10
Composer: Various. Cast: Bette Midler.

BEAR
Soundtrack (1984) .... *RCA Victor (S) CBL1-5328* 84 8-10

BEAR COUNTRY:
see WALT DISNEY'S TRUE LIFE ADVENTURES

BEAST
Soundtrack (1988) .... *A&M (S) SP-3919* 88 8-10
Composer: Mark Isham.

BEASTMASTER
Soundtrack (1983) .... *Varese Sarabande (S) STV 81174* 83 15-20
Composer: Lee Holdridge. Conductor: Lee Holdridge.

BEAT STREET
Soundtrack (1984) .... *Atlantic (S) 80154-1* 84 8-10
Volume 1.
Soundtrack (1984) .... *Atlantic (S) 80158-1* 84 8-10
Volume 2.
Cast: Jazz Jay; Juicy; Tina B; Jenny Burton; others.

BEATLEMANIA
Original Cast (1977) .... *Arista (S) AL-8501* 77 10-15
Double LP set.
Composer: John Lennon; Paul McCartney; George Harrison. Cast: Joe Pecorino; Mitch Weissman; Leslie Fradkin; Justin McNeill.

BEAU JAMES
Soundtrack (1957) .... *Imperial (M) 9041* 57 50-60
Composer: Joseph J. Lilley. Cast: Walter Winchell (narration); Bob Hope; Vera Miles; Jimmy Durante; Skylarks (with dialogue).

BEAUTY AND THE BEAST
Original Cast (1974) .... *Take Home Tunes (S) THT-775* 74 8-10
One side has music from *Snow White and the Seven Dwarfs*.
Composer: Michael Valenti; Elsa Rael. Conductor: Michael Valenti. Cast: Christine Andreas; Steve Sterner; Howard Cutler.

BEAVER VALLEY:
see WALT DISNEY'S TRUE LIFE ADVENTURES

BEBO'S GIRL
Soundtrack (1964) .... *Capitol (M) T-2316* 64 25-30
Soundtrack (1964) .... *Capitol (S) ST-2316* 64 30-35
Composer: Carlo Rustichelli.

BECAUSE THEY'RE YOUNG
Studiotrack (1960) .... *Jamie (EP) JEP-304* 60 20-30
Composer: Aaron Schroeder; Ernest Gold; Don Costa. Cast: Duane Eddy.

BECAUSE YOU'RE MINE
Soundtrack (1952) .... *RCA Victor (EP) ERA-51* 52 20-25
Soundtrack (1952) .... *RCA Victor (M) LM-7015* 52 50-70
10-inch LP.
Conductor: Ray Sinatra; Constantine Callinicos. Cast: Mario Lanza; Jeff Alexander Choir.

BECKET
Soundtrack (1964) .... *Decca (M) DL-9117*   64   **$35-40**
Soundtrack (1964) .... *Decca (S) DL7-9117*   64   **45-50**
With Gregorian chants. Has *Theme from Becket*, plus background music from the film.
Composer: Laurence Rosenthal. **Conductor:** Muir Mathieson.
Soundtrack (1964) .... *RCA Victor (M) LOC-1091*   64   **30-35**
Soundtrack (1964) .... *RCA Victor (S) LSO-1091*   64   **35-40**
Composer: Laurence Rosenthal. **Conductor:** Laurence Rosenthal. **Cast:** Richard Burton; Peter
O'Toole; Sir John Gielaud (with dialogue).

BEDAZZLED
Soundtrack (1967) .... *London (S) MS-82009*   67   **25-30**
Composer: Dudley Moore. **Conductor:** Dudley Moore.

BEDKNOBS AND BROOMSTICKS
Soundtrack (1971) .... *Buena Vista (S) 5003*   71   **15-20**
Composer: Richard M. Sherman; Robert B. Sherman. **Conductor:** Irwin Kostal. **Cast:** Angela
Lansbury; David Tomlinson.

BEETLEJUICE
Soundtrack (1988) .... *Geffen (S) GHS-24202*   88   **8-10**
Composer: Danny Elfman. **Conductor:** Danny Elfman.

BEGATTING OF THE PRESIDENT
Studio Cast (1969) .... *Mediarts (S) 41-2*   69   **10-12**
Written by Myron Roberts, Lincoln Haynes, and Sasha Gilien.
Composer: Myron Roberts. **Conductor:** Luchi De Jesus. **Cast:** Orson Welles.

BEGGAR'S OPERA
Studio Cast (1957) .... *RCA Victor (M) LPM-6048*   57   **40-45**
Double LP set.
Studio Cast (1957) .... *Everest (SE) 3127-2*   **35-45**
Double LP set.
Studio Cast (1957) ..... *Library of Recorded Masterpieces (SE) LRM-2523*   62   **30-35**
Composer: John Gay. **Conductor:** Max Goberman. **Cast:** William McAlpine; Ronald Lewis;
John Frost.
Studio Cast (1957) .... *Seraphim (SE) S-6023*   **10-15**
Double LP set.
Conductor: Sir Malcolm Sargent. **Cast:** Old Victor Company; Pro Arte Orchestra.

BEHIND THE GREAT WALL
Soundtrack (1959) .... *Monitor (M) MP-525*   59   **30-40**
Soundtrack (1959) .... *Monitor (S) MFS-525*   59   **45-60**
Chinese documentary with traditional Chinese songs.

BEHOLD A PALE HORSE
Soundtrack (1964) .... *Colpix (M) CP-519*   64   **40-50**
Soundtrack (1964) .... *Colpix (S) SCP-519*   64   **60-75**
Composer: Maurice Jarre. **Conductor:** Maurice Jarre.

BEI MIR BISTU SCHOEN
Original Cast (1961) .... *Decca (M) DL-9115*   61   **40-50**
Original Cast (1961) .... *Decca (S) DL7-9115*   61   **30-40**
Composer: Sholom Secunda; Jacob Jacobs. **Conductor:** Sholom Secunda. **Cast:** Leo Fuchs;
Jacob Jacobs; Miriam Kressyn; Charlotte Cooper; Leon Liebgold; Seymour Rexite; Rebecca
Richman.
Studio Cast (1961) .... *Tikva (M) T-72*   61   **40-50**
One side has music from *Go Fight City Hall*.
Composer: Sholom Secunda; Jacob Jacobs. **Cast:** Alan Chester; Doris Colen.

BELAFONTE (THREE FOR TONIGHT):
see THREE FOR TONIGHT

BELIEVERS
Original Cast (1968) . . . . *RCA Victor (M) LOC-1151*   68   **$20-35**
Original Cast (1968) . . . . *RCA Victor (S) LSO-1151*   68   **35-50**
    Composer: Voices, Inc. **Conductor:** Brooks Alexander. **Cast:** Benjamin Carter; Dorothy
    Dinroe; Jesse DeVore; Ladji Camara; Barry Hemphill; Jo Jackson; Shirley McKie; Don
    Oliver; Anje Ray; Veronica Redd; Ron Steward; Joseph Walker.
Soundtrack (1987) . . . . *Varese Sarabande (S) STV-81238*   87   **15-20**
    Composer: J. Peter Robinson.

BELIZAIRE THE CAJUN
Soundtrack (1987) . . . . *Arhoolie (S) 5038*   87   **8-10**
    Cast: Michael Doucet and Beausoleil.

BELL, BOOK AND CANDLE
Soundtrack (1959) . . . . *Colpix (M) CP-502*   59   **75-90**
Soundtrack (1959) . . . . *Citadel (M) CT-6006*   76   **10-12**
Soundtrack (1959) . . . . *Citadel (M) CT-7006*   79   **8-10**
    Remastered.
    Composer: George Duning. **Conductor:** George Duning.

BELLE OF AMHERST
Original Cast (1976) . . . . *Credo (S) 5*   76   **10-15**
    Double LP set. Non-musical play by William Luce.
    Cast: Julie Harris (dialogue).

BELLE OF NEW YORK
Soundtrack (1952) . . . . *MGM (EP) K-108*   52   **20-25**
    Four EP boxed set.
Soundtrack (1952) . . . . *MGM (M) E-108*   52   **40-50**
    10-inch LP.
    Composer: Harry Warren; S. Mercer. **Conductor:** Adolph Deutsch. **Cast:** Fred Astaire;
    Anita Ellis; MGM Studio Orchestra and Chorus.
Soundtrack (1952) . . . . *Stet (M) DS-15004*   Re   **10-12**
    Contains eight songs by Fred Astaire that were not included in the film.
    Composer: Harry Warren. **Conductor:** Adolph Deutsch. **Cast:** Fred Astaire; Anita Ellis;
    MGM Studio Orchestra and Chorus.

BELLS ARE RINGING
Original Cast (1956) . . . . *Columbia (M) OL-5170*   57   **15-25**
Original Cast (1956) . . . . *Columbia (SE) OS-2006*   Re   **20-30**
Original Cast (1956) . . . . *Columbia Special Products (SE) AOS-2006*   Re   **8-10**
    Composer: Jule Styne; Betty Comden; Adolph Green. **Conductor:** Milton Rosenstock.
    Cast: Judy Holliday; Sidney Chaplin; Jean Stapleton; Eddie Lawrence; Peter Gennaro.

BELLS ARE RINGING (continued)
Soundtrack (1960) .... *Capitol (M) W-1435*   60   **$20-30**
Soundtrack (1960) .... *Capitol (S) SW-1435*   60   **25-35**
Soundtrack (1960) .... *Stet (S) DS-15011*   Re   **8-10**
  Composer: Jule Styne; Betty Comden; Adolph Green. **Conductor:** Andre Previn.
  Cast: Judy Holliday; Dean Martin; Fred Clark; Eddie Foy Jr.; Jean Stapleton; Hal Linden.
Studiotrack (1960) .... *Richmond (M) B-20089*   60   **10-15**
Studiotrack (1960) .... *Richmond (S) S-30089*   60   **10-20**
  Cast: London Repertory Co.

BELLS OF ST. MARY'S:
see ACCENTUATE THE POSITIVE

BELOVED CHRISTMAS HYMNS AND CAROLS:
see ON THE TWELFTH DAY

BELOW THE BELT:
see MIXED DOUBLES/BELOW THE BELT

BEN CASEY (AND OTHER THEMES)
Studiotrack (1961) .... *Carlton (M) LP-143*   61   **10-15**
  Compilation of TV themes, including: *Ben Casey, Naked City, Bonanza, Perry Como Show, Peter Gun,
  Bell Telephone Hour, Dr. Kildare, Checkmate, G.E. Theater, Gunsmoke, Alcoa Premiere* and *Wagon
  Train.*
  Composer: Various **Cast:** Valjean Johns (piano).

BEN FRANKLIN IN PARIS
Original Cast (1964) .... *Capitol (M) VAS-2191*   64   **20-25**
Original Cast (1964) .... *Capitol (S) SVAS-2191*   64   **30-35**
  Composer: Mark Sandrich Jr.; Sidney Michaels. **Conductor:** Donald Pippin. **Cast:** Robert
  Preston; Ulla Sallert; Franklin Kiser; Jack Fletcher; Sam Greene; Bob Kaliban; Jerry Schaefer;
  Susan Watson.
Studiotrack (1964) .... *Wyncote (M) W-9033*   64   **10-15**

BEN-HUR
Soundtrack (1960) .... *MGM (M) 1E1*   60   **30-35**
Soundtrack (1960) .... *MGM (S) S-1E1*   60   **35-40**
  Deluxe boxed edition. Includes hardbound book.
Soundtrack (1960) .... *MGM (M) 1E1*   60   **15-20**
Soundtrack (1960) .... *MGM (S) S-1E1*   60   **20-25**
  With gatefold cover.
  Composer: Miklos Rozsa. **Conductor:** arlo Savina.
Soundtrack (1960) .... *Lion (M) L-70123*   **25-30**
Soundtrack (1960) .... *Lion (S) SL-70123*   **35-40**
  Composer: Miklos Rozsa. **Conductor:** Erich Kloss.
Studiotrack (1960) ....*London (S) SPC-21166*   76   **10-12**
  First recording of this score by its composer.
  Composer: Miklos Rozsa. **Conductor:** Miklos Rozsa. **Cast:** Miklos Rozsa.
Soundtrack (1960) .... *MGM (M) E-3900*   61   **35-40**
Soundtrack (1960) .... *MGM (S) SE-3900*   61   **40-45**
  Actual title: *More Music from Ben-Hur.*
  Composer: Miklos Rozsa. **Conductor:** Erich Kloss.
Soundtrack (1960) .... *Metro (M) M-503*   64   **10-15**
Soundtrack (1960) ....*Metro (S) MS-503*   64   **15-20**
  Composer: Miklos Rozsa. **Conductor:** Erich Kloss.

BENEATH THE PLANET OF THE APES
Soundtrack (1970) .... *Amos (S) AAS-8001*   70   **40-50**
  Composer: Leonard Rosenman. **Conductor:** Leonard Rosenman.
  Also see PLANET OF THE APES

BENITO CERENO
Original Cast (1964) ....*Columbia (M) DOL-319*   64 $20-30
Original Cast (1964) .... *Columbia (S) DOS-719*   64   30-40
  Complete play with background music.
  Composer: Yehudi Wyner.

BENJI
Soundtrack (1974) ....*Epic (S) KSE-33010*   74   10-12
  Composer: Euel Box. **Conductor:** Euel Box. **Cast:** Charlie Rich.

BENJI (THE STORY OF BENJI)
Studio Cast (1975) ....*Mulberry Square (S) MSR-3936*   75   10-12
  Includes color booklet.
  Composer: Euel Box. **Conductor:** Euel Box. **Cast:** Jesse Davis.

BENNY GOODMAN STORY
Soundtrack (1956) ....*Decca (EP) ED-797*   59   10-15
  Volume one.
Soundtrack (1956) ....*Decca (EP) ED-798*   59   10-15
  Volume two.
Soundtrack (1956) ....*Decca (M) DL-8252*   56   15-20
  Volume one.
Soundtrack (1956) ....*Decca (M) DL-8253*   56   15-20
  Volume two.
Soundtrack (1956) .... *Decca (SE) DL7-8252*   59   20-25
Soundtrack (1956) ....*Decca (SE) DXSB7-188*   65   30-35
Soundtrack (1956) ....*MCA (SE) 4055e*   80   10-12
  Above two are double LP sets.
  Cast: Benny Goodman; Gene Krupa; Stan Getz; Lionel Hampton; Teddy Wilson; Martha Tilton.
  (Benny Goodman actually provided the music for this film, which starred Steve Allen.)

BENNY HILL-WORDS AND MUSIC
TV Soundtrack ....*Capitol (S) SN-16139*   81   8-10
  Composer: Benny Hill. **Conductor:** Harry Robinson. **Cast:** Benny Hill.

BEOWULF
Studio Cast (1977) ..../....................*Daffodil (S) DAF-30050*   77   50-70
  Double LP set.
  Composer: Victor Davies; Betty Jane Wylie. **Conductor:** Victor Davies. **Cast:** Chad Allen;
  Doug Mallory; Christine Chandler.

BERGEN SINGS MORGAN:
see HELEN MORGAN STORY

BERLIN TO BROADWAY WITH KURT WEILL
Original Cast (1972) ....*Paramount (S) PAS-4000*   74   25-30
  Double LP set.
  Composer: Kurt Weill. **Conductor:** Newton Wayland. **Cast:** Margery Cohen; Ken Kercheval;
  Judy Lander; Jerry Lanning; Hal Watters.

BERNADETTE
Soundtrack ....*Varese Sarabande (S) STV-81116*   8-10
  One side has *Island in the Sky.*

BERNARD HERRMANN CONDUCTS
Soundtrack ....*London (S) SPC-21149*   76   15-20
  Full title: *Bernard Herrmann Conducts Great British Film Scores.* Music from: *Anna Karenina, Oliver
  Twist, The Ideal Husband, The Invaders, Escape Me Never* and *Things to Come.*
  Composer: Bernard Herrmann. **Conductor:** Bernard Herrmann. **Cast:** National Philharmonic
  Orchestra.

BERNARD HERRMANN CONDUCTS (continued)

Soundtrack ....*London (S) SPC-21177* 77 $15-20
Full title: *Bernard Herrmann Conducts Great British Film Scores, Volume 2.* Music from: *Jane Eyre, Fahrenheit 451, The Devil and Daniel Webster, The Trouble with Harry, The 7th Voyage of Sinbad, Citizen Kane* and *The 3 Worlds of Gulliver.*
Composer: Bernard Herrmann. **Conductor:** Bernard Herrmann.

BERNSTEIN'S BACKGROUNDS FOR BRANDO

Studiotrack (1958) ....*Dot (M) DLP-3107* 58   15-20
Composer: Various. **Conductor:** Elmer Bernstein.

BEST FOOT FORWARD

Original Revival Cast (1963) ....*Cadence (M) CLP-4012* 63   30-35
Original Revival Cast (1963) ....*Cadence (S) CLP-24012* 63   50-60
Original Revival Cast (1963) ....*Stet (S) DS-15003*   8-10
Indicated as stereo on the LP, but available only in mono.
Composer: Hugh Martin; Ralph Blane. **Conductor:** Buster Davis. **Cast:** Paula Wayne; Liza Minnelli; Glenn Walken; Karin Wolfe; Gene Castle; Paul Charles; Kay Cole; Edmund Gaynes; Jack Irwin; Don Slaton; Grant Walden; Ronald Walken; Renee Winters.

BEST LITTLE WHOREHOUSE IN TEXAS

Original Cast (1978) ....*MCA (S) 3049* 78   8-10
Composer: Carol Hall. **Conductor:** Robert Billig. **Cast:** Clint Allmon; Pamela Blair; Lisa Brown; Gerry Burkhardt; Jay Bursky; Henderson Forsythe; Jay Garner; Carlin Glynn; Delores Hall; Susan Mansur; Michael Scott; Paul Ukena, Jr.
Soundtrack (1982) ....*MCA (S) 6112* 82   10-12
Soundtrack (1982) ....*MCA (S) 1499* Re   8-10
Soundtrack (1982) ....*MCA (S) 37218* Re   8-10
Composer: Carol Hall. **Cast:** Dolly Parton; Burt Reynolds; Jim Nabors; Teresa Merritt; Dom De Luise; Charles Durning.

BEST OF BROADWAY 1963

Studiotrack (1963) ....*Mercury (M) MG-20757* 63   8-12
Studiotrack (1963) ....*Mercury (S) SR-60757* 63   10-15
Composer: Various. **Cast:** Harry Simeone Chorale.

BEST OF BURLESQUE

Original Cast (1957) ....*MGM (M) E-3644* 57   50-60
Original Cast (1957) ......:.....................*MGM (SE) SE-3644* 58   75-85
Conductor: Herb Harris. **Cast:** Sherry Britton; Tom Poston; Vini Faye; Sugar Glaze; Emmett Rose; Nancee Ward; Lilly White; Nelle's Belles.

BEST OF FRED ASTAIRE FROM MGM CLASSIC FILMS

Soundtrack ....*MCA (S) 25985* 87   8-10
Cast: Fred Astaire.

BEST OF GENE KELLY FROM MGM CLASSIC FILMS

Soundtrack ....*MCA (S) 25166* 87   8-10
Cast: Gene Kelly.

BEST OF JUDY GARLAND FROM MGM CLASSIC FILMS

Soundtrack ....*MCA (S) 25165* 87   8-10
Cast: Judy Garland.

BEST OF MANCINI

Composer: Henry Mancini. **Conductor:** Henry Mancini. **Cast:** Henry Mancini's Orchestra and Chorus.
Soundtrack ....*RCA Victor (M) LPM-2693* 64   10-15
Soundtrack ....*RCA Victor (S) LSP-2693* 64   15-20

Soundtrack .... *RCA Victor (M) LPM-3557* 66 **$10-15**
Soundtrack ....*RCA Victor (S) LSP-3557* 66 **15-20**
Volume two.
Composer: Henry Mancini. **Conductor:** Henry Mancini. **Cast:** Henry Mancini's Orchestra and Chorus.

BEST OF NELSON RIDDLE
Soundtrack .... *Capitol (S) SY-4603* **8-12**
Includes themes from *Route 66, The Untouchables* and *Naked City.*
Conductor: Nelson Riddle. **Cast:** Nelson Riddle and His Orchestra.

BEST OF ORIGINAL SOUNDTRACKS (AND GREAT THEMES FROM MOTION PICTURES)
Soundtrack .... *United Artists (S) UAS-6570* 67 **15-20**
Has themes from: *Hawaii, Return of the Seven, The Fortune Cookie, After the Fox, Viva Maria, Escorts Away* and *Comedy Tonight.*

BEST OF THE NEW FILM THEMES
Soundtrack .... *London (M) LL-3347* 64 **10-15**
Soundtrack ....*London (S) PS-347* 64 **15-20**
Film themes from 1962-1963, including *A New Kind of Love, The Cabinet of Dr. Caligari, Divorce Italian Style, The V.I.P.'s, Charade, 8-1/2, Lord of the Flies, Tiara Tahiti, The Victors, Mondo Canne, The Cardinal* and *Toys in the Attic.*
Composer: Various. **Conductor:** Frank Chacksfield. **Cast:** Frank Chacksfield and His Orchestra.

BEST OF TODAY'S MOTION PICTURE THEME MUSIC, VOL. 1
Studiotrack .... *Unart (S) S-21015* 67 **10-15**
Themes from: *Dr. Doolittle, Gone with the Wind, In the Heat of the Night, You Only Live Twice, The Whisperers, For a Few Dollars More, Hawaii, Triple Cross* and *The Honey Pot.*

BEST THINGS IN LIFE ARE FREE
Soundtrack (1956) .... *Capitol (EP) ECF-765* 56 **15-25**
Soundtrack (1956) .... *Capitol (M) T-765* 56 **40-50**
Composer: Buddy DeSylva; Ray Henderson; Lou Brown. **Cast:** Gordon MacRae.
Soundtrack (1958) .... *Liberty (M) LRP-3017* 58 **40-45**
Composer: Buddy DeSylva; Ray Henderson; Louis Brown. **Conductor:** Lionel Newman. **Cast:** Lionel Newman and His Orchestra.

BEST YEARS OF OUR LIVES
Soundtrack (1946) ....*Entr' acte (S) EDP-8101* 78 **10-12**
Composer: Hugo Friedhofer. **Conductor:** Frank Collura. **Cast:** London Philharmonic Orchestra.

BETJEMANIA
Original London Cast (1980) .... *That's Entertainment (S) TER-1002* 80 **8-10**
Composer: John Gould; John Betjeman. **Conductor:** Rowland Davies; John Gould; Gay Soper; Barry Stokes.

BETRAYAL
Soundtrack (1977) ....*Inner City (S) IC-4001* 77 **8-10**
Composer: Teo Jacero; Janis Ian. **Conductor:** Teo Jacero. **Cast:** Janis Ian.

BETRAYED
Soundtrack (1988) .... *Varese Sarabande (S) 704-700* 88 **8-10**
Composer: Bill Conti. **Conductor:** Bill Conti.

BETTER OFF DEAD
Soundtrack (1985) .... *A&M (S) SP-5071* 85 **8-10**
Composer: Rupert Hine; others. **Cast:** Cy Curnin; Martin Ansell; Teri Nunn; Thinkman; E.G. Daily.

BETTY BLUE
Soundtrack (1988) .... *Virgin Movie Music (S) 90913-1*   88 $8-10
 Cast: Gabriel Yared.

BETTY BOOP
Studio Cast (1930) .... *Mark '56 (M) 639*   73   10-15
 Composer: Various. Cast: Cab Calloway; Fannie Brice; Maurice Chevalier; Louis Armstrong.

BETTY BOOP: SCANDALS OF 1974
Studio Cast .... *Mark '56 (M) 658*   74   '   50-100
 Picture disc.

BEVERLY HILLBILLIES
Studio Cast (1965) .... *Columbia (M) CL-2402*   65   20-25
Studio Cast (1965) .... *Columbia (S) CS-9202*   65   20-30
 Composer: Various. Conductor: Zeke Manners. Cast: Lester Flatt; Earl Scruggs; Buddy
 Ebsen; Irene Ryan; Max Baer; Donna Douglas; Nancy Kulp; Raymond Bailey.

BEVERLY HILLS COP
Soundtrack (1984) .... *MCA (S) 5553*   84   8-10
 Composer: Harold Faltermeyer; Danny Elfman; others. Cast: Patti LaBelle; Shalamar; Junior;
 Rockie Robbins; Pointer Sisters; Glenn Frey; Danny Elfman; System; Harold Faltermeyer.

BEVERLY HILLS COP II
Soundtrack (1987) .... *MCA (S) 6207*   87   8-10
 Composer: Harold Faltermeyer; others. Cast: Bob Seger; Charlie Sexton; Corey Hart; Jets;
 Pointer Sisters; Sue Ann; Jermaine Jackson; James Ingram; George Michael; Pebbles; Ready
 for the World.

BEYOND THE FOREST
 Composer: Max Steiner. Conductor: Max Steiner.

BEYOND THE FRINGE
Original Cast (1962) .... *Capitol (M) W-1792*   62   25-30
Original Cast (1962) .... *Capitol (S) SW-1792*   62   30-35
 Composer: Dudley Moore. Cast: Alan Bennett; Peter Cook; Jonathan Miller.

BEYOND THE FRINGE '64
Original Cast (1964) .... *Capitol (M) W-2072*   64   25-30
Original Cast (1964) .... *Capitol (S) SW-2072*   64   30-35
Original Cast (1964) .... *Capitol (S) ST-11654*   77   8-10
 Composer: Dudley Moore. Cast: Alan Bennett; Peter Cook; Dudley Moore; Paxton Whitehead.

BEYOND THE GREAT WALL
Soundtrack (1965) .... *Capitol (M) T-10401*   65   40-50
 Chinese documentary with traditional Chinese songs.
 Cast: Tsin Ting Kiang Hung.

BEYOND THE MOON
Soundtrack (1966) .... *Mainstream (M) 54001*   65   30-35
Soundtrack (1966) .... *Mainstream (S) 4001*   65   35-40
 May also be shown as *Gulliver's Travels Beyond the Moon.*
 Composer: Milton Delugg; Anne Delugg. Conductor: George Brackman.

BEYOND THE SOUND BARRIER
Studio Cast .... *Varese Sarabande (S) RTS-2*   10-12
 Shown as Volume two. Music from film and opera: *Tribute to a Badman* (1956), *Star Wars* (1977),
 Boy with a Goldfish (1980).
 Composer: Miklos Rozsa; John Williams; Lee Holdridge. Conductor: Morton Gould; Lee
 Holdridge. Cast: London Symphony Orchestra.

BEYOND THE VALLEY OF THE DOLLS
Soundtrack (1970) .... *20th Century-Fox (S) TFS-4211* 70 $25-30
 Composer: Stu Phillips. Conductor: Stu Phillips. Cast: Sandpipers; Strawberry Alarm
 Clock; Carrie Nations.
 Also see VALLEY OF THE DOLLS

BIBLE ... IN THE BEGINNING
Soundtrack (1966) .... *20th Century-Fox (M) TF-3184* 66   20-25
Soundtrack (1966) .... *20th Century-Fox (S) TFS-4184* 66   25-30
 Cast: John Huston (narration).
Soundtrack (1966) .... *20th Century-Fox (M) TF-3187* 66   15-20
Soundtrack (1966) .... *20th Century-Fox (S) TFS-4187* 66   15-25
 Composer: Toshiro Mayuzumi. Conductor: Franco Ferrara. Cast: Art Linkletter (narration);
 Michael Parks; Richard Harris; John Huston; Stephen Boyd; George C. Scott; Ava Gardner;
 Peter O'Toole. (With dialogue).

BICYCLETTES DE BELSIZE, LES:
see TWISTED NERVE

BIG BAD WOLF
Soundtrack (1966) .... *RCA Victor/Camden (M) CAL-1087* 66   15-20
Soundtrack (1966) .... *RCA Victor/Camden (S) CAS-1087* 66   20-25
 Composer: Milton Delugg; Anne Delugg. Conductor: Milton Delugg. Cast: Peter Tripp
 (narration).

BIG BEAT
Soundtrack (1958) .... *RCA Victor (EP) EPA-4185*   15-20
 Cast: Gogi Grant.

BIG BLUE
Soundtrack .... *Virgin Movie Music (S) 90963-1*   8-10
 Cast: Eric Serra.

BIG BLUE MARBLE
TV Soundtrack (1974) .... *A&M (S) SP-3401* 75   8-12

BIG BOUNCE
Soundtrack (1969) .... *Warner Bros. (S) WS-1718* 69   20-25
 Composer: Mike Curb. Conductor: Mike Curb.

BIG BROADCAST OF 1936
Soundtrack (1950) .... *Decca (M) DL-6008* 50   50-60
 Composer: Rainger-Parker. Conductor: Tommy Dorsey. Cast: Bing Crosby.
 Also see EASY TO REMEMBER

BIG CHILL
Soundtrack (1983) .... *Motown (S) 6062* 83   8-10
 Composer: Various. Cast: Marvin Gaye; Three Dog Night; Rascals; Smokey Robinson
 and the Miracles; Procol Harum; Exciters; Aretha Franklin; Temptations.

BIG CIRCUS
Soundtrack (1959) .... *Todd (M) 5001* 59   50-60
Soundtrack (1959) .... *Todd (S) S-5001* 59   70-80
 Composer: Paul Sawtell; Bert Shefter; Sammy Fain; Roy Webb; Sid Cutner.
 Conductor: Kurt Graunke.

BIG COUNTRY
Soundtrack (1958) ....*United Artists (M) UAL-40004*	58	$30-35
Soundtrack (1958) .... *United Artists (SE) UAS-5004*	59	30-35
Black label.		
Soundtrack (1958) .... *United Artists (SE) UAS-5004*	68	10-15
Pink and orange label.		
Soundtrack (1958) .... *Ascot (M) UM-13504*	64	15-20
Soundtrack (1958) .... *Ascot (SE) US-16504*	64	25-30
Above two LPs also have music from *Taras Bulba, Johnny Cool* and *Dr. No.*		
Soundtrack (1958) .... *United Artists (S) UA-LA270-G*	74	10-12

Composer: Jerome Moross. **Conductor:** Jerome Moross.

BIG GUNDOWN
Soundtrack (1967) ....*United Artists (S) UAS-5190*	67	25-30
Soundtrack (1967) .... *United Artists (S) UA-LA297-G*	74	8-10

Composer: Ennio Morricone. **Conductor:** Bruno Nicolai.

BIG HITS FROM COLUMBIA PICTURES
Studiotrack (1958) ....*Tops (M) L-1632*	58	15-25
Cover pictures Kim Novak and Rita Hayworth.		
Composer: Various. **Conductor:** John Williams.		
Studiotrack ....*Golden Tone (S) 9632S*		10-15

Composer: Various. **Conductor:** John Williams.

BIG RED:
see STORY OF BIG RED

BIG RIVER (THE ADVENTURES OF HUCKLEBERRY FINN)
Original Cast (1985) ....*MCA (S) 6147*	85	8-10

Composer: Roger Miller (inspired by Mark Twain's *Adventures of Huckleberry Finn*).
Conductor: Linda Twine. **Cast:** John Goodman; Daniel Jenkins; Rene Auberjonois; William Youmans; Peggy Harmon; Andi Henig; Bob Bunton; Ron Richardson; Patti Cohenour; John Short.

BIG SCREEN/LITTLE SCREEN
Movie/TV Soundtrack ....*RCA Victor (S) LSP-4630*	72	10-12

Composer: Henry Mancini. **Conductor:** Henry Mancini. **Cast:** Henry Mancini and His Orchestra.

BIG TIME
Soundtrack (1977) .... *Tamla (S) T6-35551*	77	8-10

Composer: Smokey Robinson. **Cast:** Smokey Robinson.

BIG TOP PEE-WEE
Soundtrack (1988) .... *Arista (S) AL-8568*	88	8-10

Composer: Danny Elfman. **Cast:** Pee Wee Herman; Big Top Company; Chuck Rio; Vance the Pig.

BIG TOWN
Soundtrack (1987) .... *Atlantic (S) 81769-4* 87 **$8-10**
    Composer: Various. **Cast:** Little Willie John; Ray Charles; Johnny Cash; Jesse Belvin; LaVern
    Baker; Drifters; Ronnie Self; Bobby Darin.

BIG TROUBLE IN LITTLE CHINA
Soundtrack (1986) .... *Enigma (S) SJ-73227* 86 **8-12**
    Composer: John Carpenter. **Cast:** John Carpenter; Coup De Villes.

BIG VALLEY
TV Soundtrack (1965) .... *ABC (M) ABC-527* 65 **30-35**
TV Soundtrack (1965) .... *ABC (S) ABCS-527* 65 **35-40**
    Composer: George Duning.

BIGGEST BUNDLE OF THEM ALL
Soundtrack (1967) .... *MGM (M) E-4446* 67 **15-20**
Soundtrack (1967) .... *MGM (S) SE-4446* 67 **20-25**
    Composer: Riz Ortolani. **Conductor:** Riz Ortolani. **Cast:** Johnny Mathis; Eric Burdon and
    the Animals.

BIKINI BEACH
Soundtrack (1964) .... *Buena Vista (M) BV-3324* 64 **20-40**
Soundtrack (1964) .... *Buena Vista (S) ST-3324* 64 **20-25**
    Side two has songs by Annette (written by the Sherman Brothers, Cynthia Weil, and others).
    Composer: Jerry Styner; Guy Hemric. **Cast:** Annette Funicello.

BILL AND COO
Soundtrack (1947) .... *Mercury Miniature Playhouse (M) MMP-20* 47 **400-500**
    Double 10-inch LP set. With cloth cover.
    Conductor: Lionel Newman. **Cast:** Elizabeth Walters (narration).

BILL AND TED'S EXCELLENT ADVENTURE
Soundtrack (1989) .... *A&M (S) SP-3915* **8-10**
    Composer: Various. **Cast:** Extreme; Vital Signs; Glen Burtnick; Shark Island; Bricklin;
    Robbie Robb; Power Tool; Tora Tora.

BILLIE
Soundtrack (1965) .... *United Artists (M) UAL-4131* 65 **15-20**
Soundtrack (1965) .... *United Artists (S) UAS-5131* 65 **20-30**
    Composer: Dominic Frontiere; others. **Cast:** Patty Duke.

BILLION DOLLAR BRAIN
Soundtrack (1967) . . . .*United Artists (M) UAL-4174*   67 $15-20
Soundtrack (1967) . . . .*United Artists (S) UAS-5174*   67   20-30
  Composer: Richard Rodney Bennett. **Conductor:** Marcus Dods.

BILLY
Original Cast (1974) . . . .*CBS (S) 70133*   74   15-20
  Composer: John Barry; Don Black. **Conductor:** John Barry. **Cast:** Michael Crawford.

BILLY BARNES' REVUE
Original Cast (1959) . . . . *Decca (M) DL-9076*   59   25-30
Original Cast (1959) . . . .*Decca (S) DL7-9076*   59   40-45
  Composer: Billy Barnes. **Conductor:** Billy Barnes. **Cast:** Joyce Jameson; Bert Convy;
  Patti Regan; Jackie Joseph; Ken Berry; Ann Guilbert; Bob Rodgers; Len Weinrib.

BILLY BARNES' L.A.
Original Los Angeles Cast (1962) . . . .*B.B. Records (M) 1001*   62   25-30
Original Los Angeles Cast (1962) . . . .*AEI (S) 1134*   Re   8-10
  Composer: Billy Barnes. **Conductor:** Ray Henderson. **Cast:** Joyce Jameson; Ken Berry;
  Sylvia Lewis.

BILLY BISHOP GOES TO WAR
Original Cast (1979) . . . .*Tapestry (S) GD-7372*   79   8-10
  Composer: John Gray. **Cast:** John Gray (piano and background vocals); Eric Peterson.

BILLY BUDD
Original Radio Cast (1963) . . . . *General Electric (M) GESD-1*   25-35
  Cast: Peter Ustinov; Frank Murphy; Helen Hayes (narration).

BILLY GOLDENBERG: HIS FILM AND TELEVISION MUSIC
Studiotrack . . . .*No Label Shown (S) 20*   40-50
  Promotional issue only. Has film music: *Up the Sandbox* and *Change of Habit* and TV themes: *The
  Harness* (TV movie) and *Columbo* (*Ransom for a Dead Man* episode).
  Composer: Billy Goldenberg. **Conductor:** Billy Goldenberg.

BILLY JACK
Soundtrack (1971) . . . .*Warner Bros. (S) WS-1926*   71   15-20
Soundtrack (1971) . . . . *Warner Bros. (S) BJS-1001*   73   10-15
  Composer: Mundell Lowe. **Conductor:** Mundell Lowe. **Cast:** Coven; Teresa Kelly; Lynn
  Baker; Gwen Smith; Katy Moffatt.

BILLY NONAME
Original Cast (1970) . . . .*Roulette (S) SROC-11*   70   30-35
  Composer: Johnny Brandon. **Conductor:** Sammy Benskin. **Cast:** Donny Burks; Alan Weeks;
  Hatti Winston; Thommie Bush; Doris DeMendez; Eugene Edwards; Marilyn Johnson; Roger
  Lawson; Urylee Leonardos; Joni Palmer; Andrea Saunders;
  Andy Torres; Glory Van Scott.

BILLY SUNDAY
Studio Cast . . . . *Word (S) W-3267*   8-12
  Cast: Homer Rodeheaver; Mel Dibble (narrator).

**BING CROSBY ON BROADWAY (BING CROSBY AT THE LONDON
  PALADIUM)**
Original Cast (1976) . . . . *United Artists/K-Tel (S) NE-951*   76   10-15
  Double LP set.
  Cast: Bing Crosby; Rosemary Clooney; Crosby Family.

BING CROSBY RADIO SHOWS
Radio Cast . . . . *Golden Age (M) 5023*   8-10
  Cast: Bing Crosby; others.

BINGO LONG TRAVELING ALL-STARS AND MOTOR KINGS
Soundtrack (1976) .... *Motown (S) MCA 2094*   76   **$8-10**
Composer: William Goldstein. Conductor: William Goldstein. Cast: Thelma Houston.

BIOGRAPH GIRL
Soundtrack .... *That's Entertainment (S) TER-1003*   80   **8-10**
Composer: David Heneker. Cast: Shelia White; Jane Hardy; Bruce Barry; Kate Revill; Guy Siner.

BIRD
Soundtrack (1988) .... *Columbia (S) SC-44299*   88   **8-10**
Biography of Charlie "Bird" Parker.
Composer: Lennie Niehaus. Cast: Charlie Parker; Forest Whitaker; Diane Venora.

BIRD OF PARADISE
Soundtrack (1932) .... *Medallion (M) 305-306*   80   **10-15**
Double LP set.
Composer: Max Steiner. Conductor: Max Steiner. Cast: Joel McCrea; Dolores Del Rio; John Halliday; Skeets Gallegher; Lon Chaney Jr. (With dialogue.)
Soundtrack (1932) .... *Medallion (M) 309*   80   **20-30**
Also has music from *Santa Fe Trail, A Star Is Born* and *Life with Father.*
Composer: Max Steiner.

BIRD WITH THE CRYSTAL PLUMAGE
Soundtrack (1970) .... *Capitol (S) SW-642*   70   **75-85**
Soundtrack (1970) .... *Cerberus (S) CEMS 0108*   81   **8-10**
Composer: Ennio Moricone. Conductor: Bruno Nicolai.

BIRDS, THE BEES AND THE ITALIANS
Soundtrack (1966) .... *United Artists (M) UAL-4157*   66   **20-25**
Soundtrack (1966) .... *United Artists (S) UAS-5157*   66   **25-30**
Composer: Carlo Rustichelli. Conductor: Pier Luigi Urbini.

BIRDY
Soundtrack (1984) .... *Geffen (S) GHS-24070*   84   **8-10**
Cast: Peter Gabriel.

BITE THE BULLET
Soundtrack (1975) .... *RFO (S) RFO-102*   80   **90-100**
Composer: Alex North. Conductor: Alex North.

BITTERSWEET
Original London Cast (1929) .... *World (M) SH-179/80*   **20-25**
Original London Cast (1929) ..... *Monmouth Evergreen (SE) MES-7062/3*   **8-10**
Studio Cast (1961) .... *Angel (M) 35814*   61   **25-30**
Studio Cast (1961) .... *Angel (S) S-35814*   61   **30-35**
Composer: Noel Coward. Conductor: Michael Collins. Cast: Vanesa Lee; Roberto Cardinali; Julie Dawn; John Hauxvell.

BLACK AND WHITE IN COLOR
Soundtrack (1977) .... *Buddah (S) BDS-5698*   77   **25-30**
Composer: Pierre Bachelet. Conductor: Mat Camison.

BLACK BELLY OF THE TARANTULA
Soundtrack (1972) .... *Cerberus (S) CEMS 0116*   82   **10-15**
Has music from *My Dear Assassin,* also by Ennio Morricone.
Composer: Ennio Morricone. Conductor: Ennio Morricone.

BLACK CAESAR
Soundtrack (1973) .... *Polydor (S) PD-6014*   73   **15-20**
Composer: James Brown. Cast: James Brown.

BLACK CAULDRON
Soundtrack (1985) .... *Varese Sarabande (S) STV-81253*   85   **$10-15**
Composer: Elmer Bernstein. Conductor: Elmer Bernstein. Cast: Utah Symphony Orchestra.

BLACK FIST
Soundtrack (1976) .... *Happy Fox (S) HF-1101*   76   **8-12**

BLACK HOLE
Soundtrack (1979) .... *Buena Vista (S) 5008*   79   **8-10**
Composer: John Barry. Conductor: John Barry.
Soundtrack (1979) .... *Disneyland (S) DIS-3821*   79   **8-10**
Full title: *The Black Hole (The Story of the Black Hole).*
Composer: John Barry. Conductor: John Barry. Cast: Maximilian Schell; Anthony Perkins;
Robert Forster; Joseph Bottoms; Yvette Mimieux; Ernest Borgnine. (With dialogue.)

BLACK NATIVITY
Original Cast (1961) .... *Vee Jay (M) VJ-8503*   61   **10-15**
Original Cast (1961) .... *Vee Jay (S) VJS-8503*   61   **20-25**
Original Cast (1961) .... *Vee Jay (M) LP-5022*   61   **10-15**
Original Cast (1961) .... *Vee Jay (S) SR-5002*   61   **15-20**
Original Cast (1961) .... *Trip (S) 7022*   **10-12**
Traditional gospel songs.
Cast: Marion Williams; Stars of Faith; Princess Stewart.

BLACK ORCHID
Soundtrack (1959) .... *Dot (M) DLP-3178*   59   **50-60**
Soundtrack (1959) .... *Dot (S) DLP-25178*   59   **65-80**
Composer: Alessandro Cicognini. Conductor: Carlo Savina.

BLACK ORPHEUS (ORFEO NEGRO)
Soundtrack (1959) .... *Epic (M) LN-3672*   59   **15-25**
Soundtrack (1959) .... *Fontana (M) MFG-27520*   64   **10-15**
Soundtrack (1959) .... *Fontana (SE) SRF-67520*   64   **10-15**
Composer: Antonio Carlos Jobim; Luiz Bonfa.

BLACK RAIN
Soundtrack (1989) .... *Virgin (S) 91292-1*   89   **8-10**
Composer: Hans Zimmer; others. Conductor: Shirley Walker. Cast: Gregg Allman; UB40;
Iggy Pop; Soul II; Soul with Caron Wheeler; Les Rita Mitsouko and Sparks; Ryuichi Sakamoto.

BLACK STALLION
Soundtrack (1979) .... *United Artists (S) LOQ-1040*   80   **8-10**
Composer: Carmine Coppola. Conductor: Carmine Coppola.

BLACK STALLION RETURNS
Soundtrack (1983) .... *Liberty (S) LO-51144*   83   **8-10**
Composer: Georges Delerue. Conductor: Georges Delerue. Cast: Kelly Reno; Teri Garr;
Allen Goorwitz; Vincent Spano; Woody Strode.

BLACK TIGHTS
Soundtrack (1962) .... *RCA Victor (M) FOC-3*   62   **25-30**
Soundtrack (1962) .... *RCA Victor (S) FSO-3*   62   **40-45**
Composer: George Bizet; others. Cast: Maurice Chevalier (narration).

BLACKBEARD'S GHOST
Soundtrack (1968) .... *Disneyland (M) DQ-1305*   68   **10-12**
Cast: Peter Ustinov (narration); Dean Jones; Suzanne Pleshette. (With dialogue.)

BLACKBIRDS OF 1928

Studio Cast .... *Revue (M) 1* $15-20
  Has 12 tracks.
Studio Cast .... *Sutton (M) SU-270*   Re   20-25
  Has only 10 tracks.
Studio Cast .... *Sutton (SE) SSU-270*   20-25
Studio Cast .... *Columbia (M) OL-6770*   68   10-12
  With original cast stars. Has 14 tracks, four of which are alternate takes.
  Composer: Jimmy McHugh; Dorothy Fields. **Conductor:** Duke Ellington; Don Redmond.
  Cast: Adelaide Hall; Bill Robinson; Cab Calloway; Mills Brothers; Ethel Waters; Cecil Mack
  Choir.
Studio Cast (1953) .... *RCA Victor (EP) EPA-483*   53   10-20
Studio Cast (1953) .... *RCA Victor (M) LPM-3154*   53   30-40
  10-inch LP. One side has music from *Shuffle Along*.
  Composer: Jimmy McHugh; Dorothy Fields. SHUFFLE ALONG: Eubie Blake; Noble Sissle.
  Conductor: Lehman Engel. SHUFFLE ALONG: Eubie Blake. **Cast:** Cab Calloway; Thelma
  Carpenter. SHUFFLE ALONG: Avon Long; Thelma Carpenter; Louise Woods; Laurence
  Watson.
Studio Cast (1970) .... *Monmouth Evergreen (SE) MES-7080*   76   8-10
  Composer: Jimmy McHugh; Dorothy Fields. **Cast:** Adelaide Hall.

BLACULA

Soundtrack (1972) .... *RCA Victor (S) LSP-4806*   72   15-20
  Composer: Gene Page; Wally Holmes; Karl Russell. **Conductor:** Gene Page; Don Peake.
  Cast: 21st Century, Ltd.; Hues Corporation.

BLADE RUNNER

Soundtrack (1982) .... *Full Moon/Warner Bros. (S) 1-23748*   82   8-10
  Composer: Vangelis. **Conductor:** Jack Elliott; Patrick Williams. **Cast:** John Bahler; New
  American Orchestra.

BLAZE

Soundtrack (1989) .... *A&M (S) SP-3932*   89   8-10
  Composer: Bennie Wallace (original music); others. **Conductor:** Bennie Wallace; others.
  Cast: Bennie Wallace; Fats Domino; Hank Williams Sr., Bonnie Sheridan; Randy Newman.

BLESS THE BEASTS AND CHILDREN

Soundtrack (1971) .... *A&M (S) SP-4322*   71   25-30
  Composer: Barry DeVorzon; Perry Botkin Jr. **Cast:** Carpenters.

BLESS THE BRIDE:
see WATER GYPSIES

BLIND DATE

Soundtrack (1987) .... *Rhino (S) RNIN-70705*   87   8-10
  Composer: Various. **Cast:** Jennifer Warnes; Billy Vera and the Beaters; Keith L'Neire;
  Hubert Tubbs; Henry Mancini; Stanley Jordan.
Soundtrack (19) .... *Varese Sarabande (S) 81202*   8-10
  Cast: John Kongos.

BLISS OR MRS. BLOSSOM

Soundtrack (1968) .... *RCA Victor (S) LSP-4080*   68   25-30
  Composer: Riz Ortolani. **Cast:** New Vaudeville Band; Shirley MacLaine; Spectrum.

BLITZ

Original London Cast .... *AEI (S) 1117*   8-10
  Composer: Lionel Bart.

BLOOD AND SAND
Soundtrack (1941) .... *Decca (M) DL-5380* 52 **$50-60**
10-inch LP.
Soundtrack (1941) .... *Decca (M) DL-4629* 56 **30-40**
Soundtrack (1941) .... *Decca (SE) DL7-4629* 59 **30-40**
Composer: Vincente Gómez. Cast: Vincente Gómez Quintet; Graciela Parraga.

BLOOD ON THE SUN
Soundtrack (1945) .... *Citadel (M) CT-6031* 79 **15-20**
Composer: Miklos Rozsa. Conductor: Miklos Rozsa.

BLOODLINE
Soundtrack (1979) .... *Varese Sarabande (S) STV-81131* 79 **8-12**
Composer: Ennio Morricone. Conductor: Ennio Morricone.

BLOODY MAMA
Soundtrack (1970) .... *American Int'l (S) STA-1031* 70 **15-20**
Composer: Don Randi. Conductor: Don Randi. Cast: Bigfoot.

BLOOMER GIRL
Original Cast (1944) .... *Decca (M) DL-8015* 50 **25-40**
Original Cast (1944) .... *Decca (M) DL-9126* 65 **15-20**
Original Cast (1944) .... *Decca (SE) DL7-9126* 65 **15-20**
Original Cast (1944) .... *MCA (SE) 2072e* 72 **8-10**
Composer: Harold Arlen; E.Y. Harburg. Conductor: Leon Leonardi. Cast: Celeste Holm;
David Brooks; Toni Hart; Harold Arlen; Hubert Dilworth; Richard Huey; Joan McCracken;
Mabel Taliaferro; Dooley Wilson.

BLOOMFIELD:
see HERO

BLOSSOM TIME
Studio Cast (1947) .... *RCA Victor (M) LK-1018* **35-40**
Composer: Franz Schubert; Heinrich Berte; Dorothy Donnelly (adapted by Sigmund Romberg).
Conductor: Al Goodman. Cast: Earl Wrightson; Donald Dame; Mary Martha Briney; Blanka
Peric; Mullen Sisters; Guild Choristers.

BLOW-UP
Soundtrack (1966) .... *MGM (M) E-4447* 67 **25-30**
Soundtrack (1966) .... *MGM (S) SE-4447* 67 **30-35**
Composer: Herbie Hancock. Conductor: Herbie Hancock. Cast: Yardbirds; Herbie Hancock.

BLUE
Soundtrack (1968) .... *Dot (M) DLP-3855* 68 **20-25**
Soundtrack (1968) .... *Dot (S) DLP-25855* 68 **30-40**
Composer: Manos Hadjidakis. Conductor: Manos Hadjidakis.

BLUE CITY
Soundtrack (1986) .... *Warner Bros. (S) 1-25386* 86 **8-10**
Cast: Ry Cooder; True Believers; Pops and Timer.

BLUE COLLAR
Soundtrack (1978) .... *MCA (S) 3034* 78 **8-12**
Composer: Jack Nitzsche. Conductor: Jack Nitzsche. Cast: Captain Beefheart.

BLUE EYED BANDIT
Soundtrack .... *Cerberus (S) CEMS-0114* 82 **8-10**
Composer: Ennio Morricone. Conductor: Ennio Morricone.

BLUE HAWAII
Soundtrack (1961) .... *RCA Victor (M) LPM-2426*   61   **$75-90**
 Black label, reads "Long Play" at bottom.
Soundtrack (1961) .... *RCA Victor (S) LSP-2426*   61   **90-100**
 Black label, reads "Living Stereo" at bottom.
Soundtrack (1961) .... *RCA Victor (M) LPM-2426*   63   **40-50**
 Black label, reads "Mono" at bottom.
Soundtrack (1961) .... *RCA Victor (M) LPM-2426*   65   **25-30**
 Black label, reads "Monaural" at bottom.
Soundtrack (1961) .... *RCA Victor (S) LSP-2426*   65   **25-30**
 Black label, reads "Stereo" at bottom.
Soundtrack (1961) .... *RCA Victor (S) LSP-2426*   69   **10-20**
 Orange or tan label. (Tan label issued in 1976.)
Soundtrack (1961) .... *RCA Victor (S) AFL1-2426*   77   **8-10**
Soundtrack (1961) .... *RCA Victor (S) AYL1-3683*   81   **5-8**
 Composer: Sid Tepper; Roy C. Bennett; Fred Wise; Ben Weisman; others. **Cast:** Elvis Presley;
 Scotty Moore (guitar); Bob Moore (bass); D.J. Fontana (drums); Floyd Cramer (piano); Boots
 Randolph (sax); Hank Garland (guitar); Jordanaires (vocals); Surfers (vocals).

BLUE IGUANA
Soundtrack (1988) .... *Polydor (S) 835592-1*   88   **8-10**
 Composer: Various. **Cast:** Kurtis Blow; Zodiac Mindwarp and the Love Reaction; Fat Boys;
 Del Vikings; Chuck Brown and the Soul Searchers; James Brown; Platters; Dirge; Fela
 Anikulapo Kuti; Ethan James; White Boys.

BLUE LAGOON
Soundtrack (1980) .... *Marlin (S) 2236-X*   80   **8-10**
 Composer: Basil Poledouris.

BLUE MAX
Soundtrack (1966) .... *Mainstream (M) 56081*   66   **35-40**
Soundtrack (1966) .... *Mainstream (S) S-6081*   66   **50-75**
Soundtrack (1966) .... *Citadel (S) CT-6008*   76   **12-15**
Soundtrack (1966) .... *Citadel (S) CT-7007*   79   **15-25**
 Remastered.
 Composer: Jerry Goldsmith. **Conductor:** Jerry Goldsmith.

BLUE MONDAY
Studio Cast (1925) .... *Vox Turnabout (SE) TV-S 3463*   76   **10-12**
 Side two contains Gershwin production numbers.
 Composer: George Gershwin. **Conductor:** Gregg Smith. **Cast:** Joyce Andrews; Patrick Mason.

BLUE SKIES
Soundtrack (1946) .... *Decca (M) DLP-5042*   50   **40-50**
 10-inch LP.

BLUE SKIES (continued)
Soundtrack (1946) .... *Decca (M) DL-4259*   62 $25-30
   Also contains music from *Out of This World*. Issued as part of *Bing's Hollywood Series*.
   Composer: Irving Berlin. **Conductor:** John Scott Trotter. **Cast:** Bing Crosby; Fred Astaire;
   Trudy Erwin.

BLUE THUNDER
Soundtrack (1983) .... *MCA (S) 6122*   83   8-10
   Composer: Arthur Rubinstein. **Conductor:** Arthur Rubinstein. **Cast:** Beepers.

BLUE VELVET
Soundtrack (1986) .... *Varese Sarabande (S) STV-81292*   86   15-20
   Composer: Angelo Badalamenti; others. **Conductor:** Angelo Badalamenti. **Cast:** Julee Cruise;
   Ketty Lester; Roy Orbison.

BLUEBEARD
Soundtrack (1980) .... *Cerberus (S) CEM-S-010*   80   8-10
   Composer: Ennio Morricone. **Conductor:** Franco Tamponi.

BLUES
Soundtrack (1967) .... *Asch (M) 101*   8-10
   Cast: J.D. Short; Pink Anderson; Furry Lewis; Baby Tate; Memphis Willie B.; Gus Cannon;
   Sleepy John Estes.

BLUES, BALLADS AND SIN SONGS
Original Cast (1954) .... *Monmouth Evergreen (SE) MRS-6501*   10-15
   Cast: Libby Holman; Gerald Cook (piano).

BLUES BROTHERS
Soundtrack (1980) .... *Atlantic (S) SD-16017*   80   8-10
   Composer: Various. **Conductor:** Ira Newborn. **Cast:** Blues Brothers (John Belushi and Dan
   Aykroyd); Ray Charles; James Brown; Aretha Franklin; Cab Calloway; James Cleveland Choir.

BLUES OPERA:
see FREE AND EASY

BOB AND CAROL AND TED AND ALICE
Soundtrack (1969) .... *Bell (S) 1200*   69   15-20
   Composer: Quincy Jones. **Conductor:** Quincy Jones.

BOB AND RAY - THE TWO AND ONLY
Original Cast (1970) .... *Columbia (S) S-30412*   70   10-15
   Composer: Bob Elliot; Ray Goulding. **Cast:** Bob Elliot; Ray Goulding (comedy skits
   without music).

BOBBY DEERFIELD
Soundtrack (1977) .... *Casablanca (S) NBLP-7071*   77   8-10
   Composer: Dave Grusin. **Conductor:** Dave Grusin.

BOBO
Soundtrack (1967) .... *Warner Bros. (M) W-1711*   67   15-20
Soundtrack (1967) .... *Warner Bros. (S) WS-1711*   67   20-25
   Composer: Francis Lai. **Conductor:** Francis Lai. **Cast:** Peter Sellers.

BOCCACCIO '70
Soundtrack (1962) .... *RCA Victor (M) FOC-5*   62   40-45
Soundtrack (1962) .... *RCA Victor (S) FSO-5*   62   50-55
   Composer: Nino Rota; Armando Trovajoli. **Conductor:** Nino Rota; Armando Trovajoli;
   Franco Ferrara.

BODY BEAUTIFUL
Original Cast . . . . *Blue Pear (M) BP-1006* $25-30
  Composer: Jerry Bock; Sheldon Harnick. Cast: Mindy Carson; Jack Warden; Steve Forrest;
  Tony Atkins; Dorothy Aull; Mace Barrett; Edward Becker; Armand Boney; Richard Chitos;
  Bob Daley; Richard De Bella; Jack DeLon; Kathie Forman; Edmond Gaynes; Betty Graham;
  Buzz Halliday; Tommy Halloran; William Hickey; Louis Kosman; Mary Louise; Mara Lynn;
  Barbara McNair; Mitchell Nutick; Broc Peters; Albert Popwell; Tom Raskin; Bill Richards;
  Jeff Roberts; Harry Lee Rogers; Jane Romano; Lonnie Sattin; Helen Silver; Knute Sullivan;
  Alan Weeks; Bob Wiens.

BODY HEAT
Soundtrack (1983) . . . .*Label X (S) LXSE 1-002*   83   100-150
  This LP is the only source for John Williams' *Ladd Co. Fanfare.*
  Composer: John Barry. Conductor: John Barry.

BODY IN THE SEINE
Original Cast (1955) . . . .*Private Label-Alden-Shaw (M) VB-001*   200-400
  Has tracks from a musical that got no farther than this collection of songs. From the producers of
  The Athenian Touch.
  Composer: David Lippincott. Conductor: Buster Davis. Cast: Alice Pearce; Jim Symington;
  Barbara Ashley; George S. Irving; Laurel Selby; Terry Turner; Pat Wilkes; Don Liberto.

BODY ROCK
Soundtrack (1984) . . . .*EMI America (S) SO-17140*   84   8-10
  Composer: Various. Cast: Maria Vidal; David Lasley; Laura Branigan; others.

BODY SLAM
Soundtrack (1987) . . . .*MCA (S) 6197*   87   8-10
  Composer: Various. Cast: Moses Tyson Jr.; Bachman-Turner Overdrive; Kick; Frankie Valli
  and the 4 Seasons; Debbie Lytton; Jimmy Scarlet and the Dimensions.

BOEING, BOEING
Soundtrack (1965) . . . . *RCA Victor (M) LOC-1121*   65   20-25
Soundtrack (1965) . . . . *RCA Victor (S) LSO-1121*   65   25-30
  Composer: Neal Hefti. Conductor: Neal Hefti.

BOGIE: A SALUTE
Soundtrack . . . .*MGM (M) E-4359*   10-20
Soundtrack . . . . *MGM (S) SE-4359*   15-25

BOLD VENTURES
Studio Cast (1969) . . . . *Revell (S) 87-8162*   69   15-20
  Promotional issue from Revell, makers of toy models.
  Composer: Jack Shaindlin. Cast: James Maguire; Mike Geller; Donald Hirsh; Fred
  Clements Jr.; Walter Hoffman; Don Rickles.

BOLERO
Soundtrack (1981) . . . . *Polydor (S) PD-1-6353*   82   8-10
  Composer: Michel Legrand; Francis Lai.
Soundtrack . . . . *Varese Sarabande (S) 81228*   8-10
  Conductor: Elmer Bernstein. Cast: Elmer Bernstein and His Orchestra.

BOLSHOI BALLET '67
Soundtrack (1966) . . . .*Command (S) S-11035*   66   25-30
  Cast: Members and dancers of the Bolshoi (translation: Big) Ballet Company.

BONANZA
TV Soundtrack (1958) . . . .*MGM (M) E-3960*   61   25-35
TV Soundtrack (1958) . . . . *MGM (S) SE-3960*   61   45-60
  Composer: David Rose; Jay Livingston; Ray Evans. Conductor: David Rose.
  Cast: David Rose and His Orchestra.

BONANZA BOUND
Original Cast (1947) .... *No Label Shown (M) JJA-19764*   **$10-20**
Unreleased recordings by the original cast. Side two has *The Revuers 1938 - 1944.*
Composer: Saul Chaplin; Betty Comden; Adolph Green (lyrics). **Conductor:** Lehman Engel.
Cast: Carol Raye; Hal Hackett; Adolph Green; Allyn Ann McLerie; George Colouris.
REVUERS: Judy Holliday; Betty Comden; Adolph Green; Leonard Bernstein (piano).

BONANZA - CHRISTMAS ON THE PONDEROSA
TV Soundtrack (1963) .... *RCA Victor (M) LPM-2557*   63   **15-20**
TV Soundtrack (1963) .... *RCA Victor (S) LSP-2557*   63   **20-25**
Cast: Lorne Greene; Michael Landon; Pernell Roberts; Dan Blocker.

BONANZA - PONDEROSA PARTY TIME
TV Soundtrack (1962) .... *RCA Victor (M) LPM-2583*   62   **20-25**
TV Soundtrack (1962) .... *RCA Victor (S) LSP-2583*   62   · **25-30**
Conductor: Billy Liebert. **Cast:** Lorne Greene; Michael Landon; Pernell Roberts; Dan Blocker.

BONJOUR, TRISTESSE
Soundtrack (1958) .... *RCA Victor (M) LOC-1040*   58   **60-70**
Composer: Georges Auric. **Conductor:** Georges Auric.

BONNIE AND CLYDE
Soundtrack (1967) .... *Warner Bros. (M) W-1742*   67   **20-25**
Soundtrack (1967) .... *Warner Bros. (S) WS-1742*   67   **25-30**
Composer: Charles Strouse; others. **Cast:** Warren Beatty; Faye Dunaway; Michael J. Pollard;
Gene Hackman; Estelle Parsons.

BOOGALOO
Soundtrack (1984) .... *Polydor (S) 422-82369*   84   **8-10**

BOOK OF NUMBERS
Soundtrack (1973) .... *Brut (S) 6002*   73   .   **12-15**
Cast: Sonny Terry; Brownie McGhee.

BORA, BORA
Soundtrack (1970) .... *American Int' l (S) STA-1029*   70   **20-25**
Composer: Les Baxter. **Conductor:** Les Baxter.

BORDER
Soundtrack (1981) .... *Backstreet BSR-6105*   81   **8-10**
Composer: Ry Cooder; John Hiatt; Jim Dickinson; Sam "Sam the Sham" Samudio; Dan Penn.
Conductor: Ry Cooder. **Cast:** Ry Cooder; Willie Greene Jr.; Jim Dickinson; Sam "Sam the
Sham" Samudio; John Hiatt; Brenda Patterson; Bobby King.

BORDER RADIO
Soundtrack (1987) .... *Enigma (S) SJ-73221*   87   **8-10**
Composer: Various. **Cast:** Divine Horsemen; Green on Red; Dave Alvin; John Doe; Chris D.;
The Tonys.

BORN AGAIN
Soundtrack (1978) .... *Lamb & Lion (S) LL-1041*   78   **8-10**
Composer: Les Baxter. **Conductor:** Les Baxter. **Cast:** Larnelle Harris (with dialogue).

BORN FREE
Soundtrack (1966) .... *MGM (M) E-4368*   66   **10-15**
Soundtrack (1966) .... *MGM (S) SE-4368*   66   **15-20**
Composer: John Barry. **Conductor:** John Barry. **Cast:** Matt Monro; John Barry.

BORN LOSERS
TV Soundtrack (1967) .... *Tower (M) T-5082*   67   **15-20**
TV Soundtrack (1967) .... *Tower (S) DT-5082*   67   **20-25**
Composer: Mike Curb; others. **Cast:** Terry Stafford; Sidewalk Sounds; Summer Saxophones.

BORN ON THE FOURTH OF JULY
Soundtrack . . . .*MCA (S) 6340*   **$8-10**
    Composer: Various. **Cast:** Edie Brickell and New Bohemians; Broken Homes; Van Morrison;
    Don McLean; Temptations; Shirelles; Frankie Avalon; Henry Mancini.

BORROWERS
TV Soundtrack (1973) . . . .*Stanyan (Q) SRQ-4014*   74   **10-12**
    Composer: Rod McKuen. **Conductor:** Billy Byers. **Cast:** Rod McKuen; Shelby Flint.

BORSALINO
Soundtrack (1970) . . . .*Paramount (S) PAS-5019*   70   **25-30**
Soundtrack (1970) . . . . *Lumiere (S) L-1001*   Re   **10-12**
    Composer: Claude Bolling. **Conductor:** Claude Bolling.

BOSTONIANS
Soundtrack (1984) . . . . *Audiotrax Ltd. (S) ATXLPO-2*   84   **8-10**
    Composer: Richard Robbins. **Conductor:** Richard Robbins. **Cast:** Christopher Reeve;
    Vanessa Redgrave; Jessica Tandy; Nancy Marchand; Madeleine Potter.

BOULEVARD NIGHTS
Soundtrack (1979) . . . .*Warner Bros. (S) BSK-3328*   79   **8-10**
    Composer: Lalo Schifrin. **Conductor:** Lalo Schifrin. **Cast:** George Benson.

BOUND FOR GLORY
Soundtrack (1976) . . . . *United Artists (S) UA-LA695-H*   76   **10-12**
Soundtrack (1976) . . . . *Liberty (S) LKAO-695*   Re   **8-10**
    Composer: Woody Guthrie; Leonard Rosenman. **Conductor:** Leonard Rosenman; David
    Carradine.

BOURBON STREET BEAT
TV Soundtrack (1960) . . . . *Warner Bros. (M) W-1321*   60   **20-25**
TV Soundtrack (1960) . . . .*Warner Bros. (S) WS-1321*   60   **25-35**
    Composer: Max David; Jay Livingston; others. **Conductor:** Don Ralke. **Cast:** Don Ralke
    and His Orchestra.

BOY FRIEND
Original Cast (1954) . . . . *RCA Victor (EP) EOC-1018*   54   **15-25**
Original Cast (1954) . . . . *RCA Victor (M) LOC-1018*   54   **20-30**
    Composer: Sandy Wilson. **Conductor:** Anton Coppola. **Cast:** Julie Andrews; Ann Wakefield;
    John Hewer; Ruth Altman; Eric Berry; Paulette Girard; Geoffrey Hibbert; Dilys Lay; Bob
    Scheerer.
Original London Cast (1953) . . . .*Stanyan (M) SR-10008*   **10-15**
    Composer: Sandy Wilson. **Conductor:** Stan Edwards. **Cast:** Stan Edwards (piano).
Original Australian Cast (1968) . . . . *Ace of Clubs (S) SCL-1263*   68   **15-20**
    Composer: Sandy Wilson. **Conductor:** Peter Narroway. **Cast:** Deidre Rubenstein; Laurel
    Veitch; Julia Day.
Original Revival Cast (1970) . . . . *Decca (S) DL-79177*   70   **15-20**
Original Revival Cast (1970) . . . .*MCA (S) 2074*   70   **10-12**
Original Revival Cast (1970) . . . .*MCA (S) 1537*   Re   **8-10**
    Composer: Sandy Wilson. **Conductor:** Jerry Goldberg. **Cast:** Sandy Duncan; Ronald Young;
    Jenne Beauvais; Leon Shaw; Barbara Andres; Judy Carne; Harvey Evans; Simon McQueen;
    David Vaughn; Ronald Young.
Original Revival Cast (1970) . . . . *MGM (S) 1SE-32*   71   **12-18**
    Composer: Sandy Wilson; others. **Conductor:** Peter Maxwell Davies. **Cast:** Twiggy;
    Christopher Gable; Max Adrian.
    Also see DIVORCE ME, DARLING

BOY MEETS BOY

Original Cast (1975) .... *R&P (S) JO-13* 75 **$15-20**
  Composer: Billy Solly. **Conductor:** David Friedman. **Cast:** Joe Barrett; Bobby Bower;
  David Gallegly; Jan Crean; Rita Gordon; Monica Grignon; Richard King; Paul Ratkevich;
  Bobby Reed; Dan Rounds; Raymond Wood.
Original Cast (1975) .... *AEI (S) 1102* Re **8-10**
  Composer: Billy Solly. **Conductor:** David Friedman. **Cast:** Joe Barrett; Bobby Bower; David
  Gallegly.
Original Cast (1980) .... *Private Editions Series (S) FRC PES-1* **10-15**
  Based on the 1979 production by The Out & About Theatre, Minneapolis.
  Conductor: Brad Callahan; Patti Haight. **Cast:** Farrell Batley; Vic Campbell; Mick Isackson;
  Thomas Freiberg.

BOY NAMED CHARLIE BROWN

Soundtrack (1970) .... *Columbia (S) OS-3500* 70 **15-20**
Soundtrack (1970) .... *Columbia Special Products (S) AOS-3500* Re **8-12**
  Composer: Rod McKuen; Vince Guaraldi; John Scott Trotter. **Conductor:** John Scott Trotter.
TV Soundtrack (1970) .... *Fantasy (S) 84-30* 70 **15-20**
  Composer: Vince Guaraldi. **Cast:** Vince Guaraldi Trio.

BOY ON A DOLPHIN

Soundtrack (1957) .... *Decca (M) DL-8580* 57 **60-75**
Soundtrack (1957) .... *Varese Sarabande (M) STV-81119* 81 **8-10**
  Composer: Hugo Friedhofer. **Conductor:** Lionel Newman. **Cast:** Mary Kaye; 20th
  Century-Fox Orchestra and Chorus.

BOYS:

see SEVEN LIVELY ARTS

BOYS FROM BRAZIL

Soundtrack (1978) .... *A&M (S) SP-4731* 78 **8-10**
  Composer: Jerry Goldsmith. **Conductor:** Jerry Goldsmith.

BOYS FROM SYRACUSE

Original London Cast .... *Decca (M) DL-4564* 64 **25-30**
Original London Cast .... *Stet (S) DS-15016* Re **8-10**
  Composer: Richard Rodgers; Lorenz Hart. **Conductor:** Robert Lowe **Cast:** Bob Monkhouse;
  Denis Quilley; Pat Turner.
Original Revival Cast (1963) .... *Capitol (M) TAO-1933* 63 **25-30**
Original Revival Cast (1963) .... *Capitol (S) STAO-1933* 63 **30-40**
  Above two LPs have a gatefold cover.
  Composer: Richard Rodgers; Lorenz Hart. **Conductor:** Rene Weigert. **Cast:** Ellen Hanley;
  Danny Carroll; Cathryn Damon; Stuart Damon; Richard Nieves; Fred Kimbrough; Matt
  Tobin; Gary Oakes; Rudy Tronto; Clifford David; Julienne Marie; Karen Morrow.
Studio Cast (1954) .... *Columbia (M) ML-4837* 54 **30-35**
Studio Cast (1954) .... *Columbia (M) CL-847* 56 **20-25**
Studio Cast (1954) .... *Columbia (M) OL-7080* 64 **10-15**
Studio Cast (1954) .... *Columbia (SE) OS-2580* 64 **10-15**
Studio Cast (1954) .... *Columbia Special Products (SE) COS-2580* Re **8-10**
  Composer: Richard Rodgers; Lorenz Hart. **Conductor:** Lehman Engel. **Cast:** Portia Nelson;
  Jack Cassidy; Bob Shaver.

BOYS IN THE BAND

Original Cast (1969) .... *A&M (S) 6001* 69 **20-25**
  Double LP. A complete play.

BRAINCHILD
Original Cast (1974) .... *Demo (M) RFP-104*   74   **$75-100**
   Limited edition, only 1,000 copies pressed.
   Composer: Michel Legrand; Hal David. **Cast:** Dorian Harewood.

BRAINSTORM
Soundtrack (1983) .... *Varese Sarabande (S) STV-81197*   83   **8-12**
   Composer: James Horner. **Conductor:** James Horner. **Cast:** London Symphony Orchestra.

BRASS TARGET
Soundtrack (1978) .... *Varese Sarabande (S) VC-81082*   78   **8-10**
   Composer: Laurence Rosenthal. **Conductor:** Laurence Rosenthal. **Cast:** Laurence Rosenthal.

BRAVE ONE
Soundtrack (1956) .... *Decca (EP) ED-847*   56   **20-25**
Soundtrack (1956) .... *Decca (M) DL-8344*   56   **65-75**
Soundtrack (1956) .... *AEI (M) 3107*   81   **8-10**
   Composer: Victor Young. **Conductor:** Victor Young. **Cast:** Victor Young and His Orchestra.

BRAVO GIOVANNI!
Original Cast (1962) .... *Columbia (M) KOL-5800*   62   **30-35**
Original Cast (1962) .... *Columbia (S) KOS-2200*   62   **35-40**
   Composer: Milton Schafer; Ronny Graham. **Conductor:** Anton Coppola. **Cast:** Cesare Siepi;
   Michele Lee; Maria Karnilova; Nino Banome; Rico Froehlich; George S.
   Irving; Buzz Miller; David Opatoshu; Gene Varrone.
Studiotrack (1961) .... *Columbia (M) CL-1820*   62   **10-20**
Studiotrack (1961) .... *Columbia (S) CS-8620*   62   **15-25**
   Composer: Milton Schafer; Ronny Graham. **Conductor:** Luther Henderson. **Cast:** Luther
   Henderson Orchestra.

BREAKER MORANT
Soundtrack (1980) .... *First American (S) FA7783*   81   **8-10**
   Cast: Edward Woodward.

BREAKFAST AT TIFFANY'S
Original Cast (1966) .... *S.P.M. CO-478* **10-20**
   Cast: Richard Chamberlain; Sally Kellerman; Larry Kert; Art Lund; Mary Tyler Moore.
Soundtrack (1961) .... *RCA Victor (M) LPM-2362*   61   **20-30**
Soundtrack (1961) .... *RCA Victor (S) LSP-2362*   61   **25-35**
   Black label.
Soundtrack (1961) .... *RCA Victor (S) LSP-2362*   75   **10-15**
   Orange label.
   Composer: Henry Mancini. **Conductor:** Henry Mancini. **Cast:** Henry Mancini's Orchestra
   and Chorus.

BREAKFAST CLUB
Soundtrack (1985) .... *A&M (S) SP-3294*   85   **8-10**
   Composer: Various. **Cast:** Elizabeth Daily; Wang Chung; Jesse Johnson; Karla De Vito;
   Joyce Kennedy.

BREAKIN'
Soundtrack (1984) .... *Polydor (S) 821 919-1*   84   **8-10**
   Composer: Various. **Cast:** Bar-Kays; Carol Lynn James; Rufus; Chaka Khan; Chris Taylor
   and David Storrs; Ollie and Jerry; Hotstreak; 3V; Fire Fox; Re-Flex.

BREAKIN' 2 - ELECTRIC BOOGALOO
Soundtrack (1984) .... *Polydor (S) 823696-1*   84   **8-10**
   Composer: Various. **Cast:** Ollie and Jerry; Fire Fox; George Krantz; Steve Donn; Carol Lynn
   Townes; Mark Scott; Rags and Riches.

BREAKING GLASS
Soundtrack (1980) ....A&M (S) SP-4820   80   **$8-10**
Composer: Hazel O'Connor. Cast: Hazel O'Connor.

BREATH OF SCANDAL
Soundtrack (1959) ....Imperial (M) 9132   59   **40-50**
Soundtrack (1959) ....Imperial (S) 12068-W   59   **60-75**
Composer: Alessandro Cicognini. Cast: Maurice Chevalier.

BRECHT ON BRECHT
Original Cast (1962) ....Columbia (M) O2L-278   62   **20-25**
Double LP set.
Original Cast (1962) ....Columbia (S) O2S-203   62   **25-35**
Double LP set.
Composer: George Tabori. Cast: Dane Clark; Anne Jackson; Lotte Lenya; Viveca Lindfors.

BREEZY
Soundtrack (1973) ....MCA (S) 384   73   **15-20**
Composer: Michel Legrand. Conductor: Michel Legrand.

BREL, JACQUES:
see JACQUES BREL IS ALIVE AND WELL AND LIVING IN PARIS

BREMEN TOWN MUSICIANS
Soundtrack ....Golden (M) LP-168   **10-20**
Composer: Milton Delugg; Anne Delugg. Conductor: Lehman Engel. Cast: Paul Tripp (narration).

BREWSTER McCLOUD
Soundtrack (1970) ....MGM (S) 1SE-28   70   **15-20**
Composer: John Phillips; Gene Page. Conductor: Gene Page. Cast: Merry Clayton; John Phillips; Sally Kellerman.

BRIAN'S SONG - THEMES AND VARIATIONS
Studiotrack (1972) ....Bell (S) 6071   72   **10-15**
Also includes music from Summer of '62 and Wurthering Heights.

BRICE, FANNY:
see FANNY BRICE

BRIDE
Soundtrack .... Varese Sarabande (S) 81254   **8-10**
Composer: Maurice Jarre. Conductor: Maurice Jarre. Cast: Maurice Jarre and His Orchestra.

BRIDE WORE BLACK:
see TWISTED NERVE

BRIDE WORE YOLANDE:
see SOPHIA LOREN IN ROME

BRIDESHEAD REVISITED
TV Soundtrack (1982) ....Chrysalis (S) CHR-1367   82   **10-15**
Composer: Geoffrey Burgon. Conductor: Geoffrey Burgon. Cast: Jeremy Irons; Anthony Andrews; Diana Quick; Laurence Oliver.
TV Soundtrack (1982) ....Chrysalis (S) FV-41367   82   **8-10**
Produced by Granada Television.
Composer: Geoffrey Burgon. Conductor: Geoffrey Burgon. Cast: Sir Laurence Olivier; John Gielgud.

BRIDGE ON THE RIVER KWAI
Soundtrack (1957) ....Columbia (M) CL-1100   57   **15-20**
Soundtrack (1957) ....Columbia (SE) CS-9426   67   **10-15**
Composer: Malcolm Arnold; Kenneth Alford. Conductor: Malcolm Arnold. Cast: Mitch Miller's Orchestra and Chorus.

BRIDGE TOO FAR
Soundtrack (1977) ....*United Artists (S) UA-LA762-H*   77 $10-12
Soundtrack (1977) .... *Liberty (S) LKAO-762*   Re   8-10
  Composer: John Addison. **Conductor:** John Addison.

BRIGADOON
Original Cast (1947) .... *RCA Victor (EP) EOB-1001*   51   10-20
  Double EP set.
Original Cast (1947) .... *RCA Victor (M) LOC-1001*   51   25-35
Original Cast (1947) .... *RCA Victor (EP) WK-7*   51   20-30
  Five blue vinyl discs. Boxed set.
Original Cast (1947) .... *RCA Victor (SE) LSO-1001*   63   10-15
Original Cast (1947) .... *RCA Victor (SE) AYL1-3901*   81   8-10
  Brigadoon was RCA's first recording of an original cast, made for 78s in 1947, then issued on LP in 1951.
  Composer: Alan J. Lerner; Frederick Loewe. **Conductor:** Franz Allers. **Cast:** David Brooks;
  Marion Bell; Pamela Britton; Lee Sullivan; Delbert Anderson; Hayes Gordon; Earl Redding;
  Shirley Robbins; Jeff Warren.
London Studio Cast ....*Wing (M) WL-1051*   10-15
  One side has music from *Kiss Me Kate.*
  Conductor: John Gregory. **Cast:** KISS ME KATE: Elizabeth Larner; Barry Kent; Mike
  Sammes Singers.
Studio Cast (1958) .... *Columbia (M) CL-1132*   58   15-20
Studio Cast (1958) .... *Columbia (M) OL-7040*   65   10-20
Studio Cast (1958) ....*Columbia (SE) OS-2540e*   65   10-15
Studio Cast (1958) .... *Columbia Special Products (SE) COS-2540e*   Re   8-10
  Composer: Alan J. Lerner; Frederick Loewe. **Conductor:** Lehman Engel. **Cast:** Shirley
  Jones; Jack Cassidy; Susan Johnson; Frank Porretta.
Studio Cast (1960) .... *RCA Victor (S) LOS-2275*   60   15-25
  One side has music from *Gigi* by the same cast.
  Composer: Alan J. Lerner; Frederick Loewe. **Cast:** Jan Peerce; Jane Powell; Robert Merrill;
  Phil Harris.
Soundtrack (1954) ....*MGM (EP) X-263*   54   10-20
Soundtrack (1954) ....*MGM (M) E-3135*   54   20-30
Soundtrack (1954) .... *MCA (M) 39062*   Re   5-10
  Composer: Alan J. Lerner; Frederick Lowe. **Conductor:** Johnny Green. **Cast:** Gene Kelly;
  Van Johnson; Cyd Charisse; Carol Richards; John Gustafson.
Studiotrack (1953) ....*RCA Victor (EP) ERA-129*   53   5-10
  Conductor: Arthur Fiedler. **Cast:** Boston Pops Orchestra.
TV Soundtrack (1968) .... *Columbia Special Products (M) CSM-385*   68   35-40
  Composer: Frederick Loewe. **Conductor:** Irwin Kostal. **Cast:** Robert Goulet; Sally Ann
  Howes; Marilyn Mason; Thomas Carlisle.
  Also see FINIAN'S RAINBOW AND BRIGADOON REMEMBERED

BRIGHT LIGHTS, BIG CITY
Soundtrack (1988) .... *Warner Bros. (S) 1-25688*   88   8-10
  Composer: Various. **Cast:** Prince; New Order; Narada; Bryan Ferry; Depeche Mode;
  Donald Fagen; Noise Club; Konk; Jennifer Hall; M/A/R/R/S.

BRIGHTON BEACH MEMOIRS
Soundtrack (1987) ....*MCA (S) 6193*   87   8-10
  Composer: Various. **Cast:** Steve Clayton; George Hall Orchestra.

BRIMSTONE AND TREACLE
Soundtrack (1982) .... *A&M (S) SP-4915*   82   8-10
  Composer: Police; Sting; Go-Go's; Squeeze. **Cast:** Police; Sting; Go-Go's; Squeeze;
  Finchley Children's Music Group; Brimstone Chorale.

BRING BACK BIRDIE
Original Cast (1981) ....*Original Cast (S) OC-8132*   **$8-10**
  Composer: Charles Strouse. **Cast:** Chita Rivera; Donald O'Connor; Marcel Forestieri; Betsy
  Friday; Maurice Hines; Maria Karnilova; Robin Morse; Rebecca Renfroe.

BROADWAY
Studiotrack (1958) ....*Columbia (EP) B-11101*   58   **5-10**
Studiotrack (1958) ....*Columbia (M) CL-1110*   58   **10-15**
Studiotrack (1958) ....*Columbia (S) CS-8052*   58   **15-20**
  Composer: Various. **Cast:** Norman Luboff Orchestra and Choir.

BROADWAY BALLET
Studiotrack (1954) ....*MGM (EP) X-1026*   54   **10-15**
  Cast: Gene Kelly.

BROADWAY, BROADWAY, BROADWAY
Studiotrack .... *Longines Symphonette (S) LWS-117*   **10-15**
  Composer: Various. **Cast:** Judy Garland; Lena Horne; Jimmy Durante; Bing Crosby; Maurice
  Chevalier.

BROADWAY CAVALCADE
Studiotrack (1958) .... *Capitol (M) WBO-1079*   58   **10-20**
  Composer: Various. **Conductor:** Fred Waring. **Cast:** Fred Waring and His Orchestra.

BROADWAY CHORUS CALL
Studio Cast (1959) ....*Epic (M) LN-3546*   59   **10-15**
Studio Cast (1959) .... *Epic (S) BN-519*   59   **15-20**
  Composer: Various. **Cast:** Merrill Staton Choir.

BROADWAY CLASSICS
Studiotrack (1954) ....*RCA Victor (EP) EPA-561*   54   **10-20**
  Tunes from: *Kismet, By the Beautiful Sea, The Golden Apple* and *The Girl in Pink Tights.*
  Composer: Various. **Conductor:** Hugo Winterhalter. **Cast:** Eddie Fisher; Hugo Winterhalter
  and His Orchestra.

BROADWAY COMPLEAT
Studiotrack (1959) ....*Warner Bros. (M) B-1253*   59   **10-15**
Studiotrack (1959) .... *Warner Bros. (S) BS-1253*   59   **10-20**
  Cast: Warren Barker Orchestra.

BROADWAY EXTRAVAGANZA
Studiotrack (1987) ....*MCA (S) 6219*   87   **8-10**
  Composer: Various. **Conductor:** Paul Gerignani. **Cast:** Royal Philharmonic Orchestra.

BROADWAY '55
Studiotrack (1955) .... *Decca (EP) ED-2169*   55   **5-10**
  Volume one of three.
Studiotrack (1955) .... *Decca (EP) ED-2175*   55   **5-10**
  Volume two of three.
Studiotrack (1955) .... *Decca (EP) ED-2182*   55   **5-10**
  Volume three of three.
Studiotrack (1955) .... *Decca (M) DL-8099*   55   **10-20**
  Composer: Various. **Conductor:** Fred Waring. **Cast:** Fred Waring and His Orchestra.

BROADWAY GOES HOLLYWOOD
Studiotrack (1955) .... *Decca (EP) ED-2270*   55   **5-10**
  Volume one of three.
Studiotrack (1955) .... *Decca (EP) ED-2271*   55   **5-10**
  Volume two of three.
Studiotrack (1955) .... *Decca (EP) ED-2272*   55   **5-10**
  Volume three of three.
Studiotrack (1955) .... *Decca (M) DL-8167*   55   **10-20**
  Composer: Various. **Conductor:** Jack Pleis. **Cast:** Jack Pleis and His Orchestra.

BROADWAY GOES TO COLLEGE

Studiotrack (1959) .... *Mercury (M) MG-20456*   59   **$10-15**
Studiotrack (1959) .... *Mercury (S) SR-60139*   59   **15-20**
    Composer: Various. **Cast:** Northwestern Men's Glee Club.

BROADWAY HIGHLIGHTS

Studiotrack (1955) ....*Capitol (EP) EAP 1-583*   55   **5-10**
    Volume one of three.
Studiotrack (1955) ....*Capitol (EP) EAP 2-583*   55   **5-10**
    Volume two of three.
Studiotrack (1955) ....*Capitol (EP) EAP 3-583*   55   **5-10**
    Volume three of three.
Studiotrack (1955) .... *Capitol (M) T-583*   55   **15-25**
    Composer: Various. **Cast:** John Raitt.

BROADWAY HITS IN HI-FI

Studiotrack (1954) .... *ABC-Paramount (M) ABC-154*   54   **10-20**
    Composer: Various. **Conductor:** Irving Fields. **Cast:** Irving Fields' Orchestra.

BROADWAY HITS OF YESTERDAY

Studiotrack (1954) .... *Varsity (EP) E-20*   54   **5-10**
Studiotrack (1954) .... *Varsity (EP) E-45*   54   **5-10**
Studiotrack (1954) .... *Varsity (M) VLP-6011*   54   **10-20**
    Composer: Various. **Conductor:** Russell Bennett. **Cast:** Russell Bennett and His Orchestra.

BROADWAY MAGIC - BEST OF BROADWAY MUSICALS

Studiotrack (1979) .... *Columbia (S) JS-36282*   79   **8-10**
    Composer: Various. **Cast:** Joel Gray; Priscilla Lopez; Angela Lansbury; Elaine Stritch; Ethel
    Merman; Gwen Verdon; Larry Kert; Julie Andrews; Carol Lawrence; Betty Wolfe.

BROADWAY MELODIES

Studiotrack (1956) .... *Kapp (M) KL-1033*   56   **15-20**
    Composer: Various. **Cast:** Buddy Greco Quartet.
Studiotrack (1953) .... *London (M) LL-509*   53   **15-20**
    Composer: Various. **Conductor:** Frank Chacksfield. **Cast:** Frank Chacksfield and His Orchestra.

BROADWAY SHOWCASE

Studiotrack (1957) .... *Verve (M) MG-2033*   57   **10-20**
    Composer: Various. **Conductor:** Buddy De Franco. **Cast:** Buddy De Franco and His Orchestra.

BROADWAY SONG BOOK

Studiotrack (1959) .... *Coral (M) CRL-57274*   59   **10-15**
Studiotrack (1959) .... *Coral (S) CRL7-57274*   59   **15-20**
    Volume one.
Studiotrack (1959) .... *Coral (M) CRL-57275*   59   **10-15**
Studiotrack (1959) .... *Coral (S) CRL7-57275*   59   **15-20**
    Volume two.
Studiotrack (1959) .... *Coral (M) CX-4*   59   **15-20**
Studiotrack (1959) .... *Coral (S) CX-7*   59   **20-25**
    Combines volumes one and two. Double LP sets.
    Composer: Various. **Conductor:** Dick Jacobs. **Cast:** Dick Jacobs and His Orchestra.

BROADWAY SUCCESS STORY

Studiotrack (1955) .... *Epic (M) LN-1122*   55   **15-25**
    Composer: Various. **Cast:** Delores Hawkins and the Mellow Larks.

BROADWAY'S BEST:
see THIS IS BROADWAY'S BEST

BROADWAY'S BIG HITS
Studiotrack (1963) ....*Mercury (M) MG-20811*   63   **$10-15**
Studiotrack (1963) .... *Mercury (S) SR-60811*   63   **10-20**
  Composer: Various. Cast: Various artists.

BRONCO BILLY
Soundtrack (1980) .... *Elektra (S) 5E-512*   80   **8-10**
  Composer: Steve Dorff. Cast: Ronnie Milsap; Penny DeHaven; Merle Haggard; Clint
  Eastwood; Reinsmen.

BRONISLAW KAPER:
see KAPER: THE FILM MUSIC OF BRONISLAW

BRONTES
Original Cast .... *Vanguard (S) VRS-9176/7*   **40-50**
  Double LP set.
  Cast: Margaret Webster.

BROTHER FROM ANOTHER PLANET
Soundtrack (1984) ....*Daring (S) DR1007*   84   **10-15**
  Composer: Mason Daring; others. Cast: Joe Morton; Ren Woods; Efrain Salgado; Lee
  "Scratch" Perry; Dee Dee Bridgewater; Jeff Anderson.

BROTHER ON THE RUN
Soundtrack (1973) .... *Perception (S) PLP-45*   73   **25-30**
  Composer: Johnny Pate; Adam Wade. Conductor: Johnny Pate. Cast: Adam Wade.

BROTHERHOOD (AND OTHER THEMES)
Soundtrack (1969) ....*Dot (S) DLP 25925*   69   **10-15**
  Also has themes from: *Artists and Models, Romeo and Juliet, Anyone Can Play, Captain Carey, USA*
  and *The Caddy.*
  Composer: Lalo Schifrin; others. Cast: Creative Cast.

BROTHERS
Soundtrack (1977) .... *Warner Bros. (S) BS-3024*   77   **10-12**
  Composer: Taj Mahal. Conductor: Taj Mahal.

BROWN, MARY C.:
see MARY C. BROWN

BRUTE FORCE
Soundtrack (1947) .... *TT (Tony Thomas) (M) MR-3*   80   **8-10**
  Also contains *Naked City.*
  Composer: Miklos Rozsa (both); Frank Skinner. Conductor: Miklos Rozsa.
  Also see LUST FOR LIFE

BUBBLING BROWN SUGAR
Original Cast (1976) ....*H&L (S) HL-69011*   **8-10**
Original Cast (1986) .... *Amherst (S) 3310*   86   **8-10**
  Composer: Danny Holgate; others. Conductor: Danny Holgate. Cast: Avon Long; Vivian
  Reed; Joseph Premice; Chip Garnett; Joseph Attles; Carolyn Byrd; Ethel Beatty; Barry Preston.

BUCCANEER
Original Cast (1980) .... *AEI (S) 1114*   80   **$8-10**
   British musical.
   Composer: Sandy Wilson. **Cast:** Betty Warren; Ronald Radd.
Soundtrack (1958) .... *Columbia (M) CL-1278*   58   **35-40**
Soundtrack (1958) .... *Columbia (S) CS-8096*   58   **55-65**
Soundtrack (1958) .... *Columbia Special Products (S) ACS-8096*   Re   **8-10**
   Composer: Elmer Bernstein.

BUCK ROGERS
Soundtrack (1979) .... *MCA (S) 3097*   79   **8-10**
   Composer: Stu Phillips; Glen A. Larson. **Conductor:** Stu Phillips.

BUDDY HOLLY STORY
Soundtrack (1978) .... *Epic/American Int'l (S) SE-35412*   78   **8-12**
   A collection of songs made famous by Buddy Holly.
   Composer: Buddy Holly; others. **Cast:** Gary Busey.

BUDGIE
Original London Cast (1988) .... *MCA (S) 6035*   88   **10-12**
   Composer: Mort Shuman; Don Black. **Cast:** Adam Faith; Anita Dobson; John Turner.

BUGSY MALONE
Soundtrack (1976) .... *Polydor (S) 2442-142*   76   **20-25**
   Composer: Paul Williams.

BULL DURHAM
Soundtrack (1988) .... *Capitol (S) C1-90586*   88   **8-10**
   Composer: Various. **Cast:** George Thorogood and the Destroyers; Fabulous Thunderbirds;
   House of Schock; Los Lobos; John Fogerty; Pat Laughlin; Dr. Bennie Wallace; Blasters.

BULLET FOR A PRETTY BOY
Soundtrack (1970) .... *American Int'l (S) STA-1034*   70   **10-15**
   Composer: Harley Hatcher. **Conductor:** Harley Hatcher. **Cast:** The Source.

BULLITT
Soundtrack (1968) .... *Warner Bros. (S) WS-1777*   68   **40-45**
   Composer: Lalo Schifrin. **Conductor:** Lalo Schifrin.

BULLWHIP GRIFFIN:
see ADVENTURES OF BULLWHIP GRIFFIN

BUNDLE OF JOY
Soundtrack (1956) .... *RCA Victor (M) LPM-1399*   56   **40-50**
   Composer: Josef Myrow. **Conductor:** Hugo Montenegro; Walter Scharf. **Cast:** Eddie Fisher;
   Debbie Reynolds; Nita Talbot.

BUNNY LAKE IS MISSING
Soundtrack (1965) .... *RCA Victor (M) LOC-1115*   65   **25-35**
Soundtrack (1965) .... *RCA Victor (S) LSO-1115*   65   **40-65**
   Composer: Paul Glass. **Conductor:** Paul Glass. **Cast:** Zombies.

BUNNY O'HARE
Soundtrack (1971) .... *American Int'l (S) STA-1041*   71   **12-18**
   Composer: Mike Curb; Billy Strange. **Conductor:** Billy Strange. **Cast:** Billy Strange; Mike
   Curb Congregation; Full Circle.

BUONA SERA, MRS. CAMPBELL
Soundtrack (1969) .... *United Artists (S) UAS-5192*   69   **20-25**
   Composer: Riz Ortolani. **Conductor:** Riz Ortolani. **Cast:** Jimmy Roselli.

BURGLAR
Soundtrack (1987) . . . . *MCA (S) 6201*   87   **$8-10**

BURGLARS
Soundtrack (1971) . . . . *Bell (S) 1105*   71   **25-30**
Composer: Ennio Morricone. Conductor: Ennio Morricone.

BURKE'S LAW
TV Soundtrack (1964) . . . . *Liberty (M) LRP-3374*   64   **40-50**
TV Soundtrack (1964) . . . . *Liberty (S) LST-7374*   64   **45-60**
Composer: Herschel Burke Gilbert; others. Conductor: Herschel Burke Gilbert.

BURLESQUE SHOW
Studio Cast (1963) . . . . *Cameo (M) C-2002*   63   **30-40**
Composer: Kermit Schafer.

BURN
Soundtrack (1970) . . . . *United Artists (S) UA-LA303-G*   70   **10-15**
Composer: Ennio Morricone. Conductor: Ennio Morricone.

BURNING
Soundtrack (1981) . . . . *Varese Sarabande (S) 81162*   81   **8-10**
Cast: Rick Wakeman.

BUSTER
Soundtrack (1988) . . . . *Atlantic (S) 81905-1*   88   **8-10**
Composer: Various. Cast: Phil Collins; Gerry and the Pacemakers; Spencer Davis Group; Dusty
Springfield; London Film Orchestra; Anne Dudley; Sonny and Cher; Four Tops; Searchers.

BUSTIN' LOOSE
Soundtrack (1981) . . . . *MCA (S) 5141*   81   **8-10**
Composer: Various. Cast: Roberta Flack; Peabo Bryson; Eric Mercury; Luther Vandros; others.

BUT BEAUTIFUL
Soundtrack (1948) . . . . *Decca (M) DL-4260*   62   **30-40**
Also has music from *Welcome Stranger, The Road to Rio, The Emperor Waltz* and *Variety Girl.*
Issued as part of *Bing's Hollywood Series.*
Composer: ROAD TO RIO: James Van Heusen; John Burke. Conductor: ROAD TO RIO:
Victor Young; Vic Schoen. Cast: Bing Crosby (all). ROAD TO RIO: Andrews Sisters; Nan
Wynn. WELCOME STRANGER: Callico Kids.

BUTCH CASSIDY AND THE SUNDANCE KID
Soundtrack (1969) . . . . *A&M (S) SP-4227*   69   **8-12**
Composer: Burt Bacharach. Conductor: Burt Bacharach.

BUTTERFIELD 8
Soundtrack (1960) . . . . *MGM (M) E-3952*   60   **10-15**
Studiotrack (1960) . . . . *MGM (S) SE-3952*   61   **15-20**
Composer: Bronislau Kaper; others. Conductor: David Rose. Cast: David Rose and His
Orchestra.

BUTTERFLY
Soundtrack (1982) . . . . *Applause (S) APPL-1017*   82   **10-15**
Composer: Ennio Morricone. Conductor: Ennio Morricone.

BY JUPITER

Original Revival Cast (1967) .... *RCA Victor (M) LOC-1137*   67   **$40-50**
Original Revival Cast (1967) .... *RCA Victor (M) LSO-1137*   67   **55-70**
  Composer: Richard Rodgers; Lorenz Hart. **Conductor:** Milton Setzer. **Cast:** Bob Dishy; Jackie
  Alloway; Irene Byatt; Emory Bass; Ronnie Cunningham; Norma Doggett; Rosemarie Heyer;
  Robert R. Kaye; Richard Marshall; Sheila Doggett.
Studio Cast (1964) .... *Roulette (M) R-25278*   64   **30-40**
  One side has music from *Girl Crazy.*
  Composer: Richard Rodgers; Lorenz Hart. GIRL CRAZY: George Gershwin; Ira Gershwin.
  Cast: Jackie Cain; Roy Kral.

BY THE BEAUTIFUL SEA

Original Cast (1954) .... *Capitol (EP) EDM-531*   54   **20-30**
Original Cast (1954) .... *Capitol (M) S-531*   54   **100-125**
Original Cast (1954) .... *Capitol (M) T-11652*   77   **8-10**
  Composer: Arthur Schwartz; Dorothy Fields. **Conductor:** Jay Blackton. **Cast:** Shirley Booth;
  Wilbur Evans; Cameron Prud'homme; Richard France; Mae Barnes; Libi Staiger; Thomas
  Gleason; Mary Harmon; Larry Howard; Cindy Robbins; Eddie Roll; Gloria Smith.
Studiotrack (1954) .... *Capitol (EP) EPA-535*   54   **10-20**
  Composer: Arthur Schwartz; Dorothy Fields. **Cast:** Nat "King" Cole; Betty Hutton; Helen
  O'Connell; Les Baxter.

BY THE LIGHT OF THE SILVERY MOON

Soundtrack (1953) .... *Capitol (EP) EBF-422*   53   **20-40**
  Double EP set.
Soundtrack (1953) .... *Capitol (M) H-422*   53   **50-60**
Soundtrack (1953) .... *Capitol (EP) EAP 1-422*   55   **10-20**
  Volume one of three.
Soundtrack (1953) .... *Capitol (EP) EAP 2-422*   55   **10-20**
  Volume two of three.
Soundtrack (1953) .... *Capitol (EP) EAP 3-422*   55   **10-20**
  Volume three of three.
Soundtrack (1953) .... *Capitol (M) T-422*   55   **20-35**
  Volume three of three.
  Conductor: Axel Stordahl. **Cast:** Gordon Mac Rae; June Sutton.
Studiotrack (1953) .... *Columbia (M) CL-6248*   53   **40-50**
  10-inch LP.
  Conductor: Paul Weston. **Cast:** Doris Day; Norman Luboff Choir.

BYE BYE BIRDIE

Original Cast (1960) .... *Columbia (M) OL-5510*   60   **20-25**
Original Cast (1960) .... *Columbia (S) OS-2025*   60   **30-35**
  Conductor: Elliot Lawrence. **Cast:** Chita Rivera; Dick Van Dyke; Paul Lynde.
Original Cast (1973) .... *Columbia Special Products (S) COS-2025*   Re   **8-12**
  Composer: Charles Strouse; Lee Adams. **Conductor:** Elliot Lawrence. **Cast:** Chita Rivera;
  Dick Van Dyke; Paul Lynde; Michael J. Pollard; Jessica Albright; Johnny Borden; Dick Gautier;
  Sharon Lerit; Maricle; Susan Watson.
Original London Cast (1960) .... *Mercury (M) 13000*   60   **25-30**
Original London Cast (1960) .... *Mercury (S) 17000*   60   **30-35**
  Composer: Charles Strouse; Lee Adams. **Conductor:** Alyn Ainsworth. **Cast:** Chita Rivera;
  Peter Marshall; Angela Baddeley.

BYE BYE BIRDIE (continued)

Soundtrack (1963) . . . .*RCA Victor (M) LOC-1081*   63   **$10-20**
Soundtrack (1963) . . . .*RCA Victor (S) LSO-1081*   63   **15-25**
   On above two, Ann-Margret is not shown on cover.
Soundtrack (1963) . . . .*RCA Victor (S) LSO-1081*   63   **10-15**
   Above two picture Ann-Margret on the cover.
Soundtrack (1963) . . . .*RCA Victor (S) AYL1-3947*   81   **8-10**
   Composer: Charles Strouse; Lee Adams. **Conductor:** Johnny Green. **Cast:** Janet Leigh; Dick
   Van Dyke; Ann-Margret; Maureen Stapleton; Bobby Rydell; Paul Lynde; Jesse Pearson;
   Mary LaRoche; Bryan Russell.
Studiotrack (1961) . . . . *Columbia (M) CL-1590*   61   **10-15**
Studiotrack (1961) . . . . *Columbia (S) CS-8390*   61   **15-20**
   Composer: Charles Strouse; Lee Adams. **Cast:** Chico Hamilton Quintet.
Studio Cast (1964) . . . .*Colpix (M) CP-454*   64   **25-35**
Studio Cast (1964) . . . .*Colpix (S) SCP-454*   62   **30-40**
   Composer: Charles Strouse; Lee Adams. **Conductor:** Stu Phillips. **Cast:** James Darren;
   Marcels; Shelley Fabares; Paul Peterson.
Studiotrack (1963) . . . .*Colpix (M) CP-451*   63   **10-15**
Studiotrack (1963) . . . .*Colpix (S) SCP-451*   63   **15-20**
   Composer: Charles Strouse; Lee Adams. **Conductor:** Bill Potts. **Cast:** Bill Potts and His
   Orchestra.
Studiotrack (1963) . . . .*Cameo (M) C-1043*   63   **15-20**
Studiotrack (1963) . . . . *Cameo (S) CS-1043*   63   **15-25**
   Composer: Charles Strouse; Lee Adams. **Cast:** Bobby Rydell.
Studiotrack (1964) . . . . *Design (S) DLP-171*   64   **8-12**
  One side has music from *Hello Dolly.*
   Composer: Charles Strouse; Lee Adams.

C

C'MON, LET'S LIVE A LITTLE
Soundtrack (1966) .... *Liberty (M) LRP-3430*   66   **$15-20**
Soundtrack (1966) .... *Liberty (S) LST-7430*   66   **20-25**
   Composer: Don Crawford; others. **Conductor:** Don Ralke. **Cast:** Jackie DeShannon; Bobby
Vee; Eddie Hodges.

C.C. AND COMPANY
Soundtrack (1970) .... *Avco Embassy (S) AVE-0-110*   70   **10-12**
   Composer: Lenny Stack. **Conductor:** Lenny Stack.

CABARET
Original Cast (1966) .... *Columbia (M) KOL-6640*   66   **10-15**
Original Cast (1966) .... *Columbia (S) KOS-3040*   66   **15-20**
   Composer: John Kander; Fred Ebb. **Conductor:** Harold Hastings. **Cast:** Joel Grey; Jill Haworth;
Jack Gilford; Bert Convy; Lotte Lenya; Mary Ehara; Rita O'Connor; Robert Sharp.
Studio Cast (1966) .... *Columbia (S) CS-9375*   66   **10-15**
   Composer: John Kander; Fred·Ebb. **Conductor:** Joe Basile. **Cast:** Joe Basile Orchestra.
Soundtrack (1972) .... *ABC (S) D-752*   72   **12-18**
Soundtrack (1972) .... *MCA (S) AB-752*   **8-10**
Soundtrack (1972) .... *MCA (S) 37125*   **5-8**
   Composer: John Kander; Fred Ebb. **Conductor:** Ralph Burns. **Cast:** Liza Minnelli; Joel Grey;
Greta Keller.
Original London Cast .... *EMB (S) 31026*   **8-12**
   Composer: John Kander; Fred Ebb. **Cast:** Jodi Dench.

CABIN IN THE SKY
Original Cast (1940) .... *Columbia (M) CL-2792*   68   **10-15**
   Actual title: *Ethel Waters.*
Original Cast (1940) .... *Columbia (M) AE1-1107*   68   **10-12**
   Both Columbia CL-2792 and CCL-2792, which follows, have material originally issued on two 78 rpm
singles. This reissue has that material plus the original cast overture, all of which originally appeared on
three 78 rpm singles.
Original Cast (1940) .... *Columbia Special Products (M) CCL-2792*   76   **8-10**
   Composer: Vernon Duke; John Latouche. **Conductor:** Max Meth. **Cast:** Ethel Waters.
Original Revival Cast (1964) .... *Capitol (M) W-2073*   64   **35-40**
Original Revival (1964) .... *Capitol (S) SW-2073*   64   **45-60**
   Composer: Vernon Duke; John Latouche. **Conductor:** Sy Oliver. **Cast:** Rosetta LeNoire; Ketty
Lester; Tony Middleton; Helen Ferguson; Bernard Johnson; Sam Laws; Harold Pierson; Morton
Winston.
Soundtrack (1943) .... *Hollywood Soundstage (M) HS-5003*   **8-12**
   Composer: Vernon Duke; John Latouche.
   Also see PORGY AND BESS

CACTUS FLOWER
Soundtrack (1969) .... *Bell (S) 1201*   70   **15-20**
   Composer: Quincy Jones; Neil Diamond; others. **Conductor:** Eric W. Knight. **Cast:** Sarah
Vaughan.

CADDYSHACK
Soundtrack (1980) .... *Columbia (S) JS-36737*   80   **8-10**
   Composer: Johnny Mandel; Kenny Loggins; others. **Cast:** Kenny Loggins; Beat; Hilly Michaels.

CADDYSHACK II
Soundtrack (1988) . . . . *Columbia (S) SC-44317*   88   **$8-10**
    Composer: Various. **Cast:** Tamara Champlin; Cheap Trick; Earth, Wind and Fire; Full Force;
    Lisa Lisa and Cult Jam; Kenny Loggins; Patty Smyth; Eric Martin; Ira Newborn; Pointer Sisters.

CAGE AUX FOLLES, LA:
see LA CAGE AUX FOLLES

CAINE MUTINY
Soundtrack (1954) . . . .*RCA Victor (M) LOC-1013*   54 **5,000-10,000**
    Composer: Max Steiner. **Conductor:** Max Steiner. **Cast:** Humphrey Bogart; Jose Ferrer; Van
    Johnson; Fred MacMurray; Robert Francis; May Wynn. (With dialogue.)

CAINE MUTINY COURT MARTIAL
TV Soundtrack (1976) . . . .*Mark '56 (S) 741*   76   **40-50**
    Double LP set.
    Cast: Barry Sullivan; Lloyd Nolan; Frank Lovejoy.
TV Soundtrack (1976) . . . .*Mark '56 (S) 751*   **50-60**

CAL
Soundtrack (1984) . . . .*Mercury (S) 422-82276*   84   **8-10**
    Composer: Mark Knopfler. **Conductor:** Mark Knopfler. **Cast:** Mark Knopfler.

CALAMITY JANE
Soundtrack (1953) . . . .*Columbia (EP) B-347*   53   **15-20**
Soundtrack (1953) . . . .*Columbia (EP) B-1803*   53   **10-20**
Soundtrack (1953) . . . .*Columbia (EP) B-1804*   53   **10-20**
Soundtrack (1953) . . . . *Columbia (M) CL-6373*   53   **40-50**
    10-inch LP.
Soundtrack (1953) . . . . *Columbia Special Products (M) P-19611*   Re   **8-10**
    Composer: Sammy Fain. **Conductor:** Ray Heindorf. **Cast:** Doris Day; Howard Keel.

CALIFORNIA
Studiotrack (1949) .... *Decca (M) DL-8011*   50   **$20-30**
One side has music from *Manhattan Tower*.
Composer: Gordon Jenkins (both). MANHATTAN TOWER: Tom Adair. **Conductor:** Gordon Jenkins (both). MANHATTAN TOWER: Tom Adair. **Cast:** MANHATTAN TOWER: Lee Sweetland; Beverly Maha; Betty Brewer; Art Gentry; Elliot Lewis (narrator).
Also see MANHATTAN TOWER

CALIFORNIA DREAMING
Soundtrack (1978) .... *Casablanca/American Int' l AILP-3001*   78   **8-10**
Soundtrack (1978) .... *Casablanca/American Int' l (S) AILP-3001*   78   **8-12**
Composer: Fred Karlin. **Conductor:** Fred Karlin. **Cast:** Glynnis O'Connor; Seymour Cassel; Dorothy Tristan; Dennis Christopher; John Calvin.

CALIFORNIA SUITE
Soundtrack (1978) .... *Columbia (S) JS-35727*   79   **8-10**
Composer: Claude Bolling. **Conductor:** Claude Bolling.

CALIGULA - THE MUSIC
Soundtrack (1980) .... *Penthouse (S) 101*   80   **8-10**

CALL ME MADAM
Original Cast (1950) .... *RCA Victor (EP) EOA-438*   50   **15-25**
Original Cast (1950) .... *RCA Victor (M) LOC-1000*   50   **75-80**
Original Cast (1950) .... *RCA Victor (M) CBM1-2032*   68   **8-12**
On the preceding three releases, Dinah Shore (who did not appear in the show) sings the songs originally performed on stage by Ethel Merman. Labeled "Gems from the Original Cast Recording," the credits read: "Dinah Shore and the Original Broadway Company."
Composer: Irving Berlin. **Conductor:** Jay Blackton. **Cast:** Dinah Shore; Paul Lukas; Russell Nype; Galina Talva; Pat Harrington; Ralph Chambers; Jay Velie.
Studio Cast (1950) .... *Decca (EP) ED-806*   50   **15-20**
Studio Cast (1950) .... *Decca (M) DL-5304*   50   **50-60**
10-inch LP.
Studio Cast (1950) .... *Decca (M) DL-8035*   50   **25-30**
Studio Cast (1950) .... *Decca (M) DL-9022*   55   **15-25**
Studio Cast (1950) .... *Decca (SE) DL7-9022*   59   **10-20**
Studio Cast (1950) .... *MCA (SE) 2055e*   72   **8-10**
Composer: Irving Berlin. **Conductor:** Gordon Jenkins. **Cast:** Ethel Merman; Dick Haymes; Eileen Wilson.
Studio Cast (1951) .... *MGM (M) E-531*   51   **20-30**
Composer: Irving Berlin. **Cast:** Billy Eckstine; Johnny Desmond; Art Lund.
Studiotrack (1951) .... *Mercury (M) 25088*   51   **15-30**
10-inch LP.
Composer: Irving Berlin. **Cast:** Various Mercury artists.
Original London Cast .... *Monmouth Evergreen (SE) MES-7073*   **8-10**
Composer: Irving Berlin. **Conductor:** Cyril Ornadel. **Cast:** Billie Worth; Anton Walbrook.
Soundtrack (1953) .... *Decca (EP) ED-508*   53   **10-15**
Soundtrack (1953) .... *Decca (M) DL-5465*   53   **40-50**
Soundtrack (1953) .... *Ace of Hearts (M) AH-137*   Re   **8-10**
One side has music from *Guys and Dolls*.
Composer: Irving Berlin. **Conductor:** Alfred Newman. **Cast:** Ethel Merman; George Sanders; Donald O'Connor; Carole Richards.
Soundtrack .... *Stet (S) DS-2500*   **8-10**
Also has music from *I'll Cry Tomorrow* and *Guys and Dolls*.

CALL ME MISTER
Original Cast (1946) .... *Decca (M) DL-7005*   50   **$130-140**
  10-inch LP.
Original Cast (1946) .... *Columbia Special Products (M) X-14877*   Re   **8-12**
  Also has music from *This Is the Army.*
  Composer: Harold Rome. **Conductor:** Lehman Engel. **Cast:** Betty Garrett; Lawrence Winters;
  Paula Bane; Danny Scholl; Bill Callahan; Harry Clark; Chandler Cowles; Jules Munshin.
Studio Cast (1957) .... *Coral (M) CRL-57082*   57   **20-25**
  Composer: Harold Rome. **Conductor:** Harold Rome. **Cast:** Harold Rome (piano).

CAMELOT
Original Cast (1960) .... *Columbia (M) OL-5620*   60   **20-25**
  A three-inch record of *Camelot,* with special paper sleeve. Used as a Christmas gift certificate for this LP
  by retail stores. The value of this mini-disc is $10 to $12.
Original Cast (1960) .... *Columbia (S) OS-2031*   60   **30-35**
Original Cast (1960) .... *Columbia (S) JS-32602*   73   **8-10**
  Composer: Alan J. Lerner; Frederick Loewe. **Conductor:** Franz Allers. **Cast:** Julie Andrews;
  Richard Burton; Robert Goulet; Roddy McDowell; Bruce Yarnell; John Cullum; Mary Sue
  Berry; James Gannon.
Original London Cast (1982) .... *Varese Sarabande (S) OCV-81168*   **8-10**
London Studio Cast .... *World (S) T-851*   **15-20**
  Composer: Alan J. Lerner; Frederick Loewe. **Conductor:** Gareth Davies. **Cast:** Patrick Macnee;
  Madge Stephens; Geoffrey Chard.
London Cast .... *Stet (S) DS-15022*   **8-10**
Studio Cast .... *Ambassador (S) S98070*   **8-10**
  Composer: Alan J. Lerner; Frederick Loewe. **Conductor:** Al Goodman. **Cast:** Richard Torigi;
  Lois Winters; Earl Rogers.
Soundtrack (1967) .... *Warner Bros. (M) B-1712*   67   **10-15**
Soundtrack (1967) .... *Warner Bros. (S) BS-1712*   67   **15-20**
Soundtrack (1967) .... *Warner Bros. (S) BSK-3102*   77   **8-10**
  Composer: Alan J. Lerner; Frederick Loewe. **Conductor:** Alfred Newman. **Cast:** Richard Harris;
  Vanessa Redgrave; Franco Nero.

Soundtrack (1967) .... *Warner Bros. (S) PRO-268*   67   **$35-40**
 Promotional issue only.
Soundtrack .... *Pickwick (S) SPC-3103*   **5-10**
Studiotrack .... *Design (S) SDLP-281*   **8-10**
Studiotrack (1967) .... *Mainstream (M) 56101*   67   **8-12**
Studiotrack (1967) .... *Mainstream (S) 6101*   67   **10-15**
 Composer: Alan J. Lerner; Frederick Loewe. **Conductor:** Hugo Montenegro. **Cast:** Hugo
 Montenegro and His Orchestra.

CAN-CAN

Original Cast (1953) .... *Capitol (EP) EPM-452*   53   **15-20**
Original Cast (1953) .... *Capitol (M) S-452*   53   **30-40**
Original Cast (1953) .... *Capitol (M) W-452*   62   **15-20**
Original Cast (1953) .... *Capitol (SE) DW-452e*   62   **15-20**
 Composer: Cole Porter. **Conductor:** Milton Rosenstock. **Cast:** Lilo; Hans Conreid; Gwen
 Verdon; Erik Rhodes; Peter Cookson.
Studio Cast .... *Design (M) DLP-111*   **10-20**
Studio Cast .... *Design (S) 1009*   **15-20**
 One side has music from *Kiss Me Kate*.
 Composer: Cole Porter. **Conductor:** Warren Vincent. **Cast:** Mimi Benzell; Felix Knight.
Studio Cast .... *Halo (M) 50217*   **10-20**
 Composer: Cole Porter. **Cast:** National Strings and Orchestra.
Soundtrack (1960) .... *Capitol (M) W-1301*   60   **15-20**
Soundtrack (1960) .... *Capitol (S) SW-1301*   60   **20-25**
Soundtrack (1960) .... *Capitol (S) SM-1301*   Re   **8-10**
 Composer: Cole Porter. **Conductor:** Nelson Riddle. **Cast:** Frank Sinatra; Shirley MacLaine;
 Maurice Chevalier; Louis Jourdan.

CAN HIERONYMUS MERKIN EVER FORGET MERCY HUMPPE (AND FIND TRUE HAPPINESS)?

Soundtrack (1969) .... *Kapp (S) KRS-5509*   69   **20-25**
 Composer: Anthony Newley. **Cast:** Anthony Newley; Joan Collins; Stubby Kaye; Bruce Forsythe.

CAN'T STOP THE MUSIC

Soundtrack (1980) .... *Casablanca (S) NBLP-7220*   80   **8-10**
 Composer: Jacques Moral; others. **Conductor:** Horace Ott. **Cast:** David London; Ritchie Family;
 Village People.

CANADA

Original Cast (1977) .... *Broadway Baby Demos (S) BBD-776*   77   **8-10**
 Composer: Bruce Molloy; Zachary Morfogen. **Conductor:** Bruce Molloy. **Cast:** Carol Lee
 Gorson; Bruce Molloy Sr.

CANDIDATE

Soundtrack (1964) .... *Jubilee (M) 5029*   64   **15-20**
Soundtrack (1964) .... *Jubilee (S) 5029*   64   **20-25**
 Composer: Steve Karmen. **Conductor:** Steve Karmen.

CANDIDE

Original Cast (1956) .... *Columbia (M) OL-5180*   56   **25-30**
Original Cast (1956) .... *Columbia (SE) OS-2350*   63   **10-15**
 Has alternate takes.
Original Cast (1956) .... *Columbia (SE) PST-2350*   Re   **8-10**
 Composer: Leonard Bernstein. **Conductor:** Samuel Krachmalnick. **Cast:** Max Adrian; Robert
 Rounseville; Barbara Cook; George Blackwell; William Chapman; Robert Mesrobian; William
 Olvis; Irra Petina; Thomas Pyle; Norman Roland; Robert Rue.

CANDIDE (continued)

Original Revival Cast (1973) .... *Columbia (S) S2X-32923*   73   **$10-15**
Double LP set.
Composer: Leonard Bernstein; Stephen Sondheim. **Conductor:** John Mauceri. **Cast:** Lewis J.
Stadlen; Mark Baker; Maureen Brennan; Sam Freed; June Gable; Jim Corti; David Horwitz; Gail
Boggs; Lynne Gannaway; Chip Garnett; Robert Henderson; David Horwitz; Becky McSpadden;
Carolann Page; Deborah St. Darr; Renee Semes.

Original Revival Cast (1982) .... *New World NW-340/1*   82   **10-15**
Double LP set.
Composer: Leonard Bernstein; Stephen Sondheim. **Conductor:** John Mauceri. **Cast:** David
Eisler; Ralph Bassett; Robert Brubaker; Joyce Castle; Ivy Austin; Erie Mills; Scott Reeve; James
Billings; Rhoda Butler; Maris Clement; Jack Harrold; William Ledbetter; Don Yule; John
Lankston. (With Dialogue.)

CANDY

Soundtrack (1968) .... *ABC (S) ABCS-OC-9*   68   **20-25**
Composer: Dave Grusin. **Conductor:** Dave Grusin. **Cast:** Steppenwolf; Byrds.

CANNIBALS:
see SONNY AND JED

CANTERBURY TALES

Original Cast (1969) .... *Capitol (S) SW-229*   69   **15-20**
Original Cast (1969) .... *Capitol (S) SWCR-292(3)*   69   **35-40**
Triple LP set. Also has music from *Celebration* and *Zorba*.
Composer: Richard Hill; John Hawkins; Nevil Coghill. **Conductor:** Oscar Kosarin.
Cast: George Rose; Hermione Baddeley; Martyn Green; Roy Cooper; Sandy Duncan; Ed
Evanko; Ann Gardner; Bruce Hyde; Evelyn Page; Suzan Sidney; Edwin Steffe.

CANTOR, EDDIE, STORY:
see EDDIE CANTOR STORY

CAPER OF THE GOLDEN BULLS

Soundtrack (1967) .... *Tower (M) T-5086*   67   **15-20**
Soundtrack (1967) .... *Tower (S) ST-5086*   67   **20-25**
Composer: Vic Mizzy. **Conductor:** Vic Mizzy.

CAPRICORN ONE

Soundtrack (1978) .... *Warner Bros. (S) BSK 3201*   78   **15-25**
Composer: Jerry Goldsmith. **Conductor:** Jerry Goldsmith.

CAPTAIN BLOOD (CLASSIC FILM SCORES FROM ERROL FLYNN)

Studiotrack .... *RCA Victor (S) ARL-1-091*   75   **10-12**
Has music from: *They Died with Their Boots On, The Sun Also Rises, Dodge City, Adventures of Don
Juan, Objective Burma, The Adventures of Robin Hood, Captain Blood* and *The Sea Hawk*.
Composer: Max Steiner; Erich Wolfgang Korngold; Franz Waxman; others.
Conductor: Charles Gerhardt.

CAPTAIN FROM CASTILE

Soundtrack (1947) .... *Mercury (EP) ME-1-3041*   52   **20-40**
Soundtrack (1947) .... *Mercury (M) MG-25072*   50   **90-100**
10-inch LP.
Soundtrack (1947) .... *Mercury (M) MG-20005*   52   **50-75**
Soundtrack (1947) .... *Philips (M) 200-098*   63   **15-20**
Soundtrack (1947) .... *Delos (M) F-25411*   Re   **8-10**
Composer: Alfred Newman. **Conductor:** Alfred Newman.

Soundtrack . . . . *Citadel (S) 7-7015*   79   **$8-10**
Also has themes from: *All About Eve, Pinky, The Song of Bernadette, Wuthering Heights, A Royal Scandal, The Razor's Edge, How Green Was My Valley* and *A Letter to Three Wives.*

CAPTAIN FROM CASTILE: THE CLASSIC FILM SCORES OF ALFRED NEWMAN

Soundtrack . . . . *RCA Victor (S) ARL1-0184*   73   **8-10**
Also has music from: *How to Marry a Millionaire, Wuthering Heights, Down to the Sea in Ships, The Song of Bernadette, The Bravados, Anastasia, The Best of Everything, Airport* (1970), and *The Robe.*
Composer: Alfred Newman. **Conductor:** Alfred Newman.

CAPTAIN HORATIO HORNBLOWER

Studiotrack (1951) . . . .*Delyse (M) D-6057*   60   **100-125**
Studiotrack (1951) . . . . *Delyse (SE) DS-6057*   60   **175-200**
Studiotrack (1951) . . . .*Citadel (SE) CT-7009*   79   **15-20**
Also has *Rhapsody for Violin and Orchestra.*
Composer: Robert Farnon. **Conductor:** Robert Farnon. **Cast:** London Festival Symphony Orchestra.

CAPTAIN JINKS OF THE HORSE MARINES

Original Cast (1975) . . . . *RCA Victor (S) ARL2-1727*   75   **20-25**
Double LP set.
Composer: Jack Beeson; Sheldon Harnick. **Conductor:** Russell Patterson. **Cast:** Eugene Green; George Livings; Keith Harmon; William Latimer; James Ditsch; Robert Owens Jones; Caro Wilcox; Brian Steel; Walter Hook.

CAPTAIN KANGAROO

TV Cast . . . . *Columbia (M) CL-1012*   57   **15-20**
Actual title: *Captain Kangaroo Songs and Dances.*
Cast: Bob Keeshan.
TV Cast . . . . *Columbia (M) CL-678*   55   **20-25**
Actual title: *Captain Kangaroo - Treasure House.*
Cast: Bob Keeshan.
TV Cast . . . . *Harmony (M) HL-9520*   60   **10-20**
Cast: Bob Keeshan with Orchestra and Chorus.

CAPTAIN MIDNIGHT

Radio Cast . . . .*Golden Age (M) 5006*   78   **8-10**

CAPTIVE

Soundtrack (1987) . . . . *Virgin (S) 90609-1*   87   **10-12**
Composer: The Edge; Michael Berkeley. **Cast:** The Edge.

CAR WASH

Soundtrack (1976) . . . . *MCA (EP) 1947*   76   **10-15**
Promotional issue only. Actual title: *Mini Wash.*
Composer: Norman Whitfield; others. **Cast:** Rose Royce; Pointer Sisters.
Soundtrack (1976) . . . . *MCA (S) 2-6000*   76   **12-15**
Double LP set.
Composer: Norman Whitfield; others. **Cast:** Rose Royce; Pointer Sisters.

CARAVANS

Soundtrack (1978) . . . . *Epic (S) ASE-35787*   78   **8-10**
Composer: Mike Batt. **Conductor:** Mike Batt.

CARD

London Cast (1973) . . . .*AEI (S) 1124*   **8-10**
Reissue of 1973 U.K. release (Pye 18408).
Composer: Tony Hatch; Jackie Trent. **Cast:** Jim Dale; Millicent Martin; Joan Hickson; Marti Webb; Eleanor Bron.

CARDINAL
Soundtrack (1963) . . . .*RCA Victor (M) LOC-1084*   63 $30-35
  Composer: Jerome Moross. **Conductor:** Jerome Moross.
Soundtrack (1963) . . . .*RCA Victor (S) LSO-1084*   63   **50-55**
Soundtrack (1963) . . . . *Entr' acte (S) ERS-6518*   80   **8-10**
  Composer: Jerome Moross. **Conductor:** Jerome Moross.

CAREFREE:
see FLYING DOWN TO RIO

CAREFUL, HE MIGHT HEAR YOU
Soundtrack (1983) . . . . *Varese Sarabande (S) STV-81221*   83   **8-10**
  Cast: Ray Cook.

CARETAKERS
Soundtrack (1963) . . . .*AVA (M) A-31*   63   **25-30**
Soundtrack (1963) . . . .*AVA (S) A-31*   63   **30-35**
  Composer: Elmer Bernstein. **Conductor:** Elmer Bernstein.

CARMELINA
Original Cast (1979) . . . .*Original Cast (S) OC-8019*   79   **8-10**
  Composer: Burton Lane; Alan J. Lerner. **Conductor:** Don Jennings. **Cast:** Georgia Brown; Paul Sorvino; Jossie De Guzman; Grace Keagy; Bernie Knee; Gordon Ramsey; Howard Ross.

CARMEN
Studio Cast . . . .*Harmony (M) 2086*   10-15
  Cast: Milton Cross (narrator).

CARMEN JONES
Original Cast (1943) . . . . *Decca (EP) ED-904*   50   **15-20**
Original Cast (1943) . . . . *Decca (M) DL-8014*   50   **25-40**
Original Cast (1943) . . . . *Decca (M) DL-9021*   55   **20-30**
Original Cast (1943) . . . .*Decca (SE) DL7-9021*   59   **15-20**
Original Cast (1943) . . . .*MCA (SE) 2054e*   72   **10-12**
Original Cast (1943) . . . .*MCA (SE) 1531*   Re   **8-10**
  Composer: Oscar Hammerstein; Georges Bizet. **Conductor:** Joseph Littau. **Cast:** Muriel Smith; Luther Saxon; Cozy Cole; Glenn Bryant; Carlotta Franzell; June Hawkins; Dick Montgomery; Jessica Russell; Randall Steplight.
Soundtrack (1955) . . . . *RCA Victor (EP) ERA-233*   55   **10-15**
Soundtrack (1955) . . . .*RCA Victor (EP) ERC-1881*   55   **25-30**
  Triple EP set.
Soundtrack (1955) . . . .*RCA Victor (M) LM-1881*   55   **25-30**
Soundtrack (1955) . . . . *RCA Victor (SE) ARL1-0046*   73   **15-20**
  Composer: Georges Bizet. **Conductor:** Herschel Gilbert. **Cast:** Pearl Bailey; Marilyn Horne; LeVerne Peterson; Joe Crawford; Broc Peters; Marvin Hayes.

CARMILLA: A VAMPIRE TALE
Original Cast (1972) . . . .*Vanguard (S) VSD-79322*   72   **8-10**
  Based on a novel by J.S. Le Fanu.
  Composer: Ben Johnston; Wilford Leach. **Conductor:** Zizi Mueller. **Cast:** Margaret Benczak; Donald Harrington; Camille Tibaldeo; Sandra Johnson.

CARNEGIE HALL:
see NIGHT AT CARNEGIE HALL

CARNIVAL
Original Cast (1961) . . . .*MGM (M) E-3946*   61   **15-20**
Original Cast (1961) . . . . *MGM (S) SE-3946*   61   **15-25**
  Composer: Bob Merrill. **Conductor:** Saul Schectman. **Cast:** Anna Maria Alberghetti; James Mitchell; Kaye Ballard; Jerry Orbach; Henry Lascoe; Pierre Olaf.

CAROUSEL

Original Cast (1945) .... Decca (EP) ED-804	49	$15-20
Original Cast (1945) .... Decca (M) DL-8003	49	30-40
Original Cast (1945) .... Decca (M) DL-9020	55	20-25
Original Cast (1945) .... Decca (SE) DL7-9020	59	15-20
Original Cast (1945) .... MCA (SE) 2033	72	10-12
Original Cast (1943) .... MCA (SE) 37093	81	8-10
Original Cast (1945) .... MCA (SE) 1627	Re	8-10

  Composer: Richard Rodgers; Oscar Hammerstein II. **Conductor:** Joseph Littau. **Cast:** John
  Raitt; Jan Clayton; Jean Darling; Connie Baxter; Christine Johnson; Eric Mattson; Murvyn Vye.

Studio Cast (1953) .... RCA Victor (EP) EPA-475	53	10-20

  Composer: Richard Rodgers; Oscar Hammerstein II. **Conductor:** Al Goodman.

Studio Cast (1953) .... RCA Victor (M) LPM-3150	53	25-35

  10-inch LP. One side has music from *Oklahoma*.

Original Revival Cast (1965) .... RCA Victor (S) LSO-1114	65	10-15

  Composer: Richard Rodgers; Oscar Hammerstein II. **Conductor:** Franz Allers. **Cast:** John Raitt;
  Eileen Christy; Susan Watson; Benay Venuta; Edward Everett Horton; Katherine Hilgenberg;
  Jerry Orbach; Reid Shelton.

Studio Cast (1962) .... Command (S) RS-843-SD	62	15-20

  Composer: Richard Rodgers; Oscar Hammerstein II. **Conductor:** Jay Blackton. **Cast:** Alfred
  Drake; Roberta Peters.

Studio Cast (1960) .... Epic (M) LN-3679	60	10-20

  Composer: Richard Rodgers; Oscar Hammerstein II. **Cast:** Lois Hunt; Harry Snow.

Studio Cast (1966) .... Buena Vista (M) BV-4029	66	10-15
Studio Cast (1966) .... Buena Vista (S) STER-4029	66	15-20

  Above two LPs have a gatefold cover and bound-in booklet.
  Composer: Richard Rodgers; Oscar Hammerstein II. **Conductor:** Tutti Camarata.
  Cast: Jan Clayton.

Studio Cast (1954) .... RCA Victor (EP) EPC-1048	54	10-15
Studio Cast (54) .... RCA Victor (M) LPM-1048	54	15-20

  Composer: Richard Rodgers; Oscar Hammerstein II. **Cast:** Patrice Munsel; Robert Merrill;
  Henderson; others.

Soundtrack (1956) .... Capitol (EP) EDM-694	56	12-18
Soundtrack (1956) .... Capitol (M) W-694	56	25-30

  Has the complete version of *The Carousel Waltz*. This LP is not banded.

Soundtrack (1956) .... Capitol (SE) SW-694	62	10-15

  True stereo. Has an edited *Carousel Waltz*. This pressing is banded.

Soundtrack (1956) .... Capitol (M) TCL-1790	62	30-40
Soundtrack (1956) .... Capitol (SE) STCL-1790	62	35-45

  Triple LP set: *Rodgers and Hammerstein Deluxe Set*. Also has discs for *The King and I* and *Oklahoma*.
  Composer: Richard Rodgers; Oscar Hammerstein II. **Conductor:** Alfred Newman. **Cast:** Gordon
  MacRae; Shirley Jones; Cameron Mitchell; Robert Rounsevill; Barbara Ruick; Claramae Turner.

TV Soundtrack (1969) .... Columbia Special Products (M) CSM-479	69	35-40

  Composer: Richard Rodgers; Oscar Hammerstein II. **Conductor:** Jack Elliot. **Cast:** Robert
  Goulet; Mary Grover; Pernell Roberts; Marlyn Mason.
  Also has music from *Oklahoma*.

Studiotrack .... MCA (S) 6209	87	8-10

  Composer: Richard Rodgers; Oscar Hammerstein II. **Conductor:** Paul Gemignani.
  Cast: Royal Philharmonic Orchestra.
  Also has music from *Porgy and Bess*.

CARPETBAGGERS

Soundtrack (1964) .... Ava (M) A-45	64	25-30
Soundtrack (1964) .... Ava (S) AS-45	64	30-35

  Composer: Elmer Bernstein. **Conductor:** Elmer Bernstein.

CARRIE
Soundtrack (1976) . . . . *United Artists (S) UA-LA716-H*   76 $12-15
Composer: Pino Donaggio. Cast: Katie Irving.

CARRY IT ON
Soundtrack (1971) . . . . *Vanguard (S) 79313*   71   **8-10**
Cast: Joan Baez; David Harris.

CARRY NATION
Original Cast (1968) . . . . *Desto (S) DC-6463/64/65*   68   **20-25**
Triple LP set.
Composer: Douglas Moore; William North Jayme. Conductor: Samuel Krachmalnick.
Cast: Beverly Wolf; Ellen Faull; Julian Patrick; Arnold Voketaitis.

CASABLANCA: CLASSIC FILM SCORES FOR HUMPHREY BOGART
Soundtrack . . . . *RCA Victor (S) ARL1-0422*   74   **12-15**
Soundtrack . . . . *RCA Victor (S) ALG1-3782*   81   **8-12**
Also has music from: *Passage to Marseille, The Treasure of the Sierra Madre, The Big Sleep, The Caine Mutiny, To Have and Have Not, The Two Mrs. Carrolls, Sabrina, The Left Hand of God, Sahara, Virginia City* and *Key Largo.*
Composer: Max Steiner; Franz Waxman; Frederick Hollander; Victor Young; others.
Conductor: Charles Gerhardt. Cast: National Philharmonic Orchestra.

CASANOVA '70:
see TRIPLE FEATURE

CASEY'S SHADOW
Soundtrack (1978) . . . . *Columbia (S) PS-35344*   78   **8-10**
Composer: Patrick Williams. Conductor: Patrick Williams.

CASINO ROYALE
Soundtrack (1967) . . . . *Colgems (M) COMO 5005*   67   **30-60**
Soundtrack (1967) . . . . *Colgems (S) COSO 5005*   67   **75-150**
Composer: Burt Bacharach. Conductor: Burt Bacharach. Cast: Herb Alpert and the Tijuana Brass; Dusty Springfield.

CASSANDRA CROSSING
Soundtrack (1977) . . . . *Citadel CT-6020*   77   **15-20**
Composer: Jerry Goldsmith. Conductor: Jerry Goldsmith.

CAST A GIANT SHADOW
Soundtrack (1966) . . . . *United Artists (M) UAL-4138*   66   **20-25**
Soundtrack (1966) . . . . *United Artists (S) UAS-5138*   66   **25-30**
Soundtrack (1966) . . . . *MCA (S) 25093*   Re   **8-10**
Composer: Elmer Bernstein. Conductor: Elmer Bernstein.

CASUALTIES OF WAR
Soundtrack . . . . *MCA (S) 6340*   **8-10**
Composer: Ennio Morricone. Conductor: Ennio Morricone.

CAT AND THE FIDDLE
Original London Cast (1931) . . . . *World (M) SH-171*   **15-20**
Composer: Jerome Kern; Otto Harbach. Conductor: Carroll Gibbons. Cast: Peggy Wood.
Studio Cast (1953) . . . . *RCA Victor (EP) EPA-477*   53   **10-20**
Composer: Jerome Kern; Otto Harbach. Conductor: Lehman Engel. Cast: Patricia Neway; Stephen Douglass.
Studio Cast (1953) . . . . *RCA Victor (M) LPM-3151*   53   **20-30**
One side has music from *Show Boat.*
Composer: Jerome Kern; Otto Harbach. Conductor: Lehman Engel. Cast: Patricia Neway; Stephen Douglass.

Studio Cast (1959) .... *Epic (M) LN-3569*   59   **$25-30**
One side has music from *Hit the Deck*.
Composer: Jerome Kern; Otto Gregory. **Conductor:** Johnny Gregory. **Cast:** Doreen Hume; Denis Quilley.

CAT BALLOU
Soundtrack (1965) .... *Capitol (M) T-2340*   65   **10-12**
Soundtrack (1965) .... *Capitol (S) ST-2340*   65   **15-20**
Actual title: *Nat King Cole Sings His Songs from Cat Ballou and Other Motion Pictures.*
Cast: Nat "King" Cole.

CAT PEOPLE
Soundtrack (1982) .... *Backstreet Records BSR-6107*   82   **8-10**
Composer: Giorgio Moroder. **Conductor:** Giorgio Moroder. **Cast:** David Bowie.

CATHERINE WHEEL
Original Cast .... *Sire (S) SRK-3645*   **8-12**
Composer: David Burne.

CAT'S EYE
Soundtrack (1985) .... *Varese Sarabande (S) STV-81241*   85   **8-12**
Composer: Alan Silvestri.

CATS
Original London Cast (1981) .... *Polydor (S) CATX-001*   81   **10-15**
Original London Cast (1981) .... *Geffen (S) 2GHS-2017*   Re   **10-12**
Above two are double LP sets.
Composer: Andrew Lloyd Webber. **Conductor:** Andrew Lloyd Weber. **Cast:** Sleep; Nicholas; Lessed; Paige.
Original Cast (1981) .... *Geffen (S) GHS-2026*   82   **10-15**
Selections from the original Broadway show, on one LP.
Original Cast (1981) .... *Geffen (S) 2GHS-2031*   83   **10-15**
Double LP set.
Composer: Andrew Lloyd Webber. **Conductor:** Rene Wiegert. **Cast:** Kenneth Ard; Betty Buckley; Rene Ceballos; Wendy Edmead; Steven Gelfer; Harry Groener; Stephen Hanan; Janet L. Hubert; Reed Jones; Donna King; Anna McNeely; Terrence V. Mann; Hector Jaime Mercado; Cynthia Onrubia; Ken Page; Timothy Scott; Bonnie Simmons.

CAUGHT IN THE ACT:
see VICTOR BORGE

CELEBRATION
Original Cast (1969) .... *Capitol (S) SW-198*   69   **15-20**
Composer: Harvey Schmidt; Tom Jones. **Conductor:** Ron Dereninko. **Cast:** Keith Charles; Michael Glenn Smith; Susan Watson; Ted Thurston.
Also see CANTERBURY TALES

CERTAIN FURY
Soundtrack .... *Varese Sarabande (S) 81239*   **8-10**

CERTAIN SMILE
Soundtrack (1958) .... *Columbia (M) CL-1194*   58   **75-85**
Soundtrack (1958) .... *Columbia (S) CS-8068*   58   **90-100**
Composer: Alfred Newman. **Conductor:** Alfred Newman.

CHAIRMAN
Soundtrack (1969) .... *Tetragrammaton (S) 5007*   69   **30-35**
Soundtrack (1969) .... *AEI (S) 3110*   82   **8-10**
Composer: Jerry Goldsmith. **Conductor:** Jerry Goldsmith.

CHALIAPIN AS BORIS
Original Cast ....*RCA Victor (M) LCT-3*   49   **$20-35**
   Excerpts of performances done between 1935 and 1940.
   Conductor: Albert Coates; M. Steimann; V. Bellezza. **Cast:** Feodor Chaliapin. (With dialogue.)

CHALLENGE OF THE SALT (I'M GOING TO SET MYSELF ON FIRE)
Soundtrack (1973) ....*MVC (S) 1001*   73   **8-10**

CHAMP
Soundtrack (1979) ....*Planet (S) PL-9001*   79   **8-10**
   Composer: Dave Grusin; Carole Bayer Sager; Marvin Hamlisch. **Conductor:** Dave Grusin.
   Cast: Dave Grusin; Chris Thompson.

CHAPLIN REVUE
Soundtrack (1960) ....*Decca (M) DL-4040*   60   **50-55**
   Composer: Charlie Chaplin. **Conductor:** Eric Spears. **Cast:** Charlie Chaplin.

CHAPLIN'S ART OF COMEDY
Soundtrack (1966) ....*Mainstream (M) 56089*   66   **20-25**
Soundtrack (1966) .... *Mainstream (S) 6089*   66   **25-35**
   Score based on original Charlie Chaplin films and documentaries.
   Composer: Elias Breeskin. **Conductor:** Elias Breeskin. **Cast:** Charlie Chaplin.

CHAPMAN REPORT
Soundtrack (1962) ....*Warner Bros. (M) W-1478*   62   **25-30**
Soundtrack (1962) ....*Warner Bros. (S) WS-1478*   62   **30-35**
   Composer: Leonard Rosenman. **Conductor:** Leonard Rosenman.

CHAPPAQUA
Soundtrack (1968) ....*Columbia (S) OS-3230*   68   **15-20**
   Composer: Ravi Shankar. **Cast:** Ravi Shankar.

CHARADE
Soundtrack (1963) ....*RCA Victor (M) LPM-2755*   63   **20-25**
Soundtrack (1963) ....*RCA Victor (S) LSP-2755*   63   **25-30**
   Composer: Henry Mancini. **Conductor:** Henry Mancini. **Cast:** Henry Mancini's Orchestra and
   Chorus.

CHARGE OF THE LIGHT BRIGADE
Soundtrack (1968) ....*United Artists (S) UAS-5177*   68   **20-25**
   Composer: John Addison. **Conductor:** John Addison. **Cast:** Manfred Mann. (With dialogue.)
   Also see DEATH OF A SCOUNDREL

CHARIOT OF THE GODS
Soundtrack (1974) ....*Polydor (S) PD-6504*   74   **20-25**
   Composer: Peter Thomas. **Conductor:** Peter Thomas.

CHARIOTS OF FIRE
Soundtrack (1981) ....*Polydor (S) PD 1-6335*   81   **8-10**
   Composer: Vangelis. **Conductor:** Vangelis. **Cast:** Ambrosian Singers; Vangelis.

CHARLEY WEAVER — LETTERS FROM MAMA
TV Soundtrack ....*Coral (M) CRL-57458*   **10-15**
   From the soundtrack of the Steve Allen Show.
   Cast: Cliff Arquette.

CHARLIE AND ALGERNON
Original London Cast (1980) ....*Original Cast (S) OC-8021*   80   **8-10**
   Composer: Charles Strouse; David Rogers. **Conductor:** Alexander Farris. **Cast:** Michael
   Crawford; Cheryl Kennedy; Aubrey Woods; Ralph Nossek.

CHARLIE BROWN CHRISTMAS
TV Soundtrack (1964) ....*Fantasy (S) 8431*   70   **8-10**
   Composer: Vince Guaraldi. **Conductor:** Vince Guaraldi. **Cast:** Vince Guaraldi Trio.

CHARLIE CHAN AT THE OPERA
Soundtrack (1936) . . . . *Medallion (M) MED 310*   81   **$8-10**
  Also has *Gershwin: A Portrait by Levant and Levant - Piano Concerto.*
  Composer: Oscar Levant.

CHARLIE SENT ME
Original Cast (1984) . . . .*Glendale (S) 6035*   84   **8-10**

CHARLOTTE SWEET
 Original Cast (1982) . . . . *John Hammond (S) W2X-38680*
  Cast: Mara Beckerman; Lynn Eldredge; Jeffrey Keller; Timothy Landfield; Merle Louise;
  Michael McCormick; Polly Pen; Christopher Seppe.

CHARLOTTE'S WEB
Soundtrack (1973) . . . .*Paramount (S) 1008*   73   **20-25**
  Composer: Richard M. Sherman; Robert B. Sherman. **Conductor:** Irwin Kostal. **Cast:** Henry
  Gibson (narration); Debbie Reynolds; Paul Lynde; Agnes Morehead.

CHARLY
Soundtrack (1968) . . . . *World Pacific (S) WS-21454*   68   **20-25**
  Composer: Ravi Shankar. **Cast:** Ravi Shankar.

CHASE
Soundtrack (1978) . . . . *Casablanca (S) 20146*   78   **10-12**
  12-inch disco pressing.
Soundtrack (1966) . . . . *Columbia (M) OL-6560*   66   **35-45**
Soundtrack (1966) . . . .*Columbia (S) OS-2960*   66   **60-80**
  Composer: John Barry. **Conductor:** John Barry. **Cast:** John Barry and His Orchestra.

CHASTITY
Soundtrack (1969) . . . . *Atco (S) SD-33-302*   69   **15-18**
  Composer: Sonny Bono; Elyse Weinberg. **Cast:** Cher.

CHE!
Soundtrack (1969) . . . . *Tetragrammaton (S) T-5006*   69   **25-30**
Soundtrack (1969) . . . .*AEI (S) 3111*   82   **8-10**
  Composer: Lalo Schifrin. **Conductor:** Lalo Schifrin.

CHECKMATE
TV Soundtrack (1960) . . . . *Columbia (M) CL-1591*   60   **30-35**
TV Soundtrack (1960) . . . .*Columbia (S) CS-8391*   60   **40-45**
  Composer: John Williams. **Conductor:** John Williams.
Studiotrack (1961) . . . . *Contemporary (M) 3599*   62   **10-15**
Studiotrack (1961) . . . . *Contemporary (S) S-7599*   62   **15-20**
  Jazz, based on music from the TV show.
  Composer: Johnny Williams. **Conductor:** Shelly Manne. **Cast:** Shelly Manne.

CHEE CHEE
Studio Cast (1963) . . . . *Ava (M) A-26*   63   **30-40**
Studio Cast (1963) . . . .*Ava (S) AS-26*   63   **50-60**
  One side has music from *Treasure Girl.*
  Composer: Richard Rodgers; Lorenz Hart. **Conductor:** Richard Lewine. **Cast:** Betty Comden.

CHEECH AND CHONG'S UP IN SMOKE
see UP IN SMOKE

CHERRY, HARRY AND RAQUEL
Soundtrack . . . .*Beverly Hills (S) BHS-23*   **8-10**
  Composer: Bill Loose. **Conductor:** Bill Loose.

CHESS
  Broadway Cast (1988) . . . . *RCA Victor (S) 7700-1*   88   **$8-10**
    Composer: Benny Anderson; Bjorn Ulvaeus. **Conductor:** Paul Bogaev. **Cast:** Judy Kuhn; David
    Carroll; Philip Casnoff.

CHESS (A EUROPEAN MUSICAL)
  Original Cast (1984) . . . . *RCA Victor (S) CPL2-5340*   84   **8-10**
    Double LP set.
    Composer: Rice. **Cast:** Elaine Paige; Murray Head; others.

CHESS PIECES
  Original Cast . . . . *RCA Victor (S) AFL1-7163*   **8-10**
    Cast: Elaine Paige; Murray Head; others.

CHEYENNE AUTUMN
  Soundtrack (1963) . . . . *Label X (S) LXSE 1-003*   83   **40-60**
    All reviewers agreed on this price range, although, as of November 1990, a catalog of currently available
    LPs lists this one as in print.
    Composer: Alex North. **Conductor:** Alex North.

CHICAGO
  Original Cast (1975) . . . . *Arista (S) 9005*   75   **8-10**
    Composer: John Kander; Fred Ebb. **Conductor:** Stanley Lebowsky. **Cast:** Gwen Verdon; Chita
    Rivera; Jerry Orbach; Barney Martin; Mary McCarty; M. O'Haughey.

CHICKEN CHRONICLES
  Soundtrack (1977) . . . . *United Artists (S) UA-LA830-H*   77   **10-15**
    Composer: Ken Lauber; others. **Conductor:** Ken Lauber. **Cast:** Classics IV; Nitty Gritty Dirt
    Band; Canned Heat; Boffalongo; Kutee; Jackie De Shannon.

CHILD'S INTRODUCTION TO THE MELODY AND THE INSTRUMENTS
  OF THE ORCHESTRA
  Studio Cast (1962) . . . . *Disneyland (M) DQ-1232*   62   **8-12**

CHILDREN, CHILDREN, CHILDREN
  Original Cast (1955) . . . . *Capitol (EP) EAXP-305*   55   **15-20**
    Also has music from *Lady and the Tramp.*

CHILDREN OF A LESSER GOD
  Soundtrack (1986) . . . . *GNP/Crescendo (S) GNPS-8007*   86   **8-15**
    Composer: Michael Convertino. **Conductor:** Shirley Walker.

CHILDREN OF SANCHEZ
  Soundtrack (1978) . . . . *A&M (S) SP-6700*   78   **10-15**
    Double LP set.
    Composer: Chuck Mangione. **Conductor:** Chuck Mangione.

CHILDREN OF THE CORN
  Soundtrack (1984) . . . . *Varese Sarabande (S) STV 81203*   84   **8-15**
    Composer: Jonathan Elias. **Conductor:** Jonathan Elias.

CHILDREN'S HOUR
  Studio Cast (1950) . . . . *Decca (M) DL-8013*   50   **20-30**
    One side has music from *Cinderella.*

CHINATOWN
  Soundtrack (1974) . . . . *ABC (S) DP-848*   74   **35-50**
    Composer: Jerry Goldsmith; others. **Conductor:** Jerry Goldsmith.

CHIPMUNKS' CHRISTMAS
  Studio Cast (1981) . . . . *RCA Victor (S) AQL1-4041*   81   **8-10**

CHITTY, CHITTY, BANG, BANG
Soundtrack (1968) . . . . *United Artists (S) UAS-5188* 68   **$15-20**
  Composer: Richard M. Sherman; Robert B. Sherman. **Conductor:** Irwin Kostal. **Cast:** Dick
  VanDyke; Sally Ann Howes; Anna Quayle; Lionel Jeffries.

CHOCALONIA
Original Cast (1976) . . . .*Crissy (S) CR-2034* 76   **15-20**
  Composer: Glenn Houle. **Conductor:** Glenn Houle. **Cast:** Frankie Marshall; Dennis Lybe; Jim
  Hayes; Gary Fuller; Chris Costello.

CHOCOLATE SOLDIER
Studio Cast (1948) . . . .*Columbia (M) ML-4060* 48   **25-35**
  10-inch LP. One side has music from *The Student Prince.*
Studio Cast (1948) . . . . *Columbia Special Products (M) P-13707* Re   **8-10**
  One side has music from *The Naughty Marietta.*
  Composer: Oscar Straus. **Conductor:** Robert Armbruster. **Cast:** Rise Stevens; Nelson Eddy.
Studio Cast (1951) . . . .*RCA Victor (EP) EKB-1006* 51   **15-20**
  Double EP set.
Studio Cast (1951) . . . .*RCA Victor (M) LK-1006* 51   **25-35**
  Composer: Oscar Straus. **Conductor:** Al Goodman. **Cast:** Ann Ayars; Charles Fredericks; John
  Percival; Jimmy Carroll.
Studio Cast (1958) . . . . *RCA Victor (M) LOP-6005* 58   **20-25**
Studio Cast (1958) . . . . *RCA Victor (S) LSO-6005* 58   **30-35**
  Above two are double LP sets.
Studio Cast (1958) . . . . *RCA Victor (M) LOP-1506* 59   **15-20**
  Contains only excerpts.
Studio Cast (1958) . . . . *RCA Victor (S) LSO-1506* 59   **20-25**
  Excerpts.
  Composer: Oscar Straus. **Conductor:** Lehman Engel. **Cast:** Rise Stevens; Robert Merrill; Jo
  Sullivan; Peter Palmer.

CHOICE OF ARMS:
see CHOIX DES ARMES

CHOIRBOYS
Soundtrack (1978) . . . .*MCA (S) 2326* '78   **8-12**
  Composer: Frank De Vol. **Conductor:** Frank De Vol.

CHOIX DES ARMES (CHOICE OF ARMS)
Soundtrack (1981) . . . . *DRG (S) SL-9510* 81   **8-10**
  Conductor: Philippe Sarde. **Cast:** London Symphony Orchestra.

CHORUS LINE
Original Cast (1975) . . . . *Columbia (S) JS-33581* 75   **8-10**
Original Cast (1975) . . . .*Columbia (S) HS-43581* 81   **10-15**
  Half-speed mastered.
  Composer: Marvin Hamlisch; Edward Kleban. **Conductor:** Donald Pippin. **Cast:** Scott Allen;
  Carol Bishop; Renee Baughman; Pamela Blair; Wayne Cilento; Ronald Dennis; Kay Cole;
  Nancy Lane; Priscilla Lopez, Donna McKechnie; Don Percassi.
Soundtrack (1985) . . . .*Casablanca (S) 826306-1* 85   **8-10**

CHOSEN
Soundtrack (1978) . . . .*Cerberus (S) CEMS 0103* 79   **8-12**
  This film was originally titled *Holocaust 2000.*
  Composer: Ennio Morricone. **Conductor:** Ennio Morricone.

CHRISTIANE F.
Soundtrack (1982) . . . . *RCA Victor (S) ABL1-4239* 82   **8-10**
  Cast: David Bowie.

CHRISTINE

Original Cast (1960) .... *Columbia (M) OL-5220*   60   **$45-50**
Original Cast (1960) .... *Columbia (S) OS-2026*   60   **60-70**
 Composer: Sammy Fain; Paul Webster. **Conductor:** Jay Blackton. **Cast:** Maureen O'Hara;
 Morley Meredith; Nancy Andrews; Janet Pavek; Phil Leeds.

CHRISTINE

Soundtrack (1983) .... *Motown (S) M-6086*   83   **8-10**
 Composer: Various. **Cast:** George Thorogood and the Destroyers; Buddy Holly and the Crickets;
 Johnny Ace; Robert and Johnny; Little Richard; Dion and the Belmonts; Viscounts; Thurston
 Harris; Danny and the Juniors; Larry Williams.

CHRISTMAS CAROL

Original Cast (1980) .... *MMG (S) 3-MMG-302*   80   **20-30**
 Triple LP, boxed set. Includes 24-page booklet/libretto. From the world premiere performance.
 Composer: Thea Musgrave.
Irish Theatre Cast (1959) .... *Vanguard (M) VRS-9040*   59   **10-15**
Studio Cast (1950) .... *Decca (SE) DL-8010*   50   **30-40**
 Also contains *Mister Pickwick's Christmas.*
Studio Cast (1950) .... *MCA (M) DL-734684*   Re   **10-12**
 Composer: Victor Young; Hanns Eisler. **Conductor:** Victor Young; Hanns Eisler. **Cast:** Ronald
 Colman; Eric Snowden; Barbara Jean Wong; Lou Merrill; Hans Conreid; Cy Kendall; Gale
 Gordon; Heather Thatcher; Fred MacKaye; Stephen Muller; Duane Thompson; Ferdinand
 Munier; Charles Laughton.
Studio Cast (1961) .... *Caedmon (M) 1135*   **10-15**
 Cast: Paul Scofield (narration); Sir Ralph Richardson; Frederick Treves; David Dodimead;
 Willoughby Goddard; Norman Mitchell; Douglas Wilmer; Colette Wilde; Edgar Wreford; James
 Culliford; Pauline Jameson; John Mitchell; Michael Lewis.
Studio Cast .... *MGM (M) CH-112*   **10-15**
Studio Cast .... *MGM (SE) PMS-32*   **8-10**
 Composer: Samuel Timberg. **Conductor:** Samuel Timberg. **Cast:** Richard Hale (narration);
 Lionel Barrymore.
Studio Cast (1949) .... *Columbia (M) ML-4081*   49   **40-50**
Studiotrack (1959) .... *Harmony (M) HL-9523*   60   **10-15**
 Composer: Leith Stevens. **Conductor:** Leith Stevens. **Cast:** Basil Rathbone; Francis X.
 Bushman; Lyn Murray Singers.
TV Soundtrack (1954) .... *Unicorn (M) 850*   **8-12**
 Composer: Bernard Herrmann; Maxwell Anderson. **Cast:** Fredric March.
TV Studiotrack .... *Pepsi (M) AAB-1367*   **10-20**
 Side two has *Mister Micawber's Difficulties,* from *David Copperfield* (Laurence Olivier). Produced by
 Towers of London.
TV Studiotrack .... *Spinorama (M) XMK-4014*   **8-10**
 Reissue (side one of Pepsi AAB-1367).
 Cast: Laurence Olivier.
 Also see IT'S A WONDERFUL LIFE

CHRISTMAS RAPPINGS

Original Cast (1979) .... *Judson (S) 1002*   79   **20-30**
 Double LP set.
 Composer: Al Carmines. **Conductor:** Al Carmines. **Cast:** Judson Poets' Theatre Chorus.

CHRISTMAS STORY

Studio Cast (1954) .... *RCA Victor (EP) EPB-3199*   54   **15-20**
Studio Cast (1954) .... *RCA Victor (M) LPM-3199*   54   **20-35**
 10-inch LP.
 Cast: Jack Webb.

CHRISTMAS THAT ALMOST WASN'T

Soundtrack (1966) .... *RCA Victor/Camden (M) CAL-1086*   66   **$12-20**
Soundtrack (1966) .... *RCA Victor/Camden (S) CAS-1086*   66   **15-20**
  Composer: Ray Carter. **Cast:** Paul Tripp (narration); Mischa Auer; Sonny Fox; Rossano Brazzi.

CHRISTMAS TO ELVIS

Studio Cast (1978) .... *Classic (S) CCR-1935*   78   **15-20**
  The Jordanaires sing Christmas songs recorded by Elvis Presley. Includes studio conversations, comments, and reflections by the cast.
  Composer: Various. **Cast:** Jordanaires (Gordon Stoker, Hoyt Hawkins, Ray Walker, Neal Matthews, Louis Nunley); Scotty Moore (guitar); D.J. Fontana (drums); Gordan Stoker (organ); John Rich (guitar); Tommy Hensley (bass); Bobby Ogden (piano); Louis Nunley (bongos).

CHRISTY

Original Cast (1975) .... *Original Cast (S) OC-7913*   75   **8-10**
  Composer: Lawrence J. Blank; Bernie Spiro. **Conductor:** Robert Billig. **Cast:** Jim Elmer; Betty Forsyth; John Canary; Marie Ginnetti; Lynn Kearney; Martha T. Kearns; Bebe Sacks Landis; Gene Lefkowitz; Brian Pizer; Alexander Sokoloff; Bee Swanson.

CHRYSANTHEMUM

London Cast .... *AEI (S) 1108*   **8-10**
  Composer: Robb Stewart.

CHU CHIN CHOW

London Studio Cast .... *World (S) WRS-1007*   **10-20**
  Material from an earlier performance of this show was previously issued in England.
London Studio Cast .... *Music for Pleasure (S) MFP-1012*   **10-15**
  Composer: Fredrick Norton; Oscar Asche. **Conductor:** John Hollingsworth.

CID, EL:
see EL CID

CIMARRON (AND OTHER GREAT SONGS)

Soundtrack (1960) .... *MGM (M) E-3953*   61   **10-15**
Studiotrack (1960) .... *MGM (S) SE-3953*   61   **15-20**
  Composer: David Rose. **Cast:** David Rose and His Orchestra.

CINCINNATI KID

Soundtrack (1965) .... *MGM (M) E-4313*   65   **10-15**
Soundtrack (1965) .... *MGM (S) SE-4313*   65   **15-20**
Soundtrack (1965) .... *MCA (S) 25012*   Re   **8-10**
  Composer: Lalo Schifrin. **Conductor:** Lalo Schifrin. **Cast:** Ray Charles.

CINDERELLA

Studio Cast (1959) .... *RCA Victor (M) LPM-2012*   59   **30-35**
Studio Cast (1959) .... *RCA Victor (S) LSP-2012*   59   **35-45**
  Composer: Jerry Livingston; Norman Leyden. **Conductor:** Thomas Scherman. **Cast:** Mary Martin.
Studio Cast (1965) .... *RCA Victor/Camden (M) CAL-1057*   65   **15-20**
Studio Cast (1965) .... *RCA Victor/Camden (S) CAS-1057*   65   **20-25**
  Composer: Jerry Livingston; Norman Leyden. **Conductor:** Paul J. Smith. **Cast:** Ilene Woods; Disney cast.
Studio Cast (1962) .... *Disneyland (M) ST-3908*   **15-20**
Studio Cast (1965) .... *Disneyland (M) L-308*   65   **15-20**
  Composer: Richard Rodgers; Oscar Hammerstein II. **Cast:** Sybil Trent.
Studio Cast (1965) .... *MGM (M) CH-1007*   65   **15-20**
  Composer: Richard Rodgers; Oscar Hammerstein II. **Cast:** Sybil Trent.

CINDERELLA (continued)
Soundtrack (1949) .... *Disneyland (M) WDL-4007*   57 $25-30
   Feature length cartoon musical.
Soundtrack (1949) .... *Disneyland (M) 3107*   81   **8-12**
   Limited edition picture disc.
   Composer: Mack David; Al Hoffman; Jerry Livingston. **Conductor:** Jerry Livingston.
Studio Cast (1963) .... *Disneyland (M) DQ-1207*   **10-20**
   Composer: Jerry Livingston. **Cast:** Ilene Woods; Verna Felton; Don Barclay.
TV Soundtrack (1957) .... *Columbia (M) OL-5190*   57   **15-20**
TV Soundtrack (1957) .... *Columbia (SE) OS-2005*   59   **25-30**
TV Soundtrack (1957) .... *CBS (SE) AOS-2005*   82   **8-10**
   Composer: Richard Rodgers; Oscar Hammerstein II; with orchestrations by Robert Russell
   Bennett. **Conductor:** Alfredo Antonini. **Cast:** Julie Andrews; Bob Penn; Howard Lindsay;
   Dorothy Stickney; Ilka Chase; Kaye Ballard; Alice Ghostley; Jon Cypher; Edith Adams.
TV Soundtrack (1965) .... *Columbia (M) OL-6330*   65   **15-20**
TV Soundtrack (1965) .... *Columbia (S) OS-2730*   65   **20-25**
   Composer: Richard Rodgers; Oscar Hammerstein II. **Conductor:** John Green. **Cast:** Ginger
   Rodgers; Celeste Holm; Walter Pidgeon. (With dialogue.)
Studiotrack (1966) .... *RCA Victor/Camden (S) CAS-1085*   66   **10-20**
   Composer: Anne and Milton Delugg. **Conductor:** Milton Delugg. **Cast:** Paul Tripp (narrator).
   Also see CHILDREN'S HOUR; SLIPPER AND THE ROSE

CINDERELLA ITALIAN STYLE:
see MORE THAN MIRACLE

CINDERELLA LIBERTY
Soundtrack (1973) .... *20th Century-Fox (S) ST-100*   73   **15-20**
   Composer: John Williams. **Conductor:** John Williams.

CINDERFELLA
Soundtrack (1960) .... *Dot (M) DLP-8001*   60   **25-35**
Soundtrack (1960) .... *Dot (S) DLP-38001*   60   **40-50**
   Composer: Walter Scharf; Harry Warren. **Conductor:** Walter Scharf; Jerry Lewis.

CINDY
Original Cast (1964) .... *ABC-Paramount (M) OC-2*   64   **50-75**
Original Cast (1964) .... *ABC (S) OCS-2*   64   **75-100**
   Composer: Johnny Brandon. **Conductor:** Clark McClellan; Sammy Benskin. **Cast:** Sylvia Mann;
   Johnny Harmon; Lizabeth Pritchett; Thelma Oliver; Dena Dietrich; Mike Sawyer; Tommy
   Karaty; Joe Masiell; Jacqueline Mayro; Frank Nastasi; Lizbeth Pritchett; Mark Stone; Amelia
   Varney.

CINDY-ELLA OR I GOTTA SHOE
Soundtrack .... *Stet (S) DS-15023*   **8-10**
   Composer: Ron Grainer. **Cast:** Cleo Laine.

CINEMA '76
Studio Cast .... *Industrial (M) CILP 500*   **10-12**
   Songs of the Continental Soldiers, originally presented by at the New York World's Fair by Continental
   Insurance.
   Composer: Ray Charles.

CINEMA RHAPSODIES
Studiotrack (1953) .... *Decca (SE) DL-8051*   51   **20-30**
   Composer: Victor Young. **Conductor:** Victor Young.

CINEMA SCENE TODAY
Studiotrack (1967) .... *Mercury (M) MG-21149*   67   **8-15**
Studiotrack (1967) .... *Mercury (S) SR-61149*   67   **10-15**
   Composer: Various. **Conductor:** Marty Gold. **Cast:** Derek and Ray.

CINEMOOG
Studiotrack (1973) ....*Mercury (S) SR-61279*   73   **$8-10**
  Composer: Various. **Cast:** Electronic Concept Orchestra featuring Eddie Higgins on the Moog Synthesizer.

CINERAMA HOLIDAY
Soundtrack (1955) ....*Mercury (M) MG-20059*   55   **50-60**
  Composer: Morton Gould; Van Cleave; Jack Shaindlin; others. **Conductor:** Jack Shaindlin.
Studiotrack (1955) ....*RCA Victor (EP) ERA-258*   55   **10-15**
  Conductor: Morton Gould. **Cast:** Morton Gould and His Orchestra.

CIRCLE OF LOVE
Soundtrack (1965) ....*Monitor (M) MP-602*   65   **25-30**
Soundtrack (1965) ....*Monitor (S) MPS-602*   65   **35-40**
  Composer: Michel Magne. **Conductor:** Michel Magne.

CIRCUS OF HORRORS
Soundtrack (1960) ....*Imperial (M) 9132*   60   **100-125**
  Composer: Muir Mathieson; Franz Reizenstein; Mark Anthony. **Conductor:** Muir Mathieson. **Cast:** Gary Mills.

CIRCUS WORLD
Soundtrack (1964) ....*MGM (M) E-4252*   64   **25-30**
Soundtrack (1964) ....*MGM (S) SE-4252*   64   **30-35**
  Composer: Dimitri Tiomkin. **Conductor:** Dimitri Tiomkin.

CITIZEN KANE
Soundtrack (1941) ....*Mark '56 (M) 810*   80   **10-12**
  Double LP set of the complete film.
  Composer: Bernard Herrmann. **Conductor:** Bernard Herrmann. **Cast:** Orson Welles; Joseph Cotten; Everett Sloane; Agnes Moorehead; Dorothy Comingore; Ray Collins; George Coulouris; Ruth Warrick.
Soundtrack (1941) ....*United Artists (SE) UA-LA372-G*   75   **10-15**
  Composer: Bernard Herrmann. **Conductor:** LeRoy Holmes.
  Also see GREAT FILM CLASSICS.

CITIZEN KANE / DEVIL AND DANIEL WEBSTER
Studiotrack (1940) ....*Unicorn (SE) UN1-72008*   73   **8-10**
  Actual title: *Welles Raises Kane/The Devil and Daniel Webster*.
  Composer: Bernard Herrmann. **Conductor:** Bernard Herrmann. **Cast:** London Philharmonic Orchestra.

CITIZEN KANE: THE CLASSIC FILM SCORES OF BERNARD HERRMANN
Studiotrack ....*RCA Victor (S) ARL 1-070*   74   **10-12**
  Also has music from *On Dangerous Ground, White Witch Doctor, Hangover Square* and *Beneath the 12-Mile Reef*.
  Composer: Bernard Herrmann. **Conductor:** Charles Gerhardt. **Cast:** National Philharmonic; Kiri Te Kanawa; Joaquin Achucrro (piano).

CITIZENS ON PATROL
Soundtrack (1987) ....*Motown (S) 6235ML*   87   **8-10**
  Has music from the film *Police Academy IV*.

CITY HEAT
Soundtrack (1984) ....*Warner Bros. (S) 1-25219*   84   **8-10**
  Composer: Lennie Niehaus. **Cast:** Irene Cara; Al Jarreau; Joe Williams; Mike Lang; Pete Jolly; Clint Eastwood; Eloise Laws.

CITY OF ANGELS
Original Cast ....*Columbia (S) C-46067*   **8-10**

CIVILIZATION, PART II
Soundtrack (1988) .... *Capitol (S) C1-90205*   88   **$8-10**

CLAMBAKE
Soundtrack (1967) .... *RCA Victor (M) LPM-3893*   67   **150-200**
Black label reads "Monaural" at bottom. Includes 12" x 12" bonus photo, which represents about $40 of the value.
Soundtrack (1967) .... *RCA Victor (S) LSP-3893*   67   **60-70**
Black label reads "Stereo" at bottom. Includes 12" x 12" bonus photo, which represents about $40 of the value.
Soundtrack (1967) .... *RCA Victor (S) AFL1-2565*   77   **8-10**
Composer: Sid Tepper; Roy C. Bennett; Jerry Reed; Ben Weisman; Sid Wayne; Randy Starr; others. **Cast:** Elvis Presley; Bob Moore (bass); Floyd Cramer (piano); Jerry Reed (guitar); Buddy Harman (drums); Harold Bradley (guitar); Grady Martin (guitar); Pete Drake (steel guitar); Jordanaires (vocals); Millie Kirkham (vocals).

CLAMS ON THE HALF SHELL
Original Cast (1975) .... *Atlantic (S) SD2-9000*   75   **10-15**
Double LP set.
Conductor: Don York. **Cast:** Bette Midler; Lionel Hampton; Charlotte Crossley; Sharon Redd.
Studio Cast (1975) .... *Atlantic (S) SD-7238*   75   **8-10**
Actual title: *The Divine Miss M.* Contains seven show tunes.
Studio Cast (1975) .... *Atlantic (S) SD-18155*   76   **8-10**
Actual title: *Songs of the New Depression.* Contains three show tunes.
Studio Cast (1975) .... *Atlantic (S) SD-7270*   75   **8-10**
Actual title: *Bette Midler.* Contains four show tunes.
Conductor: Barry Manilow.
Studio Cast (1975) .... *Atlantic (S) SD-19151*   78   **8-10**
Actual title: *Broken Blossom.* Contains one show tune.

CLAN OF THE CAVE BEAR
Soundtrack (1986) .... *Varese Sarabande (S) STV-81274*   86   **8-12**
Composer: Alan Silvestri. **Conductor:** Alan Silvestri.

CLASH OF THE TITANS
Soundtrack (1981) .... *Columbia (S) JS-37386*   81   **8-10**
Composer: Laurence Rosenthal. **Conductor:** Laurence Rosenthal. **Cast:** London Symphony Orchestra; Laurence Olivier (narration).

CLASSIC FILM SCORES FOR BETTE DAVIS
Studiotrack .... *RCA Victor (S) ARL1-0183*   73   **10-12**
With booklet.
Studiotrack .... *RCA Victor (S) AGL1-3706*   80   **8-10**
Without booklet.
Composer: Max Steiner; Erich Wolfgang Korngold; Franz Waxman; Alfred Newman.
Conductor: Charles Gerhardt.

CLASSIC FILM SCORES OF ERICH WOLFGANG KORNGOLD
Studiotrack .... *RCA Victor (S) ARL 1-018*   73   **10-12**
Has music from: *The Private Lives of Elizabeth and Essex, The Prince and the Pauper, The Sea Wolf, Another Dawn, Of Human Bondage, Anthony Adverse* and *Deception.*
Composer: Erich Wolfgang Korngold. **Conductor:** Charles Gerhardt.

CLAUDINE
Soundtrack (1974) .... *Buddah (S) BDS-5602*   74   **15-20**
Composer: Curtis Mayfield. **Cast:** Curtis Mayfield; Gladys Knight and the Pips.

CLEAN SLATE:
see COUP DE TORCHON

CLEO LAINE AT CARNEGIE HALL
Original Cast (1973) .... *RCA Victor (S) LPL1-5015*   73   **$10-12**

CLEO LAINE RETURNS TO CARNEGIE HALL
Original Cast (1976) .... *RCA Victor (S) APL1-2407*   76   **8-10**
Conductor: John Dankworth. Cast: Cleo Laine.

CLEOPATRA
Studiotrack (1963) .... *RCA Victor (M) LPM-2766*   63   **20-25**
Studiotrack (1963) .... *RCA Victor (S) LSP-2766*   63   **25-30**
Composer: Alex North. Conductor: Riz Ortolani. Cast: Rome Sound Stage Orchestra.
Soundtrack (1963) .... *20th Century-Fox (M) FXG-5008*   63   **20-25**
Soundtrack (1963) .... *20th Century-Fox (S) SXG-5008*   63   **25-35**
Composer: Alex North. Conductor: Alex North.
Studiotrack (1963) .... *Design (S) 161*   63   **10-15**
Composer: Alex North.

CLOCKWORK ORANGE
Soundtrack (1971) .... *Warner Bros. (S) BS-2573*   71   **8-10**
Composer: Walter Carlos. Cast: Walter Carlos (moog synthesizer).
Soundtrack (1972) .... *Columbia (S) KC-31480*   72   **8-12**
Complete collection of Walter Carlos' music for the film.
Composer: Walter Carlos; Rachel Elkind; Beethoven; G. Rossini. Conductor: Walter Carlos.

CLOSE ENCOUNTERS OF THE THIRD KIND
Soundtrack (1977) .... *Arista (S) AL-9500*   77   **8-12**
Soundtrack (1977) .... *Arista (S) ALB6-8365*   Re   **8-10**
Composer: John Williams. Conductor: John Williams.
Studiotrack .... *Pickwick (S) SPC 3616*   **8-10**
Composer: John Williams. Conductor: Pat DeVuono.
Also see STAR WARS/CLOSE ENCOUNTERS OF THE THIRD KIND

CLOWN AND THE KIDS
Soundtrack (1968) .... *Golden (M) LP-215*   68   **20-25**
Composer: Tony Velona. Conductor: Artie Beck. Cast: Jazz Philharmonic of Sofia.

CLOWNAROUND
Original Cast (1972) .... *RCA Victor (S) LSP-4741*   72   **150-250**
Composer: Alvin Cooperman; Moose Charlap. Conductor: Harper MacKay.

CLOWNS
Soundtrack (1971) .... *Columbia (S) S-30772*   71   **30-35**
Composer: Nino Rota. Conductor: Carlos Savina.

CLUES TO A LIFE
Original Cast .... *Original Cast (S) OC-8237*   **8-12**
Composer: Alec Wilder. Conductor: Elliott Weiss. Cast: Christine Andreas; D'Jamin Bartlett;
Keith David; Craig Lucas.

CO-STAR
Studio Cast .... *Co-Star (M) CS-101*   **10-20**
Co-star with Cesar Romero. Includes script, which allows buyer to act scenes opposite the actor/actress
on the record.
Cast: Cesar Romero; You.
Studio Cast .... *Co-Star (M) CS-102*   **10-20**
Co-star with Fernando Lamas. Includes script, which allows buyer to act scenes opposite the actor/actress
on the record.
Cast: Fernando Lamas; You.

CO-STAR (continued)

Studio Cast .... *Co-Star (M) CS-103* $10-20
> Co-star with Arlene Dahl. Includes script, which allows buyer to act scenes opposite the actor/actress on the record.

Cast: Arlene Dahl; You.

Studio Cast .... *Co-Star (M) CS-104*   10-20
> Co-star with George Raft. Includes script, which allows buyer to act scenes opposite the actor/actress on the record.

Cast: George Raft; You.

Studio Cast .... *Co-Star (M) CS-105*   10-20
> Co-star with June Havoc. Includes script, which allows buyer to act scenes opposite the actor/actress on the record.

Cast: June Havoc; You.

Studio Cast .... *Co-Star (M) CS-106*   10-20
> Co-star with Sir Cedric Hardwicke. Includes script, which allows buyer to act scenes opposite the actor/actress on the record.

Cast: Sir Cedric Hardwicke; You.

Studio Cast .... *Co-Star (M) CS-107*   10-20
> Co-star with Basil Rathbone. Includes script, which allows buyer to act scenes opposite the actor/actress on the record.

Cast: Basil Rathbone; You.

Studio Cast .... *Co-Star (M) CS-108*   10-20
> Co-star with Virginia Mayo. Includes script, which allows buyer to act scenes opposite the actor/actress on the record.

Cast: Virginia Mayo; You.

Studio Cast .... *Co-Star (M) CS-109*   10-20
> Co-star with Tallulah Bankhead. Includes script, which allows buyer to act scenes opposite the actor/actress on the record.

Cast: Tallulah Bankhead; You.

Studio Cast .... *Co-Star (M) CS-110*   10-20
> Co-star with Vincent Price. Includes script, which allows buyer to act scenes opposite the actor/actress on the record.

Cast: Vincent Price; You.

Studio Cast .... *Co-Star (M) CS-111*   10-20
> Co-star with Paulette Goddard. Includes script, which allows buyer to act scenes opposite the actor/actress on the record.

Cast: Paulette Goddard; You.

Studio Cast .... *Co-Star (M) CS-112*   10-20
> Co-star with Don Ameche. Includes script, which allows buyer to act scenes opposite the actor/actress on the record.

Cast: Don Ameche; You.

Studio Cast .... *Co-Star (M) CS-113*   10-20
> Co-star with Jimmie Rodgers. Includes script, which allows buyer to act scenes opposite the actor/actress on the record.

Cast: Jimmie Rodgers; You.

Studio Cast .... *Co-Star (M) CS-114*   10-20
> Co-star with Pearl Bailey. Includes script, which allows buyer to act scenes opposite the actor/actress on the record.

Cast: Pearl Bailey; You.

Studio Cast .... *Co-Star (M) CS-115*   10-20
> Co-star with "Slapsy" Maxie Rosenbloom. Includes script, which allows buyer to act scenes opposite the actor/actress on the record.

Cast: "Slapsy" Maxie Rosenbloom; You.

COACH WITH THE SIX INSIDES

Original Cast (1967) .... *ESP Disc (M) 1019*   67   15-20
> **Composer:** Teiji Ito; James Joyce. **Conductor:** Teiji Ito. **Cast:** Sheila Roy; Van Dexter; Anita Dangler; Leonard Frey; Jean Erdman.

COAL MINER'S DAUGHTER
Soundtrack (1980) ....*MCA (S) 5107*   80   **$8-10**
Soundtrack (1980) ....*MCA (S) 1699*   Re   **5-8**
  Composer: Loretta Lynn; Willie Nelson; others. **Cast:** Sissy Spacek; Levon Helm; Beverly
  D'Angelo.

COAST TO COAST
Soundtrack (1980) .... *Full Moon (M) FM-3490*   80   **8-10**
  Cast: Rita Coolidge; Johnny Lee; Ambrosia.

COBRA
Soundtrack (1986) ....*Scotti Bros. (S) SZ-40325*   86   **8-10**
  Composer: Various. **Cast:** John Cafferty and the Beaver Brown Band; John Beauvoir; Gladys
  Knight; Bill Medley; Gary Wright; Georgia Satellites; Beach Boys; John Cougar Mellancamp;
  Ry Cooder; Preston Smith; Little Richard.

COBWEB
Soundtrack (1957) ....*MGM (M) E-3501*   57   **125-150**
  One side has music from *Edge of the City*.
  Composer: Leonard Rosenman. **Conductor:** Johnny Green.

COCKTAIL
Soundtrack (1988) .... *Elektra (S) 60806-1*   88   **8-10**
  Composer: Maurice Jarre; others. **Conductor:** Maurice Jarre; others. **Cast:** Starship; Robbie
  Nevil; Fabulous Thunderbirds; Beach Boys; Ry Cooder; Little Richard; Bobby McFerrin;
  Georgia Satellites; Preston Smith; John Cougar Mellencamp.

COCKTAIL PARTY
Original Cast (1951) .... *Decca (M) 9004*   51   **20-30**
Original Cast (1951) .... *Decca (M) 9005*   51   **20-30**
Original Cast (1951) ....*Decca (M) DX-100*   51   **40-60**
  This double LP combines DL-9004 and DL-9005.
  Cast: Sir Alec Guinness; Cathleen Nesbitt; Robert Fleming; Eileen Peel; Irene Worth; Ernest
  Clark; Grey Blake.

COCO
Original Cast (1969) .... *Paramount (S) PMS-1002*   69   **15-20**
  Composer: Andre Previn; Alan Jay Lerner. **Conductor:** Robert Emmett Dolan. **Cast:** Katharine
  Hepburn; George Rose; Gale Dixon; David Holliday; Rene Auberjonois; Jean Arnold; Will B.
  Abel; Chad Block; Jon Cypher; Jack Dabdoub; Robert Fitch; Dan Siretta.

COCOON
Soundtrack (1985) ....*Polydor (S) 827041-1*   85   **8-10**
  Composer: James Horner. **Conductor:** James Horner. **Cast:** Michael Sembello.

CODE OF SILENCE
Soundtrack (1985) .....'........................*Easy Street (S) 9900*   85   **8-10**

COFFY
Soundtrack (1973) .... *Polydor (S) 5048*   73   **15-20**
  Composer: Roy Ayers. **Cast:** Roy Ayers.

COLE
Original London Cast (1974) .... *RCA Victor (S) CRL2-5054*   74   **8-12**
  Composer: Cole Porter. **Cast:** Julie McKenzie; Kenneth Nelson; Bill Kerr; Angela Richards.

COLE PORTER AND ME
Studiotrack (1956) .... *RCA Victor (M) LPM-1340*   56   **15-25**
  Composer: Cole Porter. **Cast:** Eddie Cano (piano).

COLE PORTER REVIEW
Studiotrack (1951) ....*RCA Victor (EP) EPA-421* 51   **$10-20**
Studiotrack (1951) ....*RCA Victor (EP) EPA-158* 51   **10-20**
Studiotrack (1951) ....*RCA Victor (EP) WP-158* 51   **15-20**
Boxed set of four discs.
Studiotrack (1951) ....*RCA Victor (M) LM-32* 51   **20-30**
Based on the life of Cole Porter, as presented by Warner Brothers in the film *Night and Day*.
Composer: Cole Porter. **Conductor:** David Lore.

COLETTE
Original Cast (1970) ....*Mio (S) MCS-3001* 70   **50-60**
Composer: Harvey Schmidt; Tom Jones. **Conductor:** Harvey Schmidt. **Cast:** Zoe Caldwell; Ruth Nelson; Keith Charles; Holland Taylor.
Original London Cast ....*Sepia (S) RSR-1996*   **10-12**
Composer: John Dankworth. **Cast:** Cleo Laine.

COLLECTOR
Soundtrack (1965) ....*Mainstream (M) 56053* 65   **40-50**
Soundtrack (1965) ....*Mainstream (S) S-6053* 65   **55-65**
Composer: Maurice Jarre. **Conductor:** Maurice Jarre.

COLLEGE CONFIDENTIAL
Soundtrack (1960) ....*Chancellor (M) CHL-5016* 60   **20-30**
Soundtrack (1960) ....*Chancellor (S) CHLS-5016* 60   **30-40**
Composer: Dean Elliot. **Cast:** Shelly Manne; Bud Shank; Jimmy Rowles; Milt Bernhart; Bob Cooper.

COLOR OF MONEY
Soundtrack (1986) ....*MCA (S) 6189* 86   **8-10**
Composer: Various. **Cast:** Don Henley; Warren Zevon; Robert Palmer; Eric Clapton; Mark Knopfler; Willie Dixon; B.B. King; Robbie Robertson.

COLOR PURPLE
Soundtrack (1985) ....*Qwest (S) 25356* 85   **10-15**
"Limited Edition."
Soundtrack (1985) ....*Qwest (S) (S) 25389* 85   **8-10**
Composer: Quincy Jones. **Conductor:** Quincy Jones.

COLORS
Soundtrack (1988) ....*Warner Bros. (S) 1-25713* 88   **8-10**
Composer: Various. **Cast:** 44 Mag Mix; Decadent Dub Team; Salt-N-Pepa; Big Daddy Kane; Eric B.; Kool G.; 7A3; Roxanne Shante; M.C.; Rick James.

COLUMBO:
see BILLY GOLDENBERG: HIS FILM AND TELEVISION MUSIC

COMA
Soundtrack (1978) ....*MGM (S) MG-1-5403* 78   **10-15**
Composer: Jerry Goldsmith. **Conductor:** Jerry Goldsmith.

COMANCHE
Soundtrack (1956) ....*Coral (M) CRL-57046* 56   **250-350**
Composer: Herschel Gilbert. **Conductor:** Herschel Gilbert.

COMANCHEROS
Studiotrack ....*Varese Sarabande (S) 704-280* 85   **15-20**
Composer: Elmer Bernstein.

COME BACK CHARLESTON BLUE
Soundtrack (1972) ....*Atco (S) SD-7010* 72   **15-20**
Composer: Donny Hathaway. **Conductor:** Donny Hathaway. **Cast:** Donny Hathaway.

COME BLOW YOUR HORN
Soundtrack (1963) ....*Reprise (M) R-6071* 63   **30-40**

Soundtrack (1963) .... *Reprise (S) R9-6071* 63 **$35-50**
Composer: Nelson Riddle; James Van Heusen. **Conductor:** Nelson Riddle. **Cast:** Frank Sinatra; Nelson Riddle and His Orchestra.

COME MEET U.S.
Soundtrack .... *No Label Shown (S) No Number Used* **8-12**
Promotional album from Trans World Airlines.

COME NEXT SPRING
Soundtrack (1956) .... *Citadel (M) CT 7019* 80 **8-10**
Also has music from *The Last Command*, also by Steiner.
Composer: Max Steiner. **Conductor:** Max Steiner.

COME ON, LET'S LIVE A LITTLE:
see C'MON, LET'S LIVE A LITTLE

COME TO THE MOVIES
Studiotrack (1976) .... *Tee Vee (S) TA-1041* 76 **8-12**
Double LP set.

COME TOGETHER
Soundtrack (1971) .... *Apple (S) SW-3377* 71 **15-20**
Composer: Stelvio Cipriani; others. **Cast:** Joe South; Dells.

COMEDIANS
Soundtrack (1962) .... *MGM (M) E-4494* 62 **20-25**
Soundtrack (1962) .... *MGM (S) SE-4494* 62 **25-30**
Soundtrack (1962) .... *MCA (S) 25002* Re **8-10**
Composer: Laurence Rosenthal. **Conductor:** Laurence Rosenthal.

COMEDY IN MUSIC:
see VICTOR BORGE

COMING OF CHRIST
TV Soundtrack (1960) .... *Decca (M) DL-9093* 60 **25-30**
TV Soundtrack (1960) .... *Decca (S) DL7-9093* 60 **40-45**
Composer: Robert Russell Bennett. **Cast:** Alexander Scourby (narration).

COMING TO AMERICA
Soundtrack (1988) .... *Atco (S) 90958-1* 88 **8-10**
Composer: Nile Rodgers; others. **Cast:** System; Cover Girls; Chico DeBarge; Michael Rodgers; Laura Branigan; Joe Esposito; JJ Fad; Mell & Kim; Levert; Sister Sledge; Nona Hendrix.

COMMITTEE
Original Cast (1964) .... *Reprise (M) R-2023* 64 **20-25**
Original Cast (1964) .... *Reprise (S) FS-2023* 64 **25-30**
Composer: Ellsworth Milburn; Irene Riordan. **Cast:** Scott Beach; Hamilton Camp; Garry Goddrow; Larry Hankin.

COMPANY
Original Cast (1970) .... *Columbia (S) OS-3550* 70 **8-12**
Composer: Stephen Sondheim. **Conductor:** Harold Hastings. **Cast:** Dean Jones; Barbara Barrie; George Coe; John Cunningham; Teri Rolston; Beth Howland; Charles Braswell; Susan Browning; Steve Elmore; Charles Kimbrough; Merle Louise; Donna McKechnie; Pamela Myers; Elaine Stritch.
London Cast (1970) .... *CBS (S) 70108* **8-12**
Composer: Stephen Sondheim. **Cast:** Larry Kert (does the tunes sung by Dean Jones in the original cast); Barbara Barrie; George Coe; John Cunningham; Teri Rolston; Beth Howland.

COMPANY OF WOLVES
Soundtrack (1985) .... *Varese Sarabande (S) STV-81242* 85 **10-15**
Composer: George Fenton. **Conductor:** George Fenton.

COMPETITION
Soundtrack (1980) .... *MCA (S) 5185*   80   **$8-10**
  Composer: Randy Crawford; Lalo Schifrin. **Conductor:** Lalo Schifrin.

COMPULSION
Soundtrack (1959) .... *20th Century-Fox (EP) FEP-101*   59   **20-30**
  Cast: Orson Welles.

CONAN THE BARBARIAN
Soundtrack (1982) .... *MCA (S) 6108*   82   **8-10**
  Composer: Basil Poledouris; Zoe Poledouris. **Conductor:** Basil Poledouris.

CONAN THE DESTROYER
Soundtrack (1984) .... *MCA (S) 6135*   84   **8-10**
  Cast: Basil Poledouris.

CONFIDENTIALLY YOURS
Soundtrack (1984) .... *DRG (S) SL-9519*   83   **8-10**
  Also has music from four other Truffaut/Delerue soundtracks.
  Composer: Truffaut; Delerue.

CONNECTICUT YANKEE
Studio Cast (1927) .... *RCA Victor (EP) EKB-1026*   52   **15-20**
Studio Cast (1927) .... *RCA Victor (M) LK-1026*   52   **50-60**
  One side has music from *Rio Rita*.
  Composer: Richard Rodgers; Lorenz Hart. **Conductor:** Al Goodman. **Cast:** Earl Wrightson;
  Elaine Malbin; Guild Choristers.
Broadway Revival Cast (1943) .... *AEI (M) 1138*   **8-10**
  Composer: Richard Rodgers; Lorenz Hart. **Cast:** Vera Hart; Robert Chisholm; Dick Foran;
  Vivienne Segal; Chester Stratton; Julie Warren.

CONNECTICUT YANKEE IN KING ARTHUR'S COURT:
see SUNSHINE CAKE

CONNECTION
Original Cast (1959) .... *Blue Note (M) 4027*   59   **20-25**
Original Cast (1959) .... *Blue Note (S) 84027*   59   **30-35**
  Composer: Freddie Redd. **Conductor:** Freddie Redd.
Original Cast (1961) .... *Parker (M) PLP-806*   62   **15-20**
Original Cast (1961) .... *Parker (S) PLP-8065*   62   **20-25**
  Composer: Cecil Payne; Kenny Drew. **Conductor:** Cecil Payne.

CONQUEST OF SPACE
Studio Cast .... *Vox (M) DL-522*   **10-15**
Studio Cast .... *Vox (S) STDL-522*   **15-20**
  Cast: Dr. Wernher Von Braun; Willy Lea.

CONSUL
Original Cast (1950) .... *Decca (M) DX-101*   51   **40-50**
  Double LP set.
  Composer: Gian-Carlo Menotti.

CONTINENTAL TWIST
Soundtrack (1961) .... *Capitol (M) T-1677*   61   **15-20**
Soundtrack (1961) .... *Capitol (S) ST-1677*   61   **20-25**
  Conductor: Sam Butera. **Cast:** Sam Butera and the Witnesses.

CONVERSATION PIECE
Original London Cast (1951) .... *World (M) SH-179-80*   **15-20**
Original London Cast (1951) ..... *Monmouth Evergreen (SE) MES-7062/3*   Re   **8-10**
  Conductor: Reginald Burston. **Cast:** Noel Coward; Sidney Grammer; Yvonne Printemps;
  George Sanders.

Studio Cast . . . .*Columbia (M) SL-163*   **$50-60**
Studio Cast . . . . *Columbia Special Products (M) ASL-163*   **8-10**
  Above two are double LP sets.
  Composer: Noel Coward. **Conductor:** Lehman Engel. **Cast:** Noel Coward; Lily Pons; Richard
  Burton; Cathleen Nesbit; Ethel Griffies.

CONVOY
Soundtrack (1978) . . . .*United Artists (S) UA-LA910-H*   78   **8-10**

COOGAN'S BLUFF
Soundtrack (1968) . . . .*Temple (S) TLP-2001*   78   **50-60**
  Includes music writen but previously unreleased for *The Big Country*, conducted by Jerome Moross.
  Composer: Lalo Schiffrin. **Conductor:** Lalo Schiffrin; Jerome Moross.

COOKIE
Soundtrack . . . . *UNI (S) 600*   **8-10**
  Composer: Various. **Cast:** Holly Johnson; Transvision Vamp; Bobby Helms; Nanci Griffith;
  Thomas Newman.

COOL BREEZE
Soundtrack (1972) . . . . *MGM (S) 1SE-35*   72   **12-15**
  Composer: Solomon Burke. **Cast:** Solomon Burke.

COOL HAND LUKE
Soundtrack (1967) . . . .*Dot (M) DLP-3833*   68   **20-25**
Soundtrack (1967) . . . . *Dot (S) DLP-25833*   68   **45-65**
  Composer: Lalo Schifrin. **Conductor:** Lalo Schifrin.

COOL OF THE EVENING
Studiotrack (1951) . . . .*Decca (M) DL-4262*   62   **25-30**
  Also has music from *Mr. Music* and *Here Comes the Groom*. Issued as part of *Bing's Hollywood Series*.
  Cast: Bing Crosby.

COOL WORLD
Soundtrack (1964) . . . . *Phillips (M) 200-138*   64   **25-30**
Soundtrack (1964) . . . . *Phillips (S) 600-138*   64   **30-35**
  Composer: Mal Waldron. **Cast:** Dizzy Gillespie Quintet.

COOLEY HIGH
Soundtrack (1975) . . . .*Motown (S) M7-840R2*   75   **10-15**
  Double LP set.
  Composer: Various. **Cast:** Diana Ross and the Supremes; Stevie Wonder; Four Tops; Luther
  Allison; Martha Reeves and the Vandellas; Marvelettes; Smokey Robinson and the Miracles; Jr.
  Walker and the All-Stars; Barrett Strong; Mary Wells; Freddie Perren.

COP SHOW THEMES
TV Soundtrack (1976) . . . . *RCA Victor (S) APL1-1896*   **8-10**
  Has themes from: *NBC Mystery Movie, The Streets of San Francisco, Bumper's Theme (The Blue Knight),
  Kojak, S.W.A.T., Baretta's Theme (Keep Your Eye on the Sparrow), The Rockford Files, Hawaii Five-O*
  and *Police Woman*.
  Composer: Henry Mancini; others. **Conductor:** Henry Mancini.

COPELAND CONDUCTS COPELAND:
see QUIET CITY

CORNBREAD EARL AND ME
Soundtrack (1975) . . . .*Fantasy (S) F-9483*   75   **8-12**

CORRUPT ONES
Soundtrack (1967) . . . .*United Artists (M) UAL-4158*   67   **30-35**
Soundtrack (1967) . . . . *United Artists (S) UAS-5158*   67   **35-40**
  Composer: Georges Garvarentz. **Conductor:** Georges Garvarentz. **Cast:** Dusty Springfield.

COSA NOSTRA STORY
Studio Cast (1963) .... *Smash (M) MGS-27045*   63   **$10-20**

COSMOS
TV Soundtrack (1981) .... *.RCA Victor (S) ABL1-4003*   81   **8-10**
  Full title: *(Music of) Cosmos.* A score from a PBS television presentation.
  Cast: Vangelis.

COTTON CLUB
Soundtrack (1984) .... *Geffen (S) GHS-24062*   84   **8-10**
  Composer: John Barry; others. **Conductor:** John Barry. **Cast:** John Barry and His Orchestra.

COTTON CLUB REVUE OF 1958
Original Cast (1958) .... *Gone (M) GLP-101*   58   **50-60**
  Side two has assorted selections by Cab Calloway.
  Composer: Clay Boland; Benny Davis. **Conductor:** Eddie Barefield. **Cast:** Cab Calloway.

COTTON COMES TO HARLEM
Soundtrack (1970) .... *United Artists (S) UAS-5211*   70   **10-12**
Soundtrack (1970) .... *MCA (S) 25133*   Re   **8-10**
  Composer: Galt MacDermott. **Cast:** Melba Moore; Leta Galloway; George Tipton; Sakinah.

COTTON PATCH GOSPEL
Original Cast (1981) .... *Chapin Productions (S) CP-101*   81   **8-10**
  Composer: Harry Chapin; Tom Chapin. **Cast:** Scott Ainslie; Pete Corum; Tom Key; Jim
  Lauderdale; Michael Mark.

COUNT OF MONTE CRISTO
Studio Cast (1950) .... *Decca (M) DL-5147*   50   **40-50**
  10-inch LP.
  Composer: Victor Young. **Conductor:** Victor Young. **Cast:** Herbert Marshall; Pedro De
  Cordoba; Lou Merrill; Elliott Lewis; Frederic Worlock; Fred MacKaye; Paula Winslowe.

COUNT THREE AND PRAY:
see NO SAD SONGS FOR ME

COUNTESS FROM HONG KONG
Soundtrack (1967) .... *Decca (M) DL-1501*   67   **15-20**
Soundtrack (1967) .... *Decca (S) DL7-1501*   67   **15-25**
  Composer: Charlie Chaplin. **Conductor:** Lambert Williamson.

COUNTRY
Soundtrack (1984) .... *Windham Hill Records (S) WH-9-1039*   84   **8-10**
  Composer: Charles Gross. **Conductor:** Charles Gross. **Cast:** George Winston; Darol Anger;
  Mark Isham; Mike Marshall.

COUNTRY BEAR JAMBOREE
Soundtrack (1972) .... *Disneyland (S) 3994*   72   **$8-12**

COUNTRY COUSIN
Soundtrack (1936) .... *Disneyland (M) ST-1903*   59   **25-30**
Soundtrack (1936) .... *Disneyland (SE) DQ-1306*   67   **15-20**
Cast: Disney cast. (With dialogue.)

COUNTRY GIRL:
see ANYTHING GOES

COUNTRY MUSIC HOLIDAY
Soundtrack (1958) .... *Capitol (EP) EAP-1-921*   58   **10-20**

COUP DE TORCHON (CLEAN SLATE)
Soundtrack (1981) .... *DRG (S) SL-9511*   81   **8-10**
Conductor: Philippe Sarde. Cast: Philippe Sarde.

COUPE DE VILLE
Soundtrack (1990) .... *Cypress (S) 71334*   90   **8-10**
Composer: Various. Cast: Kingsmen; Dion; Flamingos; Temptations; Cadillacs; Joey Dee and
the Starliters; Chips; Everly Brothers; Nervous Norvous; Young MC.

COURIER
Soundtrack .... *Virgin Movie Music (S) 90954-1*   **8-10**
Composer: Various. Cast: Dangerous Games; Cry Before Dawn; Declan MacManus; Something
Happens; Hothouse Flowers; Lord John White; U2.

COURT JESTER
Soundtrack (1956) .... *Decca (M) DL-8212*   56   **50-60**
Composer: Sylvia Fine. Conductor: Vic Schoen. Cast: Danny Kaye; Notables; Lee Gordon
Singers.

COURT MARTIAL OF BILLY MITCHELL
Studio Cast (1955) .... *Mark '56 (SE) 633*   **10-15**
Composer: Dimitri Tiomkin. Conductor: Dimitri Tiomkin. Cast: Gary Cooper; Rod Steiger;
Ralph Bellamy. (With dialogue.)

COUSINS
Soundtrack (1989) .... *Warner Bros. (S) 1-25901*   89   **8-10**

COUSTEAU/AMAZON
Soundtrack .... *Varese Sarabande (S) STV-81220*   **8-10**
Conductor: John Scott. Cast: National Philharmonic Orchestra.

COWARDLY CUSTARD
Original London Cast (1973) .... *RCA Victor (S) LSO-6010*   73   **10-15**
Double LP set.
Composer: Noel Coward. Conductor: John Burrows. Cast: Olivia Breeze; Geoffrey Burridge;
Jonathan Cecil; Tudor Davies; Elaine Delmar; Peter Gale; Laura Ford; John Mohatt; Patricia
Routledge; Una Stubbs; Anna Sharkey; Derek Waring.

COWBOY
Soundtrack (1958) .... *Decca (M) DL-8684*   58   **45-50**
Composer: George Duning; Rafael Mendez. Conductor: Morris Stoloff.

CRADLE WILL ROCK
Original Cast (1937) .... *American Legacy (M) T-1001*   **75-100**
Composer: Marc Blitzstein. Cast: Howard DaSilva; Edward Fuller; Olive Stanton; Peggy
Coudray; Blanche Collins; Marc Blitzstein (piano); John Adair; Howard Bird; George Fairchild;
Dulce Fox; Maynard Holmes; Ralph MacBane; Frank Marvel; Charles Niemeyer; Marion
Rudley; Jules Schmi Schmidt; Bert Weston.

CRADLE WILL ROCK (continued)
Original Revival Cast (1964) .... *MGM (M) E-4289-2*   64   **$30-40**
Original Revival Cast (1964) .... *MGM (S) SE-4289-2*   64   **40-50**
  Above two are double LP sets.
Original Revival Cast (1964) .... *CRI (S) S-266*   Re   **8-10**
  Composer: Marc Blitzstein. **Conductor:** Gershon Kingsley. **Cast:** Jerry Orbach; Lauri Peters;
  Nancy Andrews; Hal Buckley; Gordon Clarke; Clifford David; Nichols Grimes; Joseph Bova;
  Karen Cleary; Dean Dittman; Rita Gardner; Micki Grant; Peter Meersman; Ted Scott; Wayne
  Tucker; Chris Warfield.
Original Revival Cast (1983) .... *Polydor (S) 827 937-1*   83   **8-10**
  Composer: Marc Blitzstein. **Conductor:** Michael Barrett. **Cast:** Dennis Bacigalupi; Brooks
  Baldwin; Casey Biggs; Daniel Corcoran; Leslie Geraci; Patti LuPone; Anderson Matthews;
  Randle Mell; Mary Lou Rosato; David Schramm; Norman Snow; Henry Stram; Michele-Denise
  Woods.

CREATIVE FREAKOUT
Studio Cast (1967) .... *Brief (S) No Number Used*   67   **30-35**
  10-inch LP. Promotional issue only. Issued in a paper sleeve.
  Composer: Hugh Heller; Jacques Wilson; Dave Williams; Dick Hamilton. **Cast:** Ben Chandler;
  Hellers.

CREEPERS
Soundtrack (1986) .... *Enigma (S) SJ-73205*   86   **8-10**
  Composer: Various. **Cast:** Claudio Simonetti; Ron Maiden; Goblin; Sex Gang Andi; Bill Wyman;
  Terry Taylor; Simon Boswell; Motorhead.

CREEPSHOW
Soundtrack (1982) .... *Varese Sarabande (S) STV-81160*   82   **8-10**
  Composer: John Harrison. **Conductor:** John Harrison. **Cast:** John Harrison.

CRICKET ON THE HEARTH
TV Soundtrack (1967) .... *RCA Victor (M) LSC-1140*   67   **20-25**
TV Soundtrack (1967) .... *RCA Victor (S) LSO-1140*   67   **25-30**
  Composer: Maury Laws; Bass. **Cast:** Danny Thomas; Marlo Thomas; Ed Ames; Abbe Lane;
  Norman Luboff Choir.

CRIME IN THE STREETS
Soundtrack (1956) .... *Decca (M) DL-8376*   56   **50-60**
Studiotrack .... *Entr' acte (M) 6001*   79   **8-10**
  Also has music from *Three Sketches* and *Theme, Variations and Fugato,* both by Waxman.
  Composer: Franz Waxman. **Conductor:** Franz Waxman.

CRIMES OF PASSION
Soundtrack (1986) .... *TBG/President (S) RW 3*   86   **12-15**
  Composer: Rick Wakeman. **Cast:** Maggie Bell.

CRISIS
Studio Cast (1950) .... *Decca (M) DXSA-7194*   **15-20**
Studio Cast (1950) .... *Citadel (SE) CT-7004*   **8-12**
  Composer: Miklos Rozsa. **Conductor:** Miklos Rozsa.

CRITIC
Original Cast .... *Decca (S) SL-79154*   **10-15**

CRITTERS
Soundtrack (1986) .... *Restless (S) 72154*   86   **10-12**
  Composer: David Newman. **Conductor:** David Newman.

CROCODILE DUNDEE
Soundtrack (1986) .... *Varese Sarabande (S) STV-81296*   86   **8-10**
  Composer: Peter Best. **Conductor:** Peter Best.

CROMWELL
Soundtrack (1970) ....*Capitol (S) SW-640*   70   **$35-50**
   Composer: Frank Cordell. Conductor: Frank Cordell. Cast: Richard Harris; Sir Alec Guinness;
   Robert Morley. (With dialogue.)

CROOKED MILE
Soundtrack ....*AEI (S) 1115*   **8-12**
   Composer: Peter Greenwell.

CROSBY'S RADIO SHOWS:
see BING CROSBY'S RADIO SHOWS

CROSS AND THE SWITCHBLADE
Soundtrack (1970) ....*Light (S) LS-5550*   70   **10-15**
   Composer: Ralph Carmichael. Conductor: Ralph Carmichael. Cast: Pat Boone (Biblical
   readings); Young People; John Bahler; Ron Hicklin; Stan Farber; Gene Morford.

CROSSED SWORDS
Soundtrack (1978) ....*Warner Bros. (S) BSK-3161*   78   **8-10**
   Composer: Maurice Jarre. Conductor: Maurice Jarre.

CROSSOVER DREAMS
Soundtrack (1986) .... *Elektra (S) 60470-1*   86   **8-10**
   Composer: Reuben Blades; Andy and Jerry Gonzales; Yomo Toro; Marco Rizo; Johnny Colon;
   Virgilio Marti; Ballistic Kisses; others. Cast: Reuben Blades; Virgilio Marti; Tito Puente; Chase;
   Jose Gallegos; Rooftop; Marco Rizo; Javier Vazquez.

CROSSROADS
Soundtrack (1986) .... *Warner Bros. (S) 1-25399*   86   **8-10**
   Composer: Ry Cooder.

CRUISING
Soundtrack (1980) ....*Columbia (S) JC-36410*   80   **10-12**
   Composer: Various. Cast: Willy DeVille; Cripples; John Hiatt; Madelynn Von Ritz; Mutiny;
   Rough Trade; Germs.

CRY FOR US ALL
Original Cast (1970) ....*Project 3 (S) TS-1000*   70   **25-30**
   Composer: Mitch Leigh; William Alfred; Phyllis Robinson. Conductor: Herbert Grossman.
   Cast: Joan Diener; Robert Weede; Steve Arlen; Tommy Rall; Helen Gallagher; Scott Jacoby;
   Steve Arlen; Darel Glaser; William Griffis; Todd Jones; Robert Weede.

CRY FREEDOM
Soundtrack (1987) ....*MCA (S) 6224*   87   **8-10**
   Cast: George Fenton.

CRY OF THE BANSHEE AND EDGAR ALLAN POE SUITE
Studiotrack (1970) ....*Citadel (S) CTV-7013*   80   **10-15**
   Symphonic suite based on themes from the film. Contains the *Edgar Allan Poe Suite* from the television
   special and *An Evening with Edgar Allan Poe*, starring Vincent Price.
   Composer: Les Baxter. Conductor: Les Baxter.

CRYER AND FORD
Original Cast (1975) ....*RCA Victor (S) APL1-1235*   75   **10-15**
Original Cast (1977) ....*RCA Victor (S) APL1-2146*   77   **10-12**
   A Manhattan Theatre Club performance.
   Composer: Gretchen Cryer; Nancy Ford. Cast: Gretchen Cryer; Nancy Ford (with musical
   accompaniment).

CRYSTAL HEART
Original Cast (1960) .... *Blue Pear (M) BP-1001*   **$10-15**
  Composer: Baldwin Bergersen; William Archibald. **Conductor:** Baldwin Bergersen. **Cast:** John
  Baylis; Mildred Dunnock; Bob Fitch; Margot Harley; Barbara Janezic; Katherine Litz; Byron
  Mitchell; Joe Ross; Jeanne Shea; John Stewart; Virginia Vestoff; Vincent Warren.

CURIOUS EVENING WITH GYPSY ROSE LEE
Original Cast (1961) .... *Stereoddities (S) CG-1*   61   **20-25**
Original Cast (1961) .... *Stereoddities (S) AE1-1131*   Re   **8-10**
  Composer: Bobby Kroll; Eli Basse. **Cast:** Gypsy Rose Lee.

CURTAIN GOING UP (MUSICAL GUIDE TO PLAY ACTING)
Original Cast .... *Leo (M) CH-1025*   **10-12**
  Composer: Ruth Roberts; others. **Conductor:** Frank Motis. **Cast:** Richard Kiley; Julie Harris;
  Andrea Dolin; Glen Richards.

CUSTER OF THE WEST
Soundtrack (1968) .... *ABC (M) OC-5*   68   **30-35**
Soundtrack (1968) .... *ABC (S) OCS-5*   68   **35-50**
  Composer: Bernardo Segall. **Conductor:** Bernardo Segall.

CYCLE SAVAGES
Soundtrack (1970) .... *American Int'l (S) STA-1033*   70   **10-15**
  Composer: Jerry Styner; Randy Johnson; Mike Stevens; Guy Hemric; others. **Conductor:** Jerry
  Styner.

CYRANO
Original Cast (1973) .... *A&M (S) SP-3702*   73   **15-20**
  Double LP set.
  Composer: Michael Lewis. **Conductor:** Thomas Pierson. **Cast:** Christopher Plummer; Leigh
  Berry; Mark Lamos; James Blendick; Patrick Hines; Louis Tureen; J. Kenneth Campbell; Anita
  Dangler; Arnold Soboloff.

CYRANO DE BERGERAC
Soundtrack (1950) .... *Capitol (EP) EDM-283*   51   **15-20**
Soundtrack (1950) .... *Capitol (M) S-283*   51   **40-45**
  Composer: Paul Bowles. **Conductor:** Paul Bowles. **Cast:** Edmund Trzcinski (narration); Jose
  Ferrer; Robert Carroll; Fran Letton; Vincent Donahue; Ralph Clanton; Patricia Wheel.
Studio Cast (1965) .... *Caedmon (S) TRS-306-S*   **10-20**
  Triple LP set with complete text booklet.

D

D.C. CAB
Soundtrack (1984) .... *BCA (S) 6128*   84   **$8-10**
Cast: Irene Cara; Peabo Bryson; Shalamar; others.

DAD
Soundtrack .... *MCA (S) 6359*   **8-10**
Cast: James Horner.

DAKTARI
TV Soundtrack (1967) .... *MGM (M) CH-1043*   67   **15-20**
TV Soundtrack (1967) .... *Atlantic (M) 8157*   68   **15-20**
TV Soundtrack (1967) .... *Atlantic (S) SD-8157*   68   **20-25**
Composer: Shelly Manne. Conductor: Shelly Manne. Cast: Shelly Manne and His Men.
(With dialogue.)

DALLAS
TV Soundtrack (1979) .... *First American (S) FA-780*   79   **8-10**
Themes from the TV series.
Composer: John Parker. Conductor: John Parker.
Studiotrack (1980) .... *RCA Victor (S) AHL1-3613*   80   **8-10**
Also has TV themes from: *Incredible Hulk, Taxi, All in the Family, The Waltons, Little House on the Prairie, The Restless, M*A*S*H, Laverne and Shirley* and *Knots Landing*.
Composer: Various. Conductor: Bill McElainey. Cast: Floyd Cramer.

DAMES:
see GOLDEN AGE OF THE HOLLYWOOD MUSICAL

DAMES AT SEA
Original Cast (1969) .... *Columbia (S) OS-3330*   69   **15-20**
Composer: Jim Wise; George Haimsohn; Robin Miller. Conductor: Richard J. Leonard.
Cast: David Christmas; Steve Elmore; Tamara Long; Bernadette Peters; Sally Stark;
Joseph R. Sicari.

DAMIEN - OMEN II
Soundtrack (1978) .... *20th Century-Fox (S) T-563*   78   **20-35**
Composer: Jerry Goldsmith. Conductor: Lionel Newman.

DAMN THE DEFIANT
Soundtrack (1962) .... *Colpix (M) CP-511*   62   **20-30**
Soundtrack (1962) .... *Colpix (S) SCP-511*   62   **30-40**
Composer: Clifton Parker. Conductor: Muir Mathieson.

DAMN YANKEES
Original Cast (1955) .... *RCA Victor (EP) EOC-1021*   55   **15-20**
Original Cast (1955) .... *RCA Victor (M) LOC-1021*   55   **50-60**
Green cover.
Original Cast (1955) .... *RCA Victor (M) LOC-1021*   55   **20-25**
Orange cover.
Original Cast (1955) .... *RCA Victor (SE) LSO-1021*   65   **10-12**
Composer: Richard Adler; Jerry Ross. Conductor: Hal Hastings. Cast: Gwen Verdon; Stephen
Douglass; Ray Walston; Jean Stapleton; Rae Allen; Shannon Bolin; Russ Brown; Ron Cummins;
Cherry Davis; Nathaniel Frey; Jimmie Komack; Albert Linville; Eddie Phillips; Jackie Scholle;
Robert Shafer.

DAMN YANKEES (continued)
Soundtrack (1958) . . . .*RCA Victor (M) LOC-1047*   58   **$45-50**
Soundtrack (1955) . . . . *RCA Victor (SE) AYL1-3948*   Re   **8-10**
Composer: Richard Adler; Jerry Ross. Conductor: Ray Heindorf. Cast: Gwen Verdon; Tab Hunter; Ray Walston.

DAMNED
Soundtrack (1969) . . . .*Warner Bros. (S) WS-1829*   69   **20-25**
Composer: Maurice Jarre. Conductor: Maurice Jarre.

DANCE CRAZE
Soundtrack . . . . *Chrysalis (S) PV-41299*   **8-10**
Composer: Various. Cast: Specials; English Beat; Bad Manners; Selecter; Madness; Bodysnatchers.

DANCE TO THE MUSIC OF IRVING BERLIN
Studiotrack (1959) . . . . *Vocalion (M) VL-3664*   59   **10-20**
Composer: Irving Berlin. Cast: Jimmy Smith.

DANCERS OF BALI
Original Cast (1952) . . . . *Columbia (M) ML-4618*   52   **25-30**
Original Cast (1952) . . . . *Columbia Special Products (M) AML-4618*   Re   **8-10**
Conductor: Anak Agung Gde Mandera. Cast: Gamelan Orchestra (from the village of Pliatan, Bali, Indonesia).

DANGER
TV Soundtrack (1951) . . . .*MGM (EP) X-1111*   51   **15-25**
TV Soundtrack (1951) . . . .*MGM (M) E-111*   51   **50-65**
10-inch LP.
Composer: Tony Mottola. Conductor: Tony Mottola. Cast: Ray Charles Singers.

DANGEROUS CHRISTMAS OF RED RIDING HOOD
TV Soundtrack (1965) . . . . *ABC-Paramount (M) ABC-536*   65   **25-30**
TV Soundtrack (1965) . . . . *ABC-Paramount (S) ABCS-536*   65   **30-35**
Composer: Jule Styne; Robert Merrill. Conductor: Walter Scharf. Cast: Liza Minnelli; Vic Damone; Cyril Ritchard; Animals.

DANGEROUSLY CLOSE
Soundtrack (1986) . . . . *Enigma (S) SJ-73204*   86   **8-10**
Composer: Various. Cast: Smithereens; Black Uhuru; Green on Red; T.S.O.L.; Lords of the New Church; Lost Pilots; Michael McCarty.

DANTON
Soundtrack (1983) . . . . *DRG (S) SL-9518*   83   **8-10**
Composer: Jean Prodromides. Conductor: Jan Prusak. Cast: Choral Music Society of Warsaw.

DARBY O'GILL AND THE LITTLE PEOPLE
Soundtrack (1959) . . . .*Disneyland (M) ST-1901*   59   **15-20**
Though mostly dialogue, this LP does feature the seldom heard singing voice of Sean Connery.
Composer: Lawrence Edward Watkin; Oliver Wallace. Conductor: Tutti Camarata.
Cast: Sean Connery; Arthur Shields; J. Pat O'Malley; Janet Munro.

DARK CRYSTAL
Soundtrack (1982) . . . . *Warner Bros. (S) 1-23749*   82   **8-10**
Composer: Trevor Jones. Conductor: Marcus Dods. Cast: London Symphony Orchestra.

DARK EYES
Soundtrack (1987) . . . . *DRG (S) SBL-12592*   87   **8-10**

DARK OF THE SUN
Soundtrack (1968) . . . .*MGM (M) E-4544*   68   **35-40**
Soundtrack (1968) . . . . *MGM (S) SE-4544*   68   **50-55**
Composer: Jacques Loussier.

DARK SHADOWS
TV Soundtrack (1969) .... *Philips (S) PHS-600-314*   69   **$30-40**
Composer: Robert Cobert. Conductor: Robert Cobert. Cast: Jonathan Frid (narration); David Selby.
TV Soundtrack (1966) .... *Media Sound (S) MS-00001*   86   **8-10**
Volume two.
TV Soundtrack (1966) .... *Media Sound (S0 MS-00002*   88   **8-10**
Volume three. Actual title: *Original Music from Dark Shadows.*
Composer: Robert Cobert.

DARK STAR
Soundtrack (1974) .... *Citadel (S) CT-7022*   80   **8-10**
Composer: John Carpenter. Cast: John Carpenter; Miles Watkins; "Cookie" Knapp; Dan O'Bannon; Cal Kuniholm; Brian Narelle; John Yager. (With dialogue and effects.)

DARLING:
see TRIPLE FEATURE

DARLING LILI
Soundtrack (1969) .... *RCA Victor (S) LSPX-1000*   69   **15-20**
Composer: Henry Mancini; Johnny Mercer. Conductor: Henry Mancini. Cast: Julie Andrews; Gloria Paul; Le Lycee Francais de Los Angeles Children's Choir.

DARLING OF THE DAY
Original Cast (1968) .... *RCA Victor (M) LOC-1149*   68   **30-35**
Original Cast (1968) .... *RCA Victor (S) LSO-1149*   68   **35-40**
Composer: Jule Styne; E.Y.Harburg. Conductor: Buster Davis. Cast: Vincent Price; Patricia Routledge; Brenda Forbes; Teddy Greene; Beth Howland; Mitchell Jason; Marc Jordan; Reid Klein; Joy Nichols; Charles Welch; Peter Woodthorpe.

DARWIN'S THEORIES
Original Cast (1960) .... *Town Hall Records (M) THM-1002*   60   **100-125**
Composer: Darwin Venneri. Cast: Darwin Venneri.

DAS BOOT (THE BOAT)
Soundtrack (1981) .... *Atlantic (S) SD-19348*   81   **8-10**
Composer: Klaus Doldinger. Conductor: Klaus Doldinger.

DAVID AND BATHSHEBA
Soundtrack (1951) .... *Sound of Hollywood (S) 4001*   78   **30-40**
One side has music from *How Green Was My Valley.*
Composer: Alfred Newman. Conductor: Alfred Newman.

DAVID AND LISA
Soundtrack (1963) .... *Ava (M) A-21*   63   **20-25**
Soundtrack (1963) .... *Ava (S) AS-21*   63   **25-30**
Composer: Mark Lawrence. Conductor: Norman Paris.

DAVID COPPERFIELD
TV Soundtrack (1970) .... *GRT (S) GRT-10008*   70   **45-50**
Composer: Malcolm Arnold. Conductor: Malcolm Arnold.

DAVID RAKSIN CONDUCTS HIS GREAT FILM SCORES
Studiotrack (1976) .... *RCA Victor (S) ARL1-1490*   76   **12-18**
Contains music from: *Laura, The Bad and the Beautiful* and *Forever Amber.*
Composer: David Raksin. Conductor: David Raksin. Cast: New Philharmonia Orchestra.

DAVID RAKSIN/MUSIC FOR FILMS
Soundtrack (1978) .... *Library of Congress (S) 223781*   78   **10-20**
Contains music from *Force of Evil* and *Carrie.* Distributed only with the July 1978 issue of the *Quarterly Journal of the Library of Congress.*
Composer: David Raksin. Conductor: David Raksin.

DAVID RAKSIN/MUSIC FOR FILMS (continued)

Soundtrack (1978)   *Quarterly Journal of the Library of Congress (S) 223782*   78   **$10-20**
Volume two. Contains music from *Separate Tables* and *The Redeemer*. Distributed only with the July 1978 issue of the *Quarterly Journal of the Library of Congress*.
Composer: David Raksin. **Conductor:** David Raksin.

DAVY CROCKETT

TV Soundtrack (1955) . . . . *Columbia (EP) B-2031*   55   **10-15**
Episode: *Davy Crockett, Indian Fighter*.
TV Soundtrack (1955) . . . . *Columbia (EP) B-2032*   55   **10-15**
Episode: *Davy Crockett Goes to Congress*.
TV Soundtrack (1955) . . . . *Columbia (EP) B-2033*   55   **10-15**
Episode: *Davy Crockett at the Alamo*.
TV Soundtrack (1955) . . . . *Columbia (EP) B-2073*   55   **10-15**
Episode: *Davy Crockett and Mike Fink*.
Soundtrack (1955) . . . . *Columbia (M) CL-666*   55   **40-50**
Soundtrack (1955) . . . . *Disneyland (M) WDA-3602*   62   **15-25**
Composer: George Bruns. **Conductor:** George Bruns. **Cast:** Fess Parker; Buddy Ebsen. (With dialogue.)

DAVY CROCKETT (THE REAL STORY)

Studio Cast (1955) . . . . *Folkways (M) FP-205*   55   **15-25**
Cast: Bill Hayes. (With narration.)

DAWN OF THE DEAD

Soundtrack (1979) . . . . *Varese Sarabande (S) VC-81106*   79   **8-10**
Composer: Goblin. **Cast:** David Emge; Ken Foree; Music by Goblin.

DAY AFTER HALLOWEEN

Soundtrack (1981) . . . . *Varese Sarabande (S) CTV 7020*   81   **8-10**
Composer: Brian May. **Conductor:** Brian May.

DAY IN HOLLYWOOD

Studiotrack (1955) . . . . *Columbia (EP) B-7491*   55   **10-15**
Studiotrack (1955) . . . . *Columbia (EP) B-7492*   55   **10-15**
Studiotrack (1955) . . . . *Columbia (EP) B-7493*   55   **10-15**
Studiotrack (1955) . . . . *Columbia (M) CL-749*   55   **20-30**
Cast: Doris Day.

DAY IN HOLLYWOOD/NIGHT IN THE UKRAINE

Original Cast (1980) . . . . *DRG (S) SBL-12580*   80   **8-10**
Composer: Frank Lazarus; Jerry Herman. **Conductor:** Wally Harper. **Cast:** Frank Lazarus; Priscilla Lopez; Peggy Hewett; Kate Draper; David Garrison; Stephen James.

DAY OF ANGER

Soundtrack (1969) . . . . *RCA Victor (S) LSO-1165*   69   **15-20**
Composer: Riz Ortolani. **Conductor:** Riz Ortolani.

DAY OF THE DEAD

Soundtrack (1985) . . . . *Saturn (S) SR-LP-1701*   85   **8-10**
Composer: John Harrison. **Cast:** Modern Man; Sputzy Sparacino and Delilah; others.

DAY OF THE DOLPHIN

Soundtrack (1973) . . . . *Avco Embassy (S) AV-11014*   73   **25-30**
Composer: Georges Delerue. **Conductor:** Georges Delerue.

DAY OF THE LOCUST

Soundtrack (1975) . . . . *London (S) PS-912*   75   **15-20**
Composer: John Barry; others. **Conductor:** John Barry. **Cast:** Louis Armstrong; Pamela Myers; Michael Dees; Nick Lucas.

DAY THE EARTH STOOD STILL
Soundtrack (1951) .... *Great Science Fiction Film Music (M) CSL-1001*   74 $15-20
Composer: Bernard Herrmann. Conductor: Bernard Herrmann. Cast: Bernard Herrmann and His Orchestra.
Also see: FANTASY FILM WORLD OF BERNARD HERRMANN

DAY THE FISH CAME OUT
Soundtrack (1967) .... *20th Century-Fox (M) 4194*   67   20-25
Soundtrack (1967) .... *20th Century-Fox (S) S-4194*   67   25-30
Composer: Mikis Theodorakis.

DAY TIME ENDED
Soundtrack (1981) .... *Varese Sarabande (S) STV-81140*   81   8-10
Composer: Richard Band. Conductor: Richard Band.

DAYDREAMER
Soundtrack (1966) .... *Columbia (M) OL-6540*   66   25-30
Soundtrack (1966) .... *Columbia (S) OS-2940*   66   30-35
Composer: Maury Laws; Jules Bass. Conductor: Maury Laws. Cast: Robert Goulet; Ray Bolger; Paul O'Keffe; Ed Wynn; Patty Duke; Hayley Mills.

DAYS OF HEAVEN
Soundtrack (1978) .... *Pacific Arts (S) PAC8-128*   78   8-10
Composer: Ennio Moricone; Camille Saint-Saens; Leo Kottke; Doug Kershaw. Conductor: Ennio Moricone.

DAYS OF WILFRED OWEN
Soundtrack (1966) .... *Warner Bros. (M) B-1635*   66   15-20
Soundtrack (1966) .... *Warner Bros. (S) BS-1635*   66   20-25
Composer: Richard Lewine. Conductor: Richard Lewine. Cast: Richard Burton (recitation of poems from the film).

DAYS OF WINE AND ROSES
Studiotrack (1963) .... *Columbia (M) CL-2015*   63   10-15
Studiotrack (1963) .... *Columbia (S) CS-8815*   63   12-18
Composer: Various. Cast: Andy Williams.

DAYS OF WINE AND ROSES (AND OTHER GREAT MOVIE THEMES)
Studiotrack (1963) .... *Dot (M) DLP-3504*   63   10-15
Studiotrack (1963) .... *Dot (S) DLP-25504*   63   10-20
Composer: Henry Mancini; others. Cast: Pat Boone.

DE SADE
Soundtrack (1969) .... *Tower (S) ST-5170*   69   20-25
Composer: Billy Strange. Conductor: Billy Strange.

DEAD RINGER
Soundtrack (1964) .... *Warner Bros. (M) W-1536*   64   35-40
Soundtrack (1964) .... *Warner Bros. (S) WS-1536*   64   40-50
Composer: Andre Previn. Conductor: Andre Previn.

DEADFALL
Soundtrack (1968) .... *20th Century-Fox (S) S-4203*   68   40-50
Composer: John Barry. Conductor: John Barry. Cast: Shirley Bassey.

DEADLY AFFAIR
Soundtrack (1967) .... *Verve (M) V-8679*   67   15-20
Soundtrack (1967) .... *Verve (S) V6-8679*   67   20-25
Composer: Quincy Jones. Conductor: Quincy Jones. Cast: Astrud Gilberto.

DEADLY FRIEND
Soundtrack (1986) .... *Varese Sarabande (S) STV-81291*   86   15-20
Composer: Charles Bernstein.

DEAN, JAMES, STORY:
see JAMES DEAN STORY

DEAN MARTIN SINGS:
see STOOGE

The Friars Club
presents

The DEAN MARTIN
Testimonial Dinner

In order of appearance:
Barry Mirkin
George Jessel
Jimmy Durante
Joey Bishop
Tony Martin
George Burns
Dinah Shore
Mort Sahl
Judy Garland
Sammy Cahn
Danny Thomas
Sammy Davis, Jr.
Bob Hope
Frank Sinatra
Al Hart
Eugene Debs
Glenn Wallichs
Dean Martin

Beverly Hilton
November 8, 1959

Collectors Item
$25 Donation

DEAN MARTIN TESTIMONIAL DINNER

Assembled Cast (1959) .... *Dean Martin Testimonial (M) No Number Used*   59   **$100-150**
Triple LP set (in triple-pocket cover). Sold for $25 at the door as a souvenir of the Friars Club roast of Dean Martin.
Cast: Frank Sinatra; Sammy Davis Jr.; George Jessel; Jimmy Durante; Joey Bishop; Tony Martin; Dinah Shore; Danny Thomas; Bob Hope; Barry Mirkin; George Burns; Mort Sahl; Judy Garland; Sammy Cahn; Al Hart; Eugene Debs; Glenn Wallichs; Dean Martin.

DEAN MARTIN TV SHOW

Studiotrack (1966) .... *Reprise (M) R-6223*   66   **10-20**
Studiotrack (1966) .... *Reprise (S) RS-6233*   66   **15-20**
A selection of songs performed on Dean's NBC-TV series.
Composer: Various. **Conductor:** Les Brown. **Cast:** Dean Martin; Ken Lane (piano).

DEAR JOHN

Soundtrack (1966) .... *Dunhill (M) OCD-55001*   66   **15-20**
Soundtrack (1966) .... *Dunhill (S) OCDS-5500*   66   **20-25**
Composer: Bengt Arne Wallin. **Conductor:** Bengt Arne Wallin.

DEAR WORLD

Original Cast (1969) .... *Columbia (S) BOS-3260*   69   **15-20**
Original Cast (1969) .... *Columbia Special Products (S) ABOS-3260*   Re   **8-10**
Composer: Jerry Herman. **Conductor:** Donald Pippin. **Cast:** Angela Lansbury; Jane Connell; Carmen Mathews; Milo O'Shea; Pamela Hall; Kurt Peterson.

DEATH IN VENICE

Soundtrack (1971) .... *Deutsche Grammophon (S) 25838 124*   71   **8-10**
Composer: Gustav Mahler. **Conductor:** Rafael Kubelik. **Cast:** Bavarian Radio Symphony Orchestra.

DEATH OF A SALESMAN

Original Cast (1951) .... *Decca (M) DL-9006*   51   **30-50**
Original Cast (1951) .... *Decca (M) DL-9007*   51   **30-50**

Original Cast (1951) .... *Decca (M) DX-102*   51 $60-75
Original Cast (1951) .... *MCA (M) 204182*   84   **10-12**
  Above two are double LP sets.
  Composer: Alex North. **Conductor:** Alex North. **Cast:** Thomas Mitchell; Arthur Kennedy;
  Mildred Dunnock; Cameron Mitchell.
Studio Cast .... *Caedmon (M) TRS-310*   **10-20**
  Triple LP boxed set, with script.
  Composer: Alex North. **Conductor:** Alex North. **Cast:** Lee J. Cobb; Mildred Dunnock;
  Michael Tolan; Dustin Hoffman.
Studiotrack (1951) .... *Elmer Bernstein Film Music Collection (SE) FMC-9*   77   **35-40**
  Also contains music from *Viva Zapata*.
  Composer: Alex Worth. **Conductor:** Elmer Bernstein. **Cast:** Royal Philharmonic Orchestra.

DEATH OF A SCOUNDREL
Soundtrack (1956) .... *RCA Victor (EP) EPA-919*   56   **125-140**
Soundtrack (1956) .... *Entr' acte (M) ERM-6004*   80   **8-10**
  One side has music from four other Max Steiner scores: *The Charge of the Light Brigade, Four Wives,
  The Searchers* and *A Stolen Life*. This side was previously issued as side two of *Gone with the Wind
  (and Others)*.
  Composer: Max Steiner. **Conductor:** Max Steiner.
  Also see GONE WITH THE WIND (AND OTHERS)

DEATH ON THE NILE
Soundtrack (1978) .... *Capitol (S) SW-11866*   78   **15-20**
  Composer: Nino Rota; H. Warren and B. Green; Jacob Gade; N. Brown and A. Freed.
  Conductor: Nino Rota.

DEATH WISH
Soundtrack (1974) .... *Columbia (S) PC-33199*   74   **12-15**
  Composer: Herbie Hancock. **Conductor:** Herbie Hancock. **Cast:** Herbie Hancock.

DEATH WISH II
Soundtrack (1982) .... *Swan Song (S) SS 8511*   82   **8-10**
  Composer: Jimmy Page; Gordon Edwards.

DECEIVERS
Soundtrack (1988) .... *RCA Victor (S) 7722-1*   88   **8-10**

DECLINE AND FALL OF THE ENTIRE WORLD AS SEEN THROUGH
THE EYES OF COLE PORTER
Original Cast (1965) .... *Columbia (M) OL-6410*   65   **25-30**
Original Cast (1965) .... *Columbia (S) OS-2810*   65   **30-35**
Original Cast (1965) .... *Columbia Special Products (S) COS-2810*   Re   **10-12**
Original Cast (1965) .... *Columbia Special Products (S) AOS-2810*   Re   **8-10**
  Composer: Cole Porter. **Conductor:** Skip Redwine. **Cast:** Kaye Ballard; Harold Lang;
  Carmen Alvarez.
Studio Cast (1965) .... *Ric (S) ST-3002*   65   **15-20**
  This LP inspired the off-Broadway revue. The rest of the show was issued by Columbia.
Studio Cast (1965) .... *Painted Smiles (S) PS-1340*   Re   **8-10**
  Composer: Cole Porter. **Conductor:** Norman Paris. **Cast:** Kaye Ballard; David Allen; Ronny
  Graham.

DECLINE OF WESTERN CIVILIZATION
Soundtrack (1981) .... *Slash (S) 1-23934*   81   **8-10**
  Composer: Various. **Cast:** Black Flag; X; Circle Jerks; Fear; Catholic Discipline.

DEEP
Soundtrack (1977) .... *Casablanca (S) CAL-2018*   77   **10-15**
  Blue vinyl pressing.
  Composer: John Barry. **Conductor:** John Barry; Frankie McIntosh. **Cast:** Donna Summer.

DEEP IN MY HEART
Soundtrack (1954) .... *MGM (EP) X-276*   54 $15-20
Soundtrack (1954) .... *MGM (M) E-3153*   54   40-45
  Special boxed edition.
Soundtrack (1954) .... *MGM (M) E-3153*   55   30-35
  Standard LP issue.
  Composer: Sigmund Romberg. **Conductor:** Adolph Deutsch. **Cast:** Jose Ferrer; Rosemary
  Clooney; Helen Traubel; Gene Kelly; Fred Kelly; Jane Powell; Vic Damone; Ann Miller;
  Howard Keel; Tony Martin; William Olvis.

DEEP THROAT
Soundtrack (1973) .... *DT Productions (S) No Number Used*   73   50-100
  Souvenir promotional issue given away to select theatre-goers. Has white cover with the words
  "Now for the First Time, the One and Only Deep Throat."
Soundtrack (1971) .... *Sandy Hook (M) SH 2036*   80   8-10

DEEP THROAT PART II
Soundtrack (1974) .... *Bryan (S) BRS-101*   74   20-25
  Composer: Michael Colicchio; others. **Cast:** T.J. Stone; Laura Greene.

DEER HUNTER
Soundtrack (1979) .... *Capitol (S) SOO-11940*   79   8-10
  Composer: Stanley Myers; Irving Berlin.

DELIVERANCE
Soundtrack (1972) .... *Warner Bros. (S) B-2683*   73   8-10
  Actual title: *Dueling Banjos from Deliverance.*
  Cast: Eric Weissberg; Steve Mandel.

DEMI DOZEN
Original Cast (1957) .... *Offbeat (M) O-4015*   57   25-30
  Cast: Jean Arnold; Ceil Cabot; Jane Connell; Jack Fletcher; Stan Keen; Gordon Connell;
  George Hall; Jerry Matthews.

DENNIS THE MENACE
TV Soundtrack (1960) .... *Colpix (M) CP-204*   60   20-25
  Cast: Jay North; Gloria Henry; Herbert Anderson; Joseph Kearns. (With dialogue.)

DEPUTY DAWG
TV Soundtrack (1960) .... *RCA Victor/Camden (M) CAL-1048*   60   15-20
  Cast: Dayton Allen.

DERNIER AMANT ROMANTIQUE, LE:
see LE DERNIER AMANT ROMANTIQUE

DESERT SONG
Original London Cast .... *Monmouth Evergreen (SE) MES-7054*   8-12
  One side has music from *The Student Prince.*
  Composer: Oscar Hammerstein II; Sigmund Romberg; Otto Harbach. **Conductor:** Herman
  Finck. **Cast:** Sidney Pointer; Edith Day; Harry Welchman; Dennis Hoey.

Studio Cast (1950) ....*Decca (M) DL-7000* 50 **$35-50**
10-inch LP.
Composer: Sigmund Romberg; Oscar Hammerstein II; Otto Harbach. **Conductor:** Isaac
Van Grove. **Cast:** Kitty Carlisle; Wilbur Evans; Felix Knight; Jeffry Alexander Chorus.
Studio Cast (1953) ....*Columbia (EP) A-1060* 53 **10-20**
Studio Cast (1953) ....*Columbia (M) ML-4636* 53 **30-40**
Studio Cast (1953) ....*Columbia (EP) A-1717* 56 **10-15**
Studio Cast (1953) .... *Columbia (M) CL-831* 56 **15-25**
Studio Cast (1953) ....*Columbia Special Products (M) ACL-831* Re **8-10**
Conductor: Lehman Engel. **Cast:** Nelson Eddy; Doretta Morrow; Lee Cass.
Studio Cast (1955) ....*RCA Victor (EP) EKB-1013* 55 **15-25**
Double EP set.
Studio Cast (1955) ....*RCA Victor (M) LK-1013* 55 **25-35**
Conductor: Al Goodman. **Cast:** Earl Wrightson; Francis Greer; Jimmy Carroll.
Studio Cast (1959) .... *RCA Victor (M) LOP-1000* 59 **20-25**
Studio Cast (1959) .... *RCA Victor (S) LSO-1000* 59 **35-45**
Conductor: Lehman Engel. **Cast:** Giorgio Tozzi; Kathy Barr; Peter Palmer; Warren Galjour;
Eugene Morgan.
Studio Cast (1949) ....*Decca (M) DL-7000* 49 **35-50**
10-inch LP.
Conductor: Issac Van Grove. **Cast:** Wilbur Evans; Kitty Carlisle; Felix Knight; Vicki Vale.
Studio Cast (1960) .... *RCA Victor (S) LSC-2440* 60 **15-20**
Conductor: Constantine Callinicos. **Cast:** Mario Lanza; Judith Raskin; Raymond Murcell;
Donald Arthur.
London Studio Cast (1962) ....*Angel (S) S-35905* 62 **35-40**
Conductor: Michael Collins. **Cast:** June Bronhill; Edmund Hockridge; Julie Dawn; Leonard
Weir; Bruce
Forsyth.
Studio Cast (1953) .... *Capitol (EP) EBF-351* 53 **15-20**
Studio Cast (1953) .... *Capitol (M) L-351* 53 **40-50**
10-inch LP.
Studio Cast (1953) .... *Capitol (M) T-384* 56 **25-30**
One side has music from *Roberta*.
Studio Cast (1953) ....*Capitol (M) W-1842* 63 **20-25**
Studio Cast (1953) ....*Capitol (SE) SW-1842* 63 **20-25**
Studio Cast (1953) .... *Angel (SE) S-37319* 73 **8-10**
Composer: Oscar Hammerstein II; Sigmund Romberg; Otto Harbach. **Conductor:** Van
Alexander. **Cast:** Gordon MacRae; Lucille Norman; Dorothy Kirsten; Gerald Shirkey; Lloyd
Bunnell; Roger Wagner Chorale.
Studiotrack (1953) ....*RCA Victor (EP) EPB-3105* 53 **15-20**
Double EP set.
Studiotrack (1953) .... *RCA Victor (M) LPM-3105* 53 **40-50**
10-inch LP.
Composer: Sigmund Romberg. **Conductor:** Arthur Fiedler. **Cast:** Kathryn Grayson; Tony
Martin.

DESIRE UNDER THE ELMS
Soundtrack (1958) ....*Dot (M) DLP-3095* 58 **90-100**
Composer: Elmer Bernstein. **Conductor:** Elmer Bernstein.

DESPERATE TEENAGE LOVEDOLLS
Soundtrack ....*SST (S) SST-072*   **8-10**

DESTINATION MOON
Soundtrack (1950) .... *Columbia (M) CL-6151*   50   **$125-150**
  10-inch LP.
  Composer: Leith Stevens. **Conductor:** Leith Stevens.
Soundtrack (1950) .... *Omega (M) OL-3*   58   **40-50**
Soundtrack (1950) .... *Omega (SE) OSL-3*   58   **60-75**
  Composer: Leith Stevens. **Conductor:** Henry Sandauer. **Cast:** Omega Orchestra.
Soundtrack (1950) .... *Varese Sarabande (SE) STV-81130*   80   **8-10**
  Composer: Leith Stevens. **Conductor:** Heinz Sandauer.
Soundtrack .... *Cinema (M) LP-8005*   **8-10**
  Also contains other themes.
  Composer: Leith Stevens. **Conductor:** Leith Stevens.

DESTRY RIDES AGAIN
Original Cast (1959) .... *Decca (M) DL-9075*   59   **25-30**
Original Cast (1959) .... *Decca (S) DL7-9075*   59   **40-50**
  Composer: Harold Rome. **Conductor:** Lehman Engel. **Cast:** Andy Griffith; Dolores Gray;
  Scott Brady; Don Crabtree; Rosetta LeNoire; Jack Prince; Elizabeth Watts.
Studio Cast (1959) .... *RCA Victor/Camden (M) CAL-540*   59   **10-15**
Studio Cast (1959) .... *RCA Victor/Camden (S) CAS-540*   59   **15-25**
  Composer: Harold Rome. **Conductor:** Lehman Engel. **Cast:** Louise O'Brien; Jack Haskell.
Studio Cast (1959) .... *United Artists (M) UAL-4045*   59   **10-15**
Studio Cast (1959) .... *United Artists (S) UAS-5045*   59   **15-20**
  Composer: Harold Rome. **Cast:** Randy Weston Trio; Four Trombones.

DEVIL AND DANIEL WEBSTER
Studio Cast (1939) .... *Desto (SE) 6450*   **20-25**
  Composer: Douglas Moore; Stephen Vincent Benet. **Conductor:** Armando Aliberti.
  Cast: Lawrence Winters; Joe Blankenship; Doris Young.
Soundtrack (1941) .... *Unicorn (SE) UNS-237*   **8-10**
  This film is also known as *All That Money Can Buy.*
  Composer: Bernard Herrmann. **Conductor:** Bernard Herrmann. **Cast:** Bernard Herrmann and
  His Orchestra.
  Also see GREAT FILM CLASSICS

DEVIL AT 4 O'CLOCK
Soundtrack (1962) .... *Colpix (M) CP-509*   62   **35-45**
Soundtrack (1962) .... *Colpix (S) SCP-509*   62   **50-65**
Soundtrack (1962) .... *Varese Sarabande (S) VC-81136*   80   **8-10**
  Composer: George Duning. **Conductor:** George Duning.

DEVIL IN MISS JONES
Soundtrack (1973) .... *Janus JLS-3059*   73   **10-15**
  Composer: Roy Straigis; Peter De Angelis; Alden Shuman. **Conductor:** Roy Straigis; Peter
  De Angelis; Alden Shuman.

DEVIL'S ANGELS
Soundtrack (1967) .... *Tower (M) T-5074*   67   **12-18**
Soundtrack (1967) .... *Tower (S) DT-5074*   67   **15-20**
  Composer: Mike Curb. **Conductor:** Mike Curb. **Cast:** Davie Allan and the Arrows.

DEVIL'S BRIGADE
Soundtrack (1968) .... *United Artists (M) UAL-3654*   68   **15-20**
Soundtrack (1968) .... *United Artists (S) UAS-6654*   68   **20-25**
  Composer: Alex North. **Conductor:** LeRoy Holmes.

DEVIL'S EIGHT
Soundtrack (1969) .... *Tower (S) DT-5160*   69   **15-20**
  Composer: Mike Curb; Jerry Styner.

DEVIL'S SISTERS
Radio Cast . . . .*Photon Disco (M) JOAC-X-20*   **$8-10**
  Cast: Joan Crawford.

DIAMOND HEAD
Soundtrack (1963) . . . .*Colpix (M) CP-440*   63   **40-50**
Soundtrack (1963) . . . . *Colpix (S) SCP-440*   63 ,   **60-75**
  Composer: John Williams. Conductor: John Williams.

DIAMOND STUDS
Original and Studio Cast (1975) . . . . *Pasquotank (S) PS-33 7-003*   75   **15-20**
  7-inch LP.
  Composer: Jim Wann; Bland Simpson. Cast: Jim Wann; Bland Simpson; Cass Morgan.

DIAMONDS ARE FOREVER
Soundtrack (1971) . . . . *United Artists (S) UAS-5220*   71   **15-20**
Soundtrack (1971) . . . .*United Artists (S) UA-LA301-G*   74   **8-10**
Soundtrack (1971) . . . . *Liberty (S) LT-50301*   Re   **5-8**
  Composer: John Barry. Conductor: John Barry. Cast: Shirley Bassey.

DIANA!
TV Soundtrack (1971) . . . . *Motown (S) 719*   71   **10-12**
  Cast: Diana Ross.

DIARY OF ANNE FRANK
Soundtrack (1959) . . . .*20th Century-Fox (M) TF-3012*   59   **60-75**
Soundtrack (1959) . . . . *20th Century-Fox (S) SFX-3012*   59   **85-100**
  Composer: Alfred Newman. Conductor: Alfred Newman.

DICK POWELL PRESENTS (MUSIC FROM THE ORIGINAL SOUNDTRACK
  OF FOUR STAR PRODUCTIONS)
Soundtrack (1962) . . . .*Dot (M) DLP-3421*   62   **30-50**
Soundtrack (1962) . . . . *Dot (S) DLP-25421*   62   **50-60**
  Composer: Herschel Burke Gilbert; Jerry Goldsmith; Leonard Rosenman; Leith Stevens;
  Jerry Fielding; others. Conductor: Herschel Burke Gilbert.

DICKENS' CHRISTMAS CAROL:
  see CHRISTMAS CAROL

DIGITAL TRIP DOWN BROADWAY
Studiotrack . . . .*MCA (S) 6220*   87   **8-10**
  Symphonic recollections.
  Conductor: Paul Gemignani. Cast: Royal Philharmonic Orchestra.

DILLINGER
Soundtrack (1973) . . . .*MCA (S) 360*   73   **12-15**
  Composer: Barry DeVorzon; Gus Levene.

DIME A DOZEN
Original Cast (1962) ....*Cadence (M) CLP-25063*   62   **$20-25**
  Double LP set.
  Cast: Gerry Matthew; Jack Fletcher; Mary Louise Wilson (pianos).
Original Cast (1962) ....*Cadence (S) CLP-25063*   62   **25-30**
  Cast: Gerry Matthew; Jack Fletcher; Mary Louise Wilson (pianos); Susan Browning;
  Fredricka Weber; Rex Robbins.

DINAH SHORE SINGS COLE PORTER AND RICHARD RODGERS
Studiotrack (1956) ....*Harmony (M) HL-7010*   56   **15-20**
  Cast: Dinah Shore.

DINER
Soundtrack (1982) .... *Elektra (S) E1-60107*   82   **10-12**
  Double LP set.
  Composer: Various. **Cast:** Jerry Lee Lewis; Dion and the Belmonts; Heartbeats; Eddie Cochran;
  Carl Perkins; Fleetwoods; Lowell Fulson; Clarence Henry; Del Vikings; Bobby Darin; Jane
  Morgan; Dick Haymes; Tommy Edwards; Fats Domino; Jimmy Reed; Elvis Presley; Jane
  Morgan; Jack Scott.

DINGAKA
Soundtrack (1965) ....*Mercury (M) MG-21013*   65   **20-25**
Soundtrack (1965) .... *Mercury (S) SR-61013*   65   **25-30**
  Composer: Eddie Domingo; Betha Egnos.

DINO
Soundtrack (1957) ....*Epic (M) LN-3404*   57   **50-60**
Soundtrack (1957) ....*Epic (EP) EG-7187*   57   **15-20**
  Promotional issue. Has vocal of *Dino,* written by Pockriss and Vance, but is from neither the soundtrack
  nor the album (LN-3404).
  Composer: Gerald Fried; Paul Vance; Lee Pockriss. **Conductor:** Gerald Fried; Mark Ellis.
  Cast: Sal Mineo.

DINOSAURUS!
Studiotrack (1966) .... *Leo the Lion (S) CH-1016*   66   **$8-10**
   From *The Lost World* by Arthur Conan Doyle.
   Cast: Basil Rathbone.

DIRTY DANCING
Soundtrack (1987) .... *RCA Victor (S) 6408-1*   87   **8-10**
   Composer: Various. **Cast:** Ronettes; Patrick Swayze; Maurice Wiliams and the Zodiacs; Merry Clayton; Blow Monkeys; Bruce Channel; Zappacosta; Mickey and Sylvia; Tom Johnson; Five Satins; Bill Medley; Jennifer Warnes.

DIRTY DINGUS MAGEE
Soundtrack (1970) .... *MGM (S) 1SE-24*   70   **15-20**
Soundtrack (1970) .... *MCA (S) 25095*   Re   **8-10**
   Composer: Jeff Alexander. **Conductor:** Jeff Alexander. **Cast:** Mike Curb Congregation; Jeff Alexander.

DIRTY DOZEN
Soundtrack (1967) .... *MGM (M) E-4445*   67   **15-25**
Soundtrack (1967) .... *MGM (S) SE-4445*   67   **20-25**
Soundtrack (1967) .... *MCA (S) 39064*   Re   **8-10**
   Composer: Frank DeVol. **Conductor:** Frank DeVol. **Cast:** Trini Lopez; Sibylle Siegfried.

DIRTY FEET
Soundtrack (1965) .... *Fink (M) 1007*   65   **20-25**
   Composer: M. Bartoo.

DIRTY GAME
Soundtrack (1966) .... *Laurie (M) 2034*   66   **15-20**
Soundtrack (1966) .... *Laurie (S) S-2034*   66   **20-25**
   Composer: Robert Mellin; Piero Reverberi.

DISINHAIRITED:
see HAIR

DISORDERLIES
Soundtrack (1987) .... *Tin Pan Apple (S) 833274-1*   87   **8-10**

DIVA
Soundtrack (1982) .... *DRG (S) SL-9503*   82   **8-10**
   Composer: Vladimir Cosma. **Conductor:** Vladimir Cosma. **Cast:** Wilhelmina Wiggins Fernandez.

DIVINE HAIR MASS IN F:
see HAIR

DIVINE MADNESS
Soundtrack (1979) .... *Atlantic (S) SD-16022*   79   **8-10**
   Conductor: Tony Berg; Randy Kerber. **Cast:** Bette Midler.

DIVINE NYMPH
Soundtrack (1980) .... *Cerberus (S) CEMS-0104*   80   **8-10**
   Composer: Cesare Andrea Bixio. **Conductor:** Cesare Andrea Bixio.

DIVORCE AMERICAN STYLE
Soundtrack (1967) .... *United Artists (M) UAL-5163*   67   **25-30**
Soundtrack (1967) .... *United Artists (S) UAS-5163*   67   **30-35**
   Composer: Dave Grusin. **Cast:** Debbie Reynolds; Dick Van Dyke.

DIVORCE ITALIAN STYLE
Soundtrack (1962) .... *United Artists (M) UAL-4106*   62   **$25-30**
Soundtrack (1962) .... *United Artists (S) UAS-5106*   62   **30-35**
  Composer: Carlo Rustichelli. **Conductor:** Peri Luigi Urbini.
Soundtrack (1962) .... *Ascot (M) UM-13505*   64   **15-20**
Soundtrack (1962) .... *Ascot (S) US-16505*   64   **20-30**
  Also has selections from *Phaedra, West Side Story* and *Two for the Seesaw.*
  Composer: Carlo Rustichelli. **Conductor:** Peri Luigi Urbini.

DIVORCE ME, DARLING!
Soundtrack .... *DRG (S) 15009*   **8-10**
  A continuation of Sandy Wilson's *Boy Friend.*
  Also see BOY FRIEND

DIXIE:
see SWINGING ON A STAR

DIXIELAND GOES BROADWAY
Studiotrack (1957) .... *Coral (M) CRL-57185*   57   **10-20**
  Composer: Various. **Cast:** Stan Rubin.

DO BLACK PATENT LEATHER SHOES REALLY REFLECT UP?
Original Cast (1982) .... *Columbia Special Products (S) P-18852*   86   **8-10**
  Composer: James Quinn; Alaric Jans. **Conductor:** Larry Hochman. **Cast:** Russ Thacker;
  Eileen Blackman; Carol Estey; Mary Buehrle; Louis DiCrescenzo; Susann Fletcher; Peter
  Heuchling; Patti Hoffman; Max Showalter; Don Stitt.

DO I HEAR A WALTZ?
Original Cast (1965) .... *Columbia (M) KOL-6370*   65   **10-15**
Original Cast (1965) .... *Columbia (S) KOS-2770*   65   **15-20**
Original Cast (1965) .... *Columbia Special Products (S) AKOS-2770*   Re   **8-10**
  Composer: Richard Rodgers; Stephen Sondheim. **Conductor:** Frederick Dvonch.
  Cast: Elizabeth Allen; Sergio Franchi; Madeleine Sherwood; Carol Bruce; Stuart Damon;
  Fleury D'Antonakis; Jack Manning; Julienne Marie.

DO RE MI
Original Cast (1960) .... *RCA Victor (M) LOCD-2002*   61   **25-30**
Original Cast (1960) .... *RCA Victor (S) LSOD-2002*   61   **50-55**
Original Cast (1960) .... *RCA Victor (M) LOC-1105*   65   **15-20**
Original Cast (1960) .... *RCA Victor (S) LSO-1105*   65   **25-30**
  Composer: Jule Styne; Betty Comden; Adolph Green. **Conductor:** Lehman Engel.
  Cast: Phil Silvers; Nancy Walker; John Reardon; David Burns; George Matthews;
  Nancy Dussault; George Givot.

Original London Cast (1960) ....*Decca (M) LK-4413* 60   **$50-55**
  Composer: Jule Styne; Betty Comden; Adolph Green. **Cast:** Max Bygraves; Maggie
  Fitzgibbon; Steve Arlen; Jan Waters; Danny Green.
Studio Cast (1960) .... *Capitol (M) T-1586* 61   **10-15**
Studio Cast (1960) .... *Capitol (S) ST-1586* 61   **15-20**
  Composer: Jule Styne; Betty Comden; Adolph Green. **Cast:** June Christy; Bob Cooper.
Studio Cast (1960) .... *Time (M) T-52032* 61   **10-15**
Studio Cast (1960) .... *Time (S) ST-2032* 61   **15-20**
  Composer: Jule Styne; Betty Comden; Adolph Green. **Conductor:** Maury Laws.
  Cast: Jim Tyler; Maury Laws Orchestra.

DO RE MI IN DANCE TIME
Studiotrack (1961) .... *RCA Victor (M) LPM-2375* 61   **10-15**
Studiotrack (1961) .... *RCA Victor (S) LSP-2375* 61   **12-20**
  Jazz interpretations.
  Composer: Jule Styne. **Conductor:** Jule Styne. **Cast:** Eddie Heywood (piano).

DO THE RIGHT THING
Soundtrack (1989) .... *Motown (S) MOT-6272* 89   **8-10**
  Composer: Various. **Cast:** Public Enemy; Teddy Riley; EU; Steel Pulse; Perri; Take 6;
  Keith John; Al Jarreau; Ruben Blades.

DOCTOR DETROIT
Soundtrack (1983) .... *Backstreet (S) 6120* 83   **8-10**
  Composer: Various. **Cast:** Dan Aykroyd; Devo; T. Carter; James Brown; Pattie Brooks; others.

DOCTOR DOLITTLE
Soundtrack (1967) .... *20th Century-Fox (M) TF-5101* 67   **15-20**
Soundtrack (1967) .... *20th Century-Fox (S) DTCS-5101* 67   **20-25**
Soundtrack (1967) .... *20th Century-Fox (S) WAO-91208*   **8-10**
  Composer: Leslie Bricusse. **Conductor:** Lionel Newman. **Cast:** Rex Harrison; Samantha
  Eggar; Anthony Newley; Richard Attenborough.

DOCTOR FAUSTUS
Soundtrack (1972) .... *CBS (S) S63189* 72   **150-200**
  Composer: Mario Nascimbene. **Conductor:** Mario Nascimbene. **Cast:** Richard Burton.
  (With dialogue.)

DOCTOR GOLDFOOT AND THE GIRL BOMBS
Soundtrack (1966) .... *Tower (M) T-5053* 66   **15-20**
Soundtrack (1966) .... *Tower (SE) DT-5053* 66   **15-20**
  Composer: Jerry Styner; Guy Hemric; Les Baxter; Harley Hatcher; others. **Cast:** Terry
  Stafford; Sloopys; Mad Doctors; Bobby Lile; Paul and the Pack; Candles.

DOCTOR NO
Soundtrack (1963) .... *United Artists (M) UAL-4108* 63   **25-30**
Soundtrack (1963) .... *United Artists (S) UAS-5108* 63   **35-45**
Soundtrack (1963) .... *Liberty (S) LT-50275* Re   **8-10**
  Composer: Monty Norman. **Conductor:** Monty Norman.
  Also see BIG COUNTRY

DOCTOR PEPPER - THE MOST ORIGINAL SOFT DRINK EVER
Original Cast (1974) .... *Dr. Pepper (S) No Number Used*   74   **$15-25**
Commemorative, advertising specialty issue.

DOCTOR PHIBES
Soundtrack (1971) .... *American Int'l (S) A-1040*   71   **40-50**
Also known as *The Abominable Doctor Phibes*.
Composer: Basil Kirchin; Jack Nathan; Sheldon Brooks; Johnny Mercer; others.
Conductor: Paul Frees. **Cast:** Clockwork Wizzards.

DOCTOR RHYTHM:
Also see EAST SIDE OF HEAVEN and STAR MAKER

DOCTOR SELAVY'S MAGIC THEATRE
Original Cast (1972) .... *United Artists (S) UA-LA196-G*   74   **20-25**
Composer: Tom Hendry; Stanley Silverman. **Conductor:** Stanley Silverman. **Cast:** Denise
Delapenha; Mary Delson; Jessica Harper; George McGrath; Steve Menken; Jackie Paris;
Barry Primus; Robert Schlee; Amy Taubin.

DOCTOR STRANGELOVE (AND OTHER GREAT MOVIE THEMES)
Studiotrack (1964) .... *Colpix (M) CP-464*   64   **10-15**
Studiotrack (1964) .... *Colpix (S) SCP-464*   64   **15-20**
Composer: Various. **Cast:** Laurie Johnson Orchestra; Sol Kaplan Orchestra; Leith Stevens
Orchestra; Morris Stoloff Orchestra; Norman Percival Orchestra; Muir Mathieson Orchestra.

DOCTOR ZHIVAGO
Soundtrack (1965) .... *MGM (M) 1E-6*   65   **15-20**
Soundtrack (1965) .... *MGM (S) S1E-6ST*   65   **20-25**
Above two have a gatefold cover and booklet.
Soundtrack (1965) .... *MGM (M) 1E-6ST*   66   **10-15**
Soundtrack (1965) .... *MGM (S) S1E-6ST*   66   **12-18**
Above two have gatefold cover, no booklet, and alternate music for *Yuri Writes a Poem for Lara*.
Soundtrack (1965) .... *MGM (S) S1E6-STX*   66   **10-12**
Gatefold cover. With original music for *Yuri Writes a Poem for Lara*.
Soundtrack (1965) .... *MCA (S) 89042*   86   **8-10**

DOG OF FLANDERS
Soundtrack (1959) .... *20th Century-Fox (M) TF-3026*   59   **75-100**
Soundtrack (1959) .... *20th Century-Fox (S) SFX-3026*   59   **100-125**
Composer: Paul Sawtell; Bert Shefter. **Cast:** Santa Cecilia Academy Orchestra and
Choir of Rome.

DOG'S LIFE
Soundtrack (1953) .... *Decca (M) DL-4040*   53   **30-50**
Radio Cast .... *Folkways (M) FW-5580*   **15-25**
Cast: Cast of a CBS Radio Workshop Broadcast.

DOGS IN SPACE
Soundtrack (1987) .... *Atlantic (S) 81789-1*   87   **8-10**

DOLCE VITA, LA:
see LA DOLCE VITA

DOLL'S LIFE
Original Cast (1982) .... *Original Cast (S) OC-8241*   82   **30-40**
Gatefold cover.
Composer: Larry Grossman. **Conductor:** Paul Gemignani. **Cast:** George Hearn; Betsy Joslyn;
Peter Gallagher; Barbara Lang; Norman A. Large; Edmund Lyndeck; David Vosburgh.
Original Cast (1982) .... *Columbia Special Products (S) 18846*   86   **8-12**
Composer: Larry Grossman; Betty Comden; Adolph Green. **Conductor:** Paul Gemignani.
Cast: George Hearn; Betsy Joslyn.

DOLLARS ($)
Soundtrack (1971) .... *Reprise (S) MS-2051*   71   **$15-20**
   Composer: Quincy Jones. **Cast:** Little Richard; Roberta Flack; Doug Kershaw; Don Elliott
   Voices.

DON JUAN IN HELL
Studio Cast (1952) .... *Columbia (M) SL-166*   **40-45**
   A play by Bernard Shaw, without music.
   Cast: First Drama Quartette: Charles Boyer, Charles Laughton, Cedric Hardwick, Agnes
   Moorehead.

DON'T BOTHER ME, I CAN'T COPE
Original Cast (1972) .... *Polydor (S) PD-6013*   72   **10-15**
   Composer: Micki Grant. **Conductor:** Danny Holgate. **Cast:** Alex Bradford; Hope Clarke;
   Bobby Hill; Alberta Bradford; Charles Campbell; Micki Grant; Arnold Wilkerson.

DON'T KNOCK THE TWIST
Soundtrack (1962) .... *Parkway (M) P-7011*   62   **20-25**
   Composer: Kal Mann; Bo Diddley; John Sheldon; others. **Cast:** Chubby Checker; Dovells;
   Carroll Brothers; Dee Dee Sharp.

DON'T MAKE WAVES
Soundtrack (1967) .... *MGM (M) E-4483*   67   **15-20**
Soundtrack (1967) .... *MGM (S) SE-4483*   67   **20-25**
Soundtrack (1967) .... *MCA (S) 25134*   Re   **8-10**
   Composer: Vic Mizzy. **Conductor:** Vic Mizzy. **Cast:** Byrds.

DON'T PLAY US CHEAP
Original Cast (1972) .... *Stax (S) STS 2-3006*   72   **20-25**
   Double LP set.
   Composer: Melvin Van Peebles. **Conductor:** Harold Wheeler. **Cast:** Thomas Anderson; Joshie
   Jo Armstead; Nate Barnett; Frank Carey; Robert Dunn; Rhetta Hughes; Joe Keyes, Jr.; Mabel
   King; Avon Long; George ("Ooppee") McCurn; Esther Rolle; Jay Vanleer.

DONNYBROOK!
Original Cast (1961) .... *Kapp (M) KDL-8500*   61   **20-25**
Original Cast (1961) .... *Kapp (S) KD-8500-S*   61   **25-30**
   Composer: John Burke. **Conductor:** Clay Warnick. **Cast:** Eddie Foy; Art Lund; Joan Fagan;
   Susan Johnson; Darrell Askey; Sibyl Bowan; Grace Carney; Alfred DeSio; Eddie Erickson;
   James Gannon; Art Lund; Bruce MacKay; Clarence Nordstrom; Charles C. Welch.

DOONESBURY
Original Cast (1984) .... *MCA (S) 6129*   84   **8-10**
   Composer: Elizabeth Swados; Gary Trudeau. **Conductor:** Jeff Waxman. **Cast:** Barbara Andres;
   Laura Dean; Gary Beach; Reathel Bean; Ralph Bruneau; Kate Burton; Mark Linn-Baker; Albert
   Macklin; Keith Szarabajka; Lauren Tom.

DOONESBURY'S JIMMY THUDPUCKER
TV Soundtrack (1977) .... *RCA Victor/Windsong (S) BXL1-2589*   77   **10-12**
   From an NBC-TV special. Includes eight-page cartoon storybook.
   Cast: Walden Street Rhythm Section.

DORA'S WORLD
TV Soundtrack .... *Cozy (S) PLS-0301*   **8-10**
   Cast: Dora Hall.

DOUBLE FEATURE:
see THAT MIDNIGHT KISS

DOUBLE IMPACT
Studiotrack (1960) .... *RCA Victor (M) LPM-2180*   60   **$15-20**
Studiotrack (1960) .... *RCA Victor (S) LSP-2180*   60   **20-25**
  Has TV themes from: *Riverboat, Bourbon Street Beat, Johnny Staccato, The Lineup, Twilight Zone, The
  Untouchables, Hawaiian Eye, Bonanza, International Detective, Markham, The Deputy* and *Men Into
  Space.*
  Composer: David Rose; David Livingston; Elmer Bernstein; Mack David; Jerry Goldsmith; S.J.
  Wilson; Sidney Shaw; Leroy Holmes; Bernard Herrmann. **Conductor:** Buddy Morrow.
  Cast: Buddy Morrow and His Orchestra.
  Also see IMPACT

DOUBLE OR NOTHING:
see POCKET FULL OF DREAMS

DOUBLE TROUBLE
Soundtrack (1967) .... *RCA Victor (M) LPM-3787*   67   **40-50**
  Black label reads "Monaural" at bottom. Includes 7" x 9" bonus photo, which represents about $8 of the
  value.
Soundtrack (1967) .... *RCA Victor (S) LSP-3787*   67   **40-50**
  Black label reads "Stereo" at bottom. Includes a 7" x 9" bonus photo, which represents about $8 of the
  value.
Soundtrack (1967) .... *RCA Victor (S) AFL1-2564*   69   **10-20**
  Orange or tan label. (Tan label issued in 1976.)
Soundtrack (1967) .... *RCA Victor (S) AFL1-2564*   77   **8-10**
  Composer: Doc Pomus; Mort Schuman; Randy Starr; Sid Tepper; Roy C. Bennett; Sid Wayne;
  Ben Weisman; others. **Cast:** Elvis Presley; Scotty Moore (guitar); Bob Moore (bass); D.J.
  Fontana (drums); Charlie Hodge (vocals); Jordanaires (vocals).

DOVE
Soundtrack (1974) .... *ABC (S) ABDP-852*   74   **20-25**
  Composer: John Barry. **Conductor:** John Barry. **Cast:** Lyn Paul.

DOWN AND OUT IN BEVERLY HILLS
Soundtrack (1986) ....*MCA (S) 6160*   86   **8-10**
  Composer: Various. **Cast:** Little Richard; Mariachi Vargas De Tecalitlan; David Lee Roth;
  Randy Newman.

DOWN BY LAW AND VARIETY
Soundtrack (1986) .... *Intuition (S) C1-90968*   86   **8-10**
  Cast: John Lurie.

DOWN IN THE VALLEY
Original Cast (1948) .... *Decca (M) DL-4239*   62   **20-25**
Original Cast (1948) .... *Decca (SE) DL-74239*   62   **20-25**
  Composer: Kurt Weill. **Conductor:** Maurice Levine. **Cast:** Alfred Drake; Jane Wilson; Daniel
  Slick; Norman Atkins.
TV Soundtrack (1950) .... *RCA Victor (M) LM-16*   50   **50-60**
  10-inch LP.
TV Soundtrack (1950) .... *RCA Victor (EP) WDM-1367*   50   **25-30**
  Triple EP set. Also has music from *The Lady in the Dark.*
TV Soundtrack (1950) .... *RCA Victor (M) LPV-503*   Re   **20-30**
  One side has music from *The Lady in the Dark.*
  Composer: Kurt Weill; Arnold Sundgaard. **Conductor:** Peter Herman. **Cast:** Marion Bell;
  William McGraw; Kenneth Smith; Ray Jacquemot; Richard Barrows; Robert Holland.

DOWN TO THE SEA IN SHIPS
Soundtrack (1949) ....*Entra' cte (M) ERS-6506*   77   **8-10**
  Also has music from: *Kentuckin'* (1955, Bernard Herrmann), *In Love and War* (1958, Hugo Friedhofer),
  and *Sunrise at Campobello* (1960, Franz Waxman).
  Composer: Alfred Newman.

DOWNRIVER
Original Cast (1975) . . . . *Take Home Tunes (S) THT-7811*   75   **$8-10**
   Composer: Johnny Braden. **Conductor:** Jeff Waxman. **Cast:** Richard Donne; Marcia McLain;
   Donald Arrington; Michael Corbett; Alvin Fields; Robert Price.

DRACULA
Soundtrack (1979) . . . .*MCA (S) 3166*   79   **10-15**
   Composer: John Williams. **Conductor:** John Williams.
Studiotrack (1974) . . . . *Capitol (S) ST-11340*   74   **10-12**
   Side two, "Four Faces of Evil," has music from four Hammer films: *Fear in the Night, She, The*
   Vampire Lovers and *Dr. Jekyll and Sister Hyde.*
   Composer: James Bernard; John McCabe; Harry Robinson; David Whitaker.
   Conductor: Philip Martell. **Cast:** Christopher Lee; Bill Mitchell; Hammer City Orchestra.
Studiotrack (1964) . . . . *Stamford (M) CO-1553*   **10-20**
   Double LP set.
   Cast: Christopher Lee.

DRAGNET
Original Radio Cast . . . . .· . . . .*Golden Age (M) 5003*   78   **8-10**
TV Soundtrack (1953) . . . . *RCA Victor (M) LPM-3199*   53   **50-60**
   Contains the episode *The Christmas Story.*
   Composer: Walter Schumann. **Conductor:** Walter Schumann. **Cast:** Jack Webb; Ben
   Alexander. (With dialogue.)
Soundtrack (1987) . . . .*MCA (S) 6210*   87   **8-10**
   Composer: Ira Newborn; others. **Conductor:** Ira Newborn; others. **Cast:** Dan Aykroyd;
   Tom Hanks; Art of Noise; New Edition; Peter Aykroyd; Pat Thrall; Ira Newborn.

DRAGONSLAYER
Soundtrack (1981) . . . .*Label X (S) LXSE 2-001*   83   **150-200**
   Limited edition (2,500 made) boxed set.
   Composer: Alex North. **Conductor:** Alex North.

DRANGO
Soundtrack (1957) . . . . *Liberty (M) LRP-3036*   57   **125-150**
   Composer: Elmer Bernstein. **Conductor:** Elmer Bernstein.

DRAT THE CAT
Original Broadway Cast . . . . *Blue Pear (M) BP 1005*   **25-30**
   Composer: Milton Schafer; Ira Levin. **Conductor:** Herbert Grossman. **Cast:** Lesley Ann
   Warren; Elliott Gould; Jane Connell; Jack Fletcher; Charles Durning; Sandy Ellen; David
   Gold; Lu Leonard; Gene Varrone.

DRAUGHTMAN'S CONTRACT
Soundtrack (1982) . . . . *DRG (S) SL-9513*   82   **8-10**

DREAM A LITTLE DREAM
Soundtrack (1989) . . . .*Cypress (S) YL9-0125*   89   **8-10**
   Composer: Various. **Cast:** Mike Reno; R.E.M.; Michael Damian; Fee Waybill; Chris
   Thompson; Otis Redding.

DREAM GIRLS
Original Cast (1982) . . . . . .· . . . .*Geffen (S) GHSP-2007*   82   **8-10**
   Composer: Henry Krieger. **Conductor:** Yolanda Segovia. **Cast:** Obba Babatunde; Cleavant
   Derricks; Loretta Devine; Ben Harney; Jennifer Holliday; Sheryl Lee Ralph; Deborah
   Burrell; Tony Franklin.

DREAM OF KINGS
Soundtrack (1969) . . . .*National General (S) MG-1000*   69   **20-25**
   Composer: Alex North. **Conductor:** Alex North.

DREAMS
TV Soundtrack (1984) . . . . *Columbia (S) BFC-39886*   84   **$8-10**

DREAMSCAPE
Soundtrack (1984) . . . . *Sonic Atmospheres (S) 102*   84   **15-20**
Composer: Maurice Jarre.

DRESSED TO KILL
Soundtrack (1980) . . . . *Varese Sarabande (S) STV-81148*   80   **8-10**
Composer: Pino Donaggio. Conductor: Natale Massara.

DRESSED TO THE NINES
Original Cast (1960) . . . . *MGM (M) E-3914*   60   **30-40**
Original Cast (1960) . . . . *MGM (S) SE-3914*   60   **40-50**
Composer: Various. Conductor: William Roy. Cast: Ceil Cabot; Gordon Connell; Bill Hinnant; Gerry Matthews; William Roy and Carl Norman (pianos); Pat Ruhl; Mary Louise Wilson.

DROP DEAD! (AN EXERCISE IN HORROR)
Radio Cast . . . . *Capitol (M) T-1763*   62   **30-40**
Radio Cast . . . . *Capitol (S) ST-1763*   62   **40-50**
Radio dramas.
Cast: Bea Benederet; Jack Kruschen; Junius Matthews; Mercedes McCambridge; Arch Oboler (narration).

DRUGSTORE COWBOY
Soundtrack . . . . *Novus (S) 3077-1-N9*   **8-10**
Composer: Various. Cast: Bobby Goldsboro; Abbey Lincoln; Jackie De Shannon; John Fred and Playboy Band; Desmond Dekker and Aces; others.

DUCHIN, EDDY, STORY:
see EDDY DUCHIN STORY

DUCK, YOU SUCKER
Soundtrack (1972) . . . . *United Artists (S) UAS-5221*   72   **35-45**
Composer: Ennio Morricone. Conductor: Ennio Morricone.

DUDE
Original Cast (1972) . . . . *Kilmarnock (S) KIL-72007*   72   **20-25**
Composer: Galt MacDermot; Gerome Ragini. Conductor: Galt MacDermot.
Cast: Nell Carter; Salome Bey; Nat Morris; Jim Farrell; Leta Galloway.
Studio Cast (1972) . . . . *Kilmarnock (S) KIL-72003*   72   **20-25**
Actual title: *Salome Bey Sings Dude.*
Conductor: Thomas Pierson. Cast: Salome Bey.

DUDE, THE HIGHWAY LIFE
Original Cast (1972) . . . . *Kilmarnock (S) KIL-72007*   72   **8-12**
Composer: Galt MacDermot; Gerome Ragni. Conductor: Thomas Pierson. Cast: Salome Bey; Alan Braunstein; Nell Carter; Jim Farrell; Leta Galloway; David Lasley; Nat Morris.

DUDES
Soundtrack (1987) . . . . *MCA (S) 6212*   87   **8-10**

DUEL
Original Cast (1979) . . . . *Original Cast (S) OC-7917*   79   **8-10**
Composer: Randal Wilson. Cast: Thomas Young; Randal Wilson; Kurt Yahjian; Karen Kraft; Kate DeZina; Bertilla Baker.

DUEL AT DIABLO
Soundtrack (1966) . . . . *United Artists (M) UAL-4139*   66   **15-20**
Soundtrack (1966) . . . . *United Artists (S) UAS-5139*   66   **20-25**
Composer: Neal Hefti. Conductor: Neal Hefti. Cast: Neal Hefti and His Orchestra.
Soundtrack (1966) . . . . *MCA (S) 1436*   **8-10**
Conductor: Ernie Sheldon. Cast: Ernie Sheldon.

DUEL IN THE SUN
Soundtrack (1946) .... *Sound Stage (M) 2303*   73 $20-25
  Composer: Dimitri Tomkin. **Conductor:** Dimitri Tomkin.

DUELING BANJOS FROM "DELIVERANCE":
see DELIVERANCE

DUMBO
Soundtrack (1941) .... *Disneyland (M) WDL-4013*   59   20-30
Soundtrack (1941) .... *Disneyland (M) DQ-1204*   59   10-20
  Composer: Frank Churchill; Oliver Wallace. **Cast:** Cliff Edwards.

DUNE
Soundtrack (1984) ....*Polydor (S) 422-82377*   84   8-10
  Cast: Toto.

DUNWICH HORROR
Soundtrack (1970) .... *American Int' l (S) STA-1028*   70   20-25
  Also known as "Music of the Devil God Cult."
Soundtrack (1970) ....*Varese Sarabande (S) VC-81103*   79   8-10
  Composer: Les Baxter. **Conductor:** Les Baxter. **Cast:** Les Baxter and His Orchestra.

DUSTY AND SWEETS McGEE
Soundtrack (1971) .... *Warner Bros. (S) S-1936*   71   15-20
  Composer: Various. **Cast:** Van Morrison; Monotones; Marcels; Gene Chandler; Del Shannon;
  Little Eva; Blues Image; Bruce Channel.

DYLAN
Original Cast (1964) ....*Columbia (M) DOL-301*   64   20-30
Original Cast (1964) .... *Columbia (S) DOS-701*   64   30-35
  Triple LP set. Has the complete dramatic play plus special booklet.
  Composer: Laurence Rosenthal; Teo Macero. **Cast:** Sir Alec Guinness; Kate Reid; James Ray;
  Barbara Berger; Martin Garner; Jenny O'Hara; Gordon B. Clarke; Paul Larson; Jonathan
  Moore; Carol Gustafson; Louisa Cabot; Margaret Braidwood; Ernest Graves; Grant Code; Janet
  Sarno.

DYNAMITE BROTHERS
Soundtrack (1972) .... *Prestige (S) 10082*   73   10-12
  Composer: Charles Earland.

E

E.T. - THE EXTRA-TERRESTRIAL

Soundtrack (1982) .... *MCA (S) 70000*   82   **$50-100**
  Boxed, storybook edition. Includes a 20-page program/photo booklet and a poster.
  Cast: Michael Jackson (narration and vocal).
Soundtrack (1982) .... *MCA (S) 6113*   82   **15-30**
  Picture disc. Packaged in clear plastic cover.
Soundtrack (1982) .... *MCA (S) 6109*   82   **8-10**
  Digital edition (recorded, mixed, and edited digitally).
Soundtrack (1982) .... *MCA (S) 16014*   82   **30-40**
  Audiophile edition.
Soundtrack (1982) .... *MCA (S) 37264*   88   **8-10**
  Composer: John Williams. **Conductor:** John Williams. **Cast:** John Williams and His Orchestra.

EAGLE HAS LANDED:
see FOUR MUSKETEERS / THE EAGLE HAS LANDED

EARL OF RUSTON

Original Cast (1971) .... *Capitol (S) ST-465*   71   **30-40**
  Composer: Peter Link; Ragan Courtney; C.C. Courtney. **Cast:** Peter Link; C.C. Courtney;
  Leecy R. Woods; Yolande Bavan; Boni Enten; Marta Heflin; Salvation Company.

EARTH GIRLS ARE EASY

Soundtrack (1989) .... *Sire/Reprise (S) 25835*   89   **8-10**
  Composer: Various. **Cast:** Darryl Hall; John Oates; Royalty; Information Society; Jill Jones;
  The "N"; B-52s; Depeche Mode; Jesus and Mary Chain; Stewart Copeland; Julie Brown.

EARTHA KITT SINGS SONGS FROM "NEW FACES"

Studiotrack (1954) .... *RCA Victor (EP) EPA-557*   54   **15-20**
  Composer: Leonard Sillman. **Conductor:** Henri Rene. **Cast:** Eartha Kitt; Henri Rene and
  His Orchestra.
  Also see NEW FACES OF 1952

EARTHQUAKE

Original Cast (1973) .... *Inner City (S) LRS RT-60*   73   **20-25**
  Composer: C. Bernard Jackson. **Conductor:** Larry Nash. **Cast:** Bernie Cowens; Karmello
  Brooks; Lupe Zuniga; Rod Perry; Nikki Sanz; Peter Salas; Lee Hampton.
Soundtrack (1973) .... *MCA (S) 2081*   74   **40-50**
  Limited edition, with "Sensurround" band on the *Earthquake* track, on side two.
Soundtrack (1973) .... *MCA (S) 2081*   74   **10-15**
  Composer: John Williams. **Conductor:** John Williams.

EAST OF EDEN
TV Soundtrack (1981) .... *Elektra (S) 5E-520*   81   **$8-10**
  Composer: Lee Holdridge. Conductor: Lee Holdridge.
  Also see TRIBUTE TO JAMES DEAN

EAST SIDE OF HEAVEN
Studiotrack (1939) .... *Decca (M) DL-4253*   62   **25-30**
  Also has selections from *Doctor Rhythm* and *Paris Honeymoon*. Isssued as part of *Bing's Hollywood Series*.
  Conductor: John Scott Trotter. Cast: Bing Crosby.

EAST SIDE, WEST SIDE
TV Soundtrack (1963) .... *Columbia (M) CL-2123*   63   **30-40**
TV Soundtrack (1963) .... *Columbia (S) CS-8923*   63   **25-30**
  Composer: Kenyon Hopkins. Conductor: Kenyon Hopkins.

EASTER PARADE
Soundtrack (1948) .... *MGM (EP) X-40*   50   **15-20**
Soundtrack (1948) .... *MGM (M) E-502*   50   **40-50**
  10-inch LP.
Soundtrack (1986) .... *MCA (S) 1459*   86   **8-10**
  Composer: Irving Berlin. Conductor: Johnny Green. Cast: Judy Garland; Fred Astaire; Peter Lawford; Ann Miller.
  Also see ANNIE GET YOUR GUN

EASY COME, EASY GO
Soundtrack (1967) .... *RCA Victor (EP) EPA-4387*   67   **40-50**
  Black label.
Soundtrack (1967) .... *RCA Victor (EP) EPA-4387*   67   **30-40**
  Orange label.
Soundtrack (1967) .... *RCA Victor (EP) EPA-4387*   67   **75-90**
  White label, promotional issue. Reads "EASY COME, EASY GO - Elvis Presley" at top of the label.
Soundtrack (1967) .... *RCA Victor (EP) EPA-4387*   67   **80-100**
  White label, promotional issue. Reads "RCA Victor Presents Elvis in the Original Soundtrack Recording from the Paramount Picture EASY COME, EASY GO, a Hal Wallis Production" at top of the label.
  Composer: Bill Giant; Bernie Baum; Florence Kaye; Gerald Nelson; Fred Burch; Ben Weisman; others. Cast: Elvis Presley; Scotty Moore (guitar); Bob Moore (bass); Jerry Scheff (bass); D.J. Fontana (drums); Hal Blaine (drums); Jordanaires (vocals).

EASY MONEY
Soundtrack (1983) .... *Columbia (S) JS-38968*   83   **8-10**
  Composer: Various. Cast: Billy Joel; Scandal; Heaven; Nick Lowe; Weather Girls.

EASY RIDER
Soundtrack (1969) .... *Dunhill (S) DSX-50063*   69   **20-25**
  Composer: Hoyt Axton; Jimi Hendrix; Bob Dylan; Roger McGuinn; others. Cast: Byrds; Steppenwolf; Jimi Hendrix Experience; Roger McGuinn; Fraternity of Man; Electric Prunes; Holy Modal Rounders.

EASY TO REMEMBER
Soundtrack .... *Decca (M) DL-4250*   62   **25-30**
  Has music from *Here Is My Heart, Mississippi, Two for Tonight* and *The Big Broadcast of 1936*. Issued as part of *Bing's Hollywood Series*.
  Conductor: John Scott Trotter. Cast: Bing Crosby.
  Also see BIG BROADCAST OF 1936

ECCO
Soundtrack (1965) .... *Warner Bros. (M) W-1600*   65   **10-15**
Soundtrack (1965) .... *Warner Bros. (S) WS-1600*   65   **15-20**
  Composer: Riz Ortolani. Conductor: Riz Ortolani.

ECHO PARK
Soundtrack (1986) . . . .*A&M (S) SP-5119*   86   **$8-10**
    Composer: Various. **Cast:** Jimmie Wood and the Immortals; Shandi; Dean Chamberlain;
    David Baerwald; Sights; Johnette Napolitano; David Ricketts; Patti Black; Mike Sherwood;
    Julie Christensen.

ECHOES OF ARCHY:
see SHINBONE ALLEY (ARCHY AND MEHITABEL)

EDDIE ALBERT ALBUM
Studiotrack (1967) . . . . *Columbia (M) CL-2599*   67   **10-12**
Studiotrack (1967) . . . . *Columbia (S) CS-9399*   67   **12-15**
    Includes the *Green Acres* theme.
    Composer: Various. **Cast:** Eddie Albert.

EDDIE AND THE CRUISERS
Soundtrack (1983) . . . .*Scotti Bros. (S) FZ-38929*   83   **8-10**
    Composer: John Cafferty. **Cast:** John Cafferty and the Beaver Brown Band.

EDDIE CANTOR AT CARNEGIE HALL
Original Cast (1950) . . . . *Audio Fidelity (M) AFLP-702*   **20-25**
    Cast: Eddie Cantor.

EDDIE CANTOR STORY
Soundtrack (1953) . . . . *Capitol (EP) FBF-467*   53   **25-35**
    Double EP, boxed set.
Soundtrack (1953) . . . .*Capitol (M) L-467*   53   **40-60**
    10-inch LP.
    Composer: Walter Donaldson; James J. Monaco; others. **Conductor:** Ray Heindorf.
    Cast: Eddie Cantor.
Soundtrack (1953) . . . . *Decca (EP) ED-592*   53   **15-20**
    Actual title: *Eddie Cantor Sings.*
Studiotrack (1953) . . . . *Decca (M) DL-5504*   53   **25-35**
    10-inch LP. Actual title: *Eddie Cantor Sings.*

EDDY DUCHIN STORY
Soundtrack (1956) . . . . *Decca (EP) ED-844*   56   **20-30**
    Triple disc, boxed set.
Soundtrack (1956) . . . . *Decca (M) DL-8289*   56   **25-35**
Soundtrack (1956) . . . . *Decca (SE) DL7-8289*   59   **25-30**
Soundtrack (1956) . . . . *Decca (M) DL-8396*   56   **60-75**
    Also has music from *On the Waterfront, From Here to Eternity* and *You Can't Run Away from It.*
    Composer: ON THE WATERFRONT: Leonard Bernstein. FROM HERE TO ETERNITY:
    George Duning; Fred Karger. YOU CAN'T RUN AWAY FROM IT: Johnny Mercer; Gene
    DePaul. **Conductor:** Morris Stoloff (all). **Cast:** Carmen Cavallaro. YOU CAN'T RUN
    AWAY FROM IT: Jack Lemmon; June Allyson; Stubby Kaye; Four Aces.
Soundtrack (1956) . . . . *Decca (M) DL-9121*   65   **10-15**
Soundtrack (1956) . . . .*Decca (SE) DL7-9121*   65   **10-15**
    Conductor: Morris Stoloff. **Cast:** Carmen Cavallaro.
Studiotrack (1956) . . . . *Columbia (M) CL-790*   56   **25-35**
    Composer: Various. **Cast:** Eddy Duchin (original recordings).
Studiotrack (1956) . . . .*Capitol (M) T-716*   56   **20-25**
    Actual title: *Selections from the Eddy Duchin Story.*

EDGE OF THE CITY:
see COBWEB

EDITH AND MARCEL
Soundtrack (1984) ....*Atlantic (S) 80153-1*   84   **$8-10**
Double LP set.

EDUCATION OF SONNY CARSON
Soundtrack (1974) ....*Paramount (S) PAS-1045*   74   **10-12**
Composer: Taylor Perkinson. Conductor: Taylor Perkinson.

EDWARD AND MRS. SIMPSON
TV Soundtrack (1978) ...., ... *Stet/DRG (S) DS-15019*   79   **10-12**
Mobil Showcase Network mini-series.
Composer: Ron Grainer; others. Conductor: Ron Grainer. Cast: Ron Grainer Orchestra;
Jenny Wren.

EDWARD THE KING
TV Soundtrack (1980) .... *DRG (S) DARC-2 11*   80   **10-12**
Composer: Cyril Ornadel. Conductor: Cyril Ornadel.

EDWIN DROOD
Original Broadway Cast (1985) ....*Polydor (S) 827969-1*   86   **8-12**
Composer: Rupert Holmes. Conductor: Michael Starobin. Cast: Betty Buckley; Cleo
Laine; George Rose; Patti Cottenour; Howard McGillian; others.

EGYPTIAN
Soundtrack (1954) ....*Decca (M) DL-9014*   54   **30-40**
Soundtrack (1954) .... *Decca (SE) DL7-9014*   59   **20-25**
Soundtrack (1954) ....*MCA (SE) 2029e*   72   **8-10**
Composer: Alfred Newman; Bernard Herrmann. Conductor: Alfred Newman.

EIGER SANCTION
Soundtrack (1975) ....*MCA (S) 2088*   75   **15-25**
Composer: John Williams. Conductor: John Williams.

8 AND ONE-HALF
Soundtrack (1963) .... *RCA Victor (M) FOC-6*   63   **25-30**
Soundtrack (1963) .... *RCA Victor (S) FSO-6*   63   **35-40**
Composer: Nino Rota. Conductor: Nino Rota.

EIGHT ON THE LAM
Soundtrack (1967) ....*United Artists (M) UAL-5156*   67   **12-15**
Soundtrack (1967) .... *United Artists (S) UAS-5156*   67   **15-20**
Composer: George Romanas. Conductor: Al Caiola.

EILEEN
Studio Cast (1917) .... *RCA Victor/Camden (M) CAL-210*   54   **80-100**
One side has music from *Polonaise*.
Composer: Victor Herbert; Henry Blossom. POLONAISE: Bronislaw Kaper; John Latouche.
Conductor: Harold Coates (both).

EL CID
Soundtrack (1961) ....*MGM (M) E-3977*   62   **35-40**
Soundtrack (1961) .... *MGM (S) SE-3977*   62   **45-50**
Composer: Miklos Rozsa. Conductor: Miklos Rozsa.

EL DORADO
Soundtrack (1967) ....*Epic (M) FLM-13114*   67   **40-50**
Soundtrack (1967) .... *Epic (S) FLS-15114*   67   **55-65**
Composer: Nelson Riddle. Conductor: Nelson Riddle.

EL GRANDE DE COCA COLA
Original Cast (1973) ....*Bottle Cap (S) BC-1001*   73   **50-55**
7-inch LP.
Composer: The Cast. Cast: Ron House; Allan Sherman; John Neville-Andrews; Sally Willis.

EL TOPO
Soundtrack (1972) .... *Apple (S) SWAO-3388*   72   **$25-35**
Composer: Alexandro Jodorowsky.

ELECTRA GLIDE IN BLUE
Soundtrack (1973) .... *United Artists (S) UA-LA062-H*   73   **20-25**
Gatefold cover, with 24-page booklet and two posters.
Composer: James William Guercio; others.

ELECTRIC COMPANY TV SHOW (SONGS FROM)
TV Soundtrack (1973) .... *Disneyland (S) 1350*   73   **8-12**
Cast: Tom Bahlor; Diana Lee; Idasue McCune; Jerry Whitman.

ELECTRIC DREAMS
Soundtrack (1984) .... *Virgin (S) SE-39600*   84   **8-10**
Composer: Various. Cast: Giorgio Moroder; Philip Oakey; Jeff Lynne; Culture Club; Helen
Terry; Heaven 17; P. Arnold.

ELECTRIC HORSEMAN
Soundtrack (1980) .... *Columbia (S) JS-36327*   80   **8-10**
Composer: Willie Nelson; others. Cast: Willie Nelson.

ELEPHANT CALF
Original Cast (1967) .... *Asch (M) FL-9831*   67   **15-20**
Composer: Arnold Black; Bertolt Brecht; Eric Bently. Cast: James Antonio; Hilda Brauner;
Beeson Carroll; Logan Ramsey (piano).

ELEPHANT CALLED SLOWLY:
see AN ELEPHANT CALLED SLOWLY

ELEPHANT MAN
Soundtrack (1981) .... *Pacific Arts (S) 143*   81   **10-12**
Soundtrack (1981) .... *20th Century-Fox (S) 632*   Re   **8-12**
Composer: John Morris. Conductor: John Morris.

ELEPHANT STEPS
Original Cast (1970) .... *Columbia (S) M2X-33044*   70   **15-20**
Original Cast (1970) .... *Columbia (S) 2MG-33044*   Re   **8-10**
Above two are double LP sets.
Composer: Stanley Silverman; Richard Foreman. Conductor: Michael Tilson Thomas.
Cast: Karen Altman; Susan Belling; Luther Enstad.

ELEVEN AGAINST THE ICE
TV Soundtrack (1958) .... *RCA Victor (M) LPM-1618*   58   **45-55**
Composer: Kenyon Hopkins. Conductor: Kenyon Hopkins. Cast: Jimmy Simmons.

ELIZABETH TAYLOR IN LONDON
TV Soundtrack (1963) .... *Colpix (M) CP-459*   63   **40-50**
TV Soundtrack (1963) .... *Colpix (S) SCP-459*   63   **60-75**
Composer: John Barry. Conductor: Johnnie Spence. Cast: Elizabeth Taylor (narration).

ELMER BERNSTEIN: A MAN AND HIS MOVIES
Soundtrack .... *Mainstream (M) 56094*   67   **10-15**
Soundtrack .... *Mainstream (S) S-6094*   67   **15-20**
Movie themes, including: *To Kill a Mockingbird, Walk on the Wild Side, The Man with the Golden Arm,
Mutiny on the Bounty, The Carpetbaggers, Rat Race, Sweet Smell of Success, Anna Lucasta* and *Sudden
Fear.*
Composer: Elmer Bernstein.

ELMER GANTRY
Soundtrack (1960) .... *United Artists (M) UAL-4069*   60   **50-60**
Soundtrack (1960) .... *United Artists (S) UAS-5069*   60   **60-75**

Soundtrack (1960) ....*United Artists (M) DF-6*	63	**$25-30**
Soundtrack (1960) ....*United Artists (S) DFS-56*	63	**30-40**
One side has music from *The Vikings*.		
Soundtrack (1960) ....*MCA (S) 39070*	86	**8-10**
Composer: Andre Previn. **Conductor:** Andre Previn.		

ELSA LANCHESTER HERSELF

Original Cast (1961) ....*Verve (M) MGV-15024*	61	**25-30**
Original Cast (1961) ....*Verve (S) V6-15024*	61	**35-45**
Cast: Elsa Lanchester.		
Studio Cast (1961) ....*Hi-Fi (M) R-405*	61	**15-20**
Contains only three show tunes.		
Studio Cast (1961) ....*Tradition (S) 2065*	Re	**10-12**
Studio Cast (1961) ....*Tradition (SE) 2091*		**10-12**
Cast: Elsa Lanchester.		

ELVIS

TV Soundtrack (1979) ....*Dick Clark (S) TVLP-79DC*	79	**10-20**

Composer: Various. **Cast:** Ronnie McDowell (performs the vocals of Kurt Russell, who portrayed Elvis in the film); Chip Young (guitar); Dale Sellers (guitar); David Briggs (keyboards); Bobby Ogden (keyboards); Buddy Harmon (drums); Mike Leech (bass); Charlie McCoy (harmonica); Jordanaires (vocals); Kathy Westmoreland (vocals).

ELVIS (NBC-TV SPECIAL)

TV Soundtrack (1968) ....*RCA Victor (M) LPM-4088*	68	**15-20**
Orange label. Rigid disc.		
TV Soundtrack (1968) ....*RCA Victor (M) LPM-4088*	72	**10-15**
Orange label. Flexible disc.		
TV Soundtrack (1968) ....*RCA Victor (M) LPM-4088*	76	**10-20**
Tan label.		
TV Soundtrack (1968) ....*RCA Victor (M) AFM1-4088*	77	**10-15**
TV Soundtrack (1968) ....*RCA Victor (M) AYM1-3894*	81	**5-10**

ELVIS (NBC-TV SPECIAL) (continued)

TV Soundtrack (1968) . . . . *RCA Victor (M) DVM1-0704*   85   **$25-35**
Special Products issue. Exclusive offer from HBO (Home Box Office) for cable TV subscribers. Actual title of HBO broadcast of the 1968 Burbank sessions: "Elvis—One Night With You." Includes poster. **Composer:** Elvis Presley; Jerry Leiber; Mike Stoller; W. Earl Brown; others. **Cast:** Elvis Presley; Scotty Moore (guitar); D.J. Fontana (drums); Charlie Hodge (guitar, vocals); Tom Tedesco (guitar); Hal Blaine (drums); Mike Deasy (guitar); Alan Fortas (tambourine); NBC Studio Orchestra. (With dialogue.)

ELVIS: ALOHA FROM HAWAII VIA SATELLITE

TV Soundtrack (1973) . . . . *RCA Victor (EP) DTFO-200*   73   **75-100**
Six-song, stereo EP for jukebox play. Includes 10 jukebox title strips.

TV Soundtrack (1973) . . . . *RCA Victor (Q) VPSX-6089*   73   **1,000-2,000**
With "Chicken of the Sea" sticker applied to front cover. Includes programming insert sheet Promotional issue for the Van Camps Company only.

TV Soundtrack (1973) . . . . *RCA Victor (Q) VPSX-6089*   73   **$75-90**
Song titles not printed on cover itself, but on a gold sticker applied to cover.

TV Soundtrack (1973) . . . . *RCA Victor (Q) VPSX-6089*   73   **200-250**
Promotional issue only. Titles and programming information are printed on a white sticker, applied to front cover.

TV Soundtrack (1973) . . . . *RCA Victor (Q) VPSX-6089*   73   **25-30**
Song titles are printed on back cover.

TV Soundtrack (1973) . . . . *RCA Victor (Q) CPD2-2642*   74   **10-15**
The above five are all double LP sets.

Composer: Various. **Conductor:** Joe Guercio. **Cast:** Elvis Presley; James Burton (guitar); John Wilkinson (guitar); Ronnie Tutt (drums); Jerry Scheff (bass); Glen D. Hardin (piano); Charlie Hodge (guitar, vocals); Kathy Westmoreland (vocals); Sweet Inspirations (vocals); J.D. Sumner and the Stamps (vocals); Joe Guercio and His Orchestra. (With dialogue.)

ELVIS IN CONCERT

TV Soundtrack (1977) . . . . *RCA Victor (S) APL2-2587*   77   **15-20**
Double LP set.

TV Soundtrack (1977) . . . . *RCA Victor (S) CPL2-2587*   82   **12-15**
Double LP set.

Composer: Various. **Conductor:** Joe Guercio. **Cast:** Elvis Presley; James Burton (guitar); John Wilkinson (guitar); Jerry Scheff (bass); Ronnie Tutt (drums); Glen D. Hardin (piano); Sherrill Nielsen (vocals); Vernon Presley (dialogue); J.D.Sumner and the Stamps (vocals); Sweet Inspirations (vocals); Joe Guercio and His Orchestra. (With dialogue.)

ELVIS LIVE AT THE LOUISIANA HAYRIDE

Radio Cast (1954-1956) . . . . *Louisiana Hayride (M) LH-3061*   83   **15-20**
Full title: *Elvis . . . the Beginning Years 1954 to '56 Live At the Louisiana Hayride, Where It All Began.* From KWKH radio broadcasts, Shreveport, Louisiana.

Radio Cast (1955-1956) . . . . *Music Works (M) PB-3601*   82   **10-15**
Actual title: *Elvis: The First Live Recordings.* A partial reissue of LH-3061.

Radio Cast (1954-1955) . . . . *Music Works (M) PB-3602*   82   **10-15**
Actual title: *Elvis: The Hillbilly Cat.* A partial reissue of LH-3061.

Radio Cast (1954-56) . . . . *Premore (M) PL-589*   90   **8-12**
Full title: *Early Elvis 1954-1956 Live At the Louisiana Hayride.* A mail-order only offer from the Solo Cup Co. Reissue of Louisiana Hayride LH-3061.

Composer: Various. **Cast:** Elvis Presley; Scotty Moore (guitar); Bill Black (bass); D.J. Fontana (drums); Frank Page (emcee); David Kent (narration).

EMERALD FOREST
Soundtrack (1985) . . . . *Varese Sarabande (S) STV-81244*   85   **$8-12**
Composer: Junior Homrich; Brian Gascoigne.

EMIL AND THE DETECTIVES
Soundtrack (1964) . . . . *Disneyland (M) DO-1262*   64   **12-15**
Cast: Walter Slezak (narration).

EMILY
Soundtrack (1976) . . . . *Stanyan (Q) SRQ-4025*   76   **40-45**
Composer: Rod McKuen. Conductor: Alyn Ainsworth.

EMMANUELLE
Soundtrack (1975) . . . . *Arista (S) AL-4036*   75   **20-25**
Composer: Pierre Bachelet; Herve Roy; Howard Blaikley. Conductor: Pierre Bachelet;
Herve Roy.

EMPEROR WALTZ
Studiotrack (1949) . . . . *Decca (M) DL-5272*   49   **40-50**
10-inch LP. One side has music from *Top o' the Morning*.
Composer: James VanHeusen; John Burke; others. Conductor: Victor Young; Simon Rady.
Cast: Bing Crosby; Ann Blyth; Jeff Alexander Chorus.
Also see BUT BEAUTIFUL

EMPIRE STRIKES BACK
Soundtrack (1980) . . . . *RSO (S) RS-1-3081*   80   **10-12**
Soundtrack (1980) . . . . *RSO (S) 827580-1*   Re   **8-10**
Soundtrack (1980) . . . . *RSO (S) RS-2-4201*   80   **12-15**
Double LP set.
Composer: John Williams. Cast: Malachi Throne (narration); Mark Hamill; Harrison Ford;
Carrie Fisher; Billy Dee Williams; Anthony Daniels; James Earl Jones; Frank Oz; London
Symphony Orchestra.
Soundtrack (1980) . . . . *Chalfont (S) SDG-313*   80   **15-20**
Digital recording.
Composer: John Williams. Conductor: Charles Gerhardt. Cast: National Philharmonic
Orchestra.
Soundtrack (1980) . . . . *RSO (S) RS-1-3079*   80   **8-12**
Disco version.
Composer: John Williams. Conductor: Boris Midney. Cast: London Symphony Orchestra.

ENCHANTED COTTAGE
Soundtrack (1945) . . . . *Entr' acte (M) ERM-6002*   79   **$8-10**
  Has music originally issued on 78 rpm singles. Also contains Miklos Rozsa's *Kipling's Jungle Book*
  and *The Paradine Case*, by Franz Waxman.
  Composer: Roy Webb. KIPLING'S JUNGLE BOOK: Miklos Rozsa. PARADINE CASE: Roy
  Webb; Franz Waxman. **Conductor:** KIPLING'S JUNGLE BOOK: Miklos Rozsa. PARADINE
  CASE: Constantin Bakaleinikoff; Franz Waxman. **Cast:** KIPLING'S JUNGLE BOOK: Sabu
  (narrator).

ENCORE! MORE OF THE MUSIC OF HENRY MANCINI
Studiotrack (1967) . . . . *RCA Victor (M) LPM-3887*   67   **10-15**
Studiotrack (1967) . . . . *RCA Victor (S) LSP-3887*   67   **10-20**
  Music from *Exodus, The Man with the Golden Arm, Lili, Doctor Zhivago, Captain from Castile, Laura,
  Days of Wine and Roses, Charade, Moon River, A Hard Day's Night, Born Free, Moulin Rouge, Mondo
  Cane, Black Orpheus, Zorba the Greek* and *The Umbrellas of Cherbourg*.
  Composer: Henry Mancini; others. **Conductor:** Henry Mancini.

ENDLESS LOVE
Soundtrack (1981) . . . . *Mercury (S) SRM 1-2001*   81   **10-12**
Soundtrack (1981) . . . . *Mercury (S) 826277-1*   81   **8-10**
  Composer: Jonathan Tunick; Lionel Richie. **Cast:** Diana Ross; Lionel Richie; Kiss; Cliff
  Richard.

ENDLESS SUMMER
Soundtrack (1966) . . . . *World Pacific (M) WP-1832*   66   **15-20**
Soundtrack (1966) . . . . *World Pacific (S) ST-1832*   66   **20-30**
  Composer: John Blakeley. **Cast:** Sandals.

ENEMY MINE
Soundtrack (1985) . . . . *Varese Sarabande (S) STV-81271*   85   **20-25**
  Composer: Maurice Jarre. **Conductor:** Maurice Jarre. **Cast:** Munich, West Germany,
  Studio Orchestra.

ENGLAND MADE ME
Soundtrack (1973) . . . . *East Coast (S) 1062*   **8-12**
  Composer: John Scott. **Conductor:** John Scott. **Cast:** Peter Finch; Michael York; London
  Philharmonic Orchestra; Lana Cantrell.

ENOLA GAY
TV Soundtrack (1980) . . . . *Varese Sarabande (S) STV-81149*   81   **8-12**
  Digital mix.
  Composer: Maurice Jarre. **Conductor:** Maurice Jarre.

ENTER LAUGHING
Soundtrack (1967) . . . . *Liberty (M) LOM-17004*   67   **12-15**
Soundtrack (1967) . . . . *Liberty (S) LOS-17004*   67   **15-20**
  Composer: Quincy Jones. **Conductor:** Quincy Jones.

ENTER THE DRAGON
Soundtrack (1973) . . . . *Warner Bros. (S) BS-2727*   73   **10-12**
  Composer: Lalo Schifrin. **Conductor:** Lalo Schifrin.

EQUUS
Soundtrack (1977) . . . . *United Artists (S) UA-LA839-1*   77   **10-12**
Soundtrack (1977) . . . . *Liberty (S) LT-839*   Re   **8-10**
  Composer: Richard Rodney Bennett. **Conductor:** Angela Morley. **Cast:** Richard Burton;
  Peter Firth. (With dialogue.)

ERASERHEAD
Soundtrack (1977) . . . . *I.R.S. (S) SP-70027*   82   **8-10**
  Composer: Thomas "Fats" Waller; Peter Ivers; David Lynch. **Cast:** John Nance; Charlotte
  Stewart; Allen Joseph; Jeanne Bates; Laurel Near. (With dialogue.)

ERIC SOYA'S 17
Soundtrack (1967) .... *Mercury (M) MG-21115*   67 $15-20
Soundtrack (1967) .... *Mercury (S) SR-61115*   67   20-25
  Composer: Ole Hoyer.

ERNEST IN LOVE
Original Cast (1960) .... *Columbia (M) OL-5530*   60   40-50
Original Cast (1960) .... *Columbia (S) OS-2027*   60   50-55
Original Cast (1960) .... *Columbia (M) OL-5530*   64   15-20
Original Cast (1960) .... *Columbia (S) OS-2027*   64   20-25
  Reissue identification information unavailable at this time.
  Composer: Lee Pockriss; Anne Croswell. Conductor: Liza Redfield. Cast: Leila Martin;
  John Irving; Gerrianne Raphael; Louis Edmonds; Sara Seegar; Christina Gillespie; George
  Hall; Margot Harley; Lucy Landau; Alan Shayne.

ERTEGUN'S NEW YORK - NEW YORK CABARET MUSIC
Studiotrack .... *Atlantic (S) 81817-1*   87   40-50
  Six LP boxed set. Includes 12-page booklet.
  Composer: Various. Cast: Mae Barnes; Joe Bushkin; Barbara Carroll; Eddie Condon; Chris
  Connor; Jimmy Daniels; Goldie Hawkins; Greta Keller; Jimmy Lyon; Carmen McRae; Mabel
  Mercer; Joe Mooney; Hugh Shannon; Bobby Short; Ted Straeter; Sylvia Syms; Billy Taylor;
  Mel Torme; Cy Walter; Joe Bushkin.

ESCAPE FROM NEW YORK
Soundtrack (1981) .... *Varese Sarabande (S) STV-81134*   81   8-10
  Composer: John Carpenter. Conductor: John Carpenter. Cast: John Carpenter; Alan Howarth.

ESCAPE ME NEVER:
see BERNARD HERRMANN CONDUCTS GREAT BRITISH FILM SCORES

ESCAPE TO WITCH MOUNTAIN
Soundtrack (1975) .... *Disneyland (S) DS-3809*   75   8-10
  Composer: Johnny Mandel.

ESTABLISHMENT
Original Cast (1963) .... *Riverside (M) RM-850*   63   35-50
  Skits.
  Composer: Peter Cook; The Cast. Cast: Eleanor Bron; John Bird; Original London Company.

ETERNAL SEA
Soundtrack (1955) .... *Citadel (M) CT 7021*   82   8-10
  Also contains the Elmer Bernstein soundtrack from *Make Haste to Live*.
  Composer: Elmer Bernstein. Conductor: Elmer Bernstein.

ETHEL MERMAN - A MUSICAL AUTOBIOGRAPHY
Studio Cast .... *Decca (M) DX-153*   40-60
  Double LP, boxed set. Narrated by Ethel Merman, with 34 songs from various shows.
  Composer: George Gershwin; Ira Gershwin; Cole Porter; Irving Berlin; others.
  Conductor: Buddy Cole; Jay Blackton; Gordon Jenkins; Sy Oliver. Cast: Ethel
  Merman; Buddy Cole Quartet; Joan Carroll; Harry Sosnik; Garth; Turner and Bibb;
  Ray Middleton; Ray Bolger.

ETHEL MERMAN ON STAGE
(WITH GERTRUDE NIESEN)
Original Cast (1956) ....:....................... *Vik (M) LVA-1004*   56   25-40
  Cast: Ethel Merman; Gertrude Niesen.
  Also see MERMAN IN VEGAS

ETHEL WATERS:
see CABIN IN THE SKY

EUBIE
Original Cast (1978) .... *Warner Bros. (S) HS-3267*   78   **$10-15**
  Composer: Eubie Blake; others. **Conductor:** Vicki Carter. **Cast:** Ethel Beatty; Gregory
  Hines; Lonnie McNeil; Terry Burrell; Lynnie Godfrey; Maurice Hines; Mel Johnson, Jr.;
  Janet Powell; Marion Ramsey; Alaina Reed; Jeffrey V. Thompson.

EUROPEAN HOLIDAY
  Studio Cast .... *Industrial SAS Airlines (M) TV-22216/7*   **50-60**
    10-inch LP. Gatefold cover. A Mitch Miller Musical, produced for Scandinavian Airlines. Side
    two has three native Scandinavian tunes. Promotional issue only.
   Composer: Lee Thornsby; Douglas Lance. **Conductor:** Jimmy Carroll. **Cast:** Michael
    Stewart; Jill Corey; Jerry Vale; Jonathan Winters; George Perrin; Mitch Miller and His
    Orchestra; Michael Stewart Chorus.

EUROPEANS
  Soundtrack (1980) ....*Gramavision (S) 1010*   81   **10-12**
    Composer: Stephen Foster; Clara Schumann; Franz Schubert.

EVE OF THE WAR
  Soundtrack (1980) ....*Columbia (S) 43-11148*   80   **8-10**
    12-inch disco press. One side has *Horsell Common and the Heat Ray.*

EVENING WITH, AN:
see AN EVENING WITH

EVERY GOOD BOY DESERVES FAVOR
  Original London Cast (1979) ....*RCA Victor (S) ABL1-2855*   79   **8-10**
    Composer: Andre Previn; Tom Stoppard. **Conductor:** Andre Previn. **Cast:** Ian McKellen;
    Ian Richardson; Patrick Stewart; Elizabeth Spriggs; Philip Locke; Andrew Sheldon.

EVERY WHICH WAY BUT LOOSE
  Soundtrack (1979) .... *Elektra (S) 5E-503*   79   **8-10**
    Composer: Various. **Cast:** Eddie Rabbitt; Charlie Rich; Mel Tillis.

EVERYBODY'S ALL-AMERICAN
  Soundtrack (1988) .... *Capitol (S) C1-91184*   88   **8-10**
    Composer: Various. **Cast:** Nat "King" Cole; Shirley and Lee; Lloyd Price; Jesse Hill; Hank
    Ballard and the Midnighters; Jaguars; Barbara Lynn; Smiley Lewis; Dietra Hicks and Evan
    Rogers; Don Gardner and Dee Dee Ford.

EVERYTHING I HAVE IS YOURS
Soundtrack (1952) .... *MGM (M) E-187*   53   **$40-50**
One side has music from *Lili*.
Composer: Burton Lane; Johnny Green; others. LILI: Bronislau Kaper. **Conductor:** David
Rose; Johnny Green. LILI: Bronislau Kaper. **Cast:** LILI: Leslie Caron; Mel Ferrer.
Also see I LOVE MELVIN

EVITA
Original London Cast (1976) .... *MCA (S) 2-11003*   76   **10-20**
Original concept album.
Composer: Andrew Lloyd Webber; Tim Rice. **Conductor:** Anthony Bowles. **Cast:** Paul
Jones; Julie Covington; C.T. Wilkinson; London Philharmonic Orchestra; Tony Christie;
Barbara Dickson; Mike Smith; Mike d'Abo; Christopher Neil.
Original New York Cast (1979) .... *MCA (S) 2-11007*   79   **10-15**
Above two are double LP sets. This opera is based on the life of Eva Peron.
Composer: Andrew Lloyd Webber. **Conductor:** Rene Weigert. **Cast:** Patti Lupone; Mandy
Patinkin; Bob Gunton; Jane Ohringer; Mark Syers.
Studio Cast (1978) .... *MCA (S) 3527*   78   **8-10**
Composer: Andrew Lloyd Webber; Tim Rice. **Conductor:** Anthony Dowles. **Cast:** Elaine
Page; David Essex; Joss Ackland; Siobhan McCarthy; Mark Ryan.
Studio Cast (1979) .... *RSO (S) RS-1-3061*   79   **10-12**
Disco version.
Composer: Andrew Lloyd Webber; Tim Rice. **Cast:** Festival.

EXCHANGE:
see TAMALPIAS EXCHANGE

EXCITING HONG KONG:
see HONG KONG

EXODUS
Soundtrack (1960) .... *United Artists (M) UAL-3123*   60   **10-15**
Soundtrack (1960) .... *United Artists (S) UAS-6123*   60   **15-20**
Conductor: Mitchell Powell.
Soundtrack .... *MCA (S) 39065*   Re   **8-10**
Composer: Ernest Gold. **Conductor:** Mitchell Powell. **Cast:** Hollywood Studio Orchestra.
Soundtrack (1960) .... *RCA Victor (EP) LPC-129*   60   **10-15**
Soundtrack (1960) .... *RCA Victor (M) LOC-1058*   60   **10-15**
Soundtrack (1960) .... *RCA Victor (S) LSO-1058*   60   **15-20**
Soundtrack (1960) .... *RCA Victor (S) AYL1-3872*   81   **5-10**
Composer: Ernest Gold. **Conductor:** Ernest Gold. **Cast:** Sinfonia of London Orchestra.
Studiotrack (1960) .... *United Artists (M) UAL-3125*   61   **10-15**
Studiotrack (1960) .... *United Artists (S) UAS-6125*   61   **15-20**
Also see APARTMENT

EXODUS TO JAZZ
Studiotrack (1961) .... *Vee Jay (M) VJLP-3016*   61   **15-20**
Studiotrack (1961) .... *Vee Jay (S) SR-3016*   61   **20-30**
Cast: Eddie Harris.

EXORCIST
Soundtrack (1974) .... *Warner Bros. (S) WS-2774*   74   **20-25**
Composer: Krzysztof Penderecki; Mike Oldfield; George Crumb; others.
Conductor: Leonard Slatkin.

EXORCIST II - THE HERETIC
Soundtrack (1977) .... *Warner Bros. (S) BS-3068*   77   **10-15**
Composer: Ennio Morricone. **Conductor:** Ennio Morricone.

EXPERIMENT IN TERROR

Soundtrack (1962) .... *RCA Victor (M) LPM-2442*   62   **$35-45**
Soundtrack (1962) .... *RCA Victor (S) LSP-2442*   62   **45-55**
   On above two, the cover pictures Lee Remick being attacked from behind.
Soundtrack (1962) .... *RCA Victor (M) LPM-2442*   62   **25-30**
Soundtrack (1962) .... *RCA Victor (S) LSP-2442*   62   **35-40**
   On above two, the cover pictures two mannequins.
  Composer: Henry Mancini. **Conductor:** Henry Mancini.

EXPLORERS

Soundtrack (1985) .... *MCA (S) 6148*   85   **8-10**
  Composer: Jerry Goldsmith.

EXPLORING THE UNKNOWN

Studiotrack (1955) .... *RCA Victor (EP) EPC-1025*   55   **25-35**
  Triple EP set.
Studiotrack (1955) .... *RCA Victor (M) LPC-1025*   55   **30-50**
  Composer: Leith Stevens. **Conductor:** Leith Stevens. **Cast:** Walter Schurmann Chorus;
  Paul Frees (narration).

EXPRESSO BONGO

London Cast .... *AEI (S) 1110*   **8-10**

EXTREME PREJUDICE

Soundtrack (1987) .... *Intermedia (S) MAF-7001*   87   **8-10**

EYE OF THE NEEDLE

Soundtrack (1981) .... *Varese Sarabande (S) STV-81138*   81   **8-10**
  Composer: Miklos Rozsa. **Conductor:** Miklos Rozsa . **Cast:** Nürnberg Symphony Orchestra.

EYES OF LAURA MARS

Soundtrack (1978) .... *Columbia (S) JS-35487*   78   **8-10**
  Composer: Artie Kane. **Conductor:** Artie Kane. **Cast:** Barbra Streisand; Odyssey; K.C.
  and the Sunshine Band; Michalski and Oosterveen; Michael Zager Band.

F

F.I.S.T.
Soundtrack (1978) . . . .*United Artists (S) UA-LA897-H*   79   **$8-10**
Composer: Bill Conti. Conductor: Bill Conti.

F/X
Soundtrack (1986) . . . . *Varese Sarabande (S) STV-81276*   86   **10-15**
Composer: Bill Conti.

FABULOUS BAKER BOYS
Soundtrack . . . .*GRP (S) GR-2002*   **8-10**
Composer: Dave Grusin. Cast: Dave Grusin; Michelle Pfeiffer; Duke Ellington Orchestra; Benny Goodman Orchestra; Earl Palmer Trio.

FACADE
Original Cast . . . . *London (M) A-4104*   55   **20-30**
Conductor: Anthony Collins. Cast: Dame Edith Sitwell; Peter Pears; English Opera Group Ensemble.

FACE IN THE CROWD
Soundtrack (1957) . . . . *Capitol (EP) EPA-1863*   57   **15-20**
Soundtrack (1957) . . . . *Capitol (M) W-872*   57   **40-50**
Composer: Tom Glazer. Cast: Andy Griffith; Lee Remick; Walter Matthau; Girls' Trio. (With dialogue.)

FACES
Soundtrack (1968) . . . . *Columbia (S) OS-3290*   68   **15-20**
Composer: Jack Ackerman. Cast: Jack Ackerman.

FADE OUT FADE IN
Original Cast (1964) . . . . *ABC (M) OC-3*   64   **25-30**
Original Cast (1964) . . . . *ABC (S) OCS-3*   64   **35-40**
Composer: Jule Styne; Betty Comden; Adolph Green. Conductor: Colin Romoff. Cast: Carol Burnett; Jack Cassidy; Dick Patterson; Tina Louise; Tiger Haynes; Lou Jacobi; Mitchell Jason.

FAGGOT
Original Cast (1973) . . . . *Blue Pear (M) BP-1008*   73
Composer: Al Carmines. Cast: Peggy Atkinson; Essie Borden; Lou Bullock; Al Carmines; Marilyn Child; Tony Clark; Frank Coppola; Lee Guilliatt; Bruce Hopkins; Julie Kurnitz; Philip Owens; David Pursley; Bill Reynolds; Ira Siff; David Summers.

FAHRENHEIT 451:
see FANTASY FILM WORLD OF BERNARD HERRMANN

FALCON AND THE SNOWMAN
Soundtrack (1985) .... *EMI America (S) SV-17150*   85   **$8-10**
   Composer: Pat Metheny; Lyle Mays. **Cast:** Pat Metheny Group; David Bowie.

FALL OF THE ROMAN EMPIRE
Soundtrack (1964) ....\........... *Columbia (M) OL-6060*   64   **65-75**
Soundtrack (1964) .... *Columbia (S) OS-2460*   64   **60-65**
   Composer: Dimitri Tiomkin. **Conductor:** Dimitri Tiomkin.

FAME
Soundtrack (1980) .... *RSO (S) RPO-1023*   80   **15-20**
   Limited edition, three-track sampler.
Soundtrack (1980) .... *RSO (S) 1-3080*   80   **8-12**
Soundtrack (1980) .... ,.. .... *RSO (S) 825388-1*   80   **8-10**
   Composer: Michael Gore; Dean Pitchford; others. **Cast:** Irene Cara; Paul McCrane; Linda
   Clifford; Wade Lassister; Michael Gore and Steven Margoshes (pianos).
TV Soundtrack (1982) .... *RCA Victor (S) AFL1-4259*   82   **8-12**

FAMILY AFFAIR
Original Cast (1962) .... *United Artists (M) UAL-4099*   62   **30-40**
Original Cast (1962) .... *United Artists (S) UAS-5099*   62   **40-50**
   Composer: John Kander; James Goldman; William Goldman. **Conductor:** Stanley Lebowsky.
   Cast: Shelley Berman; Eileen Heckart; Morris Carnovsky; Larry Kert; Bibi Osterwald; Gino
   Conforti; Jack De Lon; Rita Gardner; Linda Lavin; Alice Nunn; Bill McDonald; Bibi
   Osterwald; Beryl Towbin.

FAMILY WAY
Soundtrack (1967) .... *London (M) M-76007*   67   **40-50**
Soundtrack (1967) ....'............ *London (S) MS-82007*   67   **45-55**
   Counterfeit copies of this LP can be identified by the poor quality reproduction of the back cover.
   Composer: Paul McCartney.

FANNY
Original Cast (1954) .... *RCA Victor (EP) EOC-1015*   54   **15-20**
Original Cast (1954) .... *RCA Victor (EP) EOC-1015*   54   **15-25**
   Triple EP set.
Original Cast (1954) .... *RCA Victor (M) LOC-1015*   54   **20-30**
Original Cast (1954) .... *RCA Victor (SE) LSO-1015*   59   **10-20**
   Composer: Harold Rome. **Conductor:** Lehman Engel. **Cast:** Ezio Pinza; Walter Slezak;
   Florence Henderson; Nejla Ates; Mohammed El Bakkar; Edna Preston; Gerald Price; Lloyd
   Reese; William Tabbert.
Soundtrack (1961) .... *Warner Bros. (M) W-1416*   61   **20-25**
Soundtrack (1961) .... *Warner Bros. (S) WS-1416*   61   **30-35**
   Composer: Harold Rome. **Conductor:** Morris Stoloff.

FANNY BRICE: STORY IN SONG
Studiotrack (1958) .... *MGM (M) E-3704*   58   **15-20**
Studiotrack (1958) .... *MGM (S) SE-3704*   58   **20-30**
   Cast: Kaye Ballard.

FANNY HILL
Soundtrack (1971) .... *Canyon (S) S-7700*   71   **12-15**
   Composer: Clay Pitts. **Conductor:** Clay Pitts. **Cast:** Oven; Frank Thomas.

FANTASIA
Soundtrack (1940) .... *Buena Vista (M) WDS-101*   57   **25-35**
Soundtrack (1940) .... *Buena Vista (SE) WDX-101e*   57   **25-30**
   Above two are triple LP sets with gatefold covers, and color booklets.

Soundtrack .... *Buena Vista (S) STER-101*   Re   **$15-20**
Soundtrack (1982) .... *Buena Vista (S) VIS-104*   82   **15-20**
Digital recording.
Conductor: Leopold Stokowski. **Cast:** Philadelphia Orchestra.
Also see PETER AND THE WOLF

FANTASTIC FILM MUSIC OF ALBERT GLASSER, VOL.1
Soundtrack .... *Starlog (M) SR-1001*   79   **8-10**
Contains music from: *The Amazing Colossal Man, The Buckskin Lady, Beginning of the End, The Cyclops, Top of the World, The Cisco Kid, Big Town* and *The Boy and the Pirates.*
Composer: Albert Glasser. **Conductor:** Albert Glasser.

FANTASTIC PLASTIC MACHINE
Soundtrack (1969) .... *Epic (S) BN-26469*   69   **20-25**
Composer: Harry Betts. **Conductor:** Harry Betts.

FANTASTICKS
Original Cast (1960) .... *MGM (M) E-3872*   60   **10-15**
Original Cast (1960) .... *MGM (S) SE-3872*   60   **15-20**
Composer: Harvey Schmidt; Tom Jones. **Conductor:** Julian Stein. **Cast:** Kenneth Nelson; Jerry Orbach; Rita Gardner; William Larsen; Hugh Thomas.

FANTASY FILM WORLD OF BERNARD HERRMANN
Soundtrack .... *London (S) SPC-44207*   **15-20**
Has music from *Journey to the Center of the Earth, The 7th Voyage of Sinbad, The Day the Earth Stood Still* and *Fahrenheit 451.*
Composer: Bernard Herrmann. **Conductor:** Bernard Herrmann. **Cast:** National Philharmonic Orchestra.

FAR FROM THE MADDING CROWD
Soundtrack (1967) .... *MGM (M) 1E-11*   67   **20-25**
Soundtrack (1967) .... *MGM (S) S1E-11*   67   **25-30**
Composer: Richard Rodney Bennett. **Conductor:** Marcus Dods. **Cast:** Isla Cameron; Trevor Lucas.

FAR HORIZONS - THE WESTERN FILM SCORES OF HANS J. SALTER
Soundtrack .... *Medallion (M) ML-313*   82   **8-10**
Has music from: *Battle of Apache Pass, Walk the Proud Land, Man Without a Star, Bend of the River, The Spoilers, Day of the Badman, The Tall Stranger, Untamed Frontier, The Oklahoman, Four Guns to the Border* and *The Horizons.*
Composer: Hans J. Salter. **Conductor:** Hans J. Salter.

FAR NORTH
Soundtrack (1988) .... *Sugar Hill (S) SH-8502*   88   **8-10**
Cast: Red Clay Ramblers.

FAR PAVILIONS
Soundtrack (1983) .... *Chrysalis (S) FV-41464*   83   **8-10**
Composer: Carl Davis. **Conductor:** Carl Davis.

FAREWELL MY LOVELY
Soundtrack (1975) .... *United Artists (S) LT-556*   75   **10-12**
Soundtrack (1975) .... *United Artists (S) UA-LA556-G*   75   **8-10**
Composer: David Shire. **Conductor:** David Shire. **Cast:** Artie Kane (piano); Dick Nash (trombone); Justin Gordon (clarinet, saxophone); others.

FAREWELL TO ARMS
Soundtrack (1957) .... *Capitol (EP) EDM-918*   57   **15-25**
Soundtrack (1957) .... *Capitol (M) W-918*   57   **60-70**
Composer: Mario Nascimbene. **Conductor:** Franco Ferrara.

FASHIONS OF 1934:
see HOORAY FOR HOLLYWOOD

FAST TIMES AT RIDGEMONT HIGH
Soundtrack (1982) .... *Full Moon/Asylum (S) 4-60158*   82   **$10-15**
   Double LP set.
   Composer: Various. **Cast:** Jackson Browne; Jimmy Buffett; Don Felder; Go-Go's; Louise Goffin;
   Sammy Hagar; Don Henley; Gerard McMahon; Graham Nash; Oingo Boingo; Palmer-Jost; Poco;
   Quarterflash; Ravyns; Timothy B. Schmit; Stevie Nicks; Billy Squier; Donna Summer; J. Walsh.

FASTBREAK
Soundtrack (1979) .... *Motown (S) M7-915R1*   79   **8-10**
   Composer: David Shire; James DiPasquale. **Cast:** Billy Preston; Syreeta.

FASTEST GUITAR ALIVE
Soundtrack (1968) .... *MGM (M) E-4475*   68   **10-15**
Soundtrack (1968) .... *MGM (S) SE-4475*   68   **15-20**
Soundtrack (1968) .... *MCA (S) 1437*   86   **8-10**
   Composer: Roy Orbison; Bill Dees. **Conductor:** Fred Karger. **Cast:** Roy Orbison.

FATAL ATTRACTION
Soundtrack (1987) .... *GNP/Crescendo (S) GNPS-8011*   87   **8-10**
   Composer: Maurice Jarre. **Conductor:** Maurice Jarre.

FATAL BEAUTY
Soundtrack (1987) .... *Atlantic (S) 81809-1*   87   **8-10**
   Composer: Harold Faltermeyer; others. **Cast:** Donna Allen; Le Vert; Madam X; Miki Howard;
   Shannon; Debbie Gibson; War; System.

FATHOM
Soundtrack (1967) .... *20th Century-Fox (M) TFM-3195*   67   **25-30**
Soundtrack (1967) .... *20th Century-Fox (S) TFS-4195*   67   **30-35**
   Composer: John Dankworth. **Conductor:** John Dankworth.

FEAR NO EVIL
Soundtrack (1981) .... *Web (S) LP-106*   81   **8-12**
   Composer: Frank Laloggia; David Spear. **Conductor:** Frank Laloggia.

FEDORA
Soundtrack (1978) .... *Varese Sarabande (S) STV-81108*   79   **8-10**
   Composer: Miklos Rozsa. **Conductor:** Miklos Rozsa.

FEDS
Soundtrack (1988) .... *GNP/Crescendo (S) GNPS-8014*   88   **8-10**
   Cast: Albert Collins; Roy Gaines; Barry Goldberg; Electric Boys; Joe Louis Walker.

FEELING GOOD WITH ANNIE
Studio Cast .... *Columbia (S) CC-38362*   **10-12**
   Conductor: Brian Mann. **Cast:** William Woodson (narration); Robin Ignico; Brenda Baker;
   Bill Martin; Al Chalk.

FELIX THE CAT
TV Soundtrack (1959) .... *Cricket (M) CR-28*   59   **15-20**
   Composer: Win Sharples. **Cast:** Jack Mercer.

FELLINI SATYRICON
Soundtrack (1969) .... *United Artists (S) UAS-5208*   70   **15-20**
   Composer: Nino Rota. **Conductor:** Nino Rota.

FELLINI'S ROMA
Soundtrack (1972) .... *United Artists (S) UA-LA052-F*   72   **12-18**
   Composer: Nino Rota. **Conductor:** Carlo Savina.

FEMALE ANIMAL
Soundtrack (1958) .... *Canyon (M) LP-7702*   **10-15**
   Composer: Clay Pitts; Don Payne; Rick Hitchcock. **Conductor:** Clay Pitts; Don Payne;
   Rick Hitchcock.

FEMALE PRISONER
Soundtrack (1969) .... *Columbia (S) OS-3320*   69   **$20-25**
  Composer: Anton Webern; Gustav Mahler; Luciano Berio. **Conductor:** Pierre Boulez; Leonard Bernstein.

FERRY ACROSS THE MERSEY
Soundtrack (1965) .... *United Artists (M) UAL-3387*   65   **15-20**

FERRY CROSS THE MERSEY
Soundtrack (1965) .... *United Artists (S) UAS-6387*   65   **20-25**
  Composer: Gerry Marsden. **Conductor:** George Martin. **Cast:** Gerry and the Pacemakers.

FESTIVAL
Original Cast (1974) .... *Original Cast (S) OC-7916*   74   **8-10**
  Composer: Stephen Downs; Randal Martin. **Conductor:** David Spear. **Cast:** Bill Hutton; Maureen McNamara; Tina Johnson; Michael Magnusen; Lindy Nisbet; Roxann Parker; Michael Rupert; Leon Stewart; Robin Taylor; John Windsor.

FIBER McGEE AND MOLLY
Original Radio Cast .... *Golden Age (M) 5011*   78   **8-10**
  Cast: Jim and Marion Jordan.

FIDDLER ON THE ROOF
Original Cast (1964) .... *RCA Victor (M) LOC-1093*   64   **10-15**
Original Cast (1964) .... *RCA Victor (S) LSO-1093*   64   **15-20**
  Composer: Jerry Bock; Sheldon Harnick. **Conductor:** Milton Greene. **Cast:** Zero Mostel; Maria Karnilova; Beatrice Arthur; Bert Convy; Leonard Frey; Sue Babel; Tanya Everett; Michael Granger; Paul Lipson; Joanna Merlin; Julia Migenes; Austin Pendleton; Carol Sawyer.
Original London Cast (1964) .... *Columbia (S) SX-30742*   64   **10-15**
  Composer: Jerry Bock; Sheldon Harnick. **Conductor:** Gareth Davies. **Cast:** Topol; Miriam Karlin; Paul Whitsun-Jones; Cynthia Grenville; Linda Gardner.
Original German Cast (1964) .... *London (S) SW-99470*   64   **20-25**
  Composer: Jerry Bock; Sheldon Harnick. **Conductor:** Dailbor Brazda. **Cast:** Shmuel Rodensky; Lilly Towska; Eva Berthold.
London Studio Cast (1964) .... *Pickwick (S) SPC-3291*   64   **10-15**
  Composer: Jerry Bock; Sheldon Harnick. **Cast:** Gerry Grant; Rita Williams.
Studio Cast (1968) .... *London (S) SP-44121*   68   **10-15**
  Phase 4 stereo.
  Composer: Sheldon Harnick; Jerry Bock. **Conductor:** Stanley Black. **Cast:** Robert Merrill; Molly Picon; Jacob Kalich; Robert Bowman; Andy Cole; Margaret Eaves; Barbara Moore; Sylvia King; Eddie Lester; Margaret Savage; Mary Thomas; James Tullett; Patricia Whitmore.
Soundtrack (1971) .... *United Artists (S) UAS-10900*   71   **15-18**
  Double LP set.
  Cast: Topol; Norma Crane; Leonard Frey; Molly Picon; Paul Mann.
German Soundtrack (1971) .... *United Artists (S) UAS-301/2*   71   **15-20**
  Double LP set. Same film music as U.S. release, but voices are dubbed in German.
  Composer: Jerry Bock; Sheldon Harnick. **Conductor:** John Williams.
Studiotrack (1964) .... *Capitol (M) T-2216*   64   **10-15**
Studiotrack (1964) .... *Capitol (S) ST-2216*   64   **15-20**
  Cast: Jazz interpretations by Cannonball Adderley.
Studiotrack .... *Columbia (S) PST-3010*   **8-10**
  Conductor: Bernard Herschel.

50th ANNIVERSARY SHOW
TV Soundtrack (1958) .... *RCA Victor (M) LOC-1037*   58   **$20-30**
From General Motors' 50th Anniversary, an NBC-TV color special aired November 17, 1957.
Composer: Various. **Conductor:** Hugo Winterhalter. **Cast:** Pat Boone; Carol Burnett; Dan
Daily; Dinah Shore; Doretta Morrow; Steve Lawrence; Howard Keel; Cyril Ritchard; Claudia
Crawford; Hugo Winterhalter and His Orchestra.

50 YEARS OF FILM
Soundtrack .... *Warner Bros. (S) 3XX-2736*   73   **15-20**
Full title: *50 Years of Film Music (1923 - 1973)*. Triple LP, boxed set with slip-case. Inlcudes
booklet. (With dialogue.)
Soundtrack .... *Warner Bros. (M) 3XX-2737*   73   **15-20**
Triple LP, boxed set with slip-case. Includes booklet. (With dialogue.) A completely different set
than 3XX-2736.
Composer: Various. **Conductor:** Erich Wolfgang Korngold; Max Steiner; Franz Waxman;
Dimitri Tiomkin; Alex North; others. **Cast:** Ginger Rogers; Louis Armstrong; Mary Martin;
Frank Sinatra; Al Jolson; Ruby Keeler; Dick Powell; James Melton; Doris Day; Harry James;
Joan Blondel; Judy Garland; James Cagney; Frances Langford; Johnny "Scat" Davis; others.

55 DAYS AT PEKING
Soundtrack (1963) .... *Columbia (M) CL-2028*   63   **50-55**
Soundtrack (1963) .... *Columbia (S) CS-2028*   63   **65-75**
Composer: Dimitri Tiomkin. **Conductor:** Dimitri Tiomkin. **Cast:** Andy Williams.

51 GREATEST MOTION PICTURE FAVORITES
Studiotrack (1964) .... *Music Voice (M) MM-2009*   64   **10-20**
Studiotrack (1964) .... *Music Voice (S) MS-3009*   64   **15-25**
Medleys of film music.
Composer: Various. **Cast:** Vinnie Bell, his guitar and orchestra.

FIGHTER
Soundtrack (1952) .... *Decca (M) DL-5415*   52   **60-75**
10-inch LP.
Composer: Vicente Gómez. **Cast:** Vicente Gómez (guitar solos).

FILM CLASSICS
Studiotrack .... *RCA Victor (S) XRL 1-402*   81   **8-10**
Classical music as used in recent, popular films.

FILM CLASSICS: TAKE 2
Studiotrack .... *RCA Victor (S) XRL 1-431*   82   **8-10**
More classical music selections from current films.

FILM FESTIVAL
Soundtrack (1969) .... *Colgems (S) 116*   69   **15-20**
Has music from: *The Night of the Generals, Lord Jim, Behold a Pale Horse, The Victors, Murderer's
Row* and others.

FILM MUSIC

Studiotrack (1987) .... *Virgin Movie Music (S) 90674-1*   87   **$8-10**
Volume one.
Studiotrack (1988) .... *Virgin Movie Music (S) 90901-1*   88   **8-10**
Volume two.
Composer: Ennio Morricone. **Conductor:** Ennio Morricone. **Cast:** Ennio Morricone and
His Orchestra.

FILM MUSIC FROM FRANCE

Studiotrack (1962) ....*Philips (M) PHM-200-071*   62   **15-20**
Soundtrack (1962) .... *Philips (S) PHS 600-071*   62   **20-30**
Music from 12 French films.
Composer: Georges Delerue; Mikis Theodorakis; Michel Legrand; T. Albinoni.
Conductor: Georges Delerue; Mikis Theodorakis; Michel Legrand; T. Albinoni.

FILM MUSIC OF HANS J. SALTER

Soundtrack ....*Tony Thomas Productions (S) TT-HS-112*   **30-40**
Private pressing. Double LP set with soundtracks of *The Ghost of Frankenstein, The Magnificent
Doll, Bend of the River* and *Against All Flags.*
Composer: Hans J. Salter.

FILM MUSIC OF HUGO FRIEDHOFER

Soundtrack (1971) .... *Delos (S) 25420*   **10-15**
Has music from *Von Richtofen and Brown* and *Private Parts.*
Composer: Hugo Friedhofer. **Conductor:** Kurt Graunke.

FILM MUSIC OF MAX STEINER

Soundtrack .... *ML (S) 309*   79   **10-12**
Has music from *Sante Fe Trail* (1941), *Life with Father* (1947), *A Star Is Born* (1937), and *Bird
of Paradise* (1932).
Composer: Max Steiner.

FILM SPECTACULAR (VOL. 4 "THE EPIC")

Studiotrack (1972) ....*London (S) SP-44173*   72   **10-15**
Film themes from: *Stagecoach, For whom the Bell Tolls, Doctor Zhivago, Ben-Hur, 2001: A
Space Odyssey, The Sea Hawk, The Alamo* and *Patton.*
Composer: Various. **Conductor:** Stanley Black. **Cast:** London Festival Orchestra and Chorus.

FILM THEMES OF ERNEST GOLD

Studiotrack (1962) .... *London (M) LL-3320*   62   **25-30**
Studiotrack (1962) ....*London (S) PS-320*   62   **40-50**
Music from: *Pressure Point, Saddle Pals, Young Philadelphians, A Child Is Waiting, The Last Sunset*
and others.
Composer: Ernest Gold. **Conductor:** Ernest Gold. **Cast:** Ernest Gold and His Orchestra.

FILMS OF RUSS COLUMBO

Soundtrack .... *Golden Legends (S) 2000/2*   **8-10**
Contains soundtracks from *Broadway Thru a Keyhole* (1933), *Moulin Rouge* (1933), and *Wake Up
and Dream* (1934).
Composer: Russ Columbo.

FINAL COMEDOWN

Soundtrack (1972) ....*Blue Note (S) BST-84415*   72   **10-12**
Composer: Wade Marcus. **Conductor:** Wade Marcus. **Cast:** Grant Green.

FINAL CONFLICT
(THE LAST CHAPTER IN THE OMEN TRILOGY)

Soundtrack (1981) .... *Varese Sarabande (S) STV-81272*   84   **8-10**
Composer: Jerry Goldsmith. **Conductor:** Jerry Goldsmith. **Cast:** National Philharmonic
Orchestra.

FINAL COUNTDOWN
Soundtrack (1980) . . . . *Casablanca (S) NBLP-7232*   80   **$8-10**
  Composer: John Scott. **Conductor:** John Scott.

FINAL EXAM
Soundtrack (1981) . . . . *AEI (S) 3105*   81   ·   **8-10**
  Composer: Gary Scott. **Conductor:** Gary Scott.

FINE MESS
Soundtrack (1986) . . . . *Motown (S) 6180*   86   **8-10**
  Cast: Temptations; Mary Jane Girls; Chico De Barge; Henry Mancini; Smokey Robinson;
  Nick Jameson; Keith and Darryl; Los Lobos; Christine McVie.

FINEST HOURS
Soundtrack (1964) . . . . *Mercury (M) MGP2-104*   64   **25-30**
  Double LP set.
Soundtrack (1964) . . . . : *Mercury (S) SRP2-604*   64   **30-35**
  Composer: Ron Grainer. **Cast:** Orson Welles; Pat Wymark. Narration by Welles and Wymark,
  with voices of Sir Winston Churchill, Neville Chamberlain, and Franklin D. Roosevelt.

FINIAN'S RAINBOW
Original Cast (1947) . . . . *Columbia (EP) A-1520*   48   **15-20**
Original Cast (1947) . . . . *Columbia (M) ML-4062*   48   **30-35**
Original Cast (1947) . . . . *Columbia (SE) OS-2080*   63   **10-15**
Original Cast (1947) . . . . *Columbia Special Products (SE) CS-2080e*   Re   **8-10**
  Composer: Burton Lane; E.Y. Harburg. **Conductor:** Ray Charles **Cast:** Ella Logan; Donald
  Richards; David Wayne; Delores Martin; Sonny Terry; Allen Gilbert; Jerry Laws; Lorenzo Fuller.
Studio Cast (1954) . . . . *Capitol (EP) EBF-561*   54   **10-20**
  Double EP, boxed set.
Studio Cast (1954) . . . . *Capitol (M) H-561*   54   **25-30**
  10-inch LP.
  Composer: Burton Lane; E.Y. Harburg. **Cast:** Ella Logan; George Greeley (pianos).
Original Revival Cast (1960) . . . . *RCA Victor (M) LOC-1057*   40   **10-20**
Original Revival Cast (1960) . . . . *RCA Victor (S) LSO-1057*   60   **15-25**
  Composer: Burton Lane; E.Y. Harburg. **Conductor:** Max Meth. **Cast:** Jeanie Carson; Howard
  Morris; Biff McGuire; Jerry Laws; Carol Brice; Bill Glover; Sorrell Brooke; Colonel Tiger
  Haynes; Bobby Howes; Biff McGuire.
Studio Cast (1963) . . . . *Reprise (M) F-2015*   63   **15-20**
Studio Cast (1963) . . . . *Reprise (S) FS-2015*   63   **20-25**
Studio Cast . . . . *Harmony (S) HS-11286*   Re   **8-12**
  Composer: Burton Lane; E.Y. Harburg. **Conductor:** Morris Stoloff; Ken Lane. **Cast:** Dean
  Martin; Frank Sinatra; Debbie Reynolds; Sammy Davis Jr.; Bing Crosby; Rosemary
  Clooney; McGuire Sisters; Hi-Lo's; Clark Dennis; Lou Monte; Mary Kaye Singers.
Studio Cast (1951) . . . . , ... *RCA Victor (M) LKT-1000*   51   **30-40**
  Composer: Burton Lane; E.Y. Harburg. **Conductor:** Russ Case. **Cast:** Audrey Marsh;
  Jimmy Carroll; Jimmy Blair; Deep River Boys.
Soundtrack (1968) . . . . *Warner Bros. (M) B-2550*   68   **15-20**
Soundtrack (1968) . . . . *Warner Bros. (S) BS-2550*   68   **20-25**
  Composer: Burton Lane; E.Y. Harburg. **Conductor:** Ray Heindorf. **Cast:** Fred Astaire;
  Petula Clark; Tommy Steele; Keenan Wynn.
  Also see REPRISE REPERTORY THEATRE

FINIAN'S RAINBOW AND BRIGADOON REMEMBERED ·
Studiotrack (1959) . . . . *United Artists (M) UAL-3135*   59   **15-20**
Studiotrack (1959) . . . . *United Artists (S) UAS-6035*   59   **20-30**
  Jazz interpretations by Lee and Hal Schaefer.
  Cast: Lee and Hal Schaefer.

FINNEGAN'S WAKE
Soundtrack (1968) .... *RCA Victor (M) VDM-118*   68   **$15-20**
Soundtrack (1968) .... *RCA Victor (S) VDS-118*   68   **20-25**
  Composer: Elliot Kaplan. **Conductor:** Elliot Kaplan. **Cast:** Martin J. Kelly; Jane Reilly.
  (Passages from the James Joyce work.)

FIORELLO!
Original Cast (1959) .... *Capitol (M) WAO-1321*   59   **15-20**
Original Cast (1959) .... *Capitol (S) SWAO-1321*   59   **20-25**
  Composer: Jerry Bock; Sheldon Harnick. **Conductor:** Hal Hastings. **Cast:** Tom Bosley;
  Patricia Wilson; Ellen Hanley; Howard DaSilva; Pat Stanley; Nathaniel Frey; Eileen Rodgers;
  Bob Holiday.
Studio Cast .... *RCA Victor/Camden (M) CAL-599*   59   **10-15**
Studio Cast .... *RCA Victor/Camden (S) CAS-599*   59   **15-20**
  One side has *Sound of Music* by the same cast.
  Composer: Jerry Bock; Sheldon Harnick. **Cast:** Florence Henderson; Sid Bass with His
  Orchestra and Chorus.

FIRE AND ICE
Soundtrack (1987) .... *MCA (S) 6206*   87   **8-10**
  Composer: Various. **Cast:** Marietta; Gary Wright; Panarama; John Denver; Laurie Alda.

FIRE DOWN BELOW
Soundtrack (1957) .... *Decca (M) DL-8597*   57   **75-85**
  Composer: Ken Jones. **Conductor:** Muir Mathieson. **Cast:** Jeri Southern; Ned Washington;
  Lester Lee; Jack Lemmon; Vivian Comma.

FIREFLY
Studio Cast (1951) .... *RCA Victor (M) LM-121*   51   **25-35**
  Composer: Rudolf Friml; Otto Harbach. **Conductor:** Al Goodman. **Cast:** Allan Jones; Martha
  Wright; Elaine Malbin; Hayes Gordon.
Studio Cast (1959) .... *Lion (M) L-70090*   **10-15**
  Composer: Rudolf Friml; Otto Harbach. **Conductor:** Paul Britton. **Cast:** Paul Britton Orchestra.

FIRESTARTER
Soundtrack (1984) .... *MCA (S) 6131*   84   **8-10**
  Composer: Tangerine Dream. **Cast:** Tangerine Dream.

FIREWIND
Soundtrack .... *Sparrow (S) SPR-1004*   **8-10**

FIRST BLOOD
Soundtrack (1982) .... *Regency (S) 9505*   82   **8-10**
  Cast: Dan Hill.

FIRST BORN
Soundtrack (1984) .... *EMI (S) ST-17144*   84   **8-10**

FIRST FAMILY
Studio Cast (1962) . . . . *Cadence (M) CLP-3060*   62   **$15-20**
Studio Cast (1962) . . . . *Cadence (S) CLP-25060*   62   **15-25**
Studio Cast (1963) . . . . *Cadence (M) CLP-3065*   63   **15-20**
    Volume 2. Comedy skits.
   Cast: Vaughn Meader (as John F. Kennedy); Naomi Brossart (as Jackie Kennedy); others.

FIRST GREAT TRAIN ROBBERY:
see GREAT TRAIN ROBBERY

FIRST IMPRESSIONS
Original Cast (1959) . . . . *Columbia (M) OL-5400*   59   **30-40**
Original Cast (1959) . . . . *Columbia (S) OS-2014*   59   **40-50**
Original Cast (1959) . . . . *Columbia (S) AOS-2014*   Re   **8-10**
   Composer: Glenn Paxon; Robert Goldman; George Weiss. **Conductor:** Frederick Dvonch.
   Cast: Polly Bergen; Farley Granger; Hermione Gingold; Donald Madden; Phyllis Newman;
   Christopher Hewett; Lynn Ross; Ellen Hanley; Lois Bewley; Lauri Peters.

FIRST LIVE RECORDINGS:
see ELVIS LIVE AT THE LOUISIANA HAYRIDE

FIRST MEN IN THE MOON
Studiotrack . . . . *Starlog/Varese Sarabande (S) SV-95002*   80   **8-10**
   Digital recording, with *First Men in the Moon, Dr. Strangelove, Captain Kronos, Vampire Hunter* and
   Hedda.
   Composer: Laurie Johnson. **Conductor:** Laurie Johnson.

FIRST NUDIE MUSICAL
   Composer: Bruce Kimmel.
Soundtrack (1976) . . . . *Varese Sarabande (S) VC-81028*   78   **10-15**
   Composer: Bruce Kimmel. **Conductor:** Rene Hall. **Cast:** Stephen Nathan; Cindy Williams;
   Bruce Kimmel; Annette O'Toole; Debbie Shapiro; Valerie Gillett; Diana Canova.

FISH THAT SAVED PITTSBURGH
Soundtrack (1979) . . . . *Lorimar (S) SZ-36303*   80   **8-12**
   Cast: Four Tops; Phyllis Hyman; Bell and James.

FISTFUL OF DOLLARS
Soundtrack (1966) . . . . *RCA Victor (M) LOC-1135*   67   **10-15**
Soundtrack (1966) . . . . *RCA Victor (S) LSO-1135*   75   **10-15**
   Orange label.
Soundtrack (1966) . . . . *RCA Victor (S) LSO-1135*   67   **20-35**
   Black label.
   Composer: Ennio Morricone. **Conductor:** Ennio Morricone.
   Also see MUSIC FROM "A FISTFUL OF DOLLARS," "FOR A FEW DOLLARS MORE,"
   AND "THE GOOD, THE BAD AND THE UGLY"

FITZCARRALDO
Soundtrack (1982) .... *Polydor (S) H-6363*   82   **$8-10**

FITZWILLY
Soundtrack (1967) .... *United Artists (M) UAL-4173*   68   **20-25**
Soundtrack (1967) .... *United Artists (S) UAS-5173*   68   **25-30**
Soundtrack (1967) .... *MCA (S) 25098*   **8-10**
  Composer: John Williams. Conductor: John Williams.

FIVE AFTER EIGHT
Original Cast (1979) .... *Original Cast (S) OC-8027*   79   **8-12**
  Composer: Michael Bitterman. Conductor: Ron Williams. Cast: Sally Funk; James
  Handakas; Dena Olstad; Arthur Sorenson; Barbara Walker.

FIVE DAYS FROM HOME
Soundtrack (1978) .... *MCA (S) 2362*   78   **10-12**
  Composer: Bill Conti. Conductor: Bill Conti.

FIVE EASY PIECES
Soundtrack (1970) .... *Epic (S) KE-30456*   71   **25-30**
  Includes classical selections by Mozart and Chopin.
  Cast: Tammy Wynette; Pearl Kaufman; Jack Nicholson; Karen Black. (With dialogue.)

FIVE PENNIES
Soundtrack (1959) .... *Dot (M) DLP-9500*   59   **30-35**
Soundtrack (1959) .... *Dot (S) DLP-29500*   59   **40-45**
  Film biography of jazz trumpeter Red Nichols.
  Composer: Sylvia Fine; Leith Stevens; others. Conductor: Leith Stevens. Cast: Red
  Nichols; Danny Kaye; Louis Armstrong; Bob Crosby; Ray Anthony.

FLAHOOLEY
Original Cast (1951) .... *Capitol (EP) EDM-284*   51   **25-30**
Original Cast (1951) .... *Capitol (M) S-284*   51   **125-150**
Original Cast (1951) .... *Capitol (M) T-11649*   77   **12-15**
  Composer: Sammy Fain; E.Y. Harburg; Moises Vivanco. Conductor: Maurice Levine.
  Cast: Yma Sumac; Barbara Cook; Jerome Courtland; Irwin Corey; Faye DeWitt; Marilyn Ross.

FLAME AND THE FLESH
Soundtrack (1954) .... *MGM (EP) X-1080*   54   **15-25**
  Composer: Nicolos Brodsky; Jack Lawrence. Cast: Carlos Thompson.

FLAME IN THE WIND
Soundtrack (1970) .... *Unusual (S) 1004*   70   **15-20**
  Composer: Dwight Gustafson. Conductor: Dwight Gustafson.

FLAMINGO KID
Soundtrack (1984) .... *Varese Sarabande (S) 81232*   84   **8-10**
  Composer: Various. Cast: Chiffons; Jesse Frederick; Acker Bilk; Dion; Crystals; Barrett
  Strong; Impressions; Hank Ballard and Midnighters; Martha and the Vandellas.

FLASH GORDON
Original Radio Cast .... *Golden Age (M) 5007*   78   **8-10**
Soundtrack (1980) .... *Elektra (S) 5E-518*   80   **8-12**
  Cast: Queen.
Soundtrack (1938) .... *Pelican (M) LP-2006*   76   **8-12**
  Full title: *Flash Gordon's Trip to Mars.* A Universal serial.
  Composer: Franz Waxman. Conductor: Franz Waxman. Cast: Buster Crabbe; Jean Rogers;
  Frank Shannon; Charles Middleton; Beatrice Roberts; Richard Alexander; Donald Kerr;
  Wheeler Oakman; G. Montague Shaw.

FLASHDANCE
Soundtrack (1983) . . . .*Casablanca Records (S) NBLP-7278*   83   **$8-10**
  Composer: Giorgio Moroder; others. **Conductor:** Sylvestor Levay. **Cast:** Irene Cara; Shandi;
  Helen St. John; Karen Kamon; Joe Esposito; Laura Branigan; Donna Summer; Cycle V; Kim
  Carnes; Michael Sembello.
Soundtrack (1983) . . . . *Casablanca (S) 422-811492-1*   83   **8-10**
  Composer: Giorgio Moroder; others. **Conductor:** Phil Ramone. **Cast:** Irene Cara; Shandi; Helen
  St. John; Karen Kamon; Joe Esposito; Laura Branigan; Donna Summer; Cycle V; Kim Carnes;
  Michael Sembello.

FLASHER
Soundtrack (1972) . . . .*Green (S) GBS-1008*   72   **20-25**
  Composer: Pool-Pah. **Conductor:** Rupert Holmes.

FLASHPOINT
Soundtrack (1984) . . . . *EMI America (S) ST-17141*   84   **8-10**
  Cast: Tangerine; Gems.

FLEA IN HER EAR
Soundtrack (1968) . . . . *20th Century-Fox (S) TFS-4200*   68   **20-25**
  Composer: Bronislau Kaper. **Conductor:** Lionel Newman.

FLEDERMAUS
Original Cast (1951) . . . . *Columbia (S) SL-108*   **20-30**
  Metropolitan Opera Version.
  Composer: Johann Strauss. **Cast:** Lily Pons; Ljuba Welitch; Richard Tucker; Charles Kullman;
  Martha Lipton; John Brownlee.

FLESH AND BLOOD
Soundtrack (1985) . . . . *Varese Sarabande (S) STV-81256*   85   **8-10**
  Composer: Basil Poledouris. **Conductor:** Basil Poledouris.

FLETCH
Soundtrack (1985) . . . .*MCA (S) 6142*   85   **8-10**
  Composer: Harold Faltermeyer; others. **Cast:** Stephanie Mills; Dan Hartman; John Farnum;
  Fixx; Kim Wilde; Harold Faltermeyer.

FLIGHT OF THE DOVES
Soundtrack (1971) . . . .*London (S) XPS-591*   71   **15-20**
  Composer: Roy Budd. **Cast:** Roy Budd (piano).

FLINTSTONES
TV Soundtrack (1961) . . . .*Colpix (M) CP-302*   61   **15-25**
  Cast: Alan Reed; Jean Vanderpyl; Mel Blanc; Bea Benadaret. (With dialogue.)

FLIP WILSON SHOW
TV Soundtrack . . . . *Little David (S) LD-2000*   **10-15**
  Cast: Flip Wilson.

FLORA THE RED MENACE
Original Cast (1965) . . . .*RCA Victor (M) LOC-1111*   65   **25-30**
Original Cast (1965) . . . .*RCA Victor (S) LSO-1111*   65   **35-40**
Original Cast (1965) . . . . *RCA Victor (S) CBL1-2760*   Re   **15-20**
  Composer: John Kander; Fred Ebb. **Conductor:** Harold Hastings. **Cast:** Liza Minnelli; Mary
  Louise Wilson; Cathryn Damon; Robert Kaye; Stephanie Hill; Bob Dishy; Danny Carroll;
  Joe E. Marks.
Original Cast (1987) . . . .*No Label Shown (S) TER-1159*   89   **10-12**
  Off-Broadway cast.
  Composer: John Kander; Fred Ebb. **Conductor:** Hal Hastings. **Cast:** Veanne Cox; Peter
  Frechette; Lyn Greene; John Kander (piano); Danny Carroll; James Cresson; Cathryn Damon;
  Bob Dishy; Jamie Donnelly; Dortha Duckworth; Stephanie Hill; Robert Kaye; Joe E. Marks; Liza
  Minnelli; Marie Santell; Mary Louise Wilson.

FLOWER DRUM SONG
Original Cast (1958) . . . .*Columbia (EP) A-5350*   58   **$10-15**
Original Cast (1958) . . . .*Angel (M) 35886*   59   **25-30**
Original Cast (1958) . . . .*Columbia (S) OS-2009*   58   **20-25**
  Composer: Richard Rodgers; Oscar Hammerstein II. **Conductor:** Salvadtore Dell'Isola.
  Cast: Pat Suzuki; Miyoshi Umeki; Larry Blyden; Juanita Hall; Ed Kenney; Keye Luke; Jack Soo;
  Conrad Yama; Rose Quong; Pat Adiarte; Anita Ellis; Susan Lynn; Baayork Lee; Arabella Hong;
  Cely Carrillo; Luis Robert Hernandez; Linda Ribuca.
Original Cast (1958) . . . . *Columbia (M) OL-5350*   58   **15-20**
Original London Cast (1958) . . . . *Angel (S) S-35886*   59   **40-45**
  Composer: Richard Rodgers; Oscar Hammerstein II. **Conductor:** Robert Lowe.
  Cast: Kevin Scott; Ida Shepley; Yau Shang Tung; George Pastell; Yama Saki; Zed Zakari.
Soundtrack (1961) . . . .*Decca (M) DL-9098*   61   **15-20**
Soundtrack (1961) . . . .*Decca (S) DL7-9098*   61   **20-25**
Soundtrack (1961) . . . .*MCA (S) 2069*   Re   **8-10**
  Composer: Richard Rodgers; Oscar Hammerstein II. **Conductor:** Alfred Newman.
  Cast: Nancy Kwan; James Shigeta; Juanita Hall; Miyoshi Umeki; Jack Soo.
Studiotrack (1959) . . . .*Dot (M) DLP-3173*   59   **15-20**
  Jazz interpretations.
  Cast: Muriel Roberts.
Studiotrack . . . . *Crown (M) CLP-5105*   **10-15**
Studiotrack (1959) . . . .*Roost (M) LP 2231*   59   **15-20**
  Cast: Johnny Smith Quartet.
Studiotrack . . . .*Design (S) SDLP-98*   **8-12**
Studiotrack (1960) . . . . *Richmond (M) B-20081*   60   **10-15**
Studiotrack (1960) . . . . *Richmond (S) S-30081*   60   **15-20**
  Also has music from *West Side Story*.
  Cast: London Theatre Orchestra.

FLOWER DRUM SONG - ORIGINAL JAZZ PERFORMANCE
Studiotrack (1959) . . . . *Warner Bros. (M) B-1256*   59   **15-20**
  Cast: Morris Nanton Trio.

FLOWERING PEACH
Original Cast (1954) . . . . , ... *MGM (M) E-3164*   54   **75-90**
  Incidental music.
  Composer: Alan Houhaness.

FLOWERS FOR ALGERNON
London Cast (1980) . . . . *Original Cast (S) OC-8021*   80   **8-10**
  Composer: Charles Strouse. **Cast:** Michael Crawford; Cheryl Kennedy.

FLY
Soundtrack (1986) . . . . *Varese Sarabande (S) STV-81289*   86   **10-15**
  Composer: Howard Shore. **Conductor:** Howard Shore.

FLY BLACKBIRD
Original West Coast Cast (1962) . . . .*Imaginate (M) LK-1-V13786*   62   **70-80**
  Preceded original Broadway cast.
  Composer: C. Jackson; James Hatch. **Cast:** Ellen Gordon; Jack Crowder; Vera Oliver;
  George Takei.
Original Cast (1962) . . . . *Mercury (M) OCM-2206*   62   **40-50**
Original Cast (1962) . . . . *Mercury (S) OCS-6206*   62   **60-70**
  Composer: C. Jackson; James Hatch. **Conductor:** Gershon Kingsley. **Cast:** Avon Long;
  Leonard Parker; Paul Reid Roman; Jack Crowder; Jim Bailey; Robert Guillaume; Mary
  Louise; John Anania; Helen Blount; Thelma Oliver; William Sugihara; Glory Van Scott.

FLY BY NIGHT
Soundtrack (1979) ....*Parachute (S) 20525*   79   **$8-10**
  Disco press.

FLY WITH ME
Original Columbia Cast (1980) ....*Original Cast (S) OC-8023*   80   **30-40**
  Columbia University Production.
  Composer: Richard Rodgers; Lorenz Hart; Oscar Hammerstein II. **Conductor:** Howard Shanet.
  Cast: Daniel Frank; Rod Melucas; Cheryl S. Horowitz; Francis Larson; Annie Laurita; Marci
  Pliskin; Avi Simon (Columbia University students).

FLYING DOWN TO RIO
Soundtrack (1938) ....*Sandy Hook (M) SH-2010*   78   **10-15**
  One side of this LP has music from *Carefree*.
  Composer: Irving Berlin. **Cast:** Fred Astaire; Ginger Rogers.
Soundtrack ....*Spin-O-Rama (M) MK-3035*   **10-15**
  Cast: Mike Di Napoli's Trio.

FLYING NUN
Studio Cast (1967) ....*Colgems (M) COM-106*   67   **10-15**
Studio Cast (1967) ....*Colgems (S) COS-106*   67   **15-20**
  Full title of above two: *Sally Field - Star of the Flying Nun.* Contains *Who Needs Wings to Fly,* the
  film theme.
  Composer: Various. **Conductor:** Bob Mitchell. **Cast:** Sally Field; Bob Mitchell Choir.

FM
Soundtrack (1978) ....*MCA (S) 2-6900*   78   **10-12**
  Composer: Various. **Cast:** Boston; Jimmy Buffett; Doobie Brothers; Eagles; Dan Fogelberg;
  Foreigner; Billy Joel; Randy Meisner; Steve Miller; Tom Petty and Heartbreakers; Queen;
  Boz Scaggs; Bob Seger and Silver Bullet Band; Steely Dan; James Taylor; Joe Walsh.

FOG
Soundtrack (1980) ....*Varese Sarabande (S) STV-81191*   84   **10-15**
  Composer: John Carpenter.

FOLIES BERGERE
Original Cast (1964) ....*Audio Fidelity (M) 2135*   64   **10-15**
Original Cast (1964) ....*Audio Fidelity (S) AFSD-6135*   64   **8-15**
  Composer: P. Gerard; Henri Betti; others. **Conductor:** Joe Basile. **Cast:** Patachou; Georges
  Ulmer.
Soundtrack (1958) ....*Decca (M) DL-8571*   58   **35-40**
  Composer: Bernard Gerard; Henri Betti; others.

FOLLIES
Original Cast (1971) ....*Capitol (S) SO-761*   71   **10-15**
  Composer: Stephen Sondheim. **Conductor:** Harold Hastings. **Cast:** Alexis Smith; Gene
  Nelson; Dorothy Collins; John McMartin; Arnold Moss; Yvonne DeCarlo; Fifi D'Orsay;
  Mary McCarty; Ethel Shutta; Michael Bartlett; Harvey Evans; Justine Johnston; Victoria
  Mallory; Rita O'Connor; Kurt Peterson; Suzanne Rogers; others.
Original Cast (1971) ....*RCA Victor (S) HBC2-7128*   71   **15-20**
  Full title: *Follies in Concert.* Recorded live at the Lincoln Center.
  Composer: Stephen Sondheim. **Cast:** Mandy Patinkin; Barbara Cook; George Hearn; Lee
  Remick; Elaine Stritch; Carol Burnett.

FOLLOW ME
Soundtrack (1969) ....*Uni (S) 73056*   69   **15-20**
  Composer: Stu Phillips. **Conductor:** Stu Phillips. **Cast:** Dino, Desi, and Billy.

```
              COIN OPERATOR   DJ PREVUE
                     EPA 4368

              ELVIS
                  SINGS

            FOUR GREAT SONGS

        Side 1  Follow That Dream (1:36 ASCAP)
                Angel (2:40 ASCAP)
        Side 2  What A Wonderful Life (2:28 ASCAP)
                I'm Not The Marrying Kind (2:00 ASCAP)

            FROM HIS NEW MOVIE

       "FOLLOW THAT DREAM"

            AVAILABLE NOW ONLY ON 45 EP
```

FOLLOW THAT DREAM

Soundtrack (1962) .... *RCA Victor (EP) EPA-4368*   62   **$45-60**
  Black label, dog on top. If with promotional paper sleeve, add $100 to $150. Sleeve, which has red
  printing on one side, was made especially for coin (jukebox) operators and radio stations.
Soundtrack (1962) .... *RCA Victor (EP) EPA-4368*   62   **75-100**
  Black label, dog on top. Marked "Not For Sale." Promotional issue only. If with the promotional
  paper sleeve described above, add $100 to $150.
Soundtrack (1962) .... *RCA Victor (EP) EPA-4368*   65   **30-40**
  Black label, dog on side.
Soundtrack (1962) .... *RCA Victor (EP) EPA-4368*   69   **30-40**
  Orange label.
  Composer: Sid Tepper; Roy C. Bennett; Ben Weisman; Sid Wayne; Jerry Livingston; others.
  Cast: Elvis Presley; Scotty Moore (guitar); Boots Randolph (sax); Dudley Brooks (piano);
  D.J. Fontana (drums); Hal Blaine (drums); Jordanaires (vocals).

FOLLOW THAT GIRL

London Cast .... *AEI (S) 1121*   **8-10**
  Composer: Slade; Reynolds.

FOLLOW THE BOYS

Soundtrack (1962) .... *MGM (M) E-4123*   62   **15-20**
Soundtrack (1962) .... *MGM (S) SE-4123*   62   **20-25**
  Composer: Benny Davis; Ted Murry. **Conductor:** LeRoy Holmes. **Cast:** Connie Francis.

FOOL BRITANNIA

Studio Cast .... *Acappella (M) AC-1*   **20-25**
  Composer: Leslie Bricusse; Anthony Newley. **Conductor:** Marvin Holtzman. **Cast:** Peter
  Sellers; Joan Collins; Anthony Newley; Leslie Bricusse; Daniel Massey; Michael Lipton.

FOOLS

Soundtrack (1970) .... *Reprise (S) RS-6429*   71   **12-15**
  Composer: Shorty Rogers; Paul Parrish; Alex Harvey; Mimi Farina. **Conductor:** Shorty Rogers.
  Cast: Kenny Rogers and the First Edition; Mimi Farina; Shorty Rogers; Katherine Ross.

FOOTLIGHT PARADE:
see GOLDEN AGE OF THE HOLLYWOOD MUSICAL

FOOTLOOSE

Soundtrack (1983) .... *Columbia (S) JS-39242*   **8-10**
  Composer: Gore; Pitchford; Steinman; others. **Cast:** Kenny Loggins; Shalamar; Deniece
  Williams; Mike Reno and Ann Wilson; Bonnie Tyler; Sammy Hagar; Karla Bonoff;
  Moving Pictures.

FOR A FEW DOLLARS MORE
Soundtrack (1967) . . . .*United Artists (M) UAL-3608*   67   **$12-15**
Soundtrack (1967) . . . .*United Artists (S) UAS-6608*   67   **15-20**
  One side has music from *A Fistful of Dollars, Zorba the Greek, Topkapi, Viva Maria, The Train* and
  Tom Jones.
  Composer: Ennio Morricone. **Conductor:** LeRoy Holmes.
  Also see MUSIC FROM "A FISTFUL OF DOLLARS"

FOR COLORED GIRLS WHO HAVE CONSIDERED SUICIDE WHEN
THE RAINBOW IS ENUF
Original Cast (1976) . . . . *Buddah (S) BDS-95007*   76   **10-15**
  Cast: Diana Wharton (vocal); Ntozake Shange (poetry).

FOR LOVE OF IVY
Soundtrack (1968) . . . .*ABC (S) SOC-7*   68   **15-20**
  Composer: Quincy Jones. **Conductor:** Quincy Jones.

FOR ME AND MY GAL
  Conductor: George Stoll. **Cast:** Judy Garland; Gene Kelley.

FOR THE FIRST TIME
Soundtrack (1959) . . . .*RCA Victor (EP) EPA-4344*   59   **8-12**
Soundtrack (1959) . . . .*RCA Victor (M) LM-2338*   59   **15-20**
Soundtrack (1959) . . . .*RCA Victor (S) LSC-2338*   59   **25-30**
  Composer: George Stoll; others. **Conductor:** George Stoll. **Cast:** Mario Lanza (his final film).

FOR THE LOVE OF BENJI
Soundtrack (1977) . . . . *Epic (S) KSE-34867*   77   **8-12**
  Composer: Euel Box. **Conductor:** Euel Box.

FOR WHOM THE BELL TOLLS
Soundtrack (1943) . . . . *Decca (M) DL-8008*   50   **50-65**
  One side has music from *Golden Earrings.*
Soundtrack (1943) . . . . *Decca (M) DL-8481*   57   **40-50**
  One side has music from *Golden Earrings.*
  Composer: Victor Young. **Conductor:** Victor Young. **Cast:** Victor Young's Concert Orchestra.
Studiotrack (1958) . . . .*Warner Bros. (M) B-1201*   58   **20-25**
Studiotrack (1968) . . . . *Warner Bros. (S) BS-1201*   58   **25-30**
Studiotrack (1968) . . . . *Warner Bros. (Q) SRQ-4013*   73   **10-15**
  Composer: Victor Young. **Conductor:** Ray Heindorf.
Studiotrack (1957) . . . . *Jubilee (M) JLP-1034*   57   **20-30**
  Composer: Victor Young. **Cast:** Harry Sukman (piano).

FOR YOUR EYES ONLY
Soundtrack (1981) . . . .*Liberty (S) LOO-51109*   81   **8-10**
  Composer: Bill Conti. **Conductor:** Bill Conti. **Cast:** Sheena Easton; Rage; Bill Conti.

FORBIDDEN BROADWAY
Original Cast (1982) . . . .*DRG (S) SBL-12585*   84   **8-10**
  Off-Broadway parody of Broadway shows and stars.
  Composer: Gerald Alessandrini (parody lyrics). **Conductor:** Fred Barton. **Cast:** Gerard
  Alessandrini; Fred Barton; Bill Carmichael; Nora Mae Lyng; Chloe Webb.

FORBIDDEN ISLAND:
see ATLANTIS IN HI-FI

FORBIDDEN PLANET
Soundtrack (1956) . . . . *Planet (SE) PR-001*   78   **12-15**
  Composer: Louis Barron; Bebe Barron. **Cast:** Walter Pidgeon; Anne Francis.

FORBIDDEN WORLD
Soundtrack (1982) . . . .*Web (S) LP 107*   82   **8-10**
  Composer: Susan Justin. **Conductor:** Susan Justin.

FORD 50TH ANNIVERSARY TV SHOW
TV Soundtrack (1953) .... *Decca (M) DL-7027* 53 **$50-60**
. **Composer:** Irving Berlin; others. **Conductor:** Jay Blackton. **Cast:** Ethel Merman; Mary Martin.

FOREIGN INTRIGUE
Soundtrack (1956) .... *MGM (EP) X-1323* 56 **15-20**

FOREMOST COMPOSER OF THE GOLDEN AGE OF MOTION PICTURES
(ERICH WOLFGANG KORNGOLD)
Studiotrack (1962) .... *Warner Bros. (M) W-1438* 62 **20-30**
Studiotrack (1962) .... *Warner Bros. (S) WS-1438* 62 **40-60**
Music from *King's Row, Anthony Adverse, Elizabeth and Essex, The Sea Hawk, The Prince and the Pauper, The Constant Nymph* and *Robin Hood.*
Composer: Erich Wolfgang Korngold. **Conductor:** Lionel Newman.

FOREVER AMBER:
see LAURA

FOREVER YOUNG, FOREVER FREE
Soundtrack (1976) .... *MCA (S) 2093* 76 **10-12**
Composer: Lee Holdridge. **Conductor:** Lee Holdridge.

FORMULA
Soundtrack (1980) .... *Varese Sarabande (S) STV-81153* 80 **8-10**
Composer: Bill Conti. **Conductor:** Bill Conti.

FORTUNA
Studio Cast (1962) .... *Owl (M) ORLP-4* 62 **30-35**
Composer: Francis Thorne; Arnold Weinstein. **Cast:** Francis Thorne (piano).

FORTUNATE PILGRIM
Soundtrack (1988) .... *RCA Victor (S) 7788-1* 88 **8-10**

FORTUNE AND MEN'S EYES
Soundtrack (1971) .... *MGM (S) 1SE-29* 71 **10-12**
Cast: Ronnie Dyson; Galt McDermot; Leata Galloway.

FORTUNE COOKIE
Soundtrack (1966) .... *United Artists (M) UAL-4145* 66 **15-20**
Soundtrack (1966) .... *United Artists (S) UAS-5145* 66 **20-25**
Composer: Andre Previn. **Conductor:** Andre Previn.

40 POUNDS OF TROUBLE
Soundtrack (1963) .... *Mercury (M) MG-20784* 63 **25-30**
Soundtrack (1963) .... *Mercury (S) SR-60784* 63 **30-40**
Composer: Mort Lindsey. **Conductor:** Mort Lindsey.

42nd STREET
Original Cast (1980) .... *RCA Victor (S) CBL1-3891* 80 **8-10**
Conductor: John Lesko. **Cast:** Tammy Grimes; Jerry Orbach; Carole Cook; Lee Roy Ream; Joe Bova; Danny Carroll; James Congson; Jerry Kansas; Ginny King; Karen Prunczik; Wanda Richert.

FOSTER BROOKS' ROASTS
TV Soundtrack .... *Roast (S) RR-1002* 76 **10-15**
Soundtracks from the Friar's Roasts of those named in the cast.
Cast: Foster Brooks. ROASTEES: Dean Martin; Hubert Humphrey; Joe Namath; Carroll O'Connor; Johnny Carson; Ralph Nader; Don Rickles.

FOUL PLAY
Soundtrack (1978) .... *Arista (S) AL-9501* 78 **8-10**
Composer: Charles Fox. **Conductor:** Charles Fox. **Cast:** Barry Manilow.

FOUR ADVENTURES OF ZORRO
TV Soundtrack . . . . *Disneyland (M) WDA-3601*   **$10-15**
Composer: William Lava. Conductor: William Lava. Cast: Guy Williams; Henry Calvin;
Phil Ross; Jan Arvan; Jimmie Dodd.

FOUR BELOW STRIKES BACK
Original Cast (1960) . . . . *Offbeat (M) O-4017*   60   **75-85**
Composer: William Roy; others. Cast: Jenny Lou Law; Nancy Dussault; George Furth; Cy
Young; Robert Colston; Paul Trueblood (pianos).

FOUR GIRLS IN TOWN
Soundtrack (1956) . . . . *Decca (EP) ED-2486*   56   **15-25**
Soundtrack (1956) . . . . *Decca (M) DL-8424*   56   **40-50**
Soundtrack (1956) . . . . *Varese Sarabande (M) VC-81074*   **8-10**
On the above two LPs, one side has music from *Written on the Wind.*
Composer: Alex North. Conductor: Joseph Gershenson (with orchestration by Henry Mancini).
Cast: Andre Previn; Ray Linn.

FOUR HORSEMEN OF THE APOCALYPSE
Soundtrack (1962) . . . . *MGM (M) E-3993*   62   **25-30**
Soundtrack (1962) . . . . *MGM (S) SE-3993*   62   **35-40**
Composer: Andre Previn. Conductor: Andre Previn.

FOUR IN THE MORNING
Soundtrack (1966) . . . . *Roulette (M) OS-805*   66   **25-30**
Soundtrack (1966) . . . . *Roulette (S) OSS-805*   66   **35-40**
With dialogue.
Composer: John Barry. Conductor: John Barry.

FOUR MUSKETEERS / THE EAGLE HAS LANDED
Soundtrack (1978) . . . . *Entr' acte (S) ERS-6510*   **8-12**
Composer: Lalo Schifrin. Conductor: Lalo Schifrin.

FOUR SAINTS IN THREE ACTS
Original Cast (1947) . . . . *RCA Victor (M) LCT-1139*   54   **75-100**
Original Cast (1947) . . . . *RCA Victor (M) LM-2756*   64   **25-30**
Composer: Virgil Thompson; Gertrude Stein. Conductor: Virgil Thompson. Cast: Beatrice
Robinson-Wayne; Ruby Greene; Inez Matthews; Edward Matthews; Charles Holland.

FOUR SEASONS
Soundtrack (1981) . . . . *Private Stock (S) PS-7000*   81   **10-12**
Double LP set.

FOUR WIVES:
see DEATH OF A SCOUNDREL

FOURTH MAN
Soundtrack (1979) . . . . *Varese Sarabande (S) STV-81222*   84   **8-10**
Soundtrack (1979) . . . . *Varese Sarabande (S) STV-81222*   84   **8-10**
Cast: Willem Frederik Bon.

FOURTH PROTOCOL
Soundtrack (1987) . . . . *DRG (S) SBL-12591*   87   **8-10**
Composer: Lalo Schifrin. Conductor: Lalo Schifrin.

FOX
Soundtrack (1968) . . . . *Warner Bros. (S) WS-1738*   68   **35-40**
Composer: Lalo Schifrin. Conductor: Lalo Schifrin. Cast: Anne Heywood; Sally Stevens.

FOXES
Soundtrack (1980) . . . . *Casablanca (S) 7206*   80   **10-12**
Double LP set.
Composer: Giorgio Moroder.

FOXY
Original Cast (1964) . . . . *S.P.M. (M) CO-4636*   64   **$15-20**
   Composer: Robert Emmett Dolan; Johnny Mercer. **Conductor:** Donald Pippin. **Cast:** Larry
   Blyden; Cathryn Damon; John Davidson; Edward Greenhalgh; Robert H. Harris; Gerald
   Hiken; Bert Lahr; Julienne Marie.

FOXY BROWN
Soundtrack (1974) . . . . *Motown (S) 811*   74   **10-15**
   Cast: Willie Hutch.

FRANCES
Soundtrack (1983) . . . . *Southern Cross (S) SCRS-1001*   83   **15-20**
   Composer: John Barry. **Conductor:** John Barry.

FRANCES LANGFORD PRESENTS
TV Soundtrack (1959) . . . . *NBC-TV/Splendex (M)*   59   **25-35**
   Promotional issue only. Music from the TV special plus an open-end interview with Frances Langford.
   Composer: Various. **Conductor:** David Rose. **Cast:** Frances Langford; Hugh O'Brian; Julie
   London; Edgar Bergen and Charlie McCarthy; George Sanders; Jerry Colonna; Bobby Troup;
   Tony Romano; Four Freshmen; Murray McEachern; Bob Hope; David Rose and His Orchestra.

FRANCIS OF ASSISI
Soundtrack (1961) . . . . *20th Century-Fox (M) FOX-3053*   61   **125-150**
   Composer: Mario Nascimbene. **Conductor:** Franco Ferrara.
Soundtrack (1961) . . . . *20th Century-Fox (S) SFX-3053*   61   **175-200**
   With Gregorian chants.
   Composer: Mario Nascimbene. **Conductor:** Franco Ferrara.

FRANKENSTEIN:
   see WEIRD CIRCLE

FRANKIE AND JOHNNY

Soundtrack (1966) .... *RCA Victor (M) LPM-3553*   66   **$75-100**
Black label reads "Monaural" at bottom. Includes 12" x 12" color photo, which represents about $50 of the value.

Soundtrack (1966) .... *RCA Victor (S) LSP-3553*   66   **85-110**
Black label reads "Stereo" at bottom. Includes 12" x 12" color photo, which represents about $50 of the value.

Soundtrack (1965) .... *Pickwick (S) ACL-7007*   76   **10-12**
Excludes three tracks that were on the 1965 RCA Victor issues.

Soundtrack (1966) .... *RCA Victor (S) APL1-2559*   77   **10-15**
Composer: Fred Karger; Ben Weisman; Sid Tepper; Roy C. Bennett; Sid Wayne; Fred Wise; Randy Starr; Doc Pomus; Mort Schuman; Bill Giant; Bernie Baum; Florence Kaye; others.
Cast: Elvis Presley; Scotty Moore (guitar); Barney Kessel (guitar); D.J. Fontana (drums); Hal Blaine (drums); Jordanaires (vocals).

FRANKIE, DINO, AND SAMMY - SUMMIT MEETING AT THE 500 CLUB, ATLANTIC CITY, NEW JERSEY

Original Cast (1964) .... *Latimer (M) 247-17*   64   **200-300**
From a live performance. Labeled "Souvenir from the Sinatrama Room. Not for sale. Souvenir, non-published album. Not available anywhere else."

FRANTIC

Soundtrack (1958) .... *Columbia (M) CL-1268*   58   **25-30**
Soundtrack (1958) .... *Columbia Special Products (M) ACL-1268*   Re   **8-12**
Composer: Miles Davis. **Cast:** Miles Davis Quintet.

Soundtrack (1958) .... *Fontana (M) MGF-27532*   64   **15-20**
Soundtrack (1958) .... *Fontana (S) SRF-67532*   64   **20-25**
Composer: Miles Davis. **Cast:** Miles Davis Quintet.

Soundtrack (1988) .... *Elektra (S) 60782-1*   88   **8-10**
Composer: Ennio Morricone.

FRANZ LISZT STORY

Studiotrack (1960) .... *Liberty (M) LRP-3151*   60   **15-20**
Studiotrack (1960) .... *Liberty (S) LST-7151*   60   **15-25**
Cast: Harry Sukman.

Studiotrack (1960) .... *Decca (M) DL-8999*   60   **15-20**
Studiotrack (1960) .... *Decca (S) DL7-8999*   60   **15-25**
Cast: Carmen Cavallaro.

FRED ASTAIRE SINGS AND SWINGS IRVING BERLIN

TV Soundtrack .... *MGM (M) PR-1*   **10-20**
Excerpts, released in conjunction with Alcoa Premiere.
Cast: Fred Astaire; Oscar Peterson; Ray Brown; Flip Phillips.

FREE AND EASY

Studio Cast (1959) .... *Columbia (M) CL-1099*   59   **20-30**
First titled *St. Louis Woman*, rewritten as *Blues-Opera*, then titled *Free and Easy*.
Composer: Harold Arlen; Johnny Mercer. **Conductor:** Andre Kostelanetz.

FREEDOM'S FINEST HOUR

Soundtrack (1968) .... *Decca (S) DL-74943*   68   **10-15**
Documentary Soundtrack. The story of the American Revolution.
Cast: Ronald Reagan (narrator).

FRENCH LIEUTENANT'S WOMAN

Soundtrack (1981) .... *DRG (S) DRG 6106*   81   **8-10**
Composer: Carl Davis. **Conductor:** Carl Davis.

FRENCH LINE
Soundtrack (1954) .... *Mercury (EP) EP-2-318*   54   **$20-30**
  Double EP set.
Soundtrack (1954) .... *Mercury (M) MG-25182*   54   **50-60**
  Composer: Josef Myrow; Walter Scharf. **Conductor:** Constantin Bakaleinkoff.
  Cast: Jane Russell; Mary McCarty; Gilbert Roland.

FRESH HAIR:
 see HAIR

FREUD
Soundtrack (1962) .... *Citadel (S) CT-6019*   77   **25-45**
  Some music originally composed in 1962 for *Freud* was held back and later used for *Alien* in 1979.
  Composer: Jerry Goldsmith. **Conductor:** Joseph Gershenson.
Soundtrack (1962) .... *Citadel (M) CT 7011*   79   **15-20**
  Composer: Jerry Goldsmith. **Conductor:** Joseph Gershenson.
  Also see ALIEN

FRIDAY THE 13TH
Soundtrack (1983) .... *Gramavision (S) 1030*   83   **8-10**
  Has the theme from *Friday the 13th, Part 3,* plus background score from Parts 1, 2, and 3 of *Friday the 13th.*
  Composer: Harry Manfredini. **Conductor:** Harry Manfredini. **Cast:** Harry Manfredini and
  His Orchestra.

FRIENDLY PERSUASION
Soundtrack (1956) .... *Dot (EP) DEP-1054*   56   **20-25**
  Composer: Dimitri Tiomkin. **Cast:** Pat Boone.
Soundtrack (1956) .... *RKO/Unique (M) LP-110*   56   **140-150**
Soundtrack (1956) .... *Venise (M) V-7026*   60   **45-55**
  Composer: Dimitri Tiomkin. **Conductor:** Dimitri Tiomkin.
Soundtrack (1956) .... *Varese Sarabande (SE) STV-81165*   82   **8-15**
  Composer: Dimitri Tiomkin. **Conductor:** Dimitri Tiomkin.

FRIENDS
Studiotrack (1973) .... *Paramount (S) DJS-1*   73   **20-30**
  Actual title: *Paramount Records Presents an Open-end Interview with Elton John about Friends Soundtrack.* Also has song introductions by Elton. Promotional issue only.
Soundtrack (1973) .... *Paramount (S) PAS-6004*   73   **12-15**
  Composer: Elton John. **Cast:** Elton John.

FRIENDS
TV Soundtrack (1973) .... *Chelsea (S) BCL1-0332*   73   **10-12**
  Music from the TV series *Sigmund and the Sea Monsters.*
  Composer: Jansen and Hart. **Conductor:** Jimmie Haskell. **Cast:** Johnny Whitaker.

FRIGHT NIGHT
Soundtrack (1985) .... *Private I (S) SZ-40087*   85   **8-10**
  Composer: Brad Fiedel; others. **Cast:** J. Geils Band; Ian Hunter; Autograph; April Wine;
  Devo; Sparks; White Sister; Fabulous Fontaines; Evelyn "Champagne" King.

FRITZ THE CAT
Soundtrack (1972) .... *Fantasy (S) 9405*   72   **10-15**
Soundtrack (1972) .... *Fantasy (S) MPF-4532*   Re   **8-10**
  Composer: Ellas McDaniel; others. **Cast:** Bo Diddley; others.

FROM BEYOND
Soundtrack (1986) .... *Enigma (S) SJ-73240*   86   **8-10**
  Composer: Richard Band. **Conductor:** Richard Band. **Cast:** Richard Band.

FROM HERE TO ETERNITY
Soundtrack (1953) .... *Coral (M) CRL-56105*   53   **$30-45**
   10-inch LP. Hawaiian music from the soundtrack. Issued with four different covers.
   Cast: Danny Stewart and His Islanders.
Als see EDDY DUCHIN STORY

FROM ISRAEL WITH LOVE
Original Cast (1972) .... *Hed Arzi (S) BAN-14278*   72   **25-30**
   Conductor: Rafi Ben Moshe. **Cast:** Micha Adir; Dani Amihud; Chaya Arad.

FROM RUSSIA WITH LOVE
Soundtrack (1964) .... *United Artists (M) UAL-4114*   64   **10-15**
Soundtrack (1964) .... *United Artists (S) UAS-5114*   64   **15-20**
   Composer: John Barry. **Conductor:** John Barry. **Cast:** Matt Monro; John Barry and His
   Orchestra.
Studiotrack (1964) .... *Liberty (M) LRP-3356*   64   **10-15**
Soundtrack (1963) .... *Liberty (S) LST-7356*   63   **15-20**
   This Matt Monro LP has the soundtrack recording of the title song, plus 11 other film songs.
   Composer: Various. **Cast:** Matt Monro.
Studiotrack (1964) .... *Liberty (M) LRP-3353*   64   **10-15**
Studiotrack (1964) .... *Liberty (S) LST-7353*   64   **10-15**
   Full title: *From Russia with Love (and Other Themes)*. Has 12 title tracks from films.
   Composer: Various. **Conductor:** Si Zentner. **Cast:** Si Zentner and His Orchestra.
Studiotrack (1964) .... *Capitol (M) T-2075*   64   **10-15**
Studiotrack (1964) .... *Capitol (S) ST-2075*   64   **10-15**
   Has 12 assorted film title tunes.
   Composer: Various. **Conductor:** Jimmie Haskell. **Cast:** Jimmie Haskell and His Orchestra.

FROM THE SECOND CITY
Original Cast (1961) .... *Mercury (M) OCM-2201*   61   **25-35**
Original Cast (1961) .... *Mercury (S) OCS-6201*   61   **30-40**
Original Cast (1961) .... *Mercury (M) OCM-2202*   61   **25-35**
Original Cast (1961) .... *Mercury (S) OCS-6202*   61   **30-40**
Original Cast (1961) .... *Mercury (M) OCM-2203*   62   **25-35**
Original Cast (1961) .... *Mercury (S) OCS-6203*   62   **30-40**
   Composer: William Mathieu. **Conductor:** William Mathieu. **Cast:** Howard Alk; Alan Arkin;
   Roger Bowen; Severn Darden; Andrew Duncan; Barbara Harris; Mina Kolb; Paul Sand;
   Eugene Troobnick; William Mathieu (piano). (Skits.)
Original Cast .... *Mercury (S) SR-61224*   69   **20-30**
   Actual title: *The Second City Writhes Again!*
  Cast: Howard Alk; Alan Arkin; Roger Bowen; Severn Darden; Andrew Duncan; Barbara
   Harris; Mina Kolb; Paul Sand; Eugene Troobnick; Jack Burns; Avery Schrieber; Del Close;
   Omar Shapli; Ann Elder (skits).

FROM THE TERRACE
Soundtrack (1974) ....*Cinema (S) LP-8009*   74 $40-50
   Also has music from *The Liberation of L.B. Jones.*
   Composer: Elmer Bernstein. **Conductor:** Elmer Bernstein.

FRONT STREET GAIETIES
Original Cast ....*AEI (S) 1133*   ,   8-10
   Composer: Walter Willison; Jeffrey Silverman.

FROSTY THE SNOWMAN
Soundtrack (1970) .... *MGM (S) SE-4733*   70   15-20
   Composer: Steve Nelson; Jack Rollins. **Conductor:** Maury Laws. **Cast:** Jimmy Durante;
   Billy DeWolfe; Jackie Vernon; Paul Frees; June Foray.

FUGITIVE KIND
Soundtrack (1959) ....*United Artists (M) UAL-4065*   60   30-35
Soundtrack (1959) .... *United Artists (S) UAS-5065*   60   40-45
   Composer: Kenyon Hopkins. **Conductor:** Kenyon Hopkins.

FULL METAL JACKET
Soundtrack (1987) .... *Warner Bros. (S) 1-25613*   87   8-10
   Composer: Various. **Cast:** Abigail Mead; Nigel Goulding; Johnny Wright; Dixie Cups; Sam
   the Sham and the Pharoahs; Chris Kenner; Nancy Sinatra; Trashmen; Goldman Band.

FULL OF LIFE:
see NO SAD SONGS FOR ME

FUN AND FANCY FREE
Soundtrack (1947) .... *Disneyland (M) DQ-1248*   64   15-20

FUN IN ACAPULCO
Soundtrack (1963) .... *RCA Victor (M) LPM-2756*   63   40-50
   Black label, reads "Mono" at bottom.
Soundtrack (1963) ....*RCA Victor (S) LSP-2756*   63   40-50
   Black label with RCA silver top logo, reads "Stereo" at bottom.
Soundtrack (1963) .... *RCA Victor (M) LPM-2756*   65   20-30
   Black label, reads "Monaural" at bottom.
Soundtrack (1963) ....*RCA Victor (S) LSP-2756*   65   20-30
   Black label with RCA white top logo, reads "Stereo" at bottom.
Soundtrack (1963) ....*RCA Victor (S) LSP-2756*   69   10-20
   Orange label.
Soundtrack (1963) .... *RCA Victor (S) AFL1-2756*   77   8-10
   Composer: Ben Weisman; Sid Wayne; Sid Tepper; Roy C. Bennett; Bill Giant; Bernie Baum;
   Florence Kaye; Fred Wise; Don Robertson; Hal Blair; Jerry Leiber; Mike Stoller; Pepe Guizar;
   others. **Cast:** Elvis Presley; Scotty Moore (guitar); Barney Kessel (guitar); D.J. Fontana (drums);
   Hal Blaine (drums); Dudley Brooks (piano); Jordanaires (vocals); Amigos (vocals).

FUNERAL IN BERLIN
Soundtrack (1966) .... *RCA Victor (M) LOC-1136*   67   25-35
Soundtrack (1966) .... *RCA Victor (S) LSO-1136*   67   40-50
   Composer: Konrad Elfers. **Conductor:** Konrad Elfers.

FUNNY FACE
Original Cast (1927) .... *World (M) SH-144*   **$20-25**
Original Cast (1927) ....*Monmouth Evergreen (SE) MES-7037* Re   **8-12**
Original Cast (1927) ....*Smithsonian (M) R-019* Re   **8-12**
   Composer: George Gershwin; Ira Geshwin. **Conductor:** Julian Jones. **Cast:** Fred Astaire;
   Adele Astaire; Bernard Clifton; Leslie Henson; Sydney Howard; George Gershwin.
Soundtrack (1957) ....*Verve (M) MGV-15001* 57   **35-40**
Soundtrack (1957) .... *Stet (M) DS-15001* 77   **8-10**
   Composer: George Gershwin; Ira Gershwin. **Conductor:** Adolph Deutsch. **Cast:** Fred Astaire;
   Audrey Hepburn; Kay Thompson (with additional songs by Roger Edens and Leonard Gershe).

FUNNY GIRL
Original Cast (1964) .... *Capitol (M) VAS-2059* 64   **10-15**
Original Cast (1964) .... *Capitol (S) SVAS-2059* 64   **15-20**
Original Cast (1964) ....*Capitol (S) STAO-2059* Re   **8-12**
   Composer: Jule Styne; Bob Merrill. **Conductor:** Milton Rosenstock. **Cast:** Barbra Streisand;
   Sydney Chaplin; Danny Meehan; Kay Medford; Jean Stapleton; John Lankston.
London Studio Cast (1964) .... *Music for Pleasure (M) MFP-1077* 64   **20-25**
   Composer: Jule Styne; Bob Merrill.
Soundtrack (1968) ....*Columbia (S) BOS-3220* 68   **10-15**
Soundtrack (1968) ....*Columbia (Q) SQ-30992* 71   **15-20**
Soundtrack (1968) ....*Columbia (S) JS-3220* Re   **8-10**
   Composer: Jule Styne; Bob Merrill. **Conductor:** Walter Scharf. **Cast:** Barbra Streisand,
   Omar Sharif.
Studio Cast (1968) .... *Motown (S) MS-672* 68   **15-20**
   Composer: Jule Styne; Bob Merrill. **Cast:** Diana Ross and the Supremes.

FUNNY LADY
Soundtrack (1975) .... *Arista (S) AL-9004* 75   **8-10**
   Composer: John Kander; Billy Rose; others. **Conductor:** Peter Matz. **Cast:** Barbra Streisand;
   James Caan; Ben Vereen.

FUNNY THING HAPPENED ON THE WAY TO THE FORUM
Original Cast (1962) .... *Capitol (M) WAO-1717* 62   **12-15**
Original Cast (1962) .... *Capitol (S) SWAO-1717* 62   **15-20**
   Composer: Stephen Sondheim; Ken Thorne. **Conductor:** Harold Hastings. **Cast:** Zero Mostel;
   Jack Gilford; David Burns; Ruth Kobart; John Carradine; Brian Davies; Ronald Holgate;
   Preshy Marker.
Original London Cast .... *Stet (S) DS-15028*   **10-15**
   Composer: Stephen Sondheim; Ken Thorne. **Cast:** Frankie Howard; Kenneth Connor; Jon
   Pertwee; Robertson Hare; Eddie Gray.
Soundtrack (1966) ....*United Artists (M) UAL-4144* 66   **10-15**
Soundtrack (1966) ....*United Artists (S) UAS-5144* 66   **15-20**
Soundtrack (1966) .... *United Artists (S) UA-LA284-G* 74   **10-12**
   Composer: Stephen Sondheim; Ken Thorne. **Conductor:** Ken Thorne. **Cast:** Zero Mostel;
   Phil Silvers; Jack Gilford; Buster Keaton; Michael Crawford; Annette Andre; Michael
   Hordem; Leon Greene.

FURY
Soundtrack (1978) .... *Arista (S) 4175* 78   **10-15**
   Composer: John Williams. **Conductor:** John Williams.

FUZZY PINK NIGHTGOWN
Soundtrack (1957) ....*Imperial (M) LP-9042-W* 57   **40-50**
Soundtrack (1957) .... *Imperial (SE) LPS-9042-W* 59   **40-50**
   Composer: Billy May. **Conductor:** Billy May.

G

G.I. BLUES

Soundtrack (1960) . . . . *RCA Victor (M) LPM-2256*   60   **$90-110**
 Black label, reads "Long Play" at bottom.
Soundtrack (1960) . . . . *RCA Victor (S) LSP-2256*   60   **100-125**
 Black label, reads "Living Stereo" at bottom.
Soundtrack (1960) . . . . *RCA Victor (M) LPM-2256*   63   **45-55**
 Black label, reads "Mono" at bottom.
Soundtrack (1960) . . . . *RCA Victor (S) LSP-2256*   65   **25-30**
 Black label, reads "Stereo" at bottom.
Soundtrack (1960) . . . . *RCA Victor (M) LPM-2256*   65   **25-30**
 Black label, reads "Monaural" at bottom.
Soundtrack (1960) . . . . *RCA Victor (S) LSP-2256*   69   **10-20**
 Orange or tan label. (Tan label issued in 1976).
Soundtrack (1960) . . . . *RCA Victor (S) AFL1-2256*   78   **8-10**
Soundtrack (1960) . . . . *RCA Victor (S) AYL1-3735*   81   **5-8**
 Composer: Sid Wayne; Sid Tepper; Roy C. Bennett; Fred Wise; Ben Weisman; Doc Pomus;
 Mort Schuman; Carl Perkins; others. Cast: Elvis Presley; Scotty Moore (guitar); Tiny Timbrell
 (guitar); D.J. Fontana (drums); Dudley Brooks (piano); Ray Siegel (bass); Jimmie Haskell
 (accordion); Jordanaires (vocals).

GABLE AND LOMBARD

Soundtrack (1976) . . . . *MCA (S) 2091*   76   **8-10**
 Composer: Michel Legrand. Conductor: Michel Legrand.

GABRIELLA

Soundtrack (1984) . . . . *RCA Victor (S) ABL1-5186*   84   **8-10**
 Composer: Antonio Carlos Jobim. Conductor: Oscar Castro Neeves.

GAILY, GAILY

Soundtrack (1969) . . . . *United Artists (S) UAS-5202*   69   **15-20**
 Composer: Henry Mancini. Conductor: Henry Mancini. Cast: Jimmie Rodgers; Henry Mancini.

GALLANT MEN

Studio Cast (1967) . . . . *Capitol (M) T-2643*   67   **10-12**
Studio Cast (1967) . . . . *Captiol (S) ST-2643*   67   **12-15**
 Composer: John Cacavas. Conductor: John Cacavas. Cast: U.S. Senator Everett McKinley
 Dirksen.

GAME IS OVER

Soundtrack (1967) . . . .*Atco (M) 205*   67   **20-25**
Soundtrack (1967) . . . . *Atco (S) SD-205*   67   **25-30**
 Composer: Jean-Peirre Bourtayre; Jean Bouchety.

GAME OF LIFE

Soundtrack . . . . *Word (S) W-2006*   **8-12**

GAMES

Soundtrack (1970) . . . . *Viking (S) LPS-105*   70   **150-175**
 Limited Edition.
 Composer: Francis Lai. Conductor: Francis Lai. Cast: Barbara Moore Singers; Elton John.

GAMES OF XXI OLYMPIAD, MONTREAL

Assembled Cast (1976) . . . . *Polydor (S) 2424124*   76   **10-12**
 Composer: Andre Mathieu.

GANDHI
Soundtrack (1982) .... *RCA Victor (S) ABL1-4557*   82   **$8-10**
Composer: Ravi Shankar; George Fenton. Conductor: George Fenton. Cast: Ravi Shankar.

GANG'S ALL HERE
Soundtrack (1943) .... *Sandy Hook (M) SH-2009*   78   **8-10**
Composer: Harry Warren; Leo Robbin. Cast: Benny Goodman and His Orchestra.

GANGBUSTERS
Original Radio Cast .... *Golden Age (M) 5018*   78   **8-10**

GARBAGE PAIL KIDS
Soundtrack (1987) .... *MCA (S) 6221*   87   **8-10**
Composer: Various. Cast: David Lawrence; Beat Farmers; Ed Keupper; Hakim and Lady
Dianna; Jimmy Scarlett and Dimensions; Debbie Lytton; Garbage Pail Kids.

GARBO
Soundtrack .... *MGM (M) E-4201*   64   **12-18**
Music from: *Anna Christie, Susan Lennox, Mata Hari, Grand Hotel, Queen Christina, Anna Karenina,
Camille, Conquest* and *Ninotchka.*
Composer: Various. Cast: Greta Garbo; John Barrymore; Robert Taylor; Charles Boyer; others.

GARDEN OF THE FINZI-CONTINIS
Soundtrack (1971) .... *RCA Victor (S) LSP-4712*   72   **20-25**
Composer: Manuel DeSica. Conductor: Carlo Savina.

GARRETT, PAT:
see PAT GARRETT

GAS-S-S-S
Soundtrack (1970) .... *American Int'l (S) A-1038*   71   **12-15**
Cast: Robert Corff; Gourmet's Delight; Johnny and the Tornados.

GATOR
Soundtrack (1976) .... *United Artists (S) UA-LA646-G*   76   **10-12**
Soundtrack (1976) .... *United Artists (S) LT-646*   76   **8-10**
Composer: Charles Bernstein; Jerry Reed; Bobby Goldsboro. Conductor: Charles Bernstein.
Cast: Jerry Reed; Bobby Goldsboro.

GAUNTLET
Soundtrack (1978) .... *Warner Bros. (S) BSK-3144*   78   **12-15**
Cover art by Frank Frazetta.
Composer: Jerry Fielding. Conductor: Jerry Fielding.

GAY DIVORCEE
Soundtrack (1934) .... *No Label Shown (SE) STS-105*   75   **10-12**
Composer: Cole Porter. Conductor: Mac Steiner. Cast: Fred Astaire; Ginger Rogers.

GAY LIFE
Original Cast (1961) .... *Capitol (M) WAO-1560*   61   **25-30**
Original Cast (1961) .... *Capitol (S) SWAO-1560*   61   **40-50**
Composer: Arthur Schwartz; Howard Dietz. Conductor: Herbert Greene. Cast: Walter Chiari;
Barbara Cook; Jules Munshin; Loring Smith; Elizabeth Allen; Jeanne Bal; Lu Leonard.

GAY PURR-EE
Soundtrack (1963) .... *Warner Bros. (M) B-1479*   62   **25-30**
Soundtrack (1963) .... *Warner Bros. (S) BS-1479*   62   **35-40**
Composer: Harold Arlen. Conductor: Mort Lindsey. Cast: Judy Garland; Red Buttons;
Robert Goulet; Paul Frees. (Voices used in conjunction with animation.)

GEISHA BOY
Soundtrack (1958) .... *Jubilee (M) JLP-1096*   58   **$45-55**
Soundtrack (1958) .... *Jubilee (S) SDJLP-109*   58   **75-100**
  Composer: Walter Scharf. **Conductor:** Muir Mathieson.

GEMS FROM GERSHWIN
Studiotrack (1954) .... *RCA Victor (EP) EPBT-3055*   54   **10-15**
  Double EP set.
Studiotrack (1954) .... *RCA Victor (M) LPT-3055*   54   **25-35**
  10-inch LP.
  Composer: George Gershwin. **Conductor:** Nathaniel Shilkret. **Cast:** Jane Froman; Felix
  Knight; Sunny Skylar; RCA Victor Salon Group.

GENE KRUPA STORY
Soundtrack (1959) .... *Verve (M) MGV-15010*   59   **45-50**
Soundtrack (1959) .... *Verve (S) MGVS-6105*   59   **60-70**
  Composer: Leith Stevens. **Conductor:** Leith Stevens. **Cast:** Gene Krupa; Red Nichols;
  Anita O'Day; Shelly Manne; Ruby Lane.

GENERAL ELECTRIC THEATER
TV Soundtrack (1959) .... *Columbia (M) CL-1395*   59   **35-40**
TV Soundtrack (1959) .... *Columbia (S) CS-8190*   59   **60-70**
TV Soundtrack (1959) .... *Columbia Special Products (S) ACS-8190*   81   **25-35**
  Cover pictures Ronald Reagan as the General Electric spokesman.
  Composer: Elmer Bernstein. **Conductor:** Elmer Bernstein.

GENGHIS KHAN
Soundtrack (1965) .... *Liberty (M) LPR-3412*   65   **45-50**
Soundtrack (1965) .... *Liberty (S) LST-7412*   65   **65-70**
  Composer: Dusan Radic. **Conductor:** Muir Mathieson.

GENTLE RAIN
Soundtrack (1966) .... *Mercury (M) MG-21016*   66   **20-25**
Soundtrack (1966) .... *Mercury (S) SR-61016*   66   **25-30**
  Composer: Luis Bonfa. **Conductor:** Eumir Deodata.

GENTLEMEN BE SEATED (MINSTREL SHOW)
Original Cast (1957) .... *Epic (EP) PG-9011*   57   **10-15**
Original Cast (1957) .... *Epic (M) LN-3238*   57   **25-35**
  Composer: Various. **Conductor:** Allen Roth. **Cast:** Gordon Goodman; John Neher; Stanley
  Kimes; Osie Johnson; Quartones; Merrill Staton Choir; Uncle John Cole; Jimmy Leyden;
  Mac Perrin; Merrill Ostrus; Don Craig; Jay Alden Edkins.

GENTLEMEN MARRY BRUNETTES
Soundtrack (1955) . . . . *Coral (M) CRL-57013*   55   **$55-60**
  Composer: Robert Farnon. **Cast:** Jane Russell; Jeanne Crain; Rudy Vallee; Johnny Desmond;
  Anita Ellis; Robert Farnon.

GENTLEMEN PREFER BLONDES
Original Cast (1949) . . . . *Columbia (EP) A-895*   50   **30-40**
  Triple EP set.
Original Cast (1949) . . . . *Columbia (EP) A-1736*   50   **15-20**
Original Cast (1949) . . . . *Columbia (M) OL-4290*   50   **25-30**
Original Cast (1949) . . . . *Columbia (SE) OS-2310*   63   **15-20**
Original Cast (1949) . . . . *Columbia (SE) S-32610*   73   **10-12**
Original Cast (1949) . . . . *Columbia (SE) CSO-AOS-2*   Re   **8-10**
  Composer: Jule Styne; Leo Robin. **Conductor:** Milton Rosenstock. **Cast:** Carol Channing;
  Yvonne Adair; Jack McCauley; Eric Brotherson; George Irving; Rex Evans; Alice Pearce;
  Cholly Atkins; Honi Coles.
Studio Cast (1962) . . . . *Caedmon (M) TC-1148*   62   **10-15**
  Has dialogue from the original story, but original score is replaced with hit tunes from the 1920s.
  Composer: Jule Styne; Leo Robin. **Conductor:** Charlie Katz. **Cast:** Carol Channing.
Soundtrack (1953) . . . . *MGM (EP) X-208*   53   **15-20**
Soundtrack (1953) . . . . *MGM (M) E-208*   53   **40-50**
  10-inch LP.
Soundtrack (1953) . . . . *MGM (M) E-3231*   55   **25-35**
  One side has music from *Till the Clouds Roll By.*
Soundtrack (1953) . . . . *Stet (M) DS-15005*   **8-10**
  Composer: Jule Styne; Leo Robin. **Conductor:** Lionel Newman. **Cast:** Marilyn Monroe;
  Jane Russell.

GEORGE K. ARTHUR'S PRIZE PACKAGE
Soundtrack . . . . *MGM (M) E-3151*   54   **60-70**
  With scores from: *The Stranger Left No Card, Martin and Gaston* and *A Prince for Cynthia.*
  Composer: Hugo Alfven; Temple Abady. **Conductor:** Muir Mathieson.

GEORGE M.!
Original Cast (1968) . . . . *Columbia (S) KOS-3200*   68   **15-20**
  Composer: George M. Cohan. **Conductor:** Jay Blackton. **Cast:** Joel Grey; Betty Ann Grove;
  Jill O'Hara; Bernadette Peters; Loni Ackerman; Jerry Dodge; Danny Carroll; Jonelle Allen;
  Jacqueline Alloway; Susan Batson; Jamie Donnelly; Harvey Evans; Angela Martin.

GERTRUDE STEIN'S FIRST READER
Original Cast (1970) . . . . *Polydor (S) 24-7002*   70   **20-25**
  Composer: Ann Sternberg; Gertrude Stein. **Cast:** Michael Anthony; Joy Garrett; Frank
  Giordano; Sandra Thornton; Ann Sternberg (piano).

GET CRAZY
Soundtrack (1983) . . . . *Morocco (S) 6065CL*   83   **8-10**
  Composer: Various. **Cast:** Sparks; Ramones; Lou Reed; Lori Eastside & Nada; Marshall
  Crenshaw; Malcolm McDowell; Bill Henderson; Michael Boddicker; Howard Kaylan;
  Fear with Lee Ving.

GET SMART
TV Soundtrack (1965) . . . . *United Artists (M) UAL-3533*   65   **20-25**
TV Soundtrack (1965) . . . . *United Artists (S) UAS-6533*   65   **25-30**
  Cast: Don Adams. (With dialogue.)

GET YOURSELF A COLLEGE GIRL
Soundtrack (1964) . . . .*MGM (M) E-4273*   64   **$15-20**
Soundtrack (1964) . . . . *MGM (S) SE-4273*   64   **15-25**
  Conductor: Fred Karger; others. Cast: Dave Clark Five; Animals; Stan Getz; Astrude Gilberto;
  Jimmy Smith Trio; Mary Ann Mobley; Standells; Freddie Bell and the Bell Boys; Roberta Linn.

GETTING STRAIGHT
Soundtrack (1970) . . . .*Colgems (S) COSO-5010*   70   **25-30**
  Composer: Ron Stein; others. Conductor: Ron Stein; others. Cast: P.K. Limited; New
  Establishment; Elliott Gould; Candice Bergen. (With dialogue.)

GHOST AND MRS. MUIR
Soundtrack (1947) . . *Elmer Bernstein's Film Music Collection (SE) FMC-4*   75   **50-100**
  Composer: Bernard Herrmann. Conductor: Elmer Bernstein.

GHOST OF FRANKENSTEIN
Soundtrack (1942) . . . . *Private Label (Tony Thomas) (SE) HS-TT*   79   **8-10**
  Private pressing.
  Composer: Hans J. Salter. Conductor: Hans J. Salter.

GHOST STORY
Soundtrack (1981) . . . .*MCA (S) 5287*   81   **10-15**
  Composer: Philippe Sarde. Conductor: Philippe Sarde.

GHOSTBUSTERS
Soundtrack (1984) . . . .*Arista (S) AL8-8246*   84   **8-10**
  Composer: Elmer Bernstein. Conductor: Elmer Bernstein. Cast: Ray Parker Jr.; Busboys;
  Alessi; Thompson Twins; Air Supply; Laura Branigan; Mick Smiley.

GHOSTS OF THE CIVIL DEAD
Soundtrack . . . . *Mute (S) 71433-1*   **8-10**
  Cast: Blixa Bargeld; Nick Cave; Mick Harvey.

GIANT
Soundtrack (1956) . . . . *Capitol (EP) EDM-773*   56   **15-25**
Soundtrack (1956) . . . .*Capitol (M) W-773*   56   **30-40**
Soundtrack (1956) . . . .*Capitol (SE) DW-773*   63   **10-20**
  Composer: Dimitri Tiomkin. Conductor: Dimitri Tiomkin; Ray Heindorf.
  Also see TRIBUTE TO JAMES DEAN

GIFT OF LOVE
Soundtrack (1958) . . . . *Columbia (M) CL-1113*   58   **60-70**
  Composer: Cyril Mockridge; Alfred Newman; Sammy Fain. Conductor: Lionel
  Newman. Cast: Vic Damone.

GIFT OF THE MAGI
TV Soundtrack (1959) . . . .*United Artists (M) UAL-4013*   59   **40-50**
TV Soundtrack (1959) . . . . *United Artists (S) UAS-5013*   59   **65-75**
  Composer: Richard Adler. Conductor: Hal Hastings. Cast: Eli Wallach (narration); Sally
  Ann Howes; Allen Case; Bibi Osterwald; Howard St. John; Jersey Quartet.

GIGI
Original Cast (1973) . . . . *RCA Victor (S) ABL1-0404*   73   **10-15**
  Composer: Frederick Loewe; Alan J. Lerner. Conductor: Ross Reimueller. Cast: Alfred
  Drake; Agnes Moorehead; Karin Wolfe; Daniel Massy; Maria Karnilova; Howard
  Chitjian; George Gaynes.
Studio Cast (1958) . . . . *RCA Victor (M) LPM-1716*   58   **15-20**
  Composer: Frederick Loewe; Alan J. Lerner. Conductor: Dennis Farnon. Cast: Gogi
  Grant; Tony Martin.
Soundtrack (1958) . . . .*MGM (M) E-3641*   58   **15-20**
Soundtrack (1958) . . . . *MGM (S) SE-3641*   58   **20-25**

GIGI (continued)

Soundtrack (1958) .... *MCA (S) 39045* 86 **$8-10**
Composer: Frederick Loewe; Alan J. Lerner. Conductor: Andre Previn. Cast: Leslie Caron;
Louis Jourdan; Maurice Chevalier; Hermione Gingold.

Studiotrack (1958) .... *Mercury (M) MG-20367* 58 **15-20**
Composer: Frederick Loewe; Alan J. Lerner. Cast: Robert Clary.

Soundtrack .... *MGM (M) MG-1* **20-40**
Triple LP, special promotional package.
Composer: Frederick Loewe; Alan J. Lerner. Cast: Leslie Caron; Maurice Chevalier; Louis
Jourdan; Hermione Gingold; Dick Hyman Trio; David Rose.

Studiotrack .... *Saga (S) XID-5017* **10-15**
Also has music from *Porgy and Bess*.

Studio Cast (1958) .... *Waldorf Music Hall (M) MHK 33-1249* 58 **15-20**
Composer: Frederick Loewe; Alan J. Lerner. Cast: Mike Stewart; Dottie Evans; Lois
Winter; Jerry Duane; others.

Studio Cast (1958) .... *Crown (S) CST-103* 58 **15-20**
Composer: Frederick Loewe; Alan J. Lerner. Conductor: Bernie Anders. Cast: Richard Hill;
Billy Mason; Madeline Carey; Rena Ritchie; Sonny Patrick.

Studio Cast (1960) .... *Richmond (M) B-20074* 60 **10-15**
One side has music from *South Pacific*.
Composer: Frederick Loewe; Alan J. Lerner; Richard Rodgers; Oscar Hammerstein II.
Conductor: Cyril Stapleton. Cast: Bryan Johnson; Joy Worth; Ray Merril; Janet Waters;
Andy Cole; Pat Whitworth.

Original Cast (1958) .... *Columbia (M) WL-158* 58 **15-25**
French version.
Composer: Frederick Loewe; Alan J. Lerner. Cast: Maurice Chevalier; Sacha Distel;
Marie-France; Jean Marker.

Studiotrack (1958) .... *Golden Crest (M) CR-3042* 58 **15-20**
Composer: Frederick Loewe; Alan J. Lerner. Cast: Hank Jones.

Studiotrack (1958) .... *MGM (EP) X-1601* 58 **5-10**
Volume one.

Studiotrack (1958) .... *MGM (EP) X-1602* 58 **5-10**
Volume two.

Studiotrack (1958) .... *MGM (M) E-3640* 58 **10-15**
Composer: Frederick Loewe; Alan J. Lerner. Conductor: David Rose. Cast: David Rose
and His Orchestra.

Studiotrack (1958) .... *Grand Award (S) GA-215SD* 58 **10-15**
Composer: Frederick Loewe; Alan J. Lerner. Conductor: Enoch Light. Cast: Enoch Light
and His Orchestra.
Also see BRIGADOON

GIGOT

Soundtrack (1962) .... *Capitol (M) W-1754* 62 **35-40**
Soundtrack (1962) .... *Capitol (S) SW-1754* 62 **45-50**
Composer: Jackie Gleason. Conductor: Jackie Gleason. Cast: Jackie Gleason.

GILDA RADNER LIVE

Original Cast (1979) .... *Warner Bros. (S) HS-3320* 79 **10-12**
Conductor: Howard Shore. Cast: Gilda Radner.

GINGERBREAD BOY

Studio Cast (1960) .... *Harmony (M) HL-9528* 60 **10-15**
One side has music and narration from *Goldilocks and the Three Bears*.
Composer: Curtis Biever. Conductor: Curtis Biever. Cast: David Allen (narration).

GIRL CRAZY
Studio Cast (1952) .... *Columbia (M) ML-4475*   52   **$25-35**
Studio Cast (1952) .... *Columbia (M) CL-822*   56   **20-25**
Studio Cast (1952) .... *Columbia (SE) OS-2560*   59   **15-20**
Studio Cast (1952) .... *Columbia Special Products (SE) COS-2560*   Re   **8-10**
  Composer: George Gershwin; Ira Gershwin. **Cast:** Mary Martin; Louise Carlyle; Eddie Chappell.
Studio Cast (1953) .... *RCA Victor (EP) EPA-486*   53   **15-20**
Studio Cast (1953) .... *RCA Victor (M) LPM-3156*   53   **25-30**
  One side has music from *Porgy and Bess.*
  Composer: George Gershwin; Ira Gershwin. **Conductor:** Lehman Engel. **Cast:** Lisa Kirk;
  Helen Gallagher; Edith Adams.
Studio Cast (1962) .... *Reprise (M) R-6032*   62   **10-15**
Studio Cast (1962) .... *Reprise (S) RS-6032*   62   **15-20**
  Composer: George Gershwin; Ira Gershwin. **Conductor:** Morris Stoloff.
Soundtrack (1943) .... *Decca (M) DL-5412*   52   **60-70**
  10-inch LP.
  Composer: George Gershwin; Ira Gershwin. **Conductor:** George Stoll. **Cast:** Judy Garland;
  Mickey Rooney.
  Also see BY JUPITER

GIRL FRIEND
Studio Cast (1960) .... *Epic (M) LN-3685*   60   **25-30**
  Also has music from *White Horse Inn* and *The New Moon.*
  Composer: Richard Rodgers; Lorenz Hart. **Conductor:** Johnny Gregory. **Cast:** Doreen Hume;
  Bruce Trent.

GIRL FROM U.N.C.L.E.
TV Soundtrack (1966) .... *MGM (M) E-4410*   66   **15-20**
TV Soundtrack (1966) .... *MGM (S) SE-4410*   66   **20-25**
  Composer: Dave Grusin; Jerry Goldsmith; others. **Conductor:** Teddy Randazzo.

GIRL HAPPY
Soundtrack (1965) .... *RCA Victor (M) LPM-3338*   65   **40-50**
  Black label, reads "Monaural" at bottom.
Soundtrack (1965) ...., *RCA Victor (S) LSP-3338*   65   **40-50**
  Black label, reads "Stereo" at bottom.
Soundtrack (1965) .... *RCA Victor (S) LSP-3338*   69   **10-20**
  Orange or tan label. (Tan label issued in 1976.)
Soundtrack (1965) .... *RCA Victor (S) AFL1-3338*   78   **8-10**
  Composer: Doc Pomus; Bill Giant; Bernie Baum; Florence Kaye; Sid Tepper; Roy C. Bennett;
  Sid Wayne; Ben Weisman; others. **Cast:** Elvis Presley; Scotty Moore (guitar); D.J. Fontana
  (drums); Ray Siegel (bass); Jordanaires (vocals); Carole Lombard Trio (vocals); Jubilee
  Four (vocals).

GIRL HUNT BALLET:
see BAND WAGON

GIRL IN PINK TIGHTS
Original Cast (1954) .... *Columbia (EP) A-1105*   58   **20-30**
Original Cast (1954) .... *Columbia (M) ML-4890*   58   **50-60**
Original Cast (1954) .... *Columbia (SE) AOL-4890*   Re   **8-10**
  Composer: Sigmund Romberg; Leo Robin. **Conductor:** Sylvan Levin. **Cast:** Jeanmarie; Charles
  Goldner; David Atkinson; Brenda Lewis; Lydia Fredericks; Kalem Kermoyan; John Stamford.

GIRL IN THE BIKINI
Soundtrack (1952) .... *Poplar (M) 33-1002*   52   **175-225**
  Composer: Jean Yatove. **Cast:** Brigitte Bardot.

GIRL MOST LIKELY
Soundtrack (1957) . . . . *Capitol (M) W-930*   58   **$80-100**
   Composer: Hugh Martin; Ralph Blane; Nelson Riddle. **Conductor:** Nelson Riddle.
   Cast: Jane Powell; Cliff Robertson; Keith Andes; Kaye Ballard; Tommy Noonan; Jud
   Conlon Singers.

GIRL ON A MOTORCYCLE
Soundtrack (1969) . . . . *Tetragrammaton (S) T-5000*   69   **20-25**
   Composer: Les Reed. **Cast:** Douglas Gamley.

GIRL WHO CAME TO SUPPER
Original Cast (1963) . . . . *Columbia (M) KOL-6020*   63   **30-35**
Original Cast (1963) . . . . *Columbia (S) KOS-2420*   63   **40-45**
   Composer: Noel Coward. **Conductor:** Jay Blackton. **Cast:** Jose Ferrer; Florence Henderson;
   Roderick Cook; Sean Scully; Tessie O'Shea; Carey Nairnes.
Studio Cast . . . . *DRG (M) SL-5178*   **8-10**
   Noel Coward narrates and sings songs from the score.
   Composer: Noel Coward. **Conductor:** Jay Blackton. **Cast:** Noel Coward.

GIRLS, LES:
see LES GIRLS

GIRLS! GIRLS! GIRLS!
Soundtrack (1962) . . . . *RCA Victor (M) LPM-2621*   62   **75-90**
   Black label, reads "Long Play" at bottom.
Soundtrack (1962) . . . . *RCA Victor (S) LSP-2621*   62   **90-100**
   Black label, reads "Living Stereo" at bottom.
Soundtrack (1962) . . . . *RCA Victor (M) LPM-2621*   63   **40-50**
   Black label, reads "Mono" at bottom.
Soundtrack (1962) . . . . *RCA Victor (S) LSP-2621*   65   **35-45**
   Black label, reads "Stereo" at bottom.
Soundtrack (1962) . . . . *RCA Victor (M) LPM-2621*   65   **25-30**
   Black label, reads "Monaural" at bottom.
Soundtrack (1962) . . . . *RCA Victor (S) LSP-2621*   69   **10-20**
   Orange or tan label. (Tan label issued in 1976.)
Soundtrack (1962) . . . . *RCA Victor (S) AFL1-2621*   77   **8-10**
   Composer: Jerry Leiber; Mike Stoller; Bill Giant; Bernie Baum; Florence Kaye; Ruth Batchelor;
   Dudley Brooks; Sid Tepper; Roy C. Bennett; Otis Blackwell; others. **Cast:** Elvis Presley; Scotty
   Moore (guitar); Tiny Timbrell (guitar); Barney Kessel (guitar); Ray Siegel (bass); D.J. Fontana
   (drums); Dudley Brooks (piano); Boots Randolph (sax); Jordanaires (vocals); Amigos (vocals).

GIRLS JUST WANT TO HAVE FUN
Soundtrack (1985) . . . . *Mercury (S) 422-824*   85   **10-12**
Soundtrack (1985) . . . . *Mercury (S) 824510-1*   Re   **8-10**
   Composer: Various. **Cast:** Alex Brown; Chris Farren; Rainey; Q-Feel; Deborah Galli; Tami
   Holbrook; Meredith Marshall; Animotion; Amy Hart; Holland.

GIVE 'EM HELL HARRY!
Soundtrack (1975) . . . . *United Artists (S) UA-LA540-H2*   75   **20-25**
   Double LP set. Contains dialogue only.
   Cast: James Whitmore (as Harry S. Truman).

GIVE MY REGARDS TO BROAD STREET
Soundtrack (1984) . . . . *Columbia (S) SC-39613*   84   **10-12**
   Composer: Paul McCartney; John Lennon. **Cast:** Paul McCartney; Linda McCartney; Ringo Starr.

GLASS MENAGERIE
Soundtrack (1987) . . . . *MCA (S) 6222*   87   **8-10**
   Composer: Henry Mancini. **Conductor:** Henry Mancini. **Cast:** Henry Mancini and His Orchestra.

GLASS SLIPPER:
see AUNTIE MAME

GLENN MILLER STORY

Soundtrack (1954) .... *Decca (EP) ED-2124*	56	**$10-15**
Soundtrack (1954) .... *Decca (EP) ED-2125*	56	**10-15**
Soundtrack (1954) .... *Decca (M) DL-5519*	54	**40-50**
10-inch LP.		
Soundtrack (1954) .... *Decca (M) DL-8226*	56	**25-30**
Soundtrack (1954) .... *Decca (SE) DL7-8226*	59	**15-20**
Soundtrack (1954) .... *Decca (M) DL-9123*	65	**12-18**
Soundtrack (1954) .... *Decca (SE) DL7-9123*	65	**12-18**
Soundtrack (1954) .... *MCA (SE) 2036e*	72	**8-10**
Soundtrack (1954) .... *RCA Victor (EP) EPBT-3057*	54	**10-20**
Soundtrack (1954) .... *RCA Victor (M) LPT-3057*	54	**35-45**
10-inch LP.		

  Conductor: Glenn Miller. **Cast:** Glenn Miller and His Orchestra.

Studiotrack (1956) .... *RCA Victor (EP) EPA-733*	56	**10-15**
Studiotrack (1956) .... *RCA Victor (EP) EPB-1192*	56	**15-20**
Double EP set.		

  Conductor: Glenn Miller. **Cast:** Glenn Miller and His Orchestra.

Studiotrack (1956) .... *RCA Victor (M) LPM-1192*	56	**20-25**
Studiotrack (1956) .... *Decca (M) DL-5532*	56	**25-35**

  Cast: Louis Armstrong and the All Stars.

GLORY GUYS

Soundtrack (1965) .... *United Artists (M) UAL-4126*	65	**15-20**
Soundtrack (1965) .... *United Artists (S) UAS-5126*	65	**20-25**

  Composer: Riz Ortolani. **Conductor:** Riz Ortolani.

GLORY STOMPERS

Soundtrack (1968) .... *Sidewalk (S) DT-5910*	68	**15-20**

  Composer: Mike Curb; Harley Hatcher; Davie Allan. **Cast:** Davie Allan and the Arrows;
  Max Frost and the Troopers; Casey Kasem; Eddie and the Stompers; Sidewalk Sounds.

GO FIGHT CITY HALL:
see BEI MIR BISTU SCHOEN

GO FLY A KITE

Original Cast (1966) .... *General Electric (S) No Number Used*	66	**80-100**

  Double LP set. General Electric presented this show at the Fifth Electric Utility Conference, in
  Williamsburg, Virginia, September 19 - 21, 1966. The LP was distributed there as a souvenir.
  Composer: John Kander; Walter Marks; Fred Ebb. **Conductor:** Ted Simons. **Cast:** Valerie
  Harper; Henry Hamilton; Nancy Haywood; Joel Warfield.

GO, GO, GO, WORLD
Soundtrack (1965) .... *Musicor (M) MM-2059*   65 $20-30
   Composer: Bruno Nicolai; Nino Oliviero.

GO INTO YOUR DANCE
Soundtrack (1935) .... *Wunderbar (SE) SH-402*   10-15
   Composer: Various. **Cast:** Al Jolson; Ruby Keeler; Dick Powell.

GO, JOHNNY, GO!
Soundtrack (1959) .... *No Label Shown (EP) No Number Used*   60   25-50
   Composer: Various. **Conductor:** Hal Roach. **Cast:** Jimmy Clanton.
Soundtrack (1959) .... *No Label Shown (M) No Number Used*   59   500-600
   Promotional issue only.
   Composer: Various. **Cast:** Jimmy Clanton; Sandy Stewart; Jackie Wilson; Chuck Berry;
   Cadillacs; Flamingos; Eddie Cochran; Ritchie Valens; Harvey Fuqua; Jo Ann Campbell.

GOD CREATED WOMAN:
see AND GOD CREATED WOMAN

GOD'S LITTLE ACRE
Soundtrack (1958) .... *United Artists (M) UAL-40002*   58   125-150
   Composer: Elmer Bernstein. **Conductor:** Elmer Bernstein.

GODFATHER
Soundtrack (1972) .... *Paramount (S) PAS-1003*   72   15-20
   Composer: Nino Rota; Carmine Coppola; others. **Conductor:** Carmine Coppola; Carlo Savina.
   Cast: Al Martino.

GODFATHER, PART II
Soundtrack (1975) .... *ABC (S) DP-856*   75   15-20
   Composer: Nino Rota; Carmine Coppola. **Conductor:** Carmine Coppola. **Cast:** Livio Giorgi;
   Nino Palmermo; Marcia Religioso.

GODFATHER, PARTS I & II
TV Soundtrack (1972-74) .... *Sunnyvale (S) SSP2000*   77   10-20
   Has music from TV's *The Godfather Saga*.
   Composer: Carmine Coppola; Nino Rota; Francesco Pennino. **Conductor:** Carmine Coppola.
   Cast: Milan Philarmonia Orchestra.

GODS MUST BE CRAZY
Soundtrack (1981) .... *Novus (S) 3091-1-N9*   81   **$8-10**

GODSPELL
Original Cast (1971) .... *Bell (S) 1102*   71   **10-15**
Musical based on the Gospel.
Original Cast (1971) .... *Arista (S) 4001*   75   **10-12**
Original Cast (1971) .... *Arista (S) ALB6-8304*   Re   **8-10**
Composer: Stephen Schwartz. Conductor: Stephen Schwartz. Cast: Lamar Alford; Jesse Cutler;
Peggy Gordon; David Haskell; Joanna Jonas; Richard LaBonte; Robin Lamont; Gilmer
McCormick; Sonia Manzano; Jeffrey Mylett; Stephen Nathan; Steve Reinhardt; Herb Simon.
Original Australian Cast (1971) .... *Lewis Young Prod. (S) SFL-93448*   71   **25-30**
Composer: Stephen Schwartz. Conductor: Rory Thomas. Cast: Domenic Luca; Chris Sheil;
Karen Corbett; Christopher Pate; Paul Reid Roman; Colette Mann; Julian Archer; Rob Ellis.
Soundtrack (1973) .... *Arista (S) 4005*   75   **10-12**
Soundtrack (1973) .... *Bell (S) 1118*   73   **12-15**
Soundtrack (1973) .... *Arista (S) ALB6-8337*   Re   **8-10**
Composer: Stephen Schwartz. Conductor: Stephen Reinhardt. Cast: David Haskell; Victor
Garber; Robin Lamont; Joanne Jonas.

GOIN' BACK TO INDIANA
TV Soundtrack (1971) .... *Motown (S) M-742*   71   **10-12**
Composer: Various. Cast: Jackson Five; Bill Cosby; Tom Smothers.

GOING HOLLYWOOD
Soundtrack .... *Crosbyana Volume 17*   **10-12**
Soundtracks from Bing Crosby films, 1928 - 1964.
Cast: Bing Crosby.

GOING MY WAY
Studiotrack (1944) .... *Decca (M) DL-5052*   50   **40-50**
10-inch LP.
Composer: James Van Heusen; others. Conductor: John Scotty Trotter; Victor Young.
Cast: Bing Crosby; Williams Brothers; Ken Darby Singers.
Also see SWINGING ON A STAR

GOING SURFIN'
Soundtrack (1975) .... *Cowabunga (S) 1001*   75   **15-20**

GOLD
Soundtrack (1975) .... *ABC (S) ABCD-855*   75   **15-20**
Composer: Elmer Bernstein. Conductor: Elmer Bernstein. Cast: Maureen McGovern;
Jimmy Helms; Trevor Chance.

GOLD DIGGERS (OF 1933 AND 1935):
see GOLDEN AGE OF THE HOLLYWOOD MUSICAL

GOLDBERG, WHOOPI:
see WHOOPI GOLDBERG

GOLDEN AGE OF BRITISH FILM MUSIC
Soundtrack .... *Citadel (S) CT-OFI-1*   82   **15-20**
Composer: Bliss; Hopkins; Alwyn; Greenwood; Irving; others.

GOLDEN AGE OF MOVIE MUSICALS
Soundtrack (1972) .... *MGM (S) SQBO-93890*   72   **10-15**
Double LP set. Includes a 12-page guidebook.
Composer: Various. Cast: Judy Garland; Fred Astaire and Jane Powell; Ava Gardner; Gene Kelly
and Georges Guetary; Bert Lahr; Kathryn Grayson; Debbie Reynolds; Ann Miller; Howard Keel.

GOLDEN AGE OF THE HOLLYWOOD MUSICAL

Soundtrack . . . . *United Artists (S) UA-LA215-H*   72   **$10-12**
Soundtrack . . . . *Liberty (S) LKAO-215*   Re   **8-10**
Music from: *Gold Diggers of 1933, Dames, 42nd Street, Footlight Parade* and *Gold Diggers of 1935.*
Composer: Harry Warren; others. **Conductor:** Ray Heindorf; Leo F. Forbstein. **Cast:** George
Raft (narration); Joan Blondell; Ruby Keeler; Dick Powell.

GOLDEN APPLE

Original Cast (1954) . . . . *RCA Victor (EP) EOD-1014*   54   **20-30**
Original Cast (1954) . . . . *RCA Victor (M) LOC-1014*   54   **75-90**
Original Cast (1954) . . . . *Elektra (M) EKL-5000*   60   **45-60**
Composer: Jerome Moross; John Latouche. **Conductor:** Hugh Ross. **Cast:** Priscilla Gillette;
Stephen Douglass; Kaye Ballard; Bibi Osterwald; Portia Nelson; Kaye Ballard; Martha
Larrimore; Dean Michener; Geraldine Viti; Jack Whiting.

GOLDEN BOY

Original Cast (1964) . . . . *Capitol (M) VAS-2124*   64   **25-30**
Gatefold cover.
Original Cast (1964) . . . . *Capitol (S) SVAS-2124*   64   **35-40**
Gatefold cover.
Original Cast (1964) . . . . *Capitol (S) STAO-1165*   77   **10-15**
Has an alternate finale, different than heard on the original issue.
Composer: Charles Strouse; Lee Adams. **Conductor:** Elliot Lawrence. **Cast:** Sammy Davis Jr.;
Billy Daniels; Paula Wayne; Kenneth Tobey; Louis Gossett; Lola Falana; Boxers; John
Brown; Terrin Miles.
Studiotrack (1964) . . . . *Capitol (M) T-2278*   64   **10-15**
Studiotrack (1964) . . . . *Capitol (S) ST-2278*   64   **12-20**
Conductor: H.B. Barnum.
Studiotrack (1964) . . . . *Wyncote (M) W-9033*   64   **8-12**

GOLDEN BREED

Soundtrack (1967) . . . . *Capitol (S) ST-2886*   67   **12-18**
Composer: Mike Curb; Jerry Styner; Harley Hatcher. **Cast:** Mike Clifford; Davie Allen.

GOLDEN CHILD

Soundtrack (1986) . . . . *Capitol (S) SJ-12544*   87   **8-10**
Composer: John Barry; others. **Cast:** Ann Wilson; Melissa Morgan; Ashford and Simpson;
Martha Davis; Ratt; Marlon Jackson; Robbie Buchanen; John Barry.

GOLDEN COACH

Soundtrack (1952) . . . . *MGM (M) E-3111*   54   **135-150**
Composer: Antonio Vivaldi; others. **Conductor:** Gino Marinuzzi Jr.

GOLDEN EARRINGS

Soundtrack (1947) . . . . *Decca (M) DL-8008*   50   **50-60**
Composer: Victor Young. **Conductor:** Victor Young.
Also see FOR WHOM THE BELL TOLLS

GOLDEN HOLLYWOOD THEMES

Soundtrack (1963) . . . . *Decca (M) DL-4362*   63   **10-15**
Soundtrack (1963) . . . . *Decca (S) DL7-4362*   63   **15-20**

GOLDEN HORSESHOE REVIEW

Original Cast . . . . *Disneyland (M) WDL-3013*   **10-12**

GOLDEN MOTION PICTURE THEMES (AND ORIGINAL SOUNDTRACKS)
Soundtrack ....*United Artists (M) UAL-3376*   64   **$10-15**
Soundtrack .... *United Artists (S) UAS-6376*   64   **15-20**
  Composer: Various. **Conductor:** Various. **Cast:** Al Caiola; LeRoy Holmes; others.

GOLDEN RAINBOW
Original Cast (1968) ....*Calendar (M) KOM-1001*   68   **30-35**
Original Cast (1968) ....*Calendar (S) KOS-1001*   68   **40-50**
  Composer: Walter Marks. **Conductor:** Elliot Lawrence. **Cast:** Steve Lawrence; Eydie Gorme;
  Scott Jacoby; Joseph Sirola.

GOLDEN SCREW
Original Cast (1967) ....*Atco (M) 33-208*   67   **25-30**
Original Cast (1967) ....*Atco (S) SD-33-208*   67   **30-40**
  Composer: Tom Sankey. **Cast:** Tom Sankey; Jack Hooper and the Inner Sanctum.

GOLDEN SEAL
Soundtrack (1983) ....*Compleat (S) CSTR-6001*   83   **10-15**
  Composer: John Barry; Dana Kaproff. **Cast:** Glen Campbell.

GOLDEN THEMES FROM MOTION PICTURES
Studiotrack (1962) ....*United Artists (M) UAL-3210*   62   **10-15**
Studiotrack (1962) .... *United Artists (S) UAS-6210*   62   **10-20**
  Includes: *Picnic, Spellbound, Mona Lisa, As Time Goes By, Moulin Rouge, My Foolish Heart, Be*
  My Love, All the Way, Tammy, Secret Love, True Love and *The High and the Mighty.*
  Composer: Various. **Cast:** Ferrante and Teicher.

GOLDEN VOYAGE OF SINBAD
Soundtrack (1974) ....*United Artists (S) UA-LA308-G*   74   **20-25**
  Composer: Miklos Rozsa. **Conductor:** Miklos Rozsa.

GOLDFINGER
Soundtrack (1964) ....*United Artists (M) UAL-4117*   64   **10-15**
Soundtrack (1964) .... *United Artists (S) UAS-5117*   64   **15-20**
  Composer: John Barry. **Conductor:** John Barry. **Cast:** Shirley Bassey; John Barry.

GOLDFINGER (AND OTHER MUSIC FROM JAMES BOND THRILLERS)
Studiotrack (1964) .... *RCA Victor/Camden (M) CAL-913*   64   **8-12**
Studio (1965) .... *RCA Victor/Camden (S) CAS-913*   65   **10-12**
  Composer: John Barry. **Cast:** Ray Martin and His Orchestra.

GOLDILOCKS
Original Cast (1958) ....*Columbia (M) OL-5340*   58   **30-40**
Original Cast (1958) ....*Columbia (S) OS-2007*   58   **40-50**
Original Cast (1958) ./.......... *Columbia Special Products (S) COS-2007*   Re   **8-10**
  Composer: Leroy Anderson; Joan Ford; Walter Kerr; Jean Kerr. **Conductor:** Lehman Engel.
  Cast: Don Ameche; Elaine Stritch; Russell Nype; Pat Stanley; Nathaniel Frey; Margaret
  Hamilton; Gene Varrone; Richard Armbruster.
TV Soundtrack (1970) ...... *Evans-Black Carpets/Armstrong (S) DL-3511*   70   **10-12**
  Composer: Richard M. Sherman; Robert B. Sherman. **Cast:** Bing Crosby; Mary Frances
  Crosby; Kathryn Crosby; Nathaniel Crosby; Paul Winchell (narrator); Avery Schrieber.

GOLDILOCKS AND THE THREE BEARS:
see GINGERBREAD BOY

GOLIATH AND THE BARBARIANS
Soundtrack (1960) ....*American Int'l (M) 1001-M*   60   **50-65**
Soundtrack (1960) .... *American Int'l (S) 1001-S*   60   **75-85**
Soundtrack (1960) ....*Varese Sarabande (S) VC-81078*   78   **8-10**
  Composer: Les Baxter. **Conductor:** Muir Mathieson.

GONE WITH THE WAVE

Soundtrack (1965) .... *Colpix (M) CP-492*	65	**$12-15**
Soundtrack (1965) .... *Colpix (S) SCP-492*	65	**15-20**

Composer: Lalo Schifrin. **Conductor:** Lalo Schifrin. **Cast:** Shelly Manne; Laurindo Almeida.

GONE WITH THE WIND

Studio Cast (1973) .... *Chappell (S) CHP-101*	73	**50-60**

Composer: Harold Rome. **Cast:** Harold Rome (singing the complete score, including songs cut from the show); Et Tu Brutus Ensemble.

Soundtrack (1939) .... *MGM (M) 1E-10*	67	**20-25**
Soundtrack (1939) .... *MGM (SE) S1E-10*	67	**25-30**

Above two limited edition LPs came with a 32-page color booklet.

Soundtrack (1939) .... *MGM (M) 1E-10*	67	**10-15**
Soundtrack (1939) .... *MGM (SE) S1E-10*	67	**10-15**

Above two do not have the booklet.

Soundtrack (1939) .... *MGM (M) E-3954*	61	**35-40**
Soundtrack (1939) .... *MGM (SE) SE-3954*	61	**35-45**

Above two are "Commemorative editions." All above are with a gatefold cover.

Soundtrack (1939) .... *Metro (M) M-613*	66	**10-15**
Soundtrack (1939) .... *Metro (SE) MS-613*	66	**15-20**

Above two are abridged versions of MGM E/SE-3954.

Composer: Max Steiner. **Conductor:** Cyril Ornadel. **Cast:** Cyril Ornadel and the Starlight Symphony.

Soundtrack (1939) .... *MCA (SE) 39063*	Re	**8-10**

Same as MGM SE-3954. All of the above shown as stereo are in rechanneled stereo.

Studiotrack (1954) .... *RCA Victor (M) LPM-3227*	54	**50-60**

10-inch LP.

Studiotrack (1954) .... *RCA Victor/Camden (M) CAL-625*	61	**15-20**
Studiotrack (1954) .... *RCA Victor (M) LPM-3859*	67	**20-25**
Studiotrack (1954) .... *RCA Victor (SE) LPS-3859*	67	**20-25**
Studiotrack (1959) .... *Warner Bros. (M) W-1322*	59	**20-25**
Studiotrack (1959) .... *Warner Bros. (S) WS-1322*	59	**25-30**

Above two are labeled "Official Centennial" recordings. With gatefold covers, and booklet.

Studiotrack (1959) .... *Warner Bros. (M) W-1322*	61	**15-20**
Studiotrack (1959) .... *Warner Bros. (S) SW-1322*	61	**20-25**
Studiotrack (1959) .... *Warner Bros. (S) WS-1322*	72	**10-15**
Studiotrack (1959) .... *Stanyan (S) SR-10090*	73	**8-10**

Composer: Max Steiner. **Conductor:** Muir Mathieson.

Studiotrack (1939) .... *RCA Victor (SE) ARL1-0452*	74	**10-12**

Part of the *Classic Film Score Series*.

Composer: Max Steiner. **Conductor:** Charles Gerhardt.

Soundtrack .... *Pickwick (M) PC-3087*		**10-15**

Soundtrack .... *Pickwick (S) SPC-3087*   **$10-15**
  Complete original score.
  Composer: Max Steiner. **Conductor:** Walter Scott. **Cast:** London Symphonia.
  Also see PARRISH

GONE WITH THE WIND (AND OTHERS)
  Studiotrack (1954) .... *RCA Victor (M) LPM-1287* 56   **20-25**
  One side has music from four other Steiner scores: *The Charge of the Light Brigade, Four Wives,*
  The Searchers and *A Stolen Life.* This side was later issued on side two of *Death of a Scoundrel.*
  Also see DEATH OF A SCOUNDREL

GOOD COMPANIONS
  Composer: Andre Previn; Johnny Mercer. **Cast:** John Mills.

GOOD EVENING
  Original Cast (1973) .... *Island (S) ILPS-9298*   73   **15-20**
  Composer: Peter Cook; Dudley Moore. **Cast:** Peter Cook; Dudley Moore.

GOOD MORNING, VIETNAM
  Soundtrack (1987) .... *A&M (S) SP-3913* 87   **8-10**
  Composer: Various. **Cast:** Martha Reeves and Vandellas; Beach Boys; Wayne Fontana and
  Mindbenders; Searchers; Castaways; James Brown; Them; Marvelettes; Vogues; Rivieras;
  Louis Armstrong.

GOOD NEWS
  Original Cast (1974) .... *Private Label (S) SA-101/4*   **10-15**
  Double LP set, gatefold cover. Live performances.
  Composer: DeSylva; Brown; Henderson. **Cast:** Alace Faye; John Payne; Stubby Kaye.
  Studio Cast .... *World (M) WRC-7065*   **20-25**
  One side has music from *Sally.*
  Studio Cast (1974) .... *Signature (S) BSL1-0577* 74   **10-12**
  Composer: Ray Henderson; Lew Brown; Buddy DeSylva. **Cast:** Teresa Brewer.
  Soundtrack (1947) .... *MGM (EP) X-17* 50   **15-20**
  Soundtrack (1947) .... *MGM (M) E-504* 50   **40-50**
  10-inch LP.
  Soundtrack (1947) .... *MGM (M) E-3229* 55   **25-30**
  One side has music from *Three Little Words.*
  Soundtrack (1947) .... *MGM (M) E-3771* 59   **20-25**
  One side has music from *Words and Music.*
  Composer: Ray Henderson; Louis Brown; Buddy DeSylva. **Conductor:** Lennie Hayton.
  Cast: June Allyson; Peter Lawford; Pat Marshall; Joan McCracken.

GOOD OLD BAD OLD DAYS!
  London Cast .... *AEI (S) 1116*   **8-12**
  Composer: Anthony Newley; Leslie Bricusse.

GOOD, THE BAD & THE UGLY
  Soundtrack (1968) .... *United Artists (M) UAL-4172* 68   **10-15**
  Soundtrack (1968) .... *United Artists (S) UAS-5172* 68   **10-15**
  Composer: Ennio Morricone.

GOOD TIMES
  Soundtrack (1967) .... *Atco (M) 33-314* 67   **10-15**
  Soundtrack (1967) .... *Atco (S) SD-33-214* 67   **15-20**
  Composer: Sonny Bono. **Cast:** Sonny and Cher. (With dialogue.)

GOOD TO GO
Soundtrack (1986) .... *Island (S) 90509-1*   86   **$8-10**
   Composer: Various. **Cast:** Trouble Funk; Ini Kamoze; Hot Cold Sweat; Sly and Robbie;
   Wally Badarou; Chuck Brown; Donald Banks; Redds and the Boys.
   Also see MUSIC FROM "A FISTFUL OF DOLLARS"

GOODBYE AGAIN
Soundtrack (1961) .... *United Artists (M) UAL-4091*   61   **35-40**
Soundtrack (1961) .... *United Artists (S) UAS-5091*   61   **40-45**
   Composer: Georges Auric. **Cast:** Ferrante and Teicher; Diahann Carroll.

GOODBYE CHARLIE
Soundtrack (1965) .... *20th Century-Fox (M) TFM-3165*   65   **25-35**
Soundtrack (1965) .... *20th Century-Fox (S) TFS-4165*   65   **30-40**
   Composer: Andre Previn. **Conductor:** Andre Previn.

GOODBYE COLUMBUS
Soundtrack (1969) .... *Warner Bros. (S) WS-1786*   69   **15-20**
   Composer: Charles Fox; Association; others. **Cast:** Association.

GOODBYE GEMINI
Soundtrack (1971) .... *DJM (S) DJLPS-408*   71   **25-30**
   Composer: Christopher Gunning; others. **Conductor:** Marcus Dods. **Cast:** Jackie Lee;
   Peddlers; Peter Lee Stirling.

GOODBYE MR. CHIPS
Soundtrack (1969) .... *MGM (S) S1E-19*   69   **15-20**
   Composer: Leslie Bricusse. **Conductor:** John Williams. **Cast:** Petula Clark; Peter O'Toole.

GOODTIME CHARLEY
Original Cast (1975) .... *RCA Victor (S) ARL1-1011*   75   **20-25**
   Composer: Hal Hackady; Larry Grossman. **Conductor:** Arthur B. Rubinstein. **Cast:** Joel Grey;
   Ann Reinking; Louis Zorich; Ed Becker; Susan Browning; Rhoda Butler; Peggy Cooper; Jay
   Garner; Grace Keagy; Nancy Killmer; Hal Norman; Charles Rule; Richard B. Shull; Brad Tyrrell.

GOODY TWO SHOES
Studio Cast .... *MGM/Young Directional (S) YDS 301*   **8-12**
   Cast: Efrem Zimbalist Jr. (narrator).

GOONIES
Soundtrack (1985) .... *Epic (S) SE-40067*   85   **8-10**
   Composer: Dave Grusin; others. **Cast:** Cyndi Lauper; REO Speedwagon; Luther Vanderdross;
   Joseph Williams; 14K; Philip Bailey; Bangles; Dave Grusin.

GORDON'S WAR
Soundtrack (1973) .... *Buddah (S) BDS-5137*   73   **10-12**
   Cast: Barbara Mason; New Birth; Badder Than Evil.

GORILLAS IN THE MIST - THE ADVENTURES OF DIAN FOSSEY
Soundtrack (1988) ....*MCA (S) 6255*   88   **$8-10**

GORKY PARK
Soundtrack (1983) .... *Varese Sarabande (S) STV-81206*   83   **8-12**
Composer: James Horner. Conductor: James Horner.

GOSPEL
Soundtrack (1983) .... *Savoy (S) 14753*   83   **8-10**

GOSPEL ACCORDING TO ST. MATTHEW
Soundtrack (1966) .... *Mainstream (M) 54000*   66   **50-60**
Soundtrack (1966) .... *Mainstream (S) S-54000*   66   **50-60**
With African drums and traditional Negro spirituals.
Composer: Bach; Mozart; Prokofiev; others.

GOSPEL AT COLONUS
Original Cast (1985) .... *Elektra/Nonesuch (S) 97919-1*   85   **20-25**
Original Cast (1985) .... *Warner Bros. (S) 1-25182*   Re   **8-10**
Composer: Bob Tilson; Lee Breuer. Cast: Jeuetta Steele; Wille Rogers; Five Blind Boys of
Alabama.

GOSPEL ROAD
Soundtrack (1982) .... *Priority (S) UG-32253*   82   **10-15**
Double LP set. The story of Jesus Christ, told and sung by Johnny Cash.
Cast: Johnny Cash.

GOTCHA
Soundtrack (1985) ....*MCA (S) 5596*   85   **8-10**
Composer: Bill Conti; others. Cast: Thereza Bazar; Giuffra; Camelflage; Hubert Kah; Joan
Jett and the Black Hearts; Bill Conti; Bronski Beat.

GOTHIC
Soundtrack (1987) .... *Virgin (S) 90607-1*   87   **20-30**
Composer: Thomas Dolby. Conductor: Thomas Dolby. Cast: Thomas Dolby; Timothy Spall;
Screamin' Lord Byron.

GOYA
Soundtrack (1959) ....*Decca (M) DL-8236*   59   **65-75**
Film biography of painter Francisco Goya.
Composer: Vincente G"mez. Cast: Vincente G"mez (guitar).

GRAB ME A GONDOLA
London Cast ....*AEI (S) 1119*   **8-12**

GRADUATE
Soundtrack (1968) ....*Columbia (S) OS-3180*   68   **10-15**
Soundtrack (1968) .... *Columbia (S) JS-3180*   68   **10-20**
Composer: Paul Simon; Additional music by David Grusin. Cast: Paul Simon; Art Garfunkel.

GRAND CANYON SUITE
Soundtrack (1959) .... *Disneyland (M) WDL-4019*   59   **15-20**
Soundtrack (1959) .... *Disneyland (S) STER-4019*   59   **20-25**
Composer: Ferde Grofe. Conductor: Frederick Stark. Cast: Frederick Stark and the Symphonie
Orchester Graunke.
Studiotrack (1955) ....*Columbia (EP) A-1088*   55   **10-15**
Studiotrack (1955) .... *Columbia (M) CL-716*   55   **25-35**
Composer: Frede Grofe. Conductor: Andre Kostelanetz. Cast: New York Philharmonic
Orchestra.
Also see LURE OF THE GRAND CANYON

GRAND MUSIC HALL OF ISRAEL
Original Cast (1967) .... *London (S) SW-99463*   67   **$15-20**
  Recorded live at L'Olympia, Paris.

GRAND PRIX
Soundtrack (1966) .... *MGM (M) 1E-8*   66   **20-25**
Soundtrack (1966) .... *MGM (S) 1SE-8*   66   **25-30**
Soundtrack (1966) .... *MCA (S) 25101*   Re   **8-10**
  Composer: Maurice Jarre. Conductor: Maurice Jarre.

GRAND TOUR
Original Cast (1979) .... *Columbia (S) JS-35761*   79   **8-10**
  Composer: Jerry Herman. Conductor: Wally Harper. Cast: Joel Grey; Florence Lacey;
  Ronald Holgate; Chevi Colton; Travis Hudson; Gene Varrone; Stephen Vinovich.

GRANDE BOURGEOISE, LA:
see LA GRANDE BOURGEOISE

GRANDMA MOSES
Soundtrack (1950) .... *Columbia (M) ML-2185*   50   **85-100**
  10-inch LP.
  Composer: Hugh Martin. Conductor: Daniel Saidenberg. Cast: Grandma Moses.

GRASS HARP
Original Cast (1971) .... *Painted Smiles (S) PS-1354*   71   **8-10**
  Composer: Claibe Richardson; Kenward Elmslie. Conductor: Theodore Saidenberg.
  Cast: Barbara Cook; Carol Brice; Karen Morrow; Ruth Ford; Max Showalter; Russ Thacker.

GRASSHOPPER
Soundtrack (1970) .... *National General (S) NG-1001*   70   **10-12**
  Composer: Billy Goldenberg. Conductor: Billy Goldenberg. Cast: Brooklyn Bridge; Vicki
  Lawrence; Bobby Russel; David Christine.

GREASE
Original Cast (1972) .... *MGM (S) 1SE-34*   72   **10-15**
Original Cast (1972) .... *Polydor (S) 827548-1*   Re   **8-12**
  Composer: Jim Jacobs; Warren Casey. Conductor: Louis St. Louis. Cast: Adrienne Barbeau;
  Walter Bobbie; Barry Bostwick; James Canning; Carole Demas; Katie Hanley; Tom Harris; Ilene
  Kristen; Dorothy Leon; Timothy Meyers; Kathi Moss; Alan Paul; Marya Small; Garn Stephens.
Soundtrack (1978) .... *RSO (S) RS 2-4002*   78   **10-12**
  Double LP set.
  Composer: Jim Jacobs; Warren Casey. Conductor: James Getzoff; Bill Oakes. Cast: Frankie
  Valli; John Travolta; Olivia Newton-John; Frankie Avalon; Stockard Channing; Jeff Conaway;
  Cindy Bullens; Sha-Na-Na; Louis St. Louis.

GREASE 2
Soundtrack (1982) .... *RSO (S) RS-1-3803*   82   **8-10**
  Composer: Various. Cast: Four Tops; others.

GREAT ADVENTURE FILM SCORES
Soundtrack .... *Entr' acte (S) ERS-6510*   **8-10**
  Side one has the suite from *The Four Musketeers* (studiotrack). Side two has *The Eagle Has Landed*
  (soundtrack).
  Composer: Lalo Schifrin. Conductor: Lalo Schifrin.

GREAT AMERICAN BACKSTAGE MUSICAL
Original Cast (1976) .... *AEI (S) 1101*   76   **8-10**
  Composer: Billy Solly. Conductor: Billy Solly. Cast: Gaye Kruger; Jerry Clark; Tamara Long.

GREAT AMERICAN MUSICAL
Original Cast (1979) ....*Fleetwood (S) FMS-1017*   79   **$10-15**
Double LP set.

GREAT AMERICANA FILM SCORES
Studiotrack .... *Entr' acte (S) ERS-6506*   77   **8-10**
Includes: the suite from *The Kentuckian* (Bernard Herrmann), suite from *Down to the Sea in Ships*
(Alfred Newman), suite from *In Love and War* (Hugo Friedhofer), and the suite from *Sunrise at*
Campobello (Franz Waxman).
Composer: Fred Steiner; others. **Conductor:** Bernard Herrmann; Alfred Newman; Hugo
Friedhofer; Franz Waxman.

GREAT BOOKS, GREAT MOVIES, GREAT SONGS
Studiotrack (1962) .... *MGM (M) E-4132*   **10-15**
Studiotrack (1962) .... *MGM (S) SE-4132*   **10-20**
Conductor: David Rose. **Cast:** David Rose and His Orchestra.

GREAT CARUSO
Studiotrack (1951) .... *RCA Victor (M) LM-1127*   51   **25-30**
Studiotrack (1951) .... *RCA Victor (SE) LSC-1127*   59   **15-20**
Conductor: Constantine Callinicos. **Cast:** Mario Lanza.

GREAT DEBATES
Studio Cast (1979) .... *Caedmon (S) TC-2087*   **10-12**
Double LP set.
Conductor: Don Heckman. **Cast:** Fritz Weaver; Jose Ferrer.

GREAT ESCAPE
Soundtrack (1963) .... *United Artists (M) UAL-4107*   63   **10-15**
Soundtrack (1963) .... *United Artists (S) UAS-5107*   63   **20-35**
Composer: Elmer Bernstein. **Conductor:** Elmer Bernstein.

GREAT FILM CLASSICS (MUSIC FROM)
Soundtrack .... *London (S) SP-44144*   **10-12**
Has music from: *Jane Eyre, The Snows of Kilimanjaro, Citizen Kane* and *The Devil and Daniel Webster*
(also known as *All That Money Can Buy*).
Composer: Bernard Herrmann. **Conductor:** Bernard Herrmann. **Cast:** National Philharmonic
Orchestra.

GREAT GATSBY
Soundtrack (1974) .... *Paramount (S) S-3001*   74   **15-20**
Composer: Nelson Riddle. **Conductor:** Nelson Riddle. **Cast:** Nick Lucas; Bill Atherton
(vocals); Jess Stacy (piano solo).

GREAT GILDERSLEEVE
Original Radio Cast .... *Golden Age (M) 5024*   78   **8-10**
Original Radio Cast .... *Mark '56 (M) 620*   73   **8-10**
Cast: Hal Peary.

GREAT LOVE THEMES FROM MOTION PICTURES:
see MAX STEINER - GREAT LOVE THEMES FROM MOTION PICTURES

GREAT MOMENTS IN BOXING

Studio Cast .... *Coral (M) CRL-57325*   61   **$15-25**
Cast: Don Dunphy (narrator).

GREAT MOMENTS WITH MR. LINCOLN

Studio Cast (1964) .... *Buena Vista (M) BV-3981*   64   **15-20**
Studio Cast (1964) .... *Buena Vista (S) STER-3981*   64   **20-25**
Composer: Buddy Baker. Conductor: Buddy Baker. Cast: Royal Dano (narrator, as Abraham Lincoln).

GREAT MOTION PICTURE THEMES

Studiotrack (1961) .... *United Artists (M) UAL-3122*   60   **10-15**
Studiotrack (1961) .... *United Artists (S) UAS-6122*   60   **10-20**

GREAT MOTION PICTURE THEMES, VOLUME 2

Studiotrack (1961) .... *United Artists (M) UAL-3158*   61   **10-15**
Studiotrack (1961) .... *United Artists (S) UAS-6158*   61   **10-20**

GREAT MOVIE HITS OF THE FORTIES

Studiotrack (1963) .... *Kapp (M) ML-7531*   63   **10-15**
Studiotrack (1963) .... *Kapp (S) ML-7531-S*   63   **15-20**
Composer: Various. Cast: Jack Elliott Orchestra.

GREAT MOVIE HITS OF THE THIRTIES

Studiotrack (1963) .... *Kapp (M) ML-7530*   63   **10-15**
Studiotrack (1963) .... *Kapp (S) ML-7530-S*   63   **15-20**
Composer: Various. Cast: Vardi and His Orchestra.

GREAT MOVIE SOUNDS OF JOHN BARRY

Studiotrack (1967) .... *Columbia (S) CS-9293*   67   **10-15**
Includes: *Thunderball, 007 (From Russia with Love), The James Bond Theme (Dr. No), The Chase, Theme from King Rat, The Knack, Seance on a Wet Afternoon, The Ipcress File* and *Born Free.*
Composer: John Barry. Conductor: John Barry.

GREAT MOVIE THRILLERS

Soundtrack .... *London (S) SP-44126*   **8-10**
Music from Bernard Herrmann scores for these Alfred Hitchcock films: *North By Northwest, Psycho, Vertigo, Marnie* and *The Trouble with Harry.*
Composer: Bernard Herrmann. Conductor: Bernard Herrmann. Cast: London Philharmonic Orchestra.

GREAT MUPPET CAPER

Soundtrack (1981) .... *Atlantic (S) SD-16047*   81   **8-10**
Composer: Joe Raposo. Conductor: Joe Raposo. Cast: The Muppets.

GREAT MUSIC FROM A FISTFUL OF DOLLARS/FOR A FEW DOLLARS MORE/THE GOOD, THE BAD AND THE UGLY

Studiotrack (1968) .... *United Artists (S) S-21032*   68   **10-15**
Composer: Ennio Morricone. Conductor: Ennio Morricone. Cast: Hollywood Soundmakers.

GREAT MUSIC THEMES OF TELEVISION

Studiotrack (1954) .... *RCA Victor (EP) EPB-1020*   54   **10-20**
Double EP set.
Studiotrack (1954) .... *RCA Victor (M) LPM-1020*   54   **20-35**
Composer: Various. Conductor: Hugo Winterhalter. Cast: Hugo Winterhalter and His Orchestra.

GREAT NEW MOTION PICTURE THEMES
Studiotrack (1967) .... *Musicor (M) 2133*   67   **$8-12**
  Cast: Harmonicats.
Studiotrack (1967) .... *Musicor (S) 3133*   67   **10-15**
  Cast: Sounds Spectacular.

GREAT OUTDOORS
Soundtrack (1988) .... *Atlantic (S) 81859-1*   88   **8-10**
  Composer: Various. **Cast:** Joe Walsh; David Wilcox; Thomas Newman and Lazy.

GREAT PERSONALITIES OF BROADWAY
Studio Cast (1963) .... *RCA Victor/Camden (M) CAL-745*   63   **10-15**
Studiotrack (1963) .... *RCA Victor/Camden (S) CAS-745*   63   **15-20**
  Cast: George M. Cohan; Fanny Brice; Al Jolson; Rudy Valle; Ethel Merman; Pinza;
  Morgan; Lauder; Lillie.

GREAT RACE
Soundtrack (1965) .... *RCA Victor (M) LPM-3402*   65   **25-30**
Soundtrack (1965) .... *RCA Victor (S) LSP-3402*   65   **35-40**
  Composer: Henry Mancini. **Conductor:** Henry Mancini. **Cast:** Dorothy Provine.

GREAT SONGS FROM MOTION PICTURES, VOLUME I (1927 - 1937)
Studiotrack (1961) .... *Time (M) T-2044*   61   **10-15**
Studiotrack (1961) .... *Time (S) S-2044*   61   **10-20**
  Composer: Various. **Conductor:** Hugo Montenegro. **Cast:** Hugo Montenegro.

GREAT SONGS FROM MOTION PICTURES, VOLUME II (1938 - 1944)
Studiotrack (1961) .... *Time (M) T-2045*   61   **10-15**
Studiotrack (1961) .... *Time (S) S-2045*   61   **10-20**
  Composer: Various. **Conductor:** Hugo Montenegro. **Cast:** Hugo Montenegro.

GREAT SONGS FROM MOTION PICTURES, VOLUME III (1945 - 1960)
Studiotrack (1961) .... *Time (M) T-2046*   61   **10-15**
Studiotrack (1961) .... *Time (S) S-2046*   61   **10-20**
  Composer: Various. **Conductor:** Hugo Montenegro. **Cast:** Hugo Montenegro.

GREAT THEMES FROM TV AND MOTION PICTURES
Studiotrack (1967) .... *Harmony (M) 7423*   67   **8-12**
Studiotrack (1967) .... *Harmony (S) 11223*   67   **10-15**
  Cast: Harmonicats.

GREAT TRAIN ROBBERY
Soundtrack (1979) .... *United Artists (S) UA-LA962-I*   79   **8-12**
  Also known as *The First Great Train Robbery.*
Soundtrack (1978) .... *MCA (S) 25102*   78   **8-12**
  Composer: Jerry Goldsmith. **Conductor:** Jerry Goldsmith. **Cast:** National Symphony Orchestra.

GREAT WALDO PEPPER
Soundtrack (1975) .... *MCA (S) 2085*   75   **10-15**
  Composer: Henry Mancini. **Conductor:** Henry Mancini. **Cast:** Henry Mancini.

GREAT WALTZ
Original Los Angeles Revival Cast (1965) .... *Capitol (M) VAS-2426*   65   **25-30**
Original Los Angeles Revival Cast (1965) .... *Capitol (S) SVAS-2426*   65   **30-35**
  Composer: Johann Strauss Sr.; Johann Strauss Jr.; Erich Wolfgang Korngold. **Conductor:** Karl
  Kritz (musical adaptation by Erich Wolfgang Korngold, Robert Wright, and George Forrest).
  Cast: Giorgio Tozzi; Jean Fenn; Frank Porretta; Anita Gillette; Leo Fuchs; Wilbur Evans; Eric
  Brotherson; Fred Essler; Lucy Andonian.

GREAT WALTZ (continued)

London Studio Cast . . . . *World (S) S-7056*   **$12-15**
  One side has music from *Rio Rita*.
Soundtrack (1972) . . . . *MGM (S) 1SE-39*   72   **15-20**
  Conductor: Roland Shaw. **Cast:** Kenneth McKellar; Mary Costa; Ken Barrie; Joan Baxter;
  Carlos Villa (violin); Mike Sammes Singers.
Soundtrack (1938) . . . . *Private Label (SE) SR-109*   **8-10**
  Composer: Dimitri Tiomkin.

GREAT WHITE HOPE

Original Cast . . . . *Tetragrammaton (S) TDL-5200*   **15-25**
  Triple LP boxed set, with script.
  Composer: Charles Gross. **Conductor:** Charles Gross. **Cast:** James Earl Jones; Jane Alexander.

GREATEST

Soundtrack (1977) . . . . *Arista (S) AL-7000*   77   **8-10**
  Composer: Michael Masser; Linda Creed; Gerry Goffin. **Conductor:** Michael Masser.
  Cast: George Benson; Mandrill; Michael Masser.

GREATEST MOMENTS IN SPORTS

Studio Cast (1955) . . . . *Columbia (EP) AX-5000*   55   **8-12**
Studio Cast (1955) . . . . *Columbia (M) ML-5000*   55   **15-25**

GREATEST SCIENCE FICTION HITS

Studiotrack . . . . *GNP/Crescendo (S) GNPS-2128*   80   **8-10**
  Includes: *Alien, Star Wars, The Day the Earth Stood Still*, and Dominic Frontiere's *Outer Limits*.
  Composer: Various. **Conductor:** Neil Norman. **Cast:** Neil Norman.

GREATEST SCIENCE FICTION HITS, VOLUME II

Studiotrack . . . . *GNP/Crescendo (S) GNPS-2133*   81   **8-10**
  Includes: *The Twilight Zone* and *The Adventures of Superman*.
  Composer: Various. **Conductor:** Neil Norman. **Cast:** Neil Norman.

GREATEST SHOW ON EARTH

Soundtrack (1952) . . . . *RCA Victor (EP) EPB-3018*   52   **25-40**
  Double EP set.
Soundtrack (1952) . . . . *RCA Victor (M) LPM-3018*   52   **125-150**
  10-inch LP.
  Composer: Victor Young; John Ringling North; E. Ray Goetz; others. **Conductor:** Irvin
  Talbot. **Cast:** Betty Hutton.

GREATEST STORY EVER TOLD

Soundtrack (1965) . . . . *United Artists (M) UAX-5120*   65   **200-225**
  White label promotional issue. Has alternate tracks not on commercial issues.
Soundtrack (1965) . . . . *United Artists (M) UAL-4120*   65   **20-25**
Soundtrack (1965) . . . . *United Artists (S) UAS-5120*   65   **25-30**
Soundtrack (1965) . . . . *United Artists (M) UA-LA277-G*   74   **10-15**
Soundtrack (1965) . . . . *MCA (S) 39057*   Re   **8-10**
  Composer: Alfred Newman. **Conductor:** Alfred Newman.

GREEK PEARLS

Soundtrack (1968) . . . . *Lyra (M) LY-1008*   68   **20-25**
Soundtrack (1968) . . . . *Lyra (SE) LYS-1008*   68   **25-30**
  Composer: Mimis Plessas. **Conductor:** Mimis Plessas. **Cast:** Nelly Manou; Yannis Poulopoulos.

GREEN ACRES:
see EDDIE ALBERT ALBUM

GREEN DOLPHIN:
see AUNTIE MAME

GREEN HORNET
Original Radio Cast . . . .*Golden Age (M) 5010*   78   **$8-10**
TV Soundtrack (1966) . . . .*20th Century-Fox (M) TF-3186*   66   **20-25**
TV Soundtrack (1966) . . . .*20th Century-Fox (S) S-3186*   66   **30-40**
  Composer: Billy May. Conductor: Billy May.

GREEN ICE
Soundtrack (1981) . . . .*Polydor (S) POLS-1031*   81   **8-10**
  Composer: Bill Wyman. Cast: Maria Muldaur.

GREENWICH VILLAGE, U.S.A.
Original Cast (1960) . . . .*20th Century-Fox (M) TCP-105-2*   60   **75-80**
Original Cast (1960) . . . .*20th Century-Fox (S) TCF-105-2S*   60   **100-110**
  Above two are double LP sets and contain the complete show.
  Composer: Jeanne Bargy; Frank Gehrecke; Herb Corey. Conductor: Bill Costa. Cast: Jack
  Betts; Saralou Cooper; Pat Finley; Judy Guyll; Dawn Hampton; James Harwood.
Original Cast (1960) . . . .*AEI (M) 1129*   **10-15**
  Reissued in monaural only.
  Composer: Jeanne Bargy; Frank Gehrecke; Herb Corey. Conductor: Bill Costa. Cast: Jack
  Betts; Saralou Cooper; Pat Finley; Judy Guyll; Dawn Hampton; James Harwood.
Original Cast (1960) . . . .*20th Century-Fox (M) FOX-4005*   60   **30-35**
Original Cast (1960) . . . . *20th Century-Fox (S) SFX-4005*   60   **50-60**
  Composer: Jeanne Bargy; Frank Gehrecke; Herb Corey. Conductor: Bill Costa. Cast: Jack
  Betts; Saralou Cooper; Pat Finley; Judy Guyll; Dawn Hampton; James Harwood; Jane A.
  Johnston; Burke McHugh; James Pompeii; Ken Urmston.

GREENWILLOW
Original Cast (1960) . . . .*RCA Victor (M) LOC-2001*   60   **25-30**
Original Cast (1960) . . . .*RCA Victor (S) LSO-2001*   60   **40-50**
Original Cast (1960) . . . .*Columbia Special Products (S) 13974*   77   **8-10**
  Composer: Frank Loesser. Conductor: Abba Bogin. Cast: Anthony Perkins; Cecil Kellaway;
  Pert Kelton; Ellen McCown; William Chapman; Lee Cass; Saralou Cooper; Bruce MacKay;
  Jan Tucker; Brenda Harris; Lynn Brinker; John Megna.
Studio Cast (1960) . . . .*RCA Victor (M) LPM-2229*   60   **10-15**
Studio Cast (1960) . . . .*RCA Victor (S) LSP-2229*   60   **12-18**
  Composer: Frank Loesser. Conductor: George Melachrino. Cast: Melachrino Strings
  (instrumental renditions of the score).

GREMLINS
Soundtrack (1984) . . . .*Geffen (S) GHSP-24044*   84   **8-10**
  Seven track mini-album.
Soundtrack (1984) . . . .*Geffen (S) 24044*   84   **8-12**
  Composer: Jerry Goldsmith. Conductor: Jerry Goldsmith. Cast: Michael Sembello; Quarter
  Flash; Peter Gabriel.

GREY FOX
Soundtrack (1982) . . . .*DRG (S) SL-9515*   82   **8-10**

GREYFRIARS BOBBY
Soundtrack (1961) . . . .*Disneyland (M) ST-1914*   61   **20-25**
  Composer: Richard M. Sherman; Robert B. Sherman; others. Cast: Ginny Tyler; others.

GREYSTOKE - THE LEGEND OF TARZAN, LORD OF THE APES
Soundtrack (1984) . . . .*Warner Bros. (S) 1-25120*   84   **8-10**
  Composer: John Scott.

GRIND
Original Cast (1985) . . . .*Polydor (S) 827072-1*   85   **10-20**
  Composer: Larry Grossman; Ellen Fitshugh. Conductor: Paul Gemignani. Cast: Ben
  Vereen; Stubby Kaye; Leilani Jones; Timothy Nolen; Sharon Murray; Carol Woods.

GROUNDS FOR MARRIAGE
Soundtrack (1950) ....*MGM (M) E-536* 50   **$60-70**
Cast: Kathryn Grayson.

GUERRE EST FINIE, LA:
see LA GUERRE EST FINIE

GUESS WHO'S COMING TO DINNER?
Soundtrack (1967) ....*Colgems (M) COM-108* 68   **20-25**
Soundtrack (1967) ....*Colgems (S) COS-108* 68   **25-30**
Composer: Frank DeVol. Conductor: Frank DeVol. Cast: Billy Hill.

GUIDING LIGHT
Original Radio Cast ....*Golden Age (M) 5020* 78   **8-10**

GULLIVER
Soundtrack ....*Soundwings (S) SW-2101* 86   **8-10**
Conductor: Patrick Williams. Cast: Royal Philharmonic Orchestra; Sir John Gielgud (narrator).

GULLIVER'S TRAVELS BEYOND THE MOON:
see BEYOND THE MOON

GUNFIGHT AT THE O.K. CORRAL:
see LAND OF THE PHARAOHS

GUNN . . . NUMBER ONE
Soundtrack (1967) ....*RCA Victor (M) LPM-3840* 67   **12-15**
Soundtrack (1967) ....*RCA Victor (S) LSP-3840* 67   **15-20**
Composer: Henry Mancini. Conductor: Henry Mancini. Cast: Henry Mancini and His Orchestra.

GUNS FOR SAN SEBASTIAN
Soundtrack (1968) ....*MGM (M) E-4565* 68   **35-40**
Soundtrack (1968) ....*MGM (S) SE-4565* 68   **50-55**
Soundtrack (1968) ....*MCA (S) 25103* Re   **8-10**
Composer: Ennio Morricone.

GUNS OF NAVARONE
Soundtrack (1961) ....*Columbia (M) CL-1655* 61   **30-35**
Soundtrack (1961) ....*Columbia (S) CS-8455* 61   **40-45**
Composer: Dimitri Tiomkin. Conductor: Dimitri Tiomkin. Cast: Mitch Miller and His Gang.

GUNSMOKE
Original Radio Cast ....*Golden Age (M) 5004* 78   **8-10**
Cast: William Conrad (as Matt Dillion).

GURU
Soundtrack (1969) ....*RCA Victor (S) LSO-1158* 69   **15-20**
Composer: Ustad Khan. Conductor: V. Balsara.

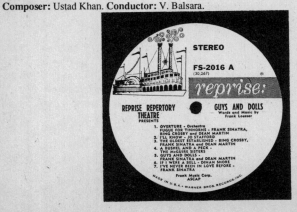

GUYS AND DOLLS

Original Cast (1950)	Decca (EP) ED-803	50	$15-20
Original Cast (1950)	Decca (M) DL-8036	50	35-40
Original Cast (1950)	Decca (M) DL-9023	55	30-35
Original Cast (1950)	Decca (SE) DL7-9023	59	15-20
Original Cast (1950)	MCA (SE) 2034e	72	10-12
Original Cast (1950)	MCA (SE) 37094	81	8-10
Original Cast (1950)	MCA (SE) 1628	Re	8-10

Composer: Frank Loesser. **Conductor:** Irving Actman. **Cast:** Robert Alda; Vivian Blaine; Sam Levene; Stubby Kaye; Johnny Silver; Isabel Bigley; Pat Rooney; Douglas Deane.

Original Revival Cast (1976)	Motown (S) M6-876S1	76	15-20

Composer: Frank Loesser. **Conductor:** Howard Roberts. **Cast:** Norma Donaldson; Robert Guillaume; Ernestine Jackson; James Randolph; Ken Page; Christopher Pierre; Bardell Connor; Irene Datcher; Sterling McQueen; Marion Moore; Emmet "Babe" Wallace.

Studio Cast (1955)	Decca (EP) ED-2308	55	10-15

Composer: Frank Loesser. **Cast:** Sammy Davis Jr.

Studio Cast (1956)	Columbia (EP) B-2077	56	10-15

Cast: Frankie Laine; Jo Stafford; Jerry Vale; Rosemary Clooney.

Studio Cast (1956)	Columbia (M) CL-2567	56	25-30

10-inch LP.

Conductor: Percy James; Harry James. **Cast:** Rosemary Clooney; Frankie Laine; Jerry Vale; Jo Stafford; Harry James.

Studiotrack (1963)	Reprise (M) F-2016	64	25-35
Studio Cast (1963)	Reprise (S) FS-2016	64	30-40

Above two have gatefold covers.

Studiotrack (1963)	Reprise (M) F-2016	64	15-25
Studio Cast (1963)	Reprise (S) FS-2016	64	20-30

Above two do not have gatefold covers.

Studio Cast (1963)	Harmony (S) HS-11374	Re	10-15

Composer: Frank Loesser. **Conductor:** Morris Stoloff. **Cast:** Frank Sinatra; Dean Martin; Sammy Davis Jr.; Bing Crosby; Dinah Shore; Alan Sherman; Debbie Reynolds; McGuire Sisters.

Studio Cast (1976)	20th Century-Fox (S) ST-514	76	10-12

Disco version.

Composer: Frank Loesser. **Conductor:** Al Capps. **Cast:** Broadway Brass.

Soundtrack (1950)	Decca (EP) ED-2332	56	10-15
Soundtrack (1955)	Brunswick (EP) ED-2332	56	10-20

Composer: Frank Loesser. **Conductor:** Jay Blackton. **Cast:** Marlon Brando; Jean Simmons. Also see CALL ME MADAM; REPRISE REPERTORY THEATRE

GYPSY

Original Cast (1959)	Columbia (EP) EPA-5420	59	10-12
Original Cast (1959)	Columbia (M) OL-5420	59	15-20
Original Cast (1959)	Columbia (S) OS-2017	59	20-25
Original Cast (1959)	Columbia (S) S-32607	73	8-10

Composer: Jule Styne; Stephen Sondheim. **Conductor:** Milton Rosenstock. **Cast:** Ethel Merman; Jack Klugman; Sandra Church; Maria Karnilova; Paul Wallace; Lane Bradbury; Faith Dane; Chotzi Foley; Jacqueline Mayro; Karen Moore.

GYPSY (continued)

Original London Cast (1974) . . . .*RCA Victor (S) LBL1-5004*   74   **$8-12**
  Partial United States issue of the original British pressing.
London Studio . . . .*Music for Pleasure (S) MFP-1308*   **20-25**
  Composer: Jule Styne; Stephen Sondheim. **Cast:** Jimmy Blackburn; Kay Medford; Sonya
  Petrie; Lorraine Smith.
Soundtrack (1962) . . . .*Warner Bros. (M) B-1480*   62   **20-25**
Soundtrack (1962) . . . . *Warner Bros. (S) BS-1480*   62   **25-30**
  Composer: Jule Styne; Stephen Sondheim. **Conductor:** Frank Perkins; Jule Styne. **Cast:** Lisa
  Kirk (actually performed the vocals of Rosalind Russell); Natalie Wood; Karl Malden; Rosalind
  Russell (dialogue).
Studiotrack (1960) . . . . *Richmond (S) S-30072*   60   **10-15**
  Also contains music from *Music Man*.
  Composer: Jule Styne; Stephen Sondheim. **Cast:** London Theatre Company.
London Cast . . . .*RCA Victor (S) SER-5686*   74   **12-15**
  Composer: Jule Styne; Stephen Sondheim. **Cast:** Angela Lansbury; Barrie Ingham; Zan Charisse.
Studiotrack (1959) . . . . *Columbia (M) CL-1352*   59   **15-20**
Studiotrack (1959) . . . . *Columbia (S) CS-8160*   59   **20-25**
  Actual title: *Teddy Wilson and His Trio Play Gypsy in Jazz*.
  Cast: Teddy Wilson and His Trio.

GYPSY GIRL

Soundtrack (1966) . . . .*Mainstream (M) 56090*   66   **15-20**
Soundtrack (1966) . . . . *Mainstream (S) 6090*   66   **20-25**
  This film was originally titled *Sky West and Crooked*.
  Composer: Milton Delugg; Anne Delugg. **Cast:** Hayley Mills.

GYPSY MOTHS

Soundtrack (1969) . . . .*Cinema (S) LP-8011*   **50-75**
  Recorded in Germany for the Film Music Collector's Society.
  Composer: Elmer Bernstein. **Conductor:** Hans Rossbach.

GYPSY ROSE LEE REMEMBERS BURLESQUE

Original Cast (1962) . . . . *Stereoddities (S) CG-1*   62   **20-25**
  Composer: Eli Basse; Bobby Kroll. **Cast:** Gypsy Rose Lee; others.

H

HAIL, HAIL, ROCK 'N' ROLL
Soundtrack (1987) ....*MCA (S) 6217*   87   **$8-10**
  Composer: Various. **Cast:** Chuck Berry; Linda Ronstadt; Robert Cray; Eric Clapton; Julian Lennon.

HAIR
Original Off-Broadway Cast (1967) .... *RCA Victor (M) LOC-1143*   67   **10-15**
Original Off-Broadway Cast (1967) .... *RCA Victor (S) LSO-1143*   67   **15-20**
Original Off-Broadway Cast (1967) .... *RCA Victor (S) ANL1-0986*   75   **8-10**
  Composer: Galt MacDermot; Gerome Ragni; James Rado. **Conductor:** John Morris.
  Cast: Walker Daniels; Gerome Ragni; Steve Dean; Sally Eaton; Marijane Maricle; Jonelle Allan; Susan Batson; Linda Compton; Suzannah Evans; Paul Jabara; Jill O'Hara; Shelley Plimpton; Alma Robinson; Arnold Wilkerson.
Original Broadway Cast (1967) .... *RCA Victor (M) LOC-1150*   68   **10-15**
Original Broadway Cast (1967) .... *RCA Victor (S) LSO-1150*   68   **10-15**
  Composer: Galt MacDermot; Gerome Ragni; James Rado. **Conductor:** Galt MacDermot.
  Cast: Ronnie Dyson; Gerome Ragni; Steve Curry; Lamont Washington; Diane Keaton; Melba Moore; James Rado.
Original London Cast (1967) .... *Atco (S) SD-7002*   69   **25-30**
Original London Cast (1967) .... *Polydor (S) 24-5501*   71   **20-25**
  Volume two. Actual title: *Fresh Hair.*
  Composer: Galt MacDermot; Gerome Ragni; James Rado. **Conductor:** Derek Wadsworth.
  Cast: Vince Edward; Oliver Tobias; Michael Feast; Paul Nicholas.
Original Japanese Cast (1971) .... *RCA Victor (S) LSO-1170*   71   **20-25**
  Conductor: Danny Hurd.
Original French Cast (1969) .... *Philips (S) PHS-600-329*   69   **10-15**
  Composer: Galt MacDermot. **Cast:** Gloria Carter; Herve Wattine; Julien Clerc; Bill Combs; Gerard Palaprat; Charles Austin; Gregory Ken; Serge Godinho; Ann Ballester; Clement Marshall; Henry Hay; Jeaniene Bennett.
Studio Cast (1969) .... *RCA Victor (M) LOC-1163*   69   **10-15**
Studio Cast (1969) .... *RCA Victor (S) LSO-1163*   69   **15-20**
  Actual title: *DisinHAIRited.* Has original cast members and composers plus future cast members doing songs written for, but not included in, the show.
  Composer: Galt MacDermot; Gerome Ragni; James Rado. **Conductor:** Galt MacDermot.
  Cast: Robin McNamara; Galt MacDermot (piano); Jim Rado; Jerry Ragni; Melba Moore; Leata Galloway.
Studio Cast .... *Kilmarnock (S) KIL-69001*   **25-30**
  Jazz instrumentals. From a Carleton University concert.
  Composer: Galt MacDermot; Jerry Ragni; James Rado. **Conductor:** Galt MacDermot.
  Cast: Galt MacDermot; Charlie Brown; Jimmy Lewis; Idris Mohammed.
Studio Cast .... *Pickwick (S) SPC-3169*   **8-12**
  Conductor: Geoff Love. **Cast:** Dave Wintour; Pat Whitmore.
Soundtrack (1979) .... *RCA Victor (S) CBL2-3274*   79   **12-18**
  Double LP set.
  Conductor: Galt MacDermot.
Studiotrack (1969) .... *RCA Victor (S) LSP-4174*   69   **12-15**
  Actual title: *Divine Hair Mass in F.*

HAIR (continued)

Studiotrack (1969) . . . .*RCA Victor (S) LSP-4174*   69   **$10-12**
Actual title: *Don Kirschner Cuts Hair*. Reissue of *Divine Hair Mass In F*.
Composer: Galt MacDermot; Gerome Ragni; James Rado. **Conductor:** Don Kirschner.
Cast: Don Kirschner (instrumental renditions).
Studiotrack (1970) . . . . *Capitol (S) ST-305*   70   **10-15**
Jazz interpretations.
Cast: Stan Kenton.

HAIRSPRAY

Soundtrack (1988) . . . .*MCA (S) 6228*   88   **8-10**
Composer: Various. **Cast:** Rachel Sweet; Ray Bryant Combo; Jan Bradley; Gene and Wendell;
Flares; Jerry Dallman and Knightcaps; Little Peggy March; Barbara Lynn; Gene Pitney; Kettes;
Toussaint McCall; Five Du-Tones.

HALF A SIXPENCE

Original Cast (1965) . . . .*RCA Victor (M) LOC-1110*   65   **20-25**
Original Cast (1965) . . . .*RCA Victor (S) LSO-1110*   65   **25-30**
Composer: David Heneker. **Conductor:** Stanley Lebowsky. **Cast:** Tommy Stelle; Grover
Dale; James Grout; Polly James; Will MacKenzie; Norman Allen; Eleanor Treiber.
London Studio Cast . . . . *World (S) T-852*   **15-20**
Composer: David Heneker. **Conductor:** Gareth Davies. **Cast:** Barbara Windsor; Marty Wilde;
Mike Sammes Singers.
Soundtrack (1967) . . . .'. . . . .*RCA Victor (M) LOC-1146*   68   **20-25**
Soundtrack (1967) . . . .*RCA Victor (S) LSO-1146*   68   **20-25**
Composer: David Heneker. **Conductor:** Irwin Kostal. **Cast:** Tommy Steele; Julia Foster.

HALF PAST WEDNESDAY

Original Cast (1962) . . . . *Columbia (M) CL-1917*   62   **25-30**
Original Cast (1962) . . . . *Columbia (S) CS-8717*   62   **30-35**
Original Cast (1962) . . . .*Harmony (M) HL-9560*   Re   **12-18**
Original Cast (1962) . . . . *Harmony (S) HS-14560*   **15-20**
Composer: Robert Colby; Nita Jones. **Conductor:** Julian Stein. **Cast:** Dom DeLuise; Sean
Garrison; Audre Johnston; Robert Fitch; David Winters.

HALL OF PRESIDENTS

Soundtrack (1972) . . . .*Disneyland (S) STER-3806*   72   **10-12**
Includes booklet.
Composer: Buddy Baker. **Conductor:** Buddy Baker. **Cast:** Lawrence Dobkin (narration);
Royal Dano (as Abraham Lincoln).

HALLELUJAH BABY!

Original Cast (1967) . . . . *Columbia (M) KOL-6690*   67   **30-35**
Original Cast (1967) . . . .*Columbia (S) KOS-3090*   67   **35-40**
Composer: Jule Styne; Betty Comden; Adolph Green. **Conductor:** Buster Davis. **Cast:** Leslie
Uggams; Robert Hooks; Allen Case; Clifford Allen; Lillian Hayman; Barbara Sharma;
Winston Dewitt Hemsley; Hope Clarke; Marilyn Cooper; Sandra Lein; Saundra McPherson;
Garrett Morris; Kenneth Scott; Alan Weeks; Justin McDonough; Lou Angel.

HALLELUJAH THE HILLS

Soundtrack (1964) . . . .*Fontana (M) F-27524*   64   **20-25**
Soundtrack (1964) :. . . . . *Fontana (S) SRF-67524*   64   **25-30**
Composer: Meyer Kupferman. **Conductor:** Meyer Kupferman.

HALLELUJAH TRAIL

Soundtrack (1965) . . . .*United Artists (M) UAL-4127*   65   **25-30**
Soundtrack (1965) . . . .*United Artists (S) UAS-5127*   65   **30-40**
Composer: Elmer Bernstein. **Conductor:** Elmer Bernstein.

HALLOWEEN
Soundtrack (1978) .... *Varese Sarabande (S) STV-81176*   83   **$8-12**
  Composer: John Carpenter. **Conductor:** John Carpenter. **Cast:** John Carpenter.

HALLOWEEN II
Soundtrack (1981) .... *Varese Sarabande (S) STV-81152*   81   **8-12**
  Composer: John Carpenter. **Conductor:** John Carpenter. **Cast:** John Carpenter; Alan Howarth;
  Chordettes.

HALLOWEEN III - SEASON OF THE WITCH
Soundtrack (1982) .... *MCA (S) 6115*   82   **8-10**
  Composer: John Carpenter; Alan Howarth. **Conductor:** John Carpenter. **Cast:** John Carpenter;
  Alan Howarth.

HAMLET
Original Cast (1964) .... *Columbia (M) OL-302*   64   **15-20**
Original Cast (1964) .... *Columbia (S) DOS-302*   64   **15-25**
  Above two shown as "John Gielgud's Hamlet." Both are boxed sets with booklets.
  Cast: Richard Burton; Hume Cronyn; Alfred Drake; Eileen Herlie; William Redfield; George
  Rose; John Gielgud; Linda Marsh; Robert Milli; John Collum; George Voskovec.
Soundtrack (1948) .... *RCA Victor (M) LCT-5*   51   **35-40**
  10-inch LP.
Soundtrack (1948) .... *RCA Victor (M) LM-1924*   55   **40-50**
  One side has music from *Henry V.*
  Composer: Sir William Walton. **Conductor:** Muir Mathieson. **Cast:** Sir Laurence Olivier.
  (With dialogue.)
TV Soundtrack (1970) .... *RCA Victor (S) VDM-119*   70   **25-30**
  Double LP set. A Hallmark production.
  Composer: John Addison. **Conductor:** John Addison. **Cast:** Richard Chamberlain; Michael
  Redgrave; Margaret Leighton; John Gielgud.
Studio Cast (1961) .... *Living Shakespeare (M) SH 5/6 A*   61   **30-35**
  Includes music, sound effects, and a booklet of the complete play.
  Composer: Desmond Leslie. **Conductor:** Cyril Ornadel. **Cast:** Michael Redgrave; Margaret
  Rawlings; Barbara Jefford; Valentine Dyall; Michael Benthall; John Phillips; David Dodimead;
  Mark Kingston; Antony Webb; Derek Francis; Irene Sutcliffe; John Humphry; Job Stewart.
  Also see MUSIC FROM SHAKESPEAREAN FILMS; WALTON CONDUCTS HIS GREAT
  FILM MUSIC

HAMMERHEAD
Soundtrack (1968) .... *Colgems (S) 110*   68   **25-30**
  Composer: David Whitaker. **Conductor:** David Whitaker. **Cast:** Madeline Bell.

HAMMERSMITH IS OUT
Soundtrack (1972) .... *Capitol (S) WS-861*   72   **20-25**
  Composer: Dominic Frontiere. **Conductor:** Dominic Frontiere. **Cast:** Sally Stevens.

HAND IS ON THE GATE
Original Cast (1966) ....*Verve (M) FV-9040-2*   66   **$20-25**
Original Cast (1966) ....*Verve (S) FVS-9040-2*   66   **25-30**
Above two are double LP sets.

Cast: Leon Bibb; Roscoe Lee Browne; Gloria Foster; Moses Gunn; James Earl Jones; Cicely
Tyson; Ellen Holly; Josephine Premice.

HANG 'EM HIGH
Soundtrack (1968) ....*United Artists (S) UAS-5179*   68   **20-25**
Soundtrack (1968) ....*MCA (S) 1435*   Re   **8-10**
Composer: Dominic Frontiere. **Conductor:** Dominic Frontiere.
Studiotrack (1968) ....*RCA Victor (S) 4022*   68   . **10-15**
Also has themes from: *In the Heat of the Night, Valley of the Dolls, The Fox, For Love of Ivy,* and others.
Composer: Various. **Conductor:** Hugo Montenegro. **Cast:** Hugo Montenegro and His Orchestra.

HANG YOUR HAT ON THE WIND
Soundtrack (1969) ....*Disneyland (M) DQ-1332*   69   **10-12**
With dialogue.
Composer: Randy Sparks. **Conductor:** Jim Helms.

HANGOVER SQUARE:
see TWISTED NERVE

HANK AARON #715
Studio Cast (1974) .... *Magnavox No Number Used*   74   **10-20**
Magnavox special products issue, commemorating Hank Aaron's 715th career home run, which broke
Babe Ruth's long-standing record.
Cast: Curt Gowdy (narrator).

HANNAH AND HER SISTERS
Soundtrack (1987) ....*MCA (S) 6190*   87   **8-10**
Composer: Various. **Cast:** Count Basie and His Orchestra; Bobby Short; Derek Smith; Harry
James; Dick Hyman; Roy Eldridge; George Malcolm; Simon Preston; Lloyd Nolan; Maureen
O'Sullivan.

HANNIBAL BROOKS
Soundtrack (1969) ....*United Artists (S) UAS-5196*   69   **10-15**
Soundtrack (1969) ....*MCA (S) 25104*   Re   **8-10**
Composer: Francis Lai. **Conductor:** Francis Lai.

HANS BRINKER
TV Soundtrack (1958) ....*Dot (M) DLP-9001*   58   **50-60**
Composer: Hugh Martin. **Conductor:** Irwin Kostal. **Cast:** Tab Hunter; Peggy King; Sheila
Smith; Jarmila Novotna; Vinny Corrod.

HANS BRINKER AND THE SILVER SKATES
Soundtrack (1972) .... *Disneyland (S) DDF-5*   72   **$10-15**
  Double LP set. Also has music from *Toby Tyler in the Circus.*
  Cast: Henry Calvin (narrator).

HANS CHRISTIAN ANDERSEN
Soundtrack (1952) .... *Decca (M) DL-5433*   52   **40-50**
Soundtrack (1952) .... *Decca (M) DL-8479*   57   **25-30**
Soundtrack (1952) .... *Decca (SE) DL-78479*   59   **20-25**
  One side has music from *Tubby the Tuba.*
  Composer: Frank Loesser. **Conductor:** Gordon Jenkins. **Cast:** Danny Kaye; Jane Wyman.

HANS CHRISTIAN ANDERSEN STORIES
Studiotrack (1963) .... *Disneyland (M) ST-3964*   63   **10-15**
  Composer: Tutti Camarata. **Conductor:** Tutti Camarata.

HANSEL AND GRETEL
Soundtrack (1955) .... *Bluebird (M) LXA-1013*   55   **35-40**
Soundtrack (1955) .... *RCA Victor (M) LBY-1024*   59   **25-30**
Soundtrack (1955) .... *RCA Victor/Camden (M) CAL-1024*   61   **15-20**
Soundtrack (1955) .... *RCA Victor/Camden (SE) CAS-1024*   61   **15-20**
  Composer: Engelbert Humperdinck. **Conductor:** Franz Allers. **Cast:** Mildred Dunnock.
TV Soundtrack (1958) .... *MGM (M) E-3690*   58   **50-60**
  Composer: Alec Wilder. **Conductor:** Glenn Osser. **Cast:** Red Buttons; Barbara Cook; Rudy
  Vallee; Stuby Kaye; Paula Laurence.
Studiotrack (1964) .... *Disneyland (M) DQ-1253*   64   **10-20**
Studiotrack (1967) .... *Disneyland (S) S-3955*   67   **10-12**

HAPPENING
Soundtrack (1967) .... *Colgems (M) COMO-5006*   67   **15-20**
Soundtrack (1967) .... *Colgems (S) COSO-5006*   67   **20-25**
  Composer: Frank DeVol. **Conductor:** Frank DeVol. **Cast:** Stephen Doyle Smith.

HAPPIEST GIRL IN THE WORLD
Original Cast (1961) .... *Columbia (M) KOL-5650*   61   **30-35**
Original Cast (1961) .... *Columbia (S) KOS-2050*   61   **45-50**
  Composer: Jacques Offenbach; E.Y. Harburg. **Conductor:** Robert Decormier. **Cast:** Cyril
  Ritchard; Janice Rule; Dran Seitz; Bruce Yarnell; Lu Leonard; Nancy Windsor.

HAPPIEST MILLIONAIRE
Soundtrack (1967) .... *Buena Vista (M) BV-5001*   67   **10-15**
Soundtrack (1967) .... *Buena Vista (S) STER-5001*   67   **15-20**
  Above two have gatefold covers and include 12-page bound-in booklets.
  Composer: Richard M. Sherman; Robert B. Sherman. **Conductor:** Jack Elliot. **Cast:** Tommy
  Steele; Lesley Ann Warren; John Davidson; Paul Petersen; Fred MacMurray; Eddie Hodges;
  Geraldine Page; Gladys Cooper; Joyce Bulifant.

HAPPY END
Original German Cast (1977) .... *Columbia (S) OS-2032*   77   **20-25**
  Performed in the German language.
Original German Cast (1977) ... *Columbia Special Products (S) COS-2032*   Re   **8-10**
  Composer: Kurt Weill; Bertolt Brecht. **Conductor:** Wilhelm Bruckner-Ruggeberg.
  Cast: Lotte Lenya.

HAPPY ENDING
Soundtrack (1969) .... *United Artists (S) UAS-5203*   69   **12-15**
Soundtrack (1969) .... *MCA (S) 25105*   Re   **8-10**
  Composer: Michel Legrand. **Conductor:** Michel Legrand. **Cast:** Michael Dees; Bill Eaton;
  Michel Legrand.

HAPPY HUNTING
Original Cast (1957) ....*RCA Victor (EP) EOC-1026*   57   **$15-20**
Original Cast (1957) ....*RCA Victor (M) LOC-1026*   57   **40-50**
  Composer: Harold Karr; Matt Dubey. **Conductor:** Jay Blackton. **Cast:** Ethel Merman;
  Fernando Lamas; Virginia Gibson; Gordon Polk; Mary Finney; Leon Belasco.

HAPPY MOTHER GOOSE (AS TOLD BY KUKLA, FRAN AND OLLIE)
Studio Cast ....*RCA Victor (EP) Y-423*   53   **10-20**
  Double 78 rpm EP set.
Studio Cast ....*RCA Victor (EP) Y-423*   53   **15-25**
  Double 45 rpm EP set.
  Composer: Jack Fascinato. **Conductor:** Jack Fascinato. **Cast:** Fran Allison; Burr Tillstrom;
  Jack Fascinato (piano).
  Also see KUKLA, FRAN AND OLLIE

HAPPY PRINCE
Studio Cast (1950) ....*Decca (M) DL-6000*   50   **30-40**
  One side has music from *The Small One*.
  Cast: Bing Crosby; Orson Welles.

HAPPY TIME
Original Cast (1968) ....*RCA Victor (M) LOC-1144*   68   **25-30**
Original Cast (1968) ....*RCA Victor (S) LSO-1144*   68   **30-35**
  Composer: John Kander; Fred Ebb. **Conductor:** Oscar Kosarin. **Cast:** Robert Goulet; David
  Wayne; Mike Rupert; Julie Gregg.

HARD COUNTRY
Soundtrack (1981) ....*Epic (S) SE-37367*   81   **8-10**
  Composer: Michael Murphey; others. **Cast:** Kim Basinger; Tanya Tucker.

HARD DAY'S NIGHT
Soundtrack (1964) ....*United Artists (M) SP-2359/60*   64   **550-650**
  Open-end interview. Includes 12-page script. Promotional issue only.
Soundtrack (1964) ....*United Artists (M) UAL-3366*   64   **40-60**
  Black label.
Soundtrack (1964) ....*United Artists (S) UAS-6366*   64   **50-75**
  Black label.
Soundtrack (1964) ....*United Artists (S) UAS-6366*   68   **25-35**
  Pink label.
Soundtrack (1964) ....*United Artists (S) UAS-6366*   71   **10-20**
  Tan label.
Soundtrack (1964) ....*United Artists (S) UAS-6366*   77   **10-12**
  Black and orange label.
Soundtrack (1964) ....*Capitol (S) SW-11921*   80   **8-12**
  Black and orange label.
Soundtrack (1964) ....*MFSL (S) 1-103*   87   **15-20**
  Half-speed mastered.
  Composer: John Lennon; Paul McCartney. **Conductor:** George Martin. **Cast:** Beatles; George
  Martin and His Orchestra.

HARD JOB BEING GOD
Studio Cast (1972) ....*GWP (S) ST-2036*   72   **25-30**
  Composer: Tom Martel. **Conductor:** John O'Reilly. **Cast:** Dorothy Lerner; Tom Martel;
  John O'Reilly; Tom Troxell; Joe Valentine; Susie Walcher.

HARD PART BEGINS
Soundtrack (1974) .... *A&M (S) SP-9016* 74   **$8-12**
Cast: Donnelly Rhodes; Paul Bradley; Nancy Bellefuller; Cliff Carol.

HARD RIDE
Soundtrack (1971) .... *Paramount (S) 6005* 71   **10-12**
Composer: Harley Hatcher. **Cast:** Bill Medley; Thelma Camacho; Junction.

HARD TO HOLD
Soundtrack (1984) .... *RCA Victor (S) ABL1-4935* 84   **8-10**
Composer: Various. **Cast:** Rick Springfield; Randy Crawford; Graham Parker; Nona Hendryx; Peter Gabriel.

HARDER THEY COME
Soundtrack (1973) .... *Mango (S) SMAS-7400* 73   **15-20**
Soundtrack (1973) .... *Mango (S) SMAS-9202* Re   **8-12**
Composer: Jimmy Cliff; others. **Cast:** Jimmy Cliff; Desmond Dekker; Slickers; Maytals.

HARK!
Original Cast (1972) .... *Private Label (S) STK-1016* 72   **130-140**
Double LP set.
Conductor: Sande Campbell.
Original Touring Cast (1972) .... *Theatre Archives (S) JGR-300* 72   **25-30**
Composer: Dan Goggin; Marvin Solley; Robert Lorick. **Cast:** Dan Goggin; Marvin Solley; Sharon Miller; Elaine Petricoff; Jack Blacton; Danny Guerreo.

HARLOW
Soundtrack (1965) .... *Columbia (M) OL-6390* 65   **20-25**
Soundtrack (1965) .... *Columbia (S) OS-2790* 65   **30-35**
From the film starring Carroll Baker.
Composer: Neal Hefti. **Conductor:** Neal Hefti.
Soundtrack (1965) .... *Warner Bros. (M) W-1599* 65   **20-25**
Soundtrack (1965) .... *Warner Bros. (S) WS-1599* 65   **30-40**
From the film starring Carol Lyney.
Composer: Nelson Riddle; Al Ham. **Conductor:** Nelson Riddle.

HARPER
Soundtrack (1966) .... *Mainstream (M) 56078* 66   **20-25**
Soundtrack (1966) .... *Mainstream (S) 6078* 66   **25-30**
Composer: Johnny Mandel; Andre Previn; Dory Previn. **Conductor:** Johnny Mandel.
Cast: Ruth Price.

HARPER VALLEY P.T.A.
Soundtrack (1978) .... *Plantation (S) PLP-700* 78   **10-15**
Green vinyl pressing.
Composer: Tom T. Hall; others. **Conductor:** Nelson Riddle. **Cast:** Barbara Eden; Nanette Fabray; Louis Nye; Pat Paulsen.

HARRAD EXPERIMENT
Soundtrack (1973) .... *Capitol (S) ST-11182* 73   **10-12**
Composer: Artie Butler. **Cast:** Ace Trucking Company; Lori Lieberman; Don Johnson.

HARRAD SUMMER
Soundtrack (1974) .... *Capitol (S) ST-11338* 74   **10-12**
Film sequel to *The Harrad Experiment*.
Composer: Artie Butler. **Cast:** Pat Williams; Gene Redding.

HARRY AND LENA
TV Soundtrack (1970) .... *RCA Victor (S) PRS-295* 70   **10-12**
Conductor: Alfred Brown. **Cast:** Harry Belafonte; Lena Horne.

HARRY AND THE HENDERSONS
Soundtrack (1987) .... *MCA (S) 6208*   87   **$8-10**
  Composer: James Honwer. **Cast:** Joe Cocker; others.

HARRY AND TONTO
Soundtrack (1974) .... *Casablanca (S) 7010*   75   **12-15**
  Cast: Art Carney; Geraldine Fitzgerald; Chief Dan George; Barbara Rhoades. (With dialogue.)

HARUM SCARUM
Soundtrack (1965) .... *RCA Victor (M) LPM-3468*   65   **75-100**
  Black label, dog on top, reads "Monaural" at bottom. Includes 12" x 12" color photo, which represents
  about $50 of the value.
Soundtrack (1965) .... *RCA Victor (S) LSP-3468*   65   **85-100**
  Black label, dog on top, reads "Stereo" at bottom. Includes 12" x 12" color photo, which represents about
  $50 of the value.
Soundtrack (1965) .... *RCA Victor (S) APL1-2558*   78   **10-15**
Soundtrack (1965) .... *RCA Victor (S) AYL1-3734*   81   **8-10**
  Composer: Bill Giant; Bernie Baum; Florence Kaye; Sid Tepper; Roy C. Bennett; others.
  Cast: Elvis Presley; Scotty Moore (guitar); D.J. Fontana (drums); Bob Moore (bass);
  Jordanaires (vocals).

HARVEY GIRLS
Soundtrack (1946) .... *Decca (M) DL-8498*   57   **60-70**
  One side has music from *Meet Me in St. Louis.*
Soundtrack (1946) .... *AEI (M) 3101*   Re   **8-10**
  Composer: Johnny Mercer; Harry Warren. **Conductor:** Lennie Hayton. **Cast:** Judy Garland;
  Kenny Baker; Virginia O'Brien; Betty Russell.

HATARI
Soundtrack (1962) .... *RCA Victor (M) LPM-2559*   62   **20-30**
Soundtrack (1962) .... *RCA Victor (S) LSP-2559*   62   **30-40**
  Composer: Henry Mancini. **Conductor:** Henry Mancini. **Cast:** Henry Mancini and His Orchestra.

HAUNTED
Soundtrack (1977) .... *Midland Int'l (S) BKL1-2131*   77   **10-12**
  Composer: Lor Crane; Freya Crane; Ronald Romano. **Conductor:** Lor Crane. **Cast:** Billy Vera;
  Carol Douglas; Herb Oscar Anderson; Freya Crane; Ronald Romano.

HAVE GUN WILL TRAVEL
TV Soundtrack (1957) .... *Cerberus (M) CST 0209*   84   **15-20**
  Composer: Bernard Herrmann. **Cast:** Ethan Allen and the Western Suite.

HAVING A WILD WEEKEND
Soundtrack (1965) .... *Epic (M) LN-24162*   65   **15-20**
Soundtrack (1965) .... *Epic (S) BN-26162*   65   **15-20**
  Has *Catch Us If You Can,* originally intended as the film title.
  Composer: Dave Clark. **Cast:** Dave Clark Five.

HAWAII
Soundtrack (1966) ....*United Artists (M) UAL-4143*	66	$15-20
Soundtrack (1966) .... *United Artists (S) UAS-5143*	66	20-25

Composer: Elmer Bernstein. **Conductor:** Elmer Bernstein.

Studiotrack (1966) .... *Liberty (M) LRP-3488*	66	10-15
Studiotrack (1966) .... *Liberty (S) LST-7488*	66	15-20

Actual title: *Hawaii, Music from the Film . . . and Other Selections.*
Composer: Elmer Bernstein; others. **Conductor:** Martin Denny. **Cast:** Martin Denny.

Studiotrack ....*Somerset (S) SF-26900*		15-20

Side 2 has five assorted Hawaiian songs.
Composer: Elmer Bernstein; J. Kuhn; others.

HAWAII FIVE-0
TV Soundtrack (1969) .... *Capitol (S) ST-410*	69	15-20
TV Soundtrack (1969) ....*Capitol (S) SM-410*	Re	8-10

Composer: Morton Stevens. **Conductor:** Morton Stevens.

HAWAIIAN EYE
TV Soundtrack (1959) .... *Warner Bros. (M) W-1355*	59	25-30
TV Soundtrack (1959) ....*Warner Bros. (S) WS-1355*	59	30-40

Composer: Jerry Livingston; Mack David; others. **Conductor:** Warren Barker. **Cast:** Connie Stevens; Robert Conrad; Poncie Ponce.

HAWAIIANS
Soundtrack (1970) .... *United Artists (S) UAS-5210*	70	10-15

Composer: Henry Mancini. **Conductor:** Henry Mancini.

HAZEL FLAGG
Original Cast (1953) ....*RCA Victor (EP) WOC-1010*	53	25-35
Original Cast (1953) .... *RCA Victor (M) LOC-1010*	53	150-160
Original Cast (1953) ....*RCA Victor (M) CBM1-2207*	Re	12-18

Composer: Jule Styne; Bob Hilliard. **Conductor:** Pembroke Davenport. **Cast:** Helen Gallagher; Benay Venuta; John Howard; Jack Whiting; Dean Campbell.

HE'S MY GIRL
Soundtrack (1987) .... *Scotti Bros. (S) SZ-40906*	87	8-10

Composer: Various. **Cast:** David Hallyday; Sylvie Vartan; Paul Revere and the Raiders; Mountain; Chambers Brothers; Mickey Barrera; Kim Bullard.

HEAD
Soundtrack (1968) .... *Colgems (S) COSO-5008*	68	40-50
Soundtrack (1968) ....*Rhino (S) RNLP-145*	Re	8-10

Composer: Ken Thorne. **Conductor:** Ken Thorne. **Cast:** Monkees (Mike Nesmith; Peter Tork; Davy Jones; Micky Dolenz). (With dialogue.)

HEAR! HEAR!
Original Cast (1955) ....*Decca (M) DL-9031*	55	50-60

Composer: Fred Waring; others. **Conductor:** Fred Culley. **Cast:** Norma Douglas; Fred Waring and His Pennsylvanians; Glee Club; Leonard Kranendonk; Bob Sands; Gordon Goodman.

HEART BEAT
Soundtrack (1980) .... *Capitol (S) SOO-12029*	80	10-12

HEART IS A LONELY HUNTER
Soundtrack (1968) .... *Warner Bros. (S) BS-1759*	68	30-35

Composer: Dave Grusin. **Cast:** Scott Davis.

HEART IS A REBEL
Soundtrack .... *Chancel (EP) CR-2005*		10-15

Conductor: Ralph Carmichael. **Cast:** Ethel Waters; Georgia Lee; Ralph Carmichael's Orchestra.

HEART OF DIXIE
Soundtrack (1989) ....*A&M (S) SP-3930*   89   **$10-15**
  Composer: Kenny Vance; Philip Namanworth; others. **Cast:** Elvis Presley; Kenny Vance; Delbert McClinton; Charlie Jacobs; Rebecca Russell; Ivory Joe Hunter; Snakes.

HEARTBREAK HOTEL
Soundtrack (1988) .... *RCA Victor (S) 8533 1-R*   88   **8-10**
  Composer: Georges Delerue (original music); others. **Cast:** Elvis Presley; David Keith and the T. Graham Brown Band; Dobie Gray; Alice Cooper; Charlie Schlatter and the Zulu Time Band.

HEARTBREAK KID
Soundtrack (1972) ....*Columbia (S) S-32155*   73   **15-20**
  Composer: Garry Sherman; Cy Coleman; others. **Conductor:** Garry Sherman. **Cast:** Bill Dean; Eddie Albert; Charles Grodin; Cybill Shepherd; Audra Lindley; Jeannie Berlin. (With dialogue.)

HEARTS OF FIRE
Soundtrack (1987) .... *Columbia (S) SC-40870*   87   **8-10**
  Cast: Bob Dylan; Fiona; Rupert Everett.

HEAT AND DUST
Soundtrack (1983) .... *Varese Sarabande (S) STV-81194*   83   **8-10**
  Cast: Harry Rabinowitz.

HEAVEN'S GATE
Soundtrack (1980) ....*Liberty (S) LOO-1073*   80   **10-15**
  Composer: David Mansfield; Ennio Morricone. **Conductor:** David Mansfield. **Cast:** Doug Kershaw.

HEAVENLY KID
Soundtrack (1985) .... *Elektra (S) 60425-1*   85   **8-10**
  Composer: Various. **Cast:** Joe Lynn Turner; Jon Fiore; Jamie Bond; Debra Laws; George Duke; Lynn Turner; Howard Hewett; Mickey Thomas; Niko-Meka.

HEAVY METAL
Soundtrack (1981) .... *Asylum (S) 5E 547*   81   **8-10**
  Composer: Elmer Bernstein. **Conductor:** Elmer Bernstein. **Cast:** Nazareth; Cheap Trick; Blue Oyster Cult; Devo; Riggs.
Soundtrack (1981) ....*Asylum (S) DP-9004*   81   **12-15**
  Double LP set.
  Composer: Elmer Bernstein. **Cast:** Black Sabbath; Blue Oyster Cult; Cheap Trick; Devo; Donald Fagen; Don Felder; Grand Funk Railroad; Sammy Hagar; Journey; Nazareth; Stevie Nicks; Riggs; Trust.

HECTOR, THE STOWAWAY PUP
TV Soundtrack (1964) ....*Disneyland (M) ST-1921*   64   **20-25**
  Composer: Richard M. Sherman; Robert B. Sherman.

HEIDI
TV Soundtrack (1968) ....*Capitol (S) SKA-02995*   68   **35-40**
  Composer: John Williams. **Conductor:** John Williams. **Cast:** Sir Michael Redgrave; Jennifer Edwards (dialogue); Carri Chase (vocal on *Heidi's Theme*).

HELEN MORGAN STORY
Soundtrack (1957) ....*RCA Victor (EP) EPA-4112*   57   **15-20**
Soundtrack (1957) .... *RCA Victor (M) LOC-1030*   57   **60-70**
  Film star Ann Blyth's songs were actually performed by Gogi Grant.
  Conductor: Ray Heindorf.
TV Soundtrack (1957) .... *Columbia (M) CL-994*   57   **25-30**
  Actual title: *Bergen Sings Morgan*.
  Conductor: Luther Henderson. **Cast:** Polly Bergen.

HELEN OF TROY
Soundtrack (1956) .... *Elmer Bernstein Film Music Collection (M) FMC-1*   74   **$35-40**
Also has music from *A Summer Place* (1958).
Composer: Max Steiner. **Conductor:** Elmer Bernstein.

HELL RAIDERS OF THE DEEP:
see ANNA / HELL RAIDERS OF THE DEEP

HELL TO ETERNITY
Soundtrack (1960) .... *Warwick (M) W-2030*   60   **50-60**
Soundtrack (1960) .... *Warwick (S) WST-2030*   60   **75-100**
Composer: Leith Stevens. **Conductor:** Leith Stevens.

HELL'S ANGELS ON WHEELS
Soundtrack (1967) .... *Smash (M) 27094*   67   **15-20**
Soundtrack (1967) .... *Smash (S) 67094*   67   **20-25**
Composer: Stu Phillips. **Conductor:** Stu Phillips.

HELL'S ANGELS '69
Soundtrack (1969) .... *Capitol (S) SKAO-303*   69   **20-25**
Cast: Tony Bruno; Sonny Valdez; Wendy Cole.

HELL'S BELLS
Soundtrack (1969) .... *Sidewalk (S) 5919*   69   **15-20**
Composer: Les Baxter. **Conductor:** Les Baxter.

HELLBOUND: HELLRAISER II - TIME TO PLAY
Soundtrack (1988) .... *GNP/Crescendo (S) GNPS-8015*   88   **8-10**
Film sequel to *Hellraiser*.
Conductor: Allan Wilson. **Cast:** Graunke Symphony Orchestra.
Also see HELLRAISER

HELLCATS
Soundtrack (1968) .... *Tower (M) T-5124*   68   **10-15**
Soundtrack (1968) .... *Tower (S) ST-5124*   68   **12-18**
Composer: Various. **Cast:** Davie Allen and the Arrows; Davy Jones.

HELLO AGAIN
Soundtrack (1987) .... *Pro-Arte (S) CDC-1004*   87   **8-10**
Conductor: William Goldstein. **Cast:** William Goldstein.

HELLO, CAROL!:
see HELLO, DOLLY!

HELLO, DOLLY!
Original Cast (1964) .... *RCA Victor (M) LOCD-1087*   64   **10-15**
Original Cast (1964) .... *RCA Victor (S) LSOD-1087*   64   **15-20**
Original Cast (1964) .... *RCA Victor (S) AYL1-3814*   81   **8-10**
Composer: Jerry Herman. **Conductor:** Shepard Coleman. **Cast:** Carol Channing; David Burns; Eileen Brennan; Sondra Lee; Charles Nelson Reilly; Jerry Dodge; Igors Gavon.
Original Cast Interview (1964) .... *RCA Victor (M) SP-33-282*   64   **15-25**
Has an interview titled *Hello, Carol!*
Cast: Carol Channing.
Original All-Black Cast (1967) .... *RCA Victor (M) LOC-1147*   67   **25-35**
Original All-Black Cast (1967) .... *RCA Victor (S) LSO-1147*   67   **30-40**
Original All-Black Cast (1967) .... *RCA Victor (S) ANL1-2849*   78   **8-10**
Composer: Jerry Herman. **Conductor:** Saul Schectman. **Cast:** Pearl Bailey; Cab Calloway; Jack Crowder; Winston DeWitt Hemsley; Chris Calloway; Roger Lawson; Emily Yancy.

HELLO DOLLY! (continued)

Original London Cast (1966) .... *RCA Victor (M) LOCD-2007*   66 $20-25
Original London Cast (1966) .... *RCA Victor (S) LSOD-2007*   66   25-30
　Composer: Jerry Herman. Conductor: Alyn Ainsworth. Cast: Mary Martin; Loring Smith;
　Marilynn Lovell; Coco Ramirez.
Original German Cast (1967) .... *Columbia (M) OL-6710*   67   25-30
Original German Cast (1967) .... *Columbia (S) OS-3110*   67   35-40
　Composer: Jerry Herman. Conductor: Klaus Doldinger. Cast: Tatjana Iwanow; Wolfgang
　Arps; Ingrid Ernest; Evelyn Balser.
London Studio Cast .... *Music for Pleasure (M) MFP-1066*   25-30
　Composer: Jerry Herman. Cast: Beryl Reid; Arthur Haynes; Patricia Routledge.
Soundtrack (1969) .... *20th Century-Fox (S) DTCS-5103*   69   15-20
Soundtrack (1969) .... *20th Century-Fox (S) 102*   74   8-10
　Composer: Jerry Herman. Conductor: Lionel Newman; Lennie Hayton. Cast: Barbra Streisand;
　Walter Matthau; Michael Crawford; Louis Armstrong.
Studiotrack (1964) .... *Kapp (M) KL-3364*   64   10-15
Studiotrack .... *Kapp (S) KS-3364*   64   10-15
　Also has songs from other shows.
　Cast: Louis Armstrong and the All Stars.
Studiotrack (1964) .... *RCA Victor (S) LPM-2916*   64   10-15
Studiotrack (1964) .... *RCA Victor (S) LSP-2916*   10-15
　Cast: Dorsey Orchestra.

HELLO OUT THERE

Studio Cast (1953) .... *Desto (SE) DST-6451*   15-20
　Composer: Jack Beeson; William Saroyan. Conductor: Frederick Waldman. Cast: John
　Reardon; Lenya Gabriele; Marvin Worden.

HELLO, SOLLY!

Original Cast (1967) .... *Capitol (M) W-2731*   67   20-30
Original Cast (1967) .... *Capitol (S) SW-2731*   67   25-35
　Conductor: Al Hausman. Cast: Mickey Katz; Larry Best; Stan Porter; Vivian Lloyd.

HELLO-GOODBYE

Soundtrack (1970) .... *20th Century-Fox (S) S-4210*   70   12-15
　Composer: Francis Lai. Conductor: Francis Lai.

HELLRAISER

Soundtrack (1987) .... *Pro-Arte (S) CDC-1001*   87   8-10
　Cast: Christopher Young.
　Also see HELLBOUND: HELLRAISER II - TIME TO PLAY

HELP!

Soundtrack (1964) .... *United Artists (M) No Number Used*   65   550-650
　Open-end interview. Includes script. Promotional issue only.
Soundtrack (1964) .... *Cicadelic (M) 002*   90   8-10
　Open-end interview. Includes script. Promotional issue, offered as a bonus to book buyers. Includes
　paper sleeve and script insert.
Soundtrack (1965) .... *Capitol (M) MAS-2386*   65   40-60
　Black label.
Soundtrack (1965) .... *Capitol (S) SMAS-2386*   65   35-45
　Black label.
Soundtrack (1965) .... *Apple (S) SMAS-2386*   68   15-20
　With Capitol logo on Apple label.
Soundtrack (1965) .... *Capitol (S) SMAS-2386*   69   20-30
　Green label.

Soundtrack (1964) .... *MFSL (S) 1-105*   85 $15-20
  Half-speed mastered.
  Composer: John Lennon; Paul McCartney; George Harrison. **Cast:** Beatles.

HEMINGWAY'S ADVENTURES OF A YOUNG MAN
Soundtrack (1962) .... *RCA Victor (M) MOC-1074*   62   **60-65**
Soundtrack (1962) .... *Label X (S) LXRS-201*   Re   **8-10**
  Composer: Franz Waxman. **Conductor:** Franz Waxman.

HENNESEY
TV Soundtrack (1959) .... *Signature (M) 1049*   59   **40-50**
TV Soundtrack (1959) .... *Signature (S) SS-1049*   59   **60-70**
  Composer: Sonny Burke. **Conductor:** Jackie Cooper.

HENRY V:
see HAMLET; KING HENRY V

HENRY VIII AND HIS SIX WIVES
Soundtrack (1972) .... *Angel (S) SFO-36895*   72   **10-15**
  Gatefold cover. Features authentic Tudor Court music and original pieces composed in a
  sixteenth-century style for the film.
  Composer: David Munrow; others. **Conductor:** David Munrow. **Cast:** Early Music
  Consort of London.

HENRY MANCINI PRESENTS THE ACADEMY AWARD SONGS
Studiotrack (1966) .... *RCA Victor (M) LPM-6013*   66   **10-15**
Studiotrack (1966) .... *RCA Victor (S) LSP-6013*   66   **15-20**
  Has 31 Oscar winning songs from 1934 - 1964.
  Composer: Various. **Conductor:** Henry Mancini. **Cast:** Henry Mancini's Orchestra and Chorus.

HENRY, SWEET HENRY
Original Cast (1967) .... *ABC (M) OC-4*   67   **25-30**
Original Cast (1967) .... *ABC (S) SOC-4*   67   **35-40**
  Composer: Robert Merrill. **Conductor:** Shepard Coleman. **Cast:** Don Ameche; Carol Bruce;
  Neva Small; Louise Lasser; Robin Wilson; Alice Playten; Laried Montgomery.

HER FIRST ROMAN
Original Cast (1968) .... *S.P.M. (M) CO-7751*   68   **10-20**
  Composer: Ervin Drake. **Conductor:** Peter Howard. **Cast:** Cal Bellini; Richard Kiley; Bruce
  MacKay; Claudia McNeil; Brooks Morton; Leslie Uggams.

HERCULES
Soundtrack (1959) .... *Bluebird (M) LBY-1036*   59   **100-125**
  Composer: Enzo Masetti. **Cast:** Conrad Nagel (narration); Steve Reeves (dialogue).
Soundtrack (1962) .... *Varese Sarabande (S) STV-81187*   **8-10**
  Background score from the film.
  Conductor: Natale Massara.

HERCULES (THE MUSIC)
Soundtrack .... *Phoenix (S) PHC AM-01*   84   **50-65**
  Composer: Enzo Masetti. **Conductor:** Enzo Masetti.

HERE COME THE WAVES:
see ACCENTUATE THE POSITIVE

HERE COMES GARFIELD
TV Soundtrack (1982) .... *Epic (S) FE 38136*   82   **8-10**

HERE COMES THE GROOM:
see COOL OF THE EVENING

HERE IS MY HEART:
see EASY TO REMEMBER; MISSISSIPPI

HERE WE GO ROUND THE MULBERRY BUSH
Soundtrack (1968) . . . .*United Artists (S) UAS-5175*   68   **$12-15**
  Composer: Traffic; Spencer Davis Group. **Cast:** Traffic; Steve Winwood; Spencer Davis Group.

HERE'S JOHNNY:
see MAGIC MOMENTS FROM THE TONIGHT SHOW

HERE'S LOVE
Original Cast (1963) . . . . *Columbia (M) KOL-6000*   63   **25-30**
Original Cast (1963) . . . .*Columbia (S) KOS-2400*   63   **40-45**
  Composer: Meredith Willson. **Conductor:** Elliot Lawrence. **Cast:** Janis Paige; Craig Stevens;
  Laurence Naismith; Fred Gwynne; Paul Reed; Cliff Hall; Arthur Rubin; Valerie Lee; Kathy Cody.

HERO
Soundtrack (1972) . . . .*Capitol (S) SW-11098*   72   **15-20**
  Composer: Johnny Harris; others. **Conductor:** Johnny Harris. **Cast:** Bloomfield's Heads Hands
  and Feet.

HERO AIN'T NOTHIN' BUT A SANDWICH
Soundtrack (1978) . . . . *Columbia (S) PS-35046*   78   **8-10**

HEROES
Soundtrack (1977) . . . .*MCA (S) 2320*   77   **10-12**
  Composer: Jack Nitzche; Richard Hazard. **Conductor:** Richard Hazard. **Cast:** Kim Carnes;
  Sounds of Sunshine.

HEROES OF TELEMARK
Soundtrack (1965) . . . .*Mainstream (M) 56064*   65   **20-25**
Soundtrack (1965) . . . .*Mainstream (S) S-6064*   65   **25-30**
  Composer: Malcolm Henry Arnold. **Conductor:** Malcolm Henry Arnold.
Soundtrack (1965) . . . . *No Label Shown (M) No Number Used*   65   **30-40**
  Open-end interview, with script. Promotional issue only.

HEY BOY, HEY GIRL
Soundtrack (1959) . . . .*Capitol (M) T-1160*   59   **20-30**
  Conductor: Nelson Riddle. **Cast:** Louis Prima; Keely Smith; Sam Butera and the Witnesses.

HEY, LET'S TWIST
Soundtrack (1961) . . . .*Roulette (M) R-25168*   62   **15-20**
Soundtrack (1961) . . . .*Roulette (S) SR-25168*   62   **25-30**
  Composer: Henry Glover. **Cast:** Joey Dee and the Starlighters; Jo Ann Campbell; Teddy
  Randazzo.

HEY THERE, IT'S YOGI BEAR
Soundtrack (1964) . . . .*Colpix (M) CP-472*   64   **15-20**
Soundtrack (1964) . . . .*Colpix (S) SCP-472*   64   **20-25**
  Composer: Ray Gilbert; Doug Goodwin; David Gates. **Conductor:** Marty Paich.
  Cast: Mel Blanc; Daws Butler; Pat O'Malley; Don Messick. (With dialogue.)

HIDING OUT
Soundtrack (1987) . . . . *Virgin (S) 90661-1*   87   **8-10**
  Composer: Various. **Cast:** Boy George; Lolita Pop; Pretty Poison; Scarlett and Black; Felix
  Cavaliere; All That Jazz; Hue and Cry; Roy Orbison; K.D. Orbison; Lee Anthony Brisdon;
  David L. Brisdon; Black Britain; Public Image Limited.

HIDING PLACE
Soundtrack (1975) . . . . *Word (S) WST-8697*   **8-10**
  Composer: Ted Smith.

HIGH AND THE MIGHTY
Soundtrack (1954) ... *Elmer Bernstein Film Music Collection (M) FMC-14*   79   **$30-40**
Also contains music from *Search for Paradise* (1957).
Composer: Dimitri Tiomkin (both); SEARCH FOR PARADISE: Ned Washington; Lowell Thomas. **Conductor:** Elmer Bernstein (both).

HIGH ANXIETY
Soundtrack (1977) .... *Asylum (S) 5E-501*   77   **8-10**
Side two has music composed by John Morris for five other Mel Brooks' films: *The Producers, Young Frankenstein, Silent Movie, Blazing Saddles* and *Twelve Chairs*.
Composer: John Morris. **Conductor:** John Morris. **Cast:** Mel Brooks.

HIGH BUTTON SHOES
Original Cast (1947) .... *RCA Victor/Camden (M) CAL-457*   58   **40-45**
Original Cast (1947) .... *RCA Victor (M) LOC-1107*   64   **35-40**
Original Cast (1947) .... *RCA Victor (SE) LSO-1107*   64   **35-40**
Composer: Jule Styne; Sammy Cahn. **Conductor:** Milton Rosenstock. **Cast:** Phil Silvers; Nanette Fabray; Lois Lee; Mark Dawson; Jack McCauley; Johnny Stewart.

HIGH ROAD TO CHINA
Soundtrack (1983) .... *Scar (S) 5003*   83   **30-40**
Composer: John Barry. **Conductor:** John Barry.

HIGH SOCIETY
Soundtrack (1956) ....,... *Capitol (45) PRO-306*   56   **10-20**
Has *True Love* on one side. Side two has interviews with Bing Crosby and Grace Kelly.
Cast: Bing Crosby; Grace Kelly.
Soundtrack (1956) .... *Capitol (EP) EDM-750*   56   **10-15**
Soundtrack (1956) .... *Capitol (M) W-750*   56   **15-25**
Soundtrack (1956) .... *Capitol (S) SW-750*   61   **10-15**
Composer: Cole Porter. **Conductor:** Johnny Green. **Cast:** Bing Crosby; Grace Kelly; Frank Sinatra; Louis Armstrong; Celeste Holm.

HIGH SPIRITS
Original Cast (1964) .... *ABC (M) OC-1*   64   **25-30**
Original Cast (1964) .... *ABC-Paramount (S) SOC-1*   64   **30-35**
Composer: Hugh Martin; Timothy Gray. **Conductor:** Fred Werner. **Cast:** Beatrice Lillie; Tammy Grimes; Edward Woodward; Timothy Gray; Louise Troy.
Soundtrack (1988) .... *SRG (S) SL-5180*   88   **8-10**
Soundtrack .... *GNP/Crescendo (S) GNPS-8016*   **8-10**
Composer: George Fenton. **Conductor:** George Fenton. **Cast:** Graunke Symphony Orchestra.

HIGH TIME
Soundtrack (1960) .... *RCA Victor (M) LPM-2314*   60   **15-20**
Soundtrack (1960) .... *RCA Victor (S) LSP-2314*   60   **25-30**
Composer: Henry Mancini; James Van Heusen. **Conductor:** Henry Mancini.
Cast: Bing Crosby; Fabian.

HIGH TOR
TV Soundtrack (1956) .... *Decca (M) DL-8272*   56   **150-175**
Composer: Arthur Schwartz; Maxwell Anderson. **Conductor:** Joseph J. Lilley.
Cast: Bing Crosby (narration); Julie Andrews; Everett Sloane. (With dialogue).

HIGHLIGHTS FROM PHANTOM OF THE OPERA:
see PHANTOM OF THE OPERA

HILLBILLY CAT:
see ELVIS LIVE AT THE LOUISIANA HAYRIDE

HINDENBERG
Soundtrack (1975) .... *MCA (S) 2090*   75   **$10-12**
    Composer: David Shire. Conductor: David Shire. Cast: Hugh Douglas (narrator of newsreel
    prologue); Peter Donat; Robert Clary; Herb Morrison (newsman from original radio broadcast).

HIS LAND
Soundtrack .... *Light (S) LS-5532*   **8-10**
    Composer: Ralph Carmichael. Conductor: Ralph Carmichael. Cast: Cliff Richard; Cliff Burrows.

HIS WIFE'S HABIT
Soundtrack (1970) .... *Capitol (S) SW-641*   70   **12-15**
    Composer: Jim Helms; Norma Green; Gary Lemel. Conductor: Jim Helms. Cast: Gary Lemel;
    Sonny Geraci.

HISTORY OF THE WORLD, PART I
Soundtrack (1981) .... *Warner Bros. (S) BSK 3579*   81   **8-10**
    Composer: John Morris; Mel Brooks; Ronny Graham. Conductor: John Morris. Cast: Mel
    Brooks; Orson Welles. (With dialogue.)

HIT THE DECK
Original London Cast .... *World (M) SH-176*   **25-30**
    One side of this LP contains music from *No No Nanette.*
    Composer: Vincent Youmans; Clifford Grey; Leo Robin. Cast: Stanley Holloway; Barry Twins;
    Ivy Tresmand.
Soundtrack (1955) .... *MGM (EP) X-287*   55   **15-20**
Soundtrack (1955) .... *MGM (M) E-3163*   55   **25-35**
Soundtrack (1955) .... *MGM (SE) 2SE-43*   **20-25**
    Double LP set.
Soundtrack (1955) .... *MCA (SE) 25033*   Re   **8-10**
    Also has music from *The Pirate* and *Pagan Love Song.* Shown as stereo, but these tracks are monaural.
    Composer: Vincent Youmans; others. Conductor: George Stoll. Cast: Jane Powell; Tony
    Martin; Debbie Reynolds; Vic Damone; Ann Miller; Kay Armen; Russ Tamblyn.
    Also see CAT AND THE FIDDLE

HIT THEMES FROM MOTION PICTURES
Studiotrack .... *United Artists (S) S-21001*   67   **10-15**

HITCH-HIKERS GUIDE TO THE GALAXY - PART ONE
BBC Radio Series (1979) .... *Hannibal (S) HNBL 2301*   82   **15-20**
    Composer: Tim Souster. Cast: Simon Jones; Geoffrey McGivern; Mark Wing-Davey; Stephen
    Moore; Cindy Oswin; Richard Vernon; Valentine Dyall; David Tate; Jim Broadbent; Bill
    Wallis; Peter Jones.

HITCHHIKER:
see OUTER SPACE SUITE

HITLER
Soundtrack (1962) .... *Medallion (S) MED-302*   80   **8-10**
    Composer: Hans J. Salter. Conductor: Hans J. Salter.

HITLER'S INFERNO
Assembled Cast .... *Audio Rarities (M) 2445*   **15-25**
    Cast: Adolph Hitler (speeches and music).

HITS FROM BROADWAY SHOWS
Studiotrack (1955) .... *RCA Victor (EP) EPA-728*   55   **8-15**
Studiotrack (1955) .... *RCA Victor (EP) EPB-728*   55   **10-20**
Studiotrack (1955) .... *RCA Victor (M) LPM-1191*   55   **15-25**
    Composer: Various. Cast: Perry Como.

HITTER
Soundtrack (1978) . . . .*Capitol (S) SW-11920*   **$8-10**
   Composer: Garfeel Ruff; others. **Cast:** Raul de Souza; Gloria Jones; Taste of Honey; Maze;
   Garfeel Ruff.

HOGAN'S HEROES
Studiotrack . . . . *Sunset (M) SUM-1137*   **10-15**
   Composer: Various. **Conductor:** Jerry Fielding. **Cast:** Robert Clary; Richard Dawson; Ivan
   Dixon; Larry Hovis.

HOLD ON!
Soundtrack (1966) . . . .*MGM (M) E-4342*   66   **10-15**
Soundtrack (1966) . . . . *MGM (S) SE-4342*   66   **15-20**
   Cast: Herman's Hermits (featuring Peter Noone); Shelley Fabares.

HOLIDAY IN MANHATTAN
Studiotrack . . . . *Design (S) SS-47*   **10-15**
   Cast: Cole Porter; Addison Bailey Orchestra.

HOLIDAY INN
Studiotrack (1942) . . . .*Decca (M) DL-5092*   50   **40-50**
Soundtrack (1942) . . . .*Decca (M) DL-4256*   62   **25-30**
   Issued as part of *Bing's Hollywood Series*.
Studiotrack (1942) . . . . *MCA (SE) 25205*   Re   **8-10**
   Composer: Irving Berlin. **Conductor:** John Scott Trotter; Bob Crosby. **Cast:** Bing Crosby;
   Fred Astaire; Margaret Lenhart; Ken Darby Singers.

HOLLY, BUDDY, STORY:
see BUDDY HOLLY STORY

HOLLYWOOD
TV Soundtrack (1979) . . . .*Stet (S) DS-15006*   80   **8-10**
   Music used to accompany classic silent films.
   Composer: Carl Davis; Charles Chaplin; others. **Conductor:** Carl Davis.

HOLLYWOOD GOLD, VOL. I
Studiotrack (1973) . . . . *Ovation (S) QVQD-1601*   73   **10-12**
   Gatefold cover.
   Composer: Various. **Cast:** Quadrastrings.

HOLLYWOOD HOTEL
Soundtrack (1937) . . . . *Hollywood Soundstage (M) HS-5004*   81   **8-10**
   Composer: Johnny Mercer; Richard Whiting. **Cast:** Dick Power; Frances Langford; Benny
   Goodman and His Orchestra; Rosemary Lane; Johnny "Scat" Davis; Mable Todd; Ted Healy;
   Jerry Cooper.
   Also see HOORAY FOR HOLLYWOOD

HOLLYWOOD KNIGHTS
Soundtrack (1980) ....*Casablanca (S) 7218*   80   **$8-10**
    Cast: Frankie Valli and the 4 Seasons; Martha and the Vandellas; Brooklyn Dreams.

HOLLYWOOD OR BUST
Soundtrack (1957) ....*Capitol (EP) EAP 1-806*   57   **25-50**
    Cast: Dean Martin.

HOLLYWOOD SONG BOOK - ACADEMY AWARD WINNERS
Studiotrack (1958) .... *Coral (M) CRL-57241*   58   **10-20**
    Volume one.
Studiotrack (1958) .... *Coral (S) CRL7-57241*   58   **15-25**
    Volume one.
Studiotrack (1958) .... *Coral (M) CRL-57242*   58   **10-20**
    Volume two.
Studiotrack (1958) .... *Coral (S) CRL7-57242*   58   **15-25**
    Volume two.
Studiotrack (1958) ....*Coral (M) CX-2*   58   **20-30**
    Volumes one and two.
Studiotrack (1958) .... *Coral (S) 7CX-2*   58   **25-35**
    Volumes one and two.
    Composer: Various. **Conductor:** Neal Hefti. **Cast:** Neal Hefti and His Orchestra.

HOLLYWOOD: THE POST WAR YEARS (1946 - 1949)
Soundtrack .... *AEI (M) 3104*   80   **8-10**
    Has music from *The Bandit of Sherwood Forest* (Hugo Friedhofer); *Time Out of Mind* (Miklos Rosza);
    A Double Life (Miklos Rosza); *Force of Evil* (David Raksin). @NOTE = **Composer:** Hugo Friedhofer;
    Miklos Rosza; David Raksin. **Conductor:** Hugo Friedhofer;
    Miklos Rosza; David Raksin.

HOLOCAUST
TV Soundtrack (1978) .... *RCA Victor (S) ARL1-2785*   78   **8-10**
    Includes synopsis insert.
    Composer: Morton Gould. **Conductor:** Morton Gould. **Cast:** National Philharmonic Orchestra.

HOME MOVIES
Soundtrack (1979) .... *Varese Sarabande (S) STV-81139*   80   **8-10**
    Composer: Pino Donaggio. **Conductor:** Pino Donaggio.

HOME OF THE BRAVE
Soundtrack (1986) ....!........ *Warner Bros. (S) 1-25400*   86   **8-10**
    Cast: Laurie Anderson.

HOMER
Soundtrack (1970) ....*Cotillion (S) SD-9037*   70   **10-12**
    Composer: Various. **Cast:** Byrds; Buffalo Springfield; Cream; Led Zeppelin; Don Scardino.

HOMETOWN U.S.A.
Soundtrack (1979) ....*KTEL (S) NU-4460*   79   **10-12**

HONEY BABY
    Cast: Diana Sands; Calvin Lockhart.

HONEY POT
Soundtrack (1967) ....*United Artists (M) UAL-4159*   67   **25-30**
Soundtrack (1967) ....*United Artists (S) UAS-5159*   67   **30-35**
Soundtrack (1967) ....*MCA (S) 25106*   Re   **8-10**
    Composer: John Addison. **Conductor:** John Addison.

HONEY WEST
TV Soundtrack (1965) . . . .*ABC-Paramount (M) 532*   65 $20-30
TV Soundtrack (1965) . . . .*ABC-Paramount (S) S-532*   65   30-40
  Composer: Joseph Mullendore. **Conductor:** Alfred Perry.

HONEYSUCKLE ROSE
Soundtrack (1980) . . . . *Columbia (S) S2-36752*   80   12-15
  Double LP set.
  Composer: Willie Nelson; others. **Cast:** Willie Nelson; Dyan Cannon; Amy Irving; Johnny
  Gimble; Jody Payne; Hank Cochran;
  Emmylou Harris; Jeannie Seely; Kenneth Threadgill.

HONG KONG
TV Soundtrack (1961) . . . .*ABC-Paramount (M) 367*   61   30-35
TV Soundtrack (1961) . . . .*ABC-Paramount (S) S-367*   61   40-45
  Full title: *Exciting Hong Kong.*
  Composer: Lionel Newman; Billy May; Frank Comstock; Marty Paich. **Conductor:** Lionel
  Newman.

HONKY TONK FREEWAY
Soundtrack (1981) . . . . *Capitol (S) ST-12160*   81   8-10
  Composer: Elmer Bernstein; George Martin. **Cast:** Russell Smith; Roger Cook; Linda Hart;
  Paul Jabara; Beverly d'Angelo.

HONKYTONK MAN
Soundtrack (1982) . . . . *Warner Bros. (S) 1-23739*   82   8-10
  Composer: Various. **Conductor:** Steve Dorff. **Cast:** Clint Eastwood; Porter Wagoner; Ray
  Price; Marty Robbins; John Anderson; Linda Hopkins; Johnny Gimble and the Texas Swing
  Band; David Frizzell and Dottie West.

HOOPER
Soundtrack (1978) . . . .*Warner Bros. (S) BSK-3234*   78   10-12
  Composer: Bill Justis. **Conductor:** Bill Justis. **Cast:** Bent Myggen; Tammy Wynette.

HOORAY FOR DAISY
London Cast . . . .*AEI (S) 1118*   8-12
  Composer: Slade; Reynolds.

HOORAY FOR HOLLYWOOD
Soundtrack . . . . *United Artists (M) UA-LA361-H*   75   8-10
  Sequel to *The Golden Age of the Hollywood Musical.* Has music from *Hollywood Hotel, Gold Diggers of*
  1935, 42nd Street, In Caliente, Gold Diggers of 1937, Wonder Bar, Fashions of 1934 and *Dames.*
  Composer: Johnny Mercer; Harry Warren; Al Dubin; Mort Dixon; Allie Wrubel; Sammy Fain;
  others. **Conductor:** Busby Berkeley. **Cast:** Busby Berkeley Girls; Frances Langford; Johnny
  "Scat" Davis; Benny Goodman and His Orchestra; Dick Powell; Gloria Stuart; Alice Brady;
  Ruby Keeler; Ginger Rogers; Judy Canova; Winifred Shaw. (With dialogue.)

HOOSIERS
Soundtrack (1987) . . . .*Polydor (S) 831475-1*   87   8-10
  Composer: Jerry Goldsmith. **Conductor:** Jerry Goldsmith.

HOOTENANNY HOOT
Soundtrack (1963) . . . .*MGM (M) E-4172*   63   12-18
Soundtrack (1963) . . . . *MGM (S) SE-4172*   63   15-20
  Composer: Various. **Cast:** Sheb Wooley; Mark Dinning; others.

HORROR EXPRESS:
see HORROR RHAPSODY

HORROR RHAPSODY
Studiotrack (1973) .... *Citadel (M) CT-7012*   78   **$8-10**
  Arranges into a suite, music from *Son of Frankenstein*, *The Mummy's Hand*, *Black Friday* and *Man Made Monster*. Also has soundtrack music from *Horror Express*, composed and conducted by John Cacavas.
  Composer: Hans J. Salter. **Conductor:** Hans J. Salter.

HORSE SOLDIERS
Soundtrack (1959) .... *United Artists (M) UAL-4035*   59   **25-35**
Soundtrack (1959) .... *United Artists (S) UAS-5035*   59   **50-60**
Soundtrack (1959) .... *Ascot (M) UM-13502*   64   **15-20**
Soundtrack (1959) .... *Ascot (S) US-16502*   64   **25-30**
  Also has selections from *Paris Blues*, *Judgment at Nuremberg* and *The Unforgiven*.
  Composer: David Buttolph; others. **Conductor:** David Buttolph.

HORSELL COMMON AND THE HEAT RAY:
see EVE OF THE WAR

HORSEMEN
Soundtrack (1971) .... *Sunflower (S) 5007*   71   **30-35**
  Composer: Georges Delerue. **Conductor:** Georges Delerue.

HOSTAGE
Soundtrack (1969) .... *MGM (S) SE-4670*   69   **10-15**
  Theme from *Z*, plus other music by Mikis Theodorakis. A promotional issue.
  Composer: Mikis Theodorakis. **Conductor:** Mikis Theodorakis. **Cast:** Mikis Theodorakis singing).

HOT BLOOD
Soundtrack (1954) .... *RCA Victor EPA-535*   54   **75-100**
  Quickly reissued and retitled *The Wild One*.
  Composer: Leith Stevens. **Conductor:** Shorty Rogers. **Cast:** Shorty Rogers and His Orchestra, featuring Bill Perkins (tenor saxophone).
  Also see WILD ONE

HOT PARTS
Soundtrack (1972) .... *Kama Sutra (S) KSBS-2054*   72   **12-15**
  Composer: Michael Brown; Bert Sommer; others. **Conductor:** Steve Martin; Bert Sommer; Alan Nicholls; Montage.

HOT ROCK
Soundtrack (1972) .... *Prophesy (S) SD-6055* 72 $10-12
  Composer: Quincy Jones. **Conductor:** Quincy Jones. **Cast:** Clark Terry; Gerry Mulligan
  Grady Tate; Ian Smith Singers.

HOT ROD GANG
Soundtrack (1958) .... *Capitol (EP) EAP-1-985* 58 100-125
  Composer: Various. **Cast:** Gene Vincent and the Blue Caps.

HOT ROD RUMBLE
Soundtrack (1957) .... *Liberty (M) LRP-3048* 57 75-100
  Composer: Alexander "Sandy" Courage. **Conductor:** Alexander "Sandy" Courage.

HOTEL
Soundtrack (1967) .... *Warner Bros. (M) W-1682* 67 20-25
Soundtrack (1967) .... *Warner Bros. (S) WS-1682* 67 25-30
  Composer: John Keating. **Conductor:** John Keating. **Cast:** Carmen McRae.

HOTEL PARIDISO
Soundtrack (1966) .... *MGM (M) E-4419* 66 10-15
  Has cover art by Frank Frazetta.
Soundtrack (1966) .... *MGM (S) SE-4419* 66 15-20
  Composer: Laurence Rosenthal. **Conductor:** Laurence Rosenthal.

HOUR OF THE GUN
Soundtrack (1967) .... *United Artists (M) UAL-4166* 67 25-35
Soundtrack (1967) .... *United Artists (S) UAS-5166* 67 50-60
  Composer: Jerry Goldsmith. **Conductor:** Jerry Goldsimth.

HOUSE IS NOT A HOME
Soundtrack (1964) .... *Ava (M) A-50* 64 10-15
Soundtrack (1964) .... *Ava (S) AS-50* 64 15-20
  Composer: Joseph Weiss; Burt Bacharach. **Conductor:** Joseph Weiss.

HOUSE OF FLOWERS
Original Cast (1954) .... *Columbia (EP) A-1113* 54 20-25
  Triple EP set.
Original Cast (1954) .... *Columbia (M) ML-4969* 54 20-25
Original Cast (1954) .... *Columbia (SE) OS-2320* 63 15-20
Original Cast (1954) .... *Columbia Special Products (S) COS-2320* Re 8-10
  Composer: Harold Arlen. **Conductor:** Jerry Arlen. **Cast:** Pearl Bailey; Diahann Carroll;
  Juanita Hall; Rawn Spearman; Ada Moore; Miriam Burton; Dolores Harper; Enid Mosier.

HOUSE OF FLOWERS (continued)
Original Revival Cast (1968) . . . . *United Artists (M) UAL-5180*   68 $25-30
Original Revival Cast (1968) . . . . *United Artists (S) UAS-5180*   68   35-40
  Composer: Harold Arlen; Truman Capote. **Conductor:** Joseph Raposo. **Cast:** Yolande Bavan;
  Thelma Oliver; Hope Clarke; Josephine Premice; Tom Helmore; Robert Jackson; Charles
  Moore; Novella Nelson; Carla Pinza.

HOUSE OF LEATHER
Studio Cast (1970) . . . . *Fontana (S) SRF-67591*   70   20-25
  Composer: Dale Menten; Frederick Gaines. **Cast:** Dale Menten; Dennis Craswell; Tom
  Hustin; Dennis Libby; Blackwood Apology.

HOUSE PARTY
Soundtrack . . . . *Motown (S) MOT-6296*   8-10
  Composer: Various. **Cast:** Arts and Crafts; Today; Force MDs; Full Force Family; Flavor
  Flav; Kid 'N' Play; Kenny Vaughan and Art of Love.

HOUSEBOAT
Soundtrack (1958) . . . . *Columbia (M) CL-1222*   58   70-80
  Composer: George Duning; Jay Livingston; Ray Evans. **Conductor:** George Duning; Frank
  DeVol. **Cast:** Sophia Loren; George Duning and His Orchestra.

HOUSEWIFE SUPERSTAR
Original Cast (1977) . . . . *Charisma (S) CAS-1123*   77   20-25
  Composer: Barry Humphries. **Cast:** Barry Humphries (piano).

HOUSEWIVES' CANTATA
Original Cast (1980) . . . . *Original Cast (S) OC-8133*   80   10-12
  Composer: Mira Spektor; June Siegel. **Conductor:** Bob Goldstone. **Cast:** Lawrence Chelsi;
  Maida Meyers; Mira J. Spektor; Sharon Talbot.

HOW GREEN WAS MY VALLEY:
  see DAVID AND BATHSHEBA

HOW NOW, DOW JONES
Original Cast (1967) . . . . *RCA Victor (M) LOC-1142*   67   20-25
Original Cast (1967) . . . . *RCA Victor (S) LSO-1142*   67   25-30
  Composer: Elmer Bernstein; Carolyn Leigh. **Conductor:** Peter Howard. **Cast:** Anthony Roberts;
  Marilyn Mason; Brenda Vaccaro; Sammy Smith; Hiram Sherman; Mara Worth; Charlotte Jones;
  Fran Stevens.

HOW SWEET IT IS
Soundtrack (1968) . . . . *RCA Victor (M) LPM-4037*   68   15-20
Soundtrack (1968) . . . . *RCA Victor (S) LSP-4037*   68   20-25
  Composer: Pat Williams; Jim Webb. **Conductor:** Pat Williams; Jim Webb. **Cast:** Picardy Singers.

HOW THE GRINCH STOLE CHRISTMAS
TV Soundtrack . . . . *Leo (S) LE-901*   8-10
  Composer: Albert Hague. **Cast:** Boris Karloff.

HOW THE WEST WAS WON
Studio Cast (1963) . . . . *Colpix (M) CP-452*   63   15-20
Studio Cast (1963) . . . . *Colpix (S) SCP-452*   63   15-20
  Cast: Burgess Meredith.
Soundtrack (1963) . . . . *MGM (M) 1E-5*   63   10-15
Soundtrack (1963) . . . . *MGM (S) S1E-5*   63   15-20
Soundtrack (1962) . . . . *MCA (S) 39043*   86   8-10
  Composer: Alfred Newman; Ken Darby; others. **Conductor:** Alfred Newman; others.
  Cast: Debbie Reynolds; Ken Darby Singers; Dave Guard; Whiskeyhill Singers.

Studiotrack (1960) .... *RCA Victor (M) LOP-6070* 60   **$15-20**
Studiotrack (1960) .... *RCA Victor (S) LSO-6070* 60   **20-30**
  Above two have gatefold covers and booklets.
  Composer: Alan Lomax; Sam Hinton; others. **Conductor:** Bob Thompson; Richard P. Condie.
  Cast: Bing Crosby; Rosemary Clooney; Sam Hinton; Jack Halloran Singers; Jimmie Driftwood;
  Tarry Town Trio; Mormon Tabernacle Choir.
Studiotrack (1963) .... *Epic (M) LN-24058* 63   **10-15**
Studiotrack (1963) .... *Epic (S) BN-26058* 63   **10-15**
  Cast: Voices Eleven.
  Also see UNDEFEATED

HOW TO BEAT THE HIGH COST OF LIVING
Soundtrack (1980) .... *Columbia (S) JS-36741* 80   **10-12**
  Composer: Patrick Williams.

HOW TO MURDER YOUR WIFE
Soundtrack (1965) .... *United Artists (M) UAL-4119* 65   **10-15**
Soundtrack (1965) .... *United Artists (S) UAS-5119* 65   **15-20**
  Composer: Neal Hefti. **Conductor:** Neal Hefti.

HOW TO SAVE A MARRIAGE AND RUIN YOUR LIFE
Soundtrack (1968) .... *Columbia (S) OS-3140* 68   **35-40**
  Composer: Michel Legrand. **Conductor:** Michel Legrand.

HOW TO STEAL A MILLION
Soundtrack (1966) .... *20th Century-Fox (M) TFM-3183* 66   **25-30**
Soundtrack (1966) .... *20th Century-Fox (S) TFS-4183* 66   **35-40**
  Composer: John Williams.

HOW TO STEAL AN ELECTION (A DIRTY POLITICS MUSICAL)
Original Cast (1968) .... *RCA Victor (S) LSO-1153* 68   **25-30**
  Composer: Oscar Brand. **Conductor:** Bhen Lanzaroni. **Cast:** Bill McCutcheon; Del Hinkley;
  Dennis Allen; Barbara Anson; Beverly Ballard; Ed Crowley; Thom Koutsoukos; Carole Demas;
  Clifton Davis.

HOW TO STUFF A WILD BIKINI
Soundtrack (1965) .... *Wand (M) 671* 65   **15-20**
Soundtrack (1965) .... *Wand (S) S-671* 65   **20-25**
  Composer: Jerry Styner; Guy Hemric; others. **Cast:** Annette Funicello; Kingsmen; Mickey
  Rooney; Lu Ann Simms; Brian Donlevy; Harvey Lembeck.

HOW TO SUCCEED IN BUSINESS WITHOUT REALLY TRYING
Original Cast (1961) .... *RCA Victor (M) LOC-1066* 61   **15-20**
Original Cast (1961) .... *RCA Victor (S) LSO-1066* 61   **20-25**
  Composer: Frank Loesser. **Conductor:** Elliot Lawrence. **Cast:** Robert Morse; Rudy Vallee;
  Bonnie Scott; Charles Nelson Rilley; Claudette Sutherland; Sammy Smith; Paul Reed; Virginia
  Martin; Ruth Kobart; Mara Landi.
Soundtrack (1967) .... *United Artists (M) UAL-4151* 67   **15-20**
Soundtrack (1967) .... *United Artists (S) UAS-5151* 67   **20-25**
  Composer: Frank Loesser. **Conductor:** Nelson Riddle. **Cast:** Robert Morse; Rudy Valee;
  Michele Lee; Sammy Smith; Anthony Teague; Kay Reynolds.
Studiotrack (1960) .... *RCA Victor (M) LPM-2493* 60   **10-15**
Studiotrack (1961) .... *RCA Victor (S) LSP-2493* 61   **10-15**
  Composer: Frank Loesser. **Conductor:** Ray Ellis. **Cast:** Ray Ellis and His Orchestra.

HOWARD THE DUCK
Soundtrack (1986) .... *MCA (S) 6173* 86   **8-10**
  Composer: John Barry. **Conductor:** John Barry. **Cast:** Dolby's Cube; Cheery Bomb; Tata Vega.

HOWLING
Soundtrack (1981) .... *Varese Sarabande (S) STV-81150*   81   **$8-10**
Composer: Pino Donaggio. Conductor: Natale Massara; Pino Donaggio.

HUCKLEBERRY FINN
Soundtrack (1974) .... *United Artists (S) UA-LA229-F*   74   **10-12**
Composer: Richard M. Sherman; Robert B. Sherman. Conductor: Fred Werner.
Cast: Roberta Flack; Paul Winfield; Jeff East; Harvey Korman; Gary Merrill; David Wayne.

HUCKLEBERRY HOUND
TV Soundtrack (1959) .... *Colpix (M) CP-202*   59   **15-25**
Cast: Daws Butler; Don Messick.

HUGHIE
Original Cast (1965) .... *Columbia (S) OS-2760*   65   **20-25**
Complete Broadway play.
Cast: Jason Robards; Jack Dodson.

HUGO MONTENEGRO - GOOD VIBRATIONS
Studiotrack (1969) .... *RCA Victor (S) LSP-4104*   69   **8-12**
Includes: *The Lady in Cement; Promises, Promises; Rosemary's Baby; The Outcasts* (TV); and *The Big Valley* (TV).
Composer: Hugo Montenegro. Conductor: Hugo Montenegro. Cast: Hugo Montenegro and His Orchestra.

HUGO THE HIPPO
Soundtrack (1976) .... *United Artists (S) UA-LA637-G*   76   **8-10**
Cartoon soundtrack.
Composer: Burt Keys. Conductor: Burt Keys. Cast: Marie Osmond; Jimmy Osmond; Burl Ives; Robert Morley; Paul Lynde.

HUMANOIDS FROM THE DEEP
Soundtrack (1980) .... *Cerberus (S) CST-0203*   81   **8-10**
Composer: James Horner. Conductor: James Horner.

HUNDRA
Soundtrack (1984) .... *Macola (S) MRC-0903*   84   **15-20**
Composer: Ennio Morricone. Conductor: Ennio Morricone.

HUNGER
Soundtrack (1983) .... *Varese Sarabande (S) STV-81184*   83   **15-20**
Composer: Michael Rubini; Denny Jaeger; others.

HURRICANE
Soundtrack (1979) .... *Elektra (S) EKL 5E-514*   79   **8-10**
Composer: Nino Rota. Conductor: Nino Rota.

HURRY SUNDOWN
Soundtrack (1967) .... *RCA Victor (M) LOC-1133*   67   **35-40**
Soundtrack (1967) .... *RCA Victor (S) LSO-1133*   67   **45-50**
Composer: Hugo Montenegro. Conductor: Hugo Montenegro.

HUSTLER
Soundtrack (1961) .... *Kapp (M) KL-1264*   61   **35-40**
Soundtrack (1961) .... *Kapp (S) KS-1264*   61   **45-50**
Composer: Kenyon Hopkins. Cast: Doc Severinsen.

I

I - A WOMAN, PART 2
Soundtrack (1969) .... *MGM (S) S1E-18* 69 $10-15
 Composer: Sven Gyldmark. **Conductor:** Sven Gyldmark.

I AND ALBERT
Original London Cast (1972) .... *No Label Shown (S) TERS-1004* 81   20-25
 Limited edition release.
 Composer: Charles Strouse; Lee Adams. **Cast:** Polly James; Sven-Bertil Taube; Lewis Fiander; Aubrey Woods; Gay Soper.

I CAN GET IT FOR YOU WHOLESALE
Original Cast (1962) ....:................. *Columbia (M) KOL-5780* 62   20-25
Original Cast (1962) .... *Columbia (S) KOS-2180* 62   30-40
Original Cast (1962) .... *Columbia Special Products (S) AKOS-2180* Re   8-10
 Composer: Harold Rome. **Conductor:** Lehman Engel. **Cast:** Lillian Roth; Jack Kruschen; Harold Lang; Barbra Streisand; Elliott Gould; Sheree North; Luba Lisa; Ken LeRoy; Marilyn Cooper; Bambi Linn; Steve Curry; Francine Bond; Kelly Brown; Wilma Curley; James Hickman; Barbara Monte; William Reilly; Pat Turner; Edward Verson.
Studio Cast (1962) .... *Columbia (M) CL-1815* 62   10-15
Studio Cast (1962) .... *Columbia (S) CS-8615* 62   15-20
 Composer: Harold Rome. **Conductor:** Sy Oliver. **Cast:** Sy Oliver and His Orchestra.

I CAN HEAR IT NOW - DAVID BEN-GURION
TV Soundtrack (1956) .... *Columbia (M) No Number Used* 56   15-20
 Cast: David Ben-Gurion. (Dialogue.)

I CAN HEAR IT NOW - GAMAL ABDEL NASSER
TV Soundtrack (1956) ......,................. *Columbia (M) ML-5110* 56   15-20
 Interview from the CBS-TV special *See It Now,* broadcast March 13, 1956.
 Cast: Gamal Abdel Nasser. (Dialogue.)

I CAN HEAR IT NOW - WINSTON CHURCHILL
TV Soundtrack (1955) .... *Columbia (EP) A-5066* 55   10-15
Studio Cast (1955) .... *Columbia (M) ML-5066* 55   15-20
 Cast: Winston Churchill. (Dialogue).

I CAN'T KEEP RUNNING IN PLACE
Original Cast (1981) .... *Painted Smiles (S) PS-1346* 81
 Composer: Barbara Schottenfeld. **Conductor:** Robert Hirschhorn. **Cast:** Evalyn Baron; Joy Franz; Helen Gallagher; Bev Larson; Phyllis Newman; Marcia Rodd.

I COULD GO ON SINGING
Soundtrack (1963) .... *Capitol (M) W-1861* 63   25-30
Soundtrack (1963) .... *Capitol (S) SW-1861* 63   35-40
 Composer: Mort Lindsey; Harold Arlen; others. **Conductor:** Mort Lindsey. **Cast:** Judy Garland.

I DO! I DO!
Original Cast (1966) .... *RCA Victor (M) LOC-1128* 66   10-15
Original Cast (1966) .... *RCA Victor (S) LSO-1128* 66   15-20
 Composer: Harvey Schmidt; Tom Jones. **Conductor:** John Lesko. **Cast:** Mary Martin; Robert Preston.

I HAD A BALL
Original Cast (1964) .... *Mercury (M) OCM-2210*   64   **$20-25**
Original Cast (1964) ....*Mercury (S) OCS-6210*   64   **25-30**
Original Cast (1964) .... *Mercury (M) OCM-2210*   64   **40-50**
  Double LP, promotional issue. Open-end interviews with cast members, plus songs by Sarah Vaughan and
  Louis Armstrong not heard in the show. Since the original cover of the cast LP was used, the mono number
  is used. Interview disc is numbered MGD-2-24.
  Composer: Jack Lawrence; Stan Freeman. **Conductor:** Pembroke Davenport. **Cast:** Buddy
  Hackett; Richard Kiley; Karen Morrow; Luba Lisa; Steve Roland; Rosetta LeNoire.

I LOVE MELVIN
Soundtrack (1953) ....*MGM (M) E-190*   53   **40-50**
  10-inch LP.
Soundtrack (1953) ....*MCA (SE) 39081*   Re   **8-10**
  Also has music from *Everything I Have Is Yours*.
  Composer: Josef Myrow. **Conductor:** George Stoll. **Cast:** Debbie Reynolds; Donald O'Connor;
  Noreen Corcoran; Marge and Gower Chamption; Monica Lewis; MGM Orchestra.

I LOVE MOVIES
Studiotrack (1958) .... *Columbia (M) CL-1178*   58   **15-20**
  Composer: Various. **Conductor:** Michel Legrand. **Cast:** Michel Legrand and his Orchestra.

I LOVE MY WIFE
Original Cast (1977) ....*Atlantic (S) SD-19107*   77   **8-10**
  Composer: Cy Coleman; Michael Stewart. **Conductor:** John Miller. **Cast:** Lenny Baker; Joanna
  Gleason; Ilene Graff; James Naughton; Ken Bichel; Michael Mark; John Miller; Joe Saulter.

I MARRIED AN ANGEL:
see NEW MOON

I NEVER SANG FOR MY FATHER
Soundtrack (1970) ....*Bell (S) 1204*   71   **60-70**
  Composer: Barry Mann; Al Gorgoni; Cynthia Weil. **Cast:** Roy Clark.

I REMEMBER MAMA
Original Cast (1979) ....*Polydor (S) 827336-1*   79   **8-10**
  Composer: Richard Rodgers; Martin Charnin; Raymond Jessel. **Conductor:** Bruce Pomahac.
  Cast: Charlotte Edwards; Joanna Borman; George Hearn; Sally Ann Howes; Ann Morrison;
  George Irving; Tom Woodman.

I SPY
TV Soundtrack (1965) .... *Warner Bros. (M) W-1637*   65   **20-25**
TV Soundtrack (1965) ....*Warner Bros. (S) WS-1637*   65   **25-30**
  Volume one.

TV Soundtrack (1965) .... *Capitol (M) T-2839*	68	**$15-20**
TV Soundtrack (1965) .... *Capitol (S) ST-2839*	68	**20-25**

Volume two.

Composer: Earle Hagen; Hugo Friedhofer. **Conductor:** Earle Hagen.

I WALK THE LINE

Soundtrack (1970) .... *Columbia (S) S-30397*	70	**15-20**

Composer: Johnny Cash. **Cast:** Johnny Cash and the Tennessee Three.

I WANT TO LIVE

Soundtrack (1958) .... *United Artists (EP) UAE-1000*	58	**15-20**
Soundtrack (1958) .... *United Artists (M) UAL-4005*	58	**20-30**
Soundtrack (1958) .... *United Artists (S) UAS-5005*	58	**30-40**

Composer: Johnny Mandel. **Conductor:** Johnny Mandel.

Soundtrack (1958) .... *United Artists (M) UAL-4006*	58	**25-35**
Soundtrack (1958) .... *United Artists (S) UAS-5006*	58	**35-50**

Above two have jazz themes from the film.

Cast: Gerry Mulligan; Shelly Manne; Art Farmer (jazz combo).

Soundtrack (1958) .... *United Artists (M) UXL-1*	58	**40-50**
Soundtrack (1958) .... *United Artists (S) UXS-51*	59	**50-60**

Above two are double LP sets, combining UAS-5005 and UAS-5006.

Soundtrack (1958) .... *United Artists (M) DF-3*	63	**15-20**
Soundtrack (1958) .... *United Artists (S) DFS-53*	63	**20-25**

One side has music from *Odds Against Tomorrow*. Part of United Artists' "Double Feature" series.

Soundtrack (1958) .... *United Artists (S) UA-LA271-G*	74	**8-10**
Soundtrack (1958) .... *Ascot (M) UM-13501*	64	**15-20**
Soundtrack (1958) .... *Ascot (S) US-16501*	64	**25-30**

Also has music from *The Vikings, Never on Sunday* and *The Wonderful Country*.

Also see JOHNNY COOL; ODDS AGAINST TOMORROW

I WAS A TEENAGE ZOMBIE

Soundtrack (1987) .... *Enigma (S) SJ-73296*	87	**8-10**

Composer: Various. **Cast:** Smithereens; Los Lobos; Alex Chilton; Ben Vaughn Group; Bob Pfeifer; Fleshtones; Del Fuegos; DB's; Dream Syndicate; Violent Femmes; Waitresses.

I'LL CRY TOMORROW

Soundtrack (1955) .... *MGM (EP) X-1180*	55	**10-15**

Composer: Alex North. **Conductor:** Alex North. **Cast:** Susan Hayward.

Also see CALL ME MADAM

I'LL NEVER FORGET WHAT'S 'IS NAME

Soundtrack (1967) .... *Decca (M) DL-9163*	68	**15-20**
Soundtrack (1967) .... *Decca (S) DL7-9163*	68	**20-25**

Composer: Francis Lai. **Conductor:** Francis Lai.

I'LL SEE YOU IN MY DREAMS

Soundtrack (1951) .... *Columbia (M) CL-6198*	51	**35-45**

10-inch LP.

Conductor: Paul Weston. **Cast:** Doris Day; Danny Thomas; Norman Luboff Choir; Lee Brothers.

I'LL TAKE SWEDEN

Soundtrack (1965) .... *United Artists (M) UAL-4121*	65	**15-20**
Soundtrack (1965) .... *United Artists (S) UAS-5121*	65	**20-25**

Composer: Jimmie Haskell; By Dunham; others. **Cast:** Frankie Avalon; Bob Hope; Tuesday Weld.

I'M GETTING MY ACT TOGETHER AND TAKING IT ON THE ROAD
Original Cast (1978) .... *Columbia Special Products (S) X-14885*   78   **$8-10**
  Composer: Nancy Ford; Gretchen Cryer. Cast: Joel Fabiani; Gretchen Cryer; Margot Rose;
  Betty Aberlin; Don Scardino.

I'M GONNA GIT YOU SUCKA
Soundtrack (1988) .... *Arista (S) AL8-8574*   88   **8-10**
  Composer: Various. Cast: Gap Band; Jennifer Holliday; Jermaine Jackson; Boogie Down
  Productions; Four Tops; Aretha Franklin; K-9 Posse; Too Nice.

IBM PRESENTS SCROOGE:
see SCROOGE

ICE CASTLES
Soundtrack (1979) .... *Arista (S) AL-9502*   79   **8-10**
  Composer: Marvin Hamlisch. Conductor: Marvin Hamlisch. Cast: Melissa Manchester;
  Alan Parsons Project.

ICE STATION ZEBRA
Soundtrack (1968) .... *MGM (S) S1E-14*   68   **40-45**
  Composer: Michel Legrand. Conductor: Michel Legrand.

ICEMAN
Soundtrack (1983) .... *Southern Cross (S) SCRS-1006*   83   **15-20**
  Composer: Bruce Smeaton. Conductor: Bruce Smeaton.

ICHABOD (THE LEGEND OF SLEEPY HOLLOW)
Studio Cast (1949) .... *Decca (M) DL-6001*   49   **50-75**
  10-inch LP. One side has *Rip Van Winkle.*
Soundtrack (1949) .... *Decca (M) DL-9106*   61   **20-25**
  One side has music from *Rip Van Winkle.*
  Composer: Victor Young. Conductor: Victor Young. Cast: Bing Crosby. RIP VAN
  WINKLE: Walter Huston.

IDEAL HUSBAND:
see BERNARD HERRMANN CONDUCTS GREAT BRITISH FILM SCORES

IDOL
Soundtrack (1966) .... *Fontana (M) MGF-27559*   66   **15-20**
Soundtrack (1966) .... *Fontana (S) SRF-67559*   66   **20-25**
  Composer: John Dankworth. Conductor: John Dankworth. Cast: Cleo Laine.

IDOLMAKER
Soundtrack (1980) .... *A&M (S) SP-4840*   80   **8-10**

IF EVER I SEE YOU AGAIN
Soundtrack (1978) .... *Warner Bros. (S) 2B-3199*   78   **8-10**
  Composer: Joe Brooks. Conductor: Joe Brooks. Cast: Kenny Karen; Debby Boone; Jamie Carr.

IF HE HOLLERS, LET HIM GO
Soundtrack (1968) .... *Tower (S) ST-5152*   68   **15-20**
  Composer: Harry Sukman; Sammy Fain; Coleridge Perkinson.

IF I HAD MY WAY:
see ROAD BEGINS

IF IT'S TUESDAY, THIS MUST BE BELGIUM
Soundtrack (1969) .... *United Artists (S) UAS-5197*   69   **15-20**
  Composer: Walter Scharf; Donovan Leitch. Conductor: Walter Scharf. Cast: J.P.Rags;
  Hopscotch.

ILLYA DARLING

Original Cast (1967) .... *United Artists (M) UAL-8901*   67   **$15-20**
A musical based on the film *Never on Sunday*.
Original Cast (1967) .... *United Artists (S) UAS-9901*   67   **20-25**
Composer: Joe Darion; Manos Hadjidakis. **Conductor:** Karen Gustafson. **Cast:** Melinda
Mercouri; Tito Vandis; Despo; Nikos Kourkoulos; Orson Bean; Hal Linden.

IMAGES

Soundtracks (1972) .... *C.I.F. (S) CIF-1002*   74   **50-75**
Composer: John Williams. **Conductor:** John Williams.

IMAGINE - THE MOTION PICTURE

Soundtrack (1988) .... *Capitol (S) C1-90803*   88   **8-10**
Composer: John Lennon; Paul McCartney. **Cast:** John Lennon; Beatles; Plastic Ono Band.

IMAGINE THAT - SONGS FROM THE TV SPECIAL

TV Soundtrack .... *Premore (S) PL-280*   **8-10**
Cast: Dora Hall.

IMITATION OF LIFE

Soundtrack (1959) .... *Decca (M) DL-8879*   59   **30-40**
Soundtrack (1959) .... *Decca (S) DL7-8879*   59   **60-70**
Composer: Frank Skinner; Sammy Fain. **Conductor:** Joseph Gershenson.

IMPACT

Studiotrack (1959) .... *RCA Victor (M) LPM-2042*   59   **15-25**
Studiotrack (1959) .... *RCA Victor (S) LSP-2042*   59   **25-35**
Has TV themes from: *Waterfront, Rawhide, Peter Gunn, Black Saddle, Highway Patrol, Richard
Diamond, Racket Squad, Sea Hunt, Mike Hammer, Perry Mason, M-Squad* and *The Naked City*.
Composer: George Duning; Ned Washington; Dimitri Tiomkin; Dave Kahn; Melvin Lenard;
Pete Rugolo; Fred Steiner; Joe Mullendore; Count Basie; Ray Llewellyn; J. Michael Hennagin;
Alexander Laszio; Henry Mancini. **Conductor:** Buddy Morrow. **Cast:** Buddy Morrow and His
Orchestra.
Also see DOUBLE IMPACT

IMPOSSIBLE DREAM - THE STORY OF THE 1967 BOSTON RED SOX

Studio Cast .... *Fleetwood (S) FCLP 3024*   **15-20**
Conductor: Bill Green. **Cast:** Ken Coleman (narrator); Ned Martin; Mel Parnell; Jess Cain.

IN CALIENTE:
see HOORAY FOR HOLLYWOOD

IN CIRCLES

Original Cast (1967) .... *Avant Garde (M) M-108*   67   **20-25**
Composer: Al Carmines; Gertrude Stein. **Cast:** Theo Barnes; Al Carmines; Jacque Lynn Colton;
David Vaughan.
Original Cast (1967) .... *Avant Garde (S) AV-108*   67   **30-40**
Composer: Al Carmines; Gertrude Stein. **Cast:** Theo Barnes; Al Carmines; Jacque Lynn Colton;
David Vaughan; Lee Crespi; Lee Guilliatt; James Hilbrandt; Julie Kurnitz; George McGrath;
Arlene Rothlein; Elaine Summers; David Tice; Arthur Williams; Nancy Zala.

IN COLD BLOOD

Soundtrack (1967) .... *Colgems (M) COM-107*   67   **20-25**
Soundtrack (1967) .... *Colgems (S) COS-107*   67   **25-35**
Composer: Quincy Jones. **Conductor:** Quincy Jones.

IN HARM'S WAY

Soundtrack (1965) .... *RCA Victor (M) LOC-1100*   65   **40-60**
Soundtrack (1965) .... *RCA Victor (S) LSO-1100*   65   **75-100**
Composer: Jerry Goldsmith. **Conductor:** Jerry Goldsmith.

IN LIKE FLINT

Soundtrack (1967) .... *20th Century-Fox (M) 4193*   67   **$40-50**
Soundtrack (1967) .... *20th Century-Fox (S) S-4193*   67   **50-75**
    Film sequel to *Our Man Flint*.
Composer: Jerry Goldsmith. **Conductor:** Jerry Goldsmith.
    Also see OUR MAN FLINT

IN PARIS:

see SOMEBODY BAD STOLE DE WEDDING BELL

IN SEARCH OF

TV Soundtrack (1977) .... *AVI (S) AVL-6008*   77   **12-15**
Composer: Laurin Rinder; W. Michael Lewis; Steve Stewart. **Conductor:** W. Michael Lewis.

IN SEARCH OF THE CASTAWAYS

Soundtrack (1962) .... *Disneyland (M) ST-3916*   62   **30-35**
Composer: Richard M. Sherman; Robert B. Sherman. **Conductor:** Muir Mathieson.
Cast: John Mills (narration); Haley Mills; Maurice Chevalier; Wilfrid Hyde White;
    George Sanders. (With dialogue.)
Soundtrack (1962) .... *Disneyland (S) DQ-1318*   68   **10-15**
    Also has music from *The Parent Trap* and *Summer Magic*.
Composer: Richard M. Sherman; Robert B. Sherman. **Conductor:** Tutti Camarata.
Cast: Hayley Mills; Maureen O'Hara; Tommy Sands; Annette; Maurice Chevalier; Burl Ives.

IN THE GOOD OLD SUMMERTIME

Soundtrack (1949) .... *MGM (M) E-3232*   55   **25-35**
Conductor: George Stoll. **Cast:** Judy Garland; King's Men.

IN THE HEAT OF THE NIGHT

Soundtrack (1967) .... *United Artists (M) UAL-4160*   67   **10-15**
Soundtrack (1967) .... *United Artists (S) UAS-5160*   67   **15-20**
Soundtrack (1967) .... *United Artists (S) UA-LA290-G*   74   **10-12**
Soundtrack (1967) .... *Liberty (S) LT-51133*   Re   **8-10**
Composer: Quincy Jones. **Conductor:** Quincy Jones. **Cast:** Ray Charles; Glen Campbell;
    Gil Bernal; Boomer and Travis.

IN THE MOOD

Soundtrack (1987) .... *Atlantic (S) 81788-1*   87   **8-10**
Composer: Various. **Conductor:** Ralph Burns. **Cast:** Ralph Burns' Big Band featuring Beverly
    D'Angelo and Jennifer Holliday.

IN TROUBLE AGAIN

Soundtrack .... *Mark '56 (M) 600*   75   **8-10**
Cast: Laurel and Hardy.

IN TROUSERS

Original Cast (1979) .... *Original Cast (S) OC-7915*   79   **8-10**
Composer: William Finn. **Conductor:** Michael Starobin. **Cast:** Alison Fraser; Joanna Green;
    Mary Testa; Chip Zien.

IN WHITE AMERICA

Original Cast (1964) .... *Columbia (M) OL-2430*   64   **15-20**
Original Cast (1964) .... *Columbia (S) OS-6030*   64   **25-35**
Conductor: Oscar Brand. **Cast:** Gloria Foster; James Greene; Moses Gunn; Claudette Nevins;
    Michael O'Sullivan; Fred Pinkard.

INCHON

Soundtrack (1982) .... *Regency (S) RI-8502*   82   **20-25**
Composer: Jerry Goldsmith.

INCREDIBLE JOURNEY
Soundtrack (1963) .... *Disneyland (M) ST-1927* 63 $20-25

INCREDIBLE WORLD OF JAMES BOND
Soundtrack (1965) .... *United Artists (S) SP-3* 65 15-20
Special Products issue only. Has music from *Dr. No, From Russia with Love* and *Goldfinger*.
Composer: John Barry; Monty Norman.

INDIANA JONES AND THE TEMPLE OF DOOM
Soundtrack (1984) .... *Polydor (S) 422-82159-1* 84 8-10
Composer: John Williams. **Conductor:** John Williams. **Cast:** John Williams and His Orchestra.

INDISCRETION OF AN AMERICAN WIFE
Soundtrack (1954) .... *Columbia (EP) B-366* 54 30-50
Double EP set.
Soundtrack (1954) .... *Columbia (M) CL-6277* 54 85-100
The first score to be transferred directly from the film soundtrack to LP.
Composer: Alessandro Cicognini. **Conductor:** Franco Ferrara.

INN OF THE SIXTH HAPPINESS
Soundtrack (1958) .... *20th Century-Fox (M) TCF-3011* 58 45-50
Soundtrack (1958) .... *20th Century-Fox (S) SFX-3011* 58 90-100
Composer: Malcolm Arnold. **Conductor:** Malcolm Arnold. **Cast:** Ingrid Bergman; Curt
Jurgens; Robert Donat.

INNER CITY
Original Cast (1971) .... *RCA Victor (S) LSO-1171* 71 20-25
Composer: Helen Miller; Eve Merriman. **Conductor:** Gordon Harrell. **Cast:** Joy Garrett; Linda
Hopkins; Carl Hall; Fluffer Hirsch; Delores Hall; Paulette Ellen Jones; Larry Marshall; Allan
Nicolls; Florence Tarlow.

INNERSPACE
Soundtrack (1987) .... *Geffen (S) GHS-24161* 87 8-10
Composer: Jerry Goldsmith; others. **Conductor:** Jerry Goldsmith. **Cast:** Rod Stewart; Wang
Chung; Narada Michael Walden; Berlin; Sam Cooke; Jerry Goldsmith.

INSIDE DAISY CLOVER
Soundtrack (1965) .... *Warner Bros. (M) W-1616* 65 30-40
Soundtrack (1965) .... *Warner Bros. (S) WS-1616* 65 35-50
Composer: Andre Previn. **Conductor:** Andre Previn.

INSIDE MOVES
Soundtrack (1980) .... *Full Moon (S) FMH-3506* 80 8-10
Composer: John Barry; others. **Cast:** Spinners; Bos Scaggs; Ambrosia; Lady Sylvia; Leo
Sayers; Eagles; Pablo Cruise.

INSIDE SINA
Studio Cast .... *Charm (M) CM-110*   **$10-20**
From the Soceity for Indecency to Naked Animals.

INSPECTOR CLOUSEAU
Soundtrack (1968) .... *United Artists (S) UAS-5186*   68   **12-18**
Soundtrack (1968) .... *MCA (S) 25107*   Re   **8-10**
Composer: Ken Thorne. Conductor: Ken Thorne.

INTERLUDE
Soundtrack (1957) .... *Coral (M) CRL-57159*   57   **70-80**
One side has music from *Tammy and the Bachelor*.
Composer: Frank Skinner (both). TAMMY AND THE BACHELOR: Jay Livingston; Ray
Evans. Conductor: Joseph Gershenson (both). Cast: TAMMY AND THE BACHELOR:
Debbie Reynolds.
Soundtrack (1968) .... *Colgems (S) COSO-5007*   68   **40-50**
Excerpts of compositions by Beethoven, Brahms, Tchaikovsky, Dvorak, and Rachmaninoff.
Composer: Georges Delerue. Conductor: Georges Delerue; Ernest Fleischmann.
Cast: Timi Yuro; Royal Philharmonic Orchestra conducted by Ernest Fleischmann.

INTERNATIONAL SOIRÉE
Original Cast (1958) .... *Audio Fidelity (M) AF-1881*   58   **15-20**
Original Cast (1958) .... *Audio Fidelity (S) AFSD-5881*   58   **20-30**
Composer: Jo Basile; others. Conductor: Jo Basile. Cast: Patachou and Co.; Jo Basile
(accordion, orchestra).

INTERNATIONAL VELVET
Soundtrack (1978) .... *MGM (S) 1-5405*   78   **8-10**
Soundtrack (1978) .... *MGM (S) 2315-400*   78   **8-10**
Composer: Francis Lai. Conductor: Francis Lai.

INTERNS (WILDEST MUSIC FROM THE WILDEST PARTY EVER FILMED!)
Soundtrack (1962) .... *Colpix (M) CP-427*   62   **25-30**
Soundtrack (1962) .... *Colpix (S) SCP-427*   62   **30-35**
Composer: Leith Stevens. Conductor: Leith Stevens; Stu Phillips.

INTERRUPTED MELODY
Soundtrack (1955) .... *MGM (EP) X-304*   55   **10-15**
Soundtrack (1955) .... *MGM (M) E-3185*   55   **40-50**
Soundtrack (1955) .... *MGM (M) E-3984*   62   **15-20**
Actual title: *The Voice of Eileen Farrell*. Film star Eleanor Parker's songs were actually sung by
Eileen Farrell.
Conductor: Walter Ducloux. Cast: Eileen Farrell; Heinz Blankenburg; Rudolf Petrak.

INTO THE NIGHT
Soundtrack (1985) .... *MCA (S) 5561*   85   **8-10**
Composer: Ira Newborn; others. Cast: B.B. King; Patti LaBelle; Thelma Houston; Marvin
Gaye; Four Tops.

INTO THE WOODS
Original Cast (1988) .... *RCA Victor (S) 6796-1*   88   **8-10**
Composer: Stephen Sondheim. Cast: Bernadette Petters; Joanna Gleason; Chip Zien.

INVADERS FROM MARS
Soundtrack (1986) .... *Enigma (S) SJ-73226*   86   **8-10**
Composer: David Storrs. Conductor: David Storrs.

INVADERS:
see BERNARD HERRMANN CONDUCTS GREAT BRITISH FILM SCORES

INVASION OF THE BODY SNATCHERS
Soundtrack (1979) .... *United Artists (S) UA-LA940-H*   79 $8-10
  Composer: Denny Zeitlin. **Conductor:** Denny Zeitlin. **Cast:** Royal Scots Dragoon Guards.

INVASION U.S.A.
Soundtrack (1985) .... *Varese Sarabande (S) 81263*   85   8-10
  Cast: Jay Chattaway.

INVESTIGATION OF A CITIZEN ABOVE SUSPICION
Soundtrack (1970) .... *Cerberus (S) GEMS-0110*   81   8-10
  Composer: Ennio Morricone. **Conductor:** Ennio Morricone.

INVITATION AU VOYAGE
Soundtrack .... *Varese Sarabande (S) STV-81189*   8-10
  Cast: Nina Scott and Lawlessness.

INVITATION TO THE DANCE
Soundtrack (1956) .... *MGM (M) E-3207*   56   40-45
Soundtrack (1956) .... *MGM (M) E-4186*   63   15-20
Soundtrack (1956) .... *MGM (SE) SE-4186*   56   15-20
  Actual title of above three: *Andre Previn: Composer, Conductor, Arranger, Pianist.*
  Composer: Andre Previn; Jacques Ibert. **Conductor:** Andre Previn; John Hollingsworth.
  Cast: Gene Kelly; Royal Philharmonic Orchestra; MGM Studio Orchestra.

INVITATION:
see AUNTIE MAME

IPCRESS FILE
Soundtrack (1965) .... *Decca (M) DL-9124*   65   15-20
Soundtrack (1965) .... *Decca (S) DL7-9124*   65   25-35
  Composer: John Barry. **Conductor:** John Barry.

BERTHA EGNOS & GAIL LAKIER'S
IPI-TOMBI
ORIGINAL CAST RECORDING

IPI-TOMBI
Original Cast (1977) .... *Ashtree (S) ASH-26000*   77   30-35
  Double LP set.
  Composer: Bertha Egnos; Gail Lakier. **Cast:** Count Wellington Judge; Dan Pule; Jabu Mbalo;
  Matthew Bodibe; Ruby Morare; Petunia Seakatsi; Joe Seakatsi; Gasta Mnguni; Andy Chabeli;
  Patrick Moletsane.

IRENE
Original London Cast (1919) ...... *Monmouth Evergreen (SE) MES-7057*   8-10
  Composer: Harry Tierney; Joseph McCarthy. **Conductor:** G.W. Byng; Frank Tours.
  Cast: Edith Day; Daisy Hancox; Winnie Collins; Robert Hale.
Original Revival Cast (1973) .... *Columbia (S) KS-32266*   73   12-15
  Composer: Harry Tierney; Joseph McCarthy; Charles Gainor; Otis Clements. **Conductor:** Jack
  Lee. **Cast:** Debbie Reynolds; Monte Markham; George S. Irving; Patsy Kelly; Ruth Warrick; Ted
  Pugh; Carmen Alvarez; Jeanne Lehman; Monte Markham; Meg Scanlon; Janie Sell; Penny Worth.

IRMA LA DOUCE

Original Cast (1960) .... *Columbia (M) OL-5560*	60	**$15-20**
Original Cast (1960) .... *Columbia (S) OS-2029*	60	**25-30**
Original Cast (1960) .... *Columbia Special Products (SE) AOS-2029*	Re	**8-10**

Composer: Marguerite Monnot. Conductor: Stanley Lebowsky. Cast: Elisabeth Seal; Michell Keith; Clive Revill; George S. Irving; Osborne Smith; Fred Gwynne; Stuart Damon; George Del Monte; Aric Lavie; Zack Matalon; Rudy Tronto.

Original London Cast (1960) .... *Philips (M) BBL-7274*	60	**30-35**

Composer: Marguerite Monnot. Conductor: Alexander Faris. Cast: Elisabeth Seal; Michell Keith; Clive Revill; Ronald Barker; John East; David Evans.

London Studio Cast (1960) .... *London (M) LL-3197*	60	**15-20**

Composer: Julian Moore; Marguerite Monnot; David Heneker. Conductor: Bob Sharples. Cast: Joyce Blair; Ian Paterson; Cliff Adams Chorus.

Soundtrack (1963) .... *United Artists (M) UAL-4109*	63	**15-20**
Soundtrack (1963) .... *United Artists (M) UAS-5109*	63	**20-25**
Soundtrack (1963) .... *United Artists (M) UAL-4134*	66	**10-15**
Soundtrack (1963) .... *United Artists (S) UAS-5134*	63	**15-20**

Above two also have music from *Tom Jones*.

Soundtrack (1963) .... *MCA (S) 39068*	Re	**8-10**

Composer: Andre Previn. Conductor: Andre Previn. Cast: Andre Previn.

Studiotrack (1963) .... *Capitol (M) T-1943*	63	**25-30**
Studiotrack (1963) .... *Capitol (S) ST-1943*	63	**35-40**

Actual title: *Jack Lemmon Plays Piano Selections from Irma La Douce.*
Conductor: Jack Marshall. Cast: Jack Lemmon (piano).

Studiotrack (1963) .... *Columbia (M) CL-1590*	63	**10-15**
Studiotrack (1963) .... *Columbia (S) CS-8390*	63	**15-20**

Cast: Chico Hamilton Quintet.

Studiotrack (1963) .... *Richmond (M) B-20089*	63	**10-15**
Studiotrack (1963) .... *Richmond (S) S-30089*	63	**10-20**

Cast: London Repertory Theatre.

IRON EAGLE

Soundtrack (1986) .... *Capitol (S) SV-12499*	86	**8-10**

Composer: Various. Cast: Queen; Katrina and the Waves; Dio; Helix; King Kobra; Eric Martin; Adrenelin; Urgent; The Jon Butcher Axis; George Clinton.

IRON EAGLE II

Soundtrack (1986) .... *Epic (S) SE-45006*	86	**8-10**

Cast: Insiders; Alice Cooper; Mike Reno; Sweet Obsession; Doug and Slugs; Britny Fox; FM/UK; Henry Lee Summer; Ruth Pointer; Billy Vera; Rick Springfield.

IRVING BERLIN: 100TH ANNIVERSARY COLLECTION

Studio Cast (1988) .... *MCA (S) 39324*	88	**8-10**

Composer: Irving Berlin. Cast: Bing Crosby; Fred Astaire; Linda Ronstadt; others.

IRVING BERLIN REVISITED

Original Cast (1967) .... *MGM (M) E-4435*	67	**20-25**
Original Cast (1967) .... *MGM (M) SE-4435*	67	**15-20**

Issued as part of "The New American Theatre Series."
Composer: Irving Berlin. Conductor: Norman Paris.

IS PARIS BURNING?

Soundtrack (1966) .... *Columbia (M) OL-6630*   66   **$30-40**
Soundtrack (1966) .... *Columbia (M) OS-3030*   66   **45-60**
  Composer: Maurice Jarre. **Conductor:** Maurice Jarre.
Soundtrack (1966) .... *No Label Shown (M) No Number Used*   66   **30-40**
  Open-end interview, with script. Promotional issue only.

IS THERE LIFE AFTER HIGH SCHOOL?

Original Cast (1982) .... *Original Cast (S) OC-8240*   82
  Composer: Craig Carnilia. **Conductor:** Bruce Coughlin. **Cast:** Raymond Baker; Cynthia Carle;
  Alma Cuervo; Sandy Faison; Harry Groener; Philip Hoffman; David Patrick Kelly; Maureen
  Shilliman; James Widdoes.

ISABEL'S A JEZEBEL

Original London Cast (1974) .... *United Artists (S) UAG-29148*   71   **50-60**
  Composer: Galt McDermott. **Conductor:** Galt McDermott.

ISADORA:
see LOVES OF ISADORA

ISLAND

Soundtrack (1979) .... *Varese Sarabande (S) VC-81147*   79   **8-10**
  Composer: Ennio Morricone. **Conductor:** Ennio Morricone.

ISLAND AT THE TOP OF THE WORLD

Soundtrack (1974) .... *Disneyland (S) DS 3814*   74   **25-35**
  Composer: Maurice Jarre. **Conductor:** Maurice Jarre. **Cast:** David Hartman; Donald Sinden.

ISLAND IN THE SKY

Soundtrack (1953) .... *Decca (M) DL-7029*   53   **175-200**
  10-inch LP.
  Composer: Emil Newman; Hugo Friedhofer; Herb Spencer. **Conductor:** Emil Newman.
  Cast: John Wayne (narration of the film's story line).
  Also see BERNADETTE

ISLAND OF DR. MOREAU

Soundtrack (1981) .... *No Label Shown (S) HG-4000*   81   **30-35**
  Promotional issue only.
  Composer: Lawrence Rosenthal. **Conductor:** Lawrence Rosenthal.

ISLANDS IN THE STREAM

Soundtrack (1977) .... *Intrada (S) RVF-6003*   **8-10**

ISRAEL NOW

Soundtrack .... *United Artists (M) UAL-3609*   68   **10-12**
  Music from *Exodus* and *Cast a Giant Shadow*, plus incidental selections.
Soundtrack .... *United Artists (S) UAS-6609*   68   **12-15**
  Composer: Ernest Gold; Elmer Berstein; Henry Sandaver. **Cast:** Elmer Bernstein; Ferrante
  and Teicher; Zemel Choir; Hollywood Studio Orchestra.

ISRAEL SPEAKS

Assembled Cast (1963) .... *United Artists (M) UAL-9002*   63   **8-12**
  Cast: Abba Eban (speech).

IT HAPPENED AT THE WORLD'S FAIR

Soundtrack (1963) .... *RCA Victor (M) LPM-2697*   63   **100-120**
  Black label, reads "Long Play" at bottom. Includes 8" x 10" color photo, which represents about
  $40 of the value.
Soundtrack (1963) .... *RCA Victor (S) LSP-2697*   63   **115-125**
  Black label, reads "Living Stereo" at bottom. Includes 8" x 10" color photo, which represents about
  $40 of the value.

IT HAPPENED AT THE WORLD'S FAIR (continued)
Soundtrack (1963) .... *RCA Victor (M) LPM-2697*   63   **$40-50**
  Black label, reads "Mono" at bottom.
Soundtrack (1963) .... *RCA Victor (S) LSP-2697*   65   **30-40**
  Black label, reads "Stereo" at bottom.
Soundtrack (1963) .... *RCA Victor (M) LPM-2697*   65   **25-30**
  Black label, reads "Monaural" at bottom.
Soundtrack (1963) .... *RCA Victor (S) APL1-2568*   78   **8-10**
  Composer: Bill Giant; Bernie Baum; Florence Kaye; Sid Wayne; Ben Weisman; Ruth
  Batchelor; Fred Wise; Sid Tepper; Roy C. Bennett; Don Robertson; Otis Blackwell; others.
  Cast: Elvis Presley; Scotty Moore (guitar); D.J. Fontana (drums); Dudley Brooks (piano);
  Jordanaires (vocals); Mellow Men (vocals).

IT HAPPENED IN BROOKLYN
Soundtrack (1947) .... *Hollywood Soundstage (M) HS-5006*   **10-12**
  Composer: Jule Styne; Sammy Cahn. **Conductor:** John Green. **Cast:** Frank Sinatra; Jimmy
  Durante; Kathryn Grayson; Peter Lawford.

IT HAPPENED ONE BITE
Soundtrack (1978) .... *Warner Bros. (S) BSK-3158*   78   **8-10**

IT STARTED IN NAPLES
Soundtrack (1960) .... *Dot (M) DLP-3324*   60   **65-70**
Soundtrack (1960) .... *Dot (S) DLP-25324*   60   **100-110**
Soundtrack (1960) .... *Varese Sarabande (S) STV-81122*   82   **8-10**
  Composer: Alessandro Cicognini; Carlo Savina. **Conductor:** Carlo Savina.

IT'S A BIRD, IT'S A PLANE, IT'S SUPERMAN
Original Cast (1966) .... *Columbia (M) KOL-6570*   66   **15-20**
Original Cast (1966) .... *Columbia (S) KOS-2970*   66   **20-25**
Original Cast (1966) .... *Columbia Special Products (M) AKOS-2970*   66   **8-10**
  Composer: Charles Strouse; Lee Adams. **Conductor:** Harold Hastings. **Cast:** Jack Cassidy;
  Bob Holliday; Eric Mason; Patricia Marand; Linda Lavin; Michael O'Sullivan; Don Chastain;
  Flying Lings.

IT'S A MAD, MAD, MAD, MAD WORLD
Soundtrack (1963) .... *United Artists (M) UAL-4110*   63   **15-20**
Soundtrack (1963) .... *United Artists (S) UAS-5110*   63   **20-25**
Soundtrack (1963) .... *United Artists (S) UA-LA276-G*   74   **8-10**
  Composer: Ernest Gold. **Conductor:** Ernest Gold.

IT'S A WHOLE NEW BALL GAME
Studio Cast (1970) .... *It's a Whole New Ball Game (M) ARA-91170*   70   **20-30**
  Promotional issue only. Includes highlights from the Phoenix Suns' 1969 - 1970 NBA season.
  Composer: Russell J. Fons (writer). **Cast:** Radio highlights with Hot Rod Hundley and
  Johnny Kerr.
  Also see SUNDERELLA PHOENIX SUNS

IT'S A WONDERFUL LIFE
Studiotrack (1988) .... *Telarc (S) Number Unknown*   88   **15-20**
  Also has original scores from *A Christmas Carol* and *Miracle on 34th Street.*
  Composer: Dimitri Tiomkin; Richard Addinsell; Cyril Mockridge. **Conductor:** David Newman.

IT'S ALIVE II (IT LIVES AGAIN)
Soundtrack (1978) .... *Starlog (S) SR-7007*   78   **10-15**
  This is the same score as *It's Alive.* It was reworked by Laurie Johnson for the sequel, after Bernard
  Herrmann's death.
  Composer: Bernard Herrmann; Laurie Johnson. **Conductor:** Laurie Johnson.

IT'S ALWAYS FAIR WEATHER
Soundtrack (1955) .... *MGM (EP) X-331*   55 $15-20
Soundtrack (1955) .... *MGM (M) E-3241*   55   40-45
Soundtrack (1955) .... *MCA (SE) 25018*   Re   8-10
   Composer: Andre Previn; Adolph Green; Betty Comden. **Conductor:** Andre Previn.
   Cast: Gene Kelly; Dan Dailey; Cyd Charisse; Delores Gray.

IT'S MY TURN
Soundtrack (1980) .... *Motown (S) M8-947M1*   80   8-10
   Composer: Patrick Williams; Michael Masser; Carole Bayer Sager; Teddy Randazzo; Tony
   Travalini; Ozone. **Conductor:** Richard Berres. **Cast:** Diana Ross; Tony Travalini; Ozone; other.

IT'S TIME TO PRAY, AMERICA!
TV Soundtrack (1976) .... *House Top (M) HTR-702*   76   8-10
   Cast: Former President Gerald R. Ford; The Honorable Jimmy Carter; Pat Boone; Johnny Cash.

ITALIAN JOB
Soundtrack (1969) .... *Paramount (S) PAS-5007*   69   15-20
   Composer: Quincy Jones. **Conductor:** Quincy Jones. **Cast:** Matt Monro.

IVANHOE
Soundtrack (1952) .... *MGM (EP) K-179*   52   25-35
   Boxed set of four singles, four sides of which have music from *Ivanhoe*. The other four contain
   music from *Plymouth Adventure*.
Soundtrack (1952) .... *MGM (M) E-179*   52   80-100
   10-inch LP.
Soundtrack (1952) .... *MGM (M) E-3507*   57   60-75
   Also has music from *Madame Bovary* and *Plymouth Adventure*.
   Composer: Miklos Rozsa. **Conductor:** Miklos Rozsa. **Cast:** MGM Studio Orchestra.

IVANOV
Original Cast (1966) .... *RCA Victor (M) VDM-109*   66   15-20
Original Cast (1966) .... *RCA Victor (S) VDS-109*   66   25-35
   A dramatic play by Anton Chekov.
   Cast: Vivien Leigh; John Gielgud; Roland Culver; Jennifer Hilary; John Merivale.

J

J.B.
Original Cast (1959) .... *RCA Victor (M) LD-6075*   59   **$80-90**
Original Cast (1959) .... *RCA Victor (S) LDS-6075*   59   **90-100**
 Double LP set. Dramatic play in verse by Archibald MacLeish.
  Composer: David Amram. **Conductor:** David Amram. **Cast:** Raymond Massey; Christopher
  Plummer; James Daly; James Olson; Ford Rainey.

JACK AND THE BEANSTALK
Studio Cast (1956) .... *RKO/Unique (M) LP-111*   56   **45-50**
 Composer: Jerry Livingston. **Conductor:** Joe Lehay. **Cast:** Bob Graybo; Lynn Roberts; Dale
  Collyer; Petticoats.
TV Soundtrack (1967) .... *HBR (M) HLP-8511*   67   **50-60**
 Composer: James Van Heusen. **Conductor:** Lennie Hayton. **Cast:** Gene Kelly; Ted Cassidy;
  Bobby Rina; Marion McNight; Marni Nixon.

JACK JOHNSON
Soundtrack (1971) .... *Columbia (S) KC-30455*   71   **15-20**
 Composer: Miles Davis. **Cast:** Jack Johnson; Miles Davis; Brock Peters. (With dialogue.)

JACK THE RIPPER
Soundtrack (1960) .... *RCA Victor (M) LPM-2199*   60   **30-40**
Soundtrack (1960) .... *RCA Victor (S) LSP-2199*   60   **60-75**
 Composer: Pete Rugolo; Jimmy McHugh. **Conductor:** Pete Rugolo.
Soundtrack (1960) .... *RCA Victor/Camden (M) CAL-590*   60   **35-50**
 Dramatic dialogue from the 1960 film.
 Composer: Stanley Black. **Cast:** Cedric Hardwicke (narration).

JACKIE GLEASON:
 see AND AWA-A-Y WE GO

JACQUES BREL IS ALIVE AND WELL AND LIVING IN PARIS
Original Cast (1968) .... *Columbia (S) D2S-779*   68   **15-20**
 Double LP set.
Original Cast (1968) .... *Columbia (S) CGK-40817*   Re   **8-10**
 Composer: Jacques Brel; Eric Blau; Mort Shuman. **Conductor:** Mort Shuman. **Cast:** Elly
  Stone; Mort Shuman; Shawn Elliott; Alice Whitfield.
Original Detroit Cast (1968) .... *Synchronicity (S) 1306*   68   **20-25**
 Composer: Jacques Brel; Eric Blau; Mort Shuman. **Conductor:** Marc Chover.
Soundtrack (1968) .... *Atlantic (S) SD-2-1000*   68   **10-20**
 Composer: Jacques Brel; Eric Blau; Mort Shuman. **Conductor:** Francois Rauber.
  Cast: Jacques Brel; Mort Shuman; Elly Stone; Shawn Elliott; Judy Lander; Joseph Neal;
  Annette Perrone; Joe Masiell.

JAGGED EDGE
Soundtrack (1985) .... *Varese Sarabande (S) 81252*   **8-10**
 Composer: John Barry. **Conductor:** John Barry.

JAILHOUSE ROCK

Soundtrack (1957) ....*RCA Victor (EP) EPA-4114*   57 $55-65
  Black label, dog on top.
Soundtrack (1957) ....*RCA Victor (EP) EPA-4114*   65   30-40
  Black label, dog on side.
Soundtrack (1957) ....*RCA Victor (EP) EPA-4114*   69   30-40
  Orange label.
  Composer: Jerry Leiber; Mike Stoller; Ben Weisman; Aaron Schroeder; others. **Cast:** Elvis
  Presley; Scotty Moore (guitar); D.J. Fontana (drums); Bill Black (bass); Dudley Brooks;
  Mike Stoller (piano); Jordanaires (vocals).

JAMAICA

Original Cast (1957) .... *RCA Victor (M) LOC-1036*   57   30-35
  Has four additional songs not included on LSO-1036 (stereo) but heard on reissues.
  Composer: Harold Arlen; E.Y. Harburg; Peter Matz. **Conductor:** Lehman Engel.
  Cast: Lena Horne; Ricardo Montalban; Josephine Premice; Adelaide Hall; Ossie
  Davis; Augustine Rios.
Original Cast (1957) .... *RCA Victor (SE) LSO-1036*   57   45-50
  Has an overture not included on other releases.
Original Cast (1957) .... *RCA Victor (M) LOC-1103*   65   25-30
Original Cast (1957) .... *RCA Victor (SE) LSO-1103*   65   40-50
  Composer: Harold Arlen; E.Y. Harburg; Peter Matz. **Conductor:** Lehman Engel.
  Cast: Lena Horne; Ricardo Montalban; Josephine Premice; Adelaide Hall; Ossie Davis;
  Augustine Rios; Joe Adams; Hugo Dilworth.
Studiotrack (1958) .... *Jubilee (EP) EP-5062*   58   10-15
Studiotrack (1956) ....*RCA Victor (EP) EPA-4038*   56   10-15
  Cast: Lena Horne.
Studiotrack (1958) .... *Jubilee (M) JLP-1062*   59   15-25
  Cast: Cy Coleman and His Orchestra.

JAMBOREE!

Soundtrack (1957) .... *Warner Bros. (M) No Number Used*   57   450-550
  Promotional issue only.
  Composer: Aaron Schroeder; Claude DeMetruis; Ernie Wilkins; Bernie Lowe; Kal Mann; Roy
  C. Bennett; Sid Tepper; Otis Blackwell; Teddy Randazzo; Leone M. Richards; Count Basie;
  Buddy Knox; Fats Domino; Dave Bartholomew. **Cast:** Fats Domino; Buddy Knox; Jimmy
  Bowen; Charlie Gracie; Slim Whitman; Jerry Lee Lewis; Connie Francis; Four Coins; Carl
  Perkins; Frankie Avalon; Jodie Sands; Count Basie; Joe Williams (Joseph Goreed); Andy
  Martin; Martha Lou Harp; Paul Carr; Lewis Lymon and the Teenchords; Ron Coby.

JAMES BLONDE (SECRET AGENT 006.95, MARKED DOWN FROM 007.00)
Studio Cast (1965) .... *Colpix (M) CP-495*   65   **$10-15**
Comedy skits based on James Bond characters.
Cast: Marty Brill; Larry Foster.

JAMES BOND - 13 ORIGINAL THEMES
Soundtrack .... *Liberty (S) LO-51138*   83   **8-10**
Includes such themes as: *The James Bond Theme, From Russia with Love, Goldfinger, Thunderball, You Only Live Twice, We Have All the Time in the World, Diamonds Are Forever, Live and Let Die.*
Composer: John Barry; others. **Conductor:** John Barry; others. **Cast:** Matt Munro; Shirley Bassey; Tom Jones; Nancy Sinatra; Louis Armstrong; Paul McCartney; Lulu; Carly Simon; Sheena Easton; Rita Coolidge.
Cast: Sounds of Screen Orchestra.

JAMES BOND - 10th ANNIVERSARY
Soundtrack (1972) .... *United Artists (S) UXS-91*   72   **20-25**
Double LP set.
Composer: John Barry; Monty Morman; Lionel Bart. **Conductor:** John Barry; Eric Rodgers.
Cast: Matt Monro; Shirley Bassey; Louis Armstrong.

JAMES BOND - 25 YEARS OF 007
Studiotrack .... *Bainbridge (S) BT-6274*   87   **8-10**

JAMES DEAN STORY
Soundtrack (1957) .... *Capitol (EP) EDM 1-881*   **40-50**
Soundtrack (1957) .... *Capitol (M) W-881*   57   **60-70**
Composer: Leith Stevens; Jay Livingston; Ray Evans. **Conductor:** Leith Stevens.
Soundtrack (1955) .... *Warner Bros. (M) BS-2843*   75   **10-12**
Actual title: *James Dean.* Has excerpts from: *Giant, East of Eden* and *Rebel Without a Cause.*
Composer: Leonard Rosenman; Dimitri Tiomkin. **Conductor:** Ray Heindorf; Dimitri Tiomkin.
Cast: James Dean; Jo Van Fleet; Raymond Massey; Julie Harris; Barbara Baxley; Jim Backus; Ann Doran; Rock Hudson; Elizabeth Taylor; Mercedes McCambridge; Charles Watts; Monte Hale; Chill Wills; Caroll Baker.
Studiotrack (1956) .... *Coral (M) CRL-57099*   56   **40-50**
Cast: Steve Allen and Bill Randle (narrators); Gigi Perreau; George Cates; Dick Jacobs.
Studiotrack (1957) .... *World Pacific (M) 2005*   57   **50-75**
Jazz interpretation.
Studiotrack (1960) .... *Kimberly (M) 2016*   60   **30-40**
Reissue of World Pacific 2005.
Cast: Chet Baker.

JANE EYRE
TV Soundtrack (1971) .... *Capitol (S) SW-749*   71   **40-50**
Composer: John Williams. **Conductor:** John Williams.

JANE, MARY:
see MARY JANE

JANIS
Soundtrack (1975) .... *Columbia (S) CGT-33345*   75   **10-12**
Cast: Janis Joplin (vocals, monologs, and interviews).

JARRE BY JARRE
Composer: Maurice Jarre. **Conductor:** Maurice Jarre. **Cast:** Royal Philharmonic Orchestra.

JAWS
Soundtrack (1975) .... *MCA (S) 2087*   75   **8-10**
Composer: John Williams. **Conductor:** John Williams. **Cast:** John Williams and His Orchestra.

JAWS 2
Soundtrack (1978) .... *MCA (S) 3045*   78   **$8-12**
Composer: John Williams. Conductor: John Williams. Cast: John Williams and His Orchestra.

JAWS 3-D
Soundtrack (1983) .... *MCA (S) 6124*   83   **8-12**
Composer: Alan Parker. Conductor: Alan Parker.

JAZZ SINGER
Soundtrack (1927) .... *Soundtrack (M) ST-102*   **10-12**
Cast: Al Jolson.
Soundtrack (1953) .... *Decca (EP) ED-2003*   53   **10-20**
Composer: Various. Conductor: Gordon Jenkins. Cast: Peggy Lee; Gordon Jenkins with His Chorus and Orchestra.
Soundtrack (1980) .... *Capitol (S) SWAV-12120*   80   **8-10**
Composer: Neil Diamond. Conductor: Neil Diamond. Cast: Neil Diamond; Laurence Olivier; Lucie Arnaz; Catlin Adams.
Studiotrack (1953) .... *RCA Victor (EP) EPB-3118*   53   **10-15**
Double EP set.
Studiotrack (1953) .... *RCA Victor (M) LPM-3118*   53   **20-30**
10-inch LP.
Cast: Danny Thomas.

JAZZ THEMES FOR COPS AND ROBBERS:
see PRIVATE HELL 36

JEANNE EAGLES
Soundtrack (1957) .... *Decca (M) DL-8574*   57   **25-30**
Actual title: *This Is Kim As Jeanne Eagles.* Has other traditional pop compositions associated with Kim Novak.
Composer: George Dunning. Conductor: Morris Stoloff. Cast: Kim Novak.

JENNIE
Original Cast (1963) .... *RCA Victor (M) LOC-1083*   63   **30-35**
Original Cast (1963) .... *RCA Victor (S) LSO-1083*   63   **45-50**
Composer: Arthur Schwartz; Howard Dietz. Conductor: John Lesko. Cast: Mary Martin; George Wallace; Ethel Shutta; Jack DeLon; Robin Bailey.

JEREMIAH JOHNSON
Soundtrack (1972) .... *Warner Bros. (S) BS-2902*   72   **10-12**
Composer: John Rubenstein; Tim McIntire.

JEREMY
Soundtrack (1973) .... *United Artists (S) UA-LA145-G*   73   **10-12**
Composer: Lee Holdridge; Joseph Brooks; Dorothea Joyce. Conductor: Lee Holdridge. Cast: Robby Benson; Glynnis O'Connor.

JERICO-JIM CROW
Original Cast (1964) .... *Folkways (M) FL-9671*   64   **15-20**
Double LP set.
Composer: Langston Hughes; Paul Campbell. Conductor: Hugh Porter. Cast: Gilbert Price; Micki Grant; Rosalie King; Joseph Attles; Dorothy Drake; William Cain; Hugh Porter Gospel Singers; Metrogene Myles.

JEROME KERN GOES TO HOLLYWOOD
Original Cast (1986) .... *Safari (S)*   86   **8-10**
Composer: Jerome Kern; Bernard Dougall; Dorothy Fields; Ira Gershwin; Oscar Hammerstein II; Otto Harbach; Jimmy McHugh; Johnny Mercer; M.E. Rourke; P.G. Wodehouse. Conductor: Clive Chaplin. Cast: Elaine Delmar; David Kernan; Liz Robertson; Elisabeth Welch.

JERRY'S GIRLS
Original Cast (1984) ....*Polydor (S) 820207-1*   84   **$20-30**
Double LP set.
Composer: Jerry Herman. **Conductor:** Janet Glazenar. **Cast:** Carol Channing; Leslie Uggams;
Andrea McArdle; Ellyn Arons; Deborah Graham; Jerry Herman; Suzanne Ishee; Diane Myron;
Laura Soltis; Helena-Joyce Wright.

JESSICA
Soundtrack (1962) ....*United Artists (M) UAL-4096*   62   **15-20**
Soundtrack (1962) ....*United Artists (S) UAS-5096*   62   **20-25**
Composer: Mario Nascimbene; Marguerite Monnot; others. **Cast:** Maurice Chevalier.

JESUS CHRIST SUPERSTAR
Original Recording (1971) ....*Decca (S) DXSA-7206*   71   **20-30**
Double LP set. Made before the show's productions. Includes a 28-page program booklet.
Composer: Andrew Lloyd Webber. **Conductor:** Andrew Lloyd Webber. **Cast:** Murray Head;
Ian Gillan; Yvonne Elliman; Brian Keith; Mike D'Abo; Paul Raven; Barry Dennen; Victor
Brox; John Gustafson; Paul Davis.
Original Recording (1971) ....*MCA (S) 10000*   72   **12-15**
Composer: Andrew Lloyd Webber; Tim Rice. **Conductor:** Andrew Lloyd Webber.
Cast: Murray Head; Ian Gillan; Yvonne Elliman; Brian Keith; Mike D'Abo; Paul Raven;
Barry Dennen; Victor Brox; John Gustafson; Paul Davis.
Original Cast (1971) ....*Decca (S) DL-71503*   71   **15-20**
Original Cast (1971) ....*MCA (S) 5000*   72   **10-12**
Composer: Andrew Lloyd Webber. **Conductor:** Marc Pressel. **Cast:** Ben Vereen; Jeff Fenholt;
Yvonne Elliman; Barry Dennen; Paul Ainsley; Bob Bingham; Phil Jethrow; Steven Bell; Alan
Braunstein; Michael Meadows.
Original London Cast (1971) ....*Decca (EP) No Number Used*   71   **20-30**
Boxed set of four stereo EPs. Promotional issue only.
Original London Cast (1971) ....*MCA (S) 2503*   71   **25-30**
Composer: Andrew Lloyd Webber; Tim Rice. **Conductor:** Anthony Bowles. **Cast:** Paul
Nichols; Stephen Tate; Dana Gillespie; John Parker.
London Studio Cast (1971) ....*Pickwick (S) SPC-3262*   71   **10-12**
Composer: Andrew Lloyd Webber; Tim Rice. **Cast:** Mike Trounce; Martin Jay; Michael Allen;
Jenny Mason.
Studio Cast ....*Springboard (S) SP-4000*   **8-10**
Composer: Andrew Lloyd Webber; Tim Rice. **Conductor:** Nick Ingram.
Soundtrack (1973) ....*MCA (S) 2-11000*   73   **10-12**
Double LP set.
Composer: Andrew Lloyd Webber; Tim Rice. **Conductor:** Andre Previn. **Cast:** Ted Neeley;
Carl Anderson; Yvonne Elliman; Barry Dennen; Bob Bingham; Larry Marshall; Joshua Mostel;
Kurt Yaghjian.

JESUS OF NAZARETH
TV Soundtrack (1977) . . . . *RCA Victor (S) CBL3-3929* 81 $25-30
   Triple LP set. Though the film premiered in April 1977, the LP was not issued until 1981.
   Composer: Maurice Jarre. **Conductor:** Maurice Jarre. **Cast:** National Philharmonic Orchestra.
   (With dialogue.)
TV Soundtrack (1982) . . . . *RCA Victor (S) ABL1-4284* 82 8-12
   Composer: Maurice Jarre. **Conductor:** Maurice Jarre.

JEWEL IN THE CROWN
TV Soundtrack (1985) . . . . *Chrysalis (S) FV-41465* 85 8-10
   14-part series, produced by Granada Television.
   Composer: George Fenton. **Conductor:** Anthony Randall; Booker Isobel Griffiths.

JEWEL OF THE NILE
Soundtrack (1985) . . . . *Jive/Arista (S) JL9-8406* 85 8-12
   Composer: Jack Nitzsche; others. **Cast:** Billy Ocean; Ruby Turner; Hugh Masekela and Jonathan
   Butler; Willesden Dodgers; Whodini; Precious Wilson; Mark Shreeve; Nubians; Jack Nitzsche.

JIMI HENDRIX
Soundtrack (1973) . . . . *Reprise (S) 2RS-6481* 73 15-25
   Double LP set.
   Composer: Jimi Hendrix; others. **Cast:** Jimi Hendrix. (Includes music and interviews.)

JIMI PLAYS MONTEREY
Soundtrack . . . . *Reprise (S) 1-25358* 8-10
   Cast: Jimi Hendrix.

JIMMY
Original Cast (1969) . . . . *RCA Victor (S) LSO-1162* 69 15-20
   Composer: Bill Jacob; Patti Jacob. **Conductor:** Milton Rosenstock. **Cast:** Frank Gorshin; Anita
   Gillette; Julie Wilson; Jack Collins; William Griffis; Dorothy Claire; Paul Forrest; Edward
   Becker; Carol Conte; Clifford Fearl; Henry Lawrence; Stanley Simmonds; Evan Thompson.

JINGLE JANGLE
Studio Cast . . . . *J.J. (S) 1001* 8-12
   Cast: Norman Wisdom.

JO JO DANCER, YOUR LIFE IS CALLING
Soundtrack (1986) . . . . *Warner Bros. (S) 1-25444* 86 8-10
   Composer: Various. **Cast:** Herbie Hancock; O'Jays; Gladys Knight and the Pips; Mahalia
   Jackson; Muddy Waters; Spinners; Chaka Khan; Junior Walker and the All Stars; Marvin Gaye.

JO STAFFORD SINGS BROADWAY'S BEST
Studiotrack (1955) . . . . *Columbia (EP) B-1660* 55 8-12
Studiotrack (1955) . . . . *Columbia (EP) B-328* 55 10-20
   Double EP set.
Studiotrack (1955) . . . . *Columbia (M) CL-584* 55 15-25
   Composer: Various. **Cast:** Jo Stafford.

JOAN
Original Cast (1971) . . . . *Judson (S) JU-1001* 71 120-130
   Double LP set.
   Composer: Al Carmines. **Conductor:** Al Carmines. **Cast:** Joe Cecil; Julie Kurnitz; Phyllis
   MacBryde; Tracy Moore; Sandy Padilla; Ira Siff; Margaret Wright; Lee Guilliant; Emily Adams;
   Jeffrey Apter; David Vaughan; Al Carmines (piano); Essie Borden; Tony Clark; Teresa King.

JOANNA
Soundtrack (1968) . . . . *20th Century-Fox (S) S-4202* 68 20-25
   Composer: Rod McKuen. **Conductor:** Arthur Greenslade. **Cast:** Rod McKuen; Michael Sarne;
   Barbara Kay.

JOE

Soundtrack (1970) .... *Mercury (S) SRM1-605*   70   **$20-25**
Soundtrack (1970) .... *Mercury (S) SRM1-607*   70   **20-25**
     Actual title *Joe Speaks*. Has dialogue in addition to music from the soundtrack.
   Composer: Bobby Scott. **Conductor:** Bobby Scott. **Cast:** Jerry Butler; Dean Michaels; Exuma;
     Peter Boyle; Dennis Patrick. (With dialogue.)

JOE COCKER: MAD DOGS AND ENGLISHMEN

Soundtrack (1970) .... *A&M (S) SP-6002*   70   **10-12**
     The "Mad Dogs and Englishmen" tour film was released in 1971.
   Cast: Joe Cocker; Leon Russell; Chris Stainton; others.

JOE LOUIS STORY

Soundtrack (1953) .... *MGM (EP) X-221*   53   **20-30**
     Double EP.
Soundtrack (1953) .... *MGM (M) E-221*   53   **50-60**
   Composer: George Bassman; others. **Conductor:** George Bassman.

JOE SPEAKS:
see JOE

JOHN AND MARY

Soundtrack (1970) .... *A&M (S) SP-4230*   70   **20-25**
     Adaptations of compositions by Bach, Mozart, Mendelssohn, and Handel.
   Composer: Quincy Jones; Alan and Marilyn Bergman; others. **Conductor:** Quincy Jones.
   Cast: Evie Sands; Strange Things; Jeff Bridges; Morgan Ames Singers.

JOHN BROWN'S BODY

Original Cast (1953) .... *Columbia (M) OSL-181*   53   **45-50**
     Double LP, boxed set.
   Composer: Walter Schumann. **Conductor:** Walter Schumann. **Cast:** Tyrone Power; Judith
     Anderson; Raymond Massey; Betty Benson; Roger Miller.

JOHN F. KENNEDY

Soundtrack (1966) .... *Capitol (M) T-2486*   66   **15-25**
     Actual title: *Years of Lightning, Day of Drums*. Produced by the U.S. Information Agency.
   Conductor: Bruce Herschenson. **Cast:** John F. Kennedy (dialogue); Gregory Peck (narration).
Studio Cast (1963) .... *Columbia (M) L2L-1017*   63   **15-20**
     Actual title: *John Fitzgerald Kennedy As We Remember Him*.
   Cast: John F. Kennedy (dialogue).
Studio Cast (1964) .... *RCA Victor (M) VDM-101*   64   **10-20**
     Actual title: *The Kennedy Wit*.
   Cast: John F. Kennedy (dialogue).
Studio Cast (1963) .... *Diplomat (M) 1000*   63   **10-15**
   Cast: John F. Kennedy (dialogue).
Studio Cast (1963) .... *20th Century-Fox (M) 3127*   63   **10-20**
     Actual title: *The Presidential Years (1960 - 1963)*.
   Cast: John F. Kennedy (dialogue).
Studio Cast (1963) .... *Pickwick (M) 1*   Re   **8-12**
     Actual title: *The Presidential Years (1960 - 1963)*.
   Cast: John F. Kennedy (dialogue).
Studio Cast (1963) .... *Colpix (M) CP-2500*   63   **10-20**
     Actual title: *Four Days That Shocked the World*.
   Cast: John F. Kennedy (dialogue).
Studio Cast (1963) .... *Decca (M) DL-2500*   63   **10-20**
     Actual title: *That Was the Week That Was*. From a British Broadcasting telecast, November 23, 1963.
Studio Cast (1963) .... *Decca (S) DL7-2500*   63   **10-20**
   Cast: John F. Kennedy (dialogue).

Studio Cast (1963) ....*Documentaries Unlimited (M) Vol. 1*   63   **$10-20**
  Actual title: *J.F.K., the Man, the President.*
  Cast: John F. Kennedy (dialogue); Barry Gray (narrator).
Studio Cast (1963) ....*Harmonica (M) HLP-3005*   63   **10-20**
  Actual title: *Kennedy Speaks.*
  Cast: John F. Kennedy (dialogue).
Studio Cast (1963) ....*Premier (M) 2099*   63   **10-20**
  Actual title: *Highlights of (Kennedy) Speeches.* Memorial tribute broadcast by WMCA, New York,
  November 22, 1963.
  Cast: John F. Kennedy (dialogue); Ed Brown (narrator).
Studio Cast (1963) ....*Somerset (M) P-16100*   63   **10-20**
  Labeled *United States' Presidents' Speeches,* has speeches by John F. Kennedy and Franklin D. Roosevelt.
  Cast: John F. Kennedy; Franklin D. Roosevelt. (With dialogue.)
Assembled Cast (1963) ....*RCA Victor (M) LMM-7030*   63   **10-20**
  Labeled *Pontifical Requiem* (Mozart Requiem).
  Cast: Cardinal Cushing; Boston Symphony and Choir.

JOHN PAUL JONES
Soundtrack (1959) ....*Warner Bros. (M) W-1293*   59   **75-85**
Soundtrack (1959) ....*Warner Bros. (S) WS-1293*   59   **100-125**
Soundtrack (1959) ....*Varese Sarabande (S) STV-81146*   81   **8-10**
  Composer: Max Steiner. **Conductor:** Muir Mathieson.

JOHNNY APPLESEED
Soundtrack (1948) ....*RCA Victor/Camden (M) CAL-1054*   64   **15-20**
Soundtrack (1948) ....*RCA Victor/Camden (SE) CAS-1054*   64   **15-20**
  One side has music from *Pecos Bill.*
  Composer: Walter Kent. **Conductor:** Ken Darby. **Cast:** Dennis Day (narration, vocals).
  PECOS BILL: Roy Rogers; Sons of the Pioneers.
Studio Cast (1964) ....*Disneyland (M) DQ-1260*   **10-12**
  Composer: Kim Gannon; Walter Kent. **Cast:** Dennis Day.

JOHNNY B. GOODE
Soundtrack (1986) ....*Capitol (S) MLP-15022*   86   **10-12**

JOHNNY BE GOOD
Soundtrack (1988) ....*Atlantic (S) 81837-1*   88   **8-10**
  Composer: Various. **Cast:** Frozen Ghost and Friends; Bernie Shanahan; Dirty Looks; Judas
  Priest; Myles Goodwyn; Kix; Fiona; Rick Astley; Saga; Ted Nugent.

JOHNNY CONCHO
Soundtrack (1956) ....*Capitol (EP) EAP 1-754*   56   **15-20**
  Composer: Nelson Riddle; Doc Stanford. **Conductor:** Nelson Riddle. **Cast:** Nelson Riddle
  and His Orchestra.

JOHNNY COOL
Soundtrack (1963) ....*United Artists (M) UAL-4111*   63   **15-20**
Soundtrack (1963) .... *United Artists (S) UAS-5111*   63   **20-25**
Soundtrack (1963) ....*Ascot (M) ALM-13012*   64   **15-20**
Soundtrack (1963) ....*Ascot (S) ALS-16012*   64   **20-25**
  Also has jazz selections from *Odds Against Tomorrow, I Want to Live, The Misfits* and *Paris Blues.*
Soundtrack (1961) ....*United Artists (S) UA-LA273-G*   74   **10-12**
  Reissue of Ascot ALS-16012.
  Composer: Alex North. **Conductor:** Alex North. **Cast:** Sammy Davis Jr.

JOHNNY GUITAR
Soundtrack (1954) ....*Citadel (M) CIT-7026*   81   **10-15**
  Composer: Victor Young. **Conductor:** Victor Young.

JOHNNY HANDSOME
Soundtrack (1989) . . . . *Warner Bros. (S) 1-25996*   89   **$8-10**
Cast: Ry Cooder.

JOHNNY JOHNSON
Studio Cast (1936) . . . .*MGM (M) E-3447*   55   **40-50**
Studio Cast (1936) . . . . *Heliodor (M) H-25024*   66   **15-20**
Studio Cast (1936) . . . . *Heliodor (SE) HS-25024*   66   **15-20**
Studio Cast (1936) . . . . *Polydor (SE) 831384*   86   **8-10**
Composer: Kurt Weill; Paul Green. Conductor: Samuel Matlowsky. Cast: Burgess Meredith;
Hiram Sherman; Evelyn Lear; Lotte Lenya; Thomas Stewart; Jane Connell; Scott Merrill.

JOHNNY TREMAINE
Soundtrack (1957) . . . . *Disneyland (M) WDL-4014*   57   **25-30**
One side, titled *Songs of Our Soldiers,* has assorted soldier-related selections.
Composer: George Bruns. Conductor: George Bruns.

JOLLY THEATRICAL SEASON
Studio Cast (1963) . . . .*Capitol (M) T-1862*   63   **10-20**
Studio Cast (1963) . . . . *Capitol (S) ST-1862*   63   **15-25**
Composer: Various. Cast: Robert Morse; Charles Nelson Reilly.

JOLSON SINGS AGAIN
Studiotrack . . . . *Decca (M) DL-5006*   49   **25-35**
10-inch LP.
Composer: Various. Conductor: Morris Stoloff; Matty Matlock. Cast: Al Jolson; Morris Stoloff
and His Orchestra; Matty Matlock and His Orchestra.

JONATHAN LIVINGSTON SEAGULL
Soundtrack (1973) . . . . *Columbia (S) KS-32550*   73   **10-12**
Soundtrack (1973) . . . . *Columbia (S) HS-42550*   81   **10-15**
Half-speed mastered.
Soundtrack (1973) . . . .*Columbia (S) JS-32550*   Re   **8-10**
Composer: Neil Diamond. Cast: Neil Diamond.
Studiotrack (1973) . . . . *Dunhill (S) DSD-50160*   73   **10-12**
From the book by Richard Bach, as told by Richard Harris.
Composer: Terry James. Conductor: Terry James. Cast: Richard Harris (narration).

JOPLIN, SCOTT:
see SCOTT JOPLIN

JOSEPH AND THE AMAZING TECHNICOLOR DREAMCOAT
Original Recording (1968) . . . . *Scepter (S) SPS-588X*   68   **20-30**
Recorded before the London show. First performed at the Colet Court School, England (1968).
Composer: Andrew Lloyd Webber. Conductor: Alan Doggett. Cast: Terry Saunders; David
Daltrey; Malcolm Parry; Tim Rice; John Cook; Bryan Watson; Colet Court Choir; Joseph
Consortium; Dr. W.S. Lloyd Webber (organ); Martin Wilcox (harpsichord).
Original London Revival Cast . . . . *Music for Pleasure (S) MFP-50455*   **20-25**
Composer: Andrew Lloyd Webber; Tim Rice. Cast: Paul Jones; Tim Rice.
Studio Cast (1973) . . . .*MCA (S) 399*   73   **8-10**
First recording of the revised complete work. (Has original London cast star.)
Composer: Andrew Lloyd Webber; Tim Rice. Conductor: Chris Hamelcooke. Cast: Gary
Bond; Peter Reeves; Maynard Williams; Gordon Waller; Roger Watson.
Original Cast (1982) . . . . *Chrysalis (S) CHR-1387*   **8-10**
Composer: Andrew Lloyd Webber; Tim Rice. Conductor: David Friedman. Cast: David
Ardao; Laurie Beechman; Kenneth Bryan; Tom Carder; Bill Hutton; Robert Hyman; Randon
Lo; Steve McNaughton; Charlie Serrano; Gordon Stanley; Harry Tarallo.

JOSEPH McCARTHY IS ALIVE AND WELL AND LIVING IN DADE COUNTY
Original Cast (1977) . . . .*AEI (S) 1103*   77   **$8-10**
   Composer: Ray Scantlin. Cast: Paul Baccus; Kim Brassner; Mary Jo Gillis; Amanda McBroom; Hal James Pederson; Jay Pevney; Daniel Trent; Gerrard Wagner; Alfred Wilson; Dennis Wood.

JOSEPHINE BAKER SHOW
Original Cast (1964) . . . . *RCA Victor (M) LOC-2427*   64   **20-25**
Original Cast (1964) . . . . *RCA Victor (S) LSO-2427*   64   **30-40**
   Conductor: Joe Bouillon. Cast: Josephine Baker.

JOURNEY THROUGH THE PAST
Soundtrack (1972) . . . . *Warner Bros. (S) 2XS-6480*   72   **12-15**
   Double LP set.
   Composer: Neil Young; others. Cast: Neil Young.

JOURNEY TO THE CENTER OF THE EARTH
Original Cast (1974) . . . . *A&M (Q) QU-53621*   74   **10-12**
   Includes booklet.
   Composer: Rick Wakeman. Conductor: David Measham. Cast: David Hemmings (narration); Rick Wakeman; Garry Pickford-Hopkins; Ashley Holt; Mike Egan; Roger Newell; Barney James; John Cleary; English Chamber Choir; others.
Soundtrack (1959) . . . .'. . . . .*Dot (EP) DEP-1091*   59   **10-15**
   Cast: Pat Boone.
   Also see FANTASY FILM WORLD OF BERNARD HERRMANN

JOY
Original Cast (1970) . . . . *RCA Victor (S) LSO-1166*   70   **15-20**
   Composer: Oscar Brown Jr.; Luiz Henrique; others. Conductor: Sivuca. Cast: Oscar Brown Jr.; Jean Pace; Sivuca; Norman Shobey.

JOYCE GRENFELL REQUESTS THE PLEASURE
Original Cast (1955) . . . . *Philips (M) BBL-7004*   **30-40**
Original Cast (1955) . . . . *DRG (M) SL-5186*   Re   **8-10**
   Composer: Joyce Grenfell; Richard Addinsell. Conductor: William Blizard. Cast: Joyce Grenfell; Beryl Kaye; Paddy Stone; Irving Davies.

JOYRIDE
Soundtrack (1977) . . . .*United Artists (S) UA-LA784-H*   77   **10-12**
   Composer: Barry Mann; Jimmie Haskell; others. Cast: Electric Light Orchestra; Barry Mann.

JUD
Soundtrack (1971) . . . .*Ampex (S) A-50101*   71   **15-20**
   Composer: Stu Phillips; Bob Dylan; others. Cast: John Hartford; American Breed; Mason Proffit; Crow; Barbara Robison.

JUDGMENT AT NUREMBERG
Soundtrack (1961) . . . .*United Artists (M) UAL-4095*   61   **25-35**
Soundtrack (1961) . . . . *United Artists (S) UAS-5095*   61   **35-45**
   Composer: Ernest Gold. Conductor: Ernest Gold. Cast: Spencer Tracy; Burt Lancaster; Maximilian Schell. (With dialogue).
   Also see HORSE SOLDIERS

JUDITH
Soundtrack (1966) ....*RCA Victor (M) LOC-1119*   66   **$25-35**
Soundtrack (1966) ....*RCA Victor (S) LSO-1119*   66   **40-50**
  Composer: Sol Kaplan. **Conductor:** Sol Kaplan.

JUDY GARLAND
Original Cast (1951) .... *Decca (M) DL-6020*   51   **50-60**
  10-inch LP. Actual title: *Judy At the Palace.*
  Composer: Harold Arlen; E.Y. Harburg; Roger Edens; James V. Monaco; Joe McCarthy.
  Conductor: Harry Sosnik; Victor Young; Georgie Stoll; David Rose; others. **Cast:** Judy
  Garland; Gene Kelly.
Original Cast (1959) ....*Capitol (M) T-1941*   59   **15-20**
Original Cast (1959) .... *Capitol (S) ST-1941*   59   **20-25**
  Above two are also known as *Our Love Letter.*
  Composer: Various. **Conductor:** Gordon Jenkins. **Cast:** Judy Garland; John Ireland.
Original Cast (1961) ....*Capitol (EP) EAP 1-1569*   **10-15**
Original Cast (1961) .... *Capitol (M) WAO-1569*   61   **12-15**
  Above two are double LP sets, titled: *Judy Garland At Carnegie Hall.*
Original Cast (1961) .... *Capitol (S) SWBO-1569*   61   **15-20**
  Conductor: Mort Lindsey. **Cast:** Judy Garland.
Original Cast (1959) ....*Capitol (M) T-1118*   59   **15-25**
Original Cast (1959) .... *Capitol (S) ST-1118*   59   **20-30**
  Actual title of above two: *Garland At the Grove.*

JUDY GARLAND - LIZA MINNELLI
LIVE AT THE LONDON PALLADIUM
Original Cast .... *Capitol (S) SWBO-2295*   **15-20**
  Double LP set. Unabridged version.
  Cast: Judy Garland; Liza Minnelli.
Original Cast .... *Capitol (S) ST-11191*   **10-12**
  Abridged version.
  Cast: Judy Garland; Liza Minnelli.

JULIE AND CAROL AT CARNEGIE HALL

Original Cast (1962) ....*Columbia (S) OL-5840*	62	**$10-15**
Original Cast (1962) ....*Columbia (S) OS-2240*	62	**15-20**

Conductor: Irwin Kostal. Cast: Julie Andrews; Carol Burnett.

JULIE AND CAROL AT LINCOLN CENTER

Original Cast (1971) .... *Columbia (S) S-31153*	71	**12-15**

Composer: Various. Conductor: Peter Matz. Cast: Julie Andrews; Carol Burnett.

JULIET OF THE SPIRITS

Soundtrack (1965) ....*Mainstream (M) 56062*	65	**30-35**
Soundtrack (1965) ....*Mainstream (S) S-6062*	65	**40-45**
Soundtrack (1965) .... *Lumiere (S) L-1000*	Re	**8-10**

Composer: Nino Rota. Conductor: Carlo Savina.

JULIUS CAESAR

Soundtrack (1953) ....*MGM (EP) X-204*	53	**20-25**
Soundtrack (1953) ....*MGM (M) E-3033*	53	**65-75**
Soundtrack (1953) .... *MCA (SE) 39055*	Re	**8-10**

Composer: Miklos Rozsa. Conductor: Miklos Rozsa. Cast: John Houseman (narrator/producer); Marlon Brando; James Mason; John Gielgud; Louis Calhern; Edmond O'Brien; Greer Garson; Deborah Kerr. (With dialogue.)

JUMBO

Studio Cast (1953) ....*RCA Victor (EP) EPA-479*	53	**10-15**

One side has music from *Babes in Arms*.

Composer: Richard Rodgers; Lorenz Hart. Conductor: Lehman Engel. Cast: Lisa Kirk; Jack Cassidy; Jordon Bentley.

Studio Cast (1953) .... *RCA Victor (M) LPM-3152*	53	**30-40**

One side has music from *Babes in Arms*.

Composer: Richard Rodgers; Lorenz Hart. Conductor: Lehman Engel. Cast: Lisa Kirk; Jack Cassidy; Jordan Bentley.

Soundtrack (1962) .... *Columbia (M) OL-5860*	62	**20-25**
Soundtrack (1962) .... *Columbia (S) OS-2260*	62	**25-30**
Soundtrack (1962) .... *Columbia Special Products (S) AOS-2260*	Re	**8-10**

Composer: Richard Rodgers; Lorenz Hart. Conductor: George Stoll. Cast: Doris Day; Stephen Boyd; Jimmy Durante; Martha Raye.

Also see BABES IN ARMS

JUMPIN' JACK FLASH

Soundtrack (1986) .... *Mercury (S) 830545-1*	86	**8-10**

Composer: Various. Cast: Rene and Angela; Bananarama; Kool and The Gang; Gwen Guthrie; Billy Branigan; Rolling Stones; Face To Face; Supremes; Thomas Newman.

JUNGLE BOOK

Soundtrack (1942) .... *RCA Victor (M) LM-2118*	60	**80-100**
Soundtrack (1942) ....*United Artists (M) UAS-29725*	Re	**10-15**

Above two also have music from *The Thief of Bagdad*.

Composer: Miklos Rozsa. Conductor: Miklos Rozsa. Cast: Leo Genn (narrator).

Soundtrack (1967) ....*Disneyland (M) 3948*	67	**12-15**
Soundtrack (1967) ....*Disneyland (S) 3948*	67	**15-20**
Soundtrack (1967) .... *Buena Vista (M) 4041*	68	**10-15**
Soundtrack (1967) .... *Buena Vista (S) ST-4041*	68	**15-20**
Soundtrack (1967) ....*Disneyland (S) 3105*	81	**8-12**

Limited edition picture disc.

Composer: Richard M. Sherman; Robert B. Sherman. Cast: Louis Prima; Phil Harris; Sterling Holloway.

JUNGLE JIM
Original Radio Cast . . . . *Golden Age (M) 5014*   78   **$8-10**

JUNO
Original Cast (1959) . . . . *Columbia (M) OL-5380*   59   **30-35**
Original Cast (1959) . . . . *Columbia (S) OS-2013*   59   **45-50**
   Composer: Marc Blitzstein. **Conductor:** Robert Emmett Dolan. **Cast:** Shirley Booth; Melvyn
   Douglas; Jack MacGowran; Jean Stapleton; Monte Amundsen; Nancy Andrews; Loren Driscoll;
   Rico Froehlich; Beulah Garrick; Robert Hoyem; Julian Patrick; Arthur Rubin; Robert Rue; Sada
   Thompson.

JUST A GIGOLO:
   see SCHONER GIGOLO - ARMER GIGOLO

JUST FOR OPENERS
Original Cast (1965) . . . . *Upstairs (S) UD-37W56*   65   **70-75**
   Conductor: Michael Cohen. **Cast:** Betty Aberlin; Richard Blair; Madeline Kahn; Fannie Flagg;
   Stockton Brigel; R.G. Brown; Michael Cohen and Edward Morris (twin pianos).

JUST FOR YOU:
   see ZING A LITTLE ZONG

JUST ONE OF THE GUYS
Soundtrack (1985) . . . .*Elektra (S) 60426-1*   85   **8-10**
   Composer: Various. **Cast:** Shalamar; Ronnie Spector; Berlin; others.

JUST TELL ME YOU LOVE ME
Soundtrack (1980) . . . . *MCA (S) 3255*   80   **8-10**
   Cast: England Dan and John Ford Coley.

JUSTINE
Soundtrack (1969) . . . .*Monument (S) SLP 18123*   69   **35-40**
   Composer: Jerry Goldsmith; others. **Conductor:** Jerry Goldsmith.

K

KA-BOOM!
Original Cast (1980) .... *CYM (S) 8130*   80   **$8-10**
  Composer: Joe Ercole; Bruce Kluger. **Conductor:** John Lehman. **Cast:** Ben Agresti; Judith
  Bro; John Hall; Ken Ward; Valerie Williams; Andrea Wright.

KALEIDOSCOPE
Soundtrack (1966) .... *Warner Bros. (M) W-1663*   66   **15-20**
Soundtrack (1966) .... *Warner Bros. (S) WS-1663*   66   **20-25**
  Composer: Stanley Myers. **Conductor:** Stanley Myers.

KAPER: THE FILM MUSIC OF BRONISLAW
Soundtrack .... *Delos (S) F-25421*   75   **8-12**
  Includes: *San Francisco, Mutiny on the Bounty, Lili, The Glass Slipper, Butterfield 8, Auntie Mame,*
  The Chocolate Soldier, Invitation, The Brothers Karamazov, Green Door, The Swan and *Lord Jim.*
  Composer: Bronislaw Kaper.

KARATE KID
Soundtrack (1984) .... *Casablanca (S) NBLP-7282*   84   **8-10**
  Composer: Various. **Cast:** Survivor; Gang of Four; Broken Edge; Commuter; Paul Davis;
  Shandi; St. Regis; Baxter Robertson; Flirts; Jan and Dean; Joe "Bean" Esposito.

KARATE KID II
Soundtrack (1986) .... *Urania (S) SW-40414*   86   **8-10**
  Cast: Peter Cetera.

KARATE KID III
Soundtrack (1989) .... *MCA (S) 6308*   89   **8-10**
  Composer: Various. **Cast:** Little River Band; Glenn Medeiros; Boys Club; Jude Cole; Pointer
  Sisters; Winger; PBF; Money Talks.

KARL MARX
Original Cast (1973) .... *Kilmarnock (S) KIL-72010*   73   **50-60**
  Actual title: *The Karl Marx Play.* With European Touring Company.
  Composer: Galt MacDermott; Rochelle Owens. **Conductor:** Galt MacDermott. **Cast:** Phyllis
  Newman; Ralph Carter; Harold Gould; Jamie Sanchez; Norman Matlock; Linda Mulrean;
  Louie Piday; Linda Swenson.

KAZABLAN
Soundtrack (1973) .... *MGM (S) 1SE-48*   73   **12-15**
  Conductor: Dow Seltzer.

KEAN
Original Cast (1961) .... *Columbia (M) KOL-5720*   61 $25-30
Original Cast (1961) .... *Columbia (S) KOS-2120*   61   40-45
  Gatefold cover.
  Composer: George Wright; Robert Forrest. **Conductor:** Pembroke Davenport. **Cast:** Alfred
  Drake; Lee Venora; Oliver Gray; Joan Weldon; Patricia Cutts; Truman Smith; Alfred Desio;
  Christopher Hewett; Robert Penn; Arthur Rubin.

KEEP UP THE GRASS
Soundtrack .... *East Coast (S) EC-10-55-S*   8-10
  Cast: Arnold Wrecking Co.

KELLY
Original Cast .... *Original Cast (S) OC-8025*   10-12

KELLY'S HEROES
Soundtrack (1970) .... *MGM (S) 1SE-23*   70   10-15
  Composer: Lalo Schifrin. **Conductor:** Lalo Schifrin. **Cast:** Hank Williams Jr; Mike Curb
  Congregation.

KELLY, PETE:
see PETE KELLY'S BLUES

KEN MURRAY'S BLACKOUTS
Original Cast (1975) .... *Mark '56 (S) 701*   8-12
  Cast: Ken Murray; Marie Wilson.

KENNEDY, JOHN F.:
see JOHN F. KENNEDY

KENT STATE
TV Soundtrack (1981) .... *RCA Victor (S) ABL1-3928*   81   8-10
  Composer: Ken Lauber. **Conductor:** Ken Lauber. **Cast:** Grace Slick; Richie Havens; John
  Sebastian.

KENTUCKIAN (GREAT AMERICAN FILM SCORES)
Soundtrack (1955) .... *Entr'acte (SE) SRS-6506*   77   25-50
  Composer: Bernard Herrmann. **Conductor:** Fred Steiner.

KEY
Soundtrack (1958) .... *Columbia (M) CL-1185*   58   80-90
  Composer: Malcolm Henry Arnold. **Conductor:** Muir Mathieson.

KHARTOUM
Soundtrack (1966) .... *United Artists (M) UAL-4140*   66   25-30
Soundtrack (1966) .... *United Artists (S) UAS-5140*   66   30-35
  Composer: Frank Cordell. **Conductor:** Frank Cordell.

KID GALAHAD
Soundtrack (1962) .... *RCA Victor (EP) EPA-4371*   62   45-60
  Black label, dog on top.
Soundtrack (1962) .... *RCA Victor (EP) EPA-4371*   65   30-40
  Black label, dog on side.
Soundtrack (1962) .... *RCA Victor (EP) EPA-4371*   69   30-40
  Orange label.
  Composer: Ben Weisman; Fred Wise; Ruth Batchelor; Hal David; others. **Cast:** Elvis Presley;
  Scotty Moore (guitar); D.J. Fontana (drums); Bob Moore (bass); Boots Randolph (sax); Dudley
  Brooks (piano); Jordanaires (vocals).

KID MILLIONS/ROMAN SCANDALS
Soundtrack .... *Classic International (M) CIF-3007* $20-25
Eddie Cantor film soundtracks.

KID POWER
TV Soundtrack (1972) .... *Pride (S) PRD-0010*   72   8-12
Cartoon soundtrack from Rankin-Bass.
Composer: Perry Botkin Jr.; Jules Bass. **Conductor:** Perry Botkin Jr.; Jules Bass. **Cast:** Jeff
and Greg Thomas; Jay Silverheels Jr.; Curbstones.

KIDNAPPED
Soundtrack (1971) ......:............... *American Int' l (S) STA-1042*   72   20-25
Composer: Roy Budd. **Conductor:** Roy Budd. **Cast:** Mary Hopkin.

KIDS ARE ALRIGHT
Soundtrack (1979) .... *MCA (S) 2-11005*   79   12-15
Soundtrack (1979) .... *MCA (S) 2-6899*   Re   10-12
Cast: The Who.

KILLER FORCE
Soundtrack (1976) .... *Audio Fidelity (S) AFSD-6277*   76   10-12
Composer: Georges Garvarentz. **Conductor:** Georges Garvarentz.

KILLERS:
see LUST FOR LIFE

KILLERS THREE
Soundtrack (1968) .... *Tower (EP) SPRO-4647/8*   68   10-15
Promotional issue only.
Soundtrack (1968) .... *Tower (S) ST-5141*   68   15-20
Composer: Harley Hatcher; Jerry Styner; others. **Cast:** Merle Haggard; Bonnie Owens; Dick
Curless; Kaye Adams.

KILLING FIELDS
Soundtrack (1984) .... *Virgin (S) V-2328*   84   10-15
Soundtrack (1984) .... *Virgin (S) 90591-1*   Re   8-10
Composer: Mike Oldfield; David Bedford. **Conductor:** Mike Oldfield. **Cast:** Orchestra of the
Bavarian State Opera and Tolzer Boys Choir (conducted by Eberhard Schoener).

KIMBERLEY JIM
Soundtrack (1965) .... *RCA Victor (M) LPM-2780*   65   20-25
Soundtrack (1965) .... *RCA Victor (S) LSP-2780*   65   25-30
Composer: Various. **Conductor:** Bill Walker. **Cast:** Jim Reeves; Madeleine Usher.

KING AND I
Original Cast (1951) .... *Decca (EP) ED-800*   51   10-20
Original Cast (1951) .... *Decca (EP) 9-260*   51   25-30
Six EP boxed set.
Original Cast (1951) .... *Decca (M) DL-9008*   51   25-35
Original Cast (1951) .... *Decca (SE) DL7-9008*   59   15-20
Original Cast (1951) .... *MCA (SE) 2028*   72   10-15
Original Cast (1951) .... *MCA (SE) 37095*   81   8-10
Original Cast (1951) .... *MCA (SE) 1629*   Re   8-10
Composer: Richard Rodgers; Oscar Hammerstein II. **Conductor:** Frederick Dvonch.
Cast: Gertrude Lawrence; Yul Brynner; Dorothy Sarnoff; Doretta Morrow; Larry Douglas.
Original Revival Cast (1964) .... *RCA Victor (M) LOC-1092*   64   10-15
Original Revival Cast (1964) .... *RCA Victor (S) LSO-1092*   64   15-20
Composer: Richard Rodgers; Oscar Hammerstein II. **Conductor:** Franz Allers. **Cast:** Rise
Stevens; Darren McGavin; Lee Venora; James Harvey; Patricia Neway; Frank Porretta.

KING AND I (continued)

Original Revival Cast (1977) .... *RCA Victor (S) ABL1-2610*   77   **$8-10**
  Composer: Richard Rodgers; Oscar Hammerstein II. **Conductor:** Milton Rosenstock.
  Cast: Yul Brynner; Constance Towers; Hye-Young Choi; Martin Vidnovic; June Angela;
  Gene Profanato; Alin Amick.

Original London Cast .... *Stet (M) DS-15014*   8-12
  Composer: Richard Rodgers; Oscar Hammerstein II. **Cast:** Valerie Hobson; Doreen Duke;
  Herbert Lom.

Studio Cast (1960) .... *Columbia (M) OL-8040*   60   **15-20**
Studio Cast (1960) .... *Columbia (S) OS-2640*   60   **20-25**
  Composer: Richard Rodgers; Oscar Hammerstein II. **Conductor:** Lehman Engel.
  Cast: Barbara Cook; Theodore Bikel; Anita Darian; Jeanette Scovotti.

Studio Cast (1977) .... *Rediffusion (S) RIM-1000*   77   **15-20**
  Composer: Richard Rodgers; Oscar Hammerstein II. **Cast:** Virginia McKenna.

Studio Cast (1955) .... *RCA Victor (EP) EKB-1022*   55   **10-20**
  Double LP set.
  Cast: Dinah Shore; Patrice Munsel; Tony Martin; Robert Merrill.

Soundtrack (1956) .... *Capitol (EP) EDM-740*   56   **10-15**
  Also known as *Shall We Dance?*

Soundtrack (1956) .... *Capitol (M) W-740*   56   **15-20**
  Mono pressings include the complete fan-dance music for *Getting to Know You.* Later issues do not.

Soundtrack (1956) .... *Capitol (SE) SW-740*   59   **15-20**
  Composer: Richard Rodgers; Oscar Hammerstein II. **Conductor:** Alfred Newman.
  Cast: Yul Brynner; Rita Moreno; Marni Nixon (actual voice on the songs performed by
  Deborah Kerr in the film); Terry Saunders; Carlos Rivas.

Studiotrack (1958) .... *Warner Bros. (M) W-1205*   58   **15-25**
Studiotrack (1958) .... *Warner Bros. (M) W-1205*   58   **15-20**
Studiotrack (1958) .... *Warner Bros. (S) WS-1205*   58   **15-25**
  Cast: Warren Barker Orchestra.

Studiotrack (1960) .... *Richmond (M) B-20065*   60   **10-20**
Studiotrack (1960) .... *Richmond (S) S-30065*   60   **10-20**
  One side has music from *My Fair Lady.*
  Cast: Cyril Stapleton and His Orchestra.

Studiotrack (1953) .... *RCA Victor (EP) EPA-411*   53   **10-15**
  Cast: Dinah Shore.

Studiotrack .... *Somerset (S) SF-2700*   **10-15**
  Also has music from *My Fair Lady.*

Studiotrack .... *Plymouth (M) P-12-39*   **10-15**
  One side has various classical tracks.
  Cast: Plymouth Players.

Studiotrack .... *Spinorama (S) MK-3045*   **10-15**
  Conductor: Al Goodman. **Cast:** Richard Torigi; Edgar Powell; Susan Shaute; Gretchen Rhoads.

Studiotrack (1960) .... *Epic (M) LN-3680*   60   **10-20**
  Cast: Lois Hunt; Charmaine Harma; Samuel Jones; Harry Snow; Irene Carroll.

Studiotrack (1959) .... *Columbia (EP) B-12522*   59   **5-10**
Studiotrack (1959) .... *Columbia (M) CL-1252*   59   **10-15**
Studiotrack (1959) .... *Columbia (S) CS-8064*   59   **15-20**
  Conductor: Ray Conniff. **Cast:** Ray Conniff and His Orchestra.

Studiotrack (1959) .... *Decca (M) DL-8305*   59   **10-20**
  Cast: Carmen Cavallaro.

Studiotrack (1954) .... *Decca (EP) ED-2057*   54   **10-15**
  Cast: Bing Crosby.

Studiotrack (1960) .... *Richmond (M) B-20071*   60   **10-15**
Studiotrack (1959) .... *Richmond (S) S-30071*   59   **10-20**
  Cast: Frank Chacksfield.

Studiotrack (1959) .... *Savoy (M) MG-12134*	59	**$10-20**
Studiotrack (1959) .... *Savoy (S) SST-13002*	59	**15-25**
Cast: Wilbur Harden.		
Studiotrack (1959) .... *World Pacific (M) 1272*	59	**10-15**
Studiotrack (1959) .... *World Pacific (S) S-1272*	59	**10-20**
Cast: Mastersounds.		

KING CREOLE

Soundtrack (1958) .... *RCA Victor (EP) EPA-5122*	59	**400-500**
Volume one. Maroon label.		
Soundtrack (1958) .... *RCA Victor (EP) EPA-4319*	58	**55-70**
Volume one. Black label, dog on top.		
Soundtrack (1958) .... *RCA Victor (EP) EPA-4319*	65	**30-40**
Volume one. Black label, dog on side.		
Soundtrack (1958) .... *RCA Victor (EP) EPA-4319*	69	**30-40**
Volume one. Orange label.		
Soundtrack (1958) .... *RCA Victor (EP) EPA-4321*	58	**55-70**
Volume two. Black label, dog on top.		
Soundtrack (1958) .... *RCA Victor (EP) EPA-4321*	65	**30-40**
Volume two. Black label, dog on side.		
Soundtrack (1958) .... *RCA Victor (EP) EPA-4321*	69	**30-40**
Orange label.		
Soundtrack (1958) .... *RCA Victor (M) LPM-1884*	58	
Black label, reads "Long Play" at bottom. Add $100 to $125 if 8" x 10" black and white photo of Elvis Presley in uniform is included.		
Soundtrack (1958) .... *RCA Victor (SE) LSP-1884e*	59	**75-85**
Black label, RCA silver-top logo. Reads "Stereo Electronically Reprocessed" at bottom.		
Soundtrack (1958) ...., *RCA Victor (M) LPM-1884*	63	**45-55**
Black label, reads "Mono" at bottom.		
Soundtrack (1958) .... *RCA Victor (SE) LSP-1884e*	60	**25-30**
Black label, RCA white-top logo.		
Soundtrack (1958) .... *RCA Victor (M) LPM-1884*	65	**25-30**
Black label, reads "Monaural" at bottom.		
Soundtrack (1958) .... *RCA Victor (SE) LSP-1884e*	69	**10-20**
Orange or tan label. (Tan label issued in 1976.)		
Soundtrack (1958) .... *RCA Victor (SE) AFL1-1884*	77	**8-10**
Soundtrack (1958) .... *RCA Victor (SE) AYL1-3733*	80	**5-8**
Composer: Fred Wise; Ben Weisman; Sid Wayne; Jerry Leiber; Mike Stoller; Sid Tepper; Roy C. Bennett; others. Cast: Elvis Presley; Scotty Moore (guitar); D.J.Fontana (drums); Bill Black (bass); Jordanaires (vocals).		

KING HENRY V

Studio Cast (1963) .... *Living Shakespeare (M) SHV 41/42 A*	63	**30-35**
Includes booklet of complete play. Contains music and sound effects.		
Composer: Desmond Leslie. Conductor: Cyril Ornadel. Cast: Richard Burton; Anna Massey; Lockwood West; Nigel Davenport; Julian Glover; Michael Goodliffe; John Moffatt; Peter Birrel; Benjamin Whitrow; Frank Williams; Kenneth Griffith; Robert Fyfe; Noel Howlett; Nancy Nevinson; Peter Woodthorpe; others.		

KING KONG

Soundtrack (1976) .... *Reprise (S) MS-2260*	76	**12-18**
Composer: John Barry. Conductor: John Barry.		
Original London/South African Cast (1961) .... *London (M) 5762*	63	**25-30**
All-African jazz opera.		
Composer: Pat Williams; Todd Matshikiza. Conductor: Stanley Glasser.		
Soundtrack (1933) .... *United Artists (SE) UA-LA373-G*	76	**15-20**
Composer: Max Steiner. Conductor: LeRoy Holmes.		

KING KONG (continued)
Soundtrack (1933) .... *Entr' acte (SE) ERS-6504*   76 $10-12
Soundtrack (1933) .... *Southern Cross (SE) SCAR-5006*   Re   8-10
  Composer: Max Steiner. **Conductor:** Fred Steiner. **Cast:** National Philharmonic Orchestra.
TV Soundtrack (1966) ....*Epic (M) LN-24231*   66   15-25
  Actual title: *Original TV Adventures of King Kong.*
TV Soundtrack (1966) .... *Epic (S) BN-26231*   66 .   25-30
  Composer: Maury Laws. **Cast:** Bob McFadden (narration).

KING KONG LIVES
Soundtrack (1987) ....*MCA (S) 6203*   87   8-10
  Composer: John Scott. **Conductor:** John Scott. **Cast:** Graunke Symphony Orchestra.

KING OF COMEDY
Soundtrack (1983) .... *Warner Bros. (S) 92-37651*   83   8-10
  Cast: Pretenders; B.B. King; Talking Heads; Bob James; Rickie Lee Jones; Robbie Robertson;
  Ric Ocasek; Ray Charles; David Sanborn; Van Morrison.

KING OF HEARTS
Soundtrack (1967) ....*United Artists (M) UAL-4150*   67   20-25
Soundtrack (1967) ....*United Artists (S) UAS-5150*   67   30-35
Soundtrack (1967) .... *United Artists (M) UA-LA287-G*   74   8-10
  Composer: Georges Delerue. **Conductor:** Georges Delerue.

KING OF HEARTS
Original Cast (1980) ....*Original Cast (S) OC-8028*   81   10-12
  Composer: Peter Link; Jacob Brackman. **Conductor:** Peter Link. **Cast:** Don Scardino;
  Millicent Martin; Pamela Blair; Bob Gunton; Michael McCarty; Gordon Weiss; Rex Hays;
  Marilyn D'Honau; A. Lacoonis.

KING OF KINGS
Soundtrack (1961) .... *MGM (M) 1E2*   61   25-30
Soundtrack (1961) .... *MGM (S) S1E2*   61   35-40
  Above two are boxed sets, each with a booklet and four 8" x 10" stills.
Soundtrack (1961) ....*MGM (M) 1E2-ST*   61   15-20
Soundtrack (1961) .... *MGM (S) S1E2-ST*   61   20-25
Soundtrack (1961) ....*MCA (S) 39056*   Re   8-10
  Composer: Miklos Rozsa. **Conductor:** Miklos Rozsa.

KING OF THE ENTIRE WORLD
Original Cast (1978) .... *4th Wall Repertory Co. (S) WRC-4*   78   20-25
  Composer: Daniel Pisello. **Conductor:** Kit McClure. **Cast:** 4th Wall Repertory Co.

KING OF THE MOUNTAIN
Soundtrack (1981) ....*No Label Shown (S) No Number Used*   81   20-25
  Promotional picture disc with two soundtrack songs.
  Cast: Deborah Van Valkenburgh.

KING RAT
Soundtrack (1965) ....*Mainstream (M) 56061*   65   30-40
Soundtrack (1965) ....*Mainstream (S) S-6061*   65   40-50
  Composer: John Barry. **Conductor:** John Barry.

KING SOLOMON'S MINES
Soundtrack (1985) .... *Restless (S) 72106-1*   85   8-10
  Composer: Jerry Goldsmith. **Conductor:** Jerry Goldsmith. **Cast:** Hungarian State Opera
  Orchestra.

KING'S ROW

Soundtrack (1942) .... *Chalfont (SE) SDG-305*   79   **$15-20**
Digital recording.
Composer: Erich Wolfgang Korngold. **Conductor:** Charles Gerhardt. **Cast:** National Philharmonic Orchestra.

KING'S STORY

Soundtrack (1967) .... *DRG (S) SL-5185*   80   **8-10**
Composer: Ivor Slaney. **Conductor:** Ivor Slaney. **Cast:** Orson Welles; Flora Robson; Patrick Wymark; David Warner. (With dialogue.)

KINGDOM OF FREE

Soundtrack .... *Custom Fidelity (S) CFS-1816*   **8-12**

KINGS GO FORTH

Soundtrack (1958) .... *Capitol (M) W-1063*   58   **150-175**
Composer: Elmer Bernstein. **Conductor:** Elmer Bernstein.

KIPLING'S JUNGLE BOOK:
see ENCHANTED COTTAGE

KIRI SINGS GERSHWIN

Studiotrack (1987) .... *EMI/Angel (S) 47454*   87   **10-12**
Composer: George Gershwin; Ira Gershwin; others. **Conductor:** John McGlinn.
Cast: Kiri Te Kanawa; New Princess Theater Orchestra.

KISMET

Original Cast (1953) .... *Columbia (EP) A-1100*   54   **10-20**
Original Cast (1953) .... *Columbia (M) ML-4850*   54   **25-30**
Original Cast (1953) .... *Columbia (SE) OS-2060*   59   **15-20**
Original Cast (1953) .... *Columbia (SE) S-32605*   73   **8-10**
Composer: Alexander Borodin; Robert Wright; George Forrest. **Conductor:** Louis Adrian.
Cast: Alfred Drake; Doretta Morrow; Joan Diener; Richard Kiley; Henry Calvin; Richard Oneto; Hal Hackett; Lucy Andonian.

Original Revival Cast (1965) .... *RCA Victor (M) LOC-1112*   65   **10-15**
Original Revival Cast (1965) .... *RCA Victor (S) LSO-1112*   65   **15-20**
Composer: Alexander Borodin; Robert Wright; George Forrest. **Conductor:** Franz Allers.
Cast: Alfred Drake; Ann Jeffreys; Henry Calvin; Don Baddoe; Lee Venora; Richard Banke; Rudy Vejar; Albert Toigo; Anita Alpert.

Studio Cast .... *London (M) PM-55001*   **10-15**
Studio Cast .... *London (S) SP-44043*   **15-20**
Composer: Alexander Borodin; Robert Wright; George Forrest. **Conductor:** Mantovani.
Cast: Robert Merrill; Regina Resnik; Kenneth McKellar; Adele Leigh; Ian Wallace; Mike Sammes Singers.

Studio Cast .... *Capitol (S) SW-2022*   64   **10-15**
Studio Cast .... *Angel (S) S-37321*   73   **8-10**
Composer: Alexander Borodin; Robert Wright; George Forrest. **Conductor:** Van Alexander.
Cast: Gordon MacRae; Dorothy Kirsten; Bunny Bishop; Salli Terri; Richard Levitt.

Soundtrack (1955) .... *MGM (EP) X-3281*   55   **10-20**
Soundtrack (1955) .... *MGM (M) E-3281*   55   **25-30**
Soundtrack (1955) .... *Metro (M) 526*   65   **15-20**
Soundtrack (1955) .... *Metro (SE) MS-526*   65   **15-20**
Soundtrack (1955) .... *MCA (SE) 1424*   Re   **8-10**
Composer: Alexander Borodin; Robert Wright; George Forrest (arranged by Robert Wright and George Forrest). **Conductor:** Andre Previn. **Cast:** Howard Keel; Ann Blyth; Dolores Gray; Vic Damone.

KISMET (continued)

Studiotrack (1952) .... Columbia (M) CL-6275	52	**$20-30**
10-inch LP.		
Studiotrack (1952) .... Columbia (EP) B-399	55	**10-15**
Double EP set.		
Studiotrack (1952) .... Columbia (M) CL-550	55	**15-20**
Conductor: Percy Faith. **Cast:** Percy Faith and His Orchestra.		
Studiotrack (1954) .... Columbia (EP) B-1800	54	**10-15**
Cast: Tony Bennett.		
Studiotrack (1954) .... Mercury (EP) EP 1-3160	54	**10-15**
Cast: Vic Damone; Ross Bagdasarian; Terry Gibbs.		
Studiotrack (1958) .... World Pacific (M) WP-1243	58	**10-15**
Cast: Four Aces; Peggy Lee; Danny Kaye.		
Studiotrack (1954) .... Decca (EP) ED-2117	54	**10-15**
Composer: Alexander Borodin; Robert Wright; George Forrest. **Cast:** Four Aces; Peggy Lee; Danny Kaye.		

KISS ME KATE

Original Cast (1948) .... Columbia (EP) A-200	49	**15-20**
Original Cast (1948) .... Columbia (M) ML-4140	48	**35-40**
Kiss Me Kate was the first original cast performance recorded especially for a long-play album.		
Original Cast (1948) .... Columbia (M) OL-4140	58	**25-30**
Cover was changed promote the TV production of the show. The back cover lists original Broadway cast.		
Original Cast (1948) .... Columbia (SE) OS-2300	63	**15-20**
Original Cast (1948) .... Columbia (SE) S-32609	73	**8-10**
Composer: Cole Porter. **Conductor:** Pembroke Davenport. **Cast:** Alfred Drake; Patricia Morison; Lisa Kirk; Harold Lang; Jack Diamond; Lorenzo Fuller; Annabelle Hill; Edwin Clay; Charles Wood; Eddie Sledge; Fred Davis.		
Original Cast (1948) .... Capitol (M) TAO-1267	59	**15-20**
Includes some members of the original cast.		
Original Cast (1948) .... Capitol (SE) STAO-1267	59	**15-25**
Composer: Cole Porter. **Conductor:** Pembroke Davenport. **Cast:** Alfred Drake; Patricia Morison; Lisa Kirk; Harold Lang; Bob Sands; Ray Drakely; Lorenzo Fuller; Aloysius Donovan; Alex Dubroff.		
London Studio Cast .... World (M) SHB-26		**20-25**
Composer: Cole Porter. **Conductor:** Freddie Bretherton. **Cast:** Patricia Morison; Bill Johnson; Julie Wilson.		
London Studio Cast .... Music for Pleasure (M) MFP-1126		**15-20**
Composer: Cole Porter. **Cast:** Patricia Routledge; David Holliday; Stella Tanner.		
German Studio Cast .... Ariola (S) S-74343		**25-30**
Composer: Cole Porter. **Conductor:** Johannes Fehring. **Cast:** Olive Moorefield; Peter Alexander.		

Studio Cast (1962) .... *Columbia (M) CL-1768*	62	**$15-20**
Studio Cast (1962) .... *Columbia (S) CS-8568*	62	**20-25**
Cast: Earl Wrightson; Lois Hunt; Mary Mayo.		
Studio Cast (1959) .... *RCA Victor (M) LPM-1984*	59	**25-30**
Studio Cast (1959) .... *RCA Victor (S) LSP-1984*	59	**35-40**
Composer: Porter. Conductor: Henri Rene. Cast: Howard Keel; Gogi Grant; Anne Jeffreys.		
Studio Cast (1964) .... *Reprise (M) F-2017*	64	**25-30**
Studio Cast (1964) .... *Reprise (S) FS-2017*	64	**30-35**
Above two have gatefold covers.		
Studio Cast (1965) .... *Reprise (M) F-2017*	65	**20-25**
Studio Cast (1964) .... *Reprise (S) FS-2017*	64	**25-30**
Above two do not have gatefold covers.		

Composer: Cole Porter. Conductor: Morris Stoloff; Ken Lane. Cast: Frank Sinatra; Dean Martin; Sammy Davis Jr.; Jo Stafford; Phyllis McGuire; Hi-Lo's; Lou Monte; Keely Smith; Johnny Prophet; Dinah Shore.

Soundtrack (1953) .... *MGM (M) E-3077*	53	**25-30**
Soundtrack (1953) .... *Metro (M) M-525*	65	**15-20**
Soundtrack (1953) .... *Metro (SE) MS-525*	65	**15-20**
Soundtrack (1953) .... *MCA (SE) 25003*	Re	**8-10**

Composer: Cole Porter. Conductor: Andre Previn. Cast: Kathryn Grayson; Howard Keel; Ann Miller; Keenan Wynn; James Whitmore; Bobby Van; Tommy Rall; Bob Fosse.

TV Soundtrack (1970) .... *Columbia (S) CSS-645*		**35-40**

Shown on cover as "Armstrong Presents Cole Porter's *Kiss Me Kate*."
Composer: Cole Porter. Conductor: Jack Elliott. Cast: Robert Goulet; Carol Lawrence; Jessica Walter; Marty Ingels; Michael Callan; Jules Munshin; Hendra and Ullett.

Soundtrack (1959) .... *Somerset (M) P-9800*	59	**10-15**
Soundtrack (1959) .... *Somerset (S) SF-9800*	59	**10-20**

Composer: Cole Porter. Cast: New World Theatre Orchestra.
Also see ANYTHING GOES; BRIGADOON; CAN-CAN; REPRISE REPERTORY THEATRE

KISS OF THE SPIDER WOMAN

Soundtrack (1985) .... *Island (S) 90475-1*	85	**8-10**
Cast: Sonia Braga; others.		

KISS THEM FOR ME

Soundtrack (1957) .... *Coral (M) CRL-57160*	57	**75-80**
Features big band music of the early '40s.		

Composer: Lionel Newman; others. Conductor: Lionel Newman.

KISSIN' COUSINS

Soundtrack (1964) .... *RCA Victor (M) LPM-2894*	64	**45-60**
Black label, reads "Mono" at bottom.		
Soundtrack (1964) .... *RCA Victor (S) LSP-2894*	64	**45-60**
Black label, RCA silver-top logo.		
Soundtrack (1964) .... *RCA Victor (M) LPM-2894*	65	**20-30**
Black label, reads "Monaural" at bottom.		
Soundtrack (1964) .... *RCA Victor (S) LSP-2894*	65	**20-30**
Black label, RCA white-top logo.		
Soundtrack (1964) .... *RCA Victor (S) LSP-2894*	69	**10-20**
Orange label.		
Soundtrack (1964) .... *RCA Victor (S) AFL1-2894*	77	**10-12**
Soundtrack (1964) .... *RCA Victor (S) AYL1-4115*	81	**8-10**

Composer: Bill Giant; Bernie Baum; Florence Kaye; Sid Tepper; Roy C. Bennett; Fred Wise; others. Conductor: Fred Karger. Cast: Elvis Presley; Scotty Moore (guitar); Harold Bradley (guitar); D.J. Fontana (drums); Floyd Cramer (piano); Bob Moore (bass); Boots Randolph (sax); Jordanaires (vocals).

KITTIWAKE ISLAND
Original Off-Broadway Cast .... *Blue Pear (M) BP-1003* $20-30
   Composer: Alec Wilder; Arnold Sundgaard. Cast: Joe Lautner; Kathleen Murray; G. Wood;
   Lainie Kazan.

KITTY FOYLE
Original Radio Cast .... *Mark '56 (M) 675*   75   8-12
   Cast: Ginger Rogers.

KLUTE
Soundtrack (1971) .... *Warner Bros. (S) WS-1940*   71   100-150
   Composer: Michael Small.

KNACK (AND HOW TO GET IT)
Soundtrack (1965) .... *United Artists (M) UAL-4129*   65   25-30
Soundtrack (1965) .... *United Artists (S) UAS-4129*   65   30-35
Soundtrack (1965) .... *United Artists (S) UA-LA270-G*   74   10-12
Soundtrack (1965) .... *MCA (S) 25109*   Re   8-10
   Composer: John Barry. Conductor: John Barry. Cast: Johnny Delittle.

KNICKERBOCKER HOLIDAY
Original Radio Cast .... *Mark '56 (M) 613*   8-12
Original Radio Cast .... *Joey (M) 7243*   8-12
   Composer: Kurt Weill; Maxwell Anderson. Cast: Walter Houston; Jeanne Madden.
   Also see MISTER IMPERIUM

KNIGHTS OF THE CITY
Soundtrack (1986) .... *Private I (S) SZ-40317*   86   8-10

KNIGHTS OF THE ROUND TABLE
Soundtrack (1953) .... *Varese Sarabande (SE) STV-81128*   80   8-10
   Composer: Miklos Rozsa. Conductor: Muir Mathieson.

KNOCK ON WOOD
Soundtrack (1954) .... *Decca (M) DL-5527*   54   50-60
   Composer: Sylvia Fine. Conductor: Vic Schoen. Cast: Danny Kaye; Lee Gordon Singers;
   Victor Young and His Singing Strings.

KOSHER WIDOW
Original Cast (1959) .... *Golden Crest (M) 4018*   59   40-50
Original Cast (1959) .... *Golden Crest (S) 4018*   59   50-60
   Composer: Sholom Secunda; Molly Picon. Conductor: Sholom Secunda. Cast: Molly Picon;
   Irving Jacobson; Mae Schoenfeld.

KOYAANISQATSI (LIFE OUT OF BALANCE)
Soundtrack (1983) .... *Antilles (S) 90626-1*   83   8-10
   Composer: Philip Glass. Conductor: Philip Glass. Cast: Philip Glass.

KRAFT TELEVISION THEATRE
TV Soundtrack (1957) .... *RKO/Unique (M) LP-127*   57   30-35
TV Soundtrack (1957) .... *RKO/Unique (SE) SLP-D1270*   58   45-50
TV Soundtrack (1957) .... *Golden Tone (M) C-4065*   20-25
   Actual title: *Profile in Music*. Though LP states "conductor Vladimir Selinsky conducts his own scores
   from TV productions," it is simply a reissue of the RKO/Unique LP.
   Composer: Vladimir Selinsky. Conductor: Vladimir Selinsky.

KRAKATOA, EAST OF JAVA
Soundtrack (1969) .... *ABC (S) SOC-8*   69   25-35
   Composer: Frank DeVol; Mack David. Conductor: Frank DeVol. Cast: Barbara Werle.

KRAMER VS. KRAMER
Soundtrack (1979) .... *Columbia (S) 35727*   79 $8-10
Soundtrack (1979) .... *Columbia (S) 35873*   79   8-10
  Composer: Antonio Vivaldi; Henry Purcell.

KRAMER VS. KRAMER (BAROQUE SUITE)
Soundtrack (1980) .... *CBS Masterworks (S) M-35873*   80   10-12
  Composer: Antonio Vivaldi; Henry Purcell. **Cast:** Raymond Leppard; English Chamber
  Orchestra and Max Goberman; New York Sinfonietta.

KRONUS
Soundtrack (1957) .... *Cacophonic (M) CLP-1001*   10-20
  Gatefold cover. Includes eight-page booklet and portrait print of the composers.
  Composer: Paul Sawtell; Bert Shefter.

KRULL
Soundtrack (1983) .... *Southern Cross (S) SCRS-1004*   83   8-12
  Composer: James Horner. **Conductor:** James Horner. **Cast:** London Symphony Orchestra.

KRUPA, GENE, STORY:
see GENE KRUPA STORY

KRUSH GROOVE
Soundtrack (1985) .... *Warner Bros. (S) 1-25295*   85   8-10
  Cast: Sheila E.; Chaka Khan; L.L.; Blow Kurtis; Fat Boys; Debbie Harry; Beastie Boys; Gap
  Band; Force M.D.'s; Run D.M.C.

KUKLA, FRAN AND OLLIE
Studio Cast .... *RCA Victor (EP) Y-425*   53   15-25
  Double 78 rpm EP set.
Studio Cast .... *RCA Victor (EP) Y-423*   53   10-20
  Double 78 rpm EP set.
  Composer: Jack Fascinato. **Conductor:** Jack Fascinato. **Cast:** Fran Allison; Burr Tillstrom;
  Jack Fascinato (piano).
Studio Cast .... *RCA Victor (EP) WY-425*   53   20-35
  Double 45 rpm EP set.
  Composer: Jack Fascinato. **Conductor:** Jack Fascinato. **Cast:** Fran Allison; Burr Tillstrom;
  Jack Fascinato (piano).
  Also see HAPPY MOTHER GOOSE

KUNG-FU
TV Soundtrack (1971) .... *Warner Bros. (S) BS-2726*   73   10-12
  Composer: Jim Helms. **Conductor:** Jim Helms. **Cast:** David Carradine; Keye Luke; Philip
  Ahn; Radames Pera. (With dialogue.)

KURT WEILL CABARET
Original Cast (1963) .... *MGM (M) E-4180*   63   15-20
Original Cast (1963) .... *MGM (S) SE-4180*   63   20-25
  Composer: Kurt Weill. **Conductor:** Abraham Stokman. **Cast:** Martha Schlamme; Will Holt.

KWAMINA
Original Cast (1961) .... *Capitol (M) W-1645*   61   40-50
Original Cast (1961) .... *Capitol (S) SW-1645*   61   60-75
  Composer: Richard Adler. **Conductor:** Colin Romoff. **Cast:** Sally Ann Howes; Terry Carter;
  Brock Peters; Robert Guillaume.
Studiotrack (1961) .... *Mercury (M) MG-20654*   10-20
Studiotrack (1961) .... *Mercury (S) SR-60654*   15-25
  Composer: Richard Adler. **Conductor:** Billy Taylor. **Cast:** Billy Taylor Orchestra.

L

LA BAMBA
Soundtrack (1987) .... *Slash (S) 1-25605*   87   **$8-10**
Composer: Ritchie Valens; Carlos Santana; Miles Goodman; others. **Cast:** Los Lobos; Marshall Crenshaw; Howard Huntsberry; Brian Setzer; Bo Diddley.

LA CAGE AUX FOLLES (BIRDS OF A FEATHER)
Original Cast (1983) .... *RCA Victor (S) HBC1-4824*   83   **8-10**
Composer: Jerry Herman. **Conductor:** Donald Pippin. **Cast:** George Hearn; Gene Barry; Jay Garner; John Weiner; Elizabeth Parrish; Leslie Stevens; William Thomas Jr.; Merle Louise; Walter Charles; Brian Kelly; others.
Soundtrack (1980) .... *Cerberus (S) 0102*   80   **10-12**
Soundtrack (1980) .... *Cerberus (S) CERS-0102*   80   **10-20**
Limited edition pink vinyl pressing.
Composer: Ennio Morricone. **Conductor:** Ennio Morricone.

LA CAGE AUX FOLLES II
Soundtrack (1981) .... *Cerberus (S) CEMS-0107*   81   **10-12**
Composer: Ennio Morricone. **Conductor:** Ennio Morricone.

LA DOLCE VITA (THE SWEET LIFE)
Soundtrack (1961) .... *RCA Victor (EP) LPC-136*   61   **10-15**
Composer: Nino Rota; others.
Soundtrack (1961) .... *RCA Victor (M) FOC-1*   61   **35-40**
Soundtrack (1961) .... *RCA Victor (S) FSO-6*   61   **45-50**
Composer: Nino Rota; others.

LA GRANDE BOURGEOISE
Soundtrack (1974) .... *Cerberus (S) CEMS-0109*   81   **8-10**
Composer: Ennio Morricone. **Conductor:** Ennio Morricone.

LA GUERRE EST FINIE
Soundtrack (1967) .... *Bell (M) 6012*   67   **15-20**
Soundtrack (1967) .... *Bell (S) 6012-S*   67   **20-25**
Composer: Giovanni Fusco. **Conductor:** Jean Gitton.

LA PERICHOLE
Original Cast .... *Met Opera Club (S) MO-713*   **8-12**
Composer: J. Offenbach. **Cast:** Patrice Munsel; Theodor Uppman; Cyril Ritchard.

L'ASSOLUTO NATURALE
Soundtrack (1980) .... *Cerberus (S) CEMS 0112*   81   **8-10**
Composer: Ennio Morricone. **Conductor:** Ennio Morricone.

LA STRADA
Studio Cast (1969) .... *United Artists (S) UAS-6688*   69   **25-30**
Cast: Sir Julian (piano).

LA TRAVIATA
Soundtrack (1983) .... *Elektra/Asylum (S) 60267-1*   83   **10-15**
Double LP set.

LA VOIX HUMAINE (THE HUMAN VOICE)
Original Cast .... *RCA Victor (S) LSS-2385*   **15-20**

LABYRINTH
Composer: Eldon Rathburn.
Soundtrack (1986) .... *EMI America (S) SV-17206*   86   **$8-10**
Composer: Trevor Jones; David Bowie. **Conductor:** Trevor Jones. **Cast:** David Bowie; Trevor Jones.

LADY AND THE TRAMP
Soundtrack (1955) .... *Decca (M) DL-5557*   55   **50-60**
10-inch LP.
Soundtrack (1955) .... *Decca (M) DL-8462*   57   **40-50**
Composer: Peggy Lee; Sonny Burke; Oliver Wallace. **Conductor:** Victor Young.
Cast: Peggy Lee; Sunny Burke (voices used in animated cartoon).
Soundtrack (1955) .... *Disneyland (M) ST-3917*   62   **15-20**
Soundtrack (1955) .... *Disneyland (M) DQ-1231*   63   **10-12**
Soundtrack (1955) .... *Disneyland (M) 3103*   80   **8-10**
Limited edition picture disc.
Composer: Peggy Lee; Sonny Burke; Oliver Wallace. **Conductor:** Sonny Burke; Oliver Wallace.
Cast: Peggy Lee; Sonny Burke; Oliver Wallace
Studiotrack (1955) .... *MGM (EP) X-1145*   55   **10-15**
Cast: Kay Armen; Marion Sisters.
Studiotrack (1955) .... *Capitol (EP) EAXP-3056*   55   **10-20**
Also see CHILDREN, CHILDREN, CHILDREN

LADY BE GOOD
Original London Cast (1924) .... *World (M) SH-124/5*   **20-25**
Original London Cast (1924) .... *Smithsonian (M) R-008*   Re   **8-12**
Original London Cast (1924) ...... *Monmouth Evergreen (SE) MES-7036*   **8-10**
Composer: George Gershwin; Ira Gershwin. **Conductor:** J. Heuvel; Carl Fenton.
Cast: Fred Astaire; Adele Astaire; George Gershwin (piano); William Kent; George Vollaire; Irving Berlin; Victor Arden and Phil Ohman (pianos); Cliff Edwards.

LADY BEWARE
Soundtrack (1987) .... *Scotti Bros. (S) SZ-40971*   87   **8-10**
Composer: Craig Safan. **Cast:** David Hallyday; LaMarca; Craig Safan.

LADY CAROLINE LAMB
Soundtrack (1972) .... *Angel (S) S-36946*   73   **20-25**
Composer: Richard Rodney Bennett. **Conductor:** Marcus Dods. **Cast:** New Philharmonic Orchestra; Peter Mark (viola).

LADY FROM PHILADELPHIA
TV Soundtrack (1957) .... *RCA Victor (M) LM-2212*   57   **25-35**
From the "See It Now" TV series.
Cast: Edward R. Murrow (narration); Marian Anderson; Franz Rupp (piano).

LADY IN CEMENT
Soundtrack (1968) .... *20th Century-Fox (S) S-4204*   68   **12-18**
Composer: Hugo Montenegro; Sammy Fain; others. **Conductor:** Hugo Montenegro.

LADY IN THE DARK
Original Cast (1941) .... *Columbia (M) CL-6249*   53   **$40-50**
Original Cast (1941) .... *Harmony (M) HL-7012*   56   **20-30**
  Composer: Maurice Abravanel. **Conductor:** Maurice Abravanel. **Cast:** Danny Kaye.
Studio Cast (1941) .... *Columbia (M) OL-5990*   63   **20-30**
Studio Cast (1941) .... *Columbia (SE) OS-2390*   63   **25-30**
Studio Cast (1941) .... *Columbia (SE) COS-2390*   Re   **8-10**
  Composer: Kurt Weill; Ira Gershwin. **Conductor:** Lehman Engel. **Cast:** Rise Stevens;
  Adolph Green; John Reardon; Stephanie Augustine; Kenneth Bridges; Roger White.
Studio Cast (1941) .... *RCA Victor (M) LRT-7001*   **30-35**
Studio Cast (1941) .... *RCA Victor (M) LPV-503*   64   **20-25**
  Composer: Kurt Weill; Ira Gershwin. **Conductor:** Leonard Joy. **Cast:** Gertrude Lawrence
  (with quartet).
Original TV Cast (1954) .... *RCA Victor (M) LM-1882*   54   **125-150**
  Composer: Kurt Weill; Ira Gershwin. **Conductor:** Charles Sanford. **Cast:** Ann Sothern;
  Carleton Carpenter; Clay-Warnick Choir.
Original Radio Cast .... *Command Performance (M) LP-10*   **8-10**
  Composer: Kurt Weill; Ira Gershwin. **Cast:** Judy Garland.
  Also see DOWN IN THE VALLEY

LADY SINGS THE BLUES
Soundtrack (1972) .... *Paramount/Dick Strout (S) 181/182*   72   **25-50**
  Labeled "An MRA (Multiple Record Album, serving the requirements of both radio and TV stations)." Has
  complete as well as open-end interviews, including a 15-minute interview with Diana Ross. Includes scripts.
Soundtrack (1972) .... *Motown (S) M-758D*   72   **12-15**
  Double LP set.
  Composer: Michel Legrand; others. **Conductor:** Michel Legrand. **Cast:** Diana Ross (sings
  songs of Billie Holliday).

LADY'S NOT FOR BURNING
Original Cast .... *Decca (M) DL-9508/9*   **50-60**
  Double LP set.

LADYHAWKE
Soundtrack (1985) .... *Atlantic (S) 81248-1*   85   **15-20**
  Composer: Andrew Powell. **Conductor:** Andrew Powell. **Cast:** Philharmonic Orchestra.

LAMBERT'S HOROSCOPE:
see RED SHOES

LAND BEFORE TIME
Soundtrack (1988) .... *MCA (S) 6266*   88   **8-10**
  Conductor: James Horner. **Cast:** James Horner; London Symphony Orchestra; King's
  College Choir; Diana Ross.

LAND OF THE PHARAOHS
Soundtrack (1955) . . . *Elmer Bernstein Film Music Collection (M) FMC-13*   78 $35-50
Also has music from *Gunfight at the O.K. Corral.*
Composer: Dimitri Tiomkin; Leonard Bernstein. **Conductor:** Leonard Bernstein.

LAND RAIDERS
Soundtrack (1970) . . . . *Beverly Hills (S) BHS-21*   70   20-25
Composer: Bruno Nicolai. **Conductor:** Bruno Nicolai.

LANDLORD
Soundtrack (1970) . . . . *United Artists (S) UAS-5209*   70   15-20
Composer: Al Kooper. **Conductor:** Al Kooper. **Cast:** Martha Stewart Singers; Lorraine
Ellison; Manny Green; Joe Farrell; Staple Singers; Al Kooper.

LANGFORD, FRANCES:
see FRANCES LANGFORD PRESENTS

LASERIUM ZODIAC
Soundtrack (1978) . . . . *Polydor (S) 1-6122*   78   8-10

LASSIE:
see MAGIC OF LASSIE

LASSITER
Soundtrack (1984) . . . . *Varese Sarabande (S) STV-81208*   84   8-12
Composer: Ken Thorne. **Conductor:** Ken Thorne. **Cast:** Danny Street.

LAST AMERICAN VIRGIN
Soundtrack (1982) . . . . *Columbia (S) JS-38279*   82   8-10
Composer: Various. **Cast:** Oingo Boingo; Phil Seymour; Tommy Tutone; others.

LAST ANGRY MAN:
see NO SAD SONGS FOR ME

LAST COMMAND:
see COME NEXT SPRING

LAST DRAGON
Soundtrack (1985) . . . . *Motown (S) 6128ML*   85   8-10
Composer: Various. **Cast:** DeBarge; Stevie Wonder; Smokey Robinson; Rockwell; Willie
Hutch: Temptations; Dwight David; Vanity; Alfie; Charlene.

LAST EMBRACE
Soundtrack (1979) . . . . *Varese Sarabande (S) STV-81166*   83   10-15
Composer: Miklos Rozsa. **Conductor:** Miklos Rozsa. **Cast:** Nürnberg Symphony Orchestra;
Albert Dominguez (piano).

LAST EMPEROR
Soundtrack (1987) . . . . *Virgin Movie Music (S) 90690-1*   87   8-10
Composer: Ryuichi Sakamoto; David Byrne; others. **Cast:** David Byrne; Cong Su; Red Guard
Accordion Band; Girls Red Guard Dancers; Ryuichi Sakamoto; Ball Orchestra of Vienna.

LAST METRO
Soundtrack (1980) . . . . *DRG (S) SL-9504*   80   8-10
Composer: Georges Delerue. **Conductor:** Georges Delerue. **Cast:** Lucienne Delyle; Rina
Ketty; Leo Marjane.

LAST OF THE AMERICAN HOBOES
Soundtrack (1978) .... *Beegee (S) BGS-1041* 70   **$15-20**
Composer: Gary Revel; Eddie Downs; others. Conductor: Judd Phillips. Cast: Gary Revel; Chapparral Brothers; Brian Mark; Wayne Storm; Noble "Kid" Chissel; Mike DeTemple.

LAST OF THE SECRET AGENTS
Soundtrack (1966) .... *Dot (M) DLP-3714* 66   **15-20**
Soundtrack (1966) .... *Dot (S) DLP-25714* 66   **20-25**
Composer: Pete King; Neal Hefti. Conductor: Frank Comstock. Cast: Steve Rossi.

LAST OF THE SKI BUMS
Soundtrack (1969) .... *World Pacific (S) WPS-21884* 69   **15-25**
  Orange cover.
Soundtrack (1969) .... *World Pacific (S) WPS-21884* 69   **10-20**
  Blue cover.
Composer: John Blakeley; Jud Strunk; others. Cast: Sandals.

LAST PICTURE SHOW
Soundtrack (1971) .... *Columbia (S) S-31143* 72   **12-15**
Composer: Various. Cast: Tony Bennett; Eddie Fisher; Pee Wee King; Hank Snow; Frankie Laine; Lefty Frizzell; Johnny Ray; Jo Stafford. (Assorted early '50s hits heard in the film).
Studiotrack (1971) .... *MGM (S) 1SE-33* 71   **12-15**
Cast: Hank Williams (collection of his early '50s recordings).

LAST PORNO FLICK
Soundtrack (1974) .... *BRS (S) 103* 75   **10-12**
Composer: Tony Bruno. Conductor: Tony Bruno.

LAST REBEL
Soundtrack (1971) .... *Capitol (S) SW-827* 71   **12-15**
Composer: Jon Lord; Tony Ashton. Cast: Ashton, Gardner and Dyke; Royal Liverpool Symphony Orchestra.

LAST RUN
Soundtrack (1971) .... *MGM (S) 1SE-30* 71   **12-15**
Soundtrack (1971) .... *MCA (S) 25116* Re   **8-10**
Composer: Jerry Goldsmith. Conductor: Jerry Goldsmith. Cast: Steve Lawrence.

LAST STARFIGHTER
Soundtrack (1984) .... *Southern Cross (S) SCRS-1007* 84   **8-10**
Conductor: Craig Safan. Cast: Craig Safan.

LAST SUMMER
Soundtrack (1969) .... *Warner Bros. (S) WS-1791* 69   **15-20**
Composer: John Simon. Conductor: John Simon.

LAST SWEET DAYS OF ISAAC
Original Cast (1970) .... *RCA Victor (S) LSO-1169* 70   **15-20**
Composer: Nancy Ford; Gretchen Cryer. Conductor: Clay Fullum. Cast: Austin Pendleton; Fredericka Weber; Charles Collins; C. David Colson; Louise Heath; John Long; Zeitgeist.

LAST TANGO IN PARIS
Soundtrack (1972) .... *United Artists (S) UA-LA045-F* 72   **10-12**
Composer: Gato Barbieri. Conductor: Gato Barbieri.

LAST TEMPTATION OF CHRIST:
see PASSION

LAST VALLEY
Soundtrack (1971) .... *Dunhill (S) X-50102* 71   **25-35**
Composer: John Barry. Conductor: John Barry.

LAST WALTZ
Soundtrack (1978) .... *Warner Bros. (S) 3WS-3146* 78 $15-20
Triple LP set.
Composer: Various. **Cast:** The Band; Paul Butterfield; Eric Clapton; Neil Diamond; Bob Dylan;
Emmylou Harris; Ronnie Hawkins; Mac "Dr. John" Rebennac; Joni Mitchell; Van Morrison;
Staples; Ringo Starr; Muddy Waters; Ron Wood; Neil Young.

LATE GREAT PLANET EARTH
Soundtrack .... *RCR Productions (S) ACAB-10022* 76 10-12
Cast: Hal Lindsey; Orson Welles.

LATE NITE COMIC (A NEW AMERICAN MUSICAL)
Original Cast .... *Original Cast (S) ORC-8843* 8-10
Cast: Brian Gari; Michael McAssey; Julie Budd; Robin Kaiser.

LAUGH-IN:
see ROWEN AND MARTIN'S LAUGH-IN

LAURA: DAVID RAKSIN CONDUCTS HIS GREAT FILM SCORES
Studiotrack .... *RCA Victor (S) ARL1-149* 76 10-12
Also has music from *The Bad and the Beautiful* and *Forever Amber*.
Composer: David Raksin. **Conductor:** David Raksin.

LAWRENCE OF ARABIA
Soundtrack (1962) .... *Colpix (M) LE-1000* 62 35-40
Soundtrack (1962) .... *Colpix (S) LES-1000* 62 40-45
Above two are boxed sets, with booklets.
Soundtrack (1962) .... *Colpix (M) CP-514* 62 20-25
Soundtrack (1962) .... *Colpix (S) SCP-514* 62 25-30
Soundtrack (1962) .... *Colgems (M) COMO-5004* 67 15-20
Soundtrack (1962) .... *Colgems (S) COSO-5004* 67 20-25
Soundtrack (1962) .... *Bell (S) B-1205* 71 10-15
Soundtrack (1962) .... *Arista (S) ABM-4009* Re 8-12
Composer: Maurice Jarre; Kenneth Alford. **Conductor:** Maurice Jarre.
Studiotrack .... *Palace (S) PST-747* 8-10
Also has *Music of the Orient*, by the Alexander Maloof Orchestra.
Composer: Maurice Jarre; Kenneth J. Alford. **Cast:** Bill Ewing (organ); Alexander Maloof
Orchestra.

LAWRENCE WELK SHOW: 10th ANNIVERSARY SPECIAL
TV Soundtrack (1965) .... *Dot (M) DLP-3591* 65 8-12
TV Soundtrack (1965) .... *Dot (S) DLP-25591* 65 10-15
Conductor: Lawrence Welk. **Cast:** Lawrence Welk and featured guests.

LE BAL
Soundtrack (1984) .... *Carrere (S) ZG-39475* 84 10-12
Double LP set.

LE DERNIER AMANT ROMANTIQUE (ROMANTIC LOVER)
Soundtrack (1978) .... *Deram (S) XDEF-160* 78 8-12

LE MANS
Soundtrack (1971) .... *Columbia (S) S-30891* 71 12-15
Composer: Michel Legrand. **Conductor:** Michel Legrand. **Cast:** Peggy Taylor Woodward;
Gene Morford.

LEADBELLY
Soundtrack (1976) .... *ABC (S) ABDP-939* 76 10-12
Composer: Huddie Ledbetter (a.k.a. "Leadbelly"). **Conductor:** Fred Karlin.

LEADER OF THE PACK
Original Cast (1985) ....*Elektra (S) 60409-1*   85   **$10-12**
   Composer: Ellie Greenwich; Jeff Barry. **Cast:** Dinah Manoff; Patrick Cassidy; Dennis Bailey;
   Annie Golden; Darlene Love; Ellie Greenwich.

LEAN ON ME
Soundtrack (1989) ....*Warner Bros. (S) 1-25843*   89   **8-10**
   Composer: Various. **Cast:** Thelma Houston; Winans; Stetsasonic; Roxanne Shante; TKA; Siedah
   Garrett; Force M.D.'s; Riff; Teen Dream; Taja Sevelle; Big Daddy Kane; Guns 'N' Roses.

LEARNING TREE
Soundtrack (1969) ....*Warner Bros. (S) WS-1812*   69   **12-15**
   Composer: Gordon Parks. **Conductor:** Tom McIntosh.

LEAVE IT TO JANE
Original Revival Cast (1959) .... *Strand (M) SL-1002*   59   **30-35**
Original Revival Cast (1959) .... *Strand (S) SLS-1002*   59   **35-40**
Original Revival Cast (1959) .... *Stet (S) DS-15002*   Re   **8-10**
   Composer: Jerome Kern; Guy Bolton; P.G. Wodehouse. **Conductor:** Joseph Stecko.
   Cast: Kathleen Murray; Dorothy Greener; George Segal; Angelo Mango; Jeanne Allen;
   Art Matthews; Ray Tudor.

LEAVE IT TO ME!
Soundtrack (1938) ....*Smithsonian (M) RO-16*   **8-10**
   Composer: Cole Porter. **Cast:** Mary Martin.

LEGAL EAGLES
Soundtrack (1986) ....*MCA (S) 6172*   86   **8-10**
   Digital recording.
   Composer: Elmer Bernstein. **Conductor:** Elmer Bernstein. **Cast:** Rascals; Darryl Hannah;
   Steppenwolf; United Kingdom Symphony.

LEGEND
Original Cast (1976) ....*Theatre Archives (M) TA-7801*   76   **8-10**
   Background music heard during the play.
   Composer: Dan Goggin. **Cast:** Tangerine Dream; Bryan Ferry; Jon Anderson.
Soundtrack (1986) ....*Moment (S) 100*   86   **25-35**
   Composer: Jerry Goldsmith. **Conductor:** Jerry Goldsmith.
Soundtrack (1986) ....*MCA (S) 6165*   86   **10-15**
   Composer: Tangerine Dream. **Cast:** Jon Anderson; Bryan Ferry; Tangerine Dream.

LEGEND OF THE LONE RANGER
Soundtrack (1981) ....*MCA (S) 5212*   81   **8-10**
   Includes Rossini's *William Tell Overture*.
   Composer: John Barry; Gioachino Rossini. **Conductor:** John Barry. **Cast:** Merle Haggard.
   Also see LONE RANGER

LEGEND OF THE SEVEN GOLDEN VAMPIRES
Soundtrack (1974) ....*Warner Bros. (S) K-56085*   74   **8-12**
   Composer: James Bernard. **Conductor:** Philip Martell. **Cast:** Peter Cushing (narration).

LEGENDS OF THE MUSICAL STAGE
Soundtrack (1980) .... *Take Two (S) TT-104*   80   **8-12**
   Warner Brothers film soundtracks, with vocals.
   Composer: Various. **Cast:** Nick Lucas; Harry Richman; Marilyn Miller; Eddie Cantor; Fanny
   Brice; Sophie Tucker; Ethel Merman; Al Jolson.

LEGS DIAMOND
Original Cast (1988) ....*RCA Victor (S) 7982-2-RC*   89   **8-10**
   Composer: Peter Allen. **Cast:** Peter Allen; Julie Wilson; Randall Edwards; Joe Silver.

LENA HORNE: THE LADY AND HER MUSIC
Original Cast (1981) . . . . *Qwest (S) 2QW-3597*   81 $10-15
  Double LP set.
  Conductor: Linda Twine; Bob Freedman. **Cast:** Lena Horne; Clare Bathe; Tyra Ferrell; Vondie
  Curtis-Hall.

LENNY
Original Cast (1971) . . . . *Blue Thumb (S) BTS-9001*   71   20-25
  Double LP set.
  Composer: Tom O'Horgan. **Cast:** Cliff Gorman; Joe Silver; Erica Yohn; Jane House; Robert
  Weil.
Soundtrack (1974) . . . . *United Artists (S) UA-LA359-H*   74   10-12
  Composer: Ralph Burns; others. **Conductor:** Ralph Burns. **Cast:** Dustin Hoffman (monologues
  from his portrayal of Lenny Bruce).

LEOPARD
Soundtrack (1963) . . . . *20th Century-Fox (M) FXG-5015*   63   25-30
Soundtrack (1963) . . . . *20th Century-Fox (S) SXG-5015*   63   40-50
  Composer: Nino Rota. **Conductor:** Franco Ferrara.

LES BICYCLETTES DE BELSIZE:
see TWISTED NERVE

LES GIRLS
Soundtrack (1957) . . . .*MGM (M) E-3590*   57   30-35
Soundtrack (1957) . . . . *MGM (SE) 2SE-S51*   73   15-20
  Double LP set.
  Composer: Cole Porter. **Conductor:** Adolph Deutsch. **Cast:** Gene Kelly; Mitzi Gaynor; Taina
  Elg.

LES LIAISONS DANGEREUSES
Soundtrack (1961) . . . .*Epic (M) LA-16022*   61   25-30
Soundtrack (1961) . . . . *Fontana (M) MGF-27539*   65   12-18
Soundtrack (1961) . . . .*Fontana (SE) SRF-67539*   65   12-18
  Composer: J. Marray. **Cast:** Art Blakey and the Jazz Messengers with Barney Wilen.
Studiotrack (1962) . . . . *Parker (M) PLP-813*   62   12-18
Studiotrack (1962) . . . . *Parker (S) PLPS-813-S*   62   15-20
  Composer: Duke Jordan. **Conductor:** Duke Jordan.

LES MISERABLES
Original Broadway Cast (1987) . . . . *Geffen (S) GHS-24151*   87   8-10

LES POUPEES DE PARIS
Original Cast (1964) . . . . *RCA Victor (M) LOC-1090*   64   20-25
  A show featuring the puppets of Sid and Marty Krofft.
Original Cast (1964) . . . . *RCA Victor (S) LSO-1090*   64   30-35
  Composer: Jimmy Van Heusen; Sammy Cahn. **Conductor:** Joe Reisman. **Cast:** Pearl Bailey;
  Milton Berle; Cyd Charisse; Annie Farge; Gene Kelly; Liberace; Jayne Mansfield; Tony Martin;
  Phil Silvers; Loretta Young; Edith Adams.

LESS THAN ZERO
Soundtrack (1987) . . . .*Def Jam/Columbia (S) SC-44042*   87   8-10
  Composer: Various. **Cast:** Aerosmith; Roy Orbison; Poison; L.; Glen Danzig and Power and
  Fury Orchestra; Slayer; Public Enemy; Black Flames; Joan Jett and Blackhearts; Oran "Juice"
  Jones; Alyson Williams; Bangles.

LET IT BE
Soundtrack (1970) .... *Apple (S) AR-34001*   70   **$15-20**
Soundtrack (1970) .... *Capitol (S) SW-11922*   79   **8-10**
Soundtrack (1970) .... *MFSL (S) 1-109*   79   **15-20**
  Half-speed mastered.
  Composer: John Lennon; Paul McCartney. **Cast:** Beatles.

LET IT RIDE
Original Cast (1961) .... *RCA Victor (M) LOC-1064*   61   **25-30**
Original Cast (1961) .... *RCA Victor (S) LSO-1064*   61   **35-40**
  Composer: Jay Livingston; Ray Evans. **Conductor:** Jay Blackton. **Cast:** George Gobel; Sam
  Levene; Barbara Nichols.

LET MY PEOPLE COME
Original Cast (1974) .... *Libra (S) LR-1069*   74   **8-10**
  Composer: Earl Wilson Jr. **Conductor:** Billy Cunningham. **Cast:** Christine Rubens; Tobie
  Columbus; Lorraine Davidson; Marty Duffy; Joe Jones; Larry Paulette; Shezwae Powell.

LET NO MAN WRITE MY EPITAPH
Soundtrack (1960) .... *Verve (M) MG-4043*   60   **20-25**
Soundtrack (1960) .... *Verve (S) V6-4043*   60   **30-35**
  Cast: Ella Fitzgerald; Paul Smith (piano).

LET THE GOOD TIMES ROLL
Soundtrack (1973) .... *Bell (S) 9002*   73   **10-15**
  Double LP set.
  Composer: Various. **Cast:** Chuck Berry; Chubby Checker; Shirelles; Little Richard; Bo Diddley;
  Coasters; Five Satins; Fats Domino; Danny and the Juniors.
Soundtrack (1974) .... *Kory (S) KK-1003*   **8-12**

LET'S BE HAPPY
Soundtrack (1957) .... *RCA Victor (EP) EPA-4060*   57   **8-15**
  Composer: Nicholas Brodszky; Paul Francis Webster. **Cast:** Tony Martin.

LET'S DO IT AGAIN
Soundtrack (1975) .... *Custom (S) CU-5005*   75   **10-12**
  Composer: Curtis Mayfield; Quinton Joseph; Phillip Upchurch; Gary Thompson; Floyd Morris;
  Joseph Scott; Rich Tufo. **Cast:** Bill Cosby; Sidney Poitier; John Amos; Calvin Lockhart; Staple
  Singers.

LET'S FACE IT
Original Cast (1941) .... *Smithsonian (SE) RO-16*   79   **10-20**
  Composer: Cole Porter. **Conductor:** Johnny Green. **Cast:** Danny Kaye; Mary Jane Walsh.

LET'S GET LOST
Soundtrack (1989) .... *Novus (S) 35054-1-N9*   89   **8-10**

LET'S HAVE A PARADE
Studio Cast (1964) .... *Disneyland (M) DQ-1261*   64   **10-15**
  Cast: Disney cast.

LET'S MAKE LOVE
Soundtrack (1960) .... *Columbia (M) CL-1527*   60   **20-25**
Soundtrack (1960) .... *Columbia (S) CS-8327*   60   **30-35**
Soundtrack (1960) .... *Columbia Special Products (S) ACS-8327*   Re   **8-10**
  Composer: James Van Heusen; others. **Conductor:** Lionel Newman. **Cast:** Marilyn Monroe;
  Yves Montand; Frankie Vaughan.

LETHAL WEAPON
Soundtrack (1987) .... *Warner Bros. (S) 1-25561* 87 **$8-10**
Composer: Michael Kamen; Eric Clapton. Cast: Eric Clapton; David Sanborn; Michael Kamen; Honeymoon Suite.

LETHAL WEAPON 2
Soundtrack (1989) .... *Warner Bros. (S) 1-25985* 89 **8-10**
Composer: Michael Kamen; Eric Clapton; Bob Dylan; George Harrison; Terry Melcher; Mike Love; David Sanborn. Conductor: Michael Kamen. Cast: George Harrison; Eric Clapton; Beach Boys; David Sanborn; Randy Crawford; Michael Kamen.

LETTER
Studiotrack (1940) .... *TT (Tony Thomas) (M) MS-12* 82 **50-75**
One side has an interview with Max Steiner.
Composer: Max Steiner. Conductor: Max Steiner. Cast: Max Steiner; Tony Thomas.

LETTER TO BREZHNEV
Soundtrack (1985) .... *MCA (S) 6162* 85 **8-10**
Cast: Redskins; Fine Young Cannibals; Carmel; Sandie Shaw; Alan Gill; Bronski Beat; Flesh; Certain Ratio; Paul Quinn; Margi Clarke.

LEVANT PLAYS GERSHWIN
Studiotrack (1955) .... *Columbia (M) CL-700* 55 **15-25**
Oscar Levant plays: *An American in Paris, Rhapsody in Blue* and *Concerto in F for Piano and Orchestra.*
Composer: George Gershwin. Conductor: Eugene Ormandy; Artur Rodzinski; Andre Kostelanetz. Cast: Oscar Levant; Philadelphia Orchestra; Philharmonic Symphony Orchestra of New York.

LIAISONS DANGEREUSES, LES:
see LES LIAISONS DANGEREUSES

LIBERACE SHOW: A PROGRAM OF TV FAVORITES
TV Soundtrack (1958) .... *Harmony (M) HL-7154* **10-20**
Cast: Liberace.

LIBERATION OF L.B. JONES:
see FROM THE TERRACE

LICENSE TO DRIVE
Soundtrack (1988) .... *MCA (S) 6241* 88 **8-10**
Composer: Various. Cast: Breakfast Club; Belinda Carlisle; Boys Club; Billy Ocean; New Edition; D.J.; Jonathan Butler; Femme Fatale; Slave Raider; Brenda K. Starr.

LICENSE TO KILL
Soundtrack (1989) .... *MCA (S) 6307* 89 **8-10**
Composer: Various. Conductor: Michael Kamen. Cast: Gladys Knight; Ivory; Tim Feehan; Michael Kamen and National Philharmonic Orchestra; Patti La Belle.

LIE OF THE MIND
Soundtrack .... *Sugar Hill (S) SH-8501* **8-10**
Cast: Red Clay Ramblers.

LIFE AND TIMES OF JUDGE ROY BEAN
Soundtrack (1972) .... *Columbia (S) S-31948* 72 **12-15**
Composer: Maurice Jarre. Conductor: Maurice Jarre. Cast: Andy Williams; Paul Newman. (With dialogue.)

LIFE OF BRIAN
Soundtrack (1979) ....*Warner Bros. (S) BSK-3396*   79   **$8-10**
  Composer: Geoffrey Burgon; Michael Palin; Andre Jacquemin; David Howman; Eric Idle.
  Conductor: Marcus Dods. **Cast:** Terry Jones; Graham Chapman; Michael Palin; John Cleese;
  Eric Idle; Terry Gilliam.

LIFEFORCE
Soundtrack (1985) ....*Varese Sarabande (S) STV-81249*   85   **15-20**
  Composer: Henry Mancini. **Conductor:** Henry Mancini. **Cast:** London Symphony Orchestra.

LIFESPAN
Soundtrack ....*STIP (S) ST-1011*   75   **10-12**
  Composer: Terry Riley.

LIGHT FANTASTIC
Soundtrack (1963) ....*20th Century-Fox (M) FXG-5016*   63   **15-20**
Soundtrack (1963) ....*20th Century-Fox (S) SXG-5016*   63   **20-25**
  Composer: Joseph Leibman. **Conductor:** Judd Woldin.

LIGHT OF DAY
Soundtrack (1987) ....*CBS Associated (S) ZK-40654*   87   **8-10**
  Composer: Various. **Cast:** Barbusters; Fabulous Thunderbirds; Ian Hunter; Dave Edmunds;
  Bon Jovi; Joan Jett and Blackhearts; Michael J. Fox; Rick Cox; Chas Smith; Jon C.

LIGHTER SIDE OF LAURITZ MELCHIOR:
see THRILL OF A ROMANCE

LI'L ABNER
Original Cast (1956) ....*Columbia (EP) A-5150*   56   **10-20**
Original Cast (1956) ....*Columbia (M) OL-5150*   56   **25-30**
  Composer: Gene DePaul; Johnny Mercer. **Conductor:** Lehman Engel. **Cast:** Edith Adams;
  Peter Palmer; Howard St. John; Stubby Kaye; Stanley Simmons; Marc Breaux; Ralph Linn;
  Jack Matthew; Carmen Alvarez; Pat Creighton; Hope Holiday; Deedee Wood.
Soundtrack (1959) ....*Columbia (M) OL-5460*   59   **20-25**
Soundtrack (1959) ....*Columbia (S) OS-2021*   59   **30-35**
  Composer: Gene DePaul; Johnny Mercer. **Conductor:** Nelson Riddle; Joseph J. Lilley.
  Cast: Peter Palmer; Stubby Kaye; Howard St. John.
Studiotrack (1959) ....*Columbia (EP) B-9551*   57   **8-12**
Studiotrack (1959) ....*Columbia (EP) B-9552*   57   **8-12**
  Volume two.
Studiotrack (1959) ....*Columbia (EP) B-9553*   57   **8-12**
  Volume three.
Studiotrack (1959) ....*Columbia (M) CL-955*   57   **15-20**
  Conductor: Percy Faith. **Cast:** Percy Faith and His Orchestra.
Studiotrack (1957) ....*Contemporary (M) C-3533*   57   **20-30**
  Actual title: *Modern Jazz Performance of Li'l Abner.*
  Cast: Shelly Mann; Andre Previn; L. Vinnegan.

LILAC TIME (BLOSSOM TIME)
London Studio (1961) . . . . *Angel (M) 35817*   61 $25-30
London Studio Cast (1961) . . . . *Angel (S) 35817*   61   35-40
   Composer: Franz Shubert; Adrian Ross. **Conductor:** Michael Collins. **Cast:** June Bronhill;
   Thomas Round; John Cameron; Rita Williams Singers.

LILI
Soundtrack (1952) . . . . *MGM (EP) X-1025*   52   10-15
   Composer: Bronislau Kaper. **Conductor:** Hans Sommer; **Cast:** MGM Studio Orchestra.
   Also see EVERYTHING I HAVE IS YOURS

LILI MARLENE
Soundtrack (1981) . . . . *DRG (S) SL 9506*   81   8-10
   Composer: Peer Raben. **Conductor:** Peer Raben.

LILIES OF THE FIELD
Soundtrack (1963) . . . . *Epic (M) LN-26094*   64   20-25
Soundtrack (1963) . . . . *Epic (S) BN-26094*   64   30-35
   Composer: Jerry Goldsmith. **Conductor:** Jerry Goldsmith. **Cast:** Jester Hairston.

LILITH
Soundtrack (1964) . . . . *Colpix (M) CP-520*   64   15-20
Soundtrack (1964) . . . . *Colpix (S) SCP-520*   64   20-25
   Composer: Kenyon Hopkins. **Conductor:** Kenyon Hopkins.

LINK
Soundtrack (1986) . . . . *Varese Sarabande (S) STV-81294*   86   10-15
   Composer: Jerry Goldsmith. **Conductor:** Jerry Goldsmith.

LINUS THE LIONHEARTED
TV Soundtrack (1964) . . . . *Post Cereals (M) No Number Used*   64   10-20
   A Post Cereal mail-order promotional LP for the cartoon show.
   Cast: Sheldon Leonard; Carl Reiner; Gerry Matthews; Bob McFadden; Ruth Buzzi; Jesse White.

LION
Soundtrack (1962) . . . . *London (M) M-76001*   62   275-325
   Composer: Malcolm Arnold. **Conductor:** Malcolm Arnold.

LION IN WINTER
Soundtrack (1968) . . . . *Columbia (S) OS-3250*   68   15-20
   Composer: John Barry. **Conductor:** John Barry. **Cast:** Jane Merrow; Voices of the Accademia
   Monteverdiana.

LION OF THE DESERT
Soundtrack (1981) . . . . *Quality (S) SV-2082*   10-12
Soundtrack (1981) . . . . *Project 3 (S) PR-5107*   81   8-10
   Composer: Maurice Jarre. **Conductor:** Maurice Jarre. **Cast:** London Symphony Orchestra.

LIONHEART
Soundtrack (1987) . . . . *Varese Sarabande (S) STV-81304*   87   10-15
   Composer: Jerry Goldsmith. **Conductor:** Jerry Goldsmith.

LIPSTICK
Soundtrack (1976) . . . . *Atlantic (S) SD-18178*   76   10-12
   Composer: Michel Polnareff. **Conductor:** Michel Polnareff; Jimmie Haskell.

LIQUID SKY
Soundtrack (1982) . . . . *Varese Sarabande (S) STV-81181*   83   10-15
   Composer: Slava Tsukerman; Brenda Hutchinson; Clive Smith.

LIQUIDATOR
Soundtrack (1966)	. . . .*MGM (M) E-4413*	66	**$12-18**
Soundtrack (1966)	. . . . *MGM (S) SE-4413*	66	**15-20**
Soundtrack (1966)	. . . . *MCA (S) 25137*	Re	**8-10**

Composer: Lalo Schifrin. **Conductor:** Lalo Schifrin. **Cast:** Shirley Bassey.

LISZTOMANIA
Soundtrack (1975)	. . . .*A&M (S) SP-4546*	75	**10-12**

Composer: Rick Wakeman; Franz Liszt; Richard Wagner. **Cast:** Roger Daltry; English Rock Ensemble; John Forsythe; Linda Lewis; George Michie; National Philharmonic Orchestra; Paul Nicholas; Rick Wakeman; David Wilde.

LITTLE ABNER:
see LI'L ABNER

LITTLE BOY LOST
Soundtrack (1953)	. . . . *Decca (EP) ED-2085*	53	**10-15**

Cast: Bing Crosby.
Also see ANYTHING GOES

LITTLE DRUMMER BOY:
see MOUSE ON THE MAYFLOWER

LITTLE FAUSS AND BIG HALSY
Soundtrack (1970)	. . . .*Columbia (S) S-30385*	70	**15-20**

Composer: Bob Dylan; Johnny Cash; others. **Cast:** Johnny Cash and the Tennessee Three; Carl Perkins.

LITTLE MARY SUNSHINE
Original Cast (1959)	. . . . *Capitol (M) WAO-1240*	60	**15-20**
Original Cast (1959)	. . . . *Capitol (S) SWAO-1240*	60	**20-25**

Composer: Rick Besoyan. **Conductor:** Glenn Osser; Arnold Goland. **Cast:** Eileen Brennan; William Graham; Elmarie Wendel; John Aniston; John McMartin; Elizabeth Parrish; Mario Siletti.

LITTLE ME
Original Cast (1962)	. . . . *RCA Victor (M) LOC-1078*	62	**15-20**
Original Cast (1962)	. . . . *RCA Victor (S) LSO-1078*	62	**20-30**

Composer: Cy Coleman; Carolyn Leigh. **Conductor:** Charles Sanford. **Cast:** Sid Caesar; Virginia Martin; Nancy Andrews; Swen Swenson; Mort Marshall; Joey Faye; Mickey Deems.
Original Cast (1962)	. . . . *RCA Victor (S) AYL1-4237*	81	**8-10**

Composer: Cy Coleman; Carolyn Leigh. **Conductor:** Charles Sanford. **Cast:** Sid Caesar; Virginia Martin; Nancy Andrews; Swen Swenson; Mort Marshall; Joey Faye; Mickey Deems.

LITTLE NIGHT MUSIC
Original Cast (1973)	. . . . *Columbia (S) KS-32265*	73	**10-12**
Original Cast (1973)	. . . . *Columbia (Q) JS-32265*	73	**10-12**

Composer: Stephen Sondheim. **Conductor:** Harold Hastings. **Cast:** Glynis Johns; Len Cariou; Hermione Gingold; Victoria Mallory; Patricia Elliott; Teri Ralston; Mark Lambert; Gene Varrone.
Original London Cast (1973)	. . . .*RCA Victor (S) LRL1-5090*	73	**8-10**

Composer: Stephen Sondheim. **Conductor:** Ray Cook. **Cast:** Jean Simmons; Hermione Gingold; Joss Ackland; Maria Aitken; Veronica Page.
Soundtrack (1978)	. . . .*Columbia (S) JS-35333*	78	**10-12**

Composer: Stephen Sondheim. **Conductor:** Jonathan Iunick. **Cast:** Elizabeth Taylor; Len Cariou; Diana Rigg; Lesley-Anne Down; Hermione Gingold; Laurence Guittard; Christopher Guard; Chloe Franks.

LITTLE PRINCE
Studio Cast (1974) .... *Pip (S) 6813*   75 $10-12
  Composer: Mort Garson. **Cast:** Richard Burton (narration); John Carradine; Billy Simpson; Jim
  Backus; Jonathan Winters; Claudine Longet; Mark Conrad (dialogue, performing the novel by
  Antoine DeSaint-Exupery).
Soundtrack (1974) .... *ABC (S) ABDP-854*   74   10-12
  Composer: Frederick Loewe; Alan J. Lerner. **Conductor:** Angela Morley. **Cast:** Richard
  Kiley; Bob Fosse; Gene Wilder.

LITTLE ROMANCE
Soundtrack (1979) .... *Varese Sarabande (S) STV-81109*   79   8-10
  Composer: Georges Delerue. **Conductor:** Georges Delerue.

LITTLE SHOP OF HORRORS
Original Cast (1982) .... *Geffen (S) GHSP-2020*   82   8-10
  Composer: Alan Menken; Howard Ashman. **Conductor:** Robert Billig. **Cast:** Ellen Greene;
  Lee Wilkof; Hy Anzell; Frane Luz; Sheila Kay Davis; Leilani Jones; Jennifer Leigh Warren;
  Martin P. Robinson; Ron Taylor.
Soundtrack (1986) .... *Geffen (S) GHS-24125*   87   8-12
  Composer: Alan Menken. **Cast:** Rick Moranis; Ellen Greene; Vincent Gardenia; Steve Martin;
  Jim Belushi; John Candy; Levi Stubbs; Christopher Guest; Bill Murray.
Soundtrack (1960) .... *Rhino (S) RNSP-304*   84   10-15

LITTLE SHOWS:
  see BAND WAGON

LITTLE WILLIE JR.'S RESURRECTION
Original Cast (1977) .... *Glori (S) JC-1044*   77   20-25
  Composer: Johnny Thompson; Oscar L. Johnson. **Conductor:** Johnny Thompson.
  Cast: Darrah Gustafson; Tom O'Neill; Belle Weil.

LITTLE WOMEN
TV Soundtrack (1958) .... *Kapp (M) KL-1104*   58   85-100
  One side of this LP has *Music for Little Women* by the Golden Strings.
  Composer: Richard Adler. **Conductor:** Hal Hastings. **Cast:** Jeanne Carson; Rise Stevens;
  Florence Henderson; Bill Hayes; Roland Winters; Zina Bethune.

LITTLEST ANGEL
Studio Cast (1950) .... *Decca (M) DLP-8009*   50   35-45
  Cover has a drawing of and angel and stable scene.
Studio Cast (1950) .... *Decca (M) DL-8009*   Re   20-30
  Cover pictures a little girl. On above two, one side has *Lullaby of Christmas*.
  Composer: C. Paul; Carmen Dragon. **Conductor:** Victor Young. **Cast:** Loretta Young.
  LULLABY OF CHRISTMAS: Gregory Peck.
TV Soundtrack (1969) .... *Mercury (S) SRM-1603*   69   20-25
  Composer: Lan O'Kun. **Cast:** Fred Gwynne (narration); Cab Calloway; Tony Randall;
  Connie Stevens; Johnnie Whitaker; Corinna Manetto.

LITTLEST OUTLAW
Soundtrack (1955) ....*Disneyland (M) DQ-1246*   64   **$8-12**
   Cast: Cliff Edwards (narration, as Jiminy Cricket).

LITTLEST REVUE
Original Cast (1956) ....*Epic (M) LN-3275*   56   **30-40**
Original Cast (1956) ....*Painted Smiles (M) PS-1361*   79   **8-10**
   Composer: Vernon Duke; others. Conductor: Will Irwin. Cast: Beverly Bozeman; Joel Grey;
   Tammy Grimes; Charlotte Rae; Larry Storch; George Marcy; Tommy Morton.

LIVE A LITTLE, STEAL A LOT
see MURPH THE SURF

LIVE AND LET DIE
Soundtrack (1973) ....*United Artists (S) UA-LA100-G*   73   **20-25**
   With none of the cover corners cut.
Soundtrack (1973) ....*United Artists (S) UA-LA100-G*   73   **8-10**
   With cut corner.
   Composer: Paul McCartney; Linda McCartney; George Martin; Monty Norman; others.
   Cast: Paul McCartney and Wings; George Martin and His Orchestra; B.J. Arnau; Harold
   A. "Duke" Degan and the Olympia Brass Band.

LIVE FOR LIFE
Soundtrack (1967) ....*United Artists (M) UAL-4165*   67   **12-15**
Soundtrack (1967) ....*United Artists (S) UAS-5165*   67   **15-20**
Soundtrack (1967) ....*United Artists (S) UA-LA291-G*   74   **8-10**
   Composer: Francis Lai. Conductor: Francis Lai. Cast: Nicole Croisille; Annie Girardot; Louis
   Aldebert.

LIVELY SET
Soundtrack (1964) ....*Decca (M) DL-9119*   64   **15-20**
Soundtrack (1964) ....*Decca (S) DL7-9119*   64   **20-25**
   Composer: Bobby Darin. Conductor: Joseph Gershenson. Cast: James Darren; Wink
   Martindale; Joanie Sommers; Ron Wilson and the Surfaris.

LIVING DESERT
Soundtrack ....*RCA Victor (EP) ERAS-1*   **10-20**
   Includes 24-page illustrated booklet.
Soundtrack (1953) ....*Buena Vista (M) STER-3326*   65   **20-30**
   One side has *The Vanishing Prairie.*
   Composer: Paul J. Smith. Conductor: Paul J. Smith. Cast: Winston Hubler (narration).

LIVING FREE
Soundtrack (1972) ....*RCA Victor (S) LSO-1172*   72   **12-15**
   Film sequel to *Born Free.*
   Composer: Sol Kaplan. Conductor: Sol Kaplan.

LIVING IT UP
Studiotrack (1954) ....*Capitol (EP) EAP 1-533*   54   **25-50**
   Composer: Jule Styne; Bob Hilliard. Conductor: Walter Scharf. Cast: Dean Martin; Jerry Lewis.

LIVING WORD
Soundtrack ....*AEI (S) 3112*   82   **8-10**
   Composer: Edward David Zeliff. Conductor: Edward David Zeliff.

LIZA MINNELLI AT THE WINTERGARDEN
Original Cast (1974) ....*Columbia (S) PC-32854*   74   **10-12**
   Composer: John Kander; Fred Ebb; others. Conductor: Jack French. Cast: Liza Minnelli.

LIZA WITH A "Z"
TV Soundtrack (1972) .... *Columbia (M) K-31762*   72 $10-12
    Includes a sequence from *Cabaret*.
    Composer: Fred Ebb; John Kander; others. **Cast:** Liza Minnelli.

LIZZIE BORDEN
Original Cast (1965) .... *Desto (S)DST-6455/6/7*   65   15-25
    Triple LP set. Original cast of the New York City Opera.
    Composer: Jack Beeson; Kenward Elmslie. **Conductor:** Anton Coppola. **Cast:** Brenda
    Lewis; Ellen Faull; Ann Elgar; Herbert Breattie; Richard Fredericks; Richard Krause.

LOCAL HERO
Soundtrack (1983) .... *Warner Bros. (S) 1-23827*   8-10
Soundtrack (1983) .... *Vertigo (S) VOG-1-3321*   83   8-10
    Composer: Mark Knopfler. **Cast:** Mark Knopfler; Gerry Rafferty.

LOCK UP YOUR DAUGHTERS
Original London Cast (1960) .... *London (M) 5766*   63   30-35
    Composer: Laurie Johnson; Lionel Bart. **Conductor:** Laurie Johnson. **Cast:** Richard
    Wordsworth; John Sharp; Terence Cooper; Robin Wentworth; Stephanie Voss; Madeline
    Newbury; Hy Hazell; Keith Marsh; Brendan Barry.

LOGAN'S RUN
Soundtrack (1976) .... *MGM (S) MG-1-5302*   76   50-60
    Composer: Jerry Goldsmith. **Conductor:** Jerry Goldsmith.

LOLA:
see VERONIKA VOSS AND LOLA

LOLITA
Soundtrack (1962) .... *MGM (M) E-4050*   62   12-15
    Composer: Nelson Riddle; Bob Harris. **Conductor:** Nelson Riddle; Bob Harris.
Soundtrack (1962) .... *MGM (S) SE-4050*   62   15-20
Soundtrack (1962) .... *MCA (S) 39067*   Re   8-10
    Composer: Nelson Riddle; Bob Harris. **Conductor:** Nelson Riddle; Bob Harris.
    Cast: Nelson Riddle and His Orchestra.

LOLLIPOP COVER

Soundtrack (1966) ....*Mainstream (M) 56067* 66   **$12-15**
Soundtrack (1966) ....*Mainstream (S) S-6067* 66   **15-20**
  Composer: Ruby Raksin. **Conductor:** Ruby Raksin. **Cast:** Carol Selfinger.

LONE RANGER

Original Radio Cast ....*Decca (M) K-29/30/31/32* 51   **60-80**
  Set of four 78s: "He Becomes the Lone Ranger" (K-29); "He Finds Silver" (K-30); "He Finds Dan
  Reid" (K-31); "He Helps the Colonel's Son" (K-32). Each disc has a color picture sleeve.
Original Radio Cast ....*Decca (M) K-29/30/31/32* 51   **75-100**
  Set of four 45s: "He Becomes the Lone Ranger" (K-29); "He Finds Silver" (K-30); "He Finds Dan
  Reid" (K-31); "He Helps the Colonel's Son" (K-32). Each disc has a color picture sleeve.
Original Radio Cast ....*Unedited Radio Programs (M) RR4M*   **8-10**
Original Radio Cast ....*Golden Age (M) 5002* 78   **8-10**
  Also see LEGEND OF THE LONE RANGER

LONELY GUY

Soundtrack (1984) ....*MCA (S) 36010* 83   **8-10**
  Composer: Jerry Goldsmith; others. **Cast:** America; Max Carl; Winston Ford; Gerard McMahon.

LONELY LADY

Soundtrack (1984) ....*Allegiance (S) 441* 84   **8-10**
  Cast: Ellis Hall Jr.; Pia Zadora; others.

LONESOME TRAIN

Studio Cast (1944) .... *Decca (M) DL-5054*   **25-40**
  Composer: Earl Robinson; Millard Campell. **Conductor:** Lyn Murray. **Cast:** Burl Ives; Earl
  Robinson; Richard Huey; Lon Clark.

LONG DUEL

Soundtrack (1967) ....*Atco (M) 228* 67   **20-25**
Soundtrack (1967) ....*Atco (S) 228* 67   **25-30**
  Composer: Patrick John Scott. **Conductor:** Patrick John Scott. **Cast:** Vince Hill.

LONG HOT SUMMER

Soundtrack (1958) ....*Roulette (M) R-25026* 58   **85-100**
  Composer: Alex North. **Conductor:** Lionel Newman. **Cast:** Jimmie Rodgers.

LONG JOHN SILVER'S RETURN TO TREASURE ISLAND

Soundtrack (1954) ....*RCA Victor (M) LPM-3279* 55   **150-200**
  10-inch LP.
  Composer: David Buttolph. **Conductor:** David Buttolph.

LONG RIDERS

Soundtrack (1980) ....*Warner Bros. (S) H-3448* 80   **8-10**
  Composer: Ry Cooder. **Cast:** Ry Cooder.

LONG SHIPS

Soundtrack (1964) ....*Colpix (M) CP-517* 64   **50-60**
Soundtrack (1964) ....*Colpix (S) SCP-517* 64   **80-90**
  Composer: Dusan Radic. **Conductor:** Borislav Pascan.

LONGEST DAY

Soundtrack (1962) ....*20th Century-Fox (M) FXG-5007* 62   **25-30**
Soundtrack (1962) ....*20th Century-Fox (S) SXG-5007* 62   **35-40**
  Composer: Paul Anka; others. **Cast:** Lowell Thomas (narration); John Wayne; Rod Steiger;
  Red Buttons; Peter Lawford (with dialogue presenting a condensed version of the film, which
  is about D-Day).

LOOK AT MONACO
TV Soundtrack (1963) .... *Columbia (M) CL-2019*   63 $30-40
  From a CBS-TV special that aired February 17, 1963.
TV Soundtrack (1963) .... *Columbia (SE) CS-8819*   63   60-80
  Composer: Percy Faith. **Conductor:** Percy Faith. **Cast:** Princess Grace [Kelly] (narrator); Percy
  Faith and the Orchestre National De L'Opera De Monte Carlo.

LOOK MA, I'M DANCIN'!
Original Cast (1948) .... *Decca (M) DL-5231*   50   150-175
  10-inch LP.
Original Cast (1948) .... *Columbia Special Products (M) X-14879*   50   8-10
  Also has music from *Arms and the Girl*.
  Composer: Hugh Martin. ARMS AND THE GIRL: Morton Gould; Nancy Fields. **Conductor:**
  Pembroke Davenport. ARMS AND THE GIRL: Frederick Dvonch. **Cast:** Nancy Walker; Harold
  Lang; Sandra Deel; Bill Shirley; Hugh Martin. ARMS AND THE GIRL: Nanette Fabray; George
  Gustaray; Pearl Bailey; Florenz Ames.

LOOKING FOR LOVE
Soundtrack (1964) .... *MGM (M) E-4229*   64   12-15
Soundtrack (1964) .... *MGM (S) SE-4229*   64   15-20
  Composer: Hank Hunter; Stan Vincent; Gary Geld; Richard Udele; Claus Ogerman; others.
  Conductor: Claus Ogerman; Joe Mazzu. **Cast:** Connie Francis.

LOOKING FOR MR. GOODBAR
Soundtrack (1977) .... *Columbia (S) JS-35029*   77   10-12
  Composer: Artie Kane; others. **Cast:** Donna Summer; Commodores with Lionel Richie; Thelma
  Houston; Diana Ross; Bill Withers.

LORD JIM
Soundtrack (1965) .... *Colpix (M) CP-521*   65   30-35
Soundtrack (1965) .... *Colpix (S) SCP-521*   65   40-45
  Composer: Bronislau Kaper. **Conductor:** Muir Mathieson.

LORD LOVE A DUCK
Soundtrack (1966) .... *United Artists (M) UAL-4137*   66   12-15
Soundtrack (1966) .... *United Artists (S) UAS-5137*   66   15-20
  Composer: Neal Hefti. **Conductor:** Neal Hefti.

LORD OF THE FLIES
Studiotrack (1963) .... *Ava (M) A-30*   63   15-20
Studiotrack (1963) .... *Ava (S) AS-30*   63   25-30
  Composer: Raymond Leppard.

LORD OF THE RINGS
Soundtrack (1978) .... *Fantasy (S) LOR-1*   78   **$10-12**
Double LP set.
Soundtrack (1978) .... *Fantasy (S) LOR-PD2*   78   **15-20**
Double picture disc set. Includes booklet.
Composer: Leonard Roseman. **Conductor:** Leonard Roseman.

LORDS OF FLATBUSH
Soundtrack (1974) .... *ABC (S) ABCD-828*   74   **12-15**
Composer: Joe Brooks.

LORELEI
Original Touring Cast (1974) .... *Verve (S) MV-5097-O*   74   **25-30**
Made before Broadway cast performance.
Composer: Jule Styne; Leo Robin. **Conductor:** Milton Rosenstock. **Cast:** Carol Channing;
Dody Goodman; Peter Palmer; John Mineo; Lee Roy Reams; Brandon
Maggart; Jean Bruno; Bob Fitch; Tamara Long.
Original Broadway Cast (1974) .... *MGM (S) M3G-55*   74   **25-30**
Composer: Jule Styne; Leo Robin. **Conductor:** Milton Rosenstock. **Cast:** Carol Channing;
Peter Palmer; Jack Fletcher; Lee Roy Reams; Bob Fitch; Tamara Long; John Mineo.

LOREN, SOPHIA:
see SOPHIA LOREN

LORETTA YOUNG SHOW
TV Soundtrack (1960) .... *Decca (M) DL-4124*   60   **25-30**
TV Soundtrack (1960) .... *Decca (S) DL7-4124*   60   **40-45**
Actual title of above two: *Music for Loretta.*
Composer: Harry Lubin. **Conductor:** Harry Lubin.

LOSS OF INNOCENCE
Soundtrack (1961) .... *Colpix (M) CP-508*   62   **60-70**
Composer: Richard Addinsell. **Conductor:** Richard Addinsell.

LOST ANGELS
Soundtrack (1989) .... *A&M (S) SP-3926*   89   **8-10**
Composer: Various. **Cast:** Apollo Smile; Happy Mondays; Cure; Soundgarden; Poghes; Toni
Childs; Soul Asylum; Raheem; Royal Court of China; John Williams; Wayne Shorter.

LOST BOYS
Soundtrack (1987) .... *Atlantic (S) 81767-1*   87   **8-10**
Composer: Various. **Cast:** Eddie and Tide; Thomas Newman; INXS and Jimmy Barnes; Roger
Daltrey; Lou Gramm; Echo and the Bunnymen; Gerard McMann; Tim Cappello; Mummy Calls.

LOST COMMAND
Soundtrack (1966) .... *Cinema (M) LP-8017*   66   **50-60**
Composer: Franz Waxman. **Conductor:** Han Rossbach.

LOST CONTINENT (ATLANTIS)
Soundtrack (1957) .... *MGM (M) E-3635*   57   **175-200**
Composer: Francesco Lavagnino. **Conductor:** Francesco Lavagnino.

LOST FILMS
(TRAILERS FROM THE FIRST YEARS OF SOUND)
Soundtrack .... *Take Two (M) TT-110*   84   **8-10**
Trailer film music from: *Gold Diggers of Broadway, My Man, Under a Texas Moon, No No Nanette,*
Queen of the Nightclubs, Honky Tonk and *Little Johnny Jones.*
Cast: Nick Lucas; Fanny Brice; Texas Guinan; Sophie Tucker; Eddie Buzzell.

LOST HORIZON
Studio Cast (1937) .... *Decca (M) DL-5154* 50 $25-35
  10-inch LP.
  Cast: Ronald Coleman; others.
Soundtrack (1973) .... *Bell (S) B-1300* 73 12-15
  Composer: Burt Bacharach; Hal David. **Conductor:** Burt Bacharach; Shawn Phillips.

LOST HORIZON: THE CLASSIC FILM SCORES OF DIMITRI TIOMKIN
Studiotrack .... *RCA Victor (S) ARL1-166* 76 10-12
  Also has music from *The Big Sky, Friendly Persuasion, Search for Paradise, The Fourposter* and
  The Guns of Navarone.
  Composer: Dimitri Tiomkin. **Conductor:** Charles Gerhardt.

LOST IN THE STARS
Original Cast (1949) .... *Decca (M) DL-8028* 49 30-40
  Unbanded (continuous play) disc.
Original Cast (1949) .... *Decca (M) DL-9120* 65 15-20
Original Cast (1949) .... *Decca (SE) 79120* 65 15-20
Original Cast (1951) .... *MCA (SE) 2071e* 72 10-12
Original Cast (1949) .... *MCA (SE) 1535* Re 8-10
  Composer: Kurt Weill; Maxwell Anderson. **Conductor:** Maurice Levin. **Cast:** Todd Duncan;
  Inez Matthews; Sheyla Guyse; Herbert Coleman; Frank Roane; Julian Mayfield; Guy Spaull.

LOST MAN
Soundtrack (1969) .... *Uni (S) 73060* 69 12-15
  Composer: Quincy Jones. **Conductor:** Stanley Wilson.

LOST WEEKEND
Soundtrack (1945) .... *TT (Tony Thomas) (M) MR-2* 80 50-100
  Composer: Miklos Rozsa. **Conductor:** Miklos Rozsa.

LOUIS, JOE, STORY:
see JOE LOUIS STORY

LOUISIANA HAYRIDE
Radio Cast (1976) .... *Louisiana Hayride (M) NR-8454* 19 600-700
  Yellow label. Issued only to subscribing radio stations. Features various artists, including guest Bobby
  G. Rice. Featured the first ever issue of Elvis Presley's version of *Tweedle Dee*, from a 1954 Louisiana
  Hayride performance.
Radio Cast (1976) .... *Louisiana Hayride (M) NR-8454* Re 300-350
  Gold label.
  Composer: Various. **Cast:** David Kent (host); Frank Page (emcee); Elvis Presley; Bill Black
  (bass); Scotty Moore (guitar); Bobby G. Rice (vocals).
  Also see ELVIS LIVE AT THE LOUISIANA HAYRIDE

LOUISIANE
Soundtrack (1984) .... *Columbia (S) FM-39353* 84 8-10
  Composer: Claude Bolling. **Cast:** Dee Dee Bridgewater; Baton Rouge Community Choir;
  Claude Bolling.

LOVE AMERICAN STYLE
Soundtrack (1973) .... *Capitol (S) ST-11250* 73 35-40
Soundtrack (1973) .... *Capitol (S) SM-11250* Re 12-15
  Composer: Charles Fox. **Conductor:** Charles Fox.

LOVE AND LET LOVE
Original Cast (1968) .... *Sam Fox (S) X4RS-0371*   68 $75-100
  With custom cover. Original issues had covers with artwork. Reissues came in white jackets. Promotional
  issue only.
Original Cast (1968) .... *Sam Fox (S) X4RS-0371*   68   **45-60**
  With plain white cover.
  Composer: Stanley Gelber; Don Christopher; John Lollos. **Cast:** Marcia Rodd; Tom Lacy;
  John Cunningham; Virginia Vestoff.

LOVE AT FIRST BITE
Soundtrack (1979) .... *Parachute (S) RRD 20526*   79   **8-20**
  12-inch single of *Love Theme.*
Soundtrack (1979) .... *Parachute (S) RRLP-9016*   79   **10-12**
  Composer: Charles Bernstein; others. **Conductor:** Charles Bernstein. **Cast:** Pat Hodges;
  Sidney Barnes.

LOVE AT LARGE
Soundtrack .... *Virgin Movie Music (S) 91359-1*   **8-10**

LOVE BUG
Soundtrack (1969) .... *Disneyland (M) ST-3986*   69   **8-12**
  Story, music, songs, and a 12-page booklet.
  Cast: Buddy Hackett (narration).

LOVE FOR LOVE
Original London Cast (1966) .... *RCA Victor (M) VDM-112*   66   **25-30**
Original London Cast (1966) .... *RCA Victor (S) VDS-112*   66   **35-40**
  Above two are triple LP sets with the complete dramatic play by William Congreve.
  Composer: Marc Wilkinson**Cast:** Sir Laurence Olivier; Lynn Redgrave; Joyce Redman;
  Anthony Hopkins; Len Whiting; Colin Blakely (dialogue).

LOVE GODDESSES
Soundtrack (1965) .... *Columbia (M) CL-2209*   65   **25-30**
Soundtrack (1965) .... *Columbia (S) CS-9009*   65   **30-35**
  Composer: Percy Faith. **Conductor:** Percy Faith. **Cast:** Percy Faith and His Orchestra.

LOVE IN 4 DIMENSIONS
Soundtrack (1966) .... *Request (M) RLP-8090*   66   **20-30**
Soundtrack (1966) .... *Request (S) SRLP-8090*   66   **30-40**
  Composer: Franco Mannio.

LOVE IN THE AFTERNOON
Soundtrack (1957) .... *Verve (EP) EPU-5055*   57   **10-15**
  Composer: Matty Malneck.

LOVE IS A BALL
Soundtrack (1963) .... *Philips (M) PHM-200-082*   63   **15-20**
Soundtrack (1963) .... *Philips (S) PHS-600-082*   63   **25-30**
  Composer: Michel Legrand. **Conductor:** Michel Legrand. **Cast:** Charles Boyer (narration).

LOVE IS A FUNNY THING
Soundtrack (1970) .... *United Artists (S) UAS-5207*   70   **12-15**
  Composer: Francis Lai. **Conductor:** Francis Lai.

LOVE IS A MANY SPLENDORED THING
Soundtrack (1956) .... *Cinema (M) LP-8013*   75   **40-50**
  Also has music from *A Walk in the Spring Rain.*
  Composer: Alfred Newman. **Conductor:** Alfred Newman.

LOVE IS A MANY SPLENDORED THING (AND ALL-TIME MOTION PICTURE THEME FAVORITES)

Studiotrack (1956) .... *Mercury (M) MG-20123* 56 $15-25
   Composer: Sammy Fain. **Conductor:** Richard Hayman. **Cast:** Richard Hayman and His Orchestra.

LOVE IS MY PROFESSION

Soundtrack (1959) ....*Everest (M) LPBR-5076* 60   **30-40**
Soundtrack (1959) .... *Everest (S) SDBR-1076* 60   **70-80**
   One side has music from *Where the Hot Wind Blows.*
   Composer: Rene Cloerec. **Conductor:** Ray Ventura.

LOVE LIFE

Studio Cast (1948) .... *Heritage (M) 0600*   **60-70**
   Composer: Alan J. Lerner; Kurt Weill. **Conductor:** Billy Taylor. **Cast:** Alan J. Lerner; Kaye Ballard; Billy Taylor Quartet.

LOVE MACHINE

Soundtrack (1971) .... *Scepter (S) SPS-595* 71   **10-12**
   Composer: Artie Butler. **Conductor:** Artie Butler. **Cast:** Dionne Warwick.

LOVE ME OR LEAVE ME

Soundtrack (1955) ....*Columbia (EP) B-540* 55   **15-25**
   Triple EP set.
Soundtrack (1955) ....*Columbia (EP) B-2090* 55   **10-15**
Soundtrack (1955) .... *Columbia (M) CL-710* 55   **25-30**
Soundtrack (1955) ....*Columbia (SE) CS-8773* 63   **15-20**
Soundtrack (1955) .... *Columbia Special Products (SE) ACS-8773* 63   **8-10**
   Conductor: Percy Faith. **Cast:** Doris Day (sings the songs of Ruth Etting).

LOVE ME TENDER

Soundtrack (1956) ....*RCA Victor (EP) EPA-4006* 56   **150-200**
   Black label, no dog on label.
Soundtrack (1956) ....*RCA Victor (EP) EPA-4006* 56   **75-80**
   Black label, dog on top. With horizontal silver line across label.
Soundtrack (1956) ....*RCA Victor (EP) EPA-4006* 56   **55-75**
   Black label, dog on top. Without horizontal silver line across label.
Soundtrack (1956) ....*RCA Victor (EP) EPA-4006* 65   **30-40**
   Black label, dog on side.
Soundtrack (1956) ....*RCA Victor (EP) EPA-4006* 69   **30-40**
   Orange label.
   Composer: Elvis Presley; Vera Matson; Ken Darby. **Cast:** Elvis Presley; Ken Darby Trio (vocals).

LOVE SCENE

Studiotrack (1959) ....:....... *Dot (M) DLP-3097* 59   **35-45**
   Has music from *Raintree County, Laura, Place in the Sun,* and others.
   Composer: Elmer Bernstein.

LOVE SONG

Original Cast (1976) .... *Original Cast (S) OC-8022* 76   **8-10**
   Composer: Michael Valenti. **Conductor:** Michael Valenti. **Cast:** Melanie Chartoff; Sigrid Heath; Jess Richards; Robert Manzari.

LOVE STORY

Soundtrack (1970) ....*Paramount (S) PAS-6002* 70   **8-10**
Soundtrack (1970) ....*Paramount (S) PAS-2-700* 71   **20-25**
   Double LP set.
   Composer: Francis Lai. **Conductor:** Francis Lai. **Cast:** Ryan O'Neal; Ali McGraw. (With dialogue.)

LOVE STORY (continued)

Soundtrack (1970) ....*RCA Victor (S) LSC-3210*   71   **$10-12**
  Classical music heard in the film, plus *The Heart Is a Lonely Hunter*, *Romeo and Juliet*, *The Thomas Crown Affair*, and others.
  Conductor: Eugene Ormandy. **Cast:** Eugene Ormandy with the Philadelphia Orchestra.

LOVE THEMES FROM MOTION PICTURES

Soundtrack (1952) ....*Decca (M) DL-5413*   52   **25-35**
  10-inch LP.
  Composer: Miklos Rosza; Franz Waxman; Jay Livingston; Ray Evans; Max Steiner; Erich Wolfgang Korngold; Hugo Friedhofer; Bronislau Kaper; Victor Young; Alfred Newman.
  Conductor: Victor Young. **Cast:** Victor Young and His Orchestra.

LOVEDOLLS SUPERSTAR

Soundtrack ....*SST (S) 062*   **8-10**
  Composer: Various. **Cast:** Redo Kross; Lovedolls; Black Flag; Sonic Youth; Painted Willie; Lawndale; Gone; Anarchy 6; Meat Puppets; Dead Kennedys.

LOVELY TO LOOK AT

Soundtrack (1952) ....*MGM (M) K-150*   52   **15-20**
  Four disc boxed set.
Soundtrack (1952) ....*MGM (M) E-150*   52   **40-50**
  10-inch LP.
Soundtrack (1952) ....*MGM (M) E-3230*   55   **25-30**
  One side of this LP has music from *Show Boat*.
  Composer: Jerome Kern; Oscar Hammerstein II; Otto Harbach. **Conductor:** Carmen Dragon. **Cast:** Howard Keel; Kathryn Grayson; Red Skelton; Ann Miller; Marge Champion; Gower Champion.

LOVERS

Original Cast (1974) ....*Golden Gloves (M) PG-723*   74   **30-35**
  LP indicates stereo but is monaural.
  Composer: Steve Sterner; Peter DelValle. **Conductor:** Steve Sterner. **Cast:** Reathel Bean; Mike Coscone; John Ingle; Martin Rivera; Robert Sevra; Gary Sneed.

LOVERS AND OTHER STRANGERS

Soundtrack (1970) ....*ABC (S) ABCS OC-15*   70   **10-12**
  Composer: Fred Karlin. **Conductor:** Fred Karlin. **Cast:** Larry Meredith; Country Coalition.

LOVES OF ISADORA

Soundtrack (1968) .... *Kapp (S) KRS-5511*   69 $25-30
    This film is also known as *Isadora*.
    Composer: Maurice Jarre. **Conductor:** Maurice Jarre.

LOVING COUPLES

Soundtrack (1980) .... *Motown (S) M8-949*   80   8-10
    Composer: Fred Karlin; Greg Wright. **Cast:** Temptations; Billy Preston; Jermaine Jackson; Syreeta.

LOVING YOU

Soundtrack (1957) .... *RCA Victor (EP) EPA-1-1515*   57   70-90
    Volume one. Black label, dog on top. With horizontal silver line across label.
Soundtrack (1957) .... *RCA Victor (EP) EPA-1-1515*   57   55-75
    Volume one. Black label, dog on top. Without horizontal silver line across label.
Soundtrack (1957) .... *RCA Victor (EP) EPA-1-1515*   65   30-40
    Volume one. Black label, dog on side.
Soundtrack (1957) .... *RCA Victor (EP) EPA-1-1515*   69   30-40
    Volume one. Orange label.
Soundtrack (1957) .... *RCA Victor (EP) EPA-2-1515*   57   70-90
    Volume two. Black label, dog on top. With horizontal silver line across label.
Soundtrack (1957) .... *RCA Victor (EP) EPA-2-1515*   57   55-75
    Volume two. Black label, dog on top. Without horizontal silver line across label.
Soundtrack (1957) .... *RCA Victor (EP) EPA-2-1515*   65   30-40
    Volume two. Black label, dog on side.
Soundtrack (1957) .... *RCA Victor (EP) EPA-2-1515*   69   30-40
    Orange label.
Soundtrack (1957) .... *RCA Victor (M) LPM-1515*   57   100-125
    Black label, reads "Long Play" at bottom.
Soundtrack (1957) .... *RCA Victor (SE) LSP-1515e*   59   75-85
    RCA silver-top logo, reads "Stereo Electronically Reprocessed" at bottom.
Soundtrack (1957) .... *RCA Victor (M) LPM-1515*   63   45-55
    Black label, reads "Mono" at bottom.
Soundtrack (1957) .... *RCA Victor (SE) LSP-1515e*   59   25-30
    Black label, RCA white-top logo.
Soundtrack (1957) .... *RCA Victor (M) LPM-1515*   57   25-30
    Black label, reads "Monaural" at bottom.
Soundtrack (1957) .... *RCA Victor (SE) LSP-1515e*   69   10-20
    Orange or tan label. (Tan label issued in 1976.)
Soundtrack (1957) .... *RCA Victor (SE) AFL1-1515e*   77   8-10
    Composer: Kal Mann; Bernie Lowe; Jerry Leiber; Mike Stoller; Sid Tepper; Roy C. Bennett; Ben Weisman; Aaron Schroeder; others. **Cast:** Elvis Presley; Scotty Moore (guitar); Bill Black (bass); D.J. Fontana (drums); Dudley Brooks (piano); Jordanaires (vocals).

LUCKY LADY

Soundtrack (1976) .... *Arista (S) AL-4069*   76   8-10
    Composer: Ralph Burns; John Kander; Fred Ebb; Cecil Masklin; Bessie Smith; others.
    Conductor: Ralph Burns. **Cast:** Liza Minnelli; Bessie Smith; Burt Reynolds.

LULLABY OF BROADWAY

Soundtrack (1951) .... *Columbia (M) CL-6168*   51   **$40-50**
  10-inch LP.
  Conductor: Frank Comstock. **Cast:** Doris Day; Norman Luboff Choir; Buddy Cole Quartet.
Studiotrack (1956) .... *Coral (M) CRL-57029*   ·56   **15-20**
  Cast: George Auld and His Orchestra.
Studiotrack (1953) .... *London (M) LL-1426*   53   **15-20**
  Cast: Woolf Phillips and His Orchestra.

LULLABY OF CHRISTMAS:
see LITTLEST ANGEL

LUM 'N ABNER

Original Radio Cast .... *Golden Age (M) 5022*   78   **8-10**

LURE OF THE GRAND CANYON

Studio Cast (1961) .... *Columbia (M) CL-1622*   61   **20-25**
Studio Cast (1961) .... *Columbia (S) CS-8422*   61   **25-35**
  Conductor: Andre Kostelanetz. **Cast:** Johnny Cash (narration); Andre Kostelanetz Orchestra.
  Also see GRAND CANYON SUITE

LUST FOR LIFE

Soundtrack (1956) .... *Decca (M) DL-10015*   56   **25-35**
Soundtrack (1956) .... *Decca (SE) DL-710015*   59   **40-45**
  One side, titled *Background to Violence*, has music from three other Roza films: *Brute Force*,
  The Killers and *The Naked City*.
  Composer: Miklos Rozsa. **Conductor:** Miklos Rozsa.

LUTE SONG

Original Cast (1946) .... *Decca (M) DL-8030*   50   **50-60**
  One side has music from *On the Town*.
  Composer: Raymond Scott; Bernard Hanighen. **Conductor:** Raymond Scott. ON THE TOWN:
  Lyn Murray; Leonard Jay; Tutti Camarata. **Cast:** Mary Martin (both). ON THE TOWN: Betty
  Comden; Adolph Green; Nancy Walker.

LUTHER

Soundtrack (1973) .... *Caedmon (S) TRS-363*   73   **25-50**
  Double LP set.

M

M*A*S*H
Soundtrack (1970) .... *Columbia (S) OS-3520*   70 $10-15
Soundtrack (1970) .... *Columbia (S) S-32753*   73   8-12
   Composer: Johnny Mandel; others. **Cast:** Donald Sutherland; Elliott Gould; Sally Kellerman;
   Robert Duvall; Tom Skerritt; Gary Burghoff; Jo Ann Pflugg; Fred Williamson. (With dialogue.)
   This issue (S-32753) has Ahmad Jamal's recording of the M*A*S*H theme, which is not on
   Columbia OS-3520.

M-SQUAD
TV Soundtrack (1958) .... *RCA Victor (M) LPM-2062*   59   20-25
TV Soundtrack (1958) .... *RCA Victor (S) LSP-2062*   59   35-40
   Composer: John Williams; Stanley Wilson; Count Basie; Benny Carter. **Conductor:** Stanley
   Wilson.

MA PERKINS
Original Radio Cast .... *Golden Age (M) 5015*   78   8-10

MAC AND ME
Soundtrack (1988) .... *Curb (S) CRB-10401*   88   8-10

MacARTHUR
Soundtrack (1977) .... *MCA (S) 2287*   77   10-15
   Composer: Jerry Goldsmith. **Conductor:** Jerry Goldsmith.

MACBETH
Studio Cast (1953) .... *RCA Victor (M) LM-6010*   53   40-50
   Double LP boxed set with booklet. Has dialogue and minimal sound effects.
   Cast: Alec Guinness; Pamela Brown; Anthony Service; Andrew Cruickshank; Robin Bailey;
   Rachel Gurney; John Bushelle; Gabrielle Blunt; Mary O'Farrell; Margaret Vines; Philip Guard;
   Stanley Van Beers; Mark Dignan; Jill Nyasa; Pat Doonan; others.
Studio Cast (1962) .... *Living Shakespeare (M) SM-1/2*   30-35
   Includes complete play booklet. Has music and sound effects.
   Composer: Desmond Leslie. **Conductor:** Cyril Ornadel. **Cast:** Michael Redgrave; Barbara
   Jefford; Michael Benthall; Irene Sutcliffe; Sylvia Coleridge; Barbara Leigh-Hunt; Michael
   Goodliffe; William McAllister; Mark Kingston; Job Stewart; Brian Spink; Roger Grainger;
   Anthony Webb; Charles West; others.

MACBIRD
Original Cast (1967) .... *Evergreen (S) EVR-004*   67   30-40
   Double LP set. A dramatic play by Barbara Garson, with music and songs by John Duffy.
   Composer: John Duffy. **Conductor:** John Duffy. **Cast:** Dalton Dearborn; Jennifer Darling;
   Cleavon Little; Paul Hecht; William Devane; Stacy Keach; Rue McClanahan; John Pleshette.

MACK
Soundtrack (1973) .... *Motown (S) M766L*   73   10-12
   Composer: Willie Hutch. **Cast:** Willie Hutch.

MACK AND MABEL
Original Cast (1974) .... *ABC (S) ABCH-830*   74   15-20
   Composer: Jerry Herman. **Conductor:** Donald Pippin. **Cast:** Robert Preston; Bernadette Peters;
   Lisa Kirk; Stanley Simmonds.

MACKENNA'S GOLD
Soundtrack (1969) .... *RCA Victor (S) LSP-4096*   69   15-25
   Composer: Quincy Jones. **Cast:** Jose Feliciano.

MACKINTOSH AND T.J.
Soundtrack (1975) .... *RCA Victor (S) APL1-1520*   76   **$8-12**
  Composer: Waylon Jennings. Cast: Waylon Jennings; Roy Rogers.

MAD ADVENTURES OF RABBI JACOB
Soundtrack (1974) .... *London (S) PS-652*   74   **8-12**
  Composer: Vladimir Cosma. Conductor: Vladimir Cosma.

MAD DOGS AND ENGLISHMEN:
see JOE COCKER: MAD DOGS AND ENGLISHMEN

MAD MAX
Soundtrack (1980) .... *Varese Sarabande (S) STV-81144*   80   **8-10**
  Composer: Brian May. Conductor: Brian May.

MAD MAX - BEYOND THUNDERDOME
Soundtrack (1985) .... *Capitol (S) SWAV-12429*   85   **8-10**
  Composer: Maurice Jarre. Conductor: Maurice Jarre. Cast: Tina Turner; Royal Philharmonic
  Orchestra.

MAD SHOW
Original Cast (1965) .... *Columbia (M) OL-6530*   65   **35-40**
Original Cast (1965) .... *Columbia (S) OS-2930*   65   **50-55**
  Composer: Mary Rodgers; Stephen Sondheim; Marshall Barer. Conductor: Sam Pottle.
  Cast: Jo Anne Worley; Linda Lavin; MacIntyre Dixon; Paul Sand; Dick Libertini.

MADAME BOVARY
Soundtrack .... *Elmer Bernstein Film Music Collection (M) FMC-12*   **25-50**
  Composer: Miklos Rozsa. Conductor: Elmer Bernstein.
  Also see IVANHOE

MADAME CLAUDE
Soundtrack (1977) .... *Philips (S) 9101-144*   77   **10-12**
  Composer: Serge Gainsbourg. Conductor: Jean Pierre Sabar. Cast: Jane Birkin.

MADAME X
Soundtrack (1966) .... *Decca (M) DL-9152*   66   **20-30**
Soundtrack (1966) .... *Decca (S) DL7-9152*   66   **30-40**
  Composer: Frank Skinner; others. Conductor: Joseph Gersheson.

MADE FOR EACH OTHER
Soundtrack (1971) .... *Buddah (S) BDS-5111*   72   **10-15**
  Composer: Trade Martin. Conductor: Trade Martin.

MADE IN HEAVEN
Soundtrack (1987) .... *Elektra (S) 60729-1*   87   **8-10**
  Composer: Various. Cast: Martha Davis; R.E.M.; Ric Ocasek; Luther Vandross; Nylons;
  Buffalo Springfield; Mark Isham.

MADEMOISELLE MODISTE
Studio Cast (1953) .... *RCA Victor (EP) EPA-480*   53   **15-20**
Studio Cast (1953) .... *RCA Victor (M) LPM-3153*   53   **30-40**
  10-inch LP. One side has music from *Naughty Marietta*.
  Composer: Victor Herbert; Henry Blossom. Conductor: Jay Blackton. Cast: Doretta Morrow;
  Felix Knight.

MADRON
Soundtrack (1970) .... *Quad (S) QUS-5001*   70   **20-30**
  Composer: Riz Ortolini. Conductor: Riz Ortolini.

MADWOMAN OF CHAILLOT
Soundtrack (1969) ....*Warner Bros. (S) WS-1805*   69 $20-25
Composer: Michael Lewis. Conductor: Michael Lewis.

MAE WEST - THE ORIGINAL VOICE TRACKS FROM HER GREATEST MOVIES
Soundtrack ....*Decca (M) DL-79176*   70   10-12
Cast: Mae West.

MAGGIE FLYNN
Original Cast (1968) ....*RCA Victor (S) LSOD-2009*   68   20-25
Gatefold cover.
Composer: Hugo Peretti; Luigi Creatore; George David Weiss. Conductor: John Lesko.
Cast: Shirley Jones; Jack Cassidy; Robert Kaye; Jennifer Darling; Sybil Bowan; Austin
Colyer; Stanley Simmonds; William James. (With dialogue.)

MAGIC CHRISTIAN
Soundtrack (1970) ....*Commonwealth United (S) CU-6004*   70   15-20
Known to have at least three sleeve and label variations.
Composer: Ken Thorne; Paul McCartney; others. Cast: Badfinger; Thunderclap Newman;
Ringo Starr; Peter Sellers; Ken Thorne. (With dialogue.)

MAGIC FIRE
Soundtrack (1956) ....*Varese Sarabande (SE) STV-81179*   8-10
Film biography of composer Richard Wagner.
Composer: Richard Wagner.

MAGIC FLUTE
Soundtrack (1976) ....*A&M (S) SP-4577*   76   10-15
Swedish performances of Mozart compositions.
Composer: Wolfgang Amadeus Mozart.

MAGIC GARDEN OF STANLEY SWEETHEART
Soundtrack (1970) ....*MGM (S) 1SE-20*   70   10-15
Composer: Michel Legrand; Bee Gees; War; others. Conductor: Jerry Styner. Cast: Bill
Medley; Eric Burdon and War; Mike Curb Congregation.

MAGIC MOMENTS FROM THE TONIGHT SHOW
TV Soundtrack ....*Casablanca (S) SPNB-1296*   76   20-40
Double LP set. Includes 25th anniversary poster.
Cast: Johnny Carson; Ed McMahon; Doc Severinsen and His Band; Jay Silverheels; Bette Midler;
Groucho Marx; George Carlin; Dean Martin; Pearl Bailey; Lenny Bruce; Billie Holiday; Judy
Garland; Aretha Franklin; Smothers Brothers; Richard M. Nixon; Peter Falk; Ike and Tina
Turner; Lucille Ball; Desi Arnaz Jr.; Buddy Hackett; Jack Benny; Glen Campbell; Don Rickles
Sammy Davis Jr.; George Burns; Joey Bishop; Jerry Lewis; others.

MAGIC OF LASSIE
Soundtrack ....*Peter Pan (M) 155*   10-15
Cast: Pat Boone; Mickey Rooney.
Composer: Richard Sherman; Robert Sherman. Cast: Alice Faye.

MAGIC SHOW
Original Cast (1974) ....*Bell (S) 9003*   74   20-25
Original Cast (1974) ....*Arista (S) 9003*   76   8-10
Composer: Stephen Schwartz. Conductor: Stephen Reinhardt. Cast: Doug Henning; Dale
Soules; David Ogden Stiers; Cheryl Barnes; Anita Morris; Annie McGreevey.

MAGICAL MYSTERY TOUR

Soundtrack (1967) . . . .*Capitol (M) MAL-2835*   67   **$60-75**
   Black label. Gatefold cover. Includes 24-page booklet.
Soundtrack (1967) . . . . *Capitol (S) SMAL-2835*   67   **30-45**
   Black label. Gatefold cover. Includes 24-page booklet.
Soundtrack (1967) . . . .*Apple (S) SMAL-2835*   68   **20-30**
   With Capitol logo on Apple label. Includes booklet.
Soundtrack (1967) . . . . *Capitol (S) SMAL-2835*   69   **20-30**
   Green label. Includes booklet.
Soundtrack (1967) . . . . *Capitol (S) SMAL-2835*   76   **10-12**
   Orange label. Includes booklet.
Soundtrack (1967) . . . . *Capitol (S) C1-48062*   88   **8-10**
Soundtrack (1967) . . . . *MFSL (S) 1-047*   80   **40-50**
   Half-speed mastered.
   Composer: John Lennon; Paul McCartney; George Harrison. **Cast:** Beatles.

MAGNAVOX PRESENTS FRANK SINATRA

TV Soundtrack (1973) . . . . *Reprise (S) PRO-578*   73   **10-15**
   Conductor: Nelson Riddle. **Cast:** Frank Sinatra; Association; Count Basie; Harpers Bizarre;
   Barbara NcNair; Don Ho.

MAGNIFICENT MOVIE MUSIC

Soundtrack . . . .*United Artists (S) UAS-5476*   70   **8-12**
   Movie themes, some from soundtracks.

MAGNIFICENT OBSESSION

Soundtrack (1954) . . . . *Decca (EP) ED-815*   54   **20-30**
   Triple disc set.
Soundtrack (1954) . . . . *Decca (M) DL-8078*   54   **90-100**
Soundtrack (1954) . . . .*Varese Sarabande (M) STV-81118*   81   **8-10**
   Composer: Frank Skinner (based on themes by Chopin, Beethoven, and Bach).
   Conductor: Joseph Gershenson. **Cast:** Universal International Orchestra and Chorus.

MAGNIFICENT ROGUE

Original Radio Cast (1956) . . . .*Radiola (M) MR-1049*   75   **10-12**
   Cast: W.C. Fields; Fred Allen (narration); Ed Wynn; Errol Flynn; Mack Sennett; Baby Leroy;
   Edgar Bergen.

MAGNIFICENT SEVEN

Soundtrack (1960) . . . .*United Artists (M) UAL-3133*   60   **15-20**
Soundtrack (1960) . . . .*United Artists (S) UAS-6133*   60   **20-25**
   Above two both have the main title plus 11 other selections which are not from the film.
   Composer: Elmer Bernstein. **Conductor:** Al Caiola. **Cast:** Al Caiola (guitar).
   Also see RETURN OF THE SEVEN.

MAHOGANY

Soundtrack (1975) . . . . *Motown (S) M6-858S1*   75   **10-12**
   Composer: Michael Masser; others. **Conductor:** Lee Holdridge. **Cast:** Diana Ross.

MAHONEY'S LAST STAND

Soundtrack (1976) . . . .*Atlantic (S) SD-36-126*   76   **8-12**
   Composer: Ron Wood; Ronnie Lane. **Cast:** Ron Wood; Ronnie Lane; Ian McLagan; Bruce
   Rowlands; Rick Grech; Ian Stewart; Kenney Jones; Pete Townshend; Bubby Keys; Jim Price;
   Benny Gallagher; Glynis Johns; Billy Nicholls.

MAID OF THE MOUNTAINS

Original London Cast (1918) . . . .*World (M) SH-169*   81   **35-50**
   Composer: Harold Fraser-Simpson; Harry Graham. **Conductor:** Merlin Morgan. **Cast:** Jose
   Collins; Thorpe Bates; Lauri DeFrece; Mable Sealby.

MAIGRET
TV Soundtrack .... *London (M) LL-3281*   63 $10-15
Themes and music from the BBC-TV show.
Composer: Ron Grainer.

MAIN EVENT
Soundtrack (1979) .... *Columbia (S) JS-36115*   79   8-10
Composer: Paul Jabara; Bob Esty; Bruce Roberts; others. **Conductor:** Bob Esty. **Cast:** Barbra
Streisand; Frankie Valli and the 4 Seasons; Loggins and Messina.

MAJOR DUNDEE
Soundtrack (1965) .... *Columbia (M) OL-6380*   65   35-40
Soundtrack (1965) .... *Columbia (S) OS-2780*   65   50-55
Composer: Daniele Amfitheatrof. **Conductor:** Daniele Amfitheatrof. **Cast:** Mitch Miller's Gang.

MAKE A WISH
Original Cast (1951) .... *RCA Victor (M) LOC-1002*   51   100-125
Original Cast (1951) .... *RCA Victor (M) CBM1-2033*   77   8-10
Composer: Hugh Martin. **Conductor:** Milton Rosenstock. **Cast:** Nanette Fabray; Stephen
Douglass; Helen Gallagher; Harold Lang; Dean Campbell.

MAKE HASTE TO LIVE:
see ETERNAL SEA

MAKE ME AN OFFER
Soundtrack (1955) .... *AEI (M) 1112*   8-10

MAKE MINE MANHATTAN
Studio Cast (1948) .... *Painted Smiles (SE) PS-1369*   79   8-10
One side has music from other revues.
Composer: Richard Lewine; Arnold Horwitt. **Conductor:** Dennis Deal. **Cast:** Nancy Andrews;
Carleton Carpenter; Helen Gallagher; Dolores Gray; Estelle Parsons; Lynn Redgrave; Arthur
Siegel; Elaine Stritch.

MAKING OF THE PRESIDENT, 1960
TV Soundtrack (1960) .... *United Artists (M) UXL-9*   60   25-30
TV Soundtrack (1960) .... *United Artists (S) UXS-59*   60   35-40
Above two are double LP sets.
Composer: Elmer Bernstein; others. **Cast:** Martin Gabel (narration); John F. Kennedy; Richard
M. Nixon (voices used in TV documentary).

MAKING THE GRADE
Soundtrack (1984) .... *Varese Sarabande (S) STV-81204*   84   8-10

MALCOLM X
Soundtrack (1972) .... *Warner Bros. (S) BS-2619*   72   10-12
Cast: Malcolm X.

MALAMONDO
Soundtrack (1964) .... *Epic (M) LN-24126*   64   25-30
Soundtrack (1964) .... *Epic (S) BN-26126*   64   35-40
Composer: Ennio Morricone. **Conductor:** Ennio Morricone. **Cast:** Ken Colman.

MAME
Original Cast (1966) .... *Columbia (M) KOL-6600*   66   10-15
Original Cast (1966) .... *Columbia (S) KOS-3000*   66   15-20
Composer: Jerry Herman. **Conductor:** Donald Pippin. **Cast:** Angela Lansbury; Beatrice Arthur;
Jane Connell; Charles Braswell; Jerry Lanning; Frankie Michaels.
London Studio .... *Musico (S) MOS-1024*   25-30
Composer: Jerry Herman. **Cast:** Beryl Reid; Joan Turner; Keith Knight; Charlie Young.

MAME (continued)
Studio Cast (1966) .... *Epic (S) 15107*   66 $20-25
  Also has music from *Sweet Charity*.
  Composer: Jerry Herman. **Cast:** Buddy Hackett; Ronnie David.
  Also see OPENING NIGHT AT THE WINTERGARDEN - MAME

MAMMY:
see 20 MILLION SWEETHEARTS

MAN AND A WOMAN
Soundtrack (1966) .... *United Artists (EP) UA-5147*   66   10-12
  Stereo EP with cover. White label, promotional issue.
Soundtrack (1966) .... *United Artists (M) UAL-4147*   66   12-15
Soundtrack (1966) .... *United Artists (S) UAS-5147*   66   15-20
  Composer: Francis Lai. **Conductor:** Francis Lai. **Cast:** Pierre Barouh; Nicole Croisille; Braden
  Powell & His Orchestra.
Studiotrack (1966) .... *Liberty (S) LST-7490*   66   8-12
  Composer: Francis Lai. **Cast:** Johnny Mann Singers.

MAN AND A WOMAN: 20 YEARS LATER
Soundtrack (1986) .... *Finnadar (S) 90562-1*   86   8-10
  Composer: Francis Lai.

MAN AND BOY
Soundtrack (1971) .... *Sussex (S) SXBS-7011*   71   10-12
  Composer: Johnny Johnson. **Conductor:** Quincy Jones. **Cast:** Bill Withers; Douglas
  Turner-Ward (monologue).

MAN CALLED ADAM
Soundtrack (1966) .... *Reprise (M) R-6180*   66   15-20
Soundtrack (1966) .... *Reprise (S) RS-6180*   66   25-30
  Composer: Benny Carter; others. **Conductor:** Benny Carter. **Cast:** Sammy Davis Jr.; Mel
  Torme; Louis Armstrong; Nat Adderley.

MAN CALLED BROWN
Original Cast ..... *Brown-Forman Distillers Corporation No Number Used*   10-20
  Produced by Brown-Forman in honor of their 100th anniversary.
  Composer: Raymond Scott; Dick Stern.

MAN CALLED DAGGER
Soundtrack (1967) .... *MGM (M) E-4516*   68   15-20
Soundtrack (1967) .... *MGM (S) SE-4516*   68   20-25
  Composer: Steve Allen; Buddy Kaye. **Conductor:** Ronald Stein. **Cast:** Maureen Arthur.

MAN CALLED FLINTSTONE
Soundtrack (1966) .... *HBR (M) HLP-2055*   67   20-25
  Composer: John McCarthy; Ted Nichols; Doug Goodwin. **Cast:** Mel Blanc; Henry Corden
  (voices heard in feature-length cartoon).

MAN CALLED HORSE
Soundtrack (1970) .... *Columbia (S) OS-3530*   70   12-15
  Composer: Leonard Rosenman. **Conductor:** Leonard Rosenman.

MAN COULD GET KILLED
Soundtrack (1966) .... *Decca (M) DL-4750*   66   15-20
Soundtrack (1966) .... *Decca (S) DL7-4750*   66   20-25
  Composer: Bert Kaempfert. **Conductor:** Bert Kaempfert.

MAN FOR ALL SEASONS
Soundtrack (1966) .... *RCA Victor (M) VDM-116*   66   35-40
  Double LP set.
  Composer: Georges Delerue. **Conductor:** Georges Delerue. **Cast:** Paul Scofield; Robert Shaw;
  Orson Welles; Wendy Hiller; Leo McKern; Susannah York. (With dialogue.)

MAN FROM INTERPOL
TV Soundtrack (1962) .... *Top Rank (M) RM-627*   62 $30-40
TV Soundtrack (1962) .... *Top Rank (S) RS-627*   62   50-60
   Composer: Tony Crombie. Conductor: Tony Crombie.

MAN FROM SHAFT
Studiotrack (1972) .... *MGM (S) 4836*   72   10-12
   Cast: Richard Roundtree.
   Also see SHAFT

MAN FROM THE EAST
Original Cast (1973) .... *Island (S) SMAS-9334*   73   25-30
   Original music from the play.
   Composer: Stomu Yamashita. Conductor: Stomu Yamashita.

MAN FROM U.N.C.L.E.
TV Soundtrack (1965) .... *RCA Victor (M) LPM-3475*   65   25-30
TV Soundtrack (1965) .... *.RCA Victor (S) LSP-3475*   65   35-40
   Composer: Jerry Goldsmith; Morton Stevens; Walter Scharf; Lalo Schifrin.
   Conductor: Hugo Montenegro.
TV Soundtrack (1965) .... *RCA Victor (M) LPM-3574*   66   30-35
   Volume two.
TV Soundtrack (1965) .... *.RCA Victor (S) LSP-3574*   66   40-45
   Volume two.
   Composer: Gerald Fried; Robert Drasnin. Conductor: Hugo Montenegro.
Studiotrack (1965) .... *MGM (S) M-544*   65   10-15
   Actual title: *Man from U.N.C.L.E. and Other Themes.* Has themes from: *Mr. Novak, Daniel Boone,*
   Flipper, Bonanza, Return to Peyton Place, Dr. Kildare, 12 O'Clock High.
   Composer: Milton DeLugg; others. Conductor: Milton DeLugg; David Rose; Leroy Holmes.
   Cast: Milton DeLugg; Richard Chamberlain.

MAN IN THE MIDDLE
Soundtrack (1965) .... *20th Century-Fox (M) TFN-3128*   65   30-40
Soundtrack (1965) .... *20th Century-Fox (S) TFS-4128*   65   40-50
   Composer: Lionel Bart. Conductor: John Barry.

MAN IN THE MOON
Original Cast (1963) .... *Golden (M) LP-104*   63   35-40
   A completely different show than the 1961 space race satire film of the same name.
   Composer: Jerry Bock; Sheldon Harnick. Cast: Marionettes of Bil Baird and Cora Baird; Frank
   Sullivan; Franz Fazakas; Cari Harms; George Baird.

MAN OF A THOUSAND FACES
Soundtrack (1957) .... *Decca (M) DL-8623*   57   85-100
   Biography of Lon Chaney, portrayed in this film by James Cagney.
Soundtrack (1957) .... *Varese Sarabande (M) STV-81121*   8-10
   Conductor: Joesph Gershenson. Cast: Universal International Orchestra.

MAN OF LA MANCHA
Original Cast (1965) .... *Kapp (M) KL-4505*   65   12-18
Original Cast (1965) .... *Kapp (S) KRS-4505*   65   15-20
Original Cast (1965) .... *MCA (S) 2018*   72   10-12
Original Cast (1965) .... *MCA (S) 1672*   Re   8-10
   Composer: Mitch Leigh; Joe Darion. Conductor: Neil Warner. Cast: Richard Kiley; Irving
   Jacobson; Ray Middleton; Robert Rounseville; Joan Diener.
Original London Cast .... *Decca (S) DXSA-7203*   68   20-25
   Double LP set.
   Conductor: Denys Rawson. Cast: Keith Michell; Joan Diener; Bernard Spear.

MAN OF LA MANCHA (continued)
Original London Cast . . . .*MCA (S) 10010* $12-18
   Double LP set. Reissue.
   Conductor: Denys Rawson. **Cast:** Keith Michell; Joan Diener; Bernard Spear.
Original Mexican Cast . . . . *Decca (M) DL-9171*   63   12-18
Studio Cast (1972) . . . .*Columbia (S) S-31237*   72   10-12
   Composer: Mitch Leigh; Joe Darion. **Conductor:** Paul Weston. **Cast:** Jim Nabors; Madeline
   Kahn; Marilyn Horne; Jack Gilford; Richard Tucker; Ron Husman; Irene Clark; David Bender.
Original Mexican Cast . . . . *Decca (S) DL7-9171*   63   15-20
   Conductor: Mario Ruiz Armengol.
Studio Cast (1972) . . . . *Golden (S) 265*   72   8-10
   Children's version.
   Composer: Mitch Leigh; Joe Darion. **Cast:** Richard Kiley.
Soundtrack (1972) . . . .*United Artists (S) UAS-9906*   72   10-12
   Composer: Mitch Leigh; Joe Darion. **Conductor:** Laurence Rosenthal. **Cast:** Peter O'Toole;
   Sophia Loren.
Studio Cast (1965) . . . .*Buena Vista (M) BV-4027*   65   10-15
Studio Cast (1965) . . . . *Buena Vista (S) STER-4027*   65   15-20
   Above two have gatefold covers and bound-in booklets. Has songs and music from the stage play.
   Conductor: Tutti Camarata. **Cast:** Mike Sammes Singers.

MAN WHO WOULD BE KING
Soundtrack (1975) . . . .*Capitol (S) SW-11474*   75   25-35
   Composer: Maurice Jarre. **Conductor:** Maurice Jarre.

MAN WITH A LOAD OF MISCHIEF
Original Cast (1966) . . . .*Kapp (M) KRL-4508*   66   25-30
Original Cast (1966) . . . .*Kapp (S) KRS-5508*   66   35-40
   Composer: John Clifton; Ben Tarver. **Conductor:** Sande Campbell. **Cast:** Alice Cannon;
   Lesslie Nicol; Tom Noel; Reid Shelton; Raymond Thorne; Virginia Vestoff.

MAN WITH BOGART'S FACE
Soundtrack (1980) . . . .*Web (S) LP 104*   81   8-12
   Composer: George Duning. **Conductor:** George Duning.

MAN WITH THE GOLDEN ARM
Soundtrack (1959) . . . . *Decca (EP) ED-2335*   59   5-10
Soundtrack (1959) . . . . *Decca (M) DL-8257*   59   25-30
Soundtrack (1959) . . . .*Decca (S) DL7-8257*   59   30-35
Soundtrack (1959) . . . .*MCA (S) 2043e*   72   8-10
Soundtrack (1959) . . . .*MCA (S) 1528*   Re   5-8
   Composer: Elmer Bernstein. **Conductor:** Elmer Bernstein. **Cast:** Shorty Rogers; Shelly Manne;
   Bud Shank (jazz renditions).

MAN WITH THE GOLDEN GUN
Soundtrack (1974) . . . . *United Artists (S) UA-LA358-G*   74   10-12
   Composer: John Barry; Monty Norman; Don Black. **Conductor:** John Barry.
   Cast: Lulu (title song).

MAN WITHOUT A COUNTRY
Studio Cast (1950) . . . . *Decca (M) DL-8020*   50   20-30
   One side has various patriotic songs.

MAN'S A MAN
Original Cast (1964) . . . .*Spoken Arts (M) 870*   64   10-12
   Musical adaptation of the Brecht play.
   Conductor: Joe Raposo. **Cast:** Joe Raposo (piano).

MANCINI GENERATION
TV Soundtrack (1972) . . . .*RCA Victor (S) LSP-4689*   72   8-12
   Composer: Henry Mancini. **Conductor:** Henry Mancini. **Cast:** Henry Mancini and His Orchestra.

MANHATTAN
Soundtrack (1979) .... *Columbia (S) JS-36020*   79   **$8-10**
   Composer: George Gershwin. **Conductor:** Zubin Mehta. **Cast:** Gary Graffman (piano); New York Philharmonic.

MANHATTAN TOWER
Studio Cast (1950) .... *Decca (EP) EDM-562*   50   **10-20**
   Composer: George Jenkins.
Studio Cast (1956) .... *Capitol (EP) EDM 1-766*   56   **8-12**
   Volume one.
Studio Cast (1956) .... *Capitol (EP) EDM 2-766*   56   **8-12**
   Volume two.
Studio Cast (1956) .... *Capitol (EP) EDM 3-766*   56   **8-12**
   Volume three.
Studio Cast (1956) .... *Capitol (M) T-766*   56   **15-25**
   Composer: Gordon Jenkins. **Cast:** Gordon Jenkins.
Studio Cast (1957) .... *Mercury (M) MG-20226*   57   **15-25**
   Composer: George Jenkins. **Cast:** Patti Page.
   Also see CALIFORNIA

MANHATTEN PROJECT
Soundtrack (1986) .... *Varese Sarabande (S) STV-81282*   86   **8-10**
   Composer: Philippe Sarde. **Conductor:** Harry Rabinowitz.

MANHUNTER
Soundtrack (1986) .... *MCA (S) 6182*   86   **8-10**
   Composer: Various. **Cast:** Iron Butterfly; Prime Movers; Reds; Red 7; Michael Rubini; Shriekback.

MANIAC
Soundtrack (1980) .... *Varese Sarabande (S) STV-81143*   80   **15-20**
   Composer: Jay Chattaway.

MANNIX
TV Soundtrack (1969) .... *Paramount (S) PAS-5004*   69   **15-20**
   Composer: Lalo Schifrin. **Conductor:** Lalo Schifrin.

MANS, LE:
   see LE MANS

MARACAIBO
Soundtrack (1958) .... *Decca (M) DL-8756*   58   **40-45**
   Composer: Laurindo Almeida; others. **Conductor:** Laurindo Almeida. **Cast:** Laurindo Almeida; Jean Wallace.

MARAT (DE) SADE
Original Cast (1966) .... *Caedmon (M) 312M*   66   **15-20**
   Triple LP set.
Original Cast (1966) .... *Caedmon (S) 312S*   66   **20-25**
   Composer: Richard Peaslee; Geoffrey Skelton; Adrian Mitchell. **Conductor:** Patrick Gowers. **Cast:** Clifford Rose; Brenda Kempner; Ruth Baker; Patrick Magee.
Soundtrack (1966) .... *United Artists (M) UAL-4153*   66   **10-15**
   Story of Jean-Paul Marat's torment and assassination.
Soundtrack (1966) .... *United Artists (S) UAS-5153*   66   **15-20**
   Composer: Richard Peaslee; Geoffrey Skelton; Adrian Mitchell. **Conductor:** Patrick Gowers. **Cast:** Glenda Jackson; John Steiner; Jeanette Landis.

MARCH OF THE FALSETTOS
Original Cast (1981) .... *DRG (S) SBL-12581*   81   **8-12**
   Composer: William Finn. **Cast:** M. Rupert; A. Fraser.

MARCO POLO
TV Soundtrack (1982) .... *Arista (S) AL-304*   82   **$8-10**
   Composer: Ennio Morricone. **Conductor:** Ennio Morricone. **Cast:** Dino Asciolla; Unione
   Musicisti di Roma.

MARCO THE MAGNIFICENT
Soundtrack (1966) .... *Columbia (M) OL-6470*   66   **25-35**
Soundtrack (1966) .... *Columbia (S) OS-2870*   66   **35-45**
   Composer: Georges Garvarentz; Charles Aznavour. **Conductor:** Georges Garvarentz.
   Cast: Jerry Vale.

MARDI GRAS
Original Cast (1965) .... *Decca (M) DL-4696*   65   **15-20**
   Music from the Jones Beach Marine Theatre Guy Lombardo musical.
Original Cast (1965) .... *Decca (S) DL7-4696*   65   **25-30**
   Composer: Carmen Lombardo; John Jacob Loeb. **Conductor:** Mitchell Ayers.
Studiotrack (1958) .... *Bell (M) LP-11*   58   **25-30**
   Composer: Sammy Fain; Paul Francis Webster. **Conductor:** Enoch Light. **Cast:** Barry Frank;
   Janet Eden; Ralph Nyland; Lois Winter; Michael Stewart Quartet.
Studiotrack (1958) .... *Waldorf Music Hall (S) MHK-SD-14*   58   **25-30**
   Composer: Sammy Fain; Paul Francis Webster. **Conductor:** Jimmy Carroll. **Cast:** Lou Mc-
   Garity; Milt Hinton; Kenny Davern; Panama Francis; Loren Becker; Dottie Evans; Jack Brown.
Soundtrack (1958) .... *Dot (EP) DEP-1075*   58   **8-15**
   Cast: Pat Boone.

MARIA GOLOVIN
Original Cast (1958) .... *RCA Victor (M) LM-6142*   58   **200-225**
   Triple LP set.
   Composer: Gian Carlo Menotti.

MARIE
Soundtrack (1985) .... *Varese Sarabande (S) STV-81265*   85   **8-10**
   Composer: Francis Lai. **Conductor:** Francis Lai.

MARIGOLD
London Cast .... *AEI (S) 1120*   **8-12**

MARILYN MONROE
Soundtrack .... *Rave (S) SH-2013*   72   **8-12**
   Cast: Marilyn Monroe.
   Also see RIVER OF NO RETURN

MARJOE
Soundtrack (1972) .... *Warner Bros. (S) BS-2667*   72   **10-15**
   Cast: Marjoe Gortner; Rev. Jerry Short; Mattie Clark; Andrae Crouch. (With dialogue.)

MARJORIE MORNINGSTAR
Soundtrack (1958) .... *RCA Victor (M) LOC-1044*   58   **90-100**
   Composer: Max Steiner; Sammy Fain; others. **Conductor:** Ray Heindorf. **Cast:** Gene Kelly.

MARK TWAIN TONIGHT
Original Cast (1959) .... *Columbia (M) OL-5440*   59 $12-15
Original Cast (1959) .... *Columbia (S) OS-2019*   59   15-20
Original Cast (1959) .... *Columbia (M) OL-5610*   61   12-15
  Volume two.
Original Cast (1959) .... *Columbia (S) OS-2030*   61   15-20
  Volume two.
TV Soundtrack (1967) .... *Columbia (M) OL-6680*   67   15-20
  Cast: Hal Holbrook (dialogue, as Mark Twain).
TV Soundtrack (1967) .... *Columbia (S) OS-3080*   67   12-15
  TV version of Holbrook's performance.

MARNIE
Soundtrack (1964) .... *Crimson (M) No Number Used*   64   75-85
  Composer: Bernard Herrmann. Conductor: Bernard Herrmann.
Soundtrack (1964) .... *Soundstage (S) 2306*   8-10
  Composer: Bernard Herrmann.
  Also see GREAT MOVIE THRILLERS

MARRIAGE ITALIAN-STYLE:
see TRIPLE FEATURE

MARRIED TO THE MOB
Soundtrack (1988) .... *Reprise (S) 1-25763*   88   8-10
  Composer: Various. Cast: Ziggy Marley and Melody Makers; New Order; Chris Isaak; Debbie
  Harry; Q. Lazzarus; Voodooist Corporation; Brian Eno; Feelies; Sinead O'Connor; Tom Tom
  Club.

MARRY ME A LITTLE (SONGS BY STEPHEN SONDHEIM)
Original Cast (1981) .... *RCA Victor (S) ABL1-4159*   81   8-10
Original Cast (1981) .... *RCA Victor (S) AGL1-7142*   Re   8-10
  Composer: Stephen Sondheim.

MARRY ME, MARRY ME
Soundtrack (1969) .... *RCA Victor (S) LSO-1160*   69   12-18
  Composer: Emil Stern; others. Conductor: Johnny Spence; Marty Manning; others.
  Cast: Jane Morgan.

MARTIN
Soundtrack (1977) .... *Varese Sarabande (S) VC-81127*   79   8-10
  Composer: Donald Rubinstein. Conductor: Donald Rubinstein.

MARTIN, DEAN:
see DEAN MARTIN

MARVIN AND TIGE
Soundtrack (1983) .... *Capitol (S) ST-12307*   83   8-10
  Composer: Patrick Williams.

MARX BROTHERS - ORIGINAL VOICE TRACKS FROM THEIR GREATEST MOVIES
Soundtrack .... *Decca (S) DL-79168*   69   10-15
  Has music from various Marx Brothers' movies.
  Conductor: Charles Bud Dant. Cast: Marx Brothers.

MARY C. BROWN AND THE HOLLYWOOD SIGN
Studio Cast (1972) .... *United Artists (S) UAS-5657*   72   12-15
  Composer: Dory Previn. Cast: Dory Previn; Joe Osborn; Peter Jameson; David Cohen; Laurindo
  Almeida; Bryan Garofolo.

MARY JANE

Soundtrack (1968) .... *Sidewalk (S) DT-5911*   68 $15-20
    Composer: Mike Curb; Lawrence Brown; Valjean Johns; Guy Hemric.

MARY POPPINS

Studio Cast (1968) .... *Caedmon (S) TC-1246*   68   10-15
    Cast: Maggie Smith; Robert Stephens (narration of stories from the original book by P.L. Travers.)
Studio Cast (1969) .... *Caedmon (S) TC-1269*   69   10-15
    Actual title: *Mary Poppins Comes Back.*
    Cast: Maggie Smith; Robert Stephens (stories from the original book).
Studio Cast (1969) .... *Caedmon (S) TC-1270*   70   10-15
    Actual title: *Mary Poppins and the Banks Family.*
    Cast: Maggie Smith; Robert Stephens (stories from the original book).
Studio Cast (1969) .... *Caedmon (S) TC-1271*   70   10-15
    Actual title: *Mary Poppins Opens the Door.*
    Cast: Maggie Smith; Robert Stephens (stories from the original book).
Studio Cast (1971) .... *Caedmon (S) TC-1348*   71   10-15
    Actual title: *Mary Poppins - Balloons and Balloons.*
    Composer: Richard M. Sherman; Robert B. Sherman. **Cast:** Maggie Smith; Robert Stephens
    (stories from the original book).
Soundtrack (1964) .... *Buena Vista (M) BV-4026*   64   10-15
Soundtrack (1964) .... *Buena Vista (S) STER-4026*   64   15-20
    Above two have gatefold covers and bound-in booklets.
Soundtrack (1964) .... *Buena Vista (S) STER-5005*   Re   8-10
Soundtrack (1964) .... *Disneyland (S) 3104*   81   8-12
    Picture disc.
    Composer: Richard Sherman; Robert Sherman. **Conductor:** Irwin Kostal. **Cast:** Julie Andrews;
    Dick Van Dyke; David Tomlinson; Glynis Johns; Ed Wynn; Karen Dotrice; Matthew Garber.
Soundtrack .... *RCA Victor (S) CSO-111*   Re   30-35
    Same soundtrack as the Buena Vista releases.
    Composer: Richard M. Sherman; Robert B. Sherman**Conductor:** Irwin Kostal. **Cast:** Julie
    Andrews; Dick Van Dyke; David Tomlinson; Glynis Johns; Ed Wynn; others.
Soundtrack (1965) .... *Buena Vista (M) BV-3335*   65   15-20
Soundtrack (1965) .... *Buena Vista (S) STER-3335*   65   20-25
    Film score performed in French.
    Cast: Christiane Legrand; Bob Martin.
Studiotrack (1964) .... *Reprise (M) R-6141*   64   10-15
Studiotrack (1964) .... *Reprise (S) RS-6141*   64   15-20
    Actual title for above two: *Duke Ellington Plays Mary Poppins.*
    Cast: Duke Ellington and His Orchestra.
Studiotrack (1964) .... *Disneyland (M) DQ-1256*   64   10-15
    Actual title: *10 Songs from Mary Poppins.*
    Cast: Marni Nixon; Bill Lee; Richard M. Sherman.
Studiotrack (1965) .... *Hamilton (M) 152*   65   8-12
Studiotrack (1965) .... *Hamilton (S) 12152*   65   10-15
    Actual title for above two: *Songs from Mary Poppins.*
    Cast: Lawrence Welk and His Orchestra.
Studiotrack (1965) .... *Monument (M) M-8034*   65   8-12
Studiotrack (1965) .... *Monument (S) SM-18034*   65   10-15
    Actual title for above two: *A Swinger's Guide to Mary Poppins.*
    Cast: Tupper Saussy Quartet; Charlie McCoy.
Studiotrack (1965) .... *Buena Vista (M) BV-3333*   65   10-12
Studiotrack (1965) .... *Buena Vista (S) STER-3333*   65   12-15
    Actual title for above two: *Let's Fly with Mary Poppins.*
    Cast: Louis Prima; Gia Malone.

Studiotrack (1965) .... *Disneyland (M) DQ-1288*   65 $10-12
    Actual title: *Marching Along with Mary Poppins.*
    Cast: University of California Bruin Band.
Studiotrack (1965) .... *Disneyland (M) L-302*   65   10-12
Studiotrack (1973) .... *RCA Victor/Camden (S) ACLI-0379*   73   8-10
    Composer: Richard M. Sherman; Robert B. Sherman. **Cast:** Living Voices.
Studiotrack .... *Happy Time (S) HT-1034*   8-10
Studiotrack (1964) .... *Vee Jay (M) VJLP-1110*   64   8-12
Studiotrack (1964) .... *Vee Jay (S) SR-1110*   64   10-15
    Actual title for above two: *Songs from Mary Poppins (and Other Songs).*
    Conductor: Ray Walston. **Cast:** Ray Walston's Children's Chorus.

MARY, QUEEN OF SCOTS
Original Cast (1978) .... *MMG (S) 3 MMG-301*   78   25-30
    Triple LP, boxed set. Includes 40-page booklet/libretto. Has the U.S. premiere performance.
    Composer: Thea Musgrave. **Conductor:** Peter Mark.
Soundtrack (1971) .... *Decca (S) 79186*   72   40-45
    Composer: John Barry. **Conductor:** John Barry. **Cast:** Vanessa Redgrave.

MASADA
TV Soundtrack (1981) .... *MCA (S) 5168*   81   8-10
TV Soundtrack (1981) .... *MCA (S) 1564*   81   5-8
    Composer: Jerry Goldsmith. **Conductor:** Jerry Goldsmith.

MASK
Soundtrack (1985) .... *MCA (S) 6140*   85   8-10
    Composer: Various. **Cast:** Steppenwolf; Gary "U.S." Bonds; Steely Dan; Little Richard;
    Lynyrd Skynyrd; Grateful Dead.

MASK AND GOWN
Original Cast (1957) .... *GNP/Crescendo (M) 602*   57   15-25
    Excerpts.
    Composer: T.C. Jones. **Cast:** T.C. Jones.

MASS
Original Cast (1971) .... *Columbia (S) M2-31008*   71   20-25
Original Cast (1971) .... *Columbia (Q) M2Q-31008*   71   20-25
    Above two are double LP, boxed sets with booklets.
    Composer: Leonard Bernstein; Stephen Schwartz. **Conductor:** Leonard Bernstein.
    Cast: Alan Titus; Norman Scribner Choir; Berkshire Boys Choir.

MASTER OF THE WORLD
Soundtrack (1961) .... *Vee Jay (M) VJLP-4000*   61   20-30
Soundtrack (1961) .... *Vee Jay (S) SR-4000*   61   40-50
Soundtrack (1961) .... *Varese Sarabande (S) VC-81070*   Re   8-10
    Composer: Les Baxter. **Conductor:** Calvin Carter.

MATEWAN
Soundtrack (1987) .... *Daring (S) DR-1011*   87   8-10
    Cast: Mason Daring.

MATING URGE
Soundtrack (1958) .... *International (M) LP-7777*   58   35-45
    Composer: Stanley Wilson. **Conductor:** Stanley Wilson.

MATTER OF INNOCENCE
Soundtrack (1968) .... *Decca (M) DL-9160*   68 $15-20
Soundtrack (1968) .... *Decca (S) DL7-9160*   68   20-25
    Composer: Michel Legrand. **Conductor:** Michel Legrand. **Cast:** Matt Monro.

MAURICE
Soundtrack (1987) .... *RCA Victor (S) 6618-1*   87   **8-10**
    Composer: Richard Robbins. **Conductor:** Richard Robbins. **Cast:** Richard Robbins.

MAX MORATH AT THE TURN OF THE CENTURY
Original Cast (1969) .... *RCA Victor (S) LSO-1159*   69   20-25
    Conductor: Fred Karlin. **Cast:** Max Morath (piano).

MAX STEINER - GREAT LOVE THEMES FROM MOTION PICTURES
Soundtrack (1955) .... *RCA Victor (EP) EPA-704*   55   **10-15**
    Includes themes from: *Johnny Belinda, The McConnell Story, The Last Command* and *Helen of Troy.*
Soundtrack (1955) .... *RCA Victor (M) LPM-1170*   55   35-40
    Composer: Max Steiner. **Conductor:** Max Steiner.

MAXIMUM OVERDRIVE:
see WHO MADE WHO

MAYA
Soundtrack (1966) .... *MGM (M) E-4376*   66   15-20
Soundtrack (1966) .... *MGM (S) SE-4376*   66   20-25
    Composer: Riz Ortolani. **Conductor:** Riz Ortolani.
TV Soundtrack (1967) .... *MGM (M) CH-1044*   67   15-20
    Composer: Hans J. Salter. **Cast:** Jay North; Sajid Khan. (With dialogue.)

MAYERLING
Soundtrack (1969) .... *Philips (S) SBL-7876*   69   100-125
    Composer: Francis Lai. **Conductor:** Francis Lai.

MAYOR
Original Cast (1985) .... *New York Music Co. (S) NYM-21*   85   10-15
    Composer: Charles Strouse. **Cast:** Lenny Wolpe; Douglas Bernstein; Marion Caffey; Keith
    Curran; Nancy Giles; Ken Jennings; Ilene Kristen; Kathryn McAteor.

MAYTIME
Original Radio Cast (1944) .... *Pelican (M) LP-121*   10-15
    With the film stars of the 1937 motion picture.
    Composer: Sigmund Romberg; Rida Johnson Young; Cyrus Wood. **Cast:** Jeanette MacDonald;
    Nelson Eddy; Edgar Barrier.

McICAR
Soundtrack (1980) .... *Polydor (S) 1-6284*   80   **8-10**
    Cast: Roger Daltrey.

McLINTOCK
Soundtrack (1963) .... *United Artists (M) UAL-4112* 63 $40-50
Soundtrack (1963) .... *United Artists (S) UAS-5112* 63 50-70
Composer: Frank DeVol. **Conductor:** Frank DeVol.

ME AND BESSIE
Original Cast (1975) .... *Columbia (S) PC-34032* 76 12-15
Conductor: Howlett Smith. **Cast:** Linda Hopkins.

ME AND JULIET
Original Cast (1953) .... *RCA Victor (EP) EOA-458* 53 15-20
Original Cast (1953) .... *RCA Victor (M) EOC-1012* 53 15-25
Original Cast (1953) .... *RCA Victor (M) LOC-1012* 53 50-60
Original Cast (1953) .... *RCA Victor (M) LOC-1098* 65 30-35
Original Cast (1953) .... *RCA Victor (SE) LSO-1098* 65 40-45
Composer: Richard Rodgers; Oscar Hammerstein. **Conductor:** Salvatore Dell'isola.
Cast: Isabel Bigley; Bill Hayes; Joan McCracken; Mark Dawson; Arthur Maxwell; Bob
Fortier; Barbara Caroll Trio.

ME AND MY GIRL
Original Cast (1981) .... *MCA (S) 6196* 81 10-12
Original Cast (1986) .... *EMI (S) PV-53030* Re 8-10
Composer: Noel Gay; Arthur Rose; Douglas Furber. **Cast:** Robert Lindsay; Maryann Plunkett;
George S. Irving.

ME AND THE COLONEL
Soundtrack (1958) .... *RCA Victor (M) LOC-1046* 58 50-60
Composer: George Duning. **Conductor:** George Duning. **Cast:** Danny Kaye.

ME NATALIE
Soundtrack (1969) .... *Columbia (S) OS-3350* 69 15-20
Composer: Henry Mancini. **Conductor:** Henry Mancini. **Cast:** Rod McKuen; Patty Duke.
(With dialogue.)

ME NOBODY KNOWS
Original Cast (1970) .... *Atlantic (S) SD-1566* 70 8-10
Composer: Gary Friedman; Will Holt. **Conductor:** Edward Strauss. **Cast:** Melanie Henderson;
Jose Fernandez; Northern J. Calloway; Beverly Bremers; Irene Cara; Gerri Dean; Douglas Grant.

MEANING OF LIFE
Soundtrack (1983) .... *A&M (S) SP-4931* 83 8-10
Soundtrack (1983) .... *MCA (S) 6121* Re 8-10
Cast: Monty Python.

MEATBALLS
Soundtrack (1979) .... *RSO (S) 1-3056* 79 8-10
Composer: Elmer Bernstein; others. **Conductor:** Elmer Bernstein. **Cast:** Bill Murray; Rick
Dees; Terry Black; Mary MacGregor; David Naughton.

MEDEA
Original Cast (1950) .... *Decca (M) DL-9000* 50 35-40
Dramatic play.
Cast: Judith Anderson.

MEDICAL CENTER
TV Soundtrack (1971) .... *MGM (S) SE-4742* 71 10-12
Also has other Lalo Schifrin scores.
Composer: Lalo Schifrin. **Conductor:** Lalo Schifrin.

MEDICINE BALL CARAVAN
Soundtrack (1971) .... *Warner Bros. (S) BS-2565* 71 **$10-12**
    Composer: Various. **Cast:** Alice Cooper; B.B. King; Youngbloods; Delaney and Bonnie; Sal Valentino and Stoneground; Doug Kershaw.

MEDITERRANEAN HOLIDAY
Soundtrack (1964) .... *London (M) M-76003* 64 **30-45**
Soundtrack (1964) .... *London (S) MS-82003* 64 **60-75**
    On U.K. issues, both film and soundtrack were titled *Flying Clipper*.
    Composer: Riz Ortolani. **Conductor:** Riz Ortolani.

MEDIUM
Original Cast (1947) .... *Columbia (M) OSL-154* 49 **40-50**
    Double LP set. One LP contains *The Telephone*.
    Composer: Gian-Carlo Menotti. **Conductor:** Emanuel Balaban. **Cast:** Marie Powers; Evelyn Keller; Beverly Dame; Frank Rogier; Catherine Mastice.
Studio Cast .... *Columbia (S) MS-7387* **8-12**
    Composer: Gian-Carlo Menotti. **Conductor:** Jorge Mester. **Cast:** Opera Society of Washington; Regina Resnik; Judith Blegen; Emily Derr; Julian Patrick; Claudine Carlson.
Soundtrack (1951) .... *Mercury (M) MGL-7* 51 **80-90**
    Double LP boxed set. Complete recording from the film.
    Composer: Gian-Carlo Menotti. **Conductor:** Thomas Schippers. **Cast:** Anna Maria Alberghetti; Marie Powers; Beverly Dame; Belva Kibler; Donald Morgan. (With dialogue.)

MEET ME IN ST. LOUIS
Studiotrack (1946) .... *Pelican (M) 118* **10-15**
    Recording of a complete dress rehearsal on Dec. 1, 1946, one day before the actual broadcast.
    Cast: Judy Garland; Margaret O'Brien; Tom Drake.
Soundtrack (1944) .... *AEI (M) 3101* Re **8-10**
    Composer: Hugh Martin; others. **Conductor:** Georgie Stoll. **Cast:** Judy Garland.

MEET ME IN ST. LOUIS:
see **HARVEY GIRLS**

MEETINGS WITH REMARKABLE MEN
Soundtrack (1979) .... *Varese Sarabande (S) VC-81129* 79 **8-10**
    Composer: Laurence Rosenthal. **Conductor:** Laurence Rosenthal.

MEGILLA OF ITZIG MANGER
Original Cast (1968) .... *Columbia (S) OS-3270* 68 **35-40**
    Composer: Dov Seltzer; Joe Darion. **Conductor:** Dov Seltzer; Max Meth. **Cast:** Pesach Burstein; Lillian Lux; Mike Burstein.

MELACHRINO ORCHESTRA PLAYS MEDLEYS
FROM "CALL ME MADAM" AND IRVING BERLIN SHOW TUNES
Studiotrack (1954) .... *RCA Victor (EP) EPA-507* 54 **10-15**
    Composer: Irving Berlin. **Conductor:** Melachrino. **Cast:** Melachrino Orchestra.

MELACHRINO ORCHESTRA PLAYS MEDLEYS
FROM "SHOW BOAT" AND "KISS ME KATE"
Studiotrack (1954) .... *RCA Victor (EP) EPA-508* 54 **10-15**
    Composer: Oscar Hammerstein II; Jerome Kern; Cole Porter. **Conductor:** Melachrino. **Cast:** Melachrino Orchestra.

MELACHRINO ORCHESTRA PLAYS MEDLEYS
FROM SHOWS
Studiotrack (1954) .... *RCA Victor (LP) LPM-1008* 54 **15-25**
    Composer: Oscar Hammerstein II; Richard Rodgers; Irving Berlin; Jerome Kern; Cole Porter. **Conductor:** Melachrino. **Cast:** Melachrino Orchestra.

**MELACHRINO ORCHESTRA PLAYS MEDLEYS
FROM "SOUTH PACIFIC" AND "CAROUSEL"**
Studiotrack (1954) ....RCA Victor (EP) EPA-509   54 $10-15
  Composer: Oscar Hammerstein II; Richard Rodgers. **Conductor:** Melachrino.
  Cast: Melachrino Orchestra.

MELBA
Soundtrack (1953) .... RCA Victor (M) LM-7012   53   **50-60**
  10-inch LP. Biography of opera star Nellie Melba.
  Cast: Patrice Munsel; Robert Morley; John McCallum.

MELINDA
Soundtrack (1972) ....Parade (S) 0006   **8-12**
  Composer: Jerry Butler.

MELODY
Soundtrack (1971) .... Atco (S) SD-33-363   71   **10-12**
  Composer: Barry Gibb; Robin Gibb; Maurice Gibb. **Cast:** Bee Gees; Crosby, Stills, Nash
  and Young; Richard Hewson Orchestra.

MEMORIES AUX BRUXELLES
Soundtrack (1959) ....Carlton (M) LP 12/112   59   **15-25**
Soundtrack (1959) .... Carlton (S) STLP 12/112   59   **20-35**
  Cast: Alexander Laszlo.

MEN IN WAR
Soundtrack (1957) ....Imperial (M) LP-9032-W   57   **125-150**
  Monaural, despite labeled as "Recorded in Stereophonic Sound."
  Composer: Elmer Bernstein. **Conductor:** Elmer Bernstein.

MERCHANT IVORY PRODUCTIONS 25th ANNIVERSARY
Soundtrack ....RCA Victor (S) 6658-1-RC16   88   **10-12**
  Double LP set. Soundtrack highlights with various artists.

MERMAN IN VEGAS
Original Cast (1963) .... Reprise (M) R-6062   63   **10-15**
Original Cast (1963) .... Reprise (M) R9-6062   63   **15-20**
  Composer: Various. **Cast:** Ethel Merman.

MERRILY WE ROLL ALONG
Original Broadway Cast (1982) .... RCA Victor (S) CBL1-4197   81   **8-10**
  Includes booklet.
  Composer: Stephen Sondheim. **Cast:** Jim Walton; Ann Morrison; Lonny Price.

MERRY ANDREW
Soundtrack (1958) .... Capitol (M) T-1016   58   **65-70**
  One side of this LP is titled *Big Top Circus Band.*
  Composer: Saul Chaplin; Johnny Mercer. **Conductor:** Nelson Riddle. **Cast:** Danny Kaye;
  Pier Angeli; Salvatore Baccaloni; Robert Coote; Rex Evans.

MERRY CHRISTMAS, MR. LAWRENCE
Soundtrack (1983) .... MCA (S) 6125   83   **8-10**
  Composer: Ryuichi Sakamoto.

MERRY WIDOW
Original Revival Cast (1964) .... RCA Victor (M) LOC-1094   64   **15-20**
Original Revival Cast (1964) .... RCA Victor (S) LSO-1094   64   **25-30**
  Composer: Franz Lehar; Paul Francis Webster. **Conductor:** Franz Allers. **Cast:** Patrice Munsel;
  Robert Wright; Sig Arno; Frank Porretta; Mischa Aver; Joan Weldon; Joseph Leon; Robert Goss.
Original London Revival Cast .... Angel (S) 35816   **20-25**
  Composer: Franz Lehar; Paul Francis Webster. **Conductor:** William Reid. **Cast:** Thomas
  Round; June Bronhill; Howell Glynne; Marion Lowe.

MERRY WIDOW (continued)

Studio Cast (1950) . . . . *Decca (M) DL-8004*   50   **$40-45**
  With 1942 revival cast star.
Studio Cast (1950) . . . . *Decca (M) DL-8819*   58   **20-25**
  Composer: Franz Lehar; Paul Francis Webster. **Conductor:** Isaac Van Grove. **Cast:** Kitty
  Carlisle; Wilbur Evans; Felix Knight.
Studio Cast (1951) . . . . *RCA Victor (M) LK-1020*   51   **25-40**
Studio Cast (1951) . . . . *RCA Victor/Camden (M) CAL-397*   57   **15-25**
  Composer: Franz Lehar; Paul Francis Webster. **Conductor:** Al Goodman. **Cast:** Donald
  Richards; Elaine Malbin; Nino Ventura; Guild Choirsters.
Studio Cast (1953) . . . . *Columbia (M) ML-4666*   53   **30-40**
  With 1943 revival cast star.
Studio Cast (1953) . . . . *Columbia (M) CL-838*   56   **20-25**
  Composer: Franz Lehar; Paul Francis Webster. **Conductor:** Lehman Engel. **Cast:** Dorothy
  Kirsten; Robert Rounseville.
Studio Cast (1964) . . . . *Columbia (M) OL-5880*   64   **10-15**
Studio Cast (1964) . . . . *Columbia (S) OS-2280*   64   **12-15**
  Composer: Franz Lehar; Paul Francis Webster. **Conductor:** Franz Allers. **Cast:** Lisa Della
  Casa; John Reardon; Laurel Hurley.
Studio Cast (1952) . . . . *Capitol (EP) EBF-335*   52   **15-25**
  Double EP set.
Studio Cast (1952) . . . . *Capitol (M) L-335*   52   **35-40**
  10-inch LP.
Studio Cast (1952) . . . . *Capitol (M) T-437*   55   **30-35**
  One side has music from *The Student Prince.*
  Composer: Franz Lehar; Forman Brown; Paul Francis Webster. **Conductor:** George Greeley.
  Cast: Gordon MacRae; Lucille Norman.
Studio Cast . . . . *London (M) A 4233*   **20-25**
  Double LP boxed set. Includes booklet.
  Composer: Franz Lehar. **Conductor:** Robert Stolz. **Cast:** Hilde Gruden; Per Gruden; Waldemar
  Kmentt; Emmy Loose; Karl Donch; Peter Klein; Kurt Equiluz; Marjan Rus; Hans Duhan; Peter
  Preses; Ljubomir Pantscheff; Edith Winkler; others.
Soundtrack (1952) . . . . *MGM (EP) X-157*   52   **15-20**
Soundtrack (1952) . . . . *MGM (M) E-157*   52   **30-35**
  10-inch LP.

Soundtrack (1952) .... *MGM (M) E-3228*   55 $25-30
   One side has music from *Rose Marie*.
   Composer: Franz Lehar (music); Paul Francis Webster (lyrics). **Conductor:** Jay Blackton.
   Cast: Fernando Lamas (with Trudy Erwin on one track and with Richard Haydn on another);
   MGM Studio Orchestra and Chorus.
Studiotrack .... *Classics International (S) CIS-1813*   8-10

MESSIAH
Soundtrack .... *Columbia (S) MS-6039*   8-12
   Conductor: Leonard Bernstein.

METROPOLIS
Soundtrack (1984) .... *Columbia (S) JS-39526*   84   8-10
Soundtrack (1984) .... *Columbia (S) CK-39526*   Re   5-8
   Composer: Giorgio Moroder; others. **Cast:** Freddie Mercury; Pat Benatar; Jon Anderson;
   Cycle V; Giorgio Moroder; Bonnie Tyler; Loverboy; Billy Squier; Adam Ant.

MEXICAN HAYRIDE
Original Cast (1944) .... *Decca (M) DL-5232*   50   150-175
Original Cast (1944) .... *Columbia (M) X-14878*   Re   8-10
   Composer: Cole Porter. **Conductor:** Harry Sosnik. **Cast:** June Havoc; Wilbur Evans; Corinna
   Mura.

MIAMI VICE
TV Soundtrack (1985) .... *MCA (S) 6150*   8-10
   Composer: Jan Hammer; others. **Conductor:** Jan Hammer; others. **Cast:** Jan Hammer; Glenn
   Frey; Chaka Khan; Phil Collins; Grandmaster Melle Mel; Tina Turner.

MIAMI VICE II
TV Soundtrack (1986) .... *MCA (S) 6192*   86   8-10
   Composer: Jan Hammer; others. **Conductor:** Jan Hammer; others. **Cast:** Jan Hammer; Phil
   Collins; Roxy Music; Jackson Browne; Damned; Patti LaBelle and Bill Champlin; Steve Jones;
   Andy Taylor.

MICKEY AND THE BEANSTALK
Studio Cast (1968) .... *Disneyland (M) ST-3974*   68   10-15
   Gatefold cover. Includes bound-in 10-page color booklet. Side two has assorted Disney-related songs.
   Composer: Jimmie Dodd; Oliver Wallace; others. **Cast:** Robbie Lester (narrator); Jim Macdonald
   (Mickey Mouse, Giant); Clarence Nash (Donald Duck); Pinto Colvig (Goofy); Marilyn Hooven
   (singing harp); Jimmie Dodd and the Mouseketeers Chorus and Orchestra.

MICKEY ONE
Soundtrack (1965) .... *MGM (M) E-4312*   65   10-15
Soundtrack (1965) .... *MGM (S) SE-4312*   65   15-20
   Composer: Eddie Sauter. **Conductor:** Eddie Sauter. **Cast:** Stan Getz.

MIDAS RUN
Soundtrack (1968) .... *Citadel (S) CT-6016*   68   100-125
   Composer: Elmer Bernstein.

MIDNIGHT COWBOY
Soundtrack (1969) .... *United Artists (S) UAS-5198*   69   10-15
Soundtrack (1969) .... *EMI America (S) E1-48409*   Re   8-10
   Composer: John Barry. **Conductor:** John Barry. **Cast:** Harry Nilsson; Groop; Leslie Miller;
   Elephant's Memory; John Barry.

MIDNIGHT EXPRESS
Soundtrack (1978) .... *Casablanca (S) NBLP-7114*   78   10-12
Soundtrack (1978) .... *Casablanca (S) 822561-1*   Re   8-10
   Composer: Giorgio Moroder. **Cast:** David Castle; Chris Bennett.

MIDNIGHT RUN
Soundtrack (1988) ....*MCA (S) 6250*   88   **$8-10**
Composer: Danny Elfman. Conductor: Danny Elfman. Cast: Danny Elfman.

MIDSUMMER NIGHT'S DREAM
Original Cast (1954) ....*RCA Victor (EP) ERB-46*   55   **20-30**
Double EP set. Has excerpts from the LP set.
Original Cast (1954) ....*RCA Victor (M) LM-6115*   55   **50-75**
Triple LP, boxed set with booklet. Based on the Old Vic 1954 production of Shakespeare's play.
Composer: Mendelssohn. Conductor: Sir Malcolm Sargent. Cast: Moira Shearer; Robert
Helpmann; Stanley Holloway; B.B.C. Orchestra
Original Cast (1978) ....*Doda (S) LPM-78D1*   78   **15-20**
Composer: Randolph Tallman. Conductor: Jim Abbott.

MIGHTY MOUSE
Studio Cast .... *Rocking Horse (M) 5042*   **5-10**

MIKADO
Studio Cast (1958) ....*Angel (M) 3573*   58   **15-25**
Studio Cast (1958) ....*Angel (S) S-3573*   58   **25-35**
Composer: William S. Gilbert; Arthur Sullivan. Conductor: Sargent. Cast: Pro Arte Orchestra.
TV Soundtrack (1960) .... *Columbia (M) OL-5480*   60   **30-35**
From an NBC-TV Bell Telephone Hour presentation.
TV Soundtrack (1960) .... *Columbia (S) OS-2022*   60   **60-65**
TV Soundtrack (1960) ....*Columbia Masterworks (S) AOL-5480*   Re   **8-12**
Composer: William S. Gilbert; Arthur Sullivan. Conductor: Donald Voorhees. Cast: Groucho
Marx; Stanley Holloway; Robert Rounseville; Barbara Meister; Dennis King; Helen Traubel;
Norman Luboff Choir; Bell Telephone Orchestra.
Studiotrack (1954) ....*RCA Victor (EP) EKL-1001*   54   **10-20**
Double EP set.
Studiotrack (1954) ....*RCA Victor (M) LK-1001*   54   **20-30**
Composer: William S. Gilbert; Arthur Sullivan. Conductor: Al Goodman. Cast: Al Goodman
and His Orchestra; Jimmy Carroll; Audrey Marsh; John Percival; Sally Sweetland; Martha
Wright; Earl Wrightson.

MIKE HAMMER
TV Soundtrack (1959) .... *RCA Victor (M) LPM-2140*   59   **15-25**
TV Soundtrack (1959) ....*RCA Victor (S) LSP-2140*   59   **25-30**
Composer: Dave Kahn; Melvyn Lenard. Conductor: Skip Martin. Cast: Skip Martin's Orchestra.

MIKE POST
Soundtrack (1984) ....*RCA Victor (S) AFL1-5183*   84   **8-10**
A collection of television and movie themes.
Composer: Mike Post; others. Conductor: Mike Post. Cast: Mike Post.
Also see MUSIC FROM L.A. LAW (AND OTHERWISE); TELEVISION THEME SONGS

MIKE'S MURDER
Soundtrack (1983) ....*A&M (S) SP-4931*   83   **8-10**
Composer: Joe Jackson. Cast: Joe Jackson.

MILANESE STORY
Soundtrack (1962) .... *Atlantic (M) 1388*   62   **10-15**
Soundtrack (1962) ....*Atlantic (S) SD-1388*   62   **15-20**
Composer: John Lewis. Conductor: John Lewis.

MILK AND HONEY

Original Cast (1961) . . . . *RCA Victor (M) LOC-1065*   61 $25-30
Original Cast (1961) . . . . *RCA Victor (S) LSO-1065*   61   **35-40**
  Above two have only text shown on their front covers.
Original Cast (1961) . . . . *RCA Victor (M) LOC-1065*   61   **20-25**
Original Cast (1961) . . . . *RCA Victor (S) LSO-1065*   61   **25-30**
  Above two have three dancers pictured on their front covers.
  Composer: Jerry Herman. **Conductor:** Max Goberman. **Cast:** Robert Weede; Mimi Benzell; Molly Picon; Tommy Rall; Juki Arkin.

MINI-WASH:
see CAR WASH

MINNIE'S BOYS

Original Cast (1970) . . . . *Project 3 (S) TS-6002-S*   70   **8-12**
  Composer: Larry Grossman; Hal Hackady. **Conductor:** John Berkman. **Cast:** Shelley Winters; Amy Freeman; Mort Marshall; Julie Kurnitz; Lewis J. Stadlen; Daniel Fortus; Irwin Pearl, Alvin Kupperman, and Gary Raucher (as the Marx Brothers).

MINOR MIRACLE

Soundtrack . . . . *Varese Sarabande (S) STV-81193*   **8-10**
  Cast: Rick Patterson.

MINSTREL DAYS

Studio Cast (1959) . . . . *Everest (M) BR-4039*   59   **15-20**
Studio Cast (1959) . . . . *Everest (S) SDBR-1039*   59   **20-30**
  Conductor: Leo Shuken; Jack Hayes. **Cast:** Eddie Foy Jr.; David Burns; Harold Adamson.

MINX

Soundtrack (1970) . . . . *Amsterdam (S) 12007*   70   **10-15**
  Composer: Tom Dawes; Don Danneman. **Cast:** Cyrkle.

MIRACLE

Soundtrack . . . . *Elmer Bernstein Film Music Collection (S) FMC-2*   **40-50**
  Also has music from *Toccata for Toy Trains*.
  Composer: Elmer Bernstein.

MIRACLE ON 34TH STREET:
see IT'S A WONDERFUL LIFE

MIRAGE

Soundtrack (1965) . . . . *Mercury (M) MG-21025*   65   **12-18**
Soundtrack (1965) . . . . *Mercury (S) SR-61025*   65   **15-20**
  Composer: Quincy Jones. **Conductor:** Quincy Jones.

MISERABLES, LES:
see LES MISERABLES

MISFITS

Soundtrack (1961) . . . .*United Artists (M) UAL-4087*   61   **20-25**
Soundtrack (1961) . . . . *United Artists (S) UAS-5087*   61   **35-40**
  Composer: Alex North. **Conductor:** Alex North.
  Also see JOHNNY COOL

MISS JULIE

Original Revival Cast (1979) . . . . *Painted Smiles (S) PS-1338*   79   **8-10**
  Composer: Ned Rorem; Kenward Elmslie. **Conductor:** Peter Leonard. **Cast:** Judith James; Ronald Madden; Veronica August.

MISS LIBERTY
Original Cast (1949) .... *Columbia (M) ML-4220*   49   **$25-30**
Original Cast (1949) .... *Columbia Special Products (M) AOL-4220*   **8-10**
  Composer: Irving Berlin. **Cast:** Eddie Albert; Allyn McLerie; Mary McCarty; Ethel Griffles; Johnny Thompson.
Studio Cast (1949) .... *Decca (M) DL-5009*   49   **40-50**
  10-inch LP.
  Composer: Irving Berlin. **Conductor:** Fred Waring. **Cast:** Joe Marine; Daisy Bernier; Gordon Goodman; Jane Wilson; Joanne Wheatley and Chorus; Fred Waring and His Pennsylvanians.

MISS SADIE THOMPSON
Soundtrack (1953) .... *Mercury (EP) 2-3147*   54   **25-40**
Soundtrack (1953) .... *Mercury (M) MG-25181*   54   **80-100**
  10-inch LP.
Soundtrack (1953) .... *Mercury (M) MG-20123*   56   **65-70**
  Composer: George Duning; Lester Lee; Ned Washington. **Conductor:** Morris Stoloff.
  Cast: Rita Hayworth; Jose Ferrer. (With dialogue.)

MISSION
Soundtrack (1986) .... *Virgin (S) 90567-1*   86   **8-12**
  Composer: Ennio Morricone. **Conductor:** Ennio Morricone. **Cast:** London Philharmonic Orchestra; Incantation (Indian instrumentation); London Voices (choir).
  Also see VIRGIN

MISSION: IMPOSSIBLE
TV Soundtrack (1967) .... *Dot (M) DLP-3831*   67   **12-15**
TV Soundtrack (1967) .... *Dot (S) DLP-25831*   67   **15-20**
  Composer: Lalo Schifrin. **Conductor:** Lalo Schifrin.
TV Soundtrack (1967) .... *Paramount (S) PAS-5002*   69   **12-18**
  Volume two.
  Composer: Lalo Schifrin. **Conductor:** Lalo Schifrin.

MISSISSIPPI
Studiotrack (1935) .... *Decca (M) DL-6008*   51   **50-60**
  10-inch LP. One side has music from *Here Is My Heart*.
Studiotrack (1935) .... *Decca (M) DL-4250*   62   **25-30**
  Also has music from *Here Is My Heart*, *Two for Tonight* and *The Big Broadcast of 1936*. Issued as part of *Bing's Hollywood Series*.
  Composer: Richard Rodgers; Lorenz Hart; Stephen Foster. **Conductor:** George Stoll. **Cast:** Bing Crosby.

MISSOURI BREAKS
Soundtrack (1976) .... *United Artists (S) UA LA623-G*   76   **20-35**
Soundtrack (1976) .... *MCA (S) 25113*   Re   **8-10**
  Composer: John Williams. **Conductor:** John Williams.

MISTER BROADWAY
TV Soundtrack (1957) . . . . *RCA Victor (M) LPM-1520*   57 $35-40
    Composer: George M. Cohan. **Conductor:** George M. Cohan. **Cast:** Mickey Rooney.
Studiotrack (1964) . . . . *Columbia (M) CL-9075*   64   10-15
Studiotrack (1964) . . . . *Columbia (S) CS-9075*   64   15-20
    Composer: Dave Brubeck. **Conductor:** Dave Brubeck. **Cast:** Dave Brubeck Quartet.

MISTER BUDDWING
Soundtrack (1966) . . . . *Verve (M) V-8638*   66   12-18
Soundtrack (1966) . . . . *Verve (S) V6-8638*   66   15-20
    Composer: Kenyon Hopkins. **Conductor:** Kenyon Hopkins. **Cast:** Kenyon Hopkins.

MISTER ED
TV Soundtrack (1962) . . . . *Colpix (M) CP-209*   62   20-30
    Cast: Alan Young; Connie Hines; Larry Keating; Edna Skinner. (Comedy skits.)

MISTER IMPERIUM
Soundtrack (1951) . . . . *RCA Victor (M) LM-61*   51   65-80
    10-inch LP. One side has music from *Knickerbocker Holiday, Roberta, One Night of Love* and
    Spring Is Here.
    Conductor: Johnny Green. **Cast:** Ezio Pinza; Fran Warren; Guadalajara Trio.

MISTER LUCKY
TV Soundtrack (1959) . . . . *RCA Victor (M) LPM-2198*   60   15-20
    Actual title: *Music from Mr. Lucky.*
TV Soundtrack (1959) . . . . *RCA Victor (S) LSP-2198*   60   20-25
    Black label.
TV Soundtrack (1959) . . . . *RCA Victor (S) LSP-2198*   72   8-10
    Orange label.
    Composer: Henry Mancini. **Conductor:** Henry Mancini. **Cast:** Henry Mancini and His Orchestra.
Studiotrack (1960) . . . . *RCA Victor/Camden (M) CAL-600*   60   10-15
Studiotrack (1960) . . . . *RCA Victor/Camden (S) CAS-600*   60   15-20
    Composer: Henry Mancini. **Conductor:** Richard Maltby. **Cast:** Richard Maltby and His
    Orchestra.

MISTER MEAN
Soundtrack . . . . *Mercury (S) SRM-3707*   8-10

MISTER MICAWBER'S DIFFICULTIES:
see CHRISTMAS CAROL

MISTER MUSIC
Soundtrack (1950) . . . . *Decca (M) DL-5284*   50   45-55
    10-inch LP.
Soundtrack (1950) . . . . *Decca (M) DL-4262*   62   25-30
    Conductor: Victor Young; Vic Schoen; Jay Blackton. **Cast:** Bing Crosby; Dorothy Kirsten;
    Andrews Sisters; Ken Lane Singers.
    Also see COOL OF THE EVENING

MISTER NOVAK
TV Soundtrack (1963) . . . . *MGM (M) E-4222*   63   15-20
TV Soundtrack (1963) . . . . *MGM (S) SE-4222*   63   20-25
    Above two have title track plus nine other high school themes.
    Conductor: Lyn Murray.

MISTER PICKWICK'S CHRISTMAS:
see CHRISTMAS CAROL

MISTER PRESIDENT

Original Cast (1962) .... *Columbia (M) KOL-5870*   62 $25-30
 Composer: Irving Berlin.
Original Cast (1962) .... *Columbia (S) KOS-2270*   62   35-40
 Above two have gatefold covers.
Original Cast (1962) .... *Columbia (M) KOL-5870*   63   15-20
Original Cast (1962) .... *Columbia (S) KOS-2270*   63   25-30
 Above two do not have gatefold covers.
Original Cast (1962) .... *Columbia Special Products (S) AKOS-2270*   Re   8-10
 Composer: Irving Berlin. **Conductor:** Jay Blackton. **Cast:** Robert Ryan; Nanette Fabray;
 Anita Gillette; Jack Haskell; Jack Washburn.
Studio Cast (1962) .... *RCA Victor (M) LPM-2630*   62   12-15
Studio Cast (1962) .... *RCA Victor (S) LSP-2630*   62   15-20
 Composer: Irving Berlin. **Conductor:** Mitchell Ayers. **Cast:** Perry Como; Kaye Ballard; Sandy
 Stewart; Ray Charles Singers.

MISTER WONDERFUL

Original Cast (1956) .... *Decca (M) DL-9032*   56   60-70
 Composer: Jerry Bock; George Weiss; Larry Holofcener. **Conductor:** Morton Stevens.
 Cast: Sammy Davis Jr.; Will Mastin Trio; Jack Carter; Chita Rivera; Pat Marshall; Olga
 James; Hal Loman.

MISTRAL'S DAUGHTERS

TV Soundtrack (1984) .... *Carrere (S) SZ-39902*   84   8-10

MISUNDERSTOOD

Soundtrack (1984) .... *Polydor (S) 821 238*   84   8-10
 Composer: Michael Hoppe; Carlos Franzetti. **Conductor:** Carlos Franzetti.

MIXED DOUBLES/BELOW THE BELT

Original Cast (1966) .... *Upstairs (S) UD-37W56*   66   80-100
 Double LP set.
 Cast: Judy Graubart; Madeline Kahn; Larry Moss; Lily Tomlin; Richard Blair; Genna Carter;
 Robert Rovin; Janie Sell; Gary Sneed.

MOAT FARM MURDERS:
see OUTER SPACE SUITE

MOBY DICK

Studio Cast (1950) .... *Decca (M) DL-5146*   50   50-75
 10-inch LP.
Soundtrack (1956) .... *RCA Victor (EP) EPB-1247*   56   20-40
 Double EP. Omits closing segment heard on the LP (LPM-1247).

Studio Cast (1950) .... *Decca (M) DL-9071*   59 $20-35
     One side has music and dialogue from *Treasure Island*.
    Composer: Victor Young. **Conductor:** Victor Young. **Cast:** Charles Laughton (*Moby Dick*);
    Thomas Mitchell (*Treasure Island*).
Soundtrack (1956) .... *RCA Victor (M) LPM-1247*   56   100-125
    Composer: Philip Sainton. **Conductor:** Louis Levy.

MODERN GIRLS
Soundtrack (1986) .... *Warner Bros. (S) 1-25526*   86   8-10

MODERN TIMES
Soundtrack (1936) .... *United Artists (M) UAL-4049*   59   25-30
Soundtrack (1936) .... *United Artists (SE) UAS-5049*   59   30-35
Soundtrack (1936) .... *United Artists (SE) UAS-5222*   71   8-10
    Composer: Charlie Chaplin. **Conductor:** Alfred Newman.

MODERNS
Soundtrack (1988) .... *Virgin Movie Music (S) 90922-1*   88   8-10
    Composer: Mark Isham; Charlelie Couture. **Conductor:** Mark Isham; Charlelie Couture.
    Cast: L'Orchestre Moderne; Charlelie Couture.

MODESTY BLAISE
Soundtrack (1966) .... *20th Century-Fox (M) 4182*   66   15-20
Soundtrack (1966) .... *20th Century-Fox (S) 4182*   66   20-25
    Composer: John Dankworth. **Conductor:** John Dankworth. **Cast:** David and Jonathan.

MOHAMMAD, MESSENGER OF GOD
Soundtrack (1977) .... *Namara (S) 79001-798*   77   10-12
    Composer: Maurice Jarre. **Conductor:** Maurice Jarre.

MOLLY MAGUIRES
Soundtrack (1970) .... *Paramount (S) PAS-6000*   70   25-35
    Composer: Henry Mancini. **Conductor:** Henry Mancini.

MOLLY'S PILGRIM
Soundtrack .... *Musicmasters (S) 20138K*   8-10

MOMENT BY MOMENT
Soundtrack (1978) .... *RSO (S) RS-1-3040*   78   8-12
    Composer: Lee Holdridge. **Cast:** Yvonne Elliman; Michael Franks; Stephen Bishop; Charles
    Lloyd; Dan Hill; 10CC.

MOMENT OF TRUTH
Soundtrack (1965) .... *Mainstream (M) 56057*   65   20-25
Soundtrack (1965) .... *Mainstream (S) S-6057*   65   30-35
     This Italian movie should not be confused with the 1952 French film of the same title.
    Composer: Piero Piccioni. **Conductor:** Piero Piccioni.

MON ONCLE D'AMERIQUE
Soundtrack (1979) .... *DRG (S) SL-9505*   79   8-10
    Composer: Arie Dzierlatka. **Conductor:** Arie Dzierlatka.

MONDO CANE
Soundtrack (1963) .... *United Artists (M) UAL-4105*   63   12-18
Soundtrack (1963) .... *United Artists (S) UAS-5105*   63   15-20
     Covers on the above two show Riz Ortolani as "Ritz Ortolani."
    Composer: Riz Ortolani; Nino Oliviero.

MONDO CANE NO. 2
Soundtrack (1964) .... *20th Century-Fox (M) TFM-3147*   64   25-30
Soundtrack (1964) .... *20th Century-Fox (S) TFS-4147*   64   35-40
    Composer: Nino Oliviero.

MONDO HOLLYWOOD
Soundtrack (1967) ....*Tower (M) T-5083*   67   **$15-20**
Soundtrack (1967) ....*Tower (S) DT-5083*   67   **20-25**
  Composer: Mike Curb; others. **Conductor:** Mike Curb. **Cast:** Davie Allan and the Arrows;
  Mugwump Establishment; Mike Clifford; Riptides; Bobby Jameson; God Pan; Darrell Dee;
  18th Century Concepts; Teddy and Darrell.

MONOLOGUES AND SONGS
Original Cast (1958) .... *Elektra (M) EKL-184*   58   **25-30**
  Composer: Joyce Grenfell; Richard Addinsell. **Cast:** Joyce Grenfell; George Bauer (piano).

MONSIEUR DE POURCEAUGNAC
Original Cast (1978) .... *Broadway Baby Demos (S) BBD-789*   78   **8-10**
  Composer: Howard Harris; Tony Schuman. **Cast:** Lisa Loomer; Tony Calabro; Homer Foil.

MONSIGNOR
Soundtrack (1982) ....*Casablanca (S) 7277*   82   **8-10**
  Composer: John Williams. **Conductor:** John Williams. **Cast:** London Symphony Orchestra.

MONTY PYTHON
Soundtrack (1975) .... *Arista (S) AB-4050*   75   **10-12**
  Actual title: *The Album of the Soundtrack of the Trailer of the Film of Monty Python and the Holy Grail.*
Soundtrack (1975) .... *Arista (S) ALB-68355*   Re   **8-10**
  Composer: Neil Innes. **Cast:** Terry Jones; Eric Idle; Graham Chapman; Terry Gilliam; John
  Cleese; Michael Palin; Douglas Adams; John Young; Bee Duffell; Connie Booth.

MOON IN THE GUTTER
Soundtrack (1983) .... *DRG (S) SL-9516*   83   **8-10**

MOON IS BLUE
Soundtrack (1953) ....*Crown (M) CLP-5095*   56   **25-30**
Soundtrack (1953) .... *Crown (SE) CST-130*   56   **40-50**
  Colored vinyl.
  Composer: Hershel Burke Gilbert; Sylvia Fine.

MOON OVER PARADOR
Soundtrack (1988) ....*MCA (S) 6249*   88   **8-10**
  Composer: Maurice Jarre. **Conductor:** Maurice Jarre.

MOON RIVER (AND OTHER GREAT MOVIE THEMES)
Studiotrack (1963) .... *Columbia (M) CL-1809*   63   **10-15**
Studiotrack (1963) .... *Columbia (S) CS-8609*   63   **12-18**
  Cast: Andy Williams.

MOON SPINNERS
Soundtrack (1964) ....*Buena Vista (M) BV-3323*   64   **35-40**
  Still in print using the original catalog number.
  Composer: Ron Grainer; Terry Gilkyson. **Conductor:** Ron Grainer.

MOONLIGHT IS SILVER:
see TONIGHT AT 8:30

MOONLIGHTING
TV Soundtrack (1987) ....*MCA (S) 6214*   87   **8-10**

MOONRAKER
Soundtrack (1979) ....*United Artists (S) UA-LA971-1*   79   **8-10**
  Composer: John Barry; Hal David. **Conductor:** John Barry. **Cast:** Shirley Bassey.

MOONSTRUCK
Soundtrack (1988) ....*Capitol (S) C1-90231*   88   **8-10**
  Composer: Various. **Cast:** Dean Martin; Dick Hyman; Vikki Carr.

MORE

Soundtrack (1968) .... *Tower (S) ST-5169*   68 $20-25
Soundtrack (1968) .... *Harvest (S) SW-11198*   73   8-10
  Composer: Pink Floyd. Cast: Pink Floyd.

MORE AMERICAN GRAFFITI

Soundtrack (1979) .... *MCA (S) 2-11006*   79   15-20
  Double LP set.
  Composer: Various. Cast: Martha and the Vandellas; Andy Williams; Byrds; Angels; Simon
  and Garfunkel; Donovan; Supremes; Cream; Bob Dylan; Aretha Franklin; Zombies; ? and the
  Mysterians; Chantays; Lenny Welch; Marvelettes; Bobby Vinton; Capitols; Country Joe and
  the Fish; Barry Sadler; Mary Wells; Doug Sahm; McCoys; Percy Sledge; Wolfman Jack.
  (With dialogue.)

MORE DIRTY DANCING

Soundtrack (1988) .... *Victor (S) 6965-1*   88   8-10

MORE FUNNY FONE CALLS:
see STEVE ALLEN'S FUNNY FONE CALLS

MORE THAN A MIRACLE

Soundtrack (1967) .... *MGM (M) E-4515*   67   15-20
  Also known as *Cinderella, Italian Style.*
Soundtrack (1967) .... *MGM (S) SE-4515*   67   20-25
  Composer: Piero Piccioni. Conductor: Piero Piccioni. Cast: Roger Williams, His Orchestra
  and Chorus.

MOSES THE LAWGIVER

Soundtrack (1976) .... *RCA Victor (S) TBL1-1106*   76   10-12
  Composer: Ennio Morricone. Conductor: Bruno Nicolai. Cast: Gianna Spagnolo.

MOSQUITO COAST

Soundtrack (1986) ...., *Fantasy (S) FSP-21005*   87   8-10
  Composer: Maurice Jarre. Conductor: Maurice Jarre.

MOST HAPPY FELLA

Original Cast (1956) .... *Columbia (EP) A-5118*   56   10-20
Original Cast (1956) .... *Columbia (M) O3L-240*   56   60-70
Original Cast (1956) .... *Columbia Special Products (M) CO3L-240*   76   15-20
  Above two are triple LP sets.
Original Cast (1956) .... *Columbia (M) OL-5118*   56   25-30
Original Cast (1956) .... *Columbia (SE) OS-2330*   63   20-25
  Composer: Frank Loesser. Conductor: Herbert Greene. Cast: Robert Weede; Jo Sullivan; Art
  Lund; Susan Johnson; Lee Cass; Shorty Long; Mona Paulee; John Henson; Alan Gilbert; Roy
  Lazarus; Arthur Rubin; Keith Kaldenberg. (With dialogue.)
Original London Cast (1961) .... *Angel (M) 35887*   61   25-30
Original London Cast (1961) .... *Angel (S) S-35887*   61   35-40
  Composer: Frank Loesser. Conductor: Kenneth Alwyn. Cast: Helena Scott; Art Lund; Inia
  Wiata; Ubi Stalger; Jack Delon; John Clifford; Ralph Farnworth; William Dickie.
London Studio Cast .... *World (M) LMP-17*   20-25
  Composer: Frank Loesser. Conductor: Jan Cervenka. Cast: Edwin Steffe; Stella Moray; Peter
  Hudson.

MOTHER EARTH

Original Cast (1972) .... *Environmental (S) SP-1001*   72   50-75
  From a pre-Broadway show.
  Composer: Toni Shearer; Ron Thronson. Conductor: Bill Hollman. Cast: Patti Austin; Dee
  Ervin; Carol Christy; Bill Hathaway; Indira Danks; Hap Palmer.

MOTHER, JUGS AND SPEED
Soundtrack (1976) .... *A&M (S) SP-4590*   76   **$10-12**
   Composer: Various. **Cast:** Paul Jabara; Steve Marriott; Peter Frampton; Billy Preston; Michelle Phillips; Brothers Johnson; Pete Jolly; Crusaders.

MOTHER OF ALL OF US
Original Revival Cast (1976) .... *New World (S) NW-288/28*   76   **12-18**
   Double LP set.
   Composer: Virgil Thompson; Gertrude Stein. **Conductor:** Raymond Leppard. **Cast:** Mignon Dunn; Philip Booth; James Atherton.

MOTION PICTURE MUSIC
Studiotrack (1953) .... *Mercury (EP) Number Unknown*   53   **10-12**
   Has: *Wuthering Heights, All About Eve, A Letter to Three Wives* and *The Razor's Edge.*
Studiotrack (1953) .... *Mercury (M) MG-20037*   53   **25-35**
   10-inch LP. One side has *Wuthering Heights,* the other has *An American in Paris.*
   Composer: Alfred Newman. **Conductor:** Alfred Newman. **Cast:** Hollywood Symphony.

MOUNTAIN:
see OMAR KHAYYAM

MOUSE ON THE MAYFLOWER
TV Soundtrack (1968) .... *No Label Shown (M) GRC-11398*   68   **50-60**
   Side two has *The Little Drummer Boy.* Promotional issue for an NBC-TV special, "Presented by Your Gas Company."
   Composer: Maury Laws; Jules Bass. **Cast:** Tennessee Ernie Ford (narration and vocals); John Gary; Eddie Albert; Joanie Sommers; Greer Garson (narration); Jose Ferrer; Teddy Eccles; Vienna Boys Choir.

MOUSE ON THE MAYFLOWER:
see LITTLE DRUMMER BOY

MOVIE MOVIE
Studiotrack (1979) .... *Filmscore Records (S) FS-7914*   **8-10**
   Composer: Ralph Burns; Buster Davis; Larry Gelbart; Sheldon Keller. **Conductor:** Buster Davis. **Cast:** Patricia Marshall; Gene Merlino; Jerry Whitman.

MOVIE STAR, AMERICAN STYLE
Soundtrack (1966) .... *Mira (M) 3007*   66 $12-15
Soundtrack (1966) .... *Mira (S) 3007*   66   15-20
   Composer: Joseph Greene. **Conductor:** Joseph Greene.

MOVIE THEMES FROM HOLLYWOOD
Soundtrack (1955) .... *Coral (M) CRL-57006*   55   30-40
   Composer: Dimitri Tiomkin. **Conductor:** Dimitri Tiomkin.

MOVIN' WITH NANCY (SINATRA)
TV Soundtrack (1967) .... *Reprise (M) 6277*   67   10-15
TV Soundtrack (1967) .... *Reprise (S) 6277*   67   15-20
   Conductor: Billy Strange. **Cast:** Nancy Sinatra; Frank Sinatra; Lee Hazelwood; Dean Martin.

MRS. BROWN, YOU'VE GOT A LOVELY DAUGHTER
Soundtrack (1968) .... *MGM (S) SE-4548*   68   15-18
   Composer: Graham Gouldman; G. Stephens; K. Young; others. **Cast:** Herman's Hermits.

MRS. PATTERSON
Original Cast (1954) .... *RCA Victor (EP) EOC-1017*   54   30-50
Original Cast (1954) .... *RCA Victor (M) LOC-1017*   54   130-150
   Composer: Charles Sebree; Greer Johnson; James Shelton. **Conductor:** Abba Bogin.
   Cast: Eartha Kitt; Enid Markey; Ruth Attaway; Terry Carter; Alonzo Basan; Helen Dowdy;
   Jay Riley; Mary Harmon; Mary Ann Hoxworth; Joan Morgan.

MRS. SOFFEL
Soundtrack (1984) .... *Windham Hill Records (S) WH-91041*   85   8-10
   Also contains music from *The Times of Harvey Milk* and *Never Cry Wolf.*
   Composer: Mark Isham.

MUCH ADO ABOUT NOTHING
Original London Cast (1965) .... *RCA Victor (M) VDM-104*   65   30-40
Original London Cast (1965) .... *RCA Victor (S) VDS-104*   65   45-55
   Above two are triple LP sets. Has Franco Zeffirelli's production of William Shakespeare's play.
   Composer: Nino Rota. **Cast:** Maggie Smith; Robert Stephens; Albert Finney; Frank Finlay;
   Lynn Redgrave; Michael York; Derek Jacobi; Gerald James. (With dialogue.)

MUNSTERS
TV Soundtrack (1964) .... *Decca (M) DL-4588*   64   15-20
TV Soundtrack (1964) .... *Decca (M) DL7-4588*   64   20-25
   Also see AT HOME WITH THE MUNSTERS

MUPPET MOVIE
Soundtrack (1979) .... *Atlantic (S) XSD-16001*   79   8-10
   Composer: Paul Williams; Kenny Ascher. **Conductor:** Ian Freebairn-Smith. **Cast:** Jim Henson;
   Frank Oz; Jerry Nelson; Richard Hunt; Dave Goelz.

MUPPET SHOW
TV Soundtrack (1977) .... *Arista (S) AB-4152*   77   8-12
   Cast: Jim Henson; Muppets.

MUPPETS TAKE MANHATTAN
Soundtrack (1984) .... *Warner Bros. (S) 1-25114*   84   8-10
   Cast: Muppets.

MURDER INC.
Soundtrack (1960) .... *Canadian-American (M) CALP-1003*   60   55-65
   Composer: Frank DeVol; George Weiss. **Conductor:** Jeff Alexander. **Cast:** Sarah Vaughan.

MURDER ON THE ORIENT EXPRESS
Soundtrack (1974) .... *Capitol (S) ST-11361*   74   20-25
   Composer: Richard Rodney Bennett. **Conductor:** Marcus Dods. **Cast:** Royal Opera House
   Orchestra.

MURDERER'S ROW
Soundtrack (1966) . . . .*Colgems (M) COMO-5003*   67   **$25-35**
Soundtrack (1966) . . . . *Colgems (S) COSO-5003*   67   **40-50**
　Composer: Lalo Schifrin. **Conductor:** Lalo Schifrin.

MURMUR OF THE HEART
Soundtrack (1972) . . . .*Roulette (S) SR-3006*   72   **15-20**
　Composer: Sidney Bechet; Dizzy Gillespie; Henri Renaud; Charlie Parker.

MURPH THE SURF
Soundtrack (1975) . . . . *Motown (S) M6-839-S1*   75   **10-12**
　This film was later titled *Live a Little, Steal a Lot*, then retitled *You Can't Steal Love*.
　Composer: Philip Lambro. **Conductor:** Philip Lambro.

MUSCLE BEACH PARTY
Soundtrack (1964) . . . .*Buena Vista (M) BV-3314*   64   **15-20**
　Cast: Frankie Avalon; Annette Funicello.
Soundtrack (1964) . . . . *Buena Vista (S) STER-3314*   64   **20-30**
　Composer: Various. **Cast:** Frankie Avalon; Annette Funicello.
Studiotrack (1964) . . . .*United Artists (M) UAL-3371*   64   **15-20**
　Full title: *Frankie Avalon Sings Songs from Muscle Beach Party.*
Studiotrack (1964) . . . .*United Artists (S) UAS-6371*   64   **20-25**
　Full title: *Frankie Avalon Sings Songs from Muscle Beach Party.*
　Composer: Various. **Cast:** Frankie Avalon.

MUSIC AND SONGS FROM ITALIAN FILMS
Soundtrack (1962) . . . . *RCA Victor (M) FOC-4*   62   **20-25**
Soundtrack . . . . *RCA Victor (S) FSO-4*   62   **25-30**
　Has 12 Italian film tracks by various artists, including *La Dolce Vita*, *Rocco and His Brothers*,
　Che Gioia Vivere, *La Grande Olimpiade* and others.

MUSIC FOR JENNIFER
Soundtrack (1953) . . . .*Columbia (EP) B-369*   53   **15-25**
　Double EP set.
Studiotrack (1953) . . . . *Columbia (M) CL-6281*   53   **40-50**
　10-inch LP. Also has tracks from; *Ruby Gentry*, *Portrait of Jennie*, *Duel in the Sun*, *Song of Bernadette*,
　Love Letters, *Since You Went Away* and *Indiscretion of an American Wife*.
　Composer: Various. **Conductor:** Paul Weston. **Cast:** Paul Weston and His Orchestra.

MUSIC FOR LITTLE WOMEN:
see LITTLE WOMEN

MUSIC FOR LORETTA:
see LORETTA YOUNG SHOW

MUSIC FROM "A FISTFUL OF DOLLARS," "FOR A FEW DOLLARS MORE," AND "THE GOOD, THE BAD AND THE UGLY"
Soundtrack . . . .*RCA Victor (S) LSP-3927*   68   **10-15**
　Composer: Ennio Morricone. **Conductor:** Hugo Montenegro. **Cast:** Hugo Montenegro and
　His Orchestra.

MUSIC FROM DISNEY MOTION PICTURES
Soundtrack . . . . *Disneyland (S) DQ-1318*   68   **10-20**
　Composer: Various. **Cast:** Hayley Mills; Burl Ives; Annette Funicello; Maurice Chevalier; others.

MUSIC FROM GREAT SHAKESPEAREAN FILMS
Soundtrack . . . .*London (S) SPC-21132*   76   **15-20**
　Has music from *Hamlet*, *Richard III* and *Julius Caesar*.
　Composer: Dimitri Shostakovich; Sir William Walton; Miklos Rozsa. **Conductor:** Bernard
　Herrmann. **Cast:** National Philharmonic Orchestra.

MUSIC FROM HOLLYWOOD
Studiotrack (1955) ....*Columbia (EP) B-1692* 55 $8-12
Studiotrack (1955) ....*Columbia (EP) B-1693* 55 8-12
Studiotrack (1955) ....*Columbia (EP) B-376* 55 10-20
  Double EP set. Combines B-1692 and B-1693.
Studiotrack (1955) .... *Columbia (M) CL-577* 55 15-25
  Composer: Various. **Conductor:** Percy Faith. **Cast:** Percy Faith and His Orchestra.

MUSIC FROM HOLLYWOOD
Studiotrack (1963) .... *Columbia (M) CL-2113* 63 30-40
Studiotrack (1963) .... *Columbia (S) CS-8913* 63 50-60
  Composer: Lionel Newman; Alex North; Miklos Rosza; Max Steiner; Dimitri Tiomkin; Franz
  Waxman; Bernard Herrmann; others. **Conductor:** Lionel Newman; Alex North; Miklos Rosza;
  Max Steiner; Dimitri Tiomkin; Franz Waxman; Bernard Herrmann; others.

MUSIC FROM L.A. LAW (AND OTHERWISE)
Soundtrack ....*Polydor (S) 833985-1* 8-10
  Composer: Mike Post; others. **Conductor:** Mike Post. **Cast:** Mike Post.
  Also see MIKE POST

MUSIC FROM MARLBORO COUNTRY
TV Soundtrack (1967) ....*United Artists (S) SP-107* 67 30-40
  Special Products issue only. Music from the Marlboro cigarette commercials.
  Composer: Elmer Bernstein. **Conductor:** Elmer Bernstein.

MUSIC FROM PETER GUNN
TV Soundtrack (1959) ....*Lion (M) L-70112* 59 10-20
  Composer: Henry Mancini. **Conductor:** Aaron Bell. **Cast:** Aaron Bell and His Orchestra.

MUSIC FROM SHAKESPEAREAN FILMS
Soundtrack ....*Angel (M) 36198* 64 20-25
Soundtrack ....*Angel (S) S-36198* 64 30-35
  Has music from *Hamlet, Henry V* and *Richard III.*
  Composer: Sir William Walton. **Conductor:** Sir William Walton.
  Also see WALTON CONDUCTS HIS GREAT FILM MUSIC

MUSIC FROM SHUBERT ALLEY
TV Soundtrack (1959) .... *Sinclair (S) OSS-2250* 59 15-25
  White label, promotional issue. From a November 13, 1959, TV show hosted by Andy Williams.
  Composer: Various. **Conductor:** Vic Shoen. **Cast:** Andy Williams; Alfred Drake; Lisa Kirk;
  Ray Walston; Doretta Morrow; Betty Comden; Adolph Green.

MUSIC FROM SIESTA
Soundtrack (1987) .... *Warner Bros. (S) 1-25655* 87 8-10
  Composer: Miles Davis; Marcus Miller.

MUSIC IN THE AIR
London Studio Cast (1932) .... *World (M) T-121* 20-25
  Cast: Marion Grimaldi; Andy Cole; Maggie Fitzgibbon; Gloria Swanson; John Boles; June Lang.
Studio Cast (1951) ....*RCA Victor (M) 39001* 51 150-250
  Picture disc.
  Composer: Jerome Kern; Oscar Hammerstein II. **Cast:** Marjorie Horton; Robert Simmons; Jack
  Parker; Conrad Thibault.
Studio Cast (1951) ....*RCA Victor (M) LK-1025* 51 125-150
  Scheduled as the original cast recording, but due to the show's unsuccessful run, only Jane Pickens' record-
  ings of the songs appear on the LP.
  Composer: Jerome Kern; Oscar Hammerstein II. **Conductor:** Al Goodman. **Cast:** Jane Pickens
  (with chorus).

MUSIC LOVERS
Soundtrack (1971) . . . .*United Artists (S) UAS-5217*   71   **$12-15**
Includes music of Tchaikovsky.
Conductor: Andre Previn. **Cast:** Andre Previn; London Symphony Orchestra.

MUSIC MAN
Original Cast (1957) . . . . *Capitol (M) WAO-990*   57   **15-20**
Original Cast (1957) . . . .*Capitol (SE) SWAO-990*   57   **25-30**
Above two have gatefold covers.
Original Cast (1957) . . . .*Capitol (SE) SW-990*   Re   **8-10**
Composer: Meredith Willson. **Conductor:** Herbert Greene. **Cast:** Robert Preston; Barbara Cook;
David Burns; Buffalo Bills; Eddie Hodges; Pert Kelton; Paul Reed; Helen Raymond; Iggie
Wolfington.
Original London Cast (1971) . . . .*Stanyan (S) SR-10039*   72   **8-10**
Composer: Meredith Willson. **Conductor:** Gareth Davies. **Cast:** Van Johnson; Patricia Lambert;
Bernard Spear; Iowa Four; Michael Malnick; Denis Waterman; Ruth Kettlewell.
Soundtrack (1962) . . . .*Warner Bros. (M) B-1459*   62   **10-15**
Soundtrack (1962) . . . .*Warner Bros. (S) BS-1459*   62   **10-20**
Still in print using the same catalog number.
Composer: Meredith Willson. **Conductor:** Ray Heindorf. **Cast:** Robert Preston; Shirley Jones;
Buddy Hackett; Hermione Gingold; Pert Kelton; Ronnie Howard; Buffalo Bills.
Studiotrack (1958) . . . . *Atlantic (M) 1276*   58   **20-30**
Studiotrack (1958) . . . .*Atlantic (S) SD-1276*   58   **30-40**
Cast: Jimmy Giuffre.
Studiotrack (1958) . . . . *Crown (M) 5062*   58   **10-20**
Conductor: Thomas M. Davis; Hans Hagan. **Cast:** Ken Harp; Donna Cook; Connie Conway;
Don Garley; Patti Steele; Jackie Allen; others.
Studiotrack (1959) . . . . *Lion (M) L-70091*   59   **10-15**
Studiotrack (1959) . . . . *Somerset/Stereo Fidelity (S) SF-7700*   59   **10-20**
Also has music from *South Pacific.*
Studio Cast . . . . *Promenade (M) 2097*   **10-15**
Conductor: Frank Meyers. **Cast:** Geri Gray; Marty Kaye; Bobby Thompson; others.
Studiotrack (1962) . . . .*MGM (M) E-4065*   62   **10-15**
Studiotrack (1962) . . . . *MGM (S) SE-4065*   62   **10-20**
Cast: Paul Smith Quartet.
Studiotrack (1962) . . . .*United Artists (M) UAL-3235*   62   **10-15**
Studiotrack (1962) . . . .*United Artists (S) UAS-6235*   62   **10-20**
Conductor: Ralph Marterie. **Cast:** Ralph Marterie and His Orchestra.
Also see GYPSY

MUSIC OF ERICH WOLFGANG KORNGOLD
Studiotrack (1938) . . . . *Warner Bros. (M) W-1438*   62   **35-45**
Soundtrack (1938) . . . .*Warner Bros. (SE) WS-1438*   62   **50-60**
Above two also known as *The Adventures of Robin Hood.*
Composer: Erich Wolfgang Korngold. **Conductor:** Lionel Newman.

MUSIC OF JEROME KERN
Studiotrack (1955) . . . .*Columbia (EP) A-1531*   55   **5-10**
Studiotrack (1955) . . . . *Columbia (M) CL-776*   55   **5-10**
Composer: Jerome Kern. **Conductor:** Andre Kostelanetz. **Cast:** Andre Kostelanetz and His
Orchestra.

MUSIC OF WALT DISNEY
Soundtrack .... *Buena Vista (M) 2000*   67 $8-12

MUSIC TO BE MURDERED BY
Studiotrack (1959) .... *DRG (S) SL-5183*   80   10-15
Conductor: Jeff Alexander. Cast: Jeff Alexander Orchestra; Alfred Hitchcock.

MUSIC TO READ "THE PRETENDERS" BY:
see PRETENDERS

MUSIC TO REMEMBER
Studiotrack .... *Mercury (EP) EP-1-3030*   8-12
Music from *Intermezzo, How Green Was My Valley, None But the Lonely Heart* and *Drink to Me Only with Thine Eyes.*
Composer: Alfred Newman; others. Conductor: Alfred Newman.

MUSICAL CHAIRS
Original Cast (1980) .... *Original Cast (S) OC-8024*   80   10-15
Composer: Tom Savage. Conductor: Barry Gordon. Cast: Brandon Maggart; Lee Meredith; Tom Urich; Patti Karr; Jess Richards; Joy Franz; Helen Blount; Leslie-Anne Wolfe; Rick Emery; Scott Ellis.

MUSICAL HISTORY OF THE BOSTON SYMPHONY AND BOSTON POPS
Studiotrack (1955) .... *RCA Victor (M) SRL-1211*   55   15-25
Composer: Hector Berlioz; Peter Tchaikovsky; Ludwig Beethoven; Richard Strauss; others.
Conductor: Karl Muck; Serge Koussevitzky; Charles Munch; Arthur Fiedler. Cast: Milton Cross; Leslie Rogers; Arthur Fiedler. (With narration.)

MUTANT
Soundtrack (1982) .... *Varese Sarabande (S) STV-81209*   8-10
This film is also known as *Forbidden World.*
Conductor: Richard Band. Cast: National Philharmonic Orchestra.

MUTINY ON THE BOUNTY
Soundtrack (1962) .... *MGM (M) 1E4*   62   30-40
Soundtrack (1962) .... *MGM (S) S1E4*   62   40-50
Above two are boxed sets. Both include a book and painting. This issue has the *Bounty Theme.*
Soundtrack (1962) .... *MGM (M) 1E4*   62   30-40
Soundtrack (1962) .... *MGM (S) S1E4*   62   40-50
Above two are boxed sets. Both include a book and painting. This issue has the *Bounty Love Theme* Tahitian chant.
Soundtrack (1962) .... *MGM (M) 1E4-ST*   62   20-25
Soundtrack (1962) .... *MGM (S) S1E4-ST*   62   25-30
Soundtrack (1962) .... *MCA (S) 25007*   Re   8-10
Composer: Bronislau Kaper. Conductor: Robert Armbruster.

MY COUSIN JOSEFA
Original Cast (1969) .... *Harlequin (S) H-3270*   69   30-35
Original Cast (1969) .... *AEI (S) 1139*   Re   8-12
Composer: Robert Austin. Conductor: Richard Braun. Cast: Carla Alberghetti; Jack Ritschel; Leslie Cozzens; Michael Hall; Walt Ritter; Graciela Franks; Nola Roeper; Ellard Davis; Asaad Kelada.

MY DEAR ASSASSIN:
see BLACK BELLY OF THE TARANTULA

MY FAIR LADY

Original Cast (1956) ....*Columbia (EP) A-5090*	56	$10-15
Original Cast (1956) .... *Columbia (M) OL-5090*	56	25-30
Original Cast (1956) ....*Columbia Special Products (M) XOL-5090*	Re	8-10

Composer: Alan J. Lerner; Frederick Loewe. **Conductor:** Franz Allers. **Cast:** Rex Harrison; Julie Andrews; Stanley Holloway; Robert Coote; Rod McLennan; John Michael King; Gordon Dilworth; Philippa Bevans.

Original London Cast (1959) ....*Columbia (S) OS-2015*	59	25-30
Original London Cast (1959) ....*Columbia (S) PS-2015*	Re	8-12

Composer: Alan J. Lerner; Frederick Loewe. **Conductor:** Cyril Ornadel. **Cast:** Rex Harrison; Julie Andrews; Stanley Holloway; Robert Coote; Leonard Weir; Robert Chisholm; Alan Dudley; Betty Woolfe.

Original London Cast (1959) .... *Avon (M) 3001*	59	15-20
Original London Cast (1959) .... *Avon (S) S-3001*	59	20-25

Composer: Alan J. Lerner; Frederick Loewe. **Conductor:** John Gregory. **Cast:** Hugert Gregg; Elizabeth Larner; John Slater; John Harvey.

Original Italian Cast (1959) ....*Columbia (M) OL-8060*		25-30
Original Italian Cast (1959) ....*Columbia (S) OS-2660*		35-40

Composer: Alan J. Lerner; Frederick Loewe. **Conductor:** Mario Migliardi. **Cast:** Delia Scala; Gianrico Tedeschi; Mario Carotenuto.

Original Revival Cast (1976) ....*Columbia (S) PS-34197*	76	10-12

20th anniversary production.

Composer: Alan J. Lerner; Frederick Loewe. **Conductor:** Theodore Saindenberg. **Cast:** Robert Coote; Ian Richardson; Christine Andreas; George Rose; Jerry Lanning; Sylvia O'Brien.

Studio Cast (1964) ....*Capitol (M) T-2173*	64	12-15
Studio Cast (1964) .... *Capitol (S) ST-2173*	64	15-20

Conductor: John Williams.

Studio Cast ....,...... *Diplomat (M) ND-2214*		10-15

Composer: Alan J. Lerner; Frederick Loewe. **Conductor:** Al Goodman. **Cast:** Lola Fisher; Richard Torigi; Edgar Powell; William Reynolds.

Original Spanish Cast .... *Columbia (S) OS-2980*		30-50

Composer: Alan J. Lerner; Frederick Loewe. **Conductor:** Mario Ruiz Armengol. **Cast:** Manolo Fabregas; Cristina Rojas; Placido Domingo; Mario Alberto Rodriquez; Miguel Suarez; Salvador Quiroz; Natalia Gentil Arcos; Tomas Saro; others.

Studio Cast ....*Spinorama (S) MK-3057*		10-15

Composer: Alan J. Lerner; Frederick Loewe. **Conductor:** Al Goodman. **Cast:** Lola Fisher; Richard Torigi; William Reynolds; Edgar Powell.

Studio Cast .... *Coronet (S) CXS-243*		10-15

Composer: Alan J. Lerner; Frederick Loewe. **Conductor:** Al Goodman. **Cast:** Lola Fisher; Richard Torigi; William Reynolds; Edgar Powell.

Studio Cast (1957) ....*Masterseal (M) MSLP-5001*	57	20-30

Composer: Alan J. Lerner; Frederick Loewe. **Conductor:** Jack Hansen. **Cast:** Lanny Ross; Marcia Neil.

Studio Cast ....*Mayfair (S) 9537-S*		15-20

Yellow vinyl.

Composer: Alan J. Lerner; Frederick Loewe. **Conductor:** Lew Raymond. **Cast:** Evelyn Sharpe; Charles Peck; Robert Back; others.

Studio Cast (1987) ....*London (S) 421 200-1*	87	8-12

Composer: Alan J. Lerner; Frederick Loewe. **Conductor:** John Mauceri. **Cast:** Kiri Te Kanawa; Jeremy Irons; John Gielgud; Warren Mitchell; Jerry Hadley; Meriel Dickenson; David Beavan; Joseph Cornwell; Lindsey Benson; Judith Rees; Susan Bickley; London Voices; Terry Edwards; London Symphony Orchestra.

Studiotrack	*La Brea (M) L-8007*		$10-15
Studiotrack	*.Design (S) DLP-212*		10-15
Soundtrack (1964)	*Columbia (M) KOL-8000*	64	12-15
Soundtrack (1964)	*Columbia (S) KOS-2600*	64	15-20
Soundtrack (1964)	*Columbia (S) JS-2600*	Re	10-12
Soundtrack (1964)	*Columbia (S) JST-20002*	Re	8-10

Composer: Alan J. Lerner; Frederick Loewe. **Conductor:** Andre Previn. **Cast:** Audrey Hepburn; Rex Harrison; Stanley Holloway; Wilfrid Hyde-White; Theodore Bikel; Marni Nixon. (With dialogue.)

Studiotrack (1959)	*Lion (M) L-70092*	59	10-15

Cast: Ann Maria Pallys; John Rvark.

Studiotrack (1959)	*RCA Victor/Camden (M) CAL-520*	60	15-20
Studiotrack (1959)	*RCA Victor/Camden (S) CAS-520*	60	20-30

Composer: Alan J. Lerner; Frederick Loewe. **Conductor:** Hill Bowen. **Cast:** Lane; Sammes; Martin; Johnson; Hill Bowen Orchestra.
Also see KING AND I; PAINT YOUR WAGON

MY FAIRFAX LADY

Original Cast (1957)	*Jubilee (M) JGM-2030*	57	40-50

Satire of *My Fair Lady* by the Los Angeles Cast.
Composer: Sid Kuller. **Conductor:** Jerry Fielding. **Cast:** Billy Gray; Bert Gordon; Carol Shannon; Kirby Stone Four.

MY FUR LADY

Original Canadian College Cast (1957)	*McGill (M) MRS LPM-3*	57	25-35
Original Canadian Cast (1957)	*McGill (M) MRS LPM-5*	57	40-50

Recorded June 12, 1957.

Composer: James Domville; Galt MacDermot; Timothy Porteous; Harry Garber; Roy Wolvin. **Conductor:** Edmund Assaly. **Cast:** Ann Golden; Jim Hugessen; Nancy Bacal; John MacLeod; Sheila McCormick; Douglas Robertson; Graham Wright.

MY GEISHA
Soundtrack (1962) ....*RCA Victor (M) LOC-1070*   62   **$60-65**
Soundtrack (1962) ....*RCA Victor (S) LSO-1070*   62   **75-80**
Composer: Franz Waxman; others. **Conductor:** Franz Waxman.

MY NAME IS NOBODY
Soundtrack (1974) .... *Cereberus (S) CEM-S 0101*   80   **8-10**
Composer: Ennio Morricone. **Conductor:** Ennio Morricone.

MY ONE AND ONLY
Original Cast (1983) .... *Atlantic (S) 80110-1*   83   **8-10**
Composer: George Gershwin; Ira Gershwin. **Cast:** Tommy Tune; Twiggy.

MY PEOPLE
Original Chicago Cast (1963) .... *Contact (M) C-1*   66   **15-20**
Original Chicago Cast (1963) ....*Contact (S) CS-1*   66   **20-25**
Original Chicago Cast (1963) ....*Flying Dutchman (S) FDS-112*   Re   **10-15**
Composer: Duke Ellington. **Conductor:** Jimmy Jones. **Cast:** Joya Sherrill; Lil Greenwood; Jimmy McPhail; Irving Bunton Singers; Bunny Briggs; Jimmy Grissom.

MY PLEASURE IS MY BUSINESS
Soundtrack (1975) ....*Daffodil (S) DAF-10051*   75   **10-15**
Composer: Thomas W. Cochrane. **Cast:** Xaviera Hollander.

MY SIDE OF THE MOUNTAIN
Soundtrack (1969) .... *Capitol (S) ST-245*   69   **20-25**
Composer: William Josephs. **Conductor:** Muir Mathieson. **Cast:** Teddy Eccles; Theodore Bikel; Tudi Wiggins. (With dialogue.)

MY SQUARE LADDIE (A LOONEY LAMPOON OF MY FAIR LADY)
Studio Cast .... *Foremost (M) FMLS-1*   **50-60**
Studio Cast .... *AEI (M) 1132*   Re   **8-10**
Composer: Max Showalter; William Howe. **Conductor:** Eddie Dunstedter. **Cast:** Reginald Gardner; Zasu Pitts; Nancy Walker.

MY STEPMOTHER IS AN ALIEN
Soundtrack (1988) ....*Polydor (S) 837798-1*   88   **8-10**
Composer: Various. **Cast:** Animotion; Marrs; Ivan Neville; Kim Basinger; Dan Aykroyd; Cameo; Jackie Jackson; Siren.

MY TURN ON EARTH
Original Cast (1977) .... *Embryo (S) ER-2003A*   77   **12-15**
Double LP set.
Composer: Lex de Azevedo; Carol Lynn Pearson. **Conductor:** Lex de Azevedo.
Cast: Candy Brand; Laurette Conkling; Shawn Engemann; Brad Murdoch; Paul Engemann.

MY UNCLE
Soundtrack (1958) ....*Fontana (EP) TFE-17175*   58   **10-15**
Cast: Jacques Tati.

MY WILD IRISH ROSE
Soundtrack (1947) .... *RCA Victor (EP) EPB-3036*   52   **15-20**
Double EP set.
Soundtrack (1947) .... *RCA Victor (M) LPM-3036*   52   **20-30**
10-inch LP.
Cast: Dennis Day.

MYRA BRECKINRIDGE
Soundtrack (1970) . . . .*20th Century-Fox (S) S-4210*   70   **$200-225**
   Promotional issue only.
  Composer: John Phillips.

MYSTERIOUS FILM WORLD OF BERNARD HERRMANN
Soundtrack . . . .*London (S) SPC-21137*   76   **10-20**
   Selections from *The Three Worlds of Gulliver* with more music from the film than the Colpix issue, which
   is mostly dialogue. Also contains music from *Mysterious Island* and *Jason and the Argonauts.*
  Composer: Bernard Herrmann. **Conductor:** Bernard Herrmann. **Cast:** National Philharmonic
   Orchestra.
   Also see THREE WORLDS OF GULLIVER

MYSTERIOUS ISLAND
Soundtrack (1961) . . . . *Cloud Nine (S) CN-4002*   84   **35-40**
  Composer: Bernard Herrmann. **Conductor:** Bernard Herrmann.

MYSTERY OF EDWIN DROOD
Original Broadway Cast (1985) . . . .*Polydor (S) 827969-1*   86   **8-10**
  Composer: Rupert Holmes. **Conductor:** M. Starobin. **Cast:** Cleo Laine; G. Rose.

N

NAGSHEAD
Original Cast (1974) ....*O. Barton (S) OBS-1114* 74 $40-45
From a Broadway demo recording, since this show did not open as planned.
Composer: Ovid Lewis. **Conductor:** Lou Toby. **Cast:** Phyllis Craig; Donald Lombardi; Lou Toby; Dick Gardner.

NAKED ANGELS
Soundtrack (1969) ....*Straight (S) STS-1056* 69 12-15
Composer: Jeffrey Simmons; Randy Steirling.

NAKED APE
Soundtrack (1973) .... *Playboy (S) PB-125* 73 10-12
Composer: Jimmy Webb; Johann Sebastian Bach. **Conductor:** Jimmy Webb. **Cast:** Donald Driver; Jimmy Webb; Clydie King; others.

NAKED CITY
TV Soundtrack (1958) ....*Colpix (S) CP-505* 59 30-35
TV Soundtrack (1958) ....*Colpix (S) SCP-505* 58 40-50
Composer: George Dunning. **Conductor:** Morris Stoloff. **Cast:** John McIntire (narration).
Also see BRUTE FORCE

NAKED MAJA
Soundtrack (1959) ....*United Artists (M) UAL-4031* 59 30-35
Soundtrack (1959) ....*United Artists (S) UAS-5031* 59 45-50
"The Naked Maja" was a model-inspired painting by Francisco Goya.
Composer: Francesco Angelo Lavagnino. **Conductor:** Francesco Angelo Lavagnino.

NAKED PREY
Soundtrack (1966) .... *Folkways (S) 3854* 8-10

NANCY GOES TO RIO
Soundtrack (1950) ....*MGM (M) E-508* 50 45-50
10-inch LP.
Composer: Ray Gilbert; others. **Conductor:** Georgie Stoll. **Cast:** Jane Powell; Ann Sothern; Carmen Miranda; Danny Scholl.

NAPOLEON
Studiotrack (1927) ....*CBS (SE) FMT-37230* 81 8-10
Composer: Carmine Coppola. **Conductor:** Carmine Coppola.

NARM'S GOLDEN DECADE
Studiotrack ....*RCA Victor (S) PRS-264* 69 20-40
Promotional souvenir disc, distributed at NARM's tenth anniversary meeting and awards banquet. Tracks were recorded in the studio but were "suggestive of the spirit of the artists' performances at the RCA parties or the NARM banquets."
Composer: Various. **Cast:** Limeliters; Ann-Margret; Al Hirt; Paul Anka; Homer and Jethro; Peter Nero; Eddy Arnold; John Gary; Chet Atkins; Floyd Cramer; Anita Kerr Singers; Boots Randolph; Myron Cohen; SSGT. Barry Sadler; Henry Mancini; Jack Jones; Harry Belafonte.

NASHVILLE
Soundtrack (1975) .... *ABC (S) ABCD-893* 75 10-15
Conductor: Richard Baskin. **Cast:** Keith Carradine.

NASHVILLE/NEW YORK
London Cast .... *That's Entertainment (S) TER-1001* $10-12
  Composer: Ogden Nash; others

NASHVILLE REBEL
Soundtrack (1966) .... *RCA Victor (M) LPM-3736*   66   12-18
Soundtrack (1966) .... *RCA Victor (S) LSP-3736e*   66   12-18
  Composer: Waylon Jennings; Paul McCartney; others. Cast: Waylon Jennings.

NATIONAL LAMPOON LEMMINGS
Original Cast (1973) .... *Blue Thumb (S) BTS-6006*   73   15-20
  Conductor: Paul Jacobs. Cast: Chevy Chase; Alice Playten; John Belushi; Gary Goodrow;
  Paul Jacobs; Christopher Guest; Mary Jennifer Mitchell.

NATIONAL LAMPOON'S ANIMAL HOUSE:
see ANIMAL HOUSE

NATIONAL LAMPOON'S VACATION
Soundtrack (1983) .... *Warner Bros. (S) 1-23909*   83   8-10
  Composer: Various. Cast: Lindsey Buckingham; Fleetwoods; Ramones; others.

NATIVE SON
Soundtrack (1986) .... *MCA (S) 6198*   87   8-10
  Cast: Mtume.

NATURAL
Soundtrack (1984) .... *Warner Bros. (S) 1-25116*   84   8-10
  Composer: Randy Newman. Conductor: Randy Newman.

NATURAL HIGH
Original Cast .... *Light (S) L5-5558-L*   10-12
  Composer: Ralph Carmichael; Kurt Kaiser.

NATURE'S HALF ACRE:
see WALT DISNEY'S TRUE LIFE ADVENTURES

NAUGHTY MARIETTA
Studio Cast (1953) .... *RCA Victor (EP) EPA-481*   53   15-20
Studio Cast (1951) .... *RCA Victor (M) LK-1005*   51   25-30
  Composer: Victor Herbert; Rida Johnson Young. Conductor: Al Goodman. Cast: Earl
  Wrightson; Elain Malbin; Jimmy Carroll.
Studio Cast (1950) .... *Columbia (M) ML-2094*   50   35-40
  Composer: Victor Herbert; Rida Johnson Young. Conductor: Robert Armbruster.
  Cast: Nelson Eddy; Nadine Conner.
Studio Cast (1954) .... *Capitol (M) L-468*   54   35-40
  10-inch LP.
Studio Cast (1954) .... *Capitol (M) P-551*   54   20-25
  One side has music from *The Red Mill*.
  Composer: Victor Herbert; Rida Johnson Young. Conductor: George Greeley. Cast: Gordon
  MacRae; Marguerite Piazza; Katherine Hilgenberg.
Studio Cast (1959) .... *Lion (M) L-70090*   59   10-15
  Composer: Victor Herbert; Rida Johnson Young. Conductor: Paul Britton.
Soundtrack (1952) .... *RCA Victor (M) LCT-16*   52   35-45
  10-inch LP.
Studiotrack (1952) .... *RCA Victor (M) LPV-526*   66   15-20
  Also contains songs from seven other films starring Nelson Eddy and Jeanette MacDonald.
  Composer: Victor Herbert; Rida Johnson Young. Conductor: Nathaniel Shilkret; Herbert
  Stothart. Cast: Nelson Eddy; Jeanette MacDonald.
  Also see CHOCOLATE SOLDIER; MADEMOISELLE MODISTE

NAVAJO JOE
Soundtrack (1966) .... *United Artists (S) UA-LA292-G*   74 $20-25
  Composer: Leo Nichols (Ennio Morricone). **Conductor:** Leo Nichols (Ennio Morricone).

NBC'S SATURDAY NIGHT LIVE
TV Soundtrack .... *Arista (S) AL-4107*   77   10-12

NED KELLY
Soundtrack (1970) .... *United Artists (S) UAS-5213*   70   15-20
Soundtrack (1970) .... *United Artists (S) UA-LA300-G*   74   10-12
  Composer: Shel Silverstein. **Cast:** Waylon Jennings; Mick Jagger; Kris Kristofferson; Tom Ghent.

NEFERTITI
Original Cast (1977) .... *Take Home Tunes (S) THT-7810*   77   8-10
  Composer: David Spangler; Christopher Gore. **Conductor:** John Demain. **Cast:** Robert Lupone;
  Andrea Marcouicci; Michael Nouri; Michael Smartt; Jane White.

NERVOUS SET
Original Cast (1959) .... *Columbia (M) OL-5430*   59   30-40
  Conductor: Tommy Wolf.
Original Cast (1959) .... *Columbia (S) OS-2018*   59   35-40
  Composer: Tommy Wolf; Fran Landesman. **Cast:** Richard Hayes; Tani Seitz; Larry Hagman;
  Del Close; Tommy Wolf (piano); William Schneider (drum); Kenny Burrell (guitar); Joe
  Benjamin (bass).

NEVADA SMITH
Soundtrack (1966) .... *Dot (M) DLP-3718*   66   30-35
Soundtrack (1966) .... *Dot (S) DLP-25718* ·66   40-50
  Composer: Alfred Newman. **Conductor:** Alfred Newman.

NEVER CRY WOLF:
see MRS. SOFFEL

NEVER ENDING STORY
Soundtrack (1984) .... *EMI America (S) ST-17139*   84   8-10
  Cast: Limahl; others.

NEVER ON SUNDAY
Soundtrack (1960) .... *United Artists (M) UAL-4070*   60 ·   10-15
Soundtrack (1960) .... *United Artists (S) UAS-5070*   60   15-20
Soundtrack (1960) .... *Liberty (S) 4N-10280*   Re   8-10
  The 1967 Broadway musical *Illya Darling*, with the same star and composer/conductor, was based on this
  film's story.
- **Composer:** Manos Hadjidakis. **Conductor:** Manos Hadjidakis. **Cast:** Melina Mercouri.
  Also see I WANT TO LIVE

NEW FACES OF 1952
Original Cast (1952) .... *RCA Victor (EP) EOA-433*   52   15-20
Original Cast (1952) .... *RCA Victor (M) LOC-1008*   52   30-40
Original Cast (1952) .... *RCA Victor (SE) LOS-1008e*   70   12-20
Original Cast (1952) .... *RCA Victor (SE) CBM1-2206*   77´   8-12
  Has one track, *Time for Tea*, not found on earlier issues.
  Composer: Ronny Graham; June Carroll; Arthur Siegel; Sheldon M. Harnick; Michael Brown;
  others. **Conductor:** Anton Coppola. **Cast:** Virgina Bosler; June Carroll; Robert Clary; Allen
  Conroy; Virginia DeLuce; Alice Ghostley; Ronny Graham; Patricia Hammerlee; Eartha Kitt;
  Joseph Lautner; Paul Lynde; Bill Mullikin; Rosemary O'Reilly.
  Also see EARTHA KITT SINGS SONGS FROM "NEW FACES"

NEW FACES OF 1956

Original Cast (1956) .... *RCA Victor (EP) EOC-1025*   56   **$15-20**
Original Cast (1956) .... *RCA Victor (M) LOC-1025*   56   **50-60**
   Composer: June Carroll; others. **Conductor:** Jay Blackton. **Cast:** T.C. Jones (host); Suzanne
   Bernard; Jane Connell; Billie Hayes; Johnny Haymer; Tiger Haynes; Ann Henry; Virginia
   Martin; John Reardon; Amru Sani; Bob Shaver; Maggie Smith; Inga Swenson.

NEW FACES OF 1968

Original Cast (1968) .... *Warner Bros. (S) BS-2551*   68   **25-30**
   Composer: Ronny Graham; others. **Conductor:** Ted Simons. **Cast:** Michael Allen; Suzanne
   Astor; Gloria Bleezarde; Trudy Carson; Marilyn Child; Elaine Giftos; Madeline Kahn; Robert
   Klein; Brandon Maggart; George Ormiston; Rod Perry; Nancie Phillips; Leonard Sillman.

NEW GIRL IN TOWN

Original Cast (1957) .... *RCA Victor (M) LOC-1027*   57   **30-35**
Original Cast (1957) .... *RCA Victor (SE) LSO-1027*   58   **45-50**
Original Cast (1957) .... *RCA Victor (M) LOC-1106*   65   **30-35**
Original Cast (1957) .... *RCA Victor (SE) LSO-1106*   65   **40-45**
   Composer: Robert Merrill. **Conductor:** Harold Hastings. **Cast:** Mark Dawson; Lulu Bates;
   Eddie Phillips; Delbert Anderson; H.F. Green; Maria Land; Gwen Verdon; Thelma Ritter;
   Cameron Prud'Homme; George Wallace.

NEW INTERNS

Soundtrack (1964) .... *Colpix (M) CP-473*   64   **20-25**
Soundtrack (1964) .... *Colpix (S) SCP-473*   64   **30-35**
   Film sequel to *The Interns.*
   Composer: Earle Hagen. **Conductor:** Earl Hagen.

NEW KIND OF LOVE

Soundtrack (1963) .... *Mercury (M) MG-20859*   63   **15-20**
Soundtrack (1963) .... *Mercury (S) SR-60859*   63   **20-25**
   Composer: Sammy Fain; Erroll Garner; others. **Conductor:** Leith Stevens. **Cast:** Erroll Garner.

NEW MOON

Original London Cast (1928) ...... *Monmouth Evergreen (SE) MES-7051*   **8-10**
   Composer: Sigmund Romberg; Oscar Hammerstein II. **Conductor:** Sigmund Romberg
   (instrumentals); Herman Finck (vocals). **Cast:** Evelyn Laye; Ben Williams; Howett Worster;
   Gene Gerrard.
Original Revival Cast (1951) .... *RCA Victor (M) EKB-1011*   51   **15-20**
   Double EP set.
Original Revival Cast (1951) .... *RCA Victor (M) LK-1011*   51   **25-35**
   Composer: Sigmund Romberg; Oscar Hammerstein II. **Conductor:** Al Goodman. **Cast:** Earl
   Wrightson; Al Goodman Orchestra; Frances Greer; Donald Dame; Earl Oxford Chorus.
Studio Cast (1950) .... *Capitol (M) T-219*   50   **25-35**
   One side has music from *Vagabond King.*
   Composer: Sigmund Romberg; Oscar Hammerstein II. **Conductor:** Paul Weston.
   Cast: Gordon MacRae; Lucille Norman.
Studio Cast (1963) .... *Capitol (M) W-1996*   63   **15-20**
Studio Cast (1963) .... *Capitol (S) SW-1996*   63   **25-30**
Studio Cast (1950) .... *Decca (EP) EP-522*   50   **15-20**
Studio Cast (1963) .... *Angel (S) S-37320*   73   **8-10**
   Composer: Sigmund Romberg; Oscar Hammerstein II. **Conductor:** Van Alexander.
   Cast: Gordon MacRae; Dorothy Kirsten; Richard Robinson.
Studio Cast (1953) .... *Decca (M) DL-5472*   53   **30-40**
   10-inch LP.
   Composer: Sigmund Romberg; Oscar Hammerstein. **Conductor:** Victor Young. **Cast:** Thomas
   Hayward; Jane Wilson; Lee Sweetland.

NEW MOON (continued)
Studio Cast (1950) .... *Columbia (M) ML-2164*   50 $35-45
  10-inch LP.
Studio Cast (1950) .... *Columbia Special Products (M) P-13878*   77   **8-10**
  One side has music from *Rose Marie*.
  Composer: Sigmund Romberg; Oscar Hammerstein II. **Conductor:** Leon Arnaud. **Cast:** Nelson
  Eddy; Eleanor Steber.
Soundtrack (1940) .... *Pelican (M) LP-103*   80   **8-12**
  One side has the original radio cast of the June 1, 1942 broadcast of *I Married an Angel*, with Jeanette
  MacDonald; Nelson Eddy; Bennie Barnes; Edward Everett Horton.
  Cast: Jeanette MacDonald; Nelson Eddy.
  Also see GIRL FRIEND

NEW YORK, NEW YORK
Soundtrack (1977) .... *United Artists (S) UA-LA750-H*   77   **12-15**
  Double LP set.
  Composer: John Kander; Fred Ebb. **Conductor:** Ralph Burns; Gary Miller. **Cast:** Shirley
  Bassey; Liza Minnelli; Larry Kert; Mary Kay Place; Dianne Abbott; Georgie Auld.

NEW YORK STORIES
Soundtrack (1989) .... *Elektra (S) 60857-1*   89   **8-10**
  Composer: Various. **Cast:** Kid Creole and Coconuts; Pianosaurus; Frankie Carle; Wilbur
  De Paris; Bernie Leighton; Procol Harum; Transvision Vamp; Hot Club of France; Bob Dylan;
  The Band.

NEXT MAN
Soundtrack (1976) .... *Buddah (S) BDS-5685*   76   **10-15**
  Composer: Michael Kamen; Rosko Mercer. **Conductor:** Michael Kamen. **Cast:** Tasha Thomas;
  Robert Fitoussi; Michael Kamen.

NICHOLAS AND ALEXANDRA
Soundtrack (1971) .... *Bell (S) B-1103*   71   **30-40**
  Composer: Richard Rodney Bennett. **Conductor:** Marcus Dods. **Cast:** New Philharmonia
  Orchestra of London.

NICHOLAS NICKLEBY
TV Soundtrack (1982) .... *DRG (S) SBL-12583*   82   **10-12**
  Composer: Stephen Oliver. **Conductor:** Harry Rabinowitz. **Cast:** Roger Rees; Jane Downs;
  Emily Richards; John Woodvine; David Threlfall; Edward Retherbridge; Susanne Bertish; Lila
  Kaye; Alun Armstrong; others.

NIGHT AND DAY:
see COLE PORTER REVIEW

NIGHT AT CARNEGIE HALL
Soundtrack (1947) .... *Columbia (M) ML-2113*   50   **45-50**
  Film title was *Carnegie Hall*.
  Composer: Mozart; Verdi; Delibes. **Conductor:** Pietro Cimara; George Sebastian; Fausto Cleva.
  Cast: Lily Pons; Ezio Pinza; Rise Stevens; Raoul Jobin.

NIGHT CROSSING
Soundtrack (1981) .... *Intrada (S) RVF-6004*   **8-10**

NIGHT DIGGER
Soundtrack (1975) .... *Cinema (S) LP-8015*   **40-60**
  Composer: Bernard Herrmann. **Conductor:** Bernard Herrmann.

NIGHT IN VENICE
Original Revival Cast (1959) . . . .*Everest (M) LPBR-6028*   59 $25-30
Original Revival Cast (1959) . . . . *Everest (S) SDBR-3028*   59   40-45
   Composer: Johann Strauss Jr.; Ruth Martin; Thomas Martin. **Conductor:** Thomas Martin.
   Cast: Enzo Stuarti; Thomas Tibbett Hayward; Norwood Smith; Jack Russell; Nola Fairbanks;
   Laurel Hurley; David Kurlan; Guen Omeron; Kenneth Schon.

NIGHT OF THE COMET
Soundtrack (1984) . . . . *Macola (S) MRCO 900*   84   10-15
   Composer: Various. **Cast:** Revolver; Diana DeWitt; Thom Pace; Skip Adams; Chris Farren;
   John Townsend; Stallion; Amy Holland.

NIGHT OF THE GENERALS
Soundtrack (1967) . . . .*Colgems (M) COMO-5002*   67   30-45
Soundtrack (1967) . . . .*Colgems (S) COSO-5002*   67   60-80
   Composer: Maurice Jarre. **Conductor:** Maurice Jarre.

NIGHT OF THE HUNTER
Soundtrack (1955) . . . .*RCA Victor (EP) EPC-1136*   55   75-125
   Triple EP set.
Soundtrack (1955) . . . . *RCA Victor (M) LPM-1136*   55   225-250
   Composer: Walter Schumann. **Conductor:** Walter Schumann. **Cast:** Charles Laughton
   (narration).

NIGHT OF THE IGUANA (AND OTHER MUSIC INSPIRED BY THE FILM)
Soundtrack (1964) . . . . *MGM (M) PR-4*   64   40-50
Soundtrack (1964) . . . .*MGM (M) E-4247*   64   20-25
Soundtrack (1964) . . . . *MGM (S) SE-4247*   64   30-35
   Composer: Benjamin Frankel. **Conductor:** Benjamin Frankel. **Cast:** John Huston
   (commentary); Richard Burton; Ava Gardner; Deborah Kerr; Sue Lyon; others.

NIGHT OF THE LIVING DEAD
Soundtrack (1968) . . . . *Varese Sarabande (M) STV-81151*   82   8-10
   An assortment of '50s recordings heard in the film.
   Composer: Spencer Moore; William Loose; George Hormel; Ib Glindemann; others.

NIGHT SHIFT
Soundtrack (1982) . . . . *Warner Bros. (S) 1-23702*   82   8-10
Soundtrack (1982) . . . . *Warner Bros. (S) 92-37021*   82   8-12
   Composer: Burt Bacharach; Carole Bayer Sager (some additional music and lyrics by Marv Ross
   and David Foster). **Cast:** Quarterflash; Burt Bacharach; Al Jarreau; Pointer Sisters; Rod Stewart;
   Marshall Crenshaw; Heaven 17; Talk Talk; Rufus with Chaka Khan.

NIGHT THE LIGHTS WENT OUT IN GEORGIA
Soundtrack (1981) . . . .*Mirage (S) XWTG-16051*   81   8-10
   Composer: David Shire. **Conductor:** Gene Armond (music coordinator). **Cast:** Tanya Tucker;
   Glen Campbell; George Jones; Tammy Wynette; Dennis Quaid; Kristy McNichol; Billy Preston;
   Syreeta.

NIGHT THEY RAIDED MINSKY'S
Soundtrack (1968) . . . . *United Artists (S) UAS-5191*   69   25-30
   Composer: Charles Strouse; Lee Adams. **Conductor:** Philip J. Lang; LeRoy Holmes.
   Cast: Rudy Vallee; Dexter Maitland; Lillian Heyman; Jason Robards; Norman Wisdom.

NIGHT TRAIN GOES TO HOLLYWOOD
Studio Cast (1962) . . . . *Mercury (M) MG-20702*   62   10-15
Studio Cast (1962) . . . . *Mercury (S) SR-60702*   62   15-20
   Songs from: *Porgy and Bess, Never on Sunday, Man with a Golden Arm, High Noon, Jailhouse Rock,*
   Exodus, The Rat Race, Dragnet, Sunset Strip and *West Side Story.*
   Composer: Various. **Conductor:** Buddy Morrow. **Cast:** Buddy Morrow.

NIGHTBREED
Soundtrack . . . . *MCA (S) 8037*   **$8-10**

NIGHTCOMERS
Soundtrack (1976) . . . . *Citadel (S) CTJF-1*   76   **150-200**
Composer: Jerry Fielding. **Conductor:** Jerry Fielding

NIGHTHAWKS
Soundtrack (1981) . . . . *Backstreet (S) 5196*   81   **10-12**
Soundtrack (1981) . . . . *MCA (S) 1521*   Re   **8-10**
Cast: Keith Emerson.

NIGHTINGALE
Original London Cast (1982) . . . . *No Label Shown (S) TER-1031*   83   **10-12**
Composer: Charles Strouse. **Cast:** Sarah Brightman; Andrew Shore; Gordon Sandison.

NIGHTMARE ON ELM STREET
Soundtrack (1984) . . . . *Varese Sarabande (S) STV-81236*   84   **15-20**
Composer: Charles Bernstein.

NIGHTMARE ON ELM STREET 4 - THE DREAM MASTER
Soundtrack (1988) . . . . *Chrysalis (S) OV-41673*   88   **8-10**
Composer: Various. **Cast:** Sea Hags; Angels from Angel City; Go West; Divinyls; Jimmy Davis and Junction; Vinnie Vincent Invasion; Vigil; Blondie; Love/Hate; Craig Safan.

NIGHTMARE ON ELM STREET 5 - THE DREAM CHILD
Soundtrack . . . . *Jive (S) 258-1J9*   **8-10**
Composer: Various. **Cast:** Bruce Dickinson; Romeo's Daughter; Samantha Fox.

NIKKI, WILD DOG OF THE NORTH
Soundtrack (1961) . . . . *Disneyland (M) DQ-1913*   62   **12-15**
Soundtrack (1961) . . . . *Disneyland (M) DQ-1281*   65   **10-12**
Composer: Paul J. Smith. **Conductor:** Paul J. Smith. **Cast:** Don Haldane; Jean Coutu; Emile Geneste. (With dialogue.)

NINE
Original Cast (1982) . . . . *Columbia (S) JS-38325*   82   **20-25**
Composer: Maurg Yeston. **Conductor:** Wally Harper. **Cast:** Raul Julia; Karen Akers; Shelly Burch; Taina Elg; Liliane Montevecchi; Anita Morris.

9½ WEEKS
Soundtrack (1986) . . . . *Capitol (S) SV-12470*   86   **8-10**
Composer: Various. **Cast:** Corey Hart; John Taylor; Eurythmics; Joe Cocker; Luba; Bryan Ferry; Dalbello; Devo; Stewart Copeland.

NINE HOURS TO RAMA
Soundtrack (1963) . . . . *London (M) M-76002*   63   **250-300**
Composer: Malcolm Arnold. **Conductor:** Malcolm Arnold.

9-30-55
Soundtrack (1977) . . . . *MCA (S) 2313*   77   **10-12**
Composer: Leonard Rosenman; others. **Conductor:** Leonard Rosenman. **Cast:** Richard Thomas (narration); Webb Pierce; Kitty Wells (with dialogue relating to James Dean). Also includes background music from *Rebel Without a Cause* and *East of Eden*, both scored by Rosenman.

NINE TO FIVE
Soundtrack (1980) . . . . *20th Century-Fox (S) 627*   80   **8-10**
Composer: Dolly Parton; Charles Fox. **Conductor:** Charles Fox. **Cast:** Dolly Parton.

1941
Soundtrack (1979) .... *Arista (S) AL-9510* 79 **$10-12**
 Composer: John Williams; others. **Conductor:** John Williams; others. **Cast:** Louis Bellson;
 Abe Most.

1963
Soundtrack (1988) .... *Polydor (S) 837362-1* 88 **8-10**
 Composer: Various. **Cast:** Jimi Hendrix; Cream; Animals; Creedence Clearwater Revival;
 Canned Heat; Zombies; Jesse Colin Young; Blind Faith; Moody Blues; Crosby, Nash and
 Young; Pretenders.

1963'S MAJOR MOTION PICTURE AND TV THEMES
Studiotrack (1963) .... *20th Century-Fox (M) TFM-3105* 63 **10-15**
Studiotrack (1963) .... *20th Century-Fox (S) TFS-4105* 63 **15-20**
 Includes: *Irma La Douce, Cleopatra, The V.I.P.'s, Papa's Delicate Condition, It's a Mad, Mad, Mad, Mad World, Phil Silvers' Show, The Lieutenant, Breaking Point, Mr. Novak, Dick Van Dyke Show*, and others.
 Composer: Various. **Conductor:** Lionel Newman. **Cast:** Lionel Newman and His Orchestra.

NO FOR AN ANSWER
Original Cast (1941) .... *Theme (M) TALP-103* 51 **500-525**
 Reissue of Musicraft 78 rpm recordings.
Original Cast (1941) .... *AEI (SE) 1140* 82 **8-10**
 Composer: Marc Blitzstein. **Cast:** Carol Channing; Olive Deering; Lloyd Gough; Marc
 Blitzstein (piano).

NO GO
Soundtrack (1976) .... *Island (S) SMAS-9333* 76 **10-15**

NO MAN CAN TAME ME
TV Soundtrack (1959) .... *Empire (M) EBC-59748* 59 **100-125**
 One-sided LP (side two is blank).
 Composer: Jay Livingston; Ray Evans. **Cast:** Gisele MacKenzie; John Raitt.

NO NO NANETTE
Original London Cast .... *Stanyan (M) SR-10035* 72 **12-15**
 One side has music from *Sunny.*
 Composer: Vincent Youmans; Otto Harbach; Irving Caesar. **Conductor:** Percival Mackey.
 Cast: Binnie Hale; Seymour Beard; Joseph Coyne; George Grossmith; Irene Brown.
Original Revival Cast (1971) .... *Columbia (S) S-30563* 71 **8-10**
Original Revival Cast (1971) .... *Columbia (S) AS-2-1023* 71 **30-35**
 Actual title: *Backstage with No No Nanette.* Lee Jordan interviews members of the cast. Also has selections
 from Columbia S-30563.
 Composer: Vincent Youmans; Otto Harbach; Irving Caesar. **Conductor:** Buster Davis.
 Cast: Ruby Keeler; Jack Gilford; Bobby Van; Helen Gallagher; Susan Watson; Patsy Kelly;
 Roger Rathburn; Irving Ceasar; others.
Studio Cast (1958) .... *Epic (M) LM-3512* 58 **25-30**
 One side has music from *Show Boat.*
 Conductor: Johnny Gregory. **Cast:** Bruce Trent; Doreen Hume.
London Studio Cast .... *Saga (S) 811* **15-20**
 Composer: Vincent Youmans; Otto Harbach; Irving Caesar. **Conductor:** Ray Cook.
 Cast: Mary Preston; John Parker; John Dane; Barry Monroe.
Studiotrack (1971) .... *RCA Victor (S) LSP-4504* 71 **10-12**
Studiotrack (1971) .... *United Artists (S) UAS-6806* 71 **10-12**
 Composer: Vincent Youmans; Otto Harbach; Irving Ceasar. **Conductor:** LeRoy Holmes.
 Cast: LeRoy Holmes Singers and Orchestra.

NO SAD SONGS FOR ME
Soundtrack (1950) .... *Web (M) ST-108*   82   **$10-12**
Also has music from *The Last Angry Man, Full of Life* and *Count Three and Pray*, all composed and
conducted by George Duning.
Composer: George Duning. **Conductor:** George Duning.

NO SMALL AFFAIR
Soundtrack (1984) .... *Atlantic (S) 78-01891*   84   **8-10**
Composer: Rupert Holmes. **Cast:** Fiona; Chrissy Faith; Rupert Holmes; Twisted Sister; Zebra;
Paul Delph; Malcolm McLaren and the McLarenettes.

NO STRINGS
Original Cast (1962) .... *Capitol (M) O-1695*   62   **20-25**
Original Cast (1962) .... *Capitol (S) SO-1695*   62   **30-35**
Composer: Richard Rodgers. **Conductor:** Peter Matz. **Cast:** Richard Kiley; Diahann Carroll;
Noelle Adam; Bernice Mass; Don Chastain; Mitchell Gregg.
Original London Cast .... *Stet (S) DS-15013*   63   **10-15**
Composer: Richard Rodgers. **Cast:** Art Lund; Beverly Todd; Hy Hazell.

NO STRINGS (WITH STRINGS)
Studiotrack .... *Epic/Columbia Special Products (S) EPSP-630*   **8-10**
Composer: Richard Rodgers. **Conductor:** Ralph Burns. **Cast:** Ralph Burns and His Orchestra.

NO SUN IN VENICE
Soundtrack (1958) .... *Atlantic (M) 1284*   58   **15-20**
Soundtrack (1958) .... *Atlantic (S) SD-1284*   58   **20-25**
Composer: John Lewis. **Conductor:** John Lewis. **Cast:** Modern Jazz Quartet.

NO WAY TO TREAT A LADY
Soundtrack (1968) .... *Dot (M) DLP-3846*   68   **10-15**
Soundtrack (1968) .... *Dot (S) DLP-25846*   68   **15-20**
Composer: Stanley Myers. **Conductor:** Stanley Myers. **Cast:** American Breed.

NOCTURNA
Soundtrack (1979) .... *MCA (S) 2-4121*   79   **10-15**
Double LP set.
Composer: Reid Whitelaw; Norman Bergen. **Cast:** Gloria Gaynor; Vicki Sue Robinson; Jay
Siegel; Heaven and Hell Orchestra and Chorus; Moment of Truth.

NORTH AND SOUTH
Soundtrack (1985) . . . . *Varese Sarabande (S) 704-150*   86 $10-12
    One side has music from *The Right Stuff*.
    Composer: Bill Conti. **Conductor:** Bill Conti. **Cast:** London Symphony Orchestra.

NORTH BY NORTHWEST
Soundtrack (1959) . . . .*Starlog/Varese Sarabande (S) SV-95001*   80   15-20
    Composer: Bernard Herrmann. **Conductor:** Laurie Johnson.

NORTH OF HOLLYWOOD
Soundtrack (1957) . . . . *RCA Victor (M) LPM-1445*   57   20-35
Soundtrack (1957) . . . . *RCA Victor (SE) LSP-1445*   57   35-50
    A collection of Alex North themes.
    Composer: Alex North.

NORWOOD
Soundtrack (1970) . . . .*Capitol (S) SW-475*   70   15-20
    Composer: Al Delory; Mac Davis; Mitchell Torok; Ramona Reed. **Cast:** Glen Campbell.

NOT SO LONG AGO
TV Soundtrack (1960) . . . . *RCA Victor (M) LOC-1055*   60   25-30
TV Soundtrack (1960) . . . . *RCA Victor (S) LSO-1055*   60   35-40
    From the NBC-TV documentary *Project Twenty*.
    Composer: Robert Russell Bennett. **Conductor:** Robert Russell Bennett. **Cast:** Bob Hope
    (narration); Harry S. Truman; Dwight D. Eisenhower; Winston Churchill; Babe Ruth; others.

NOT WITH MY WIFE, YOU DON'T
Soundtrack (1966) . . . .*Warner Bros. (M) W-1668*   66   15-20
Soundtrack (1966) . . . .*Warner Bros. (S) SW-1668*   66   20-30
    Composer: John Williams. **Conductor:** John Williams. **Cast:** Johnny Mercer.

NOTHING BUT A MAN
Soundtrack (1964) . . . . *Motown (M) MT-630*   65   12-15
Soundtrack (1964) . . . .*Motown (S) S-630*   65   15-20
    Composer: Various. **Cast:** Smokey Robinson and the Miracles; Little Stevie Wonder; Mary
    Wells; Martha Reeves and the Vandellas.

NOTHING BUT THE BEST
Soundtrack (1964) . . . . *Colpix (M) CP-477*   64   25-30
Soundtrack (1964) . . . . *Colpix (S) SCP-477*   64   30-35
    Composer: Ron Grainer. **Conductor:** Ron Grainer. **Cast:** Millicent Martin; Eagles.

NOW IS THE TIME FOR ALL GOOD MEN
Original Cast (1967) . . . . *Columbia (M) OL-6730*   67   20-25
Original Cast (1967) . . . .*Columbia (S) OS-3130*   67   30-35
    Composer: Nancy Ford; Gretchen Cryer. **Conductor:** Stephen Lawrence. **Cast:** Sally Niven;
    Judy Frank; David Cryer; Donna Curtis; David Sabin; Art Wallace; Anne Kaye; Murray Olson;
    Steve Skiles; John Bennett Perry.

NOW VOYAGER: THE CLASSIC FILM SCORES OF MAX STEINER
Studiotrack . . . .*RCA Victor (S) ARL-1-013*   73   10-12
    Has music from: *Now Voyager, King Kong, The Big Sleep, The Charge of the Light Brigade, The*
    Fountainhead, Four Wives, Since You Went Away, Saratoga Trunk, The Informer and *Johnny Belinda*.
    Composer: Max Steiner. **Conductor:** Charles Gerhardt.

NUN'S STORY
Soundtrack (1959) . . . . *Warner Bros. (M) B-1306*   59   85-95
Soundtrack (1959) . . . .*Warner Bros. (S) WS-1306*   59   120-130
Soundtrack (1959) . . . .*Stanyan (Q) SRQ-4022*   15-20
    Composer: Franz Waxman. **Conductor:** Franz Waxman. **Cast:** Dame Edith Evans; Dame
    Peggy Ashcroft.

NUNSENSE
Original Cast (1986) .... *DRG SBL-12589*   86   **$8-10**
  Composer: Dan Groggin. **Cast:** Christine Anderson; Semina DeLaurentis; Marilyn Farina; Edwina Lewis; Suzi Winson.
Original London Cast (1987) .... *Ter (S) 1132*   87   **10-12**
  Composer: Dan Groggin. **Cast:** Honor Blackman; Anna Sharkey; Pip Hinton; Louise Gold; Bronwen Stanway.

NUNZIO
Soundtrack (1978) .... *MCA (S) 2374*   78   **10-12**
  Composer: Lalo Schifrin. **Conductor:** Lalo Schifrin.

NUTCRACKER
Soundtrack (1986) .... *Telarc (S) DG-10137*   86   **15-20**
  Double LP set.
  Composer: Tchaikovsky. **Conductor:** Charles Mackerras.

NUTS
Soundtrack (1987) .... *Columbia (S) AC-40876*   87   **8-10**
  Composer: Barbra Streisand. **Conductor:** Jeremy Lubbock. **Cast:** Barbra Streisand.

O

O LUCKY MAN
Soundtrack (1973) ....*Warner Bros. (S) DS-2710* 73 **$10-12**
Composer: Alan Price. Conductor: Alan Price. Cast: Alan Price; Colin Green; Dave Markee; Clive Thacker.

O SAY CAN YOU SEE!
Original Cast (1962) ....*Sunbeam (S) XTV 87195-6* 62 **75-100**
Red cover. The original cast production ran from October 8 to November 4, 1962, at New York's Provincetown Playhouse. During that short run, about 75 private label copies were distributed.
Composer: Jack Holmes; Bill Conklin; Bob Miller. Conductor: Jack Holmes. Cast: Elmarie Wendel; Paul B. Price; Jan Chaney; Nicolas Coster; Joel Warfield; Joyce Larey; Thomas Gaines; Richard Nelson.

O'BRIEN, PAT:
see PAT O'BRIEN

OBA KOSA (THE KING DID NOT HANG)
Original Cast (1975) ....*Kaleidophone (S) KS-2201* 75 **15-20**
Composer: Duro Ladipo. Cast: Duro Ladipo National Theatre.

OBJECTIVE, BURMA!
Soundtrack (1945) .... *Cine (M) No Number Used* 75 **55-65**
Also known as "Classic Film Scores by Franz Waxman." Includes music from *Rebecca*.
Composer: Franz Waxman. Conductor: Franz Waxman.

OBSCURED BY CLOUDS
Soundtrack (1972) ....*Harvest (S) ST-11078* 72 **8-10**
From the film *The Valley*.
Composer: Roger Waters; Pink Floyd. Cast: Pink Floyd.

OBSESSION
Soundtrack (1976) ....*London (S) SPC-21160* 76 **15-20**
Composer: Bernard Herrmann. Conductor: Bernard Herrmann. Cast: National Philharmonic Orchestra.

OCTOPUSSY
Soundtrack (1983) ....*A&M (S) SP-4967* 83 **8-10**
Composer: John Barry. Conductor: John Barry. Cast: Rita Coolidge.

ODD COUPLE
Soundtrack (1968) ....*Dot (S) 25862* 68 **15-20**
Composer: Neal Hefti. Conductor: Neal Hefti. Cast: Jack Lemmon; Walter Matthau. (With dialogue.)

ODDS AGAINST TOMORROW
Soundtrack (1959) ....*United Artists (M) UAL-4061* 59 **35-40**
Soundtrack (1959) .... *United Artists (S) UAS-5061* 59 **40-50**
Composer: John Lewis. Conductor: John Lewis.
Studiotrack (1959) ....*United Artists (M) UAL-4063* 59 **15-20**
Studiotrack (1959) .... *United Artists (S) UAS-5063* 59 **20-25**
Above two have jazz interpretations of selections from the film.
Composer: John Lewis. Conductor: John Lewis. Cast: Modern Jazz Quartet.
Also see I WANT TO LIVE; JOHNNY COOL

ODE TO BILLY JOE
Soundtrack (1976) .... *Warner Bros. (S) BS-2947*   76   **$12-15**
Soundtrack (1976) .... *Warner Bros. (S) No Number Used*   76   **20-30**
   One-sided promotional issue. Actual title: *Special Radio Salute to Bobbie Gentry and Ode to Billy Joe.*
Composer: Bobbie Gentry; Michel Legrand; others. **Conductor:** Michel Legrand. **Cast:** Bobbie
Gentry.

ODESSA FILE
Soundtrack (1974) .... *MCA (S) 2084*   74   **12-15**
   Composer: Andrew Lloyd Webber; others. **Conductor:** Anthony Bowles; Alan Doggett; Adolf
Stahuber. **Cast:** Perry Como.

OF HUMAN BONDAGE (AND OTHER GREAT THEMES)
Studiotrack (1964) .... *MGM (M) E-4261*   64   **15-20**
Studiotrack (1964) .... *MGM (S) SE-4261*   64   **20-30**
   Composer: Ron Goodwin; David Rose. **Conductor:** Ron Goodwin; David Rose. **Cast:** Ron
Goodwin Orchestra; David Rose Orchestra.

OF LOVE AND DESIRE
Soundtrack (1963) .... *20th Century-Fox (M) FXG-5014*   63   **25-30**
Soundtrack (1963) .... *20th Century-Fox (S) SXG-5014*   63   **35-40**
   Composer: Ronald Stein. **Conductor:** Ronald Stein. **Cast:** Sammy Davis Jr.

OF THEE I SING
Original Revival Cast (1952) .... *Capitol (EP) EDM-350*   52   **30-45**
Original Revival Cast (1952) .... *Capitol (M) S-350*   52   **175-200**
Original Revival Cast (1952) .... *Capitol (M) T-11651*   77   **8-10**
   Composer: George Gershwin; Ira Gershwin. **Conductor:** Maurice Levine. **Cast:** Jack Carson;
Paul Hartman; Jack Whiting; Lenore Lonergan; Betty Oakes; Florenz Ames;
J. Pat O'Malley.
TV Soundtrack (1972) .... *Columbia (S) S-31763*   72   **12-15**
TV Soundtrack (1972) .... *Columbia (S) S-31763*   72   **50-60**
   Special version issued by AMF, the show's sponsor. Aired Oct. 24, 1972, on CBS-TV.
   Composer: George Gershwin; Ira Gershwin. **Conductor:** Peter Matz. **Cast:** Carroll O'Connor;
Jack Gilford; Cloris Leachman; Michelle Lee; Garrett Lewis.

OFFICER AND A GENTLEMAN
Soundtrack (1982) .... *Island (S) PR-491*   82   **10-12**
   Four track, 12-inch LP.
Soundtrack (1982) .... *Island (S) 90017-1*   82   **8-10**
   Composer: Various. **Cast:** Joe Cocker; Jennifer Warnes; Van Morrison; ZZ Top; Pat Benatar;
Sir Douglas Quintet; Dire Straits.

OFFICIAL ADVENTURES OF FLASH GORDON
Studiotrack (1966) .... *Leo the Lion (S) CH-1028*   **8-12**
   Cast: Buster Crabbe; Ronald Liss; Rita Lloyd; Corinne Orr; George Petrie; Jackson Beck
(narrator).

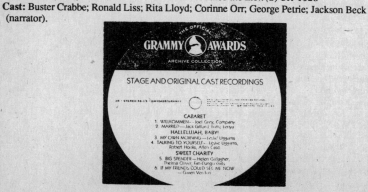

OFFICIAL GRAMMY AWARDS ARCHIVE COLLECTION
(STAGE AND ORIGINAL CAST RECORDINGS)

Original Cast .... *Franklin Mint (S) GRAM-11*   85 $75-100
Four red vinyl LPs in a boxed set. Includes 20-page booklet. Available by mail-order only, from the
Franklin Mint. Has music from: *Gypsy, Camelot, Flower Drum Song, The Sound of Music, Redhead, Bye
By Birdie, What Makes Sammy Run, Do I Hear a Waltz, Fiddler on the Roof, Half a Sixpence, Apple Tree,
Mame, Man of La Mancha, Cabaret, Hallelujah Baby, Sweet Charity, Hair, Godspell, Raisin, 1776, Annie,
Company, Chorus Line, Ain't Misbehavin', Ballroom, Sweeny Todd, I Love My Wife, One Mo' Time,* and
more.

Composer: Various. Cast: Ethel Merman; Robert Goulet; Pat Suzuki; Mary Martin; Dick Van
Dyke; Steve Lawrence; Tommy Steele; Angela Lansbury; Joel Grey; Jack Gilford; Lotte Lenya;
Leslie Uggams; Dean Jones; Hal Linden; Theodore Bikel; Sally Ann Howes; Paul Lynde; Zero
Moste Mostel; Ronnie Dyson; Andrea McArdle; Glynis Johns; Ken Page; Nell Carter; Robin
Lamont; Clifton Davis; Lynn Kellogg; Irving Jacobson; Barbara Harris; Gwen Verdon; Elizabeth
Allen; Allen Case; Robert Hooks; Charles Braswell; John Miller; others.

OH BOY!

Original London Cast (1917) .... *World (M) SHB-32*   20-25
Originally titled *Oh Joy!*

Composer: Jerome Kern; P.G. Wodehouse. Cast: Dot Temple; Tom Powers; Beatrice Lillie;
Billy Leonard.

OH, CALCUTTA!

Original Cast (1969) .... *Aidart (S) AID-9903*   69   15-20
Composer: The "Open Window." Cast: Peter Schickele; Stanley Walden; Robert Dennis; Boni
Enten; Katie Drew-Wilkinson; Mark Dempsey; Leon Russom; George Welbes; Alan Rachins;
Raina Barrett; Nancy Tribush; Margo Sappington.

OH, CAPTAIN!

Original Cast (1958) .... *Columbia (M) OL-5280*   58   35-40
Original Cast (1958) .... *Columbia Special Products (S) AOS-2002*   77   8-10
Composer: Jay Livingston; Ray Evans. Conductor: Jay Blackton. Cast: Jacquelyn McKeever;
Edward Platt; Susan Johnson; Tony Randall; Eileen Rodgers; Paul Valentine; George Ritner;
Bruce MacKay; Louis Polacek; Nolan Van Way.

Studio Cast (1958) .... *Columbia (M) CL-1167*   58   20-30
Actual title: *Hits from "Oh Captain!"*

Composer: Jay Livingston; Ray Evans. Conductor: Jose Ferrer. Cast: Johnny Mathis; Rosemary
Clooney; Vic Damone; Guy Mitchell; Tony Bennett; Jo Stafford; Stan Freeman; Norman Luboff;
Jill Corey; Don Cherry.

Studio Cast (1958) .... *MGM (M) E-3687*   58   15-20
Composer: Jay Livingston; Ray Evans. Conductor: Phil Moore. Cast: Jose Ferrer (original cast
producer); Rosemary Clooney.

OH, COWARD!

Original Cast (1972) .... *Bell (S) 9001*   72   25-30
Double LP set.

Composer: Noel Coward. Conductor: Rene Weigert. Cast: Barbara Carson; Roderick Cook;
Jamie Ross.

OH DAD, POOR DAD, MAMA'S HUNG YOU IN THE CLOSET AND
I'M FEELING SO SAD

Soundtrack (1967) .... *RCA Victor (M) LPM-3750*   67   15-20
Soundtrack (1967) .... *RCA Victor (S) LSP-3750*   67   20-25
Composer: Neal Hefti. Conductor: Neal Hefti.

OH, GOOD GRIEF!

TV Soundtrack .... *Warner Bros. (S) WS-1747*   68   15-20
Music from various "Peanuts" TV specials.

Composer: Vince Guaraldi. Conductor: Vince Guaraldi.

OH, KAY!

Original Revival Cast (1960)	20th Century-Fox (M) FXG-4003	60	$30-35
Original Revival Cast (1960)	20th Century-Fox (S) SFX-4003	60	45-50
Original Revival Cast (1960)	Stet (S) DS-15017		8-10

Composer: George Gershwin; Ira Gershwin. **Conductor:** Dorothea Freitag. **Cast:** David Daniels; Marti Stevens; Bernie West; Dorothea Freitag (piano); Reginald Beane (piano).

Original London Cast	Monmouth Evergreen (SE) MES-7043		10-15
Original London Cast	Smithsonian (SE) R-011	Re	8-12

Composer: George Gershwin; Ira Gershwin. **Cast:** Gerturde Lawrence; Harold French; Claude Hulbert.

Studio Cast	Columbia (M) OL-7050		15-20
Studio Cast	Columbia (S) OS-2550		20-25
Studio Cast (1957)	Columbia (M) CL-1050	57	15-20
Studio Cast	Columbia Special Products (M) ACL-1050	Re	8-10

Composer: George Gershwin; Ira Gershwin. **Conductor:** Lehman Engel. **Cast:** Barbara Ruick; Jack Cassidy; Allen Case; Roger White; Cy Walter (piano); Bernard Leighton (piano).

OH, ROSALINDA!

Soundtrack (1957)	Mercury (M) MG-20145	57	60-70

Composer: Johann Strauss Jr. **Cast:** Sari Barabas; Johann Strauss Light Orchestra; Weiner Symphoniker Orchestra; Alexander Young; Dennis Dowling; Walter Berry; Oska Sima; Michael Redgrave; Mel Ferrer; Anthony Quale; Anton Walbrook; Dennis Price; Ludmilla Tcherina.

OH WHAT A LOVELY WAR

Original Cast (1964)	London (M) 5906	64	25-30
Original Cast (1964)	London (S) OS-25906	64	35-40

Composer: Various. **Conductor:** Alfred Ralston. **Cast:** Charles Chilton; Pierrots.

Studio Cast	World (M) SH-130		15-20

Assorted World War I period songs heard in the stage play.

Soundtrack (1969)	Paramount (S) PAS-5008	69	15-20

Composer: Various. **Conductor:** Alfred Ralston. **Cast:** Jean Pierre Cassell; Maggie Smith; Maurice Arthur; Richard Howard; Joanne Brown; Joe Melia; Colin Redgrave; Pia Colombo.

OH YOU BEAUTIFUL DOLL

Studiotrack (1950)	RCA Victor (EP) EPA-252	50	10-15

Cast: Tony Martin; Pied Pipers.

OIL TOWN, U.S.A.

Soundtrack (1953)	RCA Victor (M) LFM-3000	53	50-60

10-inch LP.

Composer: Ralph Carmichael. **Conductor:** Ralph Carmichael. **Cast:** Billy Graham; Cindy Walker; Redd Harper.

Soundtrack (1953)	ISR (M) 10043	53	35-40

OKLAHOMA

Original Cast (1943)	Decca (EP) ED-801	49	10-15
Original Cast (1943)	Decca (M) DL-8000	49	35-40
Original Cast (1943)	Decca (M) DL-9017	55	25-30
Original Cast (1943)	Decca (SE) DL7-9017	59	20-25
Original Cast (1943)	MCA (SE) 2030e	72	8-10

Composer: Richard Rodgers; Oscar Hammerstein II. **Conductor:** Jay Blackton. **Cast:** Alfred Drake; Joan Roberts; Howard DaSilva; Celeste Holm; Lee Dixon.

Original Touring Cast (1966)	Columbia (S) OS-2610	66	10-15

Composer: Richard Rodgers; Oscar Hammerstein II. **Conductor:** Franz Allers. **Cast:** John Raitt; Florence Henderson; Phyllis Newman; Jack Elliot.

Original London Cast .... *World (M) SH-292* $10-15
Also has music from *Annie Get Your Gun* and *Carousel,* both by London casts. Includes complete scores,
whereas the Stanyan LP (listed next) has only excerpts.
  Composer: Richard Rodgers; Oscar Hammerstein II. **Conductor:** Reginald Burston.
  Cast: Howard Keel; Betty Jane Watson; Dorthea MacFarland; Walter Donahue; Henry Clarke.
Original London Cast .... *Stanyan (M) SR-10069*   8-10
One side has music from *Annie Get Your Gun.*
  Composer: Richard Rodgers; Oscar Hammerstein II. **Conductor:** Reginald Burston.
  Cast: Howard Keel; Betty Jane Watson; Dorthea MacFarland; Walter Donahue; Henry Clarke.
Original Revival Cast (1979) .... *RCA Victor (S) CBL1-3572* 79   8-10
  Composer: Richard Rodgers; Oscar Hammerstein II. **Conductor:** Jay Blackton. **Cast:** Laurence
  Guittard; Christine Andreas.
Studio Cast (1950) .... *Decca (M) DL-7002* 50   30-40
10-inch LP. Also has music from *Porgy and Bess.*
  Composer: Richard Rodgers; Oscar Hammerstein II. **Conductor:** Alfred Wallenstein.
  Cast: Philharmonic Orchestra of Los Angeles.
Studio Cast (1953) .... *RCA Victor (EP) EPA-474* 53   10-20
  Conductor: Al Goodman.
Studio Cast (1960) .... *Epic (M) LN-3678* 60   20-25
  Composer: Richard Rodgers; Oscar Hammerstein II. **Cast:** Stuart Foster; Lois Hunt; Faye DeWitt.
Studio Cast (1959) .... *Columbia (M) OL-8010* 59   10-15
  Composer: Richard Rodgers; Oscar Hammerstein II. **Conductor:** Franz Allers. **Cast:** John Raitt;
  Florence Henderson; Phyllis Newman; Jack Elliott; Irene Carroll; Leonard Stokes; Ara Berberian.
Studio Cast (1956) .... *Columbia (M) CL-828* 56   25-30
One of the most complete recordings of *Oklahoma.* The Harmony reissues are abridged versions of CL-828.
Studio Cast (1956) .... *Columbia (SE) CS-8739* 59   10-15
  Composer: Richard Rodgers; Oscar Hammerstein II. **Conductor:** Lehman Engel. **Cast:** Nelson
  Eddy; Virginia Haskins; Kaye Gallard; Portia Nelson; Lee Cass; David Atkinson; Wilton Clary;
  David Morris; others.
Studio Cast (1956) .... *Harmony (M) HL-7364* 64   10-15
Studio Cast (1956) .... *Harmony (SE) HS-11164* 64   10-15
  Composer: Richard Rodgers; Oscar Hammerstein II. **Conductor:** Lehman Engel. **Cast:** Nelson
  Eddy; Virginia Haskins; Kaye Ballard; Portia Nelson; Lee Cass; David Atkinson; Wilton Clary;
  David Morriss.
Soundtrack (1955) .... *Capitol (EP) FDM-1-595* 55   10-15
Soundtrack (1955) .... *Capitol (EP) FDM-2-595* 55   10-15
Soundtrack (1955) .... *Capitol (EP) FDM-3-595* 55   10-15
Soundtrack (1955) .... *Capitol (M) SAO-595* 55   20-30
Soundtrack (1955) .... *Capitol (SE) SWAO-595* 59   10-15
Still available using the same catalog number.
  Composer: Richard Rodgers; Oscar Hammerstein II. **Cast:** Gordon MacRae; Shirley Jones;
  Gloria Grahame; Gene Nelson; Charlotte Greenwood; James Whitmore; Rod Steiger;
  Jay C. Flippen.
Studiotrack .... *Coronet (M) CS-46*   8-12
  Cast: Coronet Studio Orchestra; Lee Carol; John Drake; Henry Cassidy; Earnscliffe Chorus.
Studiotrack (1959) .... *Lion (S) L-70094* 59   8-12
Studiotrack .... *Original Cast (S) OC-8129*   8-12
Celeste Holm gives a personal tribute.
  Cast: Celeste Holm.
Studio Cast .... *Promenade (M) 2062*   10-12
Also has music from *South Pacific.*
  Conductor: Al Goodman. **Cast:** Richard Torigi; Edgar Powell; Gretchen Rhoads; Susan Shaute;
  William Reynolds; Dolores Martin.

OKLAHOMA (continued)
Studiotrack .... *Somerset (M) P-1700*   **$10-12**
One side has music from *South Pacific.*
Conductor: D.L. Miller. **Cast:** New World Theatre Orchestra.
Also see CAROUSEL

OKLAHOMA CRUDE
Soundtrack (1973) .... *RCA Victor (S) APL1-0271* 73   **12-18**
Composer: Henry Mancini. **Conductor:** Henry Mancini.

OLD BOYFRIENDS
Soundtrack (1979) .... *Columbia (S) JS-36072* 79   **35-45**
Promotional issue given to opening night theatre patrons in Hollywood.
Conductor: David Shire. **Cast:** John Belushi.

OLD MAID AND THE THIEF
Studio Cast (1941) .... *Turnabout (SE) TV-34745*   **8-12**
Composer: Gian Carlo Menotti. **Conductor:** Jorge Mester. **Cast:** Judith Blegen; Anna Reynolds; John Reardon; Margaret Baker.

OLD MAN AND THE SEA
Soundtrack (1958) .... *Columbia (M) CL-1183* 58   **45-55**
Soundtrack (1958) .... *Columbia (S) CS-8013* 58   **60-75**
Soundtrack (1958) .... *Columbia Special Products (S) ACS-8013* Re   **8-10**
Composer: Dimitri Tiomkin. **Conductor:** Dimitri Tiomkin.

OLD YELLER
Soundtrack (1957) .... *Disneyland (M) WDL-3024* 57   **30-35**
Soundtrack (1957) .... *Disneyland (M) WDL-1024* 60   **20-25**
Soundtrack (1957) .... *Disneyland (M) DQ-1258* 64   **10-15**
Composer: Oliver G. Wallace. **Cast:** Fess Parker (narration); Dorothy McGuire; Tommy Kirk; Kevin Corcoran. (With dialogue.)

OLIVER
Original Cast (1962) .... *RCA Victor (M) LOCD-2004* 62   **15-20**
Original Cast (1962) .... *RCA Victor (S) AYL1-4113* Re   **8-10**
Composer: Lionel Bart. **Conductor:** Donald Pippin. **Cast:** Clive Revill; Georgia Brown; Bruce Prochnik; Willoughby Goddard; Hope Jackman; Michael Goodman; Alice Playten.
London Studio Cast (1962) .... *Capitol (M) T-1784* 62   **20-25**
London Studio Cast (1962) .... *Capitol (S) ST-1784* 62   **30-35**
Composer: Lionel Bart. **Conductor:** Tony Osborne. **Cast:** Stanley Holloway; Alma Cogan; Violet Carson; Denis Waterman; Tony Tanner; Leslie Fryson; Charles Granville; Williams Singers.
Studio Cast (1962) .... *Golden (M) LP 105* 62   **10-15**
Composer: Lionel Bart. **Conductor:** Jim Timmens. **Cast:** James Kenney; Myra de Groot; Janet Eden; Gene Lowell; Gene Steck.
Soundtrack (1968) .... *Colgems (S) COSD-5501* 68   **10-15**
Soundtrack (1968) .... *RCA Victor (S) COSD-5501* Re   **8-10**
Composer: Lionel Bart. **Conductor:** John Green. **Cast:** Ron Moody; Oliver Reed; Mark Lester; Harry Secombe; Shani Wallis; Peggy Mount; Jack Wild; Sheila White.

OLIVER TWIST
Studio Cast .... *Decca (M) DL-9107*   **15-20**
Studiotrack (1963) .... *Harmony (M) HL-9558* 63   **10-12**
Also has *The Three Musketeers.*
Studiotrack .... *Columbia Special Products (S) P-13902* Re   **8-10**
Conductor: Ralph Rose. THREE MUSKETEERS: Carmen Dragon. **Cast:** Basil Rathbone (narrator). THREE MUSKETEERS: Errol Flynn (narrator).
Also see BERNARD HERRMANN CONDUCTS GREAT BRITISH FILM SCORES

OLIVER'S STORY
Soundtrack (1978) .... *ABC (S) AA-1117* 78 **$8-10**
Includes Francis Lai's *Love Story* theme.
Conductor: Lee Holdridge.

OLYMPIC ELK:
see WALT DISNEY'S TRUE LIFE ADVENTURE

OLYMPUS 7-0000
TV Soundtrack (1966) .... *Command (M) CS-07* 66 **15-20**
TV Soundtrack (1966) .... *Command (S) CS-07-SD* 66 **20-25**
Composer: Richard Adler. Conductor: Philip Della Penna. Cast: Donald O'Conner; Phyllis Newman; Eddie Foy Jr.; Larry Blyden.

OMAR KHAYYAM
Soundtrack (1957) .... *Decca (M) DL-8449* 57 **70-80**
One side has music from *The Mountain.*
Composer: THE MOUNTAIN: Daniele Amfitheatrof. Conductor: THE MOUNTAIN: Daniele Amfitheatrof.
Soundtrack (1957) .... *Filmusic Records (SE) SN-2823* **30-35**
One side has *Written on the Wind.*
Composer: Victor Young (both). WRITTEN ON THE WIND: Frank Skinner, others.
Conductor: Victor Young. Cast: Victor Young and His Orchestra. WRITTEN ON THE WIND: Four Aces.
Also see MOUNTAIN

OMEN
Soundtrack (1976) .... *Tattoo (S) BJL1-1888* 76 **25-45**
Composer: Jerry Goldsmith. Conductor: Lionel Newman.

ON A CLEAR DAY YOU CAN SEE FOREVER
Original Cast (1965) .... *RCA Victor (M) LOCD-2006* 65 **15-20**
Original Cast (1965) .... *RCA Victor (S) LSOD-2006* 65 **120-25**
Above two include a souvenir theater program.
Composer: Burton Layne; Alan Jay Lerner. Conductor: Theodore Saidenberg. Cast: Barbara Harris; John Cullum; Titos Vandis; Byron Webster; William Reilly; William Daniels; Clifford David.
Soundtrack (1970) .... *Columbia (S) S-30086* 70 **15-20**
Soundtrack (1970) .... *Columbia Special Products (S) AS-30086* Re **8-10**
Composer: Burton Layne; Alan Jay Lerner. Conductor: Nelson Riddle. Cast: Barbra Streisand; Yves Montand; Bob Newhart; Larry Blyden; Jack Nicholson.

ON A NOTE OF TRIUMPH
Original Radio Cast (1975) .... *Mark '56 (M) 704* 75 **25-30**
Composer: Bernard Herrmann. Conductor: Lud Gluskin. Cast: Martin Gabel (narration).

ON ANY SUNDAY
Soundtrack (1971) .... *Bell (S) 1206* 71 **25-30**
Composer: Dominic Frontiere. Conductor: Dominic Frontiere.

ON BROADWAY
TV Soundtrack (1969) .... *Motown (S) MS-699* 69 **8-10**
Conductor: H.B. Barnum. Cast: Diana Ross and the Supremes; Temptations.

ON GOLDEN POND
Soundtrack (1981) .... *MCA (S) 6106* 82 **8-10**
Composer: Dave Grusin. Conductor: Dave Grusin. Cast: Henry Fonda; Katharine Hepburn; Dabney Coleman; Jane Fonda; Doug McKeon. (With dialogue.)

ON HER BED OF ROSES
Soundtrack (1966) .... *Mira (M) LP-3006*   66   **$25-30**
Soundtrack (1966) .... *Mira (S) LPS-3006*   66   **30-35**
   Composer: Joseph Green. **Conductor:** Joseph Green.

ON HER MAJESTY'S SECRET SERVICE
Soundtrack (1969) .... *United Artists (S) UAS-5204*   69   **15-20**
Soundtrack (1969) .... *United Artists (S) UA-LA299-G*   Re   **10-12**
  Includes Monty Norman's *James Bond Theme*.
  Composer: John Barry. **Conductor:** John Barry. **Cast:** Louis Armstrong; Nina.

ON MOONLIGHT BAY
Studiotrack (1951) .... *Columbia (M) CL-6186*   51   **35-45**
  10-inch LP.
  Cast: Doris Day.
Studiotrack (1951) .... *Coral (M) CRL-56043*   52   **15-20**
  10-inch LP.
  Cast: Lawrence Welk Orchestra.

ON THE BEACH
Soundtrack (1959) .... *Roulette (M) R-25098*   59   **75-100**
Soundtrack (1959) .... *Roulette (S) SR-25098*   59   **150-175**
  Includes Marie Cowan's *Waltzing Matilda*.
  Composer: Ernest Gold. **Conductor:** Ernest Gold.
Studiotrack (1959) .... *United Artists (M) UAL-3061*   59   **10-15**
Studiotrack (1959) .... *United Artists (S) UAS-6061*   59   **15-20**
  Also has themes from *The Vikings, The Horse Soldiers, I Want to Live, The Wonderful Country, The Naked Maja* and *The Big Country*.
  Composer: Ernest Gold; others. **Conductor:** Mitchell Powell. **Cast:** Hollywood Studio Symphony Orchestra.

ON THE BRIGHTER SIDE
Original London Cast (1963) .... *London (M) 5767*   63   **50-60**
  Conductor: Colin Beaton. **Cast:** Pip Hinton; Stanley Baxter; Betty Marsden; Ronnie Barker; David Kernan; Bob Stevenson; Judy Carnes; Alan Barnes; Victor Duret.

ON THE FLIP SIDE
TV Soundtrack (1966) .... *Decca (M) DL-4836*   66   **15-20**
TV Soundtrack (1966) .... *Decca (S) DL7-4836*   66   **20-25**
  Composer: Hal David; Burt Bacharach. **Conductor:** Peter Matz. **Cast:** Rick Nelson; Joanie Sommers; Dona Jean Young.

ON THE RECORD - EVENTS OF 1977

Studio Cast (1978) .... *Caedmon (M) TC-1572*   78   **$50-75**
  News highlights of 1977 as compiled by United Press International. Includes segments on the deaths of
  Elvis Presley, Bing Crosby, Groucho Marx, Charlie Chaplin, and Guy Lombardo.

ON THE TOWN

Original Cast (1961) .... *Columbia (M) OL-5540*   61   **20-25**
Original Cast (1961) .... *Columbia (S) OS-2028*   61   **30-35**
Original Cast (1961) .... *Columbia (S) S-31005*   70   **12-18**
  Has one song, *Carnegie Hall*, not heard on OS-2028.
  Composer: Leonard Bernstein; Betty Comden; Adolph Green. **Conductor:** Leonard Bernstein.
  Cast: Nancy Walker; Betty Comden; Adolph Green; Chris Alexander; John Reardon.
Original Cast (1961) .... *Columbia Special Products (S) AS-31005*   Re   **8-10**
  Composer: Leonard Bernstein; Betty Comden; Adolph Green. **Conductor:** Leonard Bernstein.
  Cast: Nancy Walker; Betty Comden; Adolph Green; Chris Alexander; John Reardon.
Original Cast .... *Heritage (M) 0057*   20-25
  Composer: Leonard Bernstein; Betty Comden; Adolph Green. **Cast:** Betty Comden; Adolph
  Green.
Original Cast (1954) .... *RCA Victor/Camden (M) CAL-196*   54   **25-35**
  Composer: Leonard Bernstein; Betty Comden; Adolph Green. **Conductor:** Leonard Bernstein.
Original London Cast .... *Stet (S) DS-15029*   **10-15**
  Composer: Leonard Bernstein; Betty Comden; Adolph Green. **Conductor:** Leonard Bernstein.
  Cast: Fred Lucas; Noele Gordon; Dennis Lotis; Stella Tanner; Lionel Blair; Williams Singers;
  Shane Rimmer.
  Also see LUTE SONG

ON THE TWELFTH DAY

Soundtrack (1955) .... *MGM (M) E-3223*   55   **50-60**
  One side has *Beloved Christmas Hymns and Carols*, conducted by Macklin Marrow.
  Composer: Doreen Carwithen. **Conductor:** Muir Mathieson.

ON THE TWENTIETH CENTURY

Original Cast (1978) .... *Columbia (S) JS-35330*   78   **8-12**
  Composer: Cy Coleman; Betty Comden; Adolph Green. **Cast:** Madeline Kahn; Imogene Coca;
  John Collum.

ON THE WATERFRONT:

see EDDY DUCHIN STORY; WEST SIDE STORY

ON YOUR TOES

Original Cast (1953) .... *Columbia (M) ML-4645*	53	$35-40
Original Cast .... *Polydor (S) 422-813667-1*	83	8-10
Original London Cast (1936) ......*Monmouth Evergreen (SE) MES-7049*		8-10
Cast: Jack Whiting.		
Original Revival Cast (1954) .... *Decca (EP) ED-903*	54	15-20
Original Revival Cast (1954) .... *Decca (M) DL-9015*	54	65-70
Original Revival Cast (1954) .... *Stet (M) DS-15024*	Re	8-10

Composer: Richard Rodgers; Lorenz Hart. Conductor: Salvatore Dell'Isola. Cast: Bobby Van; Elaine Stritch; Ben Astar; Kay Coulter; Joshua Shelley; Jack Williams; Eleanor Williams.

Studio Cast (1956) .... *Columbia (M) CL-837*	56	20-30
Studio Cast (1956) .... *Columbia (M) OL-7090*	Re	10-15
Studio Cast (1956) ....*Columbia (SE) OS-2590*	Re	10-20
Studio Cast (1956) .... *Columbia Special Products (SE) AOS-2590*	Re	8-10

Composer: Richard Rodgers; Lorenz Hart. Conductor: Lehman Engel. Cast: Portia Nelson; Jack Cassidy; Laurel Shelby; Ray Hyson; Robert Eckles; Zamah Cunningham.
Also see SLAUGHTER ON 10TH AVENUE

ONCE A THIEF

Soundtrack (1965) .... *Verve (M) MG-8624*	65	15-20
Soundtrack (1965) ....*Verve (S) V6-8624*	65	25-30

Above two have other Lalo Schifrin themes, such as *Joy House* and *The Man from U.N.C.L.E.*
Composer: Lalo Schifrin. Conductor: Lalo Schifrin. Cast: Irene Reid.

ONCE BITTEN

Soundtrack (1985) ....*MCA (S) 6154*	85	8-10

Composer: John Du Prez; others. Cast: 3 Speed; Hubert Kah; Real Life; Private Domain; Two of Us; Gifthorse; Maria Vidal; Moses Tyson Jr.; Kevin McKnelly.

ONCE UPON A MATTRESS

Original Cast (1959) ....*Kapp (M) KDL-7004*	59	20-25
Original Cast (1959) ....*Kapp (S) KDL-7004-S*	59	30-35
Original Cast (1959) .... *Kapp (M) KL-4507*	66	15-20
Original Cast (1959) ....*Kapp (S) KRS-5507*	66	25-30
Original Cast (1959) .... *MCA (S) 2079*	75	10-12
Original Cast (1959) ....*MCA (S) 37097*	81	8-10

Composer: Mary Rodgers; Marshall Barer. Conductor: Hal Hastings. Cast: Carol Burnett; Joseph Bova; Allen Case; Jack Gilford; Anne Jones; Harry Snow; Robert Weil; Jane White.

London Cast .... *Stet (S) DS-15026*	10-15

ONCE UPON A TIME IN AMERICA

Soundtrack (1984) .... *Mercury (S) 818697*	84	15-25

Composer: Ennio Moricone. Conductor: Ennio Moricone. Cast: Gheorghe Zamfir; Edda Dell Orso.

ONCE UPON A TIME IN THE WEST

Soundtrack (1969) ....*RCA Victor (S) LSP-4736*	72	10-15

Composer: Ennio Morricone. Conductor: Ennio Morricone.

ONCE UPON A TOUR

TV Soundtrack (1968) .... *Cozy (S) 2000*	68	12-18

Cast: Dora Hall; Phil Harris; Frank Sinatra Jr.; Oliver; Rich Little; Roosevelt Grier.

ONE AND ONLY

Soundtrack (1978) .... *ABC (S) AA-1059*	78	10-12

Composer: Patrick Williams. Conductor: Patrick Williams. Cast: Kacey Cisyk.

ONE AND ONLY, GENUINE, ORIGINAL FAMILY BAND
Soundtrack (1968) .... *Buena Vista (M) BV-5002*   68 $15-20
Soundtrack (1968) .... *Buena Vista (S) STER-5002*   68   20-25
Composer: Richard M. Sherman; Robert B. Sherman. Conductor: Jack Elliot. Cast: Walter Brennan; Buddy Ebsen; Lesley Ann Warren; John Davidson; Janet Blair; Steve Harmon; Wally Cox; Richard Deacon; John Craig.

ONE-EYED JACKS
Soundtrack (1961) .... *Liberty (M) LOM-16001*   61   35-50
Soundtrack (1961) .... *Liberty (S) LOS-17001*   61   75-85
Composer: Hugo Friedhofer. Conductor: Irving Talbot.

ONE FLEW OVER THE CUCKOO'S NEST
Soundtrack (1975) .... *Fantasy (S) F-9500*   75   10-12
Soundtrack .... *Fantasy (S) MPF-4531*   8-10
Composer: Jack Nitzsche. Conductor: Jack Nitzsche.

ONE FROM THE HEART
Soundtrack (1982) .... *Columbia (S) FC-37703*   82   8-10
Composer: Tom Waits. Cast: Tom Waits; Crystal Gayle.

ONE HUNDRED AND ONE DALMATIANS
Soundtrack (1961) .... *Disneyland (M) ST-4903*   61   15-20
Soundtrack (1961) .... *Disneyland (M) SQ-1308*   61   15-20
Composer: Mel Leven; George Bruns; others.

ONE HUNDRED AND TEN IN THE SHADE
Original Cast (1963) .... *RCA Victor (M) LOC-1085*   63   25-30
Original Cast (1963) .... *RCA Victor (S) LSO-1085*   63   35-40
Composer: Harvey Schmidt; Tom Jones. Conductor: Donald Pippin. Cast: Robert Horton; Inga Swenson; Stephen Douglass; Will Geer; Steve Roland; Scooter Teague; Lesley Warren; George Church.

ONE MO' TIME
Original Cast (1980) .... *Warner Bros. (S) HS-3454*   80   8-10
Composer: Various. Conductor: Orange Kellin. Cast: Vernel Bagneris; Topsy Chapman; Thais Clark; Sylvia "Kuumba" Williams; John Stell; Jabbo Smith.

ONE NAKED NIGHT
Soundtrack (1965) .... *Vega (S) VS-2002*   65   15-20

ONE NIGHT OF LOVE:
see MISTER IMPERIUM

ONE NIGHT STAND
Original Cast (1980) .... *Original Cast (S) OC-8134*   80   10-12
Composer: Jule Styne; Herb Gardner. Conductor: Milton Rosenstock. Cast: Jack Weston; Catherine Cox; Jeff Keller; Charles Kimbrough; William Morrison; Paul Binotto.

ONE ON ONE (THE STORY OF A WINNER)
Soundtrack (1977) .... *Warner Bros. (S) BS-3076*   77   8-10
Composer: Charles Fox; Paul Williams. Conductor: Charles Fox. Cast: Seals and Crofts.

ONE OVER THE EIGHT
Original London Cast (1961) .... *London (M) 5760*   63   50-60
Composer: Lance Mulchay; others. Cast: Kenneth Williams; Sheila Hancock; Toni Eden; Lance Percival; Sheila O'Neill; Lynda Baron; John Howard; Robin Hawdon; Frank Horrox Sextet.

ONE STEP BEYOND
TV Soundtrack (1960) .... *Decca (M) DL-8970*   60   20-25
TV Soundtrack (1960) .... *Decca (S) DL7-8970*   60   30-40
TV Soundtrack (1960) .... *Varese Sarabande (S) STV-81120*   81   8-10
Composer: Harry Lubin. Conductor: Harry Lubin.

1001 ARABIAN NIGHTS
Soundtrack (1959) .... *Colpix (M) CP-410*   59   **$55-60**
Soundtrack (1959) .... *Colpix (S) SCP-410*   59   **70-75**
Soundtrack (1959) .... *Varese Sarabande (S) STV-81138*   81   **8-10**
   Composer: George Duning. Conductor: George Duning. Cast: Jim Backus (as Mr. Magoo);
   Clark Sisters; Jud Conlin Singers.

ONE TOUCH OF VENUS
Original Cast (1943) .... *Decca (M) DL-9122*   65   **40-50**
Original Cast (1943) .... *Decca (SE) DL7-9122*   65   **40-50**
   Composer: Kurt Weill; Ogden Nash. Conductor: Maurice Abravanal. Cast: Mary Martin;
   Kenny Baker.
Original Cast (1943) .... *AEI (SE) 1136*   84   **8-10**
Studio Cast (1943) .... *Heritage (M) 0051*   65   **100-125**
   Composer: Kurt Weill; Ogden Nash.

ONE TRICK PONY
Soundtrack (1980) .... *Warner Bros. (S) XHS-3472*   80   **8-10**
   Composer: Paul Simon. Cast: Paul Simon.

ONE, TWO, THREE WALTZ
Soundtrack (1961) .... *Musicor/United Artists (M) M-2002*   **25-30**
   From the film *One, Two, Three.*
   Composer: Andre Previn. Conductor: Roger Wayne. Cast: Roger Wayne and His Orchestra.

ONE WAY TICKET TO BROADWAY
Original Cast (1979) .... *Theatre Archives (S) TA-8001*   79   **8-10**
   Composer: Dan Goggin; Robert Lorick. Cast: Katie Anders; Beth Fowler; Dan Goggin; Ann
   Hodapp; Elaine Petricoff; Marvin Solley.

ONLY FOREVER
Studiotrack .... *Decca (M) DL-4255*   62   **25-30**
   Also contains selections from: *Birth of the Blues, Rhythm on the River* and *The Road to Zanzibar.* Issued as
   part of *Bing's Hollywood Series.*
   Composer: ROAD TO ZANZIBAR: James Van Heusen; John Burke. Conductor: ROAD TO
   ZANZIBAR: John Scott Trotter. Cast: Bing Crosby; Mary Martin.

OPENING DAY CEREMONIES
TV Soundtrack (1960) .... *Century (S) No Label Shown*   **15-20**
   From the 1960 Olympic Winter Games, held in Squaw Valley, Calif.

OPENING NIGHT AT THE PALACE - SWEET CHARITY
Original Cast (1966) .... *Columbia (S) DJ-17*   66   **15-20**
   Promotional issue for The Palace and for *Sweet Charity.* Has interviews with the performers, songs from
   the play, and interviews with well-known entertainers after they attended opening night.
   Composer: Cy Coleman; Dorothy Fields. Cast: Gwen Verdon; Helen Gallagher; Neil Simon;
   Lena Horne.

OPENING NIGHT AT THE WINTERGARDEN - MAME
Original Cast (1966) .... *Columbia (M) DJ-23*   66   **15-20**
   Promotional album for The Wintergarden and *Mame.* Has interviews with the cast, plus songs from the
   play.
   Cast: Angela Lansbury; Neil Simon; Jerry Herman; Jack L. Warner; Fred Robbins (interviewer).
   Also see MAME

OPTIMISTS
Soundtrack (1973) . . . .*Paramount (S) PAS-1015*   73   **$8-12**
 Composer: Lionel Bart; George Martin. **Conductor:** Lionel Bart. **Cast:** Peter Sellers; Lionel Bart.

ORANGE BIRD
Studio Cast (1971) . . . . *Disneyland (S) STER-3991*   71   **10-12**
 Includes illustrated booklet.
 Composer: Richard M. Sherman; Robert B. Sherman. **Conductor:** Tutti Camarata.
 Cast: Anita Bryant.

ORCHESTRA WIVES
Soundtrack (1942) . . . .*RCA Victor (EP) EPBT-3065*   54   **10-20**
 Double EP set.
Soundtrack (1942) . . . .*RCA Victor (M) LPT-3065*   54   **25-30**
 10-inch LP.
Soundtrack (1942) . . . .*20th Century-Fox (M) 3020*   59   **15-20**
Soundtrack (1942) . . . .*20th Century-Fox (SE) S-3020e*   59   **15-20**
Soundtrack ((1942)) . . . .*20th Century-Fox (M) 3021*   59   **15-20**
 Volume two.
Soundtrack (1942) . . . .*20th Century-Fox (SE) S-3021e*   59   **15-20**
 Volume two.
Soundtrack (1942) . . . .*20th Century-Fox (M) TCF-100-2*   58   **20-30**
Soundtrack (1942) . . . . *20th Century-Fox (SE) TCS-100-2*   58   **20-30**
 Above two are double LP sets, combining volumes one and two.
Soundtrack (1942) . . . .*20th Century-Fox (M) 3159*   65   **10-15**
 Volume one.
Soundtrack (1942) . . . .*20th Century-Fox (SE) S-4159e*   65   **10-15**
 Volume one.
Soundtrack (1942) . . . .*20th Century-Fox (M) 3160*   65   **10-15**
 Volume two.
Soundtrack (1942) . . . .*20th Century-Fox (SE) S-4160e*   65   **10-15**
 Volume two.
Soundtrack (1942) . . . . *Movietone (SE) MTM-1003*   69   **10-12**
Soundtrack (1942) . . . .*20th Century-Fox (SE) S-72018*   73   **8-10**
 All of the above 20th Century-Fox and Movietone LPs also have music from *Sun Valley Serenade*.
 Conductor: Glenn Miller. **Cast:** Glenn Miller and His Orchestra.
 Also see SUN VALLEY SERENADE

ORDER IS LOVE
Original Cast (1961) . . . . *Trilogy (S) TA-1001*   61   **15-20**
 Composer: Lex de Azevedo; Carol Lynn Pearson. **Conductor:** Dee Winterton. **Cast:** Gordon
 Harkness; Bob Nuismer; Janey Luke; Dianne Lynne Harris; Lawrence Gardner; Doug Voet;
 Paul Miller; Bryce Chamberlain.

ORIGINAL AMATEUR HOUR - 25TH ANNIVERSARY
TV Soundtrack . . . .*United Artists (M) UXL-2*   73   **30-40**
 Double LP set.

ORIGINAL MOTION PICTURE HIT THEMES
Studio Cast (1963) . . . .*United Artists (M) UAL-3197*   63   **10-15**
Studio Cast (1963) . . . . *United Artists (S) UAS-6197*   63   **15-20**
 Composer: Various. **Conductor:** Various. **Cast:** Ferrante and Teicher; Ralph Marterie; Gene
 Pitney; Al Caiola; Roger Wayne; Nick Perito.

ORIGINAL TV ADVENTURES OF KING KONG:
see KING KONG

OSCAR
Soundtrack (1966) .... *Columbia (M) OL-6550*   66   **$25-30**
Soundtrack (1966) .... *Columbia (S) OS-2950*   66   **30-40**
 Composer: Percy Faith; Jay Livingston; Ray Evans. **Conductor:** Percy Faith; Johnny Mandel.
 Cast: Tony Bennett.

OSTERMAN WEEKEND
Soundtrack (1983) .... *Varese Sarabande (S) STV-81198*   **8-10**
 Composer: Lalo Schifrin. **Conductor:** Lalo Schifrin.

OTHER SIDE OF MIDNIGHT
Soundtrack (1977) .... *20th Century-Fox (S) T-452*   77   **10-12**
 Composer: Michel Legrand. **Conductor:** Michel Legrand.

OTHER SIDE OF THE MOUNTAIN
Soundtrack (1975) .... *MCA (S) 2086*   75   **10-12**
Soundtrack (1975) .... *MCA (S) 1539*   Re   **8-10**
 Composer: Charles Fox. **Conductor:** Charles Fox.

OTHER SIDE OF THE MOUNTAIN, PART II
Soundtrack (1978) .... *MCA (S) 2335*   78   **8-10**
 Composer: Lee Holdridge. **Conductor:** Lee Holdridge. **Cast:** Merrily Webber.

OTHER WORLD OF WINSTON CHURCHILL
TV Soundtrack (1965) .... *Mercury (M) MG-21033*   65   **20-25**
TV Soundtrack (1965) .... *Mercury (S) SR-61033*   65   **30-35**
 Above two are from NBC-TV's *Hallmark Hall of Fame*.
 Composer: Carl Davis. **Conductor:** Carl Davis. **Cast:** Paul Scofield (narration).

OTLEY
Soundtrack (1969) .... *Colgems (S) COS-112*   69   **35-40**
 Composer: Stanley Myers. **Conductor:** Stanley Myers. **Cast:** Don Partridge; Alex Keenan;
 Pete Murray.

OUR GAL SUNDAY
Original Radio Cast .... *Golden Age (M) 5017*   78   **8-10**

OUR MAN FLINT
Soundtrack (1966) .... *20th Century-Fox (M) TFM-3179*   66   **30-40**
Soundtrack (1966) .... *20th Century-Fox (S) TFS-4179*   66   **45-55**
 Composer: Jerry Goldsmith. **Conductor:** Jerry Goldsmith.
 Also see IN LIKE FLINT

OUR MAN IN HOLLYWOOD
Studiotrack (1963) .... *RCA Victor (M) LPM-2604*   63 $10-20
Studiotrack (1963) .... *RCA Victor (S) LSP-2604*   63   20-30
Black label.
Studiotrack (1963) .... *RCA Victor (S) LSP-2604*   72   8-10
Orange label.
Composer: Henry Mancini. **Conductor:** Henry Mancini. **Cast:** Henry Mancini and His Orchestra.

OUR MOTHER'S HOUSE
Soundtrack (1967) .... *MGM (M) E-4495*   67   40-50
Soundtrack (1967) .... *MGM (S) SE-4495*   67   60-70
Composer: Georges Delerue. **Conductor:** Georges Delerue.

OUR TOWN
TV Soundtrack (1956) .... *Capitol (EP) EAP-1-673*   56   10-15
Composer: James Van Heusen; Sammy Cahn. **Cast:** Frank Sinatra; Eva Marie Saint.
. Also see QUIET CITY

OUT OF AFRICA
Soundtrack (1985) .... *MCA (S) 6158*   85   10-12
Soundtrack (1985) .... *MCA (S) 39303*   Re   8-10
Composer: John Barry. **Conductor:** John Barry. **Cast:** Academy of St. Martin in the Fields.

OUT OF BOUNDS
Soundtrack (1986) .... *I.R.S. (S) 6180*   86   8-10
Composer: Various. **Cast:** Stewart Copeland; Adam Ant; Siouxsie and the Banshees; Cult;
Belinda Carlisle; Night Ranger; Tommy Keene; American Girls; Lords of the New Church.

OUT OF SIGHT
Soundtrack (1966) .... *Decca (M) DL-4751*   66   12-18
Soundtrack (1966) .... *Decca (S) DL7-4751*   66   15-20
Composer: Al DeLory; others. **Conductor:** Nick Venet. **Cast:** Gary Lewis and the Playboys;
Astronauts; Turtles; Freddie and the Dreamers; Dobie Gray; Knickerbockers.

OUT OF THIS WORLD
Original Cast (1950) .... *Columbia (M) ML-54390*   50   30-40
Disc shows ML-4390. Cover shows ML-54390.
Original Cast (1950) .... *Columbia (M) OL-4390*   Re   25-35
Original Cast (1950) .... *Columbia Special Products (M) CML-4390*   Re   8-10
Composer: Cole Porter. **Conductor:** Pembroke Davenport. **Cast:** Charlotte Greenwood;
Priscilla Gillette; William Redfield; David Burns; Barbara Ashley.
Also see BLUE SKIES

OUTER SPACE SUITE
TV Soundtrack (1957) .... *Cerberus (M) 0208*   83   20-25
Also includes *The Moat Farm Murders* and *The Hitchhiker*.
Composer: Bernard Herrmann.

OUTLAND
Soundtrack (1981) .... *Warner Bros. (S) HS-3551*   81   10-12
Composer: Jerry Goldsmith. **Conductor:** Jerry Goldsmith. **Cast:** National Philharmonic
Orchestra.

OUTLAW BLUES
Soundtrack (1977) .... *Capitol (S) ST-11691*   77   10-12
Composer: Charles Berstein; Hoyt Axton. **Conductor:** Charles Bernstein. **Cast:** Hoyt Axton;
Peter Fonda; Susan Saint James; John Crawford; James Callahan; Michael Lerner.

OUTLAW JOSEY WALES
Soundtrack (1976) .... *Warner Bros. (S) BS-2956*   76   **$15-20**
  Composer: Jerry Fielding. Conductor: Jerry Fielding.

OUTLAW RIDERS
Soundtrack (1970) .... *MGM (S) 1SE-26*   70   **10-12**
  Composer: Michael Lloyd; Simon Stokes; others. Cast: Lenny McDaniel; Horsemen; Simon
  Stokes and the Night Hawks; Bob Correll.

OUTRAGEOUS
Soundtrack (1977) .... *Polydor (S) 1-8902*   77   **8-10**
  Cast: Brenda Hoffert; Cecile Frenette; Craig Russell.

OUTSIDE IN
Soundtrack (1972) .... *MGM (S) 1SE-37*   72   **10-12**
  Composer: Randy Edelman; others. Conductor: Randy Edelman. Cast: Randy Edelman (vocal,
  piano); Five Man Electrical Band.

OVER HERE!
Original Cast (1974) .... *Columbia (S) KS-32961*   74   **30-35**
  Composer: Richard M. Sherman; Robert B. Sherman. Conductor: Joseph Klein.
  Cast: Patty Andrews; Maxene Andrews; Douglass Watson; MacIntyre Dixon; John Travolta;
  April Shawman; Janie Sell; William Griffis; Jim Weston; Phyllis Somerville; Samuel E. Wright.

OVER THE EDGE
Soundtrack (1979) .... *Warner Bros. (S) BSK-3335*   79   **8-10**
  Cast: Cheap Trick; Cars; Van Halen; Jimi Hendrix; Ramones; Little Feat; Valerie Carter.

OVER THE TOP
Soundtrack (1987) .... *Columbia (S) SC-40655*   87   **8-10**
  Cast: Sammy Hagar; Robin Zander; Larry Greene; Big Trouble; Frank Stallone; Kenny Loggins;
  Asia; Giorgio Moroder; Eddie Money.

OWL AND THE PUSSYCAT
Soundtrack (1970) .... *Columbia (S) S-30410*   70   **25-30**
  Composer: Richard Halligan. Cast: Barbra Streisand; George Segal; Blood, Sweat and Tears.

P

PACIFIC OVERTURES
Original Cast (1976) . . . . *RCA Victor (S) ARL1-1367* 76 **$8-10**
   Composer: Stephen Sondheim. **Conductor:** George Gemignani. **Cast:** Mako; Soon-Tech Oh;
   Yuki Shimoda; Sab Shimono; Isao Sato; Alvin Ing; Ernest Harada; James Dybas; Patrick
   Kinser-Lau; Jae Woo Lee; Timm Fujii; Conrad Yama; Ricardo Tobia; Gedde Watanabe.

PACKERS' GLORY YEARS
Studio Cast (1967) . . . . *Fleetwood (S) FCLP 3028* 67 **12-15**
   Narration with music and radio broadcasts.
   Cast: Ted Moore (narration).

PAGAN LOVE SONG
Soundtrack (1950) . . . .*MGM (EP) K-64* 50 **20-25**
   Triple EP boxed set.
Soundtrack (1950) . . . .*MGM (M) E-534* 50 **35-40**
   Composer: Harry Warren; Nacio Herb Brown. **Conductor:** Adolph Deutsch. **Cast:** Howard
   Keel; Esther Williams.
   Also see HIT THE DECK

PAINT YOUR WAGON
Original Cast (1951) . . . . *RCA Victor (EP) WOC-1006* 51 **15-20**
Original Cast (1951) . . . . *RCA Victor (EP) EOA-434* 51 **10-15**
Original Cast (1951) . . . . *RCA Victor (M) LOC-1006* 51 **25-30**
Original Cast (1951) . . . . *RCA Victor (SE) LSO-1006* 65 **10-15**
   Composer: Alan Jay Lerner; Frederick Loewe. **Conductor:** Franz Allers. **Cast:** James Barton;
   Olga San Juan; Tony Bavaar; Rufus Smith; Robert Penn; Dave Thomas.
Studio Cast (1951) . . . . *RCA Victor (M) LPM-6005* 60 **25-30**
Studio Cast (1951) . . . . *RCA Victor (SE) LSP-2274* 60 **25-30**
   Above two are double LP sets and also have selections from *My Fair Lady.*
   Composer: Alan Jay Lerner; Frederick Loewe. **Conductor:** Johnny Green. **Cast:** Jane Powell;
   Jan Peerce; Robert Merrill; Phil Harris.
Soundtrack (1969) . . . . *Paramount (S) PMS-1001* 69 **10-12**
   Gatefold cover.
   Composer: Alan Jay Lerner; Frederick Loewe. **Conductor:** Nelson Riddle. **Cast:** Lee Marvin;
   Clint Eastwood; Jean Seberg.
Soundtrack (1969) . . . . *Paramount (S) 1609/10* 69 **15-20**
   Promotional LP intended for radio broadcast.
   Composer: Alan Jay Lerner; Frederick Loewe; Ándre Previn. **Conductor:** Andre Previn.
   Cast: Lee Marvin; Clint Eastwood; Jean Seberg; Harve Presnell. (With dialogue.)
Soundtrack (1969) . . . .*MCA (S) 37099* **8-10**
   Cast: Nitty Gritty Dirt Band.
Studiotrack (1970) . . . . *Flying Dutchman (S) FDS-114* 70 **10-15**
   Jazz interpretations.
   Composer: Alan Jay Lerner; Frederick Loewe; Andre Previn. **Cast:** Tom Scott Quartet
   (Tom Scott, Roger Kellaway, Chuck Domanico, John Guerin).
Studiotrack . . . . *Diplomat (S) DS-2419* **8-12**

PAINTED SMILES OF COLE PORTER

Studio Cast (1972) . . . . *Painted Smiles (S) PS-1358*   72   **$20-25**
Unproduced revue, intended as a Broadway musical.
Studio Cast (1972) . . . . *Painted Smiles (S) PS-1358*   72   **20-25**
Reissue, with a different cover and seven additional songs.
Composer: Cole Porter. **Conductor:** Judd Woldin. **Cast:** Blossom Dearie; Carmen Alvarez;
Karen Morrow; Edward Earle; Laura Kenyon; Alice Playten; Charles Rydell.

PAINTING THE CLOUDS WITH SUNSHINE

Soundtrack (1951) . . . . *Capitol (M) L-291*   51   **60-70**
Cast: Gene Nelson; Dennis Morgan.

PAJAMA GAME

Original Cast (1954) . . . . *Columbia (EP) A-1098*   54   **15-20**
Original Cast (1954) . . . . *Columbia (M) ML-4840*   54   **25-35**
Original Cast (1954) . . . . *Columbia (M) S-32606*   73   **8-10**
Composer: Richard Adler; Jerry Ross. **Conductor:** Hal Hastings. **Cast:** John Raitt; Janis Paige;
Eddie Foy Jr.; Carol Haney; Reta Shaw; Stanley Prager; Buzz Miller; Peter Gennaro.
Soundtrack (1957) . . . . *Columbia (M) OL-5210*   57   **25-30**
Soundtrack (1957) . . . . *Columbia Special Products (M) AOL-5210*   Re   **8-10**
Composer: Richard Adler; Jerry Ross. **Conductor:** Ray Heindorf. **Cast:** Doris Day; John Raitt;
Carol Haney; Eddie Foy Jr.; Reta Shaw; Barbara Nichols.
Studiotrack . . . . *Somerset (S) SF-3300*   **10-12**
Also has music from *Silk Stockings*.
Composer: Richard Adler; Jerry Ross; Cole Porter; Joseph Kuhn. **Conductor:** Joseph Kuhn.
Cast: New World Theatre Orchestra.

PAJAMA PARTY

Soundtrack (1964) . . . . *Buena Vista (M) BV-3325*   64   **30-35**
Soundtrack (1964) . . . . *Buena Vista (SM) STER-332*   64   **40-45**
Composer: Jerry Styner; Guy Hemric. **Cast:** Annette Funicello; Tommy Kirk.

PAL JOEY

Original Revival Cast (1952) . . . . *Capitol (EP) EDM-310*   52   **20-25**
Original Revival Cast (1952) . . . . *Capitol (M) S-310*   52   **100-125**
Original Revival Cast (1952) . . . . *World (M) T-774*   Re   **50-60**
Composer: Richard Rodgers; Lorenz Hart. **Cast:** Helen Gallagher; Jane Froman; Patricia
Northrop; Elaine Stritch; Lewis Bolyard; Dick Beavers. Froman and Beavers were not in the
stage show.
Studio Cast (1952) . . . . *Columbia (M) ML-4364*   52   **35-40**
The success of this cast recording sparked the Broadway revival, with Vivienne Segal and Harold Lang
also starring in the show. For that reason, this LP is often mistakenly referred to as the revival cast album.
Composer: Richard Rodgers; Lorenz Hart. **Cast:** Vivienne Segal; Harold Lang; Barbara Ashley;
Beverly Fite; Kenneth Remo; Jo Hurt.
Studio Cast (1952) . . . . *Columbia (EP) A-1735*   52   **15-20**
Studio Cast (1952) . . . . *Columbia (EP) A-974*   52   **20-25**
Double EP boxed set.
Studio Cast (1952) . . . . *Columbia Special Products (M) AOL-4364*   Re   **8-10**
Composer: Richard Rodgers; Lorenz Hart. **Cast:** Vivienne Segal; Harold Lang; Barbara Ashley;
Beverly Fite; Kenneth Remo; Jo Hurt.
Studio Cast . . . . *Tops (M) L-1607*   **10-15**
Composer: Richard Rodgers; Lorenz Hart. **Conductor:** Lew Raymond. **Cast:** Martha Tilton;
June Hutton; Curt Massey; Clark Dennis; Marilyn Maxwell; Betty Baker; Clark Dennis; Bob
McKendrick.

Soundtrack (1957) .... *Capitol (EP) EDM-912*	57	**$10-15**
Soundtrack (1957) .... *Capitol (M) W-912*	57	**15-20**
Soundtrack (1957) .... *Capitol (SE) DW-912*	61	**15-20**
Soundtrack (1957) .... *Capitol (SE) SM-912e*	Re	**10-12**
Soundtrack (1957) .... *Capitol (SE) 4M-912*	Re	**8-10**

Composer: Richard Rodgers; Lorenz Hart. Conductor: Morris Stoloff. Cast: Frank Sinatra; Rita Hayworth. (With dialogue.)

Studiotrack .... *Design (S) DLP-60*   **10-12**

PALM SPRINGS WEEKEND

Soundtrack (1963) .... *Warner Bros. (M) W-1519*	63	**25-30**
Soundtrack (1963) .... *Warner Bros. (S) WS-1519*	63	**30-35**

Composer: Frank Perkins; others. Cast: Connie Stevens; Troy Donahue; Ty Hardin; Robert Conrad; Jerry Van Dyke; Modern Folk Quartet.

PANAMA HATTIE

Soundtrack (1942) .... *Sandy Hook (SE) SH-2077*   81   **8-10**
Also has music from *Babes in Arms*.
Composer: Cole Porter. Cast: Ethel Merman; Art Carney; Jack Leonard.
Also see ANYTHING GOES

PANIC BUTTON

Soundtrack (1964) .... *Musicor (M) MM-2026*	64	**30-40**
Soundtrack (1964) .... *Musicor (S) MS-3026*	64	**40-50**

Composer: Georges Garvarentz. Conductor: Georges Garvarentz.

PAPA WAS A PREACHER

Soundtrack (1985) .... *Word (S) 7-01-900210-2*   84   **8-10**
Composer: Ken Sutherland. Cast: Mac Frampton; Sandi Patti; Porter Kids; Robert Pine with Brandon Sokolosky and Choir.

PAPER MOON

Soundtrack (1973) .... *Paramount (S) PAS-1012*   73   **12-18**
Has songs from the mid-'30s by various artists.
Composer: Various. Cast: Bing Crosby; Hoagy Carmichael; Paul Whitman; Larry Stewart; Dick Powell; Jimmie Grier and His Orchestra; Boswell Sisters; Ozzie Nelson and His Orchestra; Donald Novis; Victor Young and His Orchestra; Pinky Tomlin; Leo Reisman and His Orchestra; Jimmy Davis; Tommy Dorsey and His Orchestra; Ken Darby and Ramona; Blue Sky Boys; Frank Luther.
Studiotrack .... *Harmony (SE) KH-32748*   73   **8-10**
Various songs of the '30s, but not from the film.
Composer: Various. Cast: Cliff Edwards; Sophie Tucker; Dick Powell; Buddy Clark.

PAPER TIGER

Soundtrack (1975) .... *Capitol (S) SW-11475*   75   **10-12**
Composer: Roy Budd. Conductor: Roy Budd. Cast: National Philharmonic Orchestra; Ray Conniff Singers; Mike Sammes Singers; Roy Budd (piano).

PAPILLON

Soundtrack (1973) .... *Capitol (S) ST-11260*   73   **15-20**
Composer: Jerry Goldsmith. Conductor: Jerry Goldsmith.

PARADE

Original Cast (1960) .... *Kapp (M) KDL-7005*	60	**175-200**
Original Cast (1960) .... *Kapp (S) KDS-7005*	60	**200-225**

Composer: Jerry Herman. Cast: Dody Goodman; Richard Tone; Fia Karin; Charles Nelson Reilly; Jerry Herman (piano).

PARADE (MUSIC FROM "UNDER THE CHERRY MOON")

Soundtrack (1986) .... *Warner Bros. (S) 1-25395*   86   **8-10**
Cast: Prince and the Revolution.

PARADE OF SHOW STOPPERS
Soundtrack . . . .*Columbia Special Products (S) CSP-237*   **$10-15**
  Music from various plays and films.

PARADINE CASE
Studiotrack (1948) . . . . *AEI (M) 3103*   79   **8-10**
  Also has music from *Spellbound.*
  Composer: Franz Waxman. SPELLBOUND: Miklos Rozsa. **Conductor:** Franz Waxman.
  SPELLBOUND: Miklos Rozsa.
  Also see ENCHANTED COTTAGE

PARADISE ALLEY
Soundtrack (1978) . . . . *MCA (S) 5100*   79   **8-10**
  Composer: Bill Conte; others. **Conductor:** Bob Alcivar. **Cast:** Sylvester Stallone; Tom Waits;
  Frank Stallone Jr.

PARADISE HAWAIIAN STYLE
Soundtrack (1966) . . . . *RCA Victor (M) LPM-3643*   66   **35-45**
Soundtrack (1966) . . . .*RCA Victor (S) LSP-3643*   66   **35-45**
  Black label.
Soundtrack (1966) . . . . *RCA Victor (S) LSP-3643*   69   **10-20**
  Orange or tan label. (Tan label issued in 1976.)
Soundtrack (1966) . . . . *RCA Victor (S) AFL1-3643*   77   **8-10**
  Composer: Bill Giant; Bernie Baum; Florence Kaye; Fred Wise; Randy Starr; Sid Tepper; Roy
  C. Bennett; others. **Cast:** Elvis Presley; Scotty Moore (guitar); Charlie McCoy (guitar); Barney
  Kessel (guitar); Barnal Lewis (steel); D.J. Fontana (drums); Hal Blaine (drums); Larry
  Muhoberac (keyboard); Ray Siegel (bass); Jordanaires (vocals); Mello Men (vocals).

PARAPLUIES DE CHERBOURG:
see UMBRELLAS OF CHERBOURG

PARDNERS
Studiotrack (1956) . . . . *Capitol (EP) EAP 1-752*   56   **50-75**
  Composer: Sammy Cahn; Jimmy Van Heusen. **Conductor:** Dick Stabile. **Cast:** Dean Martin;
  Jerry Lewis.

PARENT TRAP
Soundtrack (1961) . . . . *Buena Vista (M) BV-3309*   61   **25-30**
Soundtrack (1961) . . . . *Buena Vista (S) BVS-3309*   61   **35-40**
  One side of above two have music from *Intermezzo, Swiss Family Robinson, Sleeping Beauty* and *Alice in*
  Wonderland.
  Composer: Richard M. Sherman; Robert B. Sherman. **Conductor:** Tutti Camarata. **Cast:** Hayley
  Mills; Tommy Sands; Annette Funicello; Maureen O'Hara.
  Also see IN SEARCH OF THE CASTAWAYS; SUMMER MAGIC

PARENTHOOD
Soundtrack (1989) . . . . *Reprise (S) 1-26001*   89   **8-10**
  Composer: Randy Newman. **Cast:** Randy Newman.

PARIS BLUES
Soundtrack (1961) . . . . *United Artists (M) UAL-4092*   61   **20-25**
Soundtrack (1961) . . . .*United Artists (S) UAS-5092*   61   **25-30**
Soundtrack (1961) . . . . *United Artists (S) UA-LA274-G*   74   **10-12**
  Composer: Duke Ellington; others. **Cast:** Louis Armstrong.
  Also see HORSE SOLDIERS; JOHNNY COOL

PARIS HOLIDAY
Soundtrack (1958) . . . . *United Artists (M) UAL-40001*   58   **50-60**
  Composer: Joseph J. Lilley; James Van Heusen; Jerome Kern; Vernon Duke.
  Conductor: Joseph J. Lilley. **Cast:** Bob Hope; Bing Crosby.

1.

2.

3.

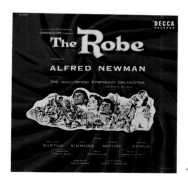

4.

5.

6.

1. He is known to TV viewers as the Sheriff of Mayberry ("The Andy Griffith Show") who became the Atlanta attorney ("Matlock"), yet his finest performance may be found in *A Face in the Crowd.* Both Andy Griffith and Lee Remick made their screen debut in this 1957 film. *2.* Decca reissued music from the 1943 Broadway production of *Carmen Jones* on this 1955 long play. The material had previously been available only on 78 rpms. *3.* This is a 1976 promotional only issue, saluting Bobbie Gentry and the film inspired by her 1967 million-seller, *Ode to Billy Joe.* *4. The Robe* featured an Oscar-nominated performance by Richard Burton. This Alfred Newman-scored, 1953 classic holds the distinction of being the first movie filmed in Cinemascope. *5.* French beauty, Jeanmaire, gave a smoldering ballet portrayal in the 1954 musical comedy, *The Girl in Pink Tights.* *6.* In 1967, a silver screen rebirth of television's "Peter Gunn" brought both Henry Mancini (composer/conductor) and Craig "Peter Gunn" Stevens together again.

1.

2.

3.

4.

5.

6.

1. Shown is the 1955 Decca issue of George Gershwin's folk opera, *Porgy and Bess;* however, *(2)* when reissued in 1959 the music was the same, but a completely different front cover was created. *3.* Kenyon Hopkins created a compelling score for the 1966 *Mister Buddwing,* portrayed on screen by James Garner. *4.* 1958's *Flower Drum Song* is just one of dozens of Rogers and Hammerstein original cast recordings found in this guide. *5.* Perhaps Ethel Merman's best known performance is that of Annie Oakley, in the 1946 *Annie Get Your Gun. 6.* Music from the 1961 version of *Back Street* is found on this Decca LP. This was the third film version of a young couple's back street affair, having previously been made in 1932 and 1941.

1. The soundtrack for *Walk on the Wild Side* appeared on two different labels in 1962: Choreo and Ava. The Ava issue is pictured here. *2. Maggie Flynn*, a musically superb 1968 show, paired real life husband and wife, Jack Cassidy and Shirley Jones. *3. Jimi Hendrix* offers a double LP of songs and dialogue from the 1973 film documentary of the life of Hendrix. *4.* Valued as high as $2,000, the Chicken of the Sea edition of *Elvis: Aloha from Hawaii Via Satellite* is second only to *The Caine Mutiny* on the list of the most valuable soundtrack and cast recordings. *5.* Jerome Moross brilliantly captured the grandeur of the Western frontier with his 1958 *Big Country* film score. *6.* Among the earliest original cast, 12-inch, long play albums is *Lost in the Stars*, a 1949 issue.

1.

2.

3.

4.

5.

6.

1. 1967's offbeat *Privilege* is billed as "a film so bizarre, so controversial, it shall crucify your mind to the tree of conscience." While perhaps not fulfilling that promise, it accurately captured the spirit of England's Mod generation. *2.* The 1968 Broadway show *Promises, Promises* was based on Billy Wilder's screen play, *The Apartment. 3.* Many original cast stars are signed to recreate their stage role on film. Such was the case with Judy Holliday, star of both the Broadway and screen showing of *Bells Are Ringing. 4.* Peter O'Toole and songbird Petula Clark co-starred in the 1969 musical reworking of *Goodbye, Mr. Chips,* 30 years after the original film release. *5.* By the time he won an Oscar for scoring *Irma La Douce* (1963), Andre Previn had accumulated ten Academy Nominations and became the first performer in the history of the Academy Awards to receive three Oscar nominations in one year. *6.* The original Broadway cast album for *How to Succeed in Business Without Really Trying* broke design tradition by giving nothing but the title on the front cover—not even a label name or number.

1.

2.

3.

4.

5.

6.

7.

8.

1. The Fighter, a 10-inch LP, features the music of Vicente Gómez, then regarded as one of the world's great classical Spanish guitarists. *2*. The 1953-issued, 10-inch *Naughty Marietta* is an example of a studio cast LP. It featured Gordon Macrae and Marguerite Piazza singing the melodies of Victor Herbert. *3*. The 1968 *Cabaret* original cast recording was deservedly a big seller, and therefore is not scarce. This LP is musically so superb that no cast/soundtrack collection is complete without it. *4*. Qualifying as a studio cast recording is *Bugs Bunny and His Friends*, which showcases the genius of the one and only Mel Blanc. *5*. *The Pajama Game* opened on Broadway in 1954 and ran for 1,063 consecutive performances. The original cast recording is pictured here—the soundtrack, picturing Doris Day, is seen on the previous page. *6*. Versatile composer Leith Stevens steeped himself in the study of space travel and science before scoring *Destination Moon*, in 1950. Stevens put us musically on the moon decades before Neil Armstrong walked there. *7*. Among the most famous of the glorious MGM musicals is Gershwin's *An American in Paris*, first issued in 1951 as a 10-inch LP. *8*. *The Desert Song*, a 10-inch, studio cast LP released in 1949, is one of Decca's earliest long-playing albums.

1.

2.

3.

4.

5.

6.

By mid-1990, most labels had ceased vinyl record production, focusing their attention instead on compact discs and cassettes. On this page are some soundtracks that are among the last issued on vinyl: *1. Lethal Weapon 2* has tracks by George Harrison, the Beach Boys, and Eric Clapton, among others. *2. Blaze* starred Paul Newman, but the soundtrack has songs by Fats Domino, Bonnie Sheridan, Randy Newman, and Hank Williams. *3.* The collectibility of *Heart of Dixie*, an obscure, 1989 soundtrack, is bolstered by the inclusion of Elvis Presley's *I Want You, I Need You, I Love You.* Presley collectors must have every release with his voice on it, thereby inflating prices on those items on which Elvis appears. *4.* Despite its recent vintage, 1983's *Valley Girl* already ranks in the Top 100 most valuable LPs. To an extent, its story is similar to that of *The Caine Mutiny*—records were manufactured but never made it into distribution. Contains such memorable tunes as *Angst in My Pants* and *Johnny Are You Queer? 5. Bad Influence*, a 1990 issue, has some assorted songs by various artists, Etta James and Skinny Puppy among them, plus some original music by Trevor Jones. *6. Sea of Love*, whose vocal theme is the 1959 hit by Phil Philips, is similar to *Bad Influence* in that it combines music from the past with some original compositions—again by Trevor Jones.

PARIS HONEYMOON
Studiotrack (1939) .... *Decca (M) DL-6012*   50   **$50-60**
10-inch LP.
Composer: Ralph Rainger; Leo Robin. **Conductor:** John Scott Trotter. **Cast:** Bing Crosby.
Also see EAST SIDE OF HEAVEN

PARIS '90
Original Cast (1952) .... *Columbia (M) ML-4619*   52   **125-150**
Composer: Kay Swift. **Conductor:** Nathaniel Shilkret. **Cast:** Cornelia Otis Skinner.

PARIS, TEXAS
Soundtrack (1984) .... *Warner Bros. (S) 1-25270*   84   **8-10**
Cast: Ry Cooder.

PARIS WHEN IT SIZZLES
Soundtrack (1964) .... *Reprise (M) R-6113*   64   **10-15**
Soundtrack (1964) .... *Reprise (S) RS-6113*   64   **15-20**
Composer: Nelson Riddle; others. **Conductor:** Nelson Riddle. **Cast:** Nelson Riddle and His
Orchestra.

PARRISH
Soundtrack (1961) .... *Warner Bros. (M) W-1413*   61   **45-55**
Soundtrack (1961) .... *Warner Bros. (S) WS-1413*   61   **65-75**
Has three love themes from *Parrish,* played by George Greeley. Also has two Max Steiner themes:
Gone with the Wind and *A Summer Place.*
Composer: Max Steiner. **Conductor:** Max Steiner. **Cast:** George Greeley (piano).

PARTY
Soundtrack (1968) .... *RCA Victor (M) LPM-3997*   68   **12-18**
Soundtrack (1968) .... *RCA Victor (S) LSP-3997*   68   **15-20**
Composer: Henry Mancini. **Conductor:** Henry Mancini.

PARTY WITH BETTY COMDEN AND ADOLPH GREEN
Original Cast (1958) .... *Capitol (M) WAO-1197*   58   **35-40**
Original Cast (1958) .... *Capitol (S) SWAO-1197*   58   **50-60**
Original Revival Cast (1977) .... *Stet (S) S2L-5177*   77   **10-15**
Double LP set.
Composer: Betty Comden; Adolph Green. **Conductor:** Peter Howard. **Cast:** Betty Comden;
Adolph Green.

PASSAGE TO INDIA
Soundtrack (1985) .... *Capitol (S) SV-12389*   85   **20-25**
Composer: Maurice Jarre. **Conductor:** Maurice Jarre.

PASSING FAIR
Original Cast (1965) .... *Proscenium (M) PR-25*   65   **30-35**
Intended for Broadway but this show never opened.
Composer: James Forbes Chapin. **Cast:** James Forbes Chapin; Valentine Pringle; Mary Louise;
Bill Dillard; Dolores Perry; Mark Donald (piano).

PASSION (MUSIC FOR "THE LAST TEMPTATION OF CHRIST")
Soundtrack (1988) .... *Real World (S) GHS-24206*   88   **10-12**
Double LP set.
Cast: Peter Gabriel.

PAT BOONE SINGS IRVING BERLIN
Studiotrack (1958) .... *Dot (M) DLP-3077*   58   **15-20**
Studiotrack (1958) .... *Dot (S) DLP-25077*   58   **10-20**
Composer: Irving Berlin. **Cast:** Pat Boone.

PAT GARRETT AND BILLY THE KID
Soundtrack (1973) ....*Columbia (S) KC-32460*   73   **$8-10**
  Composer: Bob Dylan. Cast: Bob Dylan; Brenda Patterson; Donna Weiss; Priscilla Jones;
  Byron Berline; Carol Hunter.

PAT O'BRIEN
TV Soundtrack (1964) ....*RIK (S) M-1003*   64   **10-15**
  Cast: Pat O'Brien.

PATCH OF BLUE
Soundtrack (1965) ....*Mainstream (M) 56058*   65   **30-40**
Soundtrack (1965) .... *Mainstream (S) 6058*   65   **35-50**
Soundtrack (1965) .... *Citadel (S) CT-7008*   80   **10-20**
Soundtrack (1965) .... *Citadel (S) CT-6028*   78   **10-12**
  Composer: Jerry Goldsmith. **Conductor:** Jerry Goldsmith.

PATRICK
Soundtrack (1978) ....*Varese Sarabande (S) VC-81107*   79   **8-10**
  . Composer: Brian May. **Conductor:** Brian May. **Cast:** Susan Penhaligon; Robert Helpmann.

PATTON
Soundtrack (1970) ....*20th Century-Fox (S) S-4208*   70   **12-15**
Soundtrack (1970) ....*20th Century-Fox (S) T-902*   Re   **8-10**
  Composer: Jerry Goldsmith. **Conductor:** Jerry Goldsmith. **Cast:** George C. Scott.
  (With dialogue.)

PATTY
Soundtrack (1976) ....*Stang (S) 1027*   76   **10-12**
  Composer: Al Goodman; Sammy Lowe; others. **Conductor:** Sammy Lowe. **Cast:** Moments;
  Rimshots; Chuck Jackson; Retta Young.

PATTY HEARST
Soundtrack (1988) ....*Nonesuch (S) 79186-1*   88   **8-10**

PAUL SILLS' STORY THEATRE (OF MAGICAL FOLK-ROCK FABLES)
Original Cast (1970) ....*Columbia (S) SG-30415*   70   **15-20**
  Composer: Bob Dylan; Country Joe McDonald; George Harrison; Hamid Hamilton Camp.
  Cast: Melinda Dillon; Mary Frann; Paul Sand; Richard Libertini; Peter Bonerz; Hamid Hamilton
  Camp; Valerie Harper; Richard Schaal; True Brethren. (With dialogue.)

PAWNBROKER
Soundtrack (1965) ....*Mercury (M) MG-21011*   65   **15-20**
Soundtrack (1965) .... *Mercury (S) SR-61011*   65   **20-25**
  Composer: Quincy Jones. **Conductor:** Quincy Jones. **Cast:** Rod Steiger; Marc Allen
  (With dialogue.)

PEACE
Original Cast (1969) . . . . *Metromedia (S) MP-33001*   69   **$50-55**
  Composer: Al Carmines; Tim Reynolds. Conductor: Al Carmines. Cast: Julie Kurnitz; George McGarth; Essie Borden; Ann Dunbar; David Vaughan; David Pursley; David Tice; Margaret Wright; Arlene Rothlein; Marie Santell.

PEACH THIEF
Soundtrack (1966) . . . . *Roulette (M) OS-804*   66   **15-20**
  Also has six TV soundtracks: *The Cheaters, International Detective, The Liars, The World Tomorrow, Supposin'* and *The Man from Interpol.*
Soundtrack (1966) . . . . *Roulette (S) OSS-804*   66   **20-25**
  Composer: Simeon Pirankov. Conductor: Simeon Pirankov.

PECOS BILL:
see JOHNNY APPLESEED

PELÉ
Soundtrack (1977) . . . . *Atlantic (S) SD-18231*   77   **10-12**
  Composer: Sergio Mendes; Pelé. Conductor: Sergio Mendes. Cast: Pelé.

PENELOPE
Soundtrack (1966) . . . . *MGM (M) E-4426*   66   **12-18**
Soundtrack (1966) . . . . *MGM (S) SE-4426*   66   **15-20**
  Composer: John Williams. Conductor: John Williams.

PENITENTIARY III
Soundtrack (1987) . . . . *RCA Victor (S) 6663-1*   87   **8-10**
  Composer: Various. Cast: New Choice; Gap Band; Midnight Star; Yarborough and Peoples; James Reese; Lotti Dotti; Diabolical; Larue; others.

PENNEY PROUD
Original Cast (1962) . . . . *Industrial (S) A&R-2195*   62   **15-20**
  Composer: Michael Brown. Conductor: Norman Paris. Cast: Kenneth Nelson; Ellen Martin; Walter Farrell; Cynthia Wayne; Betty Ann Busch; Michael Brown; Tom Mixon.

PENNIES FROM HEAVEN
Studiotrack (1936) . . . . *Decca (M) DL-4251*   62   **25-30**
  Also has music from *Anything Goes* and *Rhythm on the Range.* Issued as part of *Bing's Hollywood Series.*
  Conductor: John Scott Trotter. Cast: Bing Crosby.

PENNIES FROM HEAVEN
Soundtrack (1981) . . . . *Warner Bros. (SE) 2-HW-363*   81   **12-15**
  Double LP set.
  Composer: Various. Conductor: Marvin Hamlisch; Billy May. Cast: Elsie Carlisle; Sam Browne; Connie Boswell; Fred Latham; Bing Crosby; Arthur Tracy; Boswell Sisters; Ida Sue McCune; Rudy Vallee; Dolly Dawn; George Hall; Helen Kane; Walt Harrah; Gene Merlino; Vern Rowe; Robert Tebow; Irving Aaronson; Ronnie Hill.

PENTHOUSE
Soundtrack (1967) . . . . *United Artists (M) UAL-4170*   67   **20-25**
Soundtrack (1967) . . . . *United Artists (S) UAS-5170*   67   **25-30**
  Composer: John Hawksworth; others. Conductor: John Hawksworth. Cast: Lisa Shane. (With dialogue.)

PEOPLE NEXT DOOR
Soundtrack (1970) . . . . *Avco Embassy (S) AVE-0-11002*   72   **30-40**
  Composer: Don Sebesky. Conductor: Don Sebesky.

PEOPLE'S CHOICE
Studio Cast (1968) . . . . *RCA Victor (M) PRM-263*   **15-20**
  Cast: Edwin Newman (narration).

PEPE
Soundtrack (1960) .... *Colpix (M) CP-507*   61   **$25-30**
Soundtrack (1960) .... *Colpix (S) SCP-507*   61   **35-40**
  Composer: Johnny Green; others. **Conductor:** Andre Previn; Johnny Green. **Cast:** Shirley Jones;
  Maurice Chevalier; Bobby Darin; Judy Garland; Bing Crosby; Sammy Davis Jr.

PERCY FAITH PLAYS THE ACADEMY AWARD WINNER AND OTHER
  GREAT MOVIE THEMES
Studiotrack (1967) .... *Columbia (M) CL-2650*   67   **8-12**
Studiotrack (1967) .... *Columbia (S) CS-9450*   67   **10-15**
  Composer: Various. **Conductor:** Percy Faith. **Cast:** Percy Faith and His Orchestra.

PERFECT
Soundtrack (1985) .... *Arista (S) AL6-8278*   85   **8-10**
  Composer: Ralph Burns; others. **Cast:** Jermaine Jackson; Pointer Sisters; Thompson Twins;
  Wham; Berlin; Jermaine Stewart; Dan Hartman; Nona Hendrix; Lou Reed; Whitney Houston

PERFECT COUPLE
Soundtrack (1979) .... *Lion Gate (S) AQR-524*   79   **20-25**
  Composer: Tony Berg; Ted Neeley; Allan Nichols; others. **Conductor:** Tony Berg.
  Cast: Keepin' 'Em Off the Streets (Ted Neeley; Heather MacRae; Tomi-Lee Bradley;
  Steven Sharp; Marta Heflin).

PERFORMANCE
Soundtrack (1970) .... *Warner Bros. (S) BS-1846*   70   **25-30**
Soundtrack (1970) .... *Warner Bros. (S) BS-2554*   70   **12-18**
  Reissued later the same year.
  Composer: Jack Nitzsche; others. **Conductor:** Randy Newman. **Cast:** Randy Newman; Mick
  Jagger; Buffy Sainte-Marie; Merry Clayton; Merry Clayton Singers; Last Poets.

PERICHOLE, LA:
see LA PERICHOLE

PERMANENT RECORD
Soundtrack (1988) .... *Epic (S) SE-40879*   88   **8-10**
  Composer: Joe Strummer; others. **Cast:** Joe Strummer and the Latino Rockabilly War;
  Godfathers; Bodeans; J.D. Souther; Lou Reed; Stranglers.

PERRI
Soundtrack (1957) .... *Disneyland (M) ST-3902*   57   **15-25**
Soundtrack (1957) .... *Disneyland (M) ST-1909*   61   **10-15**
Soundtrack (1957) .... *Disneyland (M) DQ-1309*   67   **8-10**
  Composer: Winston Hibler; George Bruns; Paul Smith; Gil George; Ralph Wright; Tutti
  Camarata. **Cast:** Jimmy Dodd; Darlene Gillespie. (With dialogue.)

PETE KELLY'S BLUES
Soundtrack (1955) .... *Columbia (M) CL-690*   55   **25-30**
  Conductor: Ray Heindorf; Matty Matlock. **Cast:** Matty Matlock and His Jazz Band.
Soundtrack (1955) .... *Decca (M) DL-8166*   55   **20-25**
  Conductor: Harold Mooney. **Cast:** Peggy Lee; Ella Fitzgerald.
Soundtrack (1955) .... *RCA Victor (EP) EPB-1126*   55   **15-20**
  Double EP set.
Soundtrack (1955) .... *RCA Victor (EP) EPA-649*   55   **10-15**
Soundtrack (1955) .... *RCA Victor (M) LPM-1126*   55   **20-25**
Soundtrack (1955) .... *RCA Victor (M) LPM-2040*   59   **15-20**
Soundtrack (1955) .... *RCA Victor (SE) LSP-2040e*   59   **15-20**
  Cast: Jack Webb (narration); Matty Matlock; Dick Cathcart; Nick Fatool; Elmer "Moe"
  Schneider; George Van Eps; Ray Sherman; Jud DeNaut (jazz combo).
Studiotrack (1957) .... *RCA Victor (M) LPM-1413*   57   **20-25**
  Actual title: *Pete Kelly At Home.*
  Cast: Jack Webb.

TV Soundtrack (1959) ....*Warner Bros. (M) W-1303*	59	$20-25
TV Soundtrack (1959) ....*Warner Bros. (S) WS-1303*	59	30-35

Above two have assorted songs from the Roaring '20s.
Conductor: Dick Cathcart.

PETE'S DRAGON

Studio Cast (1977) ....*Disneyland (S) Storyteller 3*   77   8-12
Story of Pete's Dragon with music and dialogue from the film, plus an 11-page color booklet.
Composer: Al Kasha; Joel Hirschhorn. **Cast:** Helen Reddy; Jim Dale; Mickey Rooney; Red Buttons; Shelley Winters; Sean Marshall; Bob Holt (narrator).

Soundtrack (1977) ....*Capitol (S) SW-11704*   77   8-10
Composer: Al Kasha; Joel Hirschhorn. **Conductor:** Irwin Kostal. **Cast:** Helen Reddy; Mickey Rooney; Red Buttons; Shelly Winters; Sean Marshall; Jim Dale; Charlie Callas; Charles Tyner; Gary Morgan; Jeff Conaway; others.

PETER AND THE WOLF

Soundtrack (1946) .... *Disneyland (M) WDL-3016*		15-20
Soundtrack (1946) .... *Disneyland (M) WDL-1016*	60	10-15
Soundtrack (1946) .... *Disneyland (M) DQ-1242*	63	10-15

One side has *The Sorcerer's Apprentice* from *Fantasia.*
Composer: Serge Prokofiev. **Cast:** Sterling Holloway (narration).

Studiotrack ....*RCA Victor (S) AYL1-4450*   82   8-10
Also includes *Pinocchio.*
Cast: Sterling Holloway (narrator). PINOCCHIO: Cliff Edwards (narrator).
Also see SNOW WHITE AND THE SEVEN DWARFS

PETER GUNN

TV Soundtrack (1958) ....*RCA Victor (EP) EPA-4333*	59	10-12
TV Soundtrack (1958) ....*RCA Victor (EP) ESP-4333*	59	20-25
Stereo EP.		
TV Soundtrack (1958) .... *RCA Victor (M) LPM-1956*	59	10-15
TV Soundtrack (1958) ....*RCA Victor (S) LSP-1956*	59	15-25

Composer: Henry Mancini. **Conductor:** Henry Mancini. **Cast:** Henry Mancini and His Orchestra.

TV Soundtrack (1958) ....*RCA Victor (EP) EPA-4339*	59	10-15
Volume two.		
TV Soundtrack (1958) ....*RCA Victor (EP) ESP-4339*	59	20-25
Volume two. Stereo EP.		

PETER GUNN (continued)

TV Soundtrack (1958)	*RCA Victor (M) LPM-2040*	59	**$20-25**
TV Soundtrack (1958)	*RCA Victor (S) LSP-2040*	59	**25-35**

Above two, titled *More Music from Peter Gunn*, were issued with both a red front cover and a blue one.

Composer: Henry Mancini. **Conductor:** Henry Mancini. **Cast:** Henry Mancini and His Orchestra.

Studiotrack (1959)	*Comtemporary (M) C-3560*	59	**15-25**

Actual title *Shelly Manne and His Men Play Peter Gunn.*

Composer: Henry Mancini**Conductor:** Shelly Manne. **Cast:** Shelly Manne and His Combo.

Studiotrack (1959)	*Crown (M) 5101*	59	**10-15**
Studiotrack (1959)	*Crown (S) 138*	59	**15-20**

Composer: Henry Mancini. **Cast:** Ted Nash and His Orchestra.

Studiotrack	*Lion (M) 96112*	**10-15**

PETER PAN

Original Cast (1950)	*Columbia (EP) J-1526*	50	**15-20**
Original Cast (1950)	*Columbia (M) OL-4312*	50	**25-30**
Original Cast (1950)	*Columbia Special Products (M) AOL-4312*	Re	**8-10**

Composer: Leonard Bernstein; Alec Wilder. **Conductor:** Ben Steinberg. **Cast:** Jean Arthur; Boris Karloff; Marcia Henderson; Deg Hillias; Joe E. Marks.

Original Cast (1954)	*RCA Victor (EP) EYA-48*	54	**15-20**
Original Cast (1954)	*RCA Victor (EP) EOC-1019*	50	**15-20**
Original Cast (1954)	*RCA Victor (M) LOC-1019*	54	**40-50**
Original Cast (1954)	*RCA Victor (SE) LSO-1019*	59	**30-35**
Original Cast (1954)	*RCA Victor (SE) AYL1-3762*	Re	**8-10**

Composer: Mark Charlap; Carolyn Leigh; Jule Styne; Betty Comden; Jaye Ribanoff; Trude Rittman; Elmer Bernstein; Adolph Green. **Conductor:** Louis Adrian. **Cast:** Mary Martin; Cyril Ritchard; Kathy Nolan; Sondra Lee; Robert Harrington; Joseph Stafford; Margalo Gillmore.

Original Cast (1954)	*RCA Victor (EP) No Number Used*	**8-15**

Six track, stereo 33 EP.

Studiotrack (1960)	*Camden (M) CAL-1009*	60	**10-15**

Also has *Alice in Wonderland.*

Cast: Bobby Driscoll; Kathryn Beaumont; Norman Leyden; Henri Rene and His Orchestra.

Soundtrack (1963)	*Disneyland (M) DQ-1206*	63	**15-20**
Studiotrack	*RCA Victor (S) AYL1-4448*	82	**8-10**

Cast: Disney artists.

Studiotrack (1953)	*RCA Victor (EP) EPA-407*	53	**10-15**
Studiotrack (1954)	*Columbia (EP) B-1590*	54	**10-15**

Cast: Doris Day.

Studiotrack (1953)	*RCA Victor (M) LPM-3101*	53	**15-25**

Conductor: Hugo Winterhalter. **Cast:** Hugo Winterhalter and His Orchestra.

Studiotrack (1954)	*Columbia (EP) B-1590*	54	**10-15**

Cast: Doris Day.

PETEY WHEATSTRAW (THE DEVIL'S SON-IN-LAW)
Soundtrack (1977) .... *Magic Disc (S) MD-112*   77 $10-12
    Composer: Nat Dove; Mary Love. **Cast:** Nat Dove and the Devils.

PETTICOATS AND PETTIFOGERS
Original Cast (1969) .... *Creative Sound (S) CSS-1525*   69   25-30
    Composer: James Prigmore; Buddy Youngreen. **Cast:** Neldon Maxfield; Lynne Youngreen;
    Michael Edwards.

PETULIA
Soundtrack (1968) .... *Warner Bros. (S) WS-1755*   68   20-25
    Composer: John Barry. **Conductor:** John Barry.

PEYTON PLACE
Soundtrack (1957) .... *RCA Victor (M) LOC-1042*   58   40-50
    Reads "Long Play" at bottom of label.
Soundtrack (1957) .... *RCA Victor (S) LSO-1042*   58   85-100
    Reads "Living Stereo" at bottom of label.
Soundtrack (1957) .... *RCA Victor (M) LOC-1042*   65   20-25
    Reads "Monaural" at bottom of label.
Soundtrack (1957) .... *RCA Victor (S) LSO-1042*   65   25-35
    Reads "Stereo" at bottom of label.
Soundtrack (1957) .... *Entr' acte (S) ERS-6515*   Re   15-20
    Composer: Franz Waxman. **Conductor:** Franz Waxman.
TV Soundtrack (1965) .... *Epic (M) LN-24147*   65   20-25
TV Soundtrack (1965) .... *Epic (S) BN-26147*   65   25-30
    Composer: Randy Newman; Franz Waxman. **Conductor:** Randy Newman.

PHAEDRA
Soundtrack (1962) .... *United Artists (M) UAL-4102*   62   15-20
Soundtrack (1962) .... *United Artists (S) UAS-5102*   62   20-25
Soundtrack (1962) .... *United Artists (S) UA-LA280-G*   74   8-10
    Composer: Mikis Theodorakis. **Conductor:** Mikis Theodorakis. **Cast:** Melina Mercouri.
    Also see DIVORCE ITALIAN STYLE

PHANTASM
Soundtrack (1979) .... *Varese Sarabande (S) VC-81105*   79   8-10
    Composer: Fred Myrow; Malcolm Seagrave. **Conductor:** Fred Myrow; Malcolm Seagrave.
    Cast: Michael Baldwin; Bill Thornberry.

PHANTOM OF THE OPERA
Original London Cast (1987) .... *Polydor (S) 831273-1*   87   8-10
Original Cast (1987) .... *Polydor (S) 831563-1*   88   8-10
    Has "Highlights" from *Phantom of the Opera*.

PHANTOM OF THE PARADISE
Soundtrack (1974) .... *A&M (S) SP-3653*   74   10-12
Soundtrack (1974) .... *A&M (S) SP-3176*   82   8-10
    Composer: Paul Williams. **Cast:** Paul Williams; William Finlay; Jessica Harper; Juicy Fruits;
    Beach Bums; Undead; Ray Kennedy.

PHAR LAP
Soundtrack (1983) .... *Varese Sarabande (S) 81230*   84   8-10

PHILADELPHIA EXPERIMENT
Soundtrack (1984) .... *Rhino (S) RNSP-306*   84   10-15
    Composer: Ken Wannberg. **Conductor:** Ken Wannberg.

PHILEMON
Original Cast (1975) .... *Gallery (S) OC-1*   75   40-50
    Composer: Harvey Schmidt; Tom Jones. **Conductor:** Ken Collins. **Cast:** Michael Glenn-Smith;
    Virginia Gregory; Dick Latessa; Leila Martin; Howard Ross; Kathryn King Segal.

PIANO BAR
Original Cast (1978) ....*Original Cast (S) OC-7812*   78   **$10-15**
  Composer: Rob Fremont; Doris Willens. **Conductor:** Joel Silberman. **Cast:** Kelly Bishop; Karen
  DeVito; Steve Elmore; Jim McMahon; Richard Ryder; Joel Silberman.

PICASSO
Soundtrack (1956) ....*Folkways (M) FS-3860*   57   **8-10**
  Composer: Roman Vlad. **Conductor:** Franco Ferrara. **Cast:** Gangi (flamenco guitar).

PICASSO SUMMER:
see SUMMER OF '42

PICKWICK
Original London Cast (1965) ....*Phillips (S) SAL-3431*   65   **25-30**
  Composer: Cyril Ornadel; Leslie Bricusse. **Conductor:** Marcus Dods. **Cast:** Harry Secombe;
  Jessie Evans; Anton Rodgers; Teddy Green; Gerald James; Oscar Quitak; Julian Orchard; Hilda
  Braid; Norman Warwick; Ian Burford; Robin Wentworth; Tony Simpson.

PICNIC
Soundtrack (1955) .... *Decca (EP) ED-846*   55   **10-15**
Soundtrack (1955) .... *Decca (EP) ED-346*   55   **15-25**
  Triple disc set.
Soundtrack (1955) .... *Decca (M) DL-8320*   55   **20-25**
Soundtrack (1955) ....*Decca (SE) DL7-8320*   59   **15-20**
Soundtrack (1955) ....*MCA (SE) 2049*   72   **10-12**
Soundtrack (1955) ....*MCA (SE) 1527*   Re   **8-10**
  Composer: George Duning. **Conductor:** Morris Stoloff.

PIECES OF EIGHT
Original Cast (1959) .... *Offbeat (M) O-4016*   59   **60-65**
  Julius Monk's *Upstairs At the Downstairs* revue.
  Composer: William Roy; others. **Cast:** Ceil Cabot; Del Close; Jane Connell; Estelle Parsons;
  Gerry Matthews; William Roy and Carl Norman (pianos).
Original London Cast (1959) .... *London (M) 5761*   63   **35-40**
  Composer: Laurie Johnson. **Conductor:** Frank Horrox. **Cast:** Kenneth Williams; Fanella
  Fielding; Myra deGroot; Peter Reeves; Josephine Blake; Terence Theobald; Valerie Walsh;
  Peter Brett; Peter Cook; Frank Horrox Quintet.

PIED PIPER OF HAMELIN
TV Soundtrack (1957) .... *RCA Victor (M) LPM-1563*   57   **60-70**
  Composer: Edvard Grieg; Hal Stanley; Irving Taylor. **Conductor:** Peter Dudley King.
  Cast: Joseph Sargent (narration); Van Johnson.

PIED PIPER OF HAMLIN
Studiotrack (1968) .... *Columbia (S) CS-9572*   68 $10-12
Cast: Gene Kelly (narrator).

PINK CADILLAC
Soundtrack (1989) .... *Warner Bros. (S) 1-25922*   89   8-10
Cast: Michael Martin Murphey; Hank Williams, Jr.; Hank Williams, Sr.; Jill Hollier; Randy Travis; Southern Pacific; J.C. Crowley; Billy Hill; Dion; Robben Ford.

PINK PANTHER
Soundtrack (1964) .... *RCA Victor (M) LPM-2795*   64   10-15
Soundtrack (1964) .... *RCA Victor (S) LSP-2795*   64   15-20
Soundtrack (1964) .... *RCA Victor (S) ANL1-1389*   Re   8-10
Composer: Henry Mancini. Conductor: Henry Mancini. Cast: Meglio Stasera.

PINK PANTHER STRIKES AGAIN
Soundtrack (1976) .... *United Artists (S) UA-LA-694-G*   76   10-12
Soundtrack (1976) .... *Liberty (S) LT-51135*   8-10
Composer: Henry Mancini. Conductor: Henry Mancini. Cast: Tom Jones.

PINOCCHIO
Soundtrack (1940) .... *Disneyland (M) WDL-4002*   56   20-25
Soundtrack (1940) .... *Disneyland (M) DQ-1202*   Re   8-10
Soundtrack (1940) .... *Disneyland (M) 3102*   81   8-12
Picture disc.
Composer: Leigh Harline; Ned Washington; Paul J. Smith; Ed Plumb. Conductor: Leigh Harline; Paul J. Smith. Cast: Cliff Edwards (as Jiminy Cricket); Walter Catlett.
TV Soundtrack (1957) .... *Columbia (M) CL-1055*   57   60-65
Composer: Alec Wilder. Conductor: Glenn Osser. Cast: Mickey Rooney; Fran Allison; Jerry Colonna; Stubby Kaye; Martyn Green; Gordon B. Clarke.
Studiotrack (1950) .... *Decca (EP) ED-719*   50   10-15
Studiotrack (1950) .... *Decca (M) DL-5151*   50   20-30
10-inch LP.
Conductor: Victor Young. Cast: Cliff Edwards; Victor Young and His Orchestra.
Studiotrack (1969) .... *Disneyland (S) 3905*   69   10-12
Cast: Cliff Edwards.
Studiotrack (1940) .... *Decca (M) DL-8387*   56   20-30
One side has music from *The Wizard of Oz*.
Composer: Leigh Harline; Ned Washington; Harold Arlen; E.Y. Harburg. Conductor: Victor Young. Cast: Cliff Edwards; Julietta Novis; Ken Darby Singers; King's Men; Judy Garland; Ken Darby Singers.
Also see PETER AND THE WOLF

PINS AND NEEDLES
Studio Cast (1962) .... *Columbia (M) OL-5810*   62   20-25
Studio Cast (1962) .... *Columbia (S) OS-2210*   62   20-25
Labeled a "25th Anniversary Edition," this show was originally presented in 1937 by the International Ladies Garment Workers Union.
Studio Cast (1962) .... *Columbia Special Products (S) AOS-2210*   Re   8-10
Composer: Harold J. Rome; others. Conductor: Stan Freeman. Cast: Harold Rome; Barbra Streisand; Jack Carroll; Rose Marie Jun; Alan Sokoloff.

PIPE DREAM

Original Cast (1955) ....*RCA Victor (EP) EOC-1023* 55 **$30-40**
Triple disc set, labeled *Special Advance Edition.*

Original Cast (1955) ....*RCA Victor (M) LOC-1023* 55 **75-85**
Labeled *Special Advance Edition,* has more dramatic front cover art than the commercial issue (below).

Original Cast (1955) ....*RCA Victor (M) LOC-1023* 55 **50-60**

Original Cast (1955) ....*RCA Victor (SE) LOC-1097e* 65 **35-40**
Composer: Richard Rodgers; Oscar Hammerstein II. **Conductor:** Salvatore Dell'isola.
Cast: Helen Traubel; William Johnson; Judy Tyler; George D. Wallace; Mike Kellin.

Original Cast (1955) ....*RCA Victor (M) LOC-1097* 65 **35-40**

PIPE DREAMS

Soundtrack (1976) ....*Buddah (S) BDS-5676* 76 **10-12**
Composer: Dominic Frontiere; others. **Conductor:** Dominic Frontiere. **Cast:** Gladys Knight
and the Pips.

PIPPIN

Original Cast (1972) ....*Motown (S) M-760L* 72 **8-10**
Composer: Stephen Schwartz. **Conductor:** Stanley Lebowsky. **Cast:** Eric Berry; Jill Clayburgh;
Leland Palmer; Ben Vereen; Irene Ryan; John Rubinstein.

PIRANHA

Soundtrack (1978) ....*Varese Sarabande (S) STV-81126* 79 **8-10**
Composer: Pino Donaggio. **Conductor:** Pino Donaggio.

PIRATE

Soundtrack (1948) ....*MGM (M) E-21* 51 **35-40**
Soundtrack (1948) ....*MGM (M) E-3234* 55 **25-30**
One side of this LP contains music from *Summer Stock.*
Composer: Cole Porter. **Conductor:** Lennie Hayton. **Cast:** Judy Garland; Gene Kelly.
Also see HIT THE DECK

PIRATE MOVIE

Soundtrack (1982) ....*Polydor (S) PD-2-9503* 82 **10-15**
Double LP set.

PIRATES OF PENZANCE

Original Cast (1981) ....*Elektra (S) VE-601* 81 **12-15**
Double LP set, with a complete Gilbert and Sullivan operetta.

PIZZA HUT '73 (ANNUAL MEETING)

Assembled Cast (1973) ....*Pizza Hut (M) No Number Used* 73 **15-20**
Recorded at the Town & Country Hotel, San Diego, California, January 7 - 10, 1973.
Cast: Rich Little (doing impressions of Elvis Presley, Dean Martin, Johnny Cash, Bing Crosby,
and others).

PLACES IN THE HEART

Soundtrack (1984) ....*Varese Sarabande (S) 81229* **8-10**
Cast: Doc and Merle Watson.

PLAIN AND FANCY

Original Cast (1955) ....*Capitol (EP) EDM-603* 55 **15-20**
Original Cast (1955) ....*Capitol (M) S-603* 55 **40-45**
Original Cast (1955) ....*Capitol (SE) DW-603* 59 **25-30**
Composer: Albert Hague; Arnold Horwitt. **Conductor:** Franz Allers. **Cast:** Richard Derr;
Barbara Cook; David Daniels; Gloria Marlowe; Nancy Andrews; Elaine Lynn; Shirl Conway.

London Studio Cast (1957) ....*Dot (M) DLP-3048* 57 **75-85**
One side has music from *The Water Gypsies.*
Composer: Albert Hague; Arnold Horwitt. **Conductor:** Cyril Ornadel. **Cast:** Virginia Somers;
Jack Drummond; Grace O'Connor; Joan Hovis; Malcolm Keen.

PLANES, TRAINS, AND AUTOMOBILES
Soundtrack (1988) ....*Hughes (S) MCA-6223*   88 $8-10
  Composer: Various. Cast: Dream Academy; Steve Earl and Dukes; Dave Edmunds; Emmylou
  Harris; Silicon Teens; Stars of Heaven.

PLANET OF THE APES
Soundtrack (1968) ....*Project 3 (S) PR-5023SD*   68   8-10
  Standard cover.
Soundtrack (1968) ....*Project 3 (S) PR 5023*   68   20-25
  Gatefold cover.
  Composer: Jerry Goldsmith. Conductor: Jerry Goldsmith.
  Also see BENEATH THE PLANET OF THE APES

PLATINUM
Original Cast Live ....*No Label Shown (S) No Number Used*   78   15-25
  Composer: Gary William Friedman; Will Holt. Cast: Alexis Smith; Richard Cox; Lisa Mordente.

PLATOON (AND SONGS FROM THE ERA)
Soundtrack (1986) ....*Atlantic (S) 81742-1*   87   8-10
  Composer: Georges Delerue. Conductor: George Delerue. Cast: Vancouver Symphony
  Orchestra; Smokey Robinson; Merle Haggard; Doors; Jefferson Airplane; Aretha Franklin;
  Otis
  Redding; Percy Sledge; Rascals.

PLATOON LEADER
Soundtrack (1988) ....*GNP/Crescendo (S) GNPS-8013*   88   8-10
  Cast: George S. Clinton.

PLAY IT AGAIN, SAM
Soundtrack (1972) ....*Paramount (S) 1004*   72   15-20
  Composer: Billy Goldenberg; others. Conductor: Billy Goldenberg. Cast: Woody Allen; Diane
  Keaton; Tony Roberts; Oscar Peterson Trio.

PLAYGIRLS
Original Cast (1964) ....*Warner Bros. (M) W-1530*   64   20-25
Original Cast (1964) ....*Warner Bros. (S) WS-1530*   64   30-35
  Composer: Jackie Barnett. Conductor: Dean Elliott. Cast: Cara Williams; Kay Stevens; Julie
  Wilson; Connie Russell.

PLAYING FOR KEEPS
Soundtrack (1986) ....*Atlantic (S) 81678-1*   86   8-10
  Composer: Various. Cast: Peter Frampton; Sister Sledge; Eugene Wilde; Chris Thompson; Pete
  Townshend; Joe Cruz; Arcadia; Julian Lennon; Phil Collins.

PLEASURE SEEKERS
Soundtrack (1964) ....*RCA Victor (M) LOC-1101*   65   45-50
Soundtrack (1964) ....*RCA Victor (S) LSO-1101*   65   60-65
  Composer: James Van Heusen; Lionel Newman; others. Conductor: Lionel Newman.
  Cast: Ann-Margret.

PLOW THAT BROKE THE PLAINS:
see RIVER

PLYMOUTH ADVENTURE:
see IVANHOE

POCKET FULL OF DREAMS
Studiotrack (1938) ....*Decca (M) DL-4252*   62   25-30
  Has selections from *Waikiki Wedding, Double or Nothing* and *Sing, You Sinners*. Issued as part of *Bing's
  Hollywood Series.*
  Conductor: John Scott Trotter. Cast: Bing Crosby.

POINT
TV Soundtrack (1971) . . . .*RCA Victor (S) LSPX-1003*   71   **$10-12**
Includes eight-page storybook.
TV Soundtrack (1971) . . . .*RCA Victor (S) LSP-4417*   71   **8-10**
Without booklet.
Composer: Harry Nilsson. **Conductor:** Harry Nilsson. **Cast:** Harry Nilsson; Micky Dolenz; Davy Jones.
Original London Cast (1977) . . . .*MCA (S) 2331*   77   **8-10**

POINT OF ORDER
Soundtrack (1964) . . . .*Columbia (S) KOL-6070*   64   **15-20**
Soundtrack (1964)` . . . .*Columbia (S) KOS-2470*   64   **20-25**
Documentary of the U.S. Army/Joseph McCarthy Senate Hearings.
Cast: Eric Sevareid (narration); Joseph McCarthy; Joseph L. Welch; Robert T. Stevens; James Jullana; Roy M. Cohn; Senators: Karl E. Mundt, John G. McClellan, Henry Jackson, and Stuart Symington. (Dialogue).

POLICE ACADEMY IV - CITIZENS ON PATROL
Soundtrack (1987) . . . .*Motown (S) 6235ML*   87   **8-10**
Composer: Various. **Cast:** Darryl Duncan; S.; Stacy Lattisaw; Brian Wilson; Michael Winslow and L.; Family Dream; Chico De Barge; Garry Glenn; Southern Pacific.

POLLYANNA
Soundtrack (1960) . . . .*Disneyland (M) ST-1906*   60   **20-25**
Soundtrack (1960) . . . .*Disneyland (M) DQ-1307*   67   **8-10**
May also be shown as *The Story of Pollyana*.
Composer: Paul J. Smith; others. **Cast:** Kevin Corcoran (narration, as Jimmy Bean); Hayley Mills; Karl Malden; Jane Wyman; Adolphe Menjou; Agnes Moorehead. (With dialogue.).

POLONAISE:
see EILEEN

POLTERGEIST
Soundtrack (1982) . . . .*MGM (S) 1-5408*   82   **8-10**
Composer: Jerry Goldsmith. **Conductor:** Jerry Goldsmith.

POLTERGEIST II
Soundtrack (1986) . . . .*Intrada (S) RVF-6002*   86   **15-20**
Composer: Jerry Goldsmith. **Conductor:** Jerry Goldsmith.

POMEGRANADA
Original Cast (1966) . . . .*Patsan (M) PS-1101*   66   **80-100**
Composer: Alvin Carmines; H.M. Koutoukas. **Cast:** Alvin Carmines (piano); Michael Elias; Burton Supree; Margaret Wright; David Vaughn; Julie Kurnitz; Meredith Monk; Sandy Padilla.

PONTIFICAL REQUIEM:
see JOHN F. KENNEDY

POPEYE
Soundtrack (1980) . . . .*Boardwalk (S) SW-36880*   80   **8-10**
Composer: Harry Nilsson. **Conductor:** Van Dyke Parks. **Cast:** Robin Williams; Shelley Duvall; Ray Walston; Paul L. Smith.

POPEYE THE SAILOR
Original Radio Cast . . . .*Golden Age (M) 5008*   **8-10**

POPI
Soundtrack (1969) . . . .*United Artists (S) UAS-5194*   69   **15-20**
Soundtrack (1969) . . . .*MCA (S) 25044*   Re   **8-10**
Composer: Dominic Frontiere. **Conductor:** Dominic Frontiere.

POPPY
  Soundtrack (1936) . . . .*Columbia (M) KC-33253*   75 $8-10
  Cast: W.C. Fields.

PORGY AND BESS
  Original Cast (1940) . . . .*Decca (EP) ED-808*   50   **15-20**
  Original Cast (1940) . . . .*Decca (M) DL-7006*   50   **40-50**
    10-inch LP.
  Original Cast (1940) . . . .*Decca (M) DL-8042*   52   **30-35**
  Original Cast (1940) . . . .*Decca (M) DL-9024*   55   **25-35**
    Cover pictures artist's rendering of "Catfish Row."
  Original Cast (1940) . . . .*Decca (M) DL-9024*   59   **20-25**
    Cover pictures four cast members.
  Original Cast (1940) . . . . *Decca (SE) DL7-9024*   59   **15-20**
  Original Cast (1940) . . . .*MCA (SE) 2035e*   73   **8-12**
  Original Cast (1940) . . . . *MCA (SE) 1631*   Re   **8-10**
    Composer: George Gershwin; Ira Gershwin; DuBois Heyward. **Conductor:** Alexander Smallens.
    Cast: Todd Duncan; Anne Brown; Eva Jessye Choir; Edward Matthews; Georgette Harvey;
    Helen Dowdy; Harriett Jackson; William Woolfolk; Avon Long; Gladys Goode; Decca Sym-
    phony Orchestra.
  Original Revival Cast (1953) . . . . *RCA Victor (M) LM-2679*   63   **25-30**
  Original Revival Cast (1953) . . . . *RCA Victor (SE) LSC-2679*   63   **20-25**
    Composer: George Gershwin; Ira Gershwin; DuBois Heyward. **Conductor:** Skitch Henderson.
    Cast: Leontyne Price; William Warfield; John W. Bubbles; McHenry Boatwright.
  Original Revival Cast (1977) . . . . *RCA Victor (S) ARL3-2109*   77   **20-25**
    Triple LP set.
    Composer: George Gershwin; Ira Gershwin; DuBois Heyward. **Conductor:** John Demain.
    Cast: Donnie Ray Albert; Clamma Dale; Houston Grand Opera Company; Andrew Smith; Betty
    Lane; Carol Brice; Larry Marshall; Bernard Thacker; Glover Parhan; Melvin Wallace; Shirley
    Bains.
  Original Revival Cast (1977) . . . . *RCA Victor (S) ARL1-2109*   **8-10**
    Single LP reissue.
  Original Revival Cast (1953) . . . . *RCA Victor (EP) EPA-487*   53   **15-20**
  Studio Cast . . . . *London (S) OSA-13116*   **15-25**
    Triple LP set.
    Composer: George Gershwin; Ira Gershwin; DuBois Heyward. **Conductor:** Lorin Maazel.
    Cast: Willard White; Leona Mitchell; McHenry Boatwright; Florence Quivar; Lorin Maazel
    with the Cleveland Orchestra and Chorus.

PORGY AND BESS (continued)

Studio Cast . . . . *Columbia (M) OSL-162*   **$50-60**
Triple LP set.

Studio Cast . . . . *Columbia/Odyssey (SE) 32-36-001*   Re   **15-20**
Composer: George Gershwin; Ira Gershwin; DuBois Heyward. **Conductor:** Lehman Engel.
Cast: Lawrence Winters; Camilla Williams; Inez Matthews; Avon Long; Helen Dowdy; Eddie
Matthews; June McMechen; J. Rosamond Chorus.

Studio Cast (1962) . . . .*RCA Victor (M) LOP-1507*   62   **10-20**
Studio Cast (1962) . . . .*RCA Victor (S) LSO-1507*   62   **15-25**
Composer: George Gershwin; Ira Gershwin; DuBois Heyward. **Conductor:** Robert Corman;
Lennie Hayton. **Cast:** Lena Horne; Harry Belafonte.

Studio Cast . . . . *Bethlehem (M) EXLP-1*   **40-45**
Jazz renditions.

Studio Cast . . . . *Bethlehem (M) 3 BP-1*   Re   **8-12**
Composer: George Gershwin; Ira Gershwin. DuBois Heyward. **Cast:** Francis Faye; Mel Torme.

Studio Cast . . . . *RCA Victor (S) CPL2-1831*   76   **12-18**
Double LP set.
Composer: George Gershwin; Ira Gershwin; DuBois Heyward. **Conductor:** Frank DeVol.
Cast: Ray Charles; Cleo Laine.

Studio Cast . . . .*Verve (S) VE-2-2507*   **8-12**
Composer: George Gershwin; Ira Gershwin; DuBois Heyward. **Conductor:** Russell Garcia.
Cast: Ella Fitzgerald; Louis Armstrong.

Studio Cast (1951) . . . .*RCA Victor (M) LM-1124*   51   **25-30**
Composer: George Gershwin; Ira Gershwin; DuBois Heyward. **Conductor:** Robert Russell
Bennett. **Cast:** Rise Stevens; Robert Merrill; Robert Shaw Chorale.

Studio Cast . . . . *AEI (S) 1107*   **8-12**
Also has music from *Cabin in the Sky*.
Composer: George Gershwin; Ira Gershwin; DuBois Heyward. **Cast:** Todd Duncan; Cy Walter
(piano); Mabel Mercer.

Studio Cast (1959) . . . . *Decca (M) DL-8854*   59   **15-20**
Composer: George Gershwin; Ira Gershwin; DuBois Heyward. **Conductor:** Jack Pleis; Buddy
Bregman; Morty Stevens. **Cast:** Sammy Davis Jr.; Carmen McRae; Bill Thompson Singers.

Studio Cast . . . .*Ultraphonic (M) LP-45*   **10-15**
Composer: George Gershwin; Ira Gershwin; DuBois Heyward. **Cast:** Todd Duncan; Lawrence
Tibbett; others.

Studio Cast (1959) . . . .*United Artists (M) UAL-4021*   59   **15-20**
Studio Cast (1959) . . . .*United Artists (S) UAS-5021*   **15-25**
Composer: George Gershwin; Ira Gershwin; DuBois Heyward. **Cast:** Diahann Carroll; Andre
Previn Trio.

Soundtrack (1959) . . . . *Columbia (M) OL-5410*   59   **10-20**
Soundtrack (1959) . . . . *Columbia (S) OS-2016*   59   **8-12**
Cast: Pearl Bailey; Robert McFerrin (singing voice of Porgy, played by Sidney Poitier); Adele
Addison (singing voice of Bess, played by Dorothy Dandridge); Cab Calloway (doing songs
sung in the film by Sammy Davis Jr.).

Studiotrack . . . .*Heliodor (S) HS-25052*   **10-15**
Conductor: Kenneth Alwyn. **Cast:** Lawrence Winters; Isabelle Lucas; Ray Ellington; Barbara
Elsy; Pauline Stevens.

Studiotrack (1959) . . . . Richmond (M) B-20059   59   **10-15**
Studiotrack (1959) . . . . Richmond (S) S-30059   59   **10-15**
Above two also have music from *Show Boat*.
Conductor: Frank Chacksfield. **Cast:** Frank Chacksfield and His Orchestra.

Studiotrack (1954) . . . .*RCA Victor (EP) ERA-179*   54   **5-10**
Conductor: Arthur Fiedler. **Cast:** Arthur Feidler and the Boston Pops Orchestra.

Studiotrack (1953) . . . . *Decca (M) DL-4051*   53   **15-25**
Conductor: Johnny Green. **Cast:** Hollywood Bowl Pops Orchestra.

Studiotrack (1954) .... *MGM (M) E-3131* 54 **$10-20**
 Composer: George Gershwin; Ira Gershwin; DuBois Heyward. Cast: MGM Studio Orchestra.
 Also see CAROUSEL; GIGI; GIRL CRAZY; OKLAHOMA

PORKY'S REVENGE
 Soundtrack (1985) .... *Columbia (S) ST-39983* 85 **8-10**
 Composer: Various. Cast: Dave Edmunds; Jeff Beck; Fabulous Thunderbirds; George Harrison;
 Willie Nelson; Carl Perkins; Clarence Clemons; Crawling King Snakes.

PORTRAITS IN BRONZE
 Studio Cast (1961) .... *Liberty (M) LSM-13002* 61 **15-25**
 Studio Cast (1961) .... *Liberty (S) LSS-14002* 61 **20-30**
 Excerpts from Robert "Bumps" Blackwell's "Portraits in Bronze."
 Conductor: Robert Blackwell. Cast: Bessie Griffin; Gospel Pearls (Eddie Lee Kendrix; Joe
 Clayton; Marlene Gwynn; Tony Harris; Delores Addison).

POSTCARD FROM MOROCCO
 Original Cast (1975) .... *Desto (S) DC-7137-8* 75 **15-20**
 Double LP set.
 Composer: Dominick Argento; John Donahue. Conductor: Philip Brunelle. Cast: Barbara
 Brandt; Barry Busse; Edward Foreman; Janis Hardy; Yale Marshall; Sarita Roche; Vern Sutton
 (original cast of the Center Opera of Minnesota).

POUPEES DE PARIS, LES:
 see LES POUPEES DE PARIS

POWAQQATSI
 Soundtrack (1988) .... *Nonesuch (S) 79192-1* 88 **8-10**
 Film sequel to *Koyaanisqatsi*.
 Composer: Philip Glass. Cast: Philip Glass.

POWER
 Soundtrack (1984) .... *Cerberus (S) CST-0211* 84 **15-20**
 Composer: Chris Young. Conductor: Paul Francis Witt.

POWER IS YOU
 Studio Cast (1979) .... *Clarus (S) CL-1233* 79 **10-15**
 Composer: Rosemary Caggiano; Bernie Fass. Conductor: Marty Gold. Cast: Tony Randall;
 Lynn Redgrave; Bob Brown; Steve Clayton; Rose Marie Jun.

PRANKS
 Soundtrack (1982) .... *Citadel (S) CT-7031* 82 **8-10**
 Composer: Chris Young. Conductor: Chris Young.

PREMIER RADIO PERFORMANCES
 Studiotrack .... *Premier (M) PR-1201* **10-12**
 Has music from *A Double Life* and *Time Out of Mind* (Miklos Rozsa); *The Bandit of Sherwood Forest*
 (Hugo Friedhofer); and *Force of Evil* (David Raksin).
 Composer: Miklos Rozsa; Hugo Friedhofer; David Raksin. Conductor: Miklos Rozsa; Hugo
 Friedhofer; David Raksin.

PREMISE
 Original Cast (1960) .... *Vanguard (M) VRS-9092* 60 **35-40**
 Cast: Theodore J. Flicker; Joan Darling; George Segal; Thomas Aldredge. (With dialogue.)

PREPPIES
 Original Cast .... *Alchemy Records (S) AL-1001-D* 83 **15-20**
 Composer: Gary Portnoy; Judy Hart Angelo. Cast: Dennis Bailey; Kathleen Rowe McAllen;
 Bob Walton; Beth Fowler; Michael Ingram; David Sabin.

PRESSURE IS ON
 Soundtrack .... *Curb (S) 5E-535* **8-10**
 Cast: Hank Williams Jr.

PRETENDERS
Studiotrack (1970) . . . . *Philips (S) PHS- 600-327*   70   **$10-15**
  Full title: *Music to Read [Gwen Davis'] "The Pretenders" by.*
  Composer: Jackie Reinach. **Conductor:** Joe Reinach. **Cast:** Joe Reinach Complex.

PRETTY BABY
Soundtrack (1978) . . . . *ABC (S) AA-1076*   78   **10-12**
  Composer: Scott Joplin; Jelly Roll Morton; others. **Conductor:** Jerry Wexler.

PRETTY BELLE
Original Cast . . . .*Original Cast (S) OC-8238*   82   **25-35**
  Composer: Jule Styne; Bob Merrill. **Cast:** Angela Lansbury; Mark Dawson; Peter Lombard.

PRETTY BOY FLOYD
Soundtrack (1960) . . . . *Audio Fidelity (M) AFLP-1936*   60   **35-40**
Soundtrack (1960) . . . . *Audio Fidelity (M) AFSD-5936*   60   **45-50**
  Composer: William Sandord; Del Serino. **Conductor:** William Sandord.

PRETTY IN PINK
Soundtrack (1986) . . . . *Virgin (S) SP-17376*   86   **8-10**
  12-inch single. Has *If You Leave* on side two.
  Cast: Psychedelic Furs.
Soundtrack (1986) . . . . *A&M (S) SP-3293*   86   **8-10**
  Composer: Various. **Cast:** Psychedelic Furs; Jesse Johnson; Suzanne Vega; Orchestral
  Manoeuvres in the Dark; Smiths; Echo and Bunnymen; New Order; INXS; Belouis Some;
  Danny Hutton; Hitters.

PRETTY WOMAN
Soundtrack (1990) . . . .*EMI (S) E1-93492*   90   **8-10**
  Composer: Various. **Cast:** Roy Orbison; Natalie Cole; David Bowie; Go West; Jane Wiedlin;
  Roxette; Robert Palmer; Peter Cetera; Lauren Wood; Red Hot Chili Peppers; Christopher Otcasek.

PRIDE AND THE PASSION
Soundtrack (1957) . . . . *Capitol (M) W-873*   57   **75-85**
  Composer: George Antheil. **Conductor:** Ernest Gold.

PRIME OF MISS JEAN BRODIE
Soundtrack (1969) . . . . *20th Century-Fox (S) S-4207*   69   **12-15**
  Composer: Rod McKuen. **Conductor:** Arthur Greenslade. **Cast:** Rod McKuen; Mike Redway;
  Andrew Downey.
Soundtrack (1969) . . . .*Warner Bros. (S) WS-1787*   69   **15-20**
  Gatefold cover.
Soundtrack (1969) . . . .*Stanyan/Warner Bros. (S) WS-1853*   69   **15-20**
  Has a special overture that was played for Queen Elizabeth and her mother.
  Composer: Rod McKuen. **Conductor:** Arthur Greenslade. **Cast:** Rod McKuen.

PRINCE AND THE PAUPER
Original Cast (1963) .... *London (M) 28001* 63 $25-30
Original Cast (1963) .... *London (S) AMS-98001* 63 35-40
   Composer: George Fischoff; Verna Tomasson. **Conductor:** Burt Farber. **Cast:** Budd Mann;
   Joe Bousard; Joan Shepard; Robert McHaffey; John Davidson; Carol Blodgett; Flora Elkins.
Studio Cast (1963) .... *Disneyland (M) ST-1912* 63 20-25
Studio Cast (1963) .... *Disneyland (M) DQ-1311* 67 8-10
   Based on Mark Twain's *Prince and the Pauper*.
   Composer: Mark Twain.

PRINCE OF THE CITY
Soundtrack (1981) .... *Varese Sarabande (S) STV-81137* 81 8-10
   Composer: Paul Chihara. **Conductor:** Paul Chihara.

PRINCESS BRIDE
Soundtrack (1987) .... *Warner Bros. (S) 1-25610* 87 8-10
   Composer: Mark Knopfler. **Cast:** Mark Knopfler; Willy Deville.

PRISON
Studio Cast (1974) .... *Pacific Arts (S) PAC-101* 74 15-20
   Boxed set. Includes booklet.
   Composer: Michael Nesmith. **Cast:** Michael Nesmith; David Kempton; Red Rhodes; Michael
   Cohen; Chura; Don Whaley; Aanami Choir.

PRISONER OF ZENDA
Studiotrack .... *United Artists (S) UA-LA-374-G* 75 10-15
   Composer: Alfred Newman. **Conductor:** Leroy Holmes.

PRISONERS OF LOVE:
see PRODUCERS

PRIVATE HELL 36
Soundtrack (1954) .... *Coral (M) CRL-56122* 54 50-60
   10-inch LP.
Soundtrack (1954) .... *Coral (M) CRL-57283* 58 35-45
   Actual title: *Jazz Themes for Cops and Robbers*. Also has music from *The Thin Man, Perry Mason, Peter Gunn* and *M Squad*.
   Composer: Leith Stevens. **Conductor:** Leith Stevens.

PRIVATE LESSONS
Soundtrack (1981) .... *MCA (S) 5275* 81 8-10

PRIVATE LIVES:
see TONIGHT AT 8:30

PRIVATE PARTS
Soundtrack (1972) .... *Delos (S) DEL-25420* 79 8-12
   Includes music from 1971's *Von Richthofen and Brown*, also composed and conducted by Hugo Friedhofer.
   Composer: Hugo Friedhofer. **Conductor:** Hugo Friedhofer.

PRIVATE SCHOOL
Soundtrack (1983) .... *MCA (S) 36005* 83 8-10
   Composer: Various. **Cast:** Phoebe Cates; Men's Room; Bill Wray; Rick Springfield.

PRIVILEGE
Soundtrack (1967) .... *Uni (M) 3005* 67 15-20
Soundtrack (1967) .... *Uni (S) 73005* 67 20-25
   Composer: Mike Leander; Mark London; others. **Conductor:** Mike Leander. **Cast:** Paul Jones;
   George Bean and the Runner Beans.

PRIZE

Soundtrack (1963) .... *MGM (M) E-4192*	63	**$20-25**
Soundtrack (1963) .... *MGM (S) SE-4192*	63	**30-35**

Above two also have eight tracks from eight films, none of which are by Jerry Goldsmith.
Composer: Jerry Goldsmith. **Conductor:** Jerry Goldsmith.

PRODUCERS

Soundtrack (1968) .... *RCA Victor (M) LPM-4008*	68	**15-20**
Soundtrack (1968) .... *RCA Victor (S) LSP-4008*	68	**20-25**
Soundtrack (1968) .... *RCA Victor (S) ANL1-1132*	75	**8-10**

Also has music from *Springtime for Hitler* and *Prisoners of Love*.
Composer: John Morris; Mel Brooks; Norman Blackman. **Cast:** Gene Wilder; Zero Mostel; Dick Shawn; Kenneth Marc; Madlyn Cates; Lee Meredith; Christopher Hewett. (With dialogue.)

PROFESSIONALS

Soundtrack (1966) .... *Colgems (M) COMO-5001*	66	**50-55**
Soundtrack (1966) .... *Colgems (S) COSO-5001*	66	**65-70**

Composer: Maurice Jarre. **Conductor:** Maurice Jarre.

PROFILE IN MUSIC:
see KRAFT TELEVISION THEATRE

PROFILES IN COURAGE

Studio Cast .... *RCA Victor (M) VDM-103*	65	**8-12**

Composer: Nelson Riddle. **Cast:** Edward M. Kennedy (narration).

PROGRESS IN SOUND

Studio Cast .... *Sonic Arts Form (M) 99T645770 K8*	**20-30**

10-inch LP. Promotional issue from Motorola. Die-cut cover.
Cast: Norman Ross (narration); Jonathan Winters (dialogue).

PROMENADE

Original Cast (1969) .... *RCA Victor (S) LSO-1161*	69	**30-35**

Composer: Al Carmines; Marie Irene Fornes. **Conductor:** Susan Romann; Al Carmines.
Cast: Margot Albert; Shannon Bolin; Michael Davis; Glenn Kezer; Ty McConnell; Alice Playten; Gilbert Price; Sandra Schaeffer; Carrie Wilson; Florence Tarlow.

PROMISE AT DAWN

Soundtrack (1970) .... *Polydor (S) 24-5502*	70	**25-30**

Composer: Georges Delerue; others. **Conductor:** Georges Delerue. **Cast:** Melina Mercouri.

PROMISE HER ANYTHING

Soundtrack (1966) .... *Kapp (M) KL-1476*	66	**15-20**
Soundtrack (1966) .... *Kapp (S) KS-3476*	66	**20-25**

Composer: Lynn Murray; Burt Bacharach; Hal David; Ron Grainer. **Conductor:** John Keating.
Cast: Tom Jones; others.

PROMISED LAND

Soundtrack (1988) .... *Private Music (S) 2035-1*	88	**8-10**

Cast: James Newton Howard.

PSYCHO **363**

PROMISES, PROMISES
Original Cast (1968) . . . . *United Artists (S) UAS-9902* 68 $10-15
Original Cast (1968) . . . . *United Artists (M) SPOC-1* 68   40-50
  Cast interviews and songs. Promotional issue only.
Original Cast (1968) . . . . *EMI (S) LO-9902* Re   8-10
  Composer: Burt Bacharach; Hal David. **Conductor:** Harold Wheeler. **Cast:** Jerry Orbach; Jill
  O'Harra; Edward Winter; Donna McKechnie; A.Larry Haines; Marian Mercer; Paul Reed; Dick
  O'Neill; Norman Shelly; Vince O'Brien; Millie Slavin; Adrienne Angel.
Studio Cast . . . . *Fontana (S) SFL-13192*   20-25
  A musical based on the film *The Apartment*.
  Composer: Burt Bacharach; Hal David. **Conductor:** Keith Roberts. **Cast:** Aimi MacDonald;
  Ronnie Carroll.

PROPER TIME
Soundtrack (1960) . . . . *Contemporary (M) 3587* 60   15-20
Soundtrack (1960) . . . . *Contemporary (S) S-7587* 60   25-30
  Cast: Shelly Mann and His Men.

PROPHET
Original Cast (1974) . . . . *Atlantic (Q) QD-18120* 74   10-15
  Composer: Arif Mardin. **Conductor:** Arif Mardin. **Cast:** Richard Harris.

PROUD REBEL
Soundtrack (1958) . . . . *C.I.F. (M) 1001* 58   100-150
  Composer: Jerome Moross. **Conductor:** Jerome Moross.

PROUDLY THEY CAME
Studio Cast (1970) . . . . *Landmark (S) PR-LP-101* 70   15-20
  Double LP set.
  Composer: Various. **Cast:** Kate Smith; Bob Hope; Teresa Graves; Young Americans; Jack
  Benny; Centurymen; Dinah Shore; Glen Campbell; Dorothy Lamour; Red Skelton; Jeannie C.
  Riley; New Christy Minstrels; Pat Boone; Esther Phillips; Fred Waring; Les Brown and His
  Band; James Stewart (narration).

PROVIDENCE
Soundtrack (1977) . . . . *DRG (S) SL-9502* 80   8-10
  Composer: Miklos Rosza. **Conductor:** Miklos Rosza.

PROWLERS OF THE EVERGLADES:
see WALT DISNEY'S TRUE LIFE ADVENTURES

PRUDENCE AND THE PILL
Soundtrack (1968) . . . . *20th Century-Fox (S) S-4199* 68   15-20
  Composer: Bernard Ebbinghouse. **Conductor:** Bernard Ebbinghouse. **Cast:** Mike Sammes
  Singers.

PSYCH-OUT
Soundtrack (1968) . . . . *Sidewalk (S) ST-5913* 68   12-15
  Composer: Ron Stein; others. **Cast:** Strawberry Alarm Clock; Seeds; Storybook; Boenzee Cryque.

PSYCHO
Soundtrack (1960) . . . . *Unicorn (S) 75001* 79   10-15
  Remastered.
  Composer: Bernard Herrmann. **Conductor:** Bernard Herrmann. **Cast:** National Philharmonic
  Orchestra.
Soundtrack (1960) . . . . *Unicorn (S) RHS-336* 74   30-50

PSYCHO II
Soundtrack (1983) .... *MCA (S) 6119*   83   **$8-10**
   Composer: Jerry Goldsmith. **Conductor:** Jerry Goldsmith. **Cast:** Jerry Goldsmith and His
   Orchestra.

PSYCHO III
Soundtrack (1986) .... *MCA (S) 6174*   86   **8-10**

PUFNSTUF
Soundtrack (1970) .... *Capitol (S) SW-542*   70   **15-20**
   Composer: Charles Fox. **Conductor:** Charles Fox. **Cast:** "Mama" Cass Elliot; Martha Raye;
   Billie Hayes; Jack Wild.

PUMP BOYS AND DINETTES ON BROADWAY
Original Cast (1982) .... *Columbia (S) FM-37790*   82   **8-10**
   Composer: Jim Wann; others. **Cast:** Jim Wann; Cass Morgan; John Schimmel; Debra Monk;
   John Foley; Mark Hardwick.

PUMPING IRON 2 - THE WOMEN
Soundtrack (1985) .... *Island (S) 90273*   85   **8-10**
   Composer: Various. **Cast:** Art of Noise; Skipworth and Turner; Grace Jones; Will Powers;
   New York City Peech Boys; Black Uhuru; Roach; Fast Forward.

PURLIE
Original Cast (1970) .... *Ampex (S) A-40101*   70   **25-30**
Original Cast (1970) .... *Ampex (Q) A-40101-S*   70   **35-40**
   The Harder They Fall, heard on the stereo issue, is omitted on quad pressings.
   Composer: Gary Geld; Peter Udell. **Conductor:** Joyce Brown. **Cast:** Cleavon Little; Melba
   Moore; John Heffernan; Linda Hopkins; Sherman Hemsley; Novella Nelson; C. David Colson.

PURPLE PEOPLE EATER
Soundtrack (1988) .... *AJK (S) A227-1*   88   **8-10**
   Composer: Various. **Conductor:** Bob Summers; others. **Cast:** Little Richard; Jan and Dean;
   D.K.; Chubby Checker; Sha Na Na; Bobby Day; Mike Harris; Penny and Sondra; Longfellow;
   Happenings; Bob Summers Orchestra.

PURPLE RAIN
Soundtrack (1984) .... *Warner Bros. (S) 1-25110*   84   **8-10**
   Composer: Prince. **Cast:** Prince and the Revolution.

PURSUIT OF D.B. COOPER
Soundtrack (1981) .... *Polydor (S) PD-1-6344*   81   **8-10**
   Composer: James Horner. **Cast:** Waylon Jennings; Rita Coolidge; Jessi Coulter; Marshall Tucker
   Band.

PUTTIN' ON THE RITZ
Soundtrack (1930) .... *Meet-Patti Discs (M) PRW-1930*   **8-10**
   Also has music from *Whoopee*.
   Cast: Harry Richman. WHOOPEE: Eddie Cantor.

Q

Q THE WINGED SERPENT
Soundtrack (1983) .... *Cerberus (S) CST-0206*   83   **$10-15**
Composer: Robert O. Ragland. **Conductor:** Robert O. Ragland.

QB VII
TV Soundtrack (1974) .... *ABC (S) ABCD-822*   74   **15-25**
Composer: Jerry Goldsmith. **Conductor:** Jerry Goldsmith.

QUADROPHENIA
Soundtrack (1979) .... *Polydor (S) 2-6235*   80   **10-15**
Double LP set.
Composer: Peter Townshend; others. **Conductor:** John Entwhistle. **Cast:** The Who (Pete
Townsend; Keith Moon; Roger Daltrey; John Entwhistle).

QUANDO L'AMORE E'SENSUALITA
Soundtrack (1981) .... *Cerberus (S) CEMS-0113*   82   **8-10**
Composer: Ennio Morricone. **Conductor:** Ennio Morricone.

QUARTET
Soundtrack (1981) .... *Gramavision (S) GR 1020*   81   **8-10**
Composer: Richard Robbins. **Conductor:** Richard Robbins.

QUEST FOR FIRE
Soundtrack (1982) .... *RCA Victor (S) ABL1-4274*   82   **8-10**
Composer: Philippe Sarde. **Conductor:** Philippe Sarde.

QUICK AND THE DEAD - THE STORY OF THE ATOM BOMB
Original Radio Cast (1950) .... *RCA Victor (EP) WDM-1507*   50   **20-25**
Volume one. From an NBC public service broadcast.
Original Radio Cast (1950) .... *RCA Victor (M) LM-1129*   50   **40-60**
Volume one.
Original Radio Cast (1950) .... *RCA Victor (EP) WDM-1508*   50   **20-25**
Volume two.
Original Radio Cast (1950) .... *RCA Victor (M) LM-1130*   50   **40-60**
Volume two.
Composer: Fred Friendly (writer). **Cast:** Bob Hope; William L. Laurence; President Harry S.
Truman; Franklin D. Roosevelt; Winston Churchill; General Dwight D. Eisenhower; General
Leslie R. Groves; Admiral William S. Parsons; Captain Robert Lewis; Helen Hays; Paul Lukas;
Robert Trout.

QUICK BEFORE IT MELTS
Soundtrack (1964) .... *MGM (M) E-4285*   64   **12-18**
Soundtrack (1964) .... *MGM (S) SE-4285*   64   **15-20**
Above two also have eight David Rose selections which are not from this soundtrack.
Composer: David Rose. **Conductor:** David Rose.

QUICK DRAW MCGRAW
TV Soundtrack (1962) .... *Colpix (M) CP-203*   62   **10-15**
Cast: Daws Butler; Don Messick; Doug Young.

QUICKSILVER
Soundtrack (1986) .... *Atlantic (S) 81631*   86   **8-10**
Composer: Various. **Cast:** Roger Daltrey; Fiona; Peter Frampton; Ray Parker Jr.; Helen Terry;
Larry John McNally; Thomas Newman; Tony Banks.

QUIET CITY
Original Cast .... *Columbia (S) MS-7375*   **$8-12**
  Actual title: *Copland Conducts Copland*. Also has music from *Our Town* and other classical selections.
  Composer: Aaron Copland. **Conductor:** Aaron Copland.

QUIET DAYS IN CLICHY
Soundtrack (1970) .... *Vanguard (S) VSD-79303*   70   **10-12**
  Composer: Country Joe McDonald; Ben Webster; Andy Sundstrom. **Cast:** Country Joe
  McDonald; Ben Webster; Andy Sundstrom; Young Flowers; Papa Blue's Viking Jazz Band.

QUIET MAN
Soundtrack (1952) .... *RCA Victor (M) LPM-3089*   52   **50-65**
  10-inch LP.
  Conductor: Sydney Green. **Cast:** Merv Griffin.
Soundtrack (1952) .... *Decca (M) DL-5411*   52   **50-65**
  10-inch LP.
Soundtrack (1952) .... *Decca (M) DL-8566*   57   **60-70**
Soundtrack (1952) .... *Varese Sarabande (M) VC-81073*   77   **8-10**
  One side of above two have music from *Samson and Delilah*.
  Composer: Victor Young; others. **Conductor:** Victor Young. **Cast:** Bing Crosby; Victor Young
  and His Orchestra.

QUILLER MEMORANDUM
Soundtrack (1966) .... *Columbia (M) OL-6660*   66   **35-40**
Soundtrack (1966) .... *Columbia (S) OS-3060*   66   **55-60**
  Composer: John Barry; Tony Hatch; others. **Conductor:** John Barry. **Cast:** Matt Monro.

QUO VADIS
Soundtrack (1951) .... *MGM (EP) K-134*   51   **35-50**
  Seven disc boxed set.
Soundtrack (1951) .... *MGM (M) K-103*   57   **30-40**
  Four disc boxed set.
Soundtrack (1951) .... *MGM (M) E-103*   51   **75-85**
  10-inch LP.
Soundtrack (1951) .... *MGM (M) E-3524*   57   **40-50**
Soundtrack (1951) .... *MCA (SE) 39075*   Re   **8-10**
  Full title: *(Dramatic Highlights from) Quo Vadis*.
  Conductor: Miklos Rozsa. **Cast:** Walter Pidgeon (introduction); Robert Taylor; Deborah Kerr;
  Leo Genn; Peter Ustinov; Patricia Laffain; Felix Aylemr; Peter Miles; Finlay Currie.
  (With dialogue.)
Studiotrack (1953) .... *Capitol (EP) FAP-454*   53   **15-20**
Studiotrack (1953) .... *Capitol (EP) EBF-454*   53   **20-30**
  Double EP.
Soundtrack (1951) .... *Capitol (M) L-454*   53   **50-60**
  10-inch LP. Combines *Quo Vadis Suite* with *Spellbound Concerto*.
Studiotrack (1953) .... *Capitol (M) P-456*   53   **75-100**
  Includes the *Quo Vadis Suite*. Also has *Spellbound Concerto* and *The Red House*.
  Conductor: Erich Kloss. **Cast:** Orchestra of Nrmberg.
Studiotrack (1978) .... *London (S) SPC-21180*   78   **8-10**
  Standard cover.
Studiotrack (1978) .... *London (S) SPC-21180*   78   **20-25**
  Gatefold cover.
  Composer: Miklos Rozsa. **Conductor:** Miklos Rozsa. **Cast:** Royal Philharmonic Orchestra.

R

R.P.M.
Soundtrack (1970) . . . . *Bell (S) 1203*   70 $10-12
  Composer: Barry DeVorzon; Perry Botkin Jr; Melanie. Cast: Melanie; Chris Morgan.

R.S.V.P. THE COLE PORTERS
Original Cast (1974) . . . . *Respond (S) PMS-299*   74   50-65
  Composer: Cole Porter. Conductor: Mac Frampton. Cast: Mary Margaret McBride (prologue);
  Jack Jenkins; Sally Jenkins.

RACE FOR THE WIRE
Soundtrack . . . . *Anaconda Industrial (M) XB-491*   10-20
  From a wire industry film.
  Composer: M. Evans

RAD
Soundtrack (1986) . . . . *MCA (S) 6166*   86   8-10
  Composer: Various. Cast: John Farnham; Beat Farmers; 3-Speed; Hubert Kah; Real Life;
  Sparks; Jimmy Haddox.

RADIO DAYS
Soundtrack (1987) . . . . *Novus (S) 3917-1-N9*   87   8-10
  Full title: *Radio Days (Selections from the Soundtrack).*
  Composer: Various. Cast: Tommy Dorsey; Artie Shaw; Allan Jones; Sammy Kaye; Guy
  Lombardo; Duke Ellington; Xavier Cugat.

RAGA
Soundtrack (1971) . . . . *Apple (S) SWAO-3384*   71   15-20
  Composer: Ravi Shankar; Colin Walcott. Cast: Ravi Shankar.

RAGE TO LIVE
Soundtrack (1965) . . . . *United Artists (M) UAL-4130*   65   15-20
Soundtrack (1965) . . . . *United Artists (S) UAS-5130*   65   20-25
  Composer: Nelson Riddle; Arthur Ferrante; Louis Teicher. Conductor: Nelson Riddle.
  Cast: Ferrante and Teicher.

RAGGEDY ANN AND ANDY
Soundtrack (1977) . . . . *Columbia (S) S-34686*   77   8-12
  Composer: Joe Raposo. Conductor: Joe Raposo.

RAGTIME
Soundtrack (1981) . . . . *Electra (S) 5E-565*   81   8-10
  Composer: Randy Newman. Conductor: Randy Newman. Cast: Randy Newman; Jennifer
  Warnes.

RAGTIME YEARS
Original Cast (1978) . . . . *Vanguard (S) VSD-79391*   78   8-10
  Cast: Max Morath (piano).

RAIDERS OF THE LOST ARK
Soundtrack (1981) . . . . *Columbia (S) JS-37373*   81   8-10
Soundtrack (1981) . . . . *Polydor (S) 821-583*   84   8-10
  Composer: John Williams. Conductor: John Williams.

RAIDERS OF THE LOST ARK: THE MOVIE ON RECORD
Soundtrack (1981) ....*Columbia (S) JS-37696*   81 $10-12
   This edition includes dialogue.
  Composer: John Williams. **Conductor:** John Williams. **Cast:** Harrison Ford; Karen Allen; Paul
  Freeman; Ronald Lacey; John Rhys-Davies; Denholm Elliott. (With dialogue.)

RAILWAY CHILDREN
Soundtrack (1972) ....*Capitol (S) SW-871*   72   **25-30**
  Composer: Johnny Douglas; Vince Hill. **Conductor:** Johnny Douglas; Vince Hill.

RAIN MAN
Soundtrack (1988) ....*Capitol (S) C1-91866*   88   **8-10**
  Composer: Various. **Cast:** Delta Rhythm Boys; Etta James; Johnny Clegg and Savuka; Ian
  Gillan; Roger Glover; Bananarama; Hans Zimmer; Lou Christie; Belle Stars; Rob Wasserman;
  Aaron Neville.

RAINBOW BRIDGE
Soundtrack (1971) ....*Reprise (S) MS-2040*   71   **10-12**
  Cast: Jimi Hendrix.

RAINBOW 'ROUND MY SHOULDER
Soundtrack (1952) ....*Columbia (EP) B-1512*   52   **10-15**
  Cast: Frankie Laine.

RAINMAKER
Soundtrack (1956) ....*RCA Victor (EP) EPA-1434*   56   **25-50**
Soundtrack (1956) ....*RCA Victor (M) LPM-1434*   57   **125-150**
  Composer: Alex North. **Conductor:** Alex North.

RAINTREE COUNTY
Soundtrack (1957) ....*RCA Victor (M) LOC-1038*   58   **60-75**
Soundtrack (1957) ....*RCA Victor (S) LSO-1038*   58   **75-100**
Soundtrack (1957) ....*RCA Victor (M) LOC-6000*   57   **200-250**
Soundtrack (1957) ....*Entr' acte (S) ERS-6503-ST*   Re   **15-20**
  Above two are double LPs.
  Composer: Johnny Green. **Conductor:** Johnny Green.

RAISIN
Original Cast (1973) ....*Columbia (S) KS-32754*   73   **20-25**
  Composer: Judd Woldin; Robert Brittan. **Conductor:** Howard A. Roberts. **Cast:** Virginia
  Capers; Joe Morton; Ernestine Jackson; Robert Jackson; Deborah Allen; Helen Martin; Ralph
  Carter; Herb Downer; Marenda Perry.

RAMBO: FIRST BLOOD - PART II
Soundtrack (1985) . . . .*Jackal/Varese Sarabande (S) WOW-728*   85 $10-15
  Digital recording.
Soundtrack (1985) . . . . *Varese Sarabande (S) STV-81318*   85   **8-10**
  Composer: Jerry Goldsmith. **Conductor:** Jerry Goldsmith. **Cast:** Jerry Goldsmith and the
  National Philharmonic Orchestra; Frank Stallone.

RAMBO III
Soundtrack (1988) . . . .*Scotti Bros. (S) SZ-44319*   88   **8-10**
  Cast: Bill Medley; Jerry Goldsmith; Giorgio Moroder; Joe Pizullo.

RAMPAGE
Soundtrack (1988) . . . . *Virgin Movie Music (S) 90644-1*   88   **8-10**
  Composer: Ennio Morricone.

RANCHO DELUXE
Soundtrack (1975) . . . .*United Artists (S) UA-LA466-G*   75   **10-12**
  Composer: Jimmy Buffet. **Cast:** Jimmy Buffet.

RAPPIN'
Soundtrack (1985) . . . .*Atlantic (S) 81252-1*   85   **8-10**
  Composer: Various. **Cast:** Marion Van Peebles; Kadeem Hardison; Eriq La Salle; Tuff Inc.;
  Warren Mills.

RASHOMON
Original Cast (1959) . . . . *Carlton (M) LPX-5000*   59   **30-40**
Original Cast (1959) . . . . *Carlton (S) STLPX-500*   59   **50-65**
  Above two have incidental music from the Broadway play.
  Composer: Laurence Rosenthal. **Conductor:** Laurence Rosenthal.

RAT RACE
Soundtrack (1960) . . . .*Dot (M) DLP-3306*   60   **30-35**
Soundtrack (1960) . . . . *Dot (S) DLP-25306*   60   **60-70**
  Above two have jazz renditions of pop standards.
  Composer: Elmer Bernstein; others. **Cast:** Sam Butera and the Witnesses.

RATTLE AND HUM
Soundtrack (1988) . . . . *Island (S) 91003-1*   88   **8-10**
  Cast: U2; Jimi Hendrix.

RAW DEAL
Soundtrack (1986) . . . . *Varese Sarabande (S) STV-81286*   86   **10-12**

RAZOR'S EDGE
Soundtrack (1984) . . . . *Southern Cross (S) SCRS-1009*   84   **8-10**
  Conductor: Stanley Black. **Cast:** Stanley Black and His Orchestra.

RE-ANIMATOR
Soundtrack (1985) . . . . *Varese Sarabande (S) STV-81261*   85   **10-15**
  Composer: Richard Band. **Conductor:** Richard Band. **Cast:** Rome Philharmonic Orchestra.

REAL AMBASSADORS
Studio Cast (1963) . . . . *Columbia (M) OL-5850*   63   **15-20**
Studio Cast (1963) . . . . *Columbia (S) OS-2250*   63   **20-25**
  Composer: Dave Brubeck; Iola Brubeck. **Cast:** Louis Armstrong; Dave Brubeck; Dave Lambert;
  Jon Hendricks; Annie Ross; Carmen McRae.

REAL THING
Original Cast . . . . *Nonesuch (S) 78027-1*   84   **10-15**
  Double LP set.
  Cast: Glen Close; Jeremy Irons.

REALLY ROSIE
TV Soundtrack (1975) .... *Ode (S) SP-77027*   75 $10-12
TV Soundtrack (1975) .... *Ode (S) PE-34955*   80   8-10
   Composer: Carole King. **Conductor:** Carole King; Maurice Sendak. **Cast:** Carole King.

REBECCA:
see OBJECTIVE, BURMA!

REBEL WITHOUT A CAUSE:
see TRIBUTE TO JAMES DEAN

RED BALLOON
Soundtrack .... *Nonesuch (S) H-2001*   8-12
   Adapted from a French film classic by Albert Lamorisse.
   Composer: Al Barr. **Conductor:** Al Barr. **Cast:** Jean Vallin (story narrator).

RED DAWN
Soundtrack (1985) .... *Intrada (S) RVF-6001*   85   30-35
   Composer: Basil Poldouris. **Conductor:** Basil Poldouris.

RED GARTERS
Soundtrack (1954) .... *Columbia (EP) B-377*   54   15-20
   Double EP set.
Soundtrack (1954) .... *Columbia (M) CL-6282*   54   45-50
   10-inch LP.
   Composer: Jerry Livingston; Ray Evans. **Conductor:** Joseph J. Lilley; Percy Faith; Mitch Miller.
   Cast: Rosemary Clooney; Guy Mitchell; Joanne Gilbert.

RED HEAT
Soundtrack (1988) .... *Virgin Movie Music (S) 90891-1*   88   8-10

RED HOUSE
Soundtrack (1947) .... *Capitol (EP) FAP-2-453*   51   15-20
Soundtrack (1947) .... *Capitol (M) L-453*   51   50-60
   10-inch LP. One side has *Spellbound.*
   Composer: Miklos Rozsa. **Conductor:** Miklos Rozsa.
   Also see QUO VADIS

RED MANTLE
Soundtrack (1972) .... *RCA Victor (S) LSP-4815*   72   12-18
   Composer: Marc Fredericks. **Cast:** Judy Scott.

RED MILL
Soundtrack (1950) .... *Decca (EP) 9-165*   50   20-25
   Triple disc, boxed set.
Studio Cast (1950) .... *Decca (M) DL-8016*   50   40-50
   One side has music from *Up in Central Park.*
Studio Cast (1952) .... *RCA Victor (M) LK-1016*   52   30-40
   Composer: Victor Herbert; Henry Blossom. **Conductor:** Al Goodman. **Cast:** Earl Wightson;
   Mary Martha Briney; Donald Dame; Mullen Sisters; Guild Choristers.
Studio Cast (1952) .... *RCA Victor/Camden (M) CAL-408*   58   15-25
   Composer: Victor Herbert; Harry Blossom. **Cast:** Charles Fredericks; Marion Bell; Christina
   Lind.
   Also see BABES IN TOYLAND; NAUGHTY MARIETTA

RED PONY
Soundtrack (1949) .... *Columbia (M) ML-5983*   20-25
Soundtrack (1949) .... *Columbia (SE) MS-6583*   25-30
   Composer: Aaron Copeland. **Conductor:** Andre Previn.

RED SHOES
Soundtrack (1949) .... *Columbia (M) ML-2083* $20-30
   10-inch LP. Also has music from *Lambert's Horoscope*.
   Composer: Brian Easdale. **Conductor:** Muir Mathieson.

RED SKY AT MORNING
Soundtrack (1970) .... *Decca (S) 79180*   71   30-35
   Composer: Billy Goldberg; others. **Conductor:** Billy Goldberg; Loenard Slatkin; Vic Schoen; Benny Carter. **Cast:** Mills Brothers; Andrews Sisters; Louis Jordan; Miriam Gulager.

RED SONJA
Soundtrack (1985) .... *Varese Sarabande (S) STV-81248*   85   8-10
   Composer: Ennio Morricone. **Conductor:** Ennio Morricone.

RED TENT
Soundtrack (1971) .... *Paramount (S) PAS-6019*   71   15-25
Soundtrack (1971) .... *Paramount (S) 5019*   71   20-30
   With red cover. Promotional issue only.
   Composer: Ennio Morricone. **Conductor:** Ennio Morricone.

REDHEAD
Original Cast (1959) .... *RCA Victor (M) LOC-1048*   59   25-30
Original Cast (1959) .... *RCA Victor (S) LSO-1048*   59   40-45
Original Cast (1959) .... *RCA Victor (M) LOC-1104*   65   20-25
Original Cast (1959) .... *RCA Victor (S) LSO-1104*   65   30-35
   Composer: Albert Hague; Dorothy Fields. **Conductor:** Jay Blackton. **Cast:** Gwen Verdon; Richard Kiley; Leonard Stone; Doris Rich; Cynthia Latham; Joy Nichols; Bob Dixon; Pat Ferrier; William Le Massena; Ralph Sumpter; Buzz Miller.
Studiotrack .... *Design (S) DCF-1047*   10-15
   Composer: Albert Hague; Dorothy Fields. **Cast:** Rex Stewart Quintet.
Studiotrack (1959) .... *RCA Victor (M) LPM-2039*   59   10-15
   Actual title: *Meyer Davis Plays "Redhead" for Dancing*.
   Composer: Albert Hague; Dorothy Fields. **Conductor:** Meyer Davis. **Cast:** Meyer Davis.

REDS
Soundtrack (1981) .... *Columbia (S) BJS-37690*   81   8-10
   Includes pieces by P. Wingate; H.W. Petrie; E. Pottier; P. Degeyter & E.J. Mellinger.
   Composer: Stephen Sondheim; Dave Grusin; others. **Conductor:** Dave Grusin.
   Cast: Jean-Pierre Rampal; Claude Bolling; Moscow Radio Chorus; Heaton Vorse.

REGINA
Original Revival Cast (1959) .... *Columbia (M) O3L-260*   59   35-40
Original Revival Cast (1959) .... *Columbia (S) O3S-202*   59   50-60
   Above two are triple LP sets.
Original Revival Cast (1959) .... *Columbia/Odyssey (S) YS-35236*   Re   15-20
   Composer: Marc Blitzstein. **Conductor:** Samuel Krachmalnick. **Cast:** Brenda Lewis; Elisabeth Carron; Carol Brice; Joshua Hecht; Helen Strine; George Irving; Emil Renan.

REIVERS
Soundtrack (1969) .... *Columbia (S) OS-3510*   70   15-20
   Composer: John Williams. **Conductor:** John Williams.

RELAX WITH VICTOR HERBERT
Studiotrack (1954) .... *RCA Victor (EP) EPB-1023*   54   10-15
Studiotrack (1954) .... *RCA Victor (M) LPM-1023*   54   15-25
   Composer: Victor Herbert. **Conductor:** Al Goodman. **Cast:** Al Goodman and His Orchestra.

RELUCTANT DRAGON
TV Soundtrack .... *HBR (M) HBR-2029*   10-20
   Cast: Touche and Dum Dum (original TV stars).

REMEMBER MY NAME
Soundtrack (1978) ....*Columbia (S) JS-35553* 78 **$8-10**
  Composer: Alberta Hunter. Cast: Alberta Hunter.

REMEMBER THESE
Studio Cast (1963) .... *Ava (M) A-26* 63 **25-30**
Studio Cast (1963) .... *Ava (S) AS-26* 63 **40-50**
  Above two also have music from *Treasure Girl* and *Chee-Chee*.
  Composer: George Gershwin; Ira Gershwin. CHEE-CHEE: Richard Rodgers; Lorenz Hart.
  Conductor: Richard Lewine. Cast: Betty Comden.

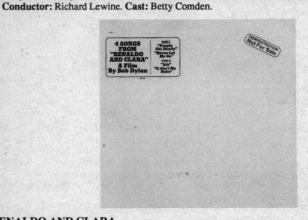

RENALDO AND CLARA
Soundtrack (1978) ....*Columbia (S) AO-422* 78 **25-35**
  Four tracks from the film. Promotional issue only.
  Composer: Bob Dylan. Cast: Bob Dylan.

RENT-A-COP
Soundtrack (1988) .... *Intrada (S) MAF-7002* 88 **8-10**

REPO MAN
Soundtrack (1984) .... *San Andreas/MCA (S) 39019* 84 **8-10**
  Composer: Various. Cast: Iggy Pop; Black Flag; Suicidal Tendencies; Plugz; Juicy Bananas;
  Circle Jerks; Burning Sensations; Fear.

REPORTER
TV Soundtrack (1963) .... *Columbia (M) CL-2269* 63 **25-30**
TV Soundtrack (1963) .... *Columbia (S) CS-9069* 63 **30-35**
  Composer: Kenyon Hopkins. Conductor: Kenyon Hopkins.

REPRISE REPERTORY THEATRE
Studio Cast (1964) .... *Reprise (S) 4FS-2019* 64 **100-150**
  Four LPs, each of which was also issued individually, in a special slip cover: *Finian's Rainbow* (FS-2015),
  Guys and Dolls (FS-2016), *Kiss Me Kate* (FS-2017), and *South Pacific* (FS-2018). Except for *Finian's
  Rainbow*, the gatefold edition is used in this set.
  Composer: See individual show listings. Conductor: Morris Stoloff; Ken Lane. Cast: See individual
  show listings.

REQUIEM FOR A CAVALIER:
see ADVENTURES OF ROBIN HOOD

RESCUERS
Soundtrack (1977) .... *Disneyland (M) S-3* $10-15
  Story, songs, and dialogue.
  Composer: Artie Butler. **Conductor:** Artie Butler. **Cast:** Shelby Flint (vocals); Bob Newhart; Eva Gabor; Joe Flynn; Geraldine Page. (With dialogue.)

RESTLESS ONES
Soundtrack (1965) .... *Grason (EP) BG-6515*   10-15
  Shown as a "Souvenier EP."
Soundtrack (1965) .... *Supreme (M) M-110*   65   15-20
Soundtrack (1965) .... *Supreme (S) MS-210*   65   25-30
  Composer: Ralph Carmichael. **Conductor:** Ralph Carmichael. **Cast:** Johnny Crawford.

RETURN OF A MAN CALLED HORSE
Soundtrack (1976) .... *United Artists (S) UA-LA692-G*   76   10-12
Soundtrack (1976) .... *Liberty (S) LT-692*   Re   8-10
  Composer: Laurence Rosenthal. **Conductor:** Laurence Rosenthal.

RETURN OF MARTIN GUERRE/JULIA
Soundtrack .... *DRG (S) SL-9514*   8-10

RETURN OF THE JEDI
Soundtrack (1983) .... *Buena Vista (S) 62103*   83   8-12
  Includes booklet.
  Composer: John Williams. **Conductor:** John Williams. **Cast:** London Symphony Orchestra. (With dialogue.)
  Also see STAR WARS - RETURN OF THE JEDI

RETURN OF THE LIVING DEAD
Soundtrack (1984) .... *Enigma (S) 72004-1*   85   8-10
  Composer: Various. **Cast:** Cramps; 45 Grave; TSOL; Flesheaters; Roky Erickson; Damned; Tall Boys; Jet Black Berries; SSQ.

RETURN OF THE LIVING DEAD, PART II
Soundtrack (1988) .... *Island (S) 90854-1*   88   8-10
  Composer: Various. **Cast:** Julian Cope; Anthrax; Mantronic; Leatherwolf; Lamont; Big O; J. Peter Robinson; Zodiac Mindwarp and the Love Reaction.

RETURN OF THE PINK PANTHER
Soundtrack (1975) .... *RCA Victor (S) ABL1-0968*   75   **$8-12**
Composer: Henry Mancini. Conductor: Henry Mancini. Cast: Henry Mancini and His Orchestra.

RETURN OF THE SEVEN
Soundtrack (1966) .... *United Artists (M) UAL-4146*   66   **10-20**
Soundtrack (1966) .... *United Artists (S) UAS-5146*   66   **15-25**
Previously issued as *The Magnificent Seven*.
Composer: Elmer Bernstein. Conductor: Elmer Bernstein.
Also see MAGNIFICENT SEVEN

RETURN TO OZ
Soundtrack (1985) .... *Sonic Atmospheres (S) 113*   85   **25-35**
Composer: David Shire. Conductor: David Shire. Cast: London Symphony Orchestra.

RETURN TO PARADISE
Soundtrack (1953) .... *Decca (EP) ED-542*   53   **20-35**
Soundtrack (1953) .... *Decca (M) DL-5489*   53   **125-150**
10-inch LP.
Composer: Dimitri Tiomkin; Charles Daufman. Conductor: Dimitri Tiomkin. Cast: Gary
Cooper (narration).

RETURN TO WATERLOO
Soundtrack (1985) .... *Arista (S) AL6-8386*   85   **8-10**
Composer: Ray Davies. Cast: Ray Davies; Mick Avery; Jim Rodford; Ian Gibbons.

REVENGE
Soundtrack (1986) .... *United Entertainment Pictures (S) UEP-6212*   86   **8-12**
Composer: Rod Slane; Jon Slazer. Cast: Michael Brewer.

REVENGE OF THE NERDS
Soundtrack (1984) .... *Scotti Bros. (S) BFZ-39599*   84   **8-12**
Composer: Various. Cast: Andrea and Hot Mink; Ya Ya; Rubinoos; others.

REVENGE OF THE PINK PANTHER
Soundtrack (1978) .... *United Artists (S) UA-LA913-H*   78   **8-10**
Composer: Henry Mancini; others. Conductor: Henry Mancini. Cast: Peter Sellers (as
Inspector Clouseau); Lon Satton.

REVOLUTION
Soundtrack (1968) .... *United Artists (S) UAS-5185*   68   **15-18**
Soundtrack (1968) .... *United Artists (S) UA-LA296-G*   74   **10-12**
Composer: Buffy St. Marie; others. Cast: Quicksilver Messenger Service; Steve Miller Band;
Mother Earth.

REVUERS 1938-1944:
see BONANZA BOUND

REX
Original Cast (1976) . . . . *RCA Victor (S) ABL1-1683* 76 $12-15
Composer: Richard Rodgers; Sheldon Harnick. **Conductor:** Jay Blackton. **Cast:** Nicol Williamson; Penny Fuller; Tom Aldredge; Barbara Andres; Glenn Close; Ed Evanko; Michael John; Merwin Goldsmith.

RHAPSODY IN BLUE
Studiotrack (1954) . . . .*RCA Victor (EP) EPA-565* 54 10-15
Composer: George Gershwin. **Conductor:** Hugo Winterhalter. **Cast:** Byron Janis (piano); Hugo Winterhalter and His Orchestra.

RHAPSODY OF STEEL
Soundtrack (1958) . . . . *US Steel (M) JB-502/3* 58 175-200
Side two has music by the Pittsburgh Symphony Orchestra.
Composer: Dimitri Tiomkin. **Conductor:** Dimitri Tiomkin. **Cast:** Gary Merrill (narration).

RHINESTONE
Soundtrack (1984) . . . . *RCA Victor (S) 1-5032* 84 8-10
Composer: Dolly Parton; others. **Cast:** Dolly Parton; Sylvester Stallone; Randy Parton; Kim Vassy.

RHYTHM ON THE RANGE
Studiotrack (1950) . . . .*Decca (M) DL-6010* 50 50-60
One side has music from *Pennies from Heaven.*
Composer: Johnny Mercer; others. **Conductor:** Jimmy Dorsey. **Cast:** Bing Crosby; Martha Raye.

RHYTHM ON THE RIVER:
see ONLY FOREVER

RICH MAN, POOR MAN
TV Soundtrack (1976) . . . .*MCA (S) 2095* 76 8-12
Composer: Alex North. **Conductor:** Alex North; Harold Mooney.

RICH, YOUNG AND PRETTY
Soundtrack (1951) . . . .*MGM (EP) K-86* 51 20-25
Four-disc, boxed set.
Soundtrack (1951) . . . .*MGM (EP) X-86* 51 12-15
Soundtrack (1951) . . . .*MGM (M) E-86* 51 40-50
10-inch LP.
Soundtrack (1951) . . . .*MGM (M) E-3236* 55 25-30
One side has music from *Singin' in the Rain.*
Composer: Nicholas Brodszky; others. **Conductor:** David Rose. **Cast:** Jane Powell; Vic Damone; Danielle Darrieux; Fernando Lamas.

RICHARD DIAMOND
TV Soundtrack (1959) . . . . *Mercury (M) MG-36162* 59 20-30
TV Soundtrack (1959) . . . .*Mercury (S) SR-80045* 59 40-50
Composer: Pete Rugulo. **Conductor:** Pete Rugulo.

RICHARD III
Soundtrack (1956) . . . . *RCA Victor (M) LM-6126* 56 35-40
Triple LP set.
Also see MUSIC FROM SHAKESPEAREAN FILMS

RIDE THE WILD SURF
Soundtrack (1964) . . . .*Liberty (M) LPR-3368* 64 20-25
Soundtrack (1964) . . . .*Liberty (S) LST-7368* 64 25-30
Composer: Roger Christian; Jan Berry; others. **Cast:** Jan and Dean; Fantastic Baggys.

RIDER ON THE RAIN
Soundtrack (1970) . . . .*Capitol (S) ST-584* 70 25-30
Composer: Francis Lai; Severine. **Conductor:** Francis Lai.

RIDES, RAPES, AND RESCUES (THEMES FROM GREAT SILENT FILMS)
Studiotrack (1961) .... *Liberty (M) LRP-3185*   61   **$10-15**
Studiotrack (1961) .... *Liberty (S) LST-7185*   61   **15-20**
  Composer: L. Jones; Carl Brandt. Cast: Hangnails Hennessey and Wingy Brubeck; Arthur
  Fiedler and the Boston Pops.

RIGHT STUFF:
see NORTH AND SOUTH

RIGHT TO HAPPINESS
Original Radio Cast .... *Golden Age (M) 5016*   78   **8-10**

RIKKY AND PETE
Soundtrack (1988) .... *DRG (S) SBL-12593*   88   **8-10**

RINK
Original Cast (1984) .... *Polydor (S) 422-823125-1*   84   **8-10**
  Composer: John Kander; Fred Ebb. Cast: Chita Rivera; Liza Minnelli.

RIO BRAVO
  Studiotrack/Soundtrack (1959) .... *Capitol (EP) PRO-1063*   59   **30-40**
    Has *Rio Bravo* and *My Rifle, My Pony and Me*, by Dean Martin, backed with *De Guello*, from the film
    soundtrack, by Nelson Riddle. Promotional issue only. Issued with a paper, picture sleeve.
  Composer: Dimitri Tiomkin; Paul Francis Webster. Conductor: Gus Levene; Nelson Riddle.
  Cast: Dean Martin; Nelson Riddle; Manny Klein (trumpet).
  Soundtrack (1959) .... *Warner Bros. (M) JB-2262*   59   **75-100**
    Actual title: *John Wayne Introduces Dean Martin and Ricky Nelson Singing "My Rifle, My Pony and Me"
    from the sound track of Warner Bros. "Rio Bravo."*
  Composer: Dimitri Tiomkin; Francis Webster. Cast: John Wayne (narration); Dean Martin;
  Ricky Nelson.

RIO GRANDE
  Soundtrack (1979) .... *Varese Sarabande (S) STV-81124*   79   **8-10**
  Composer: Victor Young. Conductor: Victor Young. Cast: Sons of the Pioneers; Ken Curtis;
  Ben Johnson; Harry Carey Jr.; Claude Jarman Jr.

RIO RITA
  Original London Cast (1927) ...... *Monmouth Evergreen (SE) MES-7058*   78   **12-15**
    Also has music from *Rose Marie* and *Show Boat*.
  Composer: Harry Tierney; Joseph McCarthy. Conductor: Jack Hilton. Cast: Edith Day;
  Geoffrey Gwyther.
  Also see CONNECTICUT YANKEE; GREAT WALTZ

RIOT ON SUNSET STRIP
Soundtrack (1967) .... *Tower (M) T-5065*   67   **$15-20**
Soundtrack (1967) ....*Tower (S) DT-5065*   67   **20-25**
  Composer: Various. **Cast:** Standells; Mugwumps; Chocolate Watch Band; Sidewalk Sounds;
  Debra Travis; Mom's Boys; Drew.

RIP VAN WINKLE:
see ICHABOD (THE LEGEND OF SLEEPY HOLLOW)

RISE AND FALL OF THE CITY OF MAHOGANY
Studio Cast (1970) .... *Columbia (M) K3L-243*   70   **15-20**
  Performed in the German language.
  Composer: Kurt Weill; Bertolt Brecht. **Conductor:** Wilhelm Bruckner-Ruggeberg. **Cast:** Lotte
  Lenya; Gisela Litz; Sigmund Roth; Richard Munch and the North German Radio Chorus
  (conducted by Max Thurn); Peter Markwort; Heinz Sauerbaum.

RISE AND FALL OF THE THIRD REICH
TV Soundtrack (1968) ....*MGM (M) 1E-12-ST*   68   **20-25**
TV Soundtrack (1968) .... *MGM (S) 1SE-12*   68   **25-30**
  Composer: Lalo Schifrin; Lili Chookasian; Alfred Perry. **Conductor:** Lawrence Foster.
  Cast: Laurence Harvey (narration); Gregg Smith Singers.

RIVER
Soundtrack (1937) .... *Desto (M) D-405*   **10-12**
Soundtrack (1937) ....*Desto (SE) DST-6405*   **10-12**
  Conductor: Walter Hendl. **Cast:** Vienna Symphony Orchestra.
Soundtrack (1937) .... *Vanguard (M) VRS-1071*   **10-12**
Soundtrack (1937) .... *Vanguard (SE) VSD-2095*   **10-12**
  One side of the above two has music from *The Plow That Broke The Plains*.
  Composer: Virgil Thomson. **Conductor:** Leopold Stokowski. **Cast:** Symphony of the Air.
Soundtrack (1937) .... *Angel (M) S-37300*   **10-20**
  Actual title: *Music from the Films*. Also includes *The Plow That Broke the Plains* and *Autumn*, a
  nine-minute concertino. Both *The River* and *The Plow That Broke the Plains* were U. S. Government
  documentary films.
  Composer: Virgil Thomson. **Conductor:** Neville Marriner. **Cast:** L.A. Chamber Orchestra.

RIVER
Soundtrack (1951) ....*Polymusic (M) PR-5003*   51   **50-75**

RIVER
Soundtrack (1984) ....*MCA (S) 6138*   84   **8-10**
  Composer: John Williams. **Conductor:** John Williams.

RIVER OF NO RETURN
Soundtrack (1954) .... *20th Century-Fox (M) FXG-5000*   59   **20-25**
Soundtrack (1954) .... *20th Century-Fox (SE) SXG-5000*   59   **25-30**
  Actual title: *Marilyn*. Also has music from *There's No Business Like Show Business* and *Gentlemen
  Prefer Blondes*.
  Composer: Lionel Newman; Ken Darby. **Conductor:** Lionel Newman. **Cast:** Marilyn Monroe.

RIVER RAT
Soundtrack (1984) .... *RCA Victor (S) CBL1-5310*   84   **8-10**
  Composer: Mike Post. **Conductor:** Mike Post. **Cast:** Alabama; Earl Thomas Conley; Deborah
  Allen; Bill Medley; Autograph; Joey Scarbury.

RIVER'S EDGE
Soundtrack (1986) .... *Enigma (S) SJ-73242*   87   **8-10**
  Composer: Various. **Cast:** Slayer; Agent Orange; Wipers; Burning Spear; Hallows Eve; Fates
  Warning.

RIVERWIND
Original Cast (1962) ....*London (M) AM-48001*   62 $55-65
Original Cast (1962) .... *London (S) AMS-78001*   62   **80-100**
  Composer: John Jennings. Conductor: Abba Bogin. Cast: Elizabeth Parrish; Helen Blount;
  Dawn Nickerson; Brooks Morton; Lovelady Powell; Martin J. Cassidy.

ROAD BEGINS
Studiotrack (1940) ....*Decca (M) DL-4254*   62   **25-30**
  Has music from *The Road to Singapore*, *The Star Maker* and *If I Had My Way*. Issued as part of *Bing's*
  Hollywood Series.
  Composer: James V. Monaco; Victor Schertzinger; John Burke. Conductor: John Scott Trotter.
  Cast: Bing Crosby; Foursome; John Scott Trotter's Frying Pan Five.

ROAD HOUSE
Soundtrack (1989) .... *Arista (S) AL9-8576*   89   **8-10**
  Composer: Various. Cast: Jeff Healey Band.

ROAD TO BALI
Studiotrack (1952) .... *Decca (M) DL-5444*   52   **55-65**
  10-inch LP.
  Composer: James Van Heusen; John Burke. Conductor: Sonny Burke; Joseph J. Lilley; Axel
  Stordahl. Cast: Bing Crosby; Bob Hope; Peggy Lee; Rhythmaires; Mellowmen.
  Also see ZING A LITTLE ZONG

ROAD TO HONG KONG
Soundtrack (1962) ....*Liberty (M) LOM-16002*   62   **20-25**
Soundtrack (1962) .... *Liberty (S) LOS-17002*   62   **30-35**
  Composer: Janes Van Heusen; Robert Farnon; Sammy Cahn. Conductor: Robert Farnon.
  Cast: Bing Crosby; Bob Hope; Dorothy Lamour; Joan Collins.

ROAD TO MOROCCO:
see SWINGING ON A STAR

ROAD TO RIO:
see BUT BEAUTIFUL

ROAD TO SINGAPORE
Studiotrack (1940) ....*Decca (M) DL-6015*   50   **50-60**
  Conductor: John Scott Trotter. Cast: Bing Crosby.
  Also see ROAD BEGINS

ROAD TO UTOPIA:
see ACCENTUATE THE POSITIVE

ROAD TO ZANZIBAR:
see ONLY FOREVER

ROAD WARRIOR
Soundtrack (1982) .... *Varese Sarabande (S) STV-81155*   82   **8-10**
  Composer: Brian May. Conductor: Brian May.

ROADIE
Soundtrack (1980) .... *Warner Bros. (S) 2HS-3441*   80   **10-12**
  Double LP set.
  Composer: Various. Cast: Cheap Trick; Pat Benatar; Teddy Pendergrass; Jay Ferguson;
  Blondie; Styx.

ROAR OF THE GREASEPAINT, THE SMELL OF THE CROWD

Original Cast (1965) .... *RCA Victor (M) LOC-1109* 65 $12-15
Original Cast (1965) .... *RCA Victor (S) LSO-1109* 65   15-20
  Composer: Anthony Newley; Leslie Bricusse. **Conductor:** Herbert Grossman. **Cast:** Anthony
  Newley; Cyril Ritchard; Sally Smith.
Studiotrack (1965) .... *RCA Victor (M) LPM-3347* 65   10-15
Studiotrack (1965) .... *.RCA Victor (S) LSP-3347* 65   15-20
  Above two are subtitled "Who Can I Turn To?"
  Composer: Anthony Newley; Leslie Bricusse. **Conductor:** Peter Knight. **Cast:** Anthony Newley.

ROARING '20s

TV Soundtrack (1960) .... *Warner Bros. (M) W-1394* 60   20-25
TV Soundtrack (1960) .... *Warner Bros. (S) WS-1394* 60   35-40
  Conductor: Alexander "Sandy" Courage. **Cast:** Dorothy Provine.
Studiotrack (1960) .... *Forum (M) F-16002* 60   15-20
Studiotrack (1960) .... *Forum (S) SF-16002* 60   25-30
  Cast: Bonnie Alden.

ROBBER BRIDEGROOM

Original Cast (1976) .... *Columbia Special Products (S) P-14589* 78   8-10
  Composer: Robert Waldman; Alfred Uhry. **Conductor:** Robert Waldman. **Cast:** Barry Bostwick;
  Rhonda Coullet; Barbara Lang; Larry Moss; Carolyn McCurry.
Studio Cast (1976) .... *Take Home Tunes (S) THT-761* 76   12-15
  Seven-inch disc.
  Composer: Robert Waldman; Alfred Uhry. **Cast:** Virginia Vestoff; Jerry Orbach.

ROBBERY

Soundtrack (1967) .... *London (M) M-76008* 67   25-30
Soundtrack (1967) .... *London (S) MS-82008* 67   30-40
  Composer: John Keating. **Conductor:** John Keating. **Cast:** Jackie Lee; John Keating and
  His Orchestra.

ROBE

Soundtrack (1953) .... *Decca (EP) ED-901* 53   12-15
Soundtrack (1953) .... *Decca (M) DL-9012* 53   25-30
Soundtrack (1953) .... *Decca (SE) DL7-9012* 59   15-20
Soundtrack (1953) .... *MCA (SE) 2052e* Re   10-12
Soundtrack (1953) .... *MCA (SE) 1529* Re   8-10
  Composer: Alfred Newman. **Conductor:** Alfred Newman. **Cast:** Hollywood Symphony
  Orchestra; Carole Richards.

ROBERT AND ELIZABETH

London Cast .... *Stet (S) SD-15021*   8-10
  Composer: Ron Grainer.

ROBERTA

Studio Cast (1933) .... *Columbia (EP) B-311* 53   12-15
Studio Cast (1933) .... *Columbia (M) CL-6220* 52   30-40
  10-inch LP.
Studio Cast (1933) .... *Columbia (M) ML-4765* 53   25-30
Studio Cast (1933) .... *Columbia (M) CL-841* 56   20-30
Studio Cast (1933) .... *Columbia (M) OL-7030* Re   10-15
Studio Cast (1933) .... *Columbia (SE) OS-2530e*   10-15
Studio Cast (1933) .... *Columbia Special Products (SE) COS-2530e* Re   8-10
  Many of the preceding Columbia releases also contain music from other film scores.
  Composer: Jerome Kern; Oscar Hammerstein II; Otto Harbach. **Conductor:** Lehman Engel.
  Cast: Joan Roberts; Jack Cassidy; Kaye Ballard; Portia Nelson; Stephen Douglass; Frank Rogier.

ROBERTA (continued)

Studio Cast (1949) . . . .*Decca (M) DLP-8007*   49   **$40-50**
  Composer: Jerome Kern; Oscar Hammerstein II; Otto Harbach. **Conductor:** Harry Sosnik; Jeff
  Alexander. **Cast:** Alfred Drake; Kitty Carlisle; Paula Lawrence; Kathryn Meisle.
Studio Cast (1952) . . . . *Capitol (EP) FBF-334*   52   **10-15**
Studio Cast (1952) . . . .*Capitol (M) L-334*   52   **35-40**
  10-inch LP.
  Composer: Jerome Kern; Oscar Hammerstein II; Otto Harbach. **Conductor:** George Greeley.
  Cast: Gordon MacRae; Lucille Norman; Anne Triola.
Studio Track (1952) . . . .*RCA Victor (EP) EKB-1007*   52   **10-15**
Studio Cast (1952) . . . .*RCA Victor (M) LK-1007*   52   **40-45**
Studio Cast (1952) . . . . *RCA Victor/Camden (M) CAL-464*   58   **25-30**
  Composer: Jerome Kern; Oscar Hammerstein II; Otto Harbach. **Conductor:** Al Goodman.
  Cast: Ray Charles; Eve Young; Jimmy Carroll; Marion Bell; Guild Choristers.
London Studio Cast . . . . . . : . . . .*World (M) T-121*   **20-25**
  Composer: Jerome Kern; Oscar Hammerstein II; Otto Harbach. **Cast:** Marion Grimaldi; Andy
  Cole; Maggie Fitzgibbon.
  Also see DESERT SONG; MISTER IMPERIUM

ROBIN AND MARIAN

Soundtrack (1976) . . . . *Sherwood (S) PRO-4345*   76   **75-100**
Soundtrack (1976) . . . . *Sherwood (S) SH-1500*   80   **30-40**
  Composer: John Barry. **Conductor:** John Barry.

ROBIN AND THE SEVEN HOODS

Soundtrack (1964) . . . . *Reprise (M) R-2021*   64   **25-35**
Soundtrack (1964) . . . . *Reprise (S) FS-2021*   64   **40-45**
  Composer: Sammy Cahn; James Van Heusen; Nelson Riddle. **Conductor:** Nelson Riddle.
  Cast: Frank Sinatra; Dean Martin; Bing Crosby; Sammy Davis Jr.; Peter Falk; Ladies of the
  Ensemble.

ROBIN HOOD

Soundtrack (1964) . . . .*Disneyland (M) DQ-1249*   64   **10-15**
  Composer: Various. **Cast:** Dal McKennon (narration); Peter Finch; Richard Todd; Elton Hayes;
  James Hayter; Robertson Justice. (With dialogue.)
Soundtrack (1973) . . . . *Disneyland (S) DQ-3810*   73   **8-10**
  From an animated cartoon.
  Composer: Roger Miller; Floyd Huddleston; George Bruns; Johnny Mercer. **Cast:** Roger Miller;
  Peter Ustinov; Phil Harris; Brian Bedford; Pat Buttram; Andy Devine; Terry Thomas; George
  Lindsay. (With dialogue.)

ROBOCOP

Soundtrack (1987) . . . . *Varese Sarabande (S) STV-81330*   87   **20-25**
  Composer: Basil Poledouris. **Conductor:** Howard Blake; Tony Britton. **Cast:** Sinfonia of
  London Orchestra.

ROCCO AND HIS BROTHERS

Soundtrack (1960) . . . . *RCA Victor (M) FOC-2*   61   **35-40**
Soundtrack (1960) . . . . *RCA Victor (S) FSO-2*   61   **50-60**
  Composer: Nino Rota. **Conductor:** Nino Rota.

ROCK ALL NIGHT

Soundtrack (1957) . . . .*Mercury (M) MG-20293*   57   **50-60**
  Composer: Various. **Cast:** Platters; Blockbusters; Eddie Beal Combo; Nora Hayes.

ROCK BABY, ROCK IT

Soundtrack (1957) . . . . *Rhino (M) RNSP-309*   **8-10**
  Composer: Various. **Cast:** Johnny Carroll and the Hot Rocks; Cell Block Seven; Don Coats and
  Bon-Aires; Five Stars; Preacher Smith and Deacons; Rosco Gordon and the Red Tops; Belew
  Twins.

ROCK JUSTICE
Original Cast (1980) . . . . *EMI America (S) SWAK-1703*   80 $8-10

ROCK 'N' ROLL HIGH SCHOOL
Soundtrack (1979) . . . . *Sire (S) SRK-6070*   79   8-10
  Composer: Various. **Cast:** Ramones; Chuck Berry; Alice Cooper; Todd Rundgren; Paley
  Brothers; Nick Lowe; Eddie and the Hot Rods; Brownsville Station; Devo; R.J. Soles; Brian Eno.

ROCK PRETTY BABY
Soundtrack (1956) . . . . *Decca (M) DL-8429*   56   75-100
  Composer: Various. **Conductor:** Joseph Gershenson. **Cast:** Jimmy Daley; Ding-A-Lings: Rod
  McKuen; Alan Copeland; Hal Dickinson.

ROCK, ROCK, ROCK
Soundtrack (1958) . . . . *Chess (M) No Number Used*   150-250
  White label, promotional issue only.
Soundtrack (1958) . . . . *Chess (M) LP-1425*   58   75-100
Soundtrack (1958) . . . . *Chess (M) 9254*   Re   8-10
  Above three have studio recordings that are heard in the film.
  Composer: Various. **Cast:** Chuck Berry; Flamingos; Moonglows.

ROCKABYE HAMLET
Studio Cast (1976) . . . . *Rising (S) RILP-103*   76   70-80
  Pre-Broadway, demonstration record.
  Composer: Cliff Jones. **Conductor:** Gordon Lowry Harrell. **Cast:** Cal Dodd; Rory Dodd; Cliff
  Jones; Lisa Hartt; Irish Rovers. Lisa Hartt and The Irish Rovers were not in the actual Broadway
  show.

ROCKERS
Soundtrack (1979) . . . . *Mango (S) 9587*   80   8-10
  Composer: Various. **Cast:** Inner Circle; Maytones; Junior Murvin; Heptones; Peter Tosh; Jacob
  Miller; Junior Byles; Bunny Wailer; Gregory Isaacs; Rockers All-Stars; Kiddus I; Burning Spear;
  Third World; Justin Hines and the Dominoes.

ROCKETSHIP X-M
Soundtrack (1950) . . . . *Starlog (M) SR-1000*   78   8-12
  Composer: Ferde Grofe Jr. **Conductor:** Albert Glasser.

ROCKY
Soundtrack (1976) . . . . *United Artists (S) UA-LA693-G*   76   8-10
  Composer: Bill Conti; others. **Conductor:** Bill Conti. **Cast:** Valentine; DeEtta Little; Nelson
  Pigford.

ROCKY II
Soundtrack (1979) . . . . *United Artists (S) UA-LA972-I*   79   8-10
  Composer: Bill Conti; others. **Conductor:** Bill Conti. **Cast:** DeEtta Little; Nelson Pigford.

ROCKY III
Soundtrack (1982) .... *Liberty (S) LO-51130*   82   **$8-10**
  Composer: Bill Conti. **Conductor:** Bill Conti. **Cast:** Survivor; Frank Stallone.

ROCKY IV
Soundtrack (1985) .... *Scotti Bros. (S) SZ-40203*   85   **8-10**
  Composer: Vince diCola; others**Cast:** Survivor; John Cafferty; Kenny Loggins; Gladys Knight;
  James Brown; Robert Tepper; Go West; Touch.

ROCKY HORROR PICTURE SHOW
Soundtrack (1975) .... *Ode (S) 9009*   78   **12-18**
Soundtrack (1975) .... *Ode (S) 78332*   78   **15-20**
  Ode label may be shown as "Ode Sound and Visions."
Soundtrack (1975) .... *Ode (S) 21653*   78   **10-12**
Soundtrack (1975) .... *Ode (S) OPD-91653*   78   **15-25**
  Picture disc.
  Composer: Richard O'Brien. **Conductor:** Richard Hartley. **Cast:** Tim Curry; Susan Sarandon;
  Barry Bostwick; Richard O'Brien; Meat Loaf.
Soundtrack (1975) .... *Rhino (S) R11H-70712*   Re   **8-10**

ROCKY HORROR SHOW
Original Cast (1975) .... *Ode (S) SP-77026*   75   **10-12**
Original Cast (1975) .... *Rhino (S) R11H-70090*   Re   **8-10**
  Composer: Richard O'Brien. **Conductor:** D'Vaughn Pershing. **Cast:** Tim Curry; Jamie
  Donnelly; Boni Enten.
Original Australian Cast (1975) .... *Elephant (S) ELA-7000*   **10-15**

RODGERS AND HART REVISITED
Studiotrack .... *Spruce (M) S-101*   **10-12**
  Composer: Richard Rodgers; Lorenz Hart. **Cast:** Dorothy Loudon; Danny Meehan; Charlotte
  Rae; Cy Young.
Studio Cast .... *Painted Smiles (S) PS-1341*   **10-12**
  Volume one.
  Composer: Richard Rodgers; Lorenz Hart. **Conductor:** Norman Paris. **Cast:** Dorothy Loudon;
  Danny Meehan; Cy Young; Charlotte Rae.
Studio Cast .... *Painted Smiles (S) PS-1343*   **10-12**
  Volume two.
  Composer: Richard Rodgers; Lorenz Hart. **Conductor:** Norman Paris. **Cast:** Blossom Dearie;
  Gloria DeHaven; Dorothy Loudon; B.B. Osterwald; Charles Rydell; Bobby Short
Studio Cast .... *Painted Smiles (S) PS-1366*   **10-12**
  Volume three.
  Composer: Richard Rodgers; Lorenz Hart. **Conductor:** Dennis Deal. **Cast:** Nancy Andrews;
  Blossom Dearie; Arthur Siegel; Johnny Desmond; Estelle Parsons; Anthony Perkins; Lynn
  Redgrave.
Studio Cast .... *Painted Smiles (S) PS-1367*   **10-12**
  Volume 4.
  Composer: Richard Rodgers; Lorenz Hart. **Conductor:** Dennis Deal. **Cast:** Nancy Andrews;
  Blossom Dearie; Johnny Desmond; Anthony Perkins; Lynn Redgrave; Elaine Stritch.

ROGUES
TV Soundtrack (1964) .... *RCA Victor (M) LPM-2976*   64   **20-30**
TV Soundtrack (1964) .... *RCA Victor (S) LSP-2976*   64   **30-40**
  Composer: Nelson Riddle. **Conductor:** Nelson Riddle.

ROLLER BALL
Soundtrack (1975) .... *United Artists (S) UA-LA470-G*   75   **$8-10**
Has music of Shostakovich, Albinoni/Giazotto, J.S. Bach, and Tchaikovsky.
Composer: Andre Previn. **Conductor:** Andre Previn. **Cast:** London Symphony Orchestra; Simon Preston (organ); John Brown (violin).

ROLLER BOOGIE
Soundtrack (1979) .... *Casablanca (S) NBLP-2-71*   80   **10-12**
Double LP set.
Composer: Various. **Conductor:** Bob Esty. **Cast:** Earth, Wind and Fire; Cher; Ron Green; Johnny Coolrock; Mavis Vegas Davis; Bob Esty and Cheeks; Michelle Aller; Emotions.

ROLLERCOASTER
Soundtrack (1977) .... *MCA (S) 2284*   77   **8-10**
Composer: Lalo Schifrin. **Conductor:** Lalo Schifrin.

ROMANCE OF A HORSETHIEF
Soundtrack (1971) .... *Allied Artists (S) AAS-110-1*   71   **40-50**
Promotional issue only.
Composer: Mort Shuman. **Conductor:** Mort Shuman. **Cast:** Yul Brynner; Lainie Kazan.

ROMANCE/ROMANCE
Original Broadway Cast (1988) .... *MCA (S) 6252*   88   **20-25**
Composer: Keith Herrmann; Barry Harman. **Conductor:** Kathy Sommer. **Cast:** Scott Bakula; Alison Fraser; Deborah Graham; Robert Hoshour.

ROME ADVENTURE
Soundtrack (1962) .... *Warner Bros. (M) W-1458*   62   **12-15**
Soundtrack (1962) .... *Warner Bros. (S) WS-1458*   62   **15-20**
One side has "Other Neapolitan Favorites," performed by the Cafe Milano Orchestra.
Composer: Max Steiner; others. **Conductor:** Max Steiner. **Cast:** Emilio Pericoli; Cafe Milano Orchestra.

ROMEO AND JULIET
Soundtrack (1954) .... *Epic (M) LC-3126*   54   **40-50**
Soundtrack (1954) .... *Epic (M) FLM-13104*   66   **30-35**
Soundtrack (1954) .... *Epic (SE) FLS-15104*   66   **30-35**
Composer: Roman Vlad. **Conductor:** Lambert Williamson. **Cast:** Sir John Gielgud (prologue); Laurence Harvey; Flora Robson; Sebastian Cabot; Susan Shentall. (With dialogue.)
Soundtrack (1968) .... *Capitol (S) ST-2993*   68   **10-12**
Instrumentals.
Soundtrack (1968) .... *Capitol (S) SWDR-289*   69   **60-65**
Four LP set. Includes music, dialogue, special effects, etc.
Composer: Nino Rota. **Cast:** Leonard Whiting; Olivia Hussey; Michael York; Milo O'Shea; John McEnry; Pat Heywood; Natasha Parry; Robert Stephens. (With dialogue.)
Soundtrack (1968) .... *Capitol (S) ST-400*   69   **10-12**
Has excerpts of Capitol SWDR-289.
Composer: Nino Rota. **Conductor:** Nino Rota. **Cast:** Leonard Whiting; Olivia Hussey; Michael York; Milo O'Shea; John McEnry; Pat Heywood; Natasha Parry; Robert Stephens.
Studiotrack (1950) .... *RCA Victor (M) LM-1019*   50   **25-50**
10-inch LP.
Composer: Peter Tchaikovsky. **Cast:** Arturo Tuscanini.

RONALD REAGAN RECOMMENDS
Studiotrack .... *Raleigh (M) No Number Used*   58   **20-40**
As TV spokesmen for General Electric, Ronald Reagan presents eight Oscar-winning tracks.

ROOFTOPS
Soundtrack (1989) .... *Capitol (S) C1-91736*　89　　**$8-10**

ROOM WITH A VIEW
Soundtrack (1985) .... *DRG (S) 12588*　86　　**8-10**
　Cast: Richard Robbins; Kiri Te Kanawa.

ROOTS
TV Soundtrack (1978) .... *Warner Bros. (S) 3WS-3048*　78　　**15-20**
　Triple LP set.
TV Soundtrack (1977) .... *A&M (S) SP-4626*　76　　**8-10**
　Composer: Quincy Jones; Gerald Fried. **Conductor:** Quincy Jones; Gerald Fried. **Cast:** Quincy
　Jones; Letta Mbulu.

ROOTS OF HEAVEN
Soundtrack (1958) .... *20th Century-Fox (M) FOX-3005*　58　　**250-300**
　Composer: Malcolm Arnold. **Conductor:** Malcolm Arnold. **Cast:** London Philharmonic
　Orchestra.

ROSE
Soundtrack (1979) .... *Atlantic (S) SD-16010*　79　　**8-10**
　Cast: Bette Midler; Rose Concert Band.

ROSE MARIE
Original London Cast .... *World (M) SHB-37*　　　**15-20**
　Composer: Rudolf Friml; Herbert Stothart; Otto Harbach. **Cast:** Edith Day; Derek Oldham; Billy
　Merson.
Studio Cast (1952) .... *RCA Victor (M) LK-1012*　52　　**30-35**
Studio Cast (1952) .... *RCA Victor/Camden (M) CAL-408*　58　　**15-20**
　Composer: Rudolf Friml; Herbert Stothart; Otto Harbach. **Conductor:** Al Goodman.
　Cast: Charles Fredericks; Marion Bell; Christina Lind; Guild Choristers.
　Also see RIO RITA
Studio Cast (1958) .... *RCA Victor (M) LOP-1001*　58　　**25-30**
Studio Cast (1958) .... *RCA Victor (S) LSO-1001*　58　　**35-40**
　Composer: Rudolf Friml; Herbert Stothart; Otto Harbach. **Conductor:** Lehman Engel.
　Cast: Julie Andrews; Giorgio Tozzi; Meier Tzelniker; Frances Day; Marion Keene; Frederick
　Harvey; Tudor Evans.
Studiotrack (1952) .... *RCA Victor (EP) ERA-220*　52　　**10-15**
Studio Cast (1950) .... *Columbia (M) ML-2178*　50　　**35-40**
　10-inch LP.
　Composer: Rudolf Friml; Herbert Stothart; Otto Harbach. **Conductor:** Leon Arnaud.
　Cast: Nelson Eddy; Dorothy Kirsten.

Soundtrack (1952) .... *RCA Victor (M) LCT-16* 52   **$35-45**
10-inch LP.
  Conductor: Nathaniel Shilkret. **Cast:** Nelson Eddy; Jeanette MacDonald.
Soundtrack (1954) .... *MGM (M) E-299* 54   **35-45**
10-inch LP.
Soundtrack (1954) .... *MGM (EP) X-299* 54   **12-15**
Soundtrack (1954) .... *MGM (M) E-3769* 60   **20-25**
  One side has music from *Seven Brides for Seven Brothers.*
Soundtrack (1954) .... *Metro (M) M-616* 67   **15-20**
Soundtrack (1954) .... *Metro (SE) MS-616* 67   **15-20**
  Composer: Rudolf Friml; Herbert Stothart; Otto Harbach. **Conductor:** George Stoll.
  Cast: Howard Keel; Ann Blyth; Bert Lahr; George Stoll; Fernando Lamas; Marjorie Main.
  Also see MERRY WIDOW; RIO RITA

ROSE ON BROADWAY
TV Soundtrack .... *Cozy (S) PL-9206*   **10-12**
  Conductor: H.B. Barnum.

ROSE TATTOO
Studio Cast (1967) .... *Caedmon (S) TRS-324* 67   **20-25**
  Triple LP set. A dramatic play.
  Cast: Maureen Stapleton; Harry Guardino.
Soundtrack (1955) .... *Columbia (EP) B-727* 55   **20-25**
Soundtrack (1955) .... *Columbia (M) CL-727* 55   **75-90**
  Composer: Alex North. **Conductor:** Alex North.

ROSEMARY'S BABY
Soundtrack (1968) .... *Dot (S) DLP-25875* 68   **25-30**
  Composer: Christopher Komeda. **Conductor:** Dick Hazard. **Cast:** Mia Farrow.

ROSENCRANTZ AND GUILDENSTERN ARE DEAD
Original London Cast (1967) .... *London (S) AMS-88003* 68   **40-50**
  Incidental music. Also has music from *The Royal Hunt of the Sun* and *As You Like It.*
  Composer: Marc Wilkinson. **Conductor:** Marc Wilkinson.

ROSZA CONDUCTS ROSZA
Studiotrack .... *Varese Sarabande (S) VC-81053* 78   **8-10**
  Contains the suite from *Lust for Life* plus *Brute Force, The Killers* and *The Naked City,* performed as the
  Background to Violence Suite.
  Composer: Miklos Rosza. **Conductor:** Miklos Rosza.

ROTHSCHILDS
Original Cast (1970) .... *Columbia (S) S-30337* 70   **40-50**
  Composer: Jerry Bock; Sheldon Harnick. **Conductor:** Milton Greene. **Cast:** Paul Hecht; Leila
  Martin; Jill Clayburgh; Hal Linden; Keen Curtis; Leo Leyden; Timothy Jerome; David Garfield;
  Allan Gruet.

ROUGH RIDERS - MUSIC FOR ON AND OFF THE ROAD
Soundtrack (1986) .... *Epic (S) FE-40248* 86   **8-10**

ROUND MIDNIGHT
Soundtrack (1986) .... *Columbia (S) SC-40464* 86   **8-10**
  Conductor: Herbie Hancock. **Cast:** Dexter Gordon.

ROUSTABOUT

Soundtrack (1964) .... *RCA Victor (M) LPM-2999*   64 $50-60
　Black label, reads "Mono" at bottom.
Soundtrack (1964) : .... *RCA Victor (S) LSP-2999*   64   500-700
　Black label, with RCA Victor logo in silver print.
Soundtrack (1964) .... *RCA Victor (M) LPM-2999*   65   20-30
　Black label, reads "Monaural" at bottom.
Soundtrack (1964) .... *RCA Victor (S) LSP-2999*   65   20-30
　Black label, with RCA Victor logo in white print.
Soundtrack (1964) .... *RCA Victor (S) LSP-2999*   69   10-20
　Orange or tan label.
Soundtrack (1964) .... *RCA Victor (S) AFL1-2999*   77   8-10
　Composer: Bill Giant; Bernie Baum; Florence Kaye; Jerry Leiber; Mike Stoller; Ben Weisman;
　Sid Wayne; Fred Wise; Randy Starr; Sid Tepper; Roy C. Bennett. **Cast:** Elvis Presley; Scotty
　Moore (guitar); Tiny Timbrell (guitar); Bob Moore (bass); Floyd Cramer (piano); D.J. Fontana
　(drums); Hal Blaine (drums); Boots Randolph (saxophone); Dudley Brooks (piano); Jordanaires
　(vocals).

ROWAN AND MARTIN'S LAUGH-IN

TV Soundtrack (1968) .... *Epic (S) 15118*   68   12-15
TV Soundtrack (1969) .... *Reprise (S) 6335*   69   10-12
　Actual title: *Laugh-In '69.*
　Cast: Dan Rowan; Dick Martin.

ROYAL HUNT OF THE SUN:
see ROSENCRANTZ AND GUILDENSTERN ARE DEAD

ROYAL WEDDING

Soundtrack (1951) .... *MGM (M) E-543*   51   35-45
　10-inch LP.
Soundtrack (1951) .... *MGM (M) E-3235*   55   25-30
　One side has music from *Seven Brides for Seven Brothers.*
　Composer: Burton Lane; Alan J. Lerner. **Conductor:** Johnny Green. **Cast:** Fred Astaire; Jane
　Powell.

RUDE AWAKENING

Soundtrack .... *Elektra (S) 60873-1*   8-10
　Composer: Various. **Cast:** Mike + Mechanics; Sigue Sigue Sputnik; Bill Medley; Franke and
　Knockouts; Kim Carnes; Georgia Satellites; Miami Sound Machine; Jefferson Airplane; Grateful
　Dean; Phoebe Snow; Bob Dylan.

RUDOLPH THE RED-NOSED REINDEER:
see STORY OF RUDOLPH THE RED-NOSED REINDEER

RUGANTINO
Original Cast (1964) .... *Warner Bros. (M) H-1528*   64 $25-30
Original Cast (1964) .... *Warner Bros. (S) HS-1528*   64   40-45
  Includes booklet. This Italian show was the first Broadway musical presented in a foreign language.
  English translation by Alfred Drake.
  Composer: Armando Trovajoli; Pietro Garinei; Sandro Giovannini. **Conductor:** Anton Coppola.
  Cast: Nino Manfredi; Ornella Vanoni; Aldo Fabrizi; Bice Valor; Lando Fiorini.

RUGGLES OF RED GAP
TV Soundtrack (1957) .... *Verve (M) MGV-15000*   57   60-70
TV Soundtrack (1957) .... *Stet (M) DS-15007*   Re   8-10
  Composer: Jule Styne; Leo Robin. **Conductor:** Buddy Bregman. **Cast:** Michael Redgrave;
  Peter Lawford; Imogene Coca; Jane Powell; David Wayne.

RULING CLASS
Soundtrack (1972) .... *Avco Embassy (S) AV-11003*   72   25-30
  Composer: John Cameron; others. **Conductor:** John Cameron. **Cast:** Peter O'Toole; Alastair
  Sim; Arthur Lowe; Harry Andrews; Carol Browne . (With dialogue.)

RUMBLE FISH
Soundtrack (1983) .... *A&M (S) SP6-4983*   83   8-10

RUN, ANGEL, RUN
Soundtrack (1969) .... *Epic (S) BN-26474*   69   15-20
  Composer: Stu Phillips; others. **Conductor:** Stu Phillips. **Cast:** Tammy Wynette; Windows.

RUN FOR YOUR WIFE
Soundtrack (1966) .... *RCA Victor (M) LOC-1129*   66   15-20
Soundtrack (1966) .... *RCA Victor (S) LSO-1129*   66   20-25
  Composer: Nino Oliviero. **Conductor:** Pier Luigi Urbini; Marty Manning. **Cast:** Frankie Randall.

RUN OF THE ARROW
Soundtrack (1957) .... *Decca (M) DL-8620*   57   65-75
Soundtrack (1957) .... *AEI (M) 3102*   78   10-15
  Composer: Victor Young; others. **Conductor:** Constantin Bakaleinikoff.

RUN WILD, RUN FREE
Soundtrack (1969) .... *SGC (S) SD-5003*   69   15-20
  Composer: David Whitaker. **Conductor:** David Whitaker. **Cast:** New Christy Minstrels.

RUNAWAY
Soundtrack (1985) .... *Varese Sarabande (S) STV-81234*   85   8-12
  Composer: Jerry Goldsmith.

RUNAWAY TRAIN
Soundtrack (1985) .... *Enigma (S) 73200-1*   86   8-12
  Composer: Trevor Jones.

RUNAWAYS
Original Cast (1978) .... *Columbia (S) JS-35410*   78   15-20
  A New York Shakespeare Festival musical.
  Composer: Elizabeth Swados. **Cast:** Bernie Allison; Trini Alvarado; Mark Anthony Butler;
  Leonard Brown; Bruce Hilbok; Diane Lane; Jossie De Guzman; Nan-Lynn Nelson; Randy Ruiz;
  Venustrak Robinson; Karen Evans; Ray Contreras.

RUNNER STUMBLES
Soundtrack (1979) .... *No Label Shown (S) EG-1001*   79   100-150
  Composer: Ernest Gold.

RUNNING MAN
Soundtrack (1987) .... *Varese Sarabande (S) STV-81356*   87   8-10
  Composer: Harold Faltermeyer.

RUNNING SCARED
Soundtrack (1986) . . . . *MCA (S) 6169*   86   **$10-12**
Soundtrack (1986) . . . . *MCA (S) 39321*   86   **8-10**
    Composer: Rod Temperton; others. **Cast:** Michael McDonald; Fee Waybill; Rod Temperton and Beat Wagon; Larry Williams; Ready for the World; Klymaxx; New Edition; Patti Labelle; Kim Wilde.

RUSH TO JUDGMENT
Soundtrack (1967) . . . .*Happening (M) 3210*   67   **15-20**
    Cast: Mark Lane (narration).
Soundtrack (1967) . . . . *Vanguard (M) 9242*   67   **15-20**
    Deliberation of the Warren Commission's findings against Lee Harvey Oswald.
    Cast: Emile De Antonio (narration).

RUSSIAN ADVENTURE
Soundtrack (1966) . . . .*Roulette (M) OS-802*   66   **30-35**
Soundtrack (1966) . . . . *Roulette (S) OSS-802*   66   **45-50**
    Above two are also known as "Cinerama's Russian Adventure."
  Conductor: Aleksandr Lokshin. **Cast:** Moscow State Symphony; Orchestra of the Moscow State Circus; Bolshoi and Moiseyev Theatre Orchestras.

RUSSIANS ARE COMING! THE RUSSIANS ARE COMING!
Soundtrack (1966) . . . .*United Artists (M) UAL-4142*   66   **12-15**
Soundtrack (1966) . . . .*United Artists (S) UAS-5142*   66   **15-20**
Soundtrack (1966) . . . .*MCA (S) 1428*   **8-10**
    Composer: Johnny Mandel; others. **Conductor:** Johnny Mandel. **Cast:** Irene Kral.

RUSTLER'S RHAPSODY
Soundtrack (1985) . . . . *Warner Bros. (S) 1-25284*   85   **8-10**
    Composer: Steve Dorff; others. **Cast:** Gary Morris; Nitty Gritty Dirt Band; John Anderson; Pinkard and Bowden; Charlie McCoy; Pam Tillis; Randy Travis; Karen Brooks; Rex Allen Jr.; Rex Allen Sr.; Roy Rogers.

RUTHLESS PEOPLE
Soundtrack (1986) . . . .*Epic (S) SE-40398*   86   **8-10**
    Composer: Various. **Cast:** Mick Jagger; Billy Joel; Machinations; Luther Vandross; Dan Hartman; Kool and the Gang; Michel Colombier; Bruce Springsteen; Nicole; Paul Young.

RUTLES
TV Soundtrack (1978) . . . . *Warner Bros. (S) HS-3151*   78   **10-12**
    Composer: Neil Innes. **Cast:** Neil Innes; Ollie Halsall; Rikki Fataar; John Halsey.

RYAN'S DAUGHTER
Soundtrack (1970) . . . .*MGM (S) 1SE-27*   70   **25-30**
    Composer: Maurice Jarre. **Conductor:** Maurice Jarre.

S

S'WONDERFUL, S'MARVELOUS, S'GERSHWIN
TV Soundtrack (1972) . . . .*Daybreak (M) DR-2009*   72 $10-15
  Composer: George Gershwin; Ira Gershwin. **Conductor:** Elliot Lawrence. **Cast:** Fred Astaire;
  Jack Lemmon; Leslie Eggams; Peter Nero; Robert Guillaume; Lary Kert; Alan Johnson.

SACCO AND VANZETTI
Soundtrack (1971) . . . .*RCA Victor (S) LSP-4612*   71   15-20
  Composer: Ennio Morricone. **Conductor:** Ennio Morricone. **Cast:** Joan Baez.

SACRED IDOL
Soundtrack (1960) . . . . *Capitol (M) T-1293*   60   30-40
Soundtrack (1960) . . . . *Capitol (S) ST-1293*   60   40-50
  Composer: Les Baxter. **Conductor:** Les Baxter.

SAGA OF THE DINGBAT
Original Cast . . . . *N.Y. Herald Tribune (S) XCSV-105844/5*   60-70
  Industrial show.
  Composer: Julian Stein; Edward Naylor. **Conductor:** Rolf Barnes. **Cast:** Ann Vivian; Hal
  Linden; Stan Page; Carole Woodruff; Mimi Vondra; Arline Woods; Gino Comforte; Don Grilley.

SAHARA
Soundtrack (1984) . . . .*Varese Sarabande (S) 81211*   84   8-10
  Composer: Ennio Morricone. **Conductor:** Ennio Morricone. **Cast:** Cathy Cole.

SAIL AWAY
Original Cast (1961) . . . .*Capitol (M) WAO-1643*   61   20-25
Original Cast (1961) . . . .*Capitol (S) SWAO-1643*   61   30-35
  Composer: Noel Coward. **Conductor:** Peter Matz. **Cast:** Elaine Stritch; James Hurst; Alice
  Pearce; Patricia Harty; Grover Dale; Charles Braswell; Paul O'Keefe.
Original London Cast . . . .*Stanyan (S) SR-10027*   72   10-15
  Composer: Noel Coward. **Conductor:** Gareth Davies. **Cast:** Elaine Stritch; David Holliday;
  Grover Dale; Sheila Forbes; John Hewer; Edith Day; Sydney Arnold.

SAINT

TV Soundtrack (1962) . . . . *RCA Victor (M) LPM-3631*   66   **$35-40**
TV Soundtrack (1962) . . . . : . . . . *RCA Victor (S) LSP-3631*   66   **60-70**
  Composer: Edwin Astley; Ken Jones. **Conductor:** Edwin Astley.

SAINT ELMO'S FIRE

Soundtrack (1985) . . . . *Atlantic (S) 78-12611*   85   **8-10**
  Composer: David Foster. **Conductor:** David Foster. **Cast:** John Parr; Billy Squier; Elefante; Jon
  Anderson; Fee Waybill; David Foster; Vikki Moss; Airplay; Donny Gerrard; Amy Holland.

SAINT JOAN

Soundtrack (1957) . . . . *Capitol (M) W-865*   57   **70-80**
  Composer: Mischa Spoliansky. **Conductor:** Mischa Spoliansky.

SAINT LOUIS BLUES

Soundtrack (1958) . . . . *Capitol (M) W-993*   58   **45-55**
  Composer: William C. Handy; Nelson Riddle. **Conductor:** Nelson Riddle. **Cast:** Nat King Cole.

SAINT LOUIS WOMAN

Original Cast (1946) . . . . *Capitol (M) L-355*   52   **60-75**
  Capitol's first original cast album. Has music reissued from 78 rpms released in 1946.
Original Cast (1946) . . . . *Capitol (SE) DW-2742*   67   **50-60**
  Composer: Harold Arlen; Johnny Mercer. **Conductor:** Leon Leonardi. **Cast:** Pearl Bailey;
  Harold Nicholas; Ruby Hill; June Hawkins; Robert Pope.

SAINT OF BLEEKER STREET

Original Cast (1954) . . . . *RCA Victor (M) LM-6032*   54   **70-80**
  Double LP boxed set, with booklet.
Original Cast (1954) . . . . *RCA Victor (M) CBM-2714*   78   **15-20**
  Composer: Gian-Carlo Menotti. **Conductor:** Thomas Schippers. **Cast:** Maria DiGerlando;
  David Aiken; Gabrielle Ruggiero; David Poleri; John Reardon; Catherine Akos; Elizabeth
  Carron; Russell Goodwin.

SALAD DAYS

Original London Cast (1958) . . . . *London (M) 5474*   58   **35-40**
  Composer: Julian Slade; Dorothy Reynolds. **Cast:** Eleanor Drew; John Warner; James
  Carincross; Cairn Cross; Michael Aldridge; Edward Rubach & Robert Docker (pianos).
Original London Cast (1958) . . . . *London (M) 5765*   63   **25-30**
Original London Cast (1958) . . . . *Embassy (M) EMB-31046*   Re   **12-15**
  Composer: Julian Slade; Dorothy Reynolds. **Cast:** Eleanor Drew; John Warner; James
  Carincross; Cairn Cross; Michael Aldridge; Edward Rubach & Robert Docker (pianos).

SALLAH

Soundtrack (1965) . . . . *Philips (M) PHM-20017*   65   **15-20**
Soundtrack (1965) . . . . *Philips (S) PHS-60017*   65   **20-25**
  Composer: Yohanan Zarai. **Conductor:** Luchi DeJesus.

SALLY
Original London Cast (1921) ...... *Monmouth Evergreen (SE) MES-7053* $8-12
  Composer: Jerome Kern; others. **Cast:** Dorothy Dickson; Gregory Stroud; Leslie Henson;
  George Grossmith; Heather Thatcher; Seymour Beard.
  Also see GOOD NEWS

SALLY FIELD:
see FLYING NUN

SALOME
Soundtrack (1953) .... *Decca (EP) ED-515*   53   25-35
Soundtrack (1953) .... *Decca (M) DL-6026*   53   125-150
  10-inch LP.
  Composer: George Dunning; Daniele Amfitheatrof. **Conductor:** Morris Stoloff. **Cast:** Rita
  Hayworth; Stewart Granger; Alan Badel. (With dialogue.)

SALSA
Soundtrack (1988) .... *MCA (S) 6232*   88   8-10

SALT AND PEPPER
Soundtrack (1968) .... *United Artists (S) UAS-5187*   68   15-20
Soundtrack (1968) .... *MCA (S) 25035*   86   8-10
  Composer: John Dankworth; Leslie Bricusse. **Cast:** Sammy Davis Jr.; George Rhodes.

SALUDOS AMIGOS (MUSIC FROM SOUTH OF THE BORDER)
Soundtrack (1943) .... *Disneyland (M) WDL-3039*   59   30-35
Soundtrack (1943) .... *Disneyland (M) WDL-1039*   60   20-25
  Composer: Ray Barroso; Augustine Lara; Charles Wolcott; others. **Conductor:** Leo Perachi.

SALUTE TO VINCENT YOUMANS: FOUR GREAT HITS FROM HIT SHOWS
Studiotrack (1954) .... *RCA Victor (EP) EPA-543*   54   15-20
  Includes: *Great Day* (from *Great Day*), *Sometimes I'm Happy* and *Hallelujah* (from *Hit the Deck*) and
  Tea for Two (from *No No Nanette*).
  Composer: Vincent Youmans. **Conductor:** Case. **Cast:** Russ Case and His Orchestra.

SALVATION
Original Cast (1969) .... *Capitol (S) SO-337*   69   20-25
  Composer: Peter Link; C.C. Courtney. **Conductor:** Kirk Nurock. **Cast:** Yolande Bavan; Peter
  Link; C.C. Courtney; Joe Morton; Martha Heflin; Boni Enten; Chapman Roberts; Annie Rachel.
Studio Cast (1969) .... *Mio International (S) MUS-5009*   69   25-30
  Promotional issue only.
  Composer: Peter Link; C.C. Courtney. **Cast:** Gallery Repertory Theatre.

SAMMY
TV Soundtrack (1973) .... *MGM (S) SE-4914*   73   10-15
  Composer: Various. **Conductor:** George Rhodes; Jack Parnell. **Cast:** Sammy Davis Jr.;
  Sammy Davis Sr.

SAMOA
Soundtrack (1956) .... *Disneyland (M) WDL-4003*   56   40-50
  One side has music from *Switzerland*.
  Composer: Oliver G. Wallace. **Conductor:** Oliver G. Wallace.

SAMSON AND DELILAH
Soundtrack (1949) .... *Decca (M) DL-6007*   52   60-70
  10-inch LP.
  Composer: Victor Young. **Conductor:** Victor Young. **Cast:** Paramount Symphony Orchestra.
  Also see QUIET MAN

SAND CASTLE
Soundtrack (1960) .... *Columbia (M) CL-1455*   61 $35-40
Soundtrack (1960) .... *Columbia (S) CS-8249*   61   65-70
  Composer: Alec Wilder. Conductor: Samuel Baron.

SAND PEBBLES
Soundtrack (1966) .... *20th Century-Fox (M) TFM-3189*   67   40-45
Soundtrack (1966) .... *20th Century-Fox (S) TFS-4189*   67   60-65
  Composer: Jerry Goldsmith. Conductor: Lionel Newman.

SANDHOG
Original Cast (1954) .... *Vanguard (M) VRS-9001*   54   275-325
  Composer: Earl Robinson; Waldo Salt. Cast: Earl Robinson (piano).

SANDPIPER
Soundtrack (1965) .... *Mercury (M) MG-21032*   65   20-25
Soundtrack (1965) .... *Mercury (S) SR-61032*   65   30-35
  Composer: Johnny Mandel. Conductor: Robert Armbruster.

SANDS OF IWO JIMA
Soundtrack (1949) .... *Citadel (M) CT-7027*   81   8-10
  Also has music from Victor Young's *The Sun Shines Bright*.
  Composer: Victor Young. Conductor: Victor Young.

SANFORD AND SON
TV Soundtrack (1972) .... *RCA Victor (M) LPM-4739*   72   12-15
  Composer: Quincy Jones. Conductor: Quincy Jones. Cast: Redd Foxx; Demond Wilson;
  Lynn Hamilton; Noam Pitlik; Hal Williams; Dick Van Patten; Harold Fong. (With dialogue.)

SANTA CLAUS IS COMIN' TO TOWN
TV Soundtrack (1970) .... *MGM (S) SE-4732*   70   15-20
  Composer: Maury Laws; Jules Bass; J. Fred Coots; Haven Gillespie. Cast: Fred Astaire
  (narration); Mickey Rooney; Keenan Wynn; Paul Frees; Joan Gardner; Robbie Lester; Gary
  White; Dina Lynn; Greg Thomas; Westminster Children's Choir. (With dialogue.)

SAP OF LIFE
Original Cast .... *Blue Pear (M) BP-1002*   25-30
  Composer: David Shire; Richard Maltby, Jr. Cast: Kenneth Nelson; Jerry Dodge; Patricia Bruder.

SARAFINA
Original Cast ....*Shanachie (S) 43052*   8-10
Original Cast .... *RCA Victor (S) 9307-1 RC9*   8-10
  Full title: *Sarafina (The Music of Liberation)*.

SARATOGA
Original Cast (1959) .... *RCA Victor (M) LOC-1051*   59   30-35
Original Cast (1959) .... *RCA Victor (S) LSO-1051*   59   40-50
  Composer: Harold Arlen; Johnny Mercer. Conductor: Jerry Arlen. Cast: Howard Keel; Carol
  Lawrence; Odette Myrtil; Carol Brice.

SARAVA
Original Cast (1979) .... *Roadshow (S) 4D-11455*   79   10-12
  12-inch, disco pressing.
  Composer: Mitch Leigh.

SATAN IN HIGH HEELS
Soundtrack (1962) .... *Parker (M) PLP-406*   62   15-20
Soundtrack (1962) .... *Parker (S) PLP-406S*   62   25-30
  Composer: Mundell Lowe. Conductor: Mundell Lowe.

SATAN'S SADISTS
Soundtrack (1969) .... *Smash (S) SRS-67127*   69   12-15
  Composer: Harley Hatcher. Conductor: Harley Hatcher.

SATCHMO THE GREAT
TV Soundtrack (1958) .... *Columbia (M) CL-1077*   58 $25-30
TV Soundtrack (1958) .... *Columbia Special Products (M) JCL-1077*   Re   8-10
    Above two have music and excerpts from the film and from the CBS-TV series *See It Now*.
   Conductor: Leonard Bernstein. **Cast:** Louis Armstrong; Edward R. Murrow; Lewishon Stadium
   Symphony Orchestra. (With dialogue.)

SATINS AND SPURS
Soundtrack (1954) .... *Capitol (EP) FBF-547*   54   15-25
TV Soundtrack (1954) .... *Capitol (M) L-547*   54   60-75
    10-inch LP.
   Composer: Jay Livingston; Ray Evans. **Cast:** Betty Hutton.

SATISFACTION
Soundtrack (1988) .... *AJK (S) A710-1*   88   8-10
   Composer: Various. **Cast:** Justine Bateman and Mystery; Michel Colombier; John Kay and
   Steppenwolf.

SATURDAY NIGHT FEVER
Soundtrack (1977) .... *RSO (S) RS-2-4001*   77   10-12
Soundtrack (1977) .... *RSO (S) 825389-1*   Re   8-10
   Composer: Barry Gibb; Robin Gibb; Maurice Gibb; others. **Conductor:** Barry Gibb; Robin Gibb;
   Maurice Gibb; David Shire; others. **Cast:** Bee Gees; Yvonne Elliman; Walter Murphy; Tavares;
   Kool and the Gang; K.C. and the Sunshine Band; Trammps; Ralph McDonald.

SATURDAY NIGHT LIVE
Original Cast (1976) .... *Arista (S) AL-4107*   76   10-12
TV Soundtrack (1976) .... *Arista (S) ALB6-8435*   Re   8-10
   Composer: Paul Shaffer; others. **Conductor:** Howard Shore. **Cast:** John Belushi; Dan Aykroyd;
   Chevy Chase; Jane Curtin; Garrett Morris; Laraine Newman; Gilda Radner; Peter Boyle; Buck
   Henry; Richard Pryor; Paul Simon; Lily Tomlin; Don Pardo; Anne Beatts; Robert King; Bill
   Wendell. (With dialogue.)

SATURDAY'S WARRIOR
Original Cast (1974) .... *Embryo (S) EM-1001*   74   8-10
   Composer: Lex de Azevedo; Doug Stewart. **Conductor:** Lex de Azevedo. **Cast:** Donna
   Conkling; Cam Clarke; Shawn Engemann.

SAVAGE
Soundtrack (1974) .... *Money (S) MS-1109*   74   12-15
   Composer: Don Julian; others.

SAVAGE SAM
Soundtrack (1963) .... *Disneyland (M) ST-1925*   63   25-30
    Sequel to *Old Yeller*.
   Cast: Thurl Ravenscroft (narration); Wellingtons; Brian Keith; Tommy Kirk; Marta Kristen; Jeff
   York; Dewey Martin; Kevin Corcoran. (With dialogue.)

SAVAGE SEVEN
Soundtrack (1968) .... *Atco (M) 33-245*   68   10-15
Soundtrack (1968) .... *Atco (S) SD-33-245*   68   10-15
   Composer: Guy Hemric; Jerry Styner. **Cast:** Cream; Iron Butterfly; Barbara Kelly; Morning
   Good.

SAVAGE STREETS
Soundtrack (1984) .... *MCA (S) L33-1206*   84   10-15
    Promotional issue only. Side 1: Justice for One. Side 2: Innocent Hearts.
   Composer: John Farnham; Sue Shifrin; Randy Bishop. **Cast:** John Farnham.
Soundtrack (1984) .... *MCA (S) 6134*   84   8-10
   Composer: Michael Lloyd; John d'Andrea. **Cast:** John Farnham; Real Life; 3 Speed; Michael
   Bradley.

SAVAGE WILD
Soundtrack (1970) . . . . *American Int'l (S) STA-1032*   70   **$15-20**
Composer: Jamie Mendoza-Nava. Conductor: Jamie Mendoza-Nava. Cast: Chris Quesada.

SAVE THE CHILDREN
Soundtrack (1973) . . . . *Motown (S) M-800-R2*   73   **12-15**
Double LP set.
Composer: Various. Cast: Matt Robinson (narration); Jackson Five; Nancy Wilson; Roberta
Flack; Brenda Lee Eager; Rev. James Cleveland; Marvin Gaye; Sammy Davis Jr.; Temptations;
Bill Withers; O'Jays; Gladys Knight and the Pips; Main Ingredient; Curtis Mayfield; Jerry Butler;
Ramsey Lewis Trio; Quincy Jones; Rev. Jesse Jackson. (With dialogue.)

SAY AMEN, SOMEBODY
Soundtrack (1983) . . . . *DRG (S) SB2L-1258*   83   **8-10**
Double LP set. Soundtrack plus concert recordings.
Composer: Various. Cast: "Mother" Willie Mae Ford Smith; "Professor" Thomas Dorsey.

SAY DARLING
Original Cast (1958) . . . .*RCA Victor (M) LOC-1045*   58   **35-40**
Original Cast (1958) . . . .*RCA Victor (S) LSO-1045*   58   **50-55**
Composer: Jule Styne; Betty Comden; Adolph Green. Conductor: Sid Ramin. Cast: David
Wayne; Vivian Blaine; Johnny Desmond; Jerome Cowan; Mitchell Gregg; Steve Condos.

SAY ONE FOR ME
Soundtrack (1959) . . . . *Columbia (M) CL-1337*   59   **25-30**
Soundtrack (1959) . . . . *Columbia (S) CS-8147*   59   **60-65**
Composer: James Van Heusen; Sammy Cahn. Conductor: Lionel Newman. Cast: Debbie
Reynolds; Bing Crosby; Robert Wagner; Buddy Cole; Judy Harriett.
Studiotrack (1959) . . . .*Buena Vista (M) BV-1302*   59   **10-20**
Cast: Rex Allen; Roberta Shore; Tony Paris.

SAYONARA
Soundtrack (1957) . . . .*RCA Victor (M) LOC-1041*   57   **50-75**
Soundtrack (1957) . . . .*RCA Victor (S) LSO-1041*   57   **75-100**
Soundtrack (1957) . . . .*Entr'acte (S) ERS-6513-ST*   Re   **8-10**
Composer: Franz Waxman; Irving Berlin; others. Conductor: Franz Waxman. Cast: Miiko
Taka.

SCALPHUNTERS
Soundtrack (1968) . . . .*United Artists (M) UAL-4176*   68   **30-35**
Soundtrack (1968) . . . .*United Artists (S) UAS-5176*   68   **40-50**
Composer: Elmer Bernstein. Conductor: Elmer Bernstein.

SCANDALOUS JOHN
Soundtrack (1971) . . . . *Buena Vista (S) STER-5004*   71   **10-12**
Composer: Rod McKuen. Cast: Rod McKuen.

SCANDALOUS LIFE OF FRANKIE AND JOHNNY
Studio Cast (1938) . . . .*Desto (M) D-408*   **8-10**
Studio Cast . . . . *Desto (S) DST-6408*   **10-12**
One side has *Indian Suite, Suite No. 2, Opus 48*, the classical work of Edward MacDowell.
Composer: Jerome Moross. Conductor: Walter Hendl. Cast: Vienna Symphony Orchestra and
Chorus.

SCARFACE
Soundtrack (1984) . . . .*MCA (S) 6126*   83   **8-12**
Composer: Giorgio Moroder. Cast: Paul Engemann; Deborah Harry; Amy Holland; Maria
Conchita; Giorgio Moroder; Elizabeth Daily; Beth Andersen.

SCARLET STREET
Soundtrack (1945) . . . . *Medallion (M) ML 303*   79   **8-10**
Composer: Hans J. Salter. Conductor: Hans J. Salter.

SCENT OF MYSTERY

Soundtrack (1960) .... *Ramrod (M) T-6001* 60 $50-60
Soundtrack (1960) .... *Ramrod (S) ST-6001* 60 75-85
Composer: Mario Nascimbene; Jordan Ramin; Harold Adamson. **Conductor:** Jack Saunders. **Cast:** Eddie Fisher.

SCHONER GIGOLO - ARMER GIGOLO (JUST A GIGOLO)

Soundtrack (1979) .... *Ariola (S) 200 462 320* 79 40-50
Composer: Various. **Conductor:** Jack Fishman; Frank Barber; John Altman. **Cast:** Marlene Dietrich; Manhattan Transfer; Ragtimers; Pasadena Roof Orchestra; Gunther Fischer Orchestra; Sydne Rome; Rebels; Barnabas Orchestra; Village People.

SCHOOL DAZE

Soundtrack (1988) .... *EMI (S) E11H-48680* 88 8-10
Composer: Various. **Cast:** E.; Tech and Effx; Rays; Jigaboo and Wannabee Ensemble; Kenny Barron and Terence Blanchard; Morehouse College Glee Club; Keith John; Phyllis Hyman; Pieces of a Dream; Portia Griffin.

SCORPIO

Composer: Jerry Fielding. **Conductor:** erry Fielding.

SCOTT JOPLIN

Soundtrack (1977) .... *MCA (S) 2098* 77 10-15
Soundtrack (1977) .... *MCA (S) 1541* Re 8-10
Composer: Scott Joplin. **Cast:** Dick Hyman.

SCRAMBLED FEET

Original Cast (1979) .... *DRG (S) 6105* 79 8-10
Composer: John Driver; Jeffrey Haddow. **Conductor:** Jimmy Wisner. **Cast:** Evalyn Baron; John Driver; Jeffrey Haddow; Roger Neil.

SCREAMERS

Soundtrack (1980) .... *Web (S) ST-101* 81 10-12
Composer: Luciano Michelini. **Conductor:** Luciano Michelini.

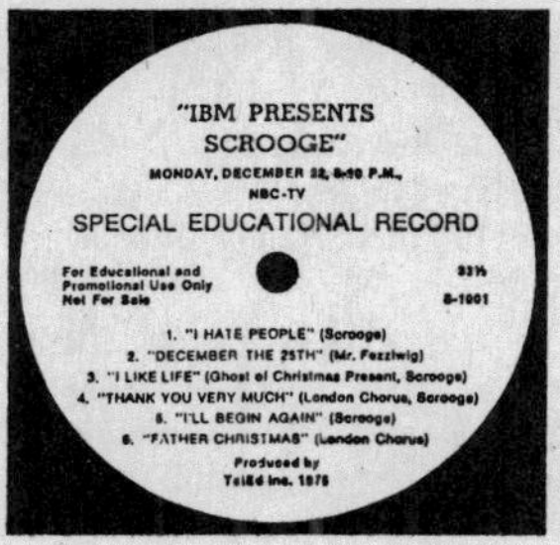

SCROOGE

Original Cast (1978) .... *Theatre Under The Stars (S) TUTS-78* 78 10-15
Seven-inch LP.
Composer: J. Bernard; Mark Holden. **Conductor:** Mark Holden.
Soundtrack (1970) .... *Columbia (S) S-30258* 70 25-30
Musical version of Charles Dickens' *A Christmas Carol*.
Soundtrack (1970) .... *Columbia Special Products (S) P-14077* Re 8-10
Composer: Leslie Bricusse. **Conductor:** Ian Fraser. **Cast:** Albert Finney; David Collins; Laurence Naismith; Sir Alec Guinness; Richard Beaumont.
TV Soundtrack (1975) .... *TelEd (S) S-1001* 75 10-20
Full title: *IBM Presents Scrooge*. Has highlights from *Scrooge*. An educational package for classroom use. Includes original sleeve, insert, and cover that serves as a classroom poster.

SEA HAWK
Soundtrack (1940) . . . . *Varese Sarabande (SE) 704-380*   87   **$10-15**
  Composer: Erich Wolfgang Korngold. **Conductor:** Varujan Kojian. **Cast:** Utah Symphony
  Orchestra and Chorus.

SEA HAWK: THE CLASSIC FILM SCORES OF ERICH WOLFGANG
KORNGOLD
Studiotrack . . . .*RCA Victor (S) LSC-3330*   72   **10-12**
  Music from: *The Sea Hawk, Kings Row, Captain Blood, The Adventures of Robin Hood, Of Human
  Bondage, Jaurez, The Constant Nymph, Anthony Adverse, Between Two Worlds, Deception, Devotion*
  and *Escape Me Never.* Includes insert liner notes.
Studiotrack . . . . *RCA Victor (S) AGL-1-370*   72   **8-10**
  Same as LSC-3330, but without insert liner notes.
  Composer: Erich Wolfgang Korngold. **Conductor:** Charles Gerhardt.

SEA OF LOVE
Soundtrack (1989) . . . . *Mercury (S) 422-842-170-1*   89   **8-10**
  Composer: Trevor Jones (original music); Phil Baptiste; George Khoury. **Conductor:** Trevor
  Jones. **Cast:** Phil Phillips and the Twilights; Tom Waits.

SEARCH FOR PARADISE
Soundtrack (1957) . . . .*RCA Victor (M) LOC-1034*   57   **75-85**
  Composer: Dimitri Tiomkin. **Conductor:** Dimitri Tiomkin. **Cast:** Robert Merrill.
  Also see HIGH AND THE MIGHTY

SEARCHERS:
see DEATH OF A SCOUNDREL

SEASIDE SWINGERS
Soundtrack (1965) . . . .*Mercury (M) MG-21031*   65   **12-18**
Soundtrack (1965) . . . . *Mercury (S) SR-61031*   65   **15-20**
  Composer: Various. **Cast:** Freddie and the Dreamers; John Leyton; Mike Sarne; Grazina Frame.

SEBASTIAN
Soundtrack (1968) . . . . *Dot (M) DLP-3845*   68   **25-30**
Soundtrack (1968) . . . .*Dot (S) DLP-25845*   68   **30-35**
  Composer: Jerry Goldsmith. **Conductor:** Jerry Goldsmith; others. **Cast:** Jimmy A. Hassell.

SECOND SHEPHERD'S PLAY
Original Cast (1976) . . . . *Broadway Baby Demos (S) BBD-774*   76   **8-10**
  Composer: Steve Kitsakos. **Cast:** Myra Quigley; Greg Cesario; Joel Stevens; Doug Holsclaw;
  Richard Woods; Karen Haas; Deborah Tilton; Natalia Chuma.

SECOND TIME AROUND
Studiotrack . . . . *RCA Victor/Camden (M) CAL-928*   66   **10-12**
Studiotrack . . . . *RCA Victor/Camden (S) CAS-928*   66   **12-15**
  Above two also have music from *High Time* and *The Great Imposter*.
  Composer: Henry Mancini. **Conductor:** Henry Mancini.

SECRET ADMIRER
Soundtrack (1985) . . . . *MCA (S) 5611*   85   **8-10**
  Composer: Jan Hammer. **Cast:** Van Stephenson; Tony Carey; Kim Wilde; Don Felder; Klymaxx;
  Nik Kershaw; Rosemary Butler; Arnold McCuller; Timothy B. Schmit; Jan Hammer.

SECRET AGENT
TV Soundtrack . . . . *RCA Victor (M) LPM-3630*   66   **30-40**
TV Soundtrack . . . .*RCA Victor (S) LSP-3630*   66   **60-70**
  Composer: Edwin Astley; others. **Conductor:** Edwin Astley.

SECRET AGENT MEETS THE SAINT
TV Soundtrack . . . . *RCA Victor (M) LPM-3467*   65 $30-40
TV Soundtrack . . . . *.RCA Victor (S) LSP-3467*   65   **50-65**
    Above two have music from *Secret Agent Man* and *The Saint*.
  Composer: Edwin Astley; others. **Conductor:** Edwin Astley.

SECRET GARDEN
Soundtrack (1988) . . . . *Columbia Special Products (S) 19920*   88   **8-10**
  Composer: Sharon Burgett. **Cast:** Barbara Cook; John Cullum; others.

SECRET LIFE OF WALTER MITTY
Original Cast (1964) . . . . *Columbia (M) OL-6320*   64   **15-20**
Original Cast (1964) . . . . *Columbia (S) OS-2720*   64   **20-25**
Original Cast (1964) . . . . *Columbia Special Products (S) AOS-2720*   Re   **8-10**
  Composer: Leon Carr, Earl Shuman. **Conductor:** Joseph Stecko. **Cast:** Mark London; Cathryn
  Damon; Eugene Roche; Christopher Norris; Charles Rydell; Rudy Tronto; Lorraine Serabian
  Rue McClanahan; Lette Rehnolds.

SECRET OF MY SUCCESS
Soundtrack (1987) . . . .*MCA (S) 6205*   87   **8-10**
  Composer: Various. **Cast:** Night Ranger; Pat Benatar; Danny Peck; Nancy Shanks; Bananarama;
  David Foster; Roger Daltrey; Restless Heart; Taxxi.

SECRET OF N.I.M.H.
Soundtrack (1982) . . . . *That's Entertainment (S) TER-1026*   82   **20-25**
  Composer: Jerry Goldsmith. **Conductor:** Jerry Goldsmith.

SECRET OF SANTA VITTORIA
Soundtrack (1969) . . . . *United Artists (S) UAS-5200*   69   **25-30**
  Composer: Ernest Gold; others. **Conductor:** Ernest Gold. **Cast:** Sergio Franchi.

SECRETS OF LIFE
Soundtrack (1956) . . . . *Disneyland (M) WDL-4006*   56   **50-60**
  Composer: Paul J. Smith. **Conductor:** Paul J. Smith.

SEDUCED AND ABANDONED
Soundtrack (1964) . . . .*CAM (M) 100001*   64   **35-40**
  Composer: Carlo Rustichelli. **Conductor:** Pier Luigi Urbini.

SEESAW
Original Cast (1973) . . . . *Buddah (S) BDS-95006*   73   **20-25**
Original Cast (1973) . . . . *Columbia Special Products (S) X-15563*   Re   **8-10**
  Composer: Cy Coleman; Dorothy Fields. **Conductor:** Donald Pippin. **Cast:** Michele Lee; Ken
  Howard; Tommy Tune; Cecelia Norfleet; Giancarol Esposito; LaMonte Des Fontaines.

SELMA
Original Cast (1976) . . . .*Cotillion (S) SD2-110*   76   **15-20**
    Double LP set.
  Composer: Tommy Butler. **Conductor:** Peggy Young. **Cast:** Tommy Butler; Denise Erwin;
  Janice Barnett; Ernie Banks; Jackie Lowe; Rubert Williams; Fred Tucks; Alzena Powell; Carlton
  Williams; Sandra Pitre; Eddie Turner; Mary Anderson; Chris Williams; Smokye Terrell; Susan
  Beaubian.

SERENADE
Soundtrack (1956) . . . . *RCA Victor (M) LM-1996*   56   **20-30**
  Composer: Various operatic composers. **Conductor:** Ray Heindorf. **Cast:** Mario Lanza; Jean
  Fenn; Licia Albanese.

SGT. PEPPER'S LONELY HEARTS CLUB BAND
Soundtrack (1979) . . . . *RSO (S) RS-2-4-41*   79   **$10-15**
   Double LP set.
  Composer: John Lennon; Paul McCartney; George Harrison. **Conductor:** George Martin.
  Cast: Bee Gees; Peter Frampton; Billy Preston; Steve Martin; Earth, Wind and Fire; Paul
  Nicholas; George Burns; Aerosmith; Alice Cooper.

SGT. PRESTON OF THE YUKON
Original Radio Cast . . . . *Golden Age (M) 5028*   78   **8-10**

SERGEANTS 3
Soundtrack (1962) . . . . *Reprise (M) R-2013*   62   **25-30**
Soundtrack (1962) . . . . *Reprise (S) R9-2013*   62   **40-45**
   Remake of *Gunga Din*, a 1939 film.
  Composer: Billy May. **Conductor:** Billy May.

SERPICO
Soundtrack (1973) . . . . *Paramount (S) PAS-1016*   73   **15-20**
  Composer: Mikis Theodorakis. **Conductor:** Mikis Theodorakis.

SESAME STREET
TV Soundtrack (1970) . . . . *Columbia (S) CS-1069*   70   **15-20**
   Includes book and poster.
  Composer: Joe Raposo; Jeffrey Moss; Jon Stone. **Cast:** Jim Henson.

SET TO MUSIC
Original Cast (1939) . . . . *JJC (M) M-3003*   **20-25**
Original Cast (1939) . . . . *JJC (SE) ST-3003*   **12-15**
Original Cast (1939) . . . . *AEI (SE) 2103*   Re   **8-10**
  Composer: Noel Coward. **Cast:** Beatrice Lillie.

SEVEN BRIDES FOR SEVEN BROTHERS
London Studio Cast . . . . *DRG (S) DS-15025*   **8-12**
Soundtrack (1954) . . . . *MGM (EP) X-244*   54   **15-20**
   Double EP set.
Soundtrack (1954) . . . . *MGM (M) E-244*   54   **35-40**
   10-inch LP.
Soundtrack (1954) . . . . *MGM (M) E-3768*   54   **20-25**
   Also has music from *Three Little Words*.
Soundtrack (1954) . . . . *MCA (SE) 25021*   Re   **8-10**
  Composer: Johnny Mercer. **Conductor:** Adolph Deutsch. **Cast:** Howard Keel; Jane Powell;
  Bill Lee; Virginia Gibson.
  Also see ROYAL WEDDING

SEVEN COME ELEVEN (A GAMING GAMBOL)
Original Cast (1961) . . . . *Columbia (M) XLP-55477*   61 $150-175
  Special pressing, sold at the theatre during the show's run.
Original Cast (1961) . . . . *Columbia (M) OL-5740*   61   100-125
  Cast: William Roy and Carl Norman at the plural pianos.

SEVEN DEADLY SINS
Studio Cast (1971) . . . . *Columbia (M) KL-5175*   71   30-35
  Performed in the German language.
  Composer: Kurt Weill; Bertolt Brecht. **Conductor:** Wilhelm Bruckner-Ruggeberg. **Cast:** Lotte
  Lenya; Julius Katona; Fritz Gollnitz; Ernest Poettgen.

SEVEN DREAMS
Studio Cast (1953) . . . . *Decca (M) DL-9011*   53   35-40
  Composer: Gordon Jenkins. **Conductor:** Gordon Jenkins. **Cast:** Bill Lee; Laurie Carroll; Jeanette
  Nolan; John McIntire; Beverly Mahr; Ernie Newton; Virginia Rees; Dick Beals; Thurl
  Ravenscroft; Keith Carver; Dave Knight; Ralph Brewster; Cornelia Davis; Ray Linn; Chuck
  Schrouder; Ralph Brewster Singers.

SEVEN GOLDEN MEN
Soundtrack (1969) . . . . *United Artists (SE) UAS-5193*   69   20-25
  Composer: Armando Trovajoli. **Conductor:** Armando Trovajoli.

SEVEN HILLS OF ROME
Soundtrack (1958) . . . .*RCA Victor (EP) EPA-4222*   58   10-15
Soundtrack (1958) . . . . *RCA Victor (M) LM-2211*   58   25-30
  One side has assorted Mario Lanza songs.
  Composer: Victor Young; Harold Adamson; others. **Cast:** Mario Lanza.

SEVEN LITTLE FOYS
Soundtrack (1955) . . . .*RCA Victor (EP) EPB-3275*   55   15-20
  Double EP set.
Soundtrack (1955) . . . . *RCA Victor (M) LPM-3275*   55   50-55
  Composer: Joesph J. Lilley. **Conductor:** Joseph J. Lilley. **Cast:** Bob Hope; James Cagney.

SEVEN LIVELY ARTS
Studio Cast . . . . *Sound Stage (S) 2305*   8-10
  Also has music from *The Boys*.

SEVENTEEN
Original Cast (1951) . . . . *RCA Victor (M) LOC-1003*   51   100-125
Original Cast (1951) . . . . *RCA Victor (M) CBM1-2034*   Re   10-12
  Composer: Walter Kent; Kim Gannon. **Conductor:** Vincent Travers. **Cast:** Ann Crowley;
  Kenneth Nelson; Doris Dalton; Frank Albertson; Dick Kallman; Helen Wood; Harrison Muller;
  Maurice Ellis; Alonzo Bonsan; Joan Bowman; Bonnie Brae; Carol Cole; Sherron McCutcheon.

1776
Original Cast (1969) . . . .*Columbia (S) BOS-3310*   69   8-12
  Conductor: Peter Howard. **Cast:** William Daniels; Paul Hecht; Clifford David; David Ford;
  Virginia Vestoff; Rex Everheart; Ken Howard; Ronald Holgate; Betty Buckley; Scott Jarvis;
  B.J.Slater; William Duell; David Vosburgh; Henry LeClair.
Soundtrack (1972) . . . . *Columbia (S) S-31741*   72   20-25
  Composer: Sherman Edwards. **Conductor:** Ray Heindorf. **Cast:** William Daniels; Howard
  DaSilva; Ken Howard; David Ford; Virginia Vestoff; Ronald Holgate; Rex Robbins; Blythe
  Danner; William Duell; Mark Montgomery; Ralston Hill.

SEVENTH DAWN
Soundtrack (1964) . . . .*United Artists (M) UAL-4115*   64   20-25
Soundtrack (1964) . . . . *United Artists (S) UAS-5115*   64   25-30
  Composer: Riz Ortolani. **Conductor:** Riz Ortolani.

SEVENTH HEAVEN
  Original Cast (1955) .... *Decca (M) DL-9001*   55   **$150-175**
    Composer: Victor Young; Stella Unger. **Conductor:** Max Meth. **Cast:** Gloria DeHaven; Ricardo
    Montalban; Robert Clary; Chita Rivera; Patricia Hammerlee; Gerianne Raphael.

7th VOYAGE OF SINBAD
  Soundtrack (1958) .... *Colpix (M) CP-504*   59   **175-200**
  Soundtrack (1958) .... *Varese Sarabande (S) STV-81135*   83   **8-10**
    Composer: Bernard Herrmann. **Conductor:** Bernard Herrmann.

70 GIRLS, 70
  Original Cast (1971) .... *Columbia (S) S-30589*   71   **35-45**
    Composer: John Kander; Fred Ebb. **Conductor:** Oscar Kosarin. **Cast:** Mildred Natwick; Hans
    Conried; Lillian Roth; Gil Lamb; Lillian Hayman; Joey Faye; Lucie Lancaster; Coley Worth;
    Ruth Gillette; Steve Mills; Abby Lewis; Lloyd Harris; Beau Tilden; Jay Velie.

77 SUNSET STRIP
  TV Soundtrack (1958) .... *Warner Bros. (M) W-1289*   59   **20-25**
  TV Soundtrack (1958) .... *Warner Bros. (S) WS-1289*   59   **35-40**
    Composer: Jerry Livingston; Alex North; Mack David; others. **Conductor:** Warren Barker.
    Cast: Warren Barker and His Orchestra.
  Studiotrack (1958) .... *Jubilee (M) J-1106*   59   **15-20**
  Studiotrack (1958) .... *Jubilee (S) SDJ-1106*   59   **25-30**
    Jazz selections.
    Cast: Frankie Ortega Trio.
  Studiotrack (1959) .... *Lion (M) L-70116*   59   **10-15**
    Actual title: *Music from 77 Sunset Strip.*
    Conductor: Aaron Bell. **Cast:** Aaron Bell and His Orchestra.

SEX AND THE SINGLE GIRL
  Soundtrack (1964) .... *Warner Bros. (M) W-1572*   64   **15-20**
  Soundtrack (1964) .... *Warner Bros. (S) WS-1572*   64   **30-35**
    Composer: Neal Hefti; others. **Conductor:** Neal Hefti. **Cast:** Fran Jeffries.

SEX LIFE OF PRIMATE (AND OTHER BITS OF GOSSIP)
  Studio Cast (1963) .... *Verve (M) 15043*   63   **20-25**
    Cast: Shelly Berman; Jerry Stiller; Anne Meara; Lovelady Powell. (Comedy, dialogue.)

SHADOW
  Original Radio Cast .... *Golden Age (M) 5029*   78   **8-10**
  Original Radio Cast (1973) .... *Mark '56 (M) 591*   **8-10**
    Promotional issue from Coca-Cola.

SHAFT
  Soundtrack (1971) .... *Enterprise (S) ENS-2-5002*   71   **12-15**
  Soundtrack (1971) .... *Stax (S) 88002*   Re   **8-12**
    Above two are double LP sets.
  Composer: Isaac Hayes. **Conductor:** Isaac Hayes. **Cast:** Isaac Hayes.
  Also see MAN FROM SHAFT

SHAFT IN AFRICA
Soundtrack (1973) .... *ABC (S) ABCX-793*   73 $15-18
   Composer: Johnny Pate; Dennis Lambert; Brian Potter. Conductor: Johnny Pate. Cast: Four
   Tops.

SHAFT'S BIG SCORE
Soundtrack (1972) .... *MGM (S) 1SE-36*   72   10-12
   Composer: Gordon Parks. Conductor: Richard Hazard. Cast: O.C. Smith.

SHAG
Soundtrack (1989) .... *Sire (S) 1-25800*   89   8-10
   Composer: Various. Cast: La Vern Baker; K.D. Lang and the Reclines; Randy Newman; Ben E.
   King; Louise Goffin; Charmettes; Hank Ballard; Chris Isaak; Tommy Page; Take 6.

SHAGGY DOG
Soundtrack (1959) .... *Disneyland (M) WDL-3044*   59   25-30
Soundtrack (1959) .... *Disneyland (M) WDL-1044*   62   15-20
   Cast: Paul Frees; Roberta Shore; Kevin Corcoran.
   Also see ABSENT-MINDED PROFESSOR; UGLY DACHSHUND

SHAKE HANDS WITH THE DEVIL
Soundtrack (1959) .... *United Artists (M) UAL-4043*   59   50-60
Soundtrack (1959) .... *United Artists (SE) UAS-5043*   59   35-40
   Composer: William Alwyn. Conductor: Muir Mathieson.

SHAKESPEARE WALLAH
Soundtrack (1966) .... *Epic (M) FLM-13110*   66   25-30
Soundtrack (1966) .... *Epic (SE) FLS-15110*   66   25-30
   Composer: Satyajit Ray; others. Conductor: Alok Dey. Cast: Mubarak Begum.

SHALAKO
Soundtrack (1968) .... *Philips (S) PHS-600-286*   68   25-30
   Composer: Robert Farnon; Muir Mathieson; Jim Dale. Conductor: Muir Mathieson.

SHANGRI-LA
Original Cast/TV Soundtrack (1956/1960) ..*Sound of Broadway (M) 300/1*   10-15
   Both the 1956 original cast and the 1960 TV soundtrack. Also has selections from *Shinbone Alley*.
   Composer: Harry Warren. Cast: Marisa Pavan; Richard Basehart; Helen Gallagher; Alice
   Ghostley; Gene Nelson.

SHARE MY LETTUCE
Original Cast .... *Nexa (S) NPL-18011*   8-12
   Composer: Keith Stratham; Patrick Gowers. Conductor: Anthony Bowles. Cast: Kenneth
   Williams; Maggie Smith; Philip Gilbert; others.

MUSIC FROM THE SOUNDTRACK OF
"SHE"
MUSIC COMPOSED BY MAX STEINER

SHARKY'S MACHINE
Soundtrack (1981) . . . . *Warner Bros. (S) BSK-3653*   81   **$8-10**
Composer: Waylon Jennings; Joe Sample; Lorenz Hart; Richard Rodgers; Snuff Garrett; others.
Conductor: Al Capps. Cast: Randy Crawford; Flora Purim; Buddy De Franco; Manhattan
Transfer; Chet Baker; Doc Severinsen; Sarah Vaughan; Joe Williams; Julie London; Peggy
Lee; Eddie Harris.

SHE
Soundtrack (1935) . . . . *Varese Sarabande (M) 80004*   **8-12**
Composer: Max Steiner.

SHE LOVES ME
Original Cast (1963) . . . . *MGM (M) E-41180C-2*   63   **30-35**
Original Cast (1963) . . . . *MGM (S) SE-41180C-2*   63   **40-45**
Above two are double LP sets.
Original Cast (1963) . . . . *Stet (S) DS-15008*   Re   **15-20**
Double LP set.
Composer: Jerry Bock; Sheldon Harnick. Conductor: Harold Hastings. Cast: Barbara Cook;
Daniel Massey; Barbara Baxley; Jack Cassidy; Nathaniel Frey; Ralph Williams; Jo Wilder; Wood
Romoff; Gino Conforti; Joe Ross; Marion Brash; Trude Adams; Peg Murray; Ludwig Donath.

SHE'S GOTTA HAVE IT
Soundtrack (1986) . . . . *Island (S) 90528-1*   86   **8-10**

SHE'S HAVING A BABY
Soundtrack (1988) . . . . *I.R.S. (S) 6211*   88   **8-10**
Composer: Various. Cast: Everything But The Girl; Bryan Ferry; Gene Loves Jezebel; Dr.;
XTC; Love and Rockets; Carmel; Dave Wakeling; Kate Bush; Kirsty MacColl.

SHE'S OUT OF CONTROL
Soundtrack (1989) . . . . *MCA (S) 6281*   89   **8-10**
Composer: Various. Cast: Troy Hinton; Brenda K. Starr; Phil Thornalley; Boys Club; Harold
Faltermeyer; Jim Ladd; Oingo Boingo; Brian Wilson; Frankie Avalon; Kinks; Jetboy.

SHEBA BABY
Soundtrack (1975) . . . . *Buddah (S) BDS-5634*   75   **10-15**
Composer: Higgins; Brown. Conductor: Higgins; Brown.

SHEENA
Soundtrack (1984) . . . . *Varesa Sarabande (S) 81225*   84   **8-10**

SHENANDOAH
Original Cast (1974) . . . . *RCA Victor (S) ARL1-1019*   74   **15-20**
Original Cast (1974) . . . . *RCA Victor (S) AGL1-3763*   81   **8-10**
Composer: Gary Geld; Peter Udell. Cast: John Cullum; Donna Theodore; Penelope Milford;
Joel Higgins; Chip Ford; Ted Agress; Gordon Halliday; Gary Harger; Charles Welch; David
Russell; Jordan Suffin.
Soundtrack (1965) . . . . *Decca (M) DL-9125*   65   **20-25**
Soundtrack (1965) . . . . *Decca (S) DL7-9125*   65   **30-35**
Composer: Frank Skinner; others. Conductor: Joseph Gershenson. Cast: James Stewart
(narration).

SHINBONE ALLEY
(ARCHY AND MEHITABEL)
Studio Cast (1954) . . . . *Columbia (M) ML-4963*   54   **25-25**
Studio Cast (1954) . . . . *Columbia (M) OL-4963*   54   **20-25**
One side is titled *Echos of Archy*.
Composer: George Klinesinger; Joe Darion. Conductor: George Klinesinger. Cast: Carol
Channing; Eddie Bracken; David Wayne; Percival Dove.
Also see SHANGRI-LA

SHINING
Soundtrack (1980) . . . . *Warner Bros. (S) HS-3449* 80 $12-15
  Composer: Wendy Carlos; Rachel Elkind; Gyorgy Ligeti; Bela Bartok; others.
  Conductor: Ernest Bour; Herbert von Karajan; others.

SHIP OF FOOLS
Soundtrack (1965) . . . . *RCA Victor (M) LM-2817* 65   **40-50**
Soundtrack (1965) . . . . *RCA Victor (S) LSC-2817* 65   **85-100**
  Composer: Ernest Gold. Conductor: Arthur Fiedler. Cast: Boston Pops Orchestra.

SHIRLEY MacLAINE LIVE AT THE PALACE
Original Cast (1976) . . . . *Columbia (S) PC-34223* 76   8-12
  From an August 19, 1976, performance.
  Composer: Various. Conductor: Donn Trenner. Cast: Shirley MacLaine; Adam Grammis;
  Candy Brown; Gary Flannery; JoAnn Lehman; Larry Vickers.

SHIRLEY TEMPLE - COMPLETE SHIRLEY TEMPLE SONG BOOK
Soundtrack . . . . *20th Century-Fox (S) TCS-103-2*   10-15
  Double LP of soundtrack songs.
  Cast: Shirley Temple.

SHOCK TREATMENT
Soundtrack (1981) . . . . *Warner Bros. (S) LLA-3615* 81   8-10
  Composer: Richard O'Brien; Richard Hartley. Conductor: Richard Hartley.

SHOCKER
Soundtrack . . . . *SBK (S) K1-93233*   8-10

SHOES OF THE FISHERMAN
Soundtrack (1968) . . . . *MGM (S) S1E-15* 68   25-30
Soundtrack (1968) . . . . *MCA (S) 25130*   8-10
  Composer: Alex North. Conductor: Alex North.

SHOESTRING '57
Original Cast (1957) . . . . *Offbeat (M) O-4012* 60   40-50
Original Cast (1957) . . . . *Painted Smiles (M) PS-1362* Re   8-10
  Composer: Shelley Mowell; Charles Strouse; Harvey Schmidt; others. Conductor: Dorothea
  Freitag. Cast: Beatrice Arthur; Fay DeWitt; Dody Goodman; Dorothy Greener; John Bartis;
  Danny Carroll; Bill McCutcheon.

SHOESTRING REVUE
Original Cast (1955) . . . . *Offbeat (M) O-4011* 59   40-45
Original Cast (1955) . . . . *Painted Smiles (M) PS-1360* Re   8-10
  Composer: Charles Strouse; David Barker; Sheldon Harnick; others. Conductor: Dorothea
  Freitag. Cast: Beatrice Arthur; Fay DeWitt; Dody Goodman; Dorothy Greener; John Bartis;
  Eddie Hilton.

SHOGUN
TV Soundtrack (1981) . . . . *RSO (S) RX-1-3088* 80   8-10
  Composer: Maurice Jarre. Conductor: Maurice Jarre.

SHOGUN ASSASSIN
Soundtrack (1980) . . . . *Baby Cart (S) 4148-49*   10-15
  Promotional Issue.
  Composer: W. Michael Lewis; Mark Lindsay; Robert Houston. Conductor: W. Michael Lewis;
  Mark Lindsay; Robert Houston.

SHOOT THE PIANO PLAYER
Soundtrack (1962) . . . . *Philips (EP) PLP-4005* 62   25-30
  Composer: Georges Delerue. Conductor: Georges Delerue.

SHOOTING PARTY
Soundtrack .... *Varese Sarabande (S) 81235*   **$8-10**
  Conductor: John Scott. Cast: Royal Philharmonic Orchestra.

SHOP ON MAIN STREET
Soundtrack (1966) .... *Mainstream (M) 56082*   67   **35-40**
Soundtrack (1966) .... *Mainstream (S) S-6082*   67   **50-60**
  Composer: Zdenek Liska.

SHORT EYES
Soundtrack (1977) .... *Curtom (S) CU-5017*   77   **10-15**
  Composer: Curtis Mayfield. Conductor: Curtis Mayfield.

SHOTGUN SLADE
TV Soundtrack (1959) .... *Mercury (M) MG-20575*   59   **30-35**
TV Soundtrack (1959) .... *Mercury (S) SR-60235*   59   **45-50**
  Composer: Gerald Fried. Conductor: Stanley Wilson.

SHOW BIZ (FROM VAUDE TO VIDEO)
Original Cast .... *RCA Victor (M) LOC-1011*   54   **25-35**
  Composer: Various. Conductor: Norman Layden. Cast: Georgie Jessel (narrator); Gene Austin;
  Ben Bernie; Bing Crosby; Fanny Brice; Eddie Cantor; George M. Cohan; Tommy Dorsey; Jimmy
  Durante; Sophie Tucker; George Gershwin; Will Rogers; Kate Smith; others.

SHOW BOAT
Original Cast .... *Columbia (M) C-55*   **15-20**
Original Cast .... *Columbia Special Products (M) AC-55*   Re   **8-10**
  Has members of the original cast, the 1932 revival cast, 1936 film cast, original London cast, and a studio
  cast.
  Composer: Jerome Kern; Oscar Hammerstein II. Conductor: Victor Young. Cast: Helen
  Morgan; James Melton; Paul Robeson; Frank Munn; Countess Albani.
Original Revival Cast (1946) .... *Columbia (M) OL-4058*   **25-30**
  Composer: Jerome Kern; Oscar Hammerstein II. Conductor: Edwin McArthur. Cast: Jan
  Clayton; Carol Bruce; Charles Fredericks; Kenneth Spencer; Helen Dowdy; Colette Lyons.
Original Revival Cast (1966) .... *RCA Victor (M) LOC-1126*   66   **10-15**
Original Revival Cast (1966) .... *RCA Victor (S) LSO-1126*   66   **12-18**
  Composer: Jerome Kern; Oscar Hammerstein II. Conductor: Franz Allers. Cast: Barbara Cook;
  Constance Towers; Stephen Douglass; David Wayne; William Warfield; Rosetta LeNoire; Allyn
  Ann McLerie; Eddie Phillips.
Original London Revival Cast .... *Stanyan (S) SR-10048*   72   **10-15**
  Double LP set.
  Composer: Jerome Kern; Oscar Hammerstein II. Conductor: Ray Cook. Cast: Andre Jobim;
  Cleo Laine; Thomas Carey; Kenneth Nelson; Lorna Dallas; Jan Hunt; Ena Cabayo.
London Studio Cast .... *Stanyan (S) SR-10036*   72   **8-10**
  Composer: Jerome Kern; Oscar Hammerstein II. Conductor: Michael Collins. Cast: Shirley
  Bassey; Marlys Watters; Don McKay; Dora Bryan; Geoffrey Webb; Isabelle Lucas; Williams
  Singers.

Studio Cast (1959) .... *RCA Victor (M) LOC-1505*	59	**$20-25**
Studio Cast (1959) .... *RCA Victor (S) LSO-1505*	59	**35-40**

Composer: Jerome Kern; Oscar Hammerstein II. Conductor: Henri Rene. Cast: Howard Keel; Anne Jeffreys; Gogi Grant.

Studio Cast (1956) .... *RCA Victor (M) LM-2008*	56	**30-35**

Composer: Jerome Kern; Oscar Hammerstein II. Conductor: Lehman Engel. Cast: Robert Merrill; Patrice Munsel; Rise Stevens; Katherine Graves; Janet Pavek.

Studio Cast (1976) .... *RCA Victor (M) AVM1-1741*	76	**8-10**
Studio Cast (1962) .... *Columbia (M) OL-5820*	62	**10-12**
Studio Cast (1962) .... *Columbia (S) OS-2220*	62	**12-15**

Composer: Jerome Kern; Oscar Hammerstein II. Conductor: Franz Allers. Cast: John Raitt; Barbara Cook; William Warfield; Anita Darian; Fay DeWitt; Louise Parker; Merrill Staton Choir.

Studio Cast (1959) .... *RCA Victor/Camden (S) CAS-488*	59	**10-20**

Composer: Jerome Kern; Oscar Hammerstein II. Conductor: Hill Bowen. Cast: Barbara Leigh; Andy Cole; Bryan Johnson; Patricia Clark; Maxine Daniels; Denis Quilley; Ivor Emmanuel.

Studio Cast (1942) .... *RCA Victor (M) LM-9002*		**10-15**

One side has various show tunes by Robert Merrill.

Composer: Jerome Kern; Oscar Hammerstein II. Conductor: John Scott Trotter. Cast: Robert Merrill; Dorothy Kirsten.

Soundtrack (1951) .... *MGM (EP) X-84*		**10-15**
Soundtrack (1951) .... *MGM (M) K-84*	51	**15-20**

Four disc, boxed set.

Soundtrack (1951) .... *MGM (M) E-559*	51	**35-40**

10-inch LP.

Soundtrack (1951) .... *Metro (M) M-527*	65	**15-20**
Soundtrack (1951) .... *Metro (SE) MS-527*	65	**15-20**
Soundtrack (1951) .... *MCA (SE) 1429*	Re	**8-10**

Composer: Jerome Kern; Oscar Hammerstein II. Conductor: Adolph Deutsch. Cast: Kathryn Grayson; Howard Keel; Marge Champion; Gower Champion; William Warfield; Ava Gardner.

Studiotrack (1960) .... *Columbia (M) CL-1419*	60	**15-20**
Studiotrack (1960) .... *Columbia (S) CS-8216*	60	**20-25**

Jazz interpretations.

Composer: Jerome Kern; Oscar Hammerstein II. Conductor: John Carisi. Cast: Guitar Choir; Bob Brookmeyer (trombone); Phil Woods (alto sax); John Carisi (trumpet).

Also see AN AMERICAN IN PARIS; CAT AND THE FIDDLE; LOVELY TO LOOK AT; PORGY AND BESS; RIO RITA.

SHOWCASE ALBUM, 1967

TV Soundtrack (1966) .... *WNDT (M) 101*   67   **$50-60**
Recordings excerpted from the 1966 - 1967 season of "Sunday Showcase" TV specials, prepared by
WNDT radio, New York.
Composer: Various. **Conductor:** Allan Miller; Abba Bogin. **Cast:** Brock Peters (narration); Rod
Steiger; Linda Lavin; Richard Morse; James Daley; Michael Tolan; Marion Williams; Clair
Bloom; Robert White; Joseph Ladone; Standwells; Suzanne Grossmann; Colleen Dewhurst; Lee
Goodman; George Tipton; Jay Berliner; K Kathleen Wideoes; Howard Da Silva; Nancy Dussault;
Kenneth Haigh. (With dialogue.)

SHOWDOWN

Soundtrack (1973) .... *National Features (EP) 2785*   73   **20-30**
Interviews with film's stars, Dean Martin and Rock Hudson. Includes script. Promotional issue only.
Cast: Dean Martin; Rock Hudson. (Dialogue.)

SHOWGIRL (CAROL CHANNING LIVE)

Original Cast (1961) .... *Roulette (M) R-80001*   61   **20-25**
Original Cast (1961) .... *Roulette (S) SR-80001*   61   **35-40**
Original Cast (1961) .... *Forum (M) F-9054*   63   **15-20**
Original Cast (1961) .... *Forum (S) FS-9054*   63   **25-30**
Composer: Charles Gaynor; others. **Conductor:** Robert Hunter. **Cast:** Carol Channing; Jules
Munshin; Les Quat' Jeudis.
Original Revue (1961) .... *Vanguard (M) D-2041*   61   **20-25**
Original Revue (1961) .... *Vanguard (S) VSD-2041*   61   **25-30**
Composer: Charles Gaynor; others. **Conductor:** George Bauer; Robert Hunter.

SHUFFLE ALONG

Original Cast (1921) .... *New World (M) NW-260*   **8-10**
Cast: Eubie Blake; Noble Sissle; Gertrude Saunders.
Studio Cast .... *Columbia (S) C2S-847*   **15-20**
Double LP set.
Composer: Eubie Blake; Noble Sissle. **Cast:** Eubie Blake; Noble Sissle.
Also see BLACKBIRDS OF 1928

SICILIAN

Soundtrack (1987) .... *Virgin Movie Music (S) 90682-1*   87   **8-10**
Conductor: David Mansfield. **Cast:** Hungarian State Symphony.

SICILIAN CLAN

Soundtrack (1970) .... *20th Century-Fox (S) TFS-4209*   70   **35-40**
Composer: Ennio Morricone. **Conductor:** Ennio Morricone.

SID AND NANCY

Soundtrack (1986) .... *MCA (S) 6181*   86   **8-10**

SIDE BY SIDE BY SONDHEIM
Original Cast (1977) . . . . *RCA Victor (S) CBL2-1851*   77   **$15-20**
    Double LP set.
    Composer: Stephen Sondheim. **Conductor:** Tim Higgs; Stuart Pedlar. **Cast:** Millicent Martin;
    Julia McKenzie; David Kernan; Tim Higgs; Stuart Pedler; Ned Sherrin.

SIDE BY SIDE 75
Original Cast (1975) . . . .*No Label Shown (S) No Number Used*   75   **10-20**
    Composer: Stanford Agency. **Cast:** Larry Muhoberac.

SIDEHACKERS
Soundtrack (1969) . . . . *Amaret (S) ST-5004*   70   **15-20**
    Composer: Jerry Styner; Guy Hemric; others. **Cast:** New Life.

SIESTA
Soundtrack (1987) . . . . *Warner Bros. (S) 1-25655*   87   **8-10**
    Full title: *(Music from) Siesta*
    Composer: Miles Davis. **Cast:** Miles Davis.

SIGMUND AND THE SEA MONSTERS:
see FRIENDS

SIGN OF AQUARIUS
Soundtrack (1969) . . . . *Adell (S) ASLP-216*   69   **25-30**
    Composer: Al Zbacinc; Tom Baker; Ed Golya; Allen Baker. **Conductor:** Tom Baker.

SILENCERS
Soundtrack (1966) . . . . *RCA Victor (M) LOC-1120*   66   **15-20**
Soundtrack (1966) . . . . *RCA Victor (S) LSO-1120*   66   **20-30**
    Composer: Elmer Bernstein. **Conductor:** Elmer Bernstein. **Cast:** Vikki Carr.
Studiotrack (1966) . . . . *Reprise (EP) SR-6211*   66   **10-15**
    Stereo jukebox EP, with six tracks.
Studiotrack (1966) . . . . *Reprise (M) R-6211*   66   **15-20**
Studiotrack (1966) . . . .*Reprise (S) RS-6211*   66   **15-20**
    Actual title: *Dean Martin as Matt Helm Sings Songs from The Silencers.*
    Composer: Elmer Bernstein; Hal David; Billy Hill; Howard Greenfield; Jerry Keller; Al Jolson;
    Charlie Chaplin; others. **Conductor:** Ernie Freeman; Gene Page. **Cast:** Dean Martin.

SILENT MOVIE
Soundtrack (1976) . . . .*United Artists (S) UA-LA672-G*   76   **10-15**
    Composer: John Morris; Jacob Gade; Margarita Lecuona. **Conductor:** Lionel Newman.

SILENT PARTNER
  Soundtrack (1979) . . . . *Pablo Today (S) 2312-103*   78   **$8-10**
    Composer: Oscar Peterson. **Cast:** Oscar Peterson; Benny Carter; Clark Terry; Zoot Sims; Milt
    Jackson; John Heard; Grady Tate.

SILENT RUNNING
  Soundtrack (1972) . . . . *Decca (S) DL7-9188*   73   **40-45**
  Soundtrack (1972) . . . . *Varese Sarabande (S) VC-81072*   Re   **15-20**
    Green vinyl.
    Composer: Peter Schickele. **Cast:** Joan Baez; Peter Schickele.

SILK STOCKINGS
  Original Cast (1955) . . . . *RCA Victor (EP) EOC-1016*   55   **12-18**
  Original Cast (1955) . . . . *RCA Victor (M) LOC-1016*   55   **40-45**
    Gatefold cover.
  Original Cast (1955) . . . . *RCA Victor (M) LOC-1102*   65   **25-30**
    Composer: Cole Porter. **Conductor:** Herbert Greene. **Cast:** Hildegarde Kneff; Don Ameche;
    Gretchen Wyler; George Tobias; Leon Belasco; Henry Lascoe; David Opatoshu.
  Original Cast (1955) . . . . *RCA Victor (SE) LSO-1102*   65   **25-30**
  Original Cast (1955) . . . . *RCA Victor (SE) CBM1-2208*   77   **8-10**
    Composer: Cole Porter. **Conductor:** Herbert Greene. **Cast:** Hildegarde Kneff; Don Ameche;
    Gretchen Wyler; George Tobias; Leon Belasco; Henry Lascoe; David Opatoshu.
  Soundtrack (1957) . . . . *MGM (M) E-3542*   57   **25-30**
  Soundtrack (1957) . . . . *MCA (SE) 39074*   **8-10**
    Composer: Cole Porter. **Conductor:** Andre Previn; Johnny Green. **Cast:** Fred Astaire; Cyd
    Charisse; Janis Paige; Carol Richards; Peter Lorre; Joseph Buloff; Jules Munshin.
    Also see PAJAMA GAME

SILKWOOD
  Soundtrack (1984) . . . . *DRG (S) 6107*   84   **8-10**
    Cast: Meryl Streep (vocal).

SILVER CHALICE
    Composer: Franz Waxman. **Conductor:** Elmer Bernstein.

SILVER LAKE
  Original Cast (1980) . . . . *Nonesuch (S) DB-79003*   80   **10-12**
    Double LP set.
    Composer: Kurt Weill. **Conductor:** Julius Rudel. **Cast:** Joel Grey; William Neill; Elizabeth
    Hynes; Elaine Bonazzi; Jack Harrold.

SILVERADO
  Soundtrack (1985) . . . . *Geffen (S) GHS-24080*   85   **12-15**
    Composer: Bruce Broughton. **Conductor:** Bruce Broughton.

SIMPLY HEAVENLY
  Original Cast (1957) . . . . *Columbia (M) OL-5240*   57   **35-40**
    Composer: David Martin; Langston Hughes. **Conductor:** David Martin. **Cast:** Claudia McNeil;
    Melvin Stewart; Anna English; Brownie McGhee; Marilyn Berry; Duke Williams; John Boule.

SINCE YOU WENT AWAY
  Soundtrack (1944) . . . . *Citadel (M) MS-3/4*   76   **75-85**
    Double LP set. Private recording, not issued commercially.
    Composer: Max Steiner. **Conductor:** Max Steiner.

SINCERELY YOURS
  Soundtrack (1955) . . . . *Columbia (M) CL-800*   56   **40-50**
    Based on the 1932 film *The Man who Played God*. Includes some classical selections.
    Composer: Various. **Conductor:** Gordon Robinson. **Cast:** Liberace (piano); Warner Bros.
    Symphony Orchestra.

SING
Soundtrack (1989) .... *Columbia (S) SC-45086*   89   **$8-10**
  Composer: Various. **Cast:** Mickey Thomas; Art Garfunkel; Patti La Belle; Laurnea Wilkerson; Joe Williams; Bill Champlin; Paul Carrack; Terri Nunn; Michael Bolton; Cast of "Sarafina"; Nia Peeples; Johnny Kemp.

SING BOY SING
Soundtrack (1958) .... *Capitol (EP) EPA-1-929*   58   **10-15**
Soundtrack (1958) .... *Capitol (EP) EPA-2-929*   58   **10-15**
Soundtrack (1958) .... *Capitol (EP) EPA-3-929*   58   **10-15**
Soundtrack (1958) .... *Capitol (M) T-929*   57   **35-40**
  Composer: Tommy Sands; Lionel Newman; others. **Conductor:** Lionel Newman. **Cast:** Tommy Sands.

SING FOR YOUR SUPPER
Studio Cast (1960) .... *Vanguard (M) VRS-9066*   60   **20-25**
  Composer: Earl Robinson; John Latouche. **Conductor:** Robert DeCormier. **Cast:** Odetta; DeCormier Chorale.
Studio Cast (1974) .... *United Artists (S) UA-LA604-G*   74   **10-12**
  Composer: Earl Robinson; John Latouche. **Conductor:** Leonard DePaur. **Cast:** Brock Peters.
Studio Cast (1976) .... *RCA Victor (M) AVM1-1739*   76   **8-10**
  Composer: Earl Robinson; John Latouche. **Conductor:** Nathaniel Shilkret. **Cast:** Paul Robeson.

SING OUT SWEET LAND
Original Cast (1944) ....*Decca (M) DL-8023*   50   **50-60**
Original Cast (1944) ....*Decca (M) DL-4304*   63   **25-30**
Original Cast (1944) .... *Decca (SE) DL-74304*   63   **25-30**
  Conductor: Elie Siegmeister. **Cast:** Burl Ives; Alma Kaye; Alfred Drake; Bibi Osterwald; Juanita Hall; Ted Tiller; Jack McCauley; Herk Armstrong.

SINGER PRESENTS TONY BENNETT
TV Soundtrack (1966) .... *Columbia (S) CSS-552*   66   **15-20**
  Composer: Various. **Conductor:** Ralph Burns. **Cast:** Tony Bennett.

SINGIN' IN THE RAIN
Original London Cast (1983) .... *Rain (S) 1*   84   **10-15**
  Composer: Nacio Herb Brown; Arthur Freed; Betty Comden; Adolf Green; Roger Edens; Dorothy Fields; Jimmy McHugh Geroge; Ira Geshwin. **Cast:** Tommy Steele; Roy Castle; Sarah Payne; Danielle Carson.
Soundtrack (1952) .... *MGM (EP) X-113*   52   **12-18**
Soundtrack (1952) .... *MGM (M) E-113*   52   **35-40**
  10-inch LP.
Soundtrack (1952) ....*MGM (M) E-3770*   60   **20-25**
  One side has music from *Till the Clouds Roll By*.
Soundtrack (1952) .... *Metro (M) M-599*   67   **15-20**
Soundtrack (1952) .... *Metro (SE) MS-599*   67   **15-20**
Soundtrack (1952) .... *MCA (SE) 39044*   86   **8-10**
  Composer: Herb Nacio Brown; others. **Conductor:** Lennie Hayton. **Cast:** Gene Kelly; Donald O'Connor; Debbie Reynolds.
  Also see RICH, YOUNG AND PRETTY

SINGING NUN
Soundtrack (1966) ....*MGM (M) 1E-7*   66   **15-20**
Soundtrack (1966) .... *MGM (S) S1E-7*   66   **25-30**
Soundtrack (1966) ....*MCA (S) 25090*   Re   **8-10**
  Composer: Randy Sparks; Soeur Sourire; others. **Conductor:** Harry Sukman. **Cast:** Debbie Reynolds.

SINGING NUN (continued)
Studiotrack (1966) . . . . *Metro (M) M-569*   66   **$10-12**
Studiotrack (1966) . . . . *Metro MS-569*   66   **10-15**
Full title: *The Singing Nun - Music from the MGM Motion Picture*. Orchestral versions of the soundtrack songs.
Composer: Randy Sparks; Soeur Sourire. **Conductor:** Joe Cain. **Cast:** Joe Cain and His Orchestra.

SINGLE ROOM FURNISHED
Soundtrack (1968) . . . . *Sidewalk (S) ST-5917*   68   **25-35**
Composer: James Sheldon. **Conductor:** James Sheldon. **Cast:** Paris Sisters; Jack Irwin.

SISTERS
Soundtrack (1973) . . . . *Entr' acte (Q) ERQ-7001*   73   **30-40**
Soundtrack (1973) . . . . *Southern Cross (S) SCAR-5004*   Re   **8-10**
Composer: Bernard Herrmann. **Conductor:** Bernard Herrmann. **Cast:** Bernard Herrmann and His Orchestra.

SIX MILLION DOLLAR MAN - BIRTH OF BIONIC
Studio Cast . . . . *Peter Pan (M) 5R-579*   **8-10**
Children's story record.

SIX PACK
Soundtrack (1982) . . . . *Alegiance (S) 430*   82   **8-10**

633 SQUADRON
Soundtrack (1964) . . . . *United Artists (S) UA-LA305-G*   74   **12-15**
Composer: Ron Goodwin. **Conductor:** Ron Goodwin.

SIXTEEN DAYS OF GLORY (1984 SUMMER OLYMPICS)
Soundtrack (1986) . . . . *DRG (S) 419386-1*   86   **8-10**
Cast: Placido Domingo.

67 MELODY LANE
TV Soundtrack (1955) . . . . *Columbia (M) CL-724*   55   **20-30**
Composer: Ken Griffin; Stephen Foster; others. **Cast:** Ken Griffin.

SKATEBOARD
Soundtrack (1977) . . . . *RCA Victor (S) ABL1-2769*   77   **8-10**
Composer: Mark Snow; others. **Conductor:** Mark Snow. **Cast:** Dr. John; Jefferson Starship; Mickey Thomas; Taro Meyer; Mona Lisa and Terry Young; Roger Jaep.

SKATEDATER
Soundtrack (1966) . . . . *Mira (M) LP-3004*   66   **12-15**
Soundtrack (1966) . . . . *Mira (S) LPS-3004*   66   **15-20**
Composer: Mike Curb. **Conductor:** Nick Venet.

SKATETOWN U.S.A.
Soundtrack (1980) . . . . *Columbia (S) JC-36292*   80   **8-10**
Composer: Various. **Cast:** Dave Mason; Earth, Wind and Fire; Emotions; Marilyn McCoo and Billy Davis Jr.; Jacksons.

SKI ON THE WILD SIDE
Soundtrack (1967) . . . . *MGM (M) E-4439*   67   **40-50**
Soundtrack (1967) . . . . *MGM (S) SE-4439*   67   **60-70**
Composer: Billy Allen.

SKIDOO
Soundtrack (1968) . . . . *RCA Victor (S) LSO-1152*   68   **15-20**
Composer: Harry Nilsson. **Conductor:** George Tipton. **Cast:** Carol Channing; Harry Nilsson.

SKYSCRAPER
Original Cast (1965) . . . . *Capitol (M) VAS-2422*   65 $15-20
Original Cast (1965) . . . . *Capitol (S) SVAS-2422*   65   25-30
    Composer: James Van Heusen; Sammy Cahn. Conductor: John Lesko. Cast: Julie Harris; Peter
    L. Marshall; Charles Nelson Reilly; Dick O'Neill; Rex Everhart; Nancy Chushman; Lesley
    Stewart.
Studiotrack (1965) . . . . *Capitol (M) T-2411*   65   10-12
Studiotrack (1965) . . . . *Capitol (S) ST-2411*   65   12-15
    Composer: James Van Heusen; Sammy Cahn. Conductor: Stu Phillips. Cast: Hollyridge Singers.

SLAM DANCE
Soundtrack (1987) . . . . *Island (S) 90662-1*   87   8-10
    Composer: Various. Cast: Stan Ridgway; Mitchell Froom; Tim Scott; Eddy Howard.

SLAPSTICK
Soundtrack (1984) . . . . *Varese Sarabande (S) STV-81163*   84   8-10
    Cast: Morton Stevens.

SLAUGHTER HOUSE FIVE
Soundtrack (1972) . . . . *Columbia (S) S-31333*   72   20-25
    Has the original Glenn Gould performances heard in the film.
    Composer: Johann Sebastian Bach. Conductor: Vladimir Golschmann; Pablo Casals.
    Cast: Glen Gould (piano); Columbia Symphony Orchestra.

SLAUGHTER ON 10TH AVENUE
Soundtrack (1957) . . . . *Decca (M) DL-8657*   57   30-40
Soundtrack (1957) . . . . *Decca (S) DL7-8657*   58   40-50
    Above two have Richard Rodgers' original ballet music from *On Your Toes*, arranged and adapted by
    Herschel Burke Gilbert.
    Composer: Richard Rodgers; others. Conductor: Joseph Gershenson.
Studiotrack (1957) . . . . *MGM (EP) X-1026*   57   10-12
    Also has music from *Words and Music* and *Singin' in the Rain*.
    Conductor: Lennie Hayton. Cast: Gene Kelly; MGM Studio Orchestra.

SLAUGHTER'S BIG RIP-OFF
Soundtrack (1973) . . . . *Polydor (S) PD-6015*   73   8-12
    Composer: James Brown; Fred Wesley. Cast: James Brown; Fred Wesley and the J.B.'s.

SLAVE TRADE IN THE WORLD TODAY
Soundtrack (1964) . . . . *London (M) M-76006*   64   75-100
    Composer: Teo Usuelli.

SLAVES
Soundtrack (1969) . . . . *Skye (S) SK-11*   69   12-15
    Composer: Bobby Scott; Bob Kessler. Conductor: Gary McFarland. Cast: Dionne Warwick.

SLEEP WARM
Soundtrack . . . . *Stanyan (S) 5081*   10-12
    Composer: Rod McKuen. Cast: Rod McKuen.

SLEEPING BEAUTY
Soundtrack (1959) . . . . *Disneyland (M) WDL-4018*   59   20-25
Soundtrack (1959) . . . . *Disneyland (S) STER-4018*   59   25-30
Soundtrack (1959) . . . . *Disneyland (M) L-301*   66   15-20
Soundtrack (1959) . . . . *Buena Vista (S) STER-4036*   70   10-12
    The Disneyland and Buena Vista releases have the music of Peter Tchaikovsky, as heard in the Disney film.
    Conductor: George Bruns.
Soundtrack (1966) . . . . *Roulette (M) OS-803*   66   20-30
Soundtrack (1966) . . . . *Roulette (S) OSS-803*   66   40-50
    Composer: Peter Ilyitch Tchaikovsky. Conductor: Boris Khaikin. Cast: Lenningrad Kirov Ballet
    Group.

SLEEPING BEAUTY (continued)
Studiotrack (1966) ....*Golden (M) 166*   66   **$8-10**
  Cast: Paul Tripp (narration).
Studiotrack (1959) .... *Disneyland (M) MM-32*   59   **15-25**
  Cast: Darlene Gillespie.
Studiotrack (1964) .... *Disneyland (M) 1228*   **10-15**

SLENDER THREAD
Soundtrack (1965) ....*Mercury (M) MG-21070*   65   **15-20**
Soundtrack (1965) .... *Mercury (S) SR-61070*   65   **20-25**
  Composer: Quincy Jones. **Conductor:** Quincy Jones.

SLEUTH
Soundtrack (1973) ....*Columbia (S) S-32154*   73   **15-20**
  Composer: John Addison. **Conductor:** John Addison. **Cast:** Michael Caine; Laurence Olivier.
  (With dialogue.)

SLIPPER AND THE ROSE (THE STORY OF CINDERELLA)
Soundtrack (1976) ....*MCA (S) 2097*   **8-10**
  Composer: Richard M. Sherman; Robert B. Sherman. **Conductor:** Angela Morley. **Cast:** Richard
  Chamberlain; Gemma Craven; Christopher Gable; Annette Crosbie; Julian Orchard; Michael
  Hordern; Kenneth More; Peter Graves.
  Also see CINDERELLA

SLIPPERY WHEN WET
Soundtrack (1959) ....*World Pacific (M) W-1265*   59   **20-25**
Soundtrack (1959) ....*World Pacific (S) WS-1265*   59   **20-25**
  Composer: Bud Shank. **Cast:** Bud Shank.

SLOW DANCING IN THE BIG CITY
Soundtrack (1978) .... *United Artists (S) UA-LA939-H*   78   **10-15**
  Composer: Bill Conti. **Conductor:** Bill Conti.

SLUMBER PARTY '57
Soundtrack (1976) ....*Mercury (S) SRM-1-109*   76   **10-12**
  Composer: Various. **Cast:** Jerry Lee Lewis; Crew Cuts; Johnny Preston; Paul and Paula; Platters;
  Angels; Bruce Channel; Danleers; Big Bopper; Phil Phillips; Jivin' Gene and the Jokers; David
  Carrol and His Orchestra.

SMALL ONE:
see HAPPY PRINCE

SMASHING TIME
Soundtrack (1967) .... *ABC (M) OC-6*   68   **12-15**
Soundtrack (1967) ....*ABC (S) ABCS OC-6*   68   **20-25**
  Composer: John Addison. **Conductor:** John Addison. **Cast:** Lynn Redgrave; Rita Tushingham.

SMILING, THE BOY FELL DEAD
Original Cast (1961) .... *Sunbeam (M) LB-549*   **25-35**
  Composer: David Baker; Sheldon Harnick. **Cast:** Danny Meehan; Joseph Macauly; Claiborne
  Cary.

SMOKEY AND THE BANDIT
Soundtrack (1977) ....*MCA (S) 2099*   77   **8-10**
  Composer: Bill Justis; Jerry Reed; Dick Feller; others. **Cast:** Jerry Reed; Burt Reynolds; Jackie
  Gleason. (With dialogue.)

SMOKEY AND THE BANDIT II
Soundtrack (1980) ....*MCA (S) 6101*   80   **8-10**
  Composer: Various. **Conductor:** Al Capps. **Cast:** Jerry Reed; Statler Brothers; Don Williams;
  Roy Rogers and the Sons of the Pioneers; Bandit Band; Tanya Tucker; Mel Tillis; Brenda Lee;
  Tommy Todesco (guitar); Herb Pedersen (banjo); Jerry Kennedy (dobro, guitar); Bobby
  Thompson (banjo); Burt Reynolds. (With dialogue.)

SMOKEY AND THE BANDIT III
Soundtrack (1983) ....*MCA (S) 36006*   83 $8-10
  Cast: John Stewart; Lee Greenwood; Ed Bruce; others.

SMOTHERS BROTHERS SHOW - TOUR DE FARCE OF AMERICAN HISTORY
TV Soundtrack (1965) ....*Mercury (M) MG-20948*   65   10-15
TV Soundtrack (1965) ....*Mercury (S) SR-60948*   65   15-20
  Cast: Smothers Brothers.

SNOOPY
Original Cast (1975) ....*DRG (S) 6103*   75   10-12
  Composer: Larry Grossman; Hal Hackady. **Conductor:** Jon Olson.
Original London Cast ....*Polydor (S) 820247-1*   8-10

SNOOPY COME HOME
Soundtrack (1972) .... *Columbia (S) S-31541*   72   15-20
  Composer: Richard M. Sherman; Robert B. Sherman. **Conductor:** Don Ralke**Cast:** Shelby Flint;
  Don Ralke; Ray Pohlman; Thurl Ravenscroft; Guy Pohlman; Linda Ercoli.

SNOOPY'S CHRISTMAS
Studio Cast ....*Diplomat (S) S-1718*   8-12

SNOW GOOSE
Studio Cast (1949) ....*Decca (M) DL-5055*   50-55
  Composer: Victor Young. **Conductor:** Victor Young. **Cast:** Herbert Marshall; Joan Loring;
  others.

SNOW QUEEN
Soundtrack (1959) ....*Decca (M) DL-8977*   59   50-60
Soundtrack (1959) ....*Decca (S) DL7-8977*   59   60-70
  Composer: Frank Skinner; Diane Lampert; Richard Loring. **Conductor:** Joseph Gershenson.
  Cast: Paul Frees (narration); Sandra Dee; Tommy Kirk; Patty McCormick. (With dialogue.)

SNOW WHITE AND ROSE RED
Soundtrack (1966) .... *RCA Victor/Camden (M) CAL-1084*   66   10-12
Soundtrack (1966) .... *RCA Victor/Camden (S) CAS-1084*   66   12-15
  Composer: Milton DeLugg; Anne DeLugg. **Conductor:** Milton DeLugg. **Cast:** Paul Tripp
  (narration).

SNOW WHITE AND THE SEVEN DWARFS
Original Radio Cast (1979) .... *Buena Vista (S) 5009*   79   15-20
  Sold only at Radio City Music Hall.
  Composer: Frank Churchill; Joe Cook; Larry Morey; Jay Blackton. **Conductor:** Donald Pippin.
  Cast: Mary Jo Salerno; Richard Bowne; Anne Francine.
Studio Cast ....*Golden (M) 5-30-A*   8-10
  Also has *Sleeping Beauty* and *Peter and the Wolf*.
Soundtrack (1937) ....*Decca (M) DL-5015*   49   60-65
  10-inch LP.
  Composer: Frank Churchill; Larry Morey; others. **Conductor:** Paul J. Smith; Leigh Harline.
Soundtrack (1937) .... *Disneyland (M) WDL-4005*   57   20-25
  This score was the first to be recorded directly from the soundtrack. It appeared originally on RCA Victor
  78 rpm singles.
Soundtrack (1937) .... *Disneyland (M) DQ-1201*   62   10-15
  Cast: Adriana Caselotti (as "Snow White"); Harry Stockwell.
Soundtrack (1937) .... *Disneyland (M) 3101*   80   8-10
  Limited edition picture disc.
Soundtrack (1937) .... *Buena Vista (M) 102*   75   15-20
  Triple LP set. Has the complete soundtrack of the film.
Studiotrack (1962) ....*Buena Vista (S) STER-4023*   62   15-20
  Conductor: Tutti Camarata.

SNOW WHITE AND THE SEVEN DWARFS (continued)
Studiotrack (1962) . . . .*Buena Vista (M) BV-4023*   62   **$10-15**
   Also see BEAUTY AND THE BEAST

SNOW WHITE AND THE THREE STOOGES
Soundtrack (1961) . . . . *Columbia (M) CL-1650*   61   **30-35**
Soundtrack (1961) . . . . *Columbia (S) CS-8450*   61   **45-50**
   Composer: Harry Harris; others. **Cast:** Carol Heiss; Three Stooges.

SNOWMAN
Soundtrack (1984) . . . . *Columbia (S) FM-39126*   84   **8-10**
   Composer: Howard Blake. **Conductor:** Howard Blake. **Cast:** Sinfonia of London; Bernard
   Cribbins (narration).

SNOWS OF KILIMANJARO:
see GREAT FILM CLASSICS

SO DEAR TO MY HEART
Soundtrack (1948) . . . .*Disneyland (M) DQ-1255*   64   **10-15**
   Cast: Bryan Russell (narration).

SO LONG, JOEY
   Conductor: Ronn Huff. **Cast:** Dave Boyer.

SO LONG, 174TH STREET
Original Cast (1976) . . . .*Original Cast (S) OC-8131*   81   **8-12**
   Based on Joseph Stein's comedy *Enter Laughing.*
   Composer: Stan Daniels. **Conductor:** Milton Rosenstock. **Cast:** Robert Morse; Kaye Ballard;
   Loni Ackerman; George S. Irving; Patti Karr.

SO THIS IS LOVE
Soundtrack (1953) . . . .*RCA Victor (M) LOC-3000*   53   **60-70**
   10-inch LP.
   Cast: Merv Griffin; Kathryn Grayson.

SO THIS IS PARIS
Soundtrack (1954) . . . . *Decca (EP) ED-700*   54   **20-25**
Soundtrack (1954) . . . . *Decca (M) DL-5553*   54   **50-60**
   10-inch LP.
   Composer: Phil Moody; Pony Sherell. **Conductor:** Joseph Gershenson. **Cast:** Gene Nelson;
   Tony Curtis; Gloria DeHaven; Paul Gilbert.

SODOM AND GOMORRAH
Soundtrack (1963) . . . .*RCA Victor (M) LOC-1076*   63   **125-150**
Soundtrack (1963) . . . .*RCA Victor (S) LSO-1076*   63   **150-175**
   Composer: Miklos Rozsa. **Conductor:** Miklos Rozsa.

SOL MADRID
Soundtrack (1968) . . . .*MGM (M) E-4541*   68   **20-25**
Soundtrack (1968) . . . .*MGM (S) SE-4541-ST*   68   **25-30**
   Composer: Lalo Schifrin. **Conductor:** Lalo Schifrin; Robert Armbruster.

SOLOMON AND SHEBA
Soundtrack (1959) . . . .*United Artists (M) UAL-4051*   59   **90-100**
   Maroon, silk cover.
Soundtrack (1959) . . . .*United Artists (S) UAS-5051*   59   **90-100**
   Maroon, silk cover.
Soundtrack (1959) . . . .*United Artists (M) UAL-4051*   59   **50-55**
   Plain cover.
Soundtrack (1959) . . . .*United Artists (S) UAS-5051*   59   **50-55**
   Plain cover.
Soundtrack (1959) . . . .*MCA (S) 1425*   80   **8-10**
   Composer: Mario Nascimbene. **Conductor:** Mario Nascimbene.

SOME CAME RUNNING
Soundtrack (1958) ....*Capitol (M) W-1109*   58   **$50-75**
Soundtrack (1958) ....*Capitol (S) SW-1109*   58   **90-100**
  Composer: Elmer Bernstein; James Van Heusen; Sammy Cahn. Conductor: Elmer Bernstein.

SOME KIND OF WONDERFUL
Soundtrack (1987) ....*MCA (S) 6200*   87   **8-10**
  Composer: Various. Cast: Furniture; Lick the Tins; Blue Room; Pete Shelley; Jesus and Mary
  Chain; Flesh for Lulu; March Violets; Stephen Duffy; Apartments; March Violets.

SOME LIKE IT HOT
Soundtrack (1959) ....*United Artists (EP) UAE-1005*   59   **10-15**
Soundtrack (1959) ....*United Artists (M) UAL-4030*   59   **25-30**
Soundtrack (1959) ....*United Artists (S) UAS-5030*   59   **40-45**
Soundtrack (1959) ....*United Artists (S) UA-LA272-G*   74   **8-10**
  Composer: Adolph Deutsch; others. Conductor: Adolph Deutsch; Matty Malneck.
  Cast: Marilyn Monroe; Society Syncopaters.
  Also see APARTMENT

SOME LIKE IT HOT - CHA CHA CHA
Studiotrack (1960) ....*United Artists (M) UAL-3029*   60   **20-25**
Studiotrack (1960) ....*United Artists (S) UAS-6029*   **20-30**
  Composer: Various. Cast: Sweet Sue and Her Society Syncopaters; Rene Hernandez and His
  Orchestra.

SOMEBODY BAD STOLE DE WEDDING BELL
Studiotrack (1954) ....*RCA Victor (EP) EPA-570*   54   **10-20**
  Music from *Who's Got De Ding Dong* (from *The New Copacabana Show of 1954*) and *In Paris*.
  Composer: Cole Porter. Conductor: Henri Rene. Cast: Eartha Kitt; Henri Rene and His
  Orchestra.

SOMEBODY LOVES ME
Soundtrack (1952) ....*RCA Victor (EP) EPB-3097*   52   **15-20**
  Double EP set.
Soundtrack (1952) ....*RCA Victor (M) LPM-3097*   52   **40-50**
  10-inch LP.
  Cast: Betty Hutton; Ralph Meeker.
Studiotrack (1952) ....*Decca (M) DL-5424*   52   **40-50**
  10-inch LP.
  Conductor: Victor Young. Cast: Blossom Seeley; Benny Fields.

SOMEBODY UP THERE LIKES ME
Soundtrack (1956) ....*RCA Victor (EP) EPA-903*   56   **10-15**
  Title theme is the only track from the film. Also has *Dream Along with Me*, Como's NBC-TV show theme.
  Composer: Various. Cast: Perry Como; Mitchell Ayres' Orchestra; Ray Charles Singers.

SOMETHING UNIQUE
Original Cast (1956) ....*RCA Victor (M) G8OP-6206*   **15-25**
  Special Products issue for the Singer Sewing Machine Company.
  Composer: Ken Hopkins. Cast: Bill Heyer; Bob Sheerer; Edith Adams.

SOMETHING WILD
Soundtrack (1986) ....*MCA (S) 6194*   86   **8-10**
  Composer: Various. Cast: Oingo Boingo; UB40; Fine Young Cannibals; Sonny Okkossun; Celia
  Cruz; Jerry Harrison; New Order; Sister Carol; Steve Jones; Jimmy Cliff.

SOMETIMES A GREAT NOTION
Soundtrack (1971) ....*Decca (S) DL-79185*   71   **20-25**
  This film was retitled *Never Give an Inch*.
  Composer: Henry Mancini. Conductor: Henry Mancini. Cast: Charley Pride.

SOMEWHERE IN TIME
Soundtrack (1980) ....*MCA (S) 5154*   80   **$10-12**
Soundtrack (1980) ....*MCA (S) 39306*   80   **8-10**
  Composer: John Barry; others. **Conductor:** John Barry. **Cast:** Roger Williams and Chet Swiatkowsky (pianos).

SON OF DRACULA
Soundtrack (1974) ....*Rapple (S) ABL1-0220*   74   **10-12**
  Composer: Harry Nilsson; others. **Cast:** Harry Nilsson.

SONDHEIM: A MUSICAL TRIBUTE
Original Cast (1973) ....*Warner Bros. (S) 2WS-2705*   73   **25-30**
  Recorded live March 11, 1973, at New York's Shubert theatre.
  Composer: Stephen Sondheim; others. **Conductor:** Paul Gemignani. **Cast:** Jack Cassidy; Dorothy Collins; Pamela Hall; Larry Kert; Angela Lansbury; Mary McCarty; Donna McKechnie; Chita Rivera; Alexis Smith; Nancy Walker; George Lee Andrews; Mark Lambert; John McMartin; Tony Steven; Larry Blyden; Pamela Myers; Stephen Sondheim.

SONG OF BERNADETTE
Studiotrack (1943) ....*Decca (M) DL-5358*   52   **130-140**
  10-inch LP. Not really a soundtrack recording. Has studio versions of the film's score.
  Composer: Alfred Newman. **Conductor:** Alfred Newman. **Cast:** Alfred Newman's Concert Orchestra.

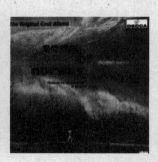

SONG OF NORWAY
Original Cast (1944) ....*Decca (EP) ED-842*   49   **15-20**
Original Cast (1944) ....*Decca (M) DL-8002*   49   **30-35**
Original Cast (1944) ....*Decca (M) DL-9019*   55   **20-25**
Original Cast (1944) ....*Decca (SE) DL7-9019*   59   **15-20**
Original Cast (1944) ....*MCA (SE) 2032e*   72   **8-10**
  Composer: Edvard Grieg; Robert Wright; George Forrest. **Conductor:** Arthur Kay. **Cast:** Robert Shafer; Lawrence Brooks; Helena Bliss; Kitty Carlisle (on the LP though not an original cast member); Sig Arno; Ivy Scott.
Original Revival Cast (1958) ....*Columbia (M) CL-1328*   59   **25-30**
Original Revival Cast (1958) ....*Columbia (S) CS-8135*   59   **40-45**
  Composer: Edvard Grieg; Robert Wright; George Forrest. **Conductor:** Lehman Engel.
  Cast: Brenda Lewis; John Reardon; Helena Scott; Sig Arno; William Olvis; Muriel O'Malley; Stan Freeman.
Soundtrack (1970) ....*ABC (S) ABCS OC-1*   70   **12-15**
  Composer: Edvard Grieg; Robert Wright; George Forrest. **Conductor:** Roland Shaw.
  Cast: Toralv Maurstad; Florence Henderson; Frank Porretta; Harry Secombe; London Symphony Orchestra.

Studio Cast . . . . *JJA (S) 19782A/B*   **$15-20**
   With Irra Petina, of the original cast, who was replaced on record by Kitty Carlisle. Also has music from
   Winged Victory and *Up in Central Park*.
  Composer: Musical adaptation by Robert Wright and George Forrest. **Conductor:** Sylvan
  Shulman. **Cast:** Irra Petina; Robert Weede.

SONG OF THE SOUTH:
see UNCLE REMUS

SONG REMAINS THE SAME
Soundtrack (1976) . . . . *Swan Song (S) SS2-201*   76   **10-12**
   Double LP set.
  Composer: Led Zeppelin (Robert Plant; Jimmy Page; John Paul Jones; John Bonham).
  Cast: Led Zeppelin.

SONG WITHOUT END
Soundtrack (1960) . . . .*Colpix (M) CP-506*   60   **15-20**
   Double this price for copies on blue vinyl.
Soundtrack (1960) . . . . *Colpix (S) SCP-506*   60   **25-30**
   Double this price for copies on blue vinyl.
  Composer: Franz Liszt; others. **Conductor:** Morris Stoloff. **Cast:** Jorge Bolet (piano); Los
  Angeles Philharmonic Orchestra.

SONGS OF OUR SOLDIERS:
see JOHNNY TREMAINE

SONGS OF THE FLINTSTONES
TV Soundtrack (1961) . . . . *Golden (M) 66*   61   **10-15**
  Cast: Mel Blanc; Alan Reed.

SONNY AND JED
Soundtrack (1973) . . . .*Cerberus (S) CEMS 0111*   81   **8-10**
   Also has music from *The Cannibals*.
  Composer: Ennio Morricone (both). **Conductor:** Ennio Morricone (both).

SONS OF KATIE ELDER
Soundtrack (1965) . . . . *Columbia (M) OL-6420*   65   **50-60**
Soundtrack (1965) . . . .*Columbia (S) OS-2820*   65   **75-85**
  Composer: Elmer Bernstein. **Conductor:** Elmer Bernstein. **Cast:** John Wayne; Johnny Cash.
  (With dialogue.)

SOPHIA LOREN IN ROME
TV Soundtrack (1964) . . . .*Columbia Special Products (M) OL-6310*   64   **25-35**
TV Soundtrack (1964) . . . .*Columbia (S) OS-2710*   64   **65-75**
TV Soundtrack (1964) . . . . *Columbia Special Products (S) CSP-172*   **8-10**
   Columbia Special Products reissue. Also has music from *The Bride Wore Yolande*.
  Composer: John Barry. **Conductor:** John Barry. **Cast:** Sophia Loren.

SOPHIE
Original Cast (1963) .... *AEI (M) 1130*   **$10-15**
Based on the life of Sophie Tucker.
Original Cast (1963) .... *AEI (M) 1130*   **20-25**
Promotional issue. Has one song, *You'd Know It* by Jenny Smith, not included on the commercial issue.
Composer: Steve Allen. **Cast:** Steve Allen; Linda Lavin; Kathy Keegan; Jerry Vale; Jenny Smith; Libi Staiser.

SOPHIE'S CHOICE
Soundtrack (1983) .. *Jackal Records/Southern Cross Records (S) WOW-726*   83   **10-12**
Soundtrack (1983) .... *Southern Cross (S) SCRS-1002*   83   **8-10**
Composer: Marvin Hamlisch. **Conductor:** Marvin Hamlisch. **Cast:** Marvin Hamlisch.

SOPHISTICATED LADIES
Original Cast (1983) .... *RCA Victor (S) DJL1-4061*   83   **8-12**
Original Cast (1983) .... *RCA Victor (S) ABL1-4693*   83   **8-12**
Full title: *Sophisticated Ladies Highlights*.
Original Cast (1981) .... *RCA Victor (S) CBL2-4053*   81   **12-15**
Double LP set. Based on the music of Duke Ellington.
Composer: Duke Ellington; others. **Conductor:** Mercer Ellington. **Cast:** Gregory Hines; Judith Jamison; Phyllis Hyman; P.J. Benjamin; Hinton Battle; Gegg Burge; Mercedes Ellington; Priscilla Baskerville; Terri Klausner.

SORCERER
Soundtrack (1977) .... *MCA (S) 2277*   77   **10-15**
Composer: Edgar Froese; Christopher Baunke; Peter Baumann. **Cast:** Tangerine Dream.

SORCERER'S APPRENTICE:
see PETER AND THE WOLF

SORRY, WRONG NUMBER
Original Radio Cast (1952) .... *Decca (M) DL-6092*   52   **60-70**
10-inch LP. Radio thriller with supporting cast and sound effects. Directed by William Spier.
Composer: Lucille Fletcher (writer). **Conductor:** William Spier. **Cast:** Agnes Moorehead.

SOUL HUSTLER
Soundtrack (1973) .... *MGM (S) SE-4943*   73   **10-15**
Composer: Harley Hatcher; others. **Conductor:** Harley Hatcher. **Cast:** Marcene Harris; Mathew Crowe and His Travelin' Band.

SOUL MAN
Soundtrack (1986) .... *A&M (S) SP-3903*   86   **8-10**
Composer: Various. **Cast:** Ricky; Rae Dawn Chong; Sly Stone; Models; Nu Shooz; Lou Reed; Vesta Williams; Tom Scott; Brenda Russell.

SOUL OF NIGGER CHARLEY
Soundtrack (1973) .... *MGM (S) 1SE-46*   73   **8-12**
Film sequel to *Legend of Nigger Charley*.
Composer: Don Costa. **Conductor:** Don Costa. **Cast:** Lou Rawls.

SOUL TO SOUL
Soundtrack (1971) .... *Atlantic (S) 7207*   71   **10-12**
Recording of an Independence Day celebration in Ghana, West Africa.
Composer: Richie Havens; Ike Cargill; others. **Cast:** Wilson Pickett; Ike and Tina Turner; Staple Singers; Eddie Harris; Les McCann; Amoa; Roberta Flack; Voices of East Harlem.

SOUND AND THE FURY
Soundtrack (1959) .... *Decca (M) DL-8885*   59   **25-30**
Soundtrack (1959) .... *Decca (S) DL7-8885*   59   **50-75**
Composer: Alex North. **Conductor:** Lionel Newman.

SOUND OF HOLLYWOOD
Studiotrack (1962) .... *Kapp (M) ML-7513* 62   **$10-15**
Studiotrack (1962) .... *Kapp (S) ML-7513-S* 62   **15-20**
  Composer: Various. **Cast:** Vardi and the Medallion Strings.

SOUND OF MUSIC
Original Cast (1959) .... *Columbia (M) KOL-5450*   59   **15-20**
Original Cast (1959) .... *Columbia (S) KOS-2020*   59   **25-30**
Original Cast (1959) .... *Columbia (S) S-32601*   73   **8-10**
  Composer: Richard Rodgers; Oscar Hammerstein II. **Conductor:** Frederick Dvonch.
  Cast: Mary Martin; Theodore Bikel; Patricia Neway; Kurt Kaszner; Marion Marlowe;
  Lauri Peters; Muriel O'Malley; Karen Shepard; Brian Davies; Elizabeth Howell.
Original London Cast (1959) .... *Regal (S) SRS-5003*   59   **35-40**
  Composer: Richard Rodgers; Oscar Hammerstein II. **Conductor:** Robert Lowe. **Cast:** Jean
  Bayless; Sylvia Beamish; Olive Gilbert; Constance Shacklock; Roger Dann; Barbara Brown;
  Eunice Gayson; Harold Kasket; Nicholas Bennett; Lynn Kennington.
London Studio Cast .... *Music for Pleasure (S) MFP-1007*   **12-15**
  Composer: Richard Rodgers; Oscar Hammerstein II. **Cast:** Maureen Hartley; Charles West;
  Shirley Chapman.
Studio Cast (1960) .... *Warner Bros. (S) WS-1377*   60   **15-20**
  Composer: Richard Rodgers; Oscar Hammerstein II. **Conductor:** Father Frank Wasner.
  Cast: Trapp Family Singers (who inspired the story).
Studio Cast (1959) .... *Richmond (M) B-20079*   59   **10-12**
Studiotrack (1959) .... *Richmond (S) S-30079*   **12-15**
  Composer: Richard Rodgers; Oscar Hammerstein II. **Cast:** London Theatre Company.
Studio Cast .... *Premier (S) PS 9017*   **10-12**
  Composer: Richard Rodgers; Oscar Hammerstein II. **Conductor:** Mitch Hacker.
Studio Cast .... *Rondo-lette (S) SA 156*   **10-15**
  Composer: Richard Rodgers; Oscar Hammerstein II. **Conductor:** Russ Cast. **Cast:** Gigi
  Durston; others.
Soundtrack (1965) .... *RCA Victor (M) LOCD-2005*   65   **15-20**
Soundtrack (1965) .... *RCA Victor (S) LSOD-2005*   65   **20-25**
  Above two do not have gatefold covers, but do have booklets.
Soundtrack (1965) .... *RCA Victor (M) LOCD-2005*   Re   **10-12**
Soundtrack (1965) .... *RCA Victor (S) LSOD-2005*   Re   **8-10**
  Above two have gatefold covers, but do not have booklets.
  Composer: Richard Rodgers; Oscar Hammerstein II. **Cast:** Julie Andrews; Christopher
  Plummer; Richard Haydn; Eleanor Parker.
Studiotrack (1961) .... *Kapp (M) KL-1175*   61   **10-12**
Studiotrack (1961) .... *Kapp (S) KS-3059*   **12-15**
  Composer: Richard Rodgers; Oscar Hammerstein II. **Cast:** Pete King Chorale.
  Also see FIORELLO!

SOUNDER
Soundtrack (1972) . . . .*Columbia (S) S-31944*   72   **$15-18**
   Composer: Various. **Cast:** Sam "Lightnin" Hopkins; Taj Mahal.

SOUNDS BROADWAY! SOUNDS HOLLYWOOD! SOUNDS GREAT!
Studiotrack (1961) . . . .*Epic (M) LN-3797*   61   **10-12**
Studio Cast (1961) . . . . *Epic (S) BN-604*   **12-15**
   Conductor: Norman Leyden; Frank Hunter (arrangers). **Cast:** Merrill Staton Voices.

SOUNDS FROM TRUE STORIES
Soundtrack . . . . *Sire (S) 1-25515*   **8-10**
   Composer: Various. **Cast:** David Byrne; Carl Finch; Panhandle Mystery Band; Kronos Quartet;
   Banda Eclipse; Steve Jordan.

SOUNDTRACK MUSIC FROM WIDE SCREEN
Studiotrack . . . .*Somerset (M) LP-16400*   **10-15**
   Has music from *El Cid*, *King of Kings* and *Ben Hur*.

SOUNDTRACKS
Soundtrack . . . . *Decca (M) DL-4362*   63   **12-15**
Soundtrack . . . .*Decca (S) DL7-4362*   63   **15-18**

SOUNDTRACKS (MUSIC FROM GREAT MOTION PICTURES)
Soundtrack . . . .*United Artists (M) UAL-3303*   63   **12-15**
Soundtrack . . . .*United Artists (S) UAS-6303*   63   **15-18**
   Composer: Various. **Cast:** LeRoy Holmes; Elmer Bernstein; others.

SOUP FOR ONE
Soundtrack (1982) . . . .*Atlantic (S) 19353*   82   **8-10**
   Composer: Nile Rodgers; Bernard Edwards; Johnny Mandel. **Cast:** Chic; Carly Simon; Teddy
   Pendergrass; others.

SOUPY SALES SHOW
TV Soundtrack (1961) . . . . *Reprise (M) R-6010*   61   **12-15**
TV Soundtrack (1961) . . . . *Reprise (S) R9-6010*   61   **15-20**
   Cast: Soupy Sales.

SOUTH PACIFIC
Original Cast (1949) . . . . *Columbia (EP) A-850*   49   **25-35**
   Boxed set with five singles and two EPs, numbered A-850-1 through A-850-14.
Original Cast (1949) . . . . *Columbia (EP) A-852*   49   **15-25**
   Triple EP set.
Original Cast (1949) . . . . *Columbia (M) ML-4180*   49   **25-30**
   A large anchor is pictured on cover.
Original Cast (1949) . . . . *Columbia (M) OL-4180*   Re   **20-25**
   Cover pictures Ezio Pinza and Mary Martin.
Original Cast (1949) . . . . *Columbia (SE) OS-2040e*   **10-12**
Original Cast (1949) . . . . *Columbia (SE) S-32604*   73   **8-10**
   Composer: Richard Rodgers; Oscar Hammerstein II. **Conductor:** Salvatore Dell'isola.
   Cast: Mary Martin; Ezio Pinza; Juanita Hall; William Tabbert; Barbara Luna.
Original Revival Cast (1967) . . . . *Columbia (M) OL-6700*   67   **10-12**
Studio Cast (1964) . . . . *Reprise (S) FS-2018*   64   **25-35**
   With gatefold cover.
Studio Cast (1964) . . . . *Reprise (M) F-2018*   64   **20-25**
Studio Cast (1964) . . . . *Reprise (S) FS-2018*   64   **25-30**
   Composer: Richard Rodgers; Oscar Hammerstein II. **Conductor:** Morris Stoloff; Ken Lane.
   Cast: Frank Sinatra; Jo Stafford; McGuire Sisters; Bing Crosby; Keely Smith; Dinah Shore;
   Debbie Reynolds; Rosemary Clooney; Sammy Davis Jr.; Hi-Los.

Original Revival Cast (1967) . . . . *Columbia (S) OS-3100*   67 $15-20
  Composer: Richard Rodgers; Oscar Hammerstein II. **Conductor:** Jonathan Anderson.
  Cast: Florence Henderson; Giorgio Tozzi; Justin McDonough; Elanor Calbes; Irene Byatt;
  David Doyle.
Studio Cast (1957) . . . . *Harmony (M) HL-7092*   57   15-25
  Composer: Richard Rodgers; Oscar Hammerstein II. **Cast:** Dino Martinelli Orchestra.
Studio Cast (1958) . . . . *RCA Victor/Camden (M) CAL-421*   58   15-25
  Composer: Richard Rodgers; Oscar Hammerstein II. **Conductor:** Al Goodman. **Cast:** Sandra
  Dee; Jimmy Carroll; Dickenson Eastham; Thelma Carpenter; Al Goodman and His Orchestra
  with the Guild Choristers.
Studio Cast (1954) . . . . *RCA Victor (M) LK-1008*   54   15-25
Soundtrack (1958) . . . . *RCA Victor (EP) EOC-1032*   58   15-20
  Triple EP set.
Soundtrack (1958) . . . . *RCA Victor (M) LOCD-2000*   57   20-25
  Deluxe edition.
Soundtrack (1958) . . . . *RCA Victor (M) LOC-1032*   57   15-20
Soundtrack (1958) . . . . *RCA Victor (S) LSO-1032*   58   20-25
Soundtrack (1958) . . . . *RCA Victor (S) AYL1-3681*   81   8-10
  Composer: Richard Rodgers; Oscar Hammerstein II. **Conductor:** Alfred Newman.
  Cast: Mitzi Gaynor; Ray Walston; Juanita Hall; Giorgio Tozzi; Ken Darby Singers.
Studiotrack . . . . *Coronet (M) CX-41*   10-20
  Cast: Coronet Studio Orchestra and Chorus.
Studiotrack . . . . *Wing (S) SRW-12502*   10-15
  Composer: Richard Rodgers; Oscar Hammerstein II. **Conductor:** Marc La Salle.
  Cast: Marc La Salle and his Orchestra.
  Also see MUSIC MAN; REPRISE REPERTORY THEATRE

SOUTH SEAS ADVENTURE
Soundtrack (1958) . . . . *Audio Fidelity (M) 189930*   59   40-50
Soundtrack (1958) . . . . *Audio Fidelity (S) AFSD-5899*   59   50-65
Soundtrack (1958) . . . . *Citadel (S) CT-7014*   81   8-10
  Also has music from *Journey into Fear*.
  Composer: Alex North. **Conductor:** Alex North.

SOUTHERN STAR
Soundtrack (1969) . . . . *Colgems (S) COSO-5009*   69   50-60
  Composer: Georges Garvarentz. **Conductor:** Georges Garvarentz. **Cast:** Matt Monro.

SPACE: 1999
TV Soundtrack (1975) . . . . *RCA Victor (S) ABL-1-1422*   75   10-15
TV Soundtrack (1975) . . . . *Power (S) 8162*   75   10-12
TV Soundtrack (1976) . . . . *Power (S) 8179*   76   10-12
  Composer: Barry Gray. **Conductor:** Barry Gray. **Cast:** Martin Landau; Barbarn Bain.

SPACEBALLS
Soundtrack (1987) . . . . *Atlantic (S) 81770-1*   87   8-10
  Composer: John Morris. **Conductor:** John Morris. **Cast:** Van Halen; Pointer Sisters; Spinners;
  Ladyfire; Berlin; Kim Charles; Jeffrey Osborn.

SPACECAMP
Soundtrack (1986) . . . . *RCA Victor (S) ABL1-5856*   86   8-10
  Composer: John Williams.

SPANISH AFFAIR
Soundtrack (1958) . . . . *Dot (M) DLP-3078*   58   75-100
  Composer: Daniele Amfitheatrof. **Conductor:** Daniele Amfitheatrof.

SPARKLE
Soundtrack (1976) . . . . *WEB Records (S) OC-105*   10-15
  Composer: Various. **Cast:** Aretha Franklin.

SPARTACUS

Soundtrack (1960) .... *Decca (M) DL-9092* 60 **$20-30**
Maroon label.
Soundtrack (1960) .... *Decca (S) DL7-9092* 60 **30-40**
Maroon label.
Soundtrack (1960) .... *Decca (S) DL7-9092* 60 **20-25**
Black label.
Soundtrack (1960) .... *Decca (M) DL-9092* 60 **15-25**
Black label.
Soundtrack (1960) .... *MCA (S) 2068* 72 **10-12**
Soundtrack (1960) .... *MCA (S) 1534* **8-10**
Composer: Alex North. **Conductor:** Alex North.

SPECTACULAR WORLD OF CLASSIC FILM SCORES

Studiotrack .... *RCA Victor (S) ARL 1-279* 78 **30-40**
Side one: "Music from the first 13 Classic Film Scores." Side two: *Julius Caesar, Peyton Place, The Thing (From Another World), King of the Khyber Rifles* and *Salome.*
Composer: Jimmy McHugh; Franz Waxman; Alfred Newman; Max Steiner; John Williams; Erich W. Korngold; Bernard Herrmann; Miklos Rosza; Dimitri Tiomkin; Daniele Amfitheatrof. **Conductor:** Charles Gerhardt.

SPEED ZONE

Soundtrack (1989) .... *Grudge (S) 4506-1-F9* 89 **8-10**
Composer: Various. **Cast:** Stevie Wonder; Richie Havens; Billy Burnette; David Wheatley; Splash; Ross Vanelli; Felix Cavaliere; Charlie Karp; Omar and Howlers; Will to Power.

SPEEDWAY

Soundtrack (1968) .... *RCA Victor (M) LPM-3989* 68 **800-1000**
Includes an 8" x 10" color photo, which represents about $10 of the value. Note: this price is only for monaural pressings.
Soundtrack (1968) .... *RCA Victor (S) LSP-3989* 68 **35-45**
Includes an 8" x 10" color photo, which represents about $10 of the value.
Soundtrack (1968) .... *RCA Victor (S) LSP-3989* 69 **10-20**
Orange or tan label. (Tan label issued in 1976.)
Soundtrack (1968) .... *RCA Victor (S) AFL1-3989* 77 **8-10**
Composer: Ben Weisman; Sid Wayne; Sid Tepper; Roy C. Bennett; others. **Cast:** Elvis Presley; Nancy Sinatra (vocals); Jordanaires (vocals).

SPELLBOUND

Soundtrack (1945) .... *REM (M) LP-1* 50 **75-100**
10-inch LP.
Soundtrack (1945) .... *Warner Bros. (M) W-1213* 58 **20-25**
Soundtrack (1945) .... *Warner Bros. (SE) WS-1213* 58 **25-35**
Soundtrack (1945) .... *Stanyan (Q) SRQ-4021* Re **10-15**
Composer: Miklos Rozsa. **Conductor:** Ray Heindorf.
Studiotrack .... *RCA Victor (S) ARL 1-091* 75 **10-12**
Music from: *Double Indemnity, Spellbound, The Lost Weekend, Knights of the Round Table, The Four Feathers, The Jungle Book, Ivanhoe, The Thief of Bagdad* and *The Red House.*
Composer: Miklos Rosza. **Conductor:** Charles Gerhardt.
Also see PARADINE CASE; QUO VADIS?; RED HOUSE

SPINOUT

Studiotrack (1966) .... *RCA Victor (M) LPM-3702* 66 **65-80**
Includes a 12" x 12" color photo, which represents about $40 of the value.
Studiotrack (1966) .... *RCA Victor (S) LSP-3702* 66 **65-80**
Includes a 12" x 12" color photo, which represents about $40 of the value.
Studiotrack (1966) .... *RCA Victor (S) AFL1-2560* 78 **8-10**
Composer: Fred Wise; Randy Starr; Sid Tepper; Roy C. Bennett; Bill Giant; Bernie Baum; Florence Kaye; Ben Weisman; Doc Pomus; Mort Shuman; Sid Wayne; others. **Cast:** Elvis Presley; Scotty Moore (guitar); D.J. Fontana (drums); Jordanaires and Imperials Quartet (vocals).

SPIRIT OF ST. LOUIS
Soundtrack (1957) . . . . *RCA Victor (M) LPM-1472*   57   **$60-70**
Soundtrack (1957) . . . . *Entr' acte (SE) ERS-6507*   Re   **8-10**
  Composer: Franz Waxman. Conductor: Franz Waxman.

SPOOK WHO SAT BY THE DOOR
Soundtrack (1973) . . . . *Columbia (S) KC-32944*   74   **8-10**
  Cast: Herbie Hancock.

SPOON RIVER ANTHOLOGY
Original Cast (1963) . . . . *Columbia (M) OL-6010*   63   **15-20**
Original Cast (1963) . . . . *Columbia (S) OS-6010*   63   **20-25**
  Theatrical presentation of Edgar Lee Masters' work, originally produced by the U.C.L.A. University
  Extension Theatre Group.
  Composer: Naomi C.Hirshhorn; Charles Aidman. Cast: Betty Garrett; Robert Elston; Joyce Van
  Patten; Naomi C. Hirshhorn; Hal Lynch. (With dialogue.)

SPOTLIGHT ON WILD BILL HICKOCK
Radio Cast . . . . *Tiara (M) TMT-7516*   **8-10**
Radio Cast . . . . *Tiara (SE) TST-7516*   **8-10**
  Cast: Guy Madison; Andy Devine.

SPRING BREAK
Soundtrack (1983) . . . . *Warner Bros. (S) 1-23826*   83   **8-10**
  Composer: Various. Cast: Cheap Trick; Gerald McMahon; Jack Mack and the Heart Attack;
  Dreamers; Hot Date; NRBQ; Big Spender.

SPRING IS HERE:
see MISTER IMPERIUM

SPRINGTIME FOR HITLER:
see PRODUCERS

SPY WHO CAME IN FROM THE COLD
Soundtrack (1965) . . . . *RCA Victor (M) LOC-1118*   65   **30-35**
Soundtrack (1965) . . . . *RCA Victor (S) LSO-1118*   65   **45-50**
  Composer: Sol Kaplan. Conductor: Sol Kaplan.

SPY WHO LOVED ME
Soundtrack (1977) . . . . *United Artists (S) UA-LA774-H*   77   **10-12**
Soundtrack (1977) . . . . *Liberty (S) LO-50774*   Re   **8-10**
  Composer: Marvin Hamlisch. Conductor: Marvin Hamlisch. Cast: Carly Simon; Marvin
  Hamlisch; Gibson Brothers.

SPY WITH A COLD NOSE
Soundtrack (1966) . . . . *Columbia (M) OL-6670*   66   **12-15**
Soundtrack (1966) . . . . *Columbia (S) OS-3070*   66   **15-20**
  Composer: Riz Ortolani. Conductor: Riz Ortolani.

SQUARE ROOT OF ZERO
Soundtrack (1966) . . . . *Mainstream (M) 56070*   66   **15-20**
Soundtrack (1966) . . . . *Mainstream (S) S-6070*   66   **20-25**
  Composer: Elliot Kaplan. Conductor: Elliot Kaplan.

STACCATO
TV Soundtrack (1959) . . . . *Capitol (M) T-1287*   59   **25-30**
TV Soundtrack (1959) . . . . *Capitol (S) ST-1287*   59   **40-45**
  Above two have music from the TV series *Johnny Staccato*.
  Composer: Elmer Bernstein. Conductor: Elmer Bernstein.

STAGE DOOR CANTEEN/HOLLYWOOD CANTEEN
Studio Cast .... *Curtain Calls (S) 100/11-12* $10-15
  Double LP set.

STAGECOACH
Soundtrack (1966) .... *Mainstream (M) 56077*   66   30-40
Soundtrack (1966) .... *Mainstream (S) S-6077*   66   50-75
  Composer: Jerry Goldsmith; others. **Conductor:** Alexander Courage.

STAGES
Original Cast (1978) .... *Varese Sarabande (S) VC-81083*   78   8-10
  Composer: Bruce Kimmell. **Conductor:** Michael Goodrow. **Cast:** Bruce Kimmell; Sammy
  Williams; Randi Kallan; Linden Waddell.

STAKEOUT
Soundtrack (1958) .... *RCA Victor (EP) EPA-4199*   58   10-20
  Composer: Irwin Schwartz; Irvin Kershner; Andrew J. Fenady. **Cast:** Hollywood Chamber Jazz
  Group.

STAN FREBERG SHOWS
Original Radio Cast .... *Capitol (M) WBO-1035*   58   55-75
  Double LP set. Actual title: *The Best of the Stan Freberg Shows.*
  Composer: Stan Freberg; Ken Sullet. **Conductor:** Billy May. **Cast:** Stan Freberg; Paul Frees
  (narration); Jesse White; Jud Conlon Singers; Peter Leeds; Byron Kane; Colleen Collins; Helen
  Kleeb.
Original Radio Cast .... *Capitol (M) T-1694*   62   30-40
  Actual title: *Face the Funnies.*
  Composer: Stan Freberg; Ken Sullet. **Conductor:** Billy May. **Cast:** Stan Freberg; Paul Frees
  (narration); Jesse White; The Jud Conlon Singers; Peter Leeds; Byron Kane; Colleen Collins;
  Helen Kleeb.
Original Radio Cast .... *Capitol (M) T-1242*   59   30-40
  Actual title: *Stan Freberg with the Original Cast.*
  Composer: Stan Freberg; Ken Sullet. **Conductor:** Billy May. **Cast:** Stan Freberg; Paul Frees
  (narration); Jesse White; Jud Conlon Singers; Peter Leeds; Byron Kane; Colleen Collins; Helen
  Kleeb.
Studio Cast (1961) .... *Capitol (M) W-1573*   61   25-35
Studio Cast (1961) .... *Capitol (S) SW-1573*   61   30-40
  Actual title for above two: *Stan Freberg Presents the United States of America Vol. 1: The Early Years.*
  A musical satire revue especially for records.
  Composer: Stan Freberg; Ken Sullet. **Conductor:** Billy May. **Cast:** Stan Freberg; Paul Frees
  (narration); Jesse White; Jud Conlon Singers; Peter Leeds; Byron Kane; Colleen Collins; Helen
  Kleeb.

STAND BY ME
Soundtrack (1986) .... *Atlantic (S) 81667-1*   86   8-10
  Composer: Various. **Cast:** Del Vikings; Buddy Holly; Silhouettes; Jerry Lee Lewis; Shirley and
  Lee; Chordettes; Coasters.

STAR
Soundtrack (1968) .... *20th Century-Fox (S) DTCS-5102*   68   10-15
  Film biography of Gertrude Lawrence.
  Conductor: Lennie Hayton. **Cast:** Julie Andrews; Daniel Massey; Bruce Forsyth; Beryl Reid;
  Garrett Lewis; Daffodils.

STAR IS BORN
Soundtrack (1954) .... *Columbia (EP) BA-1201*   54   15-20
Soundtrack (1954) .... *Columbia (M) BL-1201*   54   35-40
  Deluxe, boxed edition.
Soundtrack (1954) .... *Columbia (M) CL-1101*   58   20-25
Soundtrack (1954) .... *Columbia (SE) CS-8740*   63   25-30
Soundtrack (1954) .... *Harmony (SE) HS-11366*   69   15-20

Soundtrack (1954) .... *Columbia Special Products (SE) ACS-8740e* Re **$8-10**
  Composer: Harold Arlen; Leonard Gershe. **Conductor:** Ray Heindorf. **Cast:** Judy Garland.
Soundtrack (1937) .... *United Artists (SE) UA-LA375-G* 75 **12-15**
  Composer: Max Steiner. **Conductor:** LeRoy Holmes.
Soundtrack (1976) .... *Columbia (S) JS-34403* 76 **8-10**
  Composer: Paul Williams; Rupert Holmes. **Cast:** Barbara Streisand; Kris Kristofferson.

STAR MAKER
Studiotrack (1939) .... *Decca (M) DL-6013* 51 **50-60**
  Also has music from *Doctor Rhythm*.
  Composer: Gus Edwards; James V. Monaco; John Burke; others. **Conductor:** John Scott Trotter.
  Cast: Bing Crosby; Connee Boswell; Music Maids.
  Also see ROAD BEGINS

STAR STRUCK
Soundtrack (1983) .... *A&M (S) SP-4938* 83 **8-10**
  Composer: Various. **Cast:** Jo Kennedy; Turnaround; Swinger; Ross O'Donovan; John O'May;
  Mental As Regular.

STAR TREK
TV Soundtrack (1985) .... *GNP/Crescendo (S) 8006* 85 **8-10**
  Has the episode *The Cage*.
TV Soundtrack .... *GNP/Crescendo (S) GNPS-8010* 88 **8-10**
  Sound effects from the original TV soundtrack.
TV Soundtrack (1965) .... *Polygram (S) PDS 1-6423* 85 **8-10**
  From two episodes: *The Cage* and *Where No Man Has Gone Before*.
  Composer: Alex Courage. **Conductor:** Alex Courage. **Cast:** Alexander Courage Orchestra.

STAR TREK - THE MOTION PICTURE
Soundtrack (1979) .... *Columbia (S) JS-36334* 79 **10-12**
  Composer: Jerry Goldsmith. **Conductor:** Jerry Goldsmith.

STAR TREK II: THE WRATH OF KHAN
Soundtrack (1982) .... *Atlantic (S) SD-19363* 82 **8-10**
  Composer: James Horner. **Conductor:** James Horner.

STAR TREK III: THE SEARCH FOR SPOCK
Soundtrack (1984) .... *Capitol (S) ST-12360* 84 **10-15**
  Double LP set. Gatefold cover.
  Composer: James Horner. **Conductor:** James Horner.

STAR TREK IV: THE VOYAGE HOME
Soundtrack (1986) .... *MCA (S) L-33-17251* 87 **15-20**
  12-inch single. Promotional issue. Has *Market Street* and *Ballad of the Whale*, by the Yellowjackets.
Soundtrack (1986) .... *MCA (S) 5972* 87 **8-12**
Soundtrack (1986) .... *MCA (S) 6195* Re **8-10**
  Composer: Leonard Rosenman. **Conductor:** Leonard Rosenman.

STAR TREK THEMES
Studiotrack .... *Wonderland (S) WLP-301* **10-12**

STAR WARS
Soundtrack (1977) .... *20th Century-Fox (S) 2T-541* 77 **12-18**
  Double LP set.
Soundtrack (1977) .... *20th Century-Fox (S) 813588* Re **10-12**
Soundtrack (1977) .... *20th Century-Fox (S) T-550* 77 **10-12**
  Actual title: *The Story of Star Wars*.
Studiotrack (1980) .... *RSO (S) 1-3093* 80 **8-12**
  Composer: John Williams. **Conductor:** John Williams. **Cast:** Roscoe Lee Browne (narration);
  Mark Hamill; Alec Guinness; Carrie Fisher. (With dialogue.)
  Also see TWO CONTEMPORARY CLASSIC FILM SCORES

STAR WARS - RETURN OF THE JEDI
Soundtrack (1983) . . . . *RSO (S) 422-811767-1*   83   **$8-10**
  Composer: John Williams. Conductor: John Williams. Cast: London Symphony Orchestra.
Studiotrack (1983) . . . . *RCA Victor (S) CRC1-4748*   83   **8-12**
  Conductor: Charles Gerhardt. Cast: National Philharmonic Orchestra.
  Also see RETURN OF THE JEDI

STAR WARS/CLOSE ENCOUNTERS OF THE THIRD KIND
Studiotrack (1977) . . . . *London (S) 2M 1001*   78   **8-10**
  Has one suite devoted to each score.
  Composer: John Williams. Conductor: Zubin Mehta (arranger).

STARDUST
Soundtrack (1975) . . . . *Arista (S) A-5000*   75   **10-12**
  Double LP set. Film sequel to *That'll Be the Day*, featuring "40 Original Hit Records."
  Composer: Various. Cast: David Essex; Adam Faith.

STARLIGHT EXPRESS
Original Cast (1987) . . . . *MCA (S) 5972*   87   **8-10**
  Composer: Andrew Lloyd Webber. Cast: Josie Aiello; Peter Hewlett; Earl Jordan; Richie
  Havens; Marc Cohn; Harold Faltermeyer.

STARMAN
Soundtrack (1984) . . . . *Varese Sarabande (S) 81233*   84   **8-10**
  Composer: Jack Nitzsche.

STARS AND STRIPES FOREVER
Soundtrack (1952) . . . . *MGM (M) E-176*   52   **40-50**
  10-inch LP.
Soundtrack (1952) . . . . *MGM (M) E-3508*   57   **30-40**
  Also has four selections by the American Military Band.
  Composer: John Philip Sousa; others. Conductor: Alfred Newman. Cast: American Military
  Band.

STARS IN YOUR EYES
Studiotrack . . . . *JJC (M) ST-3004*   **8-12**
  Cast: Ethel Merman.

STARTING HERE, STARTING NOW
Original Cast (1977) . . . . *RCA Victor (S) ABL1-2360*   77   **10-12**
  Composer: David Shire; Richard Maltby Jr. Conductor: Robert W. Preston. Cast: Margery
  Cohen; George Lee Andrews; Loni Ackerman.

STATE FAIR
Soundtrack (1962) . . . . *Dot (M) DLP-9001*   62   **20-25**
Soundtrack (1962) . . . . *Dot (S) DLP-29011*   62   **30-35**
  Composer: Richard Rodgers; Oscar Hammerstein II. Conductor: Alfred Newman. Cast: Pat
  Boone; Ann-Margret; Bobby Darin; Alice Faye; Anita Gordon; Bob Smart; Tom Ewell.

STAVISKY
Soundtrack (1974) . . . . *RCA Victor (S) ARL1-0952*   75   **20-25**
  Composer: Stephen Sondheim. Conductor: Carlo Savina.

STAYING ALIVE
Soundtrack (1983) . . . . *RSO (S) 422-813-269-1*   83   **8-10**
  Gatefold cover.
  Composer: Bee Gees (Robin Gibb; Barry Gibb; Maurice Gibb); others. Cast: Bee Gees; Tommy
  Faragher; Cynthia Rhodes; Frank Stallone.

STEALING HOME
Soundtrack (1988) . . . . *Atlantic (S) 81885-1*   88   **8-10**
  Composer: Various. Cast: Jerry Lee Lewis; Bo Diddley; Everly Brothers; David Foster;
  Shirelles; Nylons; Marilyn Martin; Four Seasons.

STEELYARD BLUES
 Soundtrack (1972) .... *Warner Bros. (S) BS-2662*   72 $10-12
  Composer: Nick Gravenites; Mike Bloomfield.

STEPHEN FOSTER STORY
 Original Cast (1966) .... *XSBV (S) 111386*   66   10-20
  Show runs every summer in Kentucky, during which time the LP is available at the theatre. Though
  its run began in 1959, it is the 1966 cast on the LP.
  Composer: Stephen Foster. **Conductor:** Willis Beckett. **Cast:** Richard Silwell; Jeanette Sallee;
  William Lathon.

STEPHEN SONDHEIM EVENING
 Original Cast .... *RCA Victor (S) CBL2-4745*   83   20-25
  Composer: Stephen Sondheim. **Cast:** Liz Callaway; Cris Groenendaal; Bob Grunton; George
  Hearn; Steven Jacob; Judy Kaye; Victoria Mallory; Angela Lansbury.

STERILE CUCKOO
 Soundtrack (1969) .... *Paramount (S) PAS-5009*   69   20-25
  Composer: Fred Karlin. **Conductor:** Fred Karlin. **Cast:** Sandpipers.

STEVE ALLEN'S FUNNY FONE CALLS
 TV Soundtrack (1963) .... *Dot (M) DLP-3472*   63   15-20
  Cast: Steve Allen; Louis Nye.
 TV Soundtrack (1963) .... *Dot (M) DLP-3517*   63   15-20
  Vol. 2. Actual title: *More Funny Fone Calls.*
  Cast: Steve Allen; Louis Nye.

STEVIE
 Soundtrack (1978) .... *Epic (S) SE-37726*   78   8-10
  Composer: Patrick Gowers. **Conductor:** Marcus Dodds. **Cast:** John Williams (guitarist);
  Glenda Jackson (reading poems of Stevie Smith).

STILETTO
 Soundtrack (1969) .... *Columbia (S) OS-3360*   69   10-12
  Composer: Sid Ramin. **Conductor:** Sid Ramin.

STING
 Soundtrack (1974) .... *MCA (S) 390*   74   10-15
 Soundtrack (1974) .... *MCA (S) 370910*   81   8-12
 Soundtrack (1974) .... *MCA (S) 1625*   Re   8-10
  Composer: Marvin Hamlisch; Scott Joplin. **Conductor:** Marvin Hamlisch. **Cast:** Marvin
  Hamlisch (piano).

STING II
 Soundtrack (1983) .... *MCA (S) 6116*   83   10-15
  Composer: Lalo Schifrin. **Conductor:** Lalo Schifrin. **Cast:** Linda Hopkins.

STINGIEST MAN IN TOWN
 TV Soundtrack (1956) .... *Columbia (M) CL-950*   56   35-40
  Composer: Fred Spielman. **Conductor:** Tutti Camarata. **Cast:** Vic Damone; Johnny Desmond;
  The Four Lads; Patrice Munsel; Basil Rathbone; Robert Weede; Betty Madigan; Martyn Green;
  Robert Wright.

STIR CRAZY
 Soundtrack (1981) .... *Posse (S) 10001*   81   10-12
  Composer: Tom Scott; Michael Masser; others. **Cast:** Kiki Dee; Gene Wilder; Randy Goodrum;
  Leroy Gomez; Leata Galloway; Dorian Holley. (With dialogue.)

STOLEN LIFE:
 see DEATH OF A SCOUNDREL

STOOGE

Studiotrack (1952) .... *Capitol (EP) EBF-401*	53	**$50-75**
Double EP boxed set. Actual title: *Dean Martin Sings*.
Studiotrack (1952) ....*Capitol (EP) EAP 1-401*	53	**25-50**
Actual title: *Dean Martin Sings, Vol. 1*.
Studiotrack (1952) ....*Capitol (EP) EAP 2-401*	53	**25-50**
Actual title: *Dean Martin Sings, Vol. 2*
Soundtrack (1952) .... *Capitol (M) H-401*	53	**50-100**
10-inch LP. Actual title: *Dean Martin Sings*. Not really a soundtrack LP, but includes "Songs from the Stooge."
Studiotrack (1952) ....*Capitol (M) T-401*	55	**20-30**
Actual title: *Dean Martin Sings*. 12-inch reissue of H-401, with four tracks added. No mention anywhere about "Songs from the Stooge."
Studiotrack (1952) ....*Capitol (SE) DT-2941*	68	**10-12**
Actual title: *Dean Martin Favorites*. Reissue of *Dean Martin Sings*, but with one *Stooge* song, (*A Girl Named Mary and a Boy Named Bill*), missing.

Composer: Goering-Bernie-Hirsch; Johnny Green; E.Y. Harburg; McHugh-Fields-Oppenheimer; Mack Gordon; Harry Revel; Arthur Johnson; Sam Coslow; Richard Whiting; Leo Robin; Jerry Livingston; Mack David. **Conductor:** Dick Stabile (with special arrangements by Nelson Riddle and Gus Levene). **Cast:** Dean Martin.

STOP MAKING SENSE

Soundtrack (1984) .... *Sire (S) 1-25121*	84	**8-10**

Cast: Talking Heads.

STOP THE WORLD, I WANT TO GET OFF!

Original Cast (1962) ....*London (M) AM-58001*	62	**10-15**
Original Cast (1962) .... *London (S) AMS-88001*	62	**15-20**
Original Cast (1962) .... *Polydor (S) 820261-1*	Re	**8-10**

Composer: Anthony Newley; Leslie Bricusse. **Conductor:** Milton Rosenstock. **Cast:** Anthony Newley; Anna Quayle; Jennifer Baker; Susan Baker.

Original Revival Cast (1978) .... *Warner Bros. (S) HS-3214*	78	**8-10**

Composer: Anthony Newley; Leslie Bricusse. **Conductor:** George Rhodes. **Cast:** Sammy Davis Jr.; Marian Mercer; Shelly Burch.

Soundtrack (1966) .... *Warner Bros. (M) W-1643*	66	**20-25**
Soundtrack (1966) .... *Warner Bros. (S) BS-1643*	66	**25-30**

Composer: Anthony Newley; Leslie Bricusse; Al Ham. **Conductor:** Al Ham. **Cast:** Tony Tanner; Millicent Martin.

STORMY MONDAY

Soundtrack (1988) .... *Virgin (S) 90962-1*	88	**8-10**

Composer: Various. **Cast:** B.B. King; Mike Figgis; Krakow Jazz Ensemble; Linda Taylor; Stephanie De Sykes; Linda Allen.

STORY OF BIG RED

Soundtrack (1962) ....*Disneyland (S) ST-1916*	62	**15-20**

Composer: Richard M. Sherman; Robert B. Sherman. **Cast:** Walter Pidgeon (dialogue).

STORY OF MOBY DICK

Soundtrack (1957) .... *Dot (M) DLP-3043*	57	**35-40**

Composer: Richard Mohautt. **Conductor:** Jack Shaindlin. **Cast:** Thomas Mitchell (narration).

STORY OF POLLYANNA:

see POLLYANNA

STORY OF RUDOLPH THE RED-NOSED REINDEER
TV Soundtrack (1966) ....*Decca (M) DL-4815*   66 $12-18
TV Soundtrack (1966) ....*Decca (S) DL-74815*   66   15-20
> One side has the TV soundtrack. Side two has *Music from Rudolph the Red-Nosed Reindeer*, by the Decca Concert Orchestra, conducted by Herbert Rehbein.

Composer: Johnny Marks. Conductor: Maury Laws; Herbert Rehbein. Cast: Burl Ives; Stan Francis; Billie Richards; Paul Soles.

STORY OF STAR WARS:
see STAR WARS

STORY OF THE BLACK HOLE:
see BLACK HOLE

STORY OF THE GNOME-MOBILE
Soundtrack (1967) ....*Disneyland (S) ST-3946*   67   10-15

Composer: Buddy Baker; Robert B. Sherman; Richard M. Sherman. Conductor: Wayne Robinson. Cast: Tom Lowell (narration).

STORY OF TRON
Soundtrack (1982) ....*Disneyland (S) 2517*   82   8-10

Composer: Wendy Carlos. Cast: Chuck Riley (narration).

STORY OF TUTANKHAMEN
Studio Cast (1978) ....*Argo/Decca (S) ZNF-16*   87   8-12
> With booklet.

Composer: Gamal Salama; Kamal El Malakh; Dr. Ibrahim Ahmed.

STRADA, LA:
see LA STRADA

STRAIGHT TO HELL
Soundtrack (1987) ....*Enigma (S) SJE-73308*   87   8-10

Composer: Various. Cast: Joe Strummer; Cait O'Riordan; Pogues; Pray for Rain; Zander Schloss.

STRANGE INTERLUDE
Original Cast ....*Columbia (M) DOL-288*   20-25
Original Cast .... *Columbia (S) DOS-688*   20-30
> Recording of a play by Eugene O'Neill. Four-disc, boxed set with booklet.

Cast: Betty Field; Jane Fonda; Ben Gazzara; Pat Hingle; Geofrey Horne; Geraldine Page; William Prince; Franchot Tone; Richard Thomas.

STRANGE ONE
Soundtrack (1957) ....*Coral (M) CRL-57132*   57   50-65

Composer: Kenyon Hopkins. Conductor: Kenyon Hopkins.

STRANGER THAN PARADISE - THE RESURRECTION OF ALBERT AYLER
Soundtrack (1984) ....*Enigma (S) SJ-73213*   84   8-10

Composer: John Lurie. Cast: John Lurie.

STRAW DOGS
Studiotrack (1978) ....*Citadel (S) CTJF-2/3*   78   75-100
> Has four original scores arranged into suites. Includes *The Mechanic, Lawman* and *Chato's Land*. Gatefold cover.

Composer: Jerry Fielding. Conductor: Jerry Fielding.

STRAWBERRY BLOND
Soundtrack (1941) ....*Radiola (M) MR-1103*   10-12

Cast: James Cagney; Olivia de Havilland.

STRAWBERRY STATEMENT
Soundtrack (1970) .... *MGM (S) 2SE-14*   70   **$20-25**
Double LP set.
  Composer: Ian Freebairn-Smith; Karl Bohm. Cast: Buffy Sainte-Marie; Neil Young; Crosby,
  Stills and Nash; Thunderclap Newman; Karl Bohm; Red Mountain Jug Band; MGM Studio
  Orchestra.

STREET SCENE
Original Cast (1947) .... *Columbia (M) ML-4139*   49   **40-50**
Original Cast (1947) .... *Columbia (M) OL-4139*   Re   **35-40**
Original Cast (1947) ....*Columbia Special Products (M) COL-4139*   77   **8-10**
  Composer: Kurt Weill; Langston Hughes. Conductor: Maurice Abravanel. Cast: Anne Jeffreys;
  Polyna Stoska; Brian Sullivan; Hope Emerson; Don Saxon; Remo Lota; Beverly Janis; Creighton
  Thompson; Peggy Turnley; Ellen Carleen.

STREETCAR NAMED DESIRE
Soundtrack (1951) .... *Capitol (EP) FBF-289*   51   **30-50**
Double EP.
Soundtrack (1951) ....*Capitol (M) L-289*   51   **60-75**
10-inch LP.
  Composer: Alex North. Cast: Debra Dobkin.
Soundtrack (1951) ....*Capitol (M) T-387*   53   **65-80**
  Includes Max Steiner's Academy Award winning scores from *Since You Went Away* (1944), *Now Voyager*
  (1942), and *The Informer* (1935).
Soundtrack (1951) .... *Angel (M) S-36068*   64   **10-12**
Soundtrack (1951) .... *Allegiance (M) 439*   **8-10**
  Composer: Alex North. Conductor: Ray Heindorf. Cast: Debra Dobkin.

STREETS OF FIRE
Soundtrack (1984) ....*MCA (S) 5492*   84   **8-10**
  Composer: Various. Cast: Fire Inc.; Fix; Blasters; Marilyn Martin; Greg Phillingames; Maria
  McKee; Dan Hartman; Ry Cooder.

STROKER ACE
Soundtrack (1983) ....*MCA (S) 36003*   83   **8-10**
  Composer: Various. Cast: Marshall Tucker Band; Larry Gatlin; Terri Gibbs.

STRONG TOGETHER
Soundtrack .... *Big Tree (S) 76016*   **10-12**
  Composer: Various. Cast: Hot.

STUDENT PRINCE
Studio Cast (1950) .... *Decca (M) DL-7008*   50   **35-40**
10-inch LP.
Studio Cast (1950) .... *Decca (M) DL-8362*   52   **25-35**
10-inch LP. One side has music from *The Vagabond King*.
  Composer: Sigmund Romberg; Dorothy Donnelly. Conductor: Victor Young. Cast: Jane
  Wilson; Lee Sweetland; Gloria Lane.
Studio Cast (1962) ....*Capitol (S) SW-1841*   62   **25-30**
Studio Cast (1962) .... *Angel (S) S-37318*   73   **8-12**
  Composer: Sigmund Romberg; Dorothy Donnelly. Conductor: Van Alexander. Cast: Gordon
  MacRae; Dorothy Kirsten; Earle Wilkie; Richard Robinson; William Felber; Roger Wagner
  Chorale.
Studio Cast (1965) .... *Columbia (M) OL-5980*   65   **15-20**
Studio Cast (1965) .... *Columbia (S) OS-2380*   65   **20-25**
  Composer: Sigmund Romberg; Dorothy Donnelly. Conductor: Franz Allers. Cast: Roberta
  Peters; Jan Peerce; Giorgio Tozzi; Anita Darian; Lawrence Avery; Merrill Staton Choir.

Studio Cast (1953)	Columbia (M) ML-4592	53	$30-40
Studio Cast (1953)	Columbia (M) CL-826	56	25-30
Studio Cast (1953)	Columbia/Odyssey (M) Y-32367	Re	8-10

Composer: Sigmund Romberg; Dorothy Donnelly. Conductor: Lehman Engel. Cast: Dorothy Kirsten; Robert Rounseville; Genevieve Warner; Warner Dalton; Clifford Harvout; Brenda Miller.

Studio Cast (1951)	RCA Victor/Camden (M) CAL-382	57	15-25

Composer: Sigmund Romberg; Dorothy Donnelly. Conductor: Al Goodman. Cast: Earl Wrightson; Frances Greer; Donald Dame; Mary Martha Briney.

Studio Cast (1954)	RCA Victor (EP) ERB-1837	54	10-15

Composer: Sigmund Romberg; Dorothy Donnelly. Cast: Mario Lanza; Elizabeth Doubleday.

Studio Cast (1954)	RCA Victor (EP) LPC-117	61	10-12

Compact 33 Double.

Studio Cast (1954)	RCA Victor (M) LM-1837	54	30-35

Conductor: Constantine Callinicos.

Studiotrack (1954)	RCA Victor (M) LM-2339	60	20-25
Studio Cast (1954)	RCA Victor (SE) LSC-2339	60	10-20

Composer: Sigmund Romberg; Dorothy Donnelly. Conductor: Paul Baron. Cast: Mario Lanza; Norma Giusti.

Studio Cast (1954)	RCA Victor (SE) LSC-3216	Re	8-10

Composer: Sigmund Romberg; Dorothy Donnelly. Cast: Mario Lanza; Elizabeth Doubleday.
Also see CHOCOLATE SOLDIER; DESERT SONG; MERRY WIDOW

STUDY IN TERROR

Soundtrack (1965)	Roulette (M) OS-801	66	25-35
Soundtrack (1965)	Roulette (S) OSS-801	66	30-40

Composer: John Scott. Conductor: John Scott.

STUNT MAN

Soundtrack (1980)	20th Century-Fox (S) T-626	80	15-20

Composer: Dominic Frontiere. Conductor: Dominic Frontiere. Cast: Dusty Springfield.

SUBJECT WAS ROSES

Original Cast (1964)	Columbia (M) DOL-308	64	25-30
Original Cast (1964)	Columbia (S) DOS-708	64	35-40

Above two are triple LP sets.
Composer: Frank D. Gilroy (his dramatic play). Cast: Jack Albertson; Irene Dailey; Martin Sheen. (Dialogue.)

SUBTERRANEANS

Soundtrack (1960)	MGM (M) E-3812	60	35-40
Soundtrack (1960)	MGM (S) SE-3812	60	45-55

Composer: Andre Previn; others. Conductor: Andre Previn. Cast: Gerry Mulligan; Carmen McRae.

SUBURBIA

Soundtrack (1983)	Enigma (S) 71093-1	83	8-10

Composer: Various. Cast: Alex Gibson; Vandals; T.S.O.L.

SUBWAY

Soundtrack (1985)	Varese Sarabande (S) STV-81269	85	8-10

Composer: Eric Serra. Cast: Eric Serra.

SUBWAYS ARE FOR SLEEPING

Original Cast (1961)	Columbia (M) KOL-5730	61	30-35
Original Cast (1961)	Columbia (S) KOS-2130	61	40-45

Above two have gatefold covers.

Original Cast (1961)	Columbia Special Products (S) AOS-2130	Re	8-10

Composer: Jule Styne; Betty Comden; Adolph Green. Conductor: Milton Rosenstock. Cast: Sydney Chaplin; Carol Lawrence; Orson Bean; Phyllis Newman; Cy Young; John Sharpe; Bob Gorman; Gene Varrone.

SUBWAYS ARE FOR SLEEPING (continued)
Studio Cast (1961) .... *Coral (M) CRL-57398*   61 $20-30
Studio Cast (1961) .... *Coral (S) CRL7-57398*   61   30-40
  Composer: Jule Styne; Betty Comden; Adolph Green. Conductor: Burt Farber. Cast: McGuire
  Sisters.
Studiotrack (1961) .... *Epic (M) LN-3829*   62   20-30
Studiotrack (1961) .... *Epic (S) BN-622*   62   25-35
  Jazz renditions.
  Cast: Dave Grusin.

SUDDEN IMPACT
Soundtrack (1983) .... *Viva (S) 1-23990*   83   8-10
  Also has themes from other "Dirty Harry" films such as *Magnum Force* and *The Enforcer*.
  Composer: Lalo Schifrin. Cast: Roberta Flack; Enforcers.

SUGAR
Original Cast (1972) .... *United Artists (S) UAS-9905*   72   20-25
  Composer: Jule Styne; Robert Merrill. Conductor: Elliot Lawrence. Cast: Robert Morse; Tony
  Roberts; Cyril Ritchard; Elaine Joyce (as "Sugar"); Sheila Smith.

SUMMER AND SMOKE
Soundtrack (1961) .... *RCA Victor (M) LOC-1067*   62   60-75
Soundtrack (1961) .... *RCA Victor (S) LSO-1067*   62   75-90
Soundtrack (1961) .... *Entr' acte (S) ERS-6519*   Re   8-10
  Composer: Elmer Bernstein. Conductor: Elmer Bernstein.

SUMMER HOLIDAY
Soundtrack (1963) .... *Epic (M) LN-24063*   63   20-25
Soundtrack (1963) .... *Epic (S) BN-26063*   63   25-30
  Composer: Various. Cast: Cliff Richard and the Shadows.

SUMMER LOVE
Soundtrack (1958) .... *Decca (M) DL-8714*   58   60-70
  Composer: Henry Mancini; Rod McKuen; others. Conductor: Joseph Gershenson.
  Cast: Molly Bee; Rod McKuen; Kip Tyler; Jimmy Daley and the Ding-A-Lings.

SUMMER LOVERS
Soundtrack (1982) .... *Warner Bros. (S) 1-23695*   82   8-10
  Composer: Basil Poledouris. Conductor: Basil Poledouris. Cast: Chicago; Michael Sembello;
  Depeche Mode; Stephen Bishop; Tina Turner; Nona Hendryx; Heaven 17; Elton John.

SUMMER MAGIC
Soundtrack (1963) .... *Buena Vista (M) BV-4025*   63   15-20
Soundtrack (1963) .... *Buena Vista (S) STER-4025*   63   25-30
  Composer: Richard M. Sherman; Robert B. Sherman. Conductor: Tutti Camarata. Cast: Hayley
  Mills; Burl Ives; Eddie Hodges; Deborah Walley; Wendy Turner; Marilyn Hoover.
Soundtrack (1963) .... *Disneyland (S) DQ-1318*   68   10-15
  Also has music from *The Parent Trap* and *In Search of the Castaways*.
  Composer: Richard M. Sherman; Robert B. Sherman. Conductor: Tutti Camarata. Cast: Haley
  Mills; Maureen O'Hara; Tommy Sands; Annette; Maurice Chevalier; Burl Ives.

SUMMER OF '42
Soundtrack (1971) .... *Warner Bros. (S) WS-1925*   71   8-12
  While regarded as the *Summer of '42* soundtrack, this LP has only two tracks from that film. The
  remainder is music from *The Picasso Summer*.
  Composer: Michel Legrand. Conductor: Michel Legrand.

SUMMER PLACE (AND OTHER GREAT HITS FROM MOVIES)
Studiotrack (1959) .... *Columbia (M) 4121*   59   **$15-20**
  Also has music from: *Modern Times, Pillow Talk, On the Beach, Gigi* and *The F.B.I. Story.*
  Composer: Various. **Cast:** Percy Faith; Tony Bennett; Doris Day; Four Lads; Johnny Mathis;
  Bing Crosby; Duke Ellington; Norman Luboff Choir; Mitch Miller; Vic Damone; Richard Maltby.
  Also see HELEN OF TROY; PARRISH

SUMMER SCHOOL
Soundtrack (1987) ....*Chrysalis (S) OV-41607*   87   **8-10**
  Cast: Tami Show; Paul Engemann; Billy Burnette; Danny Elfman; Elisa Fiorillo; E.G. Daily;
  Fabulous Thunderbirds; Tone Norum; Tonio K.

SUMMER STOCK
Soundtrack (1950) ....*MGM (M) E-519*   50   **35-40**
  10-inch LP.
  Composer: Harry Warren; Harold Arlen; Saul Chaplin. **Conductor:** Johnny Green. **Cast:** Judy
  Garland; Gene Kelly; Gloria DeHaven; Phil Silvers; Pete Roberts.
  Also see PIRATE

SUMMER STORY
Soundtrack (1988) .... *Virgin Movie Music (S) 90961-1*   88   **8-10**

SUN ALSO RISES
Soundtrack (1957) .... *Kapp (M) KDL-7001*   57   **85-100**
Soundtrack (1957) .... *AEI (M) 3190*   81   **8-10**
  Composer: Hugo Friedhofer; Vincente Gomez; others. **Conductor:** Lionel Newman.

SUN SHINES BRIGHT:
see SANDS OF IWO JIMA

SUN VALLEY SERENADE
Soundtrack (1941) ....*RCA Victor (EP) EPBT-3064*   54   **15-25**
  Double EP set.
Soundtrack (1941) ....*RCA Victor (M) LPT-3064*   54   **40-50**
  10-inch LP.
  Conductor: Harry Warren; Glenn Miller. **Cast:** Glenn Miller and His Orchestra.
  Also see ORCHESTRA WIVES

SUNBURN
Soundtrack (1979) ....*Arrival (S) NU-9540*   77   **10-15**
  Composer: John Cameron; others. **Conductor:** John Cameron. **Cast:** Graham Gouldman;
  10CC; Heatwave; Kandidate; John Ferrara.

SUNDAY IN NEW YORK
Soundtrack (1963) .... *RCA Victor (M) LPM-2827*   63   **15-20**
Soundtrack (1963) ....*RCA Victor (S) LSP-2827*   63   **25-30**
  Composer: Peter Nero. **Conductor:** Peter Nero.

SUNDAY IN THE COUNTRY
Soundtrack (1984) .... *Varese Sarabande (S) 81227*   84   **8-10**

SUNDAY IN THE PARK WITH GEORGE
Original Cast (1984) ....*RCA Red Seal Digital (S) HBC1-5042*   84   **10-12**
  Includes 18-page booklet.
  Composer: Stephen Sondheim. **Conductor:** Paul Gemignani. **Cast:** Mandy Patinkin; Bernadette
  Peters.

SUNDERELLA PHOENIX SUNS
Studio Cast (1976) . . . . *Magnavox (S) FCLP-3097*   76 $15-20
  Promotional issue only. Play-by-play highlights of the Phoenix Suns' 1975-76 NBA season.
  Composer: Russ Byrnes (writer). **Cast:** Al McCoy (narrator).
  Also see IT'S A WHOLE NEW BALL GAME

SUNDOWNERS
Soundtrack (1960) . . . . *Cinema (S) LP-8014*   75   30-40
  Composer: Dimitri Tiomkin. **Conductor:** Hans Rossback.

SUNFLOWER
Soundtrack (1970) . . . . *Avco Embassy (S) AVE-0-110*   70   20-25
  Composer: Henry Mancini. **Conductor:** Henry Mancini. **Cast:** Henry Mancini and His Orchestra.

SUNNY
Original London Cast . . . . *World (M) SH-240*   20-25
  Composer: Jerome Kern; Oscar Hammerstein II; Otto Harbach. **Conductor:** Philip Braham.
  Cast: Binnie Hale (as "Sunny"); Jack Hobbs; Jack Buchanan; Elsie Randolph.
  Also see NO NO NANETTE

SUNNYSIDE
Soundtrack (1979) . . . . *American Int'l (S) AILP-3002*   79   8-10
  Composer: Steven Stahns; Stephen Longfellow; others. **Cast:** Harold Wheeler and the New York
  City Band. (With incidental music by Alan Douglas and Harold Wheeler.)

SUNSET BOULEVARD: THE CLASSIC FILM SCORES OF FRANZ WAXMAN
Studiotrack . . . . *RCA Victor (S) ARL1-0708*   74   10-20
  Includes insert with liner notes.
Studiotrack . . . . *RCA Victor (S) AGL 1-378*   80   8-10
  Without insert, liner notes. Music from: *Prince Valiant, A Place in the Sun, The Bride of Frankenstein,*
  Sunset Boulevard, Old Acquaintance, Rebecca, The Philadelphia Story and *Taras Bulba.*
  Composer: Franz Waxman. **Conductor:** Charles Gerhardt.

SUNSHINE
TV Soundtrack (1973) . . . . *MCA (S) 387*   73   10-12
  Composer: John Denver. **Cast:** Cliff DeYoung; Christina Raines. (With dialogue.)

SUNSHINE CAKE
Studiotrack (1950) . . . . *Decca (M) DL-4261*   62   25-35
  Also has selections from: *A Connecticut Yankee in King Arthur's Court, Top o' the Morning* and *Riding*
  High. Issued as part of *Bing's Hollywood Series.*
  Composer: James Van Heusen; John Burke. **Conductor:** Victor Young. **Cast:** Bing Crosby (all).
  CONNECTICUT YANKEE IN KING ARTHUR'S COURT: Rhonda Fleming; William Bendix;
  Sir Cedric Hardwicke; Ken Darby Choir; Rhythmmakers.

SUPERFLY
Soundtrack (1972) . . . . *Curtom (S) CRS-8014-ST*   72   12-15
  Composer: Curtis Mayfield. **Cast:** Curtis Mayfield.

SUPERFLY T.N.T.
Soundtrack (1973) . . . . *Buddah (S) 5136*   73   12-15

SUPERGIRL
Soundtrack (1984) . . . . *Varese Sarabande (S) STV-81231*   84   8-10
  Composer: Jerry Goldsmith. **Conductor:** Jerry Goldsmith. **Cast:** National Philharmonic
  Orchestra.

SUPERMAN
Original Radio Cast (1947) .... *Musette Records #1*   47 $50-75
Episode titled "The Flying Train." Double disc set. With 12-page storybook.
Original Radio Cast ....*Mark'56 (M) 588*   72   **8-10**
Original Radio Cast .... *Nostalgia Lane (M) 2NLR-1016*   77   **8-10**
Full title of above two: *Superman: Original Radio Broadcasts.*
Studio Cast .... *Warner Bros. (S) PRO-A-964*   81   **15-20**
Actual title: *The History of Superman - The Radio Special.* A one-hour radio show tracing the story of
Superman, from the comics, to radio and television, to films.
Also see IT'S A BIRD, IT'S A PLANE, IT'S SUPERMAN

SUPERMAN - THE MOVIE
Soundtrack (1979) ....*Warner Bros. (S) 2BSK-3257*   79   **12-15**
Double LP set.
Composer: John Williams. **Conductor:** John Williams. **Cast:** London Symphony Orchestra.
Soundtrack (1979) .... *Columbia (S) 35788*   79   **8-10**
Composer: John Williams. **Conductor:** John Williams. **Cast:** London Symphony Orchestra.

SUPERMAN II
Soundtrack (1980) ....*Warner Bros. (S) HS-3505*   80   **8-12**
Disc is laser-etched with five Superman logos circling each side.
Composer: Ken Thorne (from original material composed by John Williams). **Conductor:** Ken
Thorne.

SUPERMAN III
Soundtrack (1983) .... *Warner Bros. (S) 1-23879*   83   **8-10**
Composer: Ken Thorne; Giorgio Moroder; John Williams (original *Superman* theme).
Cast: Marshall Crenshaw; Chaka Khan; Roger Miller; Helen St. John.

SUPPER CLUB REVUE
Original Cast .... *AEI (M) 1135*   **8-10**
Cast: Sophie Tucker.

SURF PARTY
Soundtrack (1964) .... *20th Century-Fox (M) TFM-3131*   64   **15-20**
Soundtrack (1964) .... *20th Century-Fox (S) TFS-4131*   64   **25-30**
Composer: Jimmie Haskell; By Dunham. **Conductor:** Jimmie Haskell. **Cast:** Jackie DeShannon;
Astronauts; Routers; Kenny Miller; Patricia Morrow; Lory Patrick.

SURVIVAL OF ST. JOAN
Original Cast (1971) ....*Paramount (S) PAS-9000*   71   **20-25**
Double LP set.
Composer: Hank Ruffin; Gary Ruffin; James Lineberger. **Conductor:** Stephen Schwartz.
Cast: F. Murray Abraham; Willie Rook; Lenny Baker; Ronald Bishop; Richard Bright;
Elizabeth Elis; Peter Lazer; Janet Samo.

SUSPIRA
Soundtrack (1977) ....*AT LAT (S) 1042*   77   **10-12**
Composer: Dario Argento; Goblin. **Cast:** Dario Argento; Goblin.

SWALLOWS AND AMAZONS
Soundtrack (1974) .... *Merry-Go-Round (S) MFP-50155*   74   **15-20**
Composer: Wilfred Josephs. **Cast:** Virginia McKenna; Ronald Fraser. (With dialogue.)

SWAMP THING
Soundtrack (1982) .... *Varese Sarabande (S) STV-81154*   82   **8-10**
Composer: Harry Manfredini. **Conductor:** Harry Manfredini.

SWAN
Soundtrack (1956) ....*MGM (M) E-3300*   56   **75-100**
Soundtrack (1956) .... *MCA (M) 25086*   **8-10**
Composer: Bronislau Kaper. **Conductor:** Johnny Green. **Cast:** MGM Studio Orchestra.

SWAN DOWN GLOVES
Soundtrack . . . .*That's Entertainment (S) TER-1017*   **$8-12**

SWANEE RIVER
Radio Cast (1977) . . . . *Totem (S) 1028*   77   **8-10**
  Composer: Stephen Foster. Cast: Dennis Morgan; Al Jolson; Frances Gifford; Walter Huston
  (host).

SWANN IN LOVE/KATHARINA BLUM
Soundtrack . . . . *Varese Sarabande (S) 81224*   **8-10**
  Cast: Basel Radio Symphony Orchestra.

SWARM
Soundtrack (1978) . . . .*Warner Bros. (S) BSK-3208*   78   **12-15**
  Composer: Jerry Goldsmith. Conductor: Jerry Goldsmith.

SWASHBUCKLER
Soundtrack (1976) . . . .*MCA (S) 2096*   77   **15-18**
  Composer: John Addison. Conductor: John Addison.

SWEDEN, HEAVEN AND HELL
Soundtrack (1969) . . . . *Ariel (S) ARS-15000*   69   **15-20**
  Composer: Peter Umiliani. Conductor: Peter Umiliani.

SWEDISH FLY GIRLS
Soundtrack (1975) . . . .*Juno (S) S-1003*   75   **10-12**
  Music produced by Manfred Mann.
  Composer: Mose Henry; Melanie Safka.

SWEENEY TODD (THE DEMON BARBER OF FLEET STREET)
Studio Cast (1979) . . . . *RCA Victor (S) PD-11687*   79   **10-12**
  12-inch, disco pressing of *The Ballad of Sweeney Todd.* Shows RCA's Red Seal label as "Red Seals Disco."
  Cast: His Master's Fish, featuring Gordon Grody.
Original Cast (1979) . . . . *RCA Victor (S) CBL2-3379*   79   **15-20**
  Double LP set.
  Composer: Stephen Sondheim. Conductor: Paul Gemignani. Cast: Angela Lansbury; Len
  Cariou; Victor Garber; Ken Jennings; Merle Louise; Sarah Rice; Edmund Lyndeck.

SWEET BYE AND BYE
Original Cast (1974) . . . . *Desto (S) DC-7179/8*   74   **15-20**
  Composer: Jack Beeson; Kenward Elmslie. Conductor: Russell Patterson. Cast: Noel Rogers;
  Judith Anthony; Carolyn James; Paula Seibel; Robert Owen Jones; Walter Hook; Elizabeth
  Green; Dennis Howell; William Latimer.

SWEET CHARITY
Original Cast (1966) . . . .*Columbia (M) KOL-6500*   66   **10-15**
Original Cast (1966) . . . .*Columbia (S) KOS-2900*   66   **15-20**
  Composer: Cy Coleman; Dorothy Fields. Conductor: Fred Warner. Cast: Gwen Verdon; John
  McMartin; Thelma Oliver; James Luisi; Helen Gallagher; Arnold Soboloff; John Wheeler;
  Harold Pierson; Michael Davis.
Original Revival Cast (1986) . . . .*EMI (S) R-164190*   86   **8-12**
Original Revival Cast (1986) . . . .*EMI (S) SV-17196*   **8-10**
  Composer: Cy Coleman; Dorothy Fields. Cast: Deborah Allen; Michael Rupert.
Soundtrack (1969) . . . .*Decca (S) DL-71502*   69   **12-18**
  Composer: Cy Coleman; Dorothy Fields. Conductor: Joseph Gershenson. Cast: Shirley
  MacLaine; John McMartin; Chita Rivera; Paula Kelly; Stubby Kaye; Sammy
  Davis Jr.
  Also see MAME; OPENING NIGHT AT THE PALACE - SWEET CHARITY

SWEET DREAMS (THE LIFE AND TIMES OF PATSY CLINE)
Soundtrack (1985) ....*MCA (S) 6149* 85 **$8-10**
  Composer: Various. **Cast:** Patsy Cline.

SWEET LIES
Soundtrack (1988) .... *Island (S) 90855-1* 88 **8-10**
  Composer: Various. **Cast:** Compagnie Creole; Robert Palmer; Trevor Jones; Paul McGovern;
  Gold; Salif Keita; George Decimus.

SWEET LOVE, BITTER
Soundtrack (1967) .... *Impulse (M) A-9142* 67 **10-12**
  Story inspired by jazz musician Charlie "Bird" Parker.
Soundtrack (1967) ....*Impulse (S) AS-9142* 67 **12-15**
  Composer: Mal Waldron. **Cast:** Mal Waldron.

SWEET RIDE
Soundtrack (1968) ....*20th Century-Fox (S) TFS-S-419* 68 **15-20**
  Composer: Pete Rugolo; Lee Hazlewood. **Conductor:** Pete Rugolo. **Cast:** Dusty Springfield.

SWEET SMELL OF SUCCESS
Soundtrack (1957) ....*Decca (M) DL-8610* 57 **45-50**
  Composer: Elmer Bernstein; Chico Hamilton; Fred Katz. **Conductor:** Elmer Bernstein.
Studiotrack (1957) ....*Decca (M) DL-8614* 57 **25-30**
  Jazz renditions.
  Composer: Chico Hamilton; Fred Katz. **Cast:** Chico Hamilton Quintet.

SWEET SWEETBACK'S BAADASSSSS SONG
Soundtrack (1971) .... *Stax (S) STS-3001* 71 **15-20**
  Conductor: Melvin Van Peebles. **Cast:** Melvin Van Peebles; Earth, Wind and Fire; Brer Soul.

SWEETHEARTS
Studio Cast (1951) ....*RCA Victor (EP) EKB-1015* 51 **15-20**
  Double EP set.
Studio Cast (1951) ....*RCA Victor (M) LK-1015* 51 **50-60**
  Composer: Victor Herbert; Robert B. Smith. **Conductor:** Al Goodman. **Cast:** Earl Wrightson;
  Frances Greer; Jimmie Carroll; Christina Lind; Guild Choristers.
Studio Cast (1951) .... *RCA Victor/Camden (M) CAL-369* 57 **35-40**
  Composer: Victor Herbert; Robert B. Smith. **Conductor:** Al Goodman. **Cast:** Earl Wrightson;
  Frances Greer; Jimmy Carroll; Christina Lind; Guild Choristers.

SWIMMER
Soundtrack (1968) ....*Columbia (S) OS-3210* 68 **50-60**
  Composer: Marvin Hamlisch. **Conductor:** Jack Hayes.

SWINGER

Soundtrack (1966)	RCA Victor (M) LPM-3710	66	$20-25
Soundtrack (1966)	RCA Victor (S) LSP-3710	66	30-35

Has five tracks from *The Swinger*. Others include one tune from *Monde Cane* and one from *The Seven Capital Sins*.

Composer: Andre Previn; Martin Paich; Harold Arlen; Johnny Mercer. **Conductor:** Martin "Marty" Paich. **Cast:** Ann-Margret.

SWINGER'S PARADISE

Soundtrack (1965)	Epic (M) LN-24145	65	15-20
Soundtrack (1965)	Epic (S) BN-26145	65	20-25

Conductor: Stanley Black. **Cast:** Cliff Richard and the Shadows; Michael Sammes Singers; Norrie Paramor Strings.

SWINGIN' SUMMER

Soundtrack (1966)	HBR (M) HLP-8500	66	20-25
Soundtrack (1966)	HBR (M) HST-8500	66	25-30

Composer: Various. **Cast:** Donnie Brooks; Righteous Brothers; Rip Chords; Raquel Welch; Carol Conners; Swingers.

SWINGING ON A STAR

Studiotrack (1944)	Decca (M) DL-4257	62	25-30

Also has music from *The Road to Morocco*, *Dixie* and *Going My Way*. Issued as part of *Bing's Hollywood Series*.

Composer: James Van Heusen; John Burke. **Conductor:** Vic Schoen; John Scott Trotter. **Cast:** Bing Crosby; Bob Hope.

SWITZERLAND:
see SAMOA

SWORD AND THE SORCERER

Soundtrack (1982)	Varese Sarabande (S) STV-81158	82	8-10

Composer: David Whitaker. **Conductor:** David Whitaker.

SWORD IN THE STONE

Soundtrack (1963)	Disneyland (M) ST-4901	63	20-25
Soundtrack (1963)	Disneyland (M) DQ-1236	64	8-12

Composer: Richard M. Sherman; Robert B. Sherman.

SYLVESTER

Soundtrack (1985)	MCA (S) 39026	85	8-10

Composer: Various. **Cast:** Los Lobos; Gail Davies; Cruzados; Sylvester; Rank and File.

SYLVIA

Soundtrack (1965)	Mercury (M) MG-21004	65	20-25
Soundtrack (1965)	Mercury (S) SR-61004	65	25-30

Composer: David Raksin. **Conductor:** David Raksin.

SYNANON

Soundtrack (1965)	Liberty (M) LRP-3413	65	20-25
Soundtrack (1965)	Liberty (S) LST-7413	65	25-30

Composer: Neal Hefti; others. **Conductor:** Neal Hefti. **Cast:** Neal Hefti and His Orchestra.

T

T.C.B. (TAKIN' CARE OF BUSINESS)
TV Soundtrack (1968) .... *Tamla/Motown (S) MS-682* 68 **$10-12**
TV Soundtrack (1968) .... *Natural Resources (S) NR-4020T1* **8-10**
  Composer: Smokey Robinson; Holland-Dozier-Holland. **Cast:** Diana Ross and the Supremes; Temptations.

T.R. BASKIN
Soundtrack (1971) .... *Paramount (S) PAS-6018* 71 **20-25**
  Composer: Jack Elliott; June Jackson. **Conductor:** Jack Elliott.

TAI-PAN
Soundtrack (1986) .... *Varese Sarabande (S) STV-81293* 86 **8-10**
  Composer: Maurice Jarre. **Conductor:** Maurice Jarre.

TAKE FIVE
Original Cast (1958) .... *Offbeat (M) O-4013* 58 **65-75**
  With "curtain" cover.
Original Cast (1958) .... *Offbeat (M) O-4013* 58 **30-40**
  With standard (no curtain) cover.
  Conductor: Stan Keen. **Cast:** Jean Arnold; Ceil Cabot; Ellen Hanley; Ronny Graham; Gerry Matthews; Stan Keen and Gordon Connell (plural pianos).

TAKE IT FROM HERE
Original Cast (1963) .... *Columbia (M) No Number Given* 63 **45-55**
  10-inch LP. Made exclusively for Xerox from a show performed at a September 16, 1963 company meeting.
  Composer: Wilson Stone. **Conductor:** Maurice Levine.

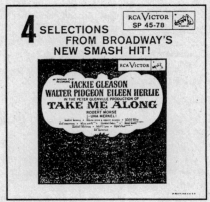

TAKE ME ALONG
Original Cast (1959) .... *RCA Victor (EP) SP-45-78* 59 **15-20**
  Promotional issue only.
Original Cast (1959) .... *RCA Victor (M) LOC-1050* 59 **25-35**
Original Cast (1959) .... *RCA Victor (S) LSO-1050* 59 **35-40**
  Composer: Robert Merrill. **Conductor:** Lehman Engel. **Cast:** Jackie Gleason; Walter Pidgeon; Eileen Herlie; Robert Morse; Una Merkel; Susan Lucky; Peter Conlow.

TAKE THIS JOB AND SHOVE IT
Soundtrack (1981) ....*Epic (S) SE-37177*   81   **$8-10**
  Cast: Johnny Paycheck.

TAKING OFF
Soundtrack (1971) ....*Decca (S) 79181*   71   **10-12**
  Composer: Various. **Cast:** Nina Hart; Susan Chafitz; 48 Girls; Carly Simon; Mary Mitchell;
  Ike and Tina Turner; Susan Cohen; Incredible String Band; Buck Henry.

TALE OF THE GIANT RAT OF SUMATRA
Original Cast (1974) ....*Columbia (S) C-32730*   74   **10-12**
  Cast: Firesign Theatre (Phil Austin, Peter Bergman, David Ossman, Philip Proctor).

TALE OF TWO CITIES
Studio Cast (1949) ....*Decca (M) DL-5153*   50   **40-50**
  10-inch LP.
  Conductor: George Wells.

TALES OF HOFFMAN
Soundtrack (1951) ....*London (M) XLLPA-4*   **40-50**
  Triple LP, boxed set. Includes booklet.
  Composer: Jacques Offenbach. **Cast:** Robert Rounseville; Pamela Brown, others.

TALES OF THE UNEXPECTED
TV Soundtrack (1979) ....*Stet (S) DS-15018*   80   **8-10**
  Also has music from: *Edward and Mrs. Simpson, Malice Aforethought, Born and Bred, Rebecca, Paul
  Temple* and *Dr. Who.*
  Composer: Ron Grainer. **Conductor:** Robert Kingston.

TAMALPAIS EXCHANGE
Original Cast (1970) ....*Atlantic (S) SD-8263*   70   **25-30**
  From the show titled *Exchange.*
  Cast: Penelope Ann Bodry; Mike Brandt; Susan Kay; Michael Knight.

TAMBOURINES TO GLORY
Studio Cast (1958) ....*Folkways (M) FG-3538*   58   **15-20**
  Composer: Jobe Huntley; Langston Hughes. **Cast:** Ernest Cook; Porter Singers.

TAMING OF THE SHREW
Soundtrack (1967) ....*RCA Victor (M) VDM-117*   67   **50-75**
  Composer: Nino Rota. **Conductor:** Nino Rota. **Cast:** Elizabeth Taylor; Richard Burton.
  (With dialogue.)

TAMMY AND THE BACHELOR:
see INTERLUDE

TAP DANCE KID
Original Cast (1984) ....*Polydor (S) 820210-1*   84   **15-20**
  Composer: Henry Krieger; Robert Lorick. **Conductor:** Don Jones.

TAPEHEADS
Soundtrack (1988) ....*Island (S) 91030-1*   88   **8-10**
  Composer: Various. **Cast:** Swanky Modes; Devo; Bo Diddley; King Cotton; Fishbone.

TARAS BULBA
Soundtrack (1962) ....*United Artists (M) UAL-4100*   62   **45-55**
Soundtrack (1962) ....*United Artists (S) UAS-5100*   62   **65-75**
  Above two have gatefold covers.
  Composer: Franz Waxman. **Conductor:** Franz Waxman.

TAROT
Original Cast (1970) ....*United Artists (S) UAS-5563*   70   **15-20**
  Composer: Touchstone. **Cast:** Touchstone (Tom Constanten; Paul Dresher; Gary Hirsh; Wes
  Steele; Art Fayer; Jim Byers). Touchstone was previously known as the Original Rubber Duck
  Band.

TARZAN AND THE EYES OF THE LION
TV Soundtrack (1966) .... *MGM (M) LE-902*   66 $12-15
TV Soundtrack (1966) .... *MGM (S) LES-902*   66   **15-20**
  Cast: Ron Ely.

TARZAN THE APE MAN
Soundtrack (1960) .... *.MGM (M) E-3798*   60   **15-20**
Soundtrack (1960) .... *MGM (S) SE-3798*   60   **20-25**
  Composer: Shorty Rogers. Conductor: Shorty Rogers.

TASTE OF HONEY
Studio Cast (1960) .... *Atlantic (M) 1355*   61   **15-20**
Studio Cast (1960) .... *Atlantic (S) SD-1355*   61   **20-30**
  Bobby Scott plays his original music for the original Broadway production.
  Composer: Bobby Scott. Cast: Bobby Scott.

TAXI DRIVER
Soundtrack (1976) .... *Arista (S) AL-1079*   76   **15-20**
  Composer: Bernard Herrmann. Conductor: Bernard Herrmann; Dave Blume. Cast: Robert
  DeNiro. (With dialogue.)

TEA DANCE
Original Cast (1976) .... *Pyramid (S) PY-9006*   76   **10-12**
  Composer: D.C. LaRue. Conductor: Adam Schefrin; Steve Tubin. Cast: D.C. LaRue; Lou
  Christie.

TEA FOR TWO
Studiotrack (1950) .... *Columbia (M) CL-6149*   50   **35-45**
  10-inch LP.
  Composer: Richard Rodgers; Lorenz Hart; George Gershwin; Ira Gershwin; Harry Warren;
  others. Conductor: Axel Stordahl. Cast: Doris Day; Gene Nelson; Ken Lane Singers; Page
  Cavanaugh Trio.
Studio Cast .... *Columbia Collectors Series (S) 17660*   **8-12**
  Also has music from *On Moonlight Bay.*

TEACHERS
Soundtrack (1984) .... *Capitol (S) SV-12371*   84   **8-10**
  Composer: Various. Cast: ZZ Top; :38 Special; Roman Holliday; Joe Cocker; Night Ranger;
  Freddie Mercury; Bob Seger and Silver Bullet Band; Eric Martin and Friends; Motels; Ian Hunter.

TEEN WOLF
Soundtrack (1985) .... *Southern Cross (S) SCRS-1010*   85   **8-10**
  Cast: Miles Goodman; Douglas Brayfield.

TEEN WOLF TOO
Soundtrack (1987) .... *Curb (S) CRB-10400*   87   **8-10**
  Sequel to *Teen Wolf.*

TEEN-AGE CRUISERS
Soundtrack (1980) .... *Rhino (S) 016*   80   **8-10**
  Composer: Various. Cast: Johnny Legend; Billy Zoom; Blasters; Ray Campi; "Wildman" Tony
  Conn; Jerry Sikorski; Alvis Wayne; Jackie Lee "Waukeen" Chochran; Charlie Feathers.

TEENAGE MUTANT NINJA TURTLES
Soundtrack (1989) .... *SBK (S) K1-91066*   89   **8-10**
  Composer: Various. Cast: Hi Tek 3; Partners in Kryme; M.C.; Riff; Spunkadelic; Johnny Kemp;
  Investiture and Crime Wave; John Du Prez; Turtles Mutate; Orchestra on the Half Shell.

TEENAGE REBELLION
Soundtrack (1967) .... *Sidewalk (M) T-5903*   67 $12-15
Soundtrack (1967) .... *Sidewalk (S) ST-5903*   67   **15-20**
  Composer: Mike Curb; Bob Summers; others. **Cast:** Burt Topper (narration).

TELEPHONE:
see MEDIUM

TELEVISION THEME SONGS
TV Soundtrack .... *Elektra (S) EL-60028*   82   **8-10**
  Has music from: *Hill Street Blues, The Greatest American Hero, The White Shadow, Richie Brockelman, Private Eye, The Rockford Files* and *Magnum P.I.*
  Composer: Mike Post. **Conductor:** Mike Post. **Cast:** Mike Post.
  Also see MIKE POST

TELL ME LIES
Soundtrack (1967) .... *Gre-Gar (M) GG-5000*   67   **12-15**
Soundtrack (1967) .... *Gre-Gar (S) GGS-5000*   67   **15-20**
  Composer: Richard Peaslee; Adrian Mitchell. **Conductor:** Tony Russell. **Cast:** Glenda Jackson; Stokely Carmichael.(Wth dialogue.)

TELL ME ON A SUNDAY
Original Cast (1980) .... *Polydor (S) PD-1-6260*   80   **8-10**
  Composer: Andrew Lloyd Webber; Don Black. **Conductor:** Harry Rabinowitz; David Caddick; Paul Maguire. **Cast:** Marti Webb; Elaine Stritch; others.

TELL ME THAT YOU LOVE ME, JUNIE MOON
Soundtrack (1970) .... *Columbia (S) OS-3540*   70   **12-18**
  Composer: Philip Springer. **Conductor:** Philip Springer. **Cast:** Pete Seeger; PG&E.

TELL TALE HEART:
see WEIRD CIRCLE

TEMPEST
Original London Cast (1964) .... *Caedmon (M) M-201*   64   **12-15**
Original London Cast (1964) .... *Caedmon (S) S-201*   64   **15-20**
  Above two are triple LP sets.

TEMPEST
Soundtrack (1982) .... *Casablanca (S) NBLPH 726*   82   **8-10**
  Composer: Stomu Yamashta. **Conductor:** Stomu Yamashta. **Cast:** Dinah Washington.

10
Soundtrack (1979) .... *Warner Bros. (S) BSK-3399*   79   **8-10**
  Composer: Henry Mancini; Maurice Ravel; others. **Conductor:** Henry Mancini. **Cast:** Henry Mancini and His Orchestra.

TEN COMMANDMENTS
Soundtrack (1956) .... *Dot (M) DLP-3054-D*   56   **60-70**
Soundtrack (1956/1960) .... *Dot (S) DLP-25054-D*   60   **45-55**
  Rerecorded in 1960 especially for stereo release. Above two are double LP sets.
  Composer: Elmer Bernstein. **Conductor:** Elmer Bernstein.
Soundtrack (1956) .... *United Artists (SE) UAS-6495*   66   **15-20**
Soundtrack (1956) .... *United Artists (SE) UA-LA304-G*   74   **8-10**
  Composer: Elmer Bernstein. **Conductor:** Elmer Bernstein.

TEN GOLDEN YEARS
Soundtrack (1968) .... *United Artists (S) UXS-68*   68   **20-25**
  Double LP set. Soundtracks and other music from 36 films.

TEN NORTH FREDERICK
Studiotrack (1958) .... *Aud (M) 33-592B*   58   **40-50**

TEN THOUSAND BEDROOMS
Studiotrack (1957) . . . .*Capitol (EP) EAP 1-840*   57 $25-50
  Composer: Nicholas Brodszky; Sammy Cahn. **Conductor:** Gus Levene. **Cast:** Dean Martin.

TEN TO MIDNIGHT
Soundtrack . . . . *Varese Sarabande (S) STV-81172*   8-10
  Cast: Robert O. Ragland.

TENDER IS THE NIGHT
Soundtrack (1962) . . . . *20th Century-Fox (M) FOX-3054*   62   125-150
Soundtrack (1962) . . . . *20th Century-Fox (S) SFX-3054*   62   175-200
  Composer: Sammy Fain; others. **Conductor:** Bernard Herrmann.

TENDER MERCIES
Soundtrack (1983) . . . .*Liberty (S) LO-51147*   83   8-10
  Composer: Various. **Cast:** Robert Duval; Charlie Craig; Sherry Grooms; Lane Brody; Criag
  Bickhardt; Gail Youngs.

TENDERLOIN
Original Cast (1960) . . . . *Capitol (M) WAO-1492*   60   30-40
Original Cast (1960) . . . .*Capitol (S) SWAO-1492*   60   40-45
  Includes theater program.
  Composer: Jerry Bock; Sheldon Harnick. **Conductor:** Hal Hastings. **Cast:** Ron Husmann; Wynne
  Miller; Eileen Rodgers; Rex Everhard; Maurice Evans; Eddie Phillips; Lee Becker; Raymond
  Bramley; Irene Kane; Nancy Emes; Carvel Caster; Margery Gray; Lanier Davis; Jack Leigh.

TENTH ANNIVERSARY JAMES BOND ALBUM
Soundtrack . . . . *United Artists (S) UXS-91*   72   20-25
  Double LP set. Music from: *Goldfinger, Dr. No, From Russia with Love, Thunderball, You Only Live
  Twice, On Her Majesty's Secret Service* and *Diamonds Are Forever.*
  Composer: John Barry; Monty Norman; Lionel Bart; Leslie Bricusse; Anthony Newley; Don
  Black; Hal David. **Conductor:** John Barry; Eric Rodgers. **Cast:** Matt Monro; Shirley Bassey.

TENTH VICTIM
Soundtrack (1965) . . . .*Mainstream (M) 56071*   65   15-20
Soundtrack (1965) . . . .*Mainstream (S) S-6071*   65   25-35
  Composer: Piero Piccioni. **Conductor:** Piero Piccioni. **Cast:** Mina.

TEPEPA
Soundtrack . . . .*Cerberus (S) CERS-0106*   82   8-10
  Composer: Ennio Morricone. **Conductor:** Ennio Morricone.

TEQUILA SUNRISE
Soundtrack (1988) . . . .*Capitol (S) C1-91185*   88   8-10
  Composer: Various. **Cast:** Ann Wilson; Robin Zander; Crowded House; Everly Brothers; Beach
  Boys; Andy Taylor; Church; Bobby Darin; Dave Grusin; Lee Ritenour; David Sanborn; Duran
  Duran; Ziggy Marley and Melody Makers.

TERMINATOR
Soundtrack (1984) . . . .*Enigma (S) 72000-1*   84   8-10
  Composer: Brad Fiedel; others. **Cast:** Tahnee Cain & Tryanglz; Jay Ferguson and 16mm; Lin
  Van Hek.

TERMS OF ENDEARMENT
Soundtrack (1984) . . . .*Capitol (S) SV-12329*   84   8-10
  Composer: Michael Gore. **Cast:** Ethel Merman; Eddie Roll, Grover Dale and the Jets; Judy
  Garland.

TERROR VISION
Soundtrack (1986) . . . .*Restless (S) 72120-1*   86   8-10
  Cast: Fibonaccis; Richard Band.

TESS
Soundtrack (1981) . . . . *MCA (S) 5193*   81   **$8-10**
   Composer: Philipe Sarde. **Conductor:** Carlo Savina. **Cast:** London Symphony Orchestra.

TEVYA AND HIS DAUGHTERS
Original Cast (1957) . . . . *Columbia (M) OL-5225*   57   **20-25**
   This show inspired *Fiddler on the Roof*.
   Composer: Serge Hovey. **Conductor:** Serge Hovey. **Cast:** Mike Kellin; Anna Vita Berger; Paul
   E. Richards; Carroll Conroy; Howard DaSilva; Joan Harvey.

TEXAS CHAINSAW MASSACRE PART 2
Soundtrack (1986) . . . . *I.R.S. (S) IRS-6184*   86   **8-10**
   Composer: Various. **Cast:** Torch Song; Lords of the New Church; Timbuk 3; Cramps; Concrete
   Blonde; Onigo Boingo; Stewart Copeland.

TEXAS LI'L DARLIN'
Original Cast (1949) . . . . *Decca (M) DL-5188*   77   **65-75**
   Composer: Robert Emmett Dolan; Johnny Mercer. **Conductor:** Will Irwin. **Cast:** Kenny Delmar;
   Danny Scholl; Mary Hatcher; Fredd Wayne; Loring Smith.

TEXAS ROMANCE, 1909:
see BAD COMPANY

THANK GOD IT'S FRIDAY
Soundtrack (1978) . . . . *Casablanca (S) NBLP-7099-3*   78   **15-20**
   Double LP set. Includes 12-inch bonus single.
   Composer: Various. **Cast:** Donna Summer; Commodores; Diana Ross; Thelma Houston; Santa
   Esmeralda; Pattie Brooks; Paul Jabara; Wright Brothers; Flying Machine; D.C. LaRue.
Soundtrack (1978) . . . . *Springboard (S) 0298*
   Composer: Various. **Cast:** Lionel Richie and the Commodores.

THAT DARN CAT
Soundtrack (1965) . . . . *Buena Vista (M) BV-3334*   65   **15-20**
Soundtrack (1965) . . . . *Buena Vista (S) STER-3334*   65   **25-30**
   Composer: Bob Brunner; Richard M. Sherman; Robert B. Sherman. **Conductor:** Bob Brunner.
   Cast: Louis Prima; Bobby Troup.

THAT MAN IN ISTANBUL
Soundtrack (1966) . . . . *Mainstream (M) 56072*   66   **20-25**
Soundtrack (1966) . . . . *Mainstream (S) S-6072*   66   **25-30**
   Composer: Georges Garvarentz; Buddy Kaye. **Cast:** Richard Anthony.

THAT MIDNIGHT KISS
Studiotrack (1949) . . . . *RCA Victor (M) LM-86*   51   **45-55**
   Actual title: *Double Feature*. Also has music from *Toast of New Orleans*.
Studiotrack (1949) . . . . *RCA Victor (M) LM-2422*   Re   **35-40**
   Composer: Various. **Conductor:** Constantine Callinicos; Ray Sinatra. **Cast:** Mario Lanza;
   Elaine Malbin.

THAT WAS THE WEEK THAT WAS
TV Soundtrack (1963) . . . . *Decca (M) DL-9116*   63   **12-15**
TV Soundtrack (1963) . . . . *Decca (S) DL7-9116*   63   **15-20**
   Chronicles events surrounding the assassination of President John F. Kennedy.
   Cast: David Frost; Dame Sybil Thorndyke.

THAT'S DANCING!
Soundtrack (1985) . . . . *EMI America (S) SJ-17149*   85   **8-10**
   Composer: Henry Mancini. **Cast:** Kim Carnes; Ruby Keeler; Wini Shaw; Dick Powell; Fred
   Astaire; Ginger Rogers; Ray Bolger; Judy Garland; Gene Kelly; Donald O'Connor; Ann Miller;
   Bobby Van; Tommy Rall; Bob Fosse; Bee Gees; Irene Cara.

THAT'S ENTERTAINMENT
Soundtrack (1974) .... *MCA (S) 2-11002*   74   **$12-15**
Double LP set.
Composer: Various. **Conductor:** Henry Mancini (overture); others. **Cast:** Fred Astaire
(narration); Bing Crosby; Gene Kelly; Frank Sinatra; James Stewart; Elizabeth Taylor;
Donald O'Connor; Peter Lawford; Debbie Reynolds; Liza Minnelli; Mickey Rooney.

THAT'S ENTERTAINMENT, PART 2
Soundtrack (1976) .... *MGM (S) MG-1-5301*   76   **10-12**
Composer: Various. **Conductor:** Nelson Riddle. **Cast:** Fred Astaire; Gene Kelly.
Soundtrack (1976) .... *MCA (S) 6155*   86   **8-10**

THAT'S THE WAY IT IS
Soundtrack (1970) .... *RCA Victor (S) LSP-4445*   70   **12-18**
Orange label.
Soundtrack (1970) .... *RCA Victor (S) AFL1-4445*   78   **10-12**
Composer: Various. **Conductor:** Joe Guercio. **Cast:** Elvis Presley; James Burton (guitar); John
Wilkinson (guitar); Jerry Scheff (bass); Ronnie Tutt (drums); Joe Guercio and His Orchestra;
Glen D. Hardin (piano); David Briggs (keyboards); Charlie Hodge (guitar, vocals); Kathy
Westmoreland (vocals); Imperials (vocals); Sweet Inspirations (vocals).

THEMES
Studiotrack (1962) .... *Capitol (M) T-1652*   62   **10-15**
Studiotrack (1962) .... *Capitol (S) ST-1652*   62   **15-20**
Conductor: Alfred Newman. **Cast:** Alfred Newman and His Orchestra.

THEMES FROM CLASSIC SCIENCE FICTION, FANTASY AND
    HORROR FILMS
Studiotrack .... *Coral (M) CRL-757240*   59   **40-45**
Music from: *The Mole People, The Creature from the Black Lagoon, This Island Earth, The Incredible
Shrinking Man, It Came from Outer Space, The Creature Walks Among Us, The House of Frankenstein,
The Horror of Dracula, Tarantula, Son of Dracula, Revenge of the Creature* and *Deadly Mantis.*
Studiotrack .... *Varese Sarabande (M) STV-81077*   78   **8-10**
Same as Coral LP except for the editing of narration and sound effects, which detracted from the original.
Remastered for improved sound quality.
Composer: Hans J. Salter; Herman Stein; Fred Carling; Ed Lawrence; Henry Mancini; Paul
Dressau; James Bernard; William Lava. **Conductor:** Dick Jacobs.

THEMES FROM MOTION PICTURES AND TV
Studiotrack (1960) .... *Carlton (M) LP 12-126*   60   **15-20**
Composer: Various. **Conductor:** Lew Douglas. **Cast:** Lew Douglas and His Orchestra.

THEMES FROM MUTINY ON THE BOUNTY (AND OTHER GREAT FILMS)
Studiotrack (1962) .... *Warner Bros. (M) W-1476*   62   **10-15**
Studiotrack (1962) .... *Warner Bros. (S) WS-1476*   62   **10-20**
Composer: Various. **Conductor:** George Greeley. **Cast:** George Greeley (piano) and His
Orchestra.

THEMES FROM THE JAMES BOND THRILLERS
Studiotrack (1965) .... *London (M) LL-3412*   65   **10-12**
Studiotrack (1965) .... *London (S) PS-412*   65   **10-15**
Music from *Goldfinger, From Russia with Love* and *Dr. No.*
Composer: Norman Barry; others. **Conductor:** Roland Shaw. **Cast:** Roland Shaw and His
Orchestra.

THEMES FROM THE MOVIES
Studiotrack (1956) .... *Tops (M) L-1519*   56   **15-25**
Composer: Various. **Conductor:** Lew Raymond. **Cast:** Lew Raymond and His Orchestra.

THEMES FROM TV'S TOP 12
Studiotrack (1962) .... *Reprise (M) R-6018*   62   **$10-15**
Studiotrack (1962) .... *Reprise (S) R9-6018*   62   **15-20**
  Composer: Various. **Conductor:** Neal Hefti. **Cast:** Neal Hefti and His Orchestra.

THERE'S NO BUSINESS LIKE SHOW BUSINESS
Soundtrack (1954) .... *Decca (EP) ED-828*   54   **15-20**
Soundtrack (1954) .... *RCA Victor (EP) EPA-593*   54   **15-20**
  Composer: Irving Berlin. **Cast:** Marilyn Monroe.
Soundtrack (1954) .... *Decca (M) DL-8091*   54   **30-40**
  Composer: Irving Berlin. **Conductor:** Alfred Newman; Lionel Newman. **Cast:** Ethel Merman;
  Donald O'Connor; Mitzi Gaynor; Johnnie Ray; Dan Dailey; Dolores Gray (performing the songs
  sung by Marilyn Monroe in the film).

THEY CALL IT AN ACCIDENT
Soundtrack .... *Island (S) WB-1457*   **10-12**
  Composer: W. DeLeon; P. Norbert.
Soundtrack (1982) .... *Island (S) XILP-9757*   82   **8-10**
  Cast: Steve Winwood; U2; Marianne Faithfull; Jess Roden; Peter Wood; Compass Point All Stars;
  Wallyu Badarou.

THEY CALL ME MISTER TIBBS
Soundtrack (1970) .... *United Artists (S) UAS-5214*   70   **12-18**
  Composer: Quincy Jones. **Conductor:** Quincy Jones.

THEY LIVE
Soundtrack (1988) .... *Enigma (S) D1-73367*   88   **8-10**
  Cast: John Carpenter; Alan Howarth.

THEY SHOOT HORSES, DON'T THEY?
Soundtrack (1969) .... *ABC (S) ABCS-OC-1*   69   **10-15**
  Composer: Johnny Green; others. **Conductor:** Johnny Green. **Cast:** Bonnie Bedelia (vocal).

THEY'RE PLAYING OUR SONG
Original Cast (1979) .... *Casablanca (S) NBLP-7141*   79   **8-12**
  Standard cover.
Original Cast (1979) .... *Casablanca (S) NBLP-7141*   79   **8-12**
  Gatefold cover.
  Composer: Marvin Hamlisch; Carol Bayer Sager. **Conductor:** Larry Blank. **Cast:** Robert
  Klein; Lucie Arnaz; Chorus.
Original London Cast (1980) .... *Chopper (S) CHOP-E-6*   80   **10-12**
Original Australian Cast (1979) .... *Festival (S) 37356*   79   **8-10**
  Composer: Marvin Hamlisch; Carole Bayer Sager. **Conductor:** Dale Ringland.
  Cast: John Waters; Jacki Weaver.
Original London Cast (1979) .... *That's Entertainment (S) TER-1035*   83   **8-10**
  Composer: Marvin Hamlisch; Carole Bayer Sager. **Conductor:** Grant Hossack.

THIEF
Soundtrack (1981) .... *Virgin (S) VL-2213*   81   **8-12**
  Composer: Tangerine Dream. **Cast:** Tangerine Dream.
Soundtrack (1981) .... *Elektra (S) 5E-521*   81   **8-10**
  Composer: Tangerine Dream (Edgar Froese, Chris Franke, Johannes Schmoelling); Craig Safan.
  Cast: Tangerine Dream.

THIEF OF BAGDAD
Studiotrack (1940) .... *Elmer Bernstein Film Music Collection (SE) FMC-8*   77   **30-35**
  Composer: Miklos Rozsa. **Conductor:** Elmer Bernstein. **Cast:** Royal Philharmonic Orchestra;
  Saltarello Choir; Bruce Ogston (baritone); Phyllis Cannan (mezzo-soprano); and Powell Jones as
  "Abu."

Studiotrack (1940) .... *Warner Bros. (SE) BSK-3183*   78   **$10-12**
  Composer: Miklos Rosza. **Conductor:** Elmer Bernstein. **Cast:** Saltarello Choir.
  Also see JUNGLE BOOK

THIEF OF HEARTS
Soundtrack (1984) ....*Casablanca (S) 422-82294*   84   **8-10**

THIEF WHO CAME TO DINNER
Soundtrack (1973) .... *Warner Bros. (S) BS-2700*   73   **12-15**
  Composer: Henry Mancini. **Conductor:** Henry Mancini.

THING
Soundtrack (1982) ....*MCA (S) 6111*   82   **8-10**
  Composer: Ennio Morricone. **Conductor:** Ennio Morricone.

THING-FISH
Original Cast (1984) .... *EMI (S) 24-0294-3*   84   **35-40**
  Triple LP, boxed set. With libretto.
  Composer: Frank Zappa. **Conductor:** Frank Zappa. **Cast:** Ike Willis; Terry Bozzio; Dale Bozzio;
  Napoleon Murphy Brock; Bob Harris; Johnny "Guitar" Watson; Ray White.

THINGS TO COME
Soundtrack (1937) ....*London (SE) STS-15112*   **10-12**
  Composer: Sir Arthur Bliss. **Conductor:** Sir Arthur Bliss. **Cast:** London Symphony Orchestra.
  Also see BERNARD HERRMANN CONDUCTS GREAT BRITISH FILM SCORES

THIRD MAN
Soundtrack (1949) .... *London (M) LL-1560*   56   **30-40**
  One side has zither duets by Fritz and Jacky.
  Cast: Anton Karas (zither).

THIRTEEN DAUGHTERS
Original Hawaiian Cast (1961) .... *Mahalo (S) M-3003*   61   **50-60**
  Composer: Eaton Magoon Jr. **Conductor:** Alvina Kaulili. **Cast:** Napua Stevens; Kam Fong
  Chun; Richard Kuga; Augustina Santiago; Tamara Long; Lordie Kaulili; Jack Annon.

30 IS A DANGEROUS AGE, CYNTHIA
Soundtrack (1968) .... *London (S) MS-82010*   68   **20-25**
  Composer: Dudley Moore. **Conductor:** Dudley Moore.

36 HOURS
Soundtrack (1964) ....*Vee Jay (M) VJLP-1131*   64   **35-40**
Soundtrack (1964) .... *Vee Jay (S) VJLPS-113*   64   **40-50**
Soundtrack (1964) ....*Varese Sarabande (S) VC-81071*   79   **8-10**
  Composer: Dimitri Tiomkin. **Conductor:** Dimitri Tiomkin.

33 GREAT WALT DISNEY MOTION PICTURE MELODIES
Studiotrack (1962) .... *Buena Vista (M) BV-3319*   62 $10-15
Studiotrack (1962) .... *Buena Vista (S) STER-3319*   62   15-20
  Conductor: Tutti Camarata.

THIS COULD BE THE NIGHT
Soundtrack (1957) .... *MGM (M) E-3530*   57   45-50
Soundtrack (1957) .... *MCA (SE) 39085*   86   8-10
  Conductor: Ray Anthony. **Cast:** Julie Wilson.

THIS EARTH IS MINE
Soundtrack (1959) .... *Decca (M) DL-8915*   59   75-100
Soundtrack (1959) .... *Decca (M) DL7-8915*   59   90-110
Soundtrack (1959) .... *Varese Sarabande (S) VC-81076*   79   8-10
  Composer: Hugo Friedhoffer; James Van Heusen; Sammy Cahn. **Conductor:** Joseph
  Gershenson. **Cast:** Bob Grabeau.

THIS IS BROADWAY'S BEST
Original Cast .... *Columbia (M) B2W-1*   25-30
Original Cast .... *Columbia (S) B2WS-1*   30-35
  Double LP set. Music from earlier Columbia original cast albums. Some tracks are in rechanneled stereo.
  Composer: Various. **Cast:** Jan Clayton; Charles Fredericks; Ella Logan; Annabelle Hill; Ezio
  Pinza; Carol Channing; Harold Lang; Beverly Fite; Carol Haney; Alfred Drake; Doretta Morrow;
  Richard Kiley; Henry Calvin; Enid Mosier; Ada Moore; Shorty Long; John Henson; Alan Gilbert;
  Roy Lazarus; Irra Petina; George Blackwell; Thomas Pyle; Barbara Cook; Judy Holliday; Carol
  Lawrence; Larry Kert; Pat Suzuki; Rex Harrison; Julie Andrews; Ethel Merman; Mary Martin;
  Robert Coote; Paul Lynde; Marijane Maricle; Clive Revill; Eliza Seal; Adolph Green; John
  Reardon; Cris Alexander.

THIS IS CINERAMA
Soundtrack (1952) .... *Peter Pan (SE) 152*   73   20-25
  Composer: Max Steiner; others. **Cast:** Lowell Thomas (narration).

THIS IS ELVIS
Soundtrack (1981) .... *RCA Victor (S) CPL2-4031*   81   12-15
  Double LP set.
  Composer: Various. **Conductor:** Joe Guercio. **Cast:** Elvis Presley; Scotty Moore (guitar); James
  Burton (guitar); John Wilkinson (guitar); Jerry Scheff (bass); Bill Black (bass); Bob Moore
  (bass); Dudley Brooks (piano); Floyd Cramer (piano); Boots Randolph (sax); D.J. Fontana
  (drums); Ronnie Tutt (drums); Jordanaires (vocals); Kathy Westmoreland (vocals); J.D.
  Summer and the Stamps (vocals); Sweet Inspirations (vocals); Joe Guercio Orchestra.

THIS IS SPINAL TAP
Soundtrack (1984) .... *Polydor (S) 817846-1*   84   8-10

THIS IS THE ARMY
Original Cast (1942) .... *Decca (M) DL-5108*   50   150-175
  10-inch LP.
  Composer: Irving Berlin. **Conductor:** Corporal Milton Rosenstock. **Cast:** Earl Oxford; Ezra
  Stone; Philip Truex; Julie Oshins; Robert Stanley; Stuart Churchill; James "Stump" Cross; Irving
  Berlin and an all-soldier cast.
Soundtrack (1942) .... *Sandy Hook (M) SH-2035*   8-12
  Composer: Irving Berlin.
  Also see CALL ME MISTER

THIS PROPERTY IS CONDEMNED
Soundtrack (1966) .... *Verve (M) V-8664*   66   20-25
Soundtrack (1966) .... *Verve (S) V6-8664*   66   30-35
  Composer: Kenyon Hopkins; Jay Livingston; Ray Evans. **Conductor:** Kenyon Hopkins.
  Cast: Mary Badham.

THIS WAS BURLESQUE
Original Cast (1962) ....*Roulette (M) R-25185*   62 $30-35
Original Cast (1962) .... *Roulette (S) SR-25185*   62   **45-50**
  Composer: Sonny Lester; Bill Grundy; others. Conductor: Sonny Lester. Cast: Ann Corio;
  Buddy Bryant; Steve Mills; Lisa Carroll; Sandy Fuller; Jackie Henkins; "Fabulous Fannie";
  "Taj Mahal"; "Mercedie Bends"; Casino Cuties.

THIS WORLD TOMORROW
Studio Cast .... *Guild Publications (S) GP-6258*   **8-12**
  Composer: Alexander Laszlo. Cast: Vincent Price (narration).

THOMAS CROWN AFFAIR
Soundtrack (1968) .... *United Artists (S) UAS-5182*   68   **12-15**
Soundtrack (1968) ....*United Artists (S) UA-LA295-G*   74   **8-10**
  Composer: Michel Legrande; Marilyn Bergman; Alan Bergman. Conductor: Michel Legrand.
  Cast: Noel Harrison; Michel Legrand.

THOROUGHLY MODERN MILLIE
Soundtrack (1967) ....*Decca (M) DL-1500*   67   **10-15**
Soundtrack (1967) ....*Decca (S) DL7-1500*   67   **15-20**
  Composer: Elmer Bernstein; James Van Heusen; others. Conductor: Andre Previn. Cast: Julie
  Andrews; Carol Channing; John Gavin; James Fox. (With dialogue.)
Studiotrack (1967) .... *Alshire (S) ST-3002A*   67   **8-12**
  Composer: Elmer Bernstein; James Van Heusen; others. Cast: Hollywood Sound Stage
  Orchestra and Chorus.
Studiotrack (1967) .... *RCA Victor/Camden (S) CAS-2165*   67   **8-12**

THOSE DARING YOUNG MEN IN THEIR JAUNTY JALOPIES
Soundtrack (1969) ....*Paramount (S) PAS-5006*   69   **25-30**
  Composer: Ron Goodwin; others. Conductor: Ron Goodwin. Cast: Jimmy Durante.

THOSE GLORIOUS MGM MUSICALS
Soundtrack .... *MGM (S) 40-ST*   73   **15-20**
  Double LP set. Has *Singin' in the Rain* and *Easter Parade*.
Soundtrack .... *MGM (S) 41-ST*   73   **15-20**
  Double LP set. Has *Seven Brides for Seven Brothers* and *Rose Marie*.
Soundtrack .... *MGM (S) 42-ST*   73   **15-20**
  Double LP set. Has *Show Boat* and *Annie Get Your Gun*.
Soundtrack .... *MGM (S) 43-ST*   73   **15-20**
  Double LP set. Has *The Pirate, Pagan Love Song* and *Hit the Deck*.
Soundtrack .... *MGM (S) 44-ST*   73   **15-20**
  Double LP set. Has *Bandwagon* and *Kiss Me Kate*.
Soundtrack .... *MGM (S) 45-ST*   73   **15-20**
  Double LP set. Has *Till the Clouds Roll By* and *Three Little Words*.
Soundtrack ....*MGM (S) 49ST*   74   **15-20**
  Double LP set. Has *Good News, In the Good Old Summertime* and *Two Weeks with Love*.
Soundtrack ....*MGM (S) 53ST*   74   **15-20**
  Double LP set. Has *Nancy Goes to Rio, Rich, Young and Pretty*, and *Royal Wedding*.
Soundtrack ....*MGM (S) 54ST*   73   **15-20**
  Double LP set. Has *Deep in My Heart* and *Words and Music*.

THOSE MAGNIFICENT MEN IN THEIR FLYING MACHINES
Soundtrack (1965) . . . . *20th Century-Fox (M) TF-3174*　65　　**$35-40**
Soundtrack (1965) . . . . *20th Century-Fox (S) TFS-4174* ·　65　　**50-55**
　Composer: Ron Goodwin. Conductor: Ron Goodwin.
Soundtrack (1965) . . . . *20th Century-Fox (M) FM-2*　65　　**40-50**
　Script and open-end radio interview with: Sarah Miles; Stuart Whitman; Terry Thomas; Irina Demick;
　James Fox; and Alberto Sordi. Promotional issue only.

THOUSAND MILES OF MOUNTAINS
Studio cast (1964) . . . . *Northern Pacific (M) KB-4368*　64　　**20-30**
　Musical adventure in railroading; Northern Pacific's centennial celebration.
　Composer: Norman Richards. Conductor: Norman Richards. Cast: Raymond Massey
　(narration); Ken Carson; Larry Douglas; Stuart Foster; Hal Linden; Lynn Roberts; Allen Swift;
　Iggie Wolfington; Mason Adams; Paul Ballantyne; Patricia Bright; John Connell; Leslie Hunter;
　Leon Janney; Bart Larsen; others.

THREADS OF GLORY
Original Cast (1976) . . . . *Desert Dramatics (S) 4741*　76　　**10-12**
　Double LP set.
　Composer: Lex de Azevedo; Doug Stewart. Conductor: Lex de Azevedo. Cast: Ric de
　Azevedo; Kent Larson; Helen McVey; Roger McKay; Candy Wilson.

THREE AMIGOS
Soundtrack (1987) . . . . *Warner Bros. (S) 1-25558*　87　　**8-10**
　Composer: Randy Newman. Cast: Chevy Chase; Steve Martin; Martin Short; Fred Asparagus;
　Randy Newman.

THREE BITES OF THE APPLE
Soundtrack (1967) . . . . *MGM (M) E-4444*　67　　**12-15**
Soundtrack (1967) . . . . *MGM (S) SE-4444*　67 ·　**15-20**
Soundtrack (1967) . . . . *MCA (S) 25010*　67　　**8-10**
　Composer: Eddy Manson; others. Conductor: Robert Armbruster. Cast: David McCallum.

THREE DAYS OF THE CONDOR
Soundtrack (1975) . . . . *Capitol (S) SW-11469*　75　　**20-25**
　Composer: Dave Grusin. Conductor: Dave Grusin. Cast: Jim Gilstrap; Marti McCall.

THREE EVENINGS WITH FRED ASTAIRE
TV Soundtrack (1958-1960) . . . . *DRG (M) S3L-5181*　82　　**20-30**
　Triple LP set, each with one of Astaire's TV specials (from 1958, 1959, and 1960).
　Composer: Various. Cast: Fred Astaire; others.

THREE FOR THE SHOW
Soundtrack (1955) . . . . *Mercury (M) MG-25204*　55　　**50-60**
　10-inch LP.
　Composer: George Duning; George Gershwin; others. Conductor: Morris Stoloff. Cast: Betty
　Grable; Marge Champion; Jack Lemmon; Jud Conlon Singers.

THREE FOR TONIGHT
Original Cast (1955) . . . . *RCA Victor (M) LPM-1150*　55　　**30-40**
Original Cast (1955) . . . . *RCA Victor (SE) LSP-1150*　59　　**20-25**
　Actual title of above two: *Belafonte*. Has seven tracks from *Three for Tonight* plus other selections.
　Conductor: Tony Scott; others. Cast: Harry Belafonte; Millard J. Thomas (guitar); Norman
　Luboff Choir.

THREE GUYS NAKED FROM THE WAIST DOWN
Original Cast (1985) . . . . *Polydor (S) 820244-1*　85　　**8-12**
　Composer: Michael Rupert; Jerry Colker. Conductor: Henry Aronson. Cast: Scott Bakula;
　Jerry Colker; John Kassir.

THREE IN THE ATTIC
Soundtrack (1968) . . . . *Sidewalk (S) ST-5918*　69　　**15-20**
　Composer: Chad Stuart; Jeremy Clyde; Wayne Irwin; others. Cast: Chad Stuart; Jeremy Clyde.

THREE IN THE CELLAR
Soundtrack (1970) . . . . *American Int'l (S) A-1036* 71 **$15-20**
From the film *Up in the Cellar*. Another LP, using that title, is nearly identical, but does have a different cover.
Composer: Don Randi; Dory Previn. **Conductor:** Don Randi. **Cast:** Hamilton Camp.
Also see UP IN THE CELLAR

THREE LITTLE PIGS
Soundtrack (1934) . . . . *Disneyland (M) ST-1910* 61 **20-25**
With dialogue.
Soundtrack (1934) . . . . *Disneyland (M) DQ-1310* Re **8-10**
Composer: Frank Churchill. **Conductor:** Frank Churchill.

THREE LITTLE WORDS
Soundtrack (1950) . . . .*MGM (EP) X-53* 50 **15-25**
Soundtrack (1950) . . . .*MGM (M) E-516* 50 **35-45**
10-inch LP.
Soundtrack (1950) . . . . *Metro (M) M-615* 67 **15-20**
Soundtrack (1950) . . . . :. . . . *Metro (SE) MS-615* 67 **15-20**
Composer: Harry Ruby; others. **Conductor:** Richard Thorpe. **Cast:** Fred Astaire; Red Skelton; Gloria DeHaven; Anita Ellis; Gale Robbins; Helen Kane.
Also see ANNIE GET YOUR GUN; GOOD NEWS; SEVEN BRIDES FOR SEVEN BROTHERS

THREE MUSKETEERS
Original London Cast (1928) . . . . . . *Monmouth Evergreen (SE) MES-7050* 72 **15-20**
Composer: Rudolf Friml; Clifford Grey; P.G. Wodehouse. **Cast:** Dennis King; Rose Marie; Adrienne Brune; Raymond Newell; Robert Woollard.
Soundtrack (1974) . . . .*Bell (S) 1310* 74 **15-20**
Composer: Michel Legrand. **Conductor:** Michel Legrand.

THREE PENNY OPERA:
see THREEPENNY OPERA

3 SAILORS AND A GIRL
Soundtrack (1953) . . . . *Capitol (EP) FBF-485* 53 **20-25**
Double EP set.
Soundtrack (1953) . . . . *Capitol (M) L-485* 54 **50-60**
10-inch LP.
Composer: Sammy Fain. **Conductor:** George Greeley. **Cast:** Gordon MacRae; Jane Powell; Gene Nelson.

3:10 TO YUMA
Soundtrack . . . .*Citadel (M) GD-2* 79 **20-25**
Composer: George Duning. **Conductor:** George Duning. **Cast:** Frankie Laine.

THREE THE HARD WAY
Soundtrack (1974) . . . .*Custom (S) CRS-8602* 74 **10-12**
Composer: Richard Tufo. **Cast:** Impressions.

THREE TO MAKE MUSIC
Original Cast (1958) . . . . *RCA Victor (M) LPM-2012* 58 **20-25**
Original Cast (1958) . . . .*RCA Victor (S) LSP-2012* 58 **25-30**
Composer: Mary Rogers; Linda R. Melnick. **Conductor:** Thomas Scherman. **Cast:** Mary Martin.

THREE TOUGH GUYS:
see TOUGH GUYS

THREE WISHES FOR JAMIE

Original Cast (1952)	.........................*Capitol (EP) EDM-317*	52	**$25-50**
Original Cast (1952)	...........................*Capitol (M) S-317*	52	**200-225**
Original Cast (1952)	.... *Stet (M) DS-15012*	Re	**8-12**

Composer: Ralph Blane. Conductor: Joseph Littau. Cast: Bert Wheeler; Anne Jeffreys; John Raitt; Charlotte Rae; Robert Halliday; Peter Conlow.

THREE WORLDS OF GULLIVER

Soundtrack (1960)	..............................*Colpix (M) CP-414*	61	**80-100**

Based on *Gulliver's Travels*.

Soundtrack (1960)	.... *Citadel (M) CT-7018*	82	**8-10**

Composer: Bernard Herrmann. Conductor: Bernard Herrmann. Cast: Kerwin Mathews; Jo Morrow; June Thorburn; Lee Patterson; Gregoire Aslan; Basil Sydney.
Also see MYSTERIOUS FILM WORLD OF BERNARD HERRMANN

THREEPENNY OPERA

Original German Cast	.........................*Telefunken (M) 97012*		**25-30**

Also has music from *Mahogany*.

Original German Cast	.........................*Telefunken (M) 641991*	Re	**8-10**

Composer: Kurt Weill; Marc Blitzstein.

Original Revival Cast (1954)	.....................*MGM (M) E-3121*	54	**20-25**
Original Revival Cast (1954)	.... *MGM (SE) SE-3121*	59	**15-20**
Original Revival Cast (1954)	...................*Polydor (SE) 820260-1*	Re	**8-10**

Composer: Kurt Weill; Marc Blitzstein. Conductor: Samuel Matlowsky. Cast: Lotte Lenya; Scott Merrill; Charlotte Rae; Beatrice Arthur; Martin Wolfson; John Astin; Jo Sullivan; Paul Dooley; George Tyne.

Studio Cast	.... *Columbia (M) O2L-257*	58	**30-35**

German language edition. Double LP set.

Original Revival Cast (1976)	..................*Columbia (Q) PS-34326*	76	**15-20**

Gatefold cover. With lyrics insert.

Composer: Kurt Weill; Marc Blitzstein. Conductor: Stanley Silverman. Cast: C.K. Alexander; Blair Brown; Ellen Greene; Raul Julia; Caroline Kava; David Sabin; Tony Azito; Elizabeth Wilson; Roy Brocksmith; Pendleton Brown; Glenn Kezer; Robert Schlee.

Studio Cast	...............................*Columbia (SE) O2S-201*	58	**30-35**
Studio Cast	.... *Columbia/Odyssey (SE) 42-32977*	Re	**8-10**

Composer: Kurt Weill; Marc Blitzstein. Conductor: Wilhelm Bruckner-Riggeberg. Cast: Lotte Lenya; Wolfgang Neuss; Willy Trenk-Trebitsch.

Studio Cast	.... *Vanguard (M) VRS-9002*		**20-25**
Studio Cast	.... *Vanguard (SE) S-273e*		**8-10**

Above two contain the German language show.

Composer: Kurt Weill; Bertolt Brecht (German lyrics). Conductor: F. Charles Adler. Cast: Helge Roswaenge; Alfred Jerger; Rosette Anday.

Soundtrack (1963) .... *RCA Victor (M) LOC-1086*	64	$20-25

Soundtrack (1963) .... *RCA Victor (M) LOC-1086* 64 $20-25
Soundtrack (1963) .... *RCA Victor (S) LSO-1086* 64 25-30
Composer: Kurt Weill; Marc Blitzstein. **Conductor:** Samuel Matlowsky. **Cast:** Sammy Davis Jr.; Curt Jurgens; Hildegarde Kneff; June Ritchie; Gert Frobe; George E. Irving. (With dialogue.)
Soundtrack (1963) .... *London (M) M-76004* 64 15-20
German language edition.
Composer: Kurt Weill; Bertolt Brecht (German lyrics). **Conductor:** Peter Sandloff. **Cast:** Hildegarde Kneff; June Ritchie; Gert Frobe.

THRILL OF A ROMANCE
Soundtrack (1945) .... *RCA Victor/Camden (M) CAL-424* 58 40-50
Actual title: *The Lighter Side of Lauritz Melchoir.* Also has three selections from *Two Sisters from Boston.* **Cast:** Lauritz Melchoir.

THRILLER
TV Soundtrack (1960) .... *Time (M) T-52034* 60 20-30
TV Soundtrack (1960) .... *Time (S) S-2034* 60 35-45
Composer: Pete Rugolo. **Conductor:** Pete Rugolo.

THUNDER ALLEY
Soundtrack (1967) .... *Sidewalk (M) T-5902* 67 15-20
Soundtrack (1967) .... *Sidewalk (S) ST-5902* 67 20-25
Composer: Mike Curb; Jerry Styner; Guy Hemric; others. **Conductor:** Mike Curb. **Cast:** Annette Funicello; Eddie Beram; Sidewalk Sounds; Band Without a Name; Lorraine Singers.

THUNDERBALL
Soundtrack (1965) .... *United Artists (M) UAL-4132* 65 20-25
Soundtrack (1965) .... *United Artists (S) UAS-5132* 65 25-30
Composer: John Barry. **Conductor:** John Barry. **Cast:** Tom Jones.
Soundtrack (1965) .... *Sunset (S) SLS-50396* 65 15-20
Composer: John Barry. **Conductor:** John Barry. **Cast:** Sean Connery; Claudine Auger; Adolfo Celi; Luciana Paluzzi; Rik Van Nutter.

THURBER CARNIVAL
Original Cast (1960) .... *Columbia (M) KOL-5500* 60 25-30
Original Cast (1960) .... *Columbia (S) KOS-2040* 60 35-40
Original Cast (1960) .... *Columbia (S) KOS-2024* Re 30-35
Original Cast (1960) .... *Columbia Special Products (S) CKOS-2024* Re 8-10
Composer: James Thurber; Don Elliott. **Cast:** Tom Ewell; Peggy Cass; Paul Ford; John McGiver; Alice Ghostley; Peter Turgeon; Wynne Miller.

TICK ... TICK ... TICK
Soundtrack (1970) .... *MGM (S) SE-4667* 70 15-20
Conductor: Mike Curb. **Cast:** Tompall and the Glaser Brothers.

TICKLE ME
Soundtrack (1965) .... *RCA Victor (EP) EPA-4383* 65 40-50
Black label, dog on side.
Soundtrack (1965) .... *RCA Victor (EP) EPA-4383* 69 30-40
Orange label.
Composer: Doc Pomus; Mort Schuman; Jerry Leiber; Mike Stoller; Fred Wise; Sid Wayne; Ben Weisman; others. **Cast:** Elvis Presley; Scotty Moore (guitar); D.J. Fontana (drums); Bob Moore (bass); Floyd Cramer (piano); Boots Randolph (sax); Millie Kirkham (vocals); Jordanaires (vocals).

TILL THE CLOUDS ROLL BY

Soundtrack (1946) .... *MGM (EP) X-1*   50   **$15-20**
Film biography of Jerome Kern. May have been MGM's first soundtrack LP and EP release.
Soundtrack (1946) .... *MGM (M) K-1*   50   **25-30**
Double disc, boxed set.
Soundtrack (1946) .... *MGM (M) E-501*   50   **35-45**
10-inch LP.
Soundtrack (1946) .... *Metro (M) M-578*   66   **15-20**
Soundtrack (1946) .... *Metro (SE) MS-578*   66   **20-25**
Soundtrack (1946) .... *MCA (SE) 25000*   Re   **8-10**
Film biography of Jerome Kern.
Composer: Jerome Kern. **Conductor:** Lennie Hayton. **Cast:** Judy Garland; Tony Martin; Lena Horne; June Allyson; Kathryn Grayson; Virgina O'Brien; Caleb Peterson.
Also see GENTLEMEN PREFER BLONDES; SINGIN' IN THE RAIN

TILT

Soundtrack (1979) .... *ABC (S) AA-1114*   79   **8-10**
Composer: Lee Holdridge. **Conductor:** Lee Holdridge. **Cast:** Brooke Shields; Ken Marshall.

TIME AFTER TIME

Soundtrack (1979) .... *Entr' acte (S) ERS-6517*   79   **8-10**
Composer: Miklos Rozsa. **Conductor:** Miklos Rozsa. **Cast:** Royal Philharmonic Orchestra.

TIME CHANGES

Original Cast (1969) .... *ABC (S) ABCS-681*   69   **25-30**
A Ford Theatre presentation.
Composer: Harry Palmer; others. **Conductor:** Bert DeCopteaux; Johnny Pate. **Cast:** John Mazzarelli; Harry Palmer; Joey Scott; Arthur "Butch" Webster; Robert Tamagni.

TIME FOR SINGING

Original Cast (1966) .... *Warner Bros. (M) W-1639*   66   **35-40**
Original Cast (1966) .... *Warner Bros. (S) HS-1639*   66   **60-70**
Based on the novel *How Green Was My Valley*.
Composer: John Morris; Gerald Freedman. **Conductor:** Jay Blackton. **Cast:** Ivor Emmanuel; Tessie O'Shea; Shani Wallis; Laurence Naismith; Frank Griso; Brian Avery; Gene Rupert.

TIME IS THEN AS WELL AS NOW

Soundtrack .... *Columbia (S) P-13246*   **8-12**

TIME MACHINE

Soundtrack (1987) .... *GNP/Crescendo (S) GNPS-8008*   87   **8-10**
Composer: Russell Garcia. **Cast:** Russell Garcia.

TIME OF DESTINY

Soundtrack (1988) .... *Virgin Movie Music (S) 90938-1*   88   **8-10**

TIME REMEMBERED

Original Cast (1957) .... *Mercury (M) MG-20380*   57   **25-35**
Original Cast (1957) .... *Mercury (S) SR-60023*   58   **40-50**
Above two have incidental music from the dramatic Broadway play.
Composer: Vernon Duke. **Conductor:** Pete Rugolo. **Cast:** Tony Travis; Vernon Duke (piano).

TIME TO KEEP

TV Soundtrack (1964) .... *RCA Victor (M) LOC-1088*   64   **15-20**
From NBC News, with Chet Huntley and David Brinkley.
Cast: Chet Huntley; David Brinkley (newscasters).

TIME TO LOVE AND A TIME TO DIE

Soundtrack (1958) .... *Decca (M) DL-8778*   58   **60-70**
Soundtrack (1958) .... *Varese Sarabande (M) VC-81075*   79   **8-10**
Composer: Miklos Rozsa. **Conductor:** Miklos Rozsa.

TIME TO RUN
Soundtrack (1973) . . . . *World Wide Recordings (S) WWR-1001*   73   **$15-20**
  Limited pressing. Not commercially available.
Soundtrack (1973) . . . . *World Wide (S) CSS-1575*   73   **10-15**
  Premier edition.
  Composer: Ted Smith; Randy Stonehill. **Conductor:** Ted Smith. **Cast:** Jerry Whitman; Randy
  Stonehill; Barbara Sigel.

TIME TO SING
Soundtrack (1968) . . . . *MGM (S) SE-4540*   68   **12-18**
Soundtrack (1986) . . . . *MCA (S) 1458*   86   **8-10**
  Composer: Hank Williams Jr.; others. **Cast:** Hank Williams Jr.; Shelley Fabares; Clara Ward
  Singers.

TIMES OF HARVEY MILK:
see MRS. SOFFEL

TIMES SQUARE
Soundtrack (1980) . . . . *RSO (S) RS-2-4203*   80   **10-12**
  Double LP set.
  Composer: Various, performing their own material. **Cast:** Suzi Quatro; Pretenders; Roxy Music;
  Gary Numan; Marcy Levy; Robin Gibb; Talking Heads; Joe Jackson; XTC; Ramones; Robin
  Johnson; Trini Alvarado; Ruts; D.L. Byron; Lou Reed; Desmond Child and Rouge; Garland
  Jeffreys; Cure; Patti Smith Group; David Johansen.

TINTYPES
Original Cast (1981) . . . . *DRG (S) S2L-5196*   81   **10-15**
  Double LP set.

TIP TOES
Original London Cast (1925) . . . . *World (M) SH-185*   **15-20**
Original London Cast (1925) . . . . . . *Monmouth Evergreen (SE) MES-7052*   **8-12**
  One side has music from *Wildflower.*
  Composer: George Gershwin; Ira Gershwin. **Conductor:** I.A. DeOrellana. **Cast:** Allen Kearns;
  Dorothy Dickson; Laddie Cliff; John Kirby; Peggy Beatty; Evan Thomas; Vera Bryer.

TO BE OR NOT TO BE
Soundtrack (1983) . . . . *Antilles (S) ASTA-2*   83   **8-12**

TO BED ... OR NOT TO BED
Soundtrack (1963) . . . . *London (M) M-76005*   63   **35-40**
  Composer: Piero Picciono. **Conductor:** Piero Picciono.

TO BROADWAY WITH LOVE
Original Cast (1964) .... *Columbia (M) OL-8030*   64   **$30-35**
Original Cast (1964) .... *Columbia (S) OS-2630*   64   **40-45**
    Original 1964 New York World's Fair cast, saluting the music of Broadway.
   Composer: Jerry Bock; Sheldon Harnick; others. **Cast:** Bob Carroll; Rod Perry; Don Liberto;
   Millie Slavin; Patti Carr; Guy Rotondo; Miriam Burton; Nancy Leighton.

TO CATCH A THIEF
Soundtrack (1955) .... *Coral (EP) EC-81083*   54   **50-75**
    Has background music later heard in the film. (EP was issued the year before the film.)
   Conductor: Lyn Murray. **Cast:** Georgie Auld; Lyn Murray (tenor sax solos).

TO KILL A MOCKINGBIRD
Soundtrack (1962) .... *Ava (M) A-20*   63   **25-35**
Soundtrack (1962) .... *Ava (S) AS-20*   63   **35-45**
Soundtrack (1962) .... *Citadel (S) CT-7029*   81   **8-10**
   Composer: Elmer Bernstein. **Conductor:** Elmer Bernstein. **Cast:** Royal Philharmonic Orchestra.
Studiotrack (1962) ..... *Elmer Bernstein Film Music Collection (S) FMC-7*   76   **30-35**
Studiotrack (1962) .... *Warner Bros. (S) BSK-3184*   78   **10-12**
   Composer: Elmer Bernstein. **Conductor:** Elmer Bernstein.

TO LIVE AND DIE IN L.A.
Soundtrack (1985) .... *Geffen (S) GHS-24081*   85   **8-10**
   Cast: Wang Chung.

TO LIVE ANOTHER SUMMER, TO PASS ANOTHER WINTER
Original Cast (1971) .... *Buddah (S) BDS-95004*   71   **20-25**
    Double LP set.
   Composer: David Paulsen; Dov Seltzer. **Conductor:** David Kirvoshel. **Cast:** Rivka Raz; Aric
   Lavie; Yona Atari; Ili Gorlizki; Hanan Goldblatt.

TO SIR WITH LOVE
Soundtrack (1967) .... *Fontana (S) MGF-18030*   67   **12-15**
Soundtrack (1967) .... *Fontana (S) SRF-67569*   67   **15-20**
   Composer: Ron Grainer; others. **Conductor:** Ron Grainer. **Cast:** Lulu; Mindbenders.

TOAST OF NEW ORLEANS
Studiotrack (1950) .... *RCA Victor (M) LM-75*   51   **45-55**
    10-inch LP.
Studiotrack (1950) .... *RCA Victor (M) LM-2422*   59   **35-40**
    One side, titled *Double Feature*, has music from *That Midnight Kiss*, plus other selections.
   Conductor: Constantine Callinicos. **Cast:** Mario Lanza; Elaine Malbin.

TOBY TYLER
Soundtrack (1960) .... *Disneyland (M) ST-1904*   60 $20-25
  Film is also known as *Ten Weeks with the Circus*.
  Composer: Richard Loring; Diane Lampert. **Cast:** Brian Corcoran; Henry Calvin; Gene Sheldon;
  Dal McKennon (narration).
  Also see TOBY TYLER IN THE CIRCUS

TOCCATA FOR TOY TRAINS:
see MIRACLE

TOGETHER
Soundtrack (1980) .... *RCA Victor (S) ABL1-3541*   80   8-10
  Composer: Burt Bacharach; Paul Anka. **Conductor:** Burt Bacharach. **Cast:** Jackie DeShannon;
  Libby Titus; Michael McDonald.

TOGETHER BROTHERS
Soundtrack (1974) .... *20th Century-Fox (S) ST-101*   74   10-12
  Composer: Barry White; Love Unlimited. **Cast:** Love Unlimited Orchestra.

TOGETHER WITH MUSIC
TV Soundtrack (1955) .... *DRG (SE) DARC2-1103*   78   10-15
  Double LP set.
  Cast: Noel Coward; Mary Martin.

TOKYO OLYMPIAD
Soundtrack (1966) .... *Monument (M) MLP-8046*   66   15-20
Soundtrack (1966) .... *Monument (S) SLP-18046*   66   20-25
  Composer: Toshiro Mayuzumi. **Conductor:** Toshiro Mayuzumi. **Cast:** Yomiuri Nihon Tokyo
  Gakudan Orchestra.

TOM JONES
Studio Cast (1964) .... *Theatre Productions (M) 59000*   64   20-25
Studio Cast (1964) .... *Theatre Productions (S) S-9000*   64   30-35
  Planned for stage production, but not done as such.
  Composer: Ruth Batchelor; Bob Roberts. **Conductor:** Peter Matz. **Cast:** Clive Revill (narration);
  Bob Roman; Karen Morrow; Carole Shaw.
Soundtrack (1963) .... *United Artists (M) UAL-4113*   63   15-20
Soundtrack (1963) .... *United Artists (S) UAS-5113*   63   20-25
  Composer: John Addison. **Conductor:** John Addison.
  Also see IRMA LA DOUCE

TOM SAWYER
Studio Cast (1972) .... *Reader's Digest/United Artists (S) UAMPG-105*   72   10-15
  "A Musical Adaptation." Boxed set. Includes lyrics booklet.
  Composer: Richard M. Sherman; Robert B. Sherman. **Cast:** Johnny Whitaker; Jeff East;
  Jodie Foster; Celeste Holm.
Studio Cast (1977) .... *TIL (S) 499*   77   10-12
  Story, music and sound effects.
  Cast: Storytime Tellers.
Soundtrack (1973) .... *United Artists (S) UA-LA057-F*   73   15-20
  Composer: Richard M. Sherman; Robert B. Sherman. **Conductor:** John Williams.
  Cast: Charley Pride; Celeste Holm and Chorus.
TV Soundtrack (1957) .... *Decca (M) DL-8432*   57   25-30
  Theatre Guild production, aired on the United States Steel Hour.
  Composer: Frank Luther. **Conductor:** Ralph Norman. **Cast:** Jimmy Boyd; John Sharpe (as
  Tom Sawyer); Bennye Gatteys; Rose Bampton; Clarence Cooper; Song Spinners.
Studiotrack (1973) .... *Golden (S) 280*   73   10-12
  Cast: Early Williams (narration).

TOM THUMB
Soundtrack (1958) .... *Lion (M) L-70084*   58   **$25-30**
Soundtrack (1958) .... *MGM (M) CA-104-ST*   68   **15-20**
Soundtrack (1958) .... *MCA (M) 25006*   Re   **8-10**
   Composer: Fred Spielman; others. **Conductor:** Muir Mathieson. **Cast:** Russ Tamblyn; Peter Sellers; Terry Thomas; Stan Freberg; Dean Jones (narration); Ian Wallace; Bernard Miles; Alan Young; Jessie Matthews; June Thorburn; Norma Zimmer. (With dialogue.)

TOMFOOLERY
Original Cast (1980) .... *Multi Media Tapes (M) MMT LP 001*   80   **30-40**
   Composer: Tom Lehrer. **Conductor:** Chris Walker. **Cast:** Robin Ray; Jonathan Adams.

TOMMY
Original Cast (1969) .... *Decca (S) DXSW-7205*   69   **15-20**
  Includes booklet.
Original Cast (1969) .... *MCA (S) 2-10005*   72   **12-15**
   Composer: The Who. **Conductor:** Pete Townshend. **Cast:** The Who.
Studio Cast (1969) .... *Ode (S) SP-99001*   69   **20-25**
  Above three are double LP sets.
   Composer: The Who. **Conductor:** David Measham. **Cast:** The Who; Ringo Starr; Rod Stewart; Richard Harris; Sandy Denny; Steve Winwood; Richie Havens; Merry Clayton; Graham Bell; Maggie Bell; London Symphony Orchestra.
Soundtrack (1975) .... *Polydor (S) PD-29502*   75   **15-18**
  Double LP set.
   Composer: The Who (Pete Townshend; John Entwistle; Keith Moon; Roger Daltrey). **Conductor:** Pete Townshend. **Cast:** The Who; Ann-Margret; Oliver Reed; Elton John; Eric Clapton; Jack Nicholson; Tina Turner; Paul Nicholas; Simon Townshend.

TONIGHT AT 8:30
Original Cast (1936) .... *RCA Victor (M) LCT-1156*   55   **45-55**
   Composer: Noel Coward. **Cast:** Noel Coward; Gertrude Lawrence; Douglas Fairbanks, Jr.
Original Cast (1936) .... *Monmouth Evergreen (SE) MES-7042*   **8-12**
  Actual title of above two: *We Were Dancing.* Also has music from *Private Lives* and *Moonlight Is Silver.*
   Composer: Noel Coward. **Cast:** Noel Coward; Gertrude Lawrence; Douglas Fairbanks Jr.

TONIGHT WE SING
Soundtrack (1953) .... *RCA Victor (M) LM-7016*   53   **60-70**
   Composer: Various classical. **Conductor:** Alfred Newman. **Cast:** Ezio Pinza; Roberta Peters; Jan Peerce; Edwin Dunning.

TOO MANY GIRLS
Studio Cast .... *Painted Smiles (S) PS-1368*   **8-10**
   Composer: Richard Rodgers; Lorenz Hart. **Conductor:** Dennis Deal. **Cast:** Nancy Andrews; Johnny Desmond; Estelle Parsons; Anthony Perkins.

TOO MUCH, TOO SOON
Soundtrack (1958) .... *Mercury (M) MG-20381*   58   **30-40**
Soundtrack (1958) .... *Mercury (S) SR-60019*   58   **65-80**
   Composer: Ernest Gold. **Conductor:** Ray Heindorf.

TOOTSIE
Soundtrack (1983) .... *Warner Bros. (S) 1-37811*   83   **8-10**
   Composer: Dave Grusin (music); Alan and Marilyn Bergman (lyrics). **Cast:** Stephen Bishop; Dave Grusin.

TOP BANANA

Original Cast (1951) . . . . *Capitol (EP) EDM-308*	52	**$20-30**
Original Cast (1951) . . . .*Capitol (M) S-308*	52	**150-160**
Limited pressing. With rainbow, color band label.		
Original Cast (1951) . . . .*Capitol (M) S-308*	52	**100-125**
Red label.		
Original Cast (1951) . . . . *Capitol (M) T-11650*	77	**8-10**

Composer: Johnny Mercer. **Conductor:** Harold Hastings. **Cast:** Phil Silvers; Judy Lynn; Jack Albertson; Rose Marie; Joey Faye; Herbie Faye; Lindy Doherty; Eddie Hanley; Ted "Sport" Morgan; Judy Lynn; Bob Scheerer; Zachary Charles; Joan Fields; Hal Loman; Bradford Hatton; Johnny Trama.

TOP CAT

TV Soundtrack (1962) . . . .*Colpix (M) CP-212*	62	**15-20**
Has *The Unscratchables* and *Top Cat Falls in Love.*		

Cast: Arnold Stang; Allen Jenkins; Leo DeLyon; Maurice Gosfield; Marvin Kaplan.

TOP GUN

Soundtrack (1986) . . . .*Columbia (S) CAS-2349*	86	**8-10**
12-inch single of *Danger Zone*, by Kenny Loggins.		

Composer: Giorgio Moroder; Tom Whitlock. **Cast:** Kenny Loggins.

Soundtrack (1986) . . . . *Columbia (S) SC-40323*	86	**8-10**

Composer: Harold Faltermeyer. **Cast:** Kenny Loggins; Loverboy; Cheap Trick; Berlin; Harold Faltermeyer and Steve Stevens; Miami Sound Machine; Teena Marie; Marietta; Larry Greene.

TOP O' THE MORNING:
see EMPEROR WALTZ; SUNSHINE CAKE

TOP SECRET

Soundtrack (1984) . . . .*Passport (S) 3603*	84	**8-10**
Cast: Val Kilmer.		
Soundtrack (1984) . . . . *Varese Sarabande (S) STV-81219*	84	**8-10**

Composer: Maurice Jarre. **Conductor:** Maurice Jarre. **Cast:** Royal Philharmonic Orchestra.

TOPKAPI

Soundtrack (1964) . . . .*United Artists (M) UAL-4118*	64	**15-20**
Soundtrack (1964) . . . . *United Artists (S) UAS-5118*	64	**20-25**
Soundtrack (1964) . . . .*MCA (S) 25118*	Re	**8-10**

Composer: Manos Hadjidakis. **Conductor:** Manos Hadjidakis. **Cast:** Melina Mercouri.

TORCH SONG

Soundtrack (1953) . . . .*MGM (M) E-214*	53	**40-50**
10-inch LP.		

Conductor: Adolph Deutsch. **Cast:** India Adams; Walter Gross (piano).

TORCH SONG TRILOGY

Soundtrack (1988) . . . .*Polydor (S) 837785-1*	88	**8-10**

Composer: Various. **Cast:** Harvey Fierstein; Charlie Haden and Quartet West; Charles Pierce; Axel Vera; Marilyn Scott; Joe Williams with Count Basie and His Orchestra; Billie Holiday; Bill Evans; Anita O'Day.

TORN CURTAIN

Soundtrack (1966) . . . .*Decca (M) DL-9155*	66	**15-20**
Soundtrack (1966) . . . .*Decca (S) DL7-9155*	66	**25-30**
Composer: John Addison; Jay Livingston; Ray Evans. **Conductor:** John Addison.		
Studiotrack (1966) . . .*Elmer Bernstein's Film Music Collection (S) FMC-10*	77	**30-35**
Studiotrack (1966) . . . .*Warner Bros. (S) BSK-3185*	78	**10-12**
Bernard Herrmann's unused score for the film.		

Composer: Bernard Herrmann. **Conductor:** Elmer Bernstein. **Cast:** Royal Philharmonic Orchestra.

TOUCH
Original Cast (1971) ....*Ampex (S) A-50102* 71 **$20-25**
  Composer: Kenn Long; Jim Crozier. **Conductor:** Jim Crozier; David Rodman. **Cast:** Norman Jacob; Barbara Ellis; Ken Long; Phyllis Gibbs; Gary Graham; Plowright Players.

TOUCH OF CLASS
Soundtrack (1973) ....*Brut (S) 6004* 73 **15-20**
  Composer: John Cameron; George Barrie; Sammy Cahn; John Lennon; Paul McCartney. **Conductor:** John Cameron.

TOUCH OF EVIL
Soundtrack (1958) ....*Challenge (M) CHL-602* 58 **60-75**
Soundtrack (1958) ....*Warner/Challenge (M) CH-615* 62 **40-50**
Soundtrack (1958) ....*Citadel (M) CT-6015* 77 **20-25**
  Also has a suite from *The Night Visitor* by Henry Mancini.
Soundtrack (1958) ....*Citadel (M) CT-7016* Re **8-10**
  Composer: Henry Mancini. **Conductor:** Joseph Gershenson.

TOUCHABLES
Soundtrack (1968) ....*20th Century-Fox (S) S-4206* 69 **15-20**
  Composer: Ken Thorne; others. **Conductor:** Ken Thorne. **Cast:** Nirvana; Ferris Wheel; Wynder K. Frog; Roy Redman.

TOUGH ENOUGH
Soundtrack (1983) ....*Liberty (S) LT-51147* 83 **8-10**
  Composer: Various. **Cast:** Mickey Gilley; T.G. Sheppard; Dennis Quaid; Blue Skies Band; Johnny Tillotson; Lane Brody.

TOUGH GUYS
Soundtrack (1974) ....*Enterprise (S) ENS-7504* 74 **10-12**
  From the film *Three Tough Guys*.
  Composer: Isaac Hayes. **Conductor:** Isaac Hayes.

TOURIST TRAP
Soundtrack (1979) ....*Varese Sarabande (S) VC-81102* 79 **8-10**
  Composer: Pino Donaggio. **Conductor:** Pino Donaggio.

TOVARICH
Original Cast (1963) ....*Capitol (M) TAO-1940* 63 **25-30**
Original Cast (1963) ....*Capitol (S) STAO-1940* 63 **30-35**
Original Cast (1963) ....*Capitol (S) STAO-1165* 77 **10-12**
  Composer: Lee Pockriss; Anne Croswell. **Conductor:** Stanley Lebowsky. **Cast:** Vivien Leigh; Jean Pierre Aumont; George S. Irving; Louise Troy; Louise Kirtland; Byron Mitchell; Margery Gray; Paul Michael; Rita Metzger.

TOWERING INFERNO
Soundtrack (1975) ....*Warner Bros. (S) BS-2840* 75 **12-15**
  Composer: John Williams; Al Kasha; Joel Hirschhorn. **Conductor:** John Williams. **Cast:** Maureen McGovern.

TOYS IN THE ATTIC
Soundtrack (1963) ....*Citadel (S) GD-1* **50-60**
  Not issued commercially.
  Composer: George Duning. **Conductor:** George Duning.

TRAIL OF THE PINK PANTHER
Soundtrack (1982) ....*Liberty (S) LT-51139* 82 **8-10**
  Also has music from other Pink Panther films.
  Composer: Henry Mancini. **Conductor:** Henry Mancini.

TRAIN
Soundtrack (1965) .... *United Artists (M) UAL-4122* 65   **$15-20**
Soundtrack (1965) .... *United Artists (S) UAS-5122* 65   **25-30**
  Composer: Maurice Jarre. **Conductor:** Maurice Jarre.

TRAIN RIDE TO HOLLYWOOD
Soundtrack (1975) .... *London (S) PS-665* 75   **10-12**
  Cast: Bloodstone. (With dialogue.)

TRANSFORMERS - THE MOVIE
Soundtrack (1986) .... *Scotti Bros. (S) SZ-40430* 86   **8-10**
  Composer: Various. **Cast:** Stan Bush; Vince Di Cola; Spectre General; Weird Al Yankovic; Lion.

TRANSYLVANIA 6-5000
Soundtrack (1985) .... *Varese Sarabande (S) 81267* 85   **8-10**
  Conductor: Lee Holdridge. **Cast:** Zagreb Symphony Orchestra.

TRAP
Soundtrack (1966) .... *Atco (M) 33-204* 66   **30-40**
Soundtrack (1966) .... *Atco (S) SD-33-204* 66   **60-70**
  Composer: Ron Goodwin. **Conductor:** Ron Goodwin.

TRAPEZE
Soundtrack (1956) .... *Columbia (M) CL-870* 56   **60-70**
  Composer: Malcolm Arnold; others. **Conductor:** Muir Mathieson.

TRAPP FAMILY
Soundtrack (1961) .... *20th Century-Fox (M) FOX-3044* 61   **20-25**
Soundtrack (1961) .... *20th Century-Fox (S) TFS-3044* 61   **30-35**
  Composer: Frank Grothe; others. **Conductor:** Kurt Graunke.

TRAVIATA, LA:
see LA TRAVIATA

TREASURE GIRL:
see CHEE CHEE

TREASURE ISLAND
Original London Cast .... *That's Entertainment (S) TER-1008* 81   **8-12**
  Composer: Corandel; N. Newell.
Studio Cast (1950) .... *Decca (M) DL-5125* 50   **50-75**
  10-inch LP.
  Composer: Victor Young. **Conductor:** Victor Young. **Cast:** Thomas Mitchell; others.
Soundtrack (1950) .... *RCA Victor (M) LY-1* 50   **50-75**
  10-inch LP. One side has music from *Alice in Wonderland.*
  Composer: Various. **Cast:** Dal McKennon (narration); Bobby Driscoll; Robert Newton; Finlay
  Currie; Basil Sydney; Walter Fitzgerald; Denis O'Dea; Geoffrey Wilkinson. (With dialogue.)
Soundtrack (1950) .... *Disneyland (M) DQ-1251* 64   **10-15**
  Cast: Dal McKennon (narration); Bobby Driscoll; Robert Newton; Finlay Currie; Basil Sydney;
  Walter Fitzgerald; Denis O'Dea; Geoffrey Wilkinson. (With dialogue.)

TREASURE OF SAN GENNARO
Soundtrack (1966) .... *Buddah (S) BDS-5011* 68   **30-35**
  Composer: Armando Trovaioli. **Conductor:** Armando Trovaioli.

TREASURY OF GREAT OPERETTAS
Studio Cast .... *Reader's Digest (S) S-40*   **35-40**
  Nine LP, boxed set.

TREE GROWS IN BROOKLYN
Original Cast (1951) .... *Columbia (EP) A-1000*   51 $15-20
Original Cast (1951) .... *Columbia (EP) A-1712*   51   15-20
Original Cast (1951) .... *Columbia (M) ML-4405*   51   30-40
Original Cast (1951) .... *Columbia Special Products (M) AML-4405*   Re   8-10
  Composer: Arthur Schwartz; Dorothy Fields. Conductor: Max Goberman. Cast: Shirley Booth;
  Marcia Van Dyke; Nathaniel Frey; Johnny Johnston; Delbert Anderson; Nomi Mitty; Claudia
  Campbell; Beverly Purvin.

TRIAL OF BILLY JACK
Soundtrack (1974) .... *ABC (S) ABCD-853*   74   10-12
  Composer: Elmer Bernstein; John Lennon; Paul McCartney. Conductor: Elmer Bernstein.
  Cast: Michelle Wilson; Teresa Laughlin; Michael Bolland; Lynn Baker.

TRIBUTE TO JAMES DEAN
Soundtrack (1955) .... *Columbia (M) CL-940*   57   40-50
  Has music from *Rebel Without a Cause, East of Eden* and *Giant*.
Soundtrack (1955) .... *Columbia Special Products (M) ACL-940*   Re   8-12
  Composer: Leonard Rosenman. Conductor: Ray Heindorf. Cast: Ray Heindorf and His
  Orchestra.
Soundtrack (1957) .... *Imperial (M) LP-9021*   57   40-50
  Has music from *East of Eden, Rebel Without a Cause* and *Giant*.
  Composer: Leonard Rosenman; Dimitri Tiomkin. Conductor: Leonard Rosenman.

TRICK OR TREAT
Soundtrack (1986) .... *Columbia (S) PC-40549*   86   8-10
  Composer: Fastway. Cast: Fastway.

TRIP
Soundtrack (1967) .... *Tower/Sidewalk (M) T-5908*   67   20-30
Soundtrack (1967) .... *Tower/Sidewalk (S) ST-5908*   67   30-40
  Composer: Mike Bloomfield; Nick Gravenites. Cast: Mike Bloomfield and the Electric Flag
  ("An American Music Band").

TRIP TO ITALY
Soundtrack (1953) .... *Mercury (EP) EP-1-3273*   53   25-35
  Composer: Renzo Rossellini. Conductor: Renzo Rossellini. Cast: Rome Symphony Orchestra.

TRIPLE CROSS
Soundtrack (1967) .... *United Artists (M) UAL-4162*   67   15-20
Soundtrack (1967) .... *United Artists (S) UAS-5162*   67   45-50
  Composer: Georges Garvarentz. Conductor: Georges Garvarentz. Cast: Tony Allen.

TRIPLE FEATURE
Soundtrack (1966) .... *Epic (M) LN-24195*   66   35-40
Soundtrack (1966) .... *Epic (S) BN-26195*   66   45-50
  Music from *Casanova '70, Marriage Italian-Style* and *Darling*.

TROCADERO LEMON BLUE
Soundtrack (1979) .... *Casablanca (S) NBLP-7117*   79   8-10
  Composer: Alec R. Constandinos. Conductor: Raymond Knehnetsky.

TROLL
Soundtrack (1986) .... *Restless (S) 72119-1*   86   8-10
  Composer: Richard Band. Conductor: Richard Band.

TRON
Soundtrack (1982) .... *CBS (S) SM-37782*   82   8-10
  Composer: Wendy Carlos. Conductor: Wendy Carlos. Cast: London Philharmonic Orchestra;
  Journey.

TROUBLE IN MIND
Soundtrack (1985) . . . .*Island/Visual Arts (S) 90501-1-E* 86 **$8-12**
  Composer: Mark Isham. Cast: Marianne Faithfull; Mark Isham.

TROUBLE IN TAHITI
TV Soundtrack (1958) . . . .*MGM (M) E-3646* 58 **30-40**
  Recorded in stereo though not issued in stereo until 1966.
TV Soundtrack (1958) . . . .*Heliodor (M) H25020* 66 **10-15**
TV Soundtrack (1958) . . . .*Heliodor (S) H25020* 66 **15-20**
  First stereo release of the 1958 recording. May also be known as *All in One*, a three-part program with a
  play, a dance program, and the show *Trouble in Tahiti*. LP has only *Trouble in Tahiti*.
  Composer: Leonard Bernstein. Conductor: Arthur Winograd. Cast: Beverly Wolff; David
  Atkinson; Miriam Workman; Earl Rogers; Robert Bollinger. (This was also the original 1952
  cast.)
TV Soundtrack (1958) . . . .*Polydor (S) 827845-1* Re **8-10**

TROUBLE MAN
Soundtrack (1972) . . . .*Tamala (S) T-322L* 72 **10-12**
  Composer: Marvin Gaye. Cast: Marvin Gaye.

TROUBLE WITH ANGELS
Soundtrack (1966) . . . .*Mainstream (M) 56073* 66 **35-45**
Soundtrack (1966) . . . .*Mainstream (S) S-6073* 66 **60-70**
  Composer: Jerry Goldsmith; Ernie Sheldon. Conductor: Jerry Goldsmith; Harry Betts.
  Cast: Devils.

TROUBLE WITH HARRY:
see GREAT MOVIE THRILLERS

TROUBLEMAKER
Soundtrack (1964) . . . . *Ava (M) A-49* 64 **12-15**
Soundtrack (1964) . . . . *Ava (S) AS-49* 64 **15-20**
  Themes from: *Walk on the Wild Side*, *The Carpetbaggers*, *Man with the Golden Arm* and *My Fair Lady*.
  Composer: Cy Coleman. Conductor: Cy Coleman.

TRUCK TURNER
Soundtrack (1974) . . . . *Enterprise (S) ENS-2-750* 74 **12-18**
  Double LP set.
  Composer: Isaac Hayes. Cast: Isaac Hayes.

TRUE CONFESSIONS
Soundtrack (1981) . . . .*Varese Sarabande (S) STV-81141* 81 **8-10**
  Composer: Georges Delerue. Conductor: Georges Delerue.

TRUE GRIT
Soundtrack (1969) . . . .*Capitol (S) ST-263* 69 **20-30**
  Composer: Elmer Bernstein; Don Black. Conductor: Elmer Bernstein; Al DeLory.
  Cast: Glen Campbell.

TRUE LOVE
Soundtrack . . . .*RCA Victor (S) 9819-1-R9* **8-10**
  Composer: Various. Cast: Graham Parker; Grayson Hugh; Betty Wright; Jim Capaldi;
  Eurythmics.

TRUE STORY OF THE CIVIL WAR
Soundtrack (1958) . . . . *Coral (M) CRL-59100*   58 $65-75
Includes booklet. From a documentary film short.
Composer: Ernest Gold; others. **Conductor:** Ernest Gold. **Cast:** Raymond Massey (narration).

TUBBY THE TUBA
Studio Cast (1950) . . . . *Columbia (M) JL-8013*   50   **40-50**
10-inch LP.
Composer: George Kleinsinger. **Conductor:** Leon Barzin. **Cast:** Victor Jory (narrator).
Also see HANS CHRISTIAN ANDERSEN

TUCKER (THE MAN AND HIS DREAM)
Soundtrack (1988) . . . . *A&M (S) SP-3917*   88   **8-10**
Cast: Joe Jackson; others.

TUFF TURF
Soundtrack (1985) . . . . *Rhino (S) RNSP-308*   85   **8-10**
Composer: Jonathon Elias; others. **Cast:** Southside Johnny; Jim Carroll Band; Jack Mack and
the Heart Attack; Lene Lovich; Marianne Faithfull; Dale Gnyea with J.R. and the 2-Men.

TUNES OF GLORY
Soundtrack (1960) . . . . *United Artists (M) UAL-4086*   61   **35-40**
Soundtrack (1960) . . . . *United Artists (S) UAS-5086*   61   **60-70**
Composer: Malcolm Arnold (uncredited on this release). **Conductor:** Malcolm Arnold
(uncredited on this release).

TURN ON, TUNE IN, DROP OUT
Soundtrack (1967) . . . . *Mercury (M) MG-21131*   67   **15-20**
Soundtrack (1967) . . . . *Mercury (S) SR-61131*   67   **20-25**
Composer: Maryvonne Giercarz. **Conductor:** Lars Eric; Richard Bond. **Cast:** Timothy Leary,
Ph.D. (With dialogue.)

TURNABOUT
Original Cast (1975) . . . . *Pelican (S) LP-142*   75   **8-10**
With original 1956 cast regrouped for "A Satirical Revue."
Composer: Forman Brown. **Cast:** Elsa Lanchester; Forman Brown (piano); Bill Buck; Harry
Burnett; Dorothy Neumann; Frances Osborne; Ray Henderson (piano).

TURNING POINT
Soundtrack (1977) . . . . *20th Century-Fox (S) T-549*   78   **8-10**
Composer: John Lanchbery. **Cast:** Lawrence Foster; Los Angeles Philharmonic Orchestra.

TUSCALOOSA'S CALLING ME (BUT I'M NOT GOING)
Original Cast (1975) . . . . *Vanguard (S) VSD-79376*   75   **15-20**
Composer: Hank Beebe; Bill Heyer. **Conductor:** Jeremy Harris. **Cast:** Len Gochman; Patti
Perkins; Renny Temple.

TV GUIDE TOP TELEVISION THEMES
TV Soundtracks (1959) . . . . *Warner Bros. (M) W-1290*   59   **30-40**
Themes from: *D.A.'s Man, Perry Mason, 77 Sunset Strip, Pete Kelly's Blues, Mickey Mouse Club,
Maverick, Peter Gunn, Have Gun Will Travel, M-Squad, Richard Diamond, Playhouse 90* and The
Real McCoys.

TV HITS
Studio Cast (1977) . . . . *Pickwick (S) SPC-3566*   **8-12**
Composer: Various. **Cast:** Birchwood Pops Orchestra.

TV SINGALONG WITH MITCH MILLER AND THE GANG
TV Soundtrack (1961) .... *Columbia (M) CL-1698*   61   **$10-12**
TV Soundtrack (1961) .... *Columbia (S) CS-8428*   61   **12-15**
  Composer: Various. **Conductor:** Mitch Miller. **Cast:** Mitch Miller and the Gang.

TV THEME SONG SINGALONG ALBUM
TV Soundtrack (1985) .... *Rhino/CBS (S) RNLP-703*   **8-10**

TWELVE CHAIRS
Soundtrack (1970) .... *Varese Sarabande (S) STV-81159*   **8-10**

TWENTIETH CENTURY OZ
Soundtrack (1978) .... *Celestial (S) 4001*   78   **10-12**
  Composer: Ross Wilson; Joy Dunstan; Graham Matters.

TWENTY MILLION SWEETHEARTS
Soundtrack (1934) .... *Milloball (M) TMSM-3403*   **8-12**
  Also contains music from *Mammy*.
  Cast: Ray Enright; Dick Powell; Ginger Rogers; Pat O'Brien; Allen Jenkins; Grant Mitchell;
  Mills Brothers. MAMMY: Al Jolson.

25th HOUR
Soundtrack (1967) .... *MGM (M) E-4464*   67   **20-25**
Soundtrack (1967) .... *MGM (S) SE-4464*   67   **25-30**
  Composer: Georges Delerue. **Conductor:** Georges Delerue.

TWENTY-FIVE YEARS OF LIFE
TV Soundtrack (1961) .... *No Label Shown (M) No number Used*   61   **40-50**
  10-inch LP. With deluxe, soft stock cover.
  Cast: Bob Hope; Mary Martin; Sid Caesar; Peggy Cass; Ray Charles Singers; others.

TWENTY-FOUR KARAT GOLD (FROM THE SOUND STAGE)
Soundtrack (1968) .... *MGM (S) SE-242-2*   68   **15-20**
  Original soundtrack music from 16 films.

20,000 LEAGUES UNDER THE SEA
Studio Cast .... *RCA Victor/Camden (M) CAL-1057*   65   **10-20**
Studio Cast .... *RCA Victor/Camden (S) CAS-1057*   65   **15-25**
  Cast: Disney cast.

TWILIGHT OF HONOR
Soundtrack (1963) .... *MGM (M) E-4185*   63   **10-20**
Soundtrack (1963) .... *MGM (S) SE-4185*   63   **15-25**
  Above two have music from six other films, plus two vocals.
  Composer: John Green; others. **Cast:** Richard Chamberlain; others.

TWILIGHT ZONE
TV Soundtrack .... *Varese Sarabande (S) STV-81171*   83   **8-10**
  Volume 1. Music from the following episodes: *The Invaders, Perchance to Dream, Walking Distance*
  and *The Sixteen Millimeter Shrine.*
  Composer: Jerry Goldsmith; Bernard Hermann; Franz Waxman.
TV Soundtrack .... *Varese Sarabande (S) STV-81178*   83   **8-10**
  Volume 2. Music from the following episodes: *Where Is Everybody?, One Hundred Yards Over the Rim,*
  The Big Tall Wish and *A Stop at Willoughby.*
  Composer: Jerry Goldsmith; Bernard Herrmann; Fred Steiner; Nathan Scott.
TV Soundtrack .... *Varese Sarabande (S) STV-81185*   83   **8-10**
  Volume 3. Music from the following episodes: *Back There, And When the Sky Was Opened, A World of*
  Difference and *The Lonely.*
  Composer: Jerry Goldsmith; Bernard Herrmann; Leonard Rosenman; Nathan Van Cleave;
  Marius Constant.

TWILIGHT ZONE (continued)

TV Soundtrack . . . . *Varese Sarabande (S) STV-81192*   84   **$8-10**
  Volume 4. Music from the following episodes: *King Nine Will Not Return, Two, Elegy* and *Nervous Man in a Four Dollar Room.*
  Composer: Jerry Goldsmith; Nathan Van Cleave; Fred Steiner; Bernard Herrmann; Rene Garriguenc.

TV Soundtrack . . . . *Varese Sarabande (S) STV-81205*   85   **8-10**
  Volume 5. Has music from the following episodes: *I Sing the Body Electric, The Passerby, The Trouble with Templeton* and *Dust.*
  Composer: Jerry Goldsmith; Nathan Van Cleave; Fred Steiner; Bernard Herrmann; Jeff Alexander.

TWILIGHT ZONE - THE MOVIE

Soundtrack (1983) . . . . *Warner Bros. (S) 1-23887*   83   **8-10**
  Composer: Jerry Goldsmith. **Conductor:** Jerry Goldsmith. **Cast:** Jennifer Warnes.

TWINS

Soundtrack (1988) . . . . *WTG (S) SP-45036*   88   **8-10**
  Composer: Various. **Cast:** Bobby McFerrin; Herbie Hancock; 2 Live Crew; Nicolette Larson; Jeff Beck; Terry Bozzio; Tony Hymas; Philip Bailey; Little Richard; Nayobe; Henry Lee Summer; Marilyn Scott; Spinners; Andrew Roachford; Peter Richardson.

TWISTED NERVE

Soundtrack . . . . *Polydor (S) 583-728*   72   **300-325**
  One side has music from *Les Bicyclettes De Belsize.*

Soundtrack . . . . *Cinema (S) LP-8006*   75   **150-200**
  Also has music from *The Bride Wore Black* and *Hangover Square.*
  Composer: Bernard Herrmann. **Conductor:** Bernard Herrmann.

TWO

Original Cast (1978) . . . . *Take Home Tunes (S) THT-788*   78   **8-10**
  Composer: Julie Mandel. **Conductor:** Donald Oliver. **Cast:** Ann Hodapp; Hal Watters.

TWO A PENNY

Soundtrack (1971) . . . . *Light (S) LS-5530*   71   **10-12**
  Composer: Mike Leander; Cliff Richard; Paul Simon; others. **Conductor:** Mike Leander. **Cast:** Cliff Richard.

TWO BY TWO

Original Cast (1970) . . . .*Columbia (S) S-30338*   70   **20-25**
  Based on the story of Noah's Ark and *The Flowering Peach.*
  Composer: Richard Rodgers; Martin Charnin. **Conductor:** Jay Blackton. **Cast:** Danny Kaye; Harry Goz; Madeline Kahn; Michael Karm; Joan Copeland; Walter Willison; Tricia O'Neil; Marilyn Cooper.

Original Cast (1970) . . . . *Columbia (S) AS-15*   70   **35-40**
  Actual title: *Backstage at Two By Two.* Promotional issue only. Has Richard Rodgers and Danny Kaye discussing the show as well as Rodgers' 50 years as a Broadway composer. Also has Rodgers' songs from other Columbia original cast recordings.
  Composer: Richard Rodgers. **Conductor:** Jay Blackton; others. **Cast:** Lee Jordan (interviewer).

Studio Cast . . . . *RCA Victor/Camden (S) CAS-2458*   **8-12**
  A tribute to Richard Rodgers.

TWO CONTEMPORARY CLASSIC FILM SCORES

Soundtrack . . . .*RCA Victor (S) ARL1-2698*   78   **15-20**

Soundtrack . . . . *RCA Victor (S) AGL1-3650*   80   **8-10**
  Above two have music from *Star Wars* and *Close Encounters of the Third Kind.*
  Composer: John Williams. **Conductor:** John Williams.

TWO FILM SCORES FOR SOLO PIANO
Soundtrack ....*Private Label (S) STK-1069*   76 $30-35
Has music from *A Texas Romance, 1909* and *Bad Company*.
Composer: Harvey Schmidt. Cast: Harvey Schmidt (piano).

TWO FOR THE ROAD
Soundtrack (1967) .... *RCA Victor (M) LPM-3802*   67   **15-20**
Soundtrack (1967) ....*RCA Victor (S) LSP-3802*   67   **20-25**
Composer: Henry Mancini. Conductor: Henry Mancini. Cast: Henry Mancini and His Orchestra.

TWO FOR THE SEESAW
Soundtrack (1962) ....*United Artists (M) UAL-4103*   62   **20-30**
Soundtrack (1962) .... *United Artists (S) UAS-5103*   62   **30-35**
Soundtrack (1962) ....*MCA (S) 25016*   Re   **8-10**
Composer: Andre Previn; Dory Langdon. Conductor: Andre Previn. Cast: Jackie Cain.
Also see DIVORCE ITALIAN STYLE

TWO FOR TONIGHT:
see ANYTHING GOES

TWO GENTLEMEN OF VERONA
Original Cast (1971) ....*ABC (S) BCSY-1001*   71   **25-30**
Double LP set.
Composer: Galt McDermot; John Guare. Conductor: Harold Wheeler. Cast: Jonelle Allen;
Diana Davila; Clifton Davis; Raul Julia; Norman Matlock.
Original Cast (1971) ....*Kilmarnock (S) KIL-72004*   71   **20-25**
Composer: Galt MacDermot; John Guare. Conductor: Galt MacDermot. Cast: Galt MacDermot;
Sheila Gibbs; Ken Lowry; P.T. Mavins.

TWO HUNDRED MOTELS
Soundtrack (1971) .... *United Artists (S) UAS-9956*   71   **15-20**
Double LP set.
Composer: Frank Zappa. Conductor: Frank Zappa; Elgar Howarth. Cast: Theodore Bikel (narration); Royal Philharmonic Orchestra.

TWO MULES FOR SISTER SARA
Soundtrack (1970) .... *Kapp (S) KRS-5512*   70   **35-45**
Composer: Ennio Morricone. Cast: Shirley MacLaine.

TWO OF A KIND
Soundtrack (1983) ....*MCA (S) 6127*   83   **8-10**
Composer: Various. Cast: Olivia Newton-John; John Travolta; Chicago; David Foster;
Magness-Ballard; Steve Kipner; Boz Scaggs; Journey.

TWO ON THE AISLE
Original Cast (1951) ....*Decca (M) DL-8040*   51   **75-85**
Composer: Jule Styne; Betty Comden; Adolph Green. Conductor: Herbert Greene. Cast: Bert
Lahr; Dolores Gray; Kathryn Mylroie; Fred Bryan.
Studio Cast (1951) ....*Columbia Special Products (M) CSP-120*   **8-10**

TWO SISTERS FROM BOSTON:
see THRILL OF ROMANCE

2001: A SPACE ODYSSEY
Soundtrack (1968) .... *MGM (S) S1E-13-ST*   68 $10-12
  Cast: Berlin Philharmonic Orchestra; Bavarian Radio Orchestra; Stuttgart Schola Cantorum; Leningrad Philharmonic Orchestra; Sudwest Funk Orchestra.
Soundtrack (1968) .... *MGM (S) S1E-13-STX*   68   10-12
  Contains the concert version of Ligeti's *Atmospheres.*
  Composer: Richard Strauss; Gyorgy Ligeti; Johann Strauss; Aram Khachaturian.

2001: A SPACE ODYSSEY (VOL. 2)
Soundtrack (1968) .... *MGM (S) SE-4722-ST*   71   10-15
  Composer: Richard Strauss; Gyorgy Ligeti; Johann Strauss; Aram Khachaturi.

2010
Soundtrack (1984) .... *A&M (S) SP-5038*   84   8-12
  Composer: David Shire. **Cast:** Andy Summers.

TWO TICKETS TO BROADWAY
Soundtrack (1951) .... *RCA Victor (M) LPM-39*   51   40-50
  10-inch LP.
  Conductor: Hugo Winterhalter; Henri Rene. **Cast:** Tony Martin; Dinah Shore.

TWO TICKETS TO PARIS
Soundtrack (1962) .... *Roulette (M) R-25182*   62   15-20
Soundtrack (1962) .... *Roulette (S) SR-25182*   62   15-20
  Composer: Henry Glover; others. **Conductor:** Henry Glover. **Cast:** Joey Dee and the Starliters; Gary Crosby; Kay Medford; Jeri Lynne Fraser.

TWO WEEKS WITH LOVE
Soundtrack (1950) .... *MGM (M) E-530*   50   40-50
  10-inch LP.
Soundtrack (1950) .... *MGM (M) E-3233*   55   25-30
  One side has music from *Words and Music.*
  Conductor: Georgie Stoll. **Cast:** Jane Powell; Debbie Reynolds; Carleton Carpenter.

TWO'S COMPANY
Original Cast (1952) .... *RCA Victor (EP) WOC-1009*   62   25-35
Original Cast (1952) .... *RCA Victor (M) LOC-1009*   52   100-125
Original Cast (1952) .... *RCA Victor (M) CBM1-2757*   78   8-10
  Composer: Vernon Duke; Ogden Nash; Sammy Cahn. **Conductor:** Milton Rosenstock.
  Cast: Bette Davis; Hiram Sherman; David Burns; George S. Irving; Bill Callahan; Ellen Hanley; Peter Kelley; Deborah Remson; Sue Hight.

U

UGLY DACHSHUND
Soundtrack (1966) .... *Disneyland (M) DQ-1290*   66   **$10-12**
  With narration. One side has music from *The Shaggy Dog.*
  Composer: Richard M. Sherman; Robert B. Sherman.

UGLY DUCKLING
Studio Cast .... *Camden (M) 1109*   ·   **8-12**
  Cast: Boris Karloff.

UHF AND OTHER STUFF
Soundtrack (1989) .... *Rock 'N Roll (S) SZ-45265*   89   **8-10**
  Composer: Various. **Cast:** "Weird Al" Yankovic.

ULYSSES
Soundtrack (1967) .... *RCA Victor (M) LOC-1138*   67   **15-20**
Soundtrack (1967) .... *RCA Victor (S) LSO-1138*   67   **20-25**
  Composer: Stanley Myers. **Conductor:** Stanley Myers.
Soundtrack (1967) .... *Caedmon (S) TMS-300*   **10-15**
  Soundtrack of the Walter Reade Jr - Joseph Strick Production.
  Cast: James Joyce; Mild O'Shea; Barbara Jefford; Maurice Roeves.

ULYSSES - THE GREEK SUITE
Studio Cast (1978) .... *20th Century-Fox (S) 2T-1101*   78   **12-18**
  Double LP set. Includes booklet.
  Composer: Michael Rapp. **Conductor:** Michael Rapp. **Cast:** David Arias (narration); Ted
  Neeley; Yvonne Iversen; Channen Junge; Grant Goracy; Cindy Snyder; others.

UMBRELLAS OF CHERBOURG (PARAPLUIES DE CHERBOURG)
Soundtrack (1964) .... *Philips (M) PCC-216*   65   **10-15**
Soundtrack (1964) .... *Philips (S) PCC-616*   65   **15-20**
  Above two are performed in French.
  Composer: Michel Legrand. **Conductor:** Michel Legrand. **Cast:** Jacques Demy. (With dialogue.)

UNBEARABLE LIGHTNESS OF BEING
Soundtrack (1988) .... *Fantasy (S) FSP-21006*   88   **8-12**
  Cast: Leo Janacek.

UNCLE JOE SHANNON
Soundtrack (1978) .... *United Artists (S) UA-LA935-H*   79   **10-12**
Soundtrack (1978) .... *Liberty (S) D1-73234*   79   **8-10**
  Composer: Bill Conti. **Conductor:** Bill Conti. **Cast:** Maynard Ferguson (trumpet).

UNCLE MEAT
Soundtrack (1968) .... *Reprise (S) RS-2024*   68   **$15-20**
Double LP set. From an unreleased film.

UNCLE REMUS
Soundtrack (1946) .... *Disneyland (EP) DBR-28*   56   **10-15**
Soundtrack (1946) .... *Disneyland (M) WDL-4001*   56   **25-30**
Soundtrack (1946) .... *Disneyland (M) DQ-1205*   63   **10-12**
Composer: Allie Wrubel; Charles Wolcott; others. **Conductor:** Paul J. Smith; Daniele Amfitheatrof. **Cast:** James Baskett (as Uncle Remus); Hattie McDaniel; Nicodemus Stewart.

UNCLE TOM'S CABIN
Soundtrack (1968) .... *Philips (S) PHS-600272*   68   **35-40**
Composer: Peter Thomas; Aldo Von Pinelli. **Conductor:** Peter Thomas. **Cast:** Juliette Greco; Eartha Kitt; George Goodman.

UNDEFEATED
Soundtrack .... *Lone Star (S) LS-1983*   83   **30-35**
One side has music from *How the West Was Won*, as conducted by Alfred Newman.
Composer: Hugo Montenegro. **Conductor:** Hugo Montenegro.

UNDER FIRE
Soundtrack (1983) .... *Warner Bros. (S) 1-23965*   83   **8-10**
Composer: Jerry Goldsmith. **Cast:** Pat Metheny.

UNDER MILK WOOD
Original Radio Cast (1954) .... *Argo (M) SW 501-2*   **15-20**
Double LP, boxed set. Includes insert.
Composer: Daniel Jones. **Cast:** Richard Burton; Richard Bebb; Hugh Griffith; Rachel Thomas; Diana Maddox; Dafydd Havard; Sybil Williams; Dilys Davies; David Close-Thomas; Ben Williams; Meredith Edwards; Gwenllian Owen; Philip Burton; Gwenyth Petty; others.
Studio Cast .... *Caedmon (M) TC-2005*   **40-50**
Double LP set. Dramatic narrative by Dylan Thomas.
Cast: Dylan Thomas; Dion Allen; Nancy Wickwire; Roy Poole; Sada Thompson; Allen F. Collins.

UNDER THE BOARDWALK
Soundtrack (1988) .... *Enigma (S) D1-73234*   88   **8-10**
Composer: Various. **Cast:** Untouchables; Surf Punks; Surf MC's; Del-Lords; Ike Willis; Smithereens; Broadcasters; Wednesday Week; Drifters.

UNDER THE CHERRY MOON:
see PARADE (MUSIC FROM "UNDER THE CHERRY MOON")

UNDERCOVER
Soundtrack (1987) .... *Enigma (S) SJ-73276*   87   **8-10**
Composer: Various. **Cast:** Wednesday Week; T.S.O.L.; Todd Rundgren; Agent Orange; Passionnel.

UNFORGIVEN
Soundtrack (1960) .... *United Artists (M) UAL-4068*   60   **60-75**
Soundtrack (1960) .... *United Artists (S) UAS-5068*   60   **75-90**
Soundtrack (1960) .... *United Artists (M) DF-7*   Re   **20-25**
One side has music from *The Wonderful Country*.
Soundtrack (1960) .... *United Artists (S) DFS-57*   Re   **35-40**
One side has music from *The Wonderful Country*.
Composer: Dimitri Tiomkin. **Conductor:** Dimitri Tiomkin.
Also see HORSE SOLDIERS

UNMARRIED WOMAN
Soundtrack (1978) . . . .*20th Century-Fox (S) T-557*   78   **$10-12**
Composer: Bill Conti. Conductor: Bill Conti. Cast: Michelle Wiley.

UNPUBLISHED COLE PORTER
Composer: Cole Porter.

UNSINKABLE MOLLY BROWN
Original Cast (1960) . . . . *Capitol (M) WAO-1509*   60   **20-25**
Original Cast (1960) . . . .*Capitol (S) SWAO-1509*   60   **30-35**
Above two contain a program insert.
Original Cast (1960) . . . .*Capitol (M) W-2152*   64   **10-12**
Original Cast (1960) . . . .*Capitol (S) SW-2152*   64   **12-15**
Composer: Meredith Willson. Conductor: Hebert Greene. Cast: Tammy Grimes; Harve
Presnell; Cameron Prud'Homme; Edith Meiser; Mony Dalmes; Jack Harrold; Mitchell Gregg.
Studio Cast (1961) . . . . *RCA Victor/Camden (M) CAL-667*   61   **10-15**
Composer: Meredith Willson. Conductor: Elliot Lawrence. Cast: Sandy Stewart; Bernie Knee;
Elliot Lawrence's Orchestra and Chorus.
Soundtrack (1964) . . . .*MGM (M) E-4232*   64   **12-15**
Soundtrack (1964) . . . . *MGM (S) SE-4232*   64   **12-15**
Soundtrack (1964) . . . .*MCA (S) 25011*   Re   **8-10**
Composer: Meredith Willson. Conductor: Robert Armbruster. Cast: Debbie Reynolds; Harve
Presnell.

UNTIL SEPTEMBER
Soundtrack (1984) . . . . *Varese Sarabande (S) STV-81226*   84   **8-10**
Composer: John Barry. Conductor: John Barry.

UNTOUCHABLES
TV Soundtrack (1960) . . . . *Capitol (M) T-1430*   60   **25-35**
Soundtrack (1987) . . . . *A&M (S) SP-3809*   87   **8-10**
Composer: Ennio Morricone. Conductor: Ennio Morricone.
TV Soundtrack (1960) . . . . *Capitol (S) ST-1430*   60   **35-50**
Composer: Nelson Riddle. Conductor: Nelson Riddle.

UP IN CENTRAL PARK:
see RED MILL; SONG OF NORWAY

UP IN SMOKE
Soundtrack (1978) . . . .*Warner Bros. (S) BSK-3249*   78   **8-10**
Composer: Tommy Chong; Cheech Marin. Cast: Cheech and Chong. (With dialogue).

UP IN THE CELLAR
Soundtrack (1970) . . . . *American Int'l (S) A-1036*   71   **15-20**
Composer: Don Randi; Dory Previn. Conductor: Don Randi. Cast: Hamilton Camp.
Also see 3 IN THE CELLAR

UP THE ACADEMY
Soundtrack (1980) . . . . *Capitol (S) SOO-12091*   80   **8-10**
Composer: Various. Cast: Blondie; Ian Hunter; Babys; Blow-Up; Jonathan Richman and the
Modern Lovers; Cheeks; Pat Benatar; Sammy Hagar.

UP THE DOWN STAIRCASE
Soundtrack (1967) . . . .*United Artists (M) UAL-4169*   67   **15-20**
Soundtrack (1967) . . . . *United Artists (S) UAS-5169*   67   **20-25**
Composer: Fred Karlin. Conductor: Fred Karlin.

UP THE JUNCTION
Soundtrack (1968) .... *Mercury (S) SP-61159*   68   **$12-15**
Composer: M. Hugg; B. Hugg; Manfred Mann. **Cast:** Manfred Mann.

UP WITH PEOPLE!
TV Soundtrack (1965) .... *Pace (S) 1101*   65   **10-15**
Volume 1.
Composer: Paul Colwell; Ralph Colwell; Steve Colwell; Herbert Allen; David Bliss Allen; others.
Cast: Colwell Brothers; Green Glenn Singers; Linda Blackmore; Wardell Woodard; others.

UPTIGHT
Soundtrack (1968) .... *Stax (S) STS-2006*   68   **10-12**
Composer: Booker T. Jones. **Cast:** Booker T. and the MGs.

URBAN COWBOY
Soundtrack (1980) .... *Asylum (S) DP-90002*   80   **12-15**
Double LP set.
Composer: Various. **Cast:** Jimmy Buffett; Joe Walsh; Dan Fogelberg; Bob Seger and the Silver
Bullet Band; Mickey Gilley; Johnny Lee; Anne Murray; Eagles; Bonnie Raitt; Charlie Daniels
Band; Gilley's Urban Cowboy Band; Kenny Rogers; Boz Scaggs; Linda Ronstadt; John David
Souther.
Soundtrack (1980) .... *Full Moon/Epic (S) SE-36921*   80   **8-10**
Actual title: *Urban Cowboy II*. Has "More Music from the Original Soundtrack."
Composer: Various. **Cast:** Bayou City Beats (plus others listed above).

URGH - A MUSIC WAR
Soundtrack (1981) .... *A&M (S) SP-6019*   81   **10-12**
Double LP set.
Composer: Various. **Cast:** Police; Wall of Voodoo; Toyah Wilcox; Orchestral Manoeuvres in the
Dark; Oingo Boingo; XTC; Members; Go-Gos; Klaus Nomi; Athletico Spizz '80; Alley Cats;
Jools Holland; Devo; Echo and Bunnymen; Au Pairs; Cramps; Joan Jett and Blackhearts; Pere
Ubu; Gary Numan; Fleshtones; Gang of Four; John Otway; 999; X; Magazine; Skafish; Steel
Pulse.

UTTER GLORY OF MORRISSEY HALL
Original Cast (1979) .... *Original Cast (S) OC-7918*   79   **8-10**
Composer: Clark Gesner. **Conductor:** John Gordon. **Cast:** Celeste Holm; Karen Gibson; Laurie
Franks; Marilyn Franks; Marilyn Caskey; Taina Elg.

UTU
Soundtrack (1983) .... *Southern Cross (S) SRCS-1008*   83   **8-10**
Conductor: William Southgate. **Cast:** New Zealand Symphony Orchestra.

V

V.I.P.s
Soundtrack (1963) .... *MGM (M) E-4152*   63 $20-25
Soundtrack (1963) .... *MGM (S) SE-4152*   63   **25-35**
Soundtrack (1963) .... *MCA (S) 25001*   Re   **8-10**
  Composer: Miklos Rozsa. **Conductor:** Miklos Rozsa. **Cast:** Rome Symphony Orchestra.

VAGABOND KING
Studio Cast (1951) .... *RCA Victor (M) LK-1010*   51   **25-35**
  Composer: Rudolf Friml; Brian Hooker. **Conductor:** Al Goodman. **Cast:** Earl Wrightson;
  Frances Greer; Guild Choristers.
Studio Cast (1956) .... *RCA Victor (M) LM-2509*   61   **15-20**
Studio Cast (1956) .... *RCA Victor (SE) LSC-2509*   61   **15-20**
  Composer: Rudolf Friml; Brian Hooker. **Conductor:** Constantine Callinicos. **Cast:** Mario Lanza;
  Judith Raskin.
Studio Cast (1951) .... *Decca (M) DL-7014*   56   **35-45**
  10-inch LP.
  Composer: Rudolf Friml; Brian Hooker. **Conductor:** Jay Blackton. **Cast:** Alfred Drake; Mimi
  Benzell; Frances Bible.
Soundtrack (1956) .... *RCA Victor (M) LM-2004*   56   **30-40**
  Composer: Rudolf Friml; Brian Hooker. **Conductor:** Henri Rene. **Cast:** Oreste; Jean Fenn.
  Also see NEW MOON; STUDENT PRINCE

VALENTINO
Studiotrack (1951) .... *Decca (M) DL-5347*   51   **30-40**
  10-inch LP. "A collection of tangos inspired by the the motion picture *Valentino—the Loves and Times
  of Rudolph Valentino.*
  Conductor: Victor Young. **Cast:** Castillians.

VALENTINO
Soundtrack (1977) .... *United Artists (S) UA-LA810-H*   77   **8-12**
  Composer: Stanley Black; Ferde Grofe. **Conductor:** Stanley Black. **Cast:** Chris Ellis.

VALIANT YEARS
TV Soundtrack (1962) .... *ABC-Paramount (M) ABC-387*   62 $25-30
TV Soundtrack (1962) .... *ABC-Paramount (S) ABCS-387*   62   35-40
  Based on the career of Winston Churchill.
  Composer: Richard Rodgers. **Conductor:** Robert Emmett Dolan.

VALLEY:
see OBSCURED BY CLOUDS

VALLEY GIRL
Soundtrack (1983) .... *Roadshow (S) RS-101*   83   125-175
  Six track mini-album. Recalled shortly after production, with very few copies making it into circulation.
  Composer: Various. **Cast:** Bonnie Hayes with the Wild Combo; Sparks; Josie Cotton; Plimsouls.

VALLEY OF THE DOLLS
Soundtrack (1967) .... *20th Century-Fox (M) TF-4196*   67   15-20
Soundtrack (1967) .... *20th Century-Fox (S) TFS-4196*   67   20-25
  Composer: Andre Previn; Dory Previn; others. **Conductor:** John Williams. **Cast:** Tony Scotti.
  Also see BEYOND THE VALLEY OF THE DOLLS
Studiotrack .... *Spector (S) SPS-568*   8-12
  Cast: Dionne Warwick.

VALMOUTH
Original Cast (1982) .... *That's Entertainment (S) TER-1019*   82   10-12
  Cast of the Chichester Festival, England.
  Composer: Sandy Wilson. **Cast:** Bertice Reading; Fenella Fielding; Doris Hare; Robert Helpman.

VAMP
Soundtrack (1986) .... *Varese Sarabande (S) STV-81288*   86   8-10
  Composer: Jonathan Elias.

VAN NUYS BLVD.
Soundtrack (1979) .... *Mercury (S) SRM-1-3794*   8-12
  Composer: Ron Wright; Ken Mansfield. **Cast:** Ron Wright; Tere Mansfield; Jump Start.

VANESSA
Original Cast (1958) .... *RCA Victor (S) ARL2-2094*   77   12-18
  Double LP set.
  Composer: Samuel Barber; Gian-Carlo Menotti. **Conductor:** Dimitri Mitropoulos. **Cast:** Eleanor
  Steber; Rosalind Elias; Regina Resnik; Nicolai Gedda; Georgio Tozzi.

VANISHING POINT
Soundtrack (1971) .... *Amos (S) AAS-8002*   71   15-20
  Composer: Various. **Conductor:** Jimmy Bowen. **Cast:** Jerry Reed; Mountain; Dalaney and
  Bonnie and Friends; J.B. Pickers; Jimmy Walker; Bobby Doyle; "Big Mama" Thornton; Doug
  Dillard Expedition.

VANISHING PRAIRIE
Soundtrack (1954) .... *Columbia (M) CL-6332*   54   35-40
  10-inch LP.
  Composer: Paul J. Smith. **Conductor:** Paul J. Smith. **Cast:** Winston Hibler (narration).
  Also see LIVING DESERT

VARIETY GIRL:
see BUT BEAUTIFUL

VELVETEEN RABBIT
Studio Cast (1985) .... *Dancing Cat (S) DC-3007*   85   8-12
  Composer: George Winston. **Conductor:** George Winston. **Cast:** Meryl Streep (narration);
  George Winston.

VERNON DUKE REVISITED
Studiotrack . . . . *Crewe (S) CR-1342* $8-12
  Composer: Vernon Duke.

VERONIKA VOSS PLUS LOLA
Soundtrack (1982) . . . . *DRG (S) SL-9508*   8-10
  Background score for the films *Veronika Voss* and *Lola*.

VERTIGO
Soundtrack (1958) . . . . *Mercury (M) MG-20384*   58   150-175
Soundtrack (1958) . . . .*Mercury (S) SRI 75117*   77   8-12
  Composer: Bernard Herrmann. **Conductor:** Muir Mathieson. **Cast:** Sinfonia of London.

VERY GOOD EDDIE
Original Revival Cast (1975) . . . .*DRG (S) DRG-6100*   75   8-12
  Composer: Jerome Kern. **Conductor:** Lynn Crigler. **Cast:** David Christmas; Spring Fairbank;
  Travis Hudson; Hal Shane.

VERY WARM FOR MAY
Studio Cast . . . . *Monmouth Evergreen (SE) MES-6808*   8-10
  Composer: Jerome Kern; Oscar Hammerstein II. **Cast:** Reid Shelton; Susan Watson; D. Carroll.

VIA GALACTICA
Studio Cast (1972) . . . .*Kilmarnock (S) KIL-72009*   72   25-30
  Composer: Galt MacDermot; Christopher Gore. **Conductor:** Galt MacDermot. **Cast:** Bill Butler
  (guitar).

VIC AND SADE
Original Radio Cast . . . .*Golden Age (M) 5027*   78   8-10

VICTOR BORGE
Original Cast (1948) . . . . *Columbia (M) CL-6013*   48   20-30
  10-inch LP. Full title: *Victor Borge Program*.
  Conductor: Paul Baron. **Cast:** Victor Borge; Paul Baron and His Orchestra.
Original Cast (1953) . . . .*MGM (EP) X-1707*   62   10-15
Original Cast (1953) . . . .*MGM (M) E-3995*   62   15-20
  Cast: Victor Borge.
Original Cast (1953) . . . . *Columbia (M) CL-646*   55   20-30
Original Cast (1953) . . . . *Columbia Special Products (M) CCL-646*   Re   8-10
  Full title: *Victor Borge (Caught in the Act)*.
  Cast: Victor Borge.
Original Cast (1953) . . . . *Columbia (M) CL-554*   54   25-30
Original Cast (1953) . . . . *Columbia Special Products (M) CCL-554*   Re   8-10
  Full title: *Victor Borge (Comedy in Music)*. From a 1953 performance at the John Golden Theatre in
  New York.
  Cast: Victor Borge.

VICTOR/VICTORIA
Soundtrack (1982) . . . .*MGM (S) MG-1-5407*   82   20-25
  Composer: Henry Mancini; Leslie Bricusse. **Conductor:** Henry Mancini. **Cast:** Julie Andrews;
  Robert Preston; Lesley Ann Warren.

VICTORS
Soundtrack (1963) . . . .*Colpix (M) CP-516*   63   15-20
Soundtrack (1963) . . . . *Colpix (S) SCP-516*   63   20-25
  Composer: Sol Kaplan; Hugh Martin; Ralph Blane. **Conductor:** Sol Kaplan. **Cast:** Frank Sinatra.
Studiotrack (1963) . . . .*Colpix (M) CP-460*   63   15-20
Studiotrack (1963) . . . . *Colpix (S) SCP-460*   63   20-25
  Cast: Jane Morgan.

VICTORY AT SEA

TV Soundtrack (1952) . . . .*RCA Victor (EP) EPC-1779*	54	**$15-25**
Triple EP set.		
TV Soundtrack (1952) . . . .*RCA Victor (M) LM-1779*	54	**15-25**
Volume one.		
TV Soundtrack (1952) . . . .*RCA Victor (M) LM-2335*	59	**15-20**
Volume one.		
TV Soundtrack (1952) . . . . *RCA Victor (SE) LSC-2335*	59	**15-20**
Volume one.		
TV Soundtrack (1952) . . . .*RCA Victor (EP) LPC-121*	61	**10-15**
Volume one. Compact 33.		
TV Soundtrack (1952) . . . . *RCA Victor (SE) ANL1-0970*	75	**8-10**
Volume one.		
TV Soundtrack (1952) . . . .*RCA Victor (M) LM-2226*	58	**15-20**
Volume two.		
TV Soundtrack (1952) . . . . *RCA Victor (SE) LSC-2226*	58	**15-25**
Volume two.		
TV Soundtrack (1952) . . . . *RCA Victor (SE) ANL1-1432*	76	**8-10**
Volume two.		
TV Soundtrack (1952) . . . .*RCA Victor (M) LM-2532*	61	**15-20**
TV Soundtrack (1952) . . . . *RCA Victor (SE) LSC-2532*	61	**12-15**
Volume three. Above two have gatefold covers and include booklets.		
TV Soundtrack (1952) . . . . *RCA Victor (EP) LPC-142*	61	**10-15**
Volume three. Compact 33.		
TV Soundtrack (1952) . . . . *RCA Victor (SE) VSC-7064*		**15-20**
Double LP set. Highlights of the 13-hour score.		
Composer: Richard Rodgers. **Conductor:** Robert Russell Bennett.		

VIDEODROME

Soundtrack (1983) . . . . *Varese Sarabande (S) 81173*	83	**8-10**

VIEW FROM THE BRIDGE

Original Cast (1966) . . . .*Mercury (M) OCM-2-221*	66	**20-25**
Original Cast (1966) . . . .*Mercury (S) OCS-2-621*	66	**30-40**
Double LP set. The complete Arthur Miller play.		

VIEW TO A KILL

Soundtrack (1985) . . . .*Capitol (S) SJ-512413*	85	**8-10**
Composer: John Barry. **Conductor:** John Barry. **Cast:** Duran Duran.		

VIKINGS
Soundtrack (1958) ....*United Artists (M) UAL-40003* 59 $30-40
Soundtrack (1958) .... *United Artists (S) UAS-5003* 59 50-60
Gatefold cover.
Composer: Mario Nascimbene. **Conductor:** Mario Nascimbene.
Also see ELMER GANTRY; I WANT TO LIVE

VILLA RIDES!
Soundtrack (1968) .... *Dot (S) DLP-25870* 68 30-40
Composer: Maurice Jarre. **Conductor:** Maurice Jarre.

VILLAGE OF EIGHT GRAVESTONES
Soundtrack (1976) ....*Varese Sarabande (S) VC-81084* 78 8-10
Composer: Yasushi Akutagawa. **Conductor:** Yasushi Akutagawa.

VIRGIN
Original Cast (1972) .... *Paramount (S) PAA-0288* 72 15-20
Promotional issue only. Also has music from *Fear No Evil, The Mission* and *Ordination Theme*.
Original Cast (1972) ....*Paramount (S) PAS-8000* 72 30-40
Double LP, boxed set.
Composer: John O'Reilly. **Cast:** Joe DeVito; Dorothy Lerner; Jim Rast; Jay Pielecki; Mission.

VIRGIN AND THE GYPSY
Soundtrack (1970) ....*Steady (S) S-122* 70 25-30
Composer: Patrick Gowers; others. **Conductor:** Patrick Gowers.

VISION QUEST
Soundtrack (1985) ....*Geffen (S) GHS-24063* 85 8-10
Composer: Various. **Cast:** Journey; Style Council; Madonna; Don Henley; Dio; John Waite; Red Rider; Sammy Hagar; Foreigner.

VISIONS OF EIGHT
Soundtrack (1973) .... *RCA Victor (S) ABL1-0231* 73 15-25
Composer: Henry Mancini. **Conductor:** Henry Mancini.

VIVA LAS VEGAS
Soundtrack (1964) ....*RCA Victor (EP) EPA-4382* 64 45-55
Black label, dog on top.
Soundtrack (1964) ....*RCA Victor (EP) EPA-4382* 65 30-40
Black label, dog on side.
Soundtrack (1964) ....*RCA Victor (EP) EPA-4382* 69 30-40
Orange label.
Composer: Doc Pomus; Mort Schuman; Bill Giant; Bernie Baum; Florence Kaye; others.
Cast: Elvis Presley; Scotty Moore (guitar); Barney Kessel (guitar); D.J. Fontana (drums); Jordanaires (vocals).

VIVA MARIA!
Soundtrack (1965) ....*United Artists (M) UAL-4135* 66 12-15
Soundtrack (1965) .... *United Artists (S) UAS-5135* 66 15-20
Composer: Georges Delerue; Louis Malle; Jean Claude Carriere. **Conductor:** Georges Delerue.
Cast: Brigitte Bardot; Jean Moreau.

VIVA MAX!
Soundtrack (1969) ....*RCA Victor (S) LSP-4275* 70 15-20

VIVA ZAPATA:
see DEATH OF A SALESMAN

VIXEN
Soundtrack (1968) . . . . *Beverly Hills (S) BHS-22*   68 $40-50
  Composer: Bill Loose. Conductor: Bill Loose.

VOICE OF EILENE FARRELL:
see INTERRUPTED MELODY

VOICE OF F.D.R.
Studio Cast (1952) . . . . *Decca (M) DL-9628*   52   30-40
  Composer: Victor Young. Conductor: Victor Young. Cast: Quentin Reynolds (narration).

VOICES
Soundtrack (1979) . . . . *Planet (S) P-9002*   79   8-10
  Composer: Jimmy Webb; others. Cast: Burton Cummings; Willie Nelson; Tom Petty and the
  Heartbreakers.

VOIX HUMAINE, LA:
see LA VOIX HUMAINE

VON RICHTHOFEN AND BROWN:
see PRIVATE PARTS

VOYAGE EN BALLON
Soundtrack (1960) . . . . *Philips (M) PHM-200-029*   60   25-30
Soundtrack (1960) . . . . *Philips (S) PHS-600-029*   60   35-40
Soundtrack (1960) . . . . *Philips (S) FDX-290*   77   8-10
  Composer: Jean Prodromides. Conductor: Andre Girard.

VOYAGE OF THE DAMNED
Soundtrack (1976) . . . . *Entr' Acte (S) ERS-6508*   77   10-15
  Composer: Lalo Schifrin. Conductor: Lalo Schifrin.

W.C. FIELDS AND ME
Soundtrack (1976) . . . .*MCA (S) 2092*   76   **$8-10**
  Composer: Henry Mancini. **Conductor:** Henry Mancini. **Cast:** Valerie Perrine; Rod Steiger.

W.W. AND THE DIXIE DANCEKINGS
Soundtrack (1975) . . . .*20th Century-Fox (S) ST-103*   75   **10-15**
  Composer: Dave Grusin; others. **Conductor:** Lionel Newman.

WACKIEST SHIP IN THE ARMY
Soundtrack (1960) . . . . *No Label Shown (45) KB-760*   60   **50-100**
  "Theatre Promotion Record." Has *Do You Know What It Means to Miss New Orleans.*
  Cast: Ricky Nelson; Jack Lemmon (piano).

WACKY WORLD OF MOTHER GOOSE
Soundtrack (1967) . . . . *Epic (M) LN-24230*   67   **35-40**
Soundtrack (1967) . . . . *Epic (S) BN-26230*   67   **45-50**
  Composer: George Wilkins; Jules Bass. **Cast:** Margaret Rutherford (as "Mother Goose").

WAGON TRAIN
TV Soundtrack (1959) . . . . *Mercury (M) MG-20502*   59   **25-30**
TV Soundtrack (1959) . . . . *Mercury (S) SR-60179*   59   **35-40**
  Composer: Jerome Moross; others. **Conductor:** Stanley Wilson.

WAIKIKI WEDDING
Studiotrack (1937) . . . .*Decca (M) DL-6011*   51   **50-60**
  10-inch LP.
  Composer: Leo Robin; Ralph Rainger; Harry Owens. **Conductor:** Lani McIntire; Jimmy Dorsey;
  Victor Young. **Cast:** Bing Crosby.
  Also see POCKET FULL OF DREAMS

WAIT A MINIM!
Original Cast (1966) . . . . *London (M) AM-58002*   66   **12-15**
Original Cast (1966) . . . . *London (S) AMS-88002*   66   **15-20**
  Composer: Andrew Tracey. **Cast:** Andrew Tracey; Paul Tracey; Kendrew Lascelles; Michel
  Martel; Nigel Pegram; Dana Valery; Sarah Atkinson.

WAITING FOR GODOT
Studio Cast (1956) . . . . *Columbia (M) O2L-238*   56   **25-35**
  Double LP set. A "Tragicomedy."
  Cast: Bert Lahr; E.G. Marshall; Kurt Kasznar.

WAKE UP AND LIVE
Soundtrack (1937) .... *Columbia (M) CL-3068*   64 $25-30
Cast: Alice Faye; Jack Haley.

WALK DON'T RUN
Soundtrack (1966) ....*Mainstream (M) 56080*   66   25-30
Soundtrack (1966) ....*Mainstream (S) S-6080*   66   30-35
Composer: Quincy Jones; Peggy Lee. Conductor: Quincy Jones. Cast: Don Elliot Voices;
Tony Clementi.

WALK IN THE SPRING RAIN:
see LOVE IS A MANY SPLENDORED THING

WALK ON THE WILD SIDE
Soundtrack (1962) ....*Choreo (M) A-4-ST*   62   25-30
Soundtrack (1962) .... *Choreo (S) AS-4-ST*   62   35-40
Soundtrack (1962) ....*Ava (M) A-4-ST*   62   25-30
Soundtrack (1962) .... *Ava (S) AS-4-ST*   62   35-40
Some Ava label discs were packaged in a Choreo cover.
Soundtrack (1962) ....*Mainstream (M) 56083*   67   20-25
Soundtrack (1962) ....*Mainstream (S) S-6083*   67   30-35
Soundtrack (1962) .... *Citadel (S) CT-7028*   82   8-10
Composer: Elmer Bernstein. Conductor: Elmer Bernstein.

WALK WITH LOVE AND DEATH
Soundtrack (1969) .... *Citadel (S) CT-6025*   69   75-100
Composer: Georges Delerue. Conductor: Georges Delerue.

WALKER
Soundtrack (1987) .... *Virgin Movie Music (S) 90686-1*   87   8-10
Cast: Joe Strummer.

WALKING HAPPY
Original Cast (1966) .... *Capitol (M) VAS-2631*   66   25-30
Original Cast (1966) .... *Capitol (S) SVAS-2631*   66   35-40
Composer: James Van Heusen; Sammy Cahn. Conductor: Herbert Grossman. Cast: Norman
Wisdom; Louise Troy; George Rose; Ed Bakey; Gordon Dilworth; Emma Trekman; Gretchen
Van Akmen; Sharon Dierking; Ian Garry; Burt Bier; Chad Black.

WALL
Original Cast (1960) .... *Folkways (M) FG-3558*   60   10-20
Cast: Rita Karin; Norbert Horowitz; Rochelle Horowitz.

WALT DISNEY'S MICKEY MOUSE CLUB
TV Soundtrack ...:.........................*Disneyland (M) DQ-1229*   62   12-15
TV Soundtrack .... *Disneyland (M) MM-24*   65   10-12

WALT DISNEY'S STORY OF PINOCCHIO - TOLD BY JIMINY CRICKET
Studio Cast (1957) .... *Disneyland (SE) ST-3905*   10-15
Includes booklet.

WALT DISNEY'S TRUE LIFE ADVENTURES
Soundtrack .... *Disneyland (M) WDL-4011*   57   40-50
Music from five Disney "True Life Adventure" film shorts: *Beaver Valley* (1950), *Bear Country* (1953),
Prowlers of the Everglades (1953), *Nature's Half Acre* (1951), and *Olympic Elk* (1952).
Composer: Paul J. Smith. Conductor: Paul J. Smith.

WALT DISNEY'S WONDERFUL WORLD OF COLOR
TV Soundtrack ....*Disneyland (M) DQ-1245*   64   12-15

WALTON CONDUCTS HIS GREAT FILM MUSIC
Soundtrack (1945) . . . .*Seraphin (SE) S-60205*   73   **$10-15**
   Reissue of *Music from Shakespearean Films.*
  Composer: Sir William Walton. **Conductor:** Sir William Walton.
  Also see MUSIC FROM SHAKESPEAREAN FILMS

WALTZING DOWN BROADWAY
Studiotrack (1958) . . . . *Warner Bros. (M) B-1218*   58   **15-20**
Studiotrack (1958) . . . . *Warner Bros. (S) BS-1218*   58   **20-25**
  Composer: Various. **Conductor:** Warren Barker. **Cast:** Warren Barker and Orchestra.

WANDERERS
Soundtrack (1979) . . . .*Warner Bros. (S) BSK-3359*   79   **8-10**
  Composer: Various. **Cast:** 4 Seasons; Lee Dorsey; Angels; Shirelles; Ben E. King; Contours;
  Isley Brothers; Dion.

WAR AND PEACE
Soundtrack (1956) . . . . *Columbia (M) CL-930*   56   **35-40**
Soundtrack (1956) . . . .*Columbia Special Products (M) ACL-930*   76   **8-10**
  Composer: Nino Rota. **Conductor:** Franco Ferrara.
Soundtrack (1968) . . . .*Capitol (S) SWAO-2918*   68   **45-50**
  Composer: Vyacheslav Ovchinnikov. **Conductor:** Vyacheslav Ovchinnikov. **Cast:** Moscow
  Symphony Orchestra and All Union Radio and TV Chorus.

WAR GAMES
Soundtrack (1983) . . . .*Polydor (S) 422-81500*   83   **8-10**
  Composer: Arthur Rubenstein.
Soundtrack (1983) . . . .*Polydor (S) 815005-1*   83   **8-10**
  Composer: Arthur B. Rubinstein. **Conductor:** Arthur B. Rubinstein. **Cast:** Yvonne Elliman;
  Beepers. (With dialogue.)

WAR LORD
Soundtrack (1965) . . . .*Decca (M) DL-9149*   65 · **30-40**
Soundtrack (1965) . . . .*Decca (S) DL7-9149*   65   **50-65**
  Composer: Jerome Moross; Hans J. Salter. **Conductor:** Joseph Gershenson.

WAR LOVER
Studiotrack (1962) . . . .*Colpix (M) CP-512*   62   **20-30**
Soundtrack (1962) . . . . *Colpix (S) SCP-512*   62   **30-40**
  Composer: Richard Addinsel. **Conductor:** Shiro Hirosaki.

WAR OF THE WORLDS
Original Radio Cast (1938) . . . .*Evolution (SE) 4001*   **12-15**
   Double LP set. "Actual broadcast by the Mercury Theatre on the Air, October 30, 1938."
  Composer: Howard Koch (radio play). **Conductor:** Bernard Herrmann (musical director).
  Cast: Orson Welles; others. (With dialogue.)
Original Radio Cast (1938) . . . . *Audio Rarities (M) LPA-2355*   **10-15**
Soundtrack (1938) . . . .*Quasi (M) PAL-1953*   **30-35**
  A "Limited Collectors Edition." One side has music from *When Worlds Collide,* also by Leith Stevens.
  Composer: Leith Stevens. **Conductor:** Leith Stevens.
Original Radio Cast (1938) . . . *Longines Symphonette (M) No Number Used*   72   **8-10**
  Composer: Howard Koch. **Cast:** Orson Welles; Mercury Theatre Cast.

WARLOCK
Soundtrack . . . . *Intrada (S) MAF-7003*   **8-10**
  Cast: Safan Craig.

WARNING SHOT
Soundtrack (1967) . . . . *Liberty (M) LRP-3498*   67   **20-30**
Soundtrack (1967) . . . . *Liberty (S) LST-7498*   67   **30-40**
  Composer: Jerry Goldsmith; Jay Livingston; Ray Evans. **Conductor:** Si Zentner.

WARRIORS
Soundtrack (1979) .... *A&M (S) SP-4761* · 79   **$10-12**
Soundtrack (1979) .... *A&M (S) SP-3151*   Re   **8-10**
   Composer: Barry DeVorzon; others. **Cast:** Barry DeVorzon; Kenny Vance; Joe Walsh; Eric Mercury; Desmond Child.

WASHINGTON BEHIND CLOSED DOORS
TV Soundtrack (1977) .... *ABC (S) AB-1044*   77   **10-12**
   Composer: Dominic Frontiere; Norman Gimble. **Conductor:** Dominic Frontiere. **Cast:** Sally Stevens; Jackie Ward; Missy Mackay; Diana Lee; Ron Hicklin; Loren S. Farber; Gene Merlino; Mitch Gordon.

WATER GYPSIES
Original London Cast (1955) .... *World (M) SH-228*   **20-25**
   Also has music from *Bless the Bride.*
   Composer: Vivian Ellis; A.P. Herbert. **Conductor:** Jack Coles. **Cast:** Dora Byan; Laurie Payne; Peter Graves; Pamela Charles; Doris Hare; Jerry Verno. (With dialogue.)
   Also see PLAIN AND FANCY

WATERHOLE #3
Soundtrack (1967) .... *Smash (M) MGS-27096*   67   **12-15**
Soundtrack (1967) .... *Smash (S) SRS-67096*   67   **15-20**
   Composer: Dave Grusin; Bob Wells. **Conductor:** Dave Grusin. **Cast:** Roger Miller (narration and vocals).

WATERLOO
Soundtrack (1971) .... *Paramount (S) PAS-6003*   71   **25-30**
   Composer: Nino Rota. **Conductor:** Bruno Nicolai.

WATERMELON MAN
Soundtrack (1970) .... *Beverly Hills (S) BHS-26*   70   **12-15**
   Composer: Melvin Van Peebles. **Conductor:** Melvin Van Peebles. **Cast:** Melvin Van Peebles; Estelle Parsons.

WATERSHIP DOWN
Soundtrack (1978) .... *Columbia (S) JS-35707*   78   **8-12**
   Composer: Angela Morley; Malcolm Williamson; Mike Batt. **Conductor:** Marcus Dods. **Cast:** Michael Hordern (prologue narration); Art Garfunkel.

WATTSTAX (THE LIVING WORD)
Soundtrack (1973) .... *Stax (S) STS-2-301*   73   **10-15**
   Volume one.
Soundtrack (1973) .... *Stax (S) STS-2-301*   73   **10-15**
   Volume two. Above two are double LP sets.
   Composer: Various. **Conductor:** Dale Warrenn. **Cast:** Isaac Hayes; Staple Singers; Luther Ingrahm; Richard Pryor; Rev. Jesse Jackson; Rufus Thomas; Carla Thomas; Bar-Kays; Johnnie Taylor; Emotions; Kim Weston; Eddie Floyd; Albert King; Soul Children.

WAVELENGTH
Soundtrack (1983) .... *Varese Sarabande (S) STV-81207*   83   **8-10**
   Composer: Tangerine Dream. **Cast:** Tangerine Dream.

WAY OF THE WORLD
Original London Cast (1968) .... *Caedmon (M) TR-339*   68   **15-20**
Original London Cast (1968) .... *Caedmon (S) TRS-339*   68   **20-25**
   Above two are triple LP sets.

WAY WE WERE
Soundtrack (1974) .... *Columbia (S) KS-32830*   74   **8-12**
   Composer: Marvin Hamlisch; Marilyn and Alan Bergman. **Conductor:** Marvin Hamlisch. **Cast:** Barbra Streisand.

WAY WEST
Soundtrack (1967)	. . . . *United Artists (M) UAL-4149*	67	$15-20
Soundtrack (1967)	. . . . *United Artists (S) UAS-5149*	67	25-30
Soundtrack (1967)	. . . .*MCA (S) 25045*	Re	8-10

Composer: Bronislau Kaper; Mack David. **Conductor:** Andre Previn. **Cast:** Serendipity Singers.

WE STILL KILL THE OLD WAY
Soundtrack (1967)	. . . . *United Artists (M) UAL-4183*	68	20-30
Soundtrack (1967)	. . . . *United Artists (S) UAS-5183*	68	30-40
Soundtrack (1967)	. . . .*MCA (S) 25039*	68	8-10

Composer: Luis Enriquez Bacalov. **Conductor:** Bruno Nicolai.

WE WERE DANCING:
see TONIGHT AT 8:30

WE'D RATHER SWITCH
Original Cast (1969)	. . . . *Varieties (M) WRS-100*	69	60-75

Composer: Larry Crane. **Conductor:** Lorenzo Fuller. **Cast:** Tricia Sandberg; Yancy Gerber; Martha Wilcox; Howard Lemay; Ron Collins.

WEILL, KURT:
see KURT WEILL CABARET

WEIRD CIRCLE
Original Radio Cast	. . . .*Golden Age (M) 5025*	78	8-10

Has *The Tell-Tale Heart* and *Frankenstein.*

WEIRD SCIENCE
Soundtrack (1985)	. . . .*MCA (S) 6146*	85	8-10

Composer: Ira Newborn; others. **Cast:** Oingo Boingo; Max Carl; Taxxi; Cheyne; Kim Wilde; Wall of Voodoo; Broken Homes; Wild Men of Wonga; Lords of the New Church; Killing Joke.

WELCOME STRANGER:
see BUT BEAUTIFUL

WELCOME TO L.A.
Soundtrack (1977)	. . . . *United Artists (S) UA-LA703-H*	77	10-12
Soundtrack (1977)	. . . .*MCA (S) 25040*	77	8-10

Composer: Richard Baskin. **Cast:** Richard Baskin; Keith Carradine.

WEST SIDE STORY
Original Cast (1957)	. . . . *Columbia (M) OL-5230*	58	15-25
Original Cast (1957)	. . . .*Columbia (S) OS-2001*	58	25-35

Columbia's first Broadway cast LP issued in true stereo.

Original Cast (1957)	. . . . *Columbia (S) S-32603*	73	10-12
Original Cast (1957)	. . . . *Columbia (S) JS-32603*	Re	8-10

Composer: Leonard Bernstein; Stephen Sondheim. **Conductor:** Max Goberman.
Cast: Carol Lawrence; Larry Kert; Chita Rivera; Mickey Calin; Grover Dale; Marilyn Cooper; Carmen Guiterrez.

Original English Cast (1959)	. . . .*Forum (M) F-9045*	59	15-20
Original English Cast (1959)	. . . .*Forum (S) SF-9045*	59	25-30

Composer: Leonard Bernsetin; Stephen Sondheim. **Conductor:** Lawrence Leonard.
Cast: George Chakiras; Bruce Trent; Lucille Graham; Mary Thomas; Joyce Berry.

Studio Cast (1961)	. . . .*Columbia (M) ML-5651*	61	10-15
Studio Cast (1961)	. . . .*Columbia (S) MS-6251*	61	15-20

One side has a suite from *On the Waterfront.*

Composer: Leonard Bernstein; Stephen Sondheim. **Conductor:** Leonard Bernstein.
Cast: Leonard Bernstein and His Orchestra.

WEST SIDE STORY (continued)

Soundtrack (1961) .... *Columbia (M) OL-5670*   61 $15-20
Soundtrack (1961) .... *Columbia (S) OS-2070*   61   20-25
Soundtrack (1961) ....*Columbia (S) JS-2070*   Re   8-10
  Composer: Leonard Bernstein; Stephen Sondheim. **Conductor:** Johnny Green. **Cast:** Marni Nixon; Jim Bryant; Betty Wand.
Studiotrack (1961) ....*United Artists (M) UAL-3166*   61   10-15
Studiotrack (1961) ....*United Artists (S) UAS-6166*   61   15-20
  One side has music from six other films.
  Composer: Leonard Bernstein. **Conductor:** Johnny Green. **Cast:** Ferrante and Teicher.
Studiotrack (1959) ....*Warner Bros. (M) B-1240*   59   10-15
Studiotrack (1959) .... *Warner Bros. (S) BS-1240*   59   15-20
  Actual title: *Ballets U.S.A.* Includes *Ballet from West Side Story.*
  Cast: Robert Prince.
  Also see DIVORCE ITALIAN STYLE

WESTWARD HO, THE WAGONS

Soundtrack (1956) .... *Disneyland (M) WDL-4008*   56   35-40
Soundtrack (1956) .... *Disneyland (M) WDL-3041*   59   20-25
Soundtrack (1956) .... *Disneyland (M) WDL-1041*   60   15-20
  Composer: George Bruns; others. **Conductor:** George Bruns; Tutti Camarata. **Cast:** Fess Parker; Bill Beeve; Kathleen Crowley.

WESTWORLD

Soundtrack (1973) .... *MGM (S) 1SE-47*   73   15-20
Soundtrack (1973) ....*MCA (S) 25004*   Re   8-10
  Composer: Fred Karlin. **Conductor:** Fred Karlin.

WHALER OUT OF NEW BEDFORD (AND OTHER SONGS OF THE WHALING ERA)

Soundtrack .... *Folkways (S) 3850*   8-10
  Cast: Peggy Seeger; Ewan MacColl; A.L. Lloyd.

WHAT A WAY TO GO!

Soundtrack (1964) .... *20th Century-Fox (M) TFM-3143*   64   20-25
Soundtrack (1964) ....*20th Century-Fox (S) TFS-4143*   64   30-35
  Composer: Nelson Riddle; Jule Styne; Betty Comden; Adolph Green. **Conductor:** Nelson Riddle.

WHAT AM I BID?

Soundtrack (1967) ....*MGM (M) E-4506*   67   12-15
  Composer: Gene Nash; others. **Conductor:** Ernie Freeman. **Cast:** Leroy Van Dyke; Faron Young; Tex Ritter; Johnny Sea.
Soundtrack (1967) .... *MGM (S) SE-4506*   67   15-20
  Composer: Gene Nash; others. **Conductor:** Ernie Freeman. **Cast:** Leroy Van Dyke; Faron Young; Tex Ritter; Johnny Sea.

WHAT DID YOU DO IN THE WAR, DADDY?

Soundtrack (1966) .... *RCA Victor (M) LPM-3648*   66   20-25
Soundtrack (1966) ....*RCA Victor (S) LSP-3648*   66   25-30
  Composer: Henry Mancini; Jay Livingston; Ray Evans. **Conductor:** Henry Mancini. **Cast:** Aldo Ray.

WHAT DO YOU SAY TO A NAKED LADY?

Soundtrack (1970) ....*United Artists (S) UAS-5206*   70   25-30
Soundtrack (1970) ....*MCA (S) 25030*   70   8-10
  Composer: Steve Karmen. **Conductor:** Steve Karmen. **Cast:** Allen Funt (narration).

WHAT DO YOU WANT TO BE WHEN YOU GROW UP?
Studio Cast (1967) .... *RCA Victor/Camden (M) CAL-1083*   67 $10-15
Studio Cast (1967) .... *RCA Victor/Camden (S) CAS-1083*   67   15-20
  Composer: Various. **Conductor:** Billy Mure. **Cast:** Ed McMahon (narrator); Jeff McMahon;
  Jackson Beck; Evelyn Juster; Dick Van Patten; Rita Lloyd; Corrine Orr; Peter Fernandez; Jack
  Grimes; Sybil Trent; Kathy Grimes.

WHAT IT WAS, WAS LOVE
Studio Cast (1969) .... *RCA Victor (S) LSP-4115*   69   15-20
  An "Original Albumusical."
  Composer: Gordon Jenkins. **Conductor:** Gordon Jenkins. **Cast:** Steve Lawrence and Eydie
  Gorme.

WHAT MAKES SAMMY RUN?
Original Cast (1964) .... *Columbia (M) KOL-6040*   64   30-35
Original Cast (1964) .... *Columbia (S) KOS-2440*   64   40-50
  Composer: Ervin Drake. **Conductor:** Lehman Engel. **Cast:** Steve Lawrence; Sally Ann Howes;
  Robert Alda; Barry Newman; Bernice Massi.

WHAT'S A NICE COUNTRY LIKE U.S. DOING IN A STATE LIKE THIS?
Original Cast (1973) .... *RMSC (S) 747003*   73   40-45
  Seven-inch LP.
  Composer: Cary Hoffman; Ira Gasman. **Cast:** Trudy Desmond; Andrea Martin; Martin Short.
Original London Cast (1973) .... *Galaxy (S) GAL-6004*   73   30-35
  Composer: Cary Hoffman; Ira Gasman. **Cast:** Peter Blake; Billy Boyle; Neil McCaul; Jacque
  Toye; Leveen Willoughby.

WHAT'S NEW PUSSYCAT?
Soundtrack (1965) .... *United Artists (M) UAL-4128*   65   12-15
Soundtrack (1965) .... *United Artists (S) UAS-5128*   65   15-20
Soundtrack (1965) .... *United Artists (S) UA-LA278-G*   74   10-12
  Composer: Burt Bacharach (music); Hal David (lyrics). **Cast:** Tom Jones; Manfred Mann;
  Dionne Warwick.

WHAT'S THE MATTER WITH HELEN?
Soundtrack (1975) .... *No Label Shown (S) DY-1200*   75   35-40
  Promotional issue only.
  Composer: David Raksin. **Conductor:** David Raksin.

WHAT'S THE MEANING OF THIS?
Original Cast (1967) .... *Lutheran (S) S7 7956*   67   20-25
  Presented by the Youth Activity Division of the American Lutheran Church. A musical made especially for
  an August 12-17, 1967 convention.
  Composer: Richard Wilson. **Conductor:** Herbert Pilhofer. **Cast:** Castle Singers; John Prigge;
  Ken Bland; Pat Maxon; Robert Lee; Tim Schumacher.

WHAT'S UP, TIGER LILY?
Soundtrack (1966) .... *Kama Sutra (M) KLP-8053*   66 $15-20
Soundtrack (1966) .... *Kama Sutra (S) KLPS-8053*   66   20-25
  Composer: John Sebastian; others. **Cast:** Woody Allen and Lenny Maxwell (narration); Lovin' Spoonful.

WHEN HARRY MET SALLY
Soundtrack (1989) .... *Columbia (S) SC-45319*   89   8-10
  Cast: Harry Connick Jr.

WHEN THE BOYS MEET THE GIRLS
Soundtrack (1965) ....*MGM (M) E-4334*   65   12-15
Soundtrack (1965) .... *MGM (S) SE-4334*   65   15-20
Soundtrack (1965) ....*MCA (S) 25013*   Re   8-10
  Composer: George Gershwin; Ira Gershwin; Liberace; others. **Conductor:** Ernie Freeman; Fred Karger. **Cast:** Connie Francis; Harve Presnell; Liberace; Louis Armstrong; Sam the Sham and the Pharaohs; Herman's Hermits.

WHEN WORLDS COLLIDE:
see WAR OF THE WORLDS

WHERE EAGLES DARE
Soundtrack (1969) .... *MGM (S) S1E-16*   69   25-35
Soundtrack (1969) ....*MCA (S) 25082*   Re   8-10
  Composer: Ron Goodwin. **Conductor:** Ron Goodwin.

WHERE THE ACTION IS
TV Soundtrack (1965) .... *ABC-Paramount (M) ABC-531*   65   20-25
TV Soundtrack (1965) .... *ABC-Paramount (M) ABCS-531*   65   25-30
  Composer: Various. **Cast:** Steve Alaimo.

WHERE THE BLUE OF THE NIGHT MEETS THE GOLD OF THE DAY
Soundtrack (1930-33) ....*Biograph (M) BLP-17-1*   77   8-10
  Music from Bing Crosby films (1930 - 1933).
  Composer: Various. **Cast:** Bing Crosby.

WHERE THE BUFFALO ROAM
Soundtrack (1980) ....*Backstreet/MCA (S) 5126*   80   8-10
  Composer: Various. **Cast:** Jimi Hendrix; Wild Bill Band of Strings; Bob Dylan; Neil Young; Four Tops; Creedence Clearwater Revival; Temptations.

WHERE THE HOT WIND BLOWS:
see LOVE IS MY PROFESSION

WHERE THE LILIES BLOOM
Soundtrack (1974) ....*Columbia (S) KC-32806*   74   10-12
  Composer: Earl Scruggs Revue. **Conductor:** Earl Scruggs Revue. **Cast:** Earl Scruggs Revue.

WHERE'S CHARLEY?
Original London Cast (1948) .... *Monmouth Evergreen (SE) MES-7029*   8-12
  Composer: Frank Loesser. **Cast:** Norma Wisdom; Pip Hinton; Marion Grimaldi; Terrance Cooper.

WHERE'S JACK?
Soundtrack (1969) ....*Paramount (S) PAS-5005*   69   25-35
  Composer: Elmer Bernstein. **Conductor:** Elmer Bernstein. **Cast:** Mary Hopkin; Danny Dolye.

WHERE'S POPPA?
Soundtrack (1970) ....*United Artists (S) UAS-5216*   70   15-20
  Composer: Jack Z. Elliott. **Cast:** Carol Carmichael; June Jackson; Bright Cheerstrap.

WHISPERERS
Soundtrack (1967) ....*United Artists (M) UAL-4161*   67   **$15-20**
Soundtrack (1967) .... *United Artists (S) UAS-5161*   67   **20-30**
Soundtrack (1967) ....*MCA (S) 25041*   **8-10**
  Composer: John Barry. **Conductor:** John Barry.

WHITE CHRISTMAS
Soundtrack (1954) ....*Decca (M) DL-8083*   54   **40-50**
  Composer: Irving Berlin. **Conductor:** Joseph J. Lilley. **Cast:** Bing Crosby; Danny Kaye; Trudy
  Stevens; Peggy Lee; Skylarks.
Studiotrack (1954) .... *Columbia (M) CL-6338*   54   **40-50**
  Composer: Irving Berlin. **Conductor:** Percy Faith; Paul Weston; Buddy Cole. **Cast:** Rosemary
  Clooney; Mellomen.

WHITE HORSE INN
Studio Cast (1961) ....*Angel (M) 35815*   61   **15-20**
Studio Cast (1961) ....*Angel (S) S-35815*   61   **25-30**
  Composer: Ralph Benatzky; Robert Stolz; Robert Gilbert; Harry Graham. **Conductor:** Tony
  Osborne. **Cast:** Andy Cole; Mary Thomas; Rita Williams; Charles Young; Peter Regan; Rita
  Williams Singers; Barney Gilbraith.
Studio Cast (1960) .... *Angel (S) SZX-3897*   60   **10-15**
  Performed in German.
  Conductor: Willy Mattes.
Studio Cast .... *Monmouth Evergreen (SE) MES-7055*   **8-10**
  Excerpts.
  Composer: Ralph Benatzky; Robert Stolz; Robert Gilbert; Harry Graham. **Conductor:** Jack
  Hylton. **Cast:** Jack Hylton and His Orchestra.
  Also see GIRL FRIEND

WHITE MANSIONS
Studio Cast (1978) ....*A&M (S) SP-6004*   78   **8-12**

WHITE NIGHTS
Soundtrack (1985) ....*Atlantic (S) 81273-1*   85   **8-10**
  Composer: Michel Colombier. **Conductor:** Phil Ramone. **Cast:** Phil Collins; Marilyn Martin;
  David Pack; Robert Plant; Roberta Flack; Sandy Stewart; Nile Rodgers; John Hiatt; Chaka Khan;
  Lou Reed; David Foster; Jenny Burton.

WHITE ROCK - INNSBRUCK WINTER GAMES
TV Soundtrack (1978) ....*A&M (S) SP-4614*   78   **8-12**
  Composer: Rick Wakeman. **Conductor:** Rick Wakeman.

WHO IS HARRY KELLERMAN AND WHY IS HE SAYING THOSE TERRIBLE THINGS ABOUT ME?
Soundtrack (1971) ....*Columbia (S) S-30791*   71   **$15-20**
  Composer: Shel Silverstein; others. **Conductor:** Ron Haffkine. **Cast:** Ray Charles; Dr. Hook and the Medicine Show; Dustin Hoffman; Barbara Harris; Jack Warden; Dom DeLuise; Betty Walker. (With dialogue.)

WHO IS KILLING THE GREAT CHEFS OF EUROPE?
Soundtrack (1978) ....*Epic (S) SE-35692*   78   **10-12**
  Composer: Henry Mancini. **Conductor:** Henry Mancini. **Cast:** National Philharmonic Orchestra.

WHO MADE WHO?
Soundtrack (1986) .... *Atlantic (S) 81650-1*   86   **8-10**
  Soundtrack of the film *Maximum Overdrive*.
  Composer: AC/DC (Malcom Young; Angus Young; Brian Johnson). **Cast:** AC/DC.

WHO'S AFRAID OF VIRGINIA WOOLF?
Studio Cast (1963) ....*Columbia (M) DOL-287*   63   **20-45**
Studio Cast (1963) ....*Columbia (S) DOS-687*   63   **30-35**
  Above two are four LP sets, with the complete dramatic play.
  Cast: Arthur Hill; Uta Hagen; George Grizzard; Melinda Dillon. (Dialogue.)
Soundtrack (1963) ....*Warner Bros. (M) B-1656*   66   **20-25**
Soundtrack (1963) .... *Warner Bros. (S) BS-1656*   66   **35-40**
  Above two have film background music, with some dialogue.
Soundtrack (1963) ....*Warner Bros. (M) 2B-1657*   66   **50-60**
  Double LP set. Issued in mono only. Mostly dialogue.
  Composer: Alex North. **Conductor:** Alex North. **Cast:** Elizabeth Taylor; Richard Burton; George Segal; Sandy Dennis.

WHO'S GOT DE DING DONG?:
see SOMEBODY BAD STOLE DE WEDDING BELL

WHO'S THAT GIRL?
Soundtrack (1987) .... *Sire (S) 1-25611*   87   **8-10**
  Composer: Various. **Cast:** Duncan Faure; Scritti Politti; Madonna; Coati Mundi; Club Nouveau; Michael Davidson.

WHOOP-UP!
Original Cast (1958) ....*MGM (M) E-3745*   58   **45-55**
  Has the "Overture" not heard on the stereo issue.
Original Cast (1958) .... *MGM (S) SE-3745*   58   **60-75**
  Does not have the "Overture" heard on the monaural issue, making it necessary to have both the mono and the stereo albums to have the complete show.
  Composer: Moose Charlap; Norman Gimble. **Conductor:** Stanley Lebowsky. **Cast:** Susan Johnson; Ralph Young; Sylvia Syms; Romo Vincent; Danny Meehan; Tony Gardell; Asia; Tom Raskin.
Original Cast (1958) ....*Polydor (S) 837196-1*   Re   **8-10**
Studio Cast (1958) ....*MGM (M) E-3746*   58   **15-20**
Studio Cast (1958) .... *MGM (S) SE-3746*   58   **20-25**
  Composer: Moose Charlap; Norman Gimbel. **Conductor:** David Rose. **Cast:** David Rose and His Orchestra.
Studio Cast (1958) ....*MGM (M) E-3747*   58   **15-20**
Studio Cast (1958) .... *MGM (S) SE-3747*   58   **20-25**
  Composer: Moose Charlap; Norman Gimble. **Cast:** Dick Hyman.

WHOOPEE!
Soundtrack .... *Smithsonian American (M) R-012*   **8-10**
  Composer: Gus Kahn; others. **Cast:** Eddie Cantor; Ruth Etting; George Olson.
  Also see PUTTIN' ON THE RITZ

WHOOPI GOLDBERG
Original Cast . . . . *Geffen (S) GHS-24065*   **$8-10**
Cast: Whoopi Goldberg.

WHY NOT?
TV Soundtrack (1960) . . . .*Grand Award (M) GA33-424*   **10-15**
Skits from the Steve Allen Show.
Cast: Dayton Allen; Steve Allen.

WICKED LADY
Soundtrack (1984) . . . .*Atlantic (S) 80073-1* 84   **20-25**
Composer: Tony Banks. Conductor: Stanley Black. Cast: National Philharmonic Orchestra of London.

WIDE, WIDE WORLD
TV Soundtrack (1956) . . . . *RCA Victor (M) LPM-1280* 56   **35-40**
Composer: David Broekman. Conductor: David Broekman.

WILD ANGELS
Soundtrack (1966) . . . . *Tower (M) T-5043* 66   **12-15**
Soundtrack (1966) . . . .*Tower (S) DT-5043* 66   **15-20**
Composer: Mike Curb; Harley Hatcher; Davie Allan. Cast: Davie Allan and the Arrows; Hands of Time; Visitors Featuring Barbara.
Soundtrack (1966) . . . . *Tower (M) T-5056* 67   **12-15**
Volume two.
Soundtrack (1966) . . . .*Tower (S) DT-5056* 67   **15-20**
Volume two.
Composer: Mike Curb; Harley Hatcher; Davie Allan. Cast: Davie Allan and the Arrows; Hands of Time; Joe Leahy.

WILD BUNCH
Soundtrack (1969) . . . .*Warner Bros. (S) WS-1814* 69   **90-100**
Soundtrack (1969) . . . . *Varese Sarabande (S) STV-81145* 80   **8-10**
Composer: Jerry Fielding. Conductor: Jerry Fielding.

WILD EYE
Soundtrack (1968) . . . . *RCA Victor (M) LPM-4003* 68   **15-25**
Soundtrack (1968) . . . .*RCA Victor (S) LSP-4003* 68   **25-30**
Composer: Gianni Marchetti. Conductor: Marty Manning. Cast: Rufus Lumley.

WILD GEESE
Soundtrack (1978) . . . .*A&M (S) SP-4730* 78   **10-15**
Composer: Roy Budd; others. Conductor: Roy Budd. Cast: Joan Armatrading; Irish Guards with Jack Watson; Jerry and Marc Donahue. (With dialogue.)

WILD IN THE STREETS
Soundtrack (1968) . . . . *Tower (S) SKAO-5099* 68   **15-20**
Soundtrack (1968) . . . . *Capitol (S) SKAO-6284* 68   **15-20**
Composer: Les Baxter; Barry Mann; Cynthis Weil; others. Conductor: Mike Curb; others. Cast: 13th Poser; Senators; Jerry Howard; Second Time; Gurus.

WILD IS THE WIND
Soundtrack (1957) . . . . *Columbia (M) CL-1090* 57   **40-50**
Composer: Dimitri Tiomkin. Conductor: Dimitri Tiomkin. Cast: Johnny Mathis.

WILD LIFE
Soundtrack (1984) . . . .*MCA (S) 5523* 84   **8-10**
Composer: Various. Cast: Edward Van Halen; Andy Summers; Three O'Clock; Louise Goffin; Charlotte Caffey; Peter Case; Bananarama; Charlie Sexton; Ron Wood; Van Stephenson; Hanover Fist.

WILD ON THE BEACH
Soundtrack (1965) .... *RCA Victor (M) LPM-3441*   65 $15-20
Soundtrack (1965) ....*RCA Victor (S) LSP-3441*   65   20-25
  Composer: Jimmy Haskell; Sonny Bono; By Dunham; others. **Conductor:** Jimmie Haskell.
  Cast: Astronauts; Frankie Randall; Sonny and Cher; Sandy Nelson; Jackie and Gayle; Cindy
  Malone.

WILD ONE
Soundtrack (1954) .... *Decca (M) DL-5515*   54   50-75
  10-inch LP.
Soundtrack (1954) .... *Decca (M) DL-8349*   56   40-50
  Composer: Leith Stevens. **Conductor:** Leith Stevens. **Cast:** Leith Stevens' All Stars.
Studiotrack (1954) .... *Decca (EP) ED-633*   54   20-35
  Double EP set. Full title: *Jazz Themes from The Wild One.*
  Composer: Leith Stevens. **Conductor:** Leith Stevens. **Cast:** Leith Stevens' All Stars.
Studiotrack (1954) ....*RCA Victor (EP) EPA-535*   54   40-60
  Previously issued with the title *Hot Blood.*
  Composer: Leith Stevens. **Conductor:** Shorty Rogers. **Cast:** Shorty Rogers and His Orchestra,
  featuring Bill Perkins (tenor saxophone).
  Also see HOT BLOOD

WILD ORCHID
Soundtrack .... *Sire (S) 1-26127*   8-10

WILD RACERS
Soundtrack (1968) .... *Sidewalk (S) ST-5914*   68   20-25
  Cast: Arrows; Sidewalk Sounds.

WILD ROVERS
Soundtrack (1971) .... *MGM (S) 1SE-31*   71   25-35
Soundtrack (1971) ....*MCA (S) 25141*   80   8-10
  Composer: Jerry Goldsmith. **Conductor:** Sydney Sax. **Cast:** Ellen Smith.

WILD WHEELS
Soundtrack (1969) ....*RCA Victor (S) LSO-1156*   69   15-20
  Composer: Harley Hatcher; others. **Cast:** Terry Stafford; Don Epperson; Thirteenth Committee;
  Billie and Blue; Saturday Revue; Three of August.

WILD, WILD WINTER
Soundtrack (1966) .... *Decca (M) DL-4699*   66   12-15
Soundtrack (1966) ....*Decca (S) DL7-4699*   66   15-20
  Composer: Jerry Long; others. **Conductor:** Frank Wilson. **Cast:** Astronauts; Jay and the
  Americans; Beau Brummels; Dick and Dee Dee; Jackie and Gayle.

WILDCAT
Original Cast (1960) .... *RCA Victor (M) LOC-1060* 60 $25-35
Original Cast (1960) .... *RCA Victor (S) LSO-1060* 60 **40-50**
　Composer: Cy Coleman; Carolyn Leigh. **Conductor:** John Morris. **Cast:** Lucille Ball; Keith Andes; Edith King; Paula Stewart; Clifford David; Swen Swenson; Charles Braswell; Bill Walker; Ray Mason; Al Lanti; Don Tomkins.
Studio Cast (1961) .... *Kapp (M) KL-1223* 61 **15-20**
Studio Cast (1961) .... *Kapp (S) KS-3223* 61 **20-25**
　Composer: Cy Coleman; Carolyn Leigh. **Conductor:** Pete King. **Cast:** Jack Jones; Beth Adlam; Pete King Choral and Orchestra.
Studio Cast (1961) .... *RCA Victor (M) LPM-2357* 61 **10-15**
Studio Cast (1961) .... *RCA Victor (S) LSP-2357* 61 **15-20**
　Composer: Cy Coleman; Carolyn Leigh. **Conductor:** Bob Thompson. **Cast:** Bob Thompson Orchestra and Chorus.

WILDCATS
Soundtrack (1986) .... *Warner Bros. (S) 1-25388* 86 **8-10**
　Composer: Various. **Cast:** Isley Brothers; Mavis Staples; Michael Jeffries; Randy Crawford; Sidney Justin; James Ingram; Tata Vega; James Newton Howard; Joe Cocker.

WILDERNESS TRAIL
TV Soundtrack .... *National Geographic Society (M) 07708* **8-12**
　Composer: Walter Scharf. **Conductor:** Walter Scharf.

WILDEST DREAMS
London Cast .... *AEI (S) 1122* **8-12**
　Composer: J. Slade. **Conductor:** D. Reynolds.

WILDFLOWER:
see TIP TOES

WILL PENNY
Soundtrack (1968) .... *Dot (M) DLP-3844* 68 **30-40**
Soundtrack (1968) .... *Dot (S) DLP-25844* 68 **30-35**
　One side has *The Film Music of David Raksin* and includes selections from *Sylvia* and *Too Late Blues*.
　Composer: David Raksin. **Conductor:** David Raksin. **Cast:** Donald Pleasance (narration); Don Cherry.

WILL ROGERS' U.S.A.
Original Cast (1971) .... *Columbia (S) SG-30546* 71 **20-25**
　Double LP set.
　Cast: James Whitmore as Will Rogers. Dialogue.

WILLIE DYNAMITE
Soundtrack (1974) .... *MCA (S) 393* 74 **12-15**
　Composer: J.J. Johnson; Gilbert Moses III. **Cast:** Martha Reeves and the Sweet Things.

WILLY WONKA AND THE CHOCOLATE FACTORY
Soundtrack (1971) .... *Paramount (S) PAS-6012* 71 **20-25**
Soundtrack (1971) .... *MCA (S) 37124* Re **8-10**
　Composer: Anthony Newley; Leslie Bricusse. **Conductor:** Walter Scharf. **Cast:** Gene Wilder; Diana Lee; Jack Albertson (with dialogue).

WIND AND THE LION
Soundtrack (1975) .... *Arista (S) AL-4048* 75 **20-40**
Soundtrack (1975) .... *Arista (S) AR-4048* Re **8-10**
　Composer: Jerry Goldsmith. **Conductor:** Jerry Goldsmith.

WINDJAMMER
Soundtrack (1958) .... *Columbia (M) CL-1158* 58 **$15-20**
Soundtrack (1958) .... *Columbia (SE) CS-8651* 59 **15-20**
  Composer: Morton Gould; Easy Riders. **Conductor:** Jack Shaindlin.

WINDS OF CHANGE
Soundtrack (1979) .... *Casablanca (S) NBLP-7167* 79 **10-12**
  Composer: Alec R. Costandinos; Enoch Anderson. **Conductor:** Raymond Knehnetsky.

WINDWALKER
Soundtrack (1980) .... *Cerberus (S) CST-0202* 81 **10-20**
  Composer: Merrill Jenson. **Conductor:** Merrill Jenson.

WINGED VICTORY:
see SONG OF NORWAY

WINNING
Soundtrack (1969) .... *Decca (S) DL-79169* 69 **15-20**
  Black label.
Soundtrack (1969) .... *Decca (S) DL-79169* 69 **20-25**
  Maroon label.
  Composer: Dave Grusin. **Conductor:** Dave Grusin.

WINSTON CHURCHILL:
see VALIANT YEARS

WISH YOU WERE HERE
Original London Cast .... *Stet (M) DS-15015* **8-10**
  Composer: Harold Rome. **Conductor:** Cyril Ornadel. **Cast:** Shani Wallis; Christopher Hewett;
  Bruce Trent; Mark Baker; Joe "Tiger" Robinson.
Original Cast (1952) .... *RCA Victor (EP) WOC-1007* 52 **15-25**
Original Cast (1952) .... *RCA Victor (EP) EOA-437* 52 **10-15**
Original Cast (1952) .... *RCA Victor (M) LOC-1007* 52 **60-75**
Original Cast (1952) .... *RCA Victor/Camden (M) CAL-621* 61 **20-25**
Original Cast (1952) .... *RCA Victor (M) LOC-1108* 65 **25-30**
Original Cast (1952) .... *RCA Victor (SE) LSO-1108* 65 **25-30**
  Conductor: Jay Blackton. **Cast:** Sheila Bond; Jack Cassidy; Patricia Marand; Sammy Smith;
  Sidney Armns; Paul Valentine.

WITCHES OF EASTWICK
Soundtrack (1987) .... *Warner Bros. (S) 1-25607* 87 **8-10**
  Composer: John Williams.

WITH A SONG IN MY HEART
Soundtrack (1952) .... *Capitol (EP) KDF-309* 52 **20-25**
  Four-disc, boxed set.
Soundtrack (1952) .... *Capitol (M) L-309* 52 **40-50**
  10-inch LP. *1955*
Soundtrack (1952) .... *Capitol (M) T-309* 52 **30-40**
Soundtrack (1952) .... *Capitol (M) 11891* 78 **8-10**
  Composer: Richard Rodgers; others. **Conductor:** George Greeley.

WITHNAIL AND I
Soundtrack (1987) .... *DRG (S) SBL-12590* 87 **8-10**

WITHOUT YOU, I'M NOTHING
Original Cast .... *Enigma (S) 73369* **8-10**
  Cast: Sandra Bernhard.

WITNESS
Soundtrack (1985) ....*Jackal/Varese Sarabande (S) WOW-727*   85   **$10-12**
Digital Recording.
Soundtrack (1985) ....*Varese Sarabande (S) STV-81237*   85   **8-10**
Composer: Maurice Jarre.

WIZ
Original Cast (1975) ....*Atlantic (S) SD-18137*   75   **8-10**
Black adaptation of *The Wizard of Oz*.
Composer: Charlie Smalls; others. **Conductor:** Charles H. Coleman. **Cast:** Stephanie Mills; Tiger Haynes; Ted Rose; Hinton Battle; Clarice Taylor; Mabel King; Andre DeShields; Tasha Thomas; Dee Dee Bridgewater.
Soundtrack (1978) ....*MCA (S) 2-14000*   78   **12-15**
Double LP set.
Composer: Charlie Smalls; others. **Conductor:** Quincy Jones; Bobby Tucker; Robert Freedman. **Cast:** Diana Ross; Michael Jackson; Lena Horne; Richard Pryor; Nipsey Russell; Thelma Carpenter; Mabel King; Theresa Merritt; Ted Ross.

WIZARD OF OZ
Soundtrack (1939) ....*MGM (M) E-3464*   56   **35-45**
Soundtrack (1939) ....*MGM (M) E-3996*   62   **15-20**
Soundtrack (1939) ....*MGM (SE) SE-3996*   62   **15-20**
Soundtrack (1939) ....*MGM (M) SPX-104*   62   **20-25**
"Merchandising Edition."
Soundtrack (1939) ....*MCA (M) 39046*   86   **8-10**
Composer: Harold Arlen; E.Y. Harburg. **Cast:** Judy Garland; Ray Bolger; Jack Haley; Bert Lahr; Frank Morgan; Billie Burke; Margaret Hamilton.
Also see PINOCCHIO
Soundtrack ....*Decca (M) DL-5152*   52   **25-35**
10-inch LP.
Conductor: Victor Young. **Cast:** Judy Garland; Ken Darby Singers; Victor Young and His Orchestra.

WOMAN CALLED MOSES
Soundtrack (1978) ....*MCA (S) 3054*   78   **8-12**
Composer: Van McCoy. **Cast:** Tommie Young.

WOMAN IN RED
Soundtrack (1984) ....*Motown (S) 6108*   84   **8-10**
Composer: Stevie Wonder; Ben Bridges. **Cast:** Stevie Wonder; Dionne Warwick.

WOMAN NEXT DOOR
Soundtrack (1981) ....*DRG (S) SL-9507*   81   **8-10**
Composer: Georges Delerue. **Conductor:** Georges Delerue.

WOMAN OF THE YEAR
Original Cast (1981) ....*Arista (S) AL-8303*   81   **8-10**
Composer: John Kander; Fred Ebb. **Conductor:** Donald Pippin. **Cast:** Lauren Bacall; Harry Guardino; Eivind Harum; Grace Keagy; Daren Kelly; Tom Avera; Rex Hays; Lawrence Raiken; Gerry Vichi; Marilyn Cooper; Rex Everhart; Jamie Ross; Roderick Cook.

WOMAN TIMES SEVEN
Soundtrack (1967) ....*Capitol (M) T-2800*   67   **25-30**
Soundtrack (1967) ....*Capitol (S) ST-2800*   67   **30-35**
A seven-episode film, with Shirley MacLaine portraying seven different characters.
Composer: Riz Ortolani. **Conductor:** Riz Ortolani. **Cast:** Shirley MacLaine.

WOMEN OF THE WORLD

Soundtrack (1963) .... *Decca (M) DL-9112*	63	**$12-15**
Soundtrack (1963) .... *Decca (S) DL7-9112*	63	**15-20**

Composer: Riz Ortolani; Nino Oliviero. **Conductor:** Riz Ortolani.

WONDER BAR:
see HOORAY FOR HOLLYWOOD

WONDERFUL COUNTRY

Soundtrack (1959) .... *United Artists (M) UAL-4050*	59	**35-50**
Soundtrack (1959) .... *United Artists (SE) UAS-5050e*	59	**50-75**

Composer: Alex North. **Conductor:** Alex North.
Also see I WANT TO LIVE; UNFORGIVEN

WONDERFUL O

Studio Cast (1963) .... *Colpix (M) CP-6000*	63	**25-30**
Studio Cast (1963) .... *Colpix (S) SCP-6000*	63	**35-40**

Cast: Burgess Meredith.

WONDERFUL TO BE YOUNG

Soundtrack (1962) .... *Dot (M) DLP-3474*	62	**20-25**
Soundtrack (1962) .... *Dot (S) DLP-25474*	62	**30-40**

Composer: Peter Myers; Burt Bacharach; Hal David. **Cast:** Cliff Richard and the Shadows; Michael Sammes Singers.

WONDERFUL TOWN

Original Cast (1953) .... *Decca (M) DL-9010*	53	**25-30**
Original Cast (1953) .... *Decca (SE) DL7-9010*	63	**20-25**
Original Cast (1953) .... *MCA (SE) 2050e*	72	**8-10**

Composer: Leonard Bernstein; Betty Comden; Adolph Green. **Conductor:** Lehman Engle.
Cast: Rosalind Russell; George Gaynes; Edith Adams; Delbert Anderson; Dort Clark; Jordan Bentley; Chris Alexander.

Original West Coast Cast .... *Location (M) 1261-368*		**35-40**

Composer: Leonard Bernstein; Betty Comden; Adolph Green. **Cast:** Veronica Lehner; Jerry Lanning; Phyllis Newman.

TV Soundtrack (1958) .... *Columbia (M) OL-5360*	58	**25-30**
TV Soundtrack (1958) .... *Columbia (S) OS-2008*	58	**40-50**

Composer: Leonard Bernstein; Betty Comden; Adolph Green. **Conductor:** Lehman Engel.
Cast: Rosalind Russell; Sydney Chaplin; Jacquelyn McKeever; Chris Alexander; Jordan Bently; Sam Kirkham.

WONDERFUL WORLD OF THE BROTHERS GRIMM

Soundtrack (1962) .... *MGM (M) 1E-3*	62	**25-30**
Soundtrack (1962) .... *MGM (M) S1E-3*	62	**25-30**

Above two are boxed editions.
Composer: Bob Merrill. **Conductor:** Gus Levene. **Cast:** Laurence Harvey; Yvette Mimieux; Russ Tamblyn; Buddy Hackett; Jim Backus; Terry Thomas; Beulah Bond; Karl Boehm; Otto Kruger; Arnold Stang. (With dialogue.)

Soundtrack (1962) .... *MGM (M) E-4077*	63	**15-20**
Soundtrack (1962) .... *MGM (S) SE-4077*	63	**20-25**

One side of the above two has instrumentals from six other films.
Composer: Bob Merrill. **Conductor:** David Rose.

WONDERWALL

Soundtrack (1968) .... *Apple (S) ST-3350*	68	**25-30**

This film was not officially released, though prints exist and have been shown.
Composer: George Harrison. **Cast:** George Harrison; John Barhami; Tommy Reilly; Colin Manley; Edward Anthony Ashton; Roy Duke. (With musicians of Bombay, India.)

WOODSTOCK
Soundtrack (1970) ....*Cotillion (S) CT3-500* 70 **$15-20**
Volume 1. Triple LP set.
Soundtrack (1970) ....*Cotillion (S) CT2-400* 71 **12-18**
Volume 2. Double LP set.
Soundtrack (1970) .... *Mobile Fidelity (S) MFSL-5-200* **20-30**
Composer: Various. Cast: Joan Baez; Richie Havens; Crosby, Stills and Nash; Jefferson Airplane; Joe Crocker; Ten Years After; Sly and the Family Stone; Country Joe and the Fish; Santana; Who; John Sebastian; Jimi Hendrix; Neil Young.

WOOLWORTH HAD A NOTION
Original Cast (1965) ....*No Label Shown (S) No Number Used* 65 **25-35**
From a company presentation, June 16, 1965 at the Biltmore Hotel Ballroom.
Composer: Michael Brown.

WORDS AND MUSIC
Original Cast (1974) .... *RCA Victor (S) LRL1-5079* 74 **15-20**
Conductor: Richard Leonard. Cast: Lorna Dallas; Terry Mitchell; Laurel Ford.
Soundtrack (1948) ....*MGM (EP) X-37* 50 **15-20**
Soundtrack (1948) ....*MGM (M) E-505* 50 **40-50**
10-inch LP.
Soundtrack (1948) .... *Metro (M) M-580* 66 **15-20**
Soundtrack (1948) .... *Metro (SE) MS-580* 66 **15-20**
Soundtrack (1948) .... *MCA (SE) 25029* **8-10**
Composer: Richard Rodgers; Lorenz Hart. Conductor: Lennie Hayton. Cast: Mickey Rooney; Judy Garland; Betty Garrett; Lena Horne; Ann Sothern; June Allyson; MGM Studio Orchestra.
Also see GOOD NEWS; TWO WEEKS WITH LOVE

WORDS AND MUSIC
Studio Cast (1974) .... *World (S) WRS-1002* 74 **12-15**
Composer: Sammy Cahn; James Van Heusen; Jule Styne; others. Cast: Sammy Cahn; Mike Sammes Singers.

WORKING
Original Cast (1978) .... *Columbia (S) JS-35411* 78 **12-15**
Composer: Stephen Schwartz; Mary Rodgers. Conductor: Stephen Reinhardt. Cast: Susan Bieglow; Arny Freeman; Bob Gunton; Robin Lamont; Matt Landers; Bobo Lewis; David Patrick Kelly; Matthew McGrath; David Langston Smyrl; Joe Mantegna.

WORKING GIRL
Soundtrack (1988) .... *Arista (S) AL6-8593* 88 **8-10**
Composer: Various. Cast: Carly Simon; others.

WORLD (ORIGINAL CAST STARRING HOWDY DOODY)
Studio Cast ....*..... *Leslee (S) PIP-6808* 72 **10-12**
Montage of world events, from 1948 to 1960, including dialogue by political personalities. Includes the original "Howdy Doody" TV cast.
Cast: Bob Smith (as "Buffalo Bob").

WORLD APART
Soundtrack (1988) .... *RCA Victor (S) 7974-1* 88 **8-10**

WORLD IN SOUND - 1977
Studio Cast (1978) .... *Associated Press (M) 1977* 78 **80-100**
News highlights of 1977, as compiled by the Associated Press. Includes segments on the deaths of both Elvis Presley and Bing Crosby.
Composer: Jim Wessel (editor). Cast: Tom Martin (narrator).

WORLD OF CHARLES AZNAVOUR
Original Cast (1965) .... *Reprise (M) 6193*   65 $12-15
Original Cast (1965) .... *Reprise (S) S-6193*   65   15-20
    Recorded at the Huntington Hartford Theatre, Hollywood, Nov. 19, 1965.
    Cast: Charles Aznavour.

WORLD OF SUSIE WONG
Soundtrack (1960) .... *RCA Victor (M) LOC-1059*   60   35-40
Soundtrack (1960) .... *RCA Victor (S) LSO-1059*   60   60-70
    Composer: George Duning; James Van Heusen; Sammy Cahn; others. **Conductor:** Muir
Mathieson. **Cast:** Nancy Kwan; Sylvia Syms.

WORLD WAR I
TV Soundtrack (1964) .... *RCA Victor (M) LM-2791*   64   20-25
TV Soundtrack (1964) .... *RCA Victor (S) LSC-2791*   64   35-40
TV Soundtrack (1964) .... *RCA Victor (S) ANL1-2334*   64   35-40
    Composer: Morton Gould. **Conductor:** Morton Gould.

WORLD'S GREATEST LOVER
Soundtrack (1978) .... *RCA Victor (S) ABL1-2709*   78   10-12
    Composer: John Morris; Harry Nilsson. **Conductor:** John Morris. **Cast:** Gene Wilder; Carol
Kane; Dom DeLuise; Fritz Feld; Carl Ballantine; Michael Huddleston; Matt Collins.

WRAITH
Soundtrack (1986) .... *Scotti Bros. (S) SZ-40429*   86   8-10
    Composer: Michael Hoenig; others. **Cast:** Tim Feehan; Honeymoon Suite; Stan Bush; LaMarca;
Jil Michaels; Ozzy Osbourne; Lion; James House; Ian Hunter; Bonie Tyler.

WRITTEN ON THE WIND
Soundtrack (1956) .... *Decca (EP) ED-2487*   56   15-25
Soundtrack (1956) .... *Decca (M) VC-81074*   Re   8-10
    Composer: Victor Young; Sammy Cahn; Frank Skinner; others. **Conductor:** Joseph Gershenson.
    Cast: Four Aces.
    Also see FOUR GIRLS IN TOWN

WRONG BOX
Soundtrack (1966) .... *Mainstream (M) 56088*   66   40-50
Soundtrack (1966) .... *Mainstream (S) 6088*   66   75-90
    Composer: John Barry; others. **Conductor:** John Barry.

WUTHERING HEIGHTS
Soundtrack (1971) .... *American Int'l (S) A-1039*   71   15-20
    Composer: Marilyn Bergman; Alan Bergman. **Conductor:** Michel LeGrand. **Cast:** Mike Curb
Congregation.
Soundtrack .... *Elmer Bernstein's Film Music Collection (S) FMC-6*   76   35-40
    Composer: Alfred Newman. **Conductor:** Elmer Bernstein.

X

XANADU
Soundtrack (1980) .... *MCA (S) 6100*   80   **$8-10**
  Composer: John Farrar; Jeff Lynne. **Cast:** Olivia Newton-John; Electric Light Orchestra; Cliff Richard; Gene Kelly; Tubes.

Y

YANKEE DOODLE DANDY
Soundtrack (1942) .... *Curtain Calls (M) CC-100/13*   **20-30**
Soundtrack (1942) .... *Radiola (M) MR-1103*   **10-12**
  Composer: George M. Cohan; Richard Rodgers; Lorenz Hart. **Cast:** James Cagney; Walter Huston; Joan Leslie; Frances Langford; Jeanne Cagney; Irene Manning; Rosemary DeCamp.

YANKS
Soundtrack (1979) .... *MCA (S) 3181*   79   **8-10**
  Composer: Richard Rodney Bennett; others. **Conductor:** Marcus Dods.

YEAR OF LIVING DANGEROUSLY
Soundtrack (1983) .... *Varese Sarabande (S) STV-81182*   83   **8-10**
  Composer: Maurice Jarre. **Cast:** Electronic realization by Spencer Lee and Maurice Jarre.

YEAR OF THE DRAGON
Soundtrack (1985) .... *Varese Sarabande (S) STV-81266*   85   **8-10**
  Composer: David Mansfield; others. **Conductor:** David Mansfield.

YEARS OF LIGHTNING, DAY OF DRUMS:
see JOHN F. KENNEDY

YELLOW CANARY
Soundtrack (1963) .... *Verve (M) MG-8548*   63   **15-20**
Soundtrack (1963) .... *Verve (S) V6-8548*   63   **25-30**
  Composer: Kenyon Hopkins. **Conductor:** Kenyon Hopkins.

YELLOW ROLLS-ROYCE
Soundtrack (1965) .... *MGM (M) E-4292*   65   **15-20**
Soundtrack (1965) .... *MGM (S) SE-4292*   65   **25-30**
  Composer: Riz Ortolani. **Conductor:** Riz Ortolani. **Cast:** Katyna Ranieri.

YELLOW SUBMARINE
Soundtrack (1968) .... *Apple (S) SW-153*   69   **20-25**
Soundtrack (1968) .... *Capitol (S) SW-153*   76   **10-12**
Soundtrack (1968) .... *Capitol (S) C1-46445*   88   **8-10**
Soundtrack (1968) .... *MFSL (S) 1-108*   87   **15-20**
  Half-speed mastered. Side one, film songs by the Beatles; side two, original film music by George Martin.
  Composer: John Lennon; Paul McCartney; George Harrison; George Martin. **Conductor:** George Martin. **Cast:** Beatles; George Martin and His Orchestra.

YENTL
Soundtrack (1983) .... *Columbia (S) JS-39152*   83   **10-15**
  Composer: Michel Legrand; Alan Bergman; Marilyn Bergman. **Conductor:** Michel Legrand. **Cast:** Barbra Streisand.

YES, GIORGIO
Soundtrack (1982) . . . .*London (S) PCV-9001*   82 $10-12
Cast: Luciano Pavarotti.

YESTERDAY, TODAY AND TOMORROW
Soundtrack (1964) . . . . *Warner Bros. (M) W-1552*   64   25-30
Soundtrack (1964) . . . .*Warner Bros. (S) WS-1552*   64   40-45
Composer: Armando Trovajoli; others. Conductor: Armando Trovajoli. Cast: Michele Mattera.

YOJIMBO
Soundtrack (1961) . . . .*MGM (M) E-4096*   62   90-100
Soundtrack (1961) . . . . *MGM (S) SE-4096*   62   120-130
Composer: Masaru Sato. Conductor: Masaru Sato.

YOL
Soundtrack (1982) . . . .*Milan (S) A120-CH002*   83   20-30
Composer: Sebastian Argol.

YOR - THE HUNTER FROM THE FUTURE
Soundtrack (1983) . . . . *Southern Cross (S) SCRS-1005*   83   8-10
Cast: John Scott.

YOU ARE WHAT YOU EAT
Soundtrack (1968) . . . . *Columbia (S) OS-3240*   68   15-20
Composer: Peter Yarrow; John Simon; Sonny Bono; others. Cast: Peter Yarrow; Timy Tim;
Paul Butterfield; Electric Flag; Rosko; John Herold; Hamsa El Din; John Simon.

YOU BET YOUR LIFE
Original Radio Cast . . . .*Golden Age (M) 5021*   78   8-10
Cast: Groucho Marx.

YOU CAN'T RUN AWAY FROM IT:
see EDDY DUCHIN STORY

YOU LIGHT UP MY LIFE
Soundtrack (1977) . . . . *Arista (S) AB-4159*   77   12-18
Composer: Joe Brooks. Conductor: Joe Brooks. Cast: Kasey Cisyk; Joe Brooks.

YOU ONLY LIVE ONCE
Soundtrack (1969) . . . . *London (S) PS-561*   69   12-15
Composer: Jacques Loussier. Conductor: Jacques Loussier. Cast: Jacques Loussier Orchestra.

YOU ONLY LIVE TWICE
Soundtrack (1967) . . . . *United Artists (M) UAL-4155*   67   15-20
Soundtrack (1967) . . . .*United Artists (S) UAS-5155*   67   20-25
Soundtrack (1967) . . . . *United Artists (S) UA-LA289-G*   74   8-10
Composer: John Barry; Leslie Bricusse. Conductor: John Barry. Cast: Nancy Sinatra.

YOU'RE A BIG BOY NOW
Soundtrack (1966) . . . . *Kama Sutra (M) KLP-8058*   67   12-15
Soundtrack (1966) . . . . *Kama Sutra (S) KLPS-8058*   67   15-20
Composer: John B. Sebastian. Conductor: Jack Lewis. Cast: Lovin' Spoonful.

YOU'RE A GOOD MAN, CHARLIE BROWN
Original Cast (1967) . . . .*MGM (M) 1E-9*   67   12-15
Original Cast (1967) . . . . *MGM (S) S1E-9*   67   15-20
Original Cast (1967) . . . .*Polydor (S) 820262-1*   Re   8-10
Composer: Clark Gesner. Conductor: Joseph Raposo. Cast: Gary Burghoff ("Charlie Brown");
Bill Hinnant; Reva Rose; Karen Johnson; Skip Hinnant; Bob Balaban.

Studio Cast (1967) .... *MGM (S) LES-9000* 67 **$25-30**
The original musical for records, which inspired the Broadway show.
Composer: Clark Gesner. **Conductor:** Jay Blackton. **Cast:** Orson Bean; Barbara Minkus; Bill Hinnant; Clark Gesner.
Studio Cast .... *Pickwick (M) PC-3069* **10-12**
Studio Cast .... *Pickwick (S) SPC-3069* **12-15**
Composer: Clark Gesner. **Conductor:** Bugs Bauer. **Cast:** Roy Marshall; Connie Zimet.
TV Soundtrack (1972) .... *Atlantic (S) SD-7252* 72 **15-20**
Composer: Clark Gesner. **Conductor:** Elliot Lawrence. **Cast:** Wendell Burton; Ruby Persson; Barry Livingston; Mark Montgomery; Bill Hinnant; Noelle Matlovsky.

YOUNG ABE LINCOLN
Original Cast (1961) .... *Golden (M) LP-76* 61 **30-40**
Children's musical with story and songs.
Original Cast (1961) .... *Wonderland (M) WLP-76* Re **20-30**
Composer: Victor Ziskin; Joan Javits; Arnold Sundgaard. **Cast:** Darrell Sandeen; Judy Foster; Lou Cutell; Tom Noel; Travis Hudson; Jack Blackton; Ray Hyson; Robert Darnell; Jack Kauflinn.

YOUNG AND RESTLESS
TV Soundtrack (1974) .... *P.I.P. (S) PIP-6812* 74 **10-15**
Composer: Don McGinnis; Jerry Winn; Bob Todd; Barry DeVorzon; Perry Botkin Jr. **Cast:** Touch Ltd.

YOUNG AT HEART
Soundtrack (1954) .... *Columbia (M) CL-6339* 54 **40-50**
Composer: Cole Porter; George Gershwin. **Conductor:** Percy Faith; Buddy Cole; Axel Stordahl; Frank Comstock. **Cast:** Frank Sinatra; Doris Day.
Studiotrack (1954) .... *Capitol (EP) EAP-1-571* 54 **10-15**
Cast: Frank Sinatra.

YOUNG BESS
Soundtrack (1953) .... *Elmer Bernstein Film Music Collection (SE) FMC-5* 76 **30-35**
Composer: Miklos Rozsa.

YOUNG BILLY YOUNG
Soundtrack (1969) .... *United Artists (S) UAS-5199* 69 **40-45**
Soundtrack (1969) .... *MCA (S) 25031* Re **8-10**
Composer: Shelly Manne. **Conductor:** Shelly Manne. **Cast:** Billy Edd Wheeler.

YOUNG FRANKENSTEIN
Soundtrack (1975) .... *ABC (S) ABCD-870* 75 **12-15**
Composer: John Morris; others. **Conductor:** John Morris. **Cast:** Gene Wilder; Peter Boyle; Marty Feldman; Cloris Leachman; Terri Garr; Madeline Kahn. (With dialogue.)

YOUNG GIRLS OF ROCHEFORT
Soundtrack (1968) .... *Philips (M) PCC-2-226* 68 **15-20**
Soundtrack (1968) .... *Philips (S) PCC-2-626* 68 **25-30**
Above two are double LP sets with the complete show.
Soundtrack (1968) .... *Philips (M) PCC-227* 68 **12-15**
Soundtrack (1968) .... *Philips (S) PCC-627* 68 **15-20**
Above two have only excerpts from the show.
Composer: Michel Legrand. **Conductor:** Michel Legrand. **Cast:** Donald Burke; Danielle Darrieux; Anne Germain; Claude Parent; Jean Stout; Jacques Revaux; Alice Herald; Christine Legrand; Claudine Meunier.
Studiotrack (1968) .... *United Artists (M) UAL-3662* 68 **15-20**
Studiotrack (1968) .... *United Artists (S) UAS-6662* 68 **20-25**
Composer: Michel Legrand. **Conductor:** Michel Legrand.

YOUNG LIONS
Soundtrack (1958) .... *Decca (M) DL-8719*   58   **$50-60**
Soundtrack (1958) .... *Decca (S) DL7-8719*   58   **75-100**
Soundtrack (1958) .... *Varese Sarabande (S) STV-81115*   81   **8-10**
  Composer: Hugo Friedhofer. **Conductor:** Lionel Newman. **Cast:** 20th Century-Fox Orchestra.

YOUNG LOVERS
Soundtrack (1964) .... *Columbia (M) OL-7010*   64   **25-30**
Soundtrack (1964) .... *Columbia (S) OS-2510*   64   **40-45**
  Composer: Sol Kaplan. **Conductor:** Sol Kaplan.

YOUNG MAN WITH A HORN
Soundtrack (1950) .... *Columbia (M) CL-6106*   50   **40-45**
  10-inch LP. Inspired by the life of Bix Beiderbecke.
Soundtrack (1950) .... *Columbia (M) CL-582*   54   **30-35**
Soundtrack (1950) .... *Columbia Collectors' Series (M) ACL-582*   81   **8-10**
  Conductor: Harry James. **Cast:** Doris Day; Harry James and His Orchestra.

YOUNG SAVAGES
Soundtrack (1961) .... *Columbia (M) CL-1672*   61   **45-50**
Soundtrack (1961) .... *Columbia (S) CS-8472*   61   **70-80**
  Composer: David Amram. **Conductor:** David Amram.

YOUNG SHERLOCK HOLMES
Soundtrack (1985) .... *MCA (S) 6159*   85   **8-10**
  Composer: Bruce Broughton. **Conductor:** Bruce Broughton. **Cast:** Sinfonia Orchestra of London.

YOUNG WARRIORS
Soundtrack (1983) .... *Varese Sarabande (S) STV-81186*   83   **8-10**
  Cast: Bob Walsh.

YOUNG WINSTON (CHURCHILL)
Soundtrack (1972) .... *Angel (S) SFO-36901*   72   **12-15**
  Composer: Alfred Ralston. **Conductor:** Alfred Ralston.

YOUNGBLOOD
Soundtrack (1978) .... *United Artists (S) UA-LA904-H*   78   **10-12**
Soundtrack (1978) .... *RCA Victor (S) ABL1-7172*   **8-10**
  Composer: Lonnie Jordan. **Cast:** War; William Orbit; Mickey Thomas; Glenn Jones; John Hiatt; Starship; Jack Gilder; Marc Jordan; Autograph.

YOUR ARMS TOO SHORT TO BOX WITH GOD
Original Cast (1976) .... *ABC (S) AB-1004*   76   **15-20**
  Composer: Alex Bradford; Micki Grant. **Conductor:** Eddie Brown; Chapman Roberts.
  Cast: Salome Bey; Clinton Derricks Carroll; Sheila Ellis; Delores Hall; Bobby Hill; Alex Bradford; William Hardy Jr.

YOUR CHEATIN' HEART
Soundtrack (1964) .... *MGM (M) E-4260*   64   **15-20**
Soundtrack (1964) .... *MGM (S) SE-4260*   64   **20-25**
Soundtrack (1964) .... *MCA (S) 1438*   87   **8-10**
  Inspired by the life of Hank Williams Sr.
  Composer: Hank Williams Sr. **Conductor:** Fred Karger. **Cast:** Hank Williams Jr.

YOUR OWN THING
Original Cast (1968) .... *RCA Victor (M) LOC-1148*   68   **15-20**
Original Cast (1968) .... *RCA Victor (S) LSO-1148*   68   **20-25**
  Composer: Hal Hester; Danny Apolinar. **Conductor:** Charles Schneider; Peter Matz.
  Cast: Rusty Thacker; Leland Palmer; Igors Gavon; Danny Apolinar; Tom Ligon; John Kuhner; Michael Valenti; Marcia Rodd.

YOURS, ANNE
Original Cast (1985) . . . . *That's Entertainment (S) TER-1118*   87 $10-12
  Composer: Michael Cohen; Enid Futterman. **Cast:** Trini Alvarado; Dana Zeller-Alexis; George Guidall.

YOURS, MINE AND OURS
Soundtrack (1968) . . . . *United Artists (S) UAS-5181*   69   12-15
Soundtrack (1968) . . . . *MCA (S) 1434*   Re   8-10
  Composer: Fred Karlin. **Conductor:** Fred Karlin.

Z

Z
Soundtrack (1969) . . . . *Columbia (S) OS-3370*   69   20-25
  Inspired by the life and assassination of Lambrakis, the Greek Deputy.
Soundtrack (1969) . . . . *Columbia Special Products (S) AOS-3370*   8-10
  Composer: Mikis Theodorakis. **Conductor:** Bernard Gerard.
  Also see HOSTAGE

ZABRISKIE POINT
Soundtrack (1970) . . . . *MGM (S) SE-4468*   70   15-20
Soundtrack (1970) . . . . *MCA (S) 25032*   Re   8-10
  Composer: Various. **Cast:** Pink Floyd; Jerry Garcia and the Grateful Dead; Youngbloods; Patti Page; John Fahey; Kaleidoscope; Roscoe Holcolmb.

ZACHARIAH
Soundtrack (1970) . . . . *ABC (S) ABCS-OC-1*   70   12-15
  Composer: Jimmie Haskell; Joe McDonald; others. **Conductor:** Jimmie Haskell. **Cast:** Country Joe and the Fish; James Gang; Doug Kershaw; White Lightnin'; New York Rock Ensemble.

ZAPPED
Soundtrack (1982) . . . . *Regency (S) 38-152*   82   8-10
  Composer: Various. **Cast:** David Pomeranz; Plain Jane; Rick Derringer; others.

ZENDA
Original Cast . . . . *Blue Pear (M) BP-1007*   25-30
  Composer: Vernon Duke; Leonard Adelson; Sid Kuller; Martin Charnin. **Cast:** Alfred Drake; Anne Rogers; Chita Rivera.

ZIEGFELD FOLLIES OF 1919
Original Cast (1919) . . . . *Smithsonian (M) R-009*   10-12

ZIEGFELD FOLLIES OF 1946
Soundtrack (1946) . . . . *Curtain Calls (M) CC-100/15-16*   20-30
  Double LP set.
  Cast: Fred Astaire; Kathryn Grayson.

ZIGGY STARDUST - THE MOTION PICTURE
Soundtrack (1983) . . . . *RCA Victor (S) CPL2-4862*   83   10-15
  Double LP set.
  Cast: David Bowie.

ZIGZAG
Soundtrack (1970) . . . . *MGM (S) 1SE-21*   70   15-20
  Composer: Oliver Nelson; others. **Conductor:** Oliver Nelson; Don Peake. **Cast:** Roy Orbison; Bobby Hatfield.

ZING A LITTLE ZONG
Studiotrack (1952) .... *Decca (M) DL-4263*   62   **$25-30**
Has music from *The Road to Bali* and *Just for You*. Issued as part of *Bing's Hollywood Series*.
Composer: James Van Heusen; John Burke. **Conductor:** Sonny Burke; Joseph J. Lilley; Axel
Stordahl. **Cast:** Bing Crosby; Bob Hope; Peggy Lee; Rhythmaires; Mellomen.

ZITA
Soundtrack (1968) .... *Philips (SE) PHS-600-2*   69   **15-20**
Composer: Francois DeRoubaix; others. **Conductor:** Francois DeRoubaix.

ZIZI
Original Cast (1964) .... *Philips (S) PHS-600-287*   64   **20-25**
Some tracks are rechanneled stereo.
Cast: Zizi Jeanmarie.

ZOOT SUIT
Soundtrack (1981) .... *MCA (S) 5287*   81   **10-12**
Soundtrack (1981) .... *MCA (S) 1522*   Re   **8-10**
Composer: Daniel Valdez. **Conductor:** Shorty Rogers. **Cast:** Daniel Valdez; Edward James
Olmos; American Zoot Band.

ZORBA
Original Cast (1968) .... *Capitol (S) SO-118*   68   **15-20**
Original Cast (1983) .... *Capitol (S) SWCR-292(3)*   69   **35-40**
Triple LP set.
Original Cast (1968) .... *Capitol (S) ST-12291*   83   **8-10**
Composer: John Kander; Fred Ebb. **Cast:** Herschel Bernardi; Maria Karnilova; John
Cunningham; Carmen Alvarez; Lorraine Serabian; Jerry Sappir.
Original Revival Cast (1983) .... *RCA Victor (S) ABL1-4732*   83   **15-20**
Composer: John Kander; Fred Ebb. **Conductor:** Randolph Mauldin. **Cast:** Anthony Quinn;
Lila Kedrova.
Also see CANTERBURY TALES

ZORBA THE GREEK
Soundtrack (1964) .... *20th Century-Fox (M) TF-3167*   65   **15-20**
Soundtrack (1964) .... *20th Century-Fox (S) S-4167*   65   **20-25**
Soundtrack (1964) .... *20th Century-Fox (S) T-903*   Re   **10-12**
Soundtrack (1964) .... *20th Century-Fox (S) 826245-1*   73   **8-10**
Composer: Mikis Theodorakis. **Conductor:** Mikis Theodorakis.

ZULU
Soundtrack (1964) .... *United Artists (M) UAL-4116*   64   **25-35**
Soundtrack (1964) .... *United Artists (S) UAS-5116*   64   **55-65**
Composer: John Barry. **Conductor:** John Barry. **Cast:** Richard Burton (narration).

ZULU AND THE ZAYDA
Original Cast (1965) .... *Columbia (M) KOL-6480*   65   **25-30**
Original Cast (1965) .... *Columbia (S) KOS-2880*   65   **35-40**
Composer: Harold Rome. **Conductor:** Meyr Kupferman. **Cast:** Menasha Skulnik; Ossie
Davis; Louis Gossett.

ZULU DAWN
Soundtrack (1979) .... *Cereberus (S) CEM-201*   79   **10-12**
Soundtrack (1979) .... *Cereberus (S) CST-0201*   81   **8-10**
Composer: Elmer Bernstein. **Conductor:** Elmer Bernstein.

DIRECTORY OF BUYERS AND SELLERS

After you have learned the current value of your records, you may wish to offer them for sale. Just as likely, you may decide you would like to purchase out-of-print records for your collection. Either way, the author recommends you do two things:

First, request a sample issue of *DISCoveries* magazine, the record collector's publication where buyers and sellers get together each month. From the pages of *DISCoveries* you'll get an idea of what's being traded and the prices being asked for music collectibles of all types, especially records and compact discs (*DISCoveries*, P.O. Box 255, Port Townsend, WA 98368. Call toll-free: 1-800-666-DISC).

Second, contact other collectors and dealers. To assist in this regard, here is a random sampling of well-known buyers and sellers of collectible music and memorabilia, any of whom may be the right one to assist you:

ACE-HIGH RECORDS
P.O. BOX 65245
W. DES MOINES, IA 50312

ANTONE'S RECORD SHOP
2928 GUADALUPE
AUSTIN, TX 78705

BAGATELLE RECORDS
260 ATLANTIC AVE.
LONG BEACH, CA 90802
213-432-7534

BLUESLAND OLDIES RECORD SHOP
P.O. BOX 391
SPANISH FORT, AL 36526
205-626-0272

CALIFORNIA ALBUMS
P.O. BOX 3426-D
HOLLYWOOD, CA 90078

COLLECTOR'S CLEARINGHOUSE
P.O. BOX 135
NORTH SYRACUSE, NY 13212

CONNOISSEUR'S GROOVY ORIGINALS
1815 EAST PARK ROW
ARLINGTON, TX 76010
817-265-8023

VERNON EDWARDS
103 YELLOWHAMMER CIRCLE
MONTEVALLO, AL 35115
205-663-5185

FINEST RECORD STORE
2400 8TH AVE
GREELEY, CO 80631
303-352-5390

GOLDEN OLDIES
201 NE 45TH ST.
SEATTLE, WA 98105

P.D. HAMLIN
P.O. BOX 1981
SUSANVILLE, CA 96130
916-257-0596

HOT PLATTERS
P.O. BOX 2793
LOS ANGELES, CA 90078
209-527-4010

JEFF'S CLASSICAL RECORD SHOP
2556 N. CAMPBELL
TUCSON, AZ 85719
602-327-0555

JELLYROLL PRODUCTIONS
P.O. BOX 29
BOYNE FALLS, MI 49713
616-582-6852
Distributor of assorted music reference publications.

JLO WEST
P.O. BOX 8892
UNIVERSAL CITY, CA 91608

HOWARD LEVINE
7736 250TH ST.
BELLEROSE-NYC, NY. 11426-2622

LYNN'S RECORDS
P.O. BOX 5321
WALNUT CREEK, CA 94521

MEMORY LANE RECORDS
1940 E UNIVERSITY DR.
TEMPE, AZ 85281
602-968-1515

MIDNIGHT RECORDS
P.O. BOX 390
NEW YORK, NY 10011
212-675-2768

SCOTT NEUMAN RECORDS
P.O. BOX 1048
HIGHTSTOWN, NJ 08520
609-426-4730

POSITIVELY 4TH STREET
208 W. 4TH ST.
OLYMPIA, WA 98501
206-SUN-TAPE

PRINCETON RECORD EXCHANGE
20 S. TULANE ST.
PRINCETON, NJ 08542
609-921-0881

RANDY'S RECORD SHOP
157 E. 900 SOUTH
SALT LAKE CITY, UT 84111
801-532-4413

RICK RANN BEATLELIST
P.O. BOX 877
OAK PARK, IL 60303
708-442-7907

RECORD ATTIC
1326 9TH ST.
MODESTO, CA 95354

RECORD EXCHANGE
5840 HAMPTON
ST. LOUIS, MO 63109
314-832-2249

RECORD SURPLUS
11609 W.PICO BLVD.
WEST LOS ANGELES, CA
213-478-4217

RECORD SHOWCASE
228 REDBANK RD.
GOOSE CREEK, SC 29445
803-553-1991

ROWE'S RARE RECORDS
54 W. SANTA CLARA ST.
SAN JOSE, CA 95113
408-294-7200

LYNN RUSSWURM
BOX 63
ELMIRA ONTARIO, N3B 2Z5 CANADA
519-669-2386

JOE SCOTT RECORDS
P.O. BOX 464
CRYSTAL RIVER, FL 32629

JOHN TEFTELLER
P.O. BOX 1727
GRANTS PASS, OR 97526

TRACKS IN WAX RECORDS
4741 N. CENTRAL AVE.
PHOENIX, AZ 85012
602-274-2660

VERY ENGLISH & ROLLING STONE
P.O. BOX 7061
LANCASTER, PA 17604
717-627-2081

VINYL VENDORS
1800 S. ROBERTSON BLVD. #279
LOS ANGELES, CA 90035

100 MOST VALUABLE SOUNDTRACK AND CAST RECORDINGS

Some of the world's most valuable albums and extended play discs are from the field of soundtrack and cast releases. Especially noteworthy in this regard is the number one entry on the list, *The Caine Mutiny* — one of music collecting's two or three most expensive records of any type.

When studying this list, remember that this Top 100 is limited to just those recordings contained in *The Official® Price Guide to Movie/TV Soundtracks and Original Cast Albums*. Though it is unlikely there are many highly valuable U.S. releases not represented here, there certainly are soundtracks and casts issued overseas that would qualify if foreign entries were within the scope of this book.

For simplicity, the prices here represent the high end of the actual dollar range shown in the guide. See the individual listings in the body of the book for the complete price range.

Variations exist for most of these records, which is why some titles appear to be on the list more than once. Actually, each listing represents a separate release. Consult the individual record listings pages — the body of the book — for specific identification of each record.

1. **CAINE MUTINY** *RCA Victor (M) LOC-1013* **$10,000**
2. **ELVIS: ALOHA FROM HAWAII VIA**
   SATELLITE *RCA Victor (Q) VPSX-6089* **2,000**
3. **SPEEDWAY** *RCA Victor (M) LPM-3989* **1,000**
4. **ROUSTABOUT** *RCA Victor (S) LSP-2999* **700**
5. **LOUISIANA HAYRIDE** *Louisiana Hayride (M) NR-8454* **700**
6. **HELP!** *United Artists (M) No Number Used* **650**
7. **HARD DAY'S NIGHT** *United Artists (M) SP-2359/60* **650**
8. **GO JOHNNY GO!** *No Label Shown (M) No Number Used* **600**
9. **JAMBOREE!** *Warner Bros. (M) No Number Used* **550**
10. **NO FOR AN ANSWER** *Theme (M) TALP-103* **525**
11. **KING CREOLE** *RCA Victor (EP) EPA-5122* **500**
12. **BILL AND COO** *Mercury Miniature Playhouse (M) MMP-20* **500**
13. **BODY IN THE SEINE** *Private Label-Alden-Shaw (M) VB-001* **400**
14. **COMANCHE** *Coral (M) CRL-57046* **350**
15. **LOUISIANA HAYRIDE** *Louisiana Hayride (M) NR-8454* **350**
16. **LION** *London (M) M-76001* . . . . **.325**
17. **SANDHOG** *Vanguard (M) VRS-9001* **325**
18. **TWISTED NERVE** *Polydor (S) 583-728* **325**
19. **BAD SEED** *RCA Victor (M) LPM-1395* . . . . **.300**
20. **NINE HOURS TO RAMA** *London (M) M-76002* **300**

21. **ROOTS OF HEAVEN** *20th Century-Fox (M) FOX-3005* $300
22. **FRANKIE, DINO, AND SAMMY - SUMMIT MEETING AT
    THE 500 CLUB, ATLANTIC CITY, NEW JERSEY** *Latimer (M) 247-17* 300
23. **ALEXANDER THE GREAT** *Mercury (M) MG-20148* 275
24. **CLOWNAROUND** *RCA Victor (S) LSP-4741* 250
25. **ELVIS: ALOHA FROM HAWAII VIA
    SATELLITE** *RCA Victor (Q) VPSX-6089* 250
26. **NIGHT OF THE HUNTER** *RCA Victor (M) LPM-1136* 250
27. **RAINTREE COUNTY** *RCA Victor (M) LOC-6000* 250
28. **MUSIC IN THE AIR** *RCA Victor (M) 39001* 250
29. **GIRL IN THE BIKINI** *Poplar (M) 33-1002* 225
30. **GREATEST STORY EVER TOLD** *United Artists (M) UAX-5120* 225
31. **MARIA GOLOVIN** *RCA Victor (M) LM-6142* 225
32. **MYRA BRECKINRIDGE** *20th Century-Fox (S) S-4210* 225
33. **PARADE** *Kapp (S) KDS-7005* 225
34. **THREE WISHES FOR JAMIE** *Capitol (M) S-317* 225
35. **CLAMBAKE** *RCA Victor (M) LPM-3893* 200
36. **FRANCIS OF ASSISI** *20th Century-Fox (S) SFX-3053* 200
37. **ISLAND IN THE SKY** *Decca (M) DL-7029* 200
38. **LONG JOHN SILVER'S RETURN TO TREASURE
    ISLAND** *RCA Victor (M) LPM-3279* 200
39. **LOST CONTINENT (ATLANTIS)** *MGM (M) E-3635* 200
40. **LOVE ME TENDER** *RCA Victor (EP) EPA-4006* 200
41. **OF THEE I SING** *Capitol (M) S-350* 200
42. **PARADE** *Kapp (M) KDL-7005* 200
43. **RHAPSODY OF STEEL** *US Steel (M) JB-502/3* 200
44. **SEVENTH VOYAGE OF SINBAD** *Colpix (M) CP-504* 200
45. **TENDER IS THE NIGHT** *20th Century-Fox (S) SFX-3054* 200
46. **DRAGONSLAYER** *Label X (S) LXSE 2-001* 200
47. **NIGHTCOMERS** *Citadel (S) CTJF-1* 200
48. **TWISTED NERVE** *Cinema (S) LP-8006* 200
49. **DOCTOR FAUSTUS** *CBS (S) S63189* 200
50. **CAPTAIN HORATIO HORNBLOWER** *Delyse (S) DS-6057* 200
51. **BE MY GUEST** *XCTV (M) 10303* 200
52. **BARBARIAN AND THE GEISHA** *20th Century-Fox (M) 3004* 175
53. **GAMES** *Viking (S) LPS-105* 175
54. **HIGH TOR** *Decca (M) DL-8272* 175
55. **KINGS GO FORTH** *Capitol (M) W-1063* 175
56. **LOOK MA I'M DANCIN'!** *Decca (M) DL-5231* 175
57. **MEXICAN HAYRIDE** *Decca (M) DL-5232* 175
58. **ON THE BEACH** *Roulette (S) SR-25098* 175
59. **SEVENTH HEAVEN** *Decca (M) DL-9001* 175
60. **SODOM AND GOMORRAH** *RCA Victor (S) LSO-1076* 175

61. **THIS IS THE ARMY** *Decca (M) DL-5108* $175
62. **VERTIGO** *Mercury (M) MG-20384* 175
63. **SEVEN COME ELEVEN (A GAMING**
    GAMBOL) *Columbia (M) XLP-55477* 175
64. **VALLEY GIRLL** *Roadshow (S) RS-101* 175
65. **ATHENIAN TOUCH** *Broad Way East (S) OCS-101* 160
66. **HAZEL FLAGG** *RCA Victor (M) LOC-1010* 160
67. **TOP BANANA** *Capitol (M) S-308* 160
68. **AARON SLICK FROM PUNKIN CRICK** *RCA Victor (M) LPM-3006* 150
69. **ARMS AND THE GIRL** *Decca (M) DL-5200* 150
70. **CASINO ROYALE** *Colgems (S) COSO 5005* 150
71. **DESTINATION MOON** *Columbia (M) CL-6151* 150
72. **COBWEB** *MGM (M) E-3501* 150
73. **FLAHOOLEY** *Capitol (M) S-284* 150
74. **GOLDEN COACH** *MGM (M) E-3111* 150
75. **FRIENDLY PERSUASION** *RKO/Unique (M) LP-110* 150
76. **FRANCIS OF ASSISI** *20th Century-Fox (M) FOX-3053* 150
77. **GOD'S LITTLE ACRE** *United Artists (M) UAL-40002* 150
78. **GREATEST SHOW ON EARTH** *RCA Victor (M) LPM-3018* 150
79. **LADY IN THE DARK** *RCA Victor (M) LM-1882* 150
80. **MEN IN WAR** *Imperial (M) LP-9032-W* 150
81. **MRS. PATTERSON** *RCA Victor (M) LOC-1017* 150
82. **MUSIC IN THE AIR** *RCA Victor (M) LK-1025* 150
83. **PARIS '90** *Columbia (M) ML-4619* 150
84. **RETURN TO PARADISE** *Decca (M) DL-5489* 150
85. **RAINMAKER** *RCA Victor (M) LPM-1434* 150
86. **SALOME** *Decca (M) DL-6026* 150
87. **SODOM AND GOMORRAH** *RCA Victor (M) LOC-1076* 150
88. **TENDER IS THE NIGHT** *20th Century-Fox (M) FOX-3054* 150
89. **BODY HEAT** *Label X (S) LXSE 1-002* 150
90. **KLUTE** *Warner Bros. (S) WS-1940* 150
91. **PROUD REBEL** *C.I.F. (M) 1001* 150
92. **RUNNER STUMBLES** *No Label Shown (S) EG-1001* 150
93. **DRANGO** *Liberty (M) LRP-3036* 150
94. **DEAN MARTIN TESTIMONIAL**
    DINNER *Dean Martin Testimonial Dinner (M) No Number Used* 150
95. **REPRISE REPERTORY THEATRE** *Reprise (S) 4FS-2019* 150
96. **AMONG FRIENDS - WAA-MU SHOW**
    OF 1960 *RCA Victor Custom (M) L70P-5670* 150
97. **DEATH OF A SCOUNDREL** *RCA Victor (EP) EPA-919* 140
98. **ATHENIAN TOUCH** *Broad Way East (M) OC-101* 140
99. **CALL ME MISTER** *Decca (M) DL-7005* 140
100. **HARK!** *Private Label (S) STK-1016* 140

COMPOSER/CONDUCTOR/CAST INDEX

A

AANAMI CHOIR
PRISON
AARONSON, IRVING
PENNIES FROM HEAVEN
ABADY, TEMPLE
GEORGE K. ARTHUR'S PRIZE
PACKAGE
ABBEY ROAD SINGERS
AMERICAN DREAMER
ABBOTT, DIANNE
NEW YORK, NEW YORK
ABBOTT, JIM
MIDSUMMER NIGHT'S DREAM
ABEL, WILL B.
COCO
ABERLIN, BETTY
I'M GETTING MY ACT TOGETHER
AND TAKING IT ON THE ROAD
JUST FOR OPENERS
ABRAHAM, F. MURRAY
SURVIVAL OF ST. JOAN
ABRAVANAL, MAURICE
LADY IN THE DARK
ONE TOUCH OF VENUS
STREET SCENE
AC/DC
WHO MADE WHO
ACADEMY OF ST. MARTIN
OUT OF AFRICA
ACE TRUCKING COMPANY
HARRAD EXPERIMENT
ACE, JOHNNY
CHRISTINE
ACHUCRRO, JOAQUIN
CITIZEN KANE: THE CLASSIC
FILM SCORES OF BERNARD
HERRMANN
ACKERMAN, JACK
FACES
ACKERMAN, LONI
GEORGE M.!
SO LONG 174TH STREET
STARTING HERE, STARTING NOW
ACKLAND, JOSS
APPLE
EVITA
LITTLE NIGHT MUSIC
ACTMAN, IRVING
GUYS AND DOLLS
ADAIR, JOHN
CRADLE WILL ROCK
ADAIR, YVONNE
GENTLEMEN PREFER BLONDES
ADAM, NOELLE
NO STRINGS
ADAMS, CATLIN
JAZZ SINGER

ADAMS, CLIFF
IRMA LA DOUCE
ADAMS, DON
GET SMART
ADAMS, DOUGLAS
MONTY PYTHON AND THE HOLY
GRAIL
ADAMS, EDITH
BAND WAGON
CINDERELLA
GIRL CRAZY
LES POUPEES DE PARIS
LI'L ABNER
SOMETHING UNIQUE
WONDERFUL TOWN
ADAMS, EMILY
JOAN
ADAMS, INDIA
BAND WAGON
TORCH SONG
ADAMS, JOE
JAMAICA
ADAMS, JONATHAN
TOMFOOLERY
ADAMS, KAYE
KILLERS THREE
ADAMS, LEE
ALL AMERICAN
APPLAUSE
BYE BYE BIRDIE
GOLDEN BOY
I AND ALBERT
IT'S A BIRD, IT'S A PLANE, IT'S
SUPERMAN
NIGHT THEY RAIDED MINSKY'S
ADAMS, MASON
THOUSAND MILES OF MOUNTAINS
ADAMS, SKIP
NIGHT OF THE COMET
ADAMS, TRUDE
SHE LOVES ME
ADAMSON, HAROLD
MINSTREL MAN
SCENT OF MYSTERY
SEVEN HILLS OF ROME
ADANO, BOBBY
ALAKAZAM THE GREAT
ADDERLEY, CANNONBALL
FIDDLER ON THE ROOF
ADDERLEY, NAT
MAN CALLED ADAM
ADDINSELL, RICHARD
IT'S A WONDERFUL LIFE
JOYCE GRENFELL REQUESTS THE
PLEASURE
LOSS OF INNOCENCE
MONOLOGUES AND SONGS
WAR LOVER
ADDISON, ADELE
PORGY AND BESS
ADDISON, DELORES
PORTRAITS IN BRONZE
ADDISON, JOHN
AMOROUS ADVENTURES OF
MOLL FLANDERS

BRIDGE TOO FAR
CHARGE OF THE LIGHT BRIGADE
HAMLET
HONEY POT
SLEUTH
SMASHING TIME
SWASHBUCKLER
TOM JONES
TORN CURTAIN
ADELSON, LEONARD
ZENDA
ADIARTE, PAT
FLOWER DRUM SONG
ADIR, MICHA
FROM ISRAEL WITH LOVE
ADLAM, BETH
WILDCAT
ADLER, F. CHARLES
THREEPENNY OPERA
ADLER, JO
ALADD
ADLER, RICHARD
DAMN YANKEES
GIFT OF THE MAGI
KWAMINA
LITTLE WOMEN
OLYMPUS 7-0000
PAJAMA GAME
ADRENELIN
IRON EAGLE
ADRIAN, LOUIS
ANNIE GET YOUR GUN
KISMET
PETER PAN
ADRIAN, MAX
BOY FRIEND
CANDIDE
ADU, SADE
ABSOLUTE BEGINNERS
AEROSMITH
LESS THAN ZERO
SGT. PEPPER'S LONELY HEARTS
BAND
AGENT ORANGE
RIVER'S EDGE
UNDERCOVER
AGRESS, TED
SHENANDOAH
AGRESTI, BEN
KA-BOOM!
AHMED, DR. IBRAHIM
STORY OF TUTANKHAMEN
AHN, PHILIP
KUNG-FU
AIDMAN, CHARLES
SPOON RIVER ANTHOLOGY
AIELLO, JOSIE
STARLIGHT EXPRESS
AIKEN, DAVID
SAINT OF BLEEKER STREET
AINSLEY, PAUL
JESUS CHRIST SUPERSTAR
AINSLIE, SCOTT
COTTON PATCH GOSPEL

AINSWORTH, ALYN
BYE BYE BIRDIE
EMILY
HELLO DOLLY!
AIR SUPPLY
GHOSTBUSTERS
AIRPLAY
SAINT ELMO'S FIRE
AITKEN, MARIA
LITTLE NIGHT MUSIC
AKERS, KAREN
NINE
AKOS, CATHERINE
SAINT OF BLEEKER STREET
AKUTAGAWA, YASUSHI
VILLAGE OF EIGHT
GRAVESTONES
ALABAMA
RIVER RAT
ALAIMO, STEVE
WHERE THE ACTION IS
ALAN
THIS IS BROADWAY'S BEST
ALARM
BACHELOR PARTY
BODY BEAUTIFUL
MUSIC MAN
ALBANESE, LICIA
SERENADE
**ALBERGHETTI, ANNA
MARIA**
ALADDIN
CARNIVAL
MEDIUM
ALBERGHETTI, CARLA
MY COUSIN JOSEFA
ALBERT, DONNIE
PORGY AND BESS
ALBERT, EDDIE
EDDIE ALBERT ALBUM
HEARTBREAK KID
MISS LIBERTY
MOUSE ON THE MAYFLOWER
ALBERT, MARGOT
PROMENADE
ALBERTSON, FRANK
SEVENTEEN
ALBERTSON, JACK
SUBJECT WAS ROSES
TOP BANANA
WILLY WONKA AND THE
CHOCOLATE FACTORY
ALBINONI, T.
FILM MUSIC FROM FRANCE
ALBRIGHT, JESSICA
BYE BYE BIRDIE
ALCIVAR, BOB
PARADISE ALLEY
ALDA, ALAN
APPLE TREE
ALDA, LAURIE
FIRE AND ICE
ALDA, ROBERT
GUYS AND DOLLS
WHAT MAKES SAMMY RUN?
ALDEBERT, LOUIS
LIVE FOR LIFE
ALDEN, BONNIE
ROARING '20s

ALDREDGE, THOMAS
PREMISE
ALDREDGE, TOM
REX
ALDRIDGE, MICHAEL
SALAD DAYS
ALESSANDRINI, GERALD
FORBIDDEN BROADWAY
ALESSI
GHOSTBUSTERS
ALEXANDER, BARBARA
ANYA
ALEXANDER, BEN
DRAGNET
ALEXANDER, BROOKS
BELIEVERS
ALEXANDER, C.K.
THREEPENNY OPERA
ALEXANDER, CHRIS
ON THE TOWN
WONDERFUL TOWN
ALEXANDER, JANE
GREAT WHITE HOPE
ALEXANDER, JEFF
BECAUSE YOU'RE MINE
DIRTY DINGUS MAGEE
EMPEROR WALTZ
MURDER INC.
MUSIC TO BE MURDERED BY
ROBERTA
TWILIGHT ZONE
ALEXANDER, PETER
KISS ME KATE
ALEXANDER, RICHARD
FLASH GORDON
ALEXANDER, VAN
BABY FACE NELSON
DESERT SONG
KISMET
NEW MOON
STUDENT PRINCE
ALEXANDER
HOT ROD RUMBLE
ROARING '20s
ALFIE
LAST DRAGON
ALFORD, KENNETH
BRIDGE ON THE RIVER KWAI
LAWRENCE OF ARABIA
ALFORD, LAMAR
GODSPELL
ALFRED, WILLIAM
CRY FOR US ALL
ALFVEN, HUGO
GEORGE K. ARTHUR'S PRIZE
PACKAGE
ALIBERTI, ARMANDO
DEVIL AND DANIEL WEBSTER
ALK, HOWARD
FROM THE SECOND CITY
ALL THAT JAZZ
HIDING OUT
ALL-STARS
COOLEY HIGH
ALLAN, DAVIE
ALBERT PECKINGPAW'S REVENGE
DEVIL'S ANGELS
GLORY STOMPERS
MONDO HOLLYWOOD

WILD ANGELS
ALLEN, BILLY
SKI ON THE WILD SIDE
ALLEN, CHAD
BEOWULF
ALLEN, CHET
AMAHL AND THE NIGHT VISITORS
ALLEN, CLIFFORD
HALLELUJAH, BABY!
ALLEN, DAVID BLISS
UP WITH PEOPLE!
ALLEN, DAVID
DECLINE AND FALL OF THE
ENTIRE WORLD AS SEEN
THROUGH THE EYES OF COLE
PORTER
GINGERBREAD BOY
ALLEN, DAVIE
GOLDEN BREED
HELLCATS
ALLEN, DAYTON
DEPUTY DAWG
WHY NOT?
ALLEN, DEBORAH
RAISIN
RIVER RAT
SWEET CHARITY
ALLEN, DENNIS
HOW TO STEAL AN ELECTION (A
DIRTY POLITICS MUSICAL)
ALLEN, DION
UNDER MILK WOOD
ALLEN, DONNA
FATAL BEAUTY
ALLEN, ELIZABETH
DO I HEAR A WALTZ?
GAY LIFE
OFFICIAL GRAMMY AWARDS
ARCHIVE COLLECTION
ALLEN, ETHAN
HAVE GUN WILL TRAVEL
ALLEN, FRED
MAGNIFICENT ROGUE
ALLEN, HERBERT
UP WITH PEOPLE!
ALLEN, JACKIE
MUSIC MAN
ALLEN, JEANNE
LEAVE IT TO JANE
ALLEN, JONELLE
GEORGE M.!
HAIR
TWO GENTLEMEN OF VERONA
ALLEN, KAREN
RAIDERS OF THE LOST ARK: THE
MOVIE ON RECORD
ALLEN, LINDA
STORMY MONDAY
ALLEN, MARC
PAWNBROKER
ALLEN, MICHAEL
JESUS CHRIST SUPERSTAR
NEW FACES OF 1968
ALLEN, NORMAN
HALF A SIXPENCE
ALLEN, PETER
ALL THAT JAZZ
LEGS DIAMOND

B

BACHARACH, BURT
AFTER THE FOX
APRIL FOOLS
BUTCH CASSIDY AND THE
SUNDANCE KID
CASINO ROYALE
HOUSE IS NOT A HOME
LOST HORIZON
NIGHT SHIFT
ON THE FLIP SIDE
PROMISE HER ANYTHING
PROMISES, PROMISES
TOGETHER
WHAT'S NEW PUSSYCAT?
WONDERFUL TO BE YOUNG
BACHELET, PIERRE
BLACK AND WHITE IN COLOR
EMMANUELLE
**BACHMAN-TURNER
OVERDRIVE**
BODY SLAM
BACIGALUPI, DENNIS
CRADLE WILL ROCK
BACK, ROBERT
MY FAIR LADY
BACKUS, JIM
JAMES DEAN STORY
LITTLE PRINCE
1001 ARABIAN NIGHTS
WONDERFUL WORLD OF THE
BROTHERS GRIMM
BACULIS, AL
ANNE OF GREEN GABLES
BAD MANNERS
DANCE CRAZE
BADALAMENTI, ANGELO
BLUE VELVET
BADAROU, WALLY
GOOD TO GO
THEY CALL IT AN ACCIDENT
BADDELEY, ANGELA
BYE BYE BIRDIE
BADDELEY, HERMIONE
CANTERBURY TALES
BADDER THAN EVIL
GORDON'S WAR
BADDOE, DON
KISMET
BADEL, ALAN
SALOME
BADFINGER
MAGIC CHRISTIAN
BADHAM, MARY
THIS PROPERTY IS CONDEMNED
BAER, MAX
BEVERLY HILLBILLIES
BAERWALD, DAVID
ECHO PARK
BAEZ, JOAN
BANJOMAN
CARRY IT ON
SACCO AND VANZETTI
SILENT RUNNING
WOODSTOCK
BAGDASARIAN, ROSS
ALVIN SHOW
KISMET
BAGNERIS, VERNEL
ONE MO' TIME

BAHLER, JOHN
BLADE RUNNER
CROSS AND THE SWITCHBLADE
BAHLOR, TOM
ELECTRIC COMPANY TV SHOW
BAILEY, ADDISON
HOLIDAY IN MANHATTAN
BAILEY, DENNIS
LEADER OF THE PACK
PREPPIES
BAILEY, JIM
FLY BLACKBIRD
BAILEY, PEARL
ARMS AND THE GIRL
CARMEN JONES
CO-STAR
HELLO DOLLY!
HOUSE OF FLOWERS
LES POUPEES DE PARIS
LOOK MA I'M DANCIN'!
MAGIC MOMENTS FROM THE
TONIGHT SHOW
PORGY AND BESS
SAINT LOUIS WOMAN
BAILEY, PHILIP
GOONIES
TWINS
BAILEY, RAYMOND
BEVERLY HILLBILLIES
BAILEY, ROBIN
JENNIE
MacBETH
BAIN, BARBARA
SPACE: 1999
BAINS, SHIRLEY
PORGY AND BESS
BAIRD, BILL
MAN IN THE MOON
BAIRD, BOBBI
AN EVENING WITH ALAN JAY
LERNER
AN EVENING WITH SAMMY CAHN
BAIRD, GEORGE
MAN IN THE MOON
**BAKALEINKOFF,
CONSTANTIN**
FRENCH LINE
RUN OF THE ARROW
BAKER, ALLEN
SIGN OF AQUARIUS
BAKER, BERTILLA
DUEL
BAKER, BETTY
PAL JOEY
BAKER, BRENDA
FEELING GOOD WITH ANNIE
BAKER, BUDDY
GREAT MOMENTS WITH MR.
LINCOLN
HALL OF PRESIDENTS
STORY OF THE GNOME-MOBILE
BAKER, CARROLL
BABY DOLL
JAMES DEAN STORY
BAKER, CHET
JAMES DEAN STORY
SHARKY'S MACHINE
BAKER, DAVID
SMILING, THE BOY FELL DEAD

BAKER, JENNIFER
STOP THE WORLD, I WANT TO
GET OFF!
BAKER, JOSEPHINE
JOSEPHINE BAKER SHOW
BAKER, KENNY
BABES IN TOYLAND
HARVEY GIRLS
ONE TOUCH OF VENUS
BAKER, LAVERN
ANGEL HEART
BIG TOWN
SHAG
BAKER, LENNY
I LOVE MY WIFE
SURVIVAL OF ST. JOAN
BAKER, LYNN
BILLY JACK
TRIAL OF BILLY JACK
BAKER, MARGARET
OLD MAID AND THE THIEF
BAKER, MARK
CANDIDE
WISH YOU WERE HERE
BAKER, RAYMOND
IS THERE LIFE AFTER HIGH
SCHOOL?
BAKER, RUTH
MARAT (DE) SADE
BAKER, SUSAN
STOP THE WORLD, I WANT TO
GET OFF!
BAKER, TOM
SIGN OF AQUARIUS
BAKEY, ED
WALKING HAPPY
BAKULA, SCOTT
ROMANCE/ROMANCE
THREE GUYS NAKED FROM THE
WAIST DOWN
BAL, JEANNE
GAY LIFE
BALABAN, BOB
YOU'RE A GOOD MAN, CHARLIE
BROWN
BALABAN, EMANUEL
MEDIUM
BALDWIN, BROOKS
CRADLE WILL ROCK
BALDWIN, MICHAEL
PHANTASM
**BALL ORCHESTRA OF
VIENNA**
LAST EMPEROR
BALL, LUCILLE
AUNTIE MAME
MAGIC MOMENTS FROM THE
TONIGHT SHOW
WILDCAT
BALL, MICHAEL
ASPECTS OF LOVE
BALLANTINE, CARL
WORLD'S GREATEST LOVER
BALLANTYNE, PAUL
THOUSAND MILES OF MOUNTAINS
BALLARD, BEVERLY
HOW TO STEAL AN ELECTION (A
DIRTY POLITICS MUSICAL)

BALLARD, HANK
EVERYBODY'S ALL-AMERICAN
FLAMINGO KID
BALLARD, KAYE
CARNIVAL
CINDERELLA
DECLINE AND FALL OF THE
ENTIRE WORLD AS SEEN
THROUGH THE EYES OF COLE
PORTER
FANNY BRICE: STORY IN SONG
GIRL MOST LIKELY
GOLDEN APPLE
LOVE LIFE
MISTER PRESIDENT
OKLAHOMA
ROBERTA
SO LONG 174TH STREET
BALLISTIC KISSES
CROSSOVER DREAMS
BALSARA, V.
GURU
BALSER, EVELYN
HELLO DOLLY!
BAMPTON, ROSE
TOM SAWYER
BANANA SPLITS
BANANA SPLITS
BANANARAMA
JUMPIN' JACK FLASH
RAIN MAN
SECRET OF MY SUCCESS
WILD LIFE
BAND WITHOUT A NAME
THUNDER ALLEY
BAND, RICHARD
DAY TIME ENDED
FROM BEYOND
MUTANT
RE-ANIMATOR
TERROR VISION
TROLL
BANDA ECLIPSE
SOUNDS FROM TRUE STORIES
BANDIT BAND
SMOKEY AND THE BANDIT II
BAND
LAST WALTZ
NEW YORK STORIES
BANE, PAULA
CALL ME MISTER
BANGLES
GOONIES
LESS THAN ZERO
BANKE, RICHARD
KISMET
BANKHEAD, TALLULAH
CO-STAR
BANKS, DONALD
GOOD TO GO
BANKS, ERNIE
SELMA
BANKS, TONY
QUICKSILVER
WICKED LADY
BANOME, NINO
BRAVO GIOVANNI!
BAPTISTE, PHIL
SEA OF LOVE

BAR-B-Q KILLERS
ATHENS, GA. - INSIDE/OUT
BAR-KAYS
BREAKIN'
WATTSTAX (THE LIVING WORD)
BARABAS, SARI
OH ROSALINDA!
BARBARA LODEN
AFTER THE FALL
BARBEAU, ADRIENNE
GREASE
BARBER, FRANK
SCHONER GIGOLO - ARMER
GIGOLO (JUST A GIGOLO)
BARBER, SAMUEL
VANESSA
BARBIERI, GATO
LAST TANGO IN PARIS
BARBUSTERS
LIGHT OF DAY
BARCLAY, DON
CINDERELLA
BARDOT, BRIGITTE
AND GOD CREATED WOMAN
GIRL IN THE BIKINI
VIVA MARIA!
BAREFIELD, EDDIE
COTTON CLUB REVUE OF 1958
BARER, MARSHALL
MAD SHOW
ONCE UPON A MATTRESS
BARGELD, BLIXA
GHOSTS OF THE CIVIL DEAD
BARGY, JEANNE
GREENWICH VILLAGE U.S.A.
BARHAMI, JOHN
WONDERWALL
BARKER, DAVID
SHOESTRING REVUE
BARKER, RONALD
IRMA LA DOUCE
ON THE BRIGHTER SIDE
BARKER, WARREN
BROADWAY COMPLEAT
HAWAIIAN EYE
KING AND I
77 SUNSET STRIP
WALTZING DOWN BROADWAY
BALLESTER, ANN
HAIR
BARNABAS
SCHONER GIGOLO - ARMER
GIGOLO (JUST A GIGOLO)
BARNES, ALAN
ON THE BRIGHTER SIDE
BARNES, BILLY
BILLY BARNES REVUE
BILLY BARNES' L.A.
BARNES, CHERYL
AMERICAN GIGOLO
MAGIC SHOW
BARNES, MAE
BY THE BEAUTIFUL SEA
ERTEGUN'S NEW YORK - NEW
YORK CABARET MUSIC
BARNES, ROLF
SAGA OF THE DINGBAT
BARNES, SIDNEY
LOVE AT FIRST BITE

BARNES, THEO
IN CIRCLES
BARNETT, JACKIE
PLAYGIRLS
BARNETT, JANICE
SELMA
BARNETT, NATE
DON'T PLAY US CHEAP
BARNUM, H.B.
BEACH BLANKET BINGO
GOLDEN BOY
ON BROADWAY
ROSE ON BROADWAY
BARON, EVALYN
I CAN'T KEEP RUNNING IN PLACE
SCRAMBLED FEET
BARON, LYNDA
ONE OVER THE EIGHT
BARON, PAUL
STUDENT PRINCE
VICTOR BORGE PROGRAM
BARON, SAMUEL
SAND CASTLE
BAROUH, PIERRE
MAN AND A WOMAN
BARR, AL
RED BALLOON
BARR, KATHY
DESERT SONG
BARRERA, MICKEY
HE'S MY GIRL
BARRETT, JOE
BOY MEETS BOY
BARRETT, MACE
BODY BEAUTIFUL
BARRETT, MICHAEL
CRADLE WILL ROCK
BARRETT, RAINA
OH CALCUTTA!
BARRIE, BARBARA
COMPANY
BARRIE, GEORGE
TOUCH OF CLASS
BARRIE, KEN
GREAT WALTZ
BARRIER, EDGAR
MAYTIME
BARRON, BEBE
FORBIDDEN PLANET
BARROSO, RAY
SALUDOS AMIGOS (MUSIC FROM
SOUTH OF THE BORDER)
BARROWS, RICHARD
DOWN IN THE VALLEY
BARRY TWINS
HIT THE DECK
BARRY, BRENDAN
LOCK UP YOUR DAUGHTERS
BARRY, BRUCE
BIOGRAPH GIRL
BARRY, GENE
LA CAGE AUX FOLLES (BIRDS OF
A FEATHER)
BARRY, JEFF
ARCHIES
LEADER OF THE PACK

BEECHMAN, LAURIE
  ANNIE
  JOSEPH AND THE AMAZING
    TECHNICOLOR DREAMCOAT
BEEPERS
  BLUE THUNDER
  WAR GAMES
BEESON, JACK
  CAPTAIN JINKS OF THE HORSE
    MARINES
  HELLO OUT THERE
  LIZZIE BORDEN
  SWEET BYE AND BYE
BEETHOVEN, LUDWIG
  CLOCKWORK ORANGE
  MUSICAL HISTORY OF THE
    BOSTON SYMPHONY AND
    BOSTON POPS
BEEVE, BILL
  WESTWARD HO, THE WAGONS
BELAFONTE, HARRY
  HARRY AND LENA
  NARM'S GOLDEN DECADE
  PORGY AND BESS
  THREE FOR TONIGHT
BELASCO, LEON
  HAPPY HUNTING
  SILK STOCKINGS
BELFIN, FRANTISEK
  ADRIFT
BELL AND JAMES
  FISH THAT SAVED PITTSBURGH
**BELL TELEPHONE
ORCHESTRA**
  MIKADO
BELL, AARON
  MUSIC FROM PETER GUNN
  77 SUNSET STRIP
BELL, FREDDIE
  GET YOURSELF A COLLEGE GIRL
BELL, GRAHAM
  TOMMY
BELL, MADELINE
  HAMMERHEAD
BELL, MAGGIE
  CRIMES OF PASSION
  TOMMY
BELL, MARION
  BRIGADOON
  DOWN IN THE VALLEY
  RED MILL
  ROBERTA
  ROSE MARIE
BELL, STEVEN
  JESUS CHRIST SUPERSTAR
BELL, VINNIE
  51 GREATEST MOTION PICTURE
    FAVORITES
BELLAMY, RALPH
  COURT MARTIAL OF BILLY
    MITCHELL
BELLE STARS
  RAIN MAN
BELLEFULLER, NANCY
  HARD PART BEGINS
BELLEZZA, V.
  CHALIAPIN AS BORIS
BELLING, SUSAN
  ELEPHANT STEPS

BELLINI, CAL
  HER FIRST ROMAN
BELLSON, LOUIS
  1941
BELOUIS SOME
  PRETTY IN PINK
BELUSHI, JIM
  LITTLE SHOP OF HORRORS
BELUSHI, JOHN
  ANIMAL HOUSE
  BLUES BROTHERS
  NATIONAL LAMPOON LEMMINGS
  OLD BOYFRIENDS
  SATURDAY NIGHT LIVE
BELVIN, JESSE
  BIG TOWN
BEN-GURION, DAVID
  I CAN HEAR IT NOW - DAVID
    BEN-GURION
BENADARET, BEA
  FLINTSTONES
BENATAR, PAT
  AMERICAN POP
  METROPOLIS
  OFFICER AND A GENTLEMAN
  ROADIE
  SECRET OF MY SUCCESS
  UP THE ACADEMY
BENATZKY, RALPH
  WHITE HORSE INN
BENCZAK, MARGARET
  CARMILLA
BENDER, DAVID
  MAN OF LA MANCHA
BENDIX, WILLIAM
  SUNSHINE CAKE
BENEDERET, BEA
  DROP DEAD! (AN EXERCISE IN
    HORROR)
BENEDICT, DIRK
  BATTLESTAR GALACTICA (THE
    SAGA OF BATTLESTAR
    GALACTICA)
BENEKE, TEX
  ALAMO
BENET, STEPHEN VINCENT
  DEVIL AND DANIEL WEBSTER
BENJAMIN, JOE
  NERVOUS SET
BENJAMIN, P.J.
  SOPHISTICATED LADIES
BENNETT, ALAN
  BEYOND THE FRINGE
  BEYOND THE FRINGE '64
BENNETT, CHRIS
  MIDNIGHT EXPRESS
BENNETT, JEANIENE
  HAIR
BENNETT, NICHOLAS
  SOUND OF MUSIC
**BENNETT, RICHARD
RODNEY**
  BILLION DOLLAR BRAIN
  EQUUS
  FAR FROM THE MADDING CROWD
  LADY CAROLINE LAMB
  MURDER ON THE ORIENT
    EXPRESS
  NICHOLAS AND ALEXANDRA
  YANKS

**BENNETT, ROBERT
RUSSELL**
  CINDERELLA
  COMING OF CHRIST
  NOT SO LONG AGO
  BROADWAY HITS OF YESTERDAY
  PORGY AND BESS
  VICTORY AT SEA
BENNETT, ROY C.
  BLUE HAWAII
  CLAMBAKE
  DOUBLE TROUBLE
  FOLLOW THAT DREAM
  FRANKIE AND JOHNNY
  FUN IN ACAPULCO
  G.I. BLUES
  GIRL HAPPY
  GIRLS! GIRLS! GIRLS!
  HARUM SCARUM
  IT HAPPENED AT THE WORLD'S
    FAIR
  JAMBOREE!
  KING CREOLE
  KISSIN' COUSINS
  LOVING YOU
  PARADISE, HAWAIIAN STYLE
  ROUSTABOUT
  SPEEDWAY
  SPINOUT
BENNETT, RUSSELL
  BROADWAY HITS OF YESTERDAY
BENNETT, TONY
  KISMET
  LAST PICTURE SHOW
  OH CAPTAIN!
  OSCAR
  SINGER PRESENTS TONY BENNETT
  SUMMER PLACE (AND OTHER
    GREAT HITS FROM MOVIES)
BENNY, JACK
  MAGIC MOMENTS FROM THE
    TONIGHT SHOW
  PROUDLY THEY CAME
BENSKIN, SAMMY
  BALLAD FOR BIMSHIRE
  BILLY NONAME
  CINDY
BENSON, BETTY
  JOHN BROWN'S BODY
BENSON, GEORGE
  ALL THAT JAZZ
  BOULEVARD NIGHTS
  GREATEST
BENSON, LINDSEY
  MY FAIR LADY
BENSON, ROBBY
  JEREMY
BENTHALL, MICHAEL
  HAMLET
  MacBETH
BENTLEY, JORDAN
  BABES IN ARMS
  JUMBO
  WONDERFUL TOWN
BENTLEY, PAUL
  ASPECTS OF LOVE
BENTLY, ERIC
  ELEPHANT CALF
BENZELL, MIMI
  CAN CAN
  MILK AND HONEY
  VAGABOND KING

CARMICHAEL, CAROL
WHERE'S POPPA?
CARMICHAEL, HOAGY
PAPER MOON
CARMICHAEL, RALPH
CROSS AND THE SWITCHBLADE
HEART IS A REBEL
HIS LAND
NATURAL HIGH
OIL TOWN, U.S.A.
RESTLESS ONES
CARMICHAEL, STOKELY
TELL ME LIES
CARMINES, AL
CHRISTMAS RAPPINGS
FAGGOT
IN CIRCLES
JOAN
PEACE
POMEGRANADA
PROMENADE
CARNES, JUDY
BOY FRIEND
ON THE BRIGHTER SIDE
CARNES, KATHLEEN
ANNIE GET YOUR GUN
CARNES, KIM
FLASHDANCE
HEROES
RUDE AWAKENING
THAT'S DANCING!
CARNEY, ART
ANYTHING GOES
HARRY AND TONTO
PANAMA HATTIE
CARNEY, GRACE
DONNYBROOK!
CARNILIA, CRAIG
IS THERE LIFE AFTER HIGH
SCHOOL?
CARNOVSKY, MORRIS
FAMILY AFFAIR
CAROL, CLIFF
HARD PART BEGINS
CAROL, LEE
OKLAHOMA
CARON, LESLIE
AN AMERICAN IN PARIS
GIGI
CAROTENUTO, MARIO
MY FAIR LADY
CARPENTER, CARLETON
LADY IN THE DARK
MAKE MINE MANHATTAN
TWO WEEKS WITH LOVE
CARPENTER, JOHN
BIG TROUBLE IN LITTLE CHINA
DARK STAR
ESCAPE FROM NEW YORK
FOG
HALLOWEEN
HALLOWEEN II
HALLOWEEN III - SEASON OF THE
WITCH
THEY LIVE
CARPENTER, THELMA
BLACKBIRDS OF 1928
SOUTH PACIFIC
WIZ

CARPENTERS
BLESS THE BEASTS AND
CHILDREN
CARR, JAMIE
IF EVER I SEE YOU AGAIN
CARR, LEON
SECRET LIFE OF WALTER MITTY
CARR, OSMOND
AN EVENING WITH W.S. GILBERT
CARR, PATTI
TO BROADWAY WITH LOVE
CARR, PAUL
JAMBOREE!
CARR, VIKKI
MOONSTRUCK
SILENCERS
CARRACK, PAUL
SING
CARRADINE, DAVID
BOUND FOR GLORY
KUNG-FU
CARRADINE, JOHN
FUNNY THING HAPPENED ON THE
WAY TO THE FORUM
LITTLE PRINCE
CARRADINE, KEITH
NASHVILLE
WELCOME TO L.A.
CARRIERE, JEAN CLAUDE
VIVA MARIA!
CARRILLO, CELY
FLOWER DRUM SONG
CARROL, RONN
ANNIE GET YOUR GUN
CARROLL BROTHERS
DON'T KNOCK THE TWIST
CARROLL, BARBARA
ERTEGUN'S NEW YORK - NEW
YORK CABARET MUSIC
ME AND JULIET
CARROLL, BEESON
ELEPHANT CALF
CARROLL, BOB
TO BROADWAY WITH LOVE
**CARROLL, CLINTON
DERRICKS**
YOUR ARMS TOO SHORT TO BOX
WITH GOD
CARROLL, DANNY
BOYS FROM SYRACUSE
FLORA THE RED MENACE
42nd STREET
GEORGE M.!
SHOESTRING '57
CARROLL, DAVID
CHESS
SLUMBER PARTY '57
CARROLL, DIAHANN
GOODBYE AGAIN
HOUSE OF FLOWERS
NO STRINGS
PORGY AND BESS
CARROLL, IRENE
KING AND I
OKLAHOMA
CARROLL, JACK
PINS AND NEEDLES

CARROLL, JIMMY
CHOCOLATE SOLDIER
DESERT SONG
EUROPEAN HOLIDAY
FINIAN'S RAINBOW
MARDI GRAS
MIKADO
NAUGHTY MARIETTA
ROBERTA
SOUTH PACIFIC
SWEETHEARTS
CARROLL, JIM
TUFF TURF
CARROLL, JOAN
ETHEL MERMAN - A MUSICAL
AUTOBIOGRAPHY
CARROLL, JOHNNY
ROCK BABY ROCK IT
CARROLL, JUNE
NEW FACES OF 1952
NEW FACES OF 1956
CARROLL, LAURIE
SEVEN DREAMS
CARROLL, LISA
THIS WAS BURLESQUE
CARROLL, ROBERT
ANDERSONVILLE TRIAL
CYRANO DE BERGERAC
CARROLL, RONNIE
PROMISES, PROMISES
CARRON, ELIZABETH
REGINA
SAINT OF BLEEKER STREET
CARSON, BARBARA
OH COWARD!
CARSON, DANIELLE
SINGIN' IN THE RAIN
CARSON, JACK
OF THEE I SING
CARSON, JEANNIE
FINIAN'S RAINBOW
LITTLE WOMEN
CARSON, JOHNNY
FOSTER BROOKS' ROASTS
MAGIC MOMENTS FROM THE
TONIGHT SHOW
CARSON, KEN
THOUSAND MILES OF MOUNTAINS
CARSON, MINDY
BODY BEAUTIFUL
CARSON, TRUDY
NEW FACES OF 1968
CARSON, VIOLET
OLIVER
CARS
OVER THE EDGE
CARTER, BENJAMIN
BELIEVERS
CARTER, BENNY
M-SQUAD
MAN CALLED ADAM
RED SKY AT MORNING
SILENT PARTNER
CARTER, CALVIN
MASTER OF THE WORLD
CARTER, GENNA
MIXED DOUBLES/BELOW THE
BELT

CHAMBERLAIN, BRYCE
ORDER IS LOVE
CHAMBERLAIN, DEAN
ECHO PARK
CHAMBERLAIN, RICHARD
BREAKFAST AT TIFFANY'S
HAMLET
MAN FROM U.N.C.L.E.
SLIPPER AND THE ROSE (THE
STORY OF CINDERELLA)
TWILIGHT OF HONOR
CHAMBERS BROTHERS
APRIL FOOLS
HE'S MY GIRL
CHAMBERS, RALPH
CALL ME MADAM
CHAMPION, GOWER
LOVELY TO LOOK AT
SHOW BOAT
CHAMPION, MARGE
I LOVE MELVIN
LOVELY TO LOOK AT
SHOW BOAT
THREE FOR THE SHOW
CHAMPLIN, BILL
MIAMI VICE II
SING
CHAMPLIN, TAMARA
CADDYSHACK II
CHAMPS
ALL AMERICAN
CHANCE, TREVOR
GOLD
CHANDLER, BEN
CREATIVE FREAKOUT
CHANDLER, CHRISTINE
BEOWULF
CHANDLER, GENE
DUSTY AND SWEETS McGEE
CHANEY, JAN
O SAY CAN YOU SEE!
CHANEY, LON, JR.
BIRD OF PARADISE
CHANNEL, BRUCE
DIRTY DANCING
DUSTY AND SWEETS McGEE
SLUMBER PARTY '57
CHANNING, CAROL
GENTLEMEN PREFER BLONDES
HELLO DOLLY!
JERRY'S GIRLS
LORELEI
NO FOR AN ANSWER
SHINBONE ALLEY (ARCHY &
MEHITABEL)
SHOWGIRL (CAROL CHANNING
LIVE)
SKIDOO
THIS IS BROADWAY'S BEST
THOROUGHLY MODERN MILLIE
CHANNING, STOCKARD
GREASE
CHANTAYS
MORE AMERICAN GRAFFITI
CHAPIN, JAMES FORBES
PASSING FAIR

CHAPLIN, CHARLIE
CHAPLIN REVUE
CHAPLIN'S ART OF COMEDY
COUNTESS FROM HONG KONG
HOLLYWOOD
MODERN TIMES
SILENCERS
CHAPLIN, CLIVE
JEROME KERN GOES TO
HOLLYWOOD
CHAPLIN, SAUL
AN AMERICAN IN PARIS
BONANZA BOUND
MERRY ANDREW
SUMMER STOCK
CHAPLIN, SYDNEY
BELLS ARE RINGING
FUNNY GIRL
SUBWAYS ARE FOR SLEEPING
WONDERFUL TOWN
CHAPMAN, GRAHAM
LIFE OF BRIAN
MONTY PYTHON AND THE HOLY
GRAIL
CHAPMAN, SHIRLEY
SOUND OF MUSIC
CHAPMAN, TOPSY
ONE MO' TIME
CHAPMAN, WILLIAM
ARABIAN NIGHTS
CANDIDE
GREENWILLOW
CHAPPARRAL BROTHERS
LAST OF THE AMERICAN HOBOES
CHAPPELL, EDDIE
GIRL CRAZY
CHARD, GEOFFREY
CAMELOT
CHARISSE, CYD
IT'S ALWAYS FAIR WEATHER
LES POUPEES DE PARIS
SILK STOCKINGS
CHARISSE, ZAN
GYPSY
CHARLAP, MARK
PETER PAN
CHARLAP, MOOSE
ALICE THROUGH THE LOOKING
GLASS
CLOWNAROUND
WHOOP-UP!
CHARLENE
LAST DRAGON
CHARLES, KEITH
CELEBRATION
COLETTE
CHARLES, KIM
SPACEBALLS
CHARLES, PAMELA
WATER GYPSIES
CHARLES, PAUL
BEST FOOT FORWARD

CHARLES, RAY
ANY WHICH WAY YOU CAN
BIG TOWN
BLUES BROTHERS
CINCINNATI KID
CINEMA '76
DANGER
FINIAN'S RAINBOW
IN THE HEAT OF THE NIGHT
KING OF COMEDY
MISTER PRESIDENT
PORGY AND BESS
ROBERTA
SOMEBODY UP THERE LIKES ME
TWENTY-FIVE YEARS OF LIFE
WHO IS HARRY KELLERMAN AND
WHY IS HE SAYING THOSE
TERRIBLE THINGS ABOUT ME?
CHARLES, WALTER
LA CAGE AUX FOLLES (BIRDS OF
A FEATHER)
CHARLES, ZACHARY
TOP BANANA
CHARLOP
KELLY
CHARLOTTE
BEI MIR BISTU SCHOEN
CHARMETTES
SHAG
CHARNIN, MARTIN
ANNIE
I REMEMBER MAMA
TWO BY TWO
ZENDA
CHARTOFF, MELANIE
LOVE SONG
CHASE, CARRI
HEIDI
CHASE, CHEVY
NATHIONAL LAMPOON
LEMMINGS
SATURDAY NIGHT LIVE
THREE AMIGOS
CHASE, ILKA
CINDERELLA
CHASE
CROSSOVER DREAMS
CHASTAIN, DON
IT'S A BIRD, IT'S A PLANE, IT'S
SUPERMAN
NO STRINGS
CHATTAWAY, JAY
INVASION U.S.A.
MANIAC
CHEAP TRICK
CADDYSHACK II
HEAVY METAL
OVER THE EDGE
ROADIE
SPRING BREAK
TOP GUN
CHECKER, CHUBBY
DON'T KNOCK THE TWIST
LET THE GOOD TIMES ROLL
PURPLE PEOPLE EATER
CHEECH AND CHONG
UP IN SMOKE

CHEEKS
UP THE ACADEMY
CHEERY BOMB
HOWARD THE DUCK
CHELSI, LAWRENCE
HOUSEWIVES' CANTATA
CHER
CHASTITY
ROLLER BOOGIE
CHERRY, DON
OH CAPTAIN!
WILL PENNY
CHERYL LYNN
ARMED AND DANGEROUS
CHESTER, ALAN
BEI MIR BISTU SCHOEN
CHESTERFIELDS
AMERICAN HOT WAX
CHEVALIER, MAURICE
BETTY BOOP
BLACK TIGHTS
BREATH OF SCANDAL
BROADWAY, BROADWAY,
   BROADWAY
CAN CAN
GIGI
IN SEARCH OF THE CASTAWAYS
JESSICA
MUSIC FROM DISNEY MOTION
   PICTURES
PEPE
SUMMER MAGIC
CHEYNE
WEIRD SCIENCE
CHIARI, WALTER
GAY LIFE
CHICAGO
SUMMER LOVERS
TWO OF A KIND
CHIC
SOUP FOR ONE
CHIDSEY, ROBERT
ALL NIGHT STRUT
CHIFFONS
FLAMINGO KID
CHIHARA, PAUL
PRINCE OF THE CITY
CHILD, DESMOND
TIMES SQUARE
WARRIORS
CHILD, MARILYN
FAGGOT
NEW FACES OF 1968
CHILDS, TONI
LOST ANGELS
CHILTON, ALEX
I WAS A TEENAGE ZOMBIE
CHILTON, CHARLES
OH WHAT A LOVELY WAR
CHING, WILLIAM
ALLEGRO
CHIPS
COUPE DE VILLE
CHISHOLM, ROBERT
CONNECTICUT YANKEE
MY FAIR LADY
CHITEN, PAUL
BAD GUYS

CHITJIAN, HOWARD
GIGI
CHITOS, RICHARD
BODY BEAUTIFUL
CHOCOLATE WATCH BAND
RIOT ON SUNSET STRIP
CHOI, HYE-YOUNG
KING AND I
CHONG, RAE DAWN
SOUL MAN
CHONG, TOMMY
UP IN SMOKE
CHOOKASIAN, LILI
RISE AND FALL OF THE THIRD
   REICH
**CHORAL MUSIC SOCIETY
   OF WARSAW**
DANTON
CHORDETTES
ARTHUR GODFREY'S TV
   CALENDAR SHOW
HALLOWEEN II
STAND BY ME
CHOVER, MARC
JACQUES BREL IS ALIVE AND
   WELL AND LIVING IN PARIS
CHRIS D.
BORDER RADIO
CHRISTENSEN, JULIE
ECHO PARK
CHRISTIAN, ROGER
RIDE THE WILD SURF
CHRISTIANSEN, BOB
BABES IN TOYLAND
CHRISTIE, DINAH
APPLE TREE
CHRISTIE, LOU
RAIN MAN
TEA DANCE
CHRISTIE, TONY
EVITA
CHRISTINE, DAVID
GRASSHOPPER
CHRISTLIEB, PETER
ADVENTURERS
CHRISTMAS, DAVID
DAMES AT SEA
VERY GOOD EDDIE
CHRISTOPHER, DENNIS
CALIFORNIA DREAMING
CHRISTOPHER, DON
LOVE AND LET LOVE
CHRISTY, CAROL
MOTHER EARTH
CHRISTY, EILEEN
CAROUSEL
CHRISTY, JUNE
DO RE MI
CHUMA, NATALIA
SECOND SHEPHERD'S PLAY
CHUN, KAM FONG
THIRTEEN DAUGHTERS
CHURA
PRISON
CHURCH
TEQUILA SUNRISE
CHURCH, GEORGE
110 IN THE SHADE

CHURCH, SANDRA
GYPSY
CHURCHILL, FRANK
BAMBI
DUMBO
SNOW WHITE AND THE SEVEN
   DWARFS
THREE LITTLE PIGS
CHURCHILL, STUART
THIS IS THE ARMY
CHURCHILL, WINSTON
I CAN HEAR IT NOW - WINSTON
   CHURCHILL
NOT SO LONG AGO
QUICK AND THE DEAD - THE
   STORY OF THE ATOM BOMB
CICOGNINI, ALESSANDRO
BLACK ORCHID
BREATH OF SCANDAL
INDISCRETION OF AN AMERICAN
   WIFE
IT STARTED IN NAPLES
CILENTO, WAYNE
CHORUS LINE
CIMARA, PIETRO
NIGHT AT CARNEGIE HALL
CIPRIANI, STELVIO
ANONYMOUS VENETIAN
COME TOGETHER
CIRCLE JERKS
DECLINE OF WESTERN
   CIVILIZATION
REPO MAN
CISYK, KASEY
ONE AND ONLY
YOU LIGHT UP MY LIFE
CLAIRE, DOROTHY
JIMMY
CLANTON, JIMMY
GO JOHNNY GO!
CLANTON, RALPH
CYRANO DE BERGERAC
CLAPTON, ERIC
BACK TO THE FUTURE
COLOR OF MONEY
HAIL HAIL ROCK 'N' ROLL
LAST WALTZ
LETHAL WEAPON
LETHAL WEAPON 2
TOMMY
CLARK SISTERS
1001 ARABIAN NIGHTS
CLARK, BARRETT
ALICE'S ADVENTURES IN
   WONDERLAND
CLARK, BUDDY
PAPER MOON
CLARK, DANE
BRECHT ON BRECHT
CLARK, DAVE
GET YOURSELF A COLLEGE GIRL
HAVING A WILD WEEKEND
CLARK, DORT
WONDERFUL TOWN
CLARK, ERNEST
CO-STAR
COCKTAIL PARTY
CLARK, FRED
BELLS ARE RINGING

DEANE, DOUGLAS
GUYS AND DOLLS

DEANGELIS, PETER
DEVIL IN MISS JONES

DEARBORN, DALTON
MAC BIRD

DEASY, MIKE
ELVIS (NBC-TV SPECIAL)

DE AZEVEDO, LEX
AGAINST A CROOKED SKY
MY TURN ON EARTH
ORDER IS LOVE
SATURDAY'S WARRIOR
THREADS OF GLORY

DEAZEVEDO, RIC
THREADS OF GLORY

DE BARGE
LAST DRAGON

DE BARGE, CHICO
COMING TO AMERICA
FINE MESS
POLICE ACADEMY IV - CITIZENS
ON PATROL

DEBELLA, RICHARD
BODY BEAUTIFUL

DEBS, EUGENE
DEAN MARTIN TESTIMONIAL
DINNER

DECADENT DUB TEAM
COLORS

DECAMP, ROSEMARY
YANKEE DOODLE DANDY

DECARLO, YVONNE
AT HOME WITH THE MUNSTERS
FOLLIES

DECIMUS, GEORGE
SWEET LIES

DECK, ROBIN
AMONG FRIENDS - WAA-MU
SHOW OF 1960

DECOPTEAUX, BERT
TIME CHANGES

DECORDOBA, PEDRO
COUNT OF MONTE CRISTO

DECORMIER CHORALE
SING FOR YOUR SUPPER

DECORMIER, ROBERT
HAPPIEST GIRL IN THE WORLD
SING FOR YOUR SUPPER

DEE, DARRELL
MONDO HOLLYWOOD

DEE, JOEY
COUPE DE VILLE
HEY LET'S TWIST
TWO TICKETS TO PARIS

DEE, KIKI
STIR CRAZY

DEE, SANDRA
SNOW QUEEN

DEEL, SANDRA
LOOK MA I'M DANCIN'!
SOUTH PACIFIC

DE EMILE, ANTONIO
RUSH TO JUDGMENT

DEEMS, MICKEY
ANYTHING GOES
LITTLE ME

DEEP RIVER BOYS
FINIAN'S RAINBOW

DEERING, OLIVE
NO FOR AN ANSWER

DEES, BILL
FASTEST GUITAR ALIVE

DEES, MICHAEL
DAY OF THE LOCUST
HAPPY ENDING

DEES, RICK
MEATBALLS

DE FRANCO, BUDDY
BROADWAY SHOWCASE
SHARKY'S MACHINE

DEFRECE, LAURI
MAID OF THE MOUNTAINS

DEGAN, HAROLD A.
LIVE AND LET DIE

DE GROOT, MYRA
OLIVER
PIECES OF EIGHT

DEGUZMAN, JOSSIE
CARMELINA
RUNAWAYS

DEHAVEN, GLORIA
RODGERS AND HART REVISITED
SEVENTH HEAVEN
SO THIS IS PARIS
SUMMER STOCK
THREE LITTLE WORDS

DEHAVEN, PENNY
BRONCO BILLY

DE HAVILLAND, OLIVIA
STRAWBERRY BLOND

DEITZ, HOWARD
BAND WAGON

DEJESUS, LUCHI
ADIOS AMIGO
BEGATTING OF THE PRESIDENT
SALLAH

DEKKER, DESMOND
DRUGSTORE COWBOY
HARDER THEY COME

DELANEY AND BONNIE
MEDICINE BALL CARAVAN
VANISHING POINT

DELAPENHA, DENISE
DOCTOR SELAVY'S MAGIC
THEATRE

DELAURENTIS, SEMINA
NUNSENSE

DELEON, W.
THEY CALLED IT AN ACCIDENT

DELERUE, GEORGES
AGNES OF GOD
ALMOST PERFECT AFFAIR
ANNE OF THE THOUSAND DAYS
BLACK STALLION RETURNS
CONFIDENTIALLY YOURS
DAY OF THE DOLPHIN
FILM MUSIC FROM FRANCE
HEARTBREAK HOTEL
HORSEMEN
INTERLUDE
KING OF HEARTS
LAST METRO
LITTLE ROMANCE
MAN FOR ALL SEASONS
OUR MOTHER'S HOUSE
PLATOON (AND SONGS FROM THE
ERA)
PROMISE AT DAWN
SHOOT THE PIANO PLAYER

TRUE CONFESSIONS
25th HOUR
VIVA MARIA!
WALK WITH LOVE AND DEATH
WOMAN NEXT DOOR

DEL FUEGOS
I WAS A TEENAGE ZOMBIE

DELIBES
NIGHT AT CARNEGIE HALL

DELIGHTS
AMERICAN HOT WAX

DELITTLE, JOHNNY
KNACK (AND HOW TO GET IT)

DELL ORSO, EDDA
ONCE UPON A TIME IN AMERICA

DELL'ISOLA, SALVATORE
ALLEGRO
FLOWER DRUM SONG
ME AND JULIET
ON YOUR TOES
PIPE DREAM
SOUTH PACIFIC

DELL, GABRIEL
ANKLES AWEIGH
ANYONE CAN WHISTLE

DEL-LORDS
UNDER THE BOARDWALK

DELLS
COME TOGETHER

DELMAR, ELAINE
COWARDLY CUSTARD
JEROME KERN GOES TO
HOLLYWOOD

DELMAR, KENNY
TEXAS LI'L DARLIN'

DEL MONTE, GEORGE
IRMA LA DOUCE

DELON, JACK
BODY BEAUTIFUL
FAMILY AFFAIR
JENNIE
MOST HAPPY FELLA

DELORY, AL
NORWOOD
OUT OF SIGHT
TRUE GRIT

DELPH, PAUL
NO SMALL AFFAIR

DEL PRETE, DUILIO
AT LONG LAST LOVE

DEL RIO, DOLORES
BIRD OF PARADISE

DELSON, MARY
DOCTOR SELAVY'S MAGIC
THEATRE

DELTA RHYTHM BOYS
RAIN MAN

DELUCA, DEBRA
ALADD

DELUCE, VIRGINIA
NEW FACES OF 1952

DELUGG, ANNE
BEYOND THE MOON
BIG BAD WOLF
BREMEN TOWN MUSICIANS
CINDERELLA
GYPSY GIRL
SNOW WHITE AND ROSE RED

FARAGHER, TOMMY
STAYING ALIVE
FARBER, BURT
PRINCE AND THE PAUPER
SUBWAYS ARE FOR SLEEPING
FARBER, LOREN S.
WASHINGTON BEHIND CLOSED
DOORS
FARBER, STAN
CROSS AND THE SWITCHBLADE
FARGE, ANNIE
LES POUPEES DE PARIS
FARINA, MARILYN
NUNSENSE
FARINA, MIMI
FOOLS
FARIS, ALEXANDER
IRMA LA DOUCE
FARMER, ART
I WANT TO LIVE
FARNHAM, JOHN
RAD
SAVAGE STREETS
FARNON, DENNIS
ARRIVEDERCI, BABY!
GIGI
FARNON, ROBERT
CAPTAIN HORATIO HORNBLOWER
GENTLEMEN MARRY BRUNETTES
ROAD TO HONG KONG
SHALAKO
FARNUM, JOHN
FLETCH
FARNWORTH, RALPH
MOST HAPPY FELLA
FARRAR, JOHN
XANADU
FARRELL, EILEEN
INTERRUPTED MELODY
FARRELL, JIM
DUDE
DUDE, THE HIGHWAY LIFE
FARRELL, JOE
LANDLORD
FARRELL, WALTER
PENNEY PROUD
FARREN, CHRIS
GIRLS JUST WANT TO HAVE FUN
NIGHT OF THE COMET
FARRIS, ALEXANDER
CHARLIE AND ALGERNON
FARROW, MIA
ROSEMARY'S BABY
FASCINATO, JACK
HAPPY MOTHER GOOSE (AS TOLD
BY KUKLA, FRAN AND OLLIE)
KUKLA, FRAN AND OLLIE
FASS, BERNIE
POWER IS YOU
FAST FORWARD
PUMPING IRON 2 - THE WOMEN
FASTWAY
TRICK OR TREAT
FAT BOYS
BLUE IGUANA
KRUSH GROOVE
FATAAR, RIKKI
RUTLES

FATES WARNING
RIVER'S EDGE
FATOOL, NICK
PETE KELLY'S BLUES
FAULL, ELLEN
CARRY NATION
LIZZIE BORDEN
FAURE, DUNCAN
WHO'S THAT GIRL?
FAYE, ALICE
GOOD NEWS
MAGIC OF LASSIE
STATE FAIR
WAKE UP AND LIVE
FAYE, FRANCIS
PORGY AND BESS
FAYE, HERBIE
TOP BANANA
FAYE, JOEY
LITTLE ME
70 GIRLS, 70
TOP BANANA
FAYE, VINI
BEST OF BURLESQUE
FAYER, ART
TAROT
FAZAKAS, FRANZ
MAN IN THE MOON
FEAR
DECLINE OF WESTERN
CIVILIZATION
GET CRAZY
REPO MAN
FEARL, CLIFFORD
JIMMY
FEAST, MICHAEL
HAIR
FEATHERS, CHARLIE
TEEN-AGE CRUISERS
FEEHAN, TIM
LICENSE TO KILL
WRAITH
FEELIES
MARRIED TO THE MOB
FEHRING, JOHANNES
KISS ME KATE
FELBER, WILLIAM
STUDENT PRINCE
FELD, FRITZ
WORLD'S GREATEST LOVER
FELDER, DON
FAST TIMES AT RIDGEMONT HIGH
HEAVY METAL
SECRET ADMIRER
FELDMAN, MARTY
YOUNG FRANKENSTEIN
FELICIANO, JOSE
MACKENNA'S GOLD
FELLER, DICK
SMOKEY AND THE BANDIT
FELTON, VERNA
CINDERELLA
FEMME FATALE
LICENSE TO DRIVE
FENADY, ANDREW J.
STAKEOUT
FENHOLT, JEFF
JESUS CHRIST SUPERSTAR

FENN, JEAN
GREAT WALTZ
SERENADE
VAGABOND KING
FENTON, CARL
LADY BE GOOD
FENTON, GEORGE
COMPANY OF WOLVES
CRY FREEDOM
GANDHI
HIGH SPIRITS
JEWEL IN THE CROWN
FENWICK, JOHN
ANNE OF GREEN GABLES
FERGUSON, HELEN
CABIN IN THE SKY
FERGUSON, JAY
BAD DREAMS
ROADIE
TERMINATOR
FERGUSON, MAYNARD
UNCLE JOE SHANNON
FERNANDEZ, JOSE
ME NOBODY KNOWS
FERNANDEZ, PETER
WHAT DO YOU WANT TO BE
WHEN YOU GROW UP?
**FERNANDEZ, WILHELMINA
WIGGINS**
DIVA
FERRANTE AND TEICHER
GOLDEN THEMES FROM MOTION
PICTURES
GOODBYE AGAIN
ISRAEL NOW
ORIGINAL MOTION PICTURE HIT
THEMES
RAGE TO LIVE
WEST SIDE STORY
FERRARA, FRANCO
BIBLE . . . IN THE BEGINNING
BOCCACCIO '70
FAREWELL TO ARMS
FRANCIS OF ASSISI
INDISCRETION OF AN AMERICAN
WIFE
LEOPARD
PICASSO
WAR AND PEACE
FERRARA, JOHN
SUNBURN
FERRELL, TYRA
LENA HORNE: THE LADY AND
HER MUSIC
FERRER, JOSE
CAINE MUTINY
CYRANO DE BERGERAC
DEEP IN MY HEART
GIRL WHO CAME TO SUPPER
GREAT DEBATES
MISS SADIE THOMPSON
MOUSE ON THE MAYFLOWER
OH CAPTAIN!
FERRER, MEL
EVERYTHING I HAVE IS YOURS
OH ROSALINDA!
FERRIER, PAT
REDHEAD
FERRIS WHEEL
TOUCHABLES

FROESE, EDGAR
SORCERER
FROG, WYNDER K.
TOUCHABLES
FROMAN, JANE
GEMS FROM GERSHWIN
PAL JOEY
FRONTIERE, DOMINIC
AVIATOR
BILLIE
HAMMERSMITH IS OUT
HANG 'EM HIGH
ON ANY SUNDAY
PIPE DREAMS
POPI
STUNT MAN
WASHINGTON BEHIND CLOSED
DOORS
FROOM, MITCHELL
SLAM DANCE
FROST, DAVID
THAT WAS THE WEEK THAT WAS
FROST, JOHN
BEGGAR'S OPERA
FROST, MAX
GLORY STOMPERS
**FROZEN GHOST AND
FRIENDS**
JOHNNY BE GOOD
FRYSON, LESLIE
OLIVER
FUCHS, LEO
BEI MIR BISTU SCHOEN
GREAT WALTZ
FUJII, TIMM
PACIFIC OVERTURES
FULL CIRCLE.
BUNNY O'HARE
FULL FORCE
CADDYSHACK II
HOUSE PARTY
FULLER, EDWARD
CRADLE WILL ROCK
FULLER, GARY
CHOCALONIA
FULLER, LORENZO
FINIAN'S RAINBOW
KISS ME KATE
WE'D RATHER SWITCH
FULLER, PENNY
APPLAUSE
REX
FULLER, SANDY
THIS WAS BURLESQUE
FULLERTON, FLONA
ALICE'S ADVENTURES IN
WONDERLAND
FULLUM, CLAY
LAST SWEET DAYS OF ISAAC
FULSON, LOWELL
DINER
FUNK, SALLY
FIVE AFTER EIGHT
FUNT, ALLEN
WHAT DO YOU SAY TO A NAKED
LADY?
FUQUA, HARVEY
GO JOHNNY GO!

FURBER, DOUGLAS
ME AND MY GIRL
FURLONG, KIRBY
AUNTIE MAME
FURNITURE
SOME KIND OF WONDERFUL
FURTH, GEORGE
FOUR BELOW STRIKES BACK
FUSCO, GIOVANNI
LA GUERRE EST FINIE
FUTTERMAN, ENID
YOURS ANNE
FYFE, ROBERT
KING HENRY V
FYSON, LESLIE
ANNIE GET YOUR GUN

G

GABEL, MARTIN
BAKER STREET
MAKING OF THE PRESIDENT, 1960
ON A NOTE OF TRIUMPH
GABLE, CHRISTOPHER
BOY FRIEND
SLIPPER AND THE ROSE (THE
STORY OF CINDERELLA)
GABLE, JUNE
CANDIDE
GABOR, EVA
RESCUERS
GABRIEL, PETER
AGAINST ALL ODDS
BIRDY
GREMLINS
HARD TO HOLD
PASSION (MUSIC FOR)
GABRIELE, LENYA
HELLO OUT THERE
GADE, JACOB
DEATH ON THE NILE
SILENT MOVIE
GAILLARD, SLIM
ABSOLUTE BEGINNERS
GAINES, FREDERICK
HOUSE OF LEATHER
GAINES, ROY
FEDS
GAINES, THOMAS
O SAY CAN YOU SEE!
GAINSBOURG, SERGE
MADAME CLAUDE
GALE, PETER
COWARDLY CUSTARD
GALJOUR, WARREN
DESERT SONG
GALLAGHER, BENNY
MAHONEY'S LAST STAND
GALLAGHER, HELEN
CRY FOR US ALL
GIRL CRAZY
HAZEL FLAGG
I CAN'T KEEP RUNNING IN PLACE
MAKE A WISH
MAKE MINE MANHATTAN
NO, NO, NANETTE

OPENING NIGHT AT THE PALACE -
SWEET CHARITY
PAL JOEY
SHANGRI-LA
SWEET CHARITY
GALLAGHER, PETER
DOLL'S LIFE
GALLAGHER, SKEETS
BIRD OF PARADISE
GALLEGLY, DAVID
BOY MEETS BOY
GALLEGOS, JOSE
CROSSOVER DREAMS
**GALLERY REPERTORY
THEATRE**
SALVATION
GALLI, DEBORAH
GIRLS JUST WANT TO HAVE FUN
GALLOWAY, LEATA
COTTON COMES TO HARLEM
DUDE
DUDE, THE HIGHWAY LIFE
FORTUNE AND MEN'S EYES
HAIR
STIR CRAZY
GAMELAN ORCHESTRA
DANCERS OF BALI
GAMLEY, DOUGLAS
ANOTHER TIME, ANOTHER PLACE
GIRL ON A MOTORCYCLE
GANG OF FOUR
KARATE KID
URGH - A MUSIC WAR
GANG, JAMES
ZACHARIAH
GANGI
PICASSO
GANNAWAY, LYNNE
CANDIDE
GANNON, JAMES
CAMELOT
DONNYBROOK!
GANNON, KIM
JOHNNY APPLESEED
SEVENTEEN
GAP BAND
I'M GONNA GIT YOU SUCKA
KRUSH GROOVE
PENITENTIARY III
GARBAGE PAIL KIDS
GARBAGE PAIL KIDS
GARBER, HARRY
MY FUR LADY
GARBER, MATTHEW
MARY POPPINS
GARBER, VICTOR
GODSPELL
SWEENEY TODD (THE DEMON
BARBER OF FLEET STREET)
GARCIA, RUSSELL
PORGY AND BESS
TIME MACHINE
GARDELL, TONY
WHOOP-UP!
GARDENIA, VINCENT
BALLROOM
LITTLE SHOP OF HORRORS
GARDNER, ANN
CANTERBURY TALES

HANNAH, DARRYL
LEGAL EAGLES
HANOVER FIST
WILD LIFE
HANSEN, JACK
AROUND THE WORLD IN 80 DAYS
MY FAIR LADY
HANSEN, RON
ATHENIAN TOUCH
HAPPENINGS
PURPLE PEOPLE EATER
HAPPY MONDAYS
LOST ANGELS
HARADA, ERNEST
PACIFIC OVERTURES
HARBACH, OTTO
AN EVENING WITH JEROME KERN
CAT AND THE FIDDLE
DESERT SONG
FIREFLY
JEROME KERN GOES TO
HOLLYWOOD
LOVELY TO LOOK AT
NO, NO, NANETTE
ROBERTA
ROSE MARIE
SUNNY
HARBURG, E.Y.
AN EVENING WITH JEROME KERN
BLOOMER GIRL
DARLING OF THE DAY
FINIAN'S RAINBOW
FLAHOOLEY
HAPPIEST GIRL IN THE WORLD
JAMAICA
JUDY GARLAND
PINOCCHIO
STOOGE
WIZARD OF OZ
HARDEN, WILBUR
KING AND I
HARDER, JAMES
ATHENIAN TOUCH
HARDIE, RUSSELL
ANDERSONVILLE TRIAL
HARDIN, GLEN D.
ELVIS IN CONCERT
ELVIS: ALOHA FROM HAWAII VIA
SATELLITE
THAT'S THE WAY IT IS
HARDIN, TY
PALM SPRINGS WEEKEND
HARDISON, KADEEM
RAPPIN'
HARDWICK, MARK
PUMP BOYS AND DINETTES ON
BROADWAY
HARDWICKE, SIR CEDRIC
CO-STAR
JACK THE RIPPER
SUNSHINE CAKE
HARDY, JANE
BIOGRAPH GIRL
HARDY, JANIS
POSTCARD FROM MOROCCO
HARDY, WILLIAM, JR.
YOUR ARMS TOO SHORT TO BOX
WITH GOD
HARE, DORIS
VALMOUTH
WATER GYPSIES

HARE, ROBERTSON
FUNNY THING HAPPENED ON THE
WAY TO THE FORUM
HAREWOOD, DORIAN
BRAINCHILD
HARGER, GARY
SHENANDOAH
HARKNESS, GORDON
ORDER IS LOVE
HARLEY, MARGOT
CRYSTAL HEART
ERNEST IN LOVE
HARLINE, LEIGH
PINOCCHIO
SNOW WHITE AND THE SEVEN
DWARFS
HARMA, CHARMAINE
KING AND I
HARMAN, BARRY
ROMANCE/ROMANCE
HARMAN, BUDDY
CLAMBAKE
ELVIS
HARMON, JOHNNY
CINDY
HARMON, KEITH
CAPTAIN JINKS OF THE HORSE
MARINES
HARMON, MARY
BY THE BEAUTIFUL SEA
MRS. PATTERSON
HARMON, PEGGY
BIG RIVER (THE ADVENTURES OF
HUCKLEBERRY FINN)
HARMON, STEVE
ONE AND ONLY, GENUINE,
ORIGINAL FAMILY BAND
HARMONICATS
GREAT NEW MOTION PICTURE
THEMES
GREAT THEMES FROM TV AND
MOTION PICTURES
HARMS, CARI
MAN IN THE MOON
HARNEY, BEN
DREAM GIRLS
HARNICK, SHELDON M.
AN EVENING WITH SHELDON
HARNICK
APPLE TREE
BODY BEAUTIFUL
CAPTAIN JINKS OF THE HORSE
MARINES
FIDDLER ON THE ROOF
FIORELLO!
MAN IN THE MOON
NEW FACES OF 1952
REX
ROTHSCHILDS
SHE LOVES ME
SHOESTRING REVUE
SMILING, THE BOY FELL DEAD
TENDERLOIN
TO BROADWAY WITH LOVE
HARP, KEN
MUSIC MAN
HARP, MARTHA LOU
JAMBOREE!
HARPER, DOLORES
HOUSE OF FLOWERS

HARPER, JESSICA
DOCTOR SELAVY'S MAGIC
THEATRE
PHANTOM OF THE PARADISE
HARPER, REDD
OIL TOWN, U.S.A.
HARPER, VALERIE
GO FLY A KITE
PAUL SILLS' STORY THEATRE (OF
MAGICAL FOLK-ROCK FABLES)
HARPER, WALLY
BARBARA COOK AT CARNEGIE
HALL
DAY IN HOLLYWOOD/NIGHT IN
THE UKRAINE
GRAND TOUR
NINE
HARPERS BIZARRE
MAGNAVOX PRESENTS FRANK
SINATRA
HARRAH, WALT
PENNIES FROM HEAVEN
**HARRELL, GORDON
LOWRY**
INNER CITY
ROCKABYE HAMLET
HARRIETT, JUDY
SAY ONE FOR ME
HARRINGTON, DONALD
CARMILLA
HARRINGTON, PAT
CALL ME MADAM
HARRINGTON, ROBERT
PETER PAN
HARRIS, ALBERT
ALAKAZAM THE GREAT
HARRIS, BARBARA
APPLE TREE
FROM THE SECOND CITY
OFFICIAL GRAMMY AWARDS
ARCHIVE COLLECTION
ON A CLEAR DAY YOU CAN SEE
FOREVER
WHO IS HARRY KELLERMAN AND
WHY IS HE SAYING THOSE
TERRIBLE THINGS ABOUT ME?
HARRIS, BOB
LOLITA
THING-FISH
HARRIS, BRENDA
GREENWILLOW
HARRIS, DAVID
CARRY IT ON
HARRIS, DIANNE LYNNE
ORDER IS LOVE
HARRIS, ED
ALAMO BAY
HARRIS, EDDIE
EXODUS TO JAZZ
SHARKY'S MACHINE
SOUL TO SOUL
HARRIS, EMMYLOU
HONEYSUCKLE ROSE
LAST WALTZ
PLANES, TRAINS, AND
AUTOMOBILES
HARRIS, HARRY
SNOW WHITE AND THE THREE
STOOGES

HOWES, BOBBY
FINIAN'S RAINBOW
HOWES, SALLY ANN
BRIGADOON
CHITTY, CHITTY, BANG, BANG
GIFT OF THE MAGI
I REMEMBER MAMA
KWAMINA
OFFICIAL GRAMMY AWARDS
ARCHIVE COLLECTION
WHAT MAKES SAMMY RUN?
HOWLAND, BETH
COMPANY
DARLING OF THE DAY
HOWLETT, NEIL
ANNIE GET YOUR GUN
HOWLETT, NOEL
KING HENRY V
HOWMAN, DAVID
LIFE OF BRIAN
HOXWORTH, MARY ANN
MRS. PATTERSON
HOYEM, ROBERT
JUNO
HOYER, OLE
ERIC SOYA'S 17
HUBERT, JANET L.
CATS
HUDDLESTON, FLOYD
ARISTOCATS
ROBIN HOOD
HUDDLESTON, MICHAEL
WORLD'S GREATEST LOVER
HUDSON, PETER
MOST HAPPY FELLA
HUDSON, ROCK
JAMES DEAN STORY
SHOWDOWN
HUDSON, TRAVIS
GRAND TOUR
VERY GOOD EDDIE
YOUNG ABE LINCOLN
HUE AND CRY
HIDING OUT
HUES CORPORATION
BLACULA
HUEY, RICHARD
BLOOMER GIRL
LONESOME TRAIN
HUFF, RONN
SO LONG JOEY
HUGESSEN, JIM
MY FUR LADY
HUGG, B.
UP THE JUNCTION
HUGH, GRAYSON
TRUE LOVE
HUGHES, LANGSTON
JERICO-JIM CROW
SIMPLY HEAVENLY
STREET SCENE
TAMBOURINES TO GLORY
HUGHES, RHETTA
DON'T PLAY US CHEAP
HULBERT, CLAUDE
OH KAY!
HUME, DOREEN
CAT AND THE FIDDLE
GIRL FRIEND

NO, NO, NANETTE
HUMPERDINCK,
ENGELBERT
HANSEL AND GRETEL
HUMPHREY, HUBERT
FOSTER BROOKS' ROASTS
HUMPHRIES, BARRY
HOUSEWIFE SUPERSTAR
HUMPHRIES, JULIA
ALLEGRO
HUMPHRY, JOHN
HAMLET
HUNDLEY, HOT ROD
IT'S A WHOLE NEW BALL GAME
HUNG, TSIN TING KIANG
BEYOND THE GREAT WALL
HUNGARIAN STATE OPERA
KING SOLOMON'S MINES
HUNGARIAN STATE
SYMPHONY
SICILIAN
HUNT, JAN
SHOW BOAT
HUNT, LOIS
CAROUSEL
KING AND I
KISS ME KATE
OKLAHOMA
HUNT, RICHARD
MUPPET MOVIE
HUNTER, ALBERTA
REMEMBER MY NAME
HUNTER, CAROL
PAT GARRETT AND BILLY THE KID
HUNTER, FRANK
SOUNDS BROADWAY! SOUNDS
HOLLYWOOD! SOUNDS GREAT!
HUNTER, HANK
LOOKING FOR LOVE
HUNTER, IAN
FRIGHT NIGHT
LIGHT OF DAY
TEACHERS
UP THE ACADEMY
WRAITH
HUNTER, IVORY JOE
HEART OF DIXIE
HUNTER, LESLIE
THOUSAND MILES OF MOUNTAINS
HUNTER, ROBERT
SHOWGIRL (CAROL CHANNING
LIVE)
HUNTER, TAB
DAMN YANKEES
HANS BRINKER
HUNTLEY, CHET
TIME TO KEEP
HUNTLEY, JOBE
TAMBOURINES TO GLORY
HUNTSBERRY, HOWARD
LA BAMBA
HURD, DANNY
HAIR
HURLEY, LAUREL
MERRY WIDOW
NIGHT IN VENICE
HURST, JAMES
SAIL AWAY

HURT, JO
PAL JOEY
HUSMANN, RON
ALL AMERICAN
MAN OF LA MANCHA
TENDERLOIN
HUSSEY, OLIVIA
ROMEO AND JULIET
HUSTIN, TOM
HOUSE OF LEATHER
HUSTON, JOHN
BIBLE . . . IN THE BEGINNING
NIGHT OF THE IGUANA (AND
OTHER MUSIC INSPIRED BY THE
FILM)
HUSTON, WALTER
ICHABOD AND MR. TOAD
SWANEE RIVER
YANKEE DOODLE DANDY
HUTCH, WILLIE
FOXY BROWN
MACK
HUTCHINSON, BRENDA
LIQUID SKY
HUTTON, BETTY
ANNIE GET YOUR GUN
BY THE BEAUTIFUL SEA
GREATEST SHOW ON EARTH
SATINS AND SPURS
SOMEBODY LOVES ME
HUTTON, BILL
FESTIVAL
JOSEPH AND THE AMAZING
TECHNICOLOR DREAMCOAT
HUTTON, DANNY
AMERICAN FLYERS
PRETTY IN PINK
HUTTON, JUNE
PAL JOEY
HYDE, BRUCE
CANTERBURY TALES
HYDE-WHITE, WILFRID
IN SEARCH OF THE CASTAWAYS
MY FAIR LADY
HYLAN, MARY
APPLE
HYLTON, JACK
WHITE HORSE INN
HYMAN, DICK
GIGI
HANNAH AND HER SISTERS
MOONSTRUCK
SCOTT JOPLIN
WHOOP-UP!
HYMAN, PHYLLIS
FISH THAT SAVED PITTSBURGH
SCHOOL DAZE
SOPHISTICATED LADIES
HYMAN, ROBERT
JOSEPH AND THE AMAZING
TECHNICOLOR DREAMCOAT
HYMAS, TONY
TWINS
HYNES, ELIZABETH
SILVER LAKE
HYSON, RAY
ON YOUR TOES
YOUNG ABE LINCOLN

I

IAN, JANIS
BETRAYAL
IANNI, RICHARD
ATHENIAN TOUCH
IBERT, JACQUES
INVITATION TO THE DANCE
IDLE, ERIC
LIFE OF BRIAN
MONTY PYTHON AND THE HOLY
GRAIL
IDOLLS
ASSAULT OF THE KILLER BIMBOS
IGNICO, ROBIN
FEELING GOOD WITH ANNIE
IMPERIALS
THAT'S THE WAY IT IS
IMPRESSIONS
FLAMINGO KID
THREE THE HARD WAY
INCANTATION
MISSION
INCREDIBLE STRING BAND
TAKING OFF
INFERNAL BLUE MACHINE
ADIOS AMIGO
INFORMATION SOCIETY
EARTH GIRLS ARE EASY
ING, ALVIN
PACIFIC OVERTURES
INGELS, MARTY
KISS ME KATE
INGHAM, BARRIE
GYPSY
INGLE, JOHN
LOVERS
INGRAHM, LUTHER
WATTSTAX (THE LIVING WORD)
INGRAM, JAMES
AMERICAN TAIL
BEVERLY HILLS COP II
WILDCATS
INGRAM, MICHAEL
PREPPIES
INGRAM, NICK
JESUS CHRIST SUPERSTAR
INGRAM, PHILIP
BACK TO SCHOOL
INNER CIRCLE
ROCKERS
INNES, NEIL
MONTY PYTHON AND THE HOLY
GRAIL
RUTLES
INSIDERS
IRON EAGLE II
**INVESTITURE AND CRIME
WAVE**
TEENAGE MUTANT NINJA
TURTLES
INXS
AMERICAN ANTHEM
LOST BOYS

PRETTY IN PINK
IOWA FOUR
MUSIC MAN
IRISH GUARDS
WILD GEESE
IRISH ROVERS
ROCKABYE HAMLET
IRON BUTTERFLY
MANHUNTER
SAVAGE SEVEN
IRONS, JEREMY
BRIDESHEAD REVISITED
MY FAIR LADY
REAL THING
IRVING, AMY
HONEYSUCKLE ROSE
IRVING, GEORGE
AN EVENING WITH RICHARD
NIXON
ANYA
BODY IN THE SEINE
BRAVO GIOVANNI!
GENTLEMEN PREFER BLONDES
I REMEMBER MAMA
IRENE
IRMA LA DOUCE
ME AND MY GIRL
REGINA
SO LONG 174TH STREET
THREEPENNY OPERA
TOVARICH
TWO'S COMPANY
IRVING, JOHN
ERNEST IN LOVE
IRVING, KATIE
CARRIE
IRWIN, JACK
BEST FOOT FORWARD
SINGLE ROOM FURNISHED
IRWIN, WAYNE
THREE IN THE ATTIC
IRWIN, WILL
LITTLEST REVUE
TEXAS LI'L DARLIN'
ISAACS, GREGORY
ROCKERS
ISAAK, CHRIS
AMERICAN FLYERS
MARRIED TO THE MOB
SHAG
ISACKSON, MICK
BOY MEETS BOY
ISHAM, MARK
BEAST
COUNTRY
MADE IN HEAVEN
MODERNS
MRS. SOFFEL
TROUBLE IN MIND
ISHEE, SUZANNE
JERRY'S GIRLS
ISLEY BROTHERS
WANDERERS
WILDCATS
ITO, TELJI
COACH WITH THE SIX INSIDES
IUNICK, JONATHAN
LITTLE NIGHT MUSIC
IVERS, PETER
ERASERHEAD

IVERSEN, YVONNE
ULYSSES - THE GREEK SUITE
IVES, BURL
HUGO THE HIPPO
IN SEARCH OF THE CASTAWAYS
LONESOME TRAIN
MUSIC FROM DISNEY MOTION
PICTURES
SING OUT SWEET LAND
STORY OF RUDOLPH THE
RED-NOSED REINDEER
SUMMER MAGIC
IVORY
LICENSE TO KILL
IWANOW, TATJANA
HELLO DOLLY!

J

JABARA, PAUL
HAIR
HONKY-TONK FREEWAY
MAIN EVENT
MOTHER, JUGS AND SPEED
THANK GOD IT'S FRIDAY
JACERO, TEO
DYLAN
**JACK AND JILL LITTLE
PEOPLE**
ANNIE GET YOUR GUN
JACKIE AND GAYLE
WILD ON THE BEACH
WILD, WILD WINTER
JACKMAN, HOPE
OLIVER
JACKSON FIVE
GOIN' BACK TO INDIANA
SAVE THE CHILDREN
SKATETOWN U.S.A.
JACKSON, ANNE
BRECHT ON BRECHT
JACKSON, C.
FLY BLACKBIRD
JACKSON, CHUCK
PATTY
JACKSON, ERNESTINE
GUYS AND DOLLS
RAISIN
JACKSON, FREDDIE
ALL DOGS GO TO HEAVEN
JACKSON, GLENDA
MARAT (DE) SADE
STEVIE
TELL ME LIES
JACKSON, HARRIETT
PORGY AND BESS
JACKSON, JACKIE
MY STEPMOTHER IS AN ALIEN
JACKSON, JERMAINE
BEVERLY HILLS COP II
I'M GONNA GIT YOU SUCKA
LOVING COUPLES
PERFECT
JACKSON, JO
BELIEVERS

KAMEN, MICHAEL
  ADVENTURES OF BARON
    MUNCHAUSEN
  LETHAL WEAPON
  LETHAL WEAPON 2
  LICENSE TO KILL
  NEXT MAN
KAMON, KAREN
  FLASHDANCE
KAMOZE, INI
  GOOD TO GO
KANDER, JOHN
  ACT
  AN EVENING WITH FRED EBB
    AND JOHN KANDER
  CABARET
  CHICAGO
  FAMILY AFFAIR
  FLORA THE RED MENACE
  FUNNY LADY
  GO FLY A KITE
  HAPPY TIME
  LIZA MINNELLI AT THE
    WINTERGARDEN
  LIZA WITH A "Z"
  LUCKY LADY
  NEW YORK, NEW YORK
  RINK
  70 GIRLS, 70
  WOMAN OF THE YEAR
  ZORBA
KANDIDATE
  SUNBURN
KANE GANG
  BAD GUYS
KANE, ARTIE
  EYES OF LAURA MARS
  FAREWELL, MY LOVELY
  LOOKING FOR MR. GOODBAR
KANE, BIG DADDY
  COLORS
  LEAN ON ME
KANE, BYRON
  STAN FREBERG SHOWS
KANE, CAROL
  WORLD'S GREATEST LOVER
KANE, HELEN
  PENNIES FROM HEAVEN
  THREE LITTLE WORDS
KANE, IRENE
  TENDERLOIN
KANSAS, JERRY
  42nd STREET
KAPER, BRONISLAU
  AUNTIE MAME
  BUTTERFIELD 8
  FLEA IN HER EAR
  GET CRAZY
  KAPER: THE FILM MUSIC OF
    BRONISLAW
  LILI
  LORD JIM
  LOVE THEMES FROM MOTION
    PICTURES
  MUTINY ON THE BOUNTY
  SWAN
  THAT'S ENTERTAINMENT
  WAY WEST
KAPLAN, ELLIOT
  FINNEGAN'S WAKE
  SQUARE ROOT OF ZERO

KAPLAN, MARVIN
  TOP CAT
KAPLAN, SOL
  DOCTOR STRANGELOVE (AND
    OTHER GREAT MOVIE THEMES)
  JUDITH
  LIVING FREE
  SPY WHO CAME IN FROM THE
    COLD
  VICTORS
  YOUNG LOVERS
KAPROFF, DANA
  GOLDEN SEAL
KARAS, ANTON
  THIRD MAN
KARATY, TOMMY
  CINDY
KAREN, KENNY
  IF EVER I SEE YOU AGAIN
KARGER, FRED
  ANGEL, ANGEL, DOWN WE GO
  EDDY DUCHIN STORY
  FASTEST GUITAR ALIVE
  FRANKIE AND JOHNNY
  GET YOURSELF A COLLEGE GIRL
  KISSIN' COUSINS
  WHEN THE BOYS MEET THE GIRLS
  YOUR CHEATIN' HEART
KARIN, FIA
  PARADE
KARIN, RITA
  WALL
KARLIN, FRED
  BABY MAKER
  CALIFORNIA DREAMING
  LEADBELLY
  LOVERS AND OTHER STRANGERS
  LOVING COUPLES
  MAX MORATH AT THE TURN OF
    THE CENTURY
  STERILE CUCKOO
  UP THE DOWN STAIRCASE
  WESTWORLD
  YOURS, MINE AND OURS
KARLIN, MIRIAM
  FIDDLER ON THE ROOF
KARLOFF, BORIS
  AN EVENING WITH BORIS
    KARLOFF AND HIS FRIENDS
  HOW THE GRINCH STOLE
    CHRISTMAS
  PETER PAN
  UGLY DUCKLING
KARLTON, SYLVIA
  ALLEGRO
KARM, MICHAEL
  TWO BY TWO
KARMEN, STEVE
  CANDIDATE
  WHAT DO YOU SAY TO A NAKED
    LADY?
KARMOYAN, MICHAEL
  ANYA
KARNILOVA, MARIA
  BRAVO GIOVANNI!
  BRING BACK BIRDIE
  FIDDLER ON THE ROOF
  GIGI
  GYPSY
  ZORBA

KARP, CHARLIE
  SPEED ZONE
KARR, HAROLD
  HAPPY HUNTING
KARR, PATTI
  MUSICAL CHAIRS
  SO LONG 174TH STREET
KASEM, CASEY
  GLORY STOMPERS
KASHA, AL
  PETE'S DRAGON
  TOWERING INFERNO
KASKET, HAROLD
  SOUND OF MUSIC
KASSIR, JOHN
  THREE GUYS NAKED FROM THE
    WAIST DOWN
KASZNAR, KURT
  ANDROCLES AND THE LION
  SOUND OF MUSIC
  WAITING FOR GODOT
KATONA, JULIUS
  SEVEN DEADLY SINS
KATRINA AND THE WAVES
  IRON EAGLE
KATZ, CHARLIE
  GENTLEMEN PREFER BLONDES
KATZ, FRED
  SWEET SMELL OF SUCCESS
KATZ, MICKEY
  HELLO SOLLY!
KAUER, GENE
  ACROSS THE GREAT DIVIDE
KAUFLINN, JACK
  YOUNG ABE LINCOLN
KAUFMAN, ERWIN
  ALADD
KAUFMAN, JEFFREY
  AMERICAN GAME
KAUFMAN, PEARL
  FIVE EASY PIECES
KAULILI, ALVINA
  THIRTEEN DAUGHTERS
KAVA, CAROLINE
  THREEPENNY OPERA
KAY, ARTHUR
  SONG OF NORWAY
KAY, BARBARA
  JOANNA
KAY, SUSAN
  TAMALPAIS EXCHANGE
KAYE, ALMA
  SING OUT SWEET LAND
KAYE, ANNE
  NOW IS THE TIME FOR ALL GOOD
    MEN
KAYE, BERYL
  JOYCE GRENFELL REQUESTS THE
    PLEASURE
KAYE, BUDDY
  MAN CALLED DAGGER
  THAT MAN IN ISTANBUL

MacMURRAY, FRED
ABSENT-MINDED PROFESSOR
APARTMENT
CAINE MUTINY
HAPPIEST MILLIONAIRE

MacNEE, PATRICK
CAMELOT

MacRAE, GORDON
BEST THINGS IN LIFE ARE FREE
BY THE LIGHT OF THE SILVERY
MOON
CAROUSEL
DESERT SONG
KISMET
MERRY WIDOW
NAUGHTY MARIETTA
NEW MOON
OKLAHOMA
ROBERTA
STUDENT PRINCE
3 SAILORS AND A GIRL

MacRAE, HEATHER
PERFECT COUPLE

MADAM X
FATAL BEAUTY

MADDEN, DONALD
FIRST IMPRESSIONS

MADDEN, JEANNE
KNICKERBOCKER HOLIDAY

MADDEN, RONALD
MISS JULIE

MADDOX, DIANA
UNDER MILK WOOD

MADIGAN, AMY
ALAMO BAY

MADIGAN, BETTY
STINGIEST MAN IN TOWN

MADISON, GUY
SPOTLIGHT ON WILD BILL
HICKOCK

MADNESS
DANCE CRAZE

MADONNA
VISION QUEST
WHO'S THAT GIRL?

MAGAZINE
URGH - A MUSIC WAR

MAGEE, PATRICK
MARAT (DE) SADE

MAGGART, BRANDON
APPLAUSE
LORELEI
MUSICAL CHAIRS
NEW FACES OF 1968

MAGNE, MICHEL
CIRCLE OF LOVE

MAGNESS-BALLARD
TWO OF A KIND

MAGNUSEN, MICHAEL
FESTIVAL

MAGOON, EATON, JR.
THIRTEEN DAUGHTERS

MAGUIRE, JAMES
BOLD VENTURES

MAGUIRE, PAUL
TELL ME ON A SUNDAY

MAHLER, GUSTAV
DEATH IN VENICE
FEMALE PRISONER

MAHR, BEVERLY
CALIFORNIA
SEVEN DREAMS

MAIDEN, RON
CREEPERS

MAIN INGREDIENT
SAVE THE CHILDREN

MAIN, MARJORIE
ROSE MARIE

MAITLAND, DEXTER
NIGHT THEY RAIDED MINSKY'S

MAKO
PACIFIC OVERTURES

MALACHI THRONE
EMPIRE STRIKES BACK

MALBIN, ELAINE
CONNECTICUT YANKEE
FIREFLY
MERRY WIDOW
NAUGHTY MARIETTA
THAT MIDNIGHT KISS
TOAST OF NEW ORLEANS

MALCOLM, GEORGE
HANNAH AND HER SISTERS

MALDEN, KARL
BABY DOLL
GYPSY
POLLYANNA

MALLE, LOUIS
VIVA MARIA!

MALLORY, DOUG
BEOWULF

MALLORY, VICTORIA
FOLLIES
LITTLE NIGHT MUSIC
STEPHEN SONDHEIM EVENING

MALNECK, MATTY
LOVE IN THE AFTERNOON
SOME LIKE IT HOT

MALNICK, MICHAEL
MUSIC MAN

MALONE, CINDY
WILD ON THE BEACH

MALONE, GIA
MARY POPPINS

MALOOF, ALEXANDER
LAWRENCE OF ARABIA

MALTBY, RICHARD, JR.
SAP OF LIFE
STARTING HERE, STARTING NOW

MALTBY, RICHARD
BABY
MISTER LUCKY
SUMMER PLACE (AND OTHER
GREAT HITS FROM MOVIES)

MAMAS AND THE PAPAS
AMERICAN POP

MAN, HENRY
THEMES FROM CLASSIC SCIENCE
FICTION, FANTASY AND
HORROR FILMS

MANCHESTER, MELISSA
ICE CASTLES

MANCINI, HENRY
ARABESQUE
BEST OF MANCINI
BEST OF MANCINI (VOL. 2)
BIG SCREEN/LITTLE SCREEN
BLIND DATE
BORN ON THE FOURTH OF JULY

BREAKFAST AT TIFFANY'S
CHARADE
COP SHOW THEMES
DARLING LILI
DAYS OF WINE AND ROSES (AND
OTHER GREAT MOVIE THEMES)
ENCORE! MORE OF THE MUSIC OF
HENRY MANCINI
EXPERIMENT IN TERROR
FINE MESS
GAILY, GAILY
GLASS MENAGERIE
GREAT RACE
GREAT WALDO PEPPER
GUNN
HATARI
HAWAIIANS
HENRY MANCINI PRESENTS THE
ACADEMY AWARD SONGS
HIGH TIME
IMPACT
LIFEFORCE
MANCINI GENERATION
ME NATALIE
MISTER LUCKY
MOLLY MAGUIRES
MUSIC FROM PETER GUNN
NARM'S GOLDEN DECADE
OKLAHOMA CRUDE
OUR MAN IN HOLLYWOOD
PARTY
PETER GUNN
PINK PANTHER
PINK PANTHER STRIKES AGAIN
RETURN OF THE PINK PANTHER
REVENGE OF THE PINK PANTHER
SECOND TIME AROUND
SOMETIMES A GREAT NOTION
SUMMER LOVE
SUNFLOWER
10
THAT'S DANCING!
THAT'S ENTERTAINMENT
THEMES FROM CLASSIC SCIENCE
FICTION, FANTASY AND
HORROR FILMS
THIEF WHO CAME TO DINNER
TOUCH OF EVIL
TRAIL OF THE PINK PANTHER
TWO FOR THE ROAD
VICTOR/VICTORIA
VISIONS OF EIGHT
W.C. FIELDS AND ME
WHAT DID YOU DO IN THE WAR,
DADDY?
WHO IS KILLING THE GREAT
CHEFS OF EUROPE?

MANDEL, JOHNNY
AGATHA
AMERICANIZATION OF EMILY
CADDYSHACK
ESCAPE TO WITCH MOUNTAIN
HARPER
I WANT TO LIVE
M*A*S*H
OSCAR
RUSSIANS ARE COMING! THE
RUSSIANS ARE COMING!
SANDPIPER
SOUP FOR ONE

MANDEL, JULIE
TWO

MANDEL, STEVE
DELIVERANCE

O

O'BANNON, DAN
DARK STAR

O'BRIAN, HUGH
FRANCES LANGFORD PRESENTS

O'BRIEN, EDMOND
JULIUS CAESAR

O'BRIEN, LOUISE
DESTRY RIDES AGAIN

O'BRIEN, MARGARET
MEET ME IN ST. LOUIS

O'BRIEN, PAT
PAT O'BRIEN
TWENTY MILLION SWEETHEARTS

O'BRIEN, RICHARD
ROCKY HORROR PICTURE SHOW
ROCKY HORROR SHOW
SHOCK TREATMENT

O'BRIEN, SYLVIA
MY FAIR LADY

O'BRIEN, VINCE
PROMISES, PROMISES

O'BRIEN, VIRGINIA
HARVEY GIRLS
TILL THE CLOUDS ROLL BY

O'CONNELL, HELEN
BY THE BEAUTIFUL SEA

O'CONNOR, CARROLL
ALL IN THE FAMILY
ALL IN THE FAMILY - 2ND ALBUM
FOSTER BROOKS' ROASTS
OF THEE I SING

O'CONNOR, DONALD
ANYTHING GOES
BRING BACK BIRDIE
CALL ME MADAM
I LOVE MELVIN
OLYMPUS 7-0000
SINGIN' IN THE RAIN
THAT'S DANCING!
THAT'S ENTERTAINMENT
THERE'S NO BUSINESS LIKE
  SHOW BUSINESS

O'CONNOR, GLYNNIS
CALIFORNIA DREAMING
JEREMY

O'CONNOR, GRACE
PLAIN AND FANCY

O'CONNOR, HAZEL
BREAKING GLASS

O'CONNOR, RITA
CABARET
FOLLIES

O'CONNOR, SINEAD
MARRIED TO THE MOB

O'DAY, ANITA
GENE KRUPA STORY
TORCH SONG TRILOGY

O'DEA, DENIS
TREASURE ISLAND

O'DONOVAN, ROSS
STAR STRUCK

O'FARRELL, MARY
MacBETH

O'HARA, JENNY
DYLAN

O'HARA, JILL
GEORGE M.!
HAIR
PROMISES, PROMISES

O'HARA, MAUREEN
CHRISTINE
IN SEARCH OF THE CASTAWAYS
PARENT TRAP
SUMMER MAGIC

O'HAUGHEY, M.
CHICAGO

O'HORGAN, TOM
LENNY

O'JAYS
JO JO DANCER, YOUR LIFE IS
  CALLING
SAVE THE CHILDREN

O'KEEFE, PAUL
DAYDREAMER
SAIL AWAY

O'KUN, LAN
LITTLEST ANGEL

O'MALLEY, J. PAT
DARBY O'GILL AND THE LITTLE
  PEOPLE
HEY THERE, IT'S YOGI BEAR
OF THEE I SING

O'MALLEY, MURIEL
ALLEGRO
SONG OF NORWAY
SOUND OF MUSIC

O'MAY, JOHN
STAR STRUCK

O'NEAL, FREDERICK
BALLAD FOR BIMSHIRE

O'NEAL, RYAN
LOVE STORY

O'NEIL, TRICIA
TWO BY TWO

O'NEILL, DICK
PROMISES, PROMISES
SKYSCRAPER

O'NEILL, SHEILA
ONE OVER THE EIGHT

O'NEILL, TOM
LITTLE WILLIE JR.'S
  RESURRECTION

O'REILLY, JOHN
HARD JOB BEING GOD
VIRGIN

O'REILLY, ROSEMARY
NEW FACES OF 1952

O'RIORDAN, CAIT
STRAIGHT TO HELL

O'SHEA, MILO
DEAR WORLD
ROMEO AND JULIET

O'SHEA, TESSIE
GIRL WHO CAME TO SUPPER
TIME FOR SINGING

O'SULLIVAN, MAUREEN
HANNAH AND HER SISTERS

O'SULLIVAN, MICHAEL
IN WHITE AMERICA
IT'S A BIRD, IT'S A PLANE, IT'S
  SUPERMAN

O'TOOLE, ANNETTE
FIRST NUDIE MUSICAL

O'TOOLE, PETER
BECKET
BIBLE . . . IN THE BEGINNING
GOODBYE MR. CHIPS
MAN OF LA MANCHA
RULING CLASS

OAKES, BETTY
OF THEE I SING

OAKES, BILL
GREASE

OAKES, GARY
BOYS FROM SYRACUSE

OAKEY, PHILIP
ELECTRIC DREAMS

OAKMAN, WHEELER
FLASH GORDON

OATES, JOHN
EARTH GIRLS ARE EASY

OBOLER, ARCH
DROP DEAD! (AN EXERCISE IN
  HORROR)

OCASEK, RIC
KING OF COMEDY
MADE IN HEAVEN

OCEAN, BILLY
JEWEL OF THE NILE
LICENSE TO DRIVE

ODDIE, BILL
CAMBRIDGE CIRCUS

ODETTA
SING FOR YOUR SUPPER

ODYSSEY
EYES OF LAURA MARS

OFFENBACH, JACQUES
HAPPIEST GIRL IN THE WORLD
LA PERICHOLE
TALES OF HOFFMAN

OGDEN, BOBBY
CHRISTMAS TO ELVIS
ELVIS

OGERMAN, CLAUS
LOOKING FOR LOVE

OGSTON, BRUCE
THIEF OF BAGDAD

OH, SOON-TECH
PACIFIC OVERTURES

OHMAN, PHIL
LADY BE GOOD

OHRINGER, JANE
EVITA

OINGO BOINGO
BACHELOR PARTY
FAST TIMES AT RIDGEMONT HIGH
LAST AMERICAN VIRGIN
SHE'S OUT OF CONTROL
SOMETHING WILD
TEXAS CHAINSAW MASSACRE
  PART 2
URGH - A MUSIC WAR
WEIRD SCIENCE

OKKOSSUN, SONNY
SOMETHING WILD

OLAF, PIERRE
CARNIVAL

OLD VICTOR COMPANY
BEGGAR'S OPERA

OLDFIELD, MIKE
EXORCIST
KILLING FIELDS

OWEN, GWENLLIAN
UNDER MILK WOOD
OWENS, BONNIE
KILLERS THREE
OWENS, HARRY
WAIKIKI WEDDING
OWENS, PHILIP
FAGGOT
OWENS, ROCHELLE
KARL MARX
OXFORD, EARL
NEW MOON
THIS IS THE ARMY
OZ, FRANK
EMPIRE STRIKES BACK
MUPPET MOVIE
OZONE
IT'S MY TURN

P

PG&E
TELL ME THAT YOU LOVE ME,
JUNIE MOON
P.K. LIMITED
GETTING STRAIGHT
PABLO CRUISE
INSIDE MOVES
PACE, JEAN
JOY
PACE, THOM
NIGHT OF THE COMET
PACK, DAVID
WHITE NIGHTS
PADILLA, SANDY
JOAN
POMEGRANADA
PAGE, CAROLANN
CANDIDE
PAGE, EVELYN
CANTERBURY TALES
PAGE, FRANK
ELVIS LIVE AT THE LOUISIANA
HAYRIDE
LOUISIANA HAYRIDE
PAGE, GENE
BLACULA
BREWSTER McCLOUD
SILENCERS
PAGE, GERALDINE
HAPPIEST MILLIONAIRE
RESCUERS
STRANGE INTERLUDE
PAGE, JIMMY
DEATH WISH II
SONG REMAINS THE SAME
PAGE, KEN
AIN'T MISBEHAVIN'
CATS
GUYS AND DOLLS
OFFICIAL GRAMMY AWARDS
ARCHIVE COLLECTION

PAGE, PATTI
MANHATTAN TOWER
ZABRISKIE POINT
PAGE, STAN
SAGA OF THE DINGBAT
PAGE, TOMMY
SHAG
PAGE, VERONICA
LITTLE NIGHT MUSIC
PAHL, MEL
ADVENTURES OF MARCO POLO
PAICH, MARTY
HEY THERE, IT'S YOGI BEAR
HONG KONG
SWINGER
PAIGE, ELAINE
CHESS (A EUROPEAN MUSICAL)
CHESS PIECES
EVITA
PAIGE, JANIS
HERE'S LOVE
PAJAMA GAME
SILK STOCKINGS
PAINTED WILLIE
LOVEDOLLS SUPERSTAR
PALAPRAT, GERARD
HAIR
PALANCE, JACK
ALICE THROUGH THE LOOKING
GLASS
PALEY BROTHERS
ROCK 'N' ROLL HIGH SCHOOL
PALIN, MICHAEL
LIFE OF BRIAN
MONTY PYTHON AND THE HOLY
GRAIL
PALLYS, ANNA MARIA
MY FAIR LADY
PALMER, EARL
FABULOUS BAKER BOYS
PALMER, HAP
MOTHER EARTH
PALMER, HARRY
TIME CHANGES
PALMER, JONI
BILLY NONAME
PALMER, LELAND
PIPPIN
YOUR OWN THING
PALMER, PETER
CHOCOLATE SOLDIER
DESERT SONG
LI'L ABNER
LORELEI
PALMER, ROBERT
COLOR OF MONEY
PRETTY WOMAN
SWEET LIES
PALMER-JOST
FAST TIMES AT RIDGEMONT HIGH
PALMERMO, NINO
GODFATHER PART II
PALUZZI, LUCIANA
THUNDERBALL

PANARAMA
FIRE AND ICE
**PANHANDLE MYSTERY
BAND**
SOUNDS FROM TRUE STORIES
PANTSCHEFF, LJUBOMIR
MERRY WIDOW
PARAMOR, NORRIE
JUDY GARLAND
SWINGER'S PARADISE
PARDO, DON
SATURDAY NIGHT LIVE
PARENT, CLAUDE
YOUNG GIRLS OF ROCHEFORT
PARHAN, GLOVER
PORGY AND BESS
PARIS SISTERS
SINGLE ROOM FURNISHED
PARIS, JACKIE
DOCTOR SELAVY'S MAGIC
THEATRE
PARIS, JUDITH
AMBASSADOR
PARIS, NORMAN
DAVID AND LISA
DECLINE AND FALL OF THE
ENTIRE WORLD AS SEEN
THROUGH THE EYES OF COLE
PORTER
IRVING BERLIN REVISITED
PENNEY PROUD
RODGERS AND HART REVISITED
PARIS, TONY
SAY ONE FOR ME
PARKER, ALAN
JAWS 3-D
PARKER, CHARLIE
BIRD
MURMUR OF THE HEART
PARKER, CLIFTON
DAMN THE DEFIANT
PARKER, ELEANOR
SOUND OF MUSIC
PARKER, FESS
DAVY CROCKETT
OLD YELLER
WESTWARD HO, THE WAGONS
PARKER, FRANK
ARTHUR GODFREY (CHRISTMAS
WITH ARTHUR GODFREY)
ARTHUR GODFREY'S TV
CALENDAR SHOW
PARKER, GRAHAM
HARD TO HOLD
TRUE LOVE
PARKER, JACK
MUSIC IN THE AIR
PARKER, JOHN
DALLAS
JESUS CHRIST SUPERSTAR
NO, NO, NANETTE
PARKER, LEONARD
FLY BLACKBIRD
PARKER, LEW
ANKLES AWEIGH

PARKER, LOUISE
SHOW BOAT
PARKER, RAY, JR.
GHOSTBUSTERS
QUICKSILVER
PARKER, ROXANN
FESTIVAL
PARKS, GORDON
LEARNING TREE
SHAFT'S BIG SCORE
PARKS, MICHAEL
BIBLE . . . IN THE BEGINNING
PARKS, VAN DYKE
POPEYE
PARNELL, JACK
SAMMY
PARNELL, MEL
IMPOSSIBLE DREAM - THE STORY
OF THE 1967 BOSTON RED SOX
PARR, JOHN
AMERICAN ANTHEM
SAINT ELMO'S FIRE
PARRAGA, GRACIELA
BLOOD AND SAND
PARRISH, ELIZABETH
LA CAGE AUX FOLLES (BIRDS OF
A FEATHER)
LITTLE MARY SUNSHINE
RIVERWIND
PARRISH, PAUL
FOOLS
PARRY, MALCOLM
JOSEPH AND THE AMAZING
TECHNICOLOR DREAMCOAT
PARRY, NATASHA
ROMEO AND JULIET
PARSONS, ADMIRAL
WILLIAM S.
QUICK AND THE DEAD - THE
STORY OF THE ATOM BOMB
PARSONS, ALAN
ICE CASTLES
PARSONS, ESTELLE
BONNIE AND CLYDE
MAKE MINE MANHATTAN
PIECES OF EIGHT
RODGERS AND HART REVISITED
TOO MANY GIRLS
WATERMELON MAN
PARTNERS IN KRYME
TEENAGE MUTANT NINJA
TURTLES
PARTON, DOLLY
BEST LITTLE WHOREHOUSE IN
TEXAS
NINE TO FIVE
RHINESTONE
PARTRIDGE, DON
OTLEY
PASADENA ROOF
ORCHESTRA
SCHONER GIGOLO - ARMER
GIGOLO (JUST A GIGOLO)
PASCAN, BORISLAV
LONG SHIPS
PASSIONNEL
UNDERCOVER

PASTELL, GEORGE
FLOWER DRUM SONG
PATACHOU
FOLIES BERGERE
INTERNATIONAL SOIREE
PATE, CHRISTOPHER
GODSPELL
PATE, JOHNNY
BROTHER ON THE RUN
SHAFT IN AFRICA
TIME CHANGES
PATERSON, IAN
IRMA LA DOUCE
PATINKIN, MANDY
EVITA
FOLLIES
SUNDAY IN THE PARK WITH
GEORGE
PATRICK, BUTCH
AT HOME WITH THE MUNSTERS
PATRICK, DENNIS
JOE
PATRICK, JULIAN
CARRY NATION
JUNO
MEDIUM
PATRICK, LORY
SURF PARTY
PATRICK, SONNY
GIGI
PATTERSON, BRENDA
BORDER
PAT GARRETT AND BILLY THE KID
PATTERSON, DICK
FADE OUT FADE IN
PATTERSON, LEE
THREE WORLDS OF GULLIVER
PATTERSON, LORNA
AIRPLANE!
PATTERSON, RICK
MINOR MIRACLE
PATTERSON, RUSSELL
CAPTAIN JINKS OF THE HORSE
MARINES
SWEET BYE AND BYE
PATTI, SANDI
PAPA WAS A PREACHER
PAUL AND PAULA
ANIMAL HOUSE
SLUMBER PARTY '57
PAUL AND THE PACK
DOCTOR GOLDFOOT AND THE
GIRL BOMBS
PAUL, ALAN
GREASE
PAUL, C.
LITTLEST ANGEL
PAUL, GLORIA
DARLING LILI
PAUL, JUSTIN
ALADD
PAUL, LYN
DOVE
PAULEE, MONA
MOST HAPPY FELLA
PAULETTE, LARRY
LET MY PEOPLE COME

PAULSEN, DAVID
TO LIVE ANOTHER SUMMER, TO
PASS ANOTHER WINTER
PAULSEN, PAT
HARPER VALLEY P.T.A.
PAVAN, MARISA
SHANGRI-LA
PAVAROTTI, LUCIANO
YES, GIORGIO
PAVEK, JANET
CHRISTINE
SHOW BOAT
PAXON, GLENN
FIRST IMPRESSIONS
PAYCHECK, JOHNNY
TAKE THIS JOB AND SHOVE IT
PAYNE, CECIL
CONNECTION
PAYNE, DON
FEMALE ANIMAL
PAYNE, JODY
HONEYSUCKLE ROSE
PAYNE, JOHN
GOOD NEWS
PAYNE, LAURIE
WATER GYPSIES
PAYNE, SARAH
SINGIN' IN THE RAIN
PAYNTER, JOHN
AMONG FRIENDS - WAA-MU
SHOW OF 1960
PBF
KARATE KID III
PEAKE, DON
BLACULA
ZIGZAG
PEANUT BUTTER
CONSPIRACY
ANGELS FROM HELL
PEARCE, ALICE
BODY IN THE SEINE
GENTLEMEN PREFER BLONDES
SAIL AWAY
PEARS, PETER
FACADE
PEARSON, CAROL LYNN
MY TURN ON EARTH
ORDER IS LOVE
PEARSON, JESSE
BYE BYE BIRDIE
PEARY, HAL
GREAT GILDERSLEEVE
PEASLEE, RICHARD
MARAT (DE) SADE
TELL ME LIES
PEBBLES
BEVERLY HILLS COP II
PECK, CHARLES
MY FAIR LADY
PECK, DANNY
SECRET OF MY SUCCESS
PECK, GREGORY
JOHN F. KENNEDY
LITTLEST ANGEL
PECK, JON
AN EVENING WITH SAMMY CAHN

PECORINO, JOE
  BEATLEMANIA
PEDDLERS
  GOODBYE GEMINI
PEDERSEN, HERB
  SMOKEY AND THE BANDIT II
PEDERSON, HAL JAMES
  JOSEPH McCARTHY IS ALIVE AND
    WELL AND LIVING IN DADE
    COUNTY
PEDLAR, STUART
  SIDE BY SIDE BY SONDHEIM
PEEL, EILEEN
  COCKTAIL PARTY
PEEPLES, NIA
  SING
PEERCE, JAN
  AN EVENING WITH LERNER AND
    LOEWE
  BRIGADOON
  PAINT YOUR WAGON
  STUDENT PRINCE
  TONIGHT WE SING
PEGRAM, NIGEL
  WAIT A MINIM!
PELÉ
  PELÉ
PEN, POLLY
  CHARLOTTE SWEET
PENDERECKI, KRZYSZTOF
  EXORCIST
PENDERGRASS, TEDDY
  ROADIE
  SOUP FOR ONE
PENDLETON, AUSTIN
  FIDDLER ON THE ROOF
  LAST SWEET DAYS OF ISAAC
PENHALIGON, SUSAN
  PATRICK
PENN, BOB
  CINDERELLA
PENN, DAN
  BORDER
PENN, ROBERT
  KEAN
  PAINT YOUR WAGON
PENNA, PHILIP DELLA
  OLYMPUS 7-0000
PENNINO, FRANCESCO
  GODFATHER, PARTS I & II
PENNY AND SONDRA
  PURPLE PEOPLE EATER
PERA, RADAMES
  KUNG-FU
PERACHI, LEO
  SALUDOS AMIGOS (MUSIC FROM
    SOUTH OF THE BORDER)
PERCASSI, DON
  CHORUS LINE
PERCIVAL, JOHN
  CHOCOLATE SOLDIER
  MIKADO
PERCIVAL, LANCE
  ONE OVER THE EIGHT
PERETTI, HUGO
  MAGGIE FLYNN
PERIC, BLANKA
  BLOSSOM TIME

PERICOLI, EMILIO
  ROME ADVENTURE
PERITO, NICK
  ORIGINAL MOTION PICTURE HIT
    THEMES
PERKINS, ANTHONY
  BLACK HOLE (THE STORY OF THE
    BLACK HOLE)
  GREENWILLOW
  RODGERS AND HART REVISITED
  TOO MANY GIRLS
PERKINS, BILL
  HOT BLOOD
PERKINS, CARL
  DINER
  G.I. BLUES
  JAMBOREE!
  LITTLE FAUSS AND BIG HALSY
  PORKY'S REVENGE
PERKINS, FRANK
  GYPSY
  PALM SPRINGS WEEKEND
PERKINS, PATTI
  TUSCALOOSA'S CALLING ME
    (BUT I'M NOT GOING)
PERKINSON, COLERIDGE
  IF HE HOLLERS, LET HIM GO
PERKINSON, TAYLOR
  EDUCATION OF SONNY CARSON
PERREAU, GIGI
  JAMES DEAN STORY
PERREN, FREDDIE
  COOLEY HIGH
PERRI
  DO THE RIGHT THING
PERRIN, GEORGE
  EUROPEAN HOLIDAY
PERRINS, VALERIE
  W.C. FIELDS AND ME
PERRONE, ANNETTE
  JACQUES BREL IS ALIVE AND
    WELL AND LIVING IN PARIS
PERRY, ALFRED
  HONEY WEST
  RISE AND FALL OF THE THIRD
    REICH
PERRY, DOLORES
  AN EVENING WITH JEROME KERN
  PASSING FAIR
PERRY, JOHN BENNETT
  NOW IS THE TIME FOR ALL GOOD
    MEN
PERRY, MARENDA
  RAISIN
PERRY, ROD
  EARTHQUAKE
  NEW FACES OF 1968
  TO BROADWAY WITH LOVE
PERSHING, D'VAUGHN
  ROCKY HORROR SHOW
PERSOFF, NEHEMIAH
  AMERICAN TAIL
PERSSON, RUBY
  YOU'RE A GOOD MAN, CHARLIE
    BROWN
PERTWEE, JON
  FUNNY THING HAPPENED ON THE
    WAY TO THE FORUM

PETER, PAUL AND MARY
  AMERICAN POP
PETERS, BERNADETTE
  ANNIE
  DAMES AT SEA
  GEORGE M.!
  INTO THE WOODS
  MACK AND MABEL
  SUNDAY IN THE PARK WITH
    GEORGE
PETERS, BROCK
  CARMEN JONES
  JACK JOHNSON
  KWAMINA
  SHOWCASE ALBUM, 1967
  SING FOR YOUR SUPPER
PETERS, LAURI
  CRADLE WILL ROCK
  FIRST IMPRESSIONS
  SOUND OF MUSIC
PETERS, ROBERTA
  CAROUSEL
  STUDENT PRINCE
  TONIGHT WE SING
PETERSEN, PAUL
  HAPPIEST MILLIONAIRE
PETERSON, CALEB
  TILL THE CLOUDS ROLL BY
PETERSON, ERIC
  BILLY BISHOP GOES TO WAR
PETERSON, KURT
  DEAR WORLD
  FOLLIES
PETERSON, LeVERNE
  CARMEN JONES
PETERSON, OSCAR
  FRED ASTAIRE SINGS AND
    SWINGS IRVING BERLIN
  PLAY IT AGAIN, SAM
  SILENT PARTNER
PETERSON, PAUL
  BYE BYE BIRDIE
PETINA, IRRA
  ANYA
  CANDIDE
  SONG OF NORWAY
PETRAK, RUDOLF
  INTERRUPTED MELODY
PETRICOFF, ELAINE
  HARK!
  ONE WAY TICKET TO BROADWAY
PETRIE, GEORGE
  OFFICIAL ADVENTURES OF
    FLASH GORDON
PETRIE, SONYA
  GYPSY
PETTICOATS
  JACK AND THE BEANSTALK
PETTY, GWENYTH
  UNDER MILK WOOD
PETTY, TOM
  FM
  VOICES
PEVNEY, JAY
  JOSEPH McCARTHY IS ALIVE AND
    WELL AND LIVING IN DADE
    COUNTY

TWENTY MILLION SWEETHEARTS
POWELL, EDGAR
KING AND I
MY FAIR LADY
OKLAHOMA
POWELL, JANE
ALICE IN WONDERLAND
AN EVENING WITH LERNER AND
LOEWE
ATHENA
BRIGADOON
DEEP IN MY HEART
GIRL MOST LIKELY
HIT THE DECK
NANCY GOES TO RIO
PAINT YOUR WAGON
RICH, YOUNG AND PRETTY
ROYAL WEDDING
RUGGLES OF RED GAP
SEVEN BRIDES FOR SEVEN
BROTHERS
3 SAILORS AND A GIRL
TWO WEEKS WITH LOVE
POWELL, JANET
EUBIE
POWELL, JERRY
ALL ABOUT LIFE
POWELL, LOVELADY
RIVERWIND
SEX LIFE OF PRIMATE (AND
OTHER BITS OF GOSSIP)
POWELL, MITCHELL
APARTMENT
EXODUS
ON THE BEACH
POWELL, SHEZWAE
LET MY PEOPLE COME
POWER TOOL
BILL AND TED'S EXCELLENT
ADVENTURE
POWER, DICK
HOLLYWOOD HOTEL
POWER, TYRONE
JOHN BROWN'S BODY
POWERS, MARIE
MEDIUM
POWERS, TOM
OH BOY!
POWERS, WILL
PUMPING IRON 2 - THE WOMEN
PRAGER, STANLEY
PAJAMA GAME
**PRAGUE SYMPHONY
ORCHESTRA**
ADRIFT
PRAY FOR RAIN
STRAIGHT TO HELL
PRECIOUS METAL
BAD GUYS
PRECIOUS WILSON
JEWEL OF THE NILE
PREMICE, JOSEPHINE
BUBBLING BROWN SUGAR
HAND IS ON THE GATE
HOUSE OF FLOWERS
JAMAICA
PRESES, PETER
MERRY WIDOW

PRESLEY, ELVIS
BLUE HAWAII
CLAMBAKE
DINER
DOUBLE TROUBLE
EASY COME, EASY GO
ELVIS (NBC-TV SPECIAL)
ELVIS IN CONCERT
ELVIS: ALOHA FROM HAWAII VIA
SATELLITE
ELVIS LIVE AT THE LOUISIANA
HAYRIDE
FOLLOW THAT DREAM
FRANKIE AND JOHNNY
FUN IN ACAPULCO
G.I. BLUES
GIRL HAPPY
GIRLS! GIRLS! GIRLS!
HARUM SCARUM
HEART OF DIXIE
HEARTBREAK HOTEL
IT HAPPENED AT THE WORLD'S
FAIR
JAILHOUSE ROCK
KID GALAHAD
KING CREOLE
KISSIN' COUSINS
LOVE ME TENDER
LOVING YOU
PARADISE, HAWAIIAN STYLE
ROUSTABOUT
SPEEDWAY
SPINOUT
THAT'S THE WAY IT IS
THIS IS ELVIS
TICKLE ME
VIVA LAS VEGAS
PRESLEY, VERNON
ELVIS IN CONCERT
PRESNELL, HARVE
PAINT YOUR WAGON
UNSINKABLE MOLLY BROWN
WHEN THE BOYS MEET THE GIRLS
PRESSEL, MARC
JESUS CHRIST SUPERSTAR
PRESTON, BARRY
BUBBLING BROWN SUGAR
PRESTON, BILLY
FASTBREAK
LOVING COUPLES
MOTHER, JUGS AND SPEED
NIGHT THE LIGHTS WENT OUT IN
GEORGIA
SGT. PEPPER'S LONELY HEARTS
BAND
PRESTON, EDNA
FANNY
PRESTON, JOHNNY
SLUMBER PARTY '57
PRESTON, MARY
NO, NO, NANETTE
PRESTON, ROBERT
AUNTIE MAME
BEN FRANKLIN IN PARIS
I DO! I DO!
MACK AND MABEL
MUSIC MAN
STARTING HERE, STARTING NOW
VICTOR/VICTORIA
PRESTON, SIMON
HANNAH AND HER SISTERS
ROLLER BALL

PRETENDERS
KING OF COMEDY
NINETEEN SIXTY-NINE
TIMES SQUARE
PRETTY POISON
HIDING OUT
PREVIN, ANDRE
BELLS ARE RINGING
COCO
DEAD RINGER
ELMER GANTRY
EVERY GOOD BOY DESERVES
FAVOR
FORTUNE COOKIE
FOUR GIRLS IN TOWN
FOUR HORSEMEN OF THE
APOCALYPSE
GIGI
GOOD COMPANIONS
GOODBYE CHARLIE
HARPER
INSIDE DAISY CLOVER
INVITATION TO THE DANCE
IRMA LA DOUCE
IT'S ALWAYS FAIR WEATHER
JESUS CHRIST SUPERSTAR
KISMET
KISS ME KATE
LI'L ABNER
MUSIC LOVERS
MY FAIR LADY
ONE, TWO, THREE, WALTZ
PAINT YOUR WAGON
PEPE
PORGY AND BESS
RED PONY
ROLLER BALL
SILK STOCKINGS
SUBTERRANEANS
SWINGER
THOROUGHLY MODERN MILLIE
TWO FOR THE SEESAW
VALLEY OF THE DOLLS
WAY WEST
PREVIN, CHARLES
AN EVENING WITH BORIS
KARLOFF AND HIS FRIENDS
PREVIN, DORY
HARPER
MARY C. BROWN AND THE
HOLLYWOOD SIGN
THREE IN THE CELLAR
UP IN THE CELLAR
VALLEY OF THE DOLLS
PRICE, ALAN
O LUCKY MAN
PRICE, DENNIS
OH ROSALINDA!
PRICE, GERALD
FANNY
PRICE, GILBERT
JERICO-JIM CROW
PROMENADE
PRICE, HANNAH
ALADD
PRICE, JIM
MAHONEY'S LAST STAND
PRICE, LEONTYNE
PORGY AND BESS
PRICE, LLOYD
EVERYBODY'S ALL-AMERICAN

Q

R

RASKIN, TOM
WHOOP-UP!
RAST, JIM
VIRGIN
RATHBONE, BASIL
ADVENTURES OF ROBIN HOOD
ALADDIN
CHRISTMAS CAROL
CO-STAR
DINOSAURUS!
OLIVER TWIST
STINGIEST MAN IN TOWN
RATHBURN, ELDON
LABYRINTH
RATHBURN, ROGER
NO, NO, NANETTE
RATKEVICH, PAUL
BOY MEETS BOY
RATT
GOLDEN CHILD
RAUBER, FRANCOIS
JACQUES BREL IS ALIVE AND
WELL AND LIVING IN PARIS
RAVEL, MAURICE
10
RAVEN, PAUL
JESUS CHRIST SUPERSTAR
RAVENSCROFT, THURL
SAVAGE SAM
SEVEN DREAMS
SNOOPY COME HOME
RAVYNS
FAST TIMES AT RIDGEMONT HIGH
RAWLINGS, MARGARET
HAMLET
RAWLS, LOU
SOUL OF NIGGER CHARLEY
RAWSON, DENYS
MAN OF LA MANCHA
RAY, ALDO
WHAT DID YOU DO IN THE WAR,
DADDY?
RAY, ANJE
BELIEVERS
RAY, JAMES
DYLAN
RAY, JOHNNIE
LAST PICTURE SHOW
THERE'S NO BUSINESS LIKE
SHOW BUSINESS
RAY, ROBIN
TOMFOOLERY
RAY, SATYAJIT
SHAKESPEARE WALLAH
RAYE, CAROL
BONANZA BOUND
RAYE, MARTHA
JUMBO
PUFNSTUF
RHYTHM ON THE RANGE
RAYMOND, HELEN
MUSIC MAN
RAYMOND, LEW
AROUND THE WORLD IN 80 DAYS
MY FAIR LADY
PAL JOEY
THEMES FROM THE MOVIES
RAYS
SCHOOL DAZE

RAZ, RIVKA
TO LIVE ANOTHER SUMMER, TO
PASS ANOTHER WINTER
RE-FLEX
BREAKIN'
READING, BERTICE
VALMOUTH
READY FOR THE WORLD
BEVERLY HILLS COP II
RUNNING SCARED
REAGAN, RONALD
FREEDOM'S FINEST HOUR
REAL LIFE
ONCE BITTEN
RAD
SAVAGE STREETS
REAMS, LEE ROY
APPLAUSE
42nd STREET
LORELEI
REARDON, JOHN
DO RE MI
HELLO OUT THERE
LADY IN THE DARK
MERRY WIDOW
NEW FACES OF 1956
OLD MAID AND THE THIEF
ON THE TOWN
SAINT OF BLEEKER STREET
SONG OF NORWAY
REBELS
SCHONER GIGOLO - ARMER
GIGOLO (JUST A GIGOLO)
RECHT, COBY
APPLE
RED 7
MANHUNTER
RED BUTTONS
GAY PURR-EE
HANSEL AND GRETEL
LONGEST DAY
PETE'S DRAGON
RED CLAY RAMBLERS
FAR NORTH
LIE OF THE MIND
**RED GUARD ACCORDION
BAND**
LAST EMPEROR
RED HOT CHILI PEPPERS
PRETTY WOMAN
RED MOUNTAIN JUG BAND
STRAWBERRY STATEMENT
RED NICHOLS
FIVE PENNIES
GENE KRUPA STORY
RED RHODES
PRISON
RED RIDER
VISION QUEST
REDD, FREDDIE
CONNECTION
REDD, SHARON
CLAMS ON THE HALF SHELL
REDD, VERONICA
BELIEVERS
REDDIN, EARL
BRIGADOON
REDDING, GENE
HARRAD SUMMER

REDDING, OTIS
DREAM A LITTLE DREAM
PLATOON (AND SONGS FROM THE
ERA)
REDDS AND THE BOYS
GOOD TO GO
REDDY, HELEN
ALL THIS AND WORLD WAR II
PETE'S DRAGON
REDFIELD, LIZA
ERNEST IN LOVE
REDFIELD, WILLIAM
HAMLET
OUT OF THIS WORLD
REDGRAVE, COLIN
OH WHAT A LOVELY WAR
REDGRAVE, LYNN
LOVE FOR LOVE
MAKE MINE MANHATTAN
MUCH ADO ABOUT NOTHING
POWER IS YOU
RODGERS AND HART REVISITED
SMASHING TIME
REDGRAVE, MICHAEL
HAMLET
HEIDI
MacBETH
OH ROSALINDA!
RUGGLES OF RED GAP
REDGRAVE, VANESSA
CAMELOT
MARY, QUEEN OF SCOTS
REDMAN, JOYCE
LOVE FOR LOVE
REDMAN, ROY
TOUCHABLES
REDMOND, DON
BLACKBIRDS OF 1928
REDO KROSS
LOVEDOLLS SUPERSTAR
REDSKINS
BAD GUYS
LETTER TO BREZHNEV
REDWAY, MIKE
PRIME OF MISS JEAN BRODIE
REDWINE, SKIP
DECLINE AND FALL OF THE
ENTIRE WORLD AS SEEN
THROUGH THE EYES OF COLÆ
PORTER
REED, ALAINA
EUBIE
REED, ALAN
FLINTSTONES
SONGS OF THE FLINTSTONES
REED, BOBBY
BOY MEETS BOY
REED, JERRY
CLAMBAKE
GATOR
SMOKEY AND THE BANDIT
SMOKEY AND THE BANDIT II
VANISHING POINT
REED, JIMMY
DINER
REED, LES
GIRL ON A MOTORCYCLE

ROMANO, RONALD
HAUNTED
ROMANO, TONY
FRANCES LANGFORD PRESENTS
ROMBERG, SIGMUND
DEEP IN MY HEART
DESERT SONG
GIRL IN PINK TIGHTS
MAYTIME
NEW MOON
STUDENT PRINCE
ROME PHILHARMONIC
RE-ANIMATOR
ROME SOUND STAGE
ORCHESTRA
CLEOPATRA
ROME SYMPHONY
ORCHESTRA
TRIP TO ITALY
V.I.P.s
ROME, HAROLD
CALL ME MISTER
DESTRY RIDES AGAIN
FANNY
GONE WITH THE WIND
I CAN GET IT FOR YOU
  WHOLESALE
PINS AND NEEDLES
WISH YOU WERE HERE
ZULU AND THE ZAYDA
ROME, SYDNE
SCHONER GIGOLO - ARMER
  GIGOLO (JUST A GIGOLO)
ROMEO'S DAUGHTER
NIGHTMARE ON ELM STREET 5 -
  THE DREAM CHILD
ROMERO, CESAR
CO-STAR
ROMOFF, COLIN
FADE OUT FADE IN
KWAMINA
ROMOFF, WOOD
SHE LOVES ME
RONETTES
DIRTY DANCING
RONSTADT, LINDA
AMERICAN TAIL
HAIL HAIL ROCK 'N' ROLL
IRVING BERLIN: 100TH
  ANNIVERSARY COLLECTION
URBAN COWBOY
ROOFTOP
CROSSOVER DREAMS
ROOK, WILLIE
SURVIVAL OF ST. JOAN
ROONEY, MICKEY
GIRL CRAZY
HOW TO STUFF A WILD BIKINI
MAGIC OF LASSIE
MISTER BROADWAY
PETE'S DRAGON
PINOCCHIO
SANTA CLAUS IS COMIN' TO
  TOWN
THAT'S ENTERTAINMENT
WORDS AND MUSIC
ROONEY, PAT
GUYS AND DOLLS
ROOSEVELT, FRANKLIN D.
JOHN F. KENNEDY

QUICK AND THE DEAD - THE
  STORY OF THE ATOM BOMB
ROQUEMORE, LARRY
ANYONE CAN WHISTLE
ROREM, NED
MISS JULIE
ROSAMOND, J.
PORGY AND BESS
ROSATO, MARY LOU
CRADLE WILL ROCK
ROSE CONCERT BAND
ROSE
ROSE ROYCE
CAR WASH
ROSE, ARTHUR
ME AND MY GIRL
ROSE, BILLY
FUNNY LADY
ROSE, CLIFFORD
MARAT (DE) SADE
ROSE, DAVID
BONANZA
BUTTERFIELD 8
CIMARRON (AND OTHER GREAT
  SONGS)
DOUBLE IMPACT
EVERYTHING I HAVE IS YOURS
FRANCES LANGFORD PRESENTS
GIGI
GREAT BOOKS, GREAT MOVIES,
  GREAT SONGS
JUDY GARLAND
MAN FROM U.N.C.L.E.
OF HUMAN BONDAGE (AND
  OTHER GREAT THEMES)
QUICK BEFORE IT MELTS
RICH, YOUNG AND PRETTY
WHOOP-UP!
WONDERFUL WORLD OF THE
  BROTHERS GRIMM
ROSE, EMMETT
BEST OF BURLESQUE
ROSE, GEORGE
CANTERBURY TALES
COCO
EDWIN DROOD
HAMLET
MY FAIR LADY
WALKING HAPPY
ROSE, MARGOT
I'M GETTING MY ACT TOGETHER
  AND TAKING IT ON THE ROAD
ROSE, RALPH
OLIVER TWIST
ROSELLI, JIMMY
BUONA SERA, MRS. CAMPBELL
ROSENMAN, LEONARD
BARRY LYNDON
BENEATH THE PLANET OF THE
  APES
BOUND FOR GLORY
CHAPMAN REPORT
COBWEB
DICK POWELL PRESENTS (MUSIC
  FROM THE ORIGINAL
  SOUNDTRACK OF FOUR STAR
  PRODUCTIONS)
JAMES DEAN STORY
LORD OF THE RINGS
MAN CALLED HORSE
9-30-55

STAR TREK IV: THE VOYAGE
  HOME
TRIBUTE TO JAMES DEAN
TWILIGHT ZONE
ROSENSTOCK, MILTON
BELLS ARE RINGING
CAN CAN
FUNNY GIRL
GENTLEMEN PREFER BLONDES
GYPSY
HIGH BUTTON SHOES
JIMMY
KING AND I
LORELEI
MAKE A WISH
ONE NIGHT STAND
SO LONG 174TH STREET
STOP THE WORLD, I WANT TO
  GET OFF!
SUBWAYS ARE FOR SLEEPING
THIS IS THE ARMY
TWO'S COMPANY
ROSENTHAL, LAURENCE
ANASTASIA - THE MYSTERY OF
  ANNA
BECKET
BRASS TARGET
CLASH OF THE TITANS
COMEDIANS
DYLAN
HOTEL PARIDISO
ISLAND OF DR. MOREAU
MAN OF LA MANCHA
MEETINGS WITH REMARKABLE
  MEN
RASHOMON
RETURN OF A MAN CALLED
  HORSE
ROSKO
YOU ARE WHAT YOU EAT
ROSS, ADRIAN
LILAC TIME (BLOSSOM TIME)
ROSS, ANNIE
REAL AMBASSADORS
ROSS, DIANA
AN EVENING WITH DIANA ROSS
COOLEY HIGH
DIANA!
ENDLESS LOVE
FUNNY GIRL
IT'S MY TURN
LADY SINGS THE BLUES
LAND BEFORE TIME
LOOKING FOR MR. GOODBAR
MAHOGANY
ON BROADWAY
T.C.B. (TAKIN' CARE OF BUSINESS)
THANK GOD IT'S FRIDAY
WIZ
ROSS, ELIZA
ALL ABOUT LIFE
ROSS, HOWARD
CARMELINA
PHILEMON
ROSS, HUGH
GOLDEN APPLE
ROSS, JAMIE
OH COWARD!
WOMAN OF THE YEAR
ROSS, JERRY
DAMN YANKEES
PAJAMA GAME

RUBINSTEIN, ARTHUR
  BLUE THUNDER
  GOODTIME CHARLEY
  WAR GAMES
RUBINSTEIN, DONALD
  MARTIN
RUBINSTEIN, JOHN
  PIPPIN
RUBY, HARRY
  THREE LITTLE WORDS
RUDEL, JULIUS
  SILVER LAKE
RUDLEY, MARION
  CRADLE WILL ROCK
RUE, ROBERT
  CANDIDE
  JUNO
RUFF, GARFEEL
  HITTER
RUFFIN, GARY
  SURVIVAL OF ST. JOAN
RUFFIN, HANK
RUFUS
  BREAKIN'
  NIGHT SHIFT
RUGGIERO, GABRIELLE
  SAINT OF BLEEKER STREET
RUGOLO, PETE
  IMPACT
  JACK THE RIPPER
  RICHARD DIAMOND
  SWEET RIDE
  THRILLER
  TIME REMEMBERED
RUGULO, PETE
  RICHARD DIAMOND
RUHL, PAT
  DRESSED TO THE NINES
RUICK, BARBARA
  CAROUSEL
  OH KAY!
RUIZ, RANDY
  RUNAWAYS
RULE, CHARLES
  GOODTIME CHARLEY
RULE, JANICE
  HAPPIEST GIRL IN THE WORLD
RUN D.M.C.
  KRUSH GROOVE
RUNDGREN, TODD
  ROCK 'N' ROLL HIGH SCHOOL
  UNDERCOVER
RUPERT, GENE
  AN EVENING WITH RICHARD
    NIXON
  TIME FOR SINGING
RUPERT, MICHAEL
  FESTIVAL
  HAPPY TIME
  MARCH OF THE FALSETTOS
  SWEET CHARITY
  THREE GUYS NAKED FROM THE
    WAIST DOWN
RUPP, FRANZ
  LADY FROM PHILADELPHIA
RUS, MARJAN
  MERRY WIDOW

RUSK, JAMES
  AMONG FRIENDS - WAA-MU
    SHOW OF 1960
RUSSEL, BOBBY
  GRASSHOPPER
RUSSELL, ANNA
  ANNA RUSSELL'S LITTLE SHOW
    (ALL BY MYSELF)
RUSSELL, BETTY
  HARVEY GIRLS
RUSSELL, BRENDA
  SOUL MAN
RUSSELL, BRYAN
  BYE BYE BIRDIE
  SO DEAR TO MY HEART
RUSSELL, CONNIE
  PLAYGIRLS
RUSSELL, CRAIG
  OUTRAGEOUS
RUSSELL, DAVID
  SHENANDOAH
RUSSELL, JACK
  NIGHT IN VENICE
RUSSELL, JANE
  FRENCH LINE
  GENTLEMEN MARRY BRUNETTES
  GENTLEMEN PREFER BLONDES
RUSSELL, JESSICA
  CARMEN JONES
RUSSELL, KARL
  BLACULA
RUSSELL, LEON
  JOE COCKER: MAD DOGS AND
    ENGLISHMEN
RUSSELL, NIPSEY
  WIZ
RUSSELL, REBECCA
  HEART OF DIXIE
RUSSELL, ROSALIND
  AUNTIE MAME
  GYPSY
  WONDERFUL TOWN
RUSSELL, TONY
  TELL ME LIES
RUSSOM, LEON
  OH CALCUTTA!
RUSTICHELLI, CARLO
  BEBO'S GIRL
  BIRDS, THE BEES AND THE
    ITALIANS
  DIVORCE ITALIAN STYLE
  SEDUCED AND ABANDONED
RUTHERFORD, MARGARET
  WACKY WORLD OF MOTHER
    GOOSE
RUTHERFORD, MIKE
  AGAINST ALL ODDS
RUTS
  TIMES SQUARE
RVARK, JOHN
  MY FAIR LADY
RYAN, IRENE
  BEVERLY HILLBILLIES
  PIPPIN
RYAN, MARK
  EVITA
RYAN, ROBERT
  MISTER PRESIDENT

RYDELL, BOBBY
  BYE BYE BIRDIE
RYDELL, CHARLES
  PAINTED SMILES OF COLE PORTER
  RODGERS AND HART REVISITED
  SECRET LIFE OF WALTER MITTY
RYDER, RICHARD
  PIANO BAR

S

SABAR, JEAN PIERRE
  MADAME CLAUDE
SABIN, DAVID
  NOW IS THE TIME FOR ALL GOOD
    MEN
  PREPPIES
  THREEPENNY OPERA
SADLER, SSGT. BARRY
  MORE AMERICAN GRAFFITI
  NARM'S GOLDEN DECADE
SAFAN, CRAIG
  LADY BEWARE
  LAST STARFIGHTER
  NIGHTMARE ON ELM STREET 4 -
    THE DREAM MASTER
  THIEF
SAFKA, MELANIE
  ALL THE RIGHT NOISES
  R.P.M.
  SWEDISH FLY GIRLS
SAGA
  JOHNNY BE GOOD
SAGER, CAROLE BAYER
  CHAMP
  IT'S MY TURN
  NIGHT SHIFT
  THEY'RE PLAYING OUR SONG
SAHL, MORT
  DEAN MARTIN TESTIMONIAL
    DINNER
SAHM, DOUG
  MORE AMERICAN GRAFFITI
SAIDENBERG, DANIEL
  GRANDMA MOSES
SAIDENBERG, THEODORE
  GRASS HARP
  MY FAIR LADY
  ON A CLEAR DAY YOU CAN SEE
    FOREVER
ST. MARIE, EVA
  OUR TOWN
SAINT JAMES, SUSAN
  OUTLAW BLUES
SAINT-SAENS, CAMILLE
  DAYS OF HEAVEN
SAINTE-MARIE, BUFFY
  PERFORMANCE
  REVOLUTION
  STRAWBERRY STATEMENT
SAINTON, PHILIP
  MOBY DICK
SAKAMOTO, RYUICHI
  BLACK RAIN
  LAST EMPEROR
  MERRY CHRISTMAS MR.
    LAWRENCE

SECOMBE, HARRY
  OLIVER
  PICKWICK
  SONG OF NORWAY
SECOND TIME
  WILD IN THE STREETS
SECUNDA, SHOLOM
  BEI MIR BISTU SCHOEN
  KOSHER WIDOW
SEEDS
  PHYCH-OUT
SEEGAR, SARA
  ERNEST IN LOVE
SEEGER, PEGGY
  WHALER OUT OF NEW BEDFORD
    (AND OTHER SONGS OF THE
    WHALING ERA)
SEEGER, PETE
  TELL ME THAT YOU LOVE ME,
    JUNIE MOON
SEELEY, BLOSSOM
  SOMEBODY LOVES ME
SEELY, JEANNIE
  HONEYSUCKLE ROSE
SEGAL, GEORGE
  LEAVE IT TO JANE
  OWL AND THE PUSSYCAT
  PREMISE
  WHO'S AFRAID OF VIRGINIA
    WOOLF?
SEGAL, KATHRYN KING
  PHILEMON
SEGAL, VIVIENNE
  CONNECTICUT YANKEE
  PAL JOEY
SEGALL, BERNARDO
  CUSTER OF THE WEST
SEGER, BOB
  BEVERLY HILLS COP II
  FM
  TEACHERS
  URBAN COWBOY
SEGOVIA, YOLANDA
  DREAM GIRLS
SEIBEL, PAULA
  SWEET BYE AND BYE
SEITZ, DRAN
  HAPPIEST GIRL IN THE WORLD
SEITZ, TANI
  NERVOUS SET
SELBY, DAVID
  DARK SHADOWS
SELBY, LAUREL
  BODY IN THE SEINE
SELECTER
  DANCE CRAZE
SELF, RONNIE
  BIG TOWN
SELFINGER, CAROL
  LOLLIPOP COVER
SELINSKY, VLADIMIR
  KRAFT TELEVISION THEATRE
SELL, JANIE
  IRENE
  MIXED DOUBLES/BELOW THE
    BELT
  OVER HERE!
SELLERS, DALE
  ELVIS

SELLERS, PETER
  AFTER THE FOX
  ALICE'S ADVENTURES IN
    WONDERLAND
  BOBO
  FOOL BRITANNIA
  MAGIC CHRISTIAN
  REVENGE OF THE PINK PANTHER
  TOM THUMB
SELTZER, DOV
  KAZABLAN
  MEGILLA OF ITZIG MANGER
  TO LIVE ANOTHER SUMMER, TO
    PASS ANOTHER WINTER
SEMBELLO, MICHAEL
  COCOON
  FLASHDANCE
  GREMLINS
  SUMMER LOVERS
SEMES, RENEE
  CANDIDE
SENATORS
  WILD IN THE STREETS
SENDAK, MAURICE
  REALLY ROSIE
SENNETT, MACK
  MAGNIFICENT ROGUE
SEPPE, CHRISTOPHER
  CHARLOTTE SWEET
SERABIAN, LORRAINE
  SECRET LIFE OF WALTER MITTY
  ZORBA
SERENDIPITY SINGERS
  WAY WEST
SERINO, DEL
  PRETTY BOY FLOYD
SERRA, ERIC
  BIG BLUE
  SUBWAY
SERRANO, CHARLIE
  JOSEPH AND THE AMAZING
    TECHNICOLOR DREAMCOAT
SERVICE, ANTHONY
  MacBETH
SETZER, BRIAN
  LA BAMBA
SETZER, MILTON
  BY JUPITER
SEVAREID, ERIC
  POINT OF ORDER
SEVELLE, TAJA
  LEAN ON ME
SEVEN-A-THREE
  COLORS
SEVERINE
  RIDER ON THE RAIN
SEVERINSEN, DOC
  HUSTLER
  MAGIC MOMENTS FROM THE
    TONIGHT SHOW
  SHARKY'S MACHINE
SEVILLE, DAVID, AND THE
  CHIPMUNKS
  ALVIN SHOW
SEVRA, ROBERT
  LOVERS
SEXTON, CHARLIE
  BEVERLY HILLS COP II
  WILD LIFE

SEYMOUR, JANE
  BATTLESTAR GALACTICA (THE
    SAGA OF BATTLESTAR
    GALACTICA)
SEYMOUR, PHIL
  LAST AMERICAN VIRGIN
SHA NA NA
  GREASE
  PURPLE PEOPLE EATER
SHACKLOCK, CONSTANCE
  SOUND OF MUSIC
SHAFER, ROBERT
  DAMN YANKEES
  SONG OF NORWAY
SHAFFER, PAUL
  SATURDAY NIGHT LIVE
SHAINDLIN, JACK
  BOLD VENTURES
  CINERAMA HOLIDAY
  STORY OF MOBY DICK
  WINDJAMMER
SHALAMAR
  BEVERLY HILLS COP
  D.C. CAB
  FOOTLOOSE
  JUST ONE OF THE GUYS
SHANAHAN, BERNIE
  JOHNNY BE GOOD
SHANDI
  ECHO PARK
  FLASHDANCE
  KARATE KID
SHANE, HAL
  VERY GOOD EDDIE
SHANE, LISA
  PENTHOUSE
SHANET, HOWARD
  FLY WITH ME
SHANGE, NTOZAKE
  FOR COLORED GIRLS WHO HAVE
    CONSIDERED SUICIDE WHEN
    THE RAINBOW IS ENUF
SHANK, BUD
  BAREFOOT ADVENTURE
  COLLEGE CONFIDENTIAL
  MAN WITH THE GOLDEN ARM
  SLIPPERY WHEN WET
SHANKAR, RAVI
  CHAPPAQUA
  CHARLY
  GANDHI
  RAGA
SHANKS, NANCY
  SECRET OF MY SUCCESS
SHANNON
  FATAL BEAUTY
SHANNON, CAROL
  MY FAIRFAX LADY
SHANNON, DEL
  DUSTY AND SWEETS McGEE
SHANNON, FRANK
  FLASH GORDON
SHANNON, HUGH
  ERTEGUN'S NEW YORK - NEW
    YORK CABARET MUSIC
SHANTE, ROXANNE
  COLORS
  LEAN ON ME
SHAPIRO, DAN
  ANKLES AWEIGH

SLATER, B.J.
1776
SLATER, JOHN
MY FAIR LADY
SLATKIN, LEONARD
EXORCIST
RED SKY AT MORNING
SLATON, DON
BEST FOOT FORWARD
SLAVE RAIDER
LICENSE TO DRIVE
SLAVIN, MILLIE
TO BROADWAY WITH LOVE
SLAYER
LESS THAN ZERO
RIVER'S EDGE
SLAZER, JON
REVENGE
SLEDGE, EDDIE
KISS ME KATE
SLEDGE, PERCY
MORE AMERICAN GRAFFITI
PLATOON (AND SONGS FROM THE
ERA)
SLEEP
CATS
SLEZAK, WALTER
EMIL AND THE DETECTIVES
FANNY
SLICK, DANIEL
DOWN IN THE VALLEY
SLICK, GRACE
KENT STATE
SLICKERS
HARDER THEY COME
SLOANE, EVERETT
CITIZEN KANE
HIGH TOR
SLOOPYS
DOCTOR GOLDFOOT AND THE
GIRL BOMBS
SLY AND ROBBIE
GOOD TO GO
**SLY AND THE FAMILY
STONE**
WOODSTOCK
SMALL, MARYA
GREASE
SMALL, MICHAEL
KLUTE
SMALL, NEVA
HENRY, SWEET HENRY
SMALLENS, ALEXANDER
BABES IN TOYLAND
PORGY AND BESS
SMALLS, CHARLIE
WIZ
SMART, BOB
STATE FAIR
SMARTT, MICHAEL
NEFERTITI
SMEATON, BRUCE
ICEMAN
SMILEY, MICK
GHOSTBUSTERS
SMITH, ALEXIS
FOLLIES
PLATINUM

SONDHEIM: A MUSICAL TRIBUTE
SMITH, ANDREW
PORGY AND BESS
SMITH, BESSIE
ANGEL HEART
LUCKY LADY
SMITH, BOB
WORLD (ORIGINAL CAST
STARRING HOWDY DOODY)
SMITH, CHAS
LIGHT OF DAY
SMITH, CLIVE
LIQUID SKY
SMITH, DEREK
HANNAH AND HER SISTERS
SMITH, ELLEN
WILD ROVERS
SMITH, GLORIA
BY THE BEAUTIFUL SEA
SMITH, GREGG
BLUE MONDAY
RISE AND FALL OF THE THIRD
REICH
SMITH, GWEN
BILLY JACK
SMITH, HOWLETT
ME AND BESSIE
SMITH, IAN
HOT ROCK
SMITH, JABBO
ONE MO' TIME
SMITH, JENNY
SOPHIE
SMITH, JIMMY
DANCE TO THE MUSIC OF IRVING
BERLIN
GET YOURSELF A COLLEGE GIRL
SMITH, JOHNNY
FLOWER DRUM SONG
SMITH, KATE
PROUDLY THEY CAME
SHOW BIZ (FROM VAUDE TO
VIDEO)
SMITH, KELLY
HEY BOY, HEY GIRL
KISS ME KATE
SOUTH PACIFIC
SMITH, KENNETH
DOWN IN THE VALLEY
SMITH, LORING
GAY LIFE
HELLO DOLLY!
TEXAS LI'L DARLIN'
SMITH, LORRAINE
GYPSY
SMITH, MAGGIE
MARY POPPINS
MUCH ADO ABOUT NOTHING
NEW FACES OF 1956
OH WHAT A LOVELY WAR
SHARE MY LETTUCE
SMITH, MICHAEL GLENN
CELEBRATION
PHILEMON
SMITH, MIKE
EVITA
SMITH, MURIEL
CARMEN JONES

SMITH, NORWOOD
NIGHT IN VENICE
SMITH, O.C.
SHAFT'S BIG SCORE
SMITH, OSBORNE
IRMA LA DOUCE
SMITH, PATTI
TIMES SQUARE
SMITH, PAUL J.
CINDERELLA
LIVING DESERT
NIKKI, WILD DOG OF THE NORTH
PINOCCHIO
POLLYANNA
POPEYE
SECRETS OF LIFE
SNOW WHITE AND THE SEVEN
DWARFS
UNCLE REMUS
VANISHING PRAIRIE
WALT DISNEY'S TRUE LIFE
ADVENTURES
SMITH, PAUL
LET NO MAN WRITE MY EPITAPH
MUSIC MAN
PERRI
SMITH, PREACHER
ROCK BABY ROCK IT
SMITH, PRESTON
COBRA
COCKTAIL
SMITH, ROBERT B.
SWEETHEARTS
SMITH, RUFUS
ANNIE GET YOUR GUN
PAINT YOUR WAGON
SMITH, RUSSELL
HONKY-TONK FREEWAY
SMITH, SALLY
ASPECTS OF LOVE
ROAR OF THE GREASEPAINT, THE
SMELL OF THE CROWD
SMITH, SAMMY
HOW NOW, DOW JONES
HOW TO SUCCEED IN BUSINESS
WITHOUT REALLY TRYING
WISH YOU WERE HERE
SMITH, SCOTT
AMONG FRIENDS - WAA-MU
SHOW OF 1960
SMITH, SHEILA
HANS BRINKER
SUGAR
SMITH, STEPHEN DOYLE
HAPPENING
SMITH, TED
HIDING PLACE
TIME TO RUN
SMITH, TRUMAN
KEAN
SMITH, TUCKER
ANYONE CAN WHISTLE
SMITHEREENS
DANGEROUSLY CLOSE
I WAS A TEENAGE ZOMBIE
UNDER THE BOARDWALK
SMITHS
PRETTY IN PINK
SMOTHERMAN, MICHAEL
ALWAYS

W

#1 ON THE CHARTS!

The Official® Price Guide to Records, written by *the* expert, Jerry Osborne, is a hit with record collectors!

- Lists every charted hit from 1950 to 1989, from Abba to Zappa and everything in between.
- Covers country, jazz, rock, and more.
- A solid-gold 8-page color insert.

With the demise of vinyl records, *all* records are increasing in value. Check out *your* records in this invaluable guide!